NUSACH ASHKENAZ — נוסח אשכנז

Published by

A PROJECT OF THE

Mesorah Heritage Foundation

The Complete Tishah B'av Service

A new translation and anthologized commentary by

Rabbi Avrohom Chaim Feuer *and* Rabbi Avie Gold

Overview: Kinnos — A trail of Tears
by Rabbi Avrohom Chaim Feuer

Designed by Rabbi Sheah Brander

FIRST EDITION
First Impression . . . June 1991
SECOND EDITION
First Impression . . . May 1992
Second Impression . . . May 2001
Third Impression . . . April 2002
Fourth Impression . . . June 2003
Fifth Impression . . . May 2005

Published and Distributed by
MESORAH PUBLICATIONS, Ltd.
Brooklyn, New York 11232

Distributed in Europe by
LEHMANNS
Unit E, Viking Business Park
Rolling Mill Road
Jarrow, Tyne & Wear NE32 3DP
England

Distributed in Australia & New Zealand by
GOLDS WORLD OF JUDAICA
3-13 William Street
Balaclava, Melbourne 3183
Victoria Australia

Distributed in Israel by
SIFRIATI / A. GITLER — BOOKS
6 Hayarkon Street
Bnei Brak 51127

Distributed in South Africa by
KOLLEL BOOKSHOP
Shop 8A Norwood Hypermarket
Norwood 2196, Johannesburg, South Africa

THE ARTSCROLL MESORAH SERIES®
"ZECHOR L'AVRAHAM / The Complete Tishah B'Av Service"
Nusach Ashkenaz

ISBN: 0-89906-878-2 (hard cover)
ISBN: 0-89906-879-0 (paperback)

Typography by CompuScribe at ArtScroll Studios, Ltd., Brooklyn, NY
Bound by **Sefercraft, Inc.,** Brooklyn, NY

כָּל שֶׁרוּחַ הַבְּרִיּוֹת נוֹחָה הֵימֶנּוּ רוּחַ הַמָּקוֹם נוֹחָה הֵימֶנּוּ

If the spirit of one's fellows is pleased with him, the spirit of the Omnipresent is pleased with him (Avos 3:13).

This volume is dedicated to the memory of

אברהם אלטר בן משה ע״ה

Abraham Vegh ע״ה

May 7, 1991 / נפטר כ״ג אייר תשנ״א

Abraham Vegh was born and raised in Apsha, and grew to manhood in Kashau. All his life he remained loyal to the teachings and teachers of those towns that are revered in Jewish memory. After surviving Auschwitz he came to Boston where he established himself as a skilled and sought after tailor.

But he worried about raising his children in the spirit of "der heim." So he moved to Williamsburg and then to Boro Park, and started all over again. For twenty-five years, his cleaning and tailoring store was a temple of honesty. He would not accept a job if it was not in the customer's best interest, and whatever he did, he did well — so well that customers requested that he do their work in his apartment after he retired.

When it seemed "impossible" in the early 50's to be a Shomer Shabbos, to wear a yarlmulka at work in the store, or to daven with a minyan three times a day — he did it. He would leave the store to go to shul, because obligation came first, to his Maker as to his customers.

Chumash, Tehillim, Pirkei Avos — these were his life and he became their living embodiment.

To the people with whom he davened at the Sfardishe Shul for close to 30 years and the Apsha Beis Medrash during the last several years, he was known as an exceptional baal tefillah, with his heart and with his voice.

All his life, he fought to be true to Torah and Middos. In his resting place in Beit Shemesh, near Jerusalem, his memory remains a monument to the eternity of the Jew.

תנצב״ה

Lovingly Dedicated by,

Mrs. Serena Vegh

Mutty and Shoshy Vegh, Chani, Tova and Yaffa

Robby and Rozzy Vegh, David Jeffrey, Shalom and Ariella

Hy and Ruthy Kislak, Golde and Yitzy

TABLE OF CONTENTS

Kinnos listed in alpabetical order

◆§ Publisher's Preface

Tishah B'Av is a day of tragedy and hope: a day of tragedy because, as Maimonides calls it, it is "the day that was designated for punishment," the day on which both Temples were destroyed and many other misfortunes occurred; and a day of hope because it is the day on which the Redemption will be — or has been — spawned. The Book of Eichah/Lamentations and the Kinnos of Tishah B'Av consume the major parts of the evening and morning services but, to say the least, they are complex and difficult. And because they are, it is quite understandable that so many people find it difficult to attain the level of inspiration that is so essential to the day. The Sages teach that those who grieve over Jerusalem will be privileged to see its consolation; that being so, it is important that the sacred and meaning-laden words of the Kinnos be made comprehensible so that they can fulfill their portentous mission. That is the reason for this Siddur for Tishah B'Av. It is meant to be a volume that will guide the supplicant from the first moment of the day until the last word of Kiddush Levanah. In addition to the translation and commentary, this volume contains the necessary directions and laws, so that the reader will spend less time on searching and groping, and more on understanding and feeling the day's services.

The volume also includes two contemporary Kinnos, memorializing Churban Europe, the destruction of European Jewry in World War II. The authors, the Bobover Rav שליט"א and HaGaon HaRav Shimon Schwab שליט"א of K'hal Adas Jeshurun, respectively, composed them for recitation by their communities and they have since been adopted by others. (See introductions to both Kinnos).

◆§ Contents *This Siddur is as complete as possible. It includes translations of all the prayers and Torah readings, and translations and commentaries on Eichah and the Kinnos. The services for the full day are self-contained so that the reader will be spared the annoying chore of turning back and forth. The Overview provides a perspective on Tishah B'Av.*

Although the Kinnos are standard in both Nusach Ashkenaz and Nusach Sefard, there are minor variations among the texts. Some of these are obviously the work of Christian censors, who removed or altered stanzas, phrases, or words they found offensive. The authors and editors of this work consulted many different editions of the Kinnos in order to arrive at the text that seemed to be correct. We emphasize, however, that the variations are relatively few.

◆§ Translation *The translation seeks to balance the lofty beauty of the heavily nuanced text and a readily understood English rendering. Where a choice had to be made, we generally preferred fidelity to the text over inaccurate simplicity, but occasionally, we had to stray from the literal translation in order to capture the essence of a phrase in an accessible English idiom. Especially in the Kinnos we had to go beyond a strictly literal translation, and sometimes rely on the commentary to clarify the meaning of the text.*

◆§ Commentary *Because ordinary Torah study is forbidden on Tishah B'Av, this volume contains no commentary on the regular prayer order or the Torah readings. There is commentary, however, on Eichah and the Kinnos, for their*

saddening content makes it permissible to study as well as recite them. In addition, each kinnah/lamentation is provided with an introduction giving its background and historical context.

☙ **Laws and Instructions** *Clear instructions are provided throughout. More complex or lengthy halachos are discussed at the end of the volume in the 'Laws' section, which the reader will find to be a very helpful guide. This section includes general halachos that are relevant to the regular prayer service. Throughout the volume, we refer to these laws by paragraph (§) number.*

☙ **Layout and Typography** *We have followed the pattern of the ArtScroll Siddur and Machzorim, which have been greatly praised for their ease of use and clarity of layout. With its clear instructions, copious subtitles, and precise page headings, this volume was designed to make the Tishah B'Av service easy for everyone to follow: The first and last phrases of the translation on each page parallel the first and last phrases of the Hebrew text; paragraphs begin with bold-type words to facilitate the individual tefillos; each paragraph in the translation is introduced with the parallel Hebrew word to ease cross-checking; portions said aloud by the chazzan are indicated by either the symbol ∴ or the word 'chazzan.' An asterisk (*) after a word indicates that that word or phrase is treated in the commentary. Numbered footnotes give the Scriptural sources of countless verses that have been melded into the prayers, as well as variant readings. A footnote beginning 'Cf.' indicates that the Scriptural source is paraphrased.*

☙ **Hebrew Grammar** *As a general rule in the Hebrew language, the accent is on the last syllable. Where the accent is on an earlier syllable, it is indicated with a messeg, a vertical line below the accented letter:* שִֽׁירוּ. *In the case of the Shema and the Song at the Sea, which are given with the cantillation [trop], the accent follows the trop. A* שְׁוָא נָע *[sh'va na] is indicated by a hyphen mark above the letter:* בָּרְכוּ; *except for a sh'va on the first letter of a word, which is always a sh'va na. In identifying a sh'va na, we have followed the rules of the Vilna Gaon and Rabbi Yaakov Emden.*

Acknowledgments

The ArtScroll Series has been privileged to benefit from the advice and support of the venerable Torah leaders of the previous and present generations. MARAN HAGAON HARAV MOSHE FEINSTEIN, MARAN HAGAON HARAV YAAKOV KAMINETSKY, MARAN HAGAON HARAV GEDALIA SCHORR *and* HARAV HAGAON HARAV SHNEUR KOTLER, זצ״ל. *Among today's gedolei Yisrael* להבחל״ח MARAN HAGAON HARAV MORDECHAI GIFTER שליט״א *has been a father and mentor from the start, and* MARAN HAGAON HARAV ZELIK EPSTEIN שליט״א *is a treasured counselor.*

We are deeply grateful to Maranan HaGeonim HARAV DAVID FEINSTEIN, HARAV DAVID COHEN and HARAV HILLEL DAVID שליט״א *for their involvement and for placing their encyclopedic scholarship at our disposal.*

We are proud that the outstanding Torah scholar, HARAV HERSH GOLDWURM זצ״ל, *has been associated with the ArtScroll Series virtually since its inception.*

In this volume Rabbi Goldwurm has contributed the 'Laws,' reviewed most of the instructions, and been available for research and guidance.

The authors of this work, RABBI AVROHOM CHAIM FEUER *and* RABBI AVIE GOLD *are familiar to ArtScroll readers. Here they have collaborated in a work that, we are confident, will place countless Jews further in their debt. Praise is superfluous; their words speak for themselves. We are proud to be associated with them.*

Among those whose guidance was invaluable are such leaders of organizational and rabbinic life as RABBI MOSHE SHERER, RABBI PINCHAS STOLPER, RABBI BORUCH B. BORCHARDT, RABBI JOSHUA FISHMAN, RABBI FABIAN SCHONFELD, RABBI BENJAMIN WALFISH, MR. DAVID H. SCHWARTZ, RABBI YISRAEL H. EIDELMAN, RABBI BURTON JAFFA, *and* RABBI MICHOEL LEVI.

This work was conceived by our very dear friend, RABBI RAPHAEL BUTLER, *whose heroic efforts on behalf of Torah propagation have earned him many admirers — and, more importantly, have brought thousands of people closer to their heritage.*

We are especially grateful to MR. PINCHAS (FRED) HERZKA, *whose unselfish and untiring efforts over many years succeeded in gathering the Kinnos for Churban Europa and having them accepted by large numbers of Kehillos.* יהיה זכור לטוב.

Special recognition and gratitude is due to the trustees of the MESORAH HERITAGE FOUNDATION, *which sponsors this and other projects that bring the classics of our heritage to English-speaking Jews.*

We are grateful to MRS. SERENA VEGH *and her children who have dedicated this volume in memory of their husband and father,* REB AVROHOM ALTER VEGH, ז״ל. *He was a man who overcame suffering and tribulation on both sides of the ocean, but never compromised his principles of faith, integrity, and compassion. Although his own tefillah was in Nusach Sefard, his primary concern was that people daven, whatever the nusach. This Tishah B'Av service, therefore, is a fitting tribute to a noble life. His paramount goal was that he leave generations that are loyal to the tradition he absorbed as he grew to maturity; in this he succeeded, as he did in preserving the legacy his forebears left him.*

The Vegh family expresses its appreciation to RABBI YAAKOV MARCUS, *Rabbi of the Young Israel of Staten Island who has been a friend, guide and role model to the family for many years. They wish him continued good health and success in his labors for Torah and its people.*

We are also grateful to the good and loyal friends who dedicated the various editions of the ArtScroll Siddur (in order of their publication): MR. *and* MRS. ZALMAN MARGULIES; MR. *and* MRS. JOSEPH BERLINER; MR. *and* MRS. AARON L. HEIMOWITZ; MRS. MALA WASSNER; MR. *and* MRS. HIRSCH WOLF; MR. *and* MRS. BEREL TENNENBAUM, MR. *and* MRS. SOLLY KROK; MR. *and* MRS. DAN SUKENIK, *and* MR. *and* MRS. MOSHE SUKENIK; *those who have dedicated the Ashkenaz Machzorim (in order of publication):* MRS. EMMA GLICK *and her sons* YITZCHAK (EDWARD) *and* NAFTALI (NORMAN); MRS. TILLIE FEDER *and her children* NORMAN *and* MAUREEN; *the* KUSHNER *and* LAULICHT *families; the sons of* ARNOLD *and* HELEN LEE; MR. AND MRS. MICHAEL GROSS; *and* MRS. ROCHELLE SORSCHER; *and to* MR. AND MRS. ELI STERN *and* MR. AND MRS. JOSEPH STERN,

who dedicated all five Nusach Sefard Machzorim.

Many other people have provided the assistance needed to produce such Torah projects. In addition to those mentioned in previous editions of the Siddur and other ArtScroll works, we are grateful to MR. *and* MRS. LOUIS GLICK, *whose sponsorship of the ArtScroll Mishnah Series with the* YAD AVRAHAM *commentary is a jewel in the crown of Torah dissemination; and* MR. *and* MRS. IRVING STONE *and* MR. *and* MRS. MORRY WEISS, *who are sponsoring the forthcoming one-volume* STONE EDITION *of the Chumash.*

We are proud and grateful that MRS. JEROME SCHOTTENSTEIN *and* MR. AND MRS. JAY SCHOTTENSTEIN *and their families are continuing to sponsor the monumental* SCHOTTENSTEIN EDITION OF THE TALMUD *in memory of our unforgettable friend* JEROME SCHOTTENSTEIN ע״ה, *and his parents* ע״ה.

The following people have been particularly helpful in making possible the publication of this Kinnos: MR. ABRAHAM FRUCHTHANDLER; RABBI CHAIM LEIBEL; RABBI YEHUDAH LEVI; MR. SHLOMO PERL; MR. ALBERT REICHMANN; MR. SHMUEL RIEDER; MR. ELLIS A. SAFDEYE; MR. LAURENCE A. TISCH; MR. WILLY WIESNER; MR. JUDAH SEPTIMUS; and MR. NATHAN SILBERMAN.

Only a fellow craftsman can perceive the excruciating hours that REB SHEAH BRANDER *expended in designing this volume for the mispallel's maximum ease. In this project he has outdone even his own standard of excellence. Moreover, his learned and incisive comments improved every aspect of this work.*

The eminent scholar RABBI AVROHOM YOSEIF ROSENBERG *reviewed the vowelization of the Kinnos. We are honored and proud to have a talmid chacham of his stature associated with this work.*

MRS. ESTIE DICKER, MRS. ESTHER FEIERSTEIN, MRS. YAFFA DANZIGER, BASSIE GOLDSTEIN, NICHIE FENDRICH, *and* YEHUDA GORDON *typed the manuscript diligently and conscientiously.* RABBI YOSEF GESSER *and* MRS. FAYGIE WEINBAUM *carefully proofread the entire work; and* MRS. JUDI DICK *assisted in compiling sources.*

The entire staff has a share in our service to the community, each in his or her area of responsibility: SHMUEL BLITZ, SHIMON GOLDING, SHEILA TENNENBAUM, *and* AVROHOM BIDERMAN, *of the sales staff;* ELI KROEN, YITZCHAK SAFTLAS, EPHRAIM ROSENSTOCK, YOSEF TIMINSKY, MICHAEL ZIVITZ, SAID KOHAN FOLAD, LEA FREIER, MRS. LIBBY GLUSTEIN, MRS. FAIGIE PERLOWITZ, ESTIE KUSHNER *and* RAIZY BRANDER. *We conclude with gratitude to Hashem Yisborach for His infinite blessings and for the opportunity to have been the quill that records His word. May He guide our work in the future for the benefit of His people.*

Rosh Chodesh Av 5751
Brooklyn, NY

Rabbis Meir Zlotowitz / Nosson Scherman

☙ *An Overview Kinnos: A Trail of Tears — From Tragedy to Triumph!*

I. Tears: The Essence of the Soul

אָמַר ר׳ יוֹחָנָן: אותו הַיּום [שֶׁחָזְרוּ הַמְּרַגְּלִים] עֶרֶב תִּשְׁעָה בְּאָב הָיָה. אָמַר הקב״ה, אַתֶּם בְּכִיתֶם בְּכִיָּה שֶׁל חִנָּם, וַאֲנִי קוֹבֵעַ לָכֶם בְּכִיָּה לְדוֹרוֹת.

Rabbi Yochanan said that this day [when the spies returned and delivered their derogatory report about Eretz Yisrael] was Tishah B'Av eve. The Holy One, Blessed is He, said, 'You wept in vain. I will establish this date for you as a time of real weeping for all generations' (*Taanis* 29a).

Tears are uniquely suited to Tishah B'Av. Special dates in the Jewish calendar have their own tangible means to convey their essence. Rosh Hashanah has its *shofar*, Pesach has its *matzoh*, and so on. The *mitzvah* of Tishah B'Av is tears.

On the afternoon before Tishah B'Av, the *Chasam Sofer* would already be sobbing bitterly in anticipation of this day of misfortune. He collected every tear in a cup, and, when he ate his final meal before the fast, he would dip his bread into his tears and into ashes, as a sign of intense mourning. Thus would he fulfill the verse כִּי אֵפֶר כַּלֶּחֶם אָכָלְתִּי וְשִׁקֻּוַי בִּבְכִי מָסָכְתִּי, *For I have eaten ashes like bread, and mixed my drink with tears* (*Psalms* 102:10).

What is the significance of tears? Real tears, meaningful tears that are shed out of deep and sincere feelings, are the most genuine expression of the essence of the human personality. *Rav Hirsch* describes tears as 'the sweat of the soul.' When man is honestly moved or agitated, he sheds tears.

Maharal (*Netzach Yisrael* ch. 8) explains that when the Jews were redeemed from Egypt, God was actually submitting them to a new process of creation, whereby a new national entity called 'Israel' was being fashioned — a nation whose collective soul would be inextricably bound up with the teachings of the Torah and with the land of the Torah, *Eretz Yisrael*. When the Jewish people accepted the negative reports of the spies, however, they dramatically transformed their essential nature and ripped the Land of Israel out of the core of their being. They didn't merely accept the spies' report intellectually; rather, they shed real tears. Thereby they expressed the depths of their soul's antipathy for *Eretz Yisrael* — and thereby they severed their soul-bond with the Holy Land.

In order to forge a new soul-bond with the holy soil, the same tears that once

dissolved our link to the Land of Israel must now be shed in love and yearning for our homeland. Once our souls are merged with the Land, the return of our bodies will follow.

II: My Soul Weeps in Secret

בְּמִסְתָּרִים תִּבְכֶּה נַפְשִׁי מִפְּנֵי גֵוָה.

My soul shall weep in secrecy for your pride (Jeremiah 13:17).

This teaches that God has a concealed place called מִסְתָּרִים, *secrecy, where He weeps over the pride of Israel that was stripped from them and given to the nations of the world . . . Some say that God weeps over the Divine glory which has been concealed from this world . . .*

But how can we say God weeps; are we not told that עֹז וְחֶדְוָה בִּמְקֹמוֹ, *strength and rejoicing are in His Presence?* (I Chronicles 16:27).

No, this is not a contradiction! On the inside [in secret], God weeps; on the outside, He appears to rejoice (Chagigah 5b).

Perceiving the Real Loss

MAHARAL (NETZACH YISRAEL CHAPTER 9) reveals the location of God's secret hideaway — it is within the soul of every Jew. For the soul is really an aspect of God concealed within man, and that fundamental soul of man cries incessantly over the Destruction of the Temple. The average person is not in touch with his inner soul, with his real self, so he is oblivious to its weeping. The average person is aware only of his external facade, the outer world of the body, where everything appears to be fine and growing better — with abundant '*strength and rejoicing.*'

The chassidic master, Reb Bunim of P'shis'cha, illustrated this concept with a parable of a king who amassed tremendous treasures and hid them in a secret storage room, deep inside his palace. One day the palace caught fire and burned down to the ground. The entire nation and the royal court cried over the loss of the beautiful palace, but the king cried more bitterly than any of them, for he alone knew the true extent of the loss. Only he knew of the enormous hidden treasure that went up in smoke.

Similarly, a person who is out of touch with his inner soul hardly appreciates the spiritual loss suffered with the Temple's destruction.

Rav Elya Lopian זצ״ל illustrated this with the following incident (see *Lev Eliahu I, Shevivei Or* 155):

Rav Moshe Isserles, the *Rama,* wrote in *Toras HaOlah,* that when King Nebuchadnezzar came to destroy the First Temple, the Greek philosopher Plato accompanied him. After the Destruction, Plato met the prophet Jeremiah near the Temple Mount, weeping and wailing bitterly over the Temple ruins. Plato asked him two questions: 1) 'Behold, you are the preeminent sage in Israel, is it befitting a man of your intellectual stature to cry over a building, which is really no more

than a pile of sticks and stones?' 2) 'This building is already in ruins; what good will your tears do now? Why cry over the past?'

Jeremiah responded, 'Plato, as a world-renowned philosopher, you surely have many perplexing questions.'

The Greek recited his long list of complicated problems. Humbly and quietly, Jeremiah solved them all in a few brief sentences. Plato was dumbfounded. 'I can't believe that any mortal man can be so wise!'

Jeremiah pointed sadly to the Temple ruins and said, 'All of this profound wisdom I derived from those "sticks and stones," and that is why I am crying. As for your second question, "Why do I cry over the past," this I cannot tell you because you will not be able to understand the answer.'

Rav Elya Lopian related that Rav Simcha Zissel of Kelm explained Jeremiah's answer. Our tears are not for the past; rather, we cry for the future, because even though all the gateways to heaven were sealed at the time of the *Churban* [Destruction], the gateway of tears always remains open (*Berachos* 32b). Every tear we shed is collected in heaven and contributes to the reconstruction of the next Temple. This concept, which is so simple for any Jew to understand, is beyond the comprehension of a 'rational,' world-renowned Plato.

❧ ❧ ❧

JEREMIAH BEGAN OUR TRAIL of tears twenty-five centuries ago. Since then, tragically, the trail has been enlarged into an expanding stream, a mighty river, a surging torrent — and the tears continue to flow even in our days.

Transcending Sadness

Jeremiah poured all of his tears into *Eichah*, the Book of *Lamentations*, wherein he painfully predicted the travails of his tormented people. In his commentary to the *Rambam*, *Yad Hamelech* asks: The rule is that our Holy Scriptures, the *Tanach*, must be written by a proven prophet while he is under the influence and inspiration of רוּחַ הַקֹּדֶשׁ, *the Divine spirit*. The Talmud (*Shabbos* 30b) clearly teaches, however, that this holy spirit cannot envelop a person while he is in a state of sorrow, because it settles only on a person whose spirit enjoys the ecstasy of performing a *mitzvah*. If so, how could Jeremiah write the Book of *Lamentations* while he was shrouded in mourning?

Yad Hamelech explains that the spirit of prophecy rests upon men of greatness, who demonstrate nobility of character and generosity of spirit. Ordinarily, people who wallow in self-pity and are consumed by their personal woes lead narrow, self-centered lives, and are remote from the qualities of a prophet. Conversely, people who exult in performing God's commandments display a purity of character. But there is another proof of sterling character, one that is valid even in the vale of tears.

Jeremiah was not sad about himself or his plight; his personal situation concerned him not at all. Rather, his tears were over the miserable plight of his fellow Jews, and over the pain of God's Presence, which had been forced into exile. Consequently, Jeremiah's sorrow proved the greatness of his selfless personality, thus making him fit for prophetic inspiration.

III: A Tear Is Never Wasted

Rabbi Eliezer said: Since the day the Temple was destroyed, the heavenly gates of prayer have been shut, as it is written, 'Though I cry out and I plead, He shuts out my prayer' (*Lam.* 3:8); *nevertheless, the gates of tears have not been sealed, as it is written, 'Hear my prayer,* HASHEM, *listen to my outcry, be not mute to my tears'* (*Psalms* 39:13) (*Berachos* 32b).

Power of Tears

THE QUESTION HAS been asked: If the gates of tears are never locked, why did God make them in the first place? The Gerrer Rebbe explained that although *sincere* tears always gain admission above, the gates are needed to shut out *false* tears, which are abominable to God. We might add that although these gates are never locked, they are closed and can be opened only as far as the flow of tears will push them! Indeed, *Yaaros Devash* (II:11) observes that the numerical value of בֶּכִי, *weeping*, equals that of לֵב, *heart*, because tears are meaningful only if they are sincere expressions of the heart. Such tears are truly priceless.

Rav Aryeh Levin of Jerusalem was a man of rare compassion and sensitivity. Once, a distraught, recently widowed woman came to his home and cried uncontrollably. All of his efforts to offer solace were to no avail, until the widow said, 'Rabbi, I will accept your words of consolation on one condition. Please tell me, what happened to all of my tears? I prayed and prayed for my late husband, I recited chapter after chapter of *Tehillim*, and shed thousands upon thousands of tears. My very soul flowed into those tears. Were they all wasted?'

Gently, Rav Aryeh replied, 'After a hundred and twenty years, when you will leave this world and ascend to the heavenly tribunal, you will see how meaningful and precious your tears were. You will discover that God himself gathered them in and counted every single teardrop and treasured it like a priceless gem. And you will discover that, whenever some harsh and evil decree was looming over the Jewish people, one of your tears came and washed the evil away, making it null and void. Even one sincere tear is a source of salvation!'

Hearing, this the woman burst into a fresh flow of tears — not tears of sorrow and grief, but tears of courage and hope.

Sometime later she came back to Reb Aryeh and said, 'Rabbi, you remember what you told me? Please tell me again.'

For the Nation's Sake

THE JEW WHO sheds tears for his personal concerns does so as the external, physical person. Deep inside the secret recesses of his soul, however, the Godly portion within him cries over one thing only, the loss of the Divine Presence, for that is the source of all other tragedies and the underlying reason for Jewish suffering.

Our personal suffering is a direct offshoot of the collective, national suffering of the Jewish people in exile. The Midrash (*Eichah Rabbasi* 1:25, see also *Sanhedrin* 104b) tells of a widow in Rabban Gamliel's neighborhood who would

weep bitterly over her plight. When Rabban Gamliel heard her cries in the night, he would arise and cry over the destruction of the Temple and the Jewish exile. HaRav Mordechai Gifter explains that Rabban Gamliel knew that her personal woes were an outgrowth of Israel's general misfortune. When Israel is delivered collectively, all personal problems will be resolved as well.

For many years, Rabbi Yoel Sirkis, known as the *Bach*, could not arrange for the publication of *Bais Chadash*, his commentary on the *Tur Shulchan Aruch*. Whenever it was about to go to print, an unforeseen circumstance would arise and delay the printing. After many years of frustration, the *Bach* was heartbroken. One midnight, as he grieved over his personal misfortune, he stopped and berated himself: 'How selfish of me to weep over my personal problems when there is a far greater tragedy in the world, the calamity of Israel in Exile!' So he took off his shoes like a mourner and recited *Tikkun Chatzos*, the midnight prayer for the Redemption of Israel.

Eventually, fatigue overcame the *Bach* and he fell asleep. A heavenly voice addressed him in a dream: 'Know that for many years they have been displeased with you in heaven, because you became so engrossed in writing *Bais Chadash* that you neglected the recitation of *Tikkun Chatzos*. As great as Torah study is, one must never lose sight of the plight of the Jewish people. Tonight, for the first time in years, you cried over the collective misery of God and Israel — so you have regained favor in heaven.'

Heart of Our Nation

TODAY'S JERUSALEM IS A magnificent urban complex replete with every type of religious institution necessary for Torah living. With its hundreds upon hundreds of synagogues, *yeshivos, kollelim, mikvaos*, charity funds etc., the rebuilt Jerusalem of our times appears to adequately serve the spiritual needs of her devout citizens. Much impressed by appearances, the casual uninformed observer might well have reason to ask, 'Why do we continue to plead so desperately for Jerusalem to be rebuilt? True, we have no Temple and we cannot sacrifice *korbanos*, but we can hardly say that the holy city still lays in ruins!'

This question can be answered with an analogy to the patient who receives a heart transplant. The patient is up and around and appears to be healthy, but he is filled with anxiety lest his new heart be rejected or malfunction. He is extremely vulnerable to infection, and distressingly susceptible to unexpected, side effects. As advanced as technology may be, the new heart is not his own.

Similarly, the heart of mankind in general and the Jews in particular is the *Beis HaMikdash*, the Holy Temple. In that location, Adam was created and there God breathed life into his nostrils. God continued to pump vitality into mankind through the Temple until it was destroyed. Now, we are still maintained, but it is not the same. We are weak and fragile, susceptible to spiritual and moral contamination and disease. We are easily worn out. The whole system can collapse at any time.

The Temple and the Holy City are the heart of our nation; when they were destroyed we suffered a national cardiac arrest. If we are crippled as a nation, how can any individual be fully healthy? Only when Jerusalem is rebuilt will Israel be healed: As King David said, *The Builder of Jerusalem is* HASHEM*, He will gather in the outcasts of Israel. He is the Healer of the broken-hearted and the One Who binds up their sorrows* (*Psalms* 147:2,3).

IV: Jeremiah the Prophet: Fighting Fire With Tears

Jeremiah cursed the ninth day of Av, Tishah B'Av, the day of his birth (Midrash Iyov).

Every time Jeremiah admonished the Jewish people, they mocked, scorned, and humiliated him (Mishlei Rabbasi 1).

Unbridled Brazenness

JEREMIAH WAS PROBABLY the most unpopular prophet in history. For forty years he fearlessly hammered away at the people of Israel and warned them of God's impending retribution. Everything he said, he said publicly, in the marketplace, for all to hear. The people despised him for his prophecies. He was not just unpopular — he was scorned, hated, threatened, and persecuted. But he was never intimidated or silenced, because he spoke the word of God — and the word of God must be heard.

The one who detested Jeremiah most was King Yehoyakim. The height of King Yehoyakim's brazen defiance is described in chapter 36 of the Book of *Jeremiah*.

In the fourth year of his reign, eighteen years before the *Churban*, God commanded Jeremiah to prepare a scroll upon which he would record God's prediction of the evil that would befall the land during the future *Churban*. Our Rabbis teach that Jeremiah, who was then in prison because of his intrepid prophecies, recorded the basic text of the Book of *Lamentations* (chapters 1,2, and 4). Because he was incarcerated, Jeremiah sent his devoted disciple Baruch ben Neriyah to the king's palace to read this prophetic warning to him. This took place on the eighth day of Kislev while the king was in his winter palace, which was warmed by a roaring fire. One of the king's officers began to read:

'*Alas — she* (Jerusalem) *sits in solitude*!' (*Lam.* 1:1).

'Who cares,' responded Yehoyakim, 'as long as I remain king!'

'*She weeps bitterly in the night*' (ibid. 1:2).

'Who cares,' he shrugged, 'as long as I remain king!'

'*Judah has gone into exile because of suffering*' (ibid. 1:3).

'Who cares! I am still king!'

'*The roads of Zion are in mourning*!' (ibid. 1:4).

'Who cares! I am still king!'

'*Her adversaries have become her ruling monarch*' (ibid. 1:5).

'That I will never accept! I must remain king!' (*Moed Katan* 26a).

Enraged Yehoyakim seized a sharp razor, and cut out every Name of God from the scroll, and then threw God's Names and the holy scroll into the roaring fire — where it burnt until everything turned to ashes.

After the king committed this sacrilege, neither he nor any of his retinue felt any remorse or fear whatsoever. Ordinarily, when a sacred Torah scroll goes up in flames and God's Name is obliterated, it is considered a calamity of the highest order, and one must tear his clothing in mourning, and fast and repent. Not so Yehoyakim and his court; they rejoiced over the conflagration of the Torah.

For this, Yehoyakim was doomed to die a terrible death, with his remains treated

like an animal's carcass, unburied and left to rot in the street. And his subjects, who tolerated his wickedness, were doomed to destruction by sword and fire.

Jeremiah's Mission

GOD TOLD JEREMIAH to take up the prophet's pen once again to rewrite the Book of *Lamentations* to which was now added chapter three, the longest and most tragic chapter of all. It begins: *I am the man who has seen affliction by the rod of His anger* (*Lam.* 3:1).

This was Jeremiah's sorrowful destiny. He saw the destruction looming closer and closer, yet he could do nothing to prevent it, because the people and their leaders refused to listen. He tried with all his might to get the people to cry, because he knew that nothing would extinguish the flame of God's fury like sincere tears of penitence; but their hearts were hardened and not a tear would they shed.

After the destruction of the Temple, Jeremiah resolved to follow the multitude of Jews who were led into captivity. When he found a blood-drenched trail, he knew he was in the right direction. All too soon, he came across dead bodies, severed limbs, and the pitiful corpses of tiny sucklings and babes. When he finally caught up with the captives, he hugged and kissed them, clung to them in warm embrace, and accompanied them all the way to the shores of the Euphrates River, in Babylonia, where he bid them farewell saying, 'I must return to comfort the remnants of Israel who remain on the holy soil.'

When the captives realized that the prophet was leaving them, they burst into tears, 'Our dear father Jeremiah, how can you leave us?' they wept. With deep compassion, Jeremiah responded, 'I hereby bring heaven and earth to testify that I tell you the absolute truth; if only you had cried sincerely but once while you were still in Zion, you never would have been exiled.' With that, Jeremiah turned toward the Holy Land, shedding bitter tears (*Pesikta Rabbasi* 26).

A Cry for All Seasons

THE TEARS OF KINNOS are a never-ending stream. When I began to translate and elucidate the *Kinnos* on the day after Succos, I called my rebbe, HaRav Mordechai Gifter, and asked, 'How can I get into the mood of writing about *Kinnos* just a day after Simchas Torah, while the happy tunes of joy still resonate in my ears and Tishah B'Av is still so far off in the future? Who can think of *Kinnos* now?'

He replied: 'You are mistaken. *Kinnos* are not only for Tishah B'Av, they are for the entire year, except that throughout the year we recite *Kinnos* in a whisper, while on Tishah B'Av we shout them out loud! Whoever neglects *Kinnos* all year long and attempts to start reciting them on Tishah B'Av will not succeed in saying them even then, because he will recite the verses without any feeling and he will become bored. We must cry and mourn over the *Churban* all year long, in every season, and then our *Kinnos* will reach their climax of pain on Tishah B'Av!'

This concept of regular mourning over the *Churban* is codified in the very first chapter of *Shulchan Aruch* (*Orach Chaim* 1:3): *It is proper for every God-fearing person to feel and anguish over the destruction of the Holy Temple.*

The *Sfas Emes* was once asked: 'And what should someone do if he feels no anguish over the *Churban* of the Temple?' The Rebbi replied, 'Then he should be consumed with pain and anguish over his own personal *Churban*. If a Jew doesn't feel real pain over the *Churban*, it shows that his soul is in a wretched, abysmal state!'

True, *kinnos* are for all year round — but when does one begin to develop a feeling for them? On Tishah B'Av. If one truly comprehends and feels the *Kinnos* he recites on this day, he will be inspired to refer back to them throughout the year. For this reason the halachah places special emphasis on understanding the meaning of every word in the *Kinnos*:

> ... the entire congregation should understand them — including the women and children — because women are obligated to hear the *Kinnos* like the men — and undoubtedly we must make certain that the young boys understand (*Tur Shulchan Aruch, Orach Chaim* §559).

V: Tishah B'Av: The Birthday of Mashiach

> כֵּיוָן שֶׁחָרַב בֵּית הַמִּקְדָּשׁ נוֹלַד הַמָּשִׁיחַ.
>
> *From the moment the Temple was destroyed Mashiach was born* (*Midrash Abba Gorion*).
>
> What is the name of the Messiah? Rav Yehudah said in the name of Rav Iva, 'His name is Menachem, as it is written: עַל אֵלֶּה אֲנִי בוֹכִיָּה עֵינִי עֵינִי יֹרְדָה מַּיִם כִּי רָחַק מִמֶּנִּי מְנַחֵם מֵשִׁיב נַפְשִׁי, *Over these things I weep; my eyes run with water because a comforter* (*Menachem*) *to revive my spirit is far from me* (*Lam*. 1:16). ... On the day the Temple was destroyed the Messianic Savior of Israel was born. What is his name? Menachem (comforter) (*Midrash Eichah Rabbasi* 1:57).

No Contradiction

ON TISHAH B'AV we recite over forty *kinnos* expressing our pain and misery over the destruction of our Temple and the exile of the Jewish people. Scores of major Jewish themes are interwoven into the rich and complex tapestry of the *kinnos*, yet one fundamental concept is missing. There is no mention of *Mashiach!* This deletion is particularly puzzling since, according to many Rabbinic sources, *Mashiach's* birthday is on this very day of Tishah B'Av!

Perhaps the solution to this enigma may be found in the Redeemer's identity. He is מָשִׁיחַ בֶּן דָּוִד, *Messiah the son of David*, an extension and an amplification of the life and accomplishments of King David, 'The Sweet Singer of Israel' (see Overview to *ArtScroll Tehillim*). The Psalmist was uniquely able to sing God's praises under even the most adverse circumstances. Indeed, the more David suffered, the more he praised God. The more intense the pain, the more intense the passion, because David extracted the precious nugget of goodness from within every grief.

For David and for the Messiah, his scion, there are no bleak, mournful *kinnos*/lamentations; there are only exultant *mizmorim*/songs. Indeed, this is precisely how *Mashiach* will redeem Israel from her travails, by teaching Jews how to discern the positive, productive forces that are encased within every negative experience. In all of the Scriptures, no one was as afflicted as David. No one was

so misunderstood, no one had so many enemies. Job's suffering was unbearable, but it lasted for a relatively short while. But David's entire life was an endless succession of misfortune.

This is the wondrous secret of *Tehillim*. David cries out in pain, yet songs of joy pour forth from his lips. His words are those of melancholy and despair, yet a spirit of happiness saturates every syllable.

David could cry out, '*Every night my bed I drench, with my tears I soak my couch'* — and still he could exult, '*HASHEM has heard my plea, HASHEM will accept my prayer'* (*Psalms* 6:7,10). There was no contradiction, because David understood that his affliction and his acceptance were one (*Tzidkas HaTzaddik* 129).

To Cope With Heartbreak

ONE OF DAVID'S GREATEST MISFORTUNES was the rebellion of Absalom, his son. Thus, the Sages of the Talmud expound on the verse: מִזְמוֹר לְדָוִד בְּבָרְחוֹ מִפְּנֵי אַבְשָׁלוֹם בְּנוֹ. ה׳ מָה רַבּוּ צָרָי רַבִּים קָמִים עָלָי. *A song of David, as he fled from Absalom his son. HASHEM, how many are my tormentors! The great rise up against me!* (*Psalms* 3:1,2). In view of the tragic circumstances under which this psalm was composed — a revolution led by the son over whom he had doted! — the title 'A **song** of David,' seems to be incongruous. It should have been called a **kinnah/lament**! Said Rabbi Shimon ben Avishalom, this may be likened to a person in debt. Before he pays, he is worried and sad, but after he pays, he rejoices. So too with David. Since God had warned him, '*I will raise up evil against you from out of your own house*' (*II Samuel* 12:11), he was saddened. Perhaps a merciless slave or an illegitimate child would rise up in vengeance, without any mercy. Now that he saw that he was menaced by his own son, who, despite his treachery, indeed hesitated to follow Ahitophel's counsel that he pursue and slaughter his father, David sang in gratitude to God (*Berachos* 7b).

Similarly we read in Psalms how the Psalmist took a different view of the destruction of the Temple. Even in this catastrophe, he found cause to sing.

> מִזְמוֹר לְאָסָף אֱלֹהִים בָּאוּ גוֹיִם בְּנַחֲלָתֶךָ טִמְּאוּ אֶת הֵיכַל קָדְשֶׁךָ שָׂמוּ אֶת יְרוּשָׁלַםִ לְעִיִּים.
>
> *A song of Assaf, O God! The nations have entered into Your estate, they defiled the Sanctuary of Your holiness, they turned Jerusalem into a heap of rubble* (*Psalms* 79:1).

Since this woeful composition describes the Temple's destruction, the *Midrash* asks here too: מִזְמוֹר? קִינָה מִיבָּעֵי לֵהּ׳, *A song? This should be titled a kinnah*!

The *Midrash* answers with a parable. A king once erected a beautiful bridal canopy for his son's nuptials. The son, however, was so stubborn and rude that he infuriated his father. The king stormed into the wedding hall and vented his rage on the gorgeous canopy, ripping it to shreds.

So too did the stubbornness of Israel exceedingly anger God. However, He was merciful, and directed His anger at the stones and beams of the Holy Temple rather than at the Jews themselves. Although the people of Israel were severely punished, only the Temple was destroyed; the nation survived (*Rashi, Kiddushin* 31b).

Clearly, David/Messiah is able to transform every *kinnah* into a *mizmor*, song. Thus, it is impossible to include the concept of the hopeful, optimistic *Mashiach* in the despairing, despondent *kinnos* of Tishah B'Av. Where there is *Mashiach*, there can be no *kinnos!*

Measure for measure, God ordained Tisha B'Av to be a day of total grief. God thundered at the unfaithful generation of the wilderness, 'You utterly betrayed me by accepting the evil reports of the spies. You drowned yourselves in tears of desperation and self-pity as if there was absolutely no possibility for salvation. Therefore, on this very day, you and your descendants shall always be entirely immersed in sorrow and despair. You will be so blinded by tears that you will see no glimmer of hope arising from the messianic future!'

Thus, Jeremiah, the prophet who was born on Tishah B'Av, said: '*Cursed be the day on which I was born, let not the day on which my mother gave birth to me have any blessing*' (*Jeremiah* 20:14). But this very tragedy shall lead us to our ultimate triumph. Because the very fact that for thousands of years Jews the world over have forgotten the woes of the present and plunged themselves into an ocean of tears over a Holy Temple that they and their parents never saw, and lamented over a Holy Land upon which their feet never trod — this is Israel's supreme merit. The very fact that we return to our lament every Tishah B'Av, year after year, shows that we remember what was and lament what was lost, that we *do* have hope and that our faith *is* strong. Thus, as the *Kinnos* end, Jeremiah's accursed birthday is transformed into *Mashiach's* blessed birthday. Once again the *kinnah* is exchanged for a *mizmor*.

Therefore, the halachah reminds us that in certain ways Tishah B'Av is actually considered a מוֹעֵד, *holiday*, and we are enjoined from reciting the *Tachanun* supplication to demonstrate that our spirits have not been entirely crushed by this day of mourning (see *Shulchan Aruch*, *Orach Chaim* 559:4,5). Indeed, we even conclude every *kinnah* on an upbeat note of נֶחָמָה, *consolation*, to demonstrate that in the merit of these bitter, heart-rending lamentations we *do* have confidence in the redemption that lies ahead!

VI: Rabbi Elazar HaKalir: A Balm for Burning Eyes

Master Paytan

PIYUT, LITURGICAL POETRY, has been a hallowed and time-honored component of our prayer service for many centuries. Rabbi Elazar HaKalir is universally accepted as 'the Father of the *Paytanim*' [liturgical poets], having achieved an unsurpassed degree of excellence in language and style, combined with a superior level of Torah scholarship.

Magen Avraham (*Orach Chaim* 68:1) quotes *Shibbolei Haleket* who writes: 'I heard from my father who heard from his teachers that when the Kalir composed the piyut "And the fiery angels face the celestial Throne," a heavenly fire encircled him. This is what my father heard from his teachers. Indeed, Rabbi Shimon HaGadol, who was a miracle-worker, would recite that *piyut* every day.'

THE GREATEST MYSTERY surrounding the Kalir is his identity. Who was this awesome person? When and where did he live?

Who Was He?

Some scholars claim that the Kalir lived in the era of *Rav Saadya Gaon* (882-942 C.E.). Another school of thought, based on the Midrash and the Pesikta, maintains that the Kalir was a Tannaitic scholar who lived in *Eretz Yisrael*. Indeed the *Tosafos* (*Chagigah* 13a s.v. *Veragli*) and *Rabbeinu Asher* (*Berachos* 3:21) cite an opinion that the Kalir was no less than the renowned Tanna, Rabbi Elazar the son of Rabbi Shimon bar Yochai, who studied Torah in a cave for thirteen years, during which the Kabbalistic mysteries of the holy *Zohar* were revealed to them.

What is the meaning of the name *Kalir*? There are various opinions. I would humbly suggest the word *Kalir* is derived from קִילוֹרִין [*killorin,*] which means 'a balm for the eyes' (see *Shabbos* 108b and *Yalkut Shimoni, Tehillim* §675). Incessant weeping and bitter tears had burned and reddened the eyes of the Jewish people. Rabbi Elazar the Kalir composed his beautiful, soul-stirring poems in order to soothe and cool the feverish eyes and hearts of his suffering brethren.

The World Survives

THE TALMUD (SHABBOS 33B) relates that when the Roman government condemned Rabbi Shimon to death, he and his son Rabbi Elazar fled and hid in a cave for twelve years. When they emerged they were on such a lofty spiritual plane that they couldn't tolerate common folk pursuing such mundane endeavors as plowing a field. 'How can people ignore the Eternal World and pursue this world?' Everyone upon whom they focused their eyes critically was immediately consumed by fire.

A Heavenly voice thundered at them, 'Did you leave the cave in order to destroy My world?'

They returned to the cave for one more year. When they emerged a second time, Rabbi Elazar remained as zealous as ever, and his eyes continued to set things afire, while his father Rabbi Shimon had mellowed, and his eyes healed and restored everything that his son's eyes had destroyed.

The Talmud does not tell us the outcome. Perhaps Rabbi Elazar finally calmed his seething emotions and soothed his fiery eyes by composing the *piyutim*, *selichos*, and *Kinnos* that expressed the passion and feelings of his great soul.

Generations upon generations of Jews have found an expression of their innermost spiritual pain and yearning in these *Kinnos* composed by those who expanded upon the original elegies and dirges of Jeremiah the Prophet. Surely the Holy One, Blessed is He, listens carefully as He collects and cherishes our tears. Surely the treasury of tears has already been filled to overflowing by countless years of Jewish suffering. Surely the time has come to call a halt to the flow of tears and to replace our weeping with laughter.

May the tears we shed this Tishah B'Av be the last tears for all time, and may we witness the fulfillment of the Talmudic blessing: כָּל הַמִּתְאַבֵּל עַל יְרוּשָׁלַיִם זוֹכֶה וְרוֹאֶה בְּשִׂמְחָתָהּ, *Whoever mourns over Jerusalem is deserving to witness her joy!* (*Taanis* 30b).

Rabbi Avrohom Chaim Feuer
Miami Beach, Florida
17 Tammuz 5751

Prologue

The All-Encompassing Aleph-Beis: From Aleph to Tav, and Back Again

(based on The Wisdom in the Hebrew Alphabet, by Rabbi Michael L. Munk)

In Jewish thought, the *Aleph-Beis* is unlike any other alphabet; it is not merely a haphazard collection of consonants whose order was determined by convention, but that could have been — or still could be — changed without loss of content. The individual letters, their names, graphic forms, *gematrios* [numerical equivalents], and respective positions in the *Aleph-Beis* are Divinely ordained. [See Overview of ArtScroll's *The Wisdom in the Hebrew Alphabet* for a discussion of the Divine forces represented by the letters and their various combinations.] A corollary of this principle is the halachic requirement that every letter in a Torah scroll, *mezuzah*, and *tefillin* must be written perfectly. No part of a letter may be omitted or distorted, nor may its individual integrity be compromised by contact with any other letter. Every word must be spelled correctly; a missing, extra, transposed, or blemished letter can invalidate the entire scroll.

In Scripture, as in our prayers and *kinnos*, we often find verses or phrases progressing through the Hebrew alphabet from *aleph* to *tav*; conversely, there are passages that reverse the order, beginning with *tav* and going back to *aleph*. What is the significance of these letter progressions?

Aleph to Tav: Completion

IN THE POPULAR IDIOM, something that is expressed or analyzed in its entirety is said to be covered מֵאָלֶף וְעַד תָּיו, *from aleph to tav*. Since the very order of the letters represents profound halachic and philosophic concepts, this expression is far more encompassing than the idiomatic 'from A to Z' or from '*alpha* to *omega*.'

The use of an alphabetical sequence to praise God, or describe a person or concept, denotes totality and perfection. For example, the passage of אֵשֶׁת חַיִל, *An Accomplished Woman* (*Proverbs* 31:10-31), describes in twenty-two alphabetically arranged verses the entire range of the woman's virtues in following the ways of Torah, the very Torah that was translated into human expression by means of these same twenty-two letters.

Complete Blessing and Tempered Curse

THE DEFINITE ARTICLE *the* is expressed in Hebrew by prefixing the letter ה to a word. Often, for extra emphasis, the word אֶת (or אֵת) is employed in addition to the prefix. Because it is spelled with the first and last letters of the *Aleph-Beis*, אֶת alludes to completion and perfection. Thus the Torah uses this emphatic article in describing the beginning of Creation: בְּרֵאשִׁית בָּרָא אֱלֹהִים אֵת הַשָּׁמַיִם וְאֵת הָאָרֶץ, *In the beginning of God's creating the heavens and*

the earth (*Genesis* 1:1). This usage indicates that the universe was created in complete perfection, 'from *aleph* to *tav*.'

The detailed blessings promised those who observe the entire Torah begin with the א of **אם** [*If you follow My decrees. . .*] (*Leviticus* 26:3) and end with the ת of **קוֹמְמִיּוּת**, (*upright* ibid. v. 13). This indicates that the commandments are as perfect as the universe in which they are to be fulfilled (*Maharal, Netzach*), and that the blessings bestowed as a reward for *mitzvah* observance are complete and all-encompassing.

Consolation Amid Tragedy

IN A LESS HAPPY USE, alphabetic acrostics are employed to symbolize totality of destruction and transgression. In the period before the destruction of the First Temple when Israel no longer deserved blessings, the prophet Jeremiah composed the Book of *Eichah* [*Lamentations*], which contains a series of lamentations. Its verses begin, respectively, with the twenty-two letters of the *Aleph-Beis*, in order to indicate that God's *full* fury was unleashed against the people of Israel, because "they transgressed the Torah, which was given them with the twenty-two letters" (*Sanhedrin* 104a).

But there is consolation even amid tragedy. Although the Temple has not been rebuilt, the Torah, symbolizing the completion and perfection of the full *Aleph-Beis*, remains the legacy of Israel. The month of tragedy, is called **מְנַחֵם אָב**, or *consolation of the Aleph-Beis* (*Kotzker*).

The Universal Cycle of Return: From Tav to Aleph

THE ENTIRE ALEPH-BEIS is a single unit in which all the letters are interrelated. Just as every part of the universe was created by God and is totally dependent on His mercy at all times, so too the *aleph* — symbol of God's uniqueness and primacy — is the root and leader of all the sacred letters. The letters can be compared to a flame; though tongues and sparks of fire spring out in many directions, they all originate from and are part of the same flame, because all forces emanate from the One God and are connected by an underlying unity.

Accordingly, Kabbalistic literature teaches that the *Aleph-Beis* — representing all Divine forces — does not culminate with the *tav*, but turns around to reunite again with the *aleph*, which symbolizes the **יְחִידוֹ שֶׁל עוֹלָם**, *the Unique One of the universe*, Who is **אֵין סוֹף**, *Infinite*. Having attained the level of *aleph* to *tav* by making his way to completion, one has not completed his task. The achievement has elevated him, given him new insights. From the vantage point of his *tav*, one looks back at his previous insights — and begins anew — because he now sees the *aleph*, the very beginning, with new eyes. He begins again, because the ladder climaxing in the *tav* has given him a new perspective on the *aleph*, which in turn leads him to ever higher levels of perfection as he ascends from letter to letter, from teaching to teaching, from aspiration to aspiration.

The Spiritual Cycle in the Universe

THE FORCE THAT DRAWS the holy letters back to the *aleph* reflects the spiritual cycle of the universe. At the beginning of Creation, nothing stood in opposition to the will of God. Heaven and earth, from the mightiest galaxies to the tiniest microbe, reflected only His will. They existed as testimony to the revelation of His Oneness. But this sublime era ceased with the creation of man. Only man has free will. Only he can accept powers other than the Divine; only he can disobey God's will. Adam and Eve did so when they let the serpent entice them into eating from the forbidden fruit in the Garden of Eden. Ever since, sin has been part of man's nature, with the result that God's Oneness is concealed [הֶסְתֵּר יחודו]. But man's aberration is not permanent; eventually the cycle will return to its starting point, when — in Messianic times — Hashem will be acknowledged by all mankind as the exclusive and absolute Ruler (*R' Moshe Chaim Luzatto*).

Every individual human being is challenged in his own life to make a spiritual cycle that will return him to his lofty origin. Thus, the cycle of striving for the *tav* and then of reinvigorating one's personal *aleph* is the mission of mankind as a whole and of every individual Jew.

The Continuous Cycle of Generations

KING SOLOMON DERIVES FROM the cycles in the universe an allegoric illustration of man's fate, which can change from darkness to light. In the words *the sun rises and the sun sets* (*Koheles* 1:5), Solomon expresses the idea of continuity. Before the 'sun' of a righteous man sets, Providence causes the sun of another righteous man to rise. Before the sun of Moses set, God caused the sun of Joshua to rise. Before Sarah's sun set, Rebeccah's rose. On the day R' Akiva died, R' Yehudah HaNassi was born. And so, on and on, generations perish and new generations are born.

Jewish history is filled with the recurring phenomenon that periods of darkness and oppression are followed by periods of light and relief. In the midst of the Egyptian exile and slavery, Pharaoh learned from his astrologers of the imminent birth of Israel's redeemer. The king tried to prevent Moses' emergence by ordering the murder of all newborn males, but in that tragic hour of Israel's history, Moses was born (*Rashi, Exodus* 1:16). Divine Providence decreed that Israel's first redeemer — the very person the Egyptian ruler wanted to annihilate — was saved by Pharaoh's own daughter and raised in the royal palace. Indeed, light emerged from darkness!

Divine Providence has assured Israel that the greater the affliction, the closer and surer the redemption (*Sotah* 11a). Thus on the darkest day of the year, Tishah B'Av [the Ninth of Av], when the Jew mourns the destruction of both Holy Temples, he is consoled by the knowledge that the Messiah will be born on this very day, and Tishah B'Av will eventually become a joyous festival (*Midrash Abba Gurion*).

Imrei Emes finds an allusion to this thought in the fact that Tishah B'Av always falls on the same day of the week as the first day of the preceding Pesach. This indicates that the day inaugurating the redemption (from Egypt) also marks its end (the destruction of the Temple). However, in the life-cycle of Israel, as well as in the letter-cycle of the *Aleph-Beis*, 'the beginning is anchored in the end and

the end in its beginning.' Thus our Sages assure us that Tishah B'Av contains in itself the spark of the final redemption, although we cannot see it in the present darkness.

This change from pain to joy is anticipated in *Eichah* (1:15), which calls the Ninth of Av a מוֹעֵד, *festival*. Hence, even during the exile, on that day Jews do not recite *Tachanun*, the weekday plea for salvation (*Orach Chaim* 559:4).

Even the stones that were retrieved from the debris of *Eretz Yisrael's* destruction and transported to Babylonia to erect new houses of worship and study will complete the cycle of Divine Providence. The synagogues and study halls of Babylonia — and, by extension, of Israel's every sojourn during the long exile — will, in the future, be established in *Eretz Yisrael (Megillah* 29a). *Maharsha* explains that the Third Temple will be as large as the entire city of Jerusalem because it will have to accommodate all the Jews returning from the Diaspora. For this purpose their synagogues and study halls will accompany them on their return to the land. These edifices will become merged with the Temple so that their combined area will cover the whole city. Thus we may conclude that spiritual intentions are never lost; they transcend all destruction and become the foundation of future redemptions.

The Celestial Order of the Holy Letters and Man's Aspiration for It

IN THE TIMELESS REALM before Creation, the letters existed in a sequence opposite that of the *Aleph-Beis*. They began with *tav* and proceeded in the backward order of ת,ש,ר,ק and so on, concluding with *aleph*. Those letters represented the pure Divine Spirit of the Almighty and were engraved with flaming fire in the כֶּתֶר, *Crown* of God (*Sefer Yetzirah*).

When the Almighty intended to create the world through the Divine letters, He did so in the order of ...ת,ש,ר,ק. Accordingly, the Midrash (*Yalkut* 1:1) relates: When the letters descended from the Crown of the Almighty and appeared before Him in order, each one to plead that the world should be created with it, the procession began with *tav* and continued until the plea of the *beis* was accepted.

א״ב for Mercy; תשר״ק for Judgment

THE ONLY DIVINE NAME FOUND in the first chapter of *Genesis* is אֱלֹהִים, *God [of Judgment*]. This teaches us that God intended the universe to be ruled by the scales of justice. Then He tempered Justice with Mercy, and this new process was indicated by the Torah in *Genesis* 2:4, where it begins to refer to God as ה׳ אֱלֹהִים, combining His Name of Mercy [י־ה־ו־ה] with His Name of Judgment [אֱלֹהִים].

The Midrash compares this to a king who wanted a warm drink, but had only very expensive and delicate stemware. The king thought, 'If I pour in the hot water first, the thin glass will expand and crack. But if I pour in the cold water first, the thin glass will contract and snap.' So he mixed the hot water with the cold and filled his glass with the warm water.

Similarly, God said, 'If I create the world on the basis of Divine Mercy alone (represented by the Name *Hashem)*, its sins will abound; on the basis of Divine

Judgment alone *[Elohim]*, it cannot endure. Therefore, I will create it on the basis of both Judgment and Mercy, and may it then stand!' Hence, the combined expression: Hashem, Elohim.

Thus, in telling of the Creation of the universe as a whole, Elohim is used and heaven is mentioned first, for, indeed, only the celestial beings can endure governance by Justice alone. But when man entered the scene, 'earth' is mentioned first and the added use of Hashem signifies that His justice must be tempered with mercy (*Kli Yakar*).

The association of Mercy with Judgment at the creation of mankind did not effect the *essence* of the celestial letters. What changed was the *order* of the letters. By reversing their order — to begin with an *aleph* instead of *tav* — God mercifully indicated that the scheme of Creation was not intended to include only the celestial beings but was planned especially for the sake of man (*Maharal*).

The *Aleph-Beis* is a ladder and a link. It binds us to the spiritual origin of creation and life. It enables us to aspire to heights and to infuse all areas of existence with the celestial summit. It illuminates us with renewed aspiration for new life and redemption. It teaches us to pull ourselves from the *alpeh* of potential life to the *tav* of achievement — and then to begin again to attain ever new levels of accomplishment until our aspirations for the Messianic times will be fulfilled.

◆§ Erev Tishah B'Av

The laws regarding Tishah B'Av and Erev Tishah B'Av appear in a separate section at the end of this volume. Some of the main points are:

- Although the fast does not begin until sundown, the mourning of Tishah B'Av is manifested in many laws and customs that are observed during the afternoon before the fast. The last meal before the fast — the *se'udah hamafsekes* — is governed by many restrictions that limit the types of foods that may be eaten and the beverages that may be drunk (see Laws §5-16). Therefore, it is customary to eat a full meal before *Minchah* to prepare oneself for the fast, and to eat the *se'udah hamafsekes* after *Minchah*. That final meal customarily consists of bread, some of which is dipped in ashes, and a hard-boiled egg. One sits on the ground while eating this meal. Regarding food after the *se'udah hamafsekes*, see Laws §17-20.
- It is also customary to restrict one's learning on the afternoon before the fast to sad subject matter, i.e. laws pertaining to Tishah B'Av and mourning, and matters relevant to the destruction of the Holy Temple. See Laws §2. Regarding learning on Tishah B'Av or its eve when they fall on a Sabbath, see Laws §29. Concerning the *se'udah hamafsekes* in such a case, see Laws §23-24.
- Just before sunset, one must remove his leather shoes for the duration of Tishah B'Av, and commence the fast. If *Maariv* is recited before sundown, the shoes must be removed before *Barchu*. If Tishah B'Av or its eve fall on the Sabbath, the congregants remove their shoes after *Barchu*, but the *chazzan* recites the formula בָּרוּךְ הַמַּבְדִּיל בֵּין קוֹדֶשׁ לְחוֹל, and removes his shoes before *Barchu*. For a short summary of activities that are prohibited because of the fast day aspect of Tishah B'Av, see Laws §31-41.
- The *Paroches* (Curtain) is removed from the Ark before *Maariv* and not replaced until *Minchah* (see p. 406).

FOR LAWS PERTAINING TO THE EVE OF TISHAH B'AV, SEE PAGE 1.

מעריב

On Saturday night the *chazzan* recites the following before *Maariv:*

בָּרוּךְ הַמַּבְדִּיל בֵּין קֹדֶשׁ לְחוֹל.

He then removes his shoes.

Congregation, then *chazzan:*

וְהוּא רַחוּם יְכַפֵּר עָוֹן וְלֹא יַשְׁחִית, וְהִרְבָּה לְהָשִׁיב אַפּוֹ, וְלֹא יָעִיר כָּל חֲמָתוֹ.[1] יהוה הוֹשִׁיעָה, הַמֶּלֶךְ יַעֲנֵנוּ בְיוֹם קָרְאֵנוּ.[2]

In some congregations the *chazzan* chants a melody during his recitation of בָּרְכוּ, so that the congregation can then recite יִתְבָּרַךְ.

Chazzan bows at בָּרְכוּ and straightens up at ה׳.

בָּרְכוּ אֶת יהוה הַמְּבֹרָךְ.

Congregation, followed by *chazzan,* responds, bowing at בָּרוּךְ and straightening up at ה׳.

בָּרוּךְ יהוה הַמְּבֹרָךְ לְעוֹלָם וָעֶד.

יִתְבָּרַךְ וְיִשְׁתַּבַּח וְיִתְפָּאַר וְיִתְרוֹמַם וְיִתְנַשֵּׂא שְׁמוֹ שֶׁל מֶלֶךְ מַלְכֵי הַמְּלָכִים, הַקָּדוֹשׁ בָּרוּךְ הוּא. שֶׁהוּא רִאשׁוֹן וְהוּא אַחֲרוֹן, וּמִבַּלְעָדָיו אֵין אֱלֹהִים.[3] סֹלּוּ, לָרֹכֵב בָּעֲרָבוֹת, בְּיָהּ שְׁמוֹ, וְעִלְזוּ לְפָנָיו.[4] וּשְׁמוֹ מְרוֹמָם עַל כָּל בְּרָכָה וּתְהִלָּה.[5] בָּרוּךְ שֵׁם כְּבוֹד מַלְכוּתוֹ לְעוֹלָם וָעֶד. יְהִי שֵׁם יהוה מְבֹרָךְ, מֵעַתָּה וְעַד עוֹלָם.[6]

On Saturday night the congregants remove their shoes at this point.

ברכות קריאת שמע

בָּרוּךְ אַתָּה יהוה אֱלֹהֵינוּ מֶלֶךְ הָעוֹלָם, אֲשֶׁר בִּדְבָרוֹ מַעֲרִיב עֲרָבִים, בְּחָכְמָה פּוֹתֵחַ שְׁעָרִים, וּבִתְבוּנָה מְשַׁנֶּה עִתִּים, וּמַחֲלִיף אֶת הַזְּמַנִּים, וּמְסַדֵּר אֶת הַכּוֹכָבִים בְּמִשְׁמְרוֹתֵיהֶם בָּרָקִיעַ כִּרְצוֹנוֹ. בּוֹרֵא יוֹם וָלָיְלָה, גּוֹלֵל אוֹר מִפְּנֵי חֹשֶׁךְ וְחֹשֶׁךְ מִפְּנֵי אוֹר. וּמַעֲבִיר יוֹם וּמֵבִיא לָיְלָה, וּמַבְדִּיל בֵּין יוֹם וּבֵין לָיְלָה, יהוה צְבָאוֹת שְׁמוֹ. ❖ אֵל חַי וְקַיָּם, תָּמִיד יִמְלוֹךְ עָלֵינוּ, לְעוֹלָם וָעֶד. בָּרוּךְ אַתָּה יהוה, הַמַּעֲרִיב עֲרָבִים. (Cong. – אָמֵן.)

אַהֲבַת עוֹלָם בֵּית יִשְׂרָאֵל עַמְּךָ אָהָבְתָּ. תּוֹרָה וּמִצְוֹת, חֻקִּים וּמִשְׁפָּטִים, אוֹתָנוּ לִמַּדְתָּ. עַל כֵּן יהוה אֱלֹהֵינוּ, בְּשָׁכְבֵנוּ וּבְקוּמֵנוּ נָשִׂיחַ בְּחֻקֶּיךָ, וְנִשְׂמַח בְּדִבְרֵי

(1) *Psalms* 78:38. (2) 20:10. (3) Cf. *Isaiah* 44:6. (4) *Psalms* 68:5. (5) Cf. *Nehemiah* 9:5. (6) *Psalms* 113.2.

FOR LAWS PERTAINING TO THE EVE OF TISHAH B'AV, SEE PAGE 1.

MAARIV

On Saturday night the *chazzan* recites the following before *Maariv:*

Blessed is He Who separates between holy and secular.

He then removes his shoes.

Congregation, then *chazzan:*

וְהוּא *He, the Merciful One, is forgiving of iniquity and does not destroy. Frequently He withdraws His anger, not arousing His entire rage.[1] HASHEM, save! May the King answer us on the day we call.[2]*

In some congregations the *chazzan* chants a melody during his recitation of *Borchu,* so that the congregation can then recite *'Blessed, praised . . .'*

Chazzan bows at *'Bless'* and straightens up at *'HASHEM.'*

Bless HASHEM, the blessed One.

Congregation, followed by *chazzan,* responds, bowing at *'Blessed'* and straightening up at *'HASHEM.'*

Blessed is HASHEM, the blessed One, for all eternity.

Blessed, praised, glorified, exalted and upraised is the Name of the King Who rules over kings — the Holy One, Blessed is He. For He is the First and He is the Last and aside from Him there is no god.[3] Extol Him — Who rides the highest heavens — with His Name, YAH, and exult before Him.[4] His Name is exalted beyond every blessing and praise.[5] Blessed is the Name of His glorious kingdom for all eternity. Blessed be the Name of HASHEM from this time and forever.[6]

On Saturday night the congregants remove their shoes at this point.

BLESSINGS OF THE SHEMA

בָּרוּךְ *Blessed are You, HASHEM, our God, King of the universe, Who by His word brings on evenings, with wisdom opens gates, with understanding alters periods, changes the seasons, and orders the stars in their heavenly constellations as He wills. He creates day and night, removing light before darkness and darkness before light. He causes day to pass and brings night, and separates between day and night — HASHEM, Master of Legions, is His Name.* Chazzan– *May the living and enduring God continuously reign over us, for all eternity. Blessed are You, HASHEM, Who brings on evenings.* (Cong.– *Amen.)*

אַהֲבַת *With an eternal love have You loved the House of Israel, Your nation. Torah and commandments, decrees and ordinances have You taught us. Therefore HASHEM, our God, upon our retiring and arising, we will discuss Your decrees and we will rejoice with the words*

§ **Laws of Maariv** (see also *Laws* §95-109 for the laws of *Shema*)

The ideal time for *Maariv* is after dark. However, if one recited *Maariv* earlier he must repeat the three chapters of *Shema* after dark.

As a general rule, no אָמֵן, *Amen,* or other prayer response may be recited between *Borchu* and *Shemoneh Esrei,* but there are exceptions. The main exception is 'between chapters' [בֵּין הַפְּרָקִים] of the *Shema Blessings* — i.e., after each of the blessings, and between the three chapters of *Shema.* At those points, אָמֵן (but not בָּרוּךְ הוּא וּבָרוּךְ שְׁמוֹ) may be said in response to any blessing. Some responses, however, are so important that they are permitted at any point in the *Shema* blessings. They are: (a) In *Kaddish,* אָמֵן יְהֵא שְׁמֵהּ רַבָּא . . . עָלְמַיָּא and the אָמֵן after דַּאֲמִירָן בְּעָלְמָא; and (b) the response to בָּרְכוּ.

No interruptions whatever are permitted during the two verses of שְׁמַע and בָּרוּךְ שֵׁם.

תּוֹרָתֶךָ, וּבְמִצְוֹתֶיךָ לְעוֹלָם וָעֶד. ❖ כִּי הֵם חַיֵּינוּ, וְאֹרֶךְ יָמֵינוּ, וּבָהֶם נֶהְגֶּה יוֹמָם וָלָיְלָה. וְאַהֲבָתְךָ, אַל תָּסִיר מִמֶּנּוּ לְעוֹלָמִים. בָּרוּךְ אַתָּה יהוה, אוֹהֵב עַמּוֹ יִשְׂרָאֵל. (אָמֵן. –Cong.)

שמע

Immediately before its recitation, concentrate on fulfilling the positive commandment of reciting the *Shema* twice daily. It is important to enunciate each word clearly and not to run words together. For this reason, vertical lines have been placed between two words that are prone to be slurred into one and are not separated by a comma or a hyphen. See *Laws* §95-109.

When praying without a *minyan,* begin with the following three-word formula:

אֵל מֶלֶךְ נֶאֱמָן.

Recite the first verse aloud, with the right hand covering the eyes, and concentrate intently upon accepting God's absolute sovereignty.

שְׁמַע | יִשְׂרָאֵל, יהוה | אֱלֹהֵינוּ, יהוה | אֶחָד:

In an undertone – בָּרוּךְ שֵׁם כְּבוֹד מַלְכוּתוֹ לְעוֹלָם וָעֶד.

While reciting the first paragraph (דברים ו:ה-ט), concentrate on accepting the commandment to love God.

וְאָהַבְתָּ אֵת | יהוה | אֱלֹהֶיךָ, בְּכָל־לְבָבְךָ, וּבְכָל־נַפְשְׁךָ, וּבְכָל־מְאֹדֶךָ: וְהָיוּ הַדְּבָרִים הָאֵלֶּה, אֲשֶׁר | אָנֹכִי מְצַוְּךָ הַיּוֹם, עַל־לְבָבֶךָ: וְשִׁנַּנְתָּם לְבָנֶיךָ, וְדִבַּרְתָּ בָּם, בְּשִׁבְתְּךָ בְּבֵיתֶךָ, וּבְלֶכְתְּךָ בַדֶּרֶךְ, וּבְשָׁכְבְּךָ וּבְקוּמֶךָ: וּקְשַׁרְתָּם לְאוֹת | עַל־יָדֶךָ, וְהָיוּ לְטֹטָפֹת בֵּין | עֵינֶיךָ: וּכְתַבְתָּם | עַל־מְזֻזוֹת בֵּיתֶךָ, וּבִשְׁעָרֶיךָ:

While reciting the second paragraph (דברים יא:יג-כא), concentrate on accepting all the commandments and the concept of reward and punishment.

וְהָיָה, אִם־שָׁמֹעַ תִּשְׁמְעוּ אֶל־מִצְוֹתַי, אֲשֶׁר | אָנֹכִי מְצַוֶּה | אֶתְכֶם הַיּוֹם, לְאַהֲבָה אֶת־יהוה | אֱלֹהֵיכֶם וּלְעָבְדוֹ, בְּכָל־לְבַבְכֶם, וּבְכָל־נַפְשְׁכֶם: וְנָתַתִּי מְטַר־אַרְצְכֶם בְּעִתּוֹ, יוֹרֶה וּמַלְקוֹשׁ, וְאָסַפְתָּ דְגָנֶךָ וְתִירֹשְׁךָ וְיִצְהָרֶךָ: וְנָתַתִּי | עֵשֶׂב | בְּשָׂדְךָ לִבְהֶמְתֶּךָ, וְאָכַלְתָּ וְשָׂבָעְתָּ: הִשָּׁמְרוּ לָכֶם, פֶּן־יִפְתֶּה לְבַבְכֶם, וְסַרְתֶּם וַעֲבַדְתֶּם | אֱלֹהִים | אֲחֵרִים, וְהִשְׁתַּחֲוִיתֶם לָהֶם: וְחָרָה | אַף־יהוה בָּכֶם, וְעָצַר | אֶת־הַשָּׁמַיִם, וְלֹא־יִהְיֶה מָטָר, וְהָאֲדָמָה

שְׁמַע / The Shema

The recitation of the three passages of *Shema* is required by the Torah, and one must have in mind that he is about to fulfill this *mitzvah.* Although one should try to concentrate on the meaning of all three passages, he must concentrate at least on the first (שְׁמַע, *Hear . . .*) and the second verses (בָּרוּךְ שֵׁם, *Blessed . . .*) because the recitation of *Shema* represents fulfillment of the paramount commandment of acceptance of God's absolute sovereignty [קַבָּלַת עוֹל מַלְכוּת שָׁמַיִם]. By declaring that God is One, Unique, and Indivisible, we subordinate every facet of our lives to His will.

We have included cantillation symbols *(trop)* for those who recite שְׁמַע as it is read from the Torah. To enable those unfamiliar with *trop* to group the words properly, we inserted commas.

שְׁמַע יִשְׂרָאֵל — *Hear, O Israel.* Although many layers of profound meaning lie in this seminal

of Your Torah and with Your commandments for all eternity. Chazzan– *For they are our life and the length of our days and about them we will meditate day and night. May You not remove Your love from us forever. Blessed are You, HASHEM, Who loves His nation Israel.* (Cong.– *Amen.*)

THE SHEMA

Immediately before its recitation, concentrate on fulfilling the positive commandment of reciting the *Shema* twice daily. It is important to enunciate each word clearly and not to run words together. See *Laws* §95-109.

When praying without a *minyan,* begin with the following three-word formula:

God, trustworthy King.

Recite the first verse aloud, with the right hand covering the eyes, and concentrate intently upon accepting God's absolute sovereignty.

Hear, O Israel: HASHEM is our God, HASHEM, the One and Only.[1]

In an undertone– *Blessed is the Name of His glorious kingdom for all eternity.*

While reciting the first paragraph (*Deuteronomy* 6:5-9), concentrate on accepting the commandment to love God.

וְאָהַבְתָּ *You shall love HASHEM, your God, with all your heart, with all your soul and with all your resources. Let these matters that I command you today be upon your heart. Teach them thoroughly to your children and speak of them while you sit in your home, while you walk on the way, when you retire and when you arise. Bind them as a sign upon your arm and let them be tefillin between your eyes. And write them on the doorposts of your house and upon your gates.*

While reciting the second paragraph (*Deuteronomy* 11:13-21), concentrate on accepting all the commandments and the concept of reward and punishment.

וְהָיָה *And it will come to pass that if you continually hearken to My commandments that I command you today, to love HASHEM, your God, and to serve Him, with all your heart and with all your soul — then I will provide rain for your land in its proper time, the early and late rains, that you may gather in your grain, your wine, and your oil. I will provide grass in your field for your cattle and you will eat and be satisfied. Beware lest your heart be seduced and you turn astray and serve gods of others and bow to them. Then the wrath of HASHEM will blaze against you. He will restrain the heaven so there will be no rain and the ground will*

(1) *Deuteronomy* 6:4.

verse, one should have at least the following points in mind during its recitation:

□ At this point in history, ה׳, HASHEM, is only אֱלֹהֵינוּ, *our God,* for He is not acknowledged universally. Ultimately, however, all will recognize Him as ה׳ אֶחָד, *the One and Only God* (*Rashi; Aruch Hashulchan* 61:4).

□ ה׳ — *HASHEM.* God is the Eternal One, Who was, is, and always will be [הָיָה הֹוֶה וְיִהְיֶה], and He is אָדוֹן, *Master,* of all.

□ אֱלֹהֵינוּ — *Our God.* He is all-Powerful (*Orach Chaim* 5).

אֶחָד — *The One and Only.* This has two connotations: (a) There is no God other than HASHEM (*Rashbam);* and, (b) though we perceive God in many roles — kind, angry, merciful, wise, judging, etc. — they are not contradictory, even though human intelligence does not comprehend their harmony.

While saying אֶחָד, draw out the ח a bit and emphasize the final ד. While drawing out the ח — a letter with the numerical value of eight — bear in mind that God is Master of the earth and the seven heavens. While clearly enunciating the final ד — which has the numerical value of four — bear in mind that God is Master in all four directions, meaning everywhere.

לֹא תִתֵּן אֶת־יְבוּלָהּ, וַאֲבַדְתֶּם | מְהֵרָה מֵעַל הָאָרֶץ הַטֹּבָה | אֲשֶׁר | יהוה נֹתֵן לָכֶם: וְשַׂמְתֶּם | אֶת־דְּבָרַי | אֵלֶּה, עַל־לְבַבְכֶם וְעַל־נַפְשְׁכֶם, וּקְשַׁרְתֶּם | אֹתָם לְאוֹת | עַל־יֶדְכֶם, וְהָיוּ לְטוֹטָפֹת בֵּין | עֵינֵיכֶם: וְלִמַּדְתֶּם | אֹתָם | אֶת־בְּנֵיכֶם, לְדַבֵּר בָּם, בְּשִׁבְתְּךָ בְּבֵיתֶךָ, וּבְלֶכְתְּךָ בַדֶּרֶךְ, וּבְשָׁכְבְּךָ וּבְקוּמֶךָ: וּכְתַבְתָּם | עַל־מְזוּזוֹת בֵּיתֶךָ, וּבִשְׁעָרֶיךָ: לְמַעַן | יִרְבּוּ | יְמֵיכֶם וִימֵי בְנֵיכֶם, עַל הָאֲדָמָה | אֲשֶׁר נִשְׁבַּע | יהוה לַאֲבֹתֵיכֶם לָתֵת לָהֶם, כִּימֵי הַשָּׁמַיִם | עַל־הָאָרֶץ:

במדבר טו:לז-מא

וַיֹּאמֶר | יהוה | אֶל־מֹשֶׁה לֵּאמֹר: דַּבֵּר | אֶל־בְּנֵי | יִשְׂרָאֵל, וְאָמַרְתָּ אֲלֵהֶם, וְעָשׂוּ לָהֶם צִיצִת, עַל־כַּנְפֵי בִגְדֵיהֶם לְדֹרֹתָם, וְנָתְנוּ | עַל־צִיצִת הַכָּנָף, פְּתִיל תְּכֵלֶת: וְהָיָה לָכֶם לְצִיצִת, וּרְאִיתֶם | אֹתוֹ, וּזְכַרְתֶּם | אֶת־כָּל־מִצְוֹת | יהוה, וַעֲשִׂיתֶם | אֹתָם, וְלֹא תָתוּרוּ | אַחֲרֵי לְבַבְכֶם וְאַחֲרֵי | עֵינֵיכֶם, אֲשֶׁר־אַתֶּם זֹנִים | אַחֲרֵיהֶם: לְמַעַן תִּזְכְּרוּ, וַעֲשִׂיתֶם | אֶת־כָּל־מִצְוֹתָי, וִהְיִיתֶם קְדֹשִׁים לֵאלֹהֵיכֶם: אֲנִי יהוה | אֱלֹהֵיכֶם, אֲשֶׁר הוֹצֵאתִי | אֶתְכֶם | מֵאֶרֶץ מִצְרַיִם, לִהְיוֹת לָכֶם לֵאלֹהִים, אֲנִי | יהוה | אֱלֹהֵיכֶם: אֱמֶת —

Concentrate on fulfilling the commandment of remembering the Exodus from Egypt.

Although the word אֱמֶת belongs to the next paragraph, it is appended to the conclusion of the previous one.

– *Chazzan* repeats **יהוה אֱלֹהֵיכֶם אֱמֶת.**

וֶאֱמוּנָה כָּל זֹאת, וְקַיָּם עָלֵינוּ, כִּי הוּא יהוה אֱלֹהֵינוּ וְאֵין זוּלָתוֹ, וַאֲנַחְנוּ יִשְׂרָאֵל עַמּוֹ. הַפּוֹדֵנוּ מִיַּד מְלָכִים, מַלְכֵּנוּ הַגּוֹאֲלֵנוּ מִכַּף כָּל הֶעָרִיצִים. הָאֵל הַנִּפְרָע לָנוּ מִצָּרֵינוּ, וְהַמְּשַׁלֵּם גְּמוּל לְכָל אֹיְבֵי נַפְשֵׁנוּ. הָעֹשֶׂה גְדֹלוֹת עַד אֵין חֵקֶר, וְנִפְלָאוֹת עַד אֵין מִסְפָּר.[1] הַשָּׂם נַפְשֵׁנוּ בַּחַיִּים, וְלֹא נָתַן לַמּוֹט רַגְלֵנוּ.[2] הַמַּדְרִיכֵנוּ עַל בָּמוֹת אוֹיְבֵינוּ, וַיָּרֶם קַרְנֵנוּ עַל כָּל שֹׂנְאֵינוּ. הָעֹשֶׂה לָּנוּ נִסִּים וּנְקָמָה בְּפַרְעֹה, אוֹתוֹת וּמוֹפְתִים בְּאַדְמַת בְּנֵי חָם. הַמַּכֶּה בְעֶבְרָתוֹ כָּל בְּכוֹרֵי מִצְרָיִם, וַיּוֹצֵא אֶת עַמּוֹ יִשְׂרָאֵל מִתּוֹכָם לְחֵרוּת עוֹלָם. הַמַּעֲבִיר בָּנָיו בֵּין גִּזְרֵי יַם סוּף, אֶת רוֹדְפֵיהֶם וְאֶת שׂוֹנְאֵיהֶם בִּתְהוֹמוֹת טִבַּע. וְרָאוּ בָנָיו גְּבוּרָתוֹ, שִׁבְּחוּ וְהוֹדוּ לִשְׁמוֹ. ❖ וּמַלְכוּתוֹ בְּרָצוֹן קִבְּלוּ עֲלֵיהֶם. מֹשֶׁה וּבְנֵי יִשְׂרָאֵל לְךָ עָנוּ שִׁירָה, בְּשִׂמְחָה רַבָּה, וְאָמְרוּ כֻלָּם:

not yield its produce. And you will swiftly be banished from the goodly land which HASHEM *gives you. Place these words of Mine upon your heart and upon your soul; bind them for a sign upon your arm and let them be tefillin between your eyes. Teach them to your children, to discuss them, while you sit in your home, while you walk on the way, when you retire and when you arise. And write them on the doorposts of your house and upon your gates. In order to prolong your days and the days of your children upon the ground that* HASHEM *has sworn to your ancestors to give them, like the days of the heaven on the earth.*

Numbers 15:37-41

וַיֹּאמֶר *And* HASHEM *said to Moses saying: Speak to the Children of Israel and say to them that they are to make themselves tzitzis on the corners of their garments, throughout their generations. And they are to place upon the tzitzis of each corner a thread of techeiles. And it shall constitute tzitzis for you, that you may see it and remember all the commandments of* HASHEM *and perform them; and not explore after your heart and after your eyes after which you stray. So that you may remember and perform all My commandments; and be holy to your God. I am* HASHEM, *your God, Who has removed you from the land of Egypt to be a God to you; I am* HASHEM *your God — it is true —*

Concentrate on fulfilling the commandment of remembering the Exodus from Egypt.

Although the word אֱמֶת, *'it is true,'* belongs to the next paragraph, it is appended to the conclusion of the previous one.

Chazzan repeats: **HASHEM, your God, is true.**

וֶאֱמוּנָה *And faithful is all this, and it is firmly established for us that He is* HASHEM *our God, and there is none but Him, and we are Israel, His nation. He redeems us from the power of kings, our King Who delivers us from the hand of all the cruel tyrants. He is the God Who exacts vengeance for us from our foes and Who brings just retribution upon all enemies of our soul; Who performs great deeds that are beyond comprehension, and wonders beyond number.*[1] *Who set our soul in life and did not allow our foot to falter.*[2] *Who led us upon the heights of our enemies and raised our pride above all who hate us; Who wrought for us miracles and vengeance upon Pharaoh; signs and wonders on the land of the offspring of Ham; Who struck with His anger all the firstborn of Egypt and removed His nation Israel from their midst to eternal freedom; Who brought His children through the split parts of the Sea of Reeds while those who pursued them and hated them He caused to sink into the depths. When His children perceived His power, they lauded and gave grateful praise to His Name.* Chazzan– *And His Kingship they accepted upon themselves willingly. Moses and the Children of Israel raised their voices to You in song with abundant gladness — and said unanimously:*

(1) *Job* 9:10. (2) *Psalms* 66:9.

מִי כָמְכָה בָּאֵלִים יהוה, מִי כָּמְכָה נֶאְדָּר בַּקֹּדֶשׁ, נוֹרָא תְהִלֹּת, עֹשֵׂה פֶלֶא.[1] ❖ מַלְכוּתְךָ רָאוּ בָנֶיךָ בּוֹקֵעַ יָם לִפְנֵי מֹשֶׁה, זֶה אֵלִי[2] עָנוּ וְאָמְרוּ:

יהוה יִמְלֹךְ לְעֹלָם וָעֶד.[3] ❖ וְנֶאֱמַר: כִּי פָדָה יהוה אֶת יַעֲקֹב, וּגְאָלוֹ מִיַּד חָזָק מִמֶּנּוּ.[4] בָּרוּךְ אַתָּה יהוה, גָּאַל יִשְׂרָאֵל.

(Cong. – אָמֵן.)

הַשְׁכִּיבֵנוּ יהוה אֱלֹהֵינוּ לְשָׁלוֹם, וְהַעֲמִידֵנוּ מַלְכֵּנוּ לְחַיִּים, וּפְרוֹשׂ עָלֵינוּ סֻכַּת שְׁלוֹמֶךָ, וְתַקְּנֵנוּ בְּעֵצָה טוֹבָה מִלְּפָנֶיךָ, וְהוֹשִׁיעֵנוּ לְמַעַן שְׁמֶךָ. וְהָגֵן בַּעֲדֵנוּ, וְהָסֵר מֵעָלֵינוּ אוֹיֵב, דֶּבֶר, וְחֶרֶב, וְרָעָב, וְיָגוֹן, וְהָסֵר שָׂטָן מִלְּפָנֵינוּ וּמֵאַחֲרֵינוּ, וּבְצֵל כְּנָפֶיךָ תַּסְתִּירֵנוּ,[5] כִּי אֵל שׁוֹמְרֵנוּ וּמַצִּילֵנוּ אָתָּה, כִּי אֵל מֶלֶךְ חַנּוּן וְרַחוּם אָתָּה.[6] ❖ וּשְׁמוֹר צֵאתֵנוּ וּבוֹאֵנוּ, לְחַיִּים וּלְשָׁלוֹם מֵעַתָּה וְעַד עוֹלָם.[7] בָּרוּךְ אַתָּה יהוה, שׁוֹמֵר עַמּוֹ יִשְׂרָאֵל לָעַד. (Cong. – אָמֵן.)

Some congregations omit the following prayers and continue with Half-*Kaddish* (p. 10).

בָּרוּךְ יהוה לְעוֹלָם, אָמֵן וְאָמֵן.[8] בָּרוּךְ יהוה מִצִּיּוֹן, שֹׁכֵן יְרוּשָׁלָיִם, הַלְלוּיָהּ.[9] בָּרוּךְ יהוה אֱלֹהִים אֱלֹהֵי יִשְׂרָאֵל, עֹשֵׂה נִפְלָאוֹת לְבַדּוֹ. וּבָרוּךְ שֵׁם כְּבוֹדוֹ לְעוֹלָם, וְיִמָּלֵא כְבוֹדוֹ אֶת כָּל הָאָרֶץ, אָמֵן וְאָמֵן.[10] יְהִי כְבוֹד יהוה לְעוֹלָם, יִשְׂמַח יהוה בְּמַעֲשָׂיו.[11] יְהִי שֵׁם יהוה מְבֹרָךְ, מֵעַתָּה וְעַד עוֹלָם.[12] כִּי לֹא יִטֹּשׁ יהוה אֶת עַמּוֹ בַּעֲבוּר שְׁמוֹ הַגָּדוֹל, כִּי הוֹאִיל יהוה לַעֲשׂוֹת אֶתְכֶם לוֹ לְעָם.[13] וַיַּרְא כָּל הָעָם וַיִּפְּלוּ עַל פְּנֵיהֶם, וַיֹּאמְרוּ, יהוה הוּא הָאֱלֹהִים, יהוה הוּא הָאֱלֹהִים.[14] וְהָיָה יהוה לְמֶלֶךְ עַל כָּל הָאָרֶץ, בַּיּוֹם הַהוּא יִהְיֶה יהוה אֶחָד וּשְׁמוֹ אֶחָד.[15] יְהִי חַסְדְּךָ יהוה עָלֵינוּ, כַּאֲשֶׁר יִחַלְנוּ לָךְ.[16] הוֹשִׁיעֵנוּ יהוה אֱלֹהֵינוּ, וְקַבְּצֵנוּ מִן הַגּוֹיִם, לְהוֹדוֹת לְשֵׁם קָדְשֶׁךָ, לְהִשְׁתַּבֵּחַ בִּתְהִלָּתֶךָ.[17] כָּל גּוֹיִם אֲשֶׁר עָשִׂיתָ יָבוֹאוּ וְיִשְׁתַּחֲווּ לְפָנֶיךָ אֲדֹנָי, וִיכַבְּדוּ לִשְׁמֶךָ. כִּי גָדוֹל אַתָּה וְעֹשֵׂה נִפְלָאוֹת, אַתָּה אֱלֹהִים לְבַדֶּךָ.[18] וַאֲנַחְנוּ עַמְּךָ וְצֹאן מַרְעִיתֶךָ, נוֹדֶה לְּךָ לְעוֹלָם, לְדוֹר וָדֹר נְסַפֵּר תְּהִלָּתֶךָ.[19] בָּרוּךְ יהוה בַּיּוֹם. בָּרוּךְ יהוה בַּלָּיְלָה. בָּרוּךְ יהוה בְּשָׁכְבֵנוּ. בָּרוּךְ יהוה בְּקוּמֵנוּ. כִּי בְיָדְךָ נַפְשׁוֹת הַחַיִּים וְהַמֵּתִים. אֲשֶׁר בְּיָדוֹ נֶפֶשׁ כָּל חָי, וְרוּחַ כָּל

מִי כָמֹכָה *Who is like You among the heavenly powers,* HASHEM*! Who is like You, mighty in holiness, too awesome for praise, doing wonders!*[1] Chazzan– *Your children beheld Your majesty, as You split the sea before Moses: 'This is my God!'*[2] *they exclaimed, then they said:*

יהוה *'*HASHEM *shall reign for all eternity!'*[3] Chazzan– *And it is further said: 'For* HASHEM *has redeemed Jacob and delivered him from a power mightier than he.'*[4] *Blessed are You,* HASHEM, *Who redeemed Israel.* (Cong.– *Amen.)*

הַשְׁכִּיבֵנוּ *Lay us down to sleep,* HASHEM *our God, in peace, raise us erect, our King, to life; and spread over us the shelter of Your peace. Set us aright with good counsel from before Your Presence, and save us for Your Name's sake. Shield us, remove from us foe, plague, sword, famine, and woe; and remove spiritual impediment from before us and behind us, and in the shadow of Your wings shelter us*[5] *— for God Who protects and rescues us are You; for God, the Gracious and Compassionate King, are You.*[6] Chazzan– *Safeguard our going and coming, for life and for peace from now to eternity.*[7] *Blessed are You,* HASHEM, *Who protects His people Israel forever.* (Cong.– *Amen.)*

Some congregations omit the following prayers and continue with Half-*Kaddish* (p. 10).

בָּרוּךְ *Blessed is* HASHEM *forever, Amen and Amen.*[8] *Blessed is* HASHEM *from Zion, Who dwells in Jerusalem, Halleluyah!*[9] *Blessed is* HASHEM, *God, the God of Israel, Who alone does wondrous things. Blessed is His glorious Name forever, and may all the earth be filled with His glory, Amen and Amen.*[10] *May the glory of* HASHEM *endure forever, let* HASHEM *rejoice in His works.*[11] *Blessed be the Name of* HASHEM *from this time and forever.*[12] *For* HASHEM *will not cast off His nation for the sake of His Great Name, for* HASHEM *has vowed to make you His own people.*[13] *Then the entire nation saw and fell on their faces and said, '*HASHEM *— only He is God!* HASHEM *— only He is God!'*[14] *Then* HASHEM *will be King over all the world, on that day* HASHEM *will be One and His Name will be One.*[15] *May Your kindness,* HASHEM, *be upon us, just as we awaited You.*[16] *Save us,* HASHEM, *our God, gather us from the nations, to thank Your Holy Name and to glory in Your praise!*[17] *All the nations that You made will come and bow before You, My Lord, and shall glorify Your Name. For You are great and work wonders; You alone, O God.*[18] *Then we, Your nation and the sheep of Your pasture, shall thank You forever; for generation after generation we will relate Your praise.*[19] *Blessed is* HASHEM *by day; Blessed is* HASHEM *by night; Blessed is* HASHEM *when we retire; Blessed is* HASHEM *when we arise. For in Your hand are the souls of the living and the dead. He in Whose hand is the soul of all the living and the spirit of every*

(1) *Exodus* 15:11. (2) 15:2. (3) 15:18. (4) *Jeremiah* 31:10. (5) Cf. *Psalms* 17:8.
(6) Cf. *Nehemiah* 9:31. (7) Cf. *Psalms* 121:8. (8) 89:53. (9) 135:21.
(10) 72:18-19. (11) 104:31. (12) 113:2. (13) *I Samuel* 12:22. (14) *I Kings* 18:39.
(15) *Zechariah* 14:9. (16) *Psalms* 33:22. (17) 106:47. (18) 86:9-10. (19) 79:13.

בְּשַׂר אִישׁ.[1] בְּיָדְךָ אַפְקִיד רוּחִי, פָּדִיתָה אוֹתִי, יהוה אֵל אֱמֶת.[2] אֱלֹהֵינוּ שֶׁבַּשָּׁמַיִם יַחֵד שִׁמְךָ, וְקַיֵּם מַלְכוּתְךָ תָּמִיד, וּמְלוֹךְ עָלֵינוּ לְעוֹלָם וָעֶד.

יִרְאוּ עֵינֵינוּ וְיִשְׂמַח לִבֵּנוּ וְתָגֵל נַפְשֵׁנוּ בִּישׁוּעָתְךָ בֶּאֱמֶת, בֶּאֱמֹר לְצִיּוֹן מָלַךְ אֱלֹהָיִךְ.[3] יהוה מֶלֶךְ,[4] יהוה מָלָךְ,[5] יהוה יִמְלֹךְ לְעֹלָם וָעֶד.[6] ❖כִּי הַמַּלְכוּת שֶׁלְּךָ הִיא, וּלְעוֹלְמֵי עַד תִּמְלוֹךְ בְּכָבוֹד, כִּי אֵין לָנוּ מֶלֶךְ אֶלָּא אָתָּה. בָּרוּךְ אַתָּה יהוה, הַמֶּלֶךְ בִּכְבוֹדוֹ תָּמִיד יִמְלוֹךְ עָלֵינוּ לְעוֹלָם וָעֶד, וְעַל כָּל מַעֲשָׂיו. (.Cong – אָמֵן.)

The *chazzan* recites חֲצִי קַדִּישׁ.

יִתְגַּדַּל וְיִתְקַדַּשׁ שְׁמֵהּ רַבָּא. (.Cong – אָמֵן.) בְּעָלְמָא דִּי בְרָא כִרְעוּתֵהּ, וְיַמְלִיךְ מַלְכוּתֵהּ, בְּחַיֵּיכוֹן וּבְיוֹמֵיכוֹן וּבְחַיֵּי דְכָל בֵּית יִשְׂרָאֵל, בַּעֲגָלָא וּבִזְמַן קָרִיב. וְאִמְרוּ: אָמֵן.

(.Cong – אָמֵן. יְהֵא שְׁמֵהּ רַבָּא מְבָרַךְ לְעָלַם וּלְעָלְמֵי עָלְמַיָּא.)

יְהֵא שְׁמֵהּ רַבָּא מְבָרַךְ לְעָלַם וּלְעָלְמֵי עָלְמַיָּא.

יִתְבָּרַךְ וְיִשְׁתַּבַּח וְיִתְפָּאַר וְיִתְרוֹמַם וְיִתְנַשֵּׂא וְיִתְהַדָּר וְיִתְעַלֶּה וְיִתְהַלָּל שְׁמֵהּ דְּקֻדְשָׁא בְּרִיךְ הוּא (.Cong – בְּרִיךְ הוּא) — לְעֵלָּא מִן כָּל בִּרְכָתָא וְשִׁירָתָא תֻּשְׁבְּחָתָא וְנֶחֱמָתָא, דַּאֲמִירָן בְּעָלְמָא. וְאִמְרוּ: אָמֵן. (.Cong – אָמֵן.)

❧ שמונה עשרה – עמידה ❧

Take three steps backward, then three steps forward. Remain standing with the feet together while reciting *Shemoneh Esrei*. Recite it with quiet devotion and without interruption, verbal or otherwise. Although its recitation should not be audible to others, one must pray loudly enough to hear himself.

אֲדֹנָי שְׂפָתַי תִּפְתָּח, וּפִי יַגִּיד תְּהִלָּתֶךָ.[7]

אבות

Bend the knees at בָּרוּךְ; bow at אַתָּה; straighten up at ה׳.

בָּרוּךְ אַתָּה יהוה אֱלֹהֵינוּ וֵאלֹהֵי אֲבוֹתֵינוּ, אֱלֹהֵי אַבְרָהָם, אֱלֹהֵי יִצְחָק, וֵאלֹהֵי יַעֲקֹב, הָאֵל הַגָּדוֹל הַגִּבּוֹר וְהַנּוֹרָא, אֵל עֶלְיוֹן, גּוֹמֵל חֲסָדִים טוֹבִים וְקוֹנֵה הַכֹּל, וְזוֹכֵר חַסְדֵי אָבוֹת, וּמֵבִיא גוֹאֵל לִבְנֵי בְנֵיהֶם, לְמַעַן שְׁמוֹ בְּאַהֲבָה. מֶלֶךְ עוֹזֵר וּמוֹשִׁיעַ וּמָגֵן.

Bend the knees at בָּרוּךְ; bow at אַתָּה; straighten up at ה׳.

בָּרוּךְ אַתָּה יהוה, מָגֵן אַבְרָהָם.

גבורות

אַתָּה גִּבּוֹר לְעוֹלָם אֲדֹנָי, מְחַיֵּה מֵתִים אַתָּה, רַב לְהוֹשִׁיעַ. מְכַלְכֵּל חַיִּים בְּחֶסֶד, מְחַיֵּה מֵתִים בְּרַחֲמִים רַבִּים,

human being.[1] *In Your hand I shall entrust my spirit, You redeemed me,* HASHEM, *God of truth.*[2] *Our God, Who is in heaven, bring unity to Your Name; establish Your kingdom forever and reign over us for all eternity.*

יִרְאוּ *May our eyes see, our heart rejoice and our soul exult in Your salvation in truth, when Zion is told, 'Your God has reigned!'*[3] HASHEM *reigns,*[4] HASHEM *has reigned,*[5] HASHEM *will reign for all eternity.*[6] Chazzan– *For the kingdom is Yours and for all eternity You will reign in glory, for we have no King but You. Blessed are You,* HASHEM, *the King in His glory — He shall constantly reign over us forever and ever, and over all His creatures.* (Cong.– *Amen.)*

The chazzan recites Half-*Kaddish.*

יִתְגַּדַּל *May His great Name grow exalted and sanctified* (Cong.– *Amen.) in the world that He created as He willed. May He give reign to His kingship in your lifetimes and in your days, and in the lifetimes of the entire Family of Israel, swiftly and soon. Now respond: Amen.*

(Cong.– *Amen. May His great Name be blessed forever and ever.)*

May His great Name be blessed forever and ever.

Blessed, praised, glorified, exalted, extolled, mighty, upraised, and lauded be the Name of the Holy One, Blessed is He (Cong.– *Blessed is He) — beyond any blessing and song, praise and consolation that are uttered in the world. Now respond: Amen.* (Cong.– *Amen.)*

SHEMONEH ESREI – AMIDAH

Take three steps backward, then three steps forward. Remain standing with the feet together while reciting *Shemoneh Esrei.* Recite it with quiet devotion and without interruption, verbal or otherwise. Although its recitation should not be audible to others, one must pray loudly enough to hear himself.

My Lord, open my lips, that my mouth may declare Your praise.[7]

PATRIARCHS

Bend the knees at *'Blessed'*; bow at *'You'*; straighten up at *'HASHEM.'*

בָּרוּךְ *Blessed are You,* HASHEM, *our God and the God of our forefathers, God of Abraham, God of Isaac, and God of Jacob; the great, mighty, and awesome God, the supreme God, Who bestows beneficial kindnesses and creates everything, Who recalls the kindnesses of the Patriarchs and brings a Redeemer to their children's children, for His Name's sake, with love. O King, Helper, Savior, and Shield.*

Bend the knees at *'Blessed'*; bow at *'You'*; straighten up at 'HASHEM.'

Blessed are You, HASHEM, *Shield of Abraham.*

GOD'S MIGHT

אַתָּה *You are eternally mighty, my Lord, the Resuscitator of the dead are You; abundantly able to save. Who sustains the living with kindness, resuscitates the dead with abundant mercy,*

(1) *Job* 12:10. (2) *Psalms* 31:6. (3) Cf. *Isaiah* 52:7. (4) *Psalms* 10:16.
(5) 93:1 et al. (6) *Exodus* 15:18. (7) *Psalms* 51:17.

סוֹמֵךְ נוֹפְלִים, וְרוֹפֵא חוֹלִים, וּמַתִּיר אֲסוּרִים, וּמְקַיֵּם אֱמוּנָתוֹ לִישֵׁנֵי עָפָר. מִי כָמְוֹךָ בַּעַל גְּבוּרוֹת, וּמִי דּוֹמֶה לָּךְ, מֶלֶךְ מֵמִית וּמְחַיֶּה וּמַצְמִיחַ יְשׁוּעָה. וְנֶאֱמָן אַתָּה לְהַחֲיוֹת מֵתִים. בָּרוּךְ אַתָּה יהוה, מְחַיֵּה הַמֵּתִים.

קדושת השם

אַתָּה קָדוֹשׁ וְשִׁמְךָ קָדוֹשׁ, וּקְדוֹשִׁים בְּכָל יוֹם יְהַלְּלְוּךָ סֶּלָה. בָּרוּךְ אַתָּה יהוה, הָאֵל הַקָּדוֹשׁ.

בינה

אַתָּה חוֹנֵן לְאָדָם דַּעַת, וּמְלַמֵּד לֶאֱנוֹשׁ בִּינָה.

After the Sabbath add [if forgotten do not repeat *Shemoneh Esrei.*]

אַתָּה חוֹנַנְתָּנוּ לְמַדַּע תּוֹרָתֶךָ, וַתְּלַמְּדֵנוּ לַעֲשׂוֹת חֻקֵּי רְצוֹנֶךָ וַתַּבְדֵּל יהוה אֱלֹהֵינוּ בֵּין קֹדֶשׁ לְחוֹל בֵּין אוֹר לְחְשֶׁךְ, בֵּין יִשְׂרָאֵל לָעַמִּים בֵּין יוֹם הַשְּׁבִיעִי לְשֵׁשֶׁת יְמֵי הַמַּעֲשֶׂה. אָבִינוּ מַלְכֵּנוּ הָחֵל עָלֵינוּ הַיָּמִים הַבָּאִים לִקְרָאתֵנוּ לְשָׁלוֹם חֲשׂוּכִים מִכָּל חֵטְא וּמְנֻקִּים מִכָּל עָוֹן וּמְדֻבָּקִים בְּיִרְאָתֶךָ. וְ ...

חָנֵּנוּ מֵאִתְּךָ דֵּעָה בִּינָה וְהַשְׂכֵּל. בָּרוּךְ אַתָּה יהוה, חוֹנֵן הַדָּעַת.

תשובה

הֲשִׁיבֵנוּ אָבִינוּ לְתוֹרָתֶךָ, וְקָרְבֵנוּ מַלְכֵּנוּ לַעֲבוֹדָתֶךָ, וְהַחֲזִירֵנוּ בִּתְשׁוּבָה שְׁלֵמָה לְפָנֶיךָ. בָּרוּךְ אַתָּה יהוה, הָרוֹצֶה בִּתְשׁוּבָה.

סליחה

Strike the left side of the chest with the right fist while reciting the words חָטָאנוּ and פָשָׁעְנוּ.

סְלַח לָנוּ אָבִינוּ כִּי חָטָאנוּ, מְחַל לָנוּ מַלְכֵּנוּ כִּי פָשָׁעְנוּ, כִּי מוֹחֵל וְסוֹלֵחַ אָתָּה. בָּרוּךְ אַתָּה יהוה, חַנּוּן הַמַּרְבֶּה לִסְלוֹחַ.

גאולה

רְאֵה בְעָנְיֵנוּ, וְרִיבָה רִיבֵנוּ, וּגְאָלֵנוּ[1] מְהֵרָה לְמַעַן שְׁמֶךָ, כִּי גּוֹאֵל חָזָק אָתָּה. בָּרוּךְ אַתָּה יהוה, גּוֹאֵל יִשְׂרָאֵל.

רפואה

רְפָאֵנוּ יהוה וְנֵרָפֵא, הוֹשִׁיעֵנוּ וְנִוָּשֵׁעָה, כִּי תְהִלָּתֵנוּ אָתָּה,[2]

supports the fallen, heals the sick, releases the confined, and maintains His faith to those asleep in the dust. Who is like You, O Master of mighty deeds, and who is comparable to You, O King Who causes death and restores life and makes salvation sprout! And You are faithful to resuscitate the dead. Blessed are You, HASHEM, *Who resuscitates the dead.*

HOLINESS OF GOD'S NAME

אַתָּה *You are holy and Your Name is holy, and holy ones praise You every day, forever. Blessed are You,* HASHEM, *the holy God.*

INSIGHT

אַתָּה *You graciously endow man with wisdom and teach insight to a frail mortal.*

After the Sabbath add [if forgotten do not repeat *Shemoneh Esrei.*]

אַתָּה *You have graced us with intelligence to study Your Torah and You have taught us to perform the decrees You have willed.* HASHEM, *our God, You have distinguished between the sacred and the secular, between light and darkness, between Israel and the peoples, between the seventh day and the six days of labor. Our Father, our King, begin for us the days approaching us for peace, free from all sin, cleansed from all iniquity and attached to fear of You. And ...*

Endow us graciously from Yourself with wisdom, insight, and discernment. Blessed are You, HASHEM, *gracious Giver of wisdom.*

REPENTANCE

הֲשִׁיבֵנוּ *Bring us back, our Father, to Your Torah, and bring us near, our King, to Your service, and influence us to return in perfect repentance before You. Blessed are You,* HASHEM, *Who desires repentance.*

FORGIVENESS

Strike the left side of the chest with the right fist while reciting the words *'erred'* and *'sinned.'*

סְלַח *Forgive us, our Father, for we have erred; pardon us, our King, for we have willfully sinned; for You pardon and forgive. Blessed are You,* HASHEM, *the gracious One Who pardons abundantly.*

REDEMPTION

רְאֵה *Behold our affliction, take up our grievance, and redeem us*[1] *speedily for Your Name's sake, for You are a powerful Redeemer. Blessed are You,* HASHEM, *Redeemer of Israel.*

HEALTH AND HEALING

רְפָאֵנוּ *Heal us,* HASHEM *— then we will be healed; save us — then we will be saved, for You are our praise.*[2] *Bring*

(1) Cf. *Psalms* 119:153-154. (2) Cf. *Jeremiah* 17:14.

וְהַעֲלֵה רְפוּאָה שְׁלֵמָה לְכָל מַכּוֹתֵינוּ, °°כִּי אֵל מֶלֶךְ רוֹפֵא נֶאֱמָן וְרַחֲמָן אָתָּה. בָּרוּךְ אַתָּה יהוה, רוֹפֵא חוֹלֵי עַמּוֹ יִשְׂרָאֵל.

ברכת השנים

בָּרֵךְ עָלֵינוּ יהוה אֱלֹהֵינוּ אֶת הַשָּׁנָה הַזֹּאת וְאֶת כָּל מִינֵי תְבוּאָתָהּ לְטוֹבָה, וְתֵן בְּרָכָה עַל פְּנֵי הָאֲדָמָה, וְשַׂבְּעֵנוּ מִטּוּבֶךָ, וּבָרֵךְ שְׁנָתֵנוּ כַּשָּׁנִים הַטּוֹבוֹת. בָּרוּךְ אַתָּה יהוה, מְבָרֵךְ הַשָּׁנִים.

קיבוץ גליות

תְּקַע בְּשׁוֹפָר גָּדוֹל לְחֵרוּתֵנוּ, וְשָׂא נֵס לְקַבֵּץ גָּלֻיּוֹתֵינוּ, וְקַבְּצֵנוּ יַחַד מֵאַרְבַּע כַּנְפוֹת הָאָרֶץ.[1] בָּרוּךְ אַתָּה יהוה, מְקַבֵּץ נִדְחֵי עַמּוֹ יִשְׂרָאֵל.

דין

הָשִׁיבָה שׁוֹפְטֵינוּ כְּבָרִאשׁוֹנָה, וְיוֹעֲצֵינוּ כְּבַתְּחִלָּה,[2] וְהָסֵר מִמֶּנּוּ יָגוֹן וַאֲנָחָה, וּמְלוֹךְ עָלֵינוּ אַתָּה יהוה לְבַדְּךָ בְּחֶסֶד וּבְרַחֲמִים, וְצַדְּקֵנוּ בַּמִּשְׁפָּט. בָּרוּךְ אַתָּה יהוה, מֶלֶךְ אוֹהֵב צְדָקָה וּמִשְׁפָּט.

ברכת המינים

וְלַמַּלְשִׁינִים אַל תְּהִי תִקְוָה, וְכָל הָרִשְׁעָה כְּרֶגַע תֹּאבֵד, וְכָל אֹיְבֶיךָ מְהֵרָה יִכָּרֵתוּ, וְהַזֵּדִים מְהֵרָה תְעַקֵּר וּתְשַׁבֵּר וּתְמַגֵּר וְתַכְנִיעַ בִּמְהֵרָה בְיָמֵינוּ. בָּרוּךְ אַתָּה יהוה, שׁוֹבֵר אֹיְבִים וּמַכְנִיעַ זֵדִים.

צדיקים

עַל הַצַּדִּיקִים וְעַל הַחֲסִידִים, וְעַל זִקְנֵי עַמְּךָ בֵּית יִשְׂרָאֵל, וְעַל פְּלֵיטַת סוֹפְרֵיהֶם, וְעַל גֵּרֵי הַצֶּדֶק וְעָלֵינוּ, יֶהֱמוּ רַחֲמֶיךָ יהוה אֱלֹהֵינוּ, וְתֵן שָׂכָר טוֹב לְכָל הַבּוֹטְחִים בְּשִׁמְךָ בֶּאֱמֶת, וְשִׂים חֶלְקֵנוּ עִמָּהֶם לְעוֹלָם, וְלֹא נֵבוֹשׁ כִּי בְךָ בָּטָחְנוּ. בָּרוּךְ אַתָּה יהוה, מִשְׁעָן וּמִבְטָח לַצַּדִּיקִים.

°°At this point one may interject a prayer for one who is ill:

יְהִי רָצוֹן מִלְּפָנֶיךָ יהוה אֱלֹהַי וֵאלֹהֵי אֲבוֹתַי, שֶׁתִּשְׁלַח מְהֵרָה רְפוּאָה שְׁלֵמָה מִן הַשָּׁמַיִם, רְפוּאַת הַנֶּפֶשׁ וּרְפוּאַת הַגּוּף

לַחוֹלֶה—for a male (patient's name) בֶּן (mother's name) בְּתוֹךְ שְׁאָר חוֹלֵי יִשְׂרָאֵל.

לַחוֹלָה—for a female (patient's name) בַּת (mother's name) בְּתוֹךְ שְׁאָר חוֹלֵי יִשְׂרָאֵל.

continue—כִּי אֵל ...

complete recovery for all our ailments, °°for You are God, King, the faithful and compassionate Healer. Blessed are You, HASHEM, Who heals the sick of His people Israel.

YEAR OF PROSPERITY

בָּרֵךְ *Bless on our behalf — O HASHEM, our God — this year and all its kinds of crops for the best, and give a blessing on the face of the earth, and satisfy us from Your bounty, and bless our year like the best years. Blessed are You, HASHEM, Who blesses the years.*

INGATHERING OF EXILES

תְּקַע *Sound the great shofar for our freedom, raise the banner to gather our exiles and gather us together from the four corners of the earth.*[1] *Blessed are You, HASHEM, Who gathers in the dispersed of His people Israel.*

RESTORATION OF JUSTICE

הָשִׁיבָה *Restore our judges as in earliest times and our counselors as at first;*[2] *remove from us sorrow and groan; and reign over us — You, HASHEM, alone — with kindness and compassion, and justify us through judgment. Blessed are You, HASHEM, the King Who loves righteousness and judgment.*

AGAINST HERETICS

וְלַמַּלְשִׁינִים *And for slanderers let there be no hope; and may all wickedness perish in an instant; and may all Your enemies be cut down speedily. May You speedily uproot, smash, cast down, and humble the wanton sinners — speedily in our days. Blessed are You, HASHEM, Who breaks enemies and humbles wanton sinners.*

THE RIGHTEOUS

עַל הַצַּדִּיקִים *On the righteous, on the devout, on the elders of Your people the Family of Israel, on the remnant of their scholars, on the righteous converts and on ourselves — may Your compassion be aroused, HASHEM, our God, and give goodly reward to all who sincerely believe in Your Name. Put our lot with them forever, and we will not feel ashamed, for we trust in You. Blessed are You, HASHEM, Mainstay and Assurance of the righteous.*

°°At this point one may interject a prayer for one who is ill:

May it be Your will, HASHEM, my God, and the God of my forefathers, that You quickly send a complete recovery from heaven, spiritual healing and physical healing to the patient (name) *son/daughter of* (mother's name) *among the other patients of Israel.* Continue: *For You are God ...*

(1) Cf. *Isaiah* 11:12. (2) Cf. 1:26.

בנין ירושלים

וְלִירוּשָׁלַיִם עִירְךָ בְּרַחֲמִים תָּשׁוּב, וְתִשְׁכּוֹן בְּתוֹכָהּ כַּאֲשֶׁר דִּבַּרְתָּ, וּבְנֵה אוֹתָהּ בְּקָרוֹב בְּיָמֵינוּ בִּנְיַן עוֹלָם, וְכִסֵּא דָוִד מְהֵרָה לְתוֹכָהּ תָּכִין. בָּרוּךְ אַתָּה יהוה, בּוֹנֵה יְרוּשָׁלָיִם.

מלכות בית דוד

אֶת צֶמַח דָּוִד עַבְדְּךָ מְהֵרָה תַצְמִיחַ, וְקַרְנוֹ תָּרוּם בִּישׁוּעָתֶךָ, כִּי לִישׁוּעָתְךָ קִוִּינוּ כָּל הַיּוֹם. בָּרוּךְ אַתָּה יהוה, מַצְמִיחַ קֶרֶן יְשׁוּעָה.

קבלת תפלה

שְׁמַע קוֹלֵנוּ יהוה אֱלֹהֵינוּ, חוּס וְרַחֵם עָלֵינוּ, וְקַבֵּל בְּרַחֲמִים וּבְרָצוֹן אֶת תְּפִלָּתֵנוּ, כִּי אֵל שׁוֹמֵעַ תְּפִלּוֹת וְתַחֲנוּנִים אָתָּה. וּמִלְּפָנֶיךָ מַלְכֵּנוּ רֵיקָם אַל תְּשִׁיבֵנוּ, °°כִּי אַתָּה שׁוֹמֵעַ תְּפִלַּת עַמְּךָ יִשְׂרָאֵל בְּרַחֲמִים. בָּרוּךְ אַתָּה יהוה, שׁוֹמֵעַ תְּפִלָּה.

עבודה

רְצֵה יהוה אֱלֹהֵינוּ בְּעַמְּךָ יִשְׂרָאֵל וּבִתְפִלָּתָם, וְהָשֵׁב אֶת הָעֲבוֹדָה לִדְבִיר בֵּיתֶךָ. וְאִשֵּׁי יִשְׂרָאֵל וּתְפִלָּתָם בְּאַהֲבָה תְּקַבֵּל בְּרָצוֹן, וּתְהִי לְרָצוֹן תָּמִיד עֲבוֹדַת יִשְׂרָאֵל עַמֶּךָ.

°°During the silent *Shemoneh Esrei* one may insert either or both of these personal prayers.

For forgiveness:

אָנָּא יהוה, חָטָאתִי עָוִיתִי וּפָשַׁעְתִּי לְפָנֶיךָ, מִיּוֹם הֱיוֹתִי עַל הָאֲדָמָה עַד הַיּוֹם הַזֶּה (וּבִפְרַט בַּחֵטְא ....). אָנָּא יהוה, עֲשֵׂה לְמַעַן שִׁמְךָ הַגָּדוֹל, וּתְכַפֶּר לִי עַל עֲוֹנַי וַחֲטָאַי וּפְשָׁעַי שֶׁחָטָאתִי וְשֶׁעָוִיתִי וְשֶׁפָּשַׁעְתִּי לְפָנֶיךָ, מִנְּעוּרַי עַד הַיּוֹם הַזֶּה. וּתְמַלֵּא כָּל הַשֵּׁמוֹת שֶׁפָּגַמְתִּי בְּשִׁמְךָ הַגָּדוֹל.

For livelihood:

אַתָּה הוּא יהוה הָאֱלֹהִים, הַזָּן וּמְפַרְנֵס וּמְכַלְכֵּל מִקַּרְנֵי רְאֵמִים עַד בֵּיצֵי כִנִּים. הַטְרִיפֵנִי לֶחֶם חֻקִּי, וְהַמְצֵא לִי וּלְכָל בְּנֵי בֵיתִי מְזוֹנוֹתַי קוֹדֶם שֶׁאֶצְטָרֵךְ לָהֶם, בְּנַחַת וְלֹא בְצַעַר, בְּהֶתֵּר וְלֹא בְאִסּוּר, בְּכָבוֹד וְלֹא בְבִזָּיוֹן, לְחַיִּים וּלְשָׁלוֹם, מִשֶּׁפַע בְּרָכָה וְהַצְלָחָה, וּמִשֶּׁפַע בְּרֵכָה עֶלְיוֹנָה, כְּדֵי שֶׁאוּכַל לַעֲשׂוֹת רְצוֹנֶךָ וְלַעֲסוֹק בְּתוֹרָתֶךָ וּלְקַיֵּם מִצְוֹתֶיךָ. וְאַל תַּצְרִיכֵנִי לִידֵי מַתְּנַת בָּשָׂר וָדָם. וִיקֻיַּם בִּי מִקְרָא שֶׁכָּתוּב: פּוֹתֵחַ אֶת יָדֶךָ, וּמַשְׂבִּיעַ לְכָל חַי רָצוֹן.[1] וְכָתוּב: הַשְׁלֵךְ עַל יהוה יְהָבְךָ וְהוּא יְכַלְכְּלֶךָ.[2]

—Continue כִּי אַתָּה . . .

REBUILDING JERUSALEM

וְלִירוּשָׁלַיִם *And to Jerusalem, Your city, may You return in compassion, and may You rest within it, as You have spoken. May You rebuild it soon in our days as an eternal structure, and may You speedily establish the throne of David within it. Blessed are You,* HASHEM, *the Builder of Jerusalem.*

DAVIDIC REIGN

אֶת צֶמַח *The offspring of Your servant David may You speedily cause to flourish, and enhance his pride through Your salvation, for we hope for Your salvation all day long. Blessed are You,* HASHEM, *Who causes the pride of salvation to flourish.*

ACCEPTANCE OF PRAYER

שְׁמַע *Hear our voice,* HASHEM *our God, pity and be compassionate to us, and accept — with compassion and favor — our prayer, for God Who hears prayers and supplications are You. From before Yourself, our King, turn us not away empty-handed,* °° *for You hear the prayer of Your people Israel with compassion. Blessed are You,* HASHEM, *Who hears prayer.*

TEMPLE SERVICE

רְצֵה *Be favorable,* HASHEM, *our God, toward Your people Israel and their prayer and restore the service to the Holy of Holies of Your Temple. The fire-offerings of Israel and their prayer accept with love and favor, and may the service of Your people Israel always be favorable to You.*

°°During the silent *Shemoneh Esrei* one may insert either or both of these personal prayers.

For forgiveness:

אָנָּא *Please, O* HASHEM, *I have erred, been iniquitous, and willfully sinned before You, from the day I have existed on earth until this very day (and especially with the sin of . . .). Please,* HASHEM, *act for the sake of Your Great Name and grant me atonement for my iniquities, my errors, and my willful sins through which I have erred, been iniquitous, and willfully sinned before You, from my youth until this day. And make whole all the Names that I have blemished in Your Great Name.*

For livelihood:

אַתָּה *It is You,* HASHEM *the God, Who nourishes, sustains, and supports, from the horns of re'eimim to the eggs of lice. Provide me with my allotment of bread; and bring forth for me and all members of my household, my food, before I have need for it; in contentment but not in pain, in a permissible but not a forbidden manner, in honor but not in disgrace, for life and for peace; from the flow of blessing and success and from the flow of the Heavenly spring, so that I be enabled to do Your will and engage in Your Torah and fulfill Your commandments. Make me not needful of people's largesse; and may there be fulfilled in me the verse that states, 'You open Your hand and satisfy the desire of every living thing'*[1] *and that states, 'Cast Your burden upon* HASHEM *and He will support you.'*[2]

Continue: *For You hear the prayer . . .*

(1) *Psalms* 145:16. (2) 55:23.

וְתֶחֱזֶינָה עֵינֵינוּ בְּשׁוּבְךָ לְצִיּוֹן בְּרַחֲמִים. בָּרוּךְ אַתָּה יהוה, הַמַּחֲזִיר שְׁכִינָתוֹ לְצִיּוֹן.

הודאה

Bow at מוֹדִים; straighten up at 'ה.

מוֹדִים אֲנַחְנוּ לָךְ שָׁאַתָּה הוּא יהוה אֱלֹהֵינוּ וֵאלֹהֵי אֲבוֹתֵינוּ לְעוֹלָם וָעֶד. צוּר חַיֵּינוּ, מָגֵן יִשְׁעֵנוּ אַתָּה הוּא לְדוֹר וָדוֹר. נוֹדֶה לְּךָ וּנְסַפֵּר תְּהִלָּתֶךָ[1] עַל חַיֵּינוּ הַמְּסוּרִים בְּיָדֶךָ, וְעַל נִשְׁמוֹתֵינוּ הַפְּקוּדוֹת לָךְ, וְעַל נִסֶּיךָ שֶׁבְּכָל יוֹם עִמָּנוּ, וְעַל נִפְלְאוֹתֶיךָ וְטוֹבוֹתֶיךָ שֶׁבְּכָל עֵת, עֶרֶב וָבֹקֶר וְצָהֳרָיִם. הַטּוֹב כִּי לֹא כָלוּ רַחֲמֶיךָ, וְהַמְּרַחֵם כִּי לֹא תַמּוּ חֲסָדֶיךָ,[2] מֵעוֹלָם קִוִּינוּ לָךְ. וְעַל כֻּלָּם יִתְבָּרַךְ וְיִתְרוֹמַם שִׁמְךָ מַלְכֵּנוּ תָּמִיד לְעוֹלָם וָעֶד.

Bend the knees at בָּרוּךְ; bow at אַתָּה; straighten up at 'ה.

וְכֹל הַחַיִּים יוֹדוּךָ סֶּלָה, וִיהַלְלוּ אֶת שִׁמְךָ בֶּאֱמֶת, הָאֵל יְשׁוּעָתֵנוּ וְעֶזְרָתֵנוּ סֶלָה. בָּרוּךְ אַתָּה יהוה, הַטּוֹב שִׁמְךָ וּלְךָ נָאֶה לְהוֹדוֹת.

שלום

שָׁלוֹם רָב עַל יִשְׂרָאֵל עַמְּךָ תָּשִׂים לְעוֹלָם, כִּי אַתָּה הוּא מֶלֶךְ אָדוֹן לְכָל הַשָּׁלוֹם. וְטוֹב בְּעֵינֶיךָ לְבָרֵךְ אֶת עַמְּךָ יִשְׂרָאֵל, בְּכָל עֵת וּבְכָל שָׁעָה בִּשְׁלוֹמֶךָ. בָּרוּךְ אַתָּה יהוה, הַמְּבָרֵךְ אֶת עַמּוֹ יִשְׂרָאֵל בַּשָּׁלוֹם.

יִהְיוּ לְרָצוֹן אִמְרֵי פִי וְהֶגְיוֹן לִבִּי לְפָנֶיךָ, יהוה צוּרִי וְגֹאֲלִי.[3]

אֱלֹהַי, נְצוֹר לְשׁוֹנִי מֵרָע, וּשְׂפָתַי מִדַּבֵּר מִרְמָה,[4] וְלִמְקַלְלַי נַפְשִׁי תִדּוֹם, וְנַפְשִׁי כֶּעָפָר לַכֹּל תִּהְיֶה. פְּתַח לִבִּי בְּתוֹרָתֶךָ, וּבְמִצְוֹתֶיךָ תִּרְדּוֹף נַפְשִׁי. וְכֹל הַחוֹשְׁבִים עָלַי רָעָה, מְהֵרָה הָפֵר עֲצָתָם וְקַלְקֵל מַחֲשַׁבְתָּם. עֲשֵׂה לְמַעַן שְׁמֶךָ, עֲשֵׂה לְמַעַן יְמִינֶךָ, עֲשֵׂה לְמַעַן קְדֻשָּׁתֶךָ, עֲשֵׂה לְמַעַן תּוֹרָתֶךָ. לְמַעַן יֵחָלְצוּן יְדִידֶיךָ, הוֹשִׁיעָה יְמִינְךָ וַעֲנֵנִי.[5]

Some recite verses pertaining to their names here. See page 480.

יִהְיוּ לְרָצוֹן אִמְרֵי פִי וְהֶגְיוֹן לִבִּי לְפָנֶיךָ, יהוה צוּרִי וְגֹאֲלִי.[3]

Bow and take three steps back. Bow left and say . . . עֹשֶׂה; bow right and say . . . הוּא יַעֲשֶׂה; bow forward and say וְעַל כָּל . . . אָמֵן.

עֹשֶׂה שָׁלוֹם בִּמְרוֹמָיו, הוּא יַעֲשֶׂה שָׁלוֹם עָלֵינוּ, וְעַל כָּל יִשְׂרָאֵל. וְאִמְרוּ: אָמֵן.

וְתֶחֱזֶינָה *May our eyes behold Your return to Zion in compassion. Blessed are You, HASHEM, Who restores His Presence to Zion.*

THANKSGIVING [MODIM]

Bow at *'We gratefully thank You'*; straighten up at *'HASHEM.'*

מוֹדִים *We gratefully thank You, for it is You Who are HASHEM, our God and the God of our forefathers for all eternity; Rock of our lives, Shield of our salvation are You from generation to generation. We shall thank You and relate Your praise*[1] *— for our lives, which are committed to Your power and for our souls that are entrusted to You; for Your miracles that are with us every day; and for Your wonders and favors in every season — evening, morning, and afternoon. The Beneficent One, for Your compassions were never exhausted, and the Compassionate One, for Your kindnesses never ended*[2] *— always have we put our hope in You.*

For all these, may Your Name be blessed and exalted, our King, continually forever and ever.

Bend the knees at *'Blessed'*; bow at *'You'*; straighten up at *'HASHEM.'*

Everything alive will gratefully acknowledge You, Selah! and praise Your Name sincerely, O God of our salvation and help, Selah! Blessed are You, HASHEM, Your Name is 'The Beneficent One' and to You it is fitting to give thanks.

PEACE

שָׁלוֹם *Establish abundant peace upon Your people Israel forever, for You are King, Master of all peace. May it be good in Your eyes to bless Your people Israel at every time and every hour with Your peace. Blessed are You, HASHEM, Who blesses His people Israel with peace.*

May the expressions of my mouth and the thoughts of my heart find favor before You, HASHEM, my Rock and my Redeemer.[3]

אֱלֹהַי *My God, guard my tongue from evil and my lips from speaking deceitfully.*[4] *To those who curse me, let my soul be silent; and let my soul be like dust to everyone. Open my heart to Your Torah, then my soul will pursue Your commandments. As for all those who design evil against me, speedily nullify their counsel and disrupt their design. Act for Your Name's sake; act for Your right hand's sake; act for Your sanctity's sake; act for Your Torah's sake. That Your beloved ones may be given rest; let Your right hand save, and respond to me.*[5]

Some recite verses pertaining to their names at this point. See page 480.

May the expressions of my mouth and the thoughts of my heart find favor before You, HASHEM, my Rock and my Redeemer.[3] *He Who makes peace in His heights, may He make peace upon us, and upon all Israel. Now respond: Amen.*

Bow and take three steps back. Bow left and say, *'He Who makes peace . . .'*; bow right and say, *'may He make peace . . .'*; bow forward and say, *'and upon . . . Amen.'*

(1) Cf. *Psalms* 79:13. (2) Cf. *Lam.* 3:22. (3) *Psalms* 19:15. (4) Cf. 34:14. (5) 60:7;108:7.

יְהִי רָצוֹן מִלְּפָנֶיךָ יהוה אֱלֹהֵינוּ וֵאלֹהֵי אֲבוֹתֵינוּ, שֶׁיִּבָּנֶה בֵּית הַמִּקְדָּשׁ בִּמְהֵרָה בְיָמֵינוּ, וְתֵן חֶלְקֵנוּ בְּתוֹרָתֶךָ. וְשָׁם נַעֲבָדְךָ בְּיִרְאָה, כִּימֵי עוֹלָם וּכְשָׁנִים קַדְמוֹנִיּוֹת. וְעָרְבָה לַיהוה מִנְחַת יְהוּדָה וִירוּשָׁלָיִם, כִּימֵי עוֹלָם וּכְשָׁנִים קַדְמוֹנִיּוֹת.[1]

SHEMONEH ESREI ENDS HERE.

Remain standing in place for at least a few moments before taking three steps forward.

קדיש שלם

The *chazzan* recites קַדִּישׁ שָׁלֵם.

יִתְגַּדַּל וְיִתְקַדַּשׁ שְׁמֵהּ רַבָּא. (Cong. – אָמֵן.) בְּעָלְמָא דִּי בְרָא כִרְעוּתֵהּ. וְיַמְלִיךְ מַלְכוּתֵהּ, בְּחַיֵּיכוֹן וּבְיוֹמֵיכוֹן וּבְחַיֵּי דְכָל בֵּית יִשְׂרָאֵל, בַּעֲגָלָא וּבִזְמַן קָרִיב. וְאִמְרוּ: אָמֵן.

(Cong. – אָמֵן. יְהֵא שְׁמֵהּ רַבָּא מְבָרַךְ לְעָלַם וּלְעָלְמֵי עָלְמַיָּא.)

יְהֵא שְׁמֵהּ רַבָּא מְבָרַךְ לְעָלַם וּלְעָלְמֵי עָלְמַיָּא.

יִתְבָּרַךְ וְיִשְׁתַּבַּח וְיִתְפָּאַר וְיִתְרוֹמַם וְיִתְנַשֵּׂא וְיִתְהַדָּר וְיִתְעַלֶּה וְיִתְהַלָּל שְׁמֵהּ דְּקֻדְשָׁא בְּרִיךְ הוּא (Cong. – בְּרִיךְ הוּא) — לְעֵלָּא מִן כָּל בִּרְכָתָא וְשִׁירָתָא תֻּשְׁבְּחָתָא וְנֶחֱמָתָא, דַּאֲמִירָן בְּעָלְמָא. וְאִמְרוּ: אָמֵן. (Cong. – אָמֵן.)

(Cong. – קַבֵּל בְּרַחֲמִים וּבְרָצוֹן אֶת תְּפִלָּתֵנוּ.)

תִּתְקַבֵּל צְלוֹתְהוֹן וּבָעוּתְהוֹן דְּכָל בֵּית יִשְׂרָאֵל קֳדָם אֲבוּהוֹן דִּי בִשְׁמַיָּא. וְאִמְרוּ: אָמֵן. (Cong. – אָמֵן.)

(Cong. – יְהִי שֵׁם יהוה מְבֹרָךְ, מֵעַתָּה וְעַד עוֹלָם.[2])

יְהֵא שְׁלָמָא רַבָּא מִן שְׁמַיָּא, וְחַיִּים עָלֵינוּ וְעַל כָּל יִשְׂרָאֵל. וְאִמְרוּ: אָמֵן. (Cong. – אָמֵן.)

(Cong. – עֶזְרִי מֵעִם יהוה, עֹשֵׂה שָׁמַיִם וָאָרֶץ.[3])

Take three steps back. Bow left and say . . . עֹשֶׂה; bow right and say . . . הוּא; bow forward and say וְעַל כָּל . . . אָמֵן. Remain standing in place for a few moments, then take three steps forward.

עֹשֶׂה שָׁלוֹם בִּמְרוֹמָיו, הוּא יַעֲשֶׂה שָׁלוֹם עָלֵינוּ, וְעַל כָּל יִשְׂרָאֵל. וְאִמְרוּ: אָמֵן. (Cong. – אָמֵן.)

On Saturday night a lit multi-wicked candle or two ordinary candles with flames touching each other are held up and the following blessing is recited.
After the blessing the fingers are held up to the flame to see the reflected light:

בָּרוּךְ אַתָּה יהוה אֱלֹהֵינוּ מֶלֶךְ הָעוֹלָם, בּוֹרֵא מְאוֹרֵי הָאֵשׁ.

יְהִי רָצוֹן *May it be Your will, HASHEM, our God and the God of our forefathers, that the Holy Temple be rebuilt, speedily in our days. Grant us our share in Your Torah, and may we serve You there with reverence, as in days of old and in former years. Then the offering of Judah and Jerusalem will be pleasing to HASHEM, as in days of old and in former years.*[1]

SHEMONEH ESREI ENDS HERE.

Remain standing in place for at least a few moments before taking three steps forward.

FULL KADDISH

The *chazzan* recites the Full *Kaddish.*

יִתְגַּדַּל *May His great Name grow exalted and sanctified* (Cong.– *Amen.*) *in the world that He created as He willed. May He give reign to His kingship in your lifetimes and in your days, and in the lifetimes of the entire Family of Israel, swiftly and soon. Now respond: Amen.*

(Cong.– *Amen. May His great Name be blessed forever and ever.)*

May His great Name be blessed forever and ever.

Blessed, praised, glorified, exalted, extolled, mighty, upraised, and lauded be the Name of the Holy One, Blessed is He (Cong.– *Blessed is He*) — *beyond any blessing and song, praise and consolation that are uttered in the world. Now respond: Amen.* (Cong.– *Amen*.)

(Cong.– *Accept our prayers with mercy and favor.*)

May the prayers and supplications of the entire Family of Israel be accepted before their Father Who is in Heaven. Now respond: Amen. (Cong.– *Amen.*)

(Cong.– *Blessed be the Name of HASHEM, from this time and forever.*[2])

May there be abundant peace from Heaven, and life, upon us and upon all Israel. Now respond: Amen. (Cong.– *Amen.*)

(Cong.– *My help is from HASHEM, Maker of heaven and earth.*[3])

Take three steps back. Bow left and say, *'He Who makes peace . . .';* bow right and say, *'may He . . .';* bow forward and say, *'and upon all Israel . . .'*
Remain standing in place for a few moments, then take three steps forward.

He Who makes peace in His heights, may He make peace upon us, and upon all Israel. Now respond: Amen. (Cong.– *Amen.*)

On Saturday night a lit multi-wicked candle or two ordinary candles with flames touching each other are held up and the following blessing is recited.
After the blessing the fingers are held up to the flame to see the reflected light:

בָּרוּךְ *Blessed are You, HASHEM, our God, King of the universe, Who creates the illuminations of the fire.*

(1) *Malachi* 3:4. (2) *Psalms* 113:2. (3) 121:2.

מגילת איכה

פרק ראשון

א אֵיכָה* | יָשְׁבָה בָדָד* הָעִיר רַבָּתִי עָם הָיְתָה כְּאַלְמָנָה* רַבָּתִי בַגּוֹיִם שָׂרָתִי בַּמְּדִינוֹת הָיְתָה לָמַס: ב בָּכוֹ תִבְכֶּה* בַּלַּיְלָה וְדִמְעָתָהּ עַל לֶחֱיָהּ אֵין־לָהּ מְנַחֵם מִכָּל־אֹהֲבֶיהָ כָּל־רֵעֶיהָ בָּגְדוּ בָהּ הָיוּ לָהּ לְאֹיְבִים: ג גָּלְתָה יְהוּדָה* מֵעֹנִי וּמֵרֹב עֲבֹדָה הִיא יָשְׁבָה בַגּוֹיִם לֹא מָצְאָה מָנוֹחַ כָּל־רֹדְפֶיהָ הִשִּׂיגוּהָ בֵּין הַמְּצָרִים:* ד דַּרְכֵי צִיּוֹן אֲבֵלוֹת מִבְּלִי בָּאֵי מוֹעֵד כָּל־שְׁעָרֶיהָ שׁוֹמֵמִין כֹּהֲנֶיהָ נֶאֱנָחִים בְּתוּלֹתֶיהָ נּוּגוֹת וְהִיא מַר־לָהּ: ה הָיוּ צָרֶיהָ לְרֹאשׁ אֹיְבֶיהָ שָׁלוּ כִּי־יְהוָה הוֹגָהּ עַל־רֹב פְּשָׁעֶיהָ* עוֹלָלֶיהָ הָלְכוּ שְׁבִי* לִפְנֵי־צָר: ו וַיֵּצֵא °מִבַּת־צִיּוֹן כָּל־הֲדָרָהּ הָיוּ שָׂרֶיהָ כְּאַיָּלִים לֹא־מָצְאוּ מִרְעֶה וַיֵּלְכוּ

°מן בת כ׳

[This commentary to *Eichah* has been abridged from that volume in the ArtScroll Tanach Series, by Rabbi Meir Zlotowitz.]

CHAPTER ONE

1. אֵיכָה — *Alas.* The prophet, Jeremiah, wrote סֵפֶר אֵיכָה, the *Book of Lamentations.* This is the Scroll which Yehoyakim burned *on the fire that was in the brazier* [*Jeremiah* 36:23].

[The book laments the fall of the Jews and Jerusalem after the חוּרְבָּן, *Destruction*, of the First Temple. Originally the book consisted of 3 acrostic chapters [1,2 and 4] which Jeremiah rewrote after the burning. He later added chapter 3 consisting of three additional acrostics, as well as chapter 5 (*Rashi; Moed Katan* 26a).

According to *Tzemach David*, the Destruction took place during the reign of King Zedekiah in the year 3338 from Creation [422 B.C.E.]. Judah was then exiled from the Land by Nebuchadnezzar. (The ten tribes had been exiled 133 years earlier.)

For a period of 52 years after the Destruction, Eretz Yisrael lay desolate: the roads and villages were uninhabited; not even cattle or birds inhabited the Land (*Yoma* 54a).

The Exile lasted 70 years until 3408, when Darius, son of Queen Esther and King Ahasuerus, permitted the rebuilding of the Temple. The Destruction of the Second Temple took place in the days of Rabban Yochanan ben Zakkai in the year 3828 (*Tzemach David*).

אֵיכָה יָשְׁבָה בָדָד — *Alas — She sits in solitude!* Three people uttered prophecies using the word אֵיכָה, *Eichah:* Moses, Isaiah, and Jeremiah. . . Rav Levi said: It is comparable to a nation that had three groomsmen: The first beheld her in her happiness; the second beheld her in her infidelity, and the third beheld her in her disgrace. Similarly, Moses beheld the Jews in their glory and happiness, and exclaimed: אֵיכָה אֶשָּׂא לְבַדִּי טָרְחֲכֶם, *How can I alone bear your cumbrance?* (*Deut.* 1:12) [they presented all the difficulties of a large, growing, and flourishing nation]. Isaiah beheld them in their infidelity and exclaimed: אֵיכָה הָיְתָה לְזוֹנָה, *How has the faithful city become a harlot* (*Isaiah* 1:21)? Jeremiah beheld them in their disgrace and said: אֵיכָה יָשְׁבָה בָדָד, *Alas — She sits in solitude!* (*Midrash*).

The Book of *Lamentations* is written in a series of alphabetical acrostics. The *Talmud* notes: Why was Israel smitten with an alphabetical dirge? — Because they transgressed the Torah from *Alef* to *Tav*, i.e., from the first to the last letter of the alphabet (*Sanhedrin* 104b).

יָשְׁבָה בָדָד — *She sits in solitude.* Bereft of her inhabitants (*Rashi*) [*she* — i.e., Jerusalem personified as a woman].

הָיְתָה כְּאַלְמָנָה — *Has become like a widow*. The *Talmud* stresses the prefix כְּ, *as:* Jerusalem's widow-hood was not total, but temporary — she is like a woman whose husband went to a foreign country, but with the intention of returning to her (*Sanhedrin* 104b).

Another interpretation: She *is* a widow — she is bereft of the ten tribes, but not of the tribes of Judah and Benjamin. . . The Rabbis said: She was widowed of *all* the tribes [all the tribes — including Judah and Benjamin were exiled, and Jerusalem was bereft of them] but she was never deserted by God (*Midrash*).

2. בָּכוֹ תִבְכֶּה — *She weeps bitterly* [lit., *weeping she weeps.*] Many interpretations are offered for the use of בָּכוֹ תִבְכֶּה, the double form of the verb בכה, *weep:*

According to the *Talmud*: Why this 'double weeping'? — Once for the First Temple; once for the Second (*Sanhedrin* 104b).

THE BOOK OF EICHAH

CHAPTER ONE

[1] *Alas* — she sits in solitude!* The city that was great with people has become like a widow.* The greatest among nations, the princess among provinces, has become a tributary.* [2] *She weeps bitterly* in the night and her tear is on her cheek. She has no comforter from all her lovers; all her friends have betrayed her, they have become her enemies.* [3] *Judah has gone into exile* because of suffering and harsh toil. She dwelt among the nations, but found no rest; all her pursuers overtook her in narrow straits.** [4] *The roads of Zion are in mourning for lack of festival pilgrims. All her gates are desolate, her priests sigh; her maidens are aggrieved, and she herself is embittered.* [5] *Her adversaries have become her master, her enemies are at ease, for HASHEM has aggrieved her for her abundant transgressions.* Her young children have gone into captivity* before the enemy.* [6] *Gone from the daughter of Zion is all her splendor. Her leaders were like deer that found no pasture, but walked on*

Other explanations of the 'double weeping' are: On account of Judah, and of Zion and Jerusalem; on account of the exile of the ten tribes, and of Judah and Benjamin.

Another interpretation: בָּכוֹ וּתְבַכֶּה, she weeps and makes others weep with her (*Midrash*).

The word בַּלַּיְלָה, *in* the *night*, refers to the *specific* night of Tishah B'Av, which, from the time of the מְרַגְּלִים, spies, has been mournfully observed as a night of weeping and meditation (*Lechem Dim'ah*)...

As the *Talmud* (*Sanhedrin* 104b) relates: When the מְרַגְּלִים (the spies sent by Moses to investigate the land of Canaan) returned with discouraging news, the *people wept that night* (*Numbers* 14:1). That night was the ninth of Av, and God said to Israel: You have wept without cause; therefore will I appoint [this date as a time of] weeping for you in future generations.

3. גָּלְתָה יְהוּדָה — *Judah has gone into exile* — from its land (*Rashi*).

Judah is a general term encompassing both the male and female members of the tribe of Judah (*Ibn Ezra*). [The term *Judah* also includes the tribe of Benjamin who was exiled together with Judah.]

The *Midrash* compares the exile of other nations to that of Israel:

Heathen nations also go into exile, however, since they eat the bread and drink the wine [of their enemies], they do not experience real exile [i.e., they do not experience privation]. For Israel, however, which is forbidden to eat their bread or drink their wine, the exile is real.

בֵּין הַמְּצָרִים — *In narrow straits*, i.e., by cornering them (*Rashi*).

Some understand this literally, but the *Midrash* understands the phrase בֵּין הַמְּצָרִים as *within the days of distress*, i.e., all who pursued her overtook her during the period between the 17th of Tammuz when the first breach in Jerusalem's walls was made and the 9th of Av [exactly 3 weeks later, when the Temple was destroyed].

[This phrase בֵּין הַמְּצָרִים, *within the days of distress*, is used today in halachic literature as well as in common Hebrew usage to refer to the period between the 17th of Tammuz and the 9th of Av.]

5. כִּי־ה׳ הוֹגָהּ עַל־רֹב פְּשָׁעֶיהָ — *For HASHEM has aggrieved her for her abundant transgressions.* The *Midrash*, as interpreted by the commentaries, notes that God's punishment was in direct proportion to Israel's many transgressions. Even הָיוּ צָרֶיהָ לְרֹאשׁ, *her enemies have become her master*, was part of the punishment.

[The word רֹב, *many*, can also mean *majority, most*. Since the phrase is רֹב פְּשָׁעֶיהָ, *her many sins*, instead of כָּל פְּשָׁעֶיהָ, *all of her sins*, it is, perhaps, possible to translate the verse: *for God has aggrieved her for the majority of her transgressions*. In the final analysis, God *was* compassionate, for had He exacted punishment at that time for *all* her transgressions, *no one* would have survived.]

Harav David Cohen points out that *Rambam* in *Hilchos Teshuvah* 2:2 discusses the evaluation of iniquities and merits and concludes: *This valuation takes into account not the number but the magnitude* [i.e., *qualitative rather than quantitative*] *of merits and iniquities. There may be a single merit that outweighs many iniquities... and there may be one iniquity that offsets many merits... God alone makes this evaluation; He alone knows how to set off merit against iniquities.*

עוֹלָלֶיהָ הָלְכוּ שְׁבִי — *Her young children have gone into captivity.* The *Midrash* stresses that the children are the most beloved to God. According to this view, the Sanhedrin went into exile, but the *Shechinah* [God's Presence] did not go into

בְּלֹא־כֹ֖חַ לִפְנֵ֥י רוֹדֵֽף׃* ז זָֽכְרָ֣ה יְרוּשָׁלַ֗͏ִם* יְמֵ֤י עָנְיָהּ֙* וּמְרוּדֶ֔יהָ כֹּ֣ל
מַחֲמֻדֶ֔יהָ אֲשֶׁ֥ר הָי֖וּ מִ֣ימֵי קֶ֑דֶם בִּנְפֹ֧ל עַמָּ֣הּ בְּיַד־צָ֗ר וְאֵ֤ין עוֹזֵר֙ לָ֔הּ
רָא֣וּהָ צָרִ֔ים שָׂחֲק֖וּ עַ֥ל מִשְׁבַּתֶּֽהָ׃ ח חֵ֤טְא חָֽטְאָה֙ יְר֣וּשָׁלַ֔͏ִם עַל־כֵּ֖ן
לְנִידָ֣ה הָיָ֑תָה כָּֽל־מְכַבְּדֶ֤יהָ הִזִּיל֙וּהָ֙ כִּֽי־רָא֣וּ עֶרְוָתָ֔הּ גַּם־הִ֥יא
נֶאֶנְחָ֖ה וַתָּ֥שָׁב אָחֽוֹר׃ ט טֻמְאָתָ֣הּ בְּשׁוּלֶ֗יהָ לֹ֤א זָֽכְרָה֙ אַחֲרִיתָ֔הּ
וַתֵּ֣רֶד פְּלָאִ֔ים אֵ֥ין מְנַחֵ֖ם לָ֑הּ רְאֵ֤ה יהוה֙ אֶת־עָנְיִ֔י כִּ֥י הִגְדִּ֖יל אוֹיֵֽב׃
י יָדוֹ֙ פָּ֣רַשׂ צָ֔ר עַ֖ל כָּל־מַחֲמַדֶּ֑יהָ כִּֽי־רָאֲתָ֤ה גוֹיִם֙ בָּ֣אוּ מִקְדָּשָׁ֔הּ
אֲשֶׁ֣ר צִוִּ֔יתָה לֹא־יָבֹ֥אוּ בַקָּהָ֖ל לָֽךְ׃* יא כָּל־עַמָּ֤הּ נֶאֱנָחִים֙ מְבַקְּשִׁ֣ים
לֶ֔חֶם נָתְנ֧וּ °מַחֲמַדֵּיהֶ֛ם בְּאֹ֖כֶל לְהָשִׁ֣יב נָ֑פֶשׁ רְאֵ֤ה יהוה֙* וְֽהַבִּ֔יטָה כִּ֥י
הָיִ֖יתִי זוֹלֵלָֽה׃ יב ל֣וֹא אֲלֵיכֶם֮ כָּל־עֹ֣בְרֵי דֶ֒רֶךְ֒ הַבִּ֣יטוּ וּרְא֗וּ אִם־יֵ֤שׁ
מַכְאוֹב֙ כְּמַכְאֹבִ֔י אֲשֶׁ֥ר עוֹלַ֖ל לִ֑י אֲשֶׁר֙ הוֹגָ֣ה יהוה בְּי֖וֹם חֲר֥וֹן אַפּֽוֹ׃*
יג מִמָּר֛וֹם שָֽׁלַח־אֵ֥שׁ בְּעַצְמֹתַ֖י* וַיִּרְדֶּ֑נָּה פָּרַ֨שׂ רֶ֤שֶׁת לְרַגְלַי֙ הֱשִׁיבַ֣נִי
אָח֔וֹר נְתָנַ֙נִי֙ שֹֽׁמֵמָ֔ה כָּל־הַיּ֖וֹם דָּוָֽה׃ יד נִשְׂקַד֩ עֹ֨ל פְּשָׁעַ֜י בְּיָד֗וֹ
יִשְׂתָּֽרְג֛וּ* עָל֥וּ עַל־צַוָּארִ֖י הִכְשִׁ֣יל כֹּחִ֑י נְתָנַ֣נִי אֲדֹנָ֔י בִּידֵ֖י לֹא־אוּכַ֥ל
קֽוּם׃ טו סִלָּ֨ה כָל־אַבִּירַ֤י ׀ אֲדֹנָי֙ בְּקִרְבִּ֔י קָרָ֥א עָלַ֛י מוֹעֵ֖ד* לִשְׁבֹּ֣ר
בַּחוּרָ֑י גַּ֚ת דָּרַ֣ךְ אֲדֹנָ֔י לִבְתוּלַ֖ת בַּת־יְהוּדָֽה׃* טז עַל־אֵ֣לֶּה ׀ אֲנִ֣י
בוֹכִיָּ֗ה* עֵינִ֣י ׀ עֵינִ֗י יֹ֣רְדָה מַּ֔יִם כִּֽי־רָחַ֥ק מִמֶּ֛נִּי מְנַחֵ֖ם מֵשִׁ֣יב נַפְשִׁ֑י

°מחמודיהם כ׳

exile with them; the priestly watches were exiled, but the *Shechinah* did not go into exile with them. However, when the children were exiled, the *Shechinah* went into exile with them. Therefore, it is written: *Her young children have gone into captivity before the enemy*. This is immediately followed by, *Gone from the daughter of Zion is all her splendor* [i.e., the *Shechinah*].

6. לִפְנֵי רוֹדֵף — *Before the pursuer. Rashi* observes that wherever else in Scripture the word רוֹדֵף appears it is spelled חָסֵר, defectively [רֹדֵף — i.e., without the ו, *vav*]. In our verse, however, the full spelling is used to imply that the Jews were pursued vigorously and fully.

7. זָכְרָה יְרוּשָׁלַםִ — *Jerusalem recalled.* While in exile (*Rashi*).

יְמֵי עָנְיָהּ — *The days of her affliction* i.e., the Destruction which was the cause of her affliction (*Rashi*).

8. [The author now attributes all of the suffering described in verses 1-7 to Divine retribution for Jerusalem's grievous sins.]

The *Midrash*, commenting on the use of the double verb, חֵטְא חָטְאָה, *sinned a sin*, explains: They sinned doubly and were punished doubly, as it is written: כִּי לָקְחָה מִיַּד ה׳ כִּפְלַיִם בְּכָל־חַטֹּאתֶיהָ *— She received from God's hand double for all her sins* (*Isaiah* 40:2); and they were comforted doubly, as it is written: נַחֲמוּ נַחֲמוּ עַמִּי, *Comfort My people, comfort* (*Isaiah* 40:1).

Meshech Chachmah interprets the double verb: *Jerusalem sinned repeatedly* and grew accustomed to the fact, viewing it naturally, and feeling no remorse. . .

[As the *Talmud* (*Moed Katan* 27b) remarks: *As soon as a person has committed a sinful act and has repeated it* — נַעֲשֵׂית לוֹ כְּהֶיתֵּר, it has become to him as though it were something permissible (see *Overview*).]

According to the Talmud, a sin consists of two parts: the sinful act itself and the thoughts and satisfaction surrounding it. Each part of the sin is evaluated separately and punished separately (*Kiddushin* 40a). Therefore, the verse uses a twin expression of sin. In the same way, the thought leading up to a good deed and the satisfaction one derives from having performed it are rewarded by God along with the good deed itself (*Hagaon Rav Moshe Feinstein*).

10. אֲשֶׁר צִוִּיתָה לֹא־יָבֹאוּ בַקָּהָל לָךְ — *About whom You had commanded that they should not enter*

*without strength before the pursuer.** [7] *Jerusalem recalled** *the days of her affliction** *and sorrow — all the treasures that were hers in the days of old. With the fall of her people into the enemy's hand and none to help her, her enemies saw her and gloated at her downfall.* [8] *Jerusalem sinned greatly, she has therefore become a wanderer. All who once respected her disparage her, for they have seen her disgrace. She herself sighs and turns away.* [9] *Her impurity is on her hems, she was heedless of the consequences. She has sunk astonishingly, there is no one to comfort her. 'Look, HASHEM, at my misery, for the enemy has acted prodigiously!'* [10] *The enemy spread out his hand on all her treasures; indeed, she saw nations invade her sanctuary — about whom You had commanded that they should not enter Your congregation.** [11] *All her people are sighing, searching for bread. They traded their enemies for food to keep alive. 'Look, HASHEM,** *and behold what a glutton I have become!'* [12] *May it not befall you — all who pass by this road. Behold and see, if there is any pain like my pain which befell me; which HASHEM has afflicted me on the day of His wrath.** [13] *From on high He sent a fire into my bones,** *and it crushed them. he spread a net for my feet hurling me backward. He made me desolate; in constant misery.* [14] *The burden of my transgressions was accumulated in His hand; they were knit** *together and thrust upon my neck — He sapped my strength. The Lord has delivered me into the hands of those I cannot withstand.* [15] *The Lord has trampled all my heroes in my midst; He proclaimed a set time against me** *to crush my young men. As in a winepress the Lord has trodden the maiden daughter of Judah.** [16] *Over these things I weep;** *my eyes run with water because a comforter to revive my spirit is far from me.*

Your congregation. When the enemies entered the Temple, Ammonites and Moabites entered among them. While the others ran to plunder the silver and gold, the Ammonites and Moabites ran to plunder the Torah itself to expunge the verse (*Deut.* 23:4): לֹא־יָבֹא עַמּוֹנִי וּמוֹאָבִי בִּקְהַל ה׳, *An Ammonite or Moabite shall not enter the Assembly of HASHEM* (*Midrash*).

11. רְאֵה ה׳ — *'Look, HASHEM.'* An impassioned plea. From this point on, Jerusalem, itself, laments. The Community of Israel says to the nations of the world: May there not occur to you what has occurred to me.

12. בְּיוֹם חֲרוֹן אַפּוֹ — *On the day of His wrath*, i.e., the Ninth of Av when so many tragedies befell Israel throughout its history (*Shaar Bas Rabim*).

The *Midrash* stresses *the day*, i.e., that particular day upon which God's fierce anger was kindled: Had Israel repented that very day they could have cooled [i.e., averted] His anger.

13. מִמָּרוֹם שָׁלַח אֵשׁ־בְּעַצְמֹתַי — *From on high He sent a fire into my bones.* The *Midrash* understands this literally: God Himself sent a fire to burn the Temple so the heathens could not boast that they themselves destroyed it.

14. נִשְׂקַד. . .יִשְׂתָּרְגוּ — *Was accumulated. . . were knit.* Instead of constantly doling out small, proportioned punishment for every one of Zion's sins whenever she transgressed, God collected all her transgressions, noting and remembering them. He then metaphorically knit them together into a heavy garment which he thrust upon her neck in one heavy, cumulative load, effectively weighing her down, and sapping her strength until she was unable to withstand the enemy.

15. קָרָא עָלַי מוֹעֵד — *He proclaimed a set time against me*, i.e., the Ninth of Av (*Taanis* 29a). [See comm. to verse 2, s.v. בַּלַּיְלָה].

[Since Tishah B'Av is referred to as מוֹעֵד, *set time, festival*, the Sages state that halachically, as on a holiday, *Tachanun* is not said during *Minchah* services on *Erev Tishah B'Av* (*Shulchan Aruch, Orach Chaim* 552).

לִבְתוּלַת בַּת־יְהוּדָה — The *maiden daughter of Judah*, i.e., Jerusalem (*Rashi*).

16. עַל־אֵלֶּה אֲנִי בוֹכִיָּה — *Over these things I weep.* The verb בוֹכִיָּה implies a constant action: *I*

הָיוּ בָנַי שׁוֹמֵמִים כִּי גָבַר אוֹיֵב: יז פֵּרְשָׂה צִיּוֹן בְּיָדֶיהָ אֵין מְנַחֵם לָהּ
צִוָּה יהוה לְיַעֲקֹב סְבִיבָיו צָרָיו הָיְתָה יְרוּשָׁלַםִ לְנִדָּה בֵּינֵיהֶם:
יח צַדִּיק הוּא יהוה כִּי פִיהוּ מָרִיתִי שִׁמְעוּ־נָא °כָל־הָעַמִּים וּרְאוּ
מַכְאֹבִי בְּתוּלֹתַי וּבַחוּרַי הָלְכוּ בַשֶּׁבִי: יט קָרָאתִי לַמְאַהֲבַי הֵמָּה
רִמּוּנִי* כֹּהֲנַי וּזְקֵנַי בָּעִיר גָּוָעוּ כִּי־בִקְשׁוּ אֹכֶל לָמוֹ וְיָשִׁיבוּ
אֶת־נַפְשָׁם: כ רְאֵה יהוה* כִּי־צַר־לִי מֵעַי חֳמַרְמָרוּ נֶהְפַּךְ לִבִּי
בְּקִרְבִּי כִּי מָרוֹ מָרִיתִי מִחוּץ שִׁכְּלָה־חֶרֶב בַּבַּיִת כַּמָּוֶת: כא שָׁמְעוּ
כִּי נֶאֱנָחָה אָנִי* אֵין מְנַחֵם לִי כָּל־אֹיְבַי שָׁמְעוּ רָעָתִי שָׂשׂוּ כִּי
אַתָּה עָשִׂיתָ* הֵבֵאתָ יוֹם־קָרָאתָ וְיִהְיוּ כָמֹנִי: כב תָּבֹא כָל־רָעָתָם
לְפָנֶיךָ וְעוֹלֵל לָמוֹ כַּאֲשֶׁר עוֹלַלְתָּ לִי עַל כָּל־פְּשָׁעָי כִּי־רַבּוֹת
אַנְחֹתַי וְלִבִּי דַוָּי:

פרק שני

א אֵיכָה °יָעִיב בְּאַפּוֹ | אֲדֹנָי אֶת־בַּת־צִיּוֹן* הִשְׁלִיךְ מִשָּׁמַיִם אֶרֶץ
תִּפְאֶרֶת יִשְׂרָאֵל* וְלֹא־זָכַר הֲדֹם־רַגְלָיו* בְּיוֹם אַפּוֹ: ב בִּלַּע אֲדֹנָי
°וְלֹא חָמַל אֵת כָּל־נְאוֹת יַעֲקֹב* הָרַס בְּעֶבְרָתוֹ מִבְצְרֵי
בַת־יְהוּדָה הִגִּיעַ לָאָרֶץ חִלֵּל מַמְלָכָה וְשָׂרֶיהָ:* ג גָּדַע* בָּחֳרִי־אַף
כֹּל קֶרֶן יִשְׂרָאֵל הֵשִׁיב אָחוֹר יְמִינוֹ מִפְּנֵי אוֹיֵב וַיִּבְעַר בְּיַעֲקֹב*
כְּאֵשׁ לֶהָבָה אָכְלָה סָבִיב: ד דָּרַךְ קַשְׁתּוֹ כְּאוֹיֵב נִצָּב יְמִינוֹ כְּצָר

°כל־עמים כ׳ °לא־חמל כ׳

weep incessantly; or *I have become known as a habitual weeper* (*Lechem Dim'ah*). Various causes for her weeping are offered in the *Midrash*, which relates many harrowing incidents of barbarous atrocities which befell the Jews at the time of the Destruction (1:16). [The post-Holocaust generation understands only too well how the Jewish people can suffer at the hands of cruel and bestial people. Indeed, the atrocities of the Nazis are also foreshadowed in the lament of Jeremiah.]

18. Zion itself resumes the lament, and confesses publicly and without reservation that God is righteous and justified in what He has done.

19. קָרָאתִי לַמְאַהֲבַי הֵמָּה רִמּוּנִי — *I called for my lovers but they deceived me. Lovers* — i.e., those who feigned friendship (*Rashi*) [i.e., the neighboring countries — Egypt, Moab, Ammon, with whom Judea had hoped to form an alliance].

The Rabbis interpret this verse as an allusion to the false prophets who made me love their idol worship. הֵמָּה רִמּוּנִי, *they deceived me*, by incessantly uttering false prophecies of reassurance decrying Jeremiah's calls for repentance, until they caused me to go into exile.

20. רְאֵה ה׳ — *See,* HASHEM. [This verse begins with a supplication to God to bear witness to the extent of Zion's affliction, and culminates with an appeal (verse 22) for Divine retribution against the enemy.]

21. שָׁמְעוּ כִּי נֶאֱנָחָה אָנִי — *They heard how I sighed,* i.e., my *lovers* [referred to above in verses 2 and 19] heard me sigh and did not even comfort me; my real enemies, on the other hand, actually rejoiced upon hearing my plight, knowing You have caused it (*Ibn Ezra*).

כִּי אַתָּה עָשִׂיתָ — *For it was You Who did it* [i.e., my misfortune emanated from Your will]. You are the cause of their hating us because You prohibited us from eating their food or marrying their children. Had we socialized and intermarried with them, would they not have compassion upon us and on their offspring? (*Midrash; Rashi*).

Lechem Dim'ah notes that here [unlike verse 12] Zion prays that the enemies be punished for rejoicing at her downfall. And lest anyone think that Zion might then rejoice at her enemies'

My children have become forlorn, because the enemy has prevailed. [17] *Zion spread out her hands; there was none to comfort her.* HASHEM *commanded against Jacob that his enemies should surround him; Jerusalem has become as one unclean in their midst.* [18] *It is* HASHEM *Who is righteous, for I disobeyed His utterance. Listen, all you peoples and behold my pain: My maidens and my youths have gone into captivity.* [19] *I called for my lovers but they deceived me.* My priests and my elders perished in the city as they sought food for themselves to keep alive.* [20] *See,* HASHEM,* *how distressed I am; my insides churn! My heart is turned over inside me for I rebelled grievously. Outside the sword bereaved, inside was death-like.* [21] *They heard how I sighed,* there was none to comfort me. All my enemies heard of my plight and rejoiced, for it was You Who did it.* O bring on the day You proclaimed and let them be like me!* [22] *Let all their wickedness come before You, and inflict them as You inflicted me for all my transgressions. For my groans are many, and my heart is sick.*

CHAPTER TWO

[1] *Alas — the Lord in His anger has clouded the daughter of Zion.* He cast down from heaven to earth the glory of Israel.* He did not remember His footstool* on the day of His wrath.* [2] *The Lord consumed without pity all the dwellings of Jacob;* in His anger He razed the fortresses of the daughter of Judah down to the ground; He profaned the kingdom and its leaders.** [3] *He cut down,* in fierce anger, all the dignity of Israel; He withdrew His right hand in the presence of the enemy. He burned through Jacob* like a flaming fire, consuming on all sides.* [4] *He bent His bow like an enemy. His right hand poised like a foe,*

---

downfall, the verse concludes: No, there is no room for rejoicing! *My groans are many, and my heart is sick.*

CHAPTER TWO

1. בַּת־צִיּוֹן — *Daughter of Zion.* A poetic form, used to denote Jerusalem; its populace.

הִשְׁלִיךְ מִשָּׁמַיִם אֶרֶץ תִּפְאֶרֶת יִשְׂרָאֵל — *He cast down from heaven to earth the glory of Israel.* After having raised up the Jews to the uppermost heavens, He cast them down to the nethermost depths — not gradually, but in one thrust (*Rashi*).

וְלֹא־זָכַר הֲדֹם־רַגְלָיו — *He did not remember His footstool,* i.e., the בֵּית הַמִּקְדָּשׁ, *the Holy Temple* (*Midrash; Rashi*).

The *Midrash* notes, homiletically, that הֲדֹם, *footstool*, has the same spelling as הַדָּם, *the blood,* i.e., God in His anger preferred not to remember Abraham's blood of circumcision or the blood in which they wallowed in Egypt, and which they put on the doorposts there (II:1).

2. אֵת כָּל־נְאוֹת יַעֲקֹב — *All the dwellings of Jacob.* The *Midrash* homiletically translates נְאוֹת יַעֲקֹב, *the beauty of Jacob* — referring to the Torah Sages who were martyred during the Destruction.

חִלֵּל מַמְלָכָה וְשָׂרֶיהָ — *He profaned the kingdom and its leaders.* This refers to Israel which is called מַמְלֶכֶת כֹּהֲנִים, *a kingdom of priests* (*Rashi*); also, to Zedekiah, King of Judah (*Midrash*).

3. גָּדַע — *He cut down,* i.e., the branches only, leaving the root intact so it could eventually grow back (*Lechem Dim'ah*).

The *Midrash* notes that when the enemy entered Jerusalem, they took the mighty men of Israel and bound their hands behind them. The Holy One, Blessed is He, saw their distress, so He, too — anthropomorphically — *withdrew His right hand behind Him* [i.e., symbolizing His endurance of the many indignities heaped upon His glory by the heathens, as if His hands, so to speak, were behind His back, powerless to avenge] (*Yefe Anaf*).

וַיִּבְעַר בְּיַעֲקֹב — *He burned through Jacob.* The *Midrash* comments: When punishment comes into the world, no one feels it as much as [the patriarch] Jacob; and when there is good in the world, no one rejoices as much as Jacob, i.e., Jacob feels it more keenly than the other patriarchs

וַיַּהֲרֹג כֹּל מַחֲמַדֵּי־עָ֫יִן* בְּאֹ֫הֶל בַּת־צִיּ֑וֹן שָׁפַךְ כָּאֵשׁ חֲמָתֽוֹ: ה הָיָ֨ה
אֲדֹנָ֤י ׀ כְּאוֹיֵב* בִּלַּ֣ע יִשְׂרָאֵ֔ל בִּלַּע֙ כָּל־אַרְמְנוֹתֶ֔יהָ שִׁחֵ֖ת מִבְצָרָ֑יו
וַיֶּ֙רֶב֙ בְּבַת־יְהוּדָ֔ה תַּאֲנִיָּ֖ה וַאֲנִיָּֽה: ו וַיַּחְמֹ֤ס כַּגַּן֙* שֻׂכּֽוֹ* שִׁחֵ֣ת
מֹֽעֲדֽוֹ* שִׁכַּ֣ח יְהֹוָ֣ה ׀ בְּצִיּוֹן֙ מוֹעֵ֣ד וְשַׁבָּ֔ת* וַיִּנְאַ֥ץ בְּזַֽעַם־אַפֹּ֖ו מֶ֣לֶךְ
וְכֹהֵֽן: ז זָנַ֨ח אֲדֹנָ֤י ׀ מִזְבְּחוֹ֙* נִאֵ֣ר מִקְדָּשֹׁ֔ו הִסְגִּ֛יר בְּיַד־אוֹיֵ֖ב
חוֹמֹ֣ת אַרְמְנוֹתֶ֑יהָ ק֛וֹל נָתְנ֥וּ בְּבֵית־יְהֹוָ֖ה כְּי֥וֹם מוֹעֵֽד:* ח חָשַׁ֨ב
יְהֹוָ֤ה ׀ לְהַשְׁחִית֙* חוֹמַ֣ת בַּת־צִיּ֔וֹן נָ֣טָה קָ֔ו לֹֽא־הֵשִׁ֥יב יָד֖וֹ
מִבַּלֵּ֑עַ וַיַּֽאֲבֶל־חֵ֥ל וְחוֹמָ֖ה יַחְדָּ֥ו אֻמְלָֽלוּ: ט טָבְע֤וּ בָאָ֙רֶץ֙ שְׁעָרֶ֔יהָ*
אִבַּ֥ד וְשִׁבַּ֖ר בְּרִיחֶ֑יהָ מַלְכָּ֨הּ וְשָׂרֶ֤יהָ בַגּוֹיִם֙ אֵ֣ין תּוֹרָ֔ה* גַּם־נְבִיאֶ֕יהָ
לֹא־מָצְא֥וּ חָז֖וֹן מֵֽיהֹוָֽה: י יֵשְׁב֨וּ לָאָ֤רֶץ יִדְּמוּ֙* זִקְנֵ֣י בַת־צִיּ֔וֹן
הֶֽעֱל֤וּ עָפָר֙ עַל־רֹאשָׁ֔ם חָגְר֖וּ שַׂקִּ֑ים הוֹרִ֤ידוּ לָאָ֙רֶץ֙ רֹאשָׁ֔ן בְּתוּלֹ֖ת
יְרֽוּשָׁלָֽ͏ִם: יא כָּל֨וּ בַדְּמָע֤וֹת עֵינַי֙ חֳמַרְמְר֣וּ מֵעַ֔י נִשְׁפַּ֤ךְ לָאָ֙רֶץ֙
כְּבֵדִ֔י עַל־שֶׁ֖בֶר בַּת־עַמִּ֑י בֵּֽעָטֵ֤ף עוֹלֵל֙ וְיוֹנֵ֔ק בִּרְחֹב֖וֹת קִרְיָֽה:
יב לְאִמֹּתָם֙ יֹֽאמְר֔וּ* אַיֵּ֖ה דָּגָ֣ן וָיָ֑יִן* בְּהִֽתְעַטְּפָ֤ם כֶּֽחָלָל֙ בִּרְחֹב֣וֹת

---

because he experienced the most tribulations in raising his family (*Torah Temimah*).

4. In this verse Hashem is depicted, not only in His passive role as One who withdrew His support, but as One who actively participated in Israel's destruction.

וַיַּהֲרֹג כֹּל מַחֲמַדֵּי־עָיִן — *He slew all who were of pleasant appearance.*

Rav Tanchum ben Yirmiyah said this refers to the children who were as dear to their parents as the apple of their eye. The Rabbis said this refers to the members of the Sanhedrin who were as dear to Israel as the apple of their eye (*Midrash*).

5. ...הָיָה ה' כְּאוֹיֵב — *The Lord became like an enemy...* After all of the above, the Jews did not repent. Still, God restrained Himself. The verse likens His anger to that of an enemy, but He did not *become* an enemy. Also, בִּלַּע יִשְׂרָאֵל, *He consumed Israel*, but not כָּל יִשְׂרָאֵל, *all of Israel;* בִּלַּע כָּל־אַרְמְנוֹתֶיהָ, *He consumed all her citadels;* and thus vented His anger by directing His actions עַל עֵצִים וַאֲבָנִים, *on wood and stone* [i.e., on inanimate objects, rather than on human lives], so as to avoid the total slaughter of the Jews themselves (*Palgei Mayim*).

6. וַיַּחְמֹס כַּגַּן שֻׂכּוֹ — *He stripped His Booth like a garden.* His Booth, related to סֻכָּה, *sukkah* (Ibn Ezra), i.e., His dwelling place (*Rashi*) — the קֹדֶשׁ קֳדָשִׁים, Holy of Holies (*Palgei Mayim*).

The *Midrash* notes that the word for booth, שֻׂכּוֹ [*sukko*], can be read שֻׂכּוֹ [*shukko*], His appeasement, i.e., when He stripped [Jerusalem] as one strips a garden, שֶׁכָּכָה חֲמָתוֹ שֶׁל הקב"ה,

God's wrath was appeased [having vented His anger on wood and stone].

כַּגַּן — *Like a garden.* I.e., as one cuts vegetables in a garden. Jerusalem became like a garden which had been deprived of its water (*Midrash*) [and nothing looks as desolate as a garden stripped of its plants].

שִׁחֵת מֹעֲדוֹ — *He destroyed His place of assembly,* i.e., the קֹדֶשׁ קֳדָשִׁים, *the Holy of Holies,* where God presents Himself [נוֹעֵד] to His children [*Exodus* 25:22] (*Rashi*).

שִׁכַּח ה' בְּצִיּוֹן מוֹעֵד וְשַׁבָּת — *HASHEM made Zion oblivious of festival and Sabbath* [i.e., as a result of God's destruction of the Temple and sacrifices, it was as if the festivals and Sabbath were forgotten].

7. זָנַח ה' מִזְבְּחוֹ — *The Lord rejected His altar.* The Holy One, Blessed is He, said to Israel: Do you provoke Me because you rely on the sacrifices which you offer to Me? Here, have them! They are thrown in your face (*Midrash*).

כְּיוֹם מוֹעֵד — *As though it were a festival* i.e., the heathens clamored joyously at the destruction of the Temple, matching the fervor of Israel's joyous chants on its holiday (*Alshich; Rashi*).

8. חָשַׁב ה' לְהַשְׁחִית — *HASHEM resolved to destroy.* The *Midrash* explains that the resolve was not new — but an old one, as it is written: כִּי עַל־אַפִּי וְעַל־חֲמָתִי הָיְתָה לִּי הָעִיר הַזֹּאת לְמִן־הַיּוֹם אֲשֶׁר בָּנוּ אוֹתָהּ, *For this city [Jerusalem] has been to Me a provocation of My fury and My anger from the day that they built it* (*Jer.* 32:31) [and God, in a

He slew all who were of pleasant appearance. In the tent of the daughter of Zion He poured out His wrath like fire.* [5] *The Lord became like an enemy.* He consumed Israel; He consumed all her citadels, He destroyed its fortresses. He increased within the daughter of Judah moaning and mourning.* [6] *He stripped His Booth like a garden,* He destroyed His place of assembly.* HASHEM made Zion oblivious of festival and Sabbath,* and in His fierce anger He spurned king and priest.* [7] *The Lord rejected His altar,* abolished His Sanctuary; He handed over to the enemy the walls of her citadels. They raised a clamor in the House of HASHEM as though it were a festival.** [8] *HASHEM resolved to destroy* the wall of the daughter of Zion. He stretched out the line and did not relent from devouring. Indeed, He made rampart and wall mourn; together they languished.* [9] *Her gates have sunk into the earth,* He has utterly shattered her bars; her king and officers are among the heathen, there is no Torah;* her prophets, too, find no vision from HASHEM.* [10] *The elders of the daughter of Zion sit on the ground in silence;* they have strewn ashes on their heads, and wear sackcloth. The maidens of Jerusalem have bowed their heads to the ground.* [11] *My eyes fail with tears, my insides churn; my liver spills on the ground at the shattering of my people, while babes and sucklings swoon in the streets of the city.* [12] *They say to their mothers,* 'Where is bread and wine?'* as they swoon like a dying man in the streets*

---

sense, restrained Himself until then].

9. טָבְעוּ בָאָרֶץ שְׁעָרֶיהָ — *Her gates have sunk into the earth.* According to the *Midrash* the gates sunk into the ground [i.e., miraculously, and were not destroyed by the enemy], because when Solomon brought the אֲרוֹן הַבְּרִית, *Ark of the Covenant*, into Jerusalem, the gates paid honor to the Ark by rising to allow the Ark to enter [*Shabbos* 30a]. *Rashi* adds that the gates were invulnerable to the enemy because they were the handiwork of King David [*Sotah* 9a].

Minchas Shay explains that the ט, *Tes*, of טָבְעוּ, *sunk*, is small to allude to ט, *the Ninth*, of Av when the Temple was destroyed.

אֵין תּוֹרָה — *There is no Torah*, i.e., no one to provide religious instruction (*Rashi*). [All the most important people — king, princes, priests — in whose hands lay the religious administration of the country are either gone or not functioning.]

Most commentators and the *Midrash* attach this clause to the preceding and translate: *Her king and her officers are among the heathen where there is no Torah.* Hence, the *Midrash* concludes: Should a person tell you there is חָכְמָה, *wisdom*, among the nations, believe it; but if he tells you there is Torah among the nations, do not believe it.

10. In this verse, the prophet depicts the elders — who no longer have a worldly occupation to keep them occupied, and who have suffered and endured so much — mourning for Zion. They have no words, no prayers, only silent resignation. Note also the poetic contrast between the זְקֵנִים, *elders*, and בְּתוּלוֹת, *maidens*, as depicting the extremes of the population spectrum (*Kol Yaakov; Lechem Dim'ah*).

יֵשְׁבוּ לָאָרֶץ יִדְּמוּ — *Sit on the ground in silence.* [The Biblical classic form of mourning includes strewing dust on the head, wearing sackcloth, and bowing the head.]

This verse is cited as a basis for the halachic custom of sitting on the ground on *Tishah B'Av.* The 12th-century *Sefer HaEshkol* says: After the final meal, we go to the synagogue without shoes and sit on the ground, as it is written: *sit on the ground in silence.*

11. [In a personal interjection of special grief, the prophet laments the tragic sight of children languishing from hunger in the streets.]

12. לְאִמֹּתָם יֹאמְרוּ — *They* [i.e., the swooning children mentioned in the last verse] *say to their mothers.*

אַיֵּה דָּגָן וָיָיִן — *Where is bread* [lit., *grain*] *and wine?* (The translation *'bread'* follows the Midrash.)

It is obvious that fine bread and good wine were not available during the siege, and the verse could not be suggesting that the children seriously expected to receive these foods during the famine; the children would have been satisfied with any morsels of food to still their hunger pangs. Rather, as they swooned from hunger,

עִיר בְּהִשְׁתַּפֵּךְ נַפְשָׁם אֶל־חֵיק אִמֹּתָם: יג °מָה־אֲעִידֵךְ מָה אֲדַמֶּה־לָּךְ* הַבַּת יְרוּשָׁלַם מָה אַשְׁוֶה־לָּךְ וַאֲנַחֲמֵךְ* בְּתוּלַת בַּת־צִיּוֹן כִּי־גָדוֹל כַּיָּם שִׁבְרֵךְ מִי יִרְפָּא־לָךְ: יד נְבִיאַיִךְ* חָזוּ לָךְ שָׁוְא וְתָפֵל וְלֹא־גִלּוּ עַל־עֲוֺנֵךְ לְהָשִׁיב °שְׁבוּתֵךְ וַיֶּחֱזוּ לָךְ מַשְׂאוֹת שָׁוְא וּמַדּוּחִים: טו סָפְקוּ עָלַיִךְ כַּפַּיִם כָּל־עֹבְרֵי דֶרֶךְ שָׁרְקוּ וַיָּנִעוּ רֹאשָׁם* עַל־בַּת יְרוּשָׁלָם הֲזֹאת הָעִיר* שֶׁיֹּאמְרוּ כְּלִילַת יֹפִי מָשׂוֹשׂ לְכָל־הָאָרֶץ: טז פָּצוּ* עָלַיִךְ פִּיהֶם כָּל־אֹיְבַיִךְ שָׁרְקוּ וַיַּחַרְקוּ־שֵׁן אָמְרוּ בִּלָּעְנוּ אַךְ זֶה הַיּוֹם שֶׁקִּוִּינֻהוּ מָצָאנוּ רָאִינוּ:* יז עָשָׂה יהוה אֲשֶׁר זָמָם* בִּצַּע אֶמְרָתוֹ אֲשֶׁר צִוָּה מִימֵי־קֶדֶם* הָרַס וְלֹא חָמָל וַיְשַׂמַּח עָלַיִךְ אוֹיֵב* הֵרִים קֶרֶן צָרָיִךְ: יח צָעַק לִבָּם אֶל־אֲדֹנָי חוֹמַת בַּת־צִיּוֹן הוֹרִידִי כַנַּחַל דִּמְעָה יוֹמָם וָלַיְלָה אַל־תִּתְּנִי פוּגַת לָךְ אַל־תִּדֹּם בַּת־עֵינֵךְ:* יט קוּמִי ׀ רֹנִּי °בַלַּיְלָה* לְרֹאשׁ אַשְׁמֻרוֹת* שִׁפְכִי כַמַּיִם לִבֵּךְ* נֹכַח פְּנֵי אֲדֹנָי שְׂאִי אֵלָיו כַּפַּיִךְ עַל־נֶפֶשׁ

°מה־אעודך כ׳ °שביתך כ׳ °בליל כ׳

they beseeched their mothers, remembering their past comforts, and saying, *'What happened to the fine food which you used to feed us?' (Lechem Dim'ah).*

13. מָה־אֲעִידֵךְ מָה אֲדַמֶּה־לָּךְ — *With what shall I bear witness for you? To what can I compare you?* I.e., what instance can I cite of any other nation that suffered a calamity equal to yours? (*Zohar; Alshich*).

The *Midrash*, interpreting the verb אֲעִידֵךְ, *witness*, by its other meaning, *warn*, translates: [God said:] How many prophets did I send to warn you [of the consequences of your evil ways]? I.e., what more could I have done for you? (*Torah Temimah*).

מָה אַשְׁוֶה־לָּךְ וַאֲנַחֲמֵךְ — *To what can I liken you to comfort you?* I.e., whose suffering and circumstances can be likened to yours, so that you can be comforted by the comparison? (*Lechem Dim'ah*).

Human nature is such that in times of trouble one finds comfort in hearing of others who experienced similar tribulations (*Rashi*) (II:12).

14. נְבִיאַיִךְ — *Your prophets*, i.e., those prophets — whom you believed to have the most spiritual and moral insight — prophesied falsely, and whitewashed your iniquities, soothing you into self-righteousness by indulging in deceptive oracles (*Rav Arama*).

Alshich concludes: Not only did your prophets not reprimand you for your transgressions — they actually led you astray from God with their vain and deceptive prophecies. Indeed, who can heal such a nation? And if you expect to derive comfort from passersby who will see your suffering and commiserate with you, you are sadly mistaken ... [see *Alshich* next verse].

15. סָפְקוּ עָלַיִךְ כַּפַּיִם ... שָׁרְקוּ וַיָּנִעוּ רֹאשָׁם — *Clap hands at you; they hiss and wag their head* — upon witnessing your disaster (*Kiflayim L'Sushiyah*).

...In mock and derision, not over your loss, Jerusalem, but for themselves, as the Sages proclaimed: Had the heathens known how much they would lose by destroying the Temple, they would not have done it. The Divine blessing that had rested upon the entire world left with the Destruction (*Alshich*).

[*Rashi* implies that this verse refers to a sincere manifestation of grief which one naturally expresses upon seeing such a precipitous decline in someone who was once great. Perhaps, in this light, we can differentiate between this verse and the next. In this verse the prophet laments the fact that Zion's state is so lamentable that *all* neutral *passersby* will be sincerely moved to commiserate at the great loss. The next verse, however, speaks of the confirmed אוֹיֵב, *enemy*, who jeers and gnashes his teeth, openly displaying *joy* at her present condition.]

... הֲזֹאת הָעִיר — *Could this be the city...?* [This is what the passersby are moved to say, remembering her past glory, and seeing her in her present state of destruction.]

16. פָּצוּ — *(They) jeered.* [*Lamentations* is written in the form of an alphabetical acrostic, but in this chapter, and also in chapters 3 and 4, the verse beginning with פ precedes that of ע. The name of the letter פ means mouth; the name of the letter ע

of the town; as their soul ebbs away in their mothers' laps. [13] *With what shall I bear witness for you? To what can I compare you,* O daughter of Jerusalem? To what can I liken you to comfort you,* O maiden daughter of Zion? — Your ruin is as vast as the sea; who can heal you?* [14] *Your prophets* envisioned for you vanity and foolishness, and they did not expose your iniquity to bring you back in repentance; they prophesied to you oracles of vanity and deception.* [15] *All who pass along the way clap hands at you; they hiss and wag their head* at the daughter of Jerusalem: 'Could this be the city* that was called Perfect in Beauty, Joy of All the Earth?'* [16] *All your enemies jeered* at you; they hiss and gnash their teeth. They say: 'We have devoured her! Indeed, this is the day we longed for; we have actually seen it!'** [17] *HASHEM has done what He planned;* He carried out His decree which He ordained long ago;* He devastated without pity. He let the enemy rejoice over you;* He raised the pride of your foes.* [18] *Their heart cried out to the Lord. O wall of the daughter of Zion: Shed tears like a river, day and night; give yourself no respite, do not let your eyes be still.** [19] *Arise, cry out at night* in the beginning of the watches!* Pour out your heart like water* in the Presence of the Lord; lift up your hands to Him for the life of*

---

means eye.] Rashi notes: Why did he place the פ before the ע? Because they [i.e., the Spies — (*Sanhedrin* 104b; see also comm. to 1:2)] spoke with their mouths what they had not seen with their eyes [thus putting one before the other].

According to *Lechem Dim'ah*, *Rashi* is referring [not to the Spies as in *Sanhedrin*, 104b, but] to the enemies who cast diatribes at Israel long before the actual Destruction took place. Hence, the sequence of the verses: First, פָּצוּ, *All your enemies jeered at you*, then, עָשָׂה ה׳ ... הָרַס, *HASHEM has done. . .has devasted.*

מָצָאנוּ רָאִינוּ — *We have actually seen it* [lit., *we have found, we have seen*]. The *Arizal* explains that the enemy had hoped for the day when they could burn the Temple themselves. They were disappointed because *'we found, we saw,'* i.e., they found that God had already sent down the fire that burned the Temple [see commentary 1:13].

17. עָשָׂה ה׳ אֲשֶׁר זָמָם — *HASHEM has done what He planned.*

Although most human plans are never executed, God's resolve was carried through in its entirety (*Lechem Dim'ah*).

אֲשֶׁר צִוָּה מִימֵי־קֶדֶם — *Which He ordained long ago* [lit. *which He commanded from ancient days*]. According to *Rashi* this refers to the warnings in the Torah of the dire results of disobedience (e.g., *Leviticus* 26:27).

וַיְשַׂמַּח עָלַיִךְ אוֹיֵב — *He let the enemy rejoice over you.* God Himself rejoices with Israel when good befalls them; but when anything bad befalls them, He lets others do the rejoicing (*Midrash*).

18. אַל־תִּתְּנִי פוּגַת לָךְ אַל־תִּדֹּם בַּת־עֵינֵךְ — *Give yourself no respite, do not let your eyes* [lit., *pupils*] *be still.*

'The greatest sin of all is that we, in our time, stopped mourning properly for Jerusalem. I am convinced that, in punishment for this, our exile has lasted so long, we have never been able to find rest, and we are always being persecuted. Historically, whenever we found some security in any of the lands of our exile, we forgot Jerusalem and did not place it at the foremost place in our minds' (*Rav Yaakov Emden*).

19. [This verse is a continuation of the last, in which the prophet exhorts the sufferers to pray unrestrainedly to God].

בַלַּיְלָה — *At night.* [See Commentary on 1:2.]

Midrash Lekach Tov comments that *night* refers to the night of *Tishah B'Av* which should be observed annually as an eve of weeping and lamentation.

The כְּתִיב, *written form*, of the *night* is לַיִל, and refers to the earlier part of the evening, which is the רֹאשׁ אַשְׁמֻרוֹת, *beginning of the first two watches*, and is the most effective time (*Lechem Dim'ah*).

לְרֹאשׁ אַשְׁמֻרוֹת — *In the beginning of the watches*, the night being divided into three equal *watches* (*Rashi*).

שִׁפְכִי כַמַּיִם לִבֵּךְ נֹכַח פְּנֵי ה׳ — *Pour out your heart like water in the Presence of the Lord.* And confess your guilt (*Ibn Yachya*).

Wherever *Hashem's* name appears as אדני, it refers to the *Shechinah*. Therefore, first *pour out* your heart like water at the 'departure' of the *Shechinah*, and then pray for the *life of your infants*, i.e., for your own needs (*Lechem Dim'ah*).

עוֹלָלַ֫יִךְ* הָעֲטוּפִ֥ים בְּרָעָ֖ב בְּרֹ֥אשׁ כָּל־חוּצֽוֹת׃ כ רְאֵ֤ה יהוה
וְֽהַבִּ֔יטָה לְמִ֖י עוֹלַ֣לְתָּ כֹּ֑ה אִם־תֹּאכַ֨לְנָה נָשִׁ֤ים פִּרְיָם֙* עֹלֲלֵ֣י
טִפֻּחִ֔ים* אִם־יֵהָרֵ֛ג בְּמִקְדַּ֥שׁ אֲדֹנָ֖י כֹּהֵ֥ן וְנָבִֽיא׃ כא שָׁכְב֨וּ לָאָ֤רֶץ
חוּצוֹת֙ נַ֣עַר וְזָקֵ֔ן בְּתוּלֹתַ֥י וּבַחוּרַ֖י נָפְל֣וּ בֶחָ֑רֶב הָרַ֙גְתָּ֙ בְּי֣וֹם
אַפֶּ֔ךָ טָבַ֖חְתָּ לֹ֥א חָמָֽלְתָּ׃* כב תִּקְרָא֩ כְי֨וֹם מוֹעֵ֤ד* מְגוּרַי֙ מִסָּבִ֔יב
וְלֹ֥א הָיָ֛ה בְּי֥וֹם אַף־יהוה פָּלִ֣יט וְשָׂרִ֑יד אֲשֶׁר־טִפַּ֥חְתִּי וְרִבִּ֖יתִי
אֹיְבִ֥י כִלָּֽם׃

פרק שלישי

א אֲנִ֤י הַגֶּ֙בֶר֙* רָאָ֣ה עֳנִ֔י בְּשֵׁ֖בֶט עֶבְרָתֽוֹ׃ ב אוֹתִ֥י נָהַ֛ג וַיֹּלַ֖ךְ חֹ֥שֶׁךְ
וְלֹא־אֽוֹר׃ ג אַ֣ךְ בִּ֥י* יָשֻׁ֛ב יַהֲפֹ֥ךְ יָד֖וֹ* כָּל־הַיּֽוֹם׃ ד בִּלָּ֤ה בְשָׂרִי֙
וְעוֹרִ֔י* שִׁבַּ֖ר עַצְמוֹתָֽי׃ ה בָּנָ֥ה עָלַ֛י וַיַּקַּ֖ף רֹ֥אשׁ וּתְלָאָֽה׃ ו בְּמַחֲשַׁכִּ֣ים
הוֹשִׁיבַ֔נִי כְּמֵתֵ֖י עוֹלָֽם׃ ז גָּדַ֧ר בַּעֲדִ֛י* וְלֹ֥א אֵצֵ֖א הִכְבִּ֥יד נְחָשְׁתִּֽי׃
ח גַּ֚ם כִּ֣י אֶזְעַק֙ וַאֲשַׁוֵּ֔עַ* שָׂתַ֖ם תְּפִלָּתִֽי׃* ט גָּדַ֤ר דְּרָכַי֙ בְּגָזִ֔ית

Since the שַׁעֲרֵי דְמָעוֹת, *gates of weeping,* were never closed [*Berachos* 32b], the prophet assured them that sincere weeping would reach פְּנֵי ה׳, the *Presence of the Lord* (*Yismach Moshe*).

עַל־נֶפֶשׁ עוֹלָלַיִךְ — *For the life* [lit., *soul*] *of your young children.* Most commentators understand *'children'* literally, referring to the starving children in verses 11 and 12. *Midrash Lekach Tov* seems to understand it as the swooning children [i.e., citizens] of personified Jerusalem — who had been exiled בְּרֹאשׁ כָּל־חוּצוֹת, in foreign heathen countries [בְּחוּץ לָאָרֶץ] throughout the world.

Lechem Dim'ah interprets the verse: *Pour out your heart like water in the Presence of the Lord,* and if that is ineffective because your merits are insufficient, then *lift up your hands to Him as if* you were praying for *the life of your innocent infants who swoon* etc.

20. [In this verse, the thoughts of the prophet revert to Hashem.]

אִם־תֹּאכַלְנָה נָשִׁים פִּרְיָם — *Should women eat their own offspring?* An incredulous question: Has it ever happened to any other nation that their afflictions should result in the ghastly extreme of mothers eating their offspring, עֹלֲלֵי טִפֻּחִים, *babes of their care* — whom they previously fondled and cared for like all compassionate mothers? Is such a thing right? (*Alshich; Palgei Mayim*).

Wouldn't it have been sufficient to let them die from starvation without having their mothers eat them? (*Ibn Yachya*).

[Apparently, not only mothers were reduced to such a state of cruelty:] Rav Yochanan said: Fathers, too, ate the flesh of their sons and daughters at the Destruction of both the First and Second Temples. Jeremiah lamented this horror by crying, *'Therefore shall fathers eat the sons in your midst, and the sons shall eat their fathers'* [*Ezek.* 5:10] (*Pesikta Rabbasi*).

עֹלֲלֵי טִפֻּחִים — *Babes of their care,* i.e., objects of their fondling, caressing (*Ibn Ezra*).

The *Talmud* relates the incident of a child, Doeg ben Yosef, whose father died and he was left in his mother's care. Everyday she would lovingly measure him בְּטִפְחָהּ, *with her handbreadth,* and give his [extra] weight in gold to the Temple. When the enemy prevailed, however, she slaughtered him and ate him. It was to her that Jeremiah referred when he lamented to God: *Shall women eat their own offspring,* עֹלֲלֵי טִפֻּחִים, *the babes they measured by handbreadths.?* [A play on *tipuchim — of their care; fondled* — read as *tefuchim — measured by handbreadths* — as a sign of love, as in this story] (*Yoma* 38b; *Midrash; Rashi*).

21. הָרַגְתָּ בְּיוֹם אַפֶּךָ טָבַחְתָּ לֹא חָמָלְתָּ — *You slew them on the day of Your wrath; You slaughtered and showed no mercy.*

Had the Destruction come on a day other than *the day of Your wrath,* i.e., Tishah B'Av, it would have been tempered with mercy and restraint. Having come on the day You specifically set aside for display of Your anger, it was untempered and complete (*Lechem Dim'ah*).

22. כְּיוֹם מוֹעֵד — *As though at festival time.* The enemy so swarmed over Jerusalem and the Temple that it was reminiscent of the throngs of Jewish pilgrims who used to swarm into Jerusalem on the festivals (*Ibn Shuib*).

your young children, who swoon from hunger at every street corner.* [20] *Look, HASHEM, and behold, whom You have treated so. Should women eat their own offspring,* the babes of their care?* Should priest and prophet be slain in the Sanctuary of the Lord?* [21] *Out on the ground, in the streets they lie, young and old; my maidens and my young men have fallen by the sword. You slew them on the day of Your wrath; You slaughtered them and showed no mercy.** [22] *You invited, as though at festival time,* my evil neighbors round about. So that, at the day of HASHEM's wrath, there were none who survived or escaped. Those who I cherished and brought up, my enemy has wiped out.*

CHAPTER THREE

[1] *I am the man* who has seen affliction by the rod of His anger.* [2] *He has driven me on and on into unrelieved darkness.* [3] *Only against me* did He turn His hand repeatedly* all day long.* [4] *He has worn away my flesh and skin;* He broke my bones.* [5] *He besieged and encircled me with bitterness and travail.* [6] *He has placed me in darkness like the eternally dead.* [7] *He has walled me in* so I cannot escape; He has weighed me down with chains.* [8] *Though I would cry out and plead,* He shut out my prayer.** [9] *He has walled up my roads with hewn stones;*

CHAPTER THREE

1. אֲנִי הַגֶּבֶר — *I am the man.* Jeremiah, in a personal statement, laments that he saw more affliction than all the other prophets who foretold the Destruction of the Temple. For it was destroyed not in their days, but in his (*Rashi*). (It had been noted that the numerical value of אֲנִי הַגֶּבֶר, *I am the man* [=271], equals יִרְמְיָהוּ, *Jeremiah* [*Tzfunos Yisrael*]).

[Chapter 3 is composed of a triple acrostic. It is written in the form of three-verse units, each verse beginning with the same letter.]

2. [In the verses 2-16 the sufferer proceeds to describe his suffering figuratively in a series of more or less isolated pictures. The translation, which already incorporates much of the exegesis of the Sages, makes the verses, for the most part, readily understandable. The commentary, in this chapter, has therefore been intended mainly to remove surface difficulties.]

3. אַךְ בִּי — *Only against me* — i.e., I alone am the constant recipient of His punishment (*Rashi*).

Sifsei Chachamim personifies the phrase as referring specifically to Jeremiah: *On no prophet but me* [see comm. 3:1].

All nations sin but toward no other nation is God so zealous in exacting retribution as toward Israel (*Rav Yosef Kara*).

יָשֻׁב יַהֲפֹךְ יָדוֹ — *Turn His hand repeatedly.* In punishment, anthropomorphically, as if — so to speak — He wants the punishment to be constant; when one hand 'tires,' He uses the other (*Toras Chesed*).

Alshich translates: He removed His compassionate hand [i.e., His protection] from me.

4. [The verse speaks of man's total physical suffering:]

בִּלָּה בְשָׂרִי וְעוֹרִי — *He has worn away my flesh and skin.* The flesh and skin — which are sensitive to pain — He wore away. The bones — which have no tactile sensation — He crushed (*Ibn Ezra*).

7. גָּדַר בַּעֲדִי — *He has walled* [lit., *hedged*] *me in.* The prophet alludes to our long exile. God has, in effect, walled us in — so that the dark exile imprisons us. The verses continue that he weighed us down with oppression and closed the door to our prayers (*Lechem Dim'ah*).

8. גַּם כִּי אֶזְעַק וַאֲשַׁוֵּעַ — *Though I would cry out and plead.* Rav Eliezer said: From the day the Temple was destroyed, the gates of prayer have been shut, as it is written: *Though I would cry out and plead, He shut out my prayer* (*Berachos* 32b).

This refers to insincere private prayer; public prayer or sincere private prayer is always accepted (*Torah Temimah*).

שָׂתַם תְּפִלָּתִי — *He shut out my prayer* by closing the 'windows' of Heaven (*Rashi*); and by placing an 'iron barrier' between Him and Israel (*Mikdash Lekach Tov*).

The *Midrash* notes that prayers said with a congregation are more acceptable than those said alone or after the congregation has finished. [This is suggested by the fact that the word תְּפִלָּתִי, my *prayer*, is in the singular; this indicating that, had a quorum prayed, their supplication would have been heard *(Torah*

נְתִיבֹתַי עִוָּה: י דֹּב אֹרֵב הוּא לִי* °אֲרִי בְּמִסְתָּרִים: יא דְּרָכַי סוֹרֵר וַיְפַשְּׁחֵנִי שָׂמַנִי שֹׁמֵם: יב דָּרַךְ קַשְׁתּוֹ וַיַּצִּיבֵנִי* כַּמַּטָּרָא לַחֵץ: יג הֵבִיא בְּכִלְיוֹתָי בְּנֵי אַשְׁפָּתוֹ: יד הָיִיתִי שְּׂחֹק לְכָל־עַמִּי* נְגִינָתָם כָּל־הַיּוֹם:* טו הִשְׂבִּיעַנִי בַמְּרוֹרִים הִרְוַנִי לַעֲנָה: טז וַיַּגְרֵס בֶּחָצָץ שִׁנָּי הִכְפִּישַׁנִי בָּאֵפֶר:* יז וַתִּזְנַח מִשָּׁלוֹם נַפְשִׁי נָשִׁיתִי טוֹבָה: יח וָאֹמַר אָבַד נִצְחִי וְתוֹחַלְתִּי מֵיהוה: יט זְכָר־עָנְיִי וּמְרוּדִי לַעֲנָה וָרֹאשׁ: כ זָכוֹר תִּזְכּוֹר °וְתָשׁוֹחַ עָלַי נַפְשִׁי: כא זֹאת אָשִׁיב אֶל־לִבִּי* עַל־כֵּן אוֹחִיל: כב חַסְדֵי יהוה כִּי לֹא־תָמְנוּ* כִּי לֹא־כָלוּ רַחֲמָיו: כג חֲדָשִׁים לַבְּקָרִים* רַבָּה אֱמוּנָתֶךָ:* כד חֶלְקִי יהוה אָמְרָה נַפְשִׁי עַל־כֵּן אוֹחִיל לוֹ: כה טוֹב יהוה לְקֹוָו לְנֶפֶשׁ תִּדְרְשֶׁנּוּ: כו טוֹב וְיָחִיל וְדוּמָם לִתְשׁוּעַת יהוֹה: כז טוֹב לַגֶּבֶר כִּי־יִשָּׂא עֹל בִּנְעוּרָיו: כח יֵשֵׁב בָּדָד וְיִדֹּם כִּי נָטַל עָלָיו: כט יִתֵּן בֶּעָפָר פִּיהוּ אוּלַי יֵשׁ תִּקְוָה:

°אריה כ׳ °ותשיח כ׳

Temimah).] If ten righteous men pray and a wicked person joins them, would Hashem say, 'I refuse to hear their prayers because of this single wicked person'? But if a person comes after the congregation is finished, and stands alone in prayer, his every deed and thought is scrutinized.

10. דֹּב אֹרֵב הוּא לִי — *He is a lurking bear to me.* [The verse does not make it clear who is referred to: God; or His delegate — the enemy.]

According to *Rashi*, the subject is the Holy One, Blessed is He, Who has become like a lurking bear.

The *Midrash* however, interprets *bear* as referring to Nebuchadnezzar or, prophetically, to Vespasian. *Lion* refers to Nebuzaradan [the general who made the final attack during the First Destruction], or to Trajan [the conquering general during the Second Destruction].

According to many commentators (*Alshich; Ibn Yachya; Kol Yehudah*), the verse refers to the enemy who lay in hiding ready to pounce upon Israel without warning.

12. דָּרַךְ קַשְׁתּוֹ וַיַּצִּיבֵנִי — *He bent his bow and set me up. Lechem Dim'ah* notes that the order is reversed. Usually one first sets up his target and then takes aim. The verse implies the enemy kept him in constant terror by keeping his bow bent and aimed at him.

[Being *'walled in without escape'* and *'weighed down with chains'* as described in verses 7-9, he was certainly an easy target!]

14. הָיִיתִי שְּׂחֹק לְכָל־עַמִּי — *I have become a laughingstock to all my people* [i.e., an object of derision]. עַמִּי, *my people*, is explained as: The people in whose midst I dwell (*Lechem Dim'ah*).

The *Targum* translates: פְּרִיצֵי, *the impudent (scorners) of my nation.*

The *Midrash* explains this as referring to 'the nations of the world who sit in theaters and circuses. After they eat and drink and become intoxicated, they sit and discuss me, scoffing at me.'

According to *Palgei Mayim*, Jeremiah is lamenting how, whenever he prophesied oracles of reproof and impending disaster, the Jews would laugh and taunt him. Because of their inattentiveness to his prophecies, disaster fell.

נְגִינָתָם כָּל־הַיּוֹם — *Their jibes* [lit., *songs*] *all day long* [i.e., I became the theme of their satirical songs].

15. The *Midrash*, linking בַמְּרוֹרִים, *bitterness*, with מָרוֹר, *the bitter herbs*, eaten at the Passover *Seder*, notes that the night of the week on which the first day of Passover occurs is always the same as the night on which Tishah B'Av falls.

16. הִכְפִּישַׁנִי בָּאֵפֶר — *He made me cower in ashes*, i.e., He covered me with ashes (*Rashi*).

The *Talmud* relates that on the eve of Tishah B'Av, after Rav would complete his regular meal, he would dip a morsel of bread into ashes and say, 'This is the essence of the Erev Tishah B'Av meal, in fulfillment of the verse:. . .*He made me cower in ashes'* (*Yerushalmi Taanis* 4:6).

20. The *Midrash* translates: זָכוֹר תִּזְכּוֹר, *You will surely remember* [O God,] the nations of the world and will punish them for oppressing me, but while waiting for the vengeance, תָשׁוּחַ עָלַי נַפְשִׁי, *my soul is despondent* [i.e., I haven't the patience to wait any longer]. A proverb declares: While the fat one grows lean, the lean one expires.

He tangled up my paths. [10] *He is a lurking bear to me,* a lion in hiding.* [11] *He has strewn my paths with thorns and made me tread carefully; He made me desolate.* [12] *He bent his bow and set me up* as a target for the arrow.* [13] *He shot into my vitals the arrows of His quiver.* [14] *I have become a laughingstock to all my people;* object of their jibes all day long.** [15] *He filled me with bitterness, sated me with wormwood.* [16] *He ground my teeth on gravel, He made me cower in ashes.** [17] *My soul despaired of having peace, I have forgotten goodness.* [18] *And I said, 'Gone is my strength and my expectation from* HASHEM.*'* [19] *Remember my afflictions and my sorrow; the wormwood and bitterness.* [20] *My soul remembers well — and makes me despondent.* [21] *Yet, this I bear in mind;* therefore I still hope:* [22] HASHEM*'s kindness surely has not ended,* nor are His mercies exhausted.* [23] *They are new every morning;* great is Your faithfulness!** [24] *'*HASHEM *is my portion,' says my soul, therefore I have hope in Him.* [25] HASHEM *is good to those who trust in Him;* to the soul that seeks Him.* [26] *It is good to hope submissively for* HASHEM*'s salvation, for He has laid it upon him.* [27] *It is good for a man that he bear a yoke in his youth.* [28] *Let one sit in solitude and be submissive, for He has laid it upon him.* [29] *Let him put his mouth to the dust — there may yet be hope.**

---

21. זאת אָשִׁיב אֶל־לִבִּי — [Yet,] *this I bear in mind.* After my heart told me that it *'lost its expectation from* HASHEM*'* [verse 18], I bore this in mind and thus restored my faith (*Rashi*).

[Verses 19-21 represent the transition from the despair (which culminates in verse 18) and the doctrine of hope which is achieved by recalling God's mercy in verses 22-38.]

In the time to come when the era of redemption arrives, God will say to Israel, 'My sons, I wonder how you waited for Me all these years.' And they will answer, 'Lord of the universe, had it not been for Your Torah which You gave us, the heathen peoples would long ago have caused us to perish.'

Therefore, it is stated: זאת אָשִׁיב אֶל־לִבִּי, *this I bear in mind,* and זאת, *this,* indicates nothing else than the Torah, as it is said וְזֹאת הַתּוֹרָה, *And this is the Torah* [*Deut.* 4:44] (*Midrash*).

22. [This verse begins the expression of faith and hope alluded to in the previous verse and continues through verse 38.]

חַסְדֵי ה׳ כִּי לֹא־תָמְנוּ — HASHEM*'s kindness surely has not ended* [i.e., is inexhaustible]. *Rashi*, whose translation we followed, gives an alternate translation: חַסְדֵי ה׳, *it is due to* HASHEM*'s kindness,* כִּי לֹא־תָמְנוּ, *that we were not annihilated for our transgressions,* כִּי לֹא־כָלוּ רַחֲמָיו — *because His mercies are not exhausted* [see *Numbers* 17-28].

23. חֲדָשִׁים לַבְּקָרִים — *They are new every morning* [i.e., Your kindnesses are renewed from day to day (*Rashi*)]. *Alshich* interprets the subject of this verse as the soul of man: *God renews man's life every morning, and I have faith that He will continue to do so in the future and redeem us.*

The *Talmud* interprets esoterically that each day God creates a band of new angels who utter a song before Him and then pass away (*Chagigah* 14a).

רַבָּה אֱמוּנָתֶךָ — *Great is your faithfulness,* i.e., great is Your promise; and it is great to believe in Your fulfilling and guarding whatever You promised (*Rashi*).

One earns great merit by believing in You (*Lechem Dim'ah*).

25. טוֹב ה׳ לְקֹוָו — HASHEM *is good to those who trust in Him.* The *Midrash* cites an apparent contradiction between this verse and the verse in *Psalms* 145:9 stating that Hashem is good to all, not only to those who trust in Him. The *Midrash* explains with a parable: When one waters his orchard, he waters all of it. When one hoes, however, he hoes only the better plants. [So, too, in normal times, God provides for everyone equally, but in a time of punishment and destruction, only those who hope in Him are worthy of individual intervention (*Torah Temimah*).]

26-27. Since we are certain that God will not eternally neglect us, the prudent thing to do is to accept God's afflictions submissively, in quiet resignation, and silently anticipate God's ultimate salvation. As for the suffering he inflicts upon us in the interim... *It is better to bear the yoke in one's youth* — while one is young and has the vigor to withstand the tribulations, rather than when old and lacking the stamina (*Alshich*).

29. אוּלַי יֵשׁ תִּקְוָה — *There may yet be hope* — that God will forgive him (*Alshich*).

When Rabbi [the compiler of the *Mishnah*] reached these verses [29-31], he wept (*Midrash*),

ל יִתֵּן לְמַכֵּהוּ לֶחִי יִשְׂבַּע בְּחֶרְפָּה: לא כִּי לֹא יִזְנַח לְעוֹלָם אֲדֹנָי:* לב כִּי אִם־הוֹגָה וְרִחַם כְּרֹב חֲסָדָו: לג כִּי לֹא עִנָּה מִלִּבּוֹ* וַיַּגֶּה בְּנֵי־אִישׁ: לד לְדַכֵּא תַּחַת רַגְלָיו כֹּל אֲסִירֵי אָרֶץ:* לה לְהַטּוֹת מִשְׁפַּט־גָּבֶר* נֶגֶד פְּנֵי עֶלְיוֹן: לו לְעַוֵּת אָדָם בְּרִיבוֹ אֲדֹנָי לֹא רָאָה: לז מִי זֶה אָמַר וַתֶּהִי אֲדֹנָי לֹא צִוָּה: לח מִפִּי עֶלְיוֹן לֹא תֵצֵא הָרָעוֹת וְהַטּוֹב:* לט מַה־יִּתְאוֹנֵן אָדָם חָי גֶּבֶר עַל־חֲטָאָו:* מ נַחְפְּשָׂה דְרָכֵינוּ וְנַחְקֹרָה* וְנָשׁוּבָה עַד־יהוה:* מא נִשָּׂא לְבָבֵנוּ אֶל־כַּפָּיִם* אֶל־אֵל בַּשָּׁמָיִם: מב נַחְנוּ פָשַׁעְנוּ* וּמָרִינוּ אַתָּה לֹא סָלָחְתָּ: מג סַכֹּתָה בָאַף וַתִּרְדְּפֵנוּ הָרַגְתָּ לֹא חָמָלְתָּ: מד סַכֹּתָה בֶעָנָן לָךְ מֵעֲבוֹר תְּפִלָּה:* מה סְחִי וּמָאוֹס תְּשִׂימֵנוּ בְּקֶרֶב הָעַמִּים: מו פָּצוּ עָלֵינוּ פִּיהֶם* כָּל־אֹיְבֵינוּ: מז פַּחַד וָפַחַת הָיָה לָנוּ הַשֵּׁאת וְהַשָּׁבֶר:

because even after all the indignities which were heaped upon Israel, the prophet still said אוּלַי, *perhaps*, as if hope was still doubtful (*Torah Temimah*).

31. [In the last several verses, the prophet exhorted man to completely debase himself in resignation before God. Now, he justifies his advice by extolling the compassion of God.]

כִּי לֹא יִזְנַח לְעוֹלָם ה׳ — *For the Lord does not reject forever,* [i.e., His anger is of limited duration] and it is therefore good to be submissive [silent] (*Rashi*).

God waits for man to repent (*Alshich*).

33. כִּי לֹא עִנָּה מִלִּבּוֹ — *For He does not torment capriciously,* i.e., He has no desire to punish capriciously; everything is in retribution for one's sins (*Rashi; Alshich*).

34. כֹּל אֲסִירֵי אָרֶץ — *All the prisoners of the earth.* This phrase is a poetic description referring to all mankind. Are we not all *prisoners* on God's *earth* with no way to escape His providence? (*Alshich*).

35. לְהַטּוֹת מִשְׁפַּט־גָּבֶר — *Nor deny a man justice.* According to *Rashi,* this verse, too, continues the theme begun in verse 33, enumerating what Hashem does not capriciously do or allow.

37-40. *Rashi* groups together three verses and explains: One should never ascribe his suffering to chance, because from whom else but from God does good and evil emanate? Therefore, why should a man complain? Let everyone put the blame on his own sins! — and [verse 40] search his ways and repent.

הָרָעוֹת וְהַטּוֹב — *Evil and good. Palgei Mayim,* in contrast to *Rashi,* takes this phrase as a statement and explains that although everything *does* emanate from God, the choice of man's actions — good or bad — is not Divine, but human...

Thus, the *Rambam* [in his *Hilchos Teshuvah* and *Eight Chapters*] writes that man is mistaken in ascribing to God his evil ways — as if they were Divinely forced upon him. When justice is meted out to him, why should someone complain that he was coerced? גֶּבֶר עַל־חֲטָאָו, he is a *strong man* over his sins! Let him conquer his evil ways! Where there is knowledge of God there is free choice.

מַה־יִּתְאוֹנֵן אָדָם חָי גֶּבֶר עַל־חֲטָאָו — *Of what shall a living man complain? A strong man for his sins!* Let him be thankful that he is alive! Rav Levi said: The Holy One, Blessed is He, declared: Your existence is in My hand, and, being alive, you complain! Rav Huna said: Let him stand up like a brave man, acknowledge his sins, and not complain. Rav Berachiah explained the verse: Why does man complain against Him who lives eternally? If a man wishes to complain, let it be about his own sins! (*Midrash*).

This כְּתִיב, *written form,* is חֶטְאוֹ, *his sin* [in the singular], while the קְרִי, *reading,* is חֲטָאָיו, *his sins. Shaar Bas Rabim* points out that someone should be particularly concerned about his *first* sin. He dare not overlook it, or take it lightly, because עֲבֵירָה גוֹרֶרֶת עֲבֵירָה, *one sin leads to another* (*Avos* 4:2), and his entire future might very well depend upon how he reacted to that first sin.

Similarly, *Rav Yonasan Eyebescheutz* points out that one should not overlook even a single transgression — however minor it appears — rather, *man should complain about every single sin.*

40. נַחְפְּשָׂה דְרָכֵינוּ וְנַחְקֹרָה — *Let us search and examine our ways.* This is the climax of the previous verses. Since man has only his own sins to blame for any misfortunes emanating from God, he should not grumble and recriminate. Instead, let us search our conduct to find the cause of our suffering — and

[30] Let one offer his cheek to his smiter, let him be filled with disgrace. [31] — For the Lord does not reject forever; [32] He first afflicts, then pities according to His abundant kindness. [33] For He does not torment capriciously, nor afflict man. [34] Nor crush under His feet all the prisoners of the earth;* [35] nor deny a man justice* in the presence of the Most High. [36] To wrong a man in his conflict — the Lord does not approve. [37] Whose decree was ever fulfilled unless the Lord ordained it? [38] It is not from the mouth of the Most High that evil and good* emanate? [39] Of what shall a living man complain? A strong man for his sins!* [40] Let us search and examine our ways* and return to HASHEM.* [41] Let us lift our hearts with our hands* to God in heaven: [42] We have transgressed* and rebelled — You have not forgiven. [43] You have enveloped Yourself in anger and pursued us; You have slain mercilessly. [44] You wrapped Yourself in a cloud that no prayer can pierce.* [45] You made us a filth and refuse among the nations.' [46] All our enemies jeered at us;* [47] panic and pitiful were ours, ravage and ruin.*

---

then repent (*Kiflayim LeSushiyah*).

As the *Talmud* advises: If a man sees that pain and suffering visit him, let him examine his conduct, as it says: *Let us examine our ways and return to HASHEM* (*Berachos* 5a).

This verse is reminiscent of *Zephaniah* 1:12: *I will search Jerusalem with candles.* One should search his ways so that his repentance will reach *up to HASHEM* — to His Throne of Glory (*Midrash Lekach Tov*).

Rav Galanti elaborates that this soul-searching must be accomplished in a manner similar to meticulous searching with the light of a candle — in every nook and crevice — as required when searching for *chametz* before Passover. The simile here refers to the soul which is likened to light [נֵר ה׳ נִשְׁמַת אָדָם, *the light of God is the soul of man*]. When one is guided by his soul and conducts the search properly throughout every nook and cranny of his being even in areas where he least suspects it — he will inevitably discover some *chametz*, the symbol of sin and improper behavior. When he removes the *chametz*, his repentance will surely reach *'up to HASHEM's* Throne of Glory.'

וְנָשׁוּבָה עַד־ה׳ — *And return* [or: *and repent*] to *HASHEM*. The *Midrash* and commentators explain the use of the more forceful עַד, *until; up to*, rather than the more direct אֶל, *to*, by quoting the Talmudic dictum [*Yoma* 86b]: גְּדוֹלָה תְּשׁוּבָה שֶׁמַּגַּעַת עַד כִּסֵּא הַכָּבוֹד, *Great is repentance for it reaches* [עַד] *up to the Throne of Glory*. Thus, the verse alludes to a concept often stressed by our Sages: A repenter rises above the status of a sinner who falls short of the ideal. Repentance raises one to the level of the most righteous.

41. נִשָּׂא לְבָבֵנוּ אֶל־כַּפָּיִם — *Let us lift our hearts with* [lit., *to*] *our hands*. The translation follows the first of *Rashi's* two interpretations: When we lift our hands [in prayer] to God, let us lift our hearts along with him [i.e., in utmost sincerity] broken-heartedly — before God.

Prayer is efficacious only when the external lifting of the hands is accompanied by the internal lifting of the heart (*Alshich*).

As the *Talmud* explains: A man's prayer is answered only if he takes his heart in his hands [i.e., is sincere] (*Taanis* 8a).

42. נַחְנוּ פָשַׁעְנוּ — *We have trangressed... You have not forgiven,* i.e., in trangressing, *we* have been true to *our* nature and Evil Inclination; but *You* have not conformed to *Your* Merciful ways — You did not forgive (*Midrash; Rashi; Alshich*).

Ibn Ezra views this verse as a separate lament: *We have transgressed* — and did not repent. Therefore, *You have not forgiven.*

44. סַכֹּתָה... מֵעֲבוֹר תְּפִלָּה — *You wrapped Yourself in a cloud that no prayer can pierce.*

Cloud is used here allegorically, as if the cloud formed a barrier between our prayers and Hashem (*Ibn Ezra*).

The *Talmud* relates that Raba would not proclaim a fast on a cloudy day because 'God wrapped Himself *in a cloud that no prayer can pierce'* (*Berachos* 32b).

46. [Verses 46-48 which begin with פ precede, rather than follow, verses 49-51 which begin with the earlier Hebrew letter ע. (See *comm.* to 2:16).]

פָּצוּ עָלֵינוּ פִּיהֶם — *(They) jeered at us.* Instead of completely ignoring us — as one would normally ignore *filth and refuse* — our enemies taunted and jeered at us, giving us no peace; not even allowing us to wallow, undisturbed, in our misery (*Ibn Yachya*).

Ibn Ezra relates שֵׁאת to שׁוֹאָה, *sudden catastrophe.*

מח פַּלְגֵי־מַיִם֙ תֵּרַ֣ד עֵינִ֔י* עַל־שֶׁ֖בֶר בַּת־עַמִּֽי: מט עֵינִ֣י נִגְּרָ֔ה וְלֹ֖א
תִדְמֶ֑ה מֵאֵ֖ין הֲפֻגֽוֹת: נ עַד־יַשְׁקִ֣יף וְיֵ֔רֶא יְהוָ֖ה מִשָּׁמָֽיִם: נא עֵינִי֙
עֽוֹלְלָ֣ה לְנַפְשִׁ֔י מִכֹּ֖ל בְּנ֥וֹת עִירִֽי: נב צ֥וֹד צָד֛וּנִי כַּצִּפֹּ֖ר אֹיְבַ֥י חִנָּֽם:
נג צָמְת֤וּ בַבּוֹר֙ חַיָּ֔י וַיַּדּוּ־אֶ֖בֶן בִּֽי: נד צָֽפוּ־מַ֥יִם עַל־רֹאשִׁ֖י* אָמַ֥רְתִּי
נִגְזָֽרְתִּי: נה קָרָ֤אתִי שִׁמְךָ֙ יְהוָ֔ה מִבּ֖וֹר תַּחְתִּיּֽוֹת: נו קוֹלִ֖י שָׁמָ֑עְתָּ
אַל־תַּעְלֵ֧ם אָזְנְךָ֛ לְרַוְחָתִ֖י לְשַׁוְעָתִֽי: נז קָרַ֙בְתָּ֙ בְּי֣וֹם אֶקְרָאֶ֔ךָּ
אָמַ֖רְתָּ אַל־תִּירָֽא:* נח רַ֧בְתָּ אֲדֹנָ֛י רִיבֵ֥י נַפְשִׁ֖י גָּאַ֥לְתָּ חַיָּֽי:
נט רָאִ֤יתָה יְהוָה֙ עַוָּ֣תָתִ֔י שָׁפְטָ֖ה מִשְׁפָּטִֽי: ס רָאִ֙יתָה֙ כָּל־נִקְמָתָ֔ם
כָּל־מַחְשְׁבֹתָ֖ם לִֽי: סא שָׁמַ֤עְתָּ חֶרְפָּתָם֙ יְהוָ֔ה* כָּל־מַחְשְׁבֹתָ֖ם עָלָֽי:
סב שִׂפְתֵ֤י קָמַי֙ וְהֶגְיוֹנָ֔ם עָלַ֖י כָּל־הַיּֽוֹם:* סג שִׁבְתָּ֤ם וְקִֽימָתָם֙ הַבִּ֔יטָה
אֲנִ֖י מַנְגִּֽינָתָֽם: סד תָּשִׁ֧יב לָהֶ֛ם גְּמ֖וּל יְהוָ֑ה כְּמַעֲשֵׂ֥ה יְדֵיהֶֽם:*
סה תִּתֵּ֤ן לָהֶם֙ מְגִנַּת־לֵ֔ב תַּאֲלָֽתְךָ֖ לָהֶֽם: סו תִּרְדֹּ֤ף בְּאַף֙ וְתַשְׁמִידֵ֔ם
מִתַּ֖חַת שְׁמֵ֥י יְהוָֽה:*

פרק רביעי

א אֵיכָה֙ יוּעַ֣ם זָהָ֔ב יִשְׁנֶ֖א הַכֶּ֣תֶם הַטּ֑וֹב* תִּשְׁתַּפֵּ֙כְנָה֙ אַבְנֵי־
קֹ֔דֶשׁ בְּרֹ֖אשׁ כָּל־חוּצֽוֹת: ב בְּנֵ֤י צִיּוֹן֙ הַיְקָרִ֔ים* הַֽמְסֻלָּאִ֖ים בַּפָּ֑ז
אֵיכָ֤ה נֶחְשְׁבוּ֙ לְנִבְלֵי־חֶ֔רֶשׂ מַעֲשֵׂ֖ה יְדֵ֥י יוֹצֵֽר: ג גַּ֤ם־°תַּנִּים֙ חָלְצוּ

°תנין כ'

---

48. פַּלְגֵי־מַיִם תֵּרַד עֵינִי — *My eye shed streams of water.* Eye is singular. If only one eye produces such streams of water, how much more so both eyes! (*Alshich*).

51. This is a personal lament of Jeremiah who was of an aristocratic, priestly family. He anguished that his weeping eye figuratively contorted his face and aggrieved his spirit more than any inhabitant of the city. His family was particularly affected, and suffered more than others because, as priests, they had been selected for holiness and the service of God (*Rashi*).

54. . . . צָפוּ־מַיִם עַל־רֹאשִׁי — *Waters flowed over my head; I thought: 'I am doomed!'* When a man is in water up to his hips, there is still hope, but when water — here allegorically referring to the heathen nations — flows over one's head, one gives up all hope. Rather, קָרָאתִי שִׁמְךָ ה', *I called on Your Name, HASHEM* (*Rashi*).

55-56. שִׁמְךָ ה' — *Your Name, HASHEM.* When one is in great anguish, drained of strength, he merely calls out the name of a passerby with such anguish that the hearer immediately discerns the gravity of the situation and responds. Here, too, he simply called God's Name hoping

that קוֹלִי שָׁמָעְתָּ, *You heard my voice,* and therefore אַל־תַּעְלֵם אָזְנְךָ לְרַוְחָתִי לְשַׁוְעָתִי, *You would not turn Your ear from my prayer for my relief when I cry out* (*Kiflayim LeSushiyah*).

As Jonah called upon You from inside the fish and from the depths of the sea, so does Israel call upon You from its exile among the nations — likened to the depths of a pit — to hear their prayers and deliver them (*Midrash Lekach Tov*).

57. אַל־תִּירָא — *Fear not!* [The utterance, *Do not be afraid!*, is a constant refrain throughout Scripture — and was said not only on segregated occasions but to virtually every one of the fathers of our people; it is a Divine promise that Israel need not fear. To mention several: *Fear not, Avram, I am your shield* (Gen. 15:1); *Fear not,* (Isaac) (Gen. 26:24); *Fear not,* (Jacob) *to go down to Egypt* (Gen. 46:3); *Fear him not,* (Moses). . . (Numbers 21:34); *Fear not,* (Children of Israel,) *nor be discouraged* (Deut. 1:21); *Fear not,* (Joshua) *nor be dismayed* (Josh. 8:1); to Gideon (Judges 6:23); to Elijah (II Kings 1:15); to Hezekiah (II Kings 19:6); to Isaiah (Isaiah 7:4); to Jeremiah (Jeremiah 1:8); Servant Yaakov (Jeremiah 30:10); to Daniel (Daniel 10:12)].

[48] My eye shed streams of water at the shattering of my people. [49] My eye will flow and will not cease — without relief — [50] until* HASHEM *looks down and takes notice from heaven. [51] My eyes have brought me grief over all the daughters of my city. [52] I have been constantly ensnared like a bird by my enemies without cause. [53] They cut off my life in a pit and threw stones at me. [54] Waters flowed over my head;* I thought, 'I am doomed!' [55] I called on Your name,* HASHEM,* *from the depths of the pit. [56] You have heard my voice; do not shut your ear from my prayer for my relief when I cry out. [57] You always drew near on the day I would call You; You said, 'Fear not!'* [58] You always championed my cause, O Lord, you redeemed my life. [59] You have seen,* HASHEM, *the injustices I suffer; judge my cause. [60] You have seen all their vengeance, all their designs against me. [61] You have heard their insults,* HASHEM;* *all their designs regarding me. [62] The speech and thoughts of my enemies are against me all day long.* [63] Look, in everything they do, I am the butt of their taunts. [64] Pay them back their due,* HASHEM, *as they have done.* [65] Give them a broken heart; may Your curse be upon them! [66] Pursue them in anger and destroy them from under the heavens of* HASHEM.*

CHAPTER FOUR

[1] Alas — the gold is dimmed! The finest gold is changed! Sacred stones are scattered at every street corner! [2] The precious children of Zion,* who are comparable to fine gold — alas, are now treated like earthen jugs, work of a potter. [3] Even tanim will offer*

61-63. שָׁמַעְתָּ חֶרְפָּתָם — *You have heard their insults,* HASHEM. *Alshich* translates the verse as referring to their blasphemies against Hashem, i.e., *You have heard how they reviled You,* HASHEM, *and how they designed against me.*

Most commentators, however, see *Israel* as being the object of their insults, and explain verses 61-63 as referring to designs of the enemy — in thought, word and action.

כָּל־הַיּוֹם — *All day long.* Even though my enemies already accomplished many of their evil plans, their mind is not at ease. They continue to plan and talk about me incessantly *all day long,* as if their power of speech was given them just to deride me (*Lechem Dim'ah*).

64-66. [In the verses that follow, Hashem is asked to mete out retribution to Israel's enemies, in kind, for all their evil.]

כְּמַעֲשֵׂה יְדֵיהֶם — *As they have done.* I.e., for having acted in consonance with, and as emissaries of, God's will in bringing about punishment to Israel — for that they are absolved. However, כְּמַעֲשֵׂה יְדֵיהֶם, for what they added *of their own hands*, i.e., of their viciousness and overzealousness beyond the bounds expected of them — for that Hashem is asked to punish them (*Lechem Dim'ah*).

וְתַשְׁמִידֵם מִתַּחַת שְׁמֵי ה׳ — *And destroy them from under the heavens of* HASHEM — Don't punish them with exile, as You punished us. Destroy them from the face of the earth (*Rav Galanti*).

The obliteration should be so complete that they should have no descendants, and that no one will be able to say, 'This tree, or camel, or lamb belongs to him' [i.e., there will be no trace of identity left] (*Midrash*).

[Thus, with the plea that God utterly wipe out the enemy, the chapter closes.]

CHAPTER FOUR

1. אֵיכָה יוּעַם זָהָב — *Alas — the gold is dimmed!* The *gold* figuratively refers to the people of Jerusalem. It has become covered over, i.e., dull only in its external appearance and brilliance, but not in substance (*Midrash; Rashi; Ibn Yachya*).

Rashi comments that this elegy was originally pronounced over יֹאשִׁיָּהוּ, King Josiah, as mentioned in *II Chronicles* 35:25. (See commentary to *Kinnah* 11, p. 182.) Jeremiah also incorporated within it the references to Zion.

2. בְּנֵי צִיּוֹן הַיְקָרִים — *The precious children of Zion.* [The verse laments how Zion's precious inhabitants, once greatly esteemed, are now

שַׁד* הֵינִיקוּ גּוּרֵיהֶן בַּת־עַמִּי לְאַכְזָר °כַּיְעֵנִים בַּמִּדְבָּר: ד דָּבַק לְשׁוֹן יוֹנֵק אֶל־חִכּוֹ בַּצָּמָא* עוֹלָלִים שָׁאֲלוּ לֶחֶם פֹּרֵשׂ אֵין לָהֶם: ה הָאֹכְלִים לְמַעֲדַנִּים נָשַׁמּוּ בַּחוּצוֹת הָאֱמֻנִים עֲלֵי תוֹלָע חִבְּקוּ אַשְׁפַּתּוֹת: ו וַיִּגְדַּל עֲוֹן בַּת־עַמִּי מֵחַטַּאת סְדֹם* הַהֲפוּכָה כְמוֹ־רָגַע* וְלֹא־חָלוּ בָהּ יָדָיִם: ז זַכּוּ נְזִירֶיהָ מִשֶּׁלֶג צַחוּ מֵחָלָב אָדְמוּ עֶצֶם מִפְּנִינִים סַפִּיר גִּזְרָתָם: ח חָשַׁךְ מִשְּׁחוֹר תָּאֳרָם לֹא נִכְּרוּ בַּחוּצוֹת* צָפַד עוֹרָם עַל־עַצְמָם יָבֵשׁ הָיָה כָעֵץ: ט טוֹבִים הָיוּ חַלְלֵי־חֶרֶב* מֵחַלְלֵי רָעָב שֶׁהֵם יָזוּבוּ מְדֻקָּרִים מִתְּנוּבֹת שָׂדָי: י יְדֵי נָשִׁים רַחֲמָנִיּוֹת בִּשְּׁלוּ יַלְדֵיהֶן* הָיוּ לְבָרוֹת לָמוֹ בְּשֶׁבֶר בַּת־עַמִּי: יא כִּלָּה יהוה אֶת־חֲמָתוֹ* שָׁפַךְ חֲרוֹן אַפּוֹ וַיַּצֶּת־אֵשׁ בְּצִיּוֹן וַתֹּאכַל יְסוֹדֹתֶיהָ: יב לֹא הֶאֱמִינוּ מַלְכֵי־אֶרֶץ* °כֹּל יֹשְׁבֵי תֵבֵל כִּי יָבֹא צַר וְאוֹיֵב בְּשַׁעֲרֵי יְרוּשָׁלִָם: יג מֵחַטֹּאת נְבִיאֶיהָ*

°כי ענים כ׳ °וכל כ׳

treated like common clay.]

Midrash Lekach Tov, commenting on the precious character of the people of Jerusalem, notes that when residents of Jerusalem sat down to eat they would hang a cloth over their door as a signal to the poor that they might come to share their meal [see also *Bava Basra* 93b].

3. גַּם־תַּנִּים חָלְצוּ שַׁד — *Even tanim will offer the breast.* [The word תַּנִּים, *tanim*, refers to a wild animal but its exact identity is unknown. The word usually means *reptile* or *fish* and in modern Hebrew, תַּן means *jackal*. Since the specific guidance of Talmudic sources is lacking, we have left the word untranslated.]

Although *tanim* are vicious, they display warmth and kindness to their young by nursing them. Jeremiah laments how, as a result of the ravages and stress of famine, the usually compassionate Jewish mothers became cruel and placed their own lives before their children's. They consumed whatever food was available, and allowed their children to go hungry, ignoring their cries for food (*Rashi*).

According to many commentators, *tanim* figuratively refers to the vicious enemy who חָלְצוּ שַׁד, *bared the breast*, i.e., forced Jewish women to nurse their enemy's children with the tragic result that the nursing mothers had no milk left for their own children. The Jewish daughters, unable to respond to the needs of their children who cried *like ostriches in the desert*, seemed to be אַכְזָר, *cruel* (*Alshich, Palgei Mayim*).

At very least, the Jews could expect that the enemy's children who were nursed by Jewish women should display some compassion for the women who reared them. This, too, was not forthcoming. They were as cruel as ostriches in the desert (*Lechem Dim'ah*).

4. לְשׁוֹן יוֹנֵק ... בַּצָּמָא — *The tongue of the suckling ... for thirst.* Since, in the previous verse, *the daughter of my people has become cruel*, the sucklings who depend on their mothers for milk are described as dying of thirst, whereas the עוֹלָלִים, *the young children*, beg for bread (*Kiflayim LeSushiyah*).

The *Midrash* relates how the enemy also destroyed the conduits which carried water through the land. Even when a father took his thirsty child to the conduit, he found no water.

5. In this verse Jeremiah further laments the fall of the people from their previous heights to the nethermost depths to which they have fallen. People, who were brought up eating *only* the finest delicacies and dressed only in the most luxurious clothing, lay faint from hunger in the streets, and scrounged through garbage heaps for the most meager scraps of food (*Lechem Dim'ah*).

6. וַיִּגְדַּל עֲוֹן ... מֵחַטַּאת סְדֹם — *The iniquity is greater ... than the sin of Sodom.* The punishment of Zion, greater than that of Sodom [see next comm.], proves that their iniquity was greater than Sodom's (*Rashi*).

הַהֲפוּכָה כְמוֹ־רָגַע — *Which was overturned in a moment*, i.e., Sodom was destroyed instantly — without the suffering of a prolonged siege. Hence its sin is considered not as grave as

the breast and suckle their young; the daughter of my people has become cruel, like ostriches in the desert.* [4] *The tongue of the suckling cleaves to its palate for thirst;* young children beg for bread, no one extends it to them.* [5] *Those who feasted extravagantly lie destitute in the streets; those who were brought up in scarlet clothing wallow garbage.* [6] *The iniquity of the daughter of my people is greater than the sin of Sodom,* which was overturned in a moment* without mortal hands being laid on her.* [7] *Her princes were purer than snow, whiter than milk; their appearance was ruddier than rubies, their outside was like sapphire.* [8] *Their appearance has become blacker than soot, they are not recognized in the streets;* their skin has shriveled on their bones, it became dry as wood.* [9] *More fortunate were the victims of the sword* than the victims of famine, for they pine away, stricken, lacking the fruits of the field.* [10] *Hands of compassionate women have boiled their own children;* they became their food when the daughter of my people was shattered.* [11] *HASHEM vented His fury,* He poured out His fierce anger; He kindled a fire in Zion which consumed its foundations.* [12] *The kings of the earth did not believe,* nor did any of the world's inhabitants, that the adversary or enemy could enter the gates of Jerusalem.* [13] *It was for the sins of her prophets,**

Jerusalem's, which was punished with famine, sieges, war — and an exile which still endures! (*Rashi; Lechem Dim'ah*).

7-8. [The dramatic 'then and now' comparisons demonstrate the ravages of famine and war upon the nobility. Formerly they were prince-like figures of grace and nobility, while now they are *blacker than soot.*]

8. לֹא נִכְּרוּ בַּחוּצוֹת — *They are not recognized in the streets.* The *Midrash* relates of Rav Zadok that the ravages of the Destruction bore so hard upon him that his body never returned to normal although he lived for many years after the Destruction.

9. טוֹבִים הָיוּ חַלְלֵי־חֶרֶב — *More fortunate were the victims of the sword* or: *The good* [people] *were the victims of the sword* because they died a swift death, one preferable to the slow agony of famine (*Alshich*).

10. [The extent of the depravity is described. (See also 2:20.)]

יְדֵי נָשִׁים רַחֲמָנִיּוֹת בִּשְּׁלוּ יַלְדֵיהֶן — *Hands of compassionate women have boiled their own children.*

The impending Destruction and the ravages and famine of war caused compassionate mothers to become so depraved that *with their own hands they boiled their children* and they consumed them without even leaving flesh for other members of the family (*Alshich*).

Rav Almosnino comments that they boiled their own *dead* children — but did not murder them.

The *Shelah* comments that this phrase also contains moralistic criticism of overly compassionate and over-indulgent mothers who, for example, let their children sleep late rather than go to synagogue or to school. With this 'misplaced compassion' they 'roast' and destroy their children's souls.

11. כִּלָּה ה׳ אֶת חֲמָתוֹ — *HASHEM vented His fury.* The fury, pent up within Him for many years [see comm. to 2:8], was vented when He exacted vengeance upon them.

12. לֹא הֶאֱמִינוּ מַלְכֵי־אֶרֶץ — *The kings of the earth did not* [or *could not*] *believe*. The miraculous defeat of Sennacherib [*II Chronicles* 32] created the impression that Jerusalem was impregnable (*Midrash Lekach Tov*).

They didn't realize that because its sanctity had been defiled, it had become vulnerable (*Alshich*).

13. מֵחַטֹּאת נְבִיאֶיהָ — *It was for the sins of her prophets*, i.e., she became vulnerable to such calamity because of the sins of her false prophets (*Rashi*).

[These prophets gave her false security by indulging in deceptive oracles, and did not exhort her to repent. Compare *Jeremiah* 8:10-12: *From prophet to priest everyone deals falsely, for they have healed the hurt of my people superficially by saying, 'Peace, peace,' when there is no peace... Therefore they shall fall*

עֲוֺנֹ֖ת כֹּֽהֲנֶ֑יהָ הַשֹּׁפְכִ֥ים בְּקִרְבָּ֖הּ דַּ֥ם צַדִּיקִֽים׃ יד נָע֤וּ עִוְרִים֙ בַּֽחוּצ֔וֹת נְגֹֽאֲל֖וּ בַּדָּ֑ם בְּלֹ֣א יֽוּכְל֔וּ יִגְּע֖וּ בִּלְבֻשֵׁיהֶֽם׃ טו ס֣וּרוּ טָמֵ֞א קָ֣רְאוּ לָ֗מוֹ ס֤וּרוּ ס֙וּרוּ֙ אַל־תִּגָּ֔עוּ כִּ֥י נָצ֖וּ גַּם־נָ֑עוּ אָֽמְרוּ֙ בַּגּוֹיִ֔ם לֹ֥א יוֹסִ֖פוּ לָגֽוּר׃ טז פְּנֵ֤י יְהוָה֙ חִלְּקָ֔ם לֹ֥א יוֹסִ֖יף לְהַבִּיטָ֑ם פְּנֵ֤י כֹֽהֲנִים֙ לֹ֣א נָשָׂ֔אוּ °וּזְקֵנִ֖ים לֹ֥א חָנָֽנוּ׃ יז °עוֹדֵ֙ינוּ֙ תִּכְלֶ֣ינָה עֵינֵ֔ינוּ אֶל־עֶזְרָתֵ֖נוּ הָ֑בֶל בְּצִפִּיָּתֵ֣נוּ צִפִּ֔ינוּ אֶל־גּ֖וֹי לֹ֥א יוֹשִֽׁעַ׃ יח צָד֣וּ צְעָדֵ֔ינוּ מִלֶּ֖כֶת בִּרְחֹבֹתֵ֑ינוּ קָרַ֥ב קִצֵּ֛נוּ מָלְא֥וּ יָמֵ֖ינוּ כִּי־בָ֥א קִצֵּֽנוּ׃ יט קַלִּ֤ים הָיוּ֙ רֹדְפֵ֔ינוּ מִנִּשְׁרֵ֖י שָׁמָ֑יִם עַל־הֶהָרִ֣ים דְּלָקֻ֔נוּ בַּמִּדְבָּ֖ר אָ֥רְבוּ לָֽנוּ׃ כ ר֤וּחַ אַפֵּ֙ינוּ֙ מְשִׁ֣יחַ יְהוָ֔ה נִלְכַּ֖ד בִּשְׁחִיתוֹתָ֑ם אֲשֶׁ֣ר אָמַ֔רְנוּ בְּצִלּ֖וֹ נִחְיֶ֥ה בַגּוֹיִֽם׃ כא שִׂ֤ישִׂי וְשִׂמְחִי֙ בַּת־אֱד֔וֹם °יוֹשֶׁ֖בֶת בְּאֶ֣רֶץ ע֑וּץ גַּם־עָלַ֙יִךְ֙ תַּֽעֲבָר־כּ֔וֹס תִּשְׁכְּרִ֖י וְתִתְעָרִֽי׃ כב תַּם־עֲוֺנֵךְ֙ בַּת־צִיּ֔וֹן לֹ֥א יוֹסִ֖יף לְהַגְלוֹתֵ֑ךְ פָּקַ֤ד עֲוֺנֵךְ֙ בַּת־אֱד֔וֹם גִּלָּ֖ה עַל־חַטֹּאתָֽיִךְ׃

°זקנים כ׳ °עודינה כ׳ °יושבתי כ׳

among the fallen. This caused the blood of the righteous to be shed in their midst.]

A different approach is taken by *Rav Alkabetz* in interpreting verses 12-13: The priests and prophets of Israel were renowned throughout the world for their holiness and sincerity. Therefore: *The kings of the earth could not believe that Jerusalem would be made vulnerable as a result of any sins*, and if it were to become subject to conquest, it could be *on the fault of her priests and prophets.*

14-15. נָעוּ עִוְרִים בַּחוּצוֹת — *The blind wandered through the streets.* This translation follows *Rashi* who explains: When the blind wandered through the streets, their feet slipped in the blood of the murdered Jews who lay throughout the city.

Ibn Ezra interprets עִוְרִים as an adverb and translates: they wandered through the streets *blindly.*

אָמְרוּ בַּגּוֹיִם לֹא יוֹסִפוּ לָגוּר — *The nations had said: 'They will not sojourn again.'* The nations predicted that the Jews will never again return to their land to dwell as before (*Ibn Ezra; Akeidas Yitzchak*) because [next verse] God is the One Who exiled them (*Alshich*).

Other commentators translate: For the nations resolved — after seeing Israel's defilement — that they will not allow her to dwell [peacefully] in their lands, and they will compel her to wander about (*Lechem Dim'ah*).

[In this chapter, too, the verse beginning with פ precedes the verse beginning with ע. See comm. to 2:16.]

16. פְּנֵי כֹהֲנִים לֹא נָשָׂאוּ — *They showed no regard for the priests.* The end of the verse gives the reason that God dispersed the Jews and avoided looking after them: Because they showed no regard for the priests and elders, God showed no regard, as it were, for them (*Alshich*).

17. עוֹדֵינוּ תִּכְלֶינָה עֵינֵינוּ אֶל־עֶזְרָתֵנוּ הָבֶל — *Our eyes still strained in vain for our deliverance.* [The verse reproduces the state of mind that prevailed in the last days of the siege, when nearly everyone sustained the hope that outside help would arrive. From *Jeremiah* 37:5-11 we know that the advance of the Egyptian army caused the Babylonians to retreat from Jerusalem, but as Jeremiah predicted, the relief was only temporary. The Egyptians never came to save them, and the Babylonians returned as Jeremiah predicted.]

18. These verses describe the miserable state of the Jews who remained in Judea under Chaldean rule (*Ibn Shuib*).

צָדוּ צְעָדֵינוּ — *They dogged our steps so we could not walk in our streets*, i.e, they ambushed us (*Rashi*), so that when a Jew went to market they would pounce upon him screaming, 'There goes a Jew!' (*Lekach Tov*).

20. רוּחַ אַפֵּינוּ מְשִׁיחַ ה׳ — *The breath of our nostrils, HASHEM's anointed.* [The expression רוּחַ אַפֵּינוּ, *the breath of our nostrils*, occurs only here, and poetically expresses the very essence of national hope and identity — its very survival

the iniquities of her priests, who had shed in her midst the blood of the righteous. [14] *The blind wandered through the streets,* defiled with blood, so that none could touch their garments.* [15] *'Away, unclean one!' people shouted at them; 'Away! Away! Don't touch! For they are loathsome and wander about.' The nations had said: 'They will not sojourn again.'** [16] *The anger of* HASHEM *has divided them, caring for them no longer; they showed no regard for the priests* nor favor for the elders.* [17] *Our eyes still strained in vain for our deliverance;* in our expectations we watched for a nation that could not save.* [18] *They dogged our steps* so we could not walk in our streets; our end drew near, out days are done, for our end has come.* [19] *Our pursuers were swifter than eagles in the sky; they chased us in the mountains, ambushed us in the desert.* [20] *The breath of our nostrils,* HASHEM*'s anointed,* was caught in their traps; he, under whose protection, we had thought, we would live among the nations.* [21] *Rejoice and exult, O daughter of Edom,* who dwells in the land of Uz;* to you, too, will the cup pass,* you will be drunk and will vomit.** [22] *Your iniquity is expiated, O daughter of Zion,* He will not exile you again;* He remembers your iniquity, daughter of Edom, He will uncover your sins.*

---

and 'breath of life' — which focused on the monarch, God's anointed.]

21. שִׂישִׂי וְשִׂמְחִי בַּת־אֱדוֹם — *Rejoice and exult, O daughter of Edom.* These words are spoken sarcastically, as if to say: Rejoice while you can, because you will not escape punishment for your sins (*Midrash Lekach Tov*).

Ibn Ezra explains that Edom is referred to here because of its implacable hatred for Israel. They rejoiced at Jerusalem's downfall, as it is written (*Psalms* 137:7): *Remember,* HASHEM*, for the sons of Edom, the day of Jerusalem, for those who say, 'Destroy it, destroy it, unto its very foundation!'* [See also *Ovadiah* 1:10-14 for a description of the malice which Edom demonstrated on the day of Jerusalem's disaster.]

According to *Rashi* and the *Midrash*, this verse refers not to contemporary Edom but prophetically to the Romans [whom the Sages identify with Biblical Edom] who Jeremiah foresaw would destroy the Second Temple.

יוֹשֶׁבֶת בְּאֶרֶץ עוּץ — *Who dwells in the land of Uz.* [The Arameans' land bordering upon Edom (see *Jeremiah* 25:20) and named after its early Edomite settler, Uz, son of Seir (*Gen.* 36:28).]

גַּם־עָלַיִךְ תַּעֲבָר־כּוֹס — *To* [lit., *upon*] *you, too, will the cup pass,* i.e., the cup of punishment (*Rashi*).

תִּשְׁכְּרִי וְתִתְעָרִי — *You will be drunk and will vomit* [i.e., you will drink so much from the cup of punishment and wrath that you will get intoxicated from its abundance, and, like a drunken man, will vomit].

Rav Yonasan Eyebesheutz notes that the curse of vomiting is that as a result of vomiting she will have room to drink more from the cup of punishment.

[It is perhaps possible to relate תִּתְעָרִי to the Edomite outcry against Jerusalem (*Psalms* 137:7: עָרוּ עָרוּ, *'destroy it! destroy it!'*). Just as you Edomites called excessively for Jerusalem's destruction, so will you drink excessively from the cup of destruction and be destroyed.]

22. תַּם־עֲוֹנֵךְ בַּת־צִיּוֹן — *Your iniquity is expiated, O daughter of Zion,* i.e., you have been punished for all your sins (*Rashi*).

You have been punished in one blow for the accumulation of all your iniquity (*Alshich*).

The *Midrash* notes that [the miseries and calamities related in] the Book of *Lamentations* were better for Israel than the forty years during which Jeremiah exhorted and prophesied. Because of the Destruction of the Temple, all Israel's sins were expiated that very day.

לֹא יוֹסִיף לְהַגְלוֹתֵךְ — *He will not exile you again*, beyond the Edomite [Roman, i.e., current] exile (*Rashi*).

[*Rashi* thus understands the subject *He* as referring to God.]

Ibn Ezra suggests that the subject is *your iniquity* [i.e., your iniquity will never again cause you to be exiled].

[The verse closes this chapter with the prophetic consolation that the worst of God's wrath upon the Jews has passed, and that now it is time for Edom's Day of Judgment.]

פרק חמישי

א זְכֹר יהוה מֶה־הָיָה לָנוּ* °הַבִּיטָה וּרְאֵה אֶת־חֶרְפָּתֵנוּ:*
ב נַחֲלָתֵנוּ נֶהֶפְכָה לְזָרִים בָּתֵּינוּ לְנָכְרִים: ג יְתוֹמִים הָיִינוּ °וְאֵין
אָב* אִמֹּתֵינוּ כְּאַלְמָנוֹת: ד מֵימֵינוּ בְּכֶסֶף שָׁתִינוּ* עֵצֵינוּ בִּמְחִיר
יָבֹאוּ: ה עַל צַוָּארֵנוּ נִרְדָּפְנוּ יָגַעְנוּ °וְלֹא הוּנַח־לָנוּ:* ו מִצְרַיִם
נָתַנּוּ יָד* אַשּׁוּר לִשְׂבֹּעַ לָחֶם: ז אֲבֹתֵינוּ חָטְאוּ °וְאֵינָם °וַאֲנַחְנוּ
עֲוֹנֹתֵיהֶם סָבָלְנוּ:* ח עֲבָדִים מָשְׁלוּ בָנוּ פֹּרֵק אֵין מִיָּדָם: ט בְּנַפְשֵׁנוּ
נָבִיא לַחְמֵנוּ מִפְּנֵי חֶרֶב הַמִּדְבָּר: י עוֹרֵנוּ כְּתַנּוּר נִכְמָרוּ מִפְּנֵי
זַלְעֲפוֹת רָעָב: יא נָשִׁים בְּצִיּוֹן עִנּוּ בְּתֻלֹת בְּעָרֵי יְהוּדָה:* יב שָׂרִים
בְּיָדָם נִתְלוּ פְּנֵי זְקֵנִים לֹא נֶהְדָּרוּ: יג בַּחוּרִים טְחוֹן נָשָׂאוּ וּנְעָרִים

°הביט כ׳ °אין כ׳ °לא כ׳ °אינם כ׳ °אנחנו כ׳

CHAPTER FIVE

[Chapter five is composed of 22 verses like chapters 1, 2, and 4 — it differs from the previous four chapters in that it is not alphabetically arranged.]

1. זְכֹר ה׳ מֶה־הָיָה לָנוּ — *Remember, HASHEM, what has befallen us* [lit., *what has been to us*], i.e., Remember the sufferings we endured before the Destruction, as well as our present disgraceful condition (*Ibn Ezra*).

Israel spoke before the Holy One, Blessed is He: We are subject to forgetfulness, but You are not. Since there is no forgetfulness before You, please remember... (*Midrash*).

Alshich interprets this as alluding not to former *suffering*, but to former *glory* (see below).

הַבִּיטָה וּרְאֵה אֶת־חֶרְפָּתֵנוּ — *Look and see our disgrace. Remember*, God, those who died at the hands of our enemies, and *look and see* the disgrace which we survivors suffer (*Lechem Dim'ah*).

Alshich explains that the suffering of a poor man who has never seen wealth cannot be compared with the greater suffering of a wealthy man who has been reduced to pauperdom — who is now publicly disgraced at having to beg for his very sustenance. Thus the exiles, who were thrust from the heights of glory to the lowest conditions of servility, commiserated over their fate and lamented: זְכֹר ה׳ מֶה־הָיָה לָנוּ, *Remember, HASHEM, what we have been* — during our time of royalty. And as You remember our former grandeur, הַבִּיט, *look*, at our present condition in exile, וּרְאֵה אֶת־חֶרְפָּתֵנוּ, *see our disgrace* now, compared with our former glory.

3. יְתוֹמִים הָיִינוּ וְאֵין אָב — *We have become orphans, fatherless. Fatherless* refers to our relationship with God who is called *our Father* — i.e. God has, in a sense, removed Himself from us, leaving us *fatherless (Alshich)*.

Lechem Dim'ah [who also interprets *father* as God] notes that the כְּתִיב, written text, has אֵין אָב, *there is no father*, without the connecting prefix ו, *and*. It is therefore intended to be understood as a separate clause: The ravages of war made us *become orphans* from our natural father; in addition to that calamity, אֵין אָב, *there is no father*, because God has hidden Himself, so to speak, from us. But this verse is not to be understood as suggesting that God is no longer the Father of Israel, ח״ו, but that *He is not there*, in the sense that He maintains a distance instead of being available and paternal to His children.

4. מֵימֵינוּ בְּכֶסֶף שָׁתִינוּ — *We pay money to drink our own water* [lit., *our water for silver we drank*]. Because, due to the enemy, they were afraid to fetch it from the river. Instead, they were forced to purchase it at a high price from the enemy (*Rashi*) who had taken possession of their wells (*Alshich*).

Even the wells and trees which had been common property were sold at exorbitant prices due to the siege (*Ibn Ezra*).

5. וְלֹא הוּנַח־לָנוּ — *But nothing is left us.* They acquired everything we had by imposing taxes and levies (*Rashi*).

The *Midrash* translates וְלֹא הוּנַח־לָנוּ, *and we were given no rest*.

6. מִצְרַיִם נָתַנּוּ יָד — *We stretched out a hand to Egypt*. The *Midrash* relates that the Jews had traded their oil with Egypt for foodstuff which they then sent to Assyria in the hope that, if the enemy were to advance, Egypt and Assyria would come to their assistance. Ultimately the pact was fruitless — when the attack came, her 'allies' ignored her [see also 4:17]. The futility of

CHAPTER FIVE

[1] Remember, HASHEM, what has befallen us; look and see our disgrace.* [2] Our inheritance has been turned over to strangers; our houses to foreigners. [3] We have become orphans, fatherless;* our mothers are like widows. [4] We pay money to drink our own water,* obtain our wood at a price. [5] Upon our necks we are pursued; we toil, but nothing is left us.* [6] We stretched out a hand to Egypt,* and to Assyria to be satisfied with bread. [7] Our fathers have sinned and are no more, and we have suffered for their iniquities.* [8] Slaves ruled us, there is no rescuer from their hands. [9] In mortal danger we bring out bread, because of the sword of the wilderness. [10] Our skin was scorched like an oven, with the fever of famine. [11] They ravaged women in Zion; maidens in the towns of Judah.* [12] Leaders were hanged by their hand, elders were shown no respect. [13] Young men drag the millstone, and youths*

---

this ill-fated arrangement is now lamented by the prophet (*Torah Temimah*).

7. אֲבֹתֵינוּ חָטְאוּ וְאֵינָם וַאֲנַחְנוּ עֲוֹנֹתֵיהֶם סָבָלְנוּ — *Our fathers have sinned and are no more, and we have suffered for their iniquities.* Several interpretations are given for this important verse. A comprehensive selection follows:

Ibn Ezra comments that our misfortune is the result of our sins which intermingled with the sins of our ancestors for which they were not punished according to the doctrine of פֹּקֵד עֲוֹן אָבֹת עַל־בָּנִים ... [לְשֹׂנְאָי], *punishing the iniquity of the fathers upon the children...[of those that hate Me]* (*Exodus* 20:5). [*Ramban*, quoting the *Talmud* (*Sanhedrin* 27b), explains that God punishes children for the sins of the fathers only if the children persist in committing those sins.]

The *Arizal* offers an interpretation to harmonize the apparent contradiction between the verses *punishing the* עֲוֹן, *inquity, of the fathers upon the children* (*Exodus* 20:5), and אִישׁ בְּחֶטְאוֹ יוּמָתוּ, *Each man will die for his own sin* (*Deut.* 24:16). He points out — in addition to the Talmudic explanation above that the verse in *Exodus* applies only when the children persist in their fathers' ways — that there is also a distinction between עֲוֹן, *iniquity*, and חֵטְא, *sin*. *Iniquity* [referring to the verse in *Exodus*] applies to מֵזִיד, *willful* transgressions, for which, according to the Torah, children share the guilt. The verse in *Deuteronomy*, however, refers to חֵטְא, *unintentional* trangressions, for which children are not punished. Thus, the *Arizal* explains our verse [as does *Ibn Yachya, Lechem Dim'ah*]: *Our fathers* חָטְאוּ, *sinned unintentionally*, וְאֵינָם, *and they are not* — i.e. we are not being held accountable for them; וַאֲנַחְנוּ עֲוֹנֹתֵיהֶם סָבָלְנוּ, *but for* עֲוֹנֹתֵיהֶם, *their intentional trangressions* — for those we *do* suffer.

[It must be stressed that the Jews were *not* suggesting that their suffering was *wholly* the result of their fathers' sins. They admitted complicity, too, as evidenced by the outcry in verse 16: אוֹי־נָא לָנוּ כִּי חָטָאנוּ, *woe to us, for we have sinned*. Rather, as suggested by *Ibn Ezra* (above), they acknowledged their share of the iniquity. Added together with the sins of their ancestors, the cumulative guilt was the cause of their present predicament.]

Lechem Dim'ah explains that it would be more appropriate for the fathers to receive their own punishment. But since אֵינָם, *they are no more*, it is only just their children — who according to halachah are enjoined to say after a father's death, אֲנִי כַּפָּרַת מִשְׁכָּבוֹ, *'I am the atonement for his repose'* — who should accept responsibility. As the *Alshich* notes, no atonement is necessary for חֲטָאִים, *the unintentional sins* of parents, because death atones for them. For עֲוֹנוֹת, *intentional trangressions*, however, death does not suffice — suffering is a required part of the atonement. Children, therefore, should accept the obligation to atone for the sins of their parents.

11. נָשִׁים בְּצִיּוֹן עִנּוּ בְּתֻלֹת בְּעָרֵי יְהוּדָה — *They ravaged women in Zion; maidens in the town of Judah.* As if the sufferings of famine were not punishment enough, the slaves [verse 8] ravaged our wives (*Ibn Ezra*).

The greater the sanctity of the place, the more heinous their sins. In Judah, the enemy limited himself to ravaging בְּתֻלֹת, *unmarried maidens;* in the higher sanctity of Zion, the environs of Jerusalem and the Temple, he was brazen and defiant enough toward God to show his comtempt and ravage נָשִׁים, *married women* (*Kiflayim LeSushiyah*).

Lechem Dim'ah explains that when the Babylonian soldiers marched on Zion, they first passed through the towns of Judah. Not yet being sure of their own strength, they limited their ravages to unmarried maidens. But by the time they reached Jerusalem, the tide of war was

בָּעֵץ כָּשָׁלוּ:* יד זְקֵנִים מִשַּׁעַר שָׁבָתוּ בַּחוּרִים מִנְּגִינָתָם:* טו שָׁבַת מְשׂוֹשׂ לִבֵּנוּ נֶהְפַּךְ לְאֵבֶל מְחוֹלֵנוּ: טז נָפְלָה עֲטֶרֶת רֹאשֵׁנוּ אוֹי־נָא לָנוּ כִּי חָטָאנוּ:* יז עַל־זֶה הָיָה דָוֶה לִבֵּנוּ עַל־אֵלֶּה חָשְׁכוּ עֵינֵינוּ:* יח עַל הַר־צִיּוֹן שֶׁשָּׁמֵם שׁוּעָלִים הִלְּכוּ־בוֹ: יט אַתָּה יהוה לְעוֹלָם תֵּשֵׁב כִּסְאֲךָ לְדֹר וָדוֹר: כ לָמָּה לָנֶצַח תִּשְׁכָּחֵנוּ תַּעַזְבֵנוּ לְאֹרֶךְ יָמִים: כא הֲשִׁיבֵנוּ יהוה | אֵלֶיךָ °וְנָשׁוּבָה* חַדֵּשׁ יָמֵינוּ כְּקֶדֶם:* כב כִּי אִם־מָאֹס מְאַסְתָּנוּ קָצַפְתָּ עָלֵינוּ עַד־מְאֹד:

The following verse is recited aloud by the congregation, then repeated by the reader:

הֲשִׁיבֵנוּ יהוה* | אֵלֶיךָ וְנָשׁוּבָה חַדֵּשׁ יָמֵינוּ כְּקֶדֶם:

°ונשוב כ׳

going with them and they were fully confident of victory. Then they stopped at nothing, even ravaging married women.

The *Targum* translates: Married women in Zion were ravaged by Arameans [Edomites; *Ibn Yachya* and *Lechem Dim'ah* version of *Targum* reads *Romans*]; *maidens in the towns of Judah* by Chaldeans (Babylonians).

13. וּנְעָרִים בָּעֵץ כָּשָׁלוּ — *And youths stumble under* [lit., *in* or *with*] the *wood.* Rav Yehoshua ben Levi said: Three hundred children were found hung by the enemy on one branch (*Midrash*).

According to *Alshich*: The children grew so weak that they would stumble over a branch lying on the road.

14. זְקֵנִים מִשַּׁעַר שָׁבָתוּ בַּחוּרִים מִנְּגִינָתָם — *The elders are gone from the gate; the young men* [*ceased*] *from their music.* [It had been the custom for elders to station themselves at the gates (see *Ruth* 4:1; *Esther* 2:21). Now the gates lie desolate (see above 1:4).]

Elders here refer to the wise men, as the *Talmud* states: כִּי אֵין זָקֵן אֶלָּא מִי שֶׁקָּנָה חָכְמָה — For זָקֵן, *elder*, means only one who has acquired wisdom [*Kiddushin* 32b]. They have departed from the *gates of Halachah.* Similarly, *young men* refers to the young students who would study Mishnah by heart, and put the words to a melody as an aid to memorization. They, too, sang no longer (*Lechem Dim'ah*).

In verses 11-14, we have a description of how the enemy attacked every segment of the population in every social strata: married women and maidens; officers and elders; young men and children (*Rav Almosnino*).

16. אוֹי־נָא לָנוּ כִּי חָטָאנוּ — *Woe to us, for we have sinned.* Now that the Temple is destroyed, how will we atone for our sins? Previously, a sinner would offer a sacrifice to atone for his sins. Now there is no longer a Temple. Woe to us! (*Lechem Dim'ah*).

[This is an obvious confession, a recognition that everything that has befallen them is the result — and just reward — for their sinful ways (see comm. to verse 7).]

17-18. עַל־זֶה הָיָה דָוֶה לִבֵּנוּ — *For this our heart was faint* [or *sick*,] etc. For what is described in the next verse (the desolation of Mount Zion with foxes prowling it) (*Rashi*).

Alshich interprets the first half of this verse as referring to remorse over her sins which were the cause of Destruction; the second half of the verse to the desolation of Mount Zion.

The *Midrash* comments: Just as a woman who separates from her husband dor a few days because of impurity is called דָּוָה, *sick* [*Leviticus* 15:33], how much more should we be called דָּוֶה, *sick*, for being separated from the 'house of our life,' the Temple, for these many years!

עַל־אֵלֶּה חָשְׁכוּ עֵינֵינוּ — *For these our eyes dimmed* from excessive weeping (*Ibn Ezra*).

For none of our other catastrophes and suffering did our hearts grow so faint or did we weep so much, as for *'Mount Zion which lies desolate, foxes prowled over it'* (Rav Yosef Kara; Palgei Mayim).

עַל הַר־צִיּוֹן שֶׁשָּׁמֵם... — *For Mount Zion which lies desolate, foxes prowled over it.* Its desolation is so utter, that foxes, which usually dwell in ruins, prowl freely and undisturbed over it (*Alshich; Ibn Ezra*).

[In this context *Mount Zion* is used poetically in place of Mount Moriah — the actual site of the Temple.]

19-20. אַתָּה ה׳ לְעוֹלָם תֵּשֵׁב — *Yet You,* HASHEM, *are enthroned forever.* Although the manifestation of Your Kingship on earth is in ruins, nevertheless, Your dominion will never cease. You are enthroned forever. So if Your incorporeality is undiminished, and our sins

*stumble under the wood.** [14] *The elders are gone from the gate, the young men from their music.** [15] *Gone is the joy of our hearts, our dancing has turned into mourning.* [16] *The crown of our head has fallen; woe to us, for we have sinned.** [17] *For this our heart was faint, for these our eyes dimmed:** [18] *for Mount Zion which lies desolate, foxes prowled over it.* [19] *Yet You, HASHEM, are enthroned forever, Your throne is ageless.* [20] *Why do You ignore us eternally, forsake us for so long?* [21] *Bring us back to You, HASHEM, and we shall return,* renew our days as of old.** [22] *For even if You had utterly rejected us, You have already raged sufficiently against us.*

The following verse is recited aloud by the congregation, then repeated by the reader:

Bring us back to You, HASHEM, and we shall return,*
renew our days as of old.

---

only affect material manifestations of Your holiness, *why do You ignore us eternally?* (*Alshich*).

[It follows that since Hashem's Kingship *is ageless*, His throne itself will ultimately be restored.] Is there enthronement without a throne; a king without a consort? [Jerusalem is the throne: Israel the consort (*Torah Temimah*)] (*Midrash*).

21. הֲשִׁיבֵנוּ ה׳ אֵלֶיךָ וְנָשׁוּבָה — *Bring us back to You, HASHEM, and we shall return* [or *repent*]. Israel addresses God: All we ask is for some Divine assistance. If You initiate the action, and draw us near to You, then we will repent our sins and return to You wholeheartedly (*Lechem Dim'ah*).

The *Midrash* relates that there is a constant dispute, so to speak, between Hashem and Israel. God insists: שׁוּבוּ אֵלַי וְאָשׁוּבָה אֲלֵיכֶם, [First] *return to Me and* [then] *I will return to you* (*Malachi* 3:7); and Israel answers: הֲשִׁיבֵנוּ ה׳ אֵלֶיךָ וְנָשׁוּבָה, [First] *bring us back to You and* [then] *we shall return.* Neither side gives in and thus the dispute, as to who will take the initiative, continues...

...The *Maggid of Kozhnitz* explains homiletically that this is why we face the Master of the universe and say: לָמָּה לָנֶצַח תִּשְׁכָּחֵנוּ, *why for the sake of* נִצָּחוֹן, *victory, do You forget us,* Your children? Whom are you defeating — Your foolish stubborn children? Concede, O Merciful God, this one time! הֲשִׁיבֵנוּ ה׳ אֵלֶיךָ וְנָשׁוּבָה, *Bring us back to You, HASHEM, and we shall return!*

Ibn Ezra translates הֲשִׁיבֵנוּ, *bring us back,* in the physical sense: *Bring us back* to the city of the Dwelling Place of Your Name, [Jerusalem,] and we will resume serving You as before.

חַדֵּשׁ יָמֵינוּ כְּקֶדֶם — *Renew our days as of old.* As it is written (*Malachi* 3:4): *Then shall the offering of Judah and Jerusalem be pleasant to* HASHEM, כִּימֵי עוֹלָם, *as in the days of old,* וּכְשָׁנִים קַדְמוֹנִיּוֹת, *and as in ancient years* (*Midrash*) — Renew our days as You did when You took us out of Egypt (*Ibn Shuib*).

22. כִּי אִם־מָאֹס מְאַסְתָּנוּ — *For even if You had utterly rejected us* [lit., *reject You rejected us*], *You have already raged sufficiently against us.* Although we sinned, You did not have to increase rage against us as much as You did (*Rashi*).

The use of the double verb מָאֹס מְאַסְתָּנוּ, *Reject, You rejected us*, is interpreted as referring prophetically to both Temples (*Alshich*).

Pesikta d'Rav Kahana translates: *If it is 'rejection,' then You completely rejected us; but You are very 'wroth' against us.* That is, if God has *rejected* Israel, then there is no hope. If, however, He is no more than *wrathful*, then there is hope, for He Who is angered is likely to become reconciled.

Rav Levi Yitzchak of Berditchev explains these verses as follows:

Someone may divorce his wife for one of two reasons: for having found in her עֶרְוַת דָּבָר, an immorality; or because she no longer finds favor in his eyes. If he divorces her for the former reason, he may never remarry her; if for the latter, he may remarry her. This is how these verses הֲשִׁיבֵנוּ, *Bring us back*, are to be understood. You did not divorce us because of עֶרְוַת דָּבָר, that our behavior was so improper that You cannot ever take us back. Rather, You divorced us, כִּי אִם־מָאֹס מְאַסְתָּנוּ, because You utterly rejected us; i.e. we no longer found favor in Your eyes. As such You may bring us back to You.

הֲשִׁיבֵנוּ ה׳ — *Bring us back ... HASHEM.* It is customary to repeat verse 21 rather than end with the words of rebuke in verse 22. We act similarly at the conclusion of *Isaiah, Malachi,* and *Ecclesiastes* [and thus end these books on a comforting note] (*Rashi*).

קינות

א.

זְכֹר יהוה* **מֶה הָיָה לָנוּ,** אוֹי,
הַבִּיטָה וּרְאֵה אֶת חֶרְפָּתֵנוּ, אוֹי, מֶה הָיָה לָנוּ.
נַחֲלָתֵנוּ נֶהֶפְכָה לְזָרִים, אוֹי,
בָּתֵּינוּ לְנָכְרִים, אוֹי, מֶה הָיָה לָנוּ.
יְתוֹמִים הָיִינוּ וְאֵין אָב, אוֹי,
אִמּוֹתֵינוּ מְקוֹנְנוֹת בְּחֹדֶשׁ אָב, אוֹי, מֶה הָיָה לָנוּ.
מֵימֵינוּ בְּכֶסֶף שָׁתִינוּ, אוֹי,
כִּי נִסּוּךְ הַמַּיִם בָּזִינוּ,* אוֹי, מֶה הָיָה לָנוּ.
עַל צַוָּארֵנוּ נִרְדָּפְנוּ, אוֹי,
כִּי שִׂנְאַת חִנָּם רָדַפְנוּ, אוֹי, מֶה הָיָה לָנוּ.
מִצְרַיִם נָתַנּוּ יָד, אוֹי,
וְאַשּׁוּר צָדוּנוּ כְּצַיָּד, אוֹי, מֶה הָיָה לָנוּ.
אֲבוֹתֵינוּ חָטְאוּ וְאֵינָם, אוֹי,
וַאֲנַחְנוּ סוֹבְלִים אֶת עֲוֹנָם, אוֹי מֶה הָיָה לָנוּ.
עֲבָדִים מָשְׁלוּ בָנוּ, אוֹי,
כִּי שִׁלּוּחַ עֲבָדִים בִּטַּלְנוּ,[1] אוֹי, מֶה הָיָה לָנוּ.
בְּנַפְשֵׁנוּ נָבִיא לַחְמֵנוּ, אוֹי,
כִּי קָפַצְנוּ מֵעֲנִי יָדֵינוּ,[2] אוֹי, מֶה הָיָה לָנוּ.
עוֹרֵנוּ כְּתַנּוּר נִכְמָרוּ, אוֹי,
כִּי כְבוֹדָם בְּקָלוֹן הֵמִירוּ,[3] אוֹי, מֶה הָיָה לָנוּ.
נָשִׁים בְּצִיּוֹן עִנּוּ, אוֹי,
כִּי אִישׁ אֶת אֵשֶׁת רֵעֵהוּ טִמְּאוּ וְזָנוּ,[4] אוֹי, מֶה הָיָה לָנוּ.

זְכֹר ה׳ — *Remember,* HASHEM. Many of the *kinnos* are arranged according to the verses of one or more chapters of *Eichah* (the Book of *Lamentations*). This first *kinnah* is based on the fifth chapter. Each stanza contains two lines. The first stich (printed in bold type) is the opening phrase of the corresponding verse in *Eichah*, followed by the word אוֹי, *O woe!* The second stich rhymes with the first and is either the *paytan's* extension of the verse's lament, or his explanation of why the tragedy described in the first stich occurred. The phrase, 'אוֹי מֶה הָיָה לָנוּ', *O woe! What has befallen us!'* is inserted at the end of the stanza. This format allows us to focus carefully on each tragedy and to respond with a personal sigh of grief, 'אוֹי, *O woe ...*' The last four verses of *Eichah* appear at the end of the *kinnah* in their entirety, without the added phrases.

KINNOS

1.

זְכֹר *Remember, HASHEM, what has befallen us,* *O woe!*
Look and see our disgrace — O woe! What has befallen us!
Our inheritance has been turned over to strangers, O woe!
Our homes to foreigners — O woe! What has befallen us!
We have become orphans, fatherless, O woe!
Our mothers lament in the month of Av — O woe! What has befallen us!
We pay money to drink our own water, O woe!
Because we scorned the water libations ceremony — O woe! What has befallen us!*

Upon our necks we are pursued, O woe!
Because we pursued purposeless hatred — O woe! What has befallen us!
We stretched out a hand to Egypt, O woe!
While Assyria trapped us like a hunter — O woe! What has befallen us!
Our fathers have sinned and are no more, O woe!
And we [who continue in their ways] bear the burden of their iniquities — O woe! What has befallen us!
Slaves rule over us, O woe!
Because we discontinued the liberation of the [Hebrew] slaves[1] *— O woe! What has befallen us!*

In mortal danger we bring our bread, O woe!
Because we have clamped our hands tightly against the poor[2] *— O woe! What has befallen us!*

Our skin was scorched like an oven, O woe!
Because they have exchanged their dignity for degradation[3] *— O woe! What has befallen us!*

They ravaged women in Zion, O woe!
Because they sullied and seduced their neighbor's wives[4] *— O woe! What has befallen us!*

(1) See *Exodus* 21:2 and *Jeremiah* 34:8ff.
(2) Cf. *Deuteronomy* 15:7. (3) Cf. *Hosea* 4:7. (4) Cf. *Ezekiel* 18:11.

In some early editions of *Kinnos* this *kinnah* does not appear. Instead, there is an instruction that reads: 'The *chazzan* repeats [the chapter beginning] זְכֹר ה׳, *Remember, HASHEM,* and inserts אוֹי, *O woe!*, in the middle of each verse, and אוֹי מֶה הָיָה לָנוּ, *O woe! What has befallen us!*, at the end. From the verse אַתָּה ה׳, *Yet You, HASHEM*, he omits the insertions . . . but recites the verses as they appear in *Eichah* . . .'

Whether this *kinnah* is recited in the words of *Eichah* or in the words of the *paytan*, the repetition of the last chapter of Jeremiah's lament emphasizes that the Destruction of the Temples did not bring an end to Jewish suffering and tragedy; on the contrary, it marked the beginning of what seems like an interminable series of exiles and massacres. Nevertheless, if we return to *Hashem*, He will return us to Him and to His Land.

כִּי נִסּוּךְ הַמַּיִם בָּזִינוּ — *Because we scorned the water libations ceremony.* It is axiomatic that

שָׂרִים בְּיָדָם נִתְלוּ, אוֹי,
כִּי גְזֵלַת הֶעָנִי חָמְסוּ וְגָזָלוּ,[1] אוֹי, מֶה הָיָה לָנוּ.
בַּחוּרִים טְחוֹן נָשָׂאוּ, אוֹי,
כִּי בְּבֵית זוֹנָה* נִמְצָאוּ, אוֹי, מֶה הָיָה לָנוּ.
זְקֵנִים מִשַּׁעַר שָׁבָתוּ, אוֹי,
כִּי מִשְׁפַּט יָתוֹם וְאַלְמָנָה עִוְּתוּ, אוֹי, מֶה הָיָה לָנוּ.
שָׁבַת מְשׂוֹשׂ לִבֵּנוּ, אוֹי,
כִּי נִבְטְלוּ עוֹלֵי רְגָלֵינוּ, אוֹי, מֶה הָיָה לָנוּ.
נָפְלָה עֲטֶרֶת רֹאשֵׁנוּ, אוֹי,
כִּי נִשְׂרַף בֵּית מִקְדָּשֵׁנוּ,[2] אוֹי, מֶה הָיָה לָנוּ.
עַל זֶה הָיָה דָוֶה לִבֵּנוּ, אוֹי,
כִּי נִבְטַל כְּבוֹד בֵּית מַאֲוַיֵּנוּ, אוֹי, מֶה הָיָה לָנוּ.
עַל הַר צִיּוֹן שֶׁשָּׁמֵם, אוֹי,
כִּי הַר הַבַּיִת מְשׁוֹמֵם, אוֹי, מֶה הָיָה לָנוּ.

אַתָּה יהוה לְעוֹלָם תֵּשֵׁב כִּסְאֲךָ לְדוֹר וָדוֹר.
לָמָּה לָנֶצַח תִּשְׁכָּחֵנוּ תַּעַזְבֵנוּ לְאֹרֶךְ יָמִים.
הֲשִׁיבֵנוּ יהוה אֵלֶיךָ וְנָשׁוּבָה חַדֵּשׁ יָמֵינוּ כְּקֶדֶם.
כִּי אִם מָאֹס מְאַסְתָּנוּ קָצַפְתָּ עָלֵינוּ עַד מְאֹד.
הֲשִׁיבֵנוּ יהוה אֵלֶיךָ וְנָשׁוּבָה חַדֵּשׁ יָמֵינוּ כְּקֶדֶם.

(1) Cf. *Isaiah* 3:14. (2) Cf. 64:10.

Leaders were hanged by their hand, *O woe!*
Because they plundered and robbed the loot of the poor[1] *—*
O woe! What has befallen us!

Young men bear the millstone, *O woe!*
Because they were found in the harlot's house —*
O woe! What has befallen us!

The elders are gone from the gate, *O woe!*
Because they twisted the judgment of the orphan and the widow —
O woe! What has befallen us!

Gone is the joy of our hearts, *O woe!*
Because the festival pilgrimage has been discontinued —
O woe! What has befallen us!

The crown of our head has fallen, *O woe!*
Because our Holy Temple has been burnt down[2] *—*
O woe! What has befallen us!

For this our heart was faint, *O woe!*
Because the glory has ceased from the House of our Aspirations —
O woe! What has befallen us!

For Mount Zion which lies desolate, *O woe!*
Because the Temple Mount is in ruins — O woe! What has befallen us!

Yet You, HASHEM, are enthroned forever, Your throne is ageless.
Why do You ignore us eternally, forsake us for so long?
Bring us back to You, HASHEM, and we shall return,
renew our days as of old.
For even if You had utterly rejected us,
You have already raged sufficiently against us.
Bring us back to You, HASHEM, and we shall return,
renew our days as of old.

God rewards and punishes מִדָּה כְּנֶגֶד מִדָּה, *measure for measure.* Therefore, when retribution is visited upon the nation, there must be a cause and effect relationship between the deed in whose wake that retribution comes and the specific form it takes. In thirteen of the next fifteen stanzas, the *paytan* traces these relationships.

טְחוֹן ... בְּבֵית זוֹנָה — *The millstone ... in the harlot's house.* The Sages understand the root טחן, literally, *grind*, as a euphemism for adultery (*Sotah* 10a; *Eichah Rabbah* 5:13). Hence, the burden of carrying a heavy millstone is apt punishment for frequenting the harlot's house.

ON SATURDAY NIGHT:

ב.

אֵיךְ מִפִּי בֵּן וּבַת, הֲגוּת קִינוֹת רַבַּת,
תְּמוּר שִׁירִים וְחֶדְוַת,
וִיהִי נֹעַם[1] נִשְׁבַּת,* בְּמוֹצָאֵי שַׁבָּת.

אוֹי, כִּי נִגְזְרָה גְזֵרָה, בָּחֳרִי אַף וְגַם עֶבְרָה,
וְאַפּוֹ בָנוּ חָרָה, וּבָעֲרָה חֲמָתוֹ כְּלַבַּת,[2]
וִיהִי נֹעַם נִשְׁבַּת, בְּמוֹצָאֵי שַׁבָּת.

אוֹי, כִּי בָתֵּינוּ שַׁמּוּ,[3] וּבְתוּלוֹתֵינוּ עֻנּוּ,[4]
וּפָנֵינוּ נִשְׁתַּנּוּ, וְגַם הוּשְׁחֲרוּ[5] כְּמַחֲבַת,
וִיהִי נֹעַם נִשְׁבַּת, בְּמוֹצָאֵי שַׁבָּת.

אוֹי, כִּי שַׁדּוּנוּ צָרִים, וְגַם הִפִּילוּ בָנוּ פְּגָרִים,
בְּנֵי צִיּוֹן הַיְּקָרִים,[6] הָיוּ נְצוּרִים כְּבָבַת,
וִיהִי נֹעַם נִשְׁבַּת, בְּמוֹצָאֵי שַׁבָּת.

אוֹי, כִּי נָפְלָה עֲטֶרֶת,[7] וְגָבְרָה כָּתֵף סוֹרֶרֶת,[8]
וְחָדַל הוֹד וְתִפְאֶרֶת, צִמְצוּם שֶׁכֵּן חִבַּת,
וִיהִי נֹעַם נִשְׁבַּת, בְּמוֹצָאֵי שַׁבָּת.

אוֹי, כִּי נֻטְּלָה מְנוֹרָה, וּקְטֹרֶת לְבוֹנָה הַטְּהוֹרָה,
וְנִבְזֶה גָּזִית מְיֻקָּרָה, אָכְלָה אֶרֶץ זָבַת,
וִיהִי נֹעַם נִשְׁבַּת, בְּמוֹצָאֵי שַׁבָּת.

וִיהִי נֹעַם נִשְׁבַּת — *The [prayer] 'May the Pleasantness' is omitted.* Although this prayer (*Psalms* 90:17-91:16) is usually recited at the departure of the Sabbath, it is omitted when Tishah B'Av follows immediately after the Sabbath. This is because the prayer was composed by Moses in honor of the completion of the מִשְׁכָּן [*Mishkan*], *Tabernacle*, in the Wilderness (*Midrash Tehillim*). Since the *Mishkan* served the same function as the *Beis HaMikdash*, it would be unseemly to recite this prayer on the anniversary of the Destruction (*Matteh Moshe* 729, cited in *Taamei HaMinhagim*).

ON SATURDAY NIGHT:

2.

אֵיךְ *O how from the mouth of son and daughter*
many lamentations resound, instead of songs and jubilation.
*The [prayer] 'May the pleasantness'[1] is omitted,**
as the Sabbath departs.

O woe! For the decree was issued
with blazing anger and with wrath;
His anger blazed against us and His fury burned like a flame![2]

The [prayer] 'May the pleasantness' is omitted,
as the Sabbath departs.

O woe! For they turned over our homes [to strangers][3]
and ravished our virgins;[4]
our faces are distorted and blackened[5]
like [the bottom of] a frying pan.

The [prayer] 'May the pleasantness' is omitted,
as the Sabbath departs.

O woe! For enemies have plundered us
and caused corpses to fall among us,
the precious children of Zion,[6]
who had been protected like the pupil [of the eye].

The [prayer] 'May the pleasantness' is omitted,
as the Sabbath departs.

O woe! For the crown[-like Temple] has fallen,[7]
because the shoulder turned away[8]
[from God's service] has prevailed;
splendor and majesty have ceased, [from the Beis HaMikdash
in which He] constricted His loving Presence.

The [prayer] 'May the pleasantness' is omitted,
as the Sabbath departs.

O woe! For the Menorah has been taken,
along with the pure frankincense offering;
the [Sanhedrin's] cherished hewn-stone [chamber] has been degraded;
and the land overflowing [with milk and honey]
has been consumed.

The [prayer] 'May the pleasantness' is omitted,
as the Sabbath departs.

(1) *Psalms* 90:17-91:16. (2) Cf. *Eichah* 2:3. (3) Cf. 5:2. (4) Cf. 5:11. (5) Cf. 4:8. (6) 4:2. (7) Cf. *Eichah* 5:16. (8) Cf. *Zechariah* 7:11; *Nehemiah* 9:29.

ג.

בְּלֵיל זֶה יִבְכָּיוּן וְיֵילִילוּ בָנַי,
בְּלֵיל זֶה חָרַב בֵּית קָדְשִׁי וְנִשְׂרְפוּ אַרְמוֹנַי,[1]
וְכָל בֵּית יִשְׂרָאֵל יֶהְגּוּ בִיגוֹנַי,
וְיִבְכּוּ אֶת הַשְּׂרֵפָה אֲשֶׁר שָׂרַף יהוה.[2]
בְּלֵיל זֶה תְּיַלֵּל מַר עֲנִיָּה נֶחְדֶּלֶת,
וּמִבֵּית אָבִיהָ בַּחַיִּים מֻבְדֶּלֶת,
וְיָצְאָה מִבֵּיתוֹ וְנִסְגַּר הַדֶּלֶת,
וְהָלְכָה בַּשִּׁבְיָה בְּכָל פֶּה נֶאֱכֶלֶת,
בְּיוֹם שֻׁלְּחָה בָּאֵשׁ בּוֹעֶרֶת וְאוֹכֶלֶת,
וְאֵשׁ עִם גַּחֶלֶת יָצְאָה מֵאֵת יהוה.[3]

בְּלֵיל זֶה יִבְכָּיוּן וְיֵילִילוּ בָנַי. . .

בְּלֵיל זֶה הַגַּלְגַּל סִבֵּב הַחוֹבָה,*
רִאשׁוֹן גַּם שֵׁנִי בֵּיתִי נֶחֱרָבָה,
וְעוֹד לֹא רֻחָמָה בַּת הַשּׁוֹבֵבָה,*[4]
הָשְׁקְתָה מֵי רוֹשׁ[5] וְאֶת בִּטְנָהּ צָבָה,*
וְשֻׁלְּחָה מִבֵּיתוֹ וְגַם נָשְׂתָה טוֹבָה,[6]
גְּדוֹלָה הַשִּׂנְאָה מֵאֵת אֲשֶׁר אֲהֵבָהּ,[7]

בְּלֵיל זֶה — *On this night.* When the Spies returned after forty days of reconnoitering the Land of Canaan, they produced a terribly slanderous report about the Land. Rather than have faith in God's promise to bring them to a land flowing with milk and honey where they would live under Divine protection, the nation chose to believe the Spies' discouraging word, and they wept that night (*Numbers* 13:25 - 14:1). God was infuriated at Israel's treachery and declared, 'Since you shed tears on this night for no reason, I shall give you many reasons to cry on this night!' (*Taanis* 29a).

Thus, the date of Tishah B'Av became a day of repeated tragedies, throughout Jewish history. The Mishnah enumerates five of these dire events: (a) Because the nation believed the Spies' malicious report, the guilty ones were sentenced to die in the wilderness, before the nation would enter the Land; (b-c) the First and Second Temples were destroyed; (d) Bar Kochba's revolt was crushed and his stronghold at Beitar was captured by the Romans [so many Jews were slain at that time that the non-Jews fertilized their vineyards for seven years with the blood of the Jews killed at Beitar (*Gittin* 57a)]; and (e) the Roman governor Turnus Rufus had the city of Jerusalem razed and plowed under (*Taanis* 26b).

The *paytan* places this lament into the mouth of either Jerusalem (which *Eichah* describes as a widow) or the nation as a whole lamenting to her children (the exiles) about the bitter tragedies which have befallen her. Alternatively, the narrator of the *kinnah* is addressing his own children to explain the reasons for the sadness of the day.

הַגַּלְגַּל סִבֵּב הַחוֹבָה — *The calendrical cycle turned to an inauspicious date.* The Mishnah states that both the First and Second Temples were destroyed on the Ninth of Av (*Taanis* 26b). The Talmud adduces verses that verify this date for the First Temple, then seeks proof that the second Destruction also occurred on Tishah B'Av. The following *baraisa* is cited: מְגַלְגְּלִין

3.

בְּלֵיל זֶה *On this night,* weep and wail, my children,*
for on this night my Holy Temple was destroyed
and my palaces were burnt down;[1]
the entire House of Israel shall lament over my agony,
and they shall bewail the conflagration
that HASHEM has ignited.[2]

On this night, the impoverished,
abandoned one [Israel] shall wail bitterly;
she who was estranged from her Father's Temple
even while He is alive;
she went forth from his house and the door
[to redemption] was sealed;
she went into captivity
where she was devoured by every mouth,
on that day she was exiled by a flaming, consuming fire —
the fire and the flaming coal that went forth from HASHEM.[3]

On this night, weep and wail, my children...

On this night, the calendrical cycle
*turned to an inauspicious date;**
my First and my Second Temple were both destroyed;
the rebellious daughter[4]
*is still unworthy of compassion;**
she was forced to drink bitter waters[5]
*and her belly was bloated;**
she was exiled from His House
and has forgotten what good is;[6]
greater is [God's] hatred [now]
than [His] love for her had been;[7]

(1) Cf. *II Chronicles* 36:19. (2) *Leviticus* 10:6. (3) Cf. *Numbers* 16:35.
(4) *Jeremiah* 31:21, 49:4. (5) Cf. 9:14. (6) Cf. *Eichah* 3:17. (7) Cf. *II Samuel* 13:15.

זְכוּת לְיוֹם זַכַּאי וְחוֹבָה לְיוֹם חַיָּיב, *They [the Heavenly Court] make a good event occur on an auspicious date, and a bad event on an inauspicious date* (ibid. 29a; *Arachin* 11b).

וְעוֹד לֹא רֻחָמָה בַּת הַשּׁוֹבֵבָה — *The rebellious daughter is still unworthy of compassion.* God appeared to the prophet Hosea in a vision and ordered him to concretize Israel's wayward lust for idolatry in a most dramatic manner: *'Take a harlot unto yourself and bear children of adultery, for the land has been adulterous in turning away from HASHEM'* (*Hosea* 1:2). The prophet did so and three children were born to him. God told him what to name each baby — names that describe His displeasure with the nation. The second child, a daughter, was to be called לֹא רֻחָמָה, *Lo-Ruchamah* [lit., *unworthy of compassion* or *unpitied*] (ibid. 1:6). When the nation will be exiled, learn its lesson and return to God's service, her name will be changed to רֻחָמָה, *Ruchamah*, i.e., worthy of compassion (ibid. 2:3).

הֻשְׁקְתָה מֵי רוֹשׁ וְאֶת בִּטְנָהּ צָבָה — *She was forced to drink bitter waters and her belly was bloated.* Although *Rashi* (*Jeremiah* 9:14) renders מֵי רֹאשׁ as *snake venom* and *Radak* translates *bitter grass*, from the context of the *kinnah* it is obvious that the *paytan* alludes to the ordeal and degradation of the סוֹטָה, *wayward wife*, as described in Scripture (*Numbers* 5:11-31).

וּכְאַלְמְנוּת חַיּוּת כְּאִשָּׁה נֶעֱזָבָה,
וַתֹּאמֶר צִיּוֹן עֲזָבַנִי יהוה.[1]

בְּלֵיל זֶה יִבְכָּיוּן וְיֵילִילוּ בָנַי. . .

בְּלֵיל זֶה קָדַרְתִּי וְחָשְׁכוּ הַמְּאוֹרוֹת,
לְחָרְבַּן בֵּית קָדְשִׁי וּבִטּוּל מִשְׁמָרוֹת,[2]
בְּלֵיל זֶה סַבְּבוּנִי אֲפָפוּנִי צָרוֹת,
וְגַם קָרָא מוֹעֵד[3] בְּדִין חָמֵשׁ גְּזֵרוֹת,
בְּכִי חִנָּם בָּכוּ וְנִקְבַּע לַדּוֹרוֹת,
יַעַן כִּי הָיְתָה סִבָּה מֵעִם יהוה.[4]

בְּלֵיל זֶה יִבְכָּיוּן וְיֵילִילוּ בָנַי. . .

בְּלֵיל זֶה אֵרְעוּ בוֹ חָמֵשׁ מְאֹרָעוֹת,
גָּזַר עַל אָבוֹת בִּפְרוֹעַ פְּרָעוֹת,[5]
וְדָבְקוּ בוֹ צָרוֹת רַבּוֹת וְרָעוֹת,[6]
יוֹם מוּכָן הָיָה בִּפְגוֹעַ פְּגָעוֹת,
וְהֶעֱמִיד הָאוֹיֵב* וְהֵרִים קוֹל זְוָעוֹת,
קוּם כִּי זֶה הַיּוֹם אֲשֶׁר אָמַר יהוה.[7]

בְּלֵיל זֶה יִבְכָּיוּן וְיֵילִילוּ בָנַי. . .

וְהֶעֱמִיד הָאוֹיֵב — *[God] set the enemy [against us].* Some commentaries understand 'the enemy' as the subject of the verb and render: *The enemy set up [an idol in the Temple].* This interpretation is difficult because the Mishnah (*Taanis* 4:6) lists that event as one of the five tragedies of the Seventeenth of Tammuz, while this stanza of the *kinnah* recounts the tragic events of Tishah B'Av.

she is like a widow of the living, like an abandoned woman.
And Zion said: HASHEM *has forsaken me.*[1]

On this night, weep and wail, my children. . .

On this night, I was blackened
and the luminaries turned dark,
because of the destruction of my Holy Temple
and the discontinuation of the [priestly] watches.[2]
On this night, troubles encircled and surrounded me,
and He proclaimed this date as a fixed time[3]
for five [harsh] decrees.
[On this night,] they cried without cause, so it was designated
[a night of weeping] for all generations;
therefore HASHEM *caused it to happen so.*[4]

On this night, weep and wail, my children. . .

On this night, five tragedies occurred:
He decreed against [our] ancestors
when they rebelled wantonly,[5]
and many terrible troubles[6] *cleaved to them this [day],*
a day destined for dreadful visitations.
[God] set the enemy [against us], and he raised a terrifying cry:*
'Arise! For this is the day of which HASHEM *has said*[7]
[that we should destroy His Temple]!'

On this night, weep and wail, My children. . .

(1) *Isaiah* 49:14. (2) See prefatory remarks to *kinnah* 10. (3) Cf. *Eichah* 1:15. (4) *I Kings* 12:15.
(5) *Judges* 5:2; see commentaries there for various other interpretations of this phrase.
(6) Some editions read מְצָרוֹת וְגַם רָעוֹת, but the meaning is the same. (7) Cf. *Judges* 4:14.

ד.

שׁוֹמְרוֹן קוֹל תִּתֵּן מְצָאוּנִי עֲוֹנַי,[1]
לְאֶרֶץ אַחֶרֶת יְצָאוּנִי בָנַי,[2]
וְאָהֳלִיבָה תִּזְעַק נִשְׂרְפוּ אַרְמוֹנַי,[3]
וַתֹּאמֶר צִיּוֹן עֲזָבַנִי יהוה.[4]

לֹא לָךְ אָהֳלִיבָה חֲשׁוֹב עָנְיֵךְ כְּעָנְיִי,
הֲתַמְשִׁילִי חָלְיֵךְ לְשִׁבְרִי וּלְחָלְיִי,
אֲנִי אָהֳלָה סוֹרָה בָּגַדְתִּי בְקָשְׁיִי,
וְקָם עָלַי כַּחֲשִׁי וְעָנָה בִי מֶרְיִי,[5]
וּלְמִקְצַת הַיָּמִים שִׁלַּמְתִּי נִשְׁיִי,
וְתִגְלַת פִּלְאֶסֶר[6] אָכַל אֶת פִּרְיִי,
חֶמְדָּתִי פָּשַׁט וְהִצִּיל אֶת עֶדְיִי,[7]*
וְלַחֲלַח וְחָבוֹר[8] נָשָׂא אֶת שִׁבְיִי,
דֹּמִּי אָהֳלִיבָה וְאַל תִּבְכִּי כְּבִכְיִי,
שְׁנוֹתַיִךְ אָרְכוּ וְלֹא אָרְכוּ שָׁנָי.*

וְאָהֳלִיבָה תִּזְעַק נִשְׂרְפוּ אַרְמוֹנַי,
וַתֹּאמֶר צִיּוֹן עֲזָבַנִי יהוה.

מְשִׁיבָה אָהֳלִיבָה אֲנִי כֵן נֶעֱקַשְׁתִּי,
וּבְאַלּוּף נְעוּרַי[9] כְּאָהֳלָה בָּגַדְתִּי,
דֹּמִּי אָהֳלָה כִּי יְגוֹנִי זָכַרְתִּי,
נָדַדְתְּ אַתְּ אַחַת וְרַבּוֹת נָדַדְתִּי,
הִנֵּה בְּיַד הַכַּשְׂדִּים פְּעָמִים נִלְכַּדְתִּי,
וּשְׁבִיָּה עֲנִיָּה לְבָבֶל יָרַדְתִּי,

שׁוֹמְרוֹן — *Shomron.* This *kinnah* is based on chapter 23 of *Ezekiel*, where God bids the prophet to expose the sins of the Jewish people. Then unfolds the shocking parable of two faithless wives who seek fulfillment of their unnatural lusts through numerous lovers. Ezekiel tells of two sisters, אָהֳלָה, *Oholah*, and אָהֳלִיבָה, *Oholivah*, who are both married to the same man. Oholah is identified as Shomron [Samaria, capital of the Northern Kingdom, also called the Kingdom of Israel, which comprised ten of the tribes] and Oholivah as Jerusalem [capital of the Southern Kingdom, also called the Kingdom of Judah, which comprised Judah and Benjamin]. Both are 'wed' to one 'husband', God, but both brazenly betray Him.

The names, אָהֳלָה, *Oholah*, and אָהֳלִיבָה, *Oholivah*, are both derived from אֹהֶל, a *tent* or *dwelling place*. However, אָהֳלָה is a contraction of הָאֹהֶל שֶׁלָּהּ, *her tent*, because God had no part in the tabernacles of Shomron. They were 'her own tents' which she had dedicated to the golden calves Jeroboam ben Nevat had erected (see *I Kings* 12:28). On the other hand, אָהֳלִיבָה is

4.

שׁוֹמְרוֹן *Shomron gives forth [her] voice,*
'The deserts of my sins have found me![1]
My children have gone forth from me[2] *to another land!'*
Then Oholivah screams, 'My palaces were burnt down!'[3]
And Zion says, 'HASHEM has abandoned me!'[4]

ל *[Oholah:] 'It is not right for you, Oholivah,*
to consider your suffering as mine!
Can you compare your sickness to my fracture and sickness?
I, Oholah, [am now] displaced, I have rebelled in my stubbornness,
but now my deceitfulness has risen against me,[5]
and my defiance has testified against me,
and after a short time I paid my debts [for my sins].
[The Assyrian king] Tiglath-pileser[6] *devoured my [womb's] fruits,*
he stripped away my precious possessions
and confiscated my jewelry,[7]***
then [his successor Shalmaneser] carried away my captives
to Halah and Habor.[8]
[Therefore,] Oholivah be silent and weep not as I weep!
Your years [in the Land] were prolonged,
*but my years were not prolonged!'**

Then Oholivah screams, 'My palaces were burnt down!'
And Zion says, 'HASHEM has abandoned me!'

מ *Oholivah responds: 'I too deviated,*
and like Oholah, I betrayed [God,] the Mentor of my youth![9]
Be still, Oholah, for I remember my agony.
You were exiled but once, while I was exiled repeatedly.
Behold, by the hands of the Chaldeans I was taken twice;
as a miserable captive I descended to Babylon;

---

(1) Cf. *II Kings* 7:9. (2) Cf. *Jeremiah* 10:20. (3) Cf. *II Chronicles* 36:19. (4) *Isaiah* 49:14. (5) Cf. *Job* 16:8. (6) *II Kings* 15:29. (7) Cf. *Exodus* 33:6. (8) See *II Kings* 17:3-6. (9) Cf. *Jeremiah* 3:4.

---

a contraction of הָאֹהֶל שֶׁלִּי בָּהּ, *My Tent is within her*, i.e., the Tent of God, the *Beis HaMikdash*. These names place Judah, in which God's Temple stood, in sharp contrast to Shomron.

The wicked city of Shomron, with the abominations of its citizens, epitomizes all of the evil of the Ten Tribes. That segment of Israel became so corrupted that to this day those tribes are lost in exile and the possibility of their ultimate return remains the subject of considerable Talmudic debate (see *Sanhedrin* 110b and *Ramban, Sefer HaGeulah, shaar* I).

In this *kinnah*, the author compares the tragedies which befell both Judah and Samaria by means of a debate raging between the two. Each capital claims — and vehemently defends its claim — that it suffered more at the hand of the marauding enemy.

The composer of the *kinnah*, R' Shlomo ibn Gabirol (11th-century Spain), used the letters of his name שְׁלֹמֹה to begin the respective stanzas.

חֶמְדָּתִי ... עֶדְיִי — *My precious possessions ... my jewelry*. Some commentators understand these expressions as allusions to the two Temples. We have rejected that interpretation because Oholah is the speaker, but the Temples had stood in Oholivah's estate.

שְׁנוֹתַיִךְ אָרְכוּ וְלֹא אָרְכוּ שָׁנָי — *Your years [in the Land] were prolonged, but my years were not prolonged!* Oholah, the Northern Kingdom of Samaria, was exiled more than one hundred

וְנִשְׂרַף הַהֵיכָל אֲשֶׁר בּוֹ נִכְבַּדְתִּי,
וּלְשִׁבְעִים שָׁנָה בְּבָבֶל נִפְקַדְתִּי,
וְשַׁבְתִּי לְצִיּוֹן עוֹד וְהֵיכָל יָסַדְתִּי,
גַּם זֹאת הַפַּעַם מְעַט לֹא עָמַדְתִּי,
עַד לְקָחַנִי אֱדוֹם וְכִמְעַט אָבַדְתִּי,
וְעַל כָּל הָאֲרָצוֹת נָפְצוּ הֲמוֹנַי,

וְאָהֳלִיבָה תִּזְעַק נִשְׂרְפוּ אַרְמוֹנַי,
וַתֹּאמֶר צִיּוֹן עֲזָבַנִי יהוה.

הַחוֹמֵל עַל דַּל חֲמוֹל עַל דַּלּוּתָם,*
וּרְאֵה שִׁמְמוֹתָם[1] וְאֹרֶךְ גָּלוּתָם,
אַל תִּקְצוֹף עַד מְאֹד[2] וּרְאֵה שִׁפְלוּתָם,
וְאַל לָעַד תִּזְכּוֹר עֲוֹנָם[2] וְסִכְלוּתָם,
רְפָא נָא אֶת שִׁבְרָם[3] וְנַחֵם אֲבֵלוּתָם,
כִּי אַתָּה סִבְרָם וְאַתָּה אֱיָלוּתָם,
חַדֵּשׁ יָמֵינוּ כִּימֵי קַדְמוֹנַי,[4]
כְּנָאֳמֶךְ בּוֹנֵה יְרוּשָׁלַיִם יהוה.[5]

(1) Cf. *Daniel* 9:18. (2) Cf. *Isaiah* 64:8. (3) Cf. *Psalms* 60:4. (4) Cf. *Eichah* 5:21. (5) *Psalms* 147:2.

and the Sanctuary by which I was honored
was burnt down.
After seventy years in Babylon I was recalled [by God];
I returned once again to Zion
and established the [Second] Temple.
This time, too, I did not last long
before Edom seized me and I was all but annihilated.
Through all the lands were my multitudes dispersed.'

Then Oholivah screams, 'My palaces were burnt down!'
And Zion says, 'HASHEM has abandoned me!'

ה *O You Who takes pity on the pauper,*
*take pity on their poverty.**
See their desolation[1] *and the length of their exile.*
Do not be overly angered,[2] *rather take note of their degradation.*
Do not eternally remember their sins[2] *and their foolishness.*
Please heal their wounds[3] *and assuage their mourning;*
for You are their Hope and You are their Strength.

Renew our days as the days of my youth;[4]
as You have said: 'The Builder of Jerusalem is HASHEM.'[5]

---

thirty years before Oholivah, the Southern Kingdom of Judah.

דַּלּוּתָם — *Their poverty.* Until this point, the *kinnah* has been a one-on-one debate between Oholah and Oholivah. Thus, the statements are all in first or second person singular. The last stanza, however, is the *paytan's* supplication for the restitution of both, and consequently is couched in third person plural. Finally, the last line prays for the reunification of the two Kingdoms with Jerusalem as the focal point as it was in 'the days of my youth.'

ה.

עַד אָנָה בְּכִיָּה בְצִיּוֹן וּמִסְפֵּד בִּירוּשָׁלָיִם,
תְּרַחֵם צִיּוֹן[1] וְתִבְנֶה חוֹמוֹת יְרוּשָׁלָיִם.[2]

אָז בַּחֲטָאֵינוּ חָרַב מִקְדָּשׁ, וּבַעֲוֹנוֹתֵינוּ נִשְׂרַף הֵיכָל.
בָּאָרֶץ חֻבְּרָה לָּהּ[3] קָשְׁרָה מִסְפֵּד,* וּצְבָא הַשָּׁמַיִם נָשְׂאוּ קִינָה.
עַד אָנָה בְּכִיָּה בְצִיּוֹן וּמִסְפֵּד בִּירוּשָׁלָיִם, תְּרַחֵם צִיּוֹן וְתִבְנֶה חוֹמוֹת יְרוּשָׁלָיִם.

גַּם בָּכוּ בְּמֶרֶר שִׁבְטֵי יַעֲקֹב, וְאַף מַזָּלוֹת יִזְּלוּ דִמְעָה.
דִּגְלֵי יְשֻׁרוּן חָפוּ רֹאשָׁם,[4] וְכִימָה וּכְסִיל[5] קָדְרוּ פְנֵיהֶם.
עַד אָנָה בְּכִיָּה בְצִיּוֹן וּמִסְפֵּד בִּירוּשָׁלָיִם, תְּרַחֵם צִיּוֹן וְתִבְנֶה חוֹמוֹת יְרוּשָׁלָיִם.

הֶעְתִּירוּ אָבוֹת וְלֹא שָׁמַע אֵל, צָעֲקוּ בָנִים וְלֹא עָנָה אָב.[6]
וְקוֹל הַתּוֹר[7]* נִשְׁמַע בַּמָּרוֹם, וְרוֹעֶה נֶאֱמָן לֹא הִטָּה אֹזֶן.
עַד אָנָה בְּכִיָּה בְצִיּוֹן וּמִסְפֵּד בִּירוּשָׁלָיִם, תְּרַחֵם צִיּוֹן וְתִבְנֶה חוֹמוֹת יְרוּשָׁלָיִם.

זֶרַע קֹדֶשׁ לָבְשׁוּ שַׂקִּים,[8] וּצְבָא הַשָּׁמַיִם גַּם הֵם שַׂק הוּשַׂם כְּסוּתָם.
חָשַׁךְ הַשֶּׁמֶשׁ וְיָרֵחַ קָדַר,[9] וְכוֹכָבִים וּמַזָּלוֹת אָסְפוּ נָגְהָם.[10]
עַד אָנָה בְּכִיָּה בְצִיּוֹן וּמִסְפֵּד בִּירוּשָׁלָיִם, תְּרַחֵם צִיּוֹן וְתִבְנֶה חוֹמוֹת יְרוּשָׁלָיִם.

טָלֶה רִאשׁוֹן* בָּכָה בְּמַר נֶפֶשׁ, עַל כִּי כְבָשָׂיו לַטֶּבַח הוּבָלוּ.[11]
יְלָלָה הִשְׁמִיעַ **שׁוֹר** בַּמְּרוֹמִים, כִּי עַל צַוָּארֵנוּ[12]* נִרְדָּפְנוּ כֻּלָּנוּ.
עַד אָנָה בְּכִיָּה בְצִיּוֹן וּמִסְפֵּד בִּירוּשָׁלָיִם, תְּרַחֵם צִיּוֹן וְתִבְנֶה חוֹמוֹת יְרוּשָׁלָיִם.

---

(1) *Psalms* 102:14. (2) Cf. 51:20. (3) Cf. 122:3. (4) Cf. *Jeremiah* 14:3.
(5) See *Ibn Ezra* to *Amos* 5:8 for the identifications and locations of these star clusters.
(6) Cf. *Exodus* 22:22. (7) *Song of Songs* 2:12. (8) Cf. *Isaiah* 50:3. (9) Cf. 13:10.
(10) Cf. *Joel* 2:10. (11) Cf. *Isaiah* 53:7. (12) Cf. *Eichah* 5:5.

עַד אָנָה — *How long?* The theme of this *kinnah* is derived from the *Midrash* which teaches that at the time of the Temple's destruction the celestial star formations called מַזָּלוֹת [*mazalos*], *constellations*, joined in Israel's mourning (*Yalkut Shimoni* II:1008). The Rabbis teach that the term מַזָּל is cognate with נוֹזֵל, *flow*, because God causes His blessings to flow to earth, with the *mazalos* acting as conduits and transformers that bring His infinite beneficence down to the finite world. The varying positions of the *mazolos* with relation to both time and earth will affect this heavenly flow in such manner that it can be said that mankind is under the influence or control of the *mazalos*. Nevertheless, the Talmud (*Shabbos* 156a) teaches that אֵין מַזָּל לְיִשְׂרָאֵל, *Mazal does not control Israel. Rashi* explains that since *mazal* is nothing more than a tool in God's hands, a Jew can overcome his *mazal* by appealing to *Hashem* through prayer or righteous deeds and He will rearrange the *mazalos* to be favorable to the petitioner. This *kinnah* describes how, on Tishah B'Av, God aligned all of the *mazalos* against Israel, so that they were all positioned in a way that would cause a negative, harmful flow upon Israel. The *paytan* records how each of the *mazalos* cried because it had a hand in this terrible tragedy.

בָּאָרֶץ חֻבְּרָה לָּהּ קָשְׁרָה מִסְפֵּד — *On earth, the people attached to it joined in eulogy.* Just as 'the angels of the multitude above join Your people Israel who are assembled below' to crown God with praises (as stated in the *Kedushah* of *Mussaf* according to the Sefardic rite), so after the Destruction, did Israel on earth and the legions of angels in heaven unite in lamenting the *Beis HaMikdash*.

Some editions read בָּעִיר שֶׁחֻבְּרָה לָּהּ, *in the city joined to it* [i.e., to Jerusalem], and refers to celestial Jerusalem which, as the Talmud (*Taanis* 5a) teaches, is joined to the terrestrial Jerusalem.

5.

How long must there be weeping in Zion and eulogy in Jerusalem? Show Zion mercy[1] *and rebuild the walls of Jerusalem!*[2]

א *At that time, through our sins, the [Beis Ha]Mikdash was destroyed, and through our iniquities the Temple was burnt down.*

ב *On earth, the people attached to it*[3] *joined in eulogy,* while the celestial legions raised a lament.*

How long must there be weeping in Zion and eulogy in Jerusalem? Show Zion mercy and rebuild the walls of Jerusalem!

ג *The tribes of Jacob also cried bitterly, and even the constellations shed tears.*

ד *The bannered tribes of Yeshurun [Israel] hid their heads [in shame];*[4] *the countenance of Pleiades and Orion*[5] *blackened.*

How long must there be weeping in Zion and eulogy in Jerusalem? Show Zion mercy and rebuild the walls of Jerusalem!

ה *The Patriarchs pleaded but God did not listen; the children screamed, but the Father did not respond.*[6]

ו *The voice of the turtledove*[7]** was heard on High, yet the Faithful Shepherd [God] did not bend an ear.*

How long must there be weeping in Zion and eulogy in Jerusalem? Show Zion mercy and rebuild the walls of Jerusalem!

ז *The sacred progeny garbed themselves in sackloth, and the celestial legions made their garments of sackcloth.*[8]

ח *The sun darkened and the moon blackened,*[9] *the stars and constellations held back their gleam.*[10]

How long must there be weeping in Zion and eulogy in Jerusalem? Show Zion mercy and rebuild the walls of Jerusalem!

ט *The Ram [טָלֶה], the first* [constellation], bleated with bitterness of soul, because his lambs were led to the slaughter.*[11]

י *The Bull [שׁוֹר] made [its] wailing heard in the heavens, because we were all pursued upon our necks.*[12]*

How long must there be weeping in Zion and eulogy in Jerusalem? Show Zion mercy and rebuild the walls of Jerusalem!

Accordingly, the *paytan* tells us that the Heavenly City united with the angels in mourning the destruction of its earthly counterpart. (See also *Rashi* to *Psalms* 122:3.)

וְקוֹל הַתּוֹר — *The voice of the turtledove.* This is variously explained as an allusion to Moses (*Shir HaShirim Rabbah* 2:12), Israel (see *Psalms* 74:19 with *Rashi*), or the Torah (some editions even read וְקוֹל הַתּוֹרָה צוֹעֵק בְּמָרָה, *the voice of the Torah cries out bitterly*).

טָלֶה רִאשׁוֹן — *The Ram, the first* ... Each of the *mazalos*, whose plaints the *paytan* now enumerates, corresponds to another month of the Hebrew calendar (*Sefer Yetzirah* 5:2). The Ram which corresponds to the first month, Nissan, is called רִאשׁוֹן, *the first.*

The *paytan* reversed the order of the tenth and eleventh constellations. Perhaps he did this to juxtapose the verses of the Rainbow and the Bucket, both of which speak of water. The chart on the following page enumerates the twelve constellations.

עַל צַוָּארֵנוּ — *Upon our necks*, i.e., with the yoke of heavy labor (*Rashi* to *Eichah* 5:5). According to the Midrash, this refers to a decree issued by the wicked Adrianus: Every Jew must shave himself bald; any Jew found with a single hair on his head or neck would be beheaded (*Eichah Rabbah* 5:5).

Others note that in another context the word צַוָּאר, *neck*, alludes to the *Beis HaMikdash* (*Megillah* 16b). Thus, the verse means that we were pursued because we acted treacherously to the Temple.

כּוֹכָב **תְּאוֹמִים** נִרְאָה חָלוּק, כִּי דַּם אַחִים נִשְׁפַּךְ כַּמַּיִם.
לָאָרֶץ בִּקֵּשׁ לִנְפּוֹל **סַרְטָן**, כִּי נִתְעַלַּפְנוּ מִפְּנֵי צָמָא.[1]
עַד אָנָה בְּכִיָּה בְּצִיּוֹן וּמִסְפֵּד בִּירוּשָׁלָיִם, תְּרַחֵם צִיּוֹן וְתִבְנֶה חוֹמוֹת יְרוּשָׁלָיִם.

מָרוֹם נִבְעַת מִקּוֹל **אַרְיֵה**, כִּי שַׁאֲגָתֵנוּ לֹא עָלְתָה לַמָּרוֹם.[2]
נֶהֶרְגוּ בְתוּלוֹת וְגַם בַּחוּרִים,[3] כִּי עַל כֵּן **בְּתוּלָה** קָדְרָה פָנֶיהָ.
עַד אָנָה בְּכִיָּה בְּצִיּוֹן וּמִסְפֵּד בִּירוּשָׁלָיִם, תְּרַחֵם צִיּוֹן וְתִבְנֶה חוֹמוֹת יְרוּשָׁלָיִם.

סִבֵּב **מֹאזְנַיִם** וּבִקֵּשׁ תְּחִנָּה, כִּי נִבְחַר לָמוֹ מָוֶת מֵחַיִּים.[4]
עַקְרָב לָבַשׁ פַּחַד וּרְעָדָה, כִּי בְּחֶרֶב וּבְרָעָב שְׁפָטָנוּ צוּרֵנוּ.
עַד אָנָה בְּכִיָּה בְּצִיּוֹן וּמִסְפֵּד בִּירוּשָׁלָיִם, תְּרַחֵם צִיּוֹן וְתִבְנֶה חוֹמוֹת יְרוּשָׁלָיִם.

פַּלְגֵי מַיִם[5] הוֹרִידוּ דִמְעָה כַּנַּחַל,[6] כִּי אוֹת **בַּקֶּשֶׁת** לֹא נִתַּן לָנוּ.*
צָפוּ מַיִם עַל רֹאשֵׁנוּ,[7] **וּבִדְלִי** מָלֵא חִכֵּנוּ יָבֵשׁ.
עַד אָנָה בְּכִיָּה בְּצִיּוֹן וּמִסְפֵּד בִּירוּשָׁלָיִם, תְּרַחֵם צִיּוֹן וְתִבְנֶה חוֹמוֹת יְרוּשָׁלָיִם.

קֵרַבְנוּ קָרְבָּן וְלֹא נִתְקַבֵּל, **וּגְדִי** פָּסַק שְׂעִיר חַטֹּאתֵנוּ.
רַחֲמָנִיּוֹת בִּשְּׁלוּ יַלְדֵיהֶן,[8] וּמַזַּל **דָּגִים** הֶעְלִים עֵינָיו.
עַד אָנָה בְּכִיָּה בְּצִיּוֹן וּמִסְפֵּד בִּירוּשָׁלָיִם, תְּרַחֵם צִיּוֹן וְתִבְנֶה חוֹמוֹת יְרוּשָׁלָיִם.

שָׁכַחְנוּ שַׁבָּת בִּלְבּוֹת שׁוֹבָבִים, שַׁדַּי שִׁכַּח כָּל צִדְקוֹתֵינוּ.
תְּקַנֵּא לְצִיּוֹן קִנְאָה גְדוֹלָה,[9] וְתָאִיר לְרַבָּתִי עָם[10] מְאוֹר נָגְהֶךָ.

תְּרַחֵם צִיּוֹן כַּאֲשֶׁר אָמַרְתָּ, וּתְכוֹנְנֶהָ כַּאֲשֶׁר דִּבַּרְתָּ, תְּמַהֵר יְשׁוּעָה וְתָחִישׁ גְּאֻלָּה, וְתָשׁוּב לִירוּשָׁלַיִם בְּרַחֲמִים רַבִּים.

כַּכָּתוּב עַל יַד נְבִיאֶךָ, לָכֵן כֹּה אָמַר יהוה, שַׁבְתִּי לִירוּשָׁלַיִם בְּרַחֲמִים, בֵּיתִי יִבָּנֶה בָּהּ, נְאֻם יהוה צְבָאוֹת, וְקָו יִנָּטֶה עַל יְרוּשָׁלָיִם.[11]

HEBREW NAME	ASTRONOMICAL NAME	MONTH
טָלֶה / RAM OR LAMB	ARIES (THE RAM)	NISSAN
שׁוֹר / BULL	TAURUS (THE BULL)	IYAR
תְּאוֹמִים / TWINS	GEMINI (THE TWINS)	SIVAN
סַרְטָן / CRAB	CANCER (THE CRAB)	TAMMUZ
אַרְיֵה / LION	LEO (THE LION)	AV
בְּתוּלָה / MAIDEN	VIRGO (THE VIRGIN)	ELUL
מֹאזְנַיִם / SCALES	LIBRA (THE SCALES)	TISHREI
עַקְרָב / SCORPION	SCORPIO (THE SCORPION)	CHESHVAN
קֶשֶׁת / RAINBOW	SAGITTARIUS (THE ARCHER)	KISLEV
גְּדִי / GOAT OR KID	CAPRICORN (THE GOAT)	TEVES
דְּלִי / BUCKET	AQUARIUS (THE WATER BEARER)	SHEVAT
דָּגִים / FISH	PISCES (THE FISH)	ADAR

כ *The constellation of the Twins [תְּאוֹמִים] appeared separated,*
because the blood of brothers was spilled like water.

ל *The Crab [סַרְטָן] was ready to fall to the earth*
because we swooned with thirst.[1]

How long must there be weeping in Zion and eulogy in Jerusalem?
Show Zion mercy and rebuild the walls of Jerusalem!

מ *The heavens were terrified by the Lion's [אַרְיֵה] voice,*
because our roaring did not ascend on high.[2]

נ *Maidens and also young men were slain,*[3]
therefore the Maiden's [בְּתוּלָה] face blackened.

How long must there be weeping in Zion and eulogy in Jerusalem?
Show Zion mercy and rebuild the walls of Jerusalem!

ס *The Scales [מֹאזְנַיִם] caused themselves to tilt [in our favor]*
and pleaded in supplication,
because, for them [Israel], death had become preferable to life.[4]

ע *The Scorpion [עַקְרָב] garbed itself in fear and trepidation,*
because with sword and hunger did our Creator condemn us.

How long must there be weeping in Zion and eulogy in Jerusalem?
Show Zion mercy and rebuild the walls of Jerusalem!

פ *[Like] streams of water,*[5] *they shed tears like a river,*[6]
*because the omen of the Rainbow [קֶשֶׁת] was not bestowed upon us.**

צ *[Endless suffering] flowed over our heads like water*[7]
and while the Bucket [דְּלִי] was full, our palate was parched.

How long must there be weeping in Zion and eulogy in Jerusalem?
Show Zion mercy and rebuild the walls of Jerusalem!

ק *We brought an offering, but it was not accepted, and*
the Goat [גְּדִי] [mourned] the discontinuation of the he-goat sin-offering.

ר *Compassionate women boiled their own children,*[8]
and the Fish [דָּגִים] constellation averted his eyes.

How long must there be weeping in Zion and eulogy in Jerusalem?
Show Zion mercy and rebuild the walls of Jerusalem!

ש *We have neglected the Sabbath, with hearts gone astray,*
so the Almighty has made all our righteousness to be forgotten.

ת *Avenge Zion with great vengeance,*[9]
illuminate [the city] 'great with people'[10] *with Your shining light.*

Show Zion mercy as You have said, and establish her as You have spoken. Hasten salvation and speed redemption and return to Jerusalem with abundant compassion.

As it is written by the hand of Your prophet: Therefore, thus says HASHEM, 'I shall return to Jerusalem with compassion, My House shall be rebuilt within it,' says HASHEM, Master of Legions, 'and a [measuring] string shall be stretched over Jerusalem.'[11]

(1) Cf. *Amos* 8:13. (2) Some editions read כִּי שַׁאֲגָתֵנוּ עָלְתָה לַמָּרוֹם, *when our roaring ascended on high.* (3) Cf. *Eichah* 2:21. (4) Cf. *Jeremiah* 8:3; some editions read לָנוּ, *for us,* instead of לָמוֹ, *for them;* some read כִּי נִכְרַע לָנוּ כַּף מָוֶת מֵחַיִּים, *because the scale of death outweighed that of life for us.* (5) Cf. *Eichah* 3:48; *Psalms* 119:136. (6) Cf. *Eichah* 2:18. (7) Cf. 3:54. (8) Cf. 4:10. (9) Cf. *Zechariah* 1:14. (10) *Eichah* 1:1. (11) *Zechariah* 1:16.

כִּי אוֹת בַּקֶּשֶׁת לֹא נִתַּן לָנוּ — *Because the omen of the Rainbow was not bestowed upon us.* As indicated by the chart, the constellation קֶשֶׁת may be rendered either *Rainbow* or *Archer's Bow;* the *paytan* uses the former. The sign of the rainbow was given to Noah as an omen that (a) the people

וְנֶאֱמַר, עוֹד קְרָא לֵאמֹר, כֹּה אָמַר יהוה צְבָאוֹת, עוֹד תְּפוּצֶנָה עָרַי מִטּוֹב, וְנִחַם יהוה עוֹד אֶת צִיּוֹן, וּבָחַר עוֹד בִּירוּשָׁלָיִם.[1] וְנֶאֱמַר, כִּי נִחַם יהוה צִיּוֹן, נִחַם כָּל חָרְבוֹתֶיהָ, וַיָּשֶׂם מִדְבָּרָהּ כְּעֵדֶן, וְעַרְבָתָהּ כְּגַן יהוה, שָׂשׂוֹן וְשִׂמְחָה יִמָּצֵא בָהּ, תּוֹדָה וְקוֹל זִמְרָה.[2]

At this point, some congregations have introduced the custom of reciting a *kinnah* lamenting the tragedy of the six million Jews murdered during the Holocaust. Two *kinnos* of this genre appear on pages 384-389.

וִיהִי נֹעַם, USUALLY RECITED ON SATURDAY NIGHT, IS NOT RECITED ON TISHAH B'AV; וְאַתָּה קָדוֹשׁ IS RECITED EVEN ON WEEKNIGHTS.

The primary part of וְאַתָּה קָדוֹשׁ is the *Kedushah* recited by the angels. These verses are presented in bold type and it is preferable that the congregation recite them aloud and in unison. However, the interpretive translation in Aramaic (which follows the verses in bold type) should be recited softly.

וְאַתָּה קָדוֹשׁ יוֹשֵׁב תְּהִלּוֹת יִשְׂרָאֵל.[3]
וְקָרָא זֶה אֶל זֶה וְאָמַר:
קָדוֹשׁ, קָדוֹשׁ, קָדוֹשׁ יהוה צְבָאוֹת, מְלֹא כָל הָאָרֶץ כְּבוֹדוֹ.[4]
וּמְקַבְּלִין דֵּין מִן דֵּין וְאָמְרִין:
קַדִּישׁ בִּשְׁמֵי מְרוֹמָא עִלָּאָה בֵּית שְׁכִינְתֵּהּ,
קַדִּישׁ עַל אַרְעָא עוֹבַד גְּבוּרְתֵּהּ,
קַדִּישׁ לְעָלַם וּלְעָלְמֵי עָלְמַיָּא, יהוה צְבָאוֹת,
מַלְיָא כָל אַרְעָא זִיו יְקָרֵהּ.[5]
❖ וַתִּשָּׂאֵנִי רוּחַ, וָאֶשְׁמַע אַחֲרַי קוֹל רַעַשׁ גָּדוֹל:
בָּרוּךְ כְּבוֹד יהוה מִמְּקוֹמוֹ.[6]
וּנְטָלַתְנִי רוּחָא, וּשְׁמָעִית בַּתְרַי קָל זִיעַ סַגִּיא דִּמְשַׁבְּחִין וְאָמְרִין:
בְּרִיךְ יְקָרָא דַיהוה מֵאֲתַר בֵּית שְׁכִינְתֵּהּ.[7]
יהוה יִמְלֹךְ לְעֹלָם וָעֶד.[8]
יהוה מַלְכוּתֵהּ קָאֵם לְעָלַם וּלְעָלְמֵי עָלְמַיָּא.[9]

יהוה אֱלֹהֵי אַבְרָהָם יִצְחָק וְיִשְׂרָאֵל אֲבֹתֵינוּ, שָׁמְרָה זֹּאת לְעוֹלָם, לְיֵצֶר מַחְשְׁבוֹת לְבַב עַמֶּךָ, וְהָכֵן לְבָבָם אֵלֶיךָ.[10] וְהוּא רַחוּם, יְכַפֵּר עָוֹן וְלֹא יַשְׁחִית, וְהִרְבָּה לְהָשִׁיב אַפּוֹ, וְלֹא יָעִיר כָּל חֲמָתוֹ.[11] כִּי אַתָּה אֲדֹנָי טוֹב וְסַלָּח, וְרַב חֶסֶד לְכָל קֹרְאֶיךָ.[12] צִדְקָתְךָ צֶדֶק לְעוֹלָם, וְתוֹרָתְךָ אֱמֶת.[13] תִּתֵּן אֱמֶת לְיַעֲקֹב, חֶסֶד לְאַבְרָהָם, אֲשֶׁר נִשְׁבַּעְתָּ לַאֲבֹתֵינוּ מִימֵי קֶדֶם.[14] בָּרוּךְ אֲדֹנָי יוֹם יוֹם יַעֲמָס לָנוּ, הָאֵל יְשׁוּעָתֵנוּ סֶלָה.[15] יהוה צְבָאוֹת עִמָּנוּ, מִשְׂגָּב לָנוּ אֱלֹהֵי יַעֲקֹב סֶלָה.[16] יהוה צְבָאוֹת, אַשְׁרֵי אָדָם בֹּטֵחַ בָּךְ.[17] יהוה הוֹשִׁיעָה, הַמֶּלֶךְ יַעֲנֵנוּ בְיוֹם קָרְאֵנוּ.[18]

And it is said: Call out again, saying, Thus says HASHEM, *Master of Legions, 'My cities shall again overflow with beneficence, and again* HASHEM *will assuage Zion and again He will choose Jerusalem.'*[1]

And it is said: For HASHEM *comforts Zion, He comforts her ruins, and He will make her wilderness like Eden, and her wastes like a garden of* HASHEM; *gladness and joy shall be found there, thanksgiving and the sound of music.*[2]

At this point, some congregations have introduced the custom of reciting a *kinnah* lamenting the tragedy of the six million Jews murdered during the Holocaust. Two *kinnos* of this genre appear on pages 384-389.

וִיהִי נֹעַם, USUALLY RECITED ON SATURDAY NIGHT, IS NOT RECITED ON TISHAH B'AV; וְאַתָּה קָדוֹשׁ IS RECITED EVEN ON WEEKNIGHTS.

The primary part of וְאַתָּה קָדוֹשׁ is the *Kedushah* recited by the angels. These verses are presented in bold type and it is preferable that the congregation recite them aloud and in unison. However, the interpretive translation in Aramaic (which follows the verses in bold type) should be recited softly.

וְאַתָּה קָדוֹשׁ *You are the Holy One, enthroned upon the praises of Israel.*[3] *And one [angel] will call another and say:*

'Holy, holy, holy is HASHEM, Master of Legions, the whole world is filled with His glory.'[4]

And they receive permission from one another and say: 'Holy in the most exalted heaven, the abode of His Presence; holy on earth, product of His strength; holy forever and ever is HASHEM, *Master of Legions — the entire world is filled with the radiance of His glory.'*[5]

∴ *And a wind lifted me; and I heard behind me the sound of a great noise:*

'Blessed is the glory of HASHEM from His place.'[6]

And a wind lifted me and I heard behind me the sound of the powerful movement of those who praised saying: 'Blessed is the honor of HASHEM *from the place of the abode of His Presence.'*[7]

HASHEM shall reign for all eternity.[8]

HASHEM — *His kingdom is established forever and ever.*[9]

HASHEM, *God of Abraham, Isaac, and Israel, our forefathers, may You preserve this forever as the realization of the thoughts in Your people's heart, and may You direct their heart to You.*[10] *He, the Merciful One, is forgiving of iniquity and does not destroy; frequently He withdraws His anger, not arousing His entire rage.*[11] *For You, my Lord, are good and forgiving, and abundantly kind to all who call upon You.*[12] *Your righteousness remains righteous forever, and Your Torah is truth.*[13] *Grant truth to Jacob, kindness to Abraham, as You swore to our forefathers from ancient times.*[14] *Blessed is my Lord for every single day, He burdens us with blessings, the God of our salvation, Selah.*[15] HASHEM, *Master of Legions, is with us, a stronghold for us is the God of Jacob, Selah.*[16] HASHEM, *Master of Legions, praiseworthy is the man who trusts in You.*[17] HASHEM, *save! May the King answer us on the day we call.*[18]

(1) *Zechariah* 1:17. (2) *Isaiah* 51:3. (3) *Psalms* 22:4. (4) *Isaiah* 6:3. (5) *Targum Yonasan* to *Isaiah* 6:3. (6) *Ezekiel* 3:12. (7) *Targum Yonasan* to *Ezekiel* 3:12. (8) *Exodus* 15:18. (9) *Targum Onkelos* to *Exodus* 15:18. (10) *I Chronicles* 29:18. (11) *Psalms* 78:38. (12) 86:5. (13) 119:142. (14) *Micah* 7:20. (15) *Psalms* 68:20. (16) 46:8. (17) 84:13. (18) 20:10.

---

have lapsed into sinfulness, and (b) even though the world deserves another Flood, it will not come because of God's promise to Noah (see *Genesis* 9:12-16). We lament because the rainbow was not sent to stop the flood of our tears.

בָּרוּךְ הוּא אֱלֹהֵינוּ שֶׁבְּרָאָנוּ לִכְבוֹדוֹ, וְהִבְדִּילָנוּ מִן הַתּוֹעִים, וְנָתַן לָנוּ תּוֹרַת אֱמֶת, וְחַיֵּי עוֹלָם נָטַע בְּתוֹכֵנוּ. הוּא יִפְתַּח לִבֵּנוּ בְּתוֹרָתוֹ, וְיָשֵׂם בְּלִבֵּנוּ אַהֲבָתוֹ וְיִרְאָתוֹ וְלַעֲשׂוֹת רְצוֹנוֹ וּלְעָבְדוֹ בְּלֵבָב שָׁלֵם, לְמַעַן לֹא נִיגַע לָרִיק, וְלֹא נֵלֵד לַבֶּהָלָה.[1]

יְהִי רָצוֹן מִלְּפָנֶיךָ יהוה אֱלֹהֵינוּ וֵאלֹהֵי אֲבוֹתֵינוּ, שֶׁנִּשְׁמֹר חֻקֶּיךָ בָּעוֹלָם הַזֶּה, וְנִזְכֶּה וְנִחְיֶה וְנִרְאֶה וְנִירַשׁ טוֹבָה וּבְרָכָה לִשְׁנֵי יְמוֹת הַמָּשִׁיחַ וּלְחַיֵּי הָעוֹלָם הַבָּא. לְמַעַן יְזַמֶּרְךָ כָבוֹד וְלֹא יִדֹּם, יהוה אֱלֹהַי לְעוֹלָם אוֹדֶךָּ.[2] בָּרוּךְ הַגֶּבֶר אֲשֶׁר יִבְטַח בַּיהוה, וְהָיָה יהוה מִבְטַחוֹ.[3] בִּטְחוּ בַיהוה עֲדֵי עַד, כִּי בְּיָהּ יהוה צוּר עוֹלָמִים.[4] ❖ וְיִבְטְחוּ בְךָ יוֹדְעֵי שְׁמֶךָ, כִּי לֹא עָזַבְתָּ דֹּרְשֶׁיךָ, יהוה.[5] יהוה חָפֵץ לְמַעַן צִדְקוֹ, יַגְדִּיל תּוֹרָה וְיַאְדִּיר.[6]

The *chazzan* recites קַדִּישׁ שָׁלֵם בְּלֹא תִּתְקַבַּל.

יִתְגַּדַּל וְיִתְקַדַּשׁ שְׁמֵהּ רַבָּא. (.Cong – אָמֵן.) בְּעָלְמָא דִּי בְרָא כִרְעוּתֵהּ. וְיַמְלִיךְ מַלְכוּתֵהּ, בְּחַיֵּיכוֹן וּבְיוֹמֵיכוֹן וּבְחַיֵּי דְכָל בֵּית יִשְׂרָאֵל, בַּעֲגָלָא וּבִזְמַן קָרִיב. וְאִמְרוּ: אָמֵן.

(.Cong – אָמֵן. יְהֵא שְׁמֵהּ רַבָּא מְבָרַךְ לְעָלַם וּלְעָלְמֵי עָלְמַיָּא.)

יְהֵא שְׁמֵהּ רַבָּא מְבָרַךְ לְעָלַם וּלְעָלְמֵי עָלְמַיָּא.

יִתְבָּרַךְ וְיִשְׁתַּבַּח וְיִתְפָּאַר וְיִתְרוֹמַם וְיִתְנַשֵּׂא וְיִתְהַדָּר וְיִתְעַלֶּה וְיִתְהַלָּל שְׁמֵהּ דְּקֻדְשָׁא בְּרִיךְ הוּא (.Cong – בְּרִיךְ הוּא) – לְעֵלָּא מִן כָּל בִּרְכָתָא וְשִׁירָתָא תֻּשְׁבְּחָתָא וְנֶחֱמָתָא, דַּאֲמִירָן בְּעָלְמָא. וְאִמְרוּ: אָמֵן. (.Cong – אָמֵן.)

יְהֵא שְׁלָמָא רַבָּא מִן שְׁמַיָּא, וְחַיִּים עָלֵינוּ וְעַל כָּל יִשְׂרָאֵל. וְאִמְרוּ: אָמֵן. (.Cong – אָמֵן.)

Take three steps back. Bow left and say . . . עֹשֶׂה; bow right and say . . . הוּא; bow forward and say וְעַל כָּל . . . אָמֵן. Remain standing in place for a few moments, then take three steps forward.

עֹשֶׂה שָׁלוֹם בִּמְרוֹמָיו, הוּא יַעֲשֶׂה שָׁלוֹם עָלֵינוּ, וְעַל כָּל יִשְׂרָאֵל. וְאִמְרוּ: אָמֵן. (.Cong – אָמֵן.)

Stand while reciting עָלֵינוּ.

עָלֵינוּ לְשַׁבֵּחַ לַאֲדוֹן הַכֹּל, לָתֵת גְּדֻלָּה לְיוֹצֵר בְּרֵאשִׁית, שֶׁלֹּא עָשָׂנוּ כְּגוֹיֵי הָאֲרָצוֹת, וְלֹא שָׂמָנוּ כְּמִשְׁפְּחוֹת הָאֲדָמָה. שֶׁלֹּא שָׂם חֶלְקֵנוּ כָּהֶם, וְגוֹרָלֵנוּ כְּכָל הֲמוֹנָם. (שֶׁהֵם מִשְׁתַּחֲוִים לְהֶבֶל וָרִיק, וּמִתְפַּלְּלִים אֶל אֵל לֹא יוֹשִׁיעַ.[7]) וַאֲנַחְנוּ כּוֹרְעִים וּמִשְׁתַּחֲוִים וּמוֹדִים, לִפְנֵי מֶלֶךְ מַלְכֵי הַמְּלָכִים הַקָּדוֹשׁ בָּרוּךְ הוּא. שֶׁהוּא נוֹטֶה שָׁמַיִם וְיֹסֵד אָרֶץ,[8]

Bow while reciting וַאֲנַחְנוּ כּוֹרְעִים וּמִשְׁתַּחֲוִים.

Blessed is He, our God, Who created us for His glory, separated us from those who stray, gave us the Torah of truth and implanted eternal life within us. May He open our heart through His Torah and imbue our heart with love and awe of Him and that we may do His will and serve Him wholeheartedly, so that we do not struggle in vain nor produce for futility.[1]

May it be Your will, HASHEM, *our God and the God of our forefathers, that we observe Your decrees in This World, and merit that we live and see and inherit goodness and blessing in the years of Messianic times and for the life of the World to Come. So that my soul might sing to You and not be stilled,* HASHEM, *my God, forever will I thank You.*[2] *Blessed is the man who trusts in* HASHEM, *then* HASHEM *will be his security.*[3] *Trust in* HASHEM *forever, for in God,* HASHEM, *is the strength of the worlds.*[4] Chazzan– *Those knowing Your Name will trust in You, and You forsake not those Who seek You,* HASHEM.[5] HASHEM *desired, for the sake of its [Israel's] righteousness, that the Torah be made great and glorious.*[6]

The chazzan recites the following *Kaddish.*

יִתְגַּדַּל *May His great Name grow exalted and sanctified* (Cong.– *Amen.*) *in the world that He created as He willed. May He give reign to His kingship in your lifetimes and in your days, and in the lifetimes of the entire Family of Israel, swiftly and soon. Now respond: Amen.*

(Cong.– *Amen. May His great Name be blessed forever and ever.*)

May His great Name be blessed forever and ever.

Blessed, praised, glorified, exalted, extolled, mighty, upraised, and lauded be the Name of the Holy One, Blessed is He (Cong.– *Blessed is He*) — *beyond any blessing and song, praise and consolation that are uttered in the world. Now respond: Amen.* (Cong.– *Amen.*)

May there be abundant peace from Heaven, and life, upon us and upon all Israel. Now respond: Amen. (Cong.– *Amen.*)

Take three steps back. Bow left and say, *'He Who makes peace . . .';* bow right and say, *'may He . . .';* bow forward and say, *'and upon all Israel . . .'* Remain standing in place for a few moments, then take three steps forward.

He Who makes peace in His heights, may He make peace upon us, and upon all Israel. Now respond: Amen. (Cong.– *Amen.*)

Stand while reciting עָלֵינוּ, *'It is our duty . . .'*

עָלֵינוּ *It is our duty to praise the Master of all, to ascribe greatness to the Molder of primeval creation, for He has not made us like the nations of the lands, and has not emplaced us like the families of the earth; for He has not assigned our portion like theirs nor our lot like all their multitudes. (For they bow to vanity and emptiness and pray to a god which helps not.*[7]*) But we bend our knees, bow, and acknowledge our thanks before the King Who reigns over kings, the Holy One, Blessed is He. He stretches out heaven and establishes earth's foundation,*[8] *the*

Bow while reciting *'But we bend our knees.'*

(1) Cf. *Isaiah* 65:23. (2) *Psalms* 30:13. (3) *Jeremiah* 17:7. (4) *Isaiah* 26:4. (5) *Psalms* 9:11. (6) *Isaiah* 42:21. (7) *Isaiah* 45:20. (8) 51:13.

וּמוֹשַׁב יְקָרוֹ בַּשָּׁמַיִם מִמַּעַל, וּשְׁכִינַת עֻזּוֹ בְּגָבְהֵי מְרוֹמִים. הוּא אֱלֹהֵינוּ, אֵין עוֹד. אֱמֶת מַלְכֵּנוּ, אֶפֶס זוּלָתוֹ, כַּכָּתוּב בְּתוֹרָתוֹ: וְיָדַעְתָּ הַיּוֹם וַהֲשֵׁבֹתָ אֶל לְבָבֶךָ, כִּי יהוה הוּא הָאֱלֹהִים בַּשָּׁמַיִם מִמַּעַל וְעַל הָאָרֶץ מִתָּחַת, אֵין עוֹד.[1]

עַל כֵּן נְקַוֶּה לְּךָ יהוה אֱלֹהֵינוּ לִרְאוֹת מְהֵרָה בְּתִפְאֶרֶת עֻזֶּךָ, לְהַעֲבִיר גִּלּוּלִים מִן הָאָרֶץ, וְהָאֱלִילִים כָּרוֹת יִכָּרֵתוּן, לְתַקֵּן עוֹלָם בְּמַלְכוּת שַׁדַּי. וְכָל בְּנֵי בָשָׂר יִקְרְאוּ בִשְׁמֶךָ, לְהַפְנוֹת אֵלֶיךָ כָּל רִשְׁעֵי אָרֶץ. יַכִּירוּ וְיֵדְעוּ כָּל יוֹשְׁבֵי תֵבֵל, כִּי לְךָ תִּכְרַע כָּל בֶּרֶךְ, תִּשָּׁבַע כָּל לָשׁוֹן.[2] לְפָנֶיךָ יהוה אֱלֹהֵינוּ יִכְרְעוּ וְיִפֹּלוּ, וְלִכְבוֹד שִׁמְךָ יְקָר יִתֵּנוּ. וִיקַבְּלוּ כֻלָּם אֶת עוֹל מַלְכוּתֶךָ, וְתִמְלֹךְ עֲלֵיהֶם מְהֵרָה לְעוֹלָם וָעֶד. כִּי הַמַּלְכוּת שֶׁלְּךָ הִיא וּלְעוֹלְמֵי עַד תִּמְלוֹךְ בְּכָבוֹד, כַּכָּתוּב בְּתוֹרָתֶךָ: יהוה יִמְלֹךְ לְעֹלָם וָעֶד.[3] ❖ וְנֶאֱמַר: וְהָיָה יהוה לְמֶלֶךְ עַל כָּל הָאָרֶץ, בַּיּוֹם הַהוּא יִהְיֶה יהוה אֶחָד וּשְׁמוֹ אֶחָד.[4]

Some congregations recite the following after עָלֵינוּ.

אַל תִּירָא מִפַּחַד פִּתְאֹם, וּמִשֹּׁאַת רְשָׁעִים כִּי תָבֹא.[5] עֻצוּ עֵצָה וְתֻפָר, דַּבְּרוּ דָבָר וְלֹא יָקוּם, כִּי עִמָּנוּ אֵל.[6] וְעַד זִקְנָה אֲנִי הוּא, וְעַד שֵׂיבָה אֲנִי אֶסְבֹּל, אֲנִי עָשִׂיתִי וַאֲנִי אֶשָּׂא, וַאֲנִי אֶסְבֹּל וַאֲמַלֵּט.[7]

קדיש יתום

In the presence of a *minyan,* mourners recite קַדִּישׁ יָתוֹם, the Mourner's *Kaddish* (see *Laws* §132-134).

יִתְגַּדַּל וְיִתְקַדַּשׁ שְׁמֵהּ רַבָּא. (.Cong – אָמֵן.) בְּעָלְמָא דִּי בְרָא כִרְעוּתֵהּ. וְיַמְלִיךְ מַלְכוּתֵהּ, בְּחַיֵּיכוֹן וּבְיוֹמֵיכוֹן וּבְחַיֵּי דְכָל בֵּית יִשְׂרָאֵל, בַּעֲגָלָא וּבִזְמַן קָרִיב. וְאִמְרוּ: אָמֵן.

(.Cong – אָמֵן. יְהֵא שְׁמֵהּ רַבָּא מְבָרַךְ לְעָלַם וּלְעָלְמֵי עָלְמַיָּא.)

יְהֵא שְׁמֵהּ רַבָּא מְבָרַךְ לְעָלַם וּלְעָלְמֵי עָלְמַיָּא.

יִתְבָּרַךְ וְיִשְׁתַּבַּח וְיִתְפָּאַר וְיִתְרוֹמַם וְיִתְנַשֵּׂא וְיִתְהַדָּר וְיִתְעַלֶּה וְיִתְהַלָּל שְׁמֵהּ דְּקֻדְשָׁא בְּרִיךְ הוּא (.Cong – בְּרִיךְ הוּא) — לְעֵלָּא מִן כָּל בִּרְכָתָא וְשִׁירָתָא תֻּשְׁבְּחָתָא וְנֶחֱמָתָא, דַּאֲמִירָן בְּעָלְמָא. וְאִמְרוּ: אָמֵן. (.Cong – אָמֵן.)

יְהֵא שְׁלָמָא רַבָּא מִן שְׁמַיָּא, וְחַיִּים עָלֵינוּ וְעַל כָּל יִשְׂרָאֵל. וְאִמְרוּ: אָמֵן. (.Cong – אָמֵן.)

Take three steps back. Bow left and say . . . עֹשֶׂה; bow right and say . . . הוּא; bow forward and say וְעַל כָּל . . . אָמֵן. Remain standing in place for a few moments, then take three steps forward.

עֹשֶׂה שָׁלוֹם בִּמְרוֹמָיו, הוּא יַעֲשֶׂה שָׁלוֹם עָלֵינוּ, וְעַל כָּל יִשְׂרָאֵל. וְאִמְרוּ: אָמֵן. (.Cong – אָמֵן.)

seat of His homage is in the heavens above and His powerful Presence is in the loftiest heights. He is our God and there is none other. True is our King, there is nothing beside Him, as it is written in His Torah: 'You are to know this day and take to your heart that HASHEM is the only God — in heaven above and on the earth below — there is none other.'[1]

עַל כֵּן *Therefore we put our hope in You, HASHEM, our God, that we may soon see Your mighty splendor, to remove detestable idolatry from the earth, and false gods will be utterly cut off, to perfect the universe through the Almighty's sovereignty. Then all humanity will call upon Your Name, to turn all the earth's wicked toward You. All the world's inhabitants will recognize and know that to You every knee should bend, every tongue should swear.*[2] *Before You, HASHEM, our God, they will bend every knee and cast themselves down and to the glory of Your Name they will render homage, and they will all accept upon themselves the yoke of Your kingship that You may reign over them soon and eternally. For the kingdom is Yours and You will reign for all eternity in glory as it is written in Your Torah: HASHEM shall reign for all eternity.*[3] Chazzan– *And it is said: HASHEM will be King over all the world — on that day HASHEM will be One and His Name will be One.*[4]

Some congregations recite the following after *Aleinu.*

אַל תִּירָא *Do not fear sudden terror, or the holocaust of the wicked when it comes.*[5] *Plan a conspiracy and it will be annulled; speak your piece and it shall not stand, for God is with us.*[6] *Even till your seniority, I remain unchanged; and even till your ripe old age, I shall endure. I created you and I shall bear you; I shall endure and rescue.*[7]

MOURNER'S KADDISH

In the presence of a *minyan,* mourners recite קַדִּישׁ יָתוֹם, the Mourner's *Kaddish* (see *Laws* 132-134).

[A transliteration of this *Kaddish* appears on page 484.]

יִתְגַּדַּל *May His great Name grow exalted and sanctified* (Cong.– *Amen.*) *in the world that He created as He willed. May He give reign to His kingship in your lifetimes and in your days, and in the lifetimes of the entire Family of Israel, swiftly and soon. Now respond: Amen.*

(Cong.– *Amen. May His great Name be blessed forever and ever.*)

May His great Name be blessed forever and ever.

Blessed, praised, glorified, exalted, extolled, mighty, upraised, and lauded be the Name of the Holy One, Blessed is He (Cong.– *Blessed is He*) *— beyond any blessing and song, praise and consolation that are uttered in the world. Now respond: Amen.* (Cong.– *Amen*).

May there be abundant peace from Heaven, and life, upon us and upon all Israel. Now respond: Amen. (Cong.– *Amen.*)

Take three steps back. Bow left and say, *'He Who makes peace . . .';* bow right and say, *'may He . . .';* bow forward and say, *'and upon all Israel . . .'* Remain standing in place for a few moments, then take three steps forward.

He Who makes peace in His heights, may He make peace upon us, and upon all Israel. Now respond: Amen. (Cong.– *Amen.*)

---

(1) *Deuteronomy* 4:39. (2) Cf. *Isaiah* 45:23. (3) *Exodus* 15:18.
(4) *Zechariah* 14:9. (5) *Proverbs* 3:25. (6) *Isaiah* 8:10. (7) 46:4.

השכמת הבוקר

A Jew should wake up with gratitude to God for having restored his faculties and with a lionlike resolve to serve his Creator. Before getting off the bed or commencing any other conversation or activity, he declares his gratitude:

מוֹדֶה אֲנִי לְפָנֶיךָ, מֶלֶךְ חַי וְקַיָּם, שֶׁהֶחֱזַרְתָּ בִּי נִשְׁמָתִי בְּחֶמְלָה – רַבָּה אֱמוּנָתֶךָ.

Wash the fingers, but not the palms, according to the ritual procedure: Pick up the vessel of water with the right hand, pass it to the left, and pour water over the right. Then with the right hand pour over the left. Follow this procedure until water has been poured over each hand three times. (When the fingers are still damp, they may be used to remove mucus from the eyes.) Then, recite:

רֵאשִׁית חָכְמָה יִרְאַת יהוה, שֵׂכֶל טוֹב לְכָל עֹשֵׂיהֶם, תְּהִלָּתוֹ עֹמֶדֶת לָעַד.[1] בָּרוּךְ שֵׁם כְּבוֹד מַלְכוּתוֹ לְעוֹלָם וָעֶד.

ציצית, טלית, ותפילין

The *tallis kattan (tzitzis)* is worn, but the blessing is omitted.
The *tallis* and *tefillin* are not worn at *Shacharis,* but are worn at *Minchah.*

SOME CONGREGATIONS OMIT CERTAIN PASSAGES OF THE PRAYERS PRECEDING אֵיזֶהוּ מְקוֹמָן (P. 92). CUSTOMS REGARDING WHETHER AND WHICH PASSAGES ARE OMITTED VARY GREATLY. THEREFORE WE HAVE NOT OMITTED ANY PASSAGES. EACH CONGREGATION SHOULD FOLLOW ITS ESTABLISHED CUSTOM.

ברכות השחר

Recite the following collection of verses upon entering the synagogue:

מַה טֹּבוּ אֹהָלֶיךָ יַעֲקֹב, מִשְׁכְּנֹתֶיךָ יִשְׂרָאֵל.[2] וַאֲנִי בְּרֹב חַסְדְּךָ אָבוֹא בֵיתֶךָ, אֶשְׁתַּחֲוֶה אֶל הֵיכַל קָדְשְׁךָ בְּיִרְאָתֶךָ.[3] יהוה אָהַבְתִּי מְעוֹן בֵּיתֶךָ, וּמְקוֹם מִשְׁכַּן כְּבוֹדֶךָ.[4] וַאֲנִי אֶשְׁתַּחֲוֶה וְאֶכְרָעָה, אֶבְרְכָה לִפְנֵי יהוה עֹשִׂי.[5] וַאֲנִי, תְפִלָּתִי לְךָ יהוה, עֵת רָצוֹן, אֱלֹהִים בְּרָב חַסְדֶּךָ, עֲנֵנִי בֶּאֱמֶת יִשְׁעֶךָ.[6]

אֲדוֹן עוֹלָם אֲשֶׁר מָלַךְ, בְּטֶרֶם כָּל יְצִיר נִבְרָא.
לְעֵת נַעֲשָׂה בְחֶפְצוֹ כֹּל, אֲזַי מֶלֶךְ שְׁמוֹ נִקְרָא.
וְאַחֲרֵי כִּכְלוֹת הַכֹּל, לְבַדּוֹ יִמְלוֹךְ נוֹרָא.
וְהוּא הָיָה וְהוּא הֹוֶה, וְהוּא יִהְיֶה בְּתִפְאָרָה.
וְהוּא אֶחָד וְאֵין שֵׁנִי, לְהַמְשִׁיל לוֹ לְהַחְבִּירָה.
בְּלִי רֵאשִׁית בְּלִי תַכְלִית, וְלוֹ הָעֹז וְהַמִּשְׂרָה.
וְהוּא אֵלִי וְחַי גֹּאֲלִי, וְצוּר חֶבְלִי בְּעֵת צָרָה.
וְהוּא נִסִּי וּמָנוֹס לִי, מְנָת כּוֹסִי בְּיוֹם אֶקְרָא.

---

(1) *Psalms* 111:10. (2) *Numbers* 24:5. (3) *Psalms* 5:8. (4) 26:8. (5) Cf. 95:6. (6) 69:14.

UPON ARISING

A Jew should wake up with gratitude to God for having restored his faculties and with a lionlike resolve to serve his Creator. Before getting off the bed or commencing any other conversation or activity, he declares his gratitude:

מוֹדֶה אֲנִי *I gratefully thank You, O living and eternal King, for You have returned my soul within me with compassion — abundant is Your faithfulness!*

Wash the fingers, but not the palms, according to the ritual procedure: Pick up the vessel of water with the right hand, pass it to the left, and pour water over the right. Then with the right hand pour over the left. Follow this procedure until water has been poured over each hand three times. (When the fingers are still damp, they may be used to remove mucus from the eyes.) Then, recite:

רֵאשִׁית חָכְמָה *The beginning of wisdom is the fear of HASHEM — good understanding to all their practitioners; His praise endures forever.*[1] *Blessed is the Name of His glorious kingdom for all eternity.*

TZITZIS, TALLIS, AND TEFILLIN

The *tallis kattan (tzitzis)* is worn, but the blessing is omitted.
The *tallis* and *tefillin* are not worn at *Shacharis,* but are worn at *Minchah.*

SOME CONGREGATIONS OMIT CERTAIN PASSAGES OF THE PRAYERS PRECEDING אֵיזֶהוּ מְקוֹמָן, *WHAT IS THE LOCATION* (P. 92). CUSTOMS REGARDING WHETHER AND WHICH PASSAGES ARE OMITTED VARY GREATLY. THEREFORE WE HAVE NOT OMITTED ANY PASSAGES. EACH CONGREGATION SHOULD FOLLOW ITS ESTABLISHED CUSTOM.

MORNING BLESSINGS

Recite the following collection of verses upon entering the synagogue:

מַה טֹּבוּ *How goodly are your tents, O Jacob, your dwelling places, O Israel.*[2] *As for me, through Your abundant kindness I will enter Your House; I will prostrate myself toward Your Holy Sanctuary in awe of You.*[3] *O HASHEM, I love the House where You dwell, and the place where Your glory resides.*[4] *I shall prostrate myself and bow, I shall kneel before HASHEM my Maker.*[5] *As for me, may my prayer to You, HASHEM, be at an opportune time; O God, in Your abundant kindness, answer me with the truth of Your salvation.*[6]

אֲדוֹן עוֹלָם *Master of the universe, Who reigned before any form was created,*
At the time when His will brought all into being —
then as 'King' was His Name proclaimed.
After all has ceased to be, He, the Awesome One, will reign alone.
It is He Who was, He Who is, and He Who shall remain, in splendor.
He is One — there is no second to compare to Him,
to declare as His equal.
Without beginning, without conclusion —
His is the power and dominion.
He is my God, my living Redeemer, Rock of my pain in time of distress.
He is my banner, a refuge for me, the portion in my cup on the day I call.

בְּיָדוֹ אַפְקִיד רוּחִי, בְּעֵת אִישַׁן וְאָעִירָה.
וְעִם רוּחִי גְּוִיָּתִי, יהוה לִי וְלֹא אִירָא.

יִגְדַּל אֱלֹהִים חַי וְיִשְׁתַּבַּח, נִמְצָא וְאֵין עֵת אֶל מְצִיאוּתוֹ.
אֶחָד וְאֵין יָחִיד כְּיִחוּדוֹ, נֶעְלָם וְגַם אֵין סוֹף לְאַחְדוּתוֹ.
אֵין לוֹ דְמוּת הַגּוּף וְאֵינוֹ גוּף, לֹא נַעֲרוֹךְ אֵלָיו קְדֻשָּׁתוֹ.
קַדְמוֹן לְכָל דָּבָר אֲשֶׁר נִבְרָא, רִאשׁוֹן וְאֵין רֵאשִׁית לְרֵאשִׁיתוֹ.
הִנּוֹ אֲדוֹן עוֹלָם לְכָל נוֹצָר, יוֹרֶה גְדֻלָּתוֹ וּמַלְכוּתוֹ.
שֶׁפַע נְבוּאָתוֹ נְתָנוֹ, אֶל אַנְשֵׁי סְגֻלָּתוֹ וְתִפְאַרְתּוֹ.
לֹא קָם בְּיִשְׂרָאֵל כְּמֹשֶׁה עוֹד, נָבִיא וּמַבִּיט אֶת תְּמוּנָתוֹ.
תּוֹרַת אֱמֶת נָתַן לְעַמּוֹ אֵל, עַל יַד נְבִיאוֹ נֶאֱמַן בֵּיתוֹ.
לֹא יַחֲלִיף הָאֵל וְלֹא יָמִיר דָּתוֹ, לְעוֹלָמִים לְזוּלָתוֹ.
צוֹפֶה וְיוֹדֵעַ סְתָרֵינוּ, מַבִּיט לְסוֹף דָּבָר בְּקַדְמָתוֹ.
גּוֹמֵל לְאִישׁ חֶסֶד כְּמִפְעָלוֹ, נוֹתֵן לְרָשָׁע רָע כְּרִשְׁעָתוֹ.
יִשְׁלַח לְקֵץ הַיָּמִין מְשִׁיחֵנוּ, לִפְדּוֹת מְחַכֵּי קֵץ יְשׁוּעָתוֹ.
מֵתִים יְחַיֶּה אֵל בְּרֹב חַסְדּוֹ, בָּרוּךְ עֲדֵי עַד שֵׁם תְּהִלָּתוֹ.

ברכות השחר

Although many hold that the blessing עַל נְטִילַת יָדָיִם should be recited immediately after the ritual washing of the hands upon arising, others customarily recite it at this point. Similarly, some recite אֲשֶׁר יָצַר immediately after relieving themselves in the morning, while others recite it here.

בָּרוּךְ אַתָּה יהוה אֱלֹהֵינוּ מֶלֶךְ הָעוֹלָם, אֲשֶׁר קִדְּשָׁנוּ בְּמִצְוֹתָיו, וְצִוָּנוּ עַל נְטִילַת יָדָיִם.

בָּרוּךְ אַתָּה יהוה אֱלֹהֵינוּ מֶלֶךְ הָעוֹלָם, אֲשֶׁר יָצַר אֶת הָאָדָם בְּחָכְמָה, וּבָרָא בוֹ נְקָבִים נְקָבִים, חֲלוּלִים חֲלוּלִים. גָּלוּי וְיָדוּעַ לִפְנֵי כִסֵּא כְבוֹדֶךָ, שֶׁאִם יִפָּתֵחַ אֶחָד מֵהֶם, אוֹ יִסָּתֵם אֶחָד מֵהֶם, אִי אֶפְשַׁר לְהִתְקַיֵּם וְלַעֲמוֹד לְפָנֶיךָ. בָּרוּךְ אַתָּה יהוה, רוֹפֵא כָל בָּשָׂר וּמַפְלִיא לַעֲשׂוֹת.

At this point, some recite אֱלֹהַי נְשָׁמָה (p. 76).

Into His hand I shall entrust my spirit when I go to sleep —
and I shall awaken!
With my spirit shall my body remain. HASHEM is with me,
I shall not fear.

יִגְדַּל *Exalted be the Living God and praised,*
He exists — unbounded by time is His existence.
He is One — and there is no unity like His Oneness.
Inscrutable and infinite is His Oneness.
He has no semblance of a body nor is He corporeal;
nor has His holiness any comparison.
He preceded every being that was created —
the First, and nothing precedes His precedence.
Behold! He is Master of the universe to every creature,
He demonstrates His greatness and His sovereignty.
He granted His flow of prophecy
to His treasured splendrous people.
In Israel none like Moses arose again —
a prophet who perceived His vision clearly.
God gave His people a Torah of truth,
by means of His prophet, the most trusted of His household.
God will never amend nor exchange His law
for any other one, for all eternity.
He scrutinizes and knows our hiddenmost secrets;
He perceives a matter's outcome at its inception.
He recompenses man with kindness according to his deed;
He places evil on the wicked according to his wickedness.
By the End of Days He will send our Messiah,
to redeem those longing for His final salvation.
God will revive the dead in His abundant kindness —
Blessed forever is His praised Name.

MORNING BLESSINGS

Although many hold that the blessing עַל נְטִילַת יָדַיִם, *'. . .regarding washing the hands,'* should be recited immediately after the ritual washing of the hands upon arising, others customarily recite it at this point. Similarly, some recite אֲשֶׁר יָצַר, *'Who fashioned . . .,'* immediately after relieving themselves in the morning, while others recite it here.

בָּרוּךְ *Blessed are You, HASHEM, our God, King of the universe, Who has sanctified us with His commandments and has commanded us regarding washing the hands.*

בָּרוּךְ *Blessed are You, HASHEM, our God, King of the universe, Who fashioned man with wisdom and created within him many openings and many cavities. It is obvious and known before Your Throne of Glory that if but one of them were to be ruptured or but one of them were to be blocked it would be impossible to survive and to stand before You. Blessed are You, HASHEM, Who heals all flesh and acts wondrously.*

At this point, some recite אֱלֹהַי נְשָׁמָה, *'My God, the soul . . .'* (p. 76).

ברכות התורה

It is forbidden to study or recite Torah passages before reciting the following blessings. Since the commandment to study Torah is in effect all day long, these blessings need not be repeated if one studies at various times of the day. Although many *siddurim* begin a new paragraph at וְהַעֲרֶב נָא, according to the vast majority of commentators the first blessing does not end until לְעַמּוֹ יִשְׂרָאֵל.

בָּרוּךְ אַתָּה יהוה אֱלֹהֵינוּ מֶלֶךְ הָעוֹלָם, אֲשֶׁר קִדְּשָׁנוּ בְּמִצְוֹתָיו, וְצִוָּנוּ לַעֲסוֹק בְּדִבְרֵי תוֹרָה. וְהַעֲרֶב נָא יהוה אֱלֹהֵינוּ אֶת דִּבְרֵי תוֹרָתְךָ בְּפִינוּ וּבְפִי עַמְּךָ בֵּית יִשְׂרָאֵל. וְנִהְיֶה אֲנַחְנוּ וְצֶאֱצָאֵינוּ וְצֶאֱצָאֵי עַמְּךָ בֵּית יִשְׂרָאֵל, כֻּלָּנוּ יוֹדְעֵי שְׁמֶךָ וְלוֹמְדֵי תוֹרָתֶךָ לִשְׁמָהּ. בָּרוּךְ אַתָּה יהוה, הַמְלַמֵּד תּוֹרָה לְעַמּוֹ יִשְׂרָאֵל.

בָּרוּךְ אַתָּה יהוה אֱלֹהֵינוּ מֶלֶךְ הָעוֹלָם, אֲשֶׁר בָּחַר בָּנוּ מִכָּל הָעַמִּים וְנָתַן לָנוּ אֶת תּוֹרָתוֹ. בָּרוּךְ אַתָּה יהוה, נוֹתֵן הַתּוֹרָה.

במדבר ו:כד־כו

יְבָרֶכְךָ יהוה וְיִשְׁמְרֶךָ. יָאֵר יהוה פָּנָיו אֵלֶיךָ וִיחֻנֶּךָּ. יִשָּׂא יהוה פָּנָיו אֵלֶיךָ, וְיָשֵׂם לְךָ שָׁלוֹם.

משנה, פאה א:א

אֵלּוּ דְבָרִים שֶׁאֵין לָהֶם שִׁעוּר: הַפֵּאָה וְהַבִּכּוּרִים וְהָרַאְיוֹן וּגְמִילוּת חֲסָדִים וְתַלְמוּד תּוֹרָה.

שבת קכז.

אֵלּוּ דְבָרִים שֶׁאָדָם אוֹכֵל פֵּרוֹתֵיהֶם בָּעוֹלָם הַזֶּה וְהַקֶּרֶן קַיֶּמֶת לוֹ לָעוֹלָם הַבָּא. וְאֵלּוּ הֵן: כִּבּוּד אָב וָאֵם, וּגְמִילוּת חֲסָדִים, וְהַשְׁכָּמַת בֵּית הַמִּדְרָשׁ שַׁחֲרִית וְעַרְבִית, וְהַכְנָסַת אוֹרְחִים, וּבִקּוּר חוֹלִים, וְהַכְנָסַת כַּלָּה, וּלְוָיַת הַמֵּת, וְעִיּוּן תְּפִלָּה, וַהֲבָאַת שָׁלוֹם בֵּין אָדָם לַחֲבֵרוֹ – וְתַלְמוּד תּוֹרָה כְּנֶגֶד כֻּלָּם.

אֱלֹהַי, נְשָׁמָה שֶׁנָּתַתָּ בִּי טְהוֹרָה הִיא. אַתָּה בְרָאתָהּ אַתָּה יְצַרְתָּהּ, אַתָּה נְפַחְתָּהּ בִּי, וְאַתָּה מְשַׁמְּרָהּ בְּקִרְבִּי, וְאַתָּה עָתִיד לִטְּלָהּ מִמֶּנִּי, וּלְהַחֲזִירָהּ בִּי לֶעָתִיד לָבֹא. כָּל זְמַן שֶׁהַנְּשָׁמָה בְקִרְבִּי, מוֹדֶה אֲנִי לְפָנֶיךָ, יהוה אֱלֹהַי וֵאלֹהֵי אֲבוֹתַי, רִבּוֹן כָּל הַמַּעֲשִׂים, אֲדוֹן כָּל הַנְּשָׁמוֹת. בָּרוּךְ אַתָּה יהוה, הַמַּחֲזִיר נְשָׁמוֹת לִפְגָרִים מֵתִים.

BLESSINGS OF THE TORAH

It is forbidden to study or recite Torah passages before reciting the following blessings. Since the commandment to study Torah is in effect all day long, these blessings need not be repeated if one studies at various times of the day. Although many *siddurim* begin a new paragraph at וְהַעֲרֶב נָא, *'Please, HASHEM,'* according to the vast majority of commentators the first blessing does not end until לְעַמּוֹ יִשְׂרָאֵל, *'. . . His people Israel.'*

בָּרוּךְ *Blessed are You, HASHEM, our God, King of the universe, Who has sanctified us with His commandments and has commanded us to engross ourselves in the words of Torah. Please, HASHEM, our God, sweeten the words of Your Torah in our mouth and in the mouth of Your people, the family of Israel. May we and our offspring and the offspring of Your people, the House of Israel — all of us — know Your Name and study Your Torah for its own sake. Blessed are You, HASHEM, Who teaches Torah to His people Israel.*

בָּרוּךְ *Blessed are You, HASHEM, our God, King of the universe, Who selected us from all the peoples and gave us His Torah. Blessed are You, HASHEM, Giver of the Torah.*

Numbers 6:24-26

יְבָרֶכְךָ *May HASHEM bless you and safeguard you. May HASHEM illuminate His countenance for you and be gracious to you. May HASHEM turn His countenance to you and establish peace for you.*

Mishnah, *Peah* 1:1

אֵלּוּ דְבָרִים *These are the precepts that have no prescribed measure: the corner of a field [which must be left for the poor], the first-fruit offering, the pilgrimage, acts of kindness, and Torah study.*

Talmud, *Shabbos* 127a

אֵלּוּ דְבָרִים *These are the precepts whose fruits a person enjoys in This World but whose principal remains intact for him in the World to Come. They are: the honor due to father and mother, acts of kindness, early attendance at the house of study morning and evening, hospitality to guests, visiting the sick, providing for a bride, escorting the dead, absorption in prayer, bringing peace between man and his fellow — and the study of Torah is equivalent to them all.*

אֱלֹהַי *My God, the soul You placed within me is pure. You created it, You fashioned it, You breathed it into me, You safeguard it within me, and eventually You will take it from me, and restore it to me in Time to Come. As long as the soul is within me, I gratefully thank You, HASHEM, my God and the God of my forefathers, Master of all works, Lord of all souls. Blessed are You, HASHEM, Who restores souls to dead bodies.*

The *chazzan* recites the following blessings aloud, and the congregation responds אָמֵן to each blessing. Nevertheless, each person must recite these blessings for himself. Some people recite the blessings aloud for one another so that each one can have the merit of responding אָמֵן many times.

בָּרוּךְ אַתָּה יהוה אֱלֹהֵינוּ מֶלֶךְ הָעוֹלָם, אֲשֶׁר נָתַן לַשֶּׂכְוִי בִינָה[1] לְהַבְחִין בֵּין יוֹם וּבֵין לָיְלָה.

בָּרוּךְ אַתָּה יהוה אֱלֹהֵינוּ מֶלֶךְ הָעוֹלָם, שֶׁלֹּא עָשַׂנִי גּוֹי.

בָּרוּךְ אַתָּה יהוה אֱלֹהֵינוּ מֶלֶךְ הָעוֹלָם, שֶׁלֹּא עָשַׂנִי עָבֶד.

Men say:

בָּרוּךְ אַתָּה יהוה אֱלֹהֵינוּ מֶלֶךְ הָעוֹלָם, שֶׁלֹּא עָשַׂנִי אִשָּׁה.

Women say:

בָּרוּךְ אַתָּה יהוה אֱלֹהֵינוּ מֶלֶךְ הָעוֹלָם, שֶׁעָשַׂנִי כִּרְצוֹנוֹ.

בָּרוּךְ אַתָּה יהוה אֱלֹהֵינוּ מֶלֶךְ הָעוֹלָם, פּוֹקֵחַ עִוְרִים.[2]

בָּרוּךְ אַתָּה יהוה אֱלֹהֵינוּ מֶלֶךְ הָעוֹלָם, מַלְבִּישׁ עֲרֻמִּים.

בָּרוּךְ אַתָּה יהוה אֱלֹהֵינוּ מֶלֶךְ הָעוֹלָם, מַתִּיר אֲסוּרִים.[3]

בָּרוּךְ אַתָּה יהוה אֱלֹהֵינוּ מֶלֶךְ הָעוֹלָם, זוֹקֵף כְּפוּפִים.[2]

בָּרוּךְ אַתָּה יהוה אֱלֹהֵינוּ מֶלֶךְ הָעוֹלָם, רוֹקַע הָאָרֶץ עַל הַמָּיִם.[4]

Some postpone the recital of this blessing until they don leather shoes after the fast has ended.

בָּרוּךְ אַתָּה יהוה אֱלֹהֵינוּ מֶלֶךְ הָעוֹלָם, שֶׁעָשָׂה לִי כָּל צָרְכִּי.

בָּרוּךְ אַתָּה יהוה אֱלֹהֵינוּ מֶלֶךְ הָעוֹלָם, הַמֵּכִין מִצְעֲדֵי גָבֶר.[5]

בָּרוּךְ אַתָּה יהוה אֱלֹהֵינוּ מֶלֶךְ הָעוֹלָם, אוֹזֵר יִשְׂרָאֵל בִּגְבוּרָה.

Some postpone the recital of this blessing until they don *tefillin* at *Minchah*.

בָּרוּךְ אַתָּה יהוה אֱלֹהֵינוּ מֶלֶךְ הָעוֹלָם, עוֹטֵר יִשְׂרָאֵל בְּתִפְאָרָה.

בָּרוּךְ אַתָּה יהוה אֱלֹהֵינוּ מֶלֶךְ הָעוֹלָם, הַנּוֹתֵן לַיָּעֵף כֹּחַ.[6]

Although many *siddurim* begin a new paragraph at וִיהִי רָצוֹן, the following is one long blessing that ends at לְעַמּוֹ יִשְׂרָאֵל.

בָּרוּךְ אַתָּה יהוה אֱלֹהֵינוּ מֶלֶךְ הָעוֹלָם, הַמַּעֲבִיר שֵׁנָה מֵעֵינָי וּתְנוּמָה מֵעַפְעַפָּי. וִיהִי רָצוֹן מִלְּפָנֶיךָ, יהוה אֱלֹהֵינוּ וֵאלֹהֵי אֲבוֹתֵינוּ, שֶׁתַּרְגִּילֵנוּ בְּתוֹרָתֶךָ וְדַבְּקֵנוּ בְּמִצְוֹתֶיךָ, וְאַל תְּבִיאֵנוּ לֹא לִידֵי חֵטְא, וְלֹא לִידֵי עֲבֵרָה וְעָוֹן, וְלֹא לִידֵי נִסָּיוֹן, וְלֹא לִידֵי בִזָּיוֹן, וְאַל תַּשְׁלֶט בָּנוּ יֵצֶר הָרָע. וְהַרְחִיקֵנוּ מֵאָדָם רָע וּמֵחָבֵר רָע. וְדַבְּקֵנוּ בְּיֵצֶר הַטּוֹב וּבְמַעֲשִׂים טוֹבִים, וְכוֹף אֶת יִצְרֵנוּ לְהִשְׁתַּעְבֶּד לָךְ. וּתְנֵנוּ הַיּוֹם וּבְכָל יוֹם לְחֵן וּלְחֶסֶד וּלְרַחֲמִים בְּעֵינֶיךָ, וּבְעֵינֵי כָל רוֹאֵינוּ, וְתִגְמְלֵנוּ חֲסָדִים טוֹבִים. בָּרוּךְ אַתָּה יהוה, גּוֹמֵל חֲסָדִים טוֹבִים לְעַמּוֹ יִשְׂרָאֵל.

---

(1) Cf. *Job* 38:36. (2) *Psalms* 146:8. (3) v. 7. (4) Cf. 136:6. (5) Cf. 37:23. (6) *Isaiah* 40:29.

The *chazzan* recites the following blessings aloud, and the congregation responds *'Amen'* to each blessing. Nevertheless, each person must recite these blessings for himself. Some people recite the blessings aloud for one another so that each one can have the merit of responding *Amen* many times.

בָּרוּךְ *Blessed are You, HASHEM, our God, King of the universe, Who gave the heart understanding[1] to distinguish between day and night.*

Blessed are You, HASHEM, our God, King of the universe, for not having made me a gentile.

Blessed are You, HASHEM, our God, King of the universe, for not having made me a slave.

Men say:	Women say:
Blessed are You, HASHEM, our God, King of the universe, for not having made me a woman.	*Blessed are You, HASHEM, our God, King of the universe, for having made me according to His will.*

Blessed are You, HASHEM, our God, King of the universe, Who gives sight to the blind.[2]

Blessed are You, HASHEM, our God, King of the universe, Who clothes the naked.

Blessed are You, HASHEM, our God, King of the universe, Who releases the bound.[3]

Blessed are You, HASHEM, our God, King of the universe, Who straightens the bent.[2]

Blessed are You, HASHEM, our God, King of the universe, Who spreads out the earth upon the waters.[4]

Some postpone the recital of this blessing until they don leather shoes after the fast has ended.

Blessed are You, HASHEM, our God, King of the universe, Who has provided me my every need.

Blessed are You, HASHEM, our God, King of the universe, Who firms man's footsteps.[5]

Blessed are You, HASHEM, our God, King of the universe, Who girds Israel with strength.

Some postpone the recital of this blessing until they don *tefillin* at *Minchah*.

Blessed are You, HASHEM, our God, King of the universe, Who crowns Israel with splendor.

Blessed are You, HASHEM, our God, King of the universe, Who gives strength to the weary.[6]

בָּרוּךְ *Blessed are You, HASHEM, our God, King of the universe, Who removes sleep from my eyes and slumber from my eyelids. And may it be Your will, HASHEM, our God, and the God of our forefathers, that You accustom us to [study] Your Torah and attach us to Your commandments. Do not bring us into the power of error, nor into the power of transgression and sin, nor into the power of challenge, nor into the power of scorn. Let not the Evil Inclination dominate us. Distance us from an evil person and an evil companion. Attach us to the Good Inclination and to good deeds and compel our Evil Inclination to be subservient to You. Grant us today and every day grace, kindness, and mercy in Your eyes and in the eyes of all who see us, and bestow beneficent kindnesses upon us. Blessed are You, HASHEM, Who bestows beneficent kindnesses upon His people Israel.*

יְהִי רָצוֹן מִלְּפָנֶיךָ, יהוה אֱלֹהַי וֵאלֹהֵי אֲבוֹתַי, שֶׁתַּצִּילֵנִי הַיּוֹם וּבְכָל יוֹם מֵעַזֵּי פָנִים וּמֵעַזּוּת פָּנִים, מֵאָדָם רָע, וּמֵחָבֵר רָע, וּמִשָּׁכֵן רָע, וּמִפֶּגַע רָע, וּמִשָּׂטָן הַמַּשְׁחִית, מִדִּין קָשֶׁה וּמִבַּעַל דִּין קָשֶׁה, בֵּין שֶׁהוּא בֶן בְּרִית, וּבֵין שֶׁאֵינוֹ בֶן בְּרִית.

עקדה

אֱלֹהֵינוּ וֵאלֹהֵי אֲבוֹתֵינוּ, זָכְרֵנוּ בְּזִכָּרוֹן טוֹב לְפָנֶיךָ, וּפָקְדֵנוּ בִּפְקֻדַּת יְשׁוּעָה וְרַחֲמִים מִשְּׁמֵי שְׁמֵי קֶדֶם. וּזְכָר לָנוּ יהוה אֱלֹהֵינוּ אַהֲבַת הַקַּדְמוֹנִים אַבְרָהָם יִצְחָק וְיִשְׂרָאֵל עֲבָדֶיךָ, אֶת הַבְּרִית וְאֶת הַחֶסֶד וְאֶת הַשְּׁבוּעָה שֶׁנִּשְׁבַּעְתָּ לְאַבְרָהָם אָבִינוּ בְּהַר הַמּוֹרִיָּה, וְאֶת הָעֲקֵדָה שֶׁעָקַד אֶת יִצְחָק בְּנוֹ עַל גַּבֵּי הַמִּזְבֵּחַ, כַּכָּתוּב בְּתוֹרָתֶךָ:

בראשית כב:א-יט

וַיְהִי אַחַר הַדְּבָרִים הָאֵלֶּה, וְהָאֱלֹהִים נִסָּה אֶת אַבְרָהָם, וַיֹּאמֶר אֵלָיו, אַבְרָהָם, וַיֹּאמֶר, הִנֵּנִי. וַיֹּאמֶר, קַח נָא אֶת בִּנְךָ, אֶת יְחִידְךָ, אֲשֶׁר אָהַבְתָּ, אֶת יִצְחָק, וְלֶךְ לְךָ אֶל אֶרֶץ הַמֹּרִיָּה, וְהַעֲלֵהוּ שָׁם לְעֹלָה עַל אַחַד הֶהָרִים אֲשֶׁר אֹמַר אֵלֶיךָ. וַיַּשְׁכֵּם אַבְרָהָם בַּבֹּקֶר, וַיַּחֲבֹשׁ אֶת חֲמֹרוֹ, וַיִּקַּח אֶת שְׁנֵי נְעָרָיו אִתּוֹ, וְאֵת יִצְחָק בְּנוֹ, וַיְבַקַּע עֲצֵי עֹלָה, וַיָּקָם וַיֵּלֶךְ אֶל הַמָּקוֹם אֲשֶׁר אָמַר לוֹ הָאֱלֹהִים. בַּיּוֹם הַשְּׁלִישִׁי, וַיִּשָּׂא אַבְרָהָם אֶת עֵינָיו, וַיַּרְא אֶת הַמָּקוֹם מֵרָחֹק. וַיֹּאמֶר אַבְרָהָם אֶל נְעָרָיו, שְׁבוּ לָכֶם פֹּה עִם הַחֲמוֹר, וַאֲנִי וְהַנַּעַר נֵלְכָה עַד כֹּה, וְנִשְׁתַּחֲוֶה וְנָשׁוּבָה אֲלֵיכֶם. וַיִּקַּח אַבְרָהָם אֶת עֲצֵי הָעֹלָה, וַיָּשֶׂם עַל יִצְחָק בְּנוֹ, וַיִּקַּח בְּיָדוֹ אֶת הָאֵשׁ וְאֶת הַמַּאֲכֶלֶת, וַיֵּלְכוּ שְׁנֵיהֶם יַחְדָּו. וַיֹּאמֶר יִצְחָק אֶל אַבְרָהָם אָבִיו, וַיֹּאמֶר, אָבִי, וַיֹּאמֶר, הִנֶּנִּי בְנִי, וַיֹּאמֶר, הִנֵּה הָאֵשׁ וְהָעֵצִים, וְאַיֵּה הַשֶּׂה לְעֹלָה. וַיֹּאמֶר אַבְרָהָם, אֱלֹהִים יִרְאֶה לּוֹ הַשֶּׂה לְעֹלָה, בְּנִי, וַיֵּלְכוּ שְׁנֵיהֶם יַחְדָּו. וַיָּבֹאוּ אֶל הַמָּקוֹם אֲשֶׁר אָמַר לוֹ הָאֱלֹהִים, וַיִּבֶן שָׁם אַבְרָהָם אֶת הַמִּזְבֵּחַ, וַיַּעֲרֹךְ אֶת הָעֵצִים, וַיַּעֲקֹד אֶת יִצְחָק בְּנוֹ, וַיָּשֶׂם אֹתוֹ עַל הַמִּזְבֵּחַ מִמַּעַל לָעֵצִים. וַיִּשְׁלַח אַבְרָהָם אֶת יָדוֹ, וַיִּקַּח אֶת הַמַּאֲכֶלֶת לִשְׁחֹט אֶת בְּנוֹ. וַיִּקְרָא אֵלָיו מַלְאַךְ יהוה מִן הַשָּׁמַיִם, וַיֹּאמֶר, אַבְרָהָם, אַבְרָהָם, וַיֹּאמֶר, הִנֵּנִי. וַיֹּאמֶר, אַל תִּשְׁלַח יָדְךָ אֶל הַנַּעַר, וְאַל תַּעַשׂ לוֹ מְאוּמָה, כִּי עַתָּה יָדַעְתִּי כִּי

יְהִי רָצוֹן *May it be Your will,* H*ASHEM, my God, and the God of my forefathers, that You rescue me today and every day from brazen men and from brazenness, from an evil man, an evil companion, an evil neighbor, an evil mishap, the destructive spiritual impediment, a harsh trial and a harsh opponent, whether he is a member of the covenant or whether he is not a member of the covenant.*

THE AKEIDAH

אֱלֹהֵינוּ *Our God and the God of our forefathers, remember us with a favorable memory before You, and recall us with a recollection of salvation and mercy from the primeval loftiest heavens. Remember on our behalf — O* H*ASHEM, our God — the love of the Patriarchs, Abraham, Isaac and Israel, Your servants; the covenant, the kindness, and the oath that You swore to our father Abraham at Mount Moriah, and the Akeidah, when he bound his son Isaac atop the altar, as it is written in Your Torah:*

Genesis 22:1-19

וַיְהִי *And it happened after these things that God tested Abraham and said to him, 'Abraham.'*

And he replied, 'Here I am.'

And He said, 'Please take your son, your only one, whom you love — Isaac — and get yourself to the Land of Moriah; bring him up there as an offering, upon one of the mountains which I shall indicate to you.'

So Abraham awoke early in the morning and he saddled his donkey; he took his two young men with him, and Isaac, his son. He split the wood for the offering, and rose and went toward the place which God had indicated to him.

On the third day, Abraham looked up, and perceived the place from afar. And Abraham said to his young men, 'Stay here by yourselves with the donkey, while I and the lad will go yonder; we will prostrate ourselves and we will return to you.'

And Abraham took the wood for the offering, and placed it on Isaac, his son. He took in his hand the fire and the knife, and the two of them went together. Then Isaac spoke to Abraham his father and said, 'Father — '

And he said, 'Here I am, my son.'

And he said, 'Here are the fire and the wood, but where is the lamb for the offering?'

And Abraham said, 'God will seek out for Himself the lamb for the offering, my son.' And the two of them went together.

They arrived at the place which God indicated to him. Abraham built the altar there, and arranged the wood; he bound Isaac, his son, and he placed him on the altar atop the wood. Abraham stretched out his hand, and took the knife to slaughter his son.

And an angel of H*ASHEM called to him from heaven, and said, 'Abraham! Abraham!'*

And he said, 'Here I am.'

And he [the angel quoting H*ASHEM] said, 'Do not stretch out your hand against the lad nor do anything to him, for now I know that you are a*

יְרֵא אֱלֹהִים אַתָּה, וְלֹא חָשַׂכְתָּ אֶת בִּנְךָ אֶת יְחִידְךָ מִמֶּנִּי. וַיִּשָּׂא אַבְרָהָם אֶת עֵינָיו וַיַּרְא, וְהִנֵּה אַיִל, אַחַר, נֶאֱחַז בַּסְּבַךְ בְּקַרְנָיו, וַיֵּלֶךְ אַבְרָהָם וַיִּקַּח אֶת הָאַיִל, וַיַּעֲלֵהוּ לְעֹלָה תַּחַת בְּנוֹ. וַיִּקְרָא אַבְרָהָם שֵׁם הַמָּקוֹם הַהוּא יהוה יִרְאֶה, אֲשֶׁר יֵאָמֵר הַיּוֹם, בְּהַר יהוה יֵרָאֶה. וַיִּקְרָא מַלְאַךְ יהוה אֶל אַבְרָהָם, שֵׁנִית מִן הַשָּׁמָיִם. וַיֹּאמֶר, בִּי נִשְׁבַּעְתִּי נְאֻם יהוה, כִּי יַעַן אֲשֶׁר עָשִׂיתָ אֶת הַדָּבָר הַזֶּה, וְלֹא חָשַׂכְתָּ אֶת בִּנְךָ אֶת יְחִידֶךָ. כִּי בָרֵךְ אֲבָרֶכְךָ, וְהַרְבָּה אַרְבֶּה אֶת זַרְעֲךָ כְּכוֹכְבֵי הַשָּׁמַיִם, וְכַחוֹל אֲשֶׁר עַל שְׂפַת הַיָּם, וְיִרַשׁ זַרְעֲךָ אֵת שַׁעַר אֹיְבָיו. וְהִתְבָּרְכוּ בְזַרְעֲךָ כֹּל גּוֹיֵי הָאָרֶץ, עֵקֶב אֲשֶׁר שָׁמַעְתָּ בְּקֹלִי. וַיָּשָׁב אַבְרָהָם אֶל נְעָרָיו, וַיָּקֻמוּ וַיֵּלְכוּ יַחְדָּו אֶל בְּאֵר שָׁבַע, וַיֵּשֶׁב אַבְרָהָם בִּבְאֵר שָׁבַע.

רִבּוֹנוֹ שֶׁל עוֹלָם, יְהִי רָצוֹן מִלְּפָנֶיךָ, יהוה אֱלֹהֵינוּ וֵאלֹהֵי אֲבוֹתֵינוּ, שֶׁתִּזְכָּר לָנוּ בְּרִית אֲבוֹתֵינוּ. כְּמוֹ שֶׁכָּבַשׁ אַבְרָהָם אָבִינוּ אֶת רַחֲמָיו מִבֶּן יְחִידוֹ, וְרָצָה לִשְׁחוֹט אוֹתוֹ כְּדֵי לַעֲשׂוֹת רְצוֹנֶךָ, כֵּן יִכְבְּשׁוּ רַחֲמֶיךָ אֶת כַּעַסְךָ מֵעָלֵינוּ, וְיָגֹלּוּ רַחֲמֶיךָ עַל מִדּוֹתֶיךָ, וְתִכָּנֵס אִתָּנוּ לִפְנִים מִשּׁוּרַת דִּינֶךָ, וְתִתְנַהֵג עִמָּנוּ, יהוה אֱלֹהֵינוּ, בְּמִדַּת הַחֶסֶד וּבְמִדַּת הָרַחֲמִים. וּבְטוּבְךָ הַגָּדוֹל, יָשׁוּב חֲרוֹן אַפְּךָ מֵעַמְּךָ וּמֵעִירְךָ וּמֵאַרְצְךָ וּמִנַּחֲלָתֶךָ. וְקַיֶּם לָנוּ, יהוה אֱלֹהֵינוּ, אֶת הַדָּבָר שֶׁהִבְטַחְתָּנוּ עַל יְדֵי מֹשֶׁה עַבְדֶּךָ, כָּאָמוּר: וְזָכַרְתִּי אֶת בְּרִיתִי יַעֲקוֹב, וְאַף אֶת בְּרִיתִי יִצְחָק, וְאַף אֶת בְּרִיתִי אַבְרָהָם אֶזְכֹּר, וְהָאָרֶץ אֶזְכֹּר.[1]

לְעוֹלָם יְהֵא אָדָם יְרֵא שָׁמַיִם בְּסֵתֶר וּבַגָּלוּי, וּמוֹדֶה עַל הָאֱמֶת, וְדוֹבֵר אֱמֶת בִּלְבָבוֹ, וְיַשְׁכֵּם וְיֹאמַר:

רִבּוֹן כָּל הָעוֹלָמִים, לֹא עַל צִדְקוֹתֵינוּ אֲנַחְנוּ מַפִּילִים תַּחֲנוּנֵינוּ לְפָנֶיךָ, כִּי עַל רַחֲמֶיךָ הָרַבִּים. מָה אֲנַחְנוּ, מֶה חַיֵּינוּ, מֶה חַסְדֵּנוּ, מַה צִּדְקוֹתֵינוּ, מַה יְּשׁוּעָתֵנוּ, מַה כֹּחֵנוּ, מַה גְּבוּרָתֵנוּ. מַה נֹּאמַר לְפָנֶיךָ, יהוה אֱלֹהֵינוּ וֵאלֹהֵי אֲבוֹתֵינוּ, הֲלֹא כָּל הַגִּבּוֹרִים כְּאַיִן לְפָנֶיךָ, וְאַנְשֵׁי הַשֵּׁם כְּלֹא הָיוּ, וַחֲכָמִים כִּבְלִי מַדָּע, וּנְבוֹנִים כִּבְלִי הַשְׂכֵּל. כִּי רוֹב מַעֲשֵׂיהֶם תֹּהוּ, וִימֵי חַיֵּיהֶם הֶבֶל לְפָנֶיךָ, וּמוֹתַר הָאָדָם מִן הַבְּהֵמָה אָיִן, כִּי הַכֹּל הָבֶל.[2]

אֲבָל אֲנַחְנוּ עַמְּךָ, בְּנֵי בְרִיתֶךָ, בְּנֵי אַבְרָהָם אֹהַבְךָ שֶׁנִּשְׁבַּעְתָּ לּוֹ בְּהַר הַמּוֹרִיָּה, זֶרַע יִצְחָק יְחִידוֹ שֶׁנֶּעֱקַד עַל גַּב הַמִּזְבֵּחַ,

God-fearing man, since you have not withheld your son, your only one, from Me.'

And Abraham looked up and saw — behold a ram! — after it had been caught in the thicket by its horns. So Abraham went and took the ram and brought it as an offering instead of his son. And Abraham named that site 'HASHEM Yireh,' as it is said this day: On the mountain HASHEM is seen.

The angel of HASHEM called to Abraham, a second time from heaven, and said, " 'By Myself I swear,' declared HASHEM, 'that since you have done this thing, and have not withheld your son, your only one, I shall surely bless you and greatly increase your offspring like the stars of the heavens and like the sand on the seashore; and your offspring shall inherit the gate of its enemy; and all the nations of the earth shall bless themselves by your offspring, because you have listened to My voice.' "

Abraham returned to his young men, and they rose and went together to Beer Sheba, and Abraham stayed at Beer Sheba.

רִבּוֹנוֹ שֶׁל עוֹלָם *Master of the universe! May it be Your will, HASHEM, our God, and the God of our forefathers, that You remember for our sake the covenant of our forefathers. Just as Abraham our forefather suppressed his mercy for his only son and wished to slaughter him in order to do Your will, so may Your mercy suppress Your anger from upon us and may Your mercy overwhelm Your attributes. May You overstep with us the line of Your law and deal with us — O HASHEM, our God — with the attribute of kindness and the attribute of mercy. In Your great goodness may You turn aside Your burning wrath from Your people, Your city, Your land, and Your heritage. Fulfill for us, HASHEM, our God, the word You pledged through Moses, Your servant, as it is said: 'I shall remember My covenant with Jacob; also My covenant with Isaac, and also My covenant with Abraham shall I remember; and the land shall I remember.'*[1]

לְעוֹלָם *Always let a person be God-fearing privately and publicly, acknowledge the truth, speak the truth within his heart, and arise early and proclaim:*

Master of all worlds! Not in the merit of our righteousness do we cast our supplications before You, but in the merit of Your abundant mercy. What are we? What is our life? What is our kindness? What is our righteousness? What is our salvation? What is our strength? What is our might? What can we say before You, HASHEM, our God, and the God of our forefathers — are not all the heroes like nothing before You, the famous as if they had never existed, the wise as if devoid of wisdom and the perceptive as if devoid of intelligence? For most of their deeds are desolate and the days of their lives are empty before You. The pre-eminence of man over beast is non-existent for all is vain.[2]

But we are Your people, members of Your covenant, children of Abraham, Your beloved, to whom You took an oath at Mount Moriah; the offspring of Isaac, his only son, who was bound atop the altar;

(1) *Leviticus* 26:42. (2) *Ecclesiastes* 3:19.

עֲדַת יַעֲקֹב בִּנְךָ בְּכוֹרֶךָ, שֶׁמֵּאַהֲבָתְךָ שֶׁאָהַבְתָּ אוֹתוֹ וּמִשִּׂמְחָתְךָ שֶׁשָּׂמַחְתָּ בּוֹ, קָרָאתָ אֶת שְׁמוֹ יִשְׂרָאֵל וִישֻׁרוּן.

לְפִיכָךְ אֲנַחְנוּ חַיָּבִים לְהוֹדוֹת לְךָ, וּלְשַׁבֵּחֲךָ, וּלְפָאֶרְךָ, וּלְבָרֵךְ וּלְקַדֵּשׁ וְלָתֵת שֶׁבַח וְהוֹדָיָה לִשְׁמֶךָ. אַשְׁרֵינוּ, מַה טּוֹב חֶלְקֵנוּ, וּמַה נָּעִים גּוֹרָלֵנוּ, וּמַה יָּפָה יְרֻשָּׁתֵנוּ. ❖ אַשְׁרֵינוּ, שֶׁאֲנַחְנוּ מַשְׁכִּימִים וּמַעֲרִיבִים, עֶרֶב וָבֹקֶר וְאוֹמְרִים פַּעֲמַיִם בְּכָל יוֹם:

שְׁמַע יִשְׂרָאֵל, יהוה אֱלֹהֵינוּ, יהוה אֶחָד.[1]

In an undertone – בָּרוּךְ שֵׁם כְּבוֹד מַלְכוּתוֹ לְעוֹלָם וָעֶד.

Some congregations complete the first chapter of the *Shema* (following paragraph) at this point, although most omit it. However if you fear that you will not recite the full *Shema* later in *Shacharis* before the prescribed time has elapsed, recite all three chapters of *Shema* (p. 118-120) here.

דברים ו:ה-ט

וְאָהַבְתָּ אֵת יהוה אֱלֹהֶיךָ, בְּכָל לְבָבְךָ, וּבְכָל נַפְשְׁךָ, וּבְכָל מְאֹדֶךָ. וְהָיוּ הַדְּבָרִים הָאֵלֶּה, אֲשֶׁר אָנֹכִי מְצַוְּךָ הַיּוֹם, עַל לְבָבֶךָ. וְשִׁנַּנְתָּם לְבָנֶיךָ, וְדִבַּרְתָּ בָּם, בְּשִׁבְתְּךָ בְּבֵיתֶךָ, וּבְלֶכְתְּךָ בַדֶּרֶךְ, וּבְשָׁכְבְּךָ וּבְקוּמֶךָ. וּקְשַׁרְתָּם לְאוֹת עַל יָדֶךָ, וְהָיוּ לְטֹטָפֹת בֵּין עֵינֶיךָ. וּכְתַבְתָּם עַל מְזֻזוֹת בֵּיתֶךָ וּבִשְׁעָרֶיךָ.

אַתָּה הוּא עַד שֶׁלֹּא נִבְרָא הָעוֹלָם, אַתָּה הוּא מִשֶּׁנִּבְרָא הָעוֹלָם, אַתָּה הוּא בָּעוֹלָם הַזֶּה, וְאַתָּה הוּא לָעוֹלָם הַבָּא. ❖ קַדֵּשׁ אֶת שִׁמְךָ עַל מַקְדִּישֵׁי שְׁמֶךָ, וְקַדֵּשׁ אֶת שִׁמְךָ בְּעוֹלָמֶךָ. וּבִישׁוּעָתְךָ תָּרִים וְתַגְבִּיהַּ קַרְנֵנוּ. בָּרוּךְ אַתָּה יהוה, מְקַדֵּשׁ אֶת שִׁמְךָ בָּרַבִּים. (Cong. – אָמֵן.)

אַתָּה הוּא יהוה אֱלֹהֵינוּ, בַּשָּׁמַיִם וּבָאָרֶץ וּבִשְׁמֵי הַשָּׁמַיִם הָעֶלְיוֹנִים. אֱמֶת, אַתָּה הוּא רִאשׁוֹן, וְאַתָּה הוּא אַחֲרוֹן, וּמִבַּלְעָדֶיךָ אֵין אֱלֹהִים.[2] קַבֵּץ קֹוֶיךָ מֵאַרְבַּע כַּנְפוֹת הָאָרֶץ. יַכִּירוּ וְיֵדְעוּ כָּל בָּאֵי עוֹלָם כִּי אַתָּה הוּא הָאֱלֹהִים לְבַדְּךָ לְכֹל מַמְלְכוֹת הָאָרֶץ. אַתָּה עָשִׂיתָ אֶת הַשָּׁמַיִם וְאֶת הָאָרֶץ,[3] אֶת הַיָּם, וְאֶת כָּל אֲשֶׁר בָּם. וּמִי בְּכָל מַעֲשֵׂה יָדֶיךָ בָּעֶלְיוֹנִים אוֹ בַתַּחְתּוֹנִים שֶׁיֹּאמַר לְךָ, מַה תַּעֲשֶׂה. אָבִינוּ שֶׁבַּשָּׁמַיִם, עֲשֵׂה עִמָּנוּ חֶסֶד בַּעֲבוּר שִׁמְךָ הַגָּדוֹל שֶׁנִּקְרָא עָלֵינוּ, וְקַיֶּם לָנוּ יהוה אֱלֹהֵינוּ מַה שֶּׁכָּתוּב: בָּעֵת הַהִיא אָבִיא אֶתְכֶם, וּבָעֵת קַבְּצִי אֶתְכֶם, כִּי אֶתֵּן אֶתְכֶם לְשֵׁם וְלִתְהִלָּה בְּכֹל עַמֵּי הָאָרֶץ, בְּשׁוּבִי אֶת שְׁבוּתֵיכֶם לְעֵינֵיכֶם, אָמַר יהוה.[4]

the community of Jacob, Your firstborn son, whom — because of the love with which You adored him and the joy with which You delighted in him — You named Israel and Jeshurun.

לְפִיכָךְ *Therefore, we are obliged to thank You, praise You, glorify You, bless, sanctify, and offer praise and thanks to Your Name. We are fortunate — how good is our portion, how pleasant our lot, and how beautiful our heritage!* Chazzan– *We are fortunate for we come early and stay late, evening and morning, and proclaim twice each day:*

Hear, O Israel: HASHEM is our God, HASHEM, the One and Only.[1]

In an undertone– *Blessed is the Name of His glorious kingdom for all eternity.*

Some congregations complete the first chapter of the *Shema* (following paragraph) at this point, although most omit it. However if you fear that you will not recite the full *Shema* later in *Shacharis* before the prescribed time has elapsed, recite all three chapters of *Shema* (p. 118-120) here.

Deuteronomy 6:5-9

וְאָהַבְתָּ *You shall love HASHEM, your God, with all your heart, with all your soul and with all your resources. Let these matters, which I command you today, be upon your heart. Teach them thoroughly to your children and speak of them while you sit in your home, while you walk on the way, when you retire and when you arise. Bind them as a sign upon your arm and let them be tefillin between your eyes. And write them on the doorposts of your house and upon your gates.*

אַתָּה *It was You before the world was created, it is You since the world was created, it is You in This World, and it is You in the World to Come.* Chazzan– *Sanctify Your Name through those who sanctify Your Name, and sanctify Your Name in Your universe. Through Your salvation may You exalt and raise our pride. Blessed are You, HASHEM, Who sanctifies Your Name among the multitudes.*

(Cong.– *Amen.*)

אַתָּה *It is You Who are HASHEM, our God, in heaven and on earth and in the loftiest heavens. True — You are the First and You are the Last, and other than You there is no God.*[2] *Gather in those who yearn for You, from the four corners of the earth. Let all who walk the earth recognize and know that You alone are the God over all the kingdoms of the earth. You have made the heavens, the earth,*[3] *the sea, and all that is in them. Who among all Your handiwork, those above and those below, can say to You, 'What are You doing?' Our Father in Heaven, do kindness with us for the sake of Your great Name that has been proclaimed upon us. Fulfill for us, HASHEM, our God, what is written: 'At that time I will bring you and at that time I will gather you in, for I will set you up for renown and praise among all the peoples of the earth, when I bring back your captivity, before your own eyes,' said HASHEM.*[4]

---

(1) *Deuteronomy* 6:4. (2) Cf. *Isaiah* 44:6. (3) *II Kings* 19:15. (4) *Zephaniah* 3:20.

SOME CONGREGATIONS OMIT CERTAIN PASSAGES OF THE PRAYERS PRECEDING אֵיזֶהוּ מְקוֹמָן (P. 92). CUSTOMS REGARDING WHETHER AND WHICH PASSAGES ARE OMITTED VARY GREATLY. THEREFORE WE HAVE NOT OMITTED ANY PASSAGES. EACH CONGREGATION SHOULD FOLLOW ITS ESTABLISHED CUSTOM.

קרבנות

הכיור

שמות ל:יז-כא

וַיְדַבֵּר יהוה אֶל מֹשֶׁה לֵּאמֹר. וְעָשִׂיתָ כִּיּוֹר נְחֹשֶׁת, וְכַנּוֹ נְחֹשֶׁת, לְרָחְצָה, וְנָתַתָּ אֹתוֹ בֵּין אֹהֶל מוֹעֵד וּבֵין הַמִּזְבֵּחַ, וְנָתַתָּ שָׁמָּה מָיִם. וְרָחֲצוּ אַהֲרֹן וּבָנָיו מִמֶּנּוּ, אֶת יְדֵיהֶם וְאֶת רַגְלֵיהֶם. בְּבֹאָם אֶל אֹהֶל מוֹעֵד יִרְחֲצוּ מַיִם וְלֹא יָמֻתוּ, אוֹ בְגִשְׁתָּם אֶל הַמִּזְבֵּחַ לְשָׁרֵת לְהַקְטִיר אִשֶּׁה לַיהוה. וְרָחֲצוּ יְדֵיהֶם וְרַגְלֵיהֶם וְלֹא יָמֻתוּ, וְהָיְתָה לָהֶם חָק עוֹלָם, לוֹ וּלְזַרְעוֹ לְדֹרֹתָם.

תרומת הדשן

ויקרא ו:א-ו

וַיְדַבֵּר יהוה אֶל מֹשֶׁה לֵּאמֹר. צַו אֶת אַהֲרֹן וְאֶת בָּנָיו לֵאמֹר, זֹאת תּוֹרַת הָעֹלָה, הִוא הָעֹלָה עַל מוֹקְדָה עַל הַמִּזְבֵּחַ כָּל הַלַּיְלָה עַד הַבֹּקֶר, וְאֵשׁ הַמִּזְבֵּחַ תּוּקַד בּוֹ. וְלָבַשׁ הַכֹּהֵן מִדּוֹ בַד, וּמִכְנְסֵי בַד יִלְבַּשׁ עַל בְּשָׂרוֹ, וְהֵרִים אֶת הַדֶּשֶׁן אֲשֶׁר תֹּאכַל הָאֵשׁ אֶת הָעֹלָה עַל הַמִּזְבֵּחַ, וְשָׂמוֹ אֵצֶל הַמִּזְבֵּחַ. וּפָשַׁט אֶת בְּגָדָיו, וְלָבַשׁ בְּגָדִים אֲחֵרִים, וְהוֹצִיא אֶת הַדֶּשֶׁן אֶל מִחוּץ לַמַּחֲנֶה, אֶל מָקוֹם טָהוֹר. וְהָאֵשׁ עַל הַמִּזְבֵּחַ תּוּקַד בּוֹ, לֹא תִכְבֶּה, וּבִעֵר עָלֶיהָ הַכֹּהֵן עֵצִים בַּבֹּקֶר בַּבֹּקֶר, וְעָרַךְ עָלֶיהָ הָעֹלָה, וְהִקְטִיר עָלֶיהָ חֶלְבֵי הַשְּׁלָמִים. אֵשׁ תָּמִיד תּוּקַד עַל הַמִּזְבֵּחַ, לֹא תִכְבֶּה.

קרבן התמיד

Some authorities hold that the following (until קְטֹרֶת) should be recited standing.

יְהִי רָצוֹן מִלְּפָנֶיךָ, יהוה אֱלֹהֵינוּ וֵאלֹהֵי אֲבוֹתֵינוּ, שֶׁתְּרַחֵם עָלֵינוּ וְתִמְחַל לָנוּ עַל כָּל חַטֹּאתֵינוּ, וּתְכַפֵּר לָנוּ אֶת כָּל עֲוֹנוֹתֵינוּ, וְתִסְלַח לְכָל פְּשָׁעֵינוּ, וְתִבְנֶה בֵּית הַמִּקְדָּשׁ בִּמְהֵרָה בְיָמֵינוּ, וְנַקְרִיב לְפָנֶיךָ קָרְבַּן הַתָּמִיד שֶׁיְּכַפֵּר בַּעֲדֵנוּ, כְּמוֹ שֶׁכָּתַבְתָּ עָלֵינוּ בְּתוֹרָתֶךָ עַל יְדֵי מֹשֶׁה עַבְדֶּךָ, מִפִּי כְבוֹדֶךָ, כָּאָמוּר:

במדבר כח:א-ח

וַיְדַבֵּר יהוה אֶל מֹשֶׁה לֵּאמֹר. צַו אֶת בְּנֵי יִשְׂרָאֵל וְאָמַרְתָּ אֲלֵהֶם, אֶת קָרְבָּנִי לַחְמִי לְאִשַּׁי, רֵיחַ נִיחֹחִי, תִּשְׁמְרוּ לְהַקְרִיב לִי בְּמוֹעֲדוֹ. וְאָמַרְתָּ לָהֶם, זֶה הָאִשֶּׁה אֲשֶׁר תַּקְרִיבוּ

SOME CONGREGATIONS OMIT CERTAIN PASSAGES OF THE PRAYERS PRECEDING אֵיזֶהוּ מְקוֹמָן, *WHAT IS THE LOCATION* (P. 92). CUSTOMS REGARDING WHETHER AND WHICH PASSAGES ARE OMITTED VARY GREATLY. THEREFORE WE HAVE NOT OMITTED ANY PASSAGES. EACH CONGREGATION SHOULD FOLLOW ITS ESTABLISHED CUSTOM.

OFFERINGS

THE LAVER

Exodus 30:17-21

וַיְדַבֵּר *HASHEM spoke to Moses, saying: Make a laver of copper, and its base of copper, for washing; and place it between the Tent of Appointment and the Altar and put water there. Aaron and his sons are to wash their hands and feet from it. When they arrive at the Tent of Appointment they are to wash with water so that they not die, or when they approach the Altar to serve, to burn a fire-offering to HASHEM. They are to wash their hands and feet so that they not die; and this shall be an eternal decree for them — for him and for his offspring — throughout their generations.*

THE TAKING OF ASHES

Leviticus 6:1-6

וַיְדַבֵּר *HASHEM spoke to Moses saying: Instruct Aaron and his sons saying: This is the teaching of the elevation-offering, it is the elevation-offering that stays on the pyre on the Altar all night until morning, and the fire of the Altar should be kept burning on it. The Kohen should don his linen garment, and he is to don linen breeches upon his flesh; he is to pick up the ashes of what the fire consumed of the elevation-offering upon the Altar and place it next to the Altar. Then he should remove his garments and don other garments; then he should remove the ashes to the outside of the camp to a pure place. The fire on the Altar shall be kept burning on it, it may not be extinguished, and the Kohen shall burn wood upon it every morning. He is to prepare the elevation-offering upon it and burn upon it the fats of the peace-offerings. A permanent fire should remain burning on the Altar; it may not be extinguished.*

THE TAMID OFFERING

Some authorities hold that the following (until קְטֹרֶת /Incense) should be recited standing.

יְהִי רָצוֹן *May it be Your will, HASHEM, our God, and the God of our forefathers, that You have mercy on us and pardon us for all our errors, atone for us all our iniquities, forgive all our willful sins; and that You rebuild the Holy Temple speedily, in our days, so that we may offer to You the continual offering that it may atone for us, as You have prescribed for us in Your Torah through Moses, Your servant, from Your glorious mouth, as it is said:*

Numbers 28:1-8

וַיְדַבֵּר *HASHEM spoke to Moses, saying: Command the Children of Israel and tell them: My offering, My food for My fires, My satisfying aroma, you are to be scrupulous to offer Me in its appointed time. And you are to tell them: 'This is the fire-offering that you are to bring*

לַיהוה, כְּבָשִׂים בְּנֵי שָׁנָה תְמִימִם, שְׁנַיִם לַיּוֹם, עֹלָה תָמִיד. אֶת הַכֶּבֶשׂ אֶחָד תַּעֲשֶׂה בַבֹּקֶר, וְאֵת הַכֶּבֶשׂ הַשֵּׁנִי תַּעֲשֶׂה בֵּין הָעַרְבָּיִם. וַעֲשִׂירִית הָאֵיפָה סֹלֶת לְמִנְחָה, בְּלוּלָה בְּשֶׁמֶן כָּתִית רְבִיעִת הַהִין. עֹלַת תָּמִיד, הָעֲשֻׂיָה בְּהַר סִינַי, לְרֵיחַ נִיחֹחַ, אִשֶּׁה לַיהוה. וְנִסְכּוֹ רְבִיעִת הַהִין לַכֶּבֶשׂ הָאֶחָד, בַּקֹּדֶשׁ הַסֵּךְ נֶסֶךְ שֵׁכָר לַיהוה. וְאֵת הַכֶּבֶשׂ הַשֵּׁנִי תַּעֲשֶׂה בֵּין הָעַרְבָּיִם, כְּמִנְחַת הַבֹּקֶר וּכְנִסְכּוֹ תַּעֲשֶׂה, אִשֵּׁה רֵיחַ נִיחֹחַ לַיהוה.

וְשָׁחַט אֹתוֹ עַל יֶרֶךְ הַמִּזְבֵּחַ צָפֹנָה לִפְנֵי יהוה, וְזָרְקוּ בְּנֵי אַהֲרֹן הַכֹּהֲנִים אֶת דָּמוֹ עַל הַמִּזְבֵּחַ סָבִיב.[1]

יְהִי רָצוֹן מִלְּפָנֶיךָ, יהוה אֱלֹהֵינוּ וֵאלֹהֵי אֲבוֹתֵינוּ, שֶׁתְּהֵא אֲמִירָה זוּ חֲשׁוּבָה וּמְקֻבֶּלֶת וּמְרֻצָּה לְפָנֶיךָ כְּאִלּוּ הִקְרַבְנוּ קָרְבַּן הַתָּמִיד בְּמוֹעֲדוֹ וּבִמְקוֹמוֹ וּכְהִלְכָתוֹ.

קטרת

אַתָּה הוּא יהוה אֱלֹהֵינוּ שֶׁהִקְטִירוּ אֲבוֹתֵינוּ לְפָנֶיךָ אֶת קְטֹרֶת הַסַּמִּים בִּזְמַן שֶׁבֵּית הַמִּקְדָּשׁ קַיָּם, כַּאֲשֶׁר צִוִּיתָ אוֹתָם עַל יְדֵי מֹשֶׁה נְבִיאֶךָ, כַּכָּתוּב בְּתוֹרָתֶךָ:

שמות ל:לד-לו, ז-ח

וַיֹּאמֶר יהוה אֶל מֹשֶׁה, קַח לְךָ סַמִּים, נָטָף וּשְׁחֵלֶת וְחֶלְבְּנָה, סַמִּים וּלְבֹנָה זַכָּה, בַּד בְּבַד יִהְיֶה. וְעָשִׂיתָ אֹתָהּ קְטֹרֶת, רֹקַח, מַעֲשֵׂה רוֹקֵחַ, מְמֻלָּח, טָהוֹר, קֹדֶשׁ. וְשָׁחַקְתָּ מִמֶּנָּה הָדֵק, וְנָתַתָּה מִמֶּנָּה לִפְנֵי הָעֵדֻת בְּאֹהֶל מוֹעֵד אֲשֶׁר אִוָּעֵד לְךָ שָׁמָּה, קֹדֶשׁ קָדָשִׁים תִּהְיֶה לָכֶם.

וְנֶאֱמַר: וְהִקְטִיר עָלָיו אַהֲרֹן קְטֹרֶת סַמִּים, בַּבֹּקֶר בַּבֹּקֶר, בְּהֵיטִיבוֹ אֶת הַנֵּרֹת יַקְטִירֶנָּה. וּבְהַעֲלֹת אַהֲרֹן אֶת הַנֵּרֹת בֵּין הָעַרְבַּיִם, יַקְטִירֶנָּה, קְטֹרֶת תָּמִיד לִפְנֵי יהוה לְדֹרֹתֵיכֶם.

כריתות ו., ירושלמי יומא ד:ה

תָּנוּ רַבָּנָן, פִּטּוּם הַקְּטֹרֶת כֵּיצַד. שְׁלֹשׁ מֵאוֹת וְשִׁשִּׁים וּשְׁמוֹנָה מָנִים הָיוּ בָהּ. שְׁלֹשׁ מֵאוֹת וְשִׁשִּׁים וַחֲמִשָּׁה כְּמִנְיַן יְמוֹת הַחַמָּה – מָנֶה לְכָל יוֹם, פְּרַס בְּשַׁחֲרִית וּפְרַס בֵּין הָעַרְבָּיִם; וּשְׁלֹשָׁה מָנִים יְתֵרִים, שֶׁמֵּהֶם מַכְנִיס כֹּהֵן גָּדוֹל מְלֹא חָפְנָיו בְּיוֹם הַכִּפֻּרִים. וּמַחֲזִירָם לְמַכְתֶּשֶׁת בְּעֶרֶב יוֹם הַכִּפֻּרִים, וְשׁוֹחֲקָן יָפֶה יָפֶה כְּדֵי שֶׁתְּהֵא דַקָּה מִן הַדַּקָּה. וְאַחַד עָשָׂר סַמָּנִים

to HASHEM: [male] first-year lambs, unblemished, two a day, as a continual elevation-offering. One lamb-service you are to perform in the morning and the second lamb-service you are to perform in the afternoon; with a tenth-ephah of fine flour as a meal-offering, mixed with a quarter-hin of crushed olive oil. It is the continual elevation-offering that was done at Mount Sinai, for a satisfying aroma, a fire-offering to HASHEM. And its libation is a quarter-hin for each lamb, to be poured on the Holy [Altar], a fermented libation to HASHEM. And the second lamb-service you are to perform in the afternoon, like the meal-offering of the morning and its libation are you to make, a fire-offering for a satisfying aroma to HASHEM.'

He is to slaughter it on the north side of the Altar before HASHEM, and Aaron's sons the Kohanim are to dash its blood upon the Altar, all around.[1]

יְהִי רָצוֹן *May it be Your will, HASHEM, our God and the God of our forefathers, that this recital be worthy and acceptable, and favorable before You as if we had offered the continual offering in its set time, in its place, and according to its requirement.*

INCENSE

אַתָּה *It is You, HASHEM, our God, before Whom our forefathers burned the incense-spices in the time when the Holy Temple stood, as You commanded them through Moses Your prophet, as is written in Your Torah:*

Exodus 30:34-36, 7-8

וַיֹּאמֶר *HASHEM said to Moses: Take yourself spices — stacte, onycha, and galbanum — spices and pure frankincense; they are all to be of equal weight. You are to make it into incense, a spice-compound, the handiwork of an expert spice-compounder, thoroughly mixed, pure and holy. You are to grind some of it finely and place some of it before the Testimony in the Tent of Appointment, where I shall designate a time to meet you; it shall be a holy of holies for you.*

It is also written: Aaron shall burn upon it the incense-spices every morning; when he cleans the lamps he is to burn it. And when Aaron ignites the lamps in the afternoon, he is to burn it, as continual incense before HASHEM throughout your generations.

Talmud, *Kereisos* 6a, *Yerushalmi Yoma* 4:5

תָּנוּ רַבָּנָן *The Rabbis taught: How is the incense mixture formulated? Three hundred sixty-eight maneh were in it: three hundred sixty-five corresponding to the days of the solar year — a maneh for each day, half in the morning and half in the afternoon; and three extra maneh, from which the Kohen Gadol would bring both his handfuls [into the Holy of Holies] on Yom Kippur. He would return them to the mortar on the day before Yom Kippur, and grind them very thoroughly so that it would be exceptionally fine. Eleven kinds of spices*

(1) *Leviticus* 1:11.

הָיוּ בָהּ, וְאֵלּוּ הֵן: (א) הַצֳּרִי, (ב) וְהַצִּפֹּרֶן, (ג) הַחֶלְבְּנָה, (ד) וְהַלְּבוֹנָה, מִשְׁקַל שִׁבְעִים שִׁבְעִים מָנֶה; (ה) מוֹר, (ו) וּקְצִיעָה, (ז) שִׁבֹּלֶת נֵרְדְּ, (ח) וְכַרְכֹּם, מִשְׁקַל שִׁשָּׁה עָשָׂר שִׁשָּׁה עָשָׂר מָנֶה; (ט) הַקֹּשְׁטְ שְׁנֵים עָשָׂר, (י) וְקִלּוּפָה שְׁלֹשָׁה, (יא) וְקִנָּמוֹן תִּשְׁעָה. בֹּרִית כַּרְשִׁינָה תִּשְׁעָה קַבִּין, יֵין קַפְרִיסִין סְאִין תְּלָתָא וְקַבִּין תְּלָתָא, וְאִם אֵין לוֹ יֵין קַפְרִיסִין, מֵבִיא חֲמַר חִוַּרְיָן עַתִּיק, מֶלַח סְדוֹמִית רֹבַע הַקָּב; מַעֲלֶה עָשָׁן כָּל שֶׁהוּא. רַבִּי נָתָן הַבַּבְלִי אוֹמֵר: אַף כִּפַּת הַיַּרְדֵּן כָּל שֶׁהוּא. וְאִם נָתַן בָּהּ דְּבַשׁ, פְּסָלָהּ. וְאִם חִסַּר אַחַת מִכָּל סַמָּנֶיהָ, חַיָּב מִיתָה.

רַבָּן שִׁמְעוֹן בֶּן גַּמְלִיאֵל אוֹמֵר: הַצֳּרִי אֵינוֹ אֶלָּא שְׂרָף הַנּוֹטֵף מֵעֲצֵי הַקְּטָף. בֹּרִית כַּרְשִׁינָה לָמָה הִיא בָאָה, כְּדֵי לְיַפּוֹת בָּהּ אֶת הַצִּפֹּרֶן, כְּדֵי שֶׁתְּהֵא נָאָה. יֵין קַפְרִיסִין לָמָה הוּא בָא, כְּדֵי לִשְׁרוֹת בּוֹ אֶת הַצִּפֹּרֶן, כְּדֵי שֶׁתְּהֵא עַזָּה. וַהֲלֹא מֵי רַגְלַיִם יָפִין לָהּ, אֶלָּא שֶׁאֵין מַכְנִיסִין מֵי רַגְלַיִם בַּמִּקְדָּשׁ מִפְּנֵי הַכָּבוֹד.

תַּנְיָא, רַבִּי נָתָן אוֹמֵר: כְּשֶׁהוּא שׁוֹחֵק, אוֹמֵר הָדֵק הֵיטֵב, הֵיטֵב הָדֵק, מִפְּנֵי שֶׁהַקּוֹל יָפֶה לַבְּשָׂמִים. פִּטְּמָהּ לַחֲצָאִין, כְּשֵׁרָה; לִשְׁלִישׁ וְלִרְבִיעַ, לֹא שָׁמָעְנוּ. אָמַר רַבִּי יְהוּדָה: זֶה הַכְּלָל – אִם כְּמִדָּתָהּ, כְּשֵׁרָה לַחֲצָאִין; וְאִם חִסַּר אַחַת מִכָּל סַמָּנֶיהָ, חַיָּב מִיתָה.

תַּנְיָא, בַּר קַפָּרָא אוֹמֵר: אַחַת לְשִׁשִּׁים אוֹ לְשִׁבְעִים שָׁנָה הָיְתָה בָאָה שֶׁל שִׁירַיִם לַחֲצָאִין. וְעוֹד תָּנֵי בַּר קַפָּרָא: אִלּוּ הָיָה נוֹתֵן בָּהּ קוֹרְטוֹב שֶׁל דְּבַשׁ, אֵין אָדָם יָכוֹל לַעֲמֹד מִפְּנֵי רֵיחָהּ. וְלָמָּה אֵין מְעָרְבִין בָּהּ דְּבַשׁ, מִפְּנֵי שֶׁהַתּוֹרָה אָמְרָה: כִּי כָל שְׂאֹר וְכָל דְּבַשׁ לֹא תַקְטִירוּ מִמֶּנּוּ אִשֶּׁה לַיהוה.[1]

The next three verses, each beginning 'ה, are recited three times each.

יהוה צְבָאוֹת עִמָּנוּ, מִשְׂגָּב לָנוּ אֱלֹהֵי יַעֲקֹב, סֶלָה.[2]

יהוה צְבָאוֹת, אַשְׁרֵי אָדָם בֹּטֵחַ בָּךְ.[3]

יהוה הוֹשִׁיעָה, הַמֶּלֶךְ יַעֲנֵנוּ בְיוֹם קָרְאֵנוּ.[4]

אַתָּה סֵתֶר לִי, מִצַּר תִּצְּרֵנִי, רָנֵּי פַלֵּט, תְּסוֹבְבֵנִי, סֶלָה.[5] וְעָרְבָה לַיהוה מִנְחַת יְהוּדָה וִירוּשָׁלָיִם, כִּימֵי עוֹלָם וּכְשָׁנִים קַדְמֹנִיּוֹת.[6]

were in it, as follows: (1) stacte, (2) onycha, (3) galbanum, (4) frankincense — each weighing seventy maneh; (5) myrrh, (6) cassia, (7) spikenard, (8) saffron — each weighing sixteen maneh; (9) costus — twelve maneh; (10) aromatic bark — three; and (11) cinnamon — nine. [Additionally] Carshina lye, nine kab; Cyprus wine, three se'ah and three kab — if he has no Cyprus wine, he brings old white wine; Sodom salt, a quarter-kab; and a minute amount of a smoke-raising herb. Rabbi Nassan the Babylonian says: Also a minute amount of Jordan amber. If he placed fruit-honey into it, he invalidated it. But if he left out any of its spices, he is liable to the death penalty.

רַבָּן שִׁמְעוֹן *Rabban Shimon ben Gamliel says: The stacte is simply the sap that drips from balsam trees. Why is Carshina lye used? To bleach the onycha, to make it pleasing. Why is Cyprus wine used? So that the onycha could be soaked in it, to make it pungent. Even though urine is more suitable for that, nevertheless they do not bring urine into the Temple out of respect.*

תַּנְיָא *It is taught, Rabbi Nassan says: As one would grind [the incense] another would say, 'Grind thoroughly, thoroughly grind,' because the sound is beneficial for the spices. If one mixed it in half-quantities, it was fit for use, but as to a third or a quarter — we have not heard the law. Rabbi Yehudah said: This is the general rule — In its proper proportion, it is fit for use in half the full amount; but if he left out any one of its spices, he is liable to the death penalty.*

תַּנְיָא *It is taught, Bar Kappara says: Once every sixty or seventy years, the accumulated leftovers reached half the yearly quantity. Bar Kappara taught further: Had one put a kortov of fruit-honey into it, no person could have resisted its scent. Why did they not mix fruit-honey into it? — because the Torah says: 'For any leaven or any fruit-honey, you are not to burn from them a fire-offering to HASHEM.'*[1]

The next three verses, each beginning *'HASHEM,'* are recited three times each.

HASHEM, Master of Legions, is with us,
a stronghold for us is the God of Jacob, Selah![2]
HASHEM, Master of Legions,
praiseworthy is the person who trusts in You.[3]
HASHEM, save! May the King answer us on the day we call![4]

You are a shelter for me; from distress You preserve me; with glad song of rescue, You envelop me, Selah![5] *May the offering of Judah and Jerusalem be pleasing to HASHEM, as in days of old and in former years.*[6]

---

(1) *Leviticus* 2:11. (2) *Psalms* 46:8. (3) 84:13. (4) 20:10. (5) 32:7. (6) *Malachi* 3:4.

יומא לג.

אַבַּיֵי הֲוָה מְסַדֵּר סֵדֶר הַמַּעֲרָכָה מִשְּׁמָא דִגְמָרָא וְאַלִּבָּא דְאַבָּא שָׁאוּל: מַעֲרָכָה גְדוֹלָה קוֹדֶמֶת לְמַעֲרָכָה שְׁנִיָּה שֶׁל קְטֹרֶת; וּמַעֲרָכָה שְׁנִיָּה שֶׁל קְטֹרֶת קוֹדֶמֶת לְסִדּוּר שְׁנֵי גִזְרֵי עֵצִים; וְסִדּוּר שְׁנֵי גִזְרֵי עֵצִים קוֹדֵם לְדִשּׁוּן מִזְבֵּחַ הַפְּנִימִי; וְדִשּׁוּן מִזְבֵּחַ הַפְּנִימִי קוֹדֵם לַהֲטָבַת חָמֵשׁ נֵרוֹת; וַהֲטָבַת חָמֵשׁ נֵרוֹת קוֹדֶמֶת לְדַם הַתָּמִיד; וְדַם הַתָּמִיד קוֹדֵם לַהֲטָבַת שְׁתֵּי נֵרוֹת; וַהֲטָבַת שְׁתֵּי נֵרוֹת קוֹדֶמֶת לִקְטֹרֶת; וּקְטֹרֶת קוֹדֶמֶת לְאֵבָרִים; וְאֵבָרִים לְמִנְחָה; וּמִנְחָה לַחֲבִתִּין; וַחֲבִתִּין לִנְסָכִין; וּנְסָכִין לְמוּסָפִין; וּמוּסָפִין לְבָזִיכִין; וּבָזִיכִין קוֹדְמִין לְתָמִיד שֶׁל בֵּין הָעַרְבָּיִם, שֶׁנֶּאֱמַר: וְעָרַךְ עָלֶיהָ הָעֹלָה, וְהִקְטִיר עָלֶיהָ חֶלְבֵי הַשְּׁלָמִים.[1] עָלֶיהָ הַשְׁלֵם כָּל הַקָּרְבָּנוֹת כֻּלָּם.

אָנָּא בְּכֹחַ גְּדֻלַּת יְמִינְךָ תַּתִּיר צְרוּרָה. — אב״ג ית״ץ
קַבֵּל רִנַּת עַמְּךָ שַׂגְּבֵנוּ טַהֲרֵנוּ נוֹרָא. — קר״ע שט״ן
נָא גִבּוֹר דּוֹרְשֵׁי יִחוּדְךָ כְּבָבַת שָׁמְרֵם. — נג״ד יכ״ש
בָּרְכֵם טַהֲרֵם רַחֲמֵם צִדְקָתְךָ תָּמִיד גָּמְלֵם. — בט״ר צת״ג
חֲסִין קָדוֹשׁ בְּרוֹב טוּבְךָ נַהֵל עֲדָתֶךָ. — חק״ב טנ״ע
יָחִיד גֵּאֶה לְעַמְּךָ פְּנֵה זוֹכְרֵי קְדֻשָּׁתֶךָ. — יג״ל פז״ק
שַׁוְעָתֵנוּ קַבֵּל וּשְׁמַע צַעֲקָתֵנוּ יוֹדֵעַ תַּעֲלֻמוֹת. — שק״ו צי״ת
בָּרוּךְ שֵׁם כְּבוֹד מַלְכוּתוֹ לְעוֹלָם וָעֶד.

רִבּוֹן הָעוֹלָמִים, אַתָּה צִוִּיתָנוּ לְהַקְרִיב קָרְבַּן הַתָּמִיד בְּמוֹעֲדוֹ, וְלִהְיוֹת כֹּהֲנִים בַּעֲבוֹדָתָם, וּלְוִיִּם בְּדוּכָנָם, וְיִשְׂרָאֵל בְּמַעֲמָדָם. וְעַתָּה בַּעֲוֹנוֹתֵינוּ חָרַב בֵּית הַמִּקְדָּשׁ וּבָטֵל הַתָּמִיד, וְאֵין לָנוּ לֹא כֹהֵן בַּעֲבוֹדָתוֹ, וְלֹא לֵוִי בְּדוּכָנוֹ, וְלֹא יִשְׂרָאֵל בְּמַעֲמָדוֹ. וְאַתָּה אָמַרְתָּ: וּנְשַׁלְּמָה פָרִים שְׂפָתֵינוּ.[1] לָכֵן יְהִי רָצוֹן מִלְּפָנֶיךָ, יהוה אֱלֹהֵינוּ וֵאלֹהֵי אֲבוֹתֵינוּ, שֶׁיְּהֵא שִׂיחַ שִׂפְתוֹתֵינוּ חָשׁוּב וּמְקֻבָּל וּמְרֻצֶּה לְפָנֶיךָ, כְּאִלּוּ הִקְרַבְנוּ קָרְבַּן הַתָּמִיד בְּמוֹעֲדוֹ, וְעָמַדְנוּ עַל מַעֲמָדוֹ.

משנה, זבחים פרק ה

[א] **אֵיזֶהוּ** מְקוֹמָן שֶׁל זְבָחִים. קָדְשֵׁי קָדָשִׁים שְׁחִיטָתָן בַּצָּפוֹן. פַּר וְשָׂעִיר שֶׁל יוֹם הַכִּפּוּרִים שְׁחִיטָתָן בַּצָּפוֹן, וְקִבּוּל דָּמָן בִּכְלֵי שָׁרֵת בַּצָּפוֹן. וְדָמָן טָעוּן הַזָּיָה עַל בֵּין הַבַּדִּים, וְעַל הַפָּרֹכֶת, וְעַל מִזְבַּח הַזָּהָב. מַתָּנָה אַחַת מֵהֶן מְעַכָּבֶת. שְׁיָרֵי הַדָּם

(1) *Leviticus* 6:5.

Talmud, *Yoma* 33a

אַבַּיֵי *Abaye listed the order of the Altar service based on the tradition and according to Abba Shaul: The arrangement of the large pyre precedes that of the secondary pyre for the incense-offering; the secondary pyre for the incense-offering precedes the placement of two logs; the placement of two logs precedes the removal of ashes from the Inner Altar; the removal of ashes from the Inner Altar precedes the cleaning of five lamps [of the Menorah]; the cleaning of the five lamps precedes the [dashing of the] blood of the continual offering; the blood of the continual offering precedes the cleaning of the [other] two lamps; the cleaning of the two lamps precedes the incense; the incense precedes the [burning of the] limbs; the [burning of the] limbs [precedes] the meal-offering; the meal-offering [precedes] the pancakes; the pancakes [precede] the wine-libations; the wine-libations [precede] the mussaf-offering; the mussaf-offering [precedes] the bowls [of frankincense]; the bowls [precede] the afternoon continual offering, for it is said: 'And he is to arrange the elevation-offering upon it and burn the fats of the peace-offerings upon it,'[1] — 'upon it' [the elevation-offering] you are to complete all the [day's] offerings.*

אָנָּא *We beg You! With the strength of Your right hand's greatness, untie the bundled sins. Accept the prayer of Your nation; strengthen us, purify us, O Awesome One. Please, O Strong One — those who foster Your Oneness, guard them like the pupil of an eye. Bless them, purify them, show them pity, may Your righteousness always recompense them. Powerful Holy One, with Your abundant goodness guide Your congregation. One and only Exalted One, turn to Your nation, which proclaims Your holiness. Accept our entreaty and hear our cry, O Knower of mysteries.*

Blessed is the Name of His glorious Kingdom for all eternity.

רִבּוֹן הָעוֹלָמִים *Master of the worlds, You commanded us to bring the continual offering at its set time, and that the Kohanim be at their assigned service, the Levites on their platform, and the Israelites at their station. But now, through our sins, the Holy Temple is destroyed, the continual offering is discontinued, and we have neither Kohen at his service, nor Levite on his platform, nor Israelite at his station. But You said: 'Let our lips compensate for the bulls'[1] — therefore may it be Your will, HASHEM, our God and the God of our forefathers, that the prayer of our lips be worthy, acceptable and favorable before You, as if we had brought the continual offering at its set time and we had stood at its station.*

Mishnah, *Zevachim* Chapter 5

[1] **אֵיזֶהוּ** *What is the location of the offerings? [Regarding] the most holy offerings, their slaughter is in the north. The slaughter of the bull and the he-goat of Yom Kippur is in the north and the reception of their blood in a service-vessel is in the north. Their blood requires sprinkling between the poles [of the Holy Ark], and toward the Curtain [of the Holy of Holies] and upon the Golden Altar. Every one of these applications [of blood] is essential. The leftover blood*

הָיָה שׁוֹפֵךְ עַל יְסוֹד מַעֲרָבִי שֶׁל מִזְבֵּחַ הַחִיצוֹן; אִם לֹא נָתַן, לֹא עִכֵּב.

[ב] **פָּרִים** הַנִּשְׂרָפִים וּשְׂעִירִים הַנִּשְׂרָפִים שְׁחִיטָתָן בַּצָּפוֹן, וְקִבּוּל דָּמָן בִּכְלִי שָׁרֵת בַּצָּפוֹן. וְדָמָן טָעוּן הַזָּיָה עַל הַפָּרֹכֶת וְעַל מִזְבַּח הַזָּהָב. מַתָּנָה אַחַת מֵהֶן מְעַכָּבֶת. שְׁיָרֵי הַדָּם הָיָה שׁוֹפֵךְ עַל יְסוֹד מַעֲרָבִי שֶׁל מִזְבֵּחַ הַחִיצוֹן; אִם לֹא נָתַן, לֹא עִכֵּב. אֵלּוּ וָאֵלּוּ נִשְׂרָפִין בְּבֵית הַדָּשֶׁן.

[ג] **חַטֹּאת** הַצִּבּוּר וְהַיָּחִיד – אֵלּוּ הֵן חַטֹּאת הַצִּבּוּר, שְׂעִירֵי רָאשֵׁי חֳדָשִׁים וְשֶׁל מוֹעֲדוֹת – שְׁחִיטָתָן בַּצָּפוֹן, וְקִבּוּל דָּמָן בִּכְלִי שָׁרֵת בַּצָּפוֹן. וְדָמָן טָעוּן אַרְבַּע מַתָּנוֹת עַל אַרְבַּע קְרָנוֹת. כֵּיצַד, עָלָה בַכֶּבֶשׁ, וּפָנָה לַסּוֹבֵב וּבָא לוֹ לְקֶרֶן דְּרוֹמִית מִזְרָחִית, מִזְרָחִית צְפוֹנִית, צְפוֹנִית מַעֲרָבִית, מַעֲרָבִית דְּרוֹמִית. שְׁיָרֵי הַדָּם הָיָה שׁוֹפֵךְ עַל יְסוֹד דְּרוֹמִי. וְנֶאֱכָלִין לִפְנִים מִן הַקְּלָעִים, לְזִכְרֵי כְהֻנָּה, בְּכָל מַאֲכָל, לְיוֹם וָלַיְלָה, עַד חֲצוֹת.

[ד] **הָעוֹלָה** קֹדֶשׁ קָדָשִׁים. שְׁחִיטָתָהּ בַּצָּפוֹן, וְקִבּוּל דָּמָהּ בִּכְלִי שָׁרֵת בַּצָּפוֹן. וְדָמָהּ טָעוּן שְׁתֵּי מַתָּנוֹת שֶׁהֵן אַרְבַּע; וּטְעוּנָה הַפְשֵׁט וְנִתּוּחַ, וְכָלִיל לָאִשִּׁים.

[ה] **זִבְחֵי** שַׁלְמֵי צִבּוּר וַאֲשָׁמוֹת, אֵלּוּ הֵן אֲשָׁמוֹת: אֲשַׁם גְּזֵלוֹת, אֲשַׁם מְעִילוֹת, אֲשַׁם שִׁפְחָה חֲרוּפָה, אֲשַׁם נָזִיר, אֲשַׁם מְצוֹרָע, אָשָׁם תָּלוּי. שְׁחִיטָתָן בַּצָּפוֹן, וְקִבּוּל דָּמָן בִּכְלִי שָׁרֵת בַּצָּפוֹן, וְדָמָן טָעוּן שְׁתֵּי מַתָּנוֹת שֶׁהֵן אַרְבַּע. וְנֶאֱכָלִין לִפְנִים מִן הַקְּלָעִים לְזִכְרֵי כְהֻנָּה, בְּכָל מַאֲכָל, לְיוֹם וָלַיְלָה, עַד חֲצוֹת.

[ו] **הַתּוֹדָה** וְאֵיל נָזִיר קָדָשִׁים קַלִּים. שְׁחִיטָתָן בְּכָל מָקוֹם בָּעֲזָרָה, וְדָמָן טָעוּן שְׁתֵּי מַתָּנוֹת שֶׁהֵן אַרְבַּע. וְנֶאֱכָלִין בְּכָל הָעִיר, לְכָל אָדָם, בְּכָל מַאֲכָל, לְיוֹם וָלַיְלָה, עַד חֲצוֹת. הַמּוּרָם מֵהֶם כַּיּוֹצֵא בָהֶם, אֶלָּא שֶׁהַמּוּרָם נֶאֱכָל לַכֹּהֲנִים, לִנְשֵׁיהֶם וְלִבְנֵיהֶם וּלְעַבְדֵיהֶם.

he would pour onto the western base of the Outer Altar; but if he failed to apply it [the leftover blood on the base], he has not prevented [atonement].

[2] **פָּרִים** *[Regarding] the bulls that are completely burned and he-goats that are completely burned, their slaughter is in the north, and the reception of their blood in a service-vessel is in the north. Their blood requires sprinkling toward the Curtain and upon the Golden Altar. Every one of these applications is essential. The leftover blood he would pour onto the western base of the Outer Altar; but if he failed to apply it [the leftover blood on the base], he has not prevented [atonement]. Both these and those [the Yom Kippur offerings] are burned in the place where the [Altar] ashes are deposited.*

[3] **חַטֹּאת** *[Regarding] sin-offerings of the community and of the individual — the communal sin-offerings are the following: the he-goats of Rosh Chodesh and festivals — their slaughter [of all sin-offerings] is in the north and the reception of their blood in a service-vessel is in the north. Their blood requires four applications, [one] on [each of] the four corners [of the Altar]. How is it done? He [the Kohen] ascended the [Altar] ramp, turned to the surrounding ledge and arrived at the southeast [corner], the northeast, the northwest, and the southwest. The leftover blood he would pour out on the southern base. They are eaten within the [Courtyard] curtains, by males of the priesthood, prepared in any manner, on the same day and that night until midnight.*

[4] **הָעוֹלָה** *The elevation-offering is among the most holy offerings. Its slaughter is in the north and the reception of its blood in a service-vessel is in the north. Its blood requires two applications that are equivalent to four. It requires flaying and dismemberment, and it is entirely consumed by the fire.*

[5] **זִבְחֵי** *[Regarding] communal peace-offerings and [personal] guilt-offerings — the guilt-offerings are as follows: the guilt-offering for thefts, the guilt-offering for misuse of sacred objects, the guilt-offering [for violating] a betrothed maidservant, the guilt-offering of a Nazirite, the guilt-offering of a metzora, and a guilt-offering in case of doubt — their slaughter is in the north and the reception of their blood in a service-vessel is in the north. Their blood requires two applications that are equivalent to four. They are eaten within the [Courtyard] curtains, by males of the priesthood, prepared in any manner, on the same day and that night until midnight.*

[6] **הַתּוֹדָה** *The thanksgiving-offering and the ram of a Nazirite are offerings of lesser holiness. Their slaughter is anywhere in the Courtyard, and their blood requires two applications that are equivalent to four. They are eaten throughout the City [of Jerusalem] by anyone, prepared in any manner, on the same day and that night until midnight. The [priestly] portion separated from them is treated like them, except that that portion may be eaten only by the Kohanim, their wives, children and slaves.*

[ז] **שְׁלָמִים** קָדָשִׁים קַלִּים. שְׁחִיטָתָן בְּכָל מָקוֹם בָּעֲזָרָה, וְדָמָן טָעוּן שְׁתֵּי מַתָּנוֹת שֶׁהֵן אַרְבַּע. וְנֶאֱכָלִין בְּכָל הָעִיר, לְכָל אָדָם, בְּכָל מַאֲכָל, לִשְׁנֵי יָמִים וְלַיְלָה אֶחָד. הַמּוּרָם מֵהֶם כַּיּוֹצֵא בָהֶם, אֶלָּא שֶׁהַמּוּרָם נֶאֱכָל לַכֹּהֲנִים, לִנְשֵׁיהֶם וְלִבְנֵיהֶם וּלְעַבְדֵיהֶם.

[ח] **הַבְּכוֹר** וְהַמַּעֲשֵׂר וְהַפֶּסַח קָדָשִׁים קַלִּים. שְׁחִיטָתָן בְּכָל מָקוֹם בָּעֲזָרָה, וְדָמָן טָעוּן מַתָּנָה אֶחָת, וּבִלְבָד שֶׁיִּתֵּן כְּנֶגֶד הַיְסוֹד. שִׁנָּה בַאֲכִילָתָן: הַבְּכוֹר נֶאֱכָל לַכֹּהֲנִים, וְהַמַּעֲשֵׂר לְכָל אָדָם. וְנֶאֱכָלִין בְּכָל הָעִיר, בְּכָל מַאֲכָל, לִשְׁנֵי יָמִים וְלַיְלָה אֶחָד. הַפֶּסַח אֵינוֹ נֶאֱכָל אֶלָּא בַלַּיְלָה, וְאֵינוֹ נֶאֱכָל אֶלָּא עַד חֲצוֹת, וְאֵינוֹ נֶאֱכָל אֶלָּא לִמְנוּיָו, וְאֵינוֹ נֶאֱכָל אֶלָּא צָלִי.

ברייתא דר׳ ישמעאל – ספרא, פתיחה

רַבִּי יִשְׁמָעֵאל אוֹמֵר: בִּשְׁלֹשׁ עֶשְׂרֵה מִדּוֹת הַתּוֹרָה נִדְרֶשֶׁת בָּהֵן. (א) מִקַּל וָחֹמֶר; (ב) וּמִגְּזֵרָה שָׁוָה; (ג) מִבִּנְיַן אָב מִכָּתוּב אֶחָד, וּמִבִּנְיַן אָב מִשְּׁנֵי כְתוּבִים; (ד) מִכְּלָל וּפְרָט; (ה) וּמִפְּרָט וּכְלָל; (ו) כְּלָל וּפְרָט וּכְלָל, אִי אַתָּה דָן אֶלָּא כְּעֵין הַפְּרָט; (ז) מִכְּלָל שֶׁהוּא צָרִיךְ לִפְרָט, וּמִפְּרָט שֶׁהוּא צָרִיךְ לִכְלָל; (ח) כָּל דָּבָר שֶׁהָיָה בִּכְלָל וְיָצָא מִן הַכְּלָל לְלַמֵּד, לֹא לְלַמֵּד עַל עַצְמוֹ יָצָא, אֶלָּא לְלַמֵּד עַל הַכְּלָל כֻּלּוֹ יָצָא; (ט) כָּל דָּבָר שֶׁהָיָה בִּכְלָל וְיָצָא לִטְעוֹן טוֹעַן אֶחָד שֶׁהוּא כְעִנְיָנוֹ, יָצָא לְהָקֵל וְלֹא לְהַחֲמִיר; (י) כָּל דָּבָר שֶׁהָיָה בִּכְלָל וְיָצָא לִטְעוֹן טְעַן אַחֵר שֶׁלֹּא כְעִנְיָנוֹ, יָצָא לְהָקֵל וּלְהַחֲמִיר; (יא) כָּל דָּבָר שֶׁהָיָה בִּכְלָל וְיָצָא לִדּוֹן בַּדָּבָר הֶחָדָשׁ, אִי אַתָּה יָכוֹל לְהַחֲזִירוֹ לִכְלָלוֹ, עַד שֶׁיַּחֲזִירֶנּוּ הַכָּתוּב לִכְלָלוֹ בְּפֵרוּשׁ; (יב) דָּבָר הַלָּמֵד מֵעִנְיָנוֹ, וְדָבָר הַלָּמֵד מִסּוֹפוֹ; (יג) וְכֵן שְׁנֵי כְתוּבִים הַמַּכְחִישִׁים זֶה אֶת זֶה, עַד שֶׁיָּבוֹא הַכָּתוּב הַשְּׁלִישִׁי וְיַכְרִיעַ בֵּינֵיהֶם.

יְהִי רָצוֹן מִלְּפָנֶיךָ, יהוה אֱלֹהֵינוּ וֵאלֹהֵי אֲבוֹתֵינוּ, שֶׁיִּבָּנֶה בֵּית הַמִּקְדָּשׁ בִּמְהֵרָה בְיָמֵינוּ, וְתֵן חֶלְקֵנוּ בְּתוֹרָתֶךָ. וְשָׁם נַעֲבָדְךָ בְּיִרְאָה כִּימֵי עוֹלָם וּכְשָׁנִים קַדְמוֹנִיּוֹת.

שְׁלָמִים *The peace-offerings are offerings of lesser holiness. Their slaughter is anywhere in the Courtyard, and their blood requires two applications that are equivalent to four. They are eaten throughout the City [of Jerusalem] by anyone, prepared in any manner, for two days and one night. The [priestly] portion separated from them is treated like them, except that that portion may be eaten only by the Kohanim, their wives, children and slaves.*

[8] **הַבְּכוֹר** *The firstborn and tithe of animals and the pesach-offering are offerings of lesser holiness. Their slaughter is anywhere in the Courtyard, and their blood requires a single application, provided he applies it above the base. They differ in their consumption: The firstborn is eaten by Kohanim, and the tithe by anyone. They are eaten throughout the City [of Jerusalem], prepared in any manner, for two days and one night. The pesach-offering is eaten only at night and it may be eaten only until midnight; it may be eaten only by those registered for it; and it may be eaten only if roasted.*

Introduction to *Sifra*

רַבִּי יִשְׁמָעֵאל *Rabbi Yishmael says: Through thirteen rules is the Torah elucidated: (1) Through a conclusion inferred from a lenient law to a strict one, and vice versa; (2) through tradition that similar words in different contexts are meant to clarify one another; (3) through a general principle derived from one verse, and a general principle derived from two verses; (4) through a general statement limited by a specification; (5) through a specification broadened by a general statement; (6) through a general statement followed by a specification followed, in turn, by another general statement — you may only infer whatever is similar to the specification; (7) when a general statement requires a specification or a specification requires a general statement to clarify its meaning; (8) anything that was included in a general statement, but was then singled out from the general statement in order to teach something, was not singled out to teach only about itself, but to apply its teaching to the entire generality; (9) anything that was included in a general statement, but was then singled out to discuss a provision similar to the general category, has been singled out to be more lenient rather than more severe; (10) anything that was included in a general statement, but was then singled out to discuss a provision not similar to the general category, has been singled out both to be more lenient and more severe; (11) anything that was included in a general statement, but was then singled out to be treated as a new case, cannot be returned to its general statement unless Scripture returns it explicitly to its general statement; (12) a matter elucidated from its context, or from the following passage; (13) similarly, two passages that contradict one another — until a third passage comes to reconcile them.*

יְהִי רָצוֹן *May it be Your will, HASHEM, our God and the God of our forefathers, that the Holy Temple be rebuilt, speedily in our days, and grant us our share in Your Torah, and may we serve You there with reverence as in days of old and in former years.*

קדיש דרבנן

Mourners recite קַדִּישׁ דְּרַבָּנָן. See *Laws* §135-136.

יִתְגַּדַּל וְיִתְקַדַּשׁ שְׁמֵהּ רַבָּא. (.Cong – אָמֵן.) בְּעָלְמָא דִּי בְרָא כִרְעוּתֵהּ. וְיַמְלִיךְ מַלְכוּתֵהּ, בְּחַיֵּיכוֹן וּבְיוֹמֵיכוֹן וּבְחַיֵּי דְכָל בֵּית יִשְׂרָאֵל, בַּעֲגָלָא וּבִזְמַן קָרִיב. וְאִמְרוּ: אָמֵן.

(.Cong – אָמֵן. יְהֵא שְׁמֵהּ רַבָּא מְבָרַךְ לְעָלַם וּלְעָלְמֵי עָלְמַיָּא.)

יְהֵא שְׁמֵהּ רַבָּא מְבָרַךְ לְעָלַם וּלְעָלְמֵי עָלְמַיָּא.

יִתְבָּרַךְ וְיִשְׁתַּבַּח וְיִתְפָּאַר וְיִתְרוֹמַם וְיִתְנַשֵּׂא וְיִתְהַדָּר וְיִתְעַלֶּה וְיִתְהַלָּל שְׁמֵהּ דְּקֻדְשָׁא בְּרִיךְ הוּא (.Cong – בְּרִיךְ הוּא) לְעֵלָּא מִן כָּל בִּרְכָתָא וְשִׁירָתָא תֻּשְׁבְּחָתָא וְנֶחֱמָתָא, דַּאֲמִירָן בְּעָלְמָא. וְאִמְרוּ: אָמֵן. (.Cong – אָמֵן.)

עַל יִשְׂרָאֵל וְעַל רַבָּנָן, וְעַל תַּלְמִידֵיהוֹן וְעַל כָּל תַּלְמִידֵי תַלְמִידֵיהוֹן, וְעַל כָּל מָאן דְּעָסְקִין בְּאוֹרַיְתָא, דִּי בְאַתְרָא הָדֵין וְדִי בְכָל אֲתַר וַאֲתַר. יְהֵא לְהוֹן וּלְכוֹן שְׁלָמָא רַבָּא, חִנָּא וְחִסְדָּא וְרַחֲמִין, וְחַיִּין אֲרִיכִין, וּמְזוֹנֵי רְוִיחֵי, וּפֻרְקָנָא מִן קֳדָם אֲבוּהוֹן דִּי בִשְׁמַיָּא (וְאַרְעָא). וְאִמְרוּ: אָמֵן. (.Cong – אָמֵן.)

יְהֵא שְׁלָמָא רַבָּא מִן שְׁמַיָּא, וְחַיִּים (טוֹבִים) עָלֵינוּ וְעַל כָּל יִשְׂרָאֵל. וְאִמְרוּ: אָמֵן. (.Cong – אָמֵן.)

Take three steps back. Bow left and say . . . עֹשֶׂה; bow right and say . . . הוּא; bow forward and say וְעַל כָּל . . . אָמֵן. Remain standing in place for a few moments, then take three steps forward.

עֹשֶׂה שָׁלוֹם בִּמְרוֹמָיו, הוּא בְּרַחֲמָיו יַעֲשֶׂה שָׁלוֹם עָלֵינוּ, וְעַל כָּל יִשְׂרָאֵל. וְאִמְרוּ: אָמֵן. (.Cong – אָמֵן.)

❧ פסוקי דזמרה ❧

INTRODUCTORY PSALM TO PESUKEI D'ZIMRAH

תהלים ל

מִזְמוֹר שִׁיר חֲנֻכַּת הַבַּיִת לְדָוִד. אֲרוֹמִמְךָ יהוה כִּי דִלִּיתָנִי, וְלֹא שִׂמַּחְתָּ אֹיְבַי לִי. יהוה אֱלֹהָי, שִׁוַּעְתִּי אֵלֶיךָ וַתִּרְפָּאֵנִי. יהוה הֶעֱלִיתָ מִן שְׁאוֹל נַפְשִׁי, חִיִּיתַנִי מִיָּרְדִי בוֹר. זַמְּרוּ לַיהוה חֲסִידָיו, וְהוֹדוּ לְזֵכֶר קָדְשׁוֹ. כִּי רֶגַע בְּאַפּוֹ, חַיִּים בִּרְצוֹנוֹ, בָּעֶרֶב יָלִין בֶּכִי וְלַבֹּקֶר רִנָּה. וַאֲנִי אָמַרְתִּי בְשַׁלְוִי, בַּל אֶמּוֹט לְעוֹלָם. יהוה בִּרְצוֹנְךָ הֶעֱמַדְתָּה לְהַרְרִי עֹז, הִסְתַּרְתָּ פָנֶיךָ הָיִיתִי נִבְהָל. אֵלֶיךָ יהוה אֶקְרָא, וְאֶל אֲדֹנָי אֶתְחַנָּן. מַה בֶּצַע בְּדָמִי, בְּרִדְתִּי אֶל שָׁחַת, הֲיוֹדְךָ עָפָר, הֲיַגִּיד אֲמִתֶּךָ. שְׁמַע יהוה וְחָנֵּנִי, יהוה הֱיֵה עֹזֵר לִי. ❖ הָפַכְתָּ מִסְפְּדִי לְמָחוֹל לִי, פִּתַּחְתָּ שַׂקִּי, וַתְּאַזְּרֵנִי שִׂמְחָה. לְמַעַן יְזַמֶּרְךָ כָבוֹד וְלֹא יִדֹּם, יהוה אֱלֹהַי לְעוֹלָם אוֹדֶךָּ.

THE RABBIS' KADDISH

Mourners recite the Rabbis' *Kaddish*. See *Laws* §135-136.
[A transliteration of this *Kaddish* appears on page 483.]

יִתְגַּדַּל *May His great Name grow exalted and sanctified* (Cong.– *Amen.*) *in the world that He created as He willed. May He give reign to His kingship in your lifetimes and in your days, and in the lifetimes of the entire Family of Israel, swiftly and soon. Now respond: Amen.*

(Cong.– *Amen. May His great Name be blessed forever and ever.*)
May His great Name be blessed forever and ever.

Blessed, praised, glorified, exalted, extolled, mighty, upraised, and lauded be the Name of the Holy One, Blessed is He (Cong.– *Blessed is He*) *— beyond any blessing and song, praise and consolation that are uttered in the world. Now respond: Amen.* (Cong.– *Amen.*)

Upon Israel, upon the teachers, their disciples and all of their disciples and upon all those who engage in the study of Torah, who are here or anywhere else; may they and you have abundant peace, grace, kindness, and mercy, long life, ample nourishment, and salvation from before their Father Who is in Heaven (and on earth). Now respond: Amen. (Cong. – *Amen.*)

May there be abundant peace from Heaven, and (good) life, upon us and upon all Israel. Now respond: Amen. (Cong.– *Amen.*)

Take three steps back. Bow left and say, *'He Who makes peace . . .'*; bow right and say, *'may He . . .'*; bow forward and say, *'and upon all Israel . . .'* Remain standing in place for a few moments, then take three steps forward.

He Who makes peace in His heights, may He, in His compassion, make peace upon us, and upon all Israel. Now respond: Amen. (Cong.– *Amen.*)

PESUKEI D'ZIMRAH

INTRODUCTORY PSALM TO PESUKEI D'ZIMRAH

Psalm 30

מִזְמוֹר *A psalm — a song for the inauguration of the Temple— by David. I will exalt You,* HASHEM, *for You have drawn me up and not let my foes rejoice over me.* HASHEM, *my God, I cried out to You and You healed me.* HASHEM, *You have raised my soul from the lower world, You have preserved me from my descent to the Pit. Make music to* HASHEM, *His devout ones, and give thanks to His Holy Name. For His anger endures but a moment; life results from His favor. In the evening one lies down weeping, but with dawn — a cry of joy! I had said in my serenity, 'I will never falter.' But,* HASHEM, *all is through Your favor — You supported my greatness with might; should You but conceal Your face, I would be confounded. To You,* HASHEM, *I would call and to my Lord I would appeal. What gain is there in my death, when I descend to the Pit? Will the dust acknowledge You? Will it declare Your truth? Hear,* HASHEM, *and favor me;* HASHEM, *be my Helper!* Chazzan– *You have changed for me my lament into dancing; You undid my sackcloth and girded me with gladness. So that my soul might make music to You and not be stilled,* HASHEM *my God, forever will I thank You.*

קדיש יתום

Mourners recite קַדִּישׁ יָתוֹם. See *Laws* §132-134.

יִתְגַּדַּל וְיִתְקַדַּשׁ שְׁמֵהּ רַבָּא. (Cong. – אָמֵן.) בְּעָלְמָא דִּי בְרָא כִרְעוּתֵהּ. וְיַמְלִיךְ מַלְכוּתֵהּ, בְּחַיֵּיכוֹן וּבְיוֹמֵיכוֹן וּבְחַיֵּי דְכָל בֵּית יִשְׂרָאֵל, בַּעֲגָלָא וּבִזְמַן קָרִיב. וְאִמְרוּ: אָמֵן.

(Cong. – אָמֵן. יְהֵא שְׁמֵהּ רַבָּא מְבָרַךְ לְעָלַם וּלְעָלְמֵי עָלְמַיָּא.)

יְהֵא שְׁמֵהּ רַבָּא מְבָרַךְ לְעָלַם וּלְעָלְמֵי עָלְמַיָּא.

יִתְבָּרַךְ וְיִשְׁתַּבַּח וְיִתְפָּאַר וְיִתְרוֹמַם וְיִתְנַשֵּׂא וְיִתְהַדָּר וְיִתְעַלֶּה וְיִתְהַלָּל שְׁמֵהּ דְּקֻדְשָׁא בְּרִיךְ הוּא (Cong. – בְּרִיךְ הוּא) – לְעֵלָּא מִן כָּל בִּרְכָתָא וְשִׁירָתָא תֻּשְׁבְּחָתָא וְנֶחֱמָתָא, דַּאֲמִירָן בְּעָלְמָא. וְאִמְרוּ: אָמֵן. (Cong. – אָמֵן.)

יְהֵא שְׁלָמָא רַבָּא מִן שְׁמַיָּא, וְחַיִּים עָלֵינוּ וְעַל כָּל יִשְׂרָאֵל. וְאִמְרוּ: אָמֵן. (Cong. – אָמֵן.)

Take three steps back. Bow left and say . . . עֹשֶׂה; bow right and say . . . הוּא; bow forward and say וְעַל כָּל . . . אָמֵן. Remain standing in place for a few moments, then take three steps forward.

עֹשֶׂה שָׁלוֹם בִּמְרוֹמָיו, הוּא יַעֲשֶׂה שָׁלוֹם עָלֵינוּ, וְעַל כָּל יִשְׂרָאֵל. וְאִמְרוּ: אָמֵן. (Cong. – אָמֵן.)

(Some recite this short Kabbalistic declaration of intent before beginning *Pesukei D'zimrah:*)

(הֲרֵינִי מְזַמֵּן אֶת פִּי לְהוֹדוֹת וּלְהַלֵּל וּלְשַׁבֵּחַ אֶת בּוֹרְאִי. לְשֵׁם יִחוּד קוּדְשָׁא בְּרִיךְ הוּא וּשְׁכִינְתֵּיהּ עַל יְדֵי הַהוּא טָמִיר וְנֶעְלָם, בְּשֵׁם כָּל יִשְׂרָאֵל.)

Pesukei D'zimrah begins with the recital of בָּרוּךְ שֶׁאָמַר, which is recited while standing. The *tzitzis* are not held during its recitation, and are not kissed at its conclusion.

בָּרוּךְ שֶׁאָמַר וְהָיָה הָעוֹלָם, בָּרוּךְ הוּא. בָּרוּךְ עֹשֶׂה בְרֵאשִׁית, בָּרוּךְ אוֹמֵר וְעֹשֶׂה, בָּרוּךְ גּוֹזֵר וּמְקַיֵּם, בָּרוּךְ מְרַחֵם עַל הָאָרֶץ, בָּרוּךְ מְרַחֵם עַל הַבְּרִיּוֹת, בָּרוּךְ מְשַׁלֵּם שָׂכָר טוֹב לִירֵאָיו, בָּרוּךְ חַי לָעַד וְקַיָּם לָנֶצַח, בָּרוּךְ פּוֹדֶה וּמַצִּיל, בָּרוּךְ שְׁמוֹ. בָּרוּךְ אַתָּה יהוה אֱלֹהֵינוּ מֶלֶךְ הָעוֹלָם, הָאֵל הָאָב הָרַחֲמָן הַמְּהֻלָּל בְּפֶה עַמּוֹ, מְשֻׁבָּח וּמְפֹאָר בִּלְשׁוֹן חֲסִידָיו וַעֲבָדָיו, וּבְשִׁירֵי דָוִד עַבְדֶּךָ. נְהַלֶּלְךָ יהוה אֱלֹהֵינוּ, בִּשְׁבָחוֹת וּבִזְמִרוֹת. נְגַדֶּלְךָ וּנְשַׁבֵּחֲךָ וּנְפָאֶרְךָ וְנַזְכִּיר שִׁמְךָ וְנַמְלִיכְךָ, מַלְכֵּנוּ אֱלֹהֵינוּ. ❖ יָחִיד, חֵי הָעוֹלָמִים, מֶלֶךְ מְשֻׁבָּח וּמְפֹאָר עֲדֵי עַד שְׁמוֹ הַגָּדוֹל. בָּרוּךְ אַתָּה יהוה, מֶלֶךְ מְהֻלָּל בַּתִּשְׁבָּחוֹת. (Cong. – אָמֵן.)

Permitted responses during *Pesukei D'zimrah*

From this point until after *Shemoneh Esrei* conversation is forbidden. During *Pesukei D'zimrah* [from בָּרוּךְ שֶׁאָמַר until יִשְׁתַּבַּח, p. 272] certain congregational and individual responses [e.g., בָּרוּךְ הוּא וּבָרוּךְ שְׁמוֹ] are omitted. The following responses, however, should be made: אָמֵן, *Amen*, after any blessing; *Kaddish; Borchu; Kedushah;* and the Rabbis' *Modim.* Additionally, one should join the congregation in reciting the first verse of the *Shema,* and may recite the אֲשֶׁר יָצַר blessing if he had to relieve himself during *Pesukei D'zimrah.*

If one is in the middle of *Pesukei D'zimrah* and the congregation has already reached the Torah

MOURNER'S KADDISH

Mourners recite the Mourners' *Kaddish. See Laws* §132-134.
[A transliteration of this *Kaddish* appears on page 484.]

יִתְגַּדַּל *May His great Name grow exalted and sanctified* (Cong.– *Amen.*) *in the world that He created as He willed. May He give reign to His kingship in your lifetimes and in your days, and in the lifetimes of the entire Family of Israel, swiftly and soon. Now respond: Amen.*

(Cong.– *Amen. May His great Name be blessed forever and ever.*)

May His great Name be blessed forever and ever.

Blessed, praised, glorified, exalted, extolled, mighty, upraised, and lauded be the Name of the Holy One, Blessed is He (Cong.– *Blessed is He*) *— beyond any blessing and song, praise and consolation that are uttered in the world. Now respond: Amen.* (Cong.– *Amen.*)

May there be abundant peace from Heaven, and life, upon us and upon all Israel. Now respond: Amen. (Cong.– *Amen.*)

Take three steps back. Bow left and say, *'He Who makes peace . . .'*; bow right and say, *'may He . . .'*; bow forward and say, *'and upon all Israel . . .'* Remain standing in place for a few moments, then take three steps forward.

He Who makes peace in His heights, may He make peace upon us, and upon all Israel. Now respond: Amen. (Cong.– *Amen.*)

(Some recite this short Kabbalistic declaration of intent before beginning *Pesukei D'zimrah:*)

(I now prepare my mouth to thank, laud, and praise my Creator. For the sake of the unification of the Holy One, Blessed is He, and His Presence, through Him Who is hidden and inscrutable — [I pray] in the name of all Israel.)

Pesukei D'zimrah begins with the recital of בָּרוּךְ שֶׁאָמַר, *Blessed is He Who spoke . . .*, which is recited while standing. The tzitzis are not held during its recitation, and are not kissed at its conclusion.

בָּרוּךְ שֶׁאָמַר *Blessed is He Who spoke, and the world came into being — blessed is He. Blessed is He Who maintains Creation; blessed is He Who speaks and does; blessed is He Who decrees and fulfills; blessed is He Who has mercy on the earth; blessed is He Who has mercy on the creatures; blessed is He Who gives goodly reward to those who fear Him; blessed is He Who lives forever and endures to eternity; blessed is He Who redeems and rescues — blessed is His Name! Blessed are You, HASHEM, our God, King of the universe, the God, the merciful Father, Who is lauded by the mouth of His people, praised and glorified by the tongue of His devout ones and His servants and through the psalms of David Your servant. We shall laud You, HASHEM, our God, with praises and songs. We shall exalt You, praise You, glorify You, mention Your Name and proclaim Your reign, our King, our God.* Chazzan– *O Unique One, Life-giver of the worlds, King Whose great Name is eternally praised and glorified. Blessed are You, HASHEM, the King Who is lauded with praises.* (Cong.– *Amen.*)

---

reading, it is preferable that he not be called to the Torah. However, if (a) one is the only *Kohen* or Levite present, or (b) the *gabbai* inadvertently called him to the Torah, then he may recite the blessings and even read the portion softly along with the Torah reader.

If after beginning *Pesukei D'zimrah* one realizes that he has forgotten to recite the morning Blessings of the Torah (p. 194), he should pause to recite them and their accompanying verses. Likewise, if he fears that he will not reach the *Shema* before the prescribed time (see *Laws* §55), he should recite all three paragraphs of *Shema.*

In all cases of permitted responses it is preferable to respond between psalms, whenever possible. Thus, for example, if one realizes that the congregation is approaching *Kedushah,* he should not begin a new psalm, but should wait

דברי הימים א טז:ח-לו

הוֹדוּ לַיהוה קִרְאוּ בִשְׁמוֹ, הוֹדִיעוּ בָעַמִּים עֲלִילֹתָיו. שִׁירוּ לוֹ, זַמְּרוּ לוֹ, שִׂיחוּ בְּכָל נִפְלְאֹתָיו. הִתְהַלְלוּ בְּשֵׁם קָדְשׁוֹ, יִשְׂמַח לֵב מְבַקְשֵׁי יהוה. דִּרְשׁוּ יהוה וְעֻזּוֹ, בַּקְּשׁוּ פָנָיו תָּמִיד. זִכְרוּ נִפְלְאֹתָיו אֲשֶׁר עָשָׂה, מֹפְתָיו וּמִשְׁפְּטֵי פִיהוּ. זֶרַע יִשְׂרָאֵל עַבְדּוֹ, בְּנֵי יַעֲקֹב בְּחִירָיו. הוּא יהוה אֱלֹהֵינוּ, בְּכָל הָאָרֶץ מִשְׁפָּטָיו. זִכְרוּ לְעוֹלָם בְּרִיתוֹ, דָּבָר צִוָּה לְאֶלֶף דּוֹר. אֲשֶׁר כָּרַת אֶת אַבְרָהָם, וּשְׁבוּעָתוֹ לְיִצְחָק. וַיַּעֲמִידֶהָ לְיַעֲקֹב לְחֹק, לְיִשְׂרָאֵל בְּרִית עוֹלָם. לֵאמֹר, לְךָ אֶתֵּן אֶרֶץ כְּנָעַן, חֶבֶל נַחֲלַתְכֶם. בִּהְיוֹתְכֶם מְתֵי מִסְפָּר, כִּמְעַט וְגָרִים בָּהּ. וַיִּתְהַלְּכוּ מִגּוֹי אֶל גּוֹי, וּמִמַּמְלָכָה אֶל עַם אַחֵר. לֹא הִנִּיחַ לְאִישׁ לְעָשְׁקָם, וַיּוֹכַח עֲלֵיהֶם מְלָכִים. אַל תִּגְּעוּ בִּמְשִׁיחָי, וּבִנְבִיאַי אַל תָּרֵעוּ. שִׁירוּ לַיהוה כָּל הָאָרֶץ, בַּשְּׂרוּ מִיּוֹם אֶל יוֹם יְשׁוּעָתוֹ. סַפְּרוּ בַגּוֹיִם אֶת כְּבוֹדוֹ, בְּכָל הָעַמִּים נִפְלְאוֹתָיו. כִּי גָדוֹל יהוה וּמְהֻלָּל מְאֹד, וְנוֹרָא הוּא עַל כָּל אֱלֹהִים. ❖ כִּי כָּל אֱלֹהֵי הָעַמִּים אֱלִילִים, (pause) וַיהוה שָׁמַיִם עָשָׂה.

הוֹד וְהָדָר לְפָנָיו, עֹז וְחֶדְוָה בִּמְקֹמוֹ. הָבוּ לַיהוה מִשְׁפְּחוֹת עַמִּים, הָבוּ לַיהוה כָּבוֹד וָעֹז. הָבוּ לַיהוה כְּבוֹד שְׁמוֹ, שְׂאוּ מִנְחָה וּבֹאוּ לְפָנָיו, הִשְׁתַּחֲווּ לַיהוה בְּהַדְרַת קֹדֶשׁ. חִילוּ מִלְּפָנָיו כָּל הָאָרֶץ, אַף תִּכּוֹן תֵּבֵל בַּל תִּמּוֹט. יִשְׂמְחוּ הַשָּׁמַיִם וְתָגֵל הָאָרֶץ, וְיֹאמְרוּ בַגּוֹיִם, יהוה מָלָךְ. יִרְעַם הַיָּם וּמְלוֹאוֹ, יַעֲלֹץ הַשָּׂדֶה וְכָל אֲשֶׁר בּוֹ. אָז יְרַנְּנוּ עֲצֵי הַיָּעַר, מִלִּפְנֵי יהוה, כִּי בָא לִשְׁפּוֹט אֶת הָאָרֶץ. הוֹדוּ לַיהוה כִּי טוֹב, כִּי לְעוֹלָם חַסְדּוֹ. וְאִמְרוּ הוֹשִׁיעֵנוּ אֱלֹהֵי יִשְׁעֵנוּ, וְקַבְּצֵנוּ וְהַצִּילֵנוּ מִן הַגּוֹיִם, לְהֹדוֹת לְשֵׁם קָדְשֶׁךָ, לְהִשְׁתַּבֵּחַ בִּתְהִלָּתֶךָ. בָּרוּךְ יהוה אֱלֹהֵי יִשְׂרָאֵל מִן הָעוֹלָם וְעַד הָעֹלָם, וַיֹּאמְרוּ כָל הָעָם, אָמֵן, וְהַלֵּל לַיהוה.

❖ רוֹמְמוּ יהוה אֱלֹהֵינוּ וְהִשְׁתַּחֲווּ לַהֲדֹם רַגְלָיו, קָדוֹשׁ הוּא.[1] רוֹמְמוּ יהוה אֱלֹהֵינוּ וְהִשְׁתַּחֲווּ לְהַר קָדְשׁוֹ, כִּי קָדוֹשׁ יהוה אֱלֹהֵינוּ.[2]

וְהוּא רַחוּם יְכַפֵּר עָוֹן וְלֹא יַשְׁחִית, וְהִרְבָּה לְהָשִׁיב אַפּוֹ, וְלֹא יָעִיר כָּל חֲמָתוֹ.[3] אַתָּה יהוה, לֹא תִכְלָא רַחֲמֶיךָ מִמֶּנִּי, חַסְדְּךָ וַאֲמִתְּךָ תָּמִיד יִצְּרוּנִי.[4] זְכֹר רַחֲמֶיךָ יהוה וַחֲסָדֶיךָ, כִּי מֵעוֹלָם הֵמָּה.[5] תְּנוּ עֹז לֵאלֹהִים, עַל יִשְׂרָאֵל גַּאֲוָתוֹ, וְעֻזּוֹ

The responses permitted above do not apply during the 'blessing' portions of בָּרוּךְ שֶׁאָמַר for the congregation to recite *Kedushah*, then continue his prayers.

I Chronicles 16:8-36

הוֹדוּ *Give thanks to HASHEM, declare His Name, make His acts known among the peoples. Sing to Him, make music to Him, speak of all His wonders. Glory in His holy Name, be glad of heart, you who seek HASHEM. Search out HASHEM and His might, seek His Presence always. Remember His wonders that He wrought, His marvels and the judgments of His mouth. O seed of Israel, His servant, O children of Jacob, His chosen ones — He is HASHEM, our God, over all the earth are His judgments. Remember His covenant forever — the word He commanded for a thousand generations — that He made with Abraham and His vow to Isaac. Then He established it for Jacob as a statute, for Israel as an everlasting covenant; saying, 'To you I shall give the Land of Canaan, the lot of your heritage.' When you were but few in number, hardly dwelling there, and they wandered from nation to nation, from one kingdom to another people. He let no man rob them, and He rebuked kings for their sake: 'Dare not touch My anointed ones, and to My prophets do no harm.' Sing to HASHEM, everyone on earth, announce His salvation daily. Relate His glory among the nations, among all the peoples His wonders. That HASHEM is great and exceedingly lauded, and awesome is He above all heavenly powers.* Chazzan– *For all the gods of the peoples are nothings — but HASHEM made heaven!*

Glory and majesty are before Him, might and delight are in His place. Render to HASHEM, O families of the peoples, render to HASHEM honor and might. Render to HASHEM honor worthy of His Name, take an offering and come before Him, prostrate yourselves before HASHEM in His intensely holy place. Tremble before Him, everyone on earth, indeed, the world is fixed so that it cannot falter. The heavens will be glad and the earth will rejoice and say among the nations, 'HASHEM has reigned!' The sea and its fullness will roar, the field and everything in it will exult. Then the trees of the forest will sing with joy before HASHEM, for He will have arrived to judge the earth. Give thanks to HASHEM, for He is good, for His kindness endures forever. And say, 'Save us, O God of our salvation, gather us and rescue us from the nations, to thank Your Holy Name and to glory in Your praise!' Blessed is HASHEM, the God of Israel, from This World to the World to Come — and let the entire people say, 'Amen and praise to God!'

Chazzan– *Exalt HASHEM, our God, and bow at His footstool; He is holy!*[1] *Exalt HASHEM, our God, and bow at His holy mountain; for holy is HASHEM, our God.*[2]

He, the Merciful One, is forgiving of iniquity and does not destroy; frequently, He withdraws His anger, not arousing His entire rage.[3] *You, HASHEM — withhold not Your mercy from me; may Your kindness and Your truth always protect me.*[4] *Remember Your mercies, HASHEM, and Your kindnesses, for they are from the beginning of the world.*[5] *Render might to God, Whose majesty hovers over Israel and Whose might is*

(1) *Psalms* 99:5. (2) 99:9. (3) 78:38. (4) 40:12. (5) 25:6.

---

and יִשְׁתַּבַּח [i.e., from the words בָּרוּךְ אַתָּה ה׳, *Blessed are You, HASHEM,* until the blessing's conclusion] where no interruptions are permitted.

בַּשְּׁחָקִים. נוֹרָא אֱלֹהִים מִמִּקְדָּשֶׁיךָ, אֵל יִשְׂרָאֵל הוּא נֹתֵן עֹז
וְתַעֲצֻמוֹת לָעָם, בָּרוּךְ אֱלֹהִים.[1] אֵל נְקָמוֹת יהוה, אֵל נְקָמוֹת
הוֹפִיעַ. הִנָּשֵׂא שֹׁפֵט הָאָרֶץ, הָשֵׁב גְּמוּל עַל גֵּאִים.[2] לַיהוה הַיְשׁוּעָה,
עַל עַמְּךָ בִרְכָתֶךָ סֶּלָה.[3] ❖ יהוה צְבָאוֹת עִמָּנוּ, מִשְׂגָּב לָנוּ אֱלֹהֵי
יַעֲקֹב סֶלָה.[4] יהוה צְבָאוֹת, אַשְׁרֵי אָדָם בֹּטֵחַ בָּךְ.[5] יהוה הוֹשִׁיעָה,
הַמֶּלֶךְ יַעֲנֵנוּ בְיוֹם קָרְאֵנוּ.[6]

הוֹשִׁיעָה אֶת עַמֶּךָ, וּבָרֵךְ אֶת נַחֲלָתֶךָ, וּרְעֵם וְנַשְּׂאֵם עַד
הָעוֹלָם.[7] נַפְשֵׁנוּ חִכְּתָה לַיהוה, עֶזְרֵנוּ וּמָגִנֵּנוּ הוּא. כִּי בוֹ יִשְׂמַח
לִבֵּנוּ, כִּי בְשֵׁם קָדְשׁוֹ בָטָחְנוּ. יְהִי חַסְדְּךָ יהוה עָלֵינוּ, כַּאֲשֶׁר יִחַלְנוּ
לָךְ.[8] הַרְאֵנוּ יהוה חַסְדֶּךָ, וְיֶשְׁעֲךָ תִּתֶּן לָנוּ.[9] קוּמָה עֶזְרָתָה לָּנוּ, וּפְדֵנוּ
לְמַעַן חַסְדֶּךָ.[10] אָנֹכִי יהוה אֱלֹהֶיךָ הַמַּעַלְךָ מֵאֶרֶץ מִצְרָיִם, הַרְחֶב
פִּיךָ וַאֲמַלְאֵהוּ.[11] אַשְׁרֵי הָעָם שֶׁכָּכָה לּוֹ, אַשְׁרֵי הָעָם שֶׁיהוה
אֱלֹהָיו.[12] ❖ וַאֲנִי בְּחַסְדְּךָ בָטַחְתִּי, יָגֵל לִבִּי בִּישׁוּעָתֶךָ, אָשִׁירָה
לַיהוה, כִּי גָמַל עָלָי.[13]

מִזְמוֹר לְתוֹדָה (Psalm 100) is recited while standing.

מִזְמוֹר לְתוֹדָה, הָרִיעוּ לַיהוה כָּל הָאָרֶץ. עִבְדוּ אֶת יהוה
בְּשִׂמְחָה, בֹּאוּ לְפָנָיו בִּרְנָנָה. דְּעוּ כִּי יהוה
הוּא אֱלֹהִים, הוּא עָשָׂנוּ, וְלוֹ אֲנַחְנוּ, עַמּוֹ וְצֹאן מַרְעִיתוֹ. בֹּאוּ
שְׁעָרָיו בְּתוֹדָה, חֲצֵרֹתָיו בִּתְהִלָּה, הוֹדוּ לוֹ, בָּרְכוּ שְׁמוֹ. כִּי טוֹב
יהוה, לְעוֹלָם חַסְדּוֹ, וְעַד דֹּר וָדֹר אֱמוּנָתוֹ.

The following prayer should be recited with special intensity.

יְהִי כְבוֹד יהוה לְעוֹלָם, יִשְׂמַח יהוה בְּמַעֲשָׂיו.[14] יְהִי שֵׁם יהוה
מְבֹרָךְ, מֵעַתָּה וְעַד עוֹלָם. מִמִּזְרַח שֶׁמֶשׁ עַד מְבוֹאוֹ, מְהֻלָּל
שֵׁם יהוה. רָם עַל כָּל גּוֹיִם יהוה, עַל הַשָּׁמַיִם כְּבוֹדוֹ.[15] יהוה
שִׁמְךָ לְעוֹלָם, יהוה זִכְרְךָ לְדֹר וָדֹר.[16] יהוה בַּשָּׁמַיִם הֵכִין כִּסְאוֹ,
וּמַלְכוּתוֹ בַּכֹּל מָשָׁלָה.[17] יִשְׂמְחוּ הַשָּׁמַיִם וְתָגֵל הָאָרֶץ, וְיֹאמְרוּ
בַגּוֹיִם יהוה מָלָךְ.[18] יהוה מֶלֶךְ,[19] יהוה מָלָךְ,[20] יהוה יִמְלֹךְ לְעֹלָם
וָעֶד.[21] יהוה מֶלֶךְ עוֹלָם וָעֶד, אָבְדוּ גוֹיִם מֵאַרְצוֹ.[22] יהוה הֵפִיר עֲצַת
גּוֹיִם, הֵנִיא מַחְשְׁבוֹת עַמִּים.[23] רַבּוֹת מַחֲשָׁבוֹת בְּלֶב אִישׁ, וַעֲצַת
יהוה הִיא תָקוּם.[24] עֲצַת יהוה לְעוֹלָם תַּעֲמֹד, מַחְשְׁבוֹת לִבּוֹ
לְדֹר וָדֹר.[25] כִּי הוּא אָמַר וַיֶּהִי, הוּא צִוָּה וַיַּעֲמֹד.[26] כִּי בָחַר יהוה
בְּצִיּוֹן, אִוָּהּ לְמוֹשָׁב לוֹ.[27] כִּי יַעֲקֹב בָּחַר לוֹ יָהּ, יִשְׂרָאֵל לִסְגֻלָּתוֹ.[28]

in the clouds. You are awesome, O God, from Your sanctuaries, O God of Israel — it is He Who grants might and power to the people, blessed is God.[1] *O God of vengeance,* HASHEM, *O God of vengeance, appear! Arise, O Judge of the earth, render recompense to the haughty.*[2] *Salvation is* HASHEM'*s, upon Your people is Your blessing, Selah.*[3] Chazzan– HASHEM, *Master of Legions, is with us, a stronghold for us is the God of Jacob, Selah.*[4] HASHEM, *Master of Legions, praiseworthy is the person who trusts in You.*[5] HASHEM, *save! May the King answer us on the day we call.*[6]

Save Your people and bless Your heritage, tend them and elevate them forever.[7] *Our soul longed for* HASHEM *— our help and our shield is He. For in Him will our hearts be glad, for in His Holy Name we trusted. May Your kindness,* HASHEM, *be upon us, just as we awaited You.*[8] *Show us Your kindness,* HASHEM, *and grant us Your salvation.*[9] *Arise — assist us, and redeem us by virtue of Your kindness.*[10] *I am* HASHEM, *your God, Who raised you from the land of Egypt, open wide your mouth and I will fill it.*[11] *Praiseworthy is the people for whom this is so, praiseworthy is the people whose God is* HASHEM.[12] Chazzan– *As for me, I trust in Your kindness; my heart will rejoice in Your salvation. I will sing to* HASHEM, *for He dealt kindly with me.*[13]

A psalm of thanksgiving (Psalm 100) is recited while standing.

מִזְמוֹר לְתוֹדָה *A psalm of thanksgiving, call out to* HASHEM, *everyone on earth. Serve* HASHEM *with gladness, come before Him with joyous song. Know that* HASHEM, *He is God, it is He Who made us and we are His, His people and the sheep of His pasture. Enter His gates with thanksgiving, His courts with praise, give thanks to Him, bless His Name.* Chazzan – *For* HASHEM *is good, His kindness endures forever, and from generation to generation is His faithfulness.*

The following prayer should be recited with special intensity.

יְהִי *May the glory of* HASHEM *endure forever, let* HASHEM *rejoice in His works.*[14] *Blessed be the Name of* HASHEM, *from this time and forever. From the rising of the sun to its setting,* HASHEM'*s Name is praised. High above all nations is* HASHEM, *above the heavens is His glory.*[15] *'*HASHEM*' is Your Name forever, '*HASHEM*' is Your memorial throughout the generations.*[16] HASHEM *has established His throne in the heavens, and His kingdom reigns over all.*[17] *The heavens will be glad and the earth will rejoice, they will proclaim among the nations, '*HASHEM *has reigned!'*[18] HASHEM *reigns,*[19] HASHEM *has reigned,*[20] HASHEM *shall reign for all eternity.*[21] HASHEM *reigns forever and ever, even when the nations will have perished from His earth.*[22] HASHEM *annuls the counsel of nations, He balks the designs of peoples.*[23] *Many designs are in man's heart, but the counsel of* HASHEM *— only it will prevail.*[24] *The counsel of* HASHEM *will endure forever, the designs of His heart throughout the generations.*[25] *For He spoke and it came to be; He commanded and it stood firm.*[26] *For* HASHEM *selected Zion, He desired it for His dwelling place.*[27] *For God selected Jacob as His own, Israel as His treasure.*[28]

(1) *Psalms* 68:35-36. (2) 94:1-2. (3) 3:9. (4) 46:8. (5) 84:13. (6) 20:10. (7) 28:9. (8) 33:20-22. (9) 85:8. (10) 44:27. (11) 81:11. (12) 144:15. (13) 13:6. (14) 104:31. (15) 113:2-4. (16) 135:13. (17) 103:19. (18) *I Chronicles* 16:31. (19) *Psalms* 10:16. (20) 93:1 et al. (21) *Exodus* 15:18. (22) *Psalms* 10:16. (23) 33:10. (24) *Proverbs* 19:21. (25) *Psalms* 33:11. (26) 33:9. (27) 132:13. (28) 135:4.

כִּי לֹא יִטֹּשׁ יהוה עַמּוֹ, וְנַחֲלָתוֹ לֹא יַעֲזֹב.[1] ❖ וְהוּא רַחוּם יְכַפֵּר עָוֹן וְלֹא יַשְׁחִית, וְהִרְבָּה לְהָשִׁיב אַפּוֹ, וְלֹא יָעִיר כָּל חֲמָתוֹ.[2] יהוה הוֹשִׁיעָה, הַמֶּלֶךְ יַעֲנֵנוּ בְיוֹם קָרְאֵנוּ.[3]

אַשְׁרֵי יוֹשְׁבֵי בֵיתֶךָ, עוֹד יְהַלְּלוּךָ סֶּלָה.[4] אַשְׁרֵי הָעָם שֶׁכָּכָה לּוֹ, אַשְׁרֵי הָעָם שֶׁיהוה אֱלֹהָיו.[5]

תהלים קמה

תְּהִלָּה לְדָוִד,

אֲרוֹמִמְךָ אֱלוֹהַי הַמֶּלֶךְ, וַאֲבָרְכָה שִׁמְךָ לְעוֹלָם וָעֶד.

בְּכָל יוֹם אֲבָרְכֶךָּ, וַאֲהַלְלָה שִׁמְךָ לְעוֹלָם וָעֶד.

גָּדוֹל יהוה וּמְהֻלָּל מְאֹד, וְלִגְדֻלָּתוֹ אֵין חֵקֶר.

דוֹר לְדוֹר יְשַׁבַּח מַעֲשֶׂיךָ, וּגְבוּרֹתֶיךָ יַגִּידוּ.

הֲדַר כְּבוֹד הוֹדֶךָ, וְדִבְרֵי נִפְלְאֹתֶיךָ אָשִׂיחָה.

וֶעֱזוּז נוֹרְאוֹתֶיךָ יֹאמֵרוּ, וּגְדוּלָּתְךָ אֲסַפְּרֶנָּה.

זֵכֶר רַב טוּבְךָ יַבִּיעוּ, וְצִדְקָתְךָ יְרַנֵּנוּ.

חַנּוּן וְרַחוּם יהוה, אֶרֶךְ אַפַּיִם וּגְדָל חָסֶד.

טוֹב יהוה לַכֹּל, וְרַחֲמָיו עַל כָּל מַעֲשָׂיו.

יוֹדוּךָ יהוה כָּל מַעֲשֶׂיךָ, וַחֲסִידֶיךָ יְבָרְכוּכָה.

כְּבוֹד מַלְכוּתְךָ יֹאמֵרוּ, וּגְבוּרָתְךָ יְדַבֵּרוּ.

לְהוֹדִיעַ לִבְנֵי הָאָדָם גְּבוּרֹתָיו, וּכְבוֹד הֲדַר מַלְכוּתוֹ.

מַלְכוּתְךָ מַלְכוּת כָּל עֹלָמִים, וּמֶמְשַׁלְתְּךָ בְּכָל דּוֹר וָדֹר.

סוֹמֵךְ יהוה לְכָל הַנֹּפְלִים, וְזוֹקֵף לְכָל הַכְּפוּפִים.

עֵינֵי כֹל אֵלֶיךָ יְשַׂבֵּרוּ, וְאַתָּה נוֹתֵן לָהֶם אֶת אָכְלָם בְּעִתּוֹ.

While reciting the verse פּוֹתֵחַ, concentrate intently on its meaning.

פּוֹתֵחַ אֶת יָדֶךָ,

וּמַשְׂבִּיעַ לְכָל חַי רָצוֹן.

צַדִּיק יהוה בְּכָל דְּרָכָיו, וְחָסִיד בְּכָל מַעֲשָׂיו.

קָרוֹב יהוה לְכָל קֹרְאָיו, לְכֹל אֲשֶׁר יִקְרָאֻהוּ בֶאֱמֶת.

רְצוֹן יְרֵאָיו יַעֲשֶׂה, וְאֶת שַׁוְעָתָם יִשְׁמַע וְיוֹשִׁיעֵם.

שׁוֹמֵר יהוה אֶת כָּל אֹהֲבָיו, וְאֵת כָּל הָרְשָׁעִים יַשְׁמִיד.

❖ **תְּ**הִלַּת יהוה יְדַבֶּר פִּי, וִיבָרֵךְ כָּל בָּשָׂר שֵׁם קָדְשׁוֹ לְעוֹלָם וָעֶד.

וַאֲנַחְנוּ נְבָרֵךְ יָהּ, מֵעַתָּה וְעַד עוֹלָם, הַלְלוּיָהּ.[6]

---

(1) *Psalms* 94:14. (2) 78:38. (3) 20:10. (4) 84:5. (5) 144:15. (6) 115:8.

For HASHEM *will not cast off His people, nor will He forsake His heritage.*[1] Chazzan – *He, the Merciful One, is forgiving of iniquity and does not destroy; frequently He withdraws His anger, not arousing His entire rage.*[2] HASHEM, *save! May the King answer us on the day we call.*[3]

אַשְׁרֵי *Praiseworthy are those who dwell in Your house; may they always praise You, Selah!*[4] *Praiseworthy is the people for whom this is so, praiseworthy is the people whose God is* HASHEM.[5]

Psalm 145 *A psalm of praise by David:*

א *I will exalt You, my God the King,*
and I will bless Your Name forever and ever.

ב *Every day I will bless You, and I will laud Your Name forever and ever.*

ג HASHEM *is great and exceedingly lauded,*
and His greatness is beyond investigation.

ד *Each generation will praise Your deeds to the next*
and of Your mighty deeds they will tell.

ה *The splendrous glory of Your power*
and Your wondrous deeds I shall discuss.

ו *And of Your awesome power they will speak,*
and Your greatness I shall relate.

ז *A recollection of Your abundant goodness they will utter*
and of Your righteousness they will sing exultantly.

ח *Gracious and merciful is* HASHEM,
slow to anger, and great in [bestowing] kindness.

ט HASHEM *is good to all; His mercies are on all His works.*

י *All Your works shall thank You,* HASHEM,
and Your devout ones will bless You.

כ *Of the glory of Your kingdom they will speak,*
and of Your power they will tell;

ל *To inform human beings of His mighty deeds,*
and the glorious splendor of His kingdom.

מ *Your kingdom is a kingdom spanning all eternities,*
and Your dominion is throughout every generation.

ס HASHEM *supports all the fallen ones and straightens all the bent.*

ע *The eyes of all look to You with hope*
and You give them their food in its proper time;

פ *You open Your hand, and satisfy*
the desire of every living thing.

While reciting the verse, *'You open . . .'* concentrate intently on its meaning.

צ *Righteous is* HASHEM *in all His ways and magnanimous in all His deeds.*

ק HASHEM *is close to all who call upon Him —*
to all who call upon Him sincerely.

ר *The will of those who fear Him He will do;*
and their cry He will hear, and save them.

ש HASHEM *protects all who love Him; but all the wicked He will destroy.*

ת Chazzan – *May my mouth declare the praise of* HASHEM
and may all flesh bless His Holy Name forever and ever.

We will bless God from this time and forever, Halleluyah![6]

תהלים קמו

הַלְלוּיָהּ, הַלְלִי נַפְשִׁי אֶת יהוה. אֲהַלְלָה יהוה בְּחַיָּי, אֲזַמְּרָה לֵאלֹהַי בְּעוֹדִי. אַל תִּבְטְחוּ בִנְדִיבִים, בְּבֶן אָדָם שֶׁאֵין לוֹ תְשׁוּעָה. תֵּצֵא רוּחוֹ, יָשֻׁב לְאַדְמָתוֹ, בַּיּוֹם הַהוּא אָבְדוּ עֶשְׁתֹּנֹתָיו. אַשְׁרֵי שֶׁאֵל יַעֲקֹב בְּעֶזְרוֹ, שִׂבְרוֹ עַל יהוה אֱלֹהָיו. עֹשֶׂה שָׁמַיִם וָאָרֶץ, אֶת הַיָּם וְאֶת כָּל אֲשֶׁר בָּם, הַשֹּׁמֵר אֱמֶת לְעוֹלָם. עֹשֶׂה מִשְׁפָּט לַעֲשׁוּקִים, נֹתֵן לֶחֶם לָרְעֵבִים, יהוה מַתִּיר אֲסוּרִים. יהוה פֹּקֵחַ עִוְרִים, יהוה זֹקֵף כְּפוּפִים, יהוה אֹהֵב צַדִּיקִים. יהוה שֹׁמֵר אֶת גֵּרִים, יָתוֹם וְאַלְמָנָה יְעוֹדֵד, וְדֶרֶךְ רְשָׁעִים יְעַוֵּת. ❖ יִמְלֹךְ יהוה לְעוֹלָם, אֱלֹהַיִךְ צִיּוֹן, לְדֹר וָדֹר, הַלְלוּיָהּ.

תהלים קמז

הַלְלוּיָהּ, כִּי טוֹב זַמְּרָה אֱלֹהֵינוּ, כִּי נָעִים נָאוָה תְהִלָּה. בּוֹנֵה יְרוּשָׁלַיִם יהוה, נִדְחֵי יִשְׂרָאֵל יְכַנֵּס. הָרוֹפֵא לִשְׁבוּרֵי לֵב, וּמְחַבֵּשׁ לְעַצְּבוֹתָם. מוֹנֶה מִסְפָּר לַכּוֹכָבִים, לְכֻלָּם שֵׁמוֹת יִקְרָא. גָּדוֹל אֲדוֹנֵינוּ וְרַב כֹּחַ, לִתְבוּנָתוֹ אֵין מִסְפָּר. מְעוֹדֵד עֲנָוִים יהוה, מַשְׁפִּיל רְשָׁעִים עֲדֵי אָרֶץ. עֱנוּ לַיהוה בְּתוֹדָה, זַמְּרוּ לֵאלֹהֵינוּ בְכִנּוֹר. הַמְּכַסֶּה שָׁמַיִם בְּעָבִים, הַמֵּכִין לָאָרֶץ מָטָר, הַמַּצְמִיחַ הָרִים חָצִיר. נוֹתֵן לִבְהֵמָה לַחְמָהּ, לִבְנֵי עֹרֵב אֲשֶׁר יִקְרָאוּ. לֹא בִגְבוּרַת הַסּוּס יֶחְפָּץ, לֹא בְשׁוֹקֵי הָאִישׁ יִרְצֶה. רוֹצֶה יהוה אֶת יְרֵאָיו, אֶת הַמְיַחֲלִים לְחַסְדּוֹ. שַׁבְּחִי יְרוּשָׁלַיִם אֶת יהוה, הַלְלִי אֱלֹהַיִךְ צִיּוֹן. כִּי חִזַּק בְּרִיחֵי שְׁעָרָיִךְ, בֵּרַךְ בָּנַיִךְ בְּקִרְבֵּךְ. הַשָּׂם גְּבוּלֵךְ שָׁלוֹם, חֵלֶב חִטִּים יַשְׂבִּיעֵךְ. הַשֹּׁלֵחַ אִמְרָתוֹ אָרֶץ, עַד מְהֵרָה יָרוּץ דְּבָרוֹ. הַנֹּתֵן שֶׁלֶג כַּצָּמֶר, כְּפוֹר כָּאֵפֶר יְפַזֵּר. מַשְׁלִיךְ קַרְחוֹ כְפִתִּים, לִפְנֵי קָרָתוֹ מִי יַעֲמֹד. יִשְׁלַח דְּבָרוֹ וְיַמְסֵם, יַשֵּׁב רוּחוֹ יִזְּלוּ מָיִם. ❖ מַגִּיד דְּבָרָיו לְיַעֲקֹב, חֻקָּיו וּמִשְׁפָּטָיו לְיִשְׂרָאֵל. לֹא עָשָׂה כֵן לְכָל גּוֹי, וּמִשְׁפָּטִים בַּל יְדָעוּם, הַלְלוּיָהּ.

תהלים קמח

הַלְלוּיָהּ, הַלְלוּ אֶת יהוה מִן הַשָּׁמַיִם, הַלְלוּהוּ בַּמְּרוֹמִים. הַלְלוּהוּ כָל מַלְאָכָיו, הַלְלוּהוּ כָּל צְבָאָיו. הַלְלוּהוּ שֶׁמֶשׁ וְיָרֵחַ, הַלְלוּהוּ כָּל כּוֹכְבֵי אוֹר. הַלְלוּהוּ שְׁמֵי הַשָּׁמָיִם, וְהַמַּיִם אֲשֶׁר מֵעַל הַשָּׁמָיִם. יְהַלְלוּ אֶת שֵׁם יהוה, כִּי הוּא צִוָּה וְנִבְרָאוּ. וַיַּעֲמִידֵם לָעַד לְעוֹלָם, חָק נָתַן וְלֹא יַעֲבוֹר. הַלְלוּ אֶת יהוה מִן הָאָרֶץ, תַּנִּינִים וְכָל תְּהֹמוֹת. אֵשׁ וּבָרָד, שֶׁלֶג וְקִיטוֹר, רוּחַ סְעָרָה

Psalm 146

הַלְלוּיָהּ *Halleluyah! Praise* HASHEM, *O my Soul! I will praise* HASHEM *while I live, I will make music to my God while I exist. Do not rely on nobles, nor on a human being for he holds no salvation. When his spirit departs he returns to his earth, on that day his plans all perish. Praiseworthy is one whose help is Jacob's God, whose hope is in* HASHEM, *his God. He is the Maker of heaven and earth, the sea and all that is in them, Who safeguards truth forever. He does justice for the exploited; He gives bread to the hungry;* HASHEM *releases the bound.* HASHEM *gives sight to the blind;* HASHEM *straightens the bent;* HASHEM *loves the righteous.* HASHEM *protects strangers; orphan and widow He encourages; but the way of the wicked He contorts.* Chazzan – HASHEM *shall reign forever — your God, O Zion — from generation to generation. Halleluyah!*

Psalm 147

הַלְלוּיָהּ *Halleluyah! For it is good to make music to our God, for praise is pleasant and befitting. The Builder of Jerusalem is* HASHEM, *the outcast of Israel He will gather in. He is the Healer of the broken-hearted, and the One Who binds up their sorrows. He counts the number of the stars, to all of them He assigns names. Great is our Lord and abundant in strength, His understanding is beyond calculation.* HASHEM *encourages the humble, He lowers the wicked down to the ground. Call out to* HASHEM *with thanks, with the harp sing to our God — Who covers the heavens with clouds, Who prepares rain for the earth, Who makes mountains sprout with grass. He gives to an animal its food, to young ravens that cry out. Not in the strength of the horse does He desire, and not in the legs of man does He favor.* HASHEM *favors those who fear Him, those who hope for His kindness. Praise* HASHEM, *O Jerusalem, laud your God, O Zion. For He has strengthened the bars of your gates, and blessed your children in your midst; He Who makes your borders peaceful, and with the cream of the wheat He sates you; He Who dispatches His utterance earthward; how swiftly His commandment runs! He Who gives snow like fleece, He scatters frost like ashes. He hurls His ice like crumbs — before His cold, who can stand? He issues His command and it melts them, He blows His wind — the waters flow.* Chazzan – *He relates His Word to Jacob, His statutes and judgments to Israel. He did not do so for any other nation, such judgments — they know them not. Halleluyah!*

Psalm 148

הַלְלוּיָהּ *Halleluyah! Praise* HASHEM *from the heavens; praise Him in the heights. Praise Him, all His angels; praise Him, all His legions. Praise Him, sun and moon; praise Him, all bright stars. Praise Him, the most exalted of the heavens and the waters that are above the heavens. Let them praise the Name of* HASHEM, *for He commanded and they were created. And He established them forever and ever, He issued a decree that will not change. Praise* HASHEM *from the earth, sea giants and all watery depths. Fire and hail, snow and vapor, stormy wind*

עֹשָׂה דְבָרוֹ. הֶהָרִים וְכָל גְּבָעוֹת, עֵץ פְּרִי וְכָל אֲרָזִים. הַחַיָּה וְכָל בְּהֵמָה, רֶמֶשׂ וְצִפּוֹר כָּנָף. מַלְכֵי אֶרֶץ וְכָל לְאֻמִּים, שָׂרִים וְכָל שֹׁפְטֵי אָרֶץ. בַּחוּרִים וְגַם בְּתוּלוֹת, זְקֵנִים עִם נְעָרִים. ❖ יְהַלְלוּ אֶת שֵׁם יהוה, כִּי נִשְׂגָּב שְׁמוֹ לְבַדּוֹ, הוֹדוֹ עַל אֶרֶץ וְשָׁמָיִם. וַיָּרֶם קֶרֶן לְעַמּוֹ, תְּהִלָּה לְכָל חֲסִידָיו, לִבְנֵי יִשְׂרָאֵל עַם קְרֹבוֹ, הַלְלוּיָהּ.

תהלים קמט

הַלְלוּיָהּ, שִׁירוּ לַיהוה שִׁיר חָדָשׁ, תְּהִלָּתוֹ בִּקְהַל חֲסִידִים. יִשְׂמַח יִשְׂרָאֵל בְּעֹשָׂיו, בְּנֵי צִיּוֹן יָגִילוּ בְמַלְכָּם. יְהַלְלוּ שְׁמוֹ בְמָחוֹל, בְּתֹף וְכִנּוֹר יְזַמְּרוּ לוֹ. כִּי רוֹצֶה יהוה בְּעַמּוֹ, יְפָאֵר עֲנָוִים בִּישׁוּעָה. יַעְלְזוּ חֲסִידִים בְּכָבוֹד, יְרַנְּנוּ עַל מִשְׁכְּבוֹתָם. רוֹמְמוֹת אֵל בִּגְרוֹנָם, וְחֶרֶב פִּיפִיּוֹת בְּיָדָם. לַעֲשׂוֹת נְקָמָה בַּגּוֹיִם, תּוֹכֵחוֹת בַּלְאֻמִּים. ❖ לֶאְסֹר מַלְכֵיהֶם בְּזִקִּים, וְנִכְבְּדֵיהֶם בְּכַבְלֵי בַרְזֶל. לַעֲשׂוֹת בָּהֶם מִשְׁפָּט כָּתוּב, הָדָר הוּא לְכָל חֲסִידָיו, הַלְלוּיָהּ.

תהלים קנ

הַלְלוּיָהּ, הַלְלוּ אֵל בְּקָדְשׁוֹ, הַלְלוּהוּ בִּרְקִיעַ עֻזּוֹ. הַלְלוּהוּ בִגְבוּרֹתָיו, הַלְלוּהוּ כְּרֹב גֻּדְלוֹ. הַלְלוּהוּ בְּתֵקַע שׁוֹפָר, הַלְלוּהוּ בְּנֵבֶל וְכִנּוֹר. הַלְלוּהוּ בְתֹף וּמָחוֹל, הַלְלוּהוּ בְּמִנִּים וְעֻגָב. הַלְלוּהוּ בְצִלְצְלֵי שָׁמַע, הַלְלוּהוּ בְּצִלְצְלֵי תְרוּעָה. ❖ כֹּל הַנְּשָׁמָה תְּהַלֵּל יָהּ, הַלְלוּיָהּ. כֹּל הַנְּשָׁמָה תְּהַלֵּל יָהּ, הַלְלוּיָהּ.

בָּרוּךְ יהוה לְעוֹלָם, אָמֵן וְאָמֵן.[1] בָּרוּךְ יהוה מִצִּיּוֹן, שֹׁכֵן יְרוּשָׁלָיִם, הַלְלוּיָהּ.[2] בָּרוּךְ יהוה אֱלֹהִים אֱלֹהֵי יִשְׂרָאֵל, עֹשֵׂה נִפְלָאוֹת לְבַדּוֹ. ❖ וּבָרוּךְ שֵׁם כְּבוֹדוֹ לְעוֹלָם, וְיִמָּלֵא כְבוֹדוֹ אֶת כָּל הָאָרֶץ, אָמֵן וְאָמֵן.[3]

One must stand from וַיְבָרֶךְ דָּוִיד, until after the phrase אַתָּה הוּא ה׳ הָאֱלֹהִים; however, there is a generally accepted custom to remain standing until after completing אָז יָשִׁיר (p. 112).

דברי הימים א כט:י-יג

וַיְבָרֶךְ דָּוִיד אֶת יהוה לְעֵינֵי כָּל הַקָּהָל, וַיֹּאמֶר דָּוִיד: בָּרוּךְ אַתָּה יהוה, אֱלֹהֵי יִשְׂרָאֵל אָבִינוּ, מֵעוֹלָם וְעַד עוֹלָם. לְךָ יהוה הַגְּדֻלָּה וְהַגְּבוּרָה וְהַתִּפְאֶרֶת וְהַנֵּצַח וְהַהוֹד, כִּי כֹל בַּשָּׁמַיִם וּבָאָרֶץ; לְךָ יהוה הַמַּמְלָכָה וְהַמִּתְנַשֵּׂא לְכֹל לְרֹאשׁ. וְהָעֹשֶׁר וְהַכָּבוֹד מִלְּפָנֶיךָ, וְאַתָּה מוֹשֵׁל בַּכֹּל, וּבְיָדְךָ כֹּחַ וּגְבוּרָה, וּבְיָדְךָ לְגַדֵּל וּלְחַזֵּק לַכֹּל. וְעַתָּה אֱלֹהֵינוּ מוֹדִים

It is customary to set aside something for charity at this point.

fulfilling His word. Mountains and all hills, fruitful trees and all cedars. Beasts and all cattle, crawling things and winged fowl. Kings of the earth and all governments, princes and all judges on earth. Young men and also maidens, old men together with youths. Chazzan– *Let them praise the Name of HASHEM, for His Name alone will have been exalted; His glory is above earth and heaven. And He will have exalted the pride of His nation, causing praise for all His devout ones, for the Children of Israel, His intimate people. Halleluyah!*

Psalm 149

הַלְלוּיָהּ *Halleluyah! Sing to HASHEM a new song, let His praise be in the congregation of the devout. Let Israel exult in its Maker, let the Children of Zion rejoice in their King. Let them praise His Name with dancing, with drums and harp let them make music to Him. For HASHEM favors His nation, He adorns the humble with salvation. Let the devout exult in glory, let them sing joyously upon their beds. The lofty praises of God are in their throats, and a double-edged sword is in their hand — to execute vengeance among the nations, rebukes among the governments.* Chazzan– *To bind their kings with chains, and their nobles with fetters of iron. To execute upon them written judgment — that will be the splendor of all His devout ones. Halleluyah!*

Psalm 150

הַלְלוּיָהּ *Halleluyah! Praise God in His Sanctuary; praise Him in the firmament of His power. Praise Him for His mighty acts; praise Him as befits His abundant greatness. Praise Him with the blast of the shofar; praise Him with lyre and harp. Praise Him with drum and dance; praise Him with organ and flute. Praise Him with clanging cymbals; praise Him with resonant trumpets.* Chazzan– *Let all souls praise God, Halleluyah! Let all souls praise God, Halleluyah!*

בָּרוּךְ *Blessed is HASHEM forever, Amen and Amen.*[1] *Blessed is HASHEM from Zion, Who dwells in Jerusalem, Halleluyah.*[2] *Blessed is HASHEM, God, the God of Israel, Who alone does wonders.* Chazzan– *Blessed is His glorious Name forever, and may all the earth be filled with His glory, Amen and Amen.*[3]

One must stand from here until after the phrase *'It is You, HASHEM the God'*; however, there is a generally accepted custom to remain standing until after completing the Song at the Sea (p. 112).

I Chronicles 29:10-13

וַיְבָרֶךְ *And David blessed HASHEM in the presence of the entire congregation; David said, 'Blessed are You, HASHEM, the God of Israel our forefather from This World to the World to Come. Yours, HASHEM, is the greatness, the strength, the splendor, the triumph, and the glory, even everything in heaven and earth; Yours, HASHEM, is the kingdom, and the sovereignty over every leader. Wealth and honor come from You and You rule everything — in Your hand is power and strength and it is in Your hand to make anyone great or strong. So now, our God, we thank*

It is customary to set aside something for charity at this point.

(1) *Psalms* 89:53. (2) 135:21. (3) 72:18-19.

אֲנַחְנוּ לָךְ, וּמְהַלְּלִים לְשֵׁם תִּפְאַרְתֶּךָ.

נחמיה ט:ו-יא

אַתָּה הוּא יהוה לְבַדֶּךָ, אַתָּה עָשִׂיתָ אֶת הַשָּׁמַיִם, שְׁמֵי הַשָּׁמַיִם וְכָל צְבָאָם, הָאָרֶץ וְכָל אֲשֶׁר עָלֶיהָ, הַיַּמִּים וְכָל אֲשֶׁר בָּהֶם, וְאַתָּה מְחַיֶּה אֶת כֻּלָּם, וּצְבָא הַשָּׁמַיִם לְךָ מִשְׁתַּחֲוִים. ❖ אַתָּה הוּא יהוה הָאֱלֹהִים אֲשֶׁר בָּחַרְתָּ בְּאַבְרָם, וְהוֹצֵאתוֹ מֵאוּר כַּשְׂדִּים, וְשַׂמְתָּ שְׁמוֹ אַבְרָהָם. וּמָצָאתָ אֶת לְבָבוֹ נֶאֱמָן לְפָנֶיךָ —

— וְכָרוֹת עִמּוֹ הַבְּרִית לָתֵת אֶת אֶרֶץ הַכְּנַעֲנִי הַחִתִּי הָאֱמֹרִי וְהַפְּרִזִּי וְהַיְבוּסִי וְהַגִּרְגָּשִׁי, לָתֵת לְזַרְעוֹ, וַתָּקֶם אֶת דְּבָרֶיךָ, כִּי צַדִּיק אָתָּה. וַתֵּרֶא אֶת עֳנִי אֲבֹתֵינוּ בְּמִצְרָיִם, וְאֶת זַעֲקָתָם שָׁמַעְתָּ עַל יַם סוּף. וַתִּתֵּן אֹתֹת וּמֹפְתִים בְּפַרְעֹה וּבְכָל עֲבָדָיו וּבְכָל עַם אַרְצוֹ, כִּי יָדַעְתָּ כִּי הֵזִידוּ עֲלֵיהֶם, וַתַּעַשׂ לְךָ שֵׁם כְּהַיּוֹם הַזֶּה. ❖ וְהַיָּם בָּקַעְתָּ לִפְנֵיהֶם, וַיַּעַבְרוּ בְתוֹךְ הַיָּם בַּיַּבָּשָׁה, וְאֶת רֹדְפֵיהֶם הִשְׁלַכְתָּ בִמְצוֹלֹת, כְּמוֹ אֶבֶן בְּמַיִם עַזִּים.

שירת הים

שמות יד:ל-טו:יט

וַיּוֹשַׁע יהוה בַּיּוֹם הַהוּא אֶת־יִשְׂרָאֵל מִיַּד מִצְרָיִם, וַיַּרְא יִשְׂרָאֵל אֶת־מִצְרַיִם מֵת עַל־שְׂפַת הַיָּם: ❖ וַיַּרְא יִשְׂרָאֵל אֶת־הַיָּד הַגְּדֹלָה אֲשֶׁר עָשָׂה יהוה בְּמִצְרַיִם, וַיִּירְאוּ הָעָם אֶת־יהוה, וַיַּאֲמִינוּ בַּיהוה וּבְמֹשֶׁה עַבְדּוֹ:

אָז יָשִׁיר־מֹשֶׁה וּבְנֵי יִשְׂרָאֵל אֶת־הַשִּׁירָה הַזֹּאת לַיהוה, וַיֹּאמְרוּ
לֵאמֹר, אָשִׁירָה לַיהוה כִּי־גָאֹה גָּאָה, סוּס
וְרֹכְבוֹ רָמָה בַיָּם: עָזִּי וְזִמְרָת יָהּ וַיְהִי־לִי
לִישׁוּעָה, זֶה אֵלִי וְאַנְוֵהוּ, אֱלֹהֵי
אָבִי וַאֲרֹמְמֶנְהוּ: יהוה אִישׁ מִלְחָמָה, יהוה
שְׁמוֹ: מַרְכְּבֹת פַּרְעֹה וְחֵילוֹ יָרָה בַיָּם, וּמִבְחַר
שָׁלִשָׁיו טֻבְּעוּ בְיַם־סוּף: תְּהֹמֹת יְכַסְיֻמוּ, יָרְדוּ בִמְצוֹלֹת כְּמוֹ־
אָבֶן: יְמִינְךָ יהוה נֶאְדָּרִי בַּכֹּחַ, יְמִינְךָ
יהוה תִּרְעַץ אוֹיֵב: וּבְרֹב גְּאוֹנְךָ תַּהֲרֹס
קָמֶיךָ, תְּשַׁלַּח חֲרֹנְךָ יֹאכְלֵמוֹ כַּקַּשׁ: וּבְרוּחַ
אַפֶּיךָ נֶעֶרְמוּ מַיִם, נִצְּבוּ כְמוֹ־נֵד

You and praise Your splendrous Name.'

Nehemiah 9:6-11

It is You alone, HASHEM, *You have made the heaven, the most exalted heaven and all their legions, the earth and everything upon it, the seas and everything in them and You give them all life; the heavenly legions bow to You.* Chazzan– *It is You,* HASHEM *the God, Who selected Abram, brought him out of Ur Kasdim and made his name Abraham. You found his heart faithful before You —*

— and You established the covenant with him to give the land of the Canaanite, Hittite, Emorite, Perizzite, Jebusite, and Girgashite, to give it to his offspring; and You affirmed Your word, for You are righteous. You observed the suffering of our forefathers in Egypt, and their outcry You heard at the Sea of Reeds. You imposed signs and wonders upon Pharaoh and upon all his servants, and upon all the people of his land. For You knew that they sinned flagrantly against them, and You brought Yourself renown as [clear as] this very day. Chazzan– *You split the Sea before them and they crossed in the midst of the Sea on dry land; but their pursuers You hurled into the depths, like a stone into turbulent waters.*

THE SONG AT THE SEA

Exodus 14:30-15:19

וַיּוֹשַׁע HASHEM *saved — on that day — Israel from the hand of Egypt, and Israel saw the Egyptians dead on the seashore.* Chazzan– *Israel saw the great hand that* HASHEM *inflicted upon Egypt and the people feared* HASHEM, *and they had faith in* HASHEM *and in Moses, His servant.*

Then Moses and the Children of Israel chose to sing this song to HASHEM, *and they said the following:*

I shall sing to HASHEM *for He is exalted above the arrogant, having hurled horse with its rider into the sea.*

God is my might and my praise, and He was a salvation for me. This is my God, and I will build Him a Sanctuary; the God of my father, and I will exalt Him.

HASHEM *is Master of war, through His Name* HASHEM.

Pharaoh's chariots and army He threw into the sea; and the pick of his officers were mired in the Sea of Reeds.

Deep waters covered them; they descended in the depths like stone.

Your right hand, HASHEM, *is adorned with strength; Your right hand,* HASHEM, *smashes the enemy.*

In Your abundant grandeur You shatter Your opponents; You dispatch Your wrath, it consumes them like straw.

At a blast from Your nostrils the waters were heaped up; straight as

נִזְּלִים, קָפְאוּ תְהֹמֹת בְּלֶב־יָם: אָמַר
אוֹיֵב, אֶרְדֹּף אַשִּׂיג אֲחַלֵּק שָׁלָל, תִּמְלָאֵמוֹ
נַפְשִׁי, אָרִיק חַרְבִּי, תּוֹרִישֵׁמוֹ יָדִי: נָשַׁפְתָּ
בְרוּחֲךָ כִּסָּמוֹ יָם, צָלְלוּ כַּעוֹפֶרֶת בְּמַיִם,
אַדִּירִים: מִי־כָמֹכָה בָּאֵלִם יהוה, מִי
כָּמֹכָה נֶאְדָּר בַּקֹּדֶשׁ, נוֹרָא תְהִלֹּת עֹשֵׂה
פֶלֶא: נָטִיתָ יְמִינְךָ, תִּבְלָעֵמוֹ אָרֶץ: נָחִיתָ
בְחַסְדְּךָ עַם־זוּ גָּאָלְתָּ, נֵהַלְתָּ בְעָזְּךָ אֶל־נְוֵה
קָדְשֶׁךָ: שָׁמְעוּ עַמִּים יִרְגָּזוּן, חִיל
אָחַז יֹשְׁבֵי פְּלָשֶׁת: אָז נִבְהֲלוּ אַלּוּפֵי
אֱדוֹם, אֵילֵי מוֹאָב יֹאחֲזֵמוֹ רָעַד, נָמֹגוּ
כֹּל יֹשְׁבֵי כְנָעַן: תִּפֹּל עֲלֵיהֶם אֵימָתָה
וָפַחַד, בִּגְדֹל זְרוֹעֲךָ יִדְּמוּ כָּאָבֶן, עַד־
יַעֲבֹר עַמְּךָ יהוה, עַד־יַעֲבֹר עַם־זוּ
קָנִיתָ: תְּבִאֵמוֹ וְתִטָּעֵמוֹ בְּהַר נַחֲלָתְךָ, מָכוֹן
לְשִׁבְתְּךָ פָּעַלְתָּ יהוה, מִקְּדָשׁ אֲדֹנָי כּוֹנְנוּ
יָדֶיךָ: יהוה | יִמְלֹךְ לְעֹלָם וָעֶד:

יהוה יִמְלֹךְ לְעֹלָם וָעֶד. (יהוה מַלְכוּתֵהּ קָאֵם, לְעָלַם וּלְעָלְמֵי עָלְמַיָּא.) כִּי בָא סוּס פַּרְעֹה בְּרִכְבּוֹ וּבְפָרָשָׁיו בַּיָּם, וַיָּשֶׁב יהוה עֲלֵהֶם אֶת מֵי הַיָּם, וּבְנֵי יִשְׂרָאֵל הָלְכוּ בַיַּבָּשָׁה בְּתוֹךְ הַיָּם. ❖ כִּי לַיהוה הַמְּלוּכָה, וּמֹשֵׁל בַּגּוֹיִם.[1] וְעָלוּ מוֹשִׁעִים בְּהַר צִיּוֹן, לִשְׁפֹּט אֶת הַר עֵשָׂו, וְהָיְתָה לַיהוה הַמְּלוּכָה.[2] וְהָיָה יהוה לְמֶלֶךְ עַל כָּל הָאָרֶץ, בַּיּוֹם הַהוּא יִהְיֶה יהוה אֶחָד וּשְׁמוֹ אֶחָד.[3] (וּבְתוֹרָתְךָ כָּתוּב לֵאמֹר: שְׁמַע יִשְׂרָאֵל יהוה אֱלֹהֵינוּ יהוה אֶחָד.[4])

Stand while reciting יִשְׁתַּבַּח . . . The fifteen expressions of praise — שִׁיר וּשְׁבָחָה . . . בְּרָכוֹת וְהוֹדָאוֹת — should be recited without pause, preferably in one breath.

יִשְׁתַּבַּח שִׁמְךָ לָעַד מַלְכֵּנוּ, הָאֵל הַמֶּלֶךְ הַגָּדוֹל וְהַקָּדוֹשׁ, בַּשָּׁמַיִם וּבָאָרֶץ. כִּי לְךָ נָאֶה יהוה אֱלֹהֵינוּ וֵאלֹהֵי אֲבוֹתֵינוּ, שִׁיר וּשְׁבָחָה, הַלֵּל וְזִמְרָה, עֹז וּמֶמְשָׁלָה, נֶצַח גְּדֻלָּה וּגְבוּרָה, תְּהִלָּה וְתִפְאֶרֶת, קְדֻשָּׁה וּמַלְכוּת, בְּרָכוֹת וְהוֹדָאוֹת מֵעַתָּה וְעַד עוֹלָם. ❖ בָּרוּךְ אַתָּה יהוה, אֵל מֶלֶךְ גָּדוֹל בַּתִּשְׁבָּחוֹת, אֵל הַהוֹדָאוֹת, אֲדוֹן הַנִּפְלָאוֹת, הַבּוֹחֵר בְּשִׁירֵי זִמְרָה, מֶלֶךְ אֵל חֵי הָעוֹלָמִים.

(.Cong. — אָמֵן)

a wall stood the running water, the deep waters congealed in the heart of the sea.

The enemy declared: 'I will pursue, I will overtake, I will divide plunder; I will satisfy my lust with them; I will unsheathe my sword, my hand will impoverish them.'

You blew with Your wind — the sea enshrouded them; the mighty ones sank like lead in the waters.

Who is like You among the heavenly powers, HASHEM! Who is like You, mighty in holiness, too awesome for praise, doing wonders!

You stretched out Your right hand — the earth swallowed them.

You guided in Your kindness this people that You redeemed; You led with Your might to Your holy abode.

Peoples heard — they were agitated; convulsive terror gripped the dwellers of Philistia.

Then the chieftains of Edom were confounded, trembling gripped the powers of Moab, all the dwellers of Canaan dissolved.

May fear and terror befall them, at the greatness of Your arm may they be still as stone; until Your people passes through, HASHEM, until this people You have acquired passes through.

You shall bring them and implant them on the mount of Your heritage, the foundation of Your dwelling-place, which You, HASHEM, have made: the Sanctuary, my Lord, that Your hands established.

HASHEM shall reign for all eternity.

HASHEM shall reign for all eternity. (HASHEM — His kingdom is established forever and ever.) When Pharaoh's cavalry came — with his chariots and horsemen — into the sea and HASHEM turned back the waters of the sea upon them, the Children of Israel walked on the dry bed amid the sea. Chazzan– *For the sovereignty is HASHEM's and He rules over nations.*[1] *The saviors will ascend Mount Zion to judge Esau's mountain, and the kingdom will be HASHEM's.*[2] *Then HASHEM will be King over all the world, on that day HASHEM will be One and His Name will be One.*[3] *(And in Your Torah it is written: Hear O Israel: HASHEM is our God, HASHEM, the One and Only.*[4])

Stand while reciting *'May Your Name be praised . . .'*
The fifteen expressions of praise — *'song and praise. . .blessings and thanksgivings'* —
should be recited without pause, preferably in one breath.

יִשְׁתַּבַּח *May Your Name be praised forever — our King, the God, the great and holy King — in heaven and on earth. Because for You is fitting — O HASHEM, our God, and the God of our forefathers — song and praise, lauding and hymns, power and dominion, triumph, greatness and strength, praise and splendor, holiness and sovereignty, blessings and thanksgivings from this time and forever.* Chazzan– *Blessed are You, HASHEM, God, King exalted through praises, God of thanksgivings, Master of wonders, Who chooses musical songs of praise — King, God, Life-giver of the world.* (Cong.– *Amen.)*

---

(1) *Psalms* 22:29. (2) *Ovadiah* 1:21. (3) *Zechariah* 14:9. (4) *Deuteronomy* 6:4.

The *chazzan* recites חֲצִי קַדִּישׁ.

יִתְגַּדַּל וְיִתְקַדַּשׁ שְׁמֵהּ רַבָּא. (Cong. – אָמֵן.) בְּעָלְמָא דִּי בְרָא כִרְעוּתֵהּ. וְיַמְלִיךְ מַלְכוּתֵהּ, בְּחַיֵּיכוֹן וּבְיוֹמֵיכוֹן וּבְחַיֵּי דְכָל בֵּית יִשְׂרָאֵל, בַּעֲגָלָא וּבִזְמַן קָרִיב. וְאִמְרוּ: אָמֵן.

(Cong. – אָמֵן. יְהֵא שְׁמֵהּ רַבָּא מְבָרַךְ לְעָלַם וּלְעָלְמֵי עָלְמַיָּא.)

יְהֵא שְׁמֵהּ רַבָּא מְבָרַךְ לְעָלַם וּלְעָלְמֵי עָלְמַיָּא.

יִתְבָּרַךְ וְיִשְׁתַּבַּח וְיִתְפָּאַר וְיִתְרוֹמַם וְיִתְנַשֵּׂא וְיִתְהַדָּר וְיִתְעַלֶּה וְיִתְהַלָּל שְׁמֵהּ דְּקֻדְשָׁא בְּרִיךְ הוּא (Cong. – בְּרִיךְ הוּא) – לְעֵלָּא מִן כָּל בִּרְכָתָא וְשִׁירָתָא תֻּשְׁבְּחָתָא וְנֶחֱמָתָא, דַּאֲמִירָן בְּעָלְמָא. וְאִמְרוּ: אָמֵן. (Cong. – אָמֵן.)

In some congregations the *chazzan* chants a melody during his recitation of בָּרְכוּ, so that the congregation can then recite יִתְבָּרַךְ.

Chazzan bows at בָּרְכוּ and straightens up at ה׳.

בָּרְכוּ אֶת יהוה הַמְּבֹרָךְ.

Congregation, followed by *chazzan*, responds, bowing at בָּרוּךְ and straightening up at ה׳.

בָּרוּךְ יהוה הַמְּבֹרָךְ לְעוֹלָם וָעֶד.

יִתְבָּרַךְ וְיִשְׁתַּבַּח וְיִתְפָּאַר וְיִתְרוֹמַם וְיִתְנַשֵּׂא שְׁמוֹ שֶׁל מֶלֶךְ מַלְכֵי הַמְּלָכִים, הַקָּדוֹשׁ בָּרוּךְ הוּא. שֶׁהוּא רִאשׁוֹן וְהוּא אַחֲרוֹן, וּמִבַּלְעָדָיו אֵין אֱלֹהִים.[1] סֹלּוּ, לָרֹכֵב בָּעֲרָבוֹת, בְּיָהּ שְׁמוֹ, וְעִלְזוּ לְפָנָיו.[2] וּשְׁמוֹ מְרוֹמָם עַל כָּל בְּרָכָה וּתְהִלָּה.[3] בָּרוּךְ שֵׁם כְּבוֹד מַלְכוּתוֹ לְעוֹלָם וָעֶד. יְהִי שֵׁם יהוה מְבֹרָךְ, מֵעַתָּה וְעַד עוֹלָם.[4]

ברכות קריאת שמע

It is preferable that one sit while reciting the following series of prayers — particularly the *Kedushah* verses, קָדוֹשׁ קָדוֹשׁ קָדוֹשׁ and בָּרוּךְ כְּבוֹד — until *Shemoneh Esrei*.

בָּרוּךְ אַתָּה יהוה אֱלֹהֵינוּ מֶלֶךְ הָעוֹלָם, יוֹצֵר אוֹר וּבוֹרֵא חֹשֶׁךְ, עֹשֶׂה שָׁלוֹם וּבוֹרֵא אֶת הַכֹּל.[5]

הַמֵּאִיר לָאָרֶץ וְלַדָּרִים עָלֶיהָ בְּרַחֲמִים, וּבְטוּבוֹ מְחַדֵּשׁ בְּכָל יוֹם תָּמִיד מַעֲשֵׂה בְרֵאשִׁית. מָה רַבּוּ מַעֲשֶׂיךָ יהוה, כֻּלָּם בְּחָכְמָה עָשִׂיתָ, מָלְאָה הָאָרֶץ קִנְיָנֶךָ.[6] הַמֶּלֶךְ הַמְּרוֹמָם לְבַדּוֹ מֵאָז, הַמְּשֻׁבָּח וְהַמְּפֹאָר וְהַמִּתְנַשֵּׂא מִימוֹת עוֹלָם. אֱלֹהֵי עוֹלָם, בְּרַחֲמֶיךָ הָרַבִּים רַחֵם עָלֵינוּ, אֲדוֹן עֻזֵּנוּ, צוּר מִשְׂגַּבֵּנוּ, מָגֵן יִשְׁעֵנוּ, מִשְׂגָּב בַּעֲדֵנוּ. אֵל בָּרוּךְ גְּדוֹל דֵּעָה, הֵכִין וּפָעַל זָהֳרֵי חַמָּה, טוֹב יָצַר כָּבוֹד לִשְׁמוֹ, מְאוֹרוֹת נָתַן סְבִיבוֹת עֻזּוֹ, פִּנּוֹת צְבָאָיו קְדוֹשִׁים רוֹמְמֵי שַׁדַּי, תָּמִיד מְסַפְּרִים כְּבוֹד אֵל

◆ Interruptions During the Blessings of the Shema

As a general rule, no אָמֵן or other prayer response may be recited between בָּרְכוּ and *Shemoneh Esrei*, but there are exceptions. The main exception is 'between chapters' [בֵּין הַפְּרָקִים] of the *Shema* Blessings — i.e., after יוֹצֵר הַמְּאוֹרוֹת and הַבּוֹחֵר ... בְּאַהֲבָה, and between the three chapters of *Shema*. At those points, אָמֵן (but not

The *chazzan* recites Half-*Kaddish*.

יִתְגַּדַּל *May His great Name grow exalted and sanctified* (Cong.– *Amen.*) *in the world that He created as He willed. May He give reign to His kingship in your lifetimes and in your days, and in the lifetimes of the entire Family of Israel, swiftly and soon. Now respond: Amen.*

(Cong.– *Amen. May His great Name be blessed forever and ever.*)

May His great Name be blessed forever and ever.

Blessed, praised, glorified, exalted, extolled, mighty, upraised, and lauded be the Name of the Holy One, Blessed is He (Cong.– *Blessed is He*) *— beyond any blessing and song, praise and consolation that are uttered in the world. Now respond: Amen.* (Cong.– *Amen.*)

In some congregations the *chazzan* chants a melody during his recitation of *Borchu*, so that the congregation can then recite *'Blessed, praised . . .'*

Chazzan bows at *'Bless'* and straightens up at *'HASHEM.'*

Bless HASHEM, the blessed One.

Congregation, followed by *chazzan*, responds, bowing at *'Blessed'* and straightening up at *'HASHEM.'*

Blessed is HASHEM, the blessed One, for all eternity.

Blessed, praised, glorified, exalted and upraised is the Name of the King Who rules over kings — the Holy One, Blessed is He. For He is the First and He is the Last and aside from Him there is no god.[1] *Extol Him — Who rides the highest heavens — with His Name, YAH, and exult before Him.*[2] *His Name is exalted beyond every blessing and praise.*[3] *Blessed is the Name of His glorious kingdom for all eternity. Blessed be the Name of HASHEM from this time and forever.*[4]

BLESSINGS OF THE SHEMA

It is preferable that one sit while reciting the following series of prayers — particularly the *Kedushah* verses, *'Holy, holy, holy . . .'* and *'Blessed is the glory . . .'* — until *Shemoneh Esrei*.

בָּרוּךְ *Blessed are You, HASHEM, our God, King of the universe, Who forms light and creates darkness, makes peace and creates all.*[5]

הַמֵּאִיר *He Who illuminates the earth and those who dwell upon it, with compassion; and in His goodness renews daily, perpetually, the work of Creation. How great are Your works, HASHEM, You make them all with wisdom, the world is full of Your possessions.*[6] *The King Who was exalted in solitude before Creation, Who is praised, glorified, and upraised since days of old. Eternal God, with Your abundant compassion be compassionate to us — O Master of our power, our rocklike stronghold, O Shield of our salvation, be a stronghold for us. The blessed God, Who is great in knowledge, prepared and worked on the rays of the sun; the Beneficent One fashioned honor for His Name, emplaced luminaries all around His power; the leaders of His legions, holy ones, exalt the Almighty, constantly relate the honor of God*

(1) Cf. *Isaiah* 44:6. (2) *Psalms* 68:5. (3) Cf. *Nehemiah* 9:5. (4) *Psalms* 113:2. (5) Cf. *Isaiah* 45:7. (6) *Psalms* 104:24.

בָּרוּךְ הוּא וּבָרוּךְ שְׁמוֹ) may be responded to any blessing. Some responses, however, are so important that they are permitted at any point in the *Shema* blessings. They are: (a) In Kaddish, אָמֵן יְהֵא שְׁמֵהּ רַבָּא . . . עָלְמַיָּא and the אָמֵן after דַּאֲמִירָן בְּעָלְמָא; (b) the response to בָּרְכוּ (even of one called to the Torah); and (c) during the *chazzan's* repetition of *Shemoneh Esrei* — 1) in *Kedushah*, the verses . . . קָדוֹשׁ קָדוֹשׁ and בָּרוּךְ כְּבוֹד ה׳ מִמְּקוֹמוֹ; 2) the אָמֵן after הָאֵל הַקָּדוֹשׁ; 3) the three words מוֹדִים אֲנַחְנוּ לָךְ.

During the recital of the two verses שְׁמַע and בָּרוּךְ שֵׁם, absolutely no interruptions are permitted.

וּקְדֻשָּׁתוֹ. תִּתְבָּרַךְ יהוה אֱלֹהֵינוּ עַל שֶׁבַח מַעֲשֵׂה יָדֶיךָ, וְעַל מְאוֹרֵי אוֹר שֶׁעָשִׂיתָ, יְפָאֲרוּךָ, סֶּלָה.

תִּתְבָּרַךְ צוּרֵנוּ מַלְכֵּנוּ וְגֹאֲלֵנוּ, בּוֹרֵא קְדוֹשִׁים. יִשְׁתַּבַּח שִׁמְךָ לָעַד מַלְכֵּנוּ, יוֹצֵר מְשָׁרְתִים, וַאֲשֶׁר מְשָׁרְתָיו כֻּלָּם עוֹמְדִים בְּרוּם עוֹלָם, וּמַשְׁמִיעִים בְּיִרְאָה יַחַד בְּקוֹל דִּבְרֵי אֱלֹהִים חַיִּים וּמֶלֶךְ עוֹלָם.[1] כֻּלָּם אֲהוּבִים, כֻּלָּם בְּרוּרִים, כֻּלָּם גִּבּוֹרִים, וְכֻלָּם עֹשִׂים בְּאֵימָה וּבְיִרְאָה רְצוֹן קוֹנָם. ❖ וְכֻלָּם פּוֹתְחִים אֶת פִּיהֶם בִּקְדֻשָּׁה וּבְטָהֳרָה, בְּשִׁירָה וּבְזִמְרָה, וּמְבָרְכִים וּמְשַׁבְּחִים וּמְפָאֲרִים וּמַעֲרִיצִים וּמַקְדִּישִׁים וּמַמְלִיכִים —

אֶת שֵׁם הָאֵל הַמֶּלֶךְ הַגָּדוֹל הַגִּבּוֹר וְהַנּוֹרָא קָדוֹשׁ הוּא.[2] ❖ וְכֻלָּם מְקַבְּלִים עֲלֵיהֶם עֹל מַלְכוּת שָׁמַיִם זֶה מִזֶּה, וְנוֹתְנִים רְשׁוּת זֶה לָזֶה, לְהַקְדִּישׁ לְיוֹצְרָם, בְּנַחַת רוּחַ בְּשָׂפָה בְרוּרָה וּבִנְעִימָה. קְדֻשָּׁה כֻּלָּם כְּאֶחָד עוֹנִים וְאוֹמְרִים בְּיִרְאָה:

Congregation recites aloud:

קָדוֹשׁ קָדוֹשׁ קָדוֹשׁ יהוה צְבָאוֹת, מְלֹא כָל הָאָרֶץ כְּבוֹדוֹ.[3]

וְהָאוֹפַנִּים וְחַיּוֹת הַקֹּדֶשׁ בְּרַעַשׁ גָּדוֹל מִתְנַשְּׂאִים לְעֻמַּת שְׂרָפִים. לְעֻמָּתָם מְשַׁבְּחִים וְאוֹמְרִים:

Congregation recites aloud:

בָּרוּךְ כְּבוֹד יהוה מִמְּקוֹמוֹ.[4]

לְאֵל בָּרוּךְ נְעִימוֹת יִתֵּנוּ. לְמֶלֶךְ אֵל חַי וְקַיָּם, זְמִרוֹת יֹאמֵרוּ, וְתִשְׁבָּחוֹת יַשְׁמִיעוּ. כִּי הוּא לְבַדּוֹ פּוֹעֵל גְּבוּרוֹת, עֹשֶׂה חֲדָשׁוֹת, בַּעַל מִלְחָמוֹת, זוֹרֵעַ צְדָקוֹת, מַצְמִיחַ יְשׁוּעוֹת, בּוֹרֵא רְפוּאוֹת, נוֹרָא תְהִלּוֹת, אֲדוֹן הַנִּפְלָאוֹת. הַמְחַדֵּשׁ בְּטוּבוֹ בְּכָל יוֹם תָּמִיד מַעֲשֵׂה בְרֵאשִׁית. כָּאָמוּר: לְעֹשֵׂה אוֹרִים גְּדֹלִים, כִּי לְעוֹלָם חַסְדּוֹ.[5] ❖ אוֹר חָדָשׁ עַל צִיּוֹן תָּאִיר, וְנִזְכֶּה כֻלָּנוּ מְהֵרָה לְאוֹרוֹ. בָּרוּךְ אַתָּה יהוה, יוֹצֵר הַמְּאוֹרוֹת. (Cong. – אָמֵן.)

אַהֲבָה רַבָּה אֲהַבְתָּנוּ יהוה אֱלֹהֵינוּ, חֶמְלָה גְדוֹלָה וִיתֵרָה חָמַלְתָּ עָלֵינוּ. אָבִינוּ מַלְכֵּנוּ, בַּעֲבוּר אֲבוֹתֵינוּ שֶׁבָּטְחוּ בְךָ, וַתְּלַמְּדֵם חֻקֵּי חַיִּים, כֵּן תְּחָנֵּנוּ וּתְלַמְּדֵנוּ. אָבִינוּ הָאָב הָרַחֲמָן הַמְרַחֵם, רַחֵם עָלֵינוּ, וְתֵן בְּלִבֵּנוּ לְהָבִין וּלְהַשְׂכִּיל, לִשְׁמֹעַ לִלְמוֹד

and His sanctity. May You be blessed, HASHEM, our God, beyond the praises of Your handiwork and beyond the bright luminaries that You have made — may they glorify You — Selah!

תִּתְבָּרַךְ *May You be blessed, our Rock, our King and our Redeemer, Creator of holy ones; may Your Name be praised forever, our King, O Fashioner of ministering angels; all of Whose ministering angels stand at the summit of the universe and proclaim — with awe, together, loudly — the words of the living God and King of the universe.*[1] *They are all beloved; they are all flawless; they are all mighty; they all do the will of their Maker with dread and reverence.* Chazzan– *And they all open their mouth in holiness and purity, in song and hymn — and bless, praise, glorify, revere, sanctify and declare the kingship of —*

אֶת שֵׁם *The Name of God, the great, mighty, and awesome King; holy is He.*[2] Chazzan– *Then they all accept upon themselves the yoke of heavenly sovereignty from one another, and grant permission to one another to sanctify the One Who formed them, with tranquillity, with clear articulation, and with sweetness. All of them as one proclaim His holiness and say with awe:*

Congregation recites aloud:

'Holy, holy, holy is HASHEM, Master of Legions, the whole world is filled with His glory.'[3]

וְהָאוֹפַנִּים *Then the Ofanim and the holy Chayos, with great noise, raise themselves towards the Seraphim. Facing them they give praise saying:*

Congregation recites aloud:

'Blessed is the glory of HASHEM from His place.'[4]

לְאֵל *To the blessed God they shall offer sweet melodies; to the King, the living and enduring God, they shall sing hymns and proclaim praises. For He alone effects mighty deeds, makes new things, is Master of wars, sows kindnesses, makes salvations flourish, creates cures, is too awesome for praise, is Lord of wonders. In His goodness He renews daily, perpetually, the work of creation. As it is said: '[Give thanks] to Him Who makes the great luminaries, for His kindness endures forever.'*[5] Chazzan– *May You shine a new light on Zion, and may we all speedily merit its light. Blessed are You, HASHEM, Who fashions the luminaries.* (Cong.– *Amen.)*

אַהֲבָה *With an abundant love have You loved us, HASHEM, our God; with exceedingly great pity have You pitied us. Our Father, our King, for the sake of our forefathers who trusted in You and whom You taught the decrees of life, may You be equally gracious to us and teach us. Our Father, the merciful Father, Who acts mercifully, have mercy upon us, instill in our hearts to understand and elucidate, to listen, learn*

(1) Cf. *Jeremiah* 10:10. (2) Cf. *Deuteronomy* 10:17; *Psalms* 99:3.
(3) *Isaiah* 6:3. (4) *Ezekiel* 3:12. (5) *Psalms* 136:7.

וּלְלַמֵּד, לִשְׁמֹר וְלַעֲשׂוֹת וּלְקַיֵּם אֶת כָּל דִּבְרֵי תַלְמוּד תּוֹרָתֶךָ בְּאַהֲבָה. וְהָאֵר עֵינֵינוּ בְּתוֹרָתֶךָ, וְדַבֵּק לִבֵּנוּ בְּמִצְוֹתֶיךָ, וְיַחֵד לְבָבֵנוּ לְאַהֲבָה וּלְיִרְאָה אֶת שְׁמֶךָ,[1] וְלֹא נֵבוֹשׁ לְעוֹלָם וָעֶד. כִּי בְשֵׁם קָדְשְׁךָ הַגָּדוֹל וְהַנּוֹרָא בָּטָחְנוּ, נָגִילָה וְנִשְׂמְחָה בִּישׁוּעָתֶךָ. וַהֲבִיאֵנוּ לְשָׁלוֹם מֵאַרְבַּע כַּנְפוֹת הָאָרֶץ, וְתוֹלִיכֵנוּ קוֹמְמִיּוּת לְאַרְצֵנוּ. כִּי אֵל פּוֹעֵל יְשׁוּעוֹת אָתָּה, וּבָנוּ בָחַרְתָּ מִכָּל עַם וְלָשׁוֹן. ❖ וְקֵרַבְתָּנוּ לְשִׁמְךָ הַגָּדוֹל סֶלָה בֶּאֱמֶת, לְהוֹדוֹת לְךָ וּלְיַחֶדְךָ בְּאַהֲבָה. בָּרוּךְ אַתָּה יהוה, הַבּוֹחֵר בְּעַמּוֹ יִשְׂרָאֵל בְּאַהֲבָה. (Cong. – אָמֵן.)

The *tzitzis* are not gathered at this point and are not kissed during the last paragraph of the *Shema*.

שמע

Immediately before its recitation concentrate on fulfilling the positive commandment of reciting the *Shema* twice daily. It is important to enunciate each word clearly and not to run words together. For this reason, vertical lines have been placed between two words that are prone to be slurred into one and are not separated by a comma or a hyphen. See *Laws* §95-109.

When praying without a *minyan,* begin with the following three-word formula:

אֵל מֶלֶךְ נֶאֱמָן.

Recite the first verse aloud, with the right hand covering the eyes, and concentrate intently upon accepting God's absolute sovereignty.

שְׁמַע | יִשְׂרָאֵל, יהוה | אֱלֹהֵינוּ, יהוה | אֶחָד:[2]

In an undertone – בָּרוּךְ שֵׁם כְּבוֹד מַלְכוּתוֹ לְעוֹלָם וָעֶד.

While reciting the first paragraph (דברים ו:ה-ט), concentrate on accepting the commandment to love God.

וְאָהַבְתָּ אֵת | יהוה | אֱלֹהֶיךָ, בְּכָל־לְבָבְךָ, וּבְכָל־נַפְשְׁךָ, וּבְכָל־מְאֹדֶךָ: וְהָיוּ הַדְּבָרִים הָאֵלֶּה, אֲשֶׁר | אָנֹכִי מְצַוְּךָ הַיּוֹם, עַל־לְבָבֶךָ: וְשִׁנַּנְתָּם לְבָנֶיךָ, וְדִבַּרְתָּ בָּם, בְּשִׁבְתְּךָ בְּבֵיתֶךָ, וּבְלֶכְתְּךָ בַדֶּרֶךְ, וּבְשָׁכְבְּךָ וּבְקוּמֶךָ: וּקְשַׁרְתָּם לְאוֹת | עַל־יָדֶךָ, וְהָיוּ לְטֹטָפֹת בֵּין | עֵינֶיךָ: וּכְתַבְתָּם | עַל־מְזֻזוֹת בֵּיתֶךָ, וּבִשְׁעָרֶיךָ:

While reciting the second paragraph (דברים יא:יג-כא), concentrate on accepting all the commandments and the concept of reward and punishment.

וְהָיָה, אִם־שָׁמֹעַ תִּשְׁמְעוּ אֶל־מִצְוֹתַי, אֲשֶׁר | אָנֹכִי מְצַוֶּה | אֶתְכֶם הַיּוֹם, לְאַהֲבָה אֶת־יהוה | אֱלֹהֵיכֶם וּלְעָבְדוֹ, בְּכָל־לְבַבְכֶם, וּבְכָל־נַפְשְׁכֶם: וְנָתַתִּי מְטַר־אַרְצְכֶם בְּעִתּוֹ, יוֹרֶה וּמַלְקוֹשׁ, וְאָסַפְתָּ דְגָנֶךָ וְתִירֹשְׁךָ וְיִצְהָרֶךָ: וְנָתַתִּי | עֵשֶׂב | בְּשָׂדְךָ לִבְהֶמְתֶּךָ, וְאָכַלְתָּ וְשָׂבָעְתָּ: הִשָּׁמְרוּ לָכֶם, פֶּן־יִפְתֶּה לְבַבְכֶם, וְסַרְתֶּם וַעֲבַדְתֶּם | אֱלֹהִים | אֲחֵרִים, וְהִשְׁתַּחֲוִיתֶם לָהֶם: וְחָרָה | אַף־יהוה בָּכֶם, וְעָצַר | אֶת־הַשָּׁמַיִם, וְלֹא־יִהְיֶה מָטָר, וְהָאֲדָמָה לֹא

teach, safeguard, perform, and fulfill all the words of Your Torah's teaching with love. Enlighten our eyes in Your Torah, attach our hearts to Your commandments, and unify our hearts to love and fear Your Name,[1] and may we not feel inner shame for all eternity. Because we have trusted in Your great and awesome holy Name, may we exult and rejoice in Your salvation. Bring us in peacefulness from the four corners of the earth and lead us with upright pride to our land. For You effect salvations, O God; You have chosen us from among every people and tongue. Chazzan– *And You have brought us close to Your great Name forever in truth, to offer praiseful thanks to You, and proclaim Your Oneness with love. Blessed are You, HASHEM, Who chooses His people Israel with love.* (Cong.– *Amen.*)

The *tzitzis* are not gathered at this point and are not kissed during the last paragraph of the *Shema.*

THE SHEMA

Immediately before its recitation concentrate on fulfilling the positive commandment of reciting the *Shema* twice daily. It is important to enunciate each word clearly and not to run words together. See *Laws* §95-109.

When praying without a *minyan,* begin with the following three-word formula:
God, trustworthy King.

Recite the first verse aloud, with the right hand covering the eyes, and concentrate intently upon accepting God's absolute sovereignty.

Hear, O Israel: HASHEM is our God, HASHEM, the One and Only.[2]

In an undertone– *Blessed is the Name of His glorious kingdom for all eternity.*

While reciting the first paragraph (*Deuteronomy* 6:5-9), concentrate on accepting the commandment to love God.

וְאָהַבְתָּ *You shall love HASHEM, your God, with all your heart, with all your soul and with all your resources. Let these matters that I command you today be upon your heart. Teach them thoroughly to your children and speak of them while you sit in your home, while you walk on the way, when you retire and when you arise. Bind them as a sign upon your arm and let them be tefillin between your eyes. And write them on the doorposts of your house and upon your gates.*

While reciting the second paragraph (*Deuteronomy* 11:13-21), concentrate on accepting all the commandments and the concept of reward and punishment.

וְהָיָה *And it will come to pass that if you continually hearken to My commandments that I command you today, to love HASHEM, your God, and to serve Him, with all your heart and with all your soul — then I will provide rain for your land in its proper time, the early and late rains, that you may gather in your grain, your wine, and your oil. I will provide grass in your field for your cattle and you will eat and be satisfied. Beware lest your heart be seduced and you turn astray and serve gods of others and bow to them. Then the wrath of HASHEM will blaze against you. He will restrain the heaven so there will be no rain and the ground will not*

(1) Cf. *Psalms* 86:11. (2) *Deuteronomy* 6:4.

תִּתֵּ֥ן אֶת־יְבוּלָ֑הּ, וַאֲבַדְתֶּ֣ם ׀ מְהֵרָ֗ה מֵעַל֙ הָאָ֣רֶץ הַטֹּבָ֔ה ׀ אֲשֶׁ֥ר ׀ יהוָ֖ה נֹתֵ֥ן לָכֶֽם: וְשַׂמְתֶּם֙ ׀ אֶת־דְּבָרַ֣י ׀ אֵ֔לֶּה, עַל־לְבַבְכֶ֖ם וְעַל־נַפְשְׁכֶ֑ם, וּקְשַׁרְתֶּ֨ם ׀ אֹתָ֤ם לְאוֹת֙ ׀ עַל־יֶדְכֶ֔ם, וְהָי֥וּ לְטוֹטָפֹ֖ת בֵּ֥ין ׀ עֵינֵיכֶֽם: וְלִמַּדְתֶּ֥ם ׀ אֹתָ֛ם ׀ אֶת־בְּנֵיכֶ֖ם, לְדַבֵּ֣ר בָּ֑ם, בְּשִׁבְתְּךָ֤ בְּבֵיתֶ֨ךָ֙, וּבְלֶכְתְּךָ֣ בַדֶּ֔רֶךְ, וּֽבְשָׁכְבְּךָ֖ וּבְקוּמֶֽךָ: וּכְתַבְתָּ֛ם ׀ עַל־מְזוּז֥וֹת בֵּיתֶ֖ךָ, וּבִשְׁעָרֶֽיךָ: לְמַ֨עַן ׀ יִרְבּ֤וּ ׀ יְמֵיכֶם֙ וִימֵ֣י בְנֵיכֶ֔ם, עַ֚ל הָאֲדָמָ֔ה ׀ אֲשֶׁ֨ר נִשְׁבַּ֧ע ׀ יהוָ֛ה לַאֲבֹתֵיכֶ֖ם לָתֵ֣ת לָהֶ֑ם, כִּימֵ֥י הַשָּׁמַ֖יִם ׀ עַל־הָאָֽרֶץ:

במדבר טו:לז-מא

The *tzitzis* are not kissed.

וַיֹּ֣אמֶר ׀ יהוָ֖ה ׀ אֶל־מֹשֶׁ֥ה לֵּאמֹֽר: דַּבֵּ֞ר ׀ אֶל־בְּנֵ֤י ׀ יִשְׂרָאֵל֙, וְאָמַרְתָּ֣ אֲלֵהֶ֔ם, וְעָשׂ֨וּ לָהֶ֥ם צִיצִ֛ת, עַל־כַּנְפֵ֥י בִגְדֵיהֶ֖ם לְדֹרֹתָ֑ם, וְנָ֥תְנ֛וּ ׀ עַל־צִיצִ֥ת הַכָּנָ֖ף, פְּתִ֥יל תְּכֵֽלֶת: וְהָיָ֣ה לָכֶם֮ לְצִיצִת֒, וּרְאִיתֶ֣ם ׀ אֹת֗וֹ, וּזְכַרְתֶּם֙ ׀ אֶת־כָּל־מִצְוֺ֣ת ׀ יהוָ֔ה, וַעֲשִׂיתֶ֖ם ׀ אֹתָ֑ם, וְלֹֽא־תָת֜וּרוּ ׀ אַחֲרֵ֤י לְבַבְכֶם֙ וְאַחֲרֵ֣י ׀ עֵינֵיכֶ֔ם, אֲשֶׁר־אַתֶּ֥ם זֹנִ֖ים ׀ אַחֲרֵיהֶֽם: לְמַ֣עַן תִּזְכְּר֔וּ, וַעֲשִׂיתֶ֖ם ׀ אֶת־כָּל־מִצְוֺתָ֑י, וִהְיִיתֶ֥ם קְדֹשִׁ֖ים לֵאלֹהֵיכֶֽם: אֲנִ֞י יהוָ֣ה ׀ אֱלֹהֵיכֶ֗ם, אֲשֶׁ֨ר הוֹצֵ֤אתִי ׀ אֶתְכֶם֙ ׀ מֵאֶ֣רֶץ מִצְרַ֔יִם, לִהְי֥וֹת לָכֶ֖ם לֵאלֹהִ֑ים, אֲנִ֖י ׀ יהוָ֥ה ׀ אֱלֹהֵיכֶֽם: אֱמֶת —

Concentrate on fulfilling the commandment of remembering the Exodus from Egypt.

Although the word אֱמֶת belongs to the next paragraph, it is appended to the conclusion of the previous one.

—*Chazzan* repeats **יהוה אֱלֹהֵיכֶם אֱמֶת.**

וְיַצִּיב וְנָכוֹן וְקַיָּם וְיָשָׁר וְנֶאֱמָן וְאָהוּב וְחָבִיב וְנֶחְמָד וְנָעִים וְנוֹרָא וְאַדִּיר וּמְתֻקָּן וּמְקֻבָּל וְטוֹב וְיָפֶה הַדָּבָר הַזֶּה עָלֵינוּ לְעוֹלָם וָעֶד. אֱמֶת אֱלֹהֵי עוֹלָם מַלְכֵּנוּ צוּר יַעֲקֹב, מָגֵן יִשְׁעֵנוּ, לְדֹר וָדֹר הוּא קַיָּם, וּשְׁמוֹ קַיָּם, וְכִסְאוֹ נָכוֹן, וּמַלְכוּתוֹ וֶאֱמוּנָתוֹ לָעַד קַיֶּמֶת. וּדְבָרָיו חָיִים וְקַיָּמִים, נֶאֱמָנִים וְנֶחֱמָדִים לָעַד וּלְעוֹלְמֵי עוֹלָמִים. ❖ עַל אֲבוֹתֵינוּ וְעָלֵינוּ, עַל בָּנֵינוּ וְעַל דּוֹרוֹתֵינוּ, וְעַל כָּל דּוֹרוֹת זֶרַע יִשְׂרָאֵל עֲבָדֶיךָ.

עַל הָרִאשׁוֹנִים וְעַל הָאַחֲרוֹנִים, דָּבָר טוֹב וְקַיָּם לְעוֹלָם וָעֶד, אֱמֶת וֶאֱמוּנָה חֹק וְלֹא יַעֲבֹר. אֱמֶת שָׁאַתָּה הוּא יהוה אֱלֹהֵינוּ וֵאלֹהֵי אֲבוֹתֵינוּ, ❖ מַלְכֵּנוּ מֶלֶךְ אֲבוֹתֵינוּ, גֹּאֲלֵנוּ גֹּאֵל אֲבוֹתֵינוּ, יוֹצְרֵנוּ צוּר יְשׁוּעָתֵנוּ, פּוֹדֵנוּ וּמַצִּילֵנוּ מֵעוֹלָם שְׁמֶךָ, אֵין אֱלֹהִים זוּלָתֶךָ.

yield its produce. And you will swiftly be banished from the goodly land which H*ASHEM gives you. Place these words of Mine upon your heart and upon your soul; bind them for a sign upon your arm and let them be tefillin between your eyes. Teach them to your children, to discuss them, while you sit in your home, while you walk on the way, when you retire and when you arise. And write them on the doorposts of your house and upon your gates. In order to prolong your days and the days of your children upon the ground that* H*ASHEM has sworn to your ancestors to give them, like the days of the heaven on the earth.*

Numbers 15:37-41

The *tzitzis* are not kissed.

וַיֹּאמֶר *And* H*ASHEM said to Moses saying: Speak to the Children of Israel and say to them that they are to make themselves tzitzis on the corners of their garments, throughout their generations. And they are to place upon the tzitzis of each corner a thread of techeiles. And it shall constitute tzitzis for you, that you may see it and remember all the commandments of* H*ASHEM and perform them; and not explore after your heart and after your eyes after which you stray. So that you may remember and perform all My commandments; and be holy to your God. I am* H*ASHEM, your God, Who has removed you from the land of Egypt to be a God to You; I am* H*ASHEM your God — it is true —*

Concentrate on fulfilling the commandment of remembering the Exodus from Egypt.

Although the word אֱמֶת, *'it is true,'* belongs to the next paragraph, it is appended to the conclusion of the previous one.

Chazzan repeats: **HASHEM, your God, is true.**

וְיַצִּיב *And certain, established and enduring, fair and faithful, beloved and cherished, delightful and pleasant, awesome and powerful, correct and accepted, good and beautiful is this affirmation to us forever and ever. True — the God of the universe is our King; the Rock of Jacob is the Shield of our salvation. From generation to generation He endures and His Name endures and His throne is well established; His sovereignty and faithfulness endure forever. His words are living and enduring, faithful and delightful forever and to all eternity;* Chazzan– *for our forefathers and for us, for our children and for our generations, and for all the generations of Your servant Israel's offspring.*

עַל *Upon the earlier and upon the later generations, this affirmation is good and enduring forever. True and faithful, it is an unbreachable decree. It is true that You are* H*ASHEM, our God and the God of our forefathers,* Chazzan– *our King and the King of our forefathers, our Redeemer, the Redeemer of our forefathers; our Molder, the Rock of our salvation; our Liberator and our Rescuer — this has ever been Your Name. There is no God but You.*

עֶזְרַת אֲבוֹתֵינוּ אַתָּה הוּא מֵעוֹלָם, מָגֵן וּמוֹשִׁיעַ לִבְנֵיהֶם אַחֲרֵיהֶם בְּכָל דּוֹר וָדוֹר. בְּרוּם עוֹלָם מוֹשָׁבֶךָ, וּמִשְׁפָּטֶיךָ וְצִדְקָתְךָ עַד אַפְסֵי אָרֶץ. אַשְׁרֵי אִישׁ שֶׁיִּשְׁמַע לְמִצְוֹתֶיךָ, וְתוֹרָתְךָ וּדְבָרְךָ יָשִׂים עַל לִבּוֹ. אֱמֶת אַתָּה הוּא אָדוֹן לְעַמֶּךָ וּמֶלֶךְ גִּבּוֹר לָרִיב רִיבָם. אֱמֶת אַתָּה הוּא רִאשׁוֹן וְאַתָּה הוּא אַחֲרוֹן, וּמִבַּלְעָדֶיךָ אֵין לָנוּ מֶלֶךְ[1] גּוֹאֵל וּמוֹשִׁיעַ. מִמִּצְרַיִם גְּאַלְתָּנוּ יהוה אֱלֹהֵינוּ, וּמִבֵּית עֲבָדִים פְּדִיתָנוּ. כָּל בְּכוֹרֵיהֶם הָרָגְתָּ, וּבְכוֹרְךָ גָּאָלְתָּ, וְיַם סוּף בָּקַעְתָּ, וְזֵדִים טִבַּעְתָּ, וִידִידִים הֶעֱבַרְתָּ, וַיְכַסּוּ מַיִם צָרֵיהֶם, אֶחָד מֵהֶם לֹא נוֹתָר.[2] עַל זֹאת שִׁבְּחוּ אֲהוּבִים וְרוֹמְמוּ אֵל, וְנָתְנוּ יְדִידִים זְמִרוֹת שִׁירוֹת וְתִשְׁבָּחוֹת, בְּרָכוֹת וְהוֹדָאוֹת, לְמֶלֶךְ אֵל חַי וְקַיָּם, רָם וְנִשָּׂא, גָּדוֹל וְנוֹרָא, מַשְׁפִּיל גֵּאִים, וּמַגְבִּיהַּ שְׁפָלִים, מוֹצִיא אֲסִירִים, וּפוֹדֶה עֲנָוִים, וְעוֹזֵר דַּלִּים, וְעוֹנֶה לְעַמּוֹ בְּעֵת שַׁוְּעָם אֵלָיו.

Rise for *Shemoneh Esrei*. Some take three steps backward here; others do so before צוּר יִשְׂרָאֵל.

❖ תְּהִלּוֹת לְאֵל עֶלְיוֹן, בָּרוּךְ הוּא וּמְבֹרָךְ. מֹשֶׁה וּבְנֵי יִשְׂרָאֵל לְךָ עָנוּ שִׁירָה בְּשִׂמְחָה רַבָּה וְאָמְרוּ כֻלָּם:

מִי כָמֹכָה בָּאֵלִם יהוה, מִי כָּמֹכָה נֶאְדָּר בַּקֹּדֶשׁ, נוֹרָא תְהִלֹּת עֹשֵׂה פֶלֶא.[3] ❖ שִׁירָה חֲדָשָׁה שִׁבְּחוּ גְאוּלִים לְשִׁמְךָ עַל שְׂפַת הַיָּם, יַחַד כֻּלָּם הוֹדוּ וְהִמְלִיכוּ וְאָמְרוּ:

יהוה יִמְלֹךְ לְעֹלָם וָעֶד.[4]

It is forbidden to interrupt or pause between גָּאַל יִשְׂרָאֵל and *Shemoneh Esrei*, even for *Kaddish*, *Kedushah* or *Borchu*.

❖ **צוּר יִשְׂרָאֵל,** קוּמָה בְּעֶזְרַת יִשְׂרָאֵל, וּפְדֵה כִנְאֻמֶךָ יְהוּדָה וְיִשְׂרָאֵל. גֹּאֲלֵנוּ יהוה צְבָאוֹת שְׁמוֹ, קְדוֹשׁ יִשְׂרָאֵל.[5] בָּרוּךְ אַתָּה יהוה, גָּאַל יִשְׂרָאֵל.

שמונה עשרה – עמידה

Take three steps backward, then three steps forward. Remain standing with feet together while reciting *Shemoneh Esrei*. Recite it with quiet devotion and without interruption, verbal or otherwise. Although it should not be audible to others, one must pray loudly enough to hear himself.

אֲדֹנָי שְׂפָתַי תִּפְתָּח, וּפִי יַגִּיד תְּהִלָּתֶךָ.[6]

אבות

Bend the knees at בָּרוּךְ; bow at אַתָּה; straighten up at ה׳.

בָּרוּךְ אַתָּה יהוה אֱלֹהֵינוּ וֵאלֹהֵי אֲבוֹתֵינוּ, אֱלֹהֵי אַבְרָהָם, אֱלֹהֵי יִצְחָק, וֵאלֹהֵי יַעֲקֹב, הָאֵל הַגָּדוֹל הַגִּבּוֹר

עֶזְרַת *The Helper of our forefathers are You alone, forever, Shield and Savior for their children after them in every generation. At the zenith of the universe is Your dwelling, and Your justice and Your righteousness extend to the ends of the earth. Praiseworthy is the person who obeys Your commandments and takes to his heart Your teaching and Your word. True — You are the Master for Your people and a mighty King to take up their grievance. True — You are the First and You are the Last, and other than You we have no king,*[1] *redeemer, or savior. From Egypt You redeemed us, HASHEM, our God, and from the house of slavery You liberated us. All their firstborn You slew, but Your firstborn You redeemed; the Sea of Reeds You split; the wanton sinners You drowned; the dear ones You brought across; and the water covered their foes — not one of them was left.*[2] *For this, the beloved praised and exalted God; the dear ones offered hymns, songs, praises, blessings, and thanksgivings to the King, the living and enduring God — exalted and uplifted, great and awesome, Who humbles the haughty and lifts the lowly; withdraws the captive, liberates the humble, and helps the poor; Who responds to His people upon their outcry to Him.*

Rise for *Shemoneh Esrei.* Some take three steps backward at this point; others do so before צוּר יִשְׂרָאֵל, *'Rock of Israel.'*

Chazzan– *Praises to the Supreme God, the blessed One Who is blessed. Moses and the Children of Israel exclaimed a song to You with great joy and they all said:*

'Who is like You among the heavenly powers, HASHEM! Who is like You, mighty in holiness, too awesome for praise, doing wonders.'[3] Chazzan– *With a new song the redeemed ones praised Your Name at the seashore, all of them in unison gave thanks, acknowledged [Your] sovereignty, and said:*

'HASHEM shall reign for all eternity.'[4]

It is forbidden to interrupt or pause between *'Who redeemed Israel'* and *Shemoneh Esrei,* even for *Kaddish, Kedushah* or *Borchu*.

צוּר יִשְׂרָאֵל Chazzan– *Rock of Israel, arise to the aid of Israel and liberate, as You pledged, Judah and Israel. Our Redeemer — HASHEM, Master of Legions, is His Name — the Holy One of Israel.*[5] *Blessed are You, HASHEM, Who redeemed Israel.*

SHEMONEH ESREI – AMIDAH

Take three steps backward, then three steps forward. Remain standing with feet together while reciting *Shemoneh Esrei.* Recite it with quiet devotion and without interruption, verbal or otherwise. Although it should not be audible to others, one must pray loudly enough to hear himself.

My Lord, open my lips, that my mouth may declare Your praise.[6]

PATRIARCHS

Bend the knees at *'Blessed'*; bow at *'You'*; straighten up at *'HASHEM.'*

בָּרוּךְ *Blessed are You, HASHEM, our God and the God of our forefathers, God of Abraham, God of Isaac, and God of Jacob; the great, mighty,*

(1) Cf. *Isaiah* 44:6. (2) *Psalms* 106:11. (3) *Exodus* 15:11. (4) 15:18. (5) *Isaiah* 47:4. (6) *Psalms* 51:17.

וְהַנּוֹרָא, אֵל עֶלְיוֹן, גּוֹמֵל חֲסָדִים טוֹבִים וְקוֹנֵה הַכֹּל, וְזוֹכֵר חַסְדֵי אָבוֹת, וּמֵבִיא גוֹאֵל לִבְנֵי בְנֵיהֶם, לְמַעַן שְׁמוֹ בְּאַהֲבָה.

Bend the knees at בָּרוּךְ; bow at אַתָּה; straighten up at ה׳.

מֶלֶךְ עוֹזֵר וּמוֹשִׁיעַ וּמָגֵן. בָּרוּךְ אַתָּה יהוה, מָגֵן אַבְרָהָם.

גבורות

אַתָּה גִּבּוֹר לְעוֹלָם אֲדֹנָי, מְחַיֵּה מֵתִים אַתָּה, רַב לְהוֹשִׁיעַ. מְכַלְכֵּל חַיִּים בְּחֶסֶד, מְחַיֵּה מֵתִים בְּרַחֲמִים רַבִּים, סוֹמֵךְ נוֹפְלִים, וְרוֹפֵא חוֹלִים, וּמַתִּיר אֲסוּרִים, וּמְקַיֵּם אֱמוּנָתוֹ לִישֵׁנֵי עָפָר. מִי כָמוֹךָ בַּעַל גְּבוּרוֹת, וּמִי דּוֹמֶה לָּךְ, מֶלֶךְ מֵמִית וּמְחַיֶּה וּמַצְמִיחַ יְשׁוּעָה. וְנֶאֱמָן אַתָּה לְהַחֲיוֹת מֵתִים. בָּרוּךְ אַתָּה יהוה, מְחַיֵּה הַמֵּתִים.

During the *chazzan's* repetition, *Kedushah* (below) is recited at this point.

קדושת השם

אַתָּה קָדוֹשׁ וְשִׁמְךָ קָדוֹשׁ, וּקְדוֹשִׁים בְּכָל יוֹם יְהַלְלוּךָ סֶּלָה. בָּרוּךְ אַתָּה יהוה, הָאֵל הַקָּדוֹשׁ.

בינה

אַתָּה חוֹנֵן לְאָדָם דַּעַת, וּמְלַמֵּד לֶאֱנוֹשׁ בִּינָה. חָנֵּנוּ מֵאִתְּךָ דֵּעָה בִּינָה וְהַשְׂכֵּל. בָּרוּךְ אַתָּה יהוה, חוֹנֵן הַדָּעַת.

קדושה

When reciting *Kedushah,* one must stand with his feet together and avoid any interruptions. One should rise on his toes when saying the words קָדוֹשׁ, קָדוֹשׁ, קָדוֹשׁ; בָּרוּךְ (of בָּרוּךְ כְּבוֹד); and יִמְלֹךְ.

Cong. then *Chazzan* – **נְקַדֵּשׁ** אֶת שִׁמְךָ בָּעוֹלָם, כְּשֵׁם שֶׁמַּקְדִּישִׁים אוֹתוֹ בִּשְׁמֵי מָרוֹם, כַּכָּתוּב עַל יַד נְבִיאֶךָ, וְקָרָא זֶה אֶל זֶה וְאָמַר:

All – קָדוֹשׁ קָדוֹשׁ קָדוֹשׁ יהוה צְבָאוֹת, מְלֹא כָל הָאָרֶץ כְּבוֹדוֹ.[1]

Chazzan – לְעֻמָּתָם בָּרוּךְ יֹאמֵרוּ:

All – בָּרוּךְ כְּבוֹד יהוה, מִמְּקוֹמוֹ.[2]

Chazzan – וּבְדִבְרֵי קָדְשְׁךָ כָּתוּב לֵאמֹר:

All – יִמְלֹךְ יהוה לְעוֹלָם, אֱלֹהַיִךְ צִיּוֹן לְדֹר וָדֹר, הַלְלוּיָהּ.[3]

Chazzan only concludes – לְדוֹר וָדוֹר נַגִּיד גָּדְלֶךָ וּלְנֵצַח נְצָחִים קְדֻשָּׁתְךָ נַקְדִּישׁ, וְשִׁבְחֲךָ אֱלֹהֵינוּ מִפִּינוּ לֹא יָמוּשׁ לְעוֹלָם וָעֶד, כִּי אֵל מֶלֶךְ גָּדוֹל וְקָדוֹשׁ אָתָּה. בָּרוּךְ אַתָּה יהוה, הָאֵל הַקָּדוֹשׁ.

Chazzan continues . . . אַתָּה חוֹנֵן (above).

and awesome God, the supreme God, Who bestows beneficial kindnesses and creates everything, Who recalls the kindnesses of the Patriarchs and brings a Redeemer to their children's children, for His Name's sake, with love. O King, Helper, Savior, and Shield.

Bend the knees at *'Blessed'*; bow at *'You'*; straighten up at *'HASHEM.'*

Blessed are You, HASHEM, Shield of Abraham.

GOD'S MIGHT

אַתָּה *You are eternally mighty, my Lord, the Resuscitator of the dead are You; abundantly able to save. Who sustains the living with kindness, resuscitates the dead with abundant mercy, supports the fallen, heals the sick, releases the confined, and maintains His faith to those asleep in the dust. Who is like You, O Master of mighty deeds, and who is comparable to You, O King Who causes death and restores life and makes salvation sprout! And You are faithful to resuscitate the dead. Blessed are You, HASHEM, Who resuscitates the dead.*

During the *chazzan's* repetition, *Kedushah* (below) is recited at this point.

HOLINESS OF GOD'S NAME

אַתָּה *You are holy and Your Name is holy, and holy ones praise You every day, forever. Blessed are You, HASHEM, the holy God.*

INSIGHT

אַתָּה *You graciously endow man with wisdom and teach insight to a frail mortal. Endow us graciously from Yourself with wisdom, insight, and discernment. Blessed are You, HASHEM, gracious Giver of wisdom.*

KEDUSHAH

When reciting *Kedushah*, one must stand with his feet together and avoid any interruptions. One should rise on his toes when saying the words *Holy, holy, holy; Blessed is;* and *HASHEM shall reign.*

Cong. then *Chazzan* – **נְקַדֵּשׁ** *We shall sanctify Your Name in this world, just as they sanctify it in heaven above, as it is written by Your prophet, "And one [angel] will call another and say:*

All – *'Holy, holy, holy is HASHEM, Master of Legions, the whole world is filled with His glory.' "*[1]

Chazzan – *Those facing them say 'Blessed':*

All – *'Blessed is the glory of HASHEM from His place.'*[2]

Chazzan – *And in Your holy Writings the following is written:*

All – *'HASHEM shall reign forever — your God, O Zion, from generation to generation — Halleluyah!'*[3]

Chazzan only concludes – *From generation to generation we shall relate Your greatness and for infinite eternities we shall proclaim Your holiness. Your praise, our God, shall not leave our mouth forever and ever, for You, O God, are a great and holy King. Blessed are You, HASHEM, the holy God.*

Chazzan continues אַתָּה חוֹנֵן, *You graciously endow . . .* (above).

---

(1) *Isaiah* 6:3. (2) *Ezekiel* 3:12. (3) *Psalms* 146:10.

תשובה

הֲשִׁיבֵנוּ אָבִינוּ לְתוֹרָתֶךָ, וְקָרְבֵנוּ מַלְכֵּנוּ לַעֲבוֹדָתֶךָ, וְהַחֲזִירֵנוּ בִּתְשׁוּבָה שְׁלֵמָה לְפָנֶיךָ. בָּרוּךְ אַתָּה יהוה, הָרוֹצֶה בִּתְשׁוּבָה.

סליחה

Strike the left side of the chest with the right fist while reciting the words חָטָאנוּ and פָּשָׁעְנוּ.

סְלַח לָנוּ אָבִינוּ כִּי חָטָאנוּ, מְחַל לָנוּ מַלְכֵּנוּ כִּי פָשָׁעְנוּ, כִּי מוֹחֵל וְסוֹלֵחַ אָתָּה. בָּרוּךְ אַתָּה יהוה, חַנּוּן הַמַּרְבֶּה לִסְלֹחַ.

גאולה

רְאֵה בְעָנְיֵנוּ, וְרִיבָה רִיבֵנוּ, וּגְאָלֵנוּ[1] מְהֵרָה לְמַעַן שְׁמֶךָ, כִּי גּוֹאֵל חָזָק אָתָּה. בָּרוּךְ אַתָּה יהוה, גּוֹאֵל יִשְׂרָאֵל.

During his repetition the *chazzan* recites עֲנֵנוּ at this point. See *Laws* §61-63. [If he forgot to recite it at this point, he may insert it in שְׁמַע קוֹלֵנוּ, p. 130].

עֲנֵנוּ יהוה עֲנֵנוּ, בְּיוֹם צוֹם תַּעֲנִיתֵנוּ, כִּי בְצָרָה גְדוֹלָה אֲנָחְנוּ. אַל תֵּפֶן אֶל רִשְׁעֵנוּ, וְאַל תַּסְתֵּר פָּנֶיךָ מִמֶּנּוּ, וְאַל תִּתְעַלַּם מִתְּחִנָּתֵנוּ. הֱיֵה נָא קָרוֹב לְשַׁוְעָתֵנוּ, יְהִי נָא חַסְדְּךָ לְנַחֲמֵנוּ, טֶרֶם נִקְרָא אֵלֶיךָ עֲנֵנוּ, כַּדָּבָר שֶׁנֶּאֱמַר: וְהָיָה טֶרֶם יִקְרָאוּ וַאֲנִי אֶעֱנֶה, עוֹד הֵם מְדַבְּרִים וַאֲנִי אֶשְׁמָע.[2] כִּי אַתָּה יהוה הָעוֹנֶה בְּעֵת צָרָה, פּוֹדֶה וּמַצִּיל בְּכָל עֵת צָרָה וְצוּקָה. בָּרוּךְ אַתָּה יהוה, הָעוֹנֶה בְּעֵת צָרָה.

רפואה

רְפָאֵנוּ יהוה וְנֵרָפֵא, הוֹשִׁיעֵנוּ וְנִוָּשֵׁעָה, כִּי תְהִלָּתֵנוּ אָתָּה,[3] וְהַעֲלֵה רְפוּאָה שְׁלֵמָה לְכָל מַכּוֹתֵינוּ, °°כִּי אֵל מֶלֶךְ רוֹפֵא נֶאֱמָן וְרַחֲמָן אָתָּה. בָּרוּךְ אַתָּה יהוה, רוֹפֵא חוֹלֵי עַמּוֹ יִשְׂרָאֵל.

ברכת השנים

בָּרֵךְ עָלֵינוּ יהוה אֱלֹהֵינוּ אֶת הַשָּׁנָה הַזֹּאת וְאֶת כָּל מִינֵי תְבוּאָתָהּ לְטוֹבָה, וְתֵן בְּרָכָה עַל פְּנֵי הָאֲדָמָה, וְשַׂבְּעֵנוּ מִטּוּבֶךָ, וּבָרֵךְ שְׁנָתֵנוּ כַּשָּׁנִים הַטּוֹבוֹת. בָּרוּךְ אַתָּה יהוה, מְבָרֵךְ הַשָּׁנִים.

°°At this point one may interject a prayer for one who is ill:

יְהִי רָצוֹן מִלְּפָנֶיךָ יהוה אֱלֹהַי וֵאלֹהֵי אֲבוֹתַי, שֶׁתִּשְׁלַח מְהֵרָה רְפוּאָה שְׁלֵמָה מִן הַשָּׁמַיִם, רְפוּאַת הַנֶּפֶשׁ וּרְפוּאַת הַגּוּף

—for a male לַחוֹלֶה (patient's name) בֶּן (mother's name) בְּתוֹךְ שְׁאָר חוֹלֵי יִשְׂרָאֵל.

—for a female לַחוֹלָה (patient's name) בַּת (mother's name) בְּתוֹךְ שְׁאָר חוֹלֵי יִשְׂרָאֵל.

Continue—כִּי אֵל . . .

REPENTANCE

הֲשִׁיבֵנוּ *Bring us back, our Father, to Your Torah, and bring us near, our King, to Your service, and influence us to return in perfect repentance before You. Blessed are You, HASHEM, Who desires repentance.*

FORGIVENESS

Strike the left side of the chest with the right fist while reciting the words *'erred'* and *'sinned.'*

סְלַח *Forgive us, our Father, for we have erred; pardon us, our King, for we have willfully sinned; for You pardon and forgive. Blessed are You, HASHEM, the gracious One Who pardons abundantly.*

REDEMPTION

רְאֵה *Behold our affliction, take up our grievance, and redeem us*[1] *speedily for Your Name's sake, for You are a powerful Redeemer. Blessed are You, HASHEM, Redeemer of Israel.*

During his repetition the *chazzan* recites עֲנֵנוּ, *'Answer us,'* at this point. See *Laws* §61-63. [If he forgot to recite it at this point, he may insert it in שְׁמַע קוֹלֵנוּ, *'Hear our voice'* (p. 130).]

עֲנֵנוּ *Answer us, HASHEM, answer us, on this day of our fast, for we are in great distress. Do not pay attention to our wickedness; do not hide Your Face from us; and do not ignore our supplication. Please be near to our outcry; please let Your kindness comfort us — before we call to You answer us, as it is said: 'And it will be that before they call, I will answer; while they yet speak, I will hear.'*[2] *For You, HASHEM, are the One Who responds in time of distress, Who redeems and rescues in every time of distress and woe. Blessed are You, HASHEM, Who responds in time of distress.*

HEALTH AND HEALING

רְפָאֵנוּ *Heal us, HASHEM — then we will be healed; save us — then we will be saved, for You are our praise.*[3] *Bring complete recovery for all our ailments,* °°*for You are God, King, the faithful and compassionate Healer. Blessed are You, HASHEM, Who heals the sick of His people Israel.*

YEAR OF PROSPERITY

בָּרֵךְ *Bless on our behalf — O HASHEM, our God — this year and all its kinds of crops for the best, and give a blessing on the face of the earth, and satisfy us from Your bounty, and bless our year like the best years. Blessed are You, HASHEM, Who blesses the years.*

°°At this point one may interject a prayer for one who is ill:

May it be Your will, HASHEM, my God, and the God of my forefathers, that You quickly send a complete recovery from heaven, spiritual healing and physical healing to the patient (name) *son/daughter of* (mother's name) *among the other patients of Israel.*

Continue: *For You are God . . .*

(1) Cf. *Psalms* 119:153-154. (2) *Isaiah* 65:24. (3) Cf. *Jeremiah* 17:14.

קיבוץ גליות

תְּקַע בְּשׁוֹפָר גָּדוֹל לְחֵרוּתֵנוּ, וְשָׂא נֵס לְקַבֵּץ גָּלֻיּוֹתֵינוּ, וְקַבְּצֵנוּ יַחַד מֵאַרְבַּע כַּנְפוֹת הָאָרֶץ.[1] בָּרוּךְ אַתָּה יהוה, מְקַבֵּץ נִדְחֵי עַמּוֹ יִשְׂרָאֵל.

דין

הָשִׁיבָה שׁוֹפְטֵינוּ כְּבָרִאשׁוֹנָה, וְיוֹעֲצֵינוּ כְּבַתְּחִלָּה,[2] וְהָסֵר מִמֶּנּוּ יָגוֹן וַאֲנָחָה, וּמְלוֹךְ עָלֵינוּ אַתָּה יהוה לְבַדְּךָ בְּחֶסֶד וּבְרַחֲמִים, וְצַדְּקֵנוּ בַּמִּשְׁפָּט. בָּרוּךְ אַתָּה יהוה, מֶלֶךְ אוֹהֵב צְדָקָה וּמִשְׁפָּט.

ברכת המינים

וְלַמַּלְשִׁינִים אַל תְּהִי תִקְוָה, וְכָל הָרִשְׁעָה כְּרֶגַע תֹּאבֵד, וְכָל אֹיְבֶיךָ מְהֵרָה יִכָּרֵתוּ, וְהַזֵּדִים מְהֵרָה תְעַקֵּר וּתְשַׁבֵּר וּתְמַגֵּר וְתַכְנִיעַ בִּמְהֵרָה בְיָמֵינוּ. בָּרוּךְ אַתָּה יהוה, שׁוֹבֵר אֹיְבִים וּמַכְנִיעַ זֵדִים.

צדיקים

עַל הַצַּדִּיקִים וְעַל הַחֲסִידִים, וְעַל זִקְנֵי עַמְּךָ בֵּית יִשְׂרָאֵל, וְעַל פְּלֵיטַת סוֹפְרֵיהֶם, וְעַל גֵּרֵי הַצֶּדֶק וְעָלֵינוּ, יֶהֱמוּ רַחֲמֶיךָ יהוה אֱלֹהֵינוּ, וְתֵן שָׂכָר טוֹב לְכָל הַבּוֹטְחִים בְּשִׁמְךָ בֶּאֱמֶת, וְשִׂים חֶלְקֵנוּ עִמָּהֶם לְעוֹלָם, וְלֹא נֵבוֹשׁ כִּי בְךָ בָּטָחְנוּ. בָּרוּךְ אַתָּה יהוה, מִשְׁעָן וּמִבְטָח לַצַּדִּיקִים.

בנין ירושלים

וְלִירוּשָׁלַיִם עִירְךָ בְּרַחֲמִים תָּשׁוּב, וְתִשְׁכּוֹן בְּתוֹכָהּ כַּאֲשֶׁר דִּבַּרְתָּ, וּבְנֵה אוֹתָהּ בְּקָרוֹב בְּיָמֵינוּ בִּנְיַן עוֹלָם, וְכִסֵּא דָוִד מְהֵרָה לְתוֹכָהּ תָּכִין. בָּרוּךְ אַתָּה יהוה, בּוֹנֵה יְרוּשָׁלָיִם.

מלכות בית דוד

אֶת צֶמַח דָּוִד עַבְדְּךָ מְהֵרָה תַצְמִיחַ, וְקַרְנוֹ תָּרוּם בִּישׁוּעָתֶךָ, כִּי לִישׁוּעָתְךָ קִוִּינוּ כָּל הַיּוֹם. בָּרוּךְ אַתָּה יהוה, מַצְמִיחַ קֶרֶן יְשׁוּעָה.

קבלת תפלה

שְׁמַע קוֹלֵנוּ יהוה אֱלֹהֵינוּ, חוּס וְרַחֵם עָלֵינוּ, וְקַבֵּל בְּרַחֲמִים וּבְרָצוֹן אֶת תְּפִלָּתֵנוּ, כִּי אֵל שׁוֹמֵעַ תְּפִלּוֹת וְתַחֲנוּנִים אָתָּה. וּמִלְּפָנֶיךָ מַלְכֵּנוּ רֵיקָם אַל תְּשִׁיבֵנוּ,

If *chazzan* forgot to say עֲנֵנוּ before, he says it at this point but omits the concluding blessing (בָּרוּךְ . . . צָרָה).

INGATHERING OF EXILES

תְּקַע *Sound the great shofar for our freedom, raise the banner to gather our exiles and gather us together from the four corners of the earth.*[1] *Blessed are You,* HASHEM, *Who gathers in the dispersed of His people Israel.*

RESTORATION OF JUSTICE

הָשִׁיבָה *Restore our judges as in earliest times and our counselors as at first;*[2] *remove from us sorrow and groan; and reign over us — You,* HASHEM, *alone — with kindness and compassion, and justify us through judgment. Blessed are You,* HASHEM, *the King Who loves righteousness and judgment.*

AGAINST HERETICS

וְלַמַּלְשִׁינִים *And for slanderers let there be no hope; and may all wickedness perish in an instant; and may all Your enemies be cut down speedily. May You speedily uproot, smash, cast down, and humble the wanton sinners — speedily in our days. Blessed are You,* HASHEM, *Who breaks enemies and humbles wanton sinners.*

THE RIGHTEOUS

עַל הַצַּדִּיקִים *On the righteous, on the devout, on the elders of Your people the Family of Israel, on the remnant of their scholars, on the righteous converts and on ourselves — may Your compassion be aroused,* HASHEM, *our God, and give goodly reward to all who sincerely believe in Your Name. Put our lot with them forever, and we will not feel ashamed, for we trust in You. Blessed are You,* HASHEM, *Mainstay and Assurance of the righteous.*

REBUILDING JERUSALEM

וְלִירוּשָׁלַיִם *And to Jerusalem, Your city, may You return in compassion, and may You rest within it, as You have spoken. May You rebuild it soon in our days as an eternal structure, and may You speedily establish the throne of David within it. Blessed are You,* HASHEM, *the Builder of Jerusalem.*

DAVIDIC REIGN

אֶת צֶמַח *The offspring of Your servant David may You speedily cause to flourish, and enhance his pride through Your salvation, for we hope for Your salvation all day long. Blessed are You,* HASHEM, *Who causes the pride of salvation to flourish.*

ACCEPTANCE OF PRAYER

שְׁמַע *Hear our voice,* HASHEM *our God, pity and be compassionate to us, and accept — with compassion and favor — our prayer, for God Who hears prayers and supplications are You. From before Yourself, our King, turn us not away empty-handed,*

---

(1) Cf. *Isaiah* 11:12. (2) Cf. 1:26.

°° כִּי אַתָּה שׁוֹמֵעַ תְּפִלַּת עַמְּךָ יִשְׂרָאֵל בְּרַחֲמִים. בָּרוּךְ אַתָּה יהוה, שׁוֹמֵעַ תְּפִלָּה.

עבודה

רְצֵה יהוה אֱלֹהֵינוּ בְּעַמְּךָ יִשְׂרָאֵל וּבִתְפִלָּתָם, וְהָשֵׁב אֶת הָעֲבוֹדָה לִדְבִיר בֵּיתֶךָ. וְאִשֵּׁי יִשְׂרָאֵל וּתְפִלָּתָם בְּאַהֲבָה תְקַבֵּל בְּרָצוֹן, וּתְהִי לְרָצוֹן תָּמִיד עֲבוֹדַת יִשְׂרָאֵל עַמֶּךָ.

וְתֶחֱזֶינָה עֵינֵינוּ בְּשׁוּבְךָ לְצִיּוֹן בְּרַחֲמִים. בָּרוּךְ אַתָּה יהוה, הַמַּחֲזִיר שְׁכִינָתוֹ לְצִיּוֹן.

הודאה

Bow at מוֹדִים; straighten up at ה׳. In his repetition the *chazzan* should recite the entire מוֹדִים aloud, while the congregation recites מוֹדִים דְּרַבָּנָן softly.

מוֹדִים אֲנַחְנוּ לָךְ, שָׁאַתָּה הוּא יהוה אֱלֹהֵינוּ וֵאלֹהֵי אֲבוֹתֵינוּ לְעוֹלָם וָעֶד. צוּר חַיֵּינוּ, מָגֵן יִשְׁעֵנוּ אַתָּה הוּא לְדוֹר וָדוֹר. נוֹדֶה לְּךָ וּנְסַפֵּר תְּהִלָּתֶךָ[1] עַל חַיֵּינוּ הַמְּסוּרִים בְּיָדֶךָ, וְעַל נִשְׁמוֹתֵינוּ הַפְּקוּדוֹת לָךְ, וְעַל נִסֶּיךָ שֶׁבְּכָל יוֹם עִמָּנוּ, וְעַל נִפְלְאוֹתֶיךָ וְטוֹבוֹתֶיךָ שֶׁבְּכָל עֵת, עֶרֶב וָבֹקֶר וְצָהֳרָיִם. הַטּוֹב כִּי לֹא כָלוּ רַחֲמֶיךָ, וְהַמְּרַחֵם כִּי לֹא תַמּוּ חֲסָדֶיךָ,[2] מֵעוֹלָם קִוִּינוּ לָךְ.

מודים דרבנן

מוֹדִים אֲנַחְנוּ לָךְ, שָׁאַתָּה הוּא יהוה אֱלֹהֵינוּ וֵאלֹהֵי אֲבוֹתֵינוּ, אֱלֹהֵי כָל בָּשָׂר, יוֹצְרֵנוּ, יוֹצֵר בְּרֵאשִׁית. בְּרָכוֹת וְהוֹדָאוֹת לְשִׁמְךָ הַגָּדוֹל וְהַקָּדוֹשׁ, עַל שֶׁהֶחֱיִיתָנוּ וְקִיַּמְתָּנוּ. כֵּן תְּחַיֵּנוּ וּתְקַיְּמֵנוּ, וְתֶאֱסוֹף גָּלֻיּוֹתֵינוּ לְחַצְרוֹת קָדְשֶׁךָ, לִשְׁמוֹר חֻקֶּיךָ וְלַעֲשׂוֹת רְצוֹנֶךָ, וּלְעָבְדְּךָ בְּלֵבָב שָׁלֵם, עַל שֶׁאֲנַחְנוּ מוֹדִים לָךְ. בָּרוּךְ אֵל הַהוֹדָאוֹת.

°°During the silent *Shemoneh Esrei* one may insert either or both of these personal prayers.

For forgiveness:

אָנָּא יהוה, חָטָאתִי עָוִיתִי וּפָשַׁעְתִּי לְפָנֶיךָ, מִיּוֹם הֱיוֹתִי עַל הָאֲדָמָה עַד הַיּוֹם הַזֶּה (וּבִפְרַט בַּחֵטְא ....). אָנָּא יהוה, עֲשֵׂה לְמַעַן שִׁמְךָ הַגָּדוֹל, וּתְכַפֶּר לִי עַל עֲוֹנַי וַחֲטָאַי וּפְשָׁעַי שֶׁחָטָאתִי וְשֶׁעָוִיתִי וְשֶׁפָּשַׁעְתִּי לְפָנֶיךָ, מִנְּעוּרַי עַד הַיּוֹם הַזֶּה. וּתְמַלֵּא כָּל הַשֵּׁמוֹת שֶׁפָּגַמְתִּי בְּשִׁמְךָ הַגָּדוֹל.

For livelihood:

אַתָּה הוּא יהוה הָאֱלֹהִים, הַזָּן וּמְפַרְנֵס וּמְכַלְכֵּל מִקַּרְנֵי רְאֵמִים עַד בֵּיצֵי כִנִּים. הַטְרִיפֵנִי לֶחֶם חֻקִּי, וְהַמְצֵא לִי וּלְכָל בְּנֵי בֵיתִי מְזוֹנוֹתַי קוֹדֶם שֶׁאֶצְטָרֵךְ לָהֶם, בְּנַחַת וְלֹא בְצַעַר, בְּהֶתֵּר וְלֹא בְאִסּוּר, בְּכָבוֹד וְלֹא בְּבִזָּיוֹן, לְחַיִּים וּלְשָׁלוֹם, מִשֶּׁפַע בְּרָכָה וְהַצְלָחָה, וּמִשֶּׁפַע בְּרֵכָה עֶלְיוֹנָה, כְּדֵי שֶׁאוּכַל לַעֲשׂוֹת רְצוֹנֶךָ וְלַעֲסוֹק בְּתוֹרָתֶךָ וּלְקַיֵּם מִצְוֹתֶיךָ. וְאַל תַּצְרִיכֵנִי לִידֵי מַתְּנַת בָּשָׂר וָדָם. וִיקֻיַּם בִּי מִקְרָא שֶׁכָּתוּב: פּוֹתֵחַ אֶת יָדֶךָ, וּמַשְׂבִּיעַ לְכָל חַי רָצוֹן.[3] וְכָתוּב: הַשְׁלֵךְ עַל יהוה יְהָבְךָ וְהוּא יְכַלְכְּלֶךָ.[4]

Continue — כִּי אַתָּה . . .

°° *for You hear the prayer of Your people Israel with compassion. Blessed are You,* HASHEM, *Who hears prayer.*

TEMPLE SERVICE

רְצֵה *Be favorable,* HASHEM, *our God, toward Your people Israel and their prayer and restore the service to the Holy of Holies of Your Temple. The fire-offerings of Israel and their prayer accept with love and favor, and may the service of Your people Israel always be favorable to You.*

וְתֶחֱזֶינָה *May our eyes behold Your return to Zion in compassion. Blessed are You,* HASHEM, *Who restores His Presence to Zion.*

THANKSGIVING [MODIM]

Bow at *'We gratefully thank You'*; straighten up at *'HASHEM.'* In his repetition the *chazzan* should recite the entire *Modim* aloud, while the congregation recites *Modim of the Rabbis* softly.

מוֹדִים *We gratefully thank You, for it is You Who are* HASHEM, *our God and the God of our forefathers for all eternity; Rock of our lives, Shield of our salvation are You from generation to generation. We shall thank You and relate Your praise*[1] *— for our lives, which are committed to Your power and for our souls that are entrusted to You; for Your miracles that are with us every day; and for Your wonders and favors in every season — evening, morning, and afternoon. The Beneficent One, for Your compassions were never exhausted, and the Compassionate One, for Your kindnesses never ended*[2] *— always have we put our hope in You.*

MODIM OF THE RABBIS

מוֹדִים *We gratefully thank You, for it is You Who are* HASHEM, *our God and the God of our forefathers, the God of all flesh, our Molder, the Molder of the universe. Blessings and thanks are due Your great and holy Name for You have given us life and sustained us. So may You continue to give us life and sustain us and gather our exiles to the Courtyards of Your Sanctuary, to observe Your decrees, to do Your will and to serve You wholeheartedly. [We thank You] for inspiring us to thank You. Blessed is the God of thanksgivings.*

°°During the silent *Shemoneh Esrei* one may insert either or both of these personal prayers.

For forgiveness:

אָנָּא *Please, O* HASHEM, *I have erred, been iniquitous, and willfully sinned before You, from the day I have existed on earth until this very day (and especially with the sin of ...). Please,* HASHEM, *act for the sake of Your Great Name and grant me atonement for my iniquities, my errors, and my willful sins through which I have erred, been iniquitous, and willfully sinned before You, from my youth until this day. And make whole all the Names that I have blemished in Your Great Name.*

For livelihood:

אַתָּה *It is You,* HASHEM *the God, Who nourishes, sustains, and supports, from the horns of re'eimim to the eggs of lice. Provide me with my allotment of bread; and bring forth for me and all members of my household, my food, before I have need for it; in contentment but not in pain, in a permissible but not a forbidden manner, in honor but not in disgrace, for life and for peace; from the flow of blessing and success and from the flow of the Heavenly spring, so that I be enabled to do Your will and engage in Your Torah and fulfill Your commandments. Make me not needful of people's largesse; and may there be fulfilled in me the verse that states, 'You open Your hand and satisfy the desire of every living thing'*[3] *and that states, 'Cast Your burden upon* HASHEM *and He will support you.'*[4]

Continue: *For You hear the prayer . . .*

(1) Cf. *Psalms* 79:13. (2) Cf. *Lamentations* 3:22. (3) *Psalms* 145:16. (4) 55:23.

וְעַל כֻּלָּם יִתְבָּרַךְ וְיִתְרוֹמַם שִׁמְךָ מַלְכֵּנוּ תָּמִיד לְעוֹלָם וָעֶד.

Bend the knees at בָּרוּךְ; bow at אַתָּה; straighten up at ה׳.

וְכֹל הַחַיִּים יוֹדְוּךָ סֶּלָה, וִיהַלְלוּ אֶת שִׁמְךָ בֶּאֱמֶת, הָאֵל יְשׁוּעָתֵנוּ וְעֶזְרָתֵנוּ סֶלָה. בָּרוּךְ אַתָּה יהוה, הַטּוֹב שִׁמְךָ וּלְךָ נָאֶה לְהוֹדוֹת.

THE CHAZZAN DOES NOT RECITE THE PRIESTLY BLESSING

שלום

שִׂים שָׁלוֹם, טוֹבָה, וּבְרָכָה, חֵן, וָחֶסֶד וְרַחֲמִים עָלֵינוּ וְעַל כָּל יִשְׂרָאֵל עַמֶּךָ. בָּרְכֵנוּ אָבִינוּ, כֻּלָּנוּ כְּאֶחָד בְּאוֹר פָּנֶיךָ, כִּי בְאוֹר פָּנֶיךָ נָתַתָּ לָּנוּ, יהוה אֱלֹהֵינוּ, תּוֹרַת חַיִּים וְאַהֲבַת חֶסֶד, וּצְדָקָה, וּבְרָכָה, וְרַחֲמִים, וְחַיִּים, וְשָׁלוֹם. וְטוֹב בְּעֵינֶיךָ לְבָרֵךְ אֶת עַמְּךָ יִשְׂרָאֵל, בְּכָל עֵת וּבְכָל שָׁעָה בִּשְׁלוֹמֶךָ. בָּרוּךְ אַתָּה יהוה, הַמְּבָרֵךְ אֶת עַמּוֹ יִשְׂרָאֵל בַּשָּׁלוֹם.

יִהְיוּ לְרָצוֹן אִמְרֵי פִי וְהֶגְיוֹן לִבִּי לְפָנֶיךָ, יהוה צוּרִי וְגֹאֲלִי.[1]

Chazzan's repetition of *Shemoneh Esrei* ends here. Individuals continue below:

אֱלֹהַי, נְצוֹר לְשׁוֹנִי מֵרָע, וּשְׂפָתַי מִדַּבֵּר מִרְמָה,[2] וְלִמְקַלְלַי נַפְשִׁי תִדּוֹם, וְנַפְשִׁי כֶּעָפָר לַכֹּל תִּהְיֶה. פְּתַח לִבִּי בְּתוֹרָתֶךָ, וּבְמִצְוֹתֶיךָ תִּרְדּוֹף נַפְשִׁי. וְכֹל הַחוֹשְׁבִים עָלַי רָעָה, מְהֵרָה הָפֵר עֲצָתָם וְקַלְקֵל מַחֲשַׁבְתָּם. עֲשֵׂה לְמַעַן שְׁמֶךָ, עֲשֵׂה לְמַעַן יְמִינֶךָ, עֲשֵׂה לְמַעַן קְדֻשָּׁתֶךָ, עֲשֵׂה לְמַעַן תּוֹרָתֶךָ. לְמַעַן יֵחָלְצוּן יְדִידֶיךָ, הוֹשִׁיעָה יְמִינְךָ וַעֲנֵנִי.[3]

Some recite verses pertaining to their names here. See page 486.

יִהְיוּ לְרָצוֹן אִמְרֵי פִי וְהֶגְיוֹן לִבִּי לְפָנֶיךָ, יהוה צוּרִי וְגֹאֲלִי.[1]

Bow and take three steps back. Bow left and say . . . עֹשֶׂה; bow right and say . . . הוּא יַעֲשֶׂה; bow forward and say וְעַל כָּל . . . אָמֵן.

עֹשֶׂה שָׁלוֹם בִּמְרוֹמָיו, הוּא יַעֲשֶׂה שָׁלוֹם עָלֵינוּ, וְעַל כָּל יִשְׂרָאֵל. וְאִמְרוּ: אָמֵן.

יְהִי רָצוֹן מִלְּפָנֶיךָ יהוה אֱלֹהֵינוּ וֵאלֹהֵי אֲבוֹתֵינוּ, שֶׁיִּבָּנֶה בֵּית הַמִּקְדָּשׁ בִּמְהֵרָה בְיָמֵינוּ, וְתֵן חֶלְקֵנוּ בְּתוֹרָתֶךָ. וְשָׁם נַעֲבָדְךָ בְּיִרְאָה, כִּימֵי עוֹלָם וּכְשָׁנִים קַדְמוֹנִיּוֹת. וְעָרְבָה לַיהוה מִנְחַת יְהוּדָה וִירוּשָׁלָיִם, כִּימֵי עוֹלָם וּכְשָׁנִים קַדְמוֹנִיּוֹת.[4]

THE INDIVIDUAL'S RECITATION OF *SHEMONEH ESREI* ENDS HERE.

The individual remains standing in place until the *chazzan* reaches *Kedushah* — or at least until the *chazzan* begins his repetition — then he takes three steps forward. The *chazzan* himself, or one who is praying alone, should remain in place for a few moments before taking three steps forward.

For all these, may Your Name be blessed and exalted, our King, continually forever and ever.

Bend the knees at *'Blessed'*; bow at *'You'*; straighten up at *'HASHEM.'*

Everything alive will gratefully acknowledge You, Selah! and praise Your Name sincerely, O God of our salvation and help, Selah! Blessed are You, HASHEM, Your Name is 'The Beneficent One' and to You it is fitting to give thanks.

THE CHAZZAN DOES NOT RECITE THE PRIESTLY BLESSING

PEACE

שִׂים שָׁלוֹם *Establish peace, goodness, blessing, graciousness, kindness, and compassion upon us and upon all of Your people Israel. Bless us, our Father, all of us as one, with the light of Your countenance, for with the light of Your countenance You gave us, HASHEM, our God, the Torah of life and a love of kindness, righteousness, blessing, compassion, life, and peace. And may it be good in Your eyes to bless Your people Israel at every time and every hour with Your peace. Blessed are You, HASHEM, Who blesses His people Israel with peace.*

May the expressions of my mouth and the thoughts of my heart find favor before You, HASHEM, my Rock and my Redeemer.[1]

Chazzan's repetition of *Shemoneh Esrei* ends here. Individuals continue below:

אֱלֹהַי *My God, guard my tongue from evil and my lips from speaking deceitfully.*[2] *To those who curse me, let my soul be silent; and let my soul be like dust to everyone. Open my heart to Your Torah, then my soul will pursue Your commandments. As for all those who design evil against me, speedily nullify their counsel and disrupt their design. Act for Your Name's sake; act for Your right hand's sake; act for Your sanctity's sake; act for Your Torah's sake. That Your beloved ones may be given rest; let Your right hand save, and respond to me.*[3]

Some recite verses pertaining to their names at this point. See page 486.

May the expressions of my mouth and the thoughts of my heart find favor before You, HASHEM, my Rock and my Redeemer.[1] °°*He Who makes peace in His heights, may He make peace upon us, and upon all Israel. Now respond: Amen.*

Bow and take three steps back. Bow left and say, *'He Who makes peace . . .'*; bow right and say, *'may He make peace . . .'*; bow forward and say, *'and upon . . . Amen.'*

יְהִי רָצוֹן *May it be Your will, HASHEM, our God and the God of our forefathers, that the Holy Temple be rebuilt, speedily in our days. Grant us our share in Your Torah, and may we serve You there with reverence, as in days of old and in former years. Then the offering of Judah and Jerusalem will be pleasing to HASHEM, as in days of old and in former years.*[4]

THE INDIVIDUAL'S RECITATION OF *SHEMONEH ESREI* ENDS HERE.

The individual remains standing in place until the *chazzan* reaches *Kedushah* — or at least until the *chazzan* begins his repetition — then he takes three steps forward. The *chazzan* himself, or one who is praying alone, should remain in place for a few moments before taking three steps forward.

---

(1) *Psalms* 19:15. (2) Cf. 34:14. (3) 60:7; 108:7. (4) *Malachi* 3:4.

The *chazzan* recites Half-*Kaddish:*

יִתְגַּדַּל וְיִתְקַדַּשׁ שְׁמֵהּ רַבָּא. (Cong. – אָמֵן.) בְּעָלְמָא דִּי בְרָא כִרְעוּתֵהּ. וְיַמְלִיךְ מַלְכוּתֵהּ, בְּחַיֵּיכוֹן וּבְיוֹמֵיכוֹן וּבְחַיֵּי דְכָל בֵּית יִשְׂרָאֵל, בַּעֲגָלָא וּבִזְמַן קָרִיב. וְאִמְרוּ: אָמֵן.

(Cong. – אָמֵן. יְהֵא שְׁמֵהּ רַבָּא מְבָרַךְ לְעָלַם וּלְעָלְמֵי עָלְמַיָּא.)

יְהֵא שְׁמֵהּ רַבָּא מְבָרַךְ לְעָלַם וּלְעָלְמֵי עָלְמַיָּא.

יִתְבָּרַךְ וְיִשְׁתַּבַּח וְיִתְפָּאַר וְיִתְרוֹמַם וְיִתְנַשֵּׂא וְיִתְהַדָּר וְיִתְעַלֶּה וְיִתְהַלָּל שְׁמֵהּ דְּקֻדְשָׁא בְּרִיךְ הוּא (Cong. – בְּרִיךְ הוּא) – לְעֵלָּא מִן כָּל בִּרְכָתָא וְשִׁירָתָא תֻּשְׁבְּחָתָא וְנֶחֱמָתָא, דַּאֲמִירָן בְּעָלְמָא. וְאִמְרוּ: אָמֵן. (Cong. – אָמֵן.)

הוצאת ספר תורה

From the moment the Ark is opened until the Torah is returned to it, one must conduct himself with the utmost respect, and avoid unnecessary conversation. It is commendable to kiss the Torah as it is carried to the *bimah* [reading table] and back to the Ark.
All rise and remain standing until the Torah is placed on the *bimah*.
The Ark is opened. Before the Torah is removed the congregation recites:

וַיְהִי בִּנְסֹעַ הָאָרֹן וַיֹּאמֶר מֹשֶׁה, קוּמָה יהוה וְיָפֻצוּ אֹיְבֶיךָ וְיָנֻסוּ מְשַׂנְאֶיךָ מִפָּנֶיךָ.[1] כִּי מִצִּיּוֹן תֵּצֵא תוֹרָה, וּדְבַר יהוה מִירוּשָׁלָיִם.[2] בָּרוּךְ שֶׁנָּתַן תּוֹרָה לְעַמּוֹ יִשְׂרָאֵל בִּקְדֻשָּׁתוֹ.

זוהר ויקהל שסט:א

בְּרִיךְ שְׁמֵהּ דְּמָרֵא עָלְמָא, בְּרִיךְ כִּתְרָךְ וְאַתְרָךְ. יְהֵא רְעוּתָךְ עִם עַמָּךְ יִשְׂרָאֵל לְעָלַם, וּפֻרְקַן יְמִינָךְ אַחֲזֵי לְעַמָּךְ בְּבֵית מַקְדְּשָׁךְ, וּלְאַמְטוּיֵי לָנָא מִטּוּב נְהוֹרָךְ, וּלְקַבֵּל צְלוֹתָנָא בְּרַחֲמִין. יְהֵא רַעֲוָא קֳדָמָךְ, דְּתוֹרִיךְ לָן חַיִּין בְּטִיבוּתָא, וְלֶהֱוֵי אֲנָא פְּקִידָא בְּגוֹ צַדִּיקַיָּא, לְמִרְחַם עָלַי וּלְמִנְטַר יָתִי וְיַת כָּל דִּי לִי, וְדִי לְעַמָּךְ יִשְׂרָאֵל. אַנְתְּ הוּא זָן לְכֹלָּא, וּמְפַרְנֵס לְכֹלָּא, אַנְתְּ הוּא שַׁלִּיט עַל כֹּלָּא. אַנְתְּ הוּא דְּשַׁלִּיט עַל מַלְכַיָּא, וּמַלְכוּתָא דִּילָךְ הִיא. אֲנָא עַבְדָּא דְקֻדְשָׁא בְּרִיךְ הוּא, דְּסָגִידְנָא קַמֵּהּ וּמִקַּמָּא דִּיקַר אוֹרַיְתֵהּ בְּכָל עִדָּן וְעִדָּן. לָא עַל אֱנָשׁ רָחִיצְנָא, וְלָא עַל בַּר אֱלָהִין סָמֵיכְנָא, אֶלָּא בֶּאֱלָהָא דִשְׁמַיָּא, דְּהוּא אֱלָהָא קְשׁוֹט, וְאוֹרַיְתֵהּ קְשׁוֹט, וּנְבִיאוֹהִי קְשׁוֹט, וּמַסְגֵּא לְמֶעְבַּד טַבְוָן וּקְשׁוֹט. בֵּהּ אֲנָא רָחִיץ, וְלִשְׁמֵהּ קַדִּישָׁא יַקִּירָא אֲנָא אֵמַר תֻּשְׁבְּחָן. יְהֵא רַעֲוָא קֳדָמָךְ, דְּתִפְתַּח לִבָּאִי בְּאוֹרַיְתָא, וְתַשְׁלִים מִשְׁאֲלִין דְּלִבָּאִי, וְלִבָּא דְכָל עַמָּךְ יִשְׂרָאֵל, לְטַב וּלְחַיִּין וְלִשְׁלָם. (אָמֵן.)

The Torah is removed from the Ark and presented to the *chazzan,* who accepts it in his right arm. He then turns to the Ark, bows while raising the Torah, and recites:

גַּדְּלוּ לַיהוה אִתִּי וּנְרוֹמְמָה שְׁמוֹ יַחְדָּו.[3]

The *chazzan* recites Half-*Kaddish*:

יִתְגַּדַּל *May His great Name grow exalted and sanctified* (Cong.– *Amen.*) *in the world that He created as He willed. May He give reign to His kingship in your lifetimes and in your days, and in the lifetimes of the entire Family of Israel, swiftly and soon. Now respond: Amen.*

(Cong.– *Amen. May His great Name be blessed forever and ever.*)

May His great Name be blessed forever and ever.

Blessed, praised, glorified, exalted, extolled, mighty, upraised, and lauded be the Name of the Holy One, Blessed is He (Cong.– *Blessed is He*) *— beyond any blessing and song, praise and consolation that are uttered in the world. Now respond: Amen.* (Cong.– *Amen.*)

REMOVAL OF THE TORAH FROM THE ARK

From the moment the Ark is opened until the Torah is returned to it, one must conduct himself with the utmost respect, and avoid unnecessary conversation. It is commendable to kiss the Torah as it is carried to the *bimah* [reading table] and back to the Ark.

All rise and remain standing until the Torah is placed on the *bimah*.

The Ark is opened. Before the Torah is removed the congregation recites:

וַיְהִי בִּנְסֹעַ *When the Ark would travel, Moses would say, 'Arise,* HASHEM, *and let Your foes be scattered, let those who hate You flee from You.'*[1] *For from Zion the Torah will come forth and the word of* HASHEM *from Jerusalem.*[2] *Blessed is He Who gave the Torah to His people Israel in His holiness.*

Zohar, Vayakhel 369a

בְּרִיךְ שְׁמֵהּ *Blessed is the Name of the Master of the universe, blessed is Your crown and Your place. May Your favor remain with Your people Israel forever; may You display the salvation of Your right hand to Your people in Your Holy Temple, to benefit us with the goodness of Your luminescence and to accept our prayers with mercy. May it be Your will that You extend our lives with goodness and that I be numbered among the righteous; that You have mercy on me and protect me, all that is mine and that is Your people Israel's. It is You Who nourishes all and sustains all; You control everything. It is You Who controls kings, and kingship is Yours. I am a servant of the Holy One, Blessed is He, and I prostrate myself before Him and before the glory of His Torah at all times. Not in any man do I put trust, nor on any angel do I rely — only on the God of heaven Who is the God of truth, Whose Torah is truth and Whose prophets are true and Who acts liberally with kindness and truth. In Him do I trust, and to His glorious and holy Name do I declare praises. May it be Your will that You open my heart to the Torah and that You fulfill the wishes of my heart and the heart of Your entire people Israel for good, for life, and for peace. (Amen.)*

The Torah is removed from the Ark and presented to the *chazzan*, who accepts it in his right arm. He turns to the Ark, bows while raising the Torah, and recites:

Declare the greatness of HASHEM with me, and let us exalt His Name together.[3]

---

(1) *Numbers* 10:35. (2) *Isaiah* 2:3. (3) *Psalms* 34:4.

The *chazzan* turns to his right and carries the Torah to the *bimah*, as the congregation responds:

לְךָ יהוה הַגְּדֻלָּה וְהַגְּבוּרָה וְהַתִּפְאֶרֶת וְהַנֵּצַח וְהַהוֹד כִּי כֹל בַּשָּׁמַיִם וּבָאָרֶץ, לְךָ יהוה הַמַּמְלָכָה וְהַמִּתְנַשֵּׂא לְכֹל לְרֹאשׁ.[1] רוֹמְמוּ יהוה אֱלֹהֵינוּ, וְהִשְׁתַּחֲווּ לַהֲדֹם רַגְלָיו, קָדוֹשׁ הוּא. רוֹמְמוּ יהוה אֱלֹהֵינוּ, וְהִשְׁתַּחֲווּ לְהַר קָדְשׁוֹ, כִּי קָדוֹשׁ יהוה אֱלֹהֵינוּ.[2]

אַב הָרַחֲמִים הוּא יְרַחֵם עַם עֲמוּסִים, וְיִזְכֹּר בְּרִית אֵיתָנִים, וְיַצִּיל נַפְשׁוֹתֵינוּ מִן הַשָּׁעוֹת הָרָעוֹת, וְיִגְעַר בְּיֵצֶר הָרָע מִן הַנְּשׂוּאִים, וְיָחֹן אוֹתָנוּ לִפְלֵיטַת עוֹלָמִים, וִימַלֵּא מִשְׁאֲלוֹתֵינוּ בְּמִדָּה טוֹבָה יְשׁוּעָה וְרַחֲמִים.

The Torah is placed on the *bimah* and prepared for reading.
The *gabbai* uses the following formula to call a *Kohen* to the Torah:

וְתִגָּלֶה וְתֵרָאֶה מַלְכוּתוֹ עָלֵינוּ בִּזְמַן קָרוֹב, וְיָחֹן פְּלֵיטָתֵנוּ וּפְלֵיטַת עַמּוֹ בֵּית יִשְׂרָאֵל לְחֵן וּלְחֶסֶד וּלְרַחֲמִים וּלְרָצוֹן. וְנֹאמַר אָמֵן. הַכֹּל הָבוּ גֹדֶל לֵאלֹהֵינוּ וּתְנוּ כָבוֹד לַתּוֹרָה. כֹּהֵן° קְרָב, יַעֲמֹד (insert name) הַכֹּהֵן.

°If no *Kohen* is present, the *gabbai* says: "אֵין כַּאן כֹּהֵן, יַעֲמֹד (name) יִשְׂרָאֵל (לֵוִי) בִּמְקוֹם כֹּהֵן".

בָּרוּךְ שֶׁנָּתַן תּוֹרָה לְעַמּוֹ יִשְׂרָאֵל בִּקְדֻשָּׁתוֹ. (תּוֹרַת יהוה תְּמִימָה מְשִׁיבַת נָפֶשׁ, עֵדוּת יהוה נֶאֱמָנָה מַחְכִּימַת פֶּתִי. פִּקּוּדֵי יהוה יְשָׁרִים מְשַׂמְּחֵי לֵב, מִצְוַת יהוה בָּרָה מְאִירַת עֵינָיִם.[3] יהוה עֹז לְעַמּוֹ יִתֵּן, יהוה יְבָרֵךְ אֶת עַמּוֹ בַשָּׁלוֹם.[4] הָאֵל תָּמִים דַּרְכּוֹ, אִמְרַת יהוה צְרוּפָה, מָגֵן הוּא לְכֹל הַחוֹסִים בּוֹ.[5])

Congregation, then *gabbai:*

וְאַתֶּם הַדְּבֵקִים בַּיהוה אֱלֹהֵיכֶם, חַיִּים כֻּלְּכֶם הַיּוֹם.[6]

The reader shows the *oleh* (person called to the Torah) the place in the Torah. The *oleh* touches the Torah with a corner of his *tallis*, or the belt or mantle of the Torah, and kisses it. He then begins the blessing, bowing at בָּרְכוּ, and straightening up at 'ה.

בָּרְכוּ אֶת יהוה הַמְּבֹרָךְ.

Congregation, followed by *oleh*, responds, bowing at בָּרוּךְ, and straightening up at 'ה.

בָּרוּךְ יהוה הַמְּבֹרָךְ לְעוֹלָם וָעֶד.

Oleh continues:

בָּרוּךְ אַתָּה יהוה אֱלֹהֵינוּ מֶלֶךְ הָעוֹלָם, אֲשֶׁר בָּחַר בָּנוּ מִכָּל הָעַמִּים, וְנָתַן לָנוּ אֶת תּוֹרָתוֹ. בָּרוּךְ אַתָּה יהוה, נוֹתֵן הַתּוֹרָה. (.Cong.– אָמֵן)

After his Torah portion has been read, the *oleh* recites:

בָּרוּךְ אַתָּה יהוה אֱלֹהֵינוּ מֶלֶךְ הָעוֹלָם, אֲשֶׁר נָתַן לָנוּ תּוֹרַת אֱמֶת, וְחַיֵּי עוֹלָם נָטַע בְּתוֹכֵנוּ. בָּרוּךְ אַתָּה יהוה, נוֹתֵן הַתּוֹרָה. (.Cong.– אָמֵן)

THE *MI SHEBIERACH* PRAYER FOR A SICK PERSON APPEARS ON PAGE 142.

The *chazzan* turns to his right and carries the Torah to the *bimah,* as the congregation responds:

לְךָ *Yours, HASHEM, is the greatness, the strength, the splendor, the triumph, and the glory; even everything in heaven and earth; Yours, HASHEM, is the kingdom, and the sovereignty over every leader.*[1] *Exalt HASHEM, our God, and bow at His footstool; He is Holy! Exalt HASHEM, our God, and bow to His holy mountain; for holy is HASHEM, our God.*[2]

אַב הָרַחֲמִים *May the Father of compassion have mercy on the nation that is borne by Him, and may He remember the covenant of the spiritually mighty. May He rescue our souls from the bad times, and upbraid the evil inclination to leave those borne by Him, graciously make us an eternal remnant, and fulfill our requests in good measure, for salvation and mercy.*

The Torah is placed on the *bimah* and prepared for reading.
The *gabbai* uses the following formula to call a *Kohen* to the Torah:

וְתִגָּלֶה *And may His kingship over us be revealed and become visible soon, and may He be gracious to our remnant and the remnant of His people the Family of Israel, for graciousness, kindness, mercy, and favor. And let us respond, Amen. All of you ascribe greatness to our God and give honor to the Torah. Kohen,° approach. Stand* (name) *son of* (father's name) *the Kohen.*

°If no *Kohen* is present, the *gabbai* says: *'There is no Kohen present, stand* (name) *son of* (father's name) *an Israelite (Levite) in place of the Kohen.'*

Blessed is He Who gave the Torah to His people Israel in His holiness. (The Torah of HASHEM is perfect, restoring the soul; the testimony of HASHEM is trustworthy, making the simple one wise. The orders of HASHEM are upright, gladdening the heart; the command of HASHEM is clear, enlightening the eyes.[3] *HASHEM will give might to His nation; HASHEM will bless His nation with peace.*[4] *The God Whose way is perfect, the promise of HASHEM is flawless, He is a shield for all who take refuge in Him.*[5]*)*

Congregation, then *gabbai:*

You who cling to HASHEM, your God, you are all alive today.[6]

The reader shows the *oleh* (person called to the Torah) the place in the Torah. The *oleh* touches the Torah with a corner of his *tallis,* or the belt or mantle of the Torah, and kisses it. He then begins the blessing, bowing at *'Bless,'* and straightening up at 'HASHEM.'

Bless HASHEM, the blessed One.

Congregation, followed by *oleh,* responds, bowing at 'Blessed,' and straightening up at 'HASHEM.'

Blessed is HASHEM, the blessed One, for all eternity.

Oleh continues:

בָּרוּךְ *Blessed are You, HASHEM, our God, King of the universe, Who selected us from all the peoples and gave us His Torah. Blessed are You, HASHEM, Giver of the Torah.* (Cong.– *Amen.)*

After his Torah portion has been read, the *oleh* recites:

בָּרוּךְ *Blessed are You, HASHEM, our God, King of the universe, Who gave us the Torah of truth and implanted eternal life within us. Blessed are You, HASHEM, Giver of the Torah.* (Cong.– *Amen.)*

THE *MI SHEBEIRACH* PRAYER FOR A SICK PERSON APPEARS ON PAGE 143.

(1) *I Chronicles* 29:11. (2) *Psalms* 99:5,9. (3) 19:8-9. (4) 29:11. (5) 18:31. (6) *Deuteronomy* 4:4.

⊰∦ קריאת התורה ∦⊱

דברים ד:כה-מ

כהן – כִּי־תוֹלִיד בָּנִים וּבְנֵי בָנִים וְנוֹשַׁנְתֶּם בָּאָרֶץ וְהִשְׁחַתֶּם וַעֲשִׂיתֶם פֶּסֶל תְּמוּנַת כֹּל וַעֲשִׂיתֶם הָרַע בְּעֵינֵי־יהוָה־אֱלֹהֶיךָ לְהַכְעִיסוֹ: הַעִידֹתִי בָכֶם הַיּוֹם אֶת־הַשָּׁמַיִם וְאֶת־הָאָרֶץ כִּי־אָבֹד תֹּאבֵדוּן מַהֵר מֵעַל הָאָרֶץ אֲשֶׁר אַתֶּם עֹבְרִים אֶת־הַיַּרְדֵּן שָׁמָּה לְרִשְׁתָּהּ לֹא־תַאֲרִיכֻן יָמִים עָלֶיהָ כִּי הִשָּׁמֵד תִּשָּׁמֵדוּן: וְהֵפִיץ יהוָה אֶתְכֶם בָּעַמִּים וְנִשְׁאַרְתֶּם מְתֵי מִסְפָּר בַּגּוֹיִם אֲשֶׁר יְנַהֵג יהוָה אֶתְכֶם שָׁמָּה: וַעֲבַדְתֶּם־שָׁם אֱלֹהִים מַעֲשֵׂה יְדֵי אָדָם עֵץ וָאֶבֶן אֲשֶׁר לֹא־יִרְאוּן וְלֹא יִשְׁמְעוּן וְלֹא יֹאכְלוּן וְלֹא יְרִיחֻן: וּבִקַּשְׁתֶּם מִשָּׁם אֶת־יהוָה אֱלֹהֶיךָ וּמָצָאתָ כִּי תִדְרְשֶׁנּוּ בְּכָל־לְבָבְךָ וּבְכָל־נַפְשֶׁךָ: לוי – בַּצַּר לְךָ וּמְצָאוּךָ כֹּל הַדְּבָרִים הָאֵלֶּה בְּאַחֲרִית הַיָּמִים וְשַׁבְתָּ עַד־יהוָה אֱלֹהֶיךָ וְשָׁמַעְתָּ בְּקֹלוֹ: כִּי אֵל רַחוּם יהוָה אֱלֹהֶיךָ לֹא יַרְפְּךָ וְלֹא יַשְׁחִיתֶךָ וְלֹא יִשְׁכַּח אֶת־בְּרִית אֲבֹתֶיךָ אֲשֶׁר נִשְׁבַּע לָהֶם: כִּי שְׁאַל־נָא לְיָמִים רִאשֹׁנִים אֲשֶׁר־הָיוּ לְפָנֶיךָ לְמִן־הַיּוֹם אֲשֶׁר בָּרָא אֱלֹהִים | אָדָם עַל־הָאָרֶץ וּלְמִקְצֵה הַשָּׁמַיִם וְעַד־קְצֵה הַשָּׁמָיִם הֲנִהְיָה כַּדָּבָר הַגָּדוֹל הַזֶּה אוֹ הֲנִשְׁמַע כָּמֹהוּ: הֲשָׁמַע עָם קוֹל אֱלֹהִים מְדַבֵּר מִתּוֹךְ־הָאֵשׁ כַּאֲשֶׁר־שָׁמַעְתָּ אַתָּה וַיֶּחִי: אוֹ | הֲנִסָּה אֱלֹהִים לָבוֹא לָקַחַת לוֹ גוֹי מִקֶּרֶב גּוֹי בְּמַסֹּת בְּאֹתֹת וּבְמוֹפְתִים וּבְמִלְחָמָה וּבְיָד חֲזָקָה וּבִזְרוֹעַ נְטוּיָה וּבְמוֹרָאִים גְּדֹלִים כְּכֹל אֲשֶׁר־עָשָׂה לָכֶם יהוָה אֱלֹהֵיכֶם בְּמִצְרַיִם לְעֵינֶיךָ: אַתָּה הָרְאֵתָ לָדַעַת כִּי יהוָה הוּא הָאֱלֹהִים אֵין עוֹד מִלְבַדּוֹ: ישראל (מפטיר) – מִן־הַשָּׁמַיִם הִשְׁמִיעֲךָ אֶת־קֹלוֹ לְיַסְּרֶךָ וְעַל־הָאָרֶץ הֶרְאֲךָ אֶת־אִשּׁוֹ הַגְּדוֹלָה וּדְבָרָיו שָׁמַעְתָּ מִתּוֹךְ הָאֵשׁ: וְתַחַת כִּי אָהַב אֶת־אֲבֹתֶיךָ וַיִּבְחַר בְּזַרְעוֹ אַחֲרָיו וַיּוֹצִאֲךָ בְּפָנָיו בְּכֹחוֹ הַגָּדֹל מִמִּצְרָיִם: לְהוֹרִישׁ גּוֹיִם גְּדֹלִים וַעֲצֻמִים מִמְּךָ מִפָּנֶיךָ לַהֲבִיאֲךָ לָתֶת־לְךָ אֶת־אַרְצָם נַחֲלָה כַּיּוֹם הַזֶּה: וְיָדַעְתָּ הַיּוֹם וַהֲשֵׁבֹתָ

❧ Torah Reading

The Torah reading of Tishah B'Av encapsules Jewish history: the spiritual sloth that leads to idolatry and exile, the encouragement that it is in our power to arouse God's mercy — and that it is surely in His power to bring about the final redemption. In his warning that exile may be impending, Moses says that the main source of tragedy is that *you will have been long in the land*. For all its imperfections, the generation that experienced the Exodus and the miracles of the Wilderness and the conquest of the Land would not be quick to sin so grievously. But as the years and generations go by, people tend to grow stale, to take their advantages for granted, to forget the sense of freshness and spiritual

TORAH READING

Deuteronomy 4:25-40

Kohen – *When you beget children and grandchildren and will have been long in the land, you will grow corrupt and make a graven image of anything, and you will do evil in the eyes of* HASHEM, *your God, to anger Him. I appoint heaven and earth this day to bear witness that you will surely perish quickly from the land that you are crossing the Jordan to possess; you will not have lengthy days upon it, for you will be utterly destroyed.* HASHEM *will scatter you among the peoples, and you will be left few in number among the nations where* HASHEM *will lead you. There you will worship gods, the handiwork of man, of wood and stone, which do not see, do not hear, do not eat, and do not smell. From there you will seek* HASHEM, *your God, and you will find Him — if you search for Him with all your heart and all your soul.*

Levi – *When you are in distress and all these things have befallen you — at the end of days — you shall return unto* HASHEM, *your God, and hearken to His voice. For* HASHEM, *your God, is a merciful God, He shall not abandon you nor destroy you, and He shall not forget the covenant of your forefathers that He swore to them. For inquire now regarding the early days that were before you, from the day when* HASHEM *created man on the earth, and from one end of heaven to the other end of heaven, has there been anything like this great thing or has anything like it been heard? Has a people ever heard the voice of God speaking from amid the fire, as you heard, and survived? Or has any god ever miraculously come to take for himself one nation from the midst of another, with challenges, with signs, with wonders, with war, with a strong hand, with an outstretched arm, and with greatly awesome deeds, like everything that* HASHEM, *your God, did for you in Egypt before your eyes? You have been shown to know that* HASHEM *— He is the God! — there is none beside Him.*

Third (Maftir) – *From heaven He caused you to hear His voice in order to discipline you, and on earth He showed you His great fire, and you heard His words from amid the fire. Because He loved your forefathers He chose their offspring after them, and took it out before Him with His great strength from Egypt; to drive away before you nations that are greater and mightier than you, to bring you, to give you their land as an inheritance, as on this day. You are to know this day and take*

---

striving that brought them to their high plateau of success. Once that happens and they begin to look for new stimuli, they will begin to explore the lifestyle of their neighbors and experiment with it. In ancient times, this meant idolatry. Today, it can mean any of the numerous isms and beliefs that have led Jews astray once they have grown weary of their eternal tradition and sought more fashionable ways of life and belief.

But the Torah assures us that even after the exile takes place, there is always hope. From its place of distress, Israel will seek God and find Him, and the nation will repent and return to God. The Torah exhorts us to remember that God redeemed us in an unprecedented display of mercy and love. His love for us stems from the covenant with the Patriarchs, a phenomenon that is eternal and can never be diminished by sin or exile. Therefore we must always be aware that redemption *will* come again, and that it is in

אֶל־לְבָבֶךָ כִּי יהוה הוּא הָאֱלֹהִים בַּשָּׁמַיִם מִמַּעַל וְעַל־הָאָרֶץ מִתָּחַת אֵין עוֹד: וְשָׁמַרְתָּ אֶת־חֻקָּיו וְאֶת־מִצְוֹתָיו אֲשֶׁר אָנֹכִי מְצַוְּךָ הַיּוֹם אֲשֶׁר יִיטַב לְךָ וּלְבָנֶיךָ אַחֲרֶיךָ וּלְמַעַן תַּאֲרִיךְ יָמִים עַל־הָאֲדָמָה אֲשֶׁר יהוה אֱלֹהֶיךָ נֹתֵן לְךָ כָּל־הַיָּמִים:

PRAYER FOR A SICK PERSON / מי שברך לחולה

מִי שֶׁבֵּרַךְ אֲבוֹתֵינוּ אַבְרָהָם יִצְחָק וְיַעֲקֹב, מֹשֶׁה אַהֲרֹן דָּוִד וּשְׁלֹמֹה,

for a man

הוּא יְבָרֵךְ וִירַפֵּא אֶת הַחוֹלֶה (patient's name) בֶּן (mother's name) בַּעֲבוּר שֶׁ(supplicant's name) יִתֵּן לִצְדָקָה בַּעֲבוּרוֹ.°° בִּשְׂכַר זֶה, הַקָּדוֹשׁ בָּרוּךְ הוּא יִמָּלֵא רַחֲמִים עָלָיו, לְהַחֲלִימוֹ וּלְרַפְּאתוֹ לְהַחֲזִיקוֹ וּלְהַחֲיוֹתוֹ, וְיִשְׁלַח לוֹ מְהֵרָה רְפוּאָה שְׁלֵמָה מִן הַשָּׁמַיִם, לִרְמַ״ח אֵבָרָיו, וּשְׁסָ״ה גִּידָיו, בְּתוֹךְ

for a woman

הוּא יְבָרֵךְ וִירַפֵּא אֶת הַחוֹלָה (patient's name) בַּת (mother's name) בַּעֲבוּר שֶׁ(supplicant's name) יִתֵּן לִצְדָקָה בַּעֲבוּרָהּ.°° בִּשְׂכַר זֶה, הַקָּדוֹשׁ בָּרוּךְ הוּא יִמָּלֵא רַחֲמִים עָלֶיהָ, לְהַחֲלִימָהּ וּלְרַפְּאתָהּ וּלְהַחֲזִיקָהּ וּלְהַחֲיוֹתָהּ, וְיִשְׁלַח לָהּ מְהֵרָה רְפוּאָה שְׁלֵמָה מִן הַשָּׁמַיִם, לְכָל אֵבָרֶיהָ, וּלְכָל גִּידֶיהָ, בְּתוֹךְ

שְׁאָר חוֹלֵי יִשְׂרָאֵל, רְפוּאַת הַנֶּפֶשׁ, וּרְפוּאַת הַגּוּף, הַשְׁתָּא, בַּעֲגָלָא וּבִזְמַן קָרִיב. וְנֹאמַר: אָמֵן. (Cong.– אָמֵן.)

°°Many congregations substitute:

בַּעֲבוּר שֶׁכָּל הַקָּהָל מִתְפַּלְּלִים בַּעֲבוּרוֹ (בַּעֲבוּרָהּ)

חצי קדיש

After the last *oleh* has completed his closing blessing, the reader recites Half-*Kaddish*.

יִתְגַּדַּל וְיִתְקַדַּשׁ שְׁמֵהּ רַבָּא. (Cong.– אָמֵן.) בְּעָלְמָא דִּי בְרָא כִרְעוּתֵהּ. וְיַמְלִיךְ מַלְכוּתֵהּ, בְּחַיֵּיכוֹן וּבְיוֹמֵיכוֹן וּבְחַיֵּי דְכָל בֵּית יִשְׂרָאֵל, בַּעֲגָלָא וּבִזְמַן קָרִיב. וְאִמְרוּ: אָמֵן.

(Cong.– אָמֵן. יְהֵא שְׁמֵהּ רַבָּא מְבָרַךְ לְעָלַם וּלְעָלְמֵי עָלְמַיָּא.)

יְהֵא שְׁמֵהּ רַבָּא מְבָרַךְ לְעָלַם וּלְעָלְמֵי עָלְמַיָּא.

יִתְבָּרַךְ וְיִשְׁתַּבַּח וְיִתְפָּאַר וְיִתְרוֹמַם וְיִתְנַשֵּׂא וְיִתְהַדָּר וְיִתְעַלֶּה וְיִתְהַלָּל שְׁמֵהּ דְּקֻדְשָׁא בְּרִיךְ הוּא (Cong.– בְּרִיךְ הוּא) — לְעֵלָּא מִן כָּל בִּרְכָתָא וְשִׁירָתָא תֻּשְׁבְּחָתָא וְנֶחֱמָתָא, דַּאֲמִירָן בְּעָלְמָא. וְאִמְרוּ: אָמֵן. (Cong.– אָמֵן.)

הגבהה וגלילה

The Torah Scroll is raised and each person looks at the Torah and recites aloud:

וְזֹאת הַתּוֹרָה אֲשֶׁר שָׂם מֹשֶׁה לִפְנֵי בְּנֵי יִשְׂרָאֵל,[1] עַל פִּי יהוה בְּיַד מֹשֶׁה.[2]

to your heart that HASHEM is the only God — in heaven above and on the earth below — there is none other. You shall observe His decrees and His commandments that I command you this day, so that He will do good to you and to your children after you, and so that you will long remain on the land that HASHEM, your God, gives you, for all the years.

PRAYER FOR A SICK PERSON

מִי שֶׁבֵּרַךְ *He Who blessed our forefathers Abraham, Isaac and Jacob, Moses and Aaron, David and Solomon — may He bless and heal the sick person (* patient's Hebrew name*) son/daughter of (* patient's mother's Hebrew name*) because (* name of supplicant*) will contribute to charity on his/her behalf.*°° *In reward for this, may the Holy One, Blessed is He, be filled with*

for a man	for a woman
compassion for him to restore his health, to heal him, to strengthen him, and to revivify him. And may He send him speedily a complete recovery from heaven for his two hundred forty-eight organs and three hundred sixty-five blood vessels, among the other	*compassion for her to restore her health, to heal her, to strengthen her, and to revivify her. And may He send her speedily a complete recovery from heaven for all her organs and all her blood vessels, among the other*

sick people of Israel, a recovery of the body and a recovery of the spirit, may a recovery come speedily, swiftly and soon. Now let us respond: Amen.

(Cong. – *Amen.*)

°°Many congregations substitute:
because the entire congregation prays for him (her)

HALF KADDISH

After the last *oleh* has completed his closing blessing, the reader recites Half-*Kaddish.*

יִתְגַּדַּל *May His great Name grow exalted and sanctified* (Cong.– *Amen.*) *in the world that He created as He willed. May He give reign to His kingship in your lifetimes and in your days, and in the lifetimes of the entire Family of Israel, swiftly and soon. Now respond: Amen.*

(Cong.– *Amen. May His great Name be blessed forever and ever.*)

May His great Name be blessed forever and ever.

Blessed, praised, glorified, exalted, extolled, mighty, upraised, and lauded be the Name of the Holy One, Blessed is He (Cong.– *Blessed is He*) *— beyond any blessing and song, praise and consolation that are uttered in the world. Now respond: Amen.* (Cong.– *Amen*.)

HAGBAHAH AND GELILAH

The Torah Scroll is raised and each person looks at the Torah and recites aloud:

This is the Torah that Moses placed before the Children of Israel,[1] upon the command of HASHEM, through Moses' hand.[2]

(1) *Deuteronomy* 4:44. (2) *Numbers* 9:23.

our hands to hasten it through repentance.

Thus, the Torah reading is a ray of hope amid the gloom and tragedy of Tishah B'Av. The Destruction of the Temple and the resultant exile are still with us, and this is the day that does not let us forget that. But exile is not more a part of our history than is redemption. The difference is that exile, long though it may be, is a temporary condition; the coming of Messiah is the permanent and natural state of Jewry, may it happen speedily in our days.

Some add:

עֵץ חַיִּים הִיא לַמַּחֲזִיקִים בָּהּ, וְתֹמְכֶיהָ מְאֻשָּׁר.[1] דְּרָכֶיהָ דַרְכֵי נֹעַם, וְכָל נְתִיבוֹתֶיהָ שָׁלוֹם.[2] אֹרֶךְ יָמִים בִּימִינָהּ, בִּשְׂמֹאלָהּ עֹשֶׁר וְכָבוֹד.[3] יהוה חָפֵץ לְמַעַן צִדְקוֹ, יַגְדִּיל תּוֹרָה וְיַאְדִּיר.[4]

After the Torah Scroll has been wound, tied and covered, the *maftir* recites the *Haftarah* blessings.

ברכה קודם ההפטרה

בָּרוּךְ אַתָּה יהוה אֱלֹהֵינוּ מֶלֶךְ הָעוֹלָם, אֲשֶׁר בָּחַר בִּנְבִיאִים טוֹבִים, וְרָצָה בְדִבְרֵיהֶם הַנֶּאֱמָרִים בֶּאֱמֶת, בָּרוּךְ אַתָּה יהוה, הַבּוֹחֵר בַּתּוֹרָה וּבְמֹשֶׁה עַבְדּוֹ, וּבְיִשְׂרָאֵל עַמּוֹ, וּבִנְבִיאֵי הָאֱמֶת וָצֶדֶק: (–Cong. אָמֵן.)

הפטרה

ירמיה ח:יג-ט:כג

אָסֹף אֲסִיפֵם נְאֻם־יהוה אֵין עֲנָבִים בַּגֶּפֶן וְאֵין תְּאֵנִים בַּתְּאֵנָה וְהֶעָלֶה נָבֵל וָאֶתֵּן לָהֶם יַעַבְרוּם: עַל־מָה אֲנַחְנוּ יֹשְׁבִים הֵאָסְפוּ וְנָבוֹא אֶל־עָרֵי הַמִּבְצָר וְנִדְּמָה־שָּׁם כִּי יהוה אֱלֹהֵינוּ הֲדִמָּנוּ וַיַּשְׁקֵנוּ מֵי־רֹאשׁ כִּי חָטָאנוּ לַיהוה: קַוֵּה לְשָׁלוֹם וְאֵין טוֹב לְעֵת מַרְפֵּה וְהִנֵּה בְעָתָה: מִדָּן נִשְׁמַע נַחְרַת סוּסָיו מִקּוֹל מִצְהֲלוֹת אַבִּירָיו רָעֲשָׁה כָּל־הָאָרֶץ וַיָּבוֹאוּ וַיֹּאכְלוּ אֶרֶץ וּמְלוֹאָהּ עִיר וְיֹשְׁבֵי בָהּ: כִּי הִנְנִי מְשַׁלֵּחַ בָּכֶם נְחָשִׁים צִפְעֹנִים אֲשֶׁר אֵין־לָהֶם לָחַשׁ וְנִשְּׁכוּ אֶתְכֶם נְאֻם־יהוה: מַבְלִיגִיתִי עֲלֵי יָגוֹן עָלַי לִבִּי דַוָּי: הִנֵּה־קוֹל שַׁוְעַת בַּת־עַמִּי מֵאֶרֶץ מַרְחַקִּים הַיהוה אֵין בְּצִיּוֹן אִם־מַלְכָּהּ אֵין בָּהּ מַדּוּעַ הִכְעִסוּנִי בִּפְסִלֵיהֶם בְּהַבְלֵי נֵכָר: עָבַר קָצִיר כָּלָה קָיִץ וַאֲנַחְנוּ לוֹא נוֹשָׁעְנוּ: עַל־שֶׁבֶר בַּת־עַמִּי הָשְׁבָּרְתִּי קָדַרְתִּי שַׁמָּה הֶחֱזִקָתְנִי: הַצֳרִי אֵין בְּגִלְעָד אִם־רֹפֵא אֵין שָׁם כִּי מַדּוּעַ לֹא עָלְתָה אֲרֻכַת בַּת־עַמִּי: מִי־יִתֵּן רֹאשִׁי מַיִם וְעֵינִי מְקוֹר דִּמְעָה וְאֶבְכֶּה יוֹמָם וָלַיְלָה אֵת חַלְלֵי בַת־עַמִּי: מִי־יִתְּנֵנִי בַמִּדְבָּר מְלוֹן

(1) *Proverbs* 3:18. (2) 3:17. (3) 3:16. (4) *Isaiah* 42:21.

❧ The Haftarah

Unlike the Torah reading, which is primarily hopeful, the *Haftarah* is an almost unrelieved dirge. Indeed, it is read with the sad cantillation of Eichah until the last two verses, which, with their brief depiction of what is worthwhile and praiseworthy in human beings, points the way toward ultimate salvation. Jeremiah, the prophet of the Destruction and the author of *Eichah*, directed this harsh prophecy at his wayward brethren, in the vain hope that it would stir them to repent.

The *Haftarah* begins with a picture of the terror that the people felt. Their towns and farms

Some add:

עֵץ *It is a tree of life for those who grasp it, and its supporters are praiseworthy.*[1] *Its ways are ways of pleasantness and all its paths are peace.*[2] *Lengthy days are at its right; at its left are wealth and honor.*[3] *HASHEM desired, for the sake of its [Israel's] righteousness, that the Torah be made great and glorious.*[4]

After the Torah Scroll has been wound, tied and covered, the *maftir* recites the *Haftarah* blessings.

BLESSING BEFORE THE HAFTARAH

בָּרוּךְ *Blessed are You, HASHEM, our God, King of the universe, Who has chosen good prophets and was pleased with their words that were uttered with truth. Blessed are You, HASHEM, Who chooses the Torah; Moses, His servant; Israel, His nation; and the prophets of truth and righteousness.* (Cong.— *Amen.)*

HAFTARAH

Jeremiah 8:13-9:23

I shall utterly destroy them, the words of HASHEM, there will be no grapes on the grapevine and no figs on the fig tree, the leaf will wither, and what I have given them will pass away. 'Why do we remain here? Let us gather and come to fortified cities, there to be silent; for HASHEM, our God, has silenced us and given us poisonous water, for we have sinned to HASHEM. We are hoping for peace, but there is no good; for a time of healing, but behold! there is terror.'

From Dan was heard the snorting of his steeds, at the sound of his mighty ones' footsteps the whole land quaked; they came and devoured the land and its fullness, the city and its inhabitants. For behold! — I shall incite against you snakes, serpents, that cannot be charmed, and they shall bite you — the words of HASHEM. I seek strength against sorrow, but my heart is sick within me. Behold! the voice of My people's daughter from distant lands: 'Is HASHEM not in Zion, is its king not within it?' Why have they angered Me with their graven idols, with their alien vanities?

'The harvest has passed, the summer has ended, but we were not saved.'

Over the collapse of my people's daughter have I been shattered; I am blackened, desolation has gripped me. Is there no balm in Gilead, is there no healer there? Why has no recovery come to my people's daughter? If only someone would turn my head to water and my eye to a spring of tears, then I would cry all day and night for the slain of my daughter's people!

If only someone would make for me in the desert an inn for

---

were desolate and they fled to the cities, but there, too, they found no refuge. Foolishly and vainly they asked, Is HASHEM not in Zion, is its king not within it?; as if the God Whom they had spurned and the king who had been shorn of his power would help them.

אָרְחִים וְאֶעֶזְבָה אֶת־עַמִּי וְאֵלְכָה מֵאִתָּם כִּי כֻלָּם מְנָאֲפִים
עֲצֶרֶת בֹּגְדִים: וַיַּדְרְכוּ אֶת־לְשׁוֹנָם קַשְׁתָּם שֶׁקֶר וְלֹא לֶאֱמוּנָה
גָּבְרוּ בָאָרֶץ כִּי מֵרָעָה אֶל־רָעָה | יָצָאוּ וְאֹתִי לֹא־יָדָעוּ
נְאֻם־יְהֹוָה: אִישׁ מֵרֵעֵהוּ הִשָּׁמֵרוּ וְעַל־כָּל־אָח אַל־תִּבְטָחוּ כִּי
כָל־אָח עָקוֹב יַעְקֹב וְכָל־רֵעַ רָכִיל יַהֲלֹךְ: וְאִישׁ בְּרֵעֵהוּ יְהָתֵלּוּ
וֶאֱמֶת לֹא יְדַבֵּרוּ לִמְּדוּ לְשׁוֹנָם דַּבֶּר־שֶׁקֶר הַעֲוֵה נִלְאוּ: שִׁבְתְּךָ
בְּתוֹךְ מִרְמָה בְּמִרְמָה מֵאֲנוּ דַעַת־אוֹתִי נְאֻם־יְהֹוָה: לָכֵן כֹּה אָמַר
יְהֹוָה צְבָאוֹת הִנְנִי צוֹרְפָם וּבְחַנְתִּים כִּי־אֵיךְ אֶעֱשֶׂה מִפְּנֵי
בַּת־עַמִּי: חֵץ °שָׁחוּט לְשׁוֹנָם מִרְמָה דִבֵּר בְּפִיו שָׁלוֹם אֶת־רֵעֵהוּ
יְדַבֵּר וּבְקִרְבּוֹ יָשִׂים אָרְבּוֹ: הַעַל־אֵלֶּה לֹא־אֶפְקָד־בָּם נְאֻם־יְהֹוָה
אִם בְּגוֹי אֲשֶׁר־כָּזֶה לֹא תִתְנַקֵּם נַפְשִׁי: עַל־הֶהָרִים אֶשָּׂא בְכִי
וָנֶהִי וְעַל־נְאוֹת מִדְבָּר קִינָה כִּי נִצְּתוּ מִבְּלִי־אִישׁ עֹבֵר וְלֹא
שָׁמְעוּ קוֹל מִקְנֶה מֵעוֹף הַשָּׁמַיִם וְעַד־בְּהֵמָה נָדְדוּ הָלָכוּ: וְנָתַתִּי
אֶת־יְרוּשָׁלַם לְגַלִּים מְעוֹן תַּנִּים וְאֶת־עָרֵי יְהוּדָה אֶתֵּן שְׁמָמָה
מִבְּלִי יוֹשֵׁב: מִי־הָאִישׁ הֶחָכָם וְיָבֵן אֶת־זֹאת וַאֲשֶׁר דִּבֶּר פִּי־יְהֹוָה
אֵלָיו וְיַגִּדָהּ עַל־מָה אָבְדָה הָאָרֶץ נִצְּתָה כַמִּדְבָּר מִבְּלִי עֹבֵר:
וַיֹּאמֶר יְהֹוָה עַל־עָזְבָם אֶת־תּוֹרָתִי אֲשֶׁר נָתַתִּי לִפְנֵיהֶם וְלֹא־
שָׁמְעוּ בְקוֹלִי וְלֹא־הָלְכוּ בָהּ: וַיֵּלְכוּ אַחֲרֵי שְׁרִרוּת לִבָּם וְאַחֲרֵי
הַבְּעָלִים אֲשֶׁר לִמְּדוּם אֲבוֹתָם: לָכֵן כֹּה־אָמַר יְהֹוָה צְבָאוֹת
אֱלֹהֵי יִשְׂרָאֵל הִנְנִי מַאֲכִילָם אֶת־הָעָם הַזֶּה לַעֲנָה וְהִשְׁקִיתִים
מֵי־רֹאשׁ: וַהֲפִצוֹתִים בַּגּוֹיִם אֲשֶׁר לֹא יָדְעוּ הֵמָּה וַאֲבוֹתָם
וְשִׁלַּחְתִּי אַחֲרֵיהֶם אֶת־הַחֶרֶב עַד כַּלּוֹתִי אוֹתָם: כֹּה אָמַר יְהֹוָה
צְבָאוֹת הִתְבּוֹנְנוּ וְקִרְאוּ לַמְקוֹנְנוֹת וּתְבוֹאֶינָה וְאֶל־הַחֲכָמוֹת
שִׁלְחוּ וְתָבוֹאנָה: וּתְמַהֵרְנָה וְתִשֶּׂנָה עָלֵינוּ נֶהִי וְתֵרַדְנָה עֵינֵינוּ

° שׁוֹחֵט כ'

Then Jeremiah speaks of his personal despair at the degradation of his people. He is
blackened. There is no balm to soothe his
hurt. He wishes his eyes had enough tears for
him to express his heartbreak. On the other
hand, when he views their grievous sins, he
wishes there were an inn in an isolated desert
where he could escape from them. They are
immoral and traitorous to God. Their tongues
are like bows shooting arrows of falsehood and
slander. Consequently, God must smelt them
and test them, in the hope that through punishment and suffering they will repent. So the
punishment comes, and it is harsh indeed — but
the behavior of the nation leaves God no
alternative.

'Why did it happen?' the prophet asks. Because they forsook the Torah, upon which the
Sages comment that God declares, 'I wish they
had forsaken Me, but not forsaken My Torah,

guests, then I would forsake my people and leave them; for they are all adulterers, a band of traitors. 'They bend their tongue with falsehood like a bow, not for good faith have they grown strong in the land, for they progress from evil to evil, but Me they did not know' — the words of HASHEM. *'Every man beware of his fellow, and do not trust any kin; for every kinsman acts perversely, and every fellow mongers slander. Every man mocks his fellow and they do not speak the truth; they train their tongue in speaking falsehood, striving to be iniquitous. Your dwelling is amid deceit, through deceit they refuse to know Me' — the words of* HASHEM.

Therefore, so says HASHEM, *Master of Legions, 'Behold! I shall smelt them and test them — for what then can I do for My people's daughter? Their tongue is a drawn arrow, speaking deceit; with his tongue one speaks peace, but in his heart he lays his ambush. Shall I not punish them for these?' — the words of* HASHEM — *'For a nation like this, shall My soul not take vengeance?'*

'For the mountains I shall raise a wailing and lament, and for the pasture of the wilderness a dirge, for they will have become desolate without a passerby and they will not have heard the sound of flocks; from the bird of heaven to cattle they have wandered off and gone. I shall make Jerusalem heaps of rubble, a lair of snakes; and the cities of Judah I shall turn to desolation, without inhabitant.'

Who is the wise man who will understand this, to whom the mouth of HASHEM *speaks — let him relate it: 'For what reason did the land perish, become parched like a desert, without passerby?'*

And HASHEM *said, 'Because they forsook My Torah that I put before them, and did not heed My voice nor follow it. They followed the wantonness of their heart, and after the baal-idols, as their fathers taught them!'*

Therefore, so says HASHEM, *Master of Legions, the God of Israel, 'Behold! — I feed this people wormwood and give them poisonous water to drink. I shall scatter them among the nations whom they did not know, neither they nor their fathers; I shall send the sword after them until I destroy them!'*

So said HASHEM, *Master of Legions, 'Contemplate, summon the dirge-women and let them come, and send for the wise women and let them come.'*

Let them hurry and raise up a lament for us, let our eyes run with

---

because its spiritual glow would have turned them back to the good.' This has remained a lesson for all time: The Torah is Israel's ultimate hope of restoration to its former position of glory.

The *Haftarah* concludes with another timeless guide to the road map of life. Let people never seek their glory in transient and inconsequential matters such as ordinary wisdom, strength and wealth. Only knowledge of God is

דִּמְעָה וְעַפְעַפֵּינוּ יִזְּלוּ־מָיִם: כִּי קוֹל נְהִי נִשְׁמַע מִצִּיּוֹן אֵיךְ שֻׁדָּדְנוּ בֹּשְׁנוּ מְאֹד כִּי־עָזַבְנוּ אָרֶץ כִּי הִשְׁלִיכוּ מִשְׁכְּנוֹתֵינוּ: כִּי־שְׁמַעְנָה נָשִׁים דְּבַר־יהוה וְתִקַּח אָזְנְכֶם דְּבַר־פִּיו וְלַמֵּדְנָה בְנוֹתֵיכֶם נֶהִי וְאִשָּׁה רְעוּתָהּ קִינָה: כִּי־עָלָה מָוֶת בְּחַלּוֹנֵינוּ בָּא בְּאַרְמְנוֹתֵינוּ לְהַכְרִית עוֹלָל מִחוּץ בַּחוּרִים מֵרְחֹבוֹת: דַּבֵּר כֹּה נְאֻם־יהוה וְנָפְלָה נִבְלַת הָאָדָם כְּדֹמֶן עַל־פְּנֵי הַשָּׂדֶה וּכְעָמִיר מֵאַחֲרֵי הַקֹּצֵר וְאֵין מְאַסֵּף: כֹּה ׀ אָמַר יהוה אַל־יִתְהַלֵּל חָכָם בְּחָכְמָתוֹ וְאַל־יִתְהַלֵּל הַגִּבּוֹר בִּגְבוּרָתוֹ אַל־יִתְהַלֵּל עָשִׁיר בְּעָשְׁרוֹ: כִּי אִם־בְּזֹאת יִתְהַלֵּל הַמִּתְהַלֵּל הַשְׂכֵּל וְיָדֹעַ אוֹתִי כִּי אֲנִי יהוה עֹשֶׂה חֶסֶד מִשְׁפָּט וּצְדָקָה בָּאָרֶץ כִּי־בְאֵלֶּה חָפַצְתִּי נְאֻם־יהוה:

ברכות לאחר ההפטרה

After the *Haftarah* is read, the *oleh* recites the following blessings.

בָּרוּךְ אַתָּה יהוה אֱלֹהֵינוּ מֶלֶךְ הָעוֹלָם, צוּר כָּל הָעוֹלָמִים, צַדִּיק בְּכָל הַדּוֹרוֹת, הָאֵל הַנֶּאֱמָן הָאוֹמֵר וְעֹשֶׂה, הַמְּדַבֵּר וּמְקַיֵּם, שֶׁכָּל דְּבָרָיו אֱמֶת וָצֶדֶק. נֶאֱמָן אַתָּה הוּא יהוה אֱלֹהֵינוּ, וְנֶאֱמָנִים דְּבָרֶיךָ, וְדָבָר אֶחָד מִדְּבָרֶיךָ אָחוֹר לֹא יָשׁוּב רֵיקָם, כִּי אֵל מֶלֶךְ נֶאֱמָן (וְרַחֲמָן) אָתָּה. בָּרוּךְ אַתָּה יהוה, הָאֵל הַנֶּאֱמָן בְּכָל דְּבָרָיו. (–Cong. אָמֵן.)

רַחֵם עַל צִיּוֹן כִּי הִיא בֵּית חַיֵּינוּ, וְלַעֲלוּבַת נֶפֶשׁ תּוֹשִׁיעַ בִּמְהֵרָה בְיָמֵינוּ. בָּרוּךְ אַתָּה יהוה, מְשַׂמֵּחַ צִיּוֹן בְּבָנֶיהָ. (–Cong. אָמֵן.)

שַׂמְּחֵנוּ יהוה אֱלֹהֵינוּ בְּאֵלִיָּהוּ הַנָּבִיא עַבְדֶּךָ, וּבְמַלְכוּת בֵּית דָּוִד מְשִׁיחֶךָ, בִּמְהֵרָה יָבֹא וְיָגֵל לִבֵּנוּ, עַל כִּסְאוֹ לֹא יֵשֵׁב זָר וְלֹא יִנְחֲלוּ עוֹד אֲחֵרִים אֶת כְּבוֹדוֹ, כִּי בְשֵׁם קָדְשְׁךָ נִשְׁבַּעְתָּ לּוֹ, שֶׁלֹּא יִכְבֶּה נֵרוֹ לְעוֹלָם וָעֶד. בָּרוּךְ אַתָּה יהוה, מָגֵן דָּוִד. (–Cong. אָמֵן.)

---

worthwhile — and if that is someone's priority, then even his wisdom, strength, and wealth are praiseworthy, because they have become his tools in the service of God.

tears and our pupils flow with water. For the sound of lament would be heard in Zion: 'How we have been plundered, how greatly we are shamed, for we have left the land, for our dwellings have cast us out! Hearken, O women, to the word of HASHEM and let your ears absorb the word of his mouth, and teach a lament to your daughters, and each woman a dirge to her friend. For death has ascended through our windows, it has come into our palaces to cut down infants from the marketplace, young men from the streets.'

Speak thus — the words of HASHEM — 'Human corpses will fall like dung on the open field and like a sheaf behind the harvester, but none shall gather them up.'

So says HASHEM, 'Let not the wise man laud himself with his wisdom, and let not the strong man laud himself with his strength, and let not the rich man laud himself with his wealth. Only with this may one laud himself — discernment in knowing Me, for I am HASHEM Who does kindness, justice, and righteousness in the land, for in these is My desire,' the words of HASHEM.

BLESSINGS AFTER THE HAFTARAH

After the *Haftarah* is read, the *oleh* recites the following blessings.

בָּרוּךְ *Blessed are You, HASHEM, King of the universe, Rock of all eternities, Righteous in all generations, the trustworthy God, Who says and does, Who speaks and fulfills, all of Whose words are true and righteous. Trustworthy are You, HASHEM, our God, and trustworthy are Your words, not one of Your words is turned back to its origin unfulfilled, for You are God, trustworthy (and compassionate) King. Blessed are You, HASHEM, the God Who is trustworthy in all His words.* (Cong.– *Amen.*)

רַחֵם *Have mercy on Zion for it is the source of our life; to the one who is deeply humiliated bring salvation speedily, in our days. Blessed are You, HASHEM, Who gladdens Zion through her children.* (Cong.– *Amen.*)

שַׂמְּחֵנוּ *Gladden us, HASHEM, our God, with Elijah the prophet, Your servant, and with the kingdom of the House of David, Your anointed, may he come speedily and cause our heart to exult. On his throne let no stranger sit nor let others continue to inherit his honor, for by Your holy Name You swore to him that his heir will not be extinguished forever and ever. Blessed are You, HASHEM, Shield of David.* (Cong.– *Amen.*)

הכנסת ספר תורה

Chazzan takes the Torah in his right arm and recites:

יְהַלְלוּ אֶת שֵׁם יהוה, כִּי נִשְׂגָּב שְׁמוֹ לְבַדּוֹ –

Congregation responds:

– הוֹדוֹ עַל אֶרֶץ וְשָׁמָיִם. וַיָּרֶם קֶרֶן לְעַמּוֹ, תְּהִלָּה לְכָל חֲסִידָיו, לִבְנֵי יִשְׂרָאֵל עַם קְרֹבוֹ, הַלְלוּיָהּ.[1]

As the Torah is carried to the Ark, the congregation recites Psalm 24, לְדָוִד מִזְמוֹר.

לְדָוִד מִזְמוֹר, לַיהוה הָאָרֶץ וּמְלוֹאָהּ, תֵּבֵל וְיֹשְׁבֵי בָהּ. כִּי הוּא עַל יַמִּים יְסָדָהּ, וְעַל נְהָרוֹת יְכוֹנְנֶהָ. מִי יַעֲלֶה בְהַר יהוה, וּמִי יָקוּם בִּמְקוֹם קָדְשׁוֹ. נְקִי כַפַּיִם וּבַר לֵבָב, אֲשֶׁר לֹא נָשָׂא לַשָּׁוְא נַפְשִׁי וְלֹא נִשְׁבַּע לְמִרְמָה. יִשָּׂא בְרָכָה מֵאֵת יהוה, וּצְדָקָה מֵאֱלֹהֵי יִשְׁעוֹ. זֶה דּוֹר דֹּרְשָׁיו, מְבַקְשֵׁי פָנֶיךָ, יַעֲקֹב, סֶלָה. שְׂאוּ שְׁעָרִים רָאשֵׁיכֶם, וְהִנָּשְׂאוּ פִּתְחֵי עוֹלָם, וְיָבוֹא מֶלֶךְ הַכָּבוֹד. מִי זֶה מֶלֶךְ הַכָּבוֹד, יהוה עִזּוּז וְגִבּוֹר, יהוה גִּבּוֹר מִלְחָמָה. שְׂאוּ שְׁעָרִים רָאשֵׁיכֶם, וּשְׂאוּ פִּתְחֵי עוֹלָם, וְיָבֹא מֶלֶךְ הַכָּבוֹד. מִי הוּא זֶה מֶלֶךְ הַכָּבוֹד, יהוה צְבָאוֹת הוּא מֶלֶךְ הַכָּבוֹד, סֶלָה.

As the Torah is placed into the Ark, the congregation recites the following verses:

וּבְנֻחֹה יֹאמַר, שׁוּבָה יהוה רִבְבוֹת אַלְפֵי יִשְׂרָאֵל.[2] קוּמָה יהוה לִמְנוּחָתֶךָ, אַתָּה וַאֲרוֹן עֻזֶּךָ. כֹּהֲנֶיךָ יִלְבְּשׁוּ צֶדֶק, וַחֲסִידֶיךָ יְרַנֵּנוּ. בַּעֲבוּר דָּוִד עַבְדֶּךָ אַל תָּשֵׁב פְּנֵי מְשִׁיחֶךָ.[3] כִּי לֶקַח טוֹב נָתַתִּי לָכֶם, תּוֹרָתִי אַל תַּעֲזֹבוּ.[4] ❖ עֵץ חַיִּים הִיא לַמַּחֲזִיקִים בָּהּ, וְתֹמְכֶיהָ מְאֻשָּׁר.[5] דְּרָכֶיהָ דַרְכֵי נֹעַם, וְכָל נְתִיבוֹתֶיהָ שָׁלוֹם.[6] הֲשִׁיבֵנוּ יהוה אֵלֶיךָ וְנָשׁוּבָה, חַדֵּשׁ יָמֵינוּ כְּקֶדֶם.[7]

---

(1) *Psalms* 148:13-14. (2) *Numbers* 10:36. (3) *Psalms* 132:8-10.
(4) *Proverbs* 4:2. (5) 3:18. (6) 3:17. (7) *Lamentations* 5:21.

RETURNING THE TORAH

Chazzan takes the Torah in his right arm and recites:

Let them praise the Name of HASHEM, for His Name alone will have been exalted –

Congregation responds:

— His glory is above earth and heaven. And He will have exalted the pride of His people, causing praise for all His devout ones, for the Children of Israel, His intimate nation. Halleluyah![1]

As the Torah is carried to the Ark, the congregation recites Psalm 24, *'Of David a psalm.'*

לְדָוִד *Of David a psalm. HASHEM's is the earth and its fullness, the inhabited land and those who dwell in it. For He founded it upon seas, and established it upon rivers. Who may ascend the mountain of HASHEM, and who may stand in the place of His sanctity? One with clean hands and pure heart, who has not sworn in vain by My soul and has not sworn deceitfully. He will receive a blessing from HASHEM and just kindness from the God of his salvation. This is the generation of those who seek Him, those who strive for Your Presence — Jacob, Selah. Raise up your heads, O gates, and be uplifted, you everlasting entrances, so that the King of Glory may enter. Who is this King of Glory? — HASHEM, the mighty and strong, HASHEM, the strong in battle. Raise up your heads, O gates, and raise up, you everlasting entrances, so that the King of Glory may enter. Who then is the King of Glory? HASHEM, Master of Legions, He is the King of Glory. Selah!*

As the Torah is placed into the Ark, the congregation recites the following verses:

וּבְנֻחֹה *And when it rested he would say, 'Return, HASHEM, to the myriad thousands of Israel.'*[2] *Arise, HASHEM, to Your resting place, You and the Ark of Your strength. Let Your priests be clothed in righteousness, and Your devout ones will sing joyously. For the sake of David, Your servant, turn not away the face of Your anointed.*[3] *For I have given you a good teaching, do not forsake My Torah.*[4] Chazzan– *It is a tree of life for those who grasp it, and its supporters are praiseworthy.*[5] *Its ways are ways of pleasantness and all its paths are peace.*[6] *Bring us back to You, HASHEM, and we shall return, renew our days as of old.*[7]

קינות

ו.

שָׁבַת* **סוּרוּ**[1] מֶנִּי שִׁמְּעוּנִי עוֹבְרַי,[2][3]
סְחִי וּמָאוּס הֶשִׁימוּנִי[4] בְּעֶדְרֵי חֲבֵרַי,[5]
סַכּוֹתָה[6] מִשְׁכַּן מִסְּכוֹת דְּבִירַי,
סַכּוֹתָ[7] וְהֶבְלְגוּ גִבּוֹרַי,
סָפְקוּ כַף[8] וּמָעֲדוּ אֵבָרַי,
כִּסְלָה כָל אַבִּירַי.[9]

נָפְלָה[10] **עוֹדֵינוּ**[11] בְּצוּל דְּכוּיָה,
עֵינִי[12] חִכְּתָה לַחֲזוֹן בֶּן בֶּרֶכְיָה,*
עַד[13] פִּלְאֵי גִּלְגָּל* חֲבוּיָה,[14]
עֵינִי[15] מְעוֹלֶלֶת בִּיוָנִית נְכוּיָה,*
עָשָׂה[16] וְנִחַם וַיִּקְרָא לִבְכִיָּה,
וְנָם עַל אֵלֶּה אֲנִי בוֹכִיָּה.[17]

עַל[18] **פְּנֵי**[19] פְּרַת נֻפְּצוּ חֲסִידֶיהָ,*
פַּלְגֵי[20] סוּף זָכְרָה כְּעָרוּ יְסוֹדֶיהָ,[21]

---

(1) *Eichah* 5:15. (2) 4:15. (3) Some editions read עוֹכְרַי, *those who besmirched me.*
(4) Cf. *Eichah* 3:45. (5) Cf. *Song of Songs* 1:7. (6) *Eichah* 3:44. (7) Cf. 3:43. (8) 2:15. (9) Cf. 1:15.
(10) 5:16. (11) Cf. 4:17. (12) 3:51. (13) 3:50. (14) Some editions read חֲכוּיָה, *awaited*.
(15) *Eichah* 3:49. (16) 2:17. (17) 1:16. (18) 5:17. (19) 4:16. (20) 3:48. (21) Cf. *Psalms* 137:7.

שָׁבַת ◆ — *Everything came to a standstill!* R' Elazar HaKalir, one of the earliest *paytanim* (composers of liturgical poems), was a master at weaving seemingly diverse elements into a well-constructed, albeit difficult to understand, whole. In this first *kinnah* of the morning service, he has linked the verses of the respective chapters of *Eichah* into an intricate chain according to the following formula:

(a) each stanza contains six lines that correspond to the six alphabets of *Eichah* (chapters one, two and four contain 22 verses each, and are arranged according to an *aleph-beis* acrostic; chapter three comprises three verses beginning with א, three with ב, and so on);

(b) the first line of each sextet begins with the opening word or phrase of the corresponding verse in chapter five of *Eichah* (these do not follow an *aleph-beis* format), and is followed by the opening word or phrase of the corresponding verse in chapter four;

(c) the next three lines correspond to the respective triad of verses in chapter three, each set in the reverse order of its appearance in *Eichah;*

(d) the fifth line of each stanza corresponds to the verses in chapter two; and

(e) the final line is taken in its entirety from chapter one, and determines the stanza's rhyme syllable. [All of the words and phrases taken from *Eichah* appear in bold type in the Hebrew text.]

The concluding stanza deviates from the established pattern. Its first five lines contain an acrostic of the author's name אֶלְעָזָר, *Elazar,* and it closes with the refrain of the following *kinnah,* thus serving as a connective between the two.

Interestingly, the *kinnah* includes only eight stanzas taken from the last eight verses (or, in chapter three, the last eight triads) of the chapter of *Eichah.* Many commentators therefore regard this *kinnah* as the conclusion of a

KINNOS

6.

ס *Everything came to a standstill!*[1]*
'Turn away[2] *from me!' those who exiled me*[3] *made me hear.*
They made me a filth and refuse[4]
amidst the flocks of my fellow [nations].[5]
You have enveloped[6] *Your [heavenly] Tabernacle,*
that it not see my [earthly] Temple.
You have enveloped Yourself,[7] *so my warriors are overpowered.*
They [my enemies] clapped their hands [in derision][8]
and my limbs faltered
as they trampled all my heroes.[9]

ע *[Jerusalem] has fallen,*[10] *it remains*[11] *sunk in the watery depths.*
My eye[12] *still longs for the vision of [Zechariah]*
*the son of Berechiah,**
but until[13] *[we are shown] miracles [like those] of Gilgal,**
[that prophecy] has been hidden.[14]
My eye[15] *brings forth tears, because we are crippled by quicksand.**
He [God] caused[16] *[the Destruction], then regretted it,*
summoning [Israel] to cry,
saying, 'Over these things I weep.'[17]

פ *On*[18] *the surface*[19] *of the Euphrates her pious ones were mutilated;**
yet she remembered the splitting[20] *of the Sea of Reeds,*
even while her foundation was being destroyed.[21]

14-stanza *kerovah* (*piyut* recited at various points during the *chazzan's* repetition of the *Shemoneh Esrei*) written by R' Elazar HaKalir, and recited by some congregations. That *kerovah* is based on the first 14 verses of *Eichah's* chapters.

לְחָזוֹן בֶּן בֶּרֶכְיָה — *For the vision of [Zechariah] the son of Berechiah.* Zechariah's prophecies are full of hope and optimism. The Talmud points especially to his proclamation: *Thus says* HASHEM, *Master of Legions, 'Elderly men and women will yet sit in the streets of Jerusalem, each with his staff in hand due to old age. And the streets of the city will be filled with boys and girls; they will be playing in the streets'* (*Zechariah* 8:4-5; see *Makkos* 24b).

פִּלְאֵי גִלְגָּל — *Miracles [like those of] Gilgal.* While the Israelites were encamped at Gilgal, they won many battles in miraculous fashion. For example, at Gibeon, God caused the sun to remain in the skies long after it should have set. Thus, Joshua and his forces were able to annihilate the enemy, before they had a chance to retreat under cover of night. Additionally, God caused a heavy hailstorm to rain upon the five armies allied against Israel so that *more had died by the hailstones than had been put to the sword by the Children of Israel* (*Joshua* 10:11).

בִּיוָנִית נְכוּיָה — *Crippled by quicksand.* The word בִּיוָנִית is derived from יָוֵן, *thick mud* (as in *Psalms* 40:3 and 69:3). Thus, the phrase means that we are lost in a quagmire of troubles.

Alternatively, the word is derived from יָוָן, *Greece,* and is an allusion to חָכְמַת יְוָנִית, *Greek wisdom,* a form of sign-language code instrumental (to a degree) in sowing the seeds that led to the Destruction of the Second Temple (see *Menachos* 64b; see also *Bava Kamma* 83a).

עַל פְּנֵי פְרָת נִפְּצוּ חֲסִידֶיהָ — *On the surface of the Euphrates her pious ones were mutilated.* The Midrash teaches that when Nebuchadnezzar saw the renowned Levite singers who once sang in the Temple, he demanded that they serenade him as he feasted merrily over his victory, *'Sing for us from Zion's song!'* (*Psalms* 137:3). Without any hesitation, the Levites hung their precious musical instruments on the trees and deliberately

פַּחַד[1] חֵטְא שִׁילֹה* תָּכַף סוֹדֶיהָ,
פָּצוּ[2] חֲזִירֵי יַעַר[3] אַיֵּה חֲסִידֶיהָ,
פָּצוּ[4] מַעֲשֵׂה עֶרְיָה לְנִדֶּיהָ,
פֵּרְשָׂה צִיּוֹן בְּיָדֶיהָ.[5]

עַל הַר צִיּוֹן[6] **צָדוּ**[7] שְׁאוֹנֵי מְדָנַי,
צָפוּ עַל רָאשֵׁי[8] צִיּוֹן זְדוֹנַי,
צָמְתוּ[9] בְּנֹב לַעֲמוֹד[10]* זְדוֹנַי,
צוֹד[11] נָצַרְתָּ לְעוֹרֵר מְדָנַי,
צָעַק[12] עַמִּי בִּימֵי בֶן דִּינַי,*
צַדִּיק הוּא יהוה.[13]

אַתָּה[14] **קַלִּים**[15] הִכְבַּדְתָּ וּמֵעֶדְיִי עֶרְמוֹנִי,
קֵרַבְתָּ[16] בֹּא אֵלַי וַיַּחֲרִימוּנִי,
קָרָאתִי[17] לְיוֹשְׁבֵי גִבְעוֹן עוֹד הֵם זֵרְמוֹנִי,
קוֹלִי לְהַשְׁמִיעַ[18] בַּעֲרַב* הַגְּרִימוֹנִי,
קוּמִי[19] עֲבוּרִי בְּהָתֵל הֶעֱרִימוּנִי,
קָרָאתִי לַמְאַהֲבַי* הֵמָּה רִמּוּנִי.[20]

לָמָּה[21] **רוּחַ אַפֵּינוּ**[22] לַטֶּבַח שְׁמָרוּ,[23]
רָאִיתָ[24] כִּי כְּתַנּוּר עוֹרָם[25] כָּמָרוּ,[26]
רָאִיתָ[27] כִּי עָמָל וָכַעַס בְּאִוּוּיךָ גָּמָרוּ,
רַבְתָּ[28] בְּיַד יְחֶזְקֵאל לִנְקוֹם כְּמוֹ מָרוּ,

(1) *Eichah* 3:47. (2) 3:46. (3) Cf. *Psalms* 80:14. (4) *Eichah* 2:16. (5) 1:17. (6) 5:18. (7) 4:18. (8) Cf. 3:54. (9) 3:53. (10) See *Isaiah* 10:32. (11) *Eichah* 3:52; some editions read צור, but that is erroneous since the corresponding verse in *Eichah* reads צוד (*Beis Levi*). (12) 2:18. (13) 1:18. (14) 5:19. (15) 4:19. (16) Cf. 3:57. (17) 3:55. (18) Cf. 3:56. (19) 2:19. (20) 1:19. (21) 5:20. (22) 4:20. (23) See prefatory comments to *kinnah* 11. (24) Cf. *Eichah* 3:60. (25) Some editions read עוֹרִי, *my skin;* some read עוֹרֵנוּ, *our skin.* (26) Cf. *Eichah* 5:10. (27) Cf. 3:59. (28) 3:58.

mutilated their fingers, making it impossible for them to play the stringed instruments. Thus they did flatly refuse to play for Nebuchadnezzar but declared, *'How can we sing the song of* HASHEM? (ibid. 137:4). We cannot make any more music with these crippled hands!' (*Pesikta Rabasi* 31).

פַּחַד חֵטְא שִׁילֹה — *The dread of the sins of Shiloh.* Jeremiah had warned the nation that just as the Tabernacle at Shiloh had come to destruction because of the sins of the sons of Eli the *Kohen Gadol*, so would the *Beis HaMikdash* be destroyed because of the people's sinfulness (see *Jeremiah* 7:12 and 26:6). And now that his message had been ignored, his dread prophecy came true.

בְּנֹב לַעֲמוֹד — *To stand [against me] at Nob.* King Saul, in his mistaken belief that the *Kohanim* of

The dread[1] of the sins of Shiloh was swiftly fulfilled*
by the conspirators against her.
They jeered,[2] those wild boars of the forest,[3]
'Where are her pious ones?'
They uncovered[4] shameful acts in order to disgrace her.
And Zion spread her hands [in despair].[5]

צ *On Mt. Zion[6] an ambush was laid[7] by the enemy hordes.*
My vicious enemies surged over the heads[8] of Zion.
My vicious enemies gathered[9]
*to stand [against me] at Nob.[10]**
You preserved [the memory of][11]
that sin in order to incite my foes.
*My nation cried out[12] in the days of the son of Dinai,**
'He, HASHEM, is righteous!'[13]

ק *You[14] elevated the lowly[15]*
and they denuded me of my jewelry.
You caused them to close in[16]
on me and they devastated me.
I called[17] to the citizens of Gibeon [for help],
but they too drowned me.
I cried out loud[18] [for relief] in Arabia, but they crushed me.*
'Arise![19] Travel through [safely]!' is how they mocked me.
I called for my lovers, but they deceived me.[20]*

ר *Why[21] did they anticipate butchering [King Josiah,][22]*
the very life breath of our nostrils?[23]
You have seen[24] how they scorched their skin[25] like a furnace.[26]
You have seen[27] how they consummated
offensive and outrageous acts within Your desirous [Temple].
You admonished[28] [Israel] through Ezekiel,
warning that Your revenge would match their rebelliousness.

---

the Tabernacle at Nob were conspiring with David against him, had eighty-five *Kohanim* slain, along with their wives, children, neighbors and cattle (*I Samuel* 22:12-19). The Talmud reports that on the day of that slaughter, God ordained that retribution for that act will take place (in a later year) on the ninth of Av (*Sanhedrin* 95a).

בֶּן דִּינַי — *The son of Dinai.* Eliezer ben Dinai was an infamous murderer (*Sotah* 47a; *Kesubos* 27a). His unsuccessful revolt against Roman domination brought swift retribution and heavy bloodshed (see *Shir HaShirim Rabbah* 2:7). Josephus (*Antiquities* XX, 8) describes how he was captured and brought to Rome for trial.

בַּעֲרָב — *In Arabia.* When the captive Israelites were led through the Ishmaelite lands of Arabia, the local populace met them and appeared interested in helping them. The Arabs pretended friendship and sympathy, and offered food and drink. However, the bread they offered had been oversalted in order to cause the Jews great and painful thirst. Then the Ishmaelites proferred leather canteens filled, not with water, but with air. When the captives raised the containers to their mouths, the hot, stagnant air entered their bodies and they died (*Tanchuma*, *Yisro* 5).

לִמְאַהֲבַי — *To my lovers.* The prophet compares alliance with foreign nations (rather than a return of God and reliance on His salvation) to an illicit affair with a pseudo-lover.

רְאֵה[1] וְנַכְחִידֵם מִגּוֹי[2] אָמָרוּ,
רְאֵה יהוה כִּי צַר לִי מֵעַי חֳמַרְמָרוּ.[3]

הֲשִׁיבֵנוּ[4] **שִׂישִׂי**[5] שְׁמַע לְגוֹי צֹאֲנִי,
שִׁבְתָּם[6] רְמוֹס חֲצֵרַי[7] לְהַדְכִּיאֵנִי,
שִׂפְתֵי[8] מְשׁוֹרְרֵי דְבִיר דָּמְמוּ לְהַדְאִיבֵנִי,
שָׁמַעְתָּ[9] זְמוֹרוֹת[10] אַף הֵכִין לְטַאטְאֵנִי,
שָׁכְבוּ[11] וְנָדוּ חָצָץ לְהַבְרִיאֵנִי,[12]*
שָׁמְעוּ כִּי נֶאֱנָחָה אָנִי.[13]

כִּי[14] **תָּם**[15] חָקְקְתָּ בְּכֵס אוֹפַנֶּיךָ,
תָּשִׁיב לָהֶם גְּמוּל[16] כְּאָז חֲזוֹת פָּנֶיךָ,
תִּרְדּוֹף[17] לְצַלְמוֹן יוֹעֲצֵי[18] עַל צְפוּנֶיךָ,[19]
תִּתֵּן[20] לְהַבְהֵב נוֹתְצֵי פְנִינֶיךָ,
תִּקְרָא[21] לְשַׁכְּרָם כּוֹס כָּמוּס בְּפְנֶיךָ,[22]
תָּבֹא כָל רָעָתָם לְפָנֶיךָ.[23]

תָּבֹא אֶל צָר אֲשֶׁר כִּלָּנוּ,
לִמְבוֹא חֲמָת[24] בְּחֵמָה נִהֲלָנוּ,
עַד לַחֲלַח וְחָבוֹר הִגְלָנוּ,[25]
זָקֵן וּבָחוּר וּבְתוּלָה כִּבְלָנוּ,[26]
רָם הַבֶּט נָא עַמְּךָ כֻלָּנוּ,[27]
זְכוֹר יהוה מֶה הָיָה לָנוּ.[28]

(1) *Eichah* 2:20. (2) *Psalms* 83:5. (3) *Eichah* 1:20. (4) 5:21. (5) 4:21.
(6) 3:63. (7) *Isaiah* 1:12. (8) *Eichah* 3:62. (9) 3:61.
(10) Cf. *Ezekiel* 8:17; see the commentaries there. (11) *Eichah* 2:21. (12) Cf. 3:17.
(13) 1:21. (14) 5:22. (15) 4:22; see *Rashi* to *Ezekiel* 1:5. (16) *Eichah* 3:64. (17) 3:66.
(18) Some editions read יוֹעֲצֵי רָע, *those who plot evil.* (19) Cf. *Psalms* 83:4.
(20) *Eichah* 3:65. (21) 2:22. (22) Some editions read בְּפָנֶיךָ, *before You.* (23) 1:22.
(24) Cf. *Amos* 6:14. (25) *II Kings* 17:6. (26) Cf. *Jeremiah* 51:22. (27) *Isaiah* 64:8. (28) *Eichah* 5:1.

חָצָץ לְהַבְרִיאֵנִי — *They [my captors] fed me pebbles.* God had told the prophet (*Ezekiel* 12:3) to prepare easily portable cooking utensils for use during the trip into exile. The purpose of the command was that others might follow his example and thus be prepared

See[1] how [our enemies] have said,
'Let us obliterate them from nationhood!'[2]
Observe, HASHEM, how distressed I am;
my insides churn![3]

ש *Bring us back to You;[4] [and fulfill the threat You made]*
to the nation which exiled us, 'Rejoice [and exult,
O daughter of Edom. . .to you too will the cup
(of punishment) pass].'[5]
[Crush] their dwelling places,[6]
just as they trampled my courtyards[7] to crush me.
They stilled the lips[8] of the Temple singers,
and made me miserable.
You heard[9] their derisive songs[10]
of how they would sweep me away.
When they [my nation] rested[11] after they had traveled,
*they [my captors] fed me pebbles.[12]**
They heard how I sighed.[13]

ת *For[14] You engraved the likeness of the perfect one [Jacob][15]*
on the throne of Your angelic Ofanim.
[Therefore] mete out their punishment[16] as on the day
[Israel] beheld Your countenance [at the Sea of Reeds];
chase[17] into the dark shadows of Hell all those who plot[18]
against [Israel,] the ones You shelter;[19]
consign[20] into the flame those who smashed
Your precious gem[like Temples].
Designate[21] [a date on which they will be forced] to drink
the intoxicating cup [of retribution] hidden in Your corners.[22]
Let all their wickedness come before You.[23]

א *May [retribution] come upon the tormentor*
who tried to destroy us completely.
ל *In fury he led us to the entrance of Hamath.[24]*
ע *Unto Halah and Habor he exiled us.[25]*
ז *Old man, youth and maiden — he shackled us [all].[26]*
ר *O Supreme One, please look down,*
for we are all Your nation.[27]
Remember, HASHEM, what has befallen us![28]

---

to cope with the rigors of the journey. But the people jeered at him and did not obey. Therefore, the exiles had to knead their dough in pits dug into the ground and their bread became mixed with grit (*Rashi* to *Eichah* 3:16).

ז.

אֵיכָה אַצְתָּ בְאַפֶּךָ,* לְאַבֵּד בְּיַד אֲדוֹמִים אֱמוּנֶיךָ,
וְלֹא זָכַרְתָּ בְּרִית בֵּין הַבְּתָרִים[1] אֲשֶׁר בֵּרַרְתָּ לִבְחוּנֶיךָ,
וּבְכֵן בִּטֵּינוּ, זְכוֹר יהוה מֶה הָיָה לָנוּ.[2]

אֵיכָה גָּעַרְתָּ בְּגַעֲרָתֶךָ, לִגְלוֹת בְּיַד גֵּאִים גְּאוּלֶיךָ,
וְלֹא זָכַרְתָּ דְּלִיגַת דִּלּוּג דֶּרֶךְ* אֲשֶׁר דָּלַגְתָּ לִדְגָלֶיךָ,
וּבְכֵן דִּבַּרְנוּ, זְכוֹר יהוה מֶה הָיָה לָנוּ.

אֵיכָה הַגְּתָּ בְּהֶגְיוֹנֶךָ, לַהֲדוֹף בְּיַד הוֹלְלִים הֲמוֹנֶיךָ,
וְלֹא זָכַרְתָּ וִעוּד וֶתֶק וֶסֶת* אֲשֶׁר וִעַדְתָּ לְוְעוּדֶיךָ,
וּבְכֵן וְקוֹנַנּוּ, זְכוֹר יהוה מֶה הָיָה לָנוּ.

אֵיכָה זָנַחְתָּ בְּזַעְמֶךָ לְזַלְזֵל בְּיַד זָרִים זְבוּלֶךָ,
וְלֹא זָכַרְתָּ חִתּוּן חֻקֵּי חוֹרֵב אֲשֶׁר חָקַקְתָּ לַחֲמוּלֶיךָ,
וּבְכֵן חִוִּינוּ, זְכוֹר יהוה מֶה הָיָה לָנוּ.

אֵיכָה טָרַחְתָּ בְּטָרְחֶךָ,* לִטְרוֹף בְּיַד טוֹרְפִים[3] טְלָאֶיךָ,
וְלֹא זָכַרְתָּ יְקַר יְדִידוּת יֹשֶׁר אֲשֶׁר יִחַדְתָּ לְיוֹדְעֶיךָ,
וּבְכֵן יָלַלְנוּ, זְכוֹר יהוה מֶה הָיָה לָנוּ.

אֵיכָה כּוֹנַנְתָּ בְּכַעְסֶךָ, לְכַלּוֹת בְּיַד כְּפִירִים כַּרְמֶךָ,
וְלֹא זָכַרְתָּ לֹא לִזְנוֹחַ לְעוֹלָם[4] אֲשֶׁר לִמַּדְתָּ לִלְקוּחֶיךָ,
וּבְכֵן לָהַגְנוּ, זְכוֹר יהוה מֶה הָיָה לָנוּ.

---

(1) *Genesis* ch. 15. (2) *Eichah* 5:1.
(3) Some editions read טְמֵאִים, *the unclean.* (4) Cf. *Eichah* 3:31.

אֵיכָה אַצְתָּ בְּאַפֶּךָ — *How did You rush in Your fury.* This *kinnah*, by R' Elazar HaKalir — who signed his name, אֶלְעָזָר, in the acrostic of the final stanza — follows a complex alphabetical form. Each of the first eleven stanzas is constructed in the following manner:

אֵיכָה א. . .תָּ בְּא. . .ךָ, לְא. . . בְּיַד א. . .יִם א. . .ךָ,
וְלֹא זָכַרְתָּ ב. . . ב. . . ב. . ., אֲשֶׁר ב. . .תָּ לִב. . .ךָ,
וּבְכֵן ב. . .נוּ זְכוֹר ה׳ מֶה הָיָה לָנוּ.
אֵיכָה ג. . .תָּ בְּג. . .ךָ, לִג. . . בְּיַד ג. . .יִם ג. . .ךָ,
וְלֹא זָכַרְתָּ ד. . . ד. . . ד. . ., אֲשֶׁר ד. . .תָּ לִד. . .ךָ,
וּבְכֵן ד. . .נוּ זְכוֹר ה׳ מֶה הָיָה לָנוּ.

The alphabet is repeated five times for odd-numbered letters (א,ג,ה . . .) and six times for even-numbered letters (ב,ד,ו . . .). This repetition alludes to the Five Books of the Torah and the Six Orders of the Mishnah. Even the merit of Torah study was ineffective in protecting Israel when its actions became degenerate (*Kol BeRamah*).

דְּלִיגַת דִּלּוּג דֶּרֶךְ — *The contraction of the road.* When the Israelites left Sinai, they traveled three days and arrived at Kadosh Barnea — an eleven-day journey under usual circumstances! (See *Rashi* to *Deut.* 1:2.) Alternatively, this refers to the four-hundred-year period of slavery prophesied in the Covenant Between the Parts (*Genesis* 15:13) that was condensed to two hundred and ten years, from Jacob's arrival in Egypt until the Exodus (see *Targum* to *Song of Songs* 2:8).

וִעוּד וֶתֶק וֶסֶת — *The Assembly Hall, the seasonal stronghold.* This alludes to the *Beis HaMikdash,*

7.

א *How did You rush in Your fury to exterminate*
Your faithful ones at the hand of the Edomites,
ב *and not recall the Covenant Between the Parts*[1]
by which You selected those whom You tested?
Therefore we have proclaimed,
'Remember, HASHEM, what has befallen us!'[2]

ג *How did You reproach with Your rebuke,*
to exile at the hand of the haughty those You had once redeemed,
ד *and not recall the contraction of the road*
You had shortened for Your flag-bearing tribes?
Therefore we have spoken,
'Remember, HASHEM, what has befallen us!'

ה *How did You plan in Your thoughts*
to push Your multitudes into the hand of the raucous,
ו *and not recall the Assembly Hall, the seasonal stronghold**
You had designated for Your meeting partners?
Therefore, we have lamented,
'Remember, HASHEM, what has befallen us!'

ז *How did You abandon Your Temples in Your rage,*
to suffer indignity at the hands of aliens,
ח *and not recall the betrothal of [Israel to the] Laws of Sinai*
that You have carved for the recipients of Your compassion?
Therefore we have related,
'Remember, HASHEM, what has befallen us!'

ט *How did You take pains in exerting Yourself* to cause*
Your sheep to be torn asunder by the hand of the predators,[3]
י *and not recall the [merit of the] precious, beloved upright [Torah]*
that You designated for those who know You?
Therefore we have wailed,
'Remember, HASHEM, what has befallen us!'

כ *How did You concentrate in Your anger, to devastate*
Your vineyard [Israel] at the hand of the vandalizing villain,
ל *and not recall that You taught Your acquired people that*
[You would] not abandon [them] forever?[4]
Therefore we have cried,
'Remember, HASHEM, what has befallen us!'

---

the spiritual stronghold at which all of Israel would assemble during three seasons (Pesach, Shavuos, Succos) each year.

אֵיכָה טָרַחְתָּ בְּטָרְחָךְ — *How did You take pains in exerting Yourself.* For eighteen years a heavenly voice resounded through the halls of Nebuchad-

אֵיכָה **מִ**לַּלְתָּ בְּ**מ**וֹאֲסֶךָ, לְ**מִ**חוֹת בְּיַד **מ**וֹנִים **מְ**נַשְּׂאֶיךָ,
וְלֹא זָכַרְתָּ **נְ**שִׂיאַת **נ**וֹצַת **נֶ**שֶׁר אֲשֶׁר **נָ**שָׂאתָ לִ**נְ**שׂוּאֶיךָ,
וּבְכֵן **נָ**הִינוּ, זְכוֹר יהוה מֶה הָיָה לָנוּ.

אֵיכָה **שַׂ**חְתָּ בְּ**סַ**עֲרֶךָ, לְ**סַ**גֵּר בְּיַד **סֵ**עֲפִים **סַ**הֲדֶיךָ,
וְלֹא זָכַרְתָּ **ע**ֹז **עֲ**דִי **עֲ**דָיִים[1]* אֲשֶׁר **עִ**טַּרְתָּ לַ**עֲ**בָדֶיךָ,
וּבְכֵן **עָ**נִינוּ, זְכוֹר יהוה מֶה הָיָה לָנוּ.

אֵיכָה **פַּ**צְתָּ בְּ**פַ**חְדֶּךָ, לְ**פַ**גֵּר בְּיַד **פָּ**רִיצִים **פְּ**לִיאֶיךָ,
וְלֹא זָכַרְתָּ **צַ**הֲלַת **צְ**בִי **צַ**דִּיק[2] אֲשֶׁר **צָ**פַנְתָּ לִ**צְ**בָאֶיךָ,
וּבְכֵן **צָ**עַקְנוּ, זְכוֹר יהוה מֶה הָיָה לָנוּ.

אֵיכָה **קָ**רָאתָ בְּ**קְ**רִיאָתֶךָ, לִ**קְ**נוֹת בְּיַד **קָ**מִים **קְ**רוּאֶיךָ,
וְלֹא זָכַרְתָּ **רֶ**גֶשׁ **רֶ**כֶב **רִ**בּוֹתַיִם[3]* אֲשֶׁר **רָ**צִיתָ לְ**רֵ**עֶיךָ,
וּבְכֵן **רָ**גַנְנוּ, זְכוֹר יהוה מֶה הָיָה לָנוּ.

אֵיכָה **שָׁ**אַפְתָּ בְּ**שַׁ**אֲפֶךָ, לְ**שַׁ**לּוֹת בְּיַד **שׁ**וֹדְדִים **שְׁ**לֵמֶיךָ,
וְלֹא זָכַרְתָּ **תְּ**קֶף **תַּ**לְתַּלֵּי **תְּ**אַר אֲשֶׁר **תִּ**כַּנְתָּ לִ**תְ**מִימֶיךָ,
וּבְכֵן **תָּ**אַנְנוּ, זְכוֹר יהוה מֶה הָיָה לָנוּ.

תָּאַנְנוּ **לִ**שְׁפּוֹךְ דְּמָעוֹת כַּמַּיִם,
עַל מֶה בְּיוֹם זֶה נִשְׁבֵּינוּ פַּעֲמַיִם,
זָכְרִי בִּהְיוֹתִי בְּשַׁלְוָה יוֹשֶׁבֶת בִּירוּשָׁלַיִם,
רָגַנְתִּי וְעַתָּה אַאֲדֶה עַד חוּג שָׁמָיִם.

(1) Cf. *Ezekiel* 16:7. (2) Cf. *Isaiah* 24:16; some editions read, צַהֲלַת צְבִי צֶדֶק, *the joyous song of the desirable [Land* (cf. *Ezekiel* 20:15) *of] righteousness* (cf. *Isaiah* 1:16). (3) Cf. *Psalms* 68:18.

nezzar's palace. It cried: 'O perpetrator of evil! Go destroy your Master's Temple, for His children do not listen to Him' (*Midrash Eichah*, intro. 23).

עֲדִי עֲדָיִים — *Twin Torah-crowns.* When Israel was asked to accept the Torah, the nation cried out, נַעֲשֶׂה וְנִשְׁמָע, *'We will do and we will hear'* (*Exodus* 24:7), placing נַעֲשֶׂה, *we will do*, before נִשְׁמָע, *we will hear.* Thus they undertook to fulfill all of God's commandments, even before they knew what was expected of them. This devotion was rewarded when 600,000 ministering angels approached Israel and placed two crowns upon each Jew's head — one for נַעֲשֶׂה, and one for נִשְׁמָע (*Shabbos* 88a).

רֶגֶשׁ רֶכֶב רִבּוֹתַיִם — *The assembly [You attended with an] entourage of [more than] twice ten thousand.* The translation and interpolation are based on a midrashic account of God's descent upon Mount Sinai. The psalmist states: *The chariot of God is twice ten thousand, thousands*

מ *How did You speak in Your contempt, to eradicate*
at the hand of tormentors those who had exalted You,
נ *and not recall the flight on eagle's feathers*
when You carried aloft those whom You had exalted?
Therefore we have moaned,
'Remember, HASHEM, what has befallen us!'

ס *How did You speak out in Your stormy rage,*
to confine Your witnesses by the hand of free thinkers,
ע *and not recall the mighty twin Torah-crowns*[1]*
with which You crowned Your servants?
Therefore we have cried out,
'Remember HASHEM, what has befallen us!'

פ *How did You utter in Your awesomeness,*
to murder Your wondrous people by the hand of law breakers,
צ *and not recall the joyous song of the desirable righteous*[2]
that You have concealed for Your legions?
Therefore we have shouted,
'Remember HASHEM, what has befallen us!'

ק *How did You proclaim in Your proclamation, to give over those*
You had once summoned to the hand of those who oppose You,
ר *and not recall the assembly [You attended with an] entourage*
of [more than] twice ten thousand,[3]*
at which You favored your friends?
Therefore we have protested,
'Remember HASHEM, what has befallen us!'

ש *How You aspire with Your aspiration,*
to disperse Your perfect ones at the hand of pillagers,
ת *and not recall the strength of the Temple Mount's stature*
which You prepared for Your wholesome ones?
Therefore we have groaned,
Remember HASHEM, what has befallen us!'

אל *We have groaned; pouring out [our hearts] like water,*
ע *because on this day we were taken captive twice.*
ז *I recall how I dwelt serenely in Jerusalem.*
ר *I have complained, but now, I shall raise aloft [my laments]*
to the sphere of heaven.

---

of angels, my Lord is among them, at Sinai in holiness (*Psalms* 68:18). R' Avudimi of Haifa explained that twenty-two thousand ['twice ten thousand' plus two thousand, the minimum that can be called 'thousands'] ministering angels accompanied God when He descended upon Mount Sinai to give the Torah to Israel (see *Rashi* to *Psalms* 68:18).

ח.

אַאֲדֶה* עַד חוּג שָׁמַיִם,
אַאֲלֶה אִתִּי שָׁמַיִם,
אֶאוֹר יוֹם מַחֲרִיבֵי פַּעֲמַיִם, אֶתְאוֹנֵן **מִי** יִתֵּן רֹאשִׁי מַיִם.[1]
אַבְחִין בִּבְכִי לֵיל מִדְבָּר,[2]
אֶבְחֲנָה לֵיל מִלֵּיל* וּמִדְבָּר מִמִּדְבָּר,*
אֲבַכֶּה אִתִּי עוֹלַת מִדְבָּר, אֶשְׁאַג **מִי** יִתְּנֵנִי בַמִּדְבָּר.[3]
אֶגְּדַע וְאֶנָּשֵׁל כְּנֹקֶף זַיִת,
אֲגָרֶה אִתִּי כָּל בְּנֵי בַיִת,
אֶגְרוֹם שֶׁיֹּאמַר בַּעַל הַבַּיִת, אֲרָשֶׁה **מִי** יִתְּנֵנִי שָׁמִיר וָשַׁיִת.[4]
אַדְוֶה בְּכָל לֵב לְהַמְצִיאֵהוּ,
אֵדְעָה מִלִּין בָּם לְאַמְּצֵהוּ.
אֶדְאַג אַיֵּה רוֹעֶה וְלֹא אֶמְצָאֵהוּ, אֲקוֹנֵן **מִי** יִתֵּן יָדַעְתִּי וְאֶמְצָאֵהוּ.[5]
אֵהָפְכָה וְאֶתְהַפְּכָה כְּאוֹפָן בְּמִלַּי,
אֶהְגֶּה פָּנִים בְּפָנִים לְתַנּוֹת עֲמָלַי,
אָהֲהוּ חֶרֶס וָסַהַר מִלְּהַגִּיהַּ לְמוּלַי,
אֶצְרַח **מִי** יִתֵּן אֵפוֹא וְיִכָּתְבוּן מִלָּי.[6]

אוֹרַח מִשְׁפְּטֵי גוֹנְבֵי עֲלִי,*
אוֹדִיעַ בִּבְצְעִי וּמַעֲלִי,
אוּמְלְלוּ מַזָּלוֹת בְּקָרְעִי מְעִילִי, אֶפְעֶה **מִי** יִתֵּן שׁוֹמֵעַ לִי.[7]
אָזְדָה כְּהוּפְרָה הָאֲבִיוֹנָה,[8]*
אֶזְכְּרָה כִּי הָיִיתִי מְחֻתָּנָה,
אַזִּיל פְּלָגִים כִּבְרֵכָה הָעֶלְיוֹנָה,[6] אֶעֱגוֹר **מִי** יִתֶּן לִי אֵבֶר כַּיּוֹנָה.[7]

☙ אַאֲדֶה — *Would that I could soar.* The translation of this rare word is based on הִנֵּה כַנֶּשֶׁר יִדְאֶה, Behold! *It shall fly as an eagle (Jeremiah* 48:40). Alternatively the word is related to אֵיד which *Targum (Job* 21:30) renders תְּבִירָא, *destruction,* and *Ibn Ezra* explains as a *dark cloud.*

אֶבְחֲנָה לֵיל מִלֵּיל — *I would differentiate between night and night.* On that first tragic night of Tishah B'Av in the wilderness, the nation heard the Spies' slanderous reports regarding the Land of Canaan, and they wept. But that was a בְּכִיָּה שֶׁל חִנָּם, *an uncalled for* (or, *needless*) *weeping.* The tragic events that occurred on later Tishah B'Avs, however, were the source of true weeping. Thus we distinguish between tonight's weeping and that first night's weeping.

וּמִדְבָּר מִמִּדְבָּר — *And between wilderness and wilderness,* i.e., between the Wilderness of Sinai where we ate the heavenly manna, drank from the Well of Miriam and were protected by the Clouds of Glory, and the wilderness of exile where we were starving, thirsty and at the mercy of the elements and both four-legged and two-legged predators.

Once, the foreign overlords of *Eretz Yisrael* forbade the bringing of *bikkurim* (first-fruit offerings) to Jerusalem and stationed sentries on the roads to prevent the Jews from doing so. Pious men of that generation arose and placed baskets of *bikkurim,* covered with dried figs, into large wooden vessels shaped like a pestle, which was used for pressing dried figs into cakes, and carried them on their shoulders to Jerusalem. When the sentries inquired about the contents, the Jews would say that they were taking the dried figs to

8.

א *Would that I could soar* to the sphere of heaven;*
I would make the heavens lament with me!
I would curse the day on which I was twice destroyed.
ת *I would lament, 'Would that my head were [a stream of] water.'*[1]
ב *I would contemplate the crying of that night in the wilderness;*[2]
*I would differentiate between night and night**
*and between wilderness and wilderness.**
I would inspire all who emerged from the wilderness to cry with me,
ש *as I would roar, 'Would that I were [once again]*
in the Wilderness [of Sinai].'[3]
ג *[I would cry,] 'My limbs are amputated, my fruits are fallen,*
like a beaten olive.'
I would provoke the entire household [to cry] with me;*
I would cause the Master of the Household Himself to say,
ר *'Would that I allowed Myself [to tread upon Israel's enemies,*
as if they were] thorns and thistles!''[4]
ד *I would cause my whole heart to grow faint*
as I [would struggle to have Him make Himself available [to me].
Would that I knew the appropriate words
to encourage Him [to forgive me].
I would worry, 'Where is the Shepherd?' — but not be able to find Him,
ק *I would lament, 'Would that I be permitted to know,*
so that I might find him.'[5]
ה *I would turn round and round with my words*
like an [ever-spinning] wheel,
I would speak with Him face to face to bemoan my woes.
The sun and moon would howl together and refuse to shine upon me,
צ *I would shriek, 'Would that my words [of lamentation]*
be recorded [for posterity].'[6]
ו *The just ways of the pestle-thieves*
I would reveal by [contrasting them with] my greed and treachery.
Even the constellations were distraught when
I ripped my [priestly] vestments [at the Temple's destruction],
פ *I would scream, 'Would that He give heed to me!'*[7]
ז *We were exiled when the desirous [Temple]* was ruined,*[8]
I would remember that I was once wed [to the holy Torah],
I would shed tears that stream forth as from a mountaintop cistern;[9]
ע *I would exclaim, 'Would that I had wings like a dove.'*[10]

(1) *Jeremiah* 8:23, see *Targum*. (2) Some editions read יְלֵל מִדְבָּר, *the wailing of the wilderness*. (3) *Jeremiah* 9:1. (4) Cf. *Isaiah* 27:4. (5) *Job* 23:3. (6) 19:23. (7) Cf. 31:35. (8) Cf. *Ecclesiates* 12:5. (9) Cf. *Isaiah* 7:3. (10) *Psalms* 55:7.

a mortar where they would press them with their pestle. Therefore, they were given the appellation *pestle-thieves* because they would *steal the hearts*, i.e., deceive the sentries with the pretext of the pestle (*Taanis* 28a).

הָאֲבִיוֹנָה — *The desirous [Temple].* The translation follows *Rashi* and *Ibn Ezra* (*Ecclesiastes* 12:5) who render 'lust for conjugal pleasures.' Some regarded this as a compound word from אָב, *father* or *patriarch*, and יוֹנָה, *dove*, i.e., Abraham, Isaac

אָח נִפְשַׁע מִקִּרְיַת עֹז[1] אֶל צוֹר,
אָחוּ בְּלִי מַיִם[2] בְּאַף לַעֲצוֹר,
אָחַז קָמוֹת לִקְצוֹר וְעוֹלֵלוֹת לִבְצוֹר,
אָשִׂיחָה **מִי** יוֹבִלֵנִי עִיר מָצוֹר.[3]
אֶטַּע אָהֳלֵי אַפַּדְנִי[4] בְּצַלְמָוֶת,
אָטוּסָה וְאֶשְׁכּוֹנָה[5] עַד חֲצַר מָוֶת,
אֶטָּפֵל אֶת הַמְחַכִּים לַמָּוֶת,*
אֶנְהֶה **מִי** גֶבֶר יִחְיֶה וְלֹא יִרְאֶה מָּוֶת.[6]
אֱיָלוּתִי לְעֶזְרָתִי[7] תַּרְתִּי חֲזוֹת,
אֵימָתַי בְּכָל שָׁנָה אוֹמֶרֶת הִיא הַשָּׁנָה הַזֹּאת,
אֵידַע לַכֹּל כִּי מוּדַעַת זֹאת,[8] **אִם** לֹא כִּי יַד יהוה עָשְׂתָה זֹּאת.[9]
אֶכּוֹף לְךָ רֹאשׁ יהוה חֵילִי,
אֶכְרַע לְךָ בֶּרֶךְ לְחַתֵּל מַחְלִי,
אֲכַתִּירְךָ בְּשִׁיר מְשִׁירֵי מְחוֹלִי,* אֲכַוֵּן **מִי** יִתֶּנְךָ כְּאָח לִי.[10]
אַל תִּשְׁכַּח צַעֲקַת אֲרִיאֵל,[11]
אֵלָיו לֶאֱגוֹר יְהוּדָה וְיִשְׂרָאֵל,
אַלְפֵי שִׁנְאָן[12] אֲשֶׁר מָסַר אֵל,
לֵאמֹר **מִי** יִתֵּן מִצִּיּוֹן יְשׁוּעַת יִשְׂרָאֵל.[13]
יִשְׂרָאֵל מֵעֵת בִּדְרָכַי לֹא הָלָכוּ,
עֲזָבוּנִי וַעֲזַבְתִּים וּפָנַי מֵהֶם נֶהְפָּכוּ,
רָגַנְתִּי וְהֵלַלְתִּי* וּמֵעַי וְלִבִּי נִשְׁפָּכוּ,
אֵיכָה תִּפְאַרְתִּי מֵרַאֲשׁוֹתַי הִשְׁלִיכוּ.

(1) *Proverbs* 18:19; see *Nazir* 23a. (2) *Job* 8:11. (3) *Psalms* 60:11. (4) Cf. *Daniel* 11:45. (5) Cf. *Psalms* 55:7. (6) 89:49. (7) 22:20. (8) *Isaiah* 12:5. (9) *Job* 12:9. (10) *Song of Songs* 8:1. (11) See commentary to *kinnah* 37. (12) *Psalms* 68:18. (13) 53:7.

and Jacob, the Patriarchs of Israel, the nation compared to a dove (see e.g., *Song of Songs* 2:14). The verse then alludes to the Talmudic teaching, תַּמּוּ זְכוּת אָבוֹת, *the merits of the Patriarchs have ended* (*Shabbos* 55a), and means that since we no longer had the merits of the אָבוֹת to protect us, the Temple was destroyed (*Matteh Levi*).

חֲצַר מָוֶת ... הַמְחַכִּים לַמָּוֶת — *Death's Courtyard ... those who wait for death.* חֲצַרְמָוֶת, *Hazarmaveth*, was a seventh-generation descendant of Noah. According to the Midrash, he was the progenitor of a tribe of impoverished people who ate animal fodder, dressed in papyrus reed garments, and eagerly anticipated death (*Bereishis Rabbah* 37:8). The *paytan* compares the plight of exiled Israel to the lives of those unfortunates.

מְחוֹלִי — *My machalas.* The מַחֲלַת, *machalas*, is a musical instrument used by the Levite orchestra in the Temple (see *Psalms* 53:1 and 88:1). The word מַחֲלַת [and מְחוֹלִי] can also be cognate with מַחֲלָה, *sickness*, and refer to Israel's heartache over the Destruction of the two Temples (*Rashi* to *Psalms* ibid.). Alternatively, the word may be related to מָחוֹל, *a circle dance*. Accordingly the stitch is based on the verse, *You have changed for me my lament into dancing* ... (*Psalms* 30:12), and means that when redemption comes

ח *Brother [Israel] separated by sinfulness from [Jerusalem]*
the mighty city[1] *and exiled to Tyre;*
like a meadow without water,[2]
because God withheld [rain] in [His] wrath.
He held [Jerusalem] in His grasp like grain standing to be reaped
and grapes ready to be harvested;
ס *I would speak, 'Would that I be brought to the fortified city!'*[3]
ט *I would pitch my palatial tents*[4] *in the very shadow of death*
[for life is worthless in exile];
I would fly off and find rest[5] *in Death's Courtyard,*
*[where] I would associate with those who wait for death.**
נ *I would whimper, '[Would that I die, for] which man lives on*
[through interminable tragedy] and will never see death?'[6]
י *I seek to witness [the fulfillment of my plea],*
'O my Strength [God], come to my assistance!'[7]
My awe-inspiring nation proclaims every year,
'This is the year [of redemption]!'
[When that time comes I shall announce to everyone,
so that it will be universally known,[8]
מ *that had the hand of God not wrought all this*
[it could not have happened]![9]
כ *I shall bow my head to You [in penitence],* HASHEM,
my source of strength;
I shall bend my knee [in supplication] to You,
to bandage my exile-wounds.
*I shall crown You with song, with the melodies of my machalas.**
I will concentrate [my prayer] to request,
'Would that You were as a brother to me!'[10]
ל *Do not forget the scream of Ariel [the Beis HaMikdash],*[11]
to assemble to him Judah and Israel.
The thousands of protective angels[12]
whom God designated [to guard Jerusalem],
saying, 'Would that out of Zion shall emerge Israel's salvations!'[13]
אל *[To this request God responds:] 'From the moment Israel ceased*
to follow My ways;
עז *they abandoned Me, so I abandoned them and*
turned My countenance away from them!'
ר *I grumbled and I groaned,* my innards and my heart*
were spilled out [in grief];
O how they have thrown my splendor from my head!

You will have changed מְחָלַי, *my exile-wounds,* into מְחוֹלִי, *my dancing.*

רָגַנְתִּי וְהֵלַלְתִּי — *I grumbled and I groaned.* The speaker here may be God continuing His lament from the previous two lines, i.e. Israel abandoned Me ... and threw My splendor [Divine crowns from the prayers of the righteous (see *Chagigah* 13b with *Tosafos*)] from My head. Alternatively, the lament may revert to Israel's words: From the time God abandoned me ... the enemy nations have thrown my splendor [the *Beis HaMikdash*] from my head [Jerusalem].

ט.

אֵיכָה תִּפְאַרְתִּי מֵרַאֲשׁוֹתַי הִשְׁלִיכוּ,*
וּכְנֶגֶד כִּסֵּא הַכָּבוֹד* צֶלֶם הִמְלִיכוּ,
בְּחַלְּלָם* תְּנַאי אֲשֶׁר חוֹזַי נִמְלָכוּ,
וְנָם **אִם בְּחֻקֹּתַי תֵּלֵכוּ.**[1]
לָמָּה[2] תָרִיבוּ אֵלַי כֻּלְּכֶם,[3] חָזְקוּ עָלַי דִּבְרֵיכֶם,[4]
מִיֶּדְכֶם הָיְתָה זֹּאת לָכֶם.[5]

בִּלַּע שׁוֹפְטַי בְּמוֹעֲצוֹת עִוְּתָם,
וּפָנִים הִסְתִּיר מֵהֶם כְּשֶׁר עֲוָתָתָם,
וַיּוֹמַר לְאָבָק מִטְרָם[6] לְהַבְעִיתָם,
חֵלֶף **וְנָתַתִּי גִשְׁמֵיכֶם בְּעִתָּם.**[7]
סְחִי וּמָאוֹס שָׂמַנִי,[8] כִּלָּה בְאַפּוֹ וַיְשֹׁמְמֵנִי,[9]
נִחוּמָיו מְהֵרָה יְשַׁעְשְׁעוּנִי.[10]

גָּדַע רוּם קַרְנָם[11] וְעִלּוּמָם הִקְצִיר,[12]
וּבְאִבְחַת חֶרֶב שַׁעֲרֵיהֶם הֵצִיר,[13]
מְזֵי רָעָב עָשׁ בַּקָּצִיר,
תְּמוּר **וְהִשִּׂיג לָכֶם דַּיִשׁ אֶת בָּצִיר.**[14]

דָּרַךְ קַשְׁתּוֹ וְכִלָּה בְּחֶרֶץ,
וְכַבַּרְזֶל עִפֵּל שְׁמֵי עֶרֶץ,[15]
פְּרָצַנִי שְׁלֹשׁ עֶשְׂרֵה פֶּרֶץ,*
תַּחַת **וְנָתַתִּי שָׁלוֹם בָּאָרֶץ.**[16]

אֵיכָה תִּפְאַרְתִּי מֵרַאֲשׁוֹתַי הִשְׁלִיכוּ ◆ — *O how they have thrown My splendor from My head. Parashas Bechukosai* (*Leviticus* chapters 26-27) begins with the idyllic blessings that await the Jewish people if they prove themselves worthy of God's esteem. The portion proceeds to the תּוֹכָחָה, *Admonition,* a terrifying prediction of the curses and plagues which will inevitably befall the Jewish people if they betray their solemn covenant with God. This composition [by R' Elazar HaKalir] vividly depicts how Israel did indeed turn away from God and progressively forfeited, one by one, the blessings which God had in store for them and ultimately their evil ways forced God to fulfill the harsh prophecies of the admonition.

Appropriately, the acrostic of this *kinnah* is arranged according to the א״ת ב״ש order of the alphabet. In this arrangement, the first letter of the *aleph-beis* is paired with the last, the second letter is exchanged for the second to last, and so on. This pattern alludes to Israel who foolishly exchanged the first and best, God, for the last and worst, the idols.

The first word of each quatrain is taken from the respective verse of the second chapter of *Eichah,* thus forming an *aleph-beis* acrostic. The second word begins with the complementary letter in the א״ת ב״ש formation. The last stitch of each stanza is the opening of the corresponding verse in *Leviticus* 26:3-24 and appears in bold type.

Throughout this *kinnah*, the *paytan* shifts back and forth between first, second and third person. This indicates a continuously changing narrator. In some stanzas, God (as it were) mourns His splendor, the *Beis HaMikdash*, that 'they' [a reference to either the wicked king Manasseh (see *II Kings* 21:4-7) during the First Temple era; or the

9.

א־ת *O how they have thrown My splendor from My head,**
when they enthroned an idol [in the Temple that is]
*correspondent to [My] Throne of Glory.**
When they [Israel] defiled the condition My prophets had advised,*
and said, 'If you will follow My decrees.'[1]
Why[2] *do you all quarrel with Me?*[3]
Your words have come strongly against Me.[4]
From your own hand has this befallen you.[5]

ב־ש *He swallowed up my judges because of their perverted advice;*
and He concealed His countenance from them
when He saw their perverseness.
He turned their rain to dust[6] *to frighten them,*
instead of [fulfilling the blessing]:
I will give you your rains in their proper season.[7]
He made me as filth and refuse [among the nations].[8]
He annihilated me with His wrath and despised me.[9]
May His comforting swiftly cheer me.[10]

ג־ר *He cut down the pinnacle of their pride*[11]
and cut short their youth;[12]
with the butchery of the sword he laid siege to their gates.[13]
He caused them to be swollen from starvation
during the [abundant] harvest;
instead of the blessing:
And your threshing shall reach for you, until the vintage.[14]

ד־ק *He bent His bow and cut down completely,*
and as with iron He solidified the heavens[15]
[to prevent them from giving rain].
*He breached me with thirteen breaches,**
instead of [the blessing], And I will make peace in the land.[16]

(1) *Leviticus* 26:3. (2) Some early editions omit this stanza. (3) *Jeremiah* 2:29. (4) *Malachi* 3:13. (5) Cf. 1:9. (6) Cf. *Deuteronomy* 28:24. (7) *Leviticus* 26:4. (8) Cf. *Eichah* 3:45. (9) Cf. *Job* 16:9. (10) Cf. *Psalms* 94:19. (11) Cf. *Eichah* 2:3. (12) Cf. *Psalms* 89:46. (13) Cf. *Ezekiel* 21:20. (14) *Leviticus* 26:5. (15) Cf. 26:19. (16) 26:6.

pagan conquerors of the Second Temple] turned into a sanctuary for idolatry. In other stanzas, Israel ruefully laments its forsaking תִּפְאַרְתִּי מְרַאֲשׁוֹתַי, *the splendor of my head,* i.e., the Torah's laws (see commentary to בְּחַלְּלָם, below). And in some stanzas the gentile nations taunt Israel in its degradation.

Alternatively, the entire *kinnah* represents the words of one speaker, so distraught in his mourning that he variously refers to himself introspectively in the first person, admonishes himself as an outsider using the second person, and hangs his guilt on a third party, but realizes that he means himself.

וּכְנֶגֶד כִּסֵּא הַכָּבוֹד — *Correspondent to [My] Throne of Glory.* The Midrash teaches that the celestial Throne of Glory rests directly above the *Beis HaMikdash* on earth (*Mechilta* cited by *Rashi* to *Exodus* 15:17; *Targum* to *Jeremiah* 17:12).

בְּחַלְּלָם — *When they defiled.* This reference to Israel in the third person indicates that God is the speaker. However, some editions read בְּחַלְּלִי, *when I defiled,* implying that Israel is the speaker. (See commentary above.)

שְׁלֹשׁ עֶשְׂרֵה פֶּרֶץ — *Thirteen breaches.* A lattice-work fence, ten handbreadths high, stood within the walls surrounding the Temple Mount. This fence, called the סוֹרֵג, *soreig,* served as a boundary, past which neither a Jew contaminated by contact with a corpse nor a gentile was permitted to enter. When the Greeks conquered the Land

הָיָה צוּרְכֶם וּמָעֻזְּכֶם וּמִשְׂגַּבְּכֶם,
הָפַךְ לְאַכְזָר וְנִלְחַם בָּכֶם,
הַנּוֹצְרְכֶם רְחַקְכֶם, חוֹשְׁקְכֶם תִּעַבְכֶם,
וְאַיֵּה הַבְטָחַת **וּרְדַפְתֶּם אֶת אוֹיְבֵיכֶם.**[1]

וַיַּחְמוֹס פִּנַּת צֶדֶק מְלֵאָה,
כִּי בְמַשְׂכִּיּוֹתָהּ מָצָא כָּל טֻמְאָה,
וּמְכַבְּדֶיהָ הִזִּילוּהָ כְּדָוָה מְטֻמְּאָה,[2]
בְּשִׁנּוּי **וְרָדְפוּ מִכֶּם חֲמִשָּׁה מֵאָה.**[3]

זָנַח עֶלְיוֹן קִרְיַת מוֹעֲדֵיכֶם,
וְהֶאֱבִיל שַׁעֲרֵי חֵיל עֲמִידַת רַגְלֵיכֶם,
מִי בִקֵּשׁ זֹאת[4] פָּץ וְהִגְלְכֶם,
וְגָמַר אֹמֶר **וּפָנִיתִי אֲלֵיכֶם.**[5]

חָשַׁב שְׂנוּא אוֹם לְקַט כַּשּׁוֹשָׁן[6]
וּמֵחֵלֶב עוֹלָלֶיהָ אוֹתָהּ דִּשֵּׁן,*
קִיטוֹר חֻפָּתָהּ הוּעֲלָה כַּכִּבְשָׁן,
וְשָׁאֲלוּ אַיֵּה דָגָן תְּמוּר **וַאֲכַלְתֶּם יָשָׁן נוֹשָׁן.**[7]

טָבְעוּ נִכְסֵי רוֹבְדֵי דוּכָנִי,*
בְּגֵיא חֲמַת כְּנִקְטַל מְכַהֲנַי,*
הֲרֵי כַּמֶּה שָׁנִים גִּלָּה יְסוֹד מְכוֹנִי,
וְסָע מִתּוֹכִי אֹמֶר **וְנָתַתִּי מִשְׁכָּנִי.**[8]

יָשְׁבוּ מְבַכִּים מִנְּאַק מְתֵיכֶם,[9]*
בְּאַרְבַּע מִיתוֹת הִפִּיל מְתֵיכֶם,
חֶרֶב וְרָעָב וְחַיָּה וְדֶבֶר* שִׁחֶתְכֶם,[10]

---

(1) *Leviticus* 26:7. (2) Cf. *Eichah* 1:8. (3) *Leviticus* 26:8. (4) *Isaiah* 1:12. (5) *Leviticus* 26:9. (6) Cf. *Song of Songs* 2:2. (7) *Leviticus* 26:10. (8) 26:11. (9) Cf. *Job* 24:12. (10) Cf. *Ezekiel* 14:21.

---

during the Second Temple era, they angrily broke through the *soreig* in thirteen places to register their indignation at being denied entrance. In subsequent years, the Hasmonean kings repaired these breaches (see *Middos* 2:3 with *Tos. Yom Tov; Shekalim* 6:8).

וּמֵחֵלֶב עוֹלָלֶיהָ אוֹתָהּ דִּשֵּׁן — *And [the enemy's soil] was enriched with the fat of her [slaughtered] infants.* The heathen farmers fertilized their vineyards for seven years with the blood of the slaughtered Jews (*Gittin* 57a).

דּוּכָנִי — *My [Temple] platform.* The *Kohanim* would ascend a platform to bless the nation with the Priestly Blessing, and the Levite orchestra to accompany the daily Altar service.

כְּנִקְטַל מְכַהֲנַי — *When ... my priests were murdered.* This refers to the tragic events following immediately after the destruction of the First Temple. Nebuzaradan, the chief executioner for the Babylonian king, captured Seraiah the *Kohen Gadol* and his deputy Zefaniah, along with seventy other officials, and transported them to Babylonia. There he delivered them into the hands of King Nebuchadnezzar who executed them at Rivlah in the land of Hamath

ה־צ *He had been your Rock, your Fortification and your Stronghold,*
but now He has become ruthless and wages war against you.
He Who once watched you closely has set you afar;
He Who once yearned for you has come to despise you.
And where is the pledge: And you shall chase after your enemies?[1]

ו־פ *He despoiled [Jerusalem,] the cornerstone [of the world,*
that had been] filled with righteousness,
because beneath her mosaic floors
He found every manner of impurity.
Those who had once respected her
disparage her like a woman unclean.[2]
Thus was perverted [the blessing]:
And five of you shall chase after one hundred [of the enemy].[3]

ז־ע *The Exalted One has rejected the metropolis*
of your festival [assemblies],
and brought mourning to the gates of the rampart
upon which you were stationed.
'Who asked you for this [to trample My courtyards]?'[4]
cried He, as He sent you into exile,
and He nullified His statement,
'And I will turn [My attention] towards you!'[5]

ח־ס *He made His plans [to show how] He despised the nation*
that He had once picked [from among the others]
like a rose [from the thorns],[6]
*and [the enemy's soil] was enriched**
with the fat of her [slaughtered] infants.
The smoke from her [burning Temple] canopy
arose as from a furnace,
and the [starving] people asked, 'Where is the grain?' in place of
[the blessing]: And you shall eat your old, well-preserved foods.[7]

ט־נ *They drowned and slaughtered [Kohanim and Leviim]*
*who once mounted the tiers of my [Temple] platform.**
*When, in the valley of Hamath, my priests were murdered.**
Behold, many years have passed since
my Temple's foundation has been laid bare,
and gone from my midst is He Who said:
'I shall make My dwelling place [among you].'[8]

י־מ *They sat down to weep because of the cry of*
those dying among you.[9]*
He struck down your people with four forms of death:
He destroyed you with the sword, starvation,
wild beast and the plague.[10]*

(see *II Kings* 25:18-21).

מְנַאַק מְתֵיכֶם — *Because of the cry of those dying among you* [lit., *the cry of your dead*]. Since the dead cannot cry, the phrase must refer to the cry of those in the throes of death. Alternatively, it means the screams of the relatives of the dead.

וְדֶבֶר — *And the plague.* This indicates that הִפִּיל, *He struck down,* refers to God, as germ warfare was unknown at that time.

כְּסָר צִלָּם פָּץ[1] **וְהִתְהַלַּכְתִּי בְּתוֹכְכֶם.**[2]
כָּלוּ לְשׁוֹד כְּרֶגַע אָהֳלֵיכֶם,
וּבָכֶם נִשְׁבָּעוּ* מְהוֹלָלֵיכֶם,[3]
לְחֵיקְכֶם נִשְׁפְּכוּ נַפְשׁוֹת עוֹלְלֵיכֶם,[4]
בְּמַאֲסְכֶם שִׂיחַ **אֲנִי יהוה אֱלֹהֵיכֶם.**[5]
לְאִמּוֹתָם כִּלְכּוּל אָנָּה שִׁוְּעוּ,
וְצוּר לְמַלְאָכָיו שָׁח מֶנִּי שְׁעוּ,[6]
אֶרֶץ הַכַּרְמֶל[7] הֲבֵאתִים וְשֶׁעֱשָׁעוּ,
וְשָׂנְאוּ מוֹכִיחַ **וְאִם לֹא תִשְׁמָעוּ.**[8]
מָה אֲעִידֵךְ* יְשִׁישַׁיִךְ[9] עִם גּוּרַיִךְ[9] בּוֹסָסוּ,
אוֹמְרִים עַל סוּס נָנוּס* עַל כֵּן נָסוּ,[10]
נִלְאֵיתִי נְשׂוֹא[11] עֲוֹנוֹתֵיכֶם כְּהוּעֲמָסוּ,
וַאֲיַסֶּרְכֶם כְּנַמְתִּי אִם **בְּחֻקֹּתַי תִּמְאָסוּ.**[12]
נְבִיאַיִךְ תָּעוּ* תַּרְמִית שָׁוְא חֲזוֹת,[13]
וָאֶדְרוֹשׁ לִסְלוֹחַ וּפַצְתִּי אֵי לְזֹאת,[14]
פְּתִיתִים וּכְנֶגְדִּי הֵשִׁיבוּ עַזּוֹת,
וְאָנַפְתִּי וְשַׁחְתִּי **אַף אֲנִי אֶעֱשֶׂה זֹּאת.**[15]
סָפְקוּ חָרְקוּ שָׁרְקוּ מוֹנַי,[16]
מִבִּפְנִים וּמִבַּחוּץ לְהַצְמִית אֱמוּנַי,[17]
כִּי בְּנֵי זֵדִים חִלְּלוּ צְפוּנַי,
לְרָעָה וְלֹא לְטוֹבָה נָם **וְנָתַתִּי פָנַי.**[18]
פָּצוּ זֵדִים לִפְנֵי מִי תְּחַלֶּה,
עִם כֹּבֶד עָוֹן פָּקַד וַיִּלְאֶה,
לֹא תְחַכּוּ עוֹד לְמוֹפֵת וָפֶלֶא,
אָנַף וְנָסַע וְנָם **וְאִם עַד אֵלֶּה.**[19]

(1) Cf. *Numbers* 14:9. (2) *Leviticus* 26:12. (3) Cf. *Psalms* 102:9. (4) Cf. *Eichah* 2:12.
(5) *Leviticus* 26:13. (6) Cf. *Isaiah* 22:4; see *Rashi* there. (7) Cf. *Jeremiah* 2:7. (8) *Leviticus* 26:14.
(9) Cf. *II Chronicles* 36:16-17. (10) Cf. *Isaiah* 30:16. (11) 1:14. (12) Cf. *Leviticus* 26:15.
(13) Cf. *Eichah* 2:14; *Micah* 3:5-7; *Ezekiel* 13:8-10. (14) *Jeremiah* 5:7. (15) *Leviticus* 26:16.
(16) Cf. *Eichah* 2:15. (17) Cf. 1:20; *Deuteronomy* 32:25. (18) *Leviticus* 26:17. (19) 26:18.

וּבָכֶם נִשְׁבְּעוּ — *Would use you as a curse*. If one of the enemy took an oath and wished to reinforce it, he would say, 'If I am not telling the truth may I be cursed in the worst possible way, in the manner which the conquered Jews suffer!' (*Rashi* to *Psalms* 12:9).

מָה אֲעִידֵךְ — *How can I admonish you ...?* The word אֲעִידֵךְ is derived from the root עוד which can mean either *warn, admonish*, or *testify*. The translation here follows *Midrash Eichah* (2:13).

And as [God] their protective shadow departed[1]
[so did His pledge], 'And I shall walk in your midst.'[2]

כ־ל *In but one moment all of your tents were totally destroyed by pillage,*
and your taunters would use you as a curse.[3]*
The blood of your infants was spilled into your bosom,[4]
because you abominated the utterance, 'I am HASHEM, *your God.'*[5]

ל־כ *To their mothers they cried out, 'The food — where is it?'*
But the Rock [God] said to His angels
[when they took up the children's cause], 'Turn away from Me![6]
For I brought them into a fertile land[7] *where they found all delights,*
but they despised the admonition, "If you will not give heed ..."'[8]

מ־י *How can I admonish you,* [when because of your obstinacy]*
they have trampled both your dignified elders and your cubs?[9]
*They would say [to those who rebuked them],**
'We will flee on horseback!' So they [were caused to] flee*
[but never returned]![10]
I am utterly exhausted from carrying[11] *your sins,*
for they are a burden [upon Me].
Therefore, I have disciplined you as I said,
'If you will abominate My decrees ...'[12]

נ־ט *Your prophets led you astray* with deceit and vain visions.*[13]
I sought to forgive you [but you refused to repent] so I cried out,
'How shall I [pardon you] for this?'[14]
I tried to persuade them [to repent],
but they answered Me with brazenness.
I was infuriated and declared, 'I will even do this to you ...'[15]

ס־ח *My tormentors clapped, gnashed (their teeth) and hissed*[16]
[as they prepared] to decimate my faithful ones
from inside and out,[17]
because the sons of the wanton desecrated my hidden treasures.
To inflict harm and not help, He said, 'I will set My face ...'[18]

פ־ז *The wanton ones jeered at us, 'Before Whom do you pray?*
[You are] a nation heavy with iniquity;
He has abandoned you and is wearied [by your sins].
Therefore, wait no longer for sign and wonder.'
He is angered and has departed, saying,
'If despite all this [you refuse to obey].'[19]

According to others, the phrase means, *Whom can I bring to testify to you* that their suffering equals yours? (*Zohar; Targum; Rashi*), for צָרַת רַבִּים חֲצִי נֶחָמָה, *general suffering is half of assuagement*, i.e., grieving and troubles are easier to bear when one knows that there are others in the same dire circumstances (*Ibn Kaspi*).

עַל סוּס נָנוּס — *We will flee on horseback!* When warned by the prophets that the only way to avert impending disaster is a combination of repentance and quiet confidence in God's salvation, the nation proudly refused to pay heed. Instead they replied, 'We will flee on horseback!' They meant, 'We will ally ourselves with Egypt who will supply us with mighty steeds. Thus shall we escape the threat of annihilation. Then, when the enemy leaves our land, we will return home safe and sound!' For this, God caused them to flee, but did not allow them to return (*Isaiah* 30:15-16 with *Rashi*).

תָּעוּ — *Led you astray* [or, *strayed*]. Since this *kinnah* follows an א״ת ב״ש pattern (see above), a word beginning with ט (the letter corresponding

עָשָׂה וַיָּרֶם קָדְקֹד בְּנֵי שָׁאוֹן,
וְדָמִי שִׁכְּרַנִי בְּגֵיא צִמָּאוֹן,
וּבְכָל שָׁנָה וְשָׁנָה הוֹסִיף יָגוֹן עַל אוֹן,
מֵעֵת כָּעַס וְנָם **וְשָׁבַרְתִּי אֶת גְּאוֹן**.[1]

צָעַק הוֹי הוֹי וְאַשְׁפָּתוֹ הֵרִיק,
מִפֹּה וּמִפֹּה הֵבִיא עָלַי מַעֲרִיק,
וּבְלַעֲגֵי מָעוֹג שִׁנֵּי צָר הֶחֱרִיק,[2]
וְכִלָּה כֹּחִי בִּנְאֻם **וְתַם לָרִיק**.[3]

קוּמִי דָּפְקִי שַׁוְּעִי אַל דֳּמִי,[4]
וּתְנִי כְּאוֹב מֵאֶרֶץ[5] קוֹלֵךְ וְדִמְי,
מֵי רוֹשׁ הִשְׁקָנִי וְהִדְמִי,
וְחָשַׁךְ הִלּוּכִי בִּנְאֻם **וְאִם תֵּלְכוּ עִמִּי**.[6]

רְאֵה גּוֹרָל אִוִּיתָ הוּשַׂם לָרוֹעִים לְעַיִת,[7]
וְלִקְאַת מִדְבָּר הָיִיתִי דְמוּיַת,
גּוֹלָה כְּנוּיַת וְסוּרָה גְנוּיַת,[8]
בְּשָׁמְעִי **וְהִשְׁלַחְתִּי בָכֶם אֶת חַיַּת**.[9]

שָׁכְבוּ בְּעִלּוּף כְּתוֹא מִכְמָר וְאֵין דּוֹלֶה,[10]
הַמְּלֵאִים גַּעַר וְאֵין מַרְפֵּא עוֹלֶה,
הֲרֵי כַּמֶּה שָׁנִים הֲמָמַנִי לְהִתְכַּלֶּה,
אֲנוּשִׁים בְּוִכּוּחַ **וְאִם בְּאֵלֶּה**.[11]

תִּקְרָא אֵיד עוֹלַלְתָּ עַל אַדְמוֹנִי,
לְסַחֲפוֹ וּלְשַׁסְּפוֹ שִׁבְעָתַיִם כְּאוֹנִי,
תָּהוֹם צָרַי בְּצֵאת קוֹל מֵאַרְמוֹנִי,
כְּנֶהֱמַמְתִּי בְּרִיב **וְהָלַכְתִּי אַף אֲנִי**.[12]

אַף אֲנִי לָכוּד* בְּיוֹקֶשׁ שִׁבָּרוֹן,
עָרְבָה שִׂמְחָה וְהִשְׁבִּית חָרוֹן,
לָאָרֶץ אֵשֵׁב וְאֶהְגֶּה בְגָרוֹן,
אֵיכָה יָשְׁבָה חֲבַצֶּלֶת הַשָּׁרוֹן.[13]

---

to נ in (אַ"תְ בַּ"ש) is expected here. Perhaps the proper reading here is טָעוּ, *caused to err* or *erred*, which is homophonous with תָּעוּ and similar in meaning. Moreover, the only appearance of the root טעה in Scriptures (*Ezekiel* 13:10) speaks of the 'prophets' whose vain visions lulled the nation into a false sense of security. Indeed, the wording of the *kinnah* seems to be based on that

ע־ו *He proceeded to raise the heads of the tempestuous ones,*
and He made me drunk on my own blood in the waterless valley;
year after year He added anguish to [my] mourning,
since the moment He was angered and said,
'And I will shatter the pride [of your strength].'[1]

צ־ה *He cried out, 'Woe! Woe!'*
even though He emptied His quiver [against me].
From here and from there He brought pursuers against me.
They mock me for the sake of a breadloaf
and cause the oppressor to gnash his teeth [at me].[2]
He drained my strength with the statement,
'And [your strength] will be used up in vain.'[3]

ק־ד *Arise and pound [on the gates of heaven],*
cry out, 'Do not be silent!'[4]
Set your voice [in prayer] as the [muffled sound of]
necromancy [arising] from the earth,[5] *then remain still.*
He silenced me by making me drink bitter waters.
He darkened my path, when He stated,
'But if you will go against Me.'[6]

ר־ג *Behold, the lot You had once desired*
has been made into rubble heaps,[7]
and I have come to resemble the [wandering] desert bird.
They nickname me 'Exile,' and humiliate me as 'Displaced,'[8]
so I have heard [the fulfillment of],
'And I will send forth wild beasts against you.'[9]

ש־ב *They lie in a swoon like a wild ox in a snare with none to release it.*[10]
[They are] steeped in rebuke, yet no healing has emerged.
Lo, [these] many years has He completely crushed me.
We are pained by the admonition, 'And if despite this . . .'[11]

ת־א *Designate a day of doom for the red one [Edom],*
as You did [when you afflicted me],
to eradicate him and to slash him seven times more than my pain.
Confound my tormentors when the cry goes forth from my palace,
as I was shocked by the rebuke, 'And I will also go [against you]'[12]

I have also been trapped in the snare of drunkenness.*
[Only after my] joy was confounded
[by the Temple's destruction] did [His] anger subside.
I will sink down to the earth and murmur in my throat,
'O how the Rose of Sharon[13] *sits!'*

(1) *Leviticus* 26:19. (2) Cf. *Psalms* 35:16. (3) *Leviticus* 26:20. (4) Cf. *Psalms* 83:2.
(5) Cf. *Isaiah* 29:4. (6) *Leviticus* 26:21. (7) Cf. *Psalms* 79:1. (8) Cf. *Isaiah* 49:21.
(9) *Leviticus* 26:22. (10) Cf. *Isaiah* 51:20. (11) *Leviticus* 26:23. (12) 26:24. (13) *Song of Songs* 2:1.

passage (ibid. 13:9-10). Nevertheless, we have retained the word תָּעוּ because in similar passages (e.g., *Michah* 3:5-7) the root תעה is used in Scriptures, and because that is how it appears in virtually all editions.

אַף אֲנִי לָכוּד — *I have also been trapped.* Many a *kinnah* of the series attributed to R' Elazar HaKalir ends with a stanza that links it with the following *kinnah,* i.e., the closing word or stich of one is identical with the opening word or stich of

י.

אֵיכָה יָשְׁבָה* חֲבַצֶּלֶת הַשָּׁרוֹן,[1]*
וְדָמַם רוֹן מִפִּי נוֹשְׂאֵי אָרוֹן,*
וְנָעוּ מִמִּשְׁמְרוֹתָם כֹּהֲנִים בְּנֵי אַהֲרֹן,
כְּנִמְסַר הַבַּיִת בְּמִסָּרְבֵי **מָרוֹן**.*

בָּכֹה תִבְכֶּה מֵחֲמֵשֶׁת סְפָרִים,*
כְּנֶהֱרַג כֹּהֵן וְנָבִיא בְּיוֹם הַכִּפּוּרִים,
וְעַל דָּמוֹ נִשְׁחֲטוּ פְּרָחִים כִּצְפִירִים,
וְנָדוּ כְּצִפֳּרִים, כֹּהֲנֵי **צִפּוֹרִים**.*

גָּלְתָה מֵאַרְצָהּ כַּלָּה מְקֻשָּׁטָה,
בַּעֲוֹן מַעַשְׂרוֹת וּשְׁמִטָּה,
וּבְאַרְבַּעַת שְׁפָטִים* הָשְׁפָּטָה,
וּמֶעֶדְיָהּ הָפְשָׁטָה, מִשְׁמֶרֶת **מִפְשָׁטָה**.

דַּרְכֵי הֵיכָל שָׁמְמוּ כְּנִפְרַץ כָּתְלוֹ,
וְהַמְּעִיל כְּנִקְרַע פְּתִילוֹ,
הוּרַד וְהֻשְׁפַּל מִתִּלּוֹ,
וְנָע מִשְּׁתִילוֹ, כֹּהֵן **עֵיתָה לוֹ**.*

---

the next. Such a linking stanza is evident between *kinnos* 7-8, 8-9, 11-12 and 19-20, and such is the nature of this stanza. However, many early editions do not contain this stanza, which leads to the contention that it is not the work of R' Elazar, but was inserted by some later *paytan* in order to connect this and the following *kinnah*. Indeed, *Maharil* argues that *kinnah* 15 was originally juxtaposed with this *kinnah* and he would recite that *kinnah* at this point (see commentary there for his reasoning). If so, this stanza could not have been part of the original *kinnah*, as it would be entirely out of place.

⁂ **אֵיכָה יָשְׁבָה חֲבַצֶּלֶת הַשָּׁרוֹן** — *O how the Rose of Sharon sits.* The Talmud (*Taanis* 26a-27a) teaches that the early prophets, David and Samuel, established twenty-four מִשְׁמְרוֹת כְּהוּנָּה, *priestly watches*, to scrupulously perform the Temple services. Each *mishmar* (watch) served for one week, on a rotation basis. The names of the watches in the First Temple are enumerated in *I Chronicles*, chapter 24. This *kinnah* describes the watches of the Second Temple which were then known under different names. According to many commentators, these new names were the names of each *mishmar's* home city. This is the approach followed in the translation and commentary. Some commentators explain the new names as pejoratives and expound on the particular offense by which each *mishmar* earned its nickname. The commentary includes only those pejorative interpretations found in the Talmud.

In composing this *kinnah*, R' Elazar HaKalir used the opening word or phrase of the respective verses in the first chapter of *Eichah* to begin each stanza. Thus, the stanzas contain an alphabetical acrostic. The name of the corresponding *mishmar* appears in the last line. The relevant words appear in bold type.

חֲבַצֶּלֶת הַשָּׁרוֹן — *The Rose of Sharon.* The *Beis HaMikdash* was affectionately called חֲבַצֶּלֶת, *Rose.* The Midrash teaches that חֲבַצֶּלֶת is a contraction of the words חֲבוּיָה בְּצֵל, *sheltered in the shade*, i.e., in good times God loved Israel and their Temple so much that he hovered over them and provided them with the most intense protection under the shade of His Divine Presence, the *Shechinah* (*Shir HaShirim Rabbah* 2).

וְדָמַם רוֹן מִפִּי נוֹשְׂאֵי אָרוֹן — *And joy has been silenced from the mouths of those who carried the*

10.

א *O how the Rose of Sharon*[1]* *sits** *[alone]*
and joy has been silenced from the mouths
*of those who carried the Ark;**
And the Kohanim, the sons of Aaron
were removed from their watches,
When the Temple was given over to the rebels of ***Maron.****

ב *The [people endowed with the] Five Books** *wept and wept,*
when the priest and prophet [Zechariah] was slain on Yom Kippur,
when in vengeance for his blood,
blossoming children were butchered like goats,
And the Kohanim of ***Sepphoris**** *wandered like birds.*

ג *The bejewelled bride was exiled from her land*
because of the iniquity of the tithes and the Sabbatical year.
*She was condemned to suffer four types of affliction,**
And the watch of ***Mifshatah*** *was stripped of her ornaments.*

ד *The roads to the Sanctuary were silenced*
when its wall was breached;
and the [bells on the High Priest's] tunic [were silenced]
when its threads were ripped apart.
[The Temple] was pulled down and lowered from its Mount,
And the Kohen from ***Aysah-Lo*** *was uprooted from his planting.*

(1) *Song of Songs* 2:1.

Ark. According to *Rambam* (*Sefer HaMitzvos, aseh* 34 and *shoresh* 3), the *Kohanim* were the bearers of the Ark throughout the generations. Only during the early years in the Wilderness, when there were very few *Kohanim*, did the *Leviim* carry the Ark. *Ramban* (ibid.) disagrees and states that the *Leviim* were charged with carrying the Ark whenever this would become necessary throughout the generations. Most commentators to *kinnos* follow *Ramban's* view. Thus, רון refers to the *joyous song* the Levite bearers of the Ark sang on the platform in the Temple courtyard. Indeed, the Talmud relates that the Levite choir was interrupted in mid-verse when the enemy conquered the *Beis HaMikdash* (*Taanis* 29a). However, the translation of רון as *joy* [see *Psalms* 30:6 where רִנָּה, synonymous with רון, is used as the opposite of בְּכִי, *weeping*], rather than *joyous song*, allows the *kinnah* to be understood even according to *Rambam's* view that the *Kohanim* bore the Ark.

בְּמַסְרְבֵי מָרוֹן — *The rebels of Maron*. The town of Maron was situated on a mountain and only could be reached by a narrow road (see *Rosh Hashanah* 18a and *Eruvin* 22b). It was the home of the first *mishmar*, יְהוֹיָרִיב, *Jehoiarib*. The Talmud states that it was during this *mishmar's* tour of duty that Jerusalem was captured (*Taanis* 29a), and expounds on the name Jehoiarib: יָ־הּ הֵרִיב עִם בָּנָיו עַל שֶׁמָּרוּ וְסָרְבוּ בוֹ, *God contended with His children because they were rebellious and defiant against Him* (*Yerushalmi Taanis* 4:5).

מֵחֲמֶשֶׁת סְפָרִים — *The [people endowed with the] Five Books*. This refers either to Israel, the Torah nation (as indicated by the interpolation), or to the Torah itself which metaphorically wept bitterly when Zechariah was assassinated (see *kinnah* 34).

כֹּהֲנֵי צִיפּוֹרִים — *The Kohanim of Sepphoris*. The city of קִיטְרוֹן, *Kitron* (see *Judges* 1:30), was also called צִיפּוֹרֵי or צִיפּוֹרִים, *Sepphoris*, because it sat on a mountaintop like a high-soaring צִיפּוֹר, *bird* (*Megillah* 6a). It was the home town of the second watch, יְדַעְיָה, *Jedaiah*, whose name the Talmud explains as 'יָדַע יָ־הּ, *God knew*, what evil was in the depths of their hearts and so He exiled them לְצִיפּוֹרִין, *to Sepphoris*,' or, in a variant reading, 'כְּצִיפּוֹרִים, *like birds*' (*Yerushalmi Taanis* 4:5). The *paytan* merges both readings.

וּבְאַרְבַּעַת שְׁפָטִים — *Four types of affliction:* sword, starvations, wild beast and plague (see *Ezekiel* 14:21; see also *kinnah* 9).

עֵיתָה לוֹ — *Aysah-Lo*. This was the city of the fourth watch, שְׂעוֹרִים, *Seorim*. Perhaps it is identical with עַיָּת, *Aiath*, the first city taken by Sennacherib when he moved against Jerusalem (*Isaiah* 10:28 with *Rashi*). The *Vilna Gaon* identifies that place with Gilgal.

הָיוּ אוֹיְבִים מַלְעִיבִים בְּלוֹחֲמֵי לֶחֶם,[1]
כְּבִטְּלוּ הֲלֹא פָרוֹס לָרָעֵב לֶחֶם,[2]
וְהִרְעָבוּ וְהִצְמָאוּ מִמַּיִם וּמִלֶּחֶם,
כְּבִטְּלוּ שְׁתֵּי הַלֶּחֶם, מִבֵּית **לֶחֶם.***

וַיֵּצֵא הֲדַר אוֹם בַּכֶּסֶף נֶחְפַּת,[3]
וּתְמוּרוֹ אֵפֶר עַל רֹאשָׁהּ חִפַּת,
וְנֵרוֹת נִכְבּוּ וּמְנוֹרָה נִכְפַּת,
כְּפָשְׁעוּ בְּלֶחֶם וּפַת, נִלְכְּדָה **יוֹדְפַת.**[4]*

זָכְרָה זְמַן אֲשֶׁר נַעֲשֶׂה וְנִשְׁמַע[5] הֵשִׁיבוּ,
וְעַתָּה עֲנוֹת אָמֵן לֹא אָבוּ,
לַעֲנָה וָרוֹשׁ[6] שָׂבְעוּ וְרָווּ,
וְהֶקְצוּ וְהֶלְעָבוּ, כֹּהֲנֵי **עֵילְבוּ.**

חֵטְא חָטְאָה וְאָמְרָה לֶאֱלִיל זֶה אֵל,
וְהִלְעִיגָה וְתִעְתְּעָה בְּחוֹזֵי אֵל,
עֲבוּר כֵּן הֻקְנְאָה בְּמַרְגִּיזֵי אֵל,
וַיֵּצֵא מִמְּעוֹן אֵל, **כְּפַר עֻזִּיאֵל.**

טֻמְאָתָהּ הֶחֱנִיפָה תֵּבֵל,
וְנַעֲלָה רַב הַחוֹבֵל,
וְעָנָן אֲבַק רַגְלָיו כְּאָבֵל,
וְאֵין מִתְכַּרְבֵּל, בְּכֹהֲנֵי **אַרְבֵּל.**

יָדוֹ פָּרַשׂ צָר בְּבֵית זְבוּל,
כִּי כְלָיָה חִיַּבְתִּי כְּדוֹר הַמַּבּוּל,
כִּסְאוֹ הֵשִׁית לְחִבּוּל וְנִבּוּל,
וַיֵּצֵא בְּכֶבֶל כָּבוּל, כֹּהֵן **כָּבוּל.**[7]*

כָּל עַמָּהּ קוֹנְנוּ קִינָה,
כִּי הִכְעִיסוּ לְאֵל קַנָּא,
בְּגוֹי נָבָל אוֹתָם קִנֵּא,
וְנָדְדָה מִקִּנָּהּ, מִשְׁמֶרֶת **אֶלְקָנָה.**

בֵּית לֶחֶם — *Bethlehem.* The fifth watch, מַלְכִּיָּה, *Malciah*, was headquartered in Bethlehem. Additionally, בֵּית לֶחֶם, literally, *House of Bread*, alludes to the *Beis HaMikdash*. For as the Midrash teaches, as long as the Show Bread was placed on the שֻׁלְחָן, *Table*, each Sabbath, and the Two Loaves were brought every Shavuos in the Temple, the nation's flour and bread would

ה *They ridiculed those who fought in the battle [for Torah observance],*[1]
when they ignored [the verse],
'Shall you not break bread with the hungry?'[2]
Thus, they hungered and thirsted for water and for bread,
when the offering of the two loaves
was discontinued, from ***Bethlehem.****

ו *Beauty has left the nation once sheltered by the silver[like Torah],*[3]
in its place ashes cover her head.
The candles have been extinguished
and the Menorah has been bent [to the ground].
When they willfully sinned with [their failure
to give the poor] portions of bread,
the [fortress] of ***Yodpath***[4] *was captured.*

ז *Remember the moment when they replied,*
'We shall do and we shall listen!'[5]
But now [when they are admonished] they do not confirm [their sins].
They were sated and filled with wormwood and bitter gall;[6]
The Kohanim of ***Aylevu*** *were shunned and shamed.*

ח *She sinned greatly when she addressed the idol*
and said, 'This is God!'
She mocked and ridiculed God's seers,
therefore He took revenge through those who infuriated God,
and [Kohanim from] ***Kfar Uziel*** *had to depart from God's dwelling.*

ט *Her contamination has defiled the inhabited world,*
and the Captain of the ship has ascended [to his heavenly dwelling].
Clouds are on His feet like dust on [the bare feet of the] mourner,
and there is none among the Kohanim of ***Arbel***
who clads himself in the [priestly] vestments.

י *The enemy spread out his hand against the [Divine] dwelling,*
for I was culpable to extinction like the generation of the Flood.
The enemy subjected God's throne to mutilation and degradation,
And the Kohanim of ***Cabul***[7]*
went out [into exile] chained in leg irons.

כ *Her entire nation chanted a lamentation,*
because they angered the zealous God;
He took revenge against them through a degenerate nation,
And the watch of ***Elkanah*** *wandered [into exile] from its nest.*

---

(1) Cf. *Proverbs* 9:5; *Chagigah* 14a. (2) *Isaiah* 58:7. (3) Cf. *Psalms* 68:14 with *Rashi*. (4) Some editions read יוּרְפַּת, *Yurfath*. (5) *Exodus* 24:7. (6) Cf. *Eichah* 3:15. (7) See *Joshua* 19:27 and *I Kings* 9:13.

---

be blessed. But since these were stopped, blessing no longer lies in the bread. Nonetheless, in the future they will be restored (*Yalkut Shimoni* II:565).

יוֹדְפַת — *Yodpath.* A Galilean fortress, mentioned in *Arachin* (32a) as a city that was walled from the time Joshua entered the land.

כָּבוּל — *Cabul.* In return for supplying many of the materials for the *Beis HaMikdash* and Solomon's Palace, King Hiram of Tyre was presented with twenty cities in the land of Cabul, but he was not satisfied (*I Kings* 9:10-13). The Talmud explains that the inhabitants of this area of the Galilee were so wealthy that they would attire themselves in silver and gold. If so,

לֹא לַמָּרוֹם עַיִן צָפַת,
וְכֶסֶף עַל חֶרֶשׂ חִפַּת,
וּבְחִזּוּק מוּסָר הֶרְפַּת,
וְנֶהֱרַס וְנִלְפַּת, כֹּהֵן **צְפַת.**

מִמָּרוֹם הִשְׁמִיעַ נִלְאֵתִי טְעוֹן,[1]
וְהִכַּנִי בְּעִוָּרוֹן וּבְשִׁגָּעוֹן,
וּפָקַד עָלַי עֲוֹן נוֹב וְגִבְעוֹן,[2]
וְנָעָה מִמָּעוֹן, מִשְׁמֶרֶת **בֵּית** כֹּהֵן **מָעוֹן.**

נִשְׂקַד עוֹל עָוֹן וְנִכְאָב,
כְּהוֹשַׁבְתִּי אֲנוּנָה מִבְּלִי אָב,
וְנִמְנַעְתִּי מִלְּצַפְצֵף בְּמִנִּים וְעֻגָב,
וְנָשְׂאָה עָלַי קִינָה, מִשְׁמֶרֶת **יֶשֶׁבְאָב.***

סִלָּה אַבִּירַי מוֹרֵי הוֹרָיָה,
וְלֹא נִזְכַּר לִי עֲקֵדַת מוֹרִיָּה,
וּמֵרֹב מֶרֶד וּמְרִיָה,
הוּצָגָה עֵרוֹם וְעֶרְיָה,[4] מִשְׁמֶרֶת **מַעַדְיָה.**[3]

עַל גַּבִּי חָרְשׁוּ חוֹרְשִׁים וְהֶאֱרִיכוּ מַעֲנִית,[5]
וְהֵרִיקוּ עָלַי חֶרֶב וַחֲנִית,[6]
וְהִרְבֵּיתִי צוֹמוֹת וְתַעֲנִית,
וּמְצוּרַת תָּכְנִית,[7] יָצְאָה **יְוָנִית.**

פֵּרְשָׂה וְאֵין יָד שׁוֹלֵחַ,
כִּי לֹא הֶאֱמִינָה בְּהַשְׁכֵּם וְשָׁלוֹחַ,[8]
וְהִשְׁבַּתָּה בְּרִית מֶלַח,[9]
וְאֵין שֶׁמֶן מִמֻּלָּח, בְּרֹאשׁ **מַמְלָח.**

צַדִּיק הוּא יהוה כִּי פִיהוּ מָרַת,[10]
וְעָרוּ עָרוּ עַד הַיְסוֹד בָּהּ[11] הוּעֲרַת,
וּתְמוּר עָזִּי וְזִמְרָת,[12]
קִינִים עָלֶיהָ נֶחֱרַת, וּבְקַצְוֵי אֶרֶץ נִזְרַת **נִצְרַת.**

---

(1) Cf. *Isaiah* 1:14. (2) See *I Samuel* 22:19. (3) Some editions read מַעַרְיָה, *Maariah.* (4) Cf. *Hosea* 2:5. (5) Cf. *Psalms* 129:3. (6) Cf. *Ezekiel* 28:7. (7) 43:11. (8) Cf. *Jeremiah* 25:4; 29:19. (9) Cf. *Leviticus* 2:13. (10) Cf. *Eichah* 1:18. (11) Cf. *Psalms* 137:7. (12) *Exodus* 15:2.

ל *Not heavenward did [their] eye peer;*
[Their external piety was like] silverplate overlaid on earthenware.
And as [God's] admonition intensified, [their strength] waned.
The Kohanim of ***Safed*** *were knocked down and captured.*

מ *From on high He sounded [the cry],*
'I am exhausted from carrying [the burden of your sins].'[1]
Then He afflicted me with blindness and madness.
He visited upon me the iniquity
of [the massacre] of Nob and Gibeon,[2]
and the watch from ***Beis Ma'on*** *departed from the Temple.*

נ *The burden of my iniquities has accumulated and causes me pain.*
When I was forced to sit like a mourning daughter,
without [my] Father,
and I was silenced from playing the organ and flute,
the watch of ***Jeshebeab**** *raised a lament for me.*

ס *He has trampled all of my heroes, the teachers of God's Law,*
And the [merit of Abraham's] binding [Isaac as an offering]
on Mount Moriah was not recalled on my behalf;
Because of the enormity of my rebellion and insurrection,
the watch of ***Maadiah***[3] *has been put on display, naked and bare.*[4]

ע *On my back the plowers plowed, they lengthened the furrow,*[5]
they bared sword and spear against me;[6]
so I have increased fasts and afflictions;
and the [watch of] ***Yevanis*** *departed from*
the perfectly formed design [of the Temple].[7]

פ *She [Israel] spread [her hands in prayer],*
but no [helping hand] was sent.
Because she did not believe [in God's prophets]
who arose early and were sent [to admonish her].[8]
The [sacrificial service's] Covenant of Salt was discontinued,[9]
and the well-blended oil of anointment is no longer
on the head [of the Kohen Gadol] from ***Mamlah.***

צ *It is* HASHEM *Who is righteous for His utterance was disobeyed.*[10]
[Therefore the enemy cried,] 'Destroy! Destroy!
Bare it to its very foundation!'[11]
Instead of singing, 'God is my might and my praise,'[12]
laments were engraved for her,
and the watch of ***Nitzrath*** *was scattered to the ends of the earth.*

---

why was Hiram displeased? Because such wealthy people would not serve him properly (*Shabbos* 54a). According to the Talmud, Cabul was destroyed because there was strife among its citizens (*Yerushalmi Taanis* 4:5).

יֶשֶׁבְאָב — *Jeshebeab.* Although the *paytan* does not refer to any of the other watches by their Scriptural names as recorded in *I Chronicles* (24:7-18), in this case he makes an exception. According to those who interpret the names used by the *paytan* as geographical locations (see the opening comment to this *kinnah*), it is not unreasonable to assume that this *mishmar* lived in a town that bore its name. Following the opinion that these names are allusions to the sins of the *Kohanim* (see ibid.), *Beis Levi* surmises that this *mishmar* was righteous in all its deeds. Thus, it was not given a pejorative nickname.

קָרָאתִי לְצוּרִי וְקוֹלִי לֹא עָרַב,
וְקוֹנַנְתִּי בַּיַּעַר בַּעֲרָב,
וְכָבָה נֵר הַדּוֹלֵק בְּמַעֲרָב,
וְרֵיחוֹ לֹא עָרַב, **מֵאֶכְלָה עָרַב.**

רְאֵה כִּי הֻסְעַרְתִּי כָּאֳנִיָּה,
בְּתַאֲנִיָּה וַאֲנִיָּה,[1]
וּקְהָלִי כַּצֹּאן לַטֶּבַח[2] מְנוּיָה,
וְנָעָה מֵחֲנוּיָה, **מִגְדַּל נוּנִיָּה.**

שָׁמְעוּ כִּי יָצָאתִי בַּשִּׁבְיָה,
וְנִשְׂרְפָה דַּת מָרוֹם שְׁבוּיָה,[3]*
וְהוּשַׁתִּי לְשַׁמָּה וַעֲרְבוּבְיָה,
וּמֵהֶסְתֵּר חֲבוּיָה, נָדָה בֵּית **חוּבִיָּה.**

שָׁמְעוּ כִּי נִזְהַמְתִּי בְּצַחֲנָה,
וְסָתַם מֶנִּי תְּחִנָּה,
וְלֹא נָתַן לִי רַחֲמִים וַחֲנִינָה,
וּמִקִּרְיַת חָנָה,[4] נָעָה **כְּפַר יוֹחֲנָה.**

תָּבֹא רָעַת שְׁמוֹנֵי הַדָּמִין,
וְשָׁתוּ שְׁעָרַי שׁוֹמֵמִין,[5]
וְהֵשִׁיב אָחוֹר יָמִין,[6]
וּבַעֲוֹן פְּסִילִים נָעָה **גִּנְּתוֹן צַלְמִין.**

תָּבֹא תַמְרִיחַ, וְחָשְׁכֵי תַּזְרִיחַ,
וְכַדֶּשֶׁא עַצְמוֹתֵינוּ תַּפְרִיחַ,[7]
וְרֵיחַ נִיחוֹחֵינוּ כְּקֶדֶם תָּרִיחַ,
וּמִשֻּׁלְחָנְךָ תַּאֲרִיחַ, שׁוּלֵי **חֲמַת אָרִיחַ.**

(וַיְקוֹנֵן יִרְמְיָהוּ עַל יֹאשִׁיָּהוּ.)*

This view is borne out by the Talmud's statement (*Succah* 56b) that Bilgah, the *mishmar* following Jeshebeab, would arrive late (or not at all) when it was their week to serve in the Temple. At those times, the *Kohanim* of Jeshebeab would dutifully remain at their posts. For this, Bilgah's watch was punished (see ibid.) and Jeshebeab was rewarded.

דַּת מָרוֹם שְׁבוּיָה — *The Law captured from heaven.* During the forty-day period that Moses was atop Mount Sinai, he ascended to heaven to receive the Torah to bring it down to Israel. When the ministering angels complained to God that a mortal did not belong among them, He replied, 'He has ascended to take the Torah.'

The angels argued, 'This precious treasure, which was hidden away for the equivalent of 974 generations before the world was created, should not be given to mortal man.'

ק *I called out to my Rock [of salvation], but my voice was not pleasing.*
I lamented in the Arabian forest,
for the Western Lamp [which burnt wondrously
in the Temple] was extinguished,
and the fragrance [of the incense offered in the Temple
by the watch] from **Achalah Arav** *was not pleasing.*

ר *Behold, I am storm tossed like a [floundering] ship,*
moaning and mourning;[1]
my congregation resembles a flock of sheep prepared for slaughter,[2]
[the watch from] **Migdal Nuniyah** *was made*
to wander from Chanuyah [in Jerusalem].

ש *[When] they heard that I went forth into captivity,*
the Law captured from heaven[3]* *was burnt.*
I was placed in abandonment and chaos,
and [the watch] from **Hoviah** *was exiled from [the Temple]*
where God's concealed Presence was once hidden.

ש *They heard that I was befouled by the stench [of my sins],*
and that [God] had sealed [the gates of prayer] to my supplication,
and bestowed upon me neither compassion nor grace.
So [the watch] from **Kfar Yohanah** *was made to wander*
from [Jerusalem,] the City of [David's] encampment.[4]

ת *May evil befall those who cut my limbs to pieces,*
and desolated my gateways;[5]
[God] has now withdrawn His right hand,[6]
and for the iniquity of idols, [the watch from]
Ginthon-tzalmin *was made to wander.*

ת *O come and spread soothing balm [on my wounds]*
and illuminate my darkness,
and let our [dry] bones blossom forth as verdure.[7]
Accept graciously the fragrance of our pleasing offerings
as in days of yore;
and offer [the] final [watch] from **Hamath-Ariach**
hospitality at your Altar-table.

*(And Jeremiah lamented over Josiah.)**

(1) *Eichah* 2:5. (2) Cf. *Jeremiah* 12:3. (3) Cf. *Psalms* 68:19. (4) Cf. *Isaiah* 29:1.
(5) Cf. *Eichah* 1:4. (6) Cf. 2:3. (7) Cf. *Isaiah* 66:14.

God then summoned Moses to counter the arguments of the angels. Moses reasoned with them, 'Angels do not need the Torah. You have no parents to honor, no possibility of conforming to the requirements of *kashrus*, and no Egyptian bondage to remember.'

The holy angels admitted the truth of Moses' words and consented to allow the Torah out of the heavenly domain, for they realized that its precepts apply only to man and to his world (*Shabbos* 88b).

Since the angels sought to keep the Torah captive in the heavens until Moses captured it for mankind by his convincing arguments, the *paytan* describes the Torah as 'captured from heaven.'

וַיְקוֹנֵן ... יֹאשִׁיָּהוּ — *And Jeremiah lamented over Josiah.* Although this verse is printed at the end of this *kinnah* in many editions, the consensus of the commentators considers it a mistake. It is really the opening verse of the next *kinnah*, and that is how it appears in most early editions.

יא.

וַיְקוֹנֵן יִרְמְיָהוּ עַל יֹאשִׁיָּהוּ.[1]*

אֵיכָה אֵלִי* קוֹנְנוּ מֵאֵלָיו,
בֶּן שְׁמוֹנֶה שָׁנָה הֵחֵל לִדְרוֹשׁ מֵאֱלֹהָיו,[2]*
בְּנֵי חָם* בְּעָבְרָם חָנוּ עָלָיו,
וְלֹא הֻזְכַּר לוֹ שִׁגּוּי מִפְעָלָיו.

גַּם בְּכָל מַלְכֵי יִשְׂרָאֵל אֲשֶׁר קָמוּ לִגְדּוֹר,
לֹא קָם כָּמוֹהוּ מִימוֹת אֲבִיגְדּוֹר,[3]*
דָּבַק בּוֹ חֵטְא לֵיצָנֵי הַדּוֹר,
אֲשֶׁר קָמוּ אַחַר הַדֶּלֶת לִסְדּוֹר.[4]

וַיְקוֹנֵן יִרְמְיָהוּ עַל יֹאשִׁיָּהוּ — *And Jeremiah lamented over Josiah.* This *kinnah* is the most important and authentic lament we recite on Tishah B'Av (except for the Book of *Eichah*) because its recitation was ordained by the prophet Jeremiah [Yirmeyahu] himself following the tragic death of King Josiah [Yoshiyahu]: *...And all of Judah and Jerusalem mourned over Yoshiyahu. And Yirmeyahu lamented over Yoshiyahu; and all of the male singers and the female singers have mentioned Yoshiyahu in their laments to this day and made them a statute in Israel, and behold, they are written in the Book of Lamentations* (*II Chronicles* 35:24,25).

Why was the death of Yoshiyahu considered a tragedy of such proportion that it must be remembered by *all* of Israel for *all* time? Because *never* in all of Jewish history was there a leader as great as this king who sparked a massive nationwide wave of *teshuvah*, repentance, which had such a positive effect on Israel that the First Temple was almost saved from doom and preserved for future generations — as Scripture states: *And like him there was no king before him who returned to HASHEM with all his heart and all his soul and with all his resources in accordance with all the Torah teachings of Moses, nor did anyone equal to him ever arise afterwards* (*II Kings* 23:25).

Yoshiyahu's grandfather, the notorious King Menashe, had fanatically dedicated the early years of his reign to a campaign of utterly stripping the Jewish people of every vestige of true faith in God. With single-minded devotion, Menashe planted idols in every corner of his kingdom, even in the Holy of Holies itself! Although Menashe repented in his later years, it was beyond his ability to rip out the bitter root of idolatry he had planted so deeply within the heart of the Jewish people.

Amon, Menashe's son, was an idolater who corrupted Judah for two years until he was assassinated by his palace guards. His son *Yoshiyahu was eight years old when he began his reign and he reigned thirty-one years in Jerusalem* (*II Kings* 22:1).

So thoroughly had Yoshiyahu's predecessors eradicated the Torah's influence from the Jewish people that it appears that the king of the Jewish people *never saw a Sefer Torah* for the first eighteen years of his reign. In the eighteenth year, the *Kohen Gadol*, Hilkiah [Chilkiyahu, father of the prophet Yirmeyahu], began to make long overdue repairs on the Temple structure. In the course of this work, he discovered a Torah Scroll which had been hidden for generations — since the time of the wicked King Ahaz, father of Hezekiah [Chizkiyahu] and grandfather of Menashe (*Metzudas David*). Chilkiyahu was shocked when he opened the Scroll to the תּוֹכָחָה, *Admonition*, recorded in *Deuteronomy* (chs. 27 and 28), *HASHEM will carry off [to captivity] both you and the king whom you shall raise over yourself, to a nation which neither you nor your fathers have known* (*Deut.* 28:36); and, אָרוּר אֲשֶׁר לֹא־יָקִים אֶת דִּבְרֵי הַתּוֹרָה־הַזֹּאת לַעֲשׂוֹת אוֹתָם, *Cursed be he who does not uphold all the words of this Torah, to fulfill them* (*Deut.* 27:26). When King Yoshiyahu heard this, he was so shaken that he ripped his clothing (*II Chron.* 34:19) in anguish over all the years he had neglected the Torah out of sheer ignorance. Then he cried out, 'עָלֵינוּ לְהָקִים, *It is incumbent upon us to uphold [the Torah]!*' (*Yerushalmi Sotah* 5:4; *Midrash HaGadol, Devarim* 27:26).

Yoshiyahu swiftly convened a massive assembly of all the leaders and elders of Judah and Jerusalem and read to them from this new-found treasure, the Torah Scroll. Together, they entered a solemn covenant to keep all the teachings of the Torah with all their heart and soul. Yoshiyahu appointed agents to search out and destroy every vestige of idolatry in the land. They were successful in eradicating every *apparent* heathen

11.

'And Jeremiah lamented over Josiah.'[1]*

א *Arouse the lament of 'Eichah'* for one of the mightiest [kings], who after eight years began to search for His God.*[2]*

ב *Yet when the sons of Ham* passed through and encamped against him, none of his meritorious deeds were recalled [to stand] in his favor.*

ג *Also, of all the kings who arose to defend [against idolatry], no one like him arose since the days of Avigdor [Moses].*[3]*

ד *The sin of that generation's scorners clung to him — those who stood [idols] behind the door.*[4]

(1) *II Chronicles* 35:25. (2) Cf. 34:3. (3) Cf. *II Kings* 23:25. (4) Cf. *Isaiah* 57:8.

image and the vast majority of people did join in Yoshiyahu's penitence, but a stubborn minority persisted in the pagan beliefs that had taken such firm root over the generations. They invented an ingenious method for concealing their idols. They split their doors in two and they split their idols in two, down the middle. They attached one half of the idol to each half door in such a way that when the doors were closed the two idol halves came together to be whole, but when the doors were opened the idol was split in half and each piece was concealed behind the open door. When Yoshiyahu's detectives came to search for idols they opened the doors and found nothing (*Eichah Rabbah* 1:53). This *kinnah* laments that these surreptitious idolaters undermined all of Yoshiyahu's efforts to purify Israel.

In the last year of Yoshiyahu's reign, Pharaoh Necho, the king of Egypt, which is southwest of Israel, decided to wage war against Assyria which lies northeast of Israel. He asked Yoshiyahu for permission to march his troops through his land as this was the fastest and shortest route to Assyria. However, Yoshiyahu refused because God promised that when the Jewish people do His will, *'... a sword will not pass through your land'* (*Leviticus* 26:6). This means that the blessing of peace will be so pervasive that (a) foreign armies will not even attempt to use *Eretz Yisrael* en route to battle with a different country (*Sifra* and *Rashi* ibid.), and (b) the Jews will be so strong and meritorious that no army would be able to force its way through (see *Taanis* 22a,b).

Yirmeyahu the prophet sent word to Yoshiyahu to allow Pharaoh to pass through. He warned Yoshiyahu that his generation was not as righteous as he imagined and that there were still significant groups of secret idolaters. Tragically, Yoshiyahu, in his righteous zeal, refused to face reality and continued to entertain illusions of total perfection for the Jewish people (*Eichah Rabbah* 1:53). He ignored the prophet's harsh warning and instead sought advice from the prophetess Huldah whom he felt would see things in a more sympathetic light. This was a fatal mistake — to ignore the advice of the leading prophet of God and to accuse him of excessive harshness.

This *kinnah* describes King Yoshiyahu's tragic and untimely death when he went out to battle Pharaoh Necho to prevent him from crossing his territory. With his last breath, Yoshiyahu repented his sin against Yirmeyahu but it was too late. Not only was Yoshiyahu personally doomed, but the entire kingdom of Judah was now set on a course of irrevocable, ultimate destruction. Hence, the enormous tragedy of Yoshiyahu's death, because with him died the very last hope and opportunity to save the Temple and the Jewish people.

אֵיכָה אֱלִי — *The lament of 'Eichah.'* Specifically, this refers to the fourth chapter of the Book of *Eichah* which also begins with the word אֵיכָה. That elegy was originally pronounced over Yoshiyahu's death and is the *kinnah* referred to in the verse from *II Chronicles* that introduces this *kinnah* (*Rashi* to *Eichah* 4:1). For this reason the *paytan* begins each line of this *kinnah* with the first word of the corresponding verse in *Eichah* 4.

בֶּן שְׁמוֹנֶה שָׁנָה הֵחֵל לִדְרוֹשׁ מֵאֱלֹהָיו — *Who after eight years* [lit., *at eight years old*] *began to search for His God.* Actually, it was Yoshiyahu's reign that began when he was eight years old. And it was in the eighth year of his reign (when he was sixteen years old) that Yoshiyahu felt the first stirrings of *teshuvah* in his heart and *began to search for the God of David, his ancestor* (*II Chronicles* 34:3, see *Malbim*). Nevertheless, since a newly crowned king is considered like a new-born baby (see *Yoma* 22b), the *paytan* refers to Yoshiyahu in the eighth year of his reign as an eight-year-old.

בְּנֵי חָם — *The sons of Ham.* This refers to Pharaoh Necho (see above) of Egypt. מִצְרַיִם, *Mitzrayim,* the progenitor of Egypt was a son of חָם, *Ham,* the son of Noah (see *Genesis* 10:6).

אֲבִיגְדוֹר — *Avigdor [Moses].* The Talmud (*Megillah* 13a) and Midrash (*Vayikra Rabbah* 1:3) record ten names by which Moses was known: Moshe, Toviah, Yered, Avi Gedor (or Avigdor), Chaver, Avi Socho, Yekusiel, Avi Zanoach, Shemayah and Nesanel (see *I Chronicles* 4:18, 24:6).

הָאוֹכְלִים זֶרַע שִׁיחוֹר,
כְּתְמוֹ הַטּוֹב פִּחֲמוֹ מִשְּׁחוֹר,
וַיִּגְדַּל עֲוֹן וְהֵשִׁיב יְמִין אָחוֹר,[1]
וְעוֹד לֹא שָׁלַח יָדוֹ מִן הַחוֹר.[2]

זַכּוּ אֲמָרָיו כְּנָם דַּת לְהָקִים,
בִּצַּע אֶמְרָתוֹ[3] בְּאָרוּר אֲשֶׁר לֹא יָקִים,[4]
חָשַׁךְ תָּאֳרוֹ כְּנִאֲצוּ רְחוֹקִים,
בְּבֶצַע מוֹאֲסֵי דַּת וְחֻקִּים.

טוֹבִים רָעִים[5] נִקְרְאוּ בְּשָׁלְחוֹ מַלְאָךְ,
מַה לִּי וָלָךְ הַיּוֹם לְתַלְאָךְ,[6]
יְדֵי עַם הָאָרֶץ דָּמִים בִּמְלָאךְ,
תֵּעָנֵשׁ בְּבִצְעִי אֶת פְּנֵי פִלְאָךְ.

כְּלָה הֲמוֹנֵי לֶכֶת אֲרַם נַהֲרַיִם,
לְמַעַן לֹא תַעֲבוֹר חֶרֶב[7] כָּל שֶׁהוּא בְּאֶפְרַיִם,
וְלֹא שָׁמַע לַחוֹזֶה לָשׁוּב אֲחוֹרַיִם,
כִּי גְזֵרָה נִגְזְרָה לְסַכְסֵךְ מִצְרַיִם בְּמִצְרָיִם.[8]*

מֵחַטֹּאת סְתִירַת מְזוּזוֹת,
חֲזוֹן עַנְּתוֹתִי[9] הֵחֵלּוּ לְבַזּוֹת,
נָעוּ עֲנָמִים לְחוּמוֹ לְהַבְזוֹת.
וְלֹא הֵסֵב פָּנָיו[10] וְסָפְדוּ עַל זֹאת.*

סוֹרוּ הֵעִידוּ עַד לֹא שְׁאִיָּה,
וַיְמָאֲנוּ סוּר וּמָט יְסוֹד* נְשִׁיָּה,
פְּנֵי קְרָב כְּקָרֵב וְלֹא עָלְתָה לוֹ רְטִיָּה,[11]
וַיּוֹרוּ הַמּוֹרִים לַמֶּלֶךְ יֹאשִׁיָּה.[12]

עוֹדֶנּוּ עוֹצֵם עֵינָיו בְּגֵוָיו נוֹחֲצִים,
חֵץ אַחַר חֵץ מוֹרִים וְלוֹחֲצִים,

מִצְרַיִם בְּמִצְרָיִם — *Egyptian . . . against Egyptian.* According to the prophecy of Isaiah (19:2), Egypt would be destroyed through internal strife as *I will cause Egyptian to contend against Egyptian; each man to wage battle against his brother and against his friend; city against city and kingdom against kingdom.*

על זאת — *'For this . . .'* Yirmeyahu bemoaned the death of Yoshiyahu with the words: על זאת . . . , *For this shall you all gird yourselves in*

ה *[Thus] those who ate the produce of the Nile*
darkened [Josiah's] handsome,
glowing countenance blacker than charcoal.

ו *[As] iniquity increased, He withdrew His right hand;*[1]
and He has not yet returned His hand through the opening.[2]

ז *Pure were his words when he spoke of upholding the Law;*
and he carried out His decree,[3]
'Cursed be he who upholds not [the Torah].'[4]

ח *His features darkened [in anger] when the estranged [Jews]*
were defiant [of God]; through the corruption
of those who despised the Law and the statutes.

ט *The bad ones were called good*[5] *when he [Pharaoh Necho]*
sent a messenger [saying],
'Why should you and I do battle today?[6]

י *'You will be filling the hands of your countrymen with blood;*
and you will be punished [for preventing me] from
fulfilling the desire of your miracle worker [God].'

כ *[But] he [Josiah] stopped his [Pharaoh's] hordes*
from marching to Mesopotamia, so that
not even one sword would pass through[7] *Ephraim.*

ל *He failed to heed the seer [Jeremiah] who said to turn back,*
for it was [divinely] decreed that Egyptian should
contend against Egyptian.[8]*

מ *This resulted from the sin of concealing [idols behind] the doorposts,*
when they began to scoff at [the prophecies of Jeremiah,]
the seer from Anathoth.[9]

נ *The Anamite [Egyptians] moved onward to mutilate*
his [Josiah's] flesh; yet he did not turn his face [in retreat][10]
*and they eulogized him with, 'For this . . .'**

ס *'Turn back!' they warned him before the disaster would strike,*
but he refused to turn back, and [Josiah]
*the righteous foundation** *of the world collapsed.*

פ *When the vanguard of the battle lines approached,*
healing [salvation][11] *was not available to him,*
when the archers shot at King Josiah.[12]

ע *While he was yet closing his eyes, they continued,*
swiftly shooting and driving arrow after arrow into his body.

---

(1) Cf. *Eichah* 2:3. (2) Cf. *Song of Songs* 5:4. (3) *Eichah* 2:17. (4) *Deuteronomy* 27:26. (5) Some editions read טוֹבִים רֵעִים נִקְרְאוּ, *They were called good friends.* (6) Cf. *II Chronicles* 35:21. (7) Cf. *Leviticus* 26:6. (8) Cf. *Isaiah* 19:2. (9) See *Jeremiah* 1:1. (10) Cf. *II Chronicles* 35:22. (11) Some editions read שְׁעִיָּה which can mean either *salvation* or *prayer.* (12) Cf. *II Chronicles* 35:23; some editions read הַיֹּרִים (as in the Scriptural verse), rather than הַמּוֹרִים, but the meaning is the same.

---

sackloth, lament and wail, for HASHEM's burning anger has not turned from us (Jeremiah 4:8).

יְסוֹד — *[Josiah] the [righteous] foundation.* The interpolations are based on the verse: וְצַדִּיק יְסוֹד

צְדָוּהוּ וְשָׂמוּהוּ כַּמַּטָּרָה לַחִצִּים,
וַיִּזְרְקוּ בוֹ שְׁלֹשׁ מֵאוֹת חִצִּים.[1]

קַלִּים[2] הִטּוּ אַחֲרָיו אֱזוֹן מוֹצָא פִיהוּ,
וְעַד מִצּוּי נֶפֶשׁ מַעֲשָׂיו הֶפִיהוּ,
רְוּחַ שְׂפָתָיו הִפְצָה מִפִּיהוּ,
צַדִּיק הוּא יהוה* כִּי מָרִיתִי פִּיהוּ.[3]

שִׁישִׁי נוֹף* כִּי קִנֵּא זָעַם,
לְשַׁלֵּם שְׁאוֹנָם בַּעֲוֹן בִּצְעָם,[4]
תַּם כֶּתֶם הַטּוֹב עַם זוּ* בְּפָשְׁעָם,
וַיְקוֹנֵן עָלָיו כָּל אֵיכָה יוֹעַם.[5]

תָּם בְּמִקְרֶה אֶחָד* כּוֹס מְגִדּוֹ לִשְׁתּוֹת,
בְּמוֹעֵד שְׁנַת הַשְּׁמִטָּה[6] כְּגָע הַקְּהֵל לֶאֱתוֹת,
תָּלָה בְּעֶשְׂרִים וּשְׁתַּיִם* מֵהֲרוֹס שָׁתוֹת,
כִּי סָפְדוּ לוֹ אֵיכָה בְּעֶשְׂרִים וּשְׁתַּיִם אוֹתִיּוֹת.

אוֹתוֹת קִינוֹת* לְבָטָּה מְחוֹלִי,
עֵת כִּי שָׁכַחְתִּי מְחוֹלְלִי,[7]
זַמּוֹתִי כִּי לָעַד יַאֲהִילִי,
רָשַׁעְתִּי וְנָסַעְתִּי וְנֻטַּשׁ אָהֳלִי.

(1) *Eichah Rabbah* 1:53; cf. *Sanhedrin* 48b. (2) Cf. *Isaiah* 18:2. (3) Cf. *Eichah* 1:18; *Eichah Rabbah* 1:53. (4) Alternatively: *Because God's fury has avenged, repaying [Israel's] multitudes for the sin of their corruption.* (5) *Eichah* ch. 4. (6) *Deuteronomy* 31:10; see *Sotah* 41a. (7) Cf. *Deuteronomy* 32:18.

עוֹלָם, *a righteous person is the foundation of the world* (*Proverbs* 10:25; see *Chagigah* 12b).

צַדִּיק הוּא ה׳ . . . — *'It is* HASHEM *Who is righteous . . .'* With three hundred well-aimed arrows, the Egyptians pierced Yoshiyahu's body like a sieve. As the king breathed his last, Yirmeyahu swiftly ran over to his side to catch the dying words of this great *tzaddik*. Yoshiyahu completely accepted the punishment that God had meted out to him and realized that he deserved it. *'It is* HASHEM *Who is righteous, for I disobeyed His utterance* — and I disobeyed the utterances of His representative, the prophet Yirmeyahu!' (*Midrash Eichah* 1:53).

נוֹף — *Nof*, an Egyptian city mentioned in *Isaiah* (19:13), *Jeremiah* (2:16 et al.) and *Ezekiel* (30:13,16) and usually identified with Memphis.

צ *They trapped him, made him a target for [their] arrows,*
and shot three hundred arrows into him.[1]

ק *The swift-footed [emissary Jeremiah]*[2] *inclined behind him,*
to hear his [final] words;
and until his soul was forced out of him,
his deeds adorned him.

ר *The breath of his lips burst forth from his mouth,*
'It is HASHEM *Who is righteous,**
for I have disobeyed His utterance.'[3]

ש *Rejoice [while you can], O Nof,**
because [God's] fury shall avenge,
repaying [your] hordes for the sin of their corruption.[4]

ת *The good, golden one [Joshiah] has died*
because of this nation's guilt,*
and [Jeremiah] lamented him: 'Alas, the gold is dimmed . . .'[5]

[The righteous Josiah] died under the same circumstances
[as the wicked Ahab], when he drank the cup [of retribution]*
at Megiddo;
it was the Festival [of Succos in a year following a] Sabbatical year[6]
when the time of national assembly arrived.
For twenty-two [years, God] suspended*
the utter destruction of the Temple
because they eulogized [Josiah with the lament of] 'Eichah,'
[composed] in the order of the twenty-two letters
[of the aleph-beis].

א-ל *My dance degenerated into signs of lament,**
ע *at the time I forgot my Creator;*[7]
ז *I expected that He would eternally shelter me,*
ר *but I was wicked and was forced to depart,*
for my Tent was abandoned [by God].

עם זו — *This nation.* In the Song of the Sea, Israel is called עַם זוּ גָּאָלְתָּ, *'this nation' that You redeemed* (*Exodus* 15:13), and עַם זוּ קָנִיתָ, *'this nation' that You have acquired* (ibid. 15:16). Moreover, Isaiah (43:21) calls Israel, עַם זוּ יָצַרְתִּי לִי, *'this nation' which I have fashioned for Myself.* Based on these passages, the *paytanim* often refer to Israel as עַם זוּ, *this nation.*

בְּמִקְרֶה אֶחָד — *Under the same circumstances [as the wicked Ahab],* who also succumbed to an enemy archer's arrow on the battlefield (see *I King* 22:34-35).

בְּעֶשְׂרִים וּשְׁתַּיִם — *For twenty-two [years].* The calculation of these years is as follows: After the death of Yoshiyahu, his son Jehoahaz [Yehoachaz] reigned for three months, Jehoiakim [Yehoyakim] for eleven years, Jehoiachim [Yehoyachin] for three months and ten days, and the last king of Judah, Zedekiah [Zidkiyahu], for eleven years, for a total of twenty-two years, six months and ten days (*Beis Levi*).

אותות קינות — *Signs of lament.* The singular noun אות can mean either *letter of the alphabet* or *sign.* Usually the plural אותות is used for *signs* and the plural אוֹתִיוֹת for *letters.* But sometimes they are interchanged. Thus, some render this phrase *alphabetically arranged lamentations.*

יב.

אָהֳלִי אֲשֶׁר תָּאַבְתָּ עַד לֹא בְרֵאשִׁית*
עִם כִּסֵּא כָבוֹד לְצָרְפוֹ,*
לָמָּה לָנֶצַח[1] שֻׁדַּד בְּיַד שׁוֹדְדִים,
וְנִהְיֵיתָ כְּרוֹעֶה בְּעֹטְיָה[2] וְרָעַשְׁתָּ וְרָגַנְתָּ,
וְעַתָּה מַה לִּי פֹה.[3]

אָהֳלִי אֲשֶׁר קוֹמַמְתָּ לְאֵיתָנֵי אֶרֶץ.[4]
בְּחֶרְדַּת מִי אֵיפֹא,[5]*
לָמָּה לָנֶצַח צֻמַּת בְּיַד צָרִים,
וְנִהְיֵיתָ כְּצִפּוֹר בּוֹדֵד עַל גָּג[6] מַר צוֹרֵחַ, מַה לִּידִידִי פֹּה.[7]

אָהֳלִי אֲשֶׁר פַּצְתָּ לְמַעֲנוֹ לְצִיר,
וְאַתָּה עֲמוֹד עִמָּדִי פֹה,[8]
לָמָּה לָנֶצַח עֹרְעַר בְּיַד עֲרֵלִים,[9]
וְנִהְיֵיתָ כְּשׂוֹנֵא וְצָר,[10] וְאַיֵּה אִוּוּי מוֹשָׁב פֹּה.[11]

אָהֳלִי אֲשֶׁר נָחִיתָ בְּעַנְנֵי הוֹד,
לְזֹאת אֲשֶׁר יֶשְׁנוֹ פֹה וְאֵינֶנּוּ פֹה,[12]
לָמָּה לָנֶצַח מוּאַס בְּיַד מוֹרְדִים,
וְנִהְיֵיתָ כְּגִבּוֹר לֹא יוּכַל לְהוֹשִׁיעַ,[13]
מַה לְּךָ פֹה וּמִי לְךָ פֹּה.[14]

אָהֳלִי אֲשֶׁר כּוֹנַנְתָּ מוּל מָכוֹן לְשִׁבְתְּךָ[15]*
לְחוֹפֵף לְחֶפּוֹ,

אָהֳלִי ❧ — *My Tent.* Each stanza begins אָהֳלִי, *My Tent,* which variously alludes to either the *Mishkan* (Tabernacle) that accompanied Israel through the Wilderness for forty years, or to one or the other of the two Temples. According to *Ibn Ezra* (*Eichah* 2:4), the *Beis HaMikdash* is referred to as a tent, because just as when fire touches a tent, it begins to burn instantly, so did the *Beis HaMikdash* catch fire in an instant.

The *kinnah* is a series of triplets, each of which follows the same pattern: (a) The first line begins אָהֳלִי אֲשֶׁר, *My Tent that,* followed by a letter of the reverse alphabetical arrangement known as תַּשְׁרַ״ק; and ends with the syllable פו or פּוֹ; (b) the second line begins לָמָּה לָנֶצַח, *why is it forever ...,* followed by the next letter of תַּשְׁרַ״ק; and ends with the syllable ־ִים; (c) the third line begins וְנִהְיֵיתָ כְּ־, *And why have You become ...,* followed by a תַּשְׁרַ״ק letter; (d) the second part of the line is a Scriptural passage that ends with the word פה or פֹּה.

The final stanza contains an acrostic of the author's name אֶלְעָזָר, *Elazar.*

עַד לֹא בְרֵאשִׁית — *Even before Creation* [lit., *when there was no beginning*]. The Talmud states that the *Beis HaMikdash* is one of seven things (or concepts) created before the world. The other six are: תּוֹרָה, *Torah;* תְּשׁוּבָה, *repentance;* גַּן עֵדֶן, *the Garden of Eden;* גֵּיהִנֹּם, *Hell;*

12.

ת *My Tent,* that You yearned, even before Creation,**
*to align with Your [celestial] Throne of Glory,**
ש *why is it forever[1] plundered by the hand of plunderers?*
ר *And why have You become like a shepherd veiled*
[in mourning over his lost flocks],[2]
as You stormed and grumbled, 'And now, what have I here?'[3]

ק *My Tent that You erected for the powerful [Patriarchs] of the Land,[4]*
with [Isaac's] shudder [when he wondered],
*'Who is this then [that will dare to destroy the Temple]?'[5]**
צ *why is it forever slashed to pieces by tormentors?*
And why have You become like a lonely bird on a rooftop,[6]
screeching bitterly, 'What is My beloved doing here?'[7]

פ *My Tent that You spoke about to the emissary [Moses], saying,*
'You stand with me here [so I may teach you
about the Tabernacle],'[8]
ע *why is it forever stripped bare by the hand of the uncircumcised?[9]*
ס *And why have You become like an enemy and tormentor?[10]*
What has become of [Your] desire
that Your habitation be here [in Zion]?[11]

נ *My Tent that You guided with clouds of splendor,*
for the sake of those who are here and for those who are not here,[12]
מ *why is it forever made contemptuous by the hand of rebels?*
ל *And why have You become like a warrior unable to save,[13]*
[while the enemy mocks,]
'What have You here and whom have You here?'[14]

כ *My Tent that You positioned as a foundation*
for Your [celestial] dwelling[15] that hovers over it like a canopy,*

(1) *Eichah* 5:20. (2) Cf. *Song of Songs* 1:7. (3) *Isaiah* 52:5. (4) Some editions read לְאֵיתָנֵי עוֹלָם, *the powerful of the world,* or, *the powerful of yore.* (5) Cf. *Genesis* 27:33. (6) *Psalms* 102:8. (7) Cf. *Jeremiah* 11:15. (8) Cf. *Deuteronomy* 5:28. (9) Some editions read עוֹבְדֵי כּוֹכָבִים, *star worshipers,* some read נָכְרִים, *strangers,* and some read אוֹיְבִים, *enemies.* Obviously, the hand of the censor has been at work here, and the whims of the various censors had to be adhered to by the printing shops. (10) Cf. *Eichah* 2:5. (11) Cf. *Psalms* 132:13. (12) Cf. *Deuteronomy* 29:14. (13) *Jeremiah* 14:9. (14) *Isaiah* 22:16. (15) Cf. *Exodus* 15:17.

כִּסֵּא הַכָּבוֹד, *God's Throne of Glory;* and שְׁמוֹ שֶׁל מָשִׁיחַ, *the name of the Messiah* (*Pesachim* 54a; *Nedarim* 39b).

עִם כִּסֵּא כָבוֹד לְצָרְפוֹ — *To align with Your [celestial] Throne of Glory.* According to the Midrash, the *Throne of Glory* in heaven is directly above the *Beis HaMikdash* on earth (*Mechilta* cited by *Rashi* to *Exodus* 15:17; *Targum* to Jeremiah 17:12).

בְּחֶרְדַּת מִי אֵיפֹא — *With [Isaac's] shudder [when he wondered], 'Who is this then [that will dare to destroy the Temple]?'* According to the *paytan*, Isaac did not tremble because Jacob had pre-empted Esau's blessing. Rather, Isaac saw in a prophetic vision that descendants of the one standing before him would someday destroy the *Beis HaMikdash.*

כּוֹנַנְתָּ מוּל מָכוֹן לְשִׁבְתְּךָ — *That You positioned as a foundation for Your [celestial] dwelling.* The Midrash teaches that the celestial *Beis HaMikdash* is aligned with the terrestrial *Beis HaMik-*

לָמָּה לָנֶצַח יוֹעָה בְּיַד יְהִירִים,
וְנִהְיֵיתָ כְּטָס בְּחָלָל וְאֵין עוֹד נָבִיא, וְנָמְתָ הַאֵין פֹּה.[1]

אָהֳלִי אֲשֶׁר חָנִיתָ מֵאָז
בְּתָאָיו מִפֹּה וּמִפֹּה,[2]
לָמָּה לָנֶצַח זֻנַּח בְּיַד זָרִים,
וְנִהְיֵיתָ כְּוָתִיק יוֹצֵא חוּצָה, וְלֹא עָבַר פֹּה.

אָהֳלִי אֲשֶׁר הֵכַנְתָּ לְהַשְׁלִיךְ בּוֹ לְפָנֶיךָ
גּוֹרָל* פֹּה,[3]
לָמָּה לָנֶצַח דּוּחָה בְּיַד דָּמִים,[4]
וְנִהְיֵיתָ כְּגֵר בָּאָרֶץ, וְנַמְתָּ כִּי לֹא נָסוֹב עַד בּוֹאוֹ פֹּה.[5]

אָהֳלִי אֲשֶׁר בָּעֲוֹן בִּצְעִי,
חָשְׁכוּ כּוֹכְבֵי נִשְׁפּוֹ,[6]*
לָמָּה לָנֶצַח אֻפַּל בְּיַד אֻמּוֹת,
וְנִהְיֵיתָ כְּאֹרֵחַ בַּמָּלוֹן, וְעוֹד מִי לְךָ פֹּה.[7]

אָחוֹר וָקֶדֶם[8] מִפֹּה וּמִפֹּה,*
לְכָל דּוֹר וָדוֹר נוֹדַע קִצְפּוֹ וְחֶפּוֹ,
עַל מֶה מִכָּל אוֹם שָׁת עָלַי כַּפּוֹ,
זֹאת בַּעֲלִיל כִּי פִיד חָקוּק בְּכַפּוֹ,
רְפוּאָתִי בְטוּחָה כִּי רֶגַע בְּאַפּוֹ,[9]
וְעַד עַתָּה אֵיכָה יָעִיב בְּאַפּוֹ.[10]

(1) *I Kings* 22:7. (2) Cf. *Ezekiel* 40:21. (3) Cf. *Joshua* 18:6. (4) Some editions read either דּוּמִים (see *Rashi* to *Isaiah* 21:11) or דּוֹמִים (a contraction of אֲדוֹמִים), both of which mean *Edomites*; some editions read אֲחֵרִים, *others*. Once again, the censors have left their stamp on this *kinnah*. (5) *I Samuel* 16:11. (6) Cf. *Job* 3:8. (7) *Genesis* 19:12. (8) Cf. *Psalms* 139:5. (9) 30:6. (10) *Eichah* 2:1.

dash (*Tanchuma, Mishpatim* 18, cited by *Rashi* to *Exodus* 28:17).

גּוֹרָל — *Lots.* Four times each day the *Kohanim* would assemble in the *Beis HaMikdash.* At those times lots would be drawn to determine who would perform the various aspects of the Altar service. The method by which the selections were made and the particular tasks assigned at each lottery are discussed in chapter two of tractate *Yoma.*

כּוֹכְבֵי נִשְׁפּוֹ — *[Evening-]star-like luster.* The word נֶשֶׁף alludes to brightness shining through the dark, and can mean both morning and evening (*Pesachim* 2b). The interpolation of

י *why is it forever shoveled aside by the hand of the arrogant?*
ט *And why have You become like [a bird] flying in an empty void?*
And why is there no longer any prophet, as You have said,
'Is there no [prophet] here?'[1]

ח *My Tent where You encamped since yore in the chambers*
flanking this side and that,[2]
ז *why is it forsaken forever [and left] in the hand of aliens?*
ו *And why have You become like a brave veteran*
who [suddenly] runs out [in terror],
unable to return [to his place] here?

ה *My Tent where You established the casting of lots**
in Your Presence,[3]
ד *why is it forever pushed into the hand of the bloodthirsty?*[4]
ג *And why have You become like a foreigner in the land,*
and announced
that You would not return [to Your celestial Temple]
until [Israel] returns here [to terrestrial Jerusalem]?[5]

ב *My Tent that, because of the sin of my avarice,*
has had its [evening-]star-like luster darkened,*[6]
א *why is it forever blackened at the hand of the nations?*
And why have You become like a transient at an inn [begging],
'Do you have anyplace else here [for me to rest]?'[7]

א *After and before*[8] *[the Temple's destruction],*
*both this time and that,**
ל *in each and every generation God's anger*
and protective shelter are made known.
ע *So why, of all nations,*
has He pressed His [punishing] hand upon me?
ז *This is evident, although my destruction is engraved on His Palm,*
ר *nevertheless, my healing is certain,*
for His anger is but for a moment.[9]
Still, [I wonder,] how has He clouded me
until now in His anger?[10]

'evening' into the translation is thus arbitrary and could just as well read 'morning.' The meaning remains unchanged.

אָחוֹר וָקֶדֶם מִפֹּה וּמִפֹּה — *After and before ... both this time and that.* The translation of this phrase in a temporal sense follows *Matteh Levi* who understands it as an allusion to the generations following and preceding the Destruction. Alternatively, the phrase is spatial in meaning and is translated, *West and east, from here and from there* (see *Targum* to *Isaiah* 9:11 and *Job* 23:8).

יג.

אֵי **כֹּה*** **אֹ**מֶר כּוֹרֵת לְאָב בְּפֶצַח,
בִּבְרִית בֵּין הַבְּתָרִים **כֹּה** יִהְיֶה[1] לָנֶצַח,
וְהֵן עַתָּה **בִּ**לְּעוּ עֲצָמַי בְּרֶצַח,
לָמָה אֱלֹהִים זָנַחְתָּ לָנֶצַח.[2]

אֵי **כֹּה גָּ**שׁ כְּשֶׂה לְעוֹלָה לִרְצוֹתֶךָ,
נֵלְכָה עַד **כֹּה**[3] פִּתּוּ בְּעֵדוֹתֶיךָ,
וְהֵן עַתָּה **דָּ**קְּרוּ כְּפֶלַח רַעְיָתֶךָ,
יֶעְשַׁן אַפְּךָ בְּצֹאן מַרְעִיתֶךָ.[2]

אֵי **כֹּה הַ**בְטָחַת עֲקֻדִּים נְקֻדִּים[4] בִּמְשׁוּאוֹת,
אִם **כֹּה** יֹאמַר[5] כֹּה יוּחַשׁ אוֹת,
וְהֵן עַתָּה **וּ**כַּחְתָּ עִיר מְלֵאָה תְּשׁוּאוֹת,[6]
הָרִימָה פְעָמֶיךָ לְמַשֻּׁאוֹת.[7]

אֵי **כֹּה זָ**ם וְהָרַג מִצְרִי בְּגַן נָעוּל[8] בַּקֹּדֶשׁ,
וַיִּפֶן **כֹּה** וָכֹה[9] חֲתָם בַּעֲדַת קֹדֶשׁ,
וְהֵן עַתָּה **חֶ**לְקָם אָכַל חֹדֶשׁ,[10]
כָּל הֵרַע אוֹיֵב בַּקֹּדֶשׁ.[7]

---

(1) *Genesis* 15:5. (2) *Psalms* 74:1. (3) *Genesis* 22:5. (4) 31:11-13. (5) 31:8.
(6) Cf. *Isaiah* 22:2. (7) *Psalms* 74:3. (8) Cf. *Song of Songs* 4:12; see *Shemos Rabbah* 1:29.
(9) *Exodus* 2:12. (10) Cf. *Hosea* 5:7, see *Rashi* there.

⁂ אֵי כֹּה . . . — *Where is* [*the merit of the word*] *'so.' The* Midrash teaches that the *mitzvah* of *Bircas Kohanim* (the Priestly Blessing), which is introduced with the word כֹּה, *'so' shall you bless the Children of Israel,* was given in the merit of the three Patriarchs, about each of whom Scripture uses the word כֹּה, *so.* Regarding Abraham it is written, כֹּה, *so shall your offspring be* (*Genesis* 15:5); about Isaac it is said, *I and the lad* [i.e., Isaac] *will go* כֹּה, *so far* [i.e., yonder] (ibid. 22:5); and of Jacob the Torah states, כֹּה, *so shall you say to the House of Jacob* (*Exodus* 19:3; *Bereishis Rabbah* 43:8).

When God utilizes the term כֹּה, He demonstrates an intense degree of הַשְׁגָּחָה פְּרָטִית, *Divine Providence,* and reveals manifest love for His Chosen People. This *kinnah* laments that all the merits of the Patriarchs, the *Kohanim,* and various other personages and events that Scripture describes with the word כֹּה, *so,* could not prevent the Temple's destruction when Israel turned away from God's service, and God concealed His Presence from the nation.

The events recalled are: בְּרִית בֵּין הַבְּתָרִים, *the Covenant Between the Parts* (*Genesis* ch. 15); עֲקֵדַת יִצְחָק, *the offering of Isaac* (ibid., ch. 22); the dream in which Jacob was promised prosperity despite Laban's dishonesty in paying Jacob's wages (ibid. 31:1-16); Moses' killing an Egyptian taskmaster who had been beating a Jew (*Exodus* 2:11-12); Moses' encounter with God at the Burning Bush, where he was charged with redeeming the Israelite slaves from Egypt (ibid. 3:1-4:17); the Covenant of Circumcision and the *pesach* offering (ibid. 12:43-50); the Giving of the Torah at Mount Sinai (ibid. chs. 19-20); the Priestly Blessing (*Numbers* 6:22-27); Balaam's attempted curses that were transformed into blessings (ibid. chs. 22-24); the selection of the Tribe of Levi to minister in the

13.

א *Where is [the merit of the word] '**so**,'**
promised with a proclamation to [our] father [Abraham]
at the Covenant Between the Parts,
*'**So** shall [your offspring] always be [as numerous as the stars]?'*[1]

ב *Behold now, how my bones are swallowed up murderously.*
Why, O God, have you abandoned us
[for what seems like an] eternity?[2]

ג *Where is [the merit of the word] '**so**,' [mentioned*
when Abraham] approached [with his son] as with a sheep
for a burnt offering to please You?
They persuaded [the others to stay behind, saying],
*'We shall go **so** far,'*[3] *[in order to fulfill] Your testimonies.*

ד *Behold now, how Your beloved ones are speared like a piece of fruit.*
Why does Your wrath smolder against the sheep of Your pasture?[2]

ה *Where is [the merit of the word] '**so**,' in the promise [to Jacob]*
in the dark of night [when you promised him an abundance of]
striped and spotted [sheep]?[4]
When [Laban] would say,
*'[With sheep marked] **so** [I will reward you],'*[5]
so was the sign swiftly fulfilled.

ו *Behold now, how You admonished [Jerusalem,]*
the city once filled with a chorus of jubilation.[6]
Lift Your footsteps to wreak [eternal] ruin[7]
[upon the enemy who destroyed this holy city].

ז *Where is [the merit of the word] '**so**,' when [Moses]*
intentionally killed an Egyptian [who was beating a Jew]
in [view of the Israelites, who are like] a garden locked in[8]
*with holiness? He turned like **so** and like **so**,*[9] *and the matter*
[of the Egyptian's death] was kept sealed
within the holy congregation [of Israel].

ח *Behold now, how their portion was devoured in the month*
[of tragedy, Av],[10] *when all of the enemy's wickedness*
was wreaked in the Sanctuary.[7]

Sanctuary (ibid. 8:5-22); the conquest of Jericho (*Joshua* ch. 6); and the more than four hundred prophecies recorded in Scriptures that begin with the words כֹּה אָמַר ה׳, *so said* HASHEM.

The first line of each stanza begins אֵי כֹּה, *Where is [the merit of the word] 'so,'* followed by the respective letter of the *aleph-beis*. The third line begins וְהֵן עַתָּה, *Behold now, how . . .*, followed by the next letter of the alphabet. The last stitch of each stanza is taken from the first ten verses of psalm 74. The author of the *kinnah*, R' Elazar HaKalir (whose name, atypically, does not appear), draws upon the verses of this psalm to express Israel's bewilderment and confusion over the drastic change in their relationship with God, that brought about their ruination.

אֵי כֹּה טוֹב* כְּשִׁלַּח גְּאוּל עֲבָדֶיךָ,
כֹּה תֹאמַר[1] לְשַׁלַּח עַם לְעָבְדֶךָ,
וְהֵן עַתָּה יָשְׁבוּ בוֹגְדִים בְּבֵית וִעוּדֶיךָ,
שָׁאֲגוּ צוֹרְרֶיךָ בְּקֶרֶב מוֹעֲדֶיךָ.[2]

אֵי כֹּה כְּרִיתוּת חֲדָשׁוֹת בְּרִיתוֹת,*
בְּכֹה אָמַר כַּחֲצוֹת לַיְלָה בְּמוֹפְתֵי אוֹתוֹת,[3]
וְהֵן עַתָּה לְהֵקוּ בְּנַעֲלֵיהֶם לֶאֱתוֹת,
שָׂמוּ אוֹתוֹתָם אוֹתוֹת.[2]*

אֵי כֹּה מִשְׁמַע וּמֹשֶׁה עָלָה,
כֹּה תֹאמַר[4] לִנְוַת בַּיִת מְעֻלָּה,
וְהֵן עַתָּה נֶאֶסְוּהָ בְּנֵי עַוְלָה,
יִוָּדַע כְּמֵבִיא לְמָעְלָה.[5]

אֵי כֹּה שִׂיחַ שִׁשִּׁים אוֹתִיּוֹת הַקְּדוּמוֹת,*
כֹּה תְבָרְכוּ[6] לְשִׁשִּׁים גִּבּוֹרִים[7] דּוֹמוֹת,
וְהֵן עַתָּה עָתְקוּ רְדוּמוֹת,
בִּסְבָךְ עֵץ קַרְדֻּמּוֹת.[5]*

---

(1) *Exodus* 3:14. (2) *Psalms* 74:4. (3) *Exodus* 11:4. (4) 19:3. (5) *Psalms* 74:5; some editions read, וְהֵן עַד עַתָּה לֹא שָׁבוּ בְּנֵי גוֹלָה, *Behold how, until now, the exiles have not returned,* but this fits neither the alphabetic nor the repetitive aspects of the *kinnah*. It may be the result of a censor's whim. (6) *Numbers* 6:23. (7) Cf. *Song of Songs* 3:7.

טוב — *Tov[iah, Moses*]. Expounding on the verse that describes the birth of Moses, *And she [Yocheved] saw that he [her newborn son] was* טוב, *good* (*Exodus* 2:2), the Talmud explains that she named him טוֹבִיָּה, which means *God is good* (*Sotah* 12a). Pharaoh's daughter named him מֹשֶׁה, *Moses*, three months later when she drew him out of the waters of the Nile (*Exodus* 2:10).

[Although popularly pronounced as if it were spelled טוּבִיָּה, *Tuvyah*, lit., *goodness of God*, the proper vowelization of this name is טוֹבִיָּה (see for example, *Zechariah* 6:10 and *Ezra* 2:60).]

כְּרִיתוּת חֲדָשׁוֹת בְּרִיתוֹת — *When new [blood-] covenants were sealed.* When the Israelites were to be set free from Egyptian slavery, they had no merits by which to be redeemed. So God gave them the *mitzvah* of the *pesach* offering, but forbade the uncircumcised from partaking of it (*Exodus* 12:44,48). Since most of them had not been circumcised in Egypt, they had to submit to the covenant of *milah* before they could offer the *pesach*. Then the blood of the *milah* and the blood of the offerings mingled. And it was in the merit of these two blood-related *mitzvos* that the nation was redeemed (*Shemos Rabbah* 19:5). The *paytan* refers to these *mitzvos* as 'new covenants,' since one, the *pesach*, was indeed new, and the other, *milah*, had fallen into disuse and was then renewed.

שָׂמוּ אוֹתוֹתָם אוֹתוֹת — *They have made their signs for signs.* These words refer to the destruction of the First *Beis HaMikdash* at the hands of Nebuchadnezzar. He received heavenly signs which were meant to encourage his assault on Jerusalem and he was wise enough to pay heed to those messages. Thus *they* [the attackers] *made their* [Heaven-sent] *signs for* [meaningful] *signs*.

Nebuchadnezzar had not been sure whether to attack Israel or Ammon, so he had consulted seers, who foretold victory over Israel. He then shot arrows into the air, aimed in all directions. He observed that all of the arrows flew towards the south, in the direction of the Holy Land

ט *Where is [the merit of the word]* ***'so,'*** *when Tov[iah, Moses]**
was sent to redeem Your servants?
[When You said,] ***'So*** *shall you say*
[unto the Children of Israel]'[1]
this nation must be sent out to serve You.

י *Behold now, how traitors occupy Your House of Meeting,*
[as it is written,] Your enemies have roared
amidst Your meeting place.[2]

כ *Where is [the merit of the word]* ***'so,'*** *when new*
*[blood-]covenants were sealed**
[when the Jews were redeemed from Egypt]?
[Moses said,] ***'So*** *says [HASHEM]:*
About midnight [I shall go out among the Egyptians]
with miraculous signs!'[3]

ל *Behold, now, how they have gathered to come into [the Temple]*
in their shoes; They have made their signs for signs![2]*

מ *Where is [the merit of the word]* ***'so,'*** *which was heard*
when Moses ascended [Mount Sinai
and God told him to tell Israel],
'So *shall you say unto [the women,]*[4]
the distinguished homemakers?'

נ *Behold, now, how the sons of iniquity blaspheme Him*
and it is regarded as an attack on [God] above.[5]

ס *Where is [the merit of the the word]* ***'so,'*** *mentioned at*
*[the beginning of] the sixty-letter premier [benediction],**
'So *shall you bless'*[6] *which is like sixty mighty warriors?*[7]

ע *But, now, behold, the once slumbering [Babylonian Empire]*
has reawakened [and ascended] to power
and its axes are in the wooden thicket.[5]*

(Babylon is in the north). Thus assured, he confidently marched to Jerusalem (*Midrash Shocher Tov* 74:4).

Others interpret the passage as an allusion to the Destruction of the Second *Beis HaMikdash.* The Talmud describes how Titus entered the Temple, unsheathed his sword and stabbed the holy פָּרוֹכֶת, *curtain,* for he imagined that he could thereby cut God away from Israel. Blood began to flow from the curtain. Titus interpreted this as an אוֹת, *sign,* that he had slain God Himself (*Gittin* 56b). The blood was actually a Divine sign to Israel that God was 'suffering' over their tragic plight. Thus, *they* [the Romans] made אוֹתוֹתָם, *their signs* [the ones intended for encouraging Israel], for אוֹתוֹת, *signs* [for themselves and in their own favor] (*Sforno*).

שִׁשִּׁים אוֹתִיּוֹת הַקְּדוּמוֹת — *The sixty-letter premier [benediction].* בִּרְכַּת כֹּהֲנִים, *the Priestly Blessing,* contains exactly sixty letters. These are alluded to in the verse, *Behold the couch of the King of Peace, sixty of Israel's mightiest warriors surround it* (*Song of Songs* 3:7). Since all the blessings promised in the Torah are contingent upon Israel's fulfillment of the *mitzvos* (see, e.g., *Leviticus* 22:3-13 and *Deuteronomy* 28:1-14), while the Priestly Blessing is given with no conditions attached, it is called 'the premier benediction' (*Beis Levi*).

בִּסְבָךְ עֵץ קַרְדֻּמּוֹת — *Its axes are in the wooden thicket.* The Talmud (*Sanhedrin* 96b) relates that when the Babylonian multitudes laid siege to Jerusalem, King Nebuchadnezzar sent to his general Nebuzaradan three hundred mules laden with axes made of specially hardened iron which could smash through barriers of iron. At

אֵי **כֹּה** **פֶּץ** לָקוֹב עָם וּבֵרַךְ עַם קְדוֹשֶׁיךָ,
בְּשׁוּב **וְכֹה** תְדַבֵּר[1] הוּמַר לִקְדוֹשֶׁיךָ,
וְהֵן עַתָּה **צָרוּ** עַל עִיר קָדְשֶׁךָ,
שִׁלְּחוּ בָאֵשׁ מִקְדָּשֶׁיךָ.[2]

אֵי **כֹּה** קִיהַת לְוִיִּם שְׁלֵמֶיךָ,
כֹּה תַעֲשֶׂה לָהֶם לְטַהֲרָם[3] לְבֵית עוֹלָמֶיךָ,
וְהֵן עַתָּה **רָעֲשׁוּ** וְהִרְעִישׁוּ שָׁמֶיךָ,
לָאָרֶץ חִלְּלוּ מִשְׁכַּן שְׁמֶךָ.[2]

אֵי **כֹּה** **שִׁבְעַת** שׁוֹפְרוֹת עֶרֶץ,
כֹּה תַעֲשֶׂה שֵׁשֶׁת יָמִים[4] לְהַפִּיל חוֹמָה לָאָרֶץ,
וְהֵן עַתָּה שְׁעָרִים טָבְעוּ בָאָרֶץ,[5]
שָׂרְפוּ כָל מוֹעֲדֵי אֵל בָּאָרֶץ.[6]

אֵי **כֹּה** **תְּ**שׁוּעוֹת אֲסָמֵי אוֹצָר,
בְּכֹה אָמַר אֲשֶׁר לַחוֹזִים נָצָר,[7]
וְהֵן עַתָּה תְּפִּחוּ פִּרְחֵי בְּחָצֵר,
עַד מָתַי אֱלֹהִים יְחָרֶף צָר.[8]

(1) *Numbers* 23:5. (2) *Psalms* 74:7. (3) Cf. *Numbers* 8:7. (4) *Joshua* 6:3. (5) Cf. *Eichah* 2:9. (6) *Psalms* 74:8. (7) Some editions read אֲשֶׁר לַדּוֹרוֹת נָצָר, *designated for the generations.* (8) *Psalms* 74:10.

first the Babylonians were entirely unsuccessful and they wasted this entire stock of unique weapons on an assault on just one of Jerusalem's many gates, all to no avail; the axes shattered while the gate held firm. Nebuzaradan was completely demoralized and he wished to lift the siege and retreat, for he feared that he would meet the disastrous fate of Sennacherib whose vast army perished to a man when he besieged the Holy City. But a בַּת קוֹל, *heavenly voice,* resounded and said to Nebuzaradan: 'Don't be hasty. The moment has just arrived for the Temple to be destroyed and the Sanctuary to be consumed in fire.' Nebuzaradan had but one axe left in his arsenal. He threw it at the gate and it didn't even strike it with its metal head, but with its dull wooden handle, yet it smashed the iron gate wide open! This fulfilled King David's prophetic lamentation, *'It is regarded as an attack on [God] above, its axes are in the wooden*

פ *Where is [the merit of the word]* ***'so,'*** *when*
[the wicked Balaam] opened his mouth to curse —
but instead blessed — Your holy nation?
[You commanded Balaam,] 'Return
[to Balak, the king who hired you]
and ***so*** *shall you say,'*[1] *[that the curses were]*
transformed [into blessings] for Your holy ones.

צ *Behold, now, how they have set upon Your holy city;*
they have sent Your Sanctuary up in flames.[2]

ק *Where is [the merit of the word]* ***'so,'*** *when the Levites,*
Your perfect [attendants], were taken
[into Your service with the words],
*'****So*** *you shall do unto them, to purify them'*[3]
for your Eternal Temple?

ר *Behold, now, how they have stormed [the earthly Temple]*
and thereby caused Your heaven[ly Temple] to tremble;
to the ground have they desecrated the Abode of Your Name.[2]

ש *Where is [the merit of the word)* ***'so,'*** *[when the Jews circled*
the walls of Jericho and seven priests sounded]
seven powerful ram's horns? [For You had said,]
*'****So*** *shall you do for six days,*[4] *to topple the wall to the ground.'*

ש *Behold, now, how the gates [of our Holy Temple]*
have sunk into the ground;[5] *[and] they have burned*
all of God's meeting places on earth.[6]

ת *Where is [the merit of the word]* ***'so,'***
[which assured] salvation emanating from
[the Holy Temple described as]
the storehouse brimming with abundance.
[The prophecies of future redemption which God]
designated for His visionaries[7] *[all began with the words],*
*'****So*** *says [HASHEM].'*

ת *Behold, now, how my flower[-like children]*
lie bloated [from starvation] in each courtyard.
How long, O God, will the tormentor revile?[8]

---

thicket' (*Psalms* 74:5), i.e., this wondrous assault on the gates of the earthly Temple below was tantamount to an attack on the celestial Temple Above (*Rashi* ibid.).

יד.

אֵיכָה* אֵת אֲשֶׁר כְּבָר עָשְׂוּהוּ,[1]
תָּבַע מֶנִּי לִגְבוֹת נְשִׁיֵּהוּ,
אֲשֶׁר עַד לֹא שְׁחָקִים נִמְתָּחוּ,
בְּשֶׁלִּי רָמַז הֱיוֹת אֶרֶץ תֹּהוּ.[2]

בְּלַע בְּאוֹת עַרְבִית וְשַׁחֲרִית,[3]
גֵּאֶה מַגִּיד מֵרֵאשִׁית אַחֲרִית,[4]
בָּנוּי וְחָרֵב וּבָנוּי בְּאַחֲרִית,
וּמֵחוֹבִי קַלְקָלָתוֹ הֶחֱרִית.

הֶחֱרִית **אִ**ישׁוֹן חֹשֶׁךְ מִיְּדַע,
וְקַדְמוֹנִים חָזוּהוּ מְגֻדָּע,
אָז לְרָאשֵׁי דוֹרוֹת נִתּוּצוֹ נוֹדַע,
עַד לֹא עָשׂוּי קַרְנוֹתָיו גָּדַע.[5]

גָּדַע גֹּבַהּ קוֹמַת יְצִיר צָר,*
זֶה סֵפֶר[6] לְפָנָיו הוּבְצָר,
גָּלְמִי רָאוּ עֵינֶיךָ[7] הָפְצָר,
כְּהֶעֱבִיר לְפָנָיו כָּל נֶעֱצָר.*

דָּרַךְ דֹּחֵף מִבֵּית הָאוֹצָר,
וְהֶרְאָהוּ כִּי הַמַּצָּע קָצָר,[8]*

(1) *Ecclesiastes* 2:12. (2) *Genesis* 1:2. (3) Cf. 1:5. (4) *Isaiah* 46:10.
(5) *Eichah* 2:3. (6) *Genesis* 5:1. (7) *Psalms* 139:16. (8) Cf. *Isaiah* 28:20.

אֵיכָה ◆ — *Alas.* From the very beginning of Creation, God foresaw that the *Beis HaMikdash* would be built, destroyed, and rebuilt. Thus, the Torah states: בְּרֵאשִׁית בָּרָא אֱלֹהִים, *In the beginning God created* (*Genesis* 1:1), an allusion to building . . .; then, וְהָאָרֶץ הָיְתָה תֹהוּ וָבֹהוּ, *the earth was astonishingly empty* (1:2), a hint of destruction . . .; finally, וַיֹּאמֶר אֱלֹהִים יְהִי אוֹר, *God said, 'Let there be light'* (1:3), indicating a rebuilding (*Midrash Bereishis Rabbah* 2:5). This *kinnah* describes how all the Patriarchs and forebears of the Jewish people were privy to foreknowledge regarding the first two phases, but were not permitted to learn the secret of the third phase — the time of the End — when the Temple will be rebuilt.

R' Moshe Chaim Luzzatto explains in *Daas Tevunos* that God created the forces of evil in this world — and allows them to temporarily overpower the good — to provide the good with an opportunity to summon forth all of its latent inner strength and to ultimately obliterate evil. The triumph of the dark forces over those of light is always temporary, because the light is destined to burst out with hitherto untapped brilliance to ultimately wash away the stain of darkness. The Midrash (ibid.) concludes that the prophet Isaiah also had this idea in mind when he proclaimed: *Arise and shine, for your light has arrived, and the glory of* HASHEM *has dawned upon you. For, behold, darkness shall shroud the earth and deep gloom the nations, but* HASHEM *will dawn over you and His glory will be visible over you. And the nations shall walk by your shining light and kings by the brightness of your rising!* (*Isaiah* 60:1-3).

In the intricate tapestry of this *kinnah*, R' Elazar HaKalir wove together a triple *aleph-beis* and his signature (for the most part doubled). Each group of three stanzas is arranged in the following format: The first words of stanzas one and two are taken from the respective verses in

14.

א *Alas* — that it has already been done;*[1]
He [God] demanded payment of His debt from me.
א *For before the heavens had been spread out,*
He alluded to my [Temple's Destruction in the verse],
'And the earth was astonishingly empty.'[2]
ב *He intimated an omen [symbolizing the Destruction as] evening and [the future rebuilding as] morning;*[3]
thus did the Glorious One announce the final outcome at the very beginning.[4]
ב *It would be built and destroyed and then rebuilt in the end,*
yet it was because of my guilt that its ruination was inscribed.
א *God inscribed [in the Torah] the blackness and dark so that it would be known, and the ancient [Patriarchs and prophets] had visions of it having been cut down.*
א *From early times the leaders of the generations knew that it would be shattered. Even before [the Temple] was completed, its dignity was already cut down [in the Divine design].*[5]
ג *He cut down the towering stature of [Adam,]*
*the creature He had fashioned [with His own hands];**
this very book [of generations of mankind][6]
was revealed before him;
ג *additional proof [of this revelation is in the verse],*
Your eyes saw my as yet unshaped future
[and in your book all were recorded],'[7]
as You passed before him all [the souls]
*stored [in heaven until their time to be born].**
ד *He had just stepped into the treasure house [of Eden]*
when he was evicted. Thus God demonstrated to him
that the couch is too short.[8]*

---

chapter two of *Eichah;* the next word and the first word of line three begin with the same letter as that word; the third stanzas of the respective group contain a double acrostic of the author's name, אֶלְעָזָר בִּירַבִּי קַלִּיר, *Elazar son of R' Kalir;* the last word of the second stanza is repeated as the first word of the third, and the last word of the third is repeated as the first word of the following stanza.

גָּדַע גֹּבַהּ קוֹמַת יְצִיר צָר — *He cut down the towering stature of [Adam,] the creature He had fashioned [with His own hands].* Before Adam sinned by eating the forbidden fruit, He stood from the earth to heaven (see *Chagigah* 12a). His spiritual capacity was virtually limitless. There was no facet of creation, from the most mundane to the most sublime, that Adam did not encompass. Nothing was hidden from him. More — no one ever comprehended better than he how each of his actions could determine the course of creation. However, after Adam sinned, God laid His hand upon him and diminished his stature until he was able to hide *among the trees of the Garden* (*Genesis* 3:8; *Bereishis Rabbah* 19:9).

כְּהֶעֱבִיר לְפָנָיו כָּל נֶעֱצָר — *As You passed before him all [the souls] stored [in heaven until their time to be born].* Adam foresaw the fate of all future generations, as Scripture relates: זֶה סֵפֶר תּוֹלְדֹת אָדָם, *This is the account* [lit., *book*] *of the descendants of Adam* (*Genesis* 5:1). The Talmud (*Avodah Zarah* 5a) explains that this verse implies that God showed Adam every generation with its expositors, sages and leaders.

כִּי הַמַּצָּע קָצַר — *That the couch is too short,* i.e., when man arrogantly defies God there is no room for both of them to dwell together, and man must

דָּוֶה לִבּוֹ כְּבַט בְּיַאת צָר,
וַיְקוֹנֵן עָלָיו אֵיכָה בְּאַיֶּכָּה[1]* בְּעֵת צָר.

צוּר הֶרְאָה **לוֹ** מַה שֶּׁהָיָה,
נְתַץ קִיר נָטוּי וְגָדֵר הַדְּחוּיָה,[2]
לְדוֹרוֹת לְמֵד נְהוֹת נְהִי נִהְיָה,
עַל שֶׁבֶר אֲשֶׁר הָיָה.

הָיָה הַנּוֹעֵר מִמִּזְרָח,[3]
בֵּין בְּתָרִים[4] אוֹרוֹ כְּזָרַח,
וְהֶרְאָהוּ אַרְבַּע מַלְכֻיּוֹת בְּרֶדֶם וְצָרַח,
כִּי טָבַע שַׁעַר הַמִּזְרָח.[5]

וַיִּחְמוּס וַיְנַצֵּל זֶרַע,
וַיַּרְא הַשְׁלָכַת נִזְרָה,*
וְאֵימָה נוֹפֶלֶת עָלָיו כְּבִזָּרָה,[6]
וְצִדֵּק מִדַּת הַדִּין כְּאָז רָאָה.

רָאָה עֵרוֹם וְעֶרְיָה[7] וְנֶאֱנַח,
וְלַעֲקוּדוֹ סוֹד זֶה פִּעֲנַח,
עָשְׁשָׁה מִכַּעַס עֵינוֹ[8] וְלֹא נָח,
מֵרְאוֹת גִּזְעוֹ טוֹב זָנַח.[9]

זָנַח זֹהַר תָּם בַּמַּחֲזֶה,
כִּי לֹא הֶאֱמִין בִּנְאֻם זֶה,
זָן עֵינוֹ בַּמָּקוֹם הַזֶּה,
וְשָׁר שִׁמּוּמוֹ וַיְקוֹנֵן אֵין זֶה.[10]

(1) *Genesis* 3:9. (2) Cf. *Psalms* 62:4. (3) Cf. *Isaiah* 41:2. (4) See *Genesis* 15. (5) Cf. *Eichah* 2:9. (6) Cf. *Genesis* 15:12. (7) Cf. *Ezekiel* 16:7. (8) Cf. *Psalms* 6:8. (9) Cf. *Hosea* 8:3. (10) *Genesis* 28:17.

be dismissed. Interestingly, this verse also alludes to the Destruction of the *Beis HaMikdash*. The Talmud (*Sanhedrin* 103b; *Yoma* 9b) relates that when the sinful King Menashe placed an idol in the Sanctuary, God said, 'The couch is too short to support a man and his two wives,' i.e., the *Beis HaMikdash*, in which God made His Presence rest, could not tolerate the rival, idolatrous worship. And so it was to be destroyed.

אֵיכָה בְּאַיֶּכָּה — *'Eichah! Alas!' [as alluded to] in . . . 'Where are you?'* When Adam and Eve tried to hide their nakedness after eating the forbidden fruit, God approached to admonish them with the word, 'אַיֶּכָּה, *Where are you?*' The *paytan* plays on the similarity between that word and אֵיכָה, *alas*. Both words are spelled with the same letters and differ only in vowelization. Thus, they are taken as an allusion that the ultimate cause of the Destruction was Adam's initial sin. The commentators disagree regarding the speaker of the word אֵיכָה in this comparison. Either it was said by God after the actual Destruction, or it was spoken by Adam when he was shown the vision of the Destruction.

ד *His [Adam's] heart ached upon foreseeing the entry of the enemy [into the Temple]; and he lamented in time of distress over [the destroyed Temple] with the word, 'Eichah! Alas!' [as alluded to] in [God's call to him], 'Where are you?'*[1]*

ל *[Similarly,] God showed [the enemy that the Destruction of the Temple was] an accomplished fact; thus, he [merely] smashed an already crumbled wall and an already toppled fence;*[2]

ל *nevertheless, God taught all future generations to mourn the actual destruction with doleful lament over the Destruction when it actually happened.*

ה *[The Patriarch Abraham] was inspired to arise from [Ur-kasdim in] the East,*[3] *until his light shone forth [in the Holy Land] at the Covenant Between the Parts.*[4]

ה *In his sleep, [God] showed [Abraham a vision of] the Four Kingdoms [which would subjugate his descendants in exile], and he screamed when the Eastern [Temple] Gate sank [into the earth].*[5]

ו *He ripped apart [the Temple] and confiscated her tiara. [Abraham] saw the throwing-away of her crown;**

ו *and he was seized with terror when [he saw his children] scattered.*[6] *Nevertheless, he affirmed the righteousness of the Divine Attribute of Strict Justice, despite all that he foresaw.*

ע *He foresaw [his children exiled] bare and naked*[7] *and he groaned, and to his sacrificially bound [son Isaac] he revealed this secret [of the future exile];*

ע *his eye dimmed with anguish*[8] *and he could not rest, because he saw his offspring abandoned by the One Who is Good.*[9]

ז *The illustrious perfect [Patriarch Jacob] abandoned what he saw in the vision [of Israel's future descent] and would not believe this pronouncement;*

ז *but when his eyes totally absorbed [all that was destined to transpire on] this place, he foresaw its desolation and lamented, 'This cannot be!'*[10]

נִזְרָה ... זֶרָה — *Her tiara ... her crown.* Some commentators understand this as an allusion to the three crowns spoken of in *Avos* (4:17). They are the crowns of Torah scholarship, priesthood, and kingship. When the *Beis HaMikdash* was destroyed, Israel had to forfeit these three crowns. This interpretation is difficult because only two crowns are mentioned in the *kinnah*.

Perhaps the *paytan* means to teach that although the crown of priesthood was lost with the Destruction, and the crown of kingship was lost with the Exile, the crown of Torah can never be removed from the Jewish people, despite their centuries-long homeless wandering through the Diaspora.

Alternatively, this refers to the three 'crowned' vessels in the Sanctuary: הָאָרוֹן, *the Ark*, in which the Tablets of the Ten Commandments rested (see *Exodus* 25:11); הַשֻּׁלְחָן, *the Table*, for the *Panim* Loaves (ibid. 25:24); and הַמִּזְבֵּחַ, *the* Golden *Altar*, upon which the Incense was

חָשַׁב חֲשׁוֹשׁ בְּעוֹלִים וְיוֹרְדִים,
וַיָּבֶן כִּי בוֹ יְהוּ רוֹדִים,
חֲנִיכָיו עַל מֶה בְּדִינוֹ חֲרֵדִים,
וּמֵהֶם תֶּבַע זְבוּל מוֹרְדִים.

מוֹרְדִים **זְ**בוּל וּמַצְפּוּנָיו נִבְעוּ,[1]
וּמַסְמְרוֹת נְעָלֵימוֹ* בְּקַרְקָעִיתוֹ קָבְעוּ,
זִיו שְׁעָרָיו מֶנִּי מַה נִּתְבָּעוּ,
וְהִנָּם טְמוּנִים בָּאָרֶץ כִּי טָבְעוּ.[2]

טָבְעוּ טוֹרְדִים לֵידַע זְמָן,
כִּי לְגַלּוֹת קֵץ אָב זִמֵּן,[3]
טוֹב מִשֶּׁגִּלָּה לוֹ קֵץ מְזֻמָּן,
הֵשַׁע וְהִבְלִיג[4] וְקֵץ כָּמָן.

יָשְׁבוּ וְשָׁאֲלוּ לְאָב לֵידַע,
זְמַן קֵץ הַפְּלָאוֹת מָתַי יִתְוַדַּע,[5]
יָקַו לְיוֹם יְשׁוּעָה וְלֹא נוֹדַע,
עַד כִּי בְּעִתּוֹ יוּחַשׁ[6] וְיִתְוַדַּע.

יִתְוַדַּע **רָ**ז לִבָּם נִסְתַּכָּלוּ,
וְנִכְסָה מֵהֶם וְלֹא יוּכָלוּ,
רֵעֶיךָ מִקִּנְאַת בֵּיתְךָ נֶאֱכָלוּ,[7]
וּבְיָגוֹן חַיֵּימוֹ כָּלוּ.[8]

כָּלוּ כִּסְלֵי צִיר כְּשֻׁלָּח,
וְנָם שְׁלַח נָא בְּיַד תִּשְׁלָח,[9]
כִּי מַה בֶּצַע לִי לְהִשְׁתַּלָּח,
וְאַחֲרַי גִּלְעָדִי יְשֻׁלָּח.

לְאִמּוֹתָם לִבְּבוּ עוֹלְלֵי סוּף,
אֵיזֶה יוֹם הַכָּסוּף,

---

offered (ibid. 30:3). The Talmud correlates: (a) the Altar's crown with the crown of priesthood that Aaron merited and took for his descendants; (b) the Table's crown with the crown of kingship (as in the expression, שֻׁלְחָן שֶׁל מְלָכִים, *a royal table*) that David merited and took for his offspring; and (c) the Ark's crown with the crown of Torah scholarship, but that crown is still available and whoever desires to wear it can attain it [through diligent study] (*Yoma* 72b).

ח *He pondered and grew apprehensive about*
[the angels] who ascended and descended [the celestial ladder],
for he understood [that the heathen nations would ascend to power
and then come down] to oppress [Israel].

ח *O why does He [God] terrify His disciples [Israel]*
with such retribution, then exact punishment from them
[for the Destruction of] the Temple by [the heathen] rebels?

ז *[Heathen] rebels stripped bare Your Temple*
and its hidden [treasures],[1] *they riddled the [Temple] floor*
*with their hob-nailed shoes.**

ז *Why were its shining gates demanded*
[as punishment for my sins]? Behold them,
hidden in the earth for they have sunk.[2]

ט *[Jacob's sons] probed deeply and exerted themselves*
to discover the time [appointed for the final redemption],
and their father was on the verge of disclosing the End of Days].[3]

ט *But He Who is Good after revealing the End [to Jacob],*
turned it away [from him] and reinforced [this removal],[4]
thus He hid [knowledge of] the End.

י *They sat and beseeched their father to inform [them]*
when the inscrutable End would be disclosed;[5]

י *they waited hopefully for the day of salvation,*
but it will not be made known until its designated time,
or it will be made known earlier [if Israel has special merits].[6]

ר *Their hearts sought to discover the secret [of the End],*
but they were unable to for it was
absolutely concealed from them.

ר *Your beloved ones [Israel] are consumed with vengeance*
for [the Destruction of] Your House,[7]
and their lives are spent in sorrow.[8]

כ *Spent were the hopes of the emissary [Moses] when he was sent forth*
[and foresaw that the Jews would again be exiled], so he said,
'Send, please, through the agency of another messenger;[9]

כ *for what is there for me to gain by being sent*
[since the Jews will be exiled again anyway],
and after me [Elijah] the Gileadite will have to be sent
out [to announce the final redemption]?

ל *The infants at the [Sea of] Reeds asked their mothers*
with heartfelt sincerity, 'Which is that yearned-for day?'

(1) Cf. *Obadiah* 1:6. (2) Cf. *Eichah* 2:9. (3) See *Rashi* to *Genesis* 49:1. (4) Cf. *Psalms* 39:14. (5) Cf. *Daniel* 12:6. (6) Cf. *Isaiah* 60:22. (7) Cf. *Psalms* 69:10. (8) Cf. 31:11. (9) *Exodus* 4:13.

וּמַסְמְרוֹת נְעָלֵימוֹ — *With their hob-nailed shoes.* In the place so holy that the *Kohanim* were prohibited from wearing shoes while performing the Temple Service, these brazen hea-

לְבָם הֵכִין לְשׁוֹרֵר מִסּוּף,[1]
יהוה יִמְלוֹךְ בִּזְרְוֹעַ חָשׂוּף.[2]

חָשׂוּף זְרוֹעוֹ **בְּ**יַד רָמָה,
וְנִגְלָה בִּימִין רוֹמֵמָה,[3]
בָּנִים כְּשָׁרוּ חֵמָה זְרוּמָה,
קָצְרָה נַפְשָׁם בְּגֵיא אֱדוֹם לָדַעַת עַל מָה.

מַה מָּצָאתָ עַוְלָתָה בִּי,
כִּי בָגוֹד בָּגַדְתָּ בִּי,[4]
מִמִּדְבָּר הֵמַרְתָּ בִּי,[5]
וְעַד עַתָּה לֹא הֶאֱמַנְתָּ בִּי.

נְבִיאַיִךְ נִטְעֵי אֲבִיגְדוֹר,[6]
נִשְׁתַּבְּרוּ פְּרָצוֹת לִגְדּוֹר,
נִגְלֵיתִי בְּיוֹם נָקָם[7] לִסְדּוֹר,
וְלֹא קִדְּשׁוּ פָּרִיצֵי הַדּוֹר.

הַדּוֹר **יָ**זְמוּ דַּעַת סוֹד וְדָפְקוּ,
הִשְׁבַּעְתִּי אֶתְכֶם[8]* שָׁמְעוּ וּפָקְקוּ,
יַחַד כְּשָׁמְעָם כֵּן נִתְמַקְמָקוּ,
וְעַל כַּפַּיִם סָפָקוּ.

סָפְקוּ שָׂשׂוּ בָּאֵי הָאָרֶץ,
כְּנָפְלוּ בְּיָדָם מַלְכֵי אָרֶץ,
סִבְּרוּ כִּי יִשְׁעָם יָרֶץ,
וְעַל יָדָם יִתְכּוֹנֵן מְשׂוֹשׂ כָּל הָאָרֶץ.[9]

פָּצוּ פִּיהֶם חַג לַיהוה בְּשִׁילֹה,[10]
דִּמּוּ כִּי לָעַד יִהְיֶה שָׁם מוֹשְׁלוֹ,
פָּעֲלוּ שֶׁקֶר וְהֶשִׁילוּ,
עַד כִּי יָבֹא שִׁילֹה.[11]*

---

thens came tramping in with their nail-studded shoes.

הִשְׁבַּעְתִּי אֶתְכֶם — *I adjure you.* This phrase appears four times in *Song of Songs* (2:7, 3:5, 5:8, 8:4). According to the Midrash, God made Israel take four oaths: That it would not rebel against the sovereign governments; that it would not seek to hasten the End; that it would not reveal the Torah's mysteries to other nations; and that it would not attempt to ascend from the Diaspora by force (*Shir Rabbah* 2:7). When these

ל *So He prepared their hearts to sing at the Sea of Reeds,*[1]
'HASHEM shall reign, through [the power of] His uncovered arm!'[2]

ב *His arm is uncovered and His hand is lifted on high,*
and [His strength] is revealed through
[His] upraised right hand.[3]

ב *When [His] sons witnessed [His] wrath streaming down,*
their spirits were anxious, in the [exile of the] valley
of Edom, to know why [they were so severely punished].

מ *[God responded,] 'What wrong did you find in Me*
that caused you to defy Me?[4]

מ *Since the Wilderness you have rebelled against Me*[5]
and to this very day you still do not believe in Me!'

נ *Your prophets, the plantings of Avigdor [Moses],*[6]
[were sent,] but they were broken by the many breaches
[in Torah observance] that they had to mend.

נ *I revealed Myself [to them and told them] to arrange*
[prophecy regarding] a day of retribution,[7]
but the unbridled sinners of the generation
[did not heed their warnings and]
did not sanctify themselves [with repentance].

י *[The Sages of every] generation desired to know the secret*
[time of Messiah's advent] and pushed [to hasten] it,
*but then they heard [God cry out], 'I adjure you,**
[O Israel, not to attempt to force the Messiah's arrival,]'[8]
and they sealed [their mouths].

י *When they all heard this together, their [hearts] melted,*
and they clapped their hands [in anguish].

ס *But those who entered the Land [with Joshua] clapped for joy*
when the kings of the land [of Canaan] fell into their hands;

ס *because they hoped their Savior would show them favor,*
and, that by their hand, [Jerusalem] the joy of all the earth[9]
would be established.

פ *They opened their mouths and announced,*
'A festival for HASHEM in Shiloh!'[10]
They imagined that His reign would continue there forever;

פ *but they acted deceitfully, so they were thrown out*
until the advent of Shiloh [the Messiah].[11]*

---

(1) See *Sotah* 30b. (2) Cf. *Isaiah* 52:10. (3) Cf. *Psalms* 118:16. (4) Cf. *Jeremiah* 5:11. (5) Cf. 2:11. (6) See commentary to *kinnah* 11. (7) Cf. Isaiah 63:4. (8) *Song of Songs* 2:7; 3:5; 5:8; 8:4. (9) *Psalms* 48:3. (10) Cf. *Judges* 21:19. (11) *Genesis* 49:10.

---

oaths were demanded of them, the people's hearts melted in anguish.

שִׁילֹה — *Shiloh [the Messiah.]* The Talmud states four opinions regarding the Messiah's given

שִׁילֹה **רָ**צָה כַּחַלָּה מֵעִסָּה,*
וְנִמְאַס כַּאֲשֶׁר בּוֹ נַעֲשָׂה,[1]
רְאוּ מַה עֲבֵרָה עוֹשָׂה,
לְכֹל אֲשֶׁר חָפֵץ עָשָׂה.[2]

עָשָׂה עִמִּי אוֹת[3] בְּצִבְיוֹן,
וּלְעִתּוֹ חָשׁ עָלַי קִשְׁיוֹן,
עֻלַּפְתִּי כְּחֹרֶב בְּצָיוֹן,[4]
עַד אֲשֶׁר יוֹפִיעַ אֱלֹהִים מִצִּיּוֹן.[5]

צָעַק צִיּוֹן אֵיךְ נָתָן,
לָשׂוּם עָלַי גּוֹי אֵיתָן,[6]
צָהַל וְרָקַע עַל הַמִּפְתָּן,
וּבַחֲמָתוֹ חִתִּיתוֹ נָתָן.[7]

נָתָן **בְּ**עֲתוּתוֹ עֵת הוֹבִילַנִי רוֹקְמִי,
תַּרְתִּי לָעַד בָּהּ לְקוֹמְמִי,
בֹּשְׁתִּי וְגַם נִכְלַמְתִּי[8] בֵּל בַּהֲקִימִי,
וּבָחֲרִי אַף נָם לִי קוּמִי.

קוּמִי קָשַׁבְתִּי בְּהַזְנָחָה,
קוּמִי וּלְכִי כִּי לֹא זֹאת הַמְּנוּחָה,[9]
קַצְתִּי בְחַיַּי[10] מֵאֲנָחָה,
וְהִגַּשְׁתִּי וְלֹא עָרְבָה מִנְחָה.[11]

רְאֵה רֹעַ נַפְשִׁי זְנוּחָה,
מִשָּׁלוֹם וּמִשַּׁלְוָה וּמֵהֲנָחָה,
רְטוּשָׁה בַּהֲרֵי נֶשֶׁף[12] זְנוּחָה,
גַּם שָׁם לֹא נָחָה.

נָחָה **יָ**דוֹ בָּם וּבָהּ נִכְווּ,
אֲנוּשִׁים* עַל רֹאשָׁם כְּרָכְבוּ,[13]

שִׁילֹה רָצָה כַּחַלָּה מֵעִסָּה — *He [God] showed favor to Shiloh, as if it were challah from the dough.* Shiloh was the site of the first permanent Tabernacle. The *paytan* compares this to *chal-*

name: מְנַחֵם, *Menachem;* שִׁילֹה, *Shiloh;* יִנּוֹן, *Yinon;* and חֲנִינָה, *Chaninah* (*Sanhedrin* 98b). It is noteworthy that the initial letters of these four names spell מָשִׁיחַ, *Messiah.*

ר *He [God] showed favor to Shiloh, as if it were challah from the dough,* but [later] abominated it because of what was committed there [by the officiating priests].*[1]

ר *Observe what sin accomplishes, with the One Who does Whatever He pleases.*[2]

ע *He offered me a sign [of hope]*[3] *when He was pleased; but when the time called for it, He hastened [retribution] for [our] stubborn defiance.*

ע *I fell faint, as if from the dry heat of a parched land,*[4] *[not to be revived] until God appears from Zion.*[5]

צ *Zion cried out, 'How did [God] permit me to be dominated by a powerful nation*[6]

צ *that gleefully trampled on the [Temple's] threshold, and sowed terror in its fury?*[7]

ב *He Who fashioned me cast His awe [upon the heathen nations] when He brought me [into the land of Canaan] and I imagined that I would be established within it for eternity.*

ב *But I was shamed and humiliated*[8] *when the idol of Bel was erected [inside the Temple]; and with angry fury He told me, 'Arise [and leave this land]!'*

ק *'Arise!' is what I heard in abandonment, 'Arise, and go forth! For this is not the resting place!'*[9]

ק *I have become disgusted with my life,*[10] *because of [my incessant] groaning, I approached [God with offerings] but my gift proved undesirable.*[11]

ר *Behold the sorry state of my forlorn spirit, bereft of peace, serenity and composure,*

ר *torn apart and forsaken in [Exile's] mountains of darkness,*[12] *and there too finding no rest.*

י *[God] laid His hand [heavily] upon them [Israel] and they were burnt by it, as weaklings* rode over their heads.*[13]

(1) See *I Samuel* 2:11 ff. (2) Cf. *Psalms* 115:3. (3) Cf. 86:17. (4) *Isaiah* 25:5. (5) Cf. *Psalms* 50:2. (6) Cf. *Jeremiah* 5:15. (7) Cf. *Ezekiel* 32:26. (8) *Jeremiah* 31:18. (9) Cf. *Micah* 2:10. (10) *Genesis* 27:46. (11) Cf. *Malachi* 3:3-4. (12) Cf. *Jeremiah* 13:16. (13) Cf. *Psalms* 66:12.

lah, the first portion of dough separated from each batch and presented to a *Kohen.*

אֲנוּשִׁים — *Weaklings.* The translation follows *Rashi* (*Jeremiah* 17:9) who renders אָנֻשׁ as *sickly.* According to *Targum* (ibid.) the word means *powerful.* Some editions of *Kinnos* read אֱנוֹשִׁים, *frail mortals.*

יָגְעוּ עַל נַהֲרוֹת בָּבֶל[1] כְּנִתְעַכְּבוּ,*
וּכְעוֹלְלוּ עוֹלָלַי חוּצָה שָׁכְבוּ.[2]

שָׁכְבוּ שׁוֹבִים גּוֹיִם מַדְקִירִים,[3]
מִתְעוֹלְלִים בָּמוֹ כְּמוֹ בְקָרִים,
שֶׁהֵם יָזֻבוּ מְדֻקָּרִים,[4]
וּמֵי פְרָת קְרָבֵימוֹ דּוֹקְרִים.*

תִּקְרָא תְּקֶף טֶבַח וּמֶסֶךְ לְמַבְקִירִים,
קִיר עֵרָה מְקַרְקְרִים,
וְכָל עַם וְלָשׁוֹן בָּם סוֹקְרִים,
וַעֲלֵיהֶם מְקוֹנְנִים בְּנֵי צִיּוֹן הַיְקָרִים.[5]

הַיְקָרִים **קוֹל** בְּרָמָה הִשְׁמִיעוּ לִבְכֹּה,[6]
לָמָּה זֶה וְעַל מַה זֶּה הִקְרָנוּ כֹּה,
יַחַד זֶה אוֹמֵר בְּכֹה וְזֶה אוֹמֵר בְּכֹה,
רָגְנוּ לְהָמִיר לְשׁוֹן אֵיכָה בִּלְשׁוֹן אֵי כֹּה.[7]

יָגְעוּ עַל נַהֲרוֹת בָּבֶל כְּנִתְעַכְּבוּ — *They were worn down when detained along the rivers of Babylon.* When the Jewish captives arrived at the Euphrates River, Nebuchadnezzar and his retinue were sailing leisurely on the river while being entertained by musicians. The nobles of Israel trudged by the river bank, naked and chained together with heavy iron shackles. Nebuchadnezzar noticed them and asked of his attendants, 'Why are these captives allowed to walk with noble, upright bearing? Is there no burden we can place on them to bend them over?' The cruel overseers filled huge casks with sand and placed them on the captives' backs until they doubled over from the weight. At that moment all the Jews burst out in tears and their anguished cries arose to the highest heavens (*Midrash Tehillim* 137).

י *They were worn down when detained*
along the rivers of Babylon;[1]*
for they were repaid in kind for their deeds,
lying [asleep] out in the open.[2]

ש *The captors slept [peacefully], having stabbed*
their [Jewish captives'] bodies,[3]
treating them as if they were cattle.

ש *Now they pine away, stricken,*[4]
*while the waters of the Euphrates ulcerate their innards.**

ת *Summon forth, O Powerful One,*
the [day of] slaughter and the cup [of agony]
for those who repudiate You,
those who shattered the ruined wall,
while all nations and tongues [stood by and] watched;
for [only] the precious sons of Zion[5]
lamented over these [Jewish tragedies].

ק *The precious [Patriarchs] let a voice of weeping be heard on high,*[6]

ל *[crying,] 'Why is this? And why did it happen so?'*

י *In unison, one said, 'This is the reason,'*
and the other said, 'That is the reason.'

ר *but all lamented that they had been made*
to transform the expression, 'How?' into the expression,
'Where is [the Divine promise], "So [says HASHEM]"?'[7]

(1) *Psalms* 137:1. (2) Cf. *Eichah* 2:21. (3) Some editions read גְּוִיָּם מַבְקִירִים, *having left their bodies to the elements.* (4) *Eichah* 4:9. (5) 4:2. (6) Cf. *Jeremiah* 31:14. (7) See commentary to *kinnah* 13.

Many editions read גָּעוּ, *they cried,* in place of יָגְעוּ, *they were worn down.* Both versions allude to the same Midrash. However, the format of the *kinnah* indicates that this verse should begin with the letter י.

וּמֵי פְרָת קְרָבֵימוֹ דוּקְרִים — *While the waters of the Euphrates ulcerate their innards.* Why did the Jews weep so bitterly by the river of Babylon? R' Yochanan taught that the Jews were entirely unaccustomed to the harsh, sharp nature of the waters of the Euphrates River, so it had a lethal effect on them. Far more Jews died as a result of drinking these foreign waters than fell to the sword of Nebuchadnezzar! (*Midrash Tehillim* 137).

טו.

אֵיכָה אַשְׁפָּתוֹ פָּתְוּחַ כְּקֶבֶר,[1]
וּלְרוֹדִי בְּאַף הוֹסִיף אֵבֶר, **אֲנִי הַגֶּבֶר.**
אֵיכָה אֶשָּׂא עֲוֹן הָגַ,
וְחֻסַּם פִּי מִפֶּלֶל לַהַג, **אוֹתִי נָהַג.**
אֵיכָה אָץ וַעֲמוֹ לִשְׁפּוֹךְ,
הָכִיל נִלְאֵיתִי וְנָם שְׁפוֹךְ,[2] **אַךְ כִּי יָשׁוּב יַהֲפוֹךְ.**
זְכוֹר אֲפִיפָתִי בְּשָׁרָב,
וְנָם כִּי יִנָּטוּ צִלְלֵי עָרֶב,[3]
וְהֵבֵאתִי עֲלֵיכֶם חָרֶב.
בָּכֹה תִבְכֶּה בְּעֵת כֹּל חֲסָרִי,
וּכְעָזְבִי אֹרַח יִסְּרִי,[4] **בִּלָּה בְשָׂרִי וְעוֹרִי.**
בִּלַּע בַּיִת לָרוּם מְזֻקָּף,
וְכַבַּרְזֶל סִבְּכִי נִקַּף,[5] **בָּנָה עָלַי וַיַּקַּף.**
בְּנֵי בִטְנִי לֶאֱכוֹל[6] הִקְשִׁיבָנִי,
מִנִּי צָר אָחוֹר הֱשִׁיבָנִי,[7] **בְּמַחֲשַׁכִּים הוֹשִׁיבָנִי.**
נַחֲלוֹתֵינוּ כְּנֶטְּשׁוּ בְּיַד לוֹחֵם,
נָם לֹא אָחוּס וְלֹא אֲרַחֵם,
בְּשִׁבְרִי לָכֶם מַטֵּה לֶחֶם.
גָּלְתָה גְּהוּצָה לַעֲטוֹת עֶדִי,
מֶחֻפָּה לְגָלוּת בְּהִתְעַתְּדִי, **גָּדַר בַּעֲדִי.**
גָּדַע גְּאוֹן נָדִיב וָשׁוֹעַ,
וְהֵשִׁיב יָמִין אָחוֹר[8] מִלְּהוֹשִׁיעַ, **גַּם כִּי אֶזְעַק וַאֲשַׁוֵּעַ.**
גַּם גָּבַר עָלַי פּוֹרְכִי,
וּבְנַאֲקִי סָתַם חֲרַכִּי, **גָּדַר דְּרָכַי.**

אֵיכָה אַשְׁפָּתוֹ — *Alas! For His arrow case.* The longest and most intricate of our Tishah B'Av recitations, this *kinnah* was composed by R' Elazar HaKalir, based on two Scriptural sources. As explained in the Overview, the longest and the most sorrowful section of Jeremiah's *Eichah* is the third chapter which he composed after King Yehoyakim brazenly burnt the original version of *Eichah.* That chapter vividly foretells the impending *Churban* in alphabetic sequence, using three verses for every letter of the Hebrew alphabet. Essential segments of all those verses are cited in this *kinnah.* The second major component of this lament is the *Tochachah / Admonition* recorded in *Leviticus* (ch. 26), in which Moses graphically predicted the Destruction of the First Temple which came to pass in Jeremiah's day some nine hundred years later. *Ramban* in his commentary on the Torah (ibid.) demonstrates how each and every one of Moses'

15.

א *Alas! For His arrow case is open like a grave*[1] *[waiting for death],*
and He has added a wing to my furious attacker.
I am the man [who has seen affliction by the rod of His anger].

א *[God] said, 'Alas! How can I bear sin?'*
Thus, my mouth was sealed from uttering prayer.
He has driven me [into unrelieved darkness].

א *Alas! For He has rushed to pour out His wrath,*
[saying,] 'I have tired of [exercising restraint]!'
And He said, 'Pour forth!'[2]
But only against me did He turn [His hand].
Remembering [how I sinned with the Golden Calf]
during my wandering in the parched Wilderness,
He said, 'The shadows of [Exiles's] evening shall be drawn out,[3]
and I will bring a sword against you [to avenge My covenant]!'

ב *She [Zion] weeps and weeps, 'At the time I lost all,*
and when I abandoned the [righteous] path of my admonition,[4]
He wore away my flesh and skin.'

ב *He consumed the Temple which rose to lofty heights,*
and with iron have my branches been pruned.[5]
He besieged and encircled me [with bitterness and travail].

ב *He [Moses] informed me that [a time would come when]*
I would be forced to eat the children of my womb.[6]
[And this occurred when] He caused us
to retreat before the oppressor,[7]
[and] He placed me in darkness [like the eternally dead].
When our heritage [the Temple] was abandoned
into the hand of the [enemy] soldier,
He said, 'I will neither pity nor show compassion [for you],
When I break the staff of bread for you!'

ג *Exiled is she who cleansed herself [of sin in order]*
to adorn herself with [spiritual] crowns [at Sinai].
From the bridal canopy she was destined to be exiled
[for serving the Golden Calf].
[She cries,] 'He has made a wall for me
[so that I cannot return to my land].'

ג *He cut down the pride of noble and chief,*
and turned His right hand back,[8] *not to save,*
even as I would cry out and plead.

ג *Even [when] those who broke my back overpowered me,*
and when I screamed [in prayer], He sealed
the windows [of heaven to my pleas];
He walled up my roads.

---

(1) Cf. *Jeremiah* 5:16. (2) Cf. 6:11. (3) 6:4. (4) Cf. *Proverbs* 15:10. (5) Cf. *Isaiah* 10:34.
(6) Cf. *Deuteronomy* 28:53. (7) Cf. *Psalms* 44:11. (8) Cf. *Eichah* 2:3.

יְתוֹמִים גְּרוּשִׁים מֵאֲחֻזּוֹת,
וְלֹא שָׁב אַפּוֹ בְּכָל זֹאת,[1]
וְאָמַר אִם בְּזֹאת.

דַּרְכֵי דִּיץ סָךְ לְהַאֲבִילִי,
וּלְגָלוּת שֵׁשַׁךְ הוֹבִילִי, **דֹּב אֹרֵב הוּא לִי.**

דָּרַךְ דּוֹחֵק עַל בָּמוֹתַי לְהִשְׂתָּרֵר,
שְׁעוּ מִנִּי בִּבְכִי אֲמָרֵר,[2] **דְּרָכַי סוֹרֵר.**

דָּבַק דּוֹלְקִי וְצָדָנִי בְּרִשְׁתּוֹ,
עָלַי לִלְטוֹשׁ מַחֲרַשְׁתּוֹ,[3] **דָּרַךְ קַשְׁתּוֹ.**

מֵימֵינוּ דָּלַח[4] וְנָם אֲשִׁימְכֶם,
גֵּיא גָלוּת אֲטִילְכֶם לְהַכְלִימְכֶם,
וְהָלַכְתִּי עִמָּכֶם.

הָיוּ הָהּ לְיוֹם בִּכְיוֹתַי,
וְצָרֶבֶת אֵשׁ כְּוִיּוֹתַי, **הֵבִיא בְּכִלְיוֹתָי.**

הָיָה הוֹלֵךְ לְפָנַי מַזְעִימִי,
וְכֶעָסִיס דָּמִי הִטְעִימִי,[5] **הָיִיתִי שְּׂחוֹק לְכָל עַמִּי.**

הָאוֹכְלִים הֶקְדֵּשׁ פֶּסַח בְּלֵיל שִׁמּוּרִים,
הֶאֱכִילָם בְּכָפָן רָאשֵׁי חֲמוֹרִים,[6]
הִשְׂבִּיעַנִי בַמְּרוֹרִים.

עַל צַוָּארֵנוּ הִשְׂרִיג וְחִלֵּל שֶׁכֶם,
וְנָם אֶפְקוֹד עַל עֲוֹנוֹתֵיכֶם,
וַאֲכַלְתֶּם בְּשַׂר בְּנֵיכֶם.

וַיֵּצֵא וְקָדְקֹד סִפַּח[7] וְרִצֵּץ,
וְחִזַּק מוּסָרַי בִּי וָאֶתְלוֹצָץ,[7] **וַיַּגְרֵס בֶּחָצָץ.**

וַיַּחְמֹס וַיְנַצֵּל מֶעֲדָיִי[9] לְהַכְפִּישִׁי,
וּמִגָּבְהָהּ לִתְהוֹם הִרְפִּישִׁי, **וַתִּזְנַח מִשָּׁלוֹם נַפְשִׁי.**

וַיַּגְדֵּל וְכָבֵד נַאַק רִצְחִי,
וּבְקָדְקֳדִי עָלָה צְוָחִי, **וָאֹמַר אָבַד נִצְחִי.**

(1) Cf. *Isaiah* 5:25. (2) Cf. *Isaiah* 22:4. (3) *I Samuel* 13:20. (4) *Ezekiel* 32:2. (5) Cf. *Isaiah* 49:26. (6) Cf. *II Kings* 6:25. (7) Cf. *Isaiah* 3:17. (8) Cf. 28:22. (9) Cf. *Exodus* 33:6.

warnings came true when Israel's sins finally forced God to unleash His anger against them.

Thus, after every three verses from the Book of *Eichah*, the *kinnah* cites the corresponding verse

[We were] like orphans banished from ancestral estates,
yet, despite all this [suffering], His anger has not subsided,[1]
rather He said, 'If in spite of this [you fail to hearken to Me
. . .I will chastise you seven-fold for your sins]!'

ד *He has filled with thorns the roads once jubilant [with pilgrims],*
to cause me to mourn. And He led me into
the Babylonian exile [on these very same roads].
He is [like] a lurking bear to me.

ד *The attacker trampled on my neck to display his sovereignty.*
[Please] turn from me, that I may express
[my] bitterness with weeping.[2]
He has strewn my paths with thorns.

ד *My pursuer caught up to me and snared me in his net,*
he honed his plow blade [as a weapon] against me;[3]
he bent his bow [and set me as a target for his arrow].
He muddied our waters[4] and said, 'I will devastate you!
I will cast you into the valley of exile
to utterly degrade you.
I will behave toward you [with a fury of indifference].'

ה *There were [cries of] 'Ho' on the day of my weeping,*
[and the hot tears] scalded [my face] with a fiery blister.
He shot [His arrows] into my vitals.

ה *He who enraged me stood [arrogantly] in front of me,*
and he forced me to taste my own blood
as if it were sweet nectar.[5]
[Thus] have I become a laughingstock to all my people.

ה *Those who would eat the sacred flesh of*
the Pesach offering on the guarded night,
He fed donkey heads during famine.[6]
He filled me with bitterness.
He braided ropes [of our sins] upon our necks
and crippled our shoulder[-like Temple], for He said,
'I shall visit [upon you] retribution for your iniquities!
And you shall eat the flesh of your sons.'

ו *And He went forth afflicting and smashing heads with leprosy,[7]*
and it was smashed and He tightened my bonds,
because I scorned [the admonitions of His prophets],[8]
He ground my teeth on gravel.

ו *He pillaged [the Holy Temple] and stripped me of*
my [spiritual] adornments,[9] covering me with dust,
[He lowered me] from the loftiest heights to
[muddy me in] the depths.
My soul despaired of having peace.

ו *The cry of my murdered one grew louder and stronger,*
until my scream reverberated in my skull
And I said, 'Gone is my strength!'

מִצְרַיִם וְכוּשׁ שָׂח אֲשִׁיבְכֶם,[1]
וְאֶשְׁפּוֹטְכֶם כְּזִמּוֹתֵיכֶם,
וְהִשְׁמַדְתִּי אֶת בָּמוֹתֵיכֶם.

זָכְרָה זֹאת כִּי נִבְאַשׁ נִרְדִּי,
וּלְכַלָּה פָּץ מִכָּבוֹד רְדִי, **זְכָר עָנְיִי וּמְרוּדִי.**
זָנַח זְבוּל וְלֵב הִקְשִׁיחַ,
וּבְהִתְעַבְּרוֹ עִם מָשִׁיחַ,[2] **זָכוֹר תִּזְכּוֹר וְתָשִׂיחַ.**[3]
זְכוּת זְקֵנַי וּפָעֳלָם אָבִיא,
כִּי בְּכֵן פָּרַץ נְתִיבִי, **זֹאת אָשִׁיב אֶל לִבִּי.**

אֲבוֹתֵינוּ זָעֲקוּ וְכָלוּ מִדִּבָּה,
וְשָׂח עַל רָעָתֵנוּ כִּי רַבָּה,
וְנָתַתִּי אֶת עָרֵיכֶם חָרְבָּה.

חֵטְא חָז כִּי בֶּעָוֹן נִכְתָּמְנוּ,[4]
תְּמוּר כִּי בְצִחְיוֹן נִזְהָמְנוּ, **חַסְדֵי יהוה כִּי לֹא תָמְנוּ.**
חָשַׁב חוֹרְשֵׁי לְקַרְקֵר (קִיר)[5] יְקָרִים,
וּמַר יִבְכָּיוּן[6] מַכָּתִי סוֹקְרִים, **חֲדָשִׁים לַבְּקָרִים.**
חָשַׁךְ חֲזוֹן מַגִּישֵׁי אִשִּׁי,
קִיר כְּעִוֵּר לְגַשְּׁשִׁי,[7] **חֶלְקִי יהוה אָמְרָה נַפְשִׁי.**

עֲבָדִים חִסְּמוּנִי מִלִּגְדּוֹר פֶּרֶץ,
וְתוֹכָחוֹת קָשׁוֹת פָּץ בְּחֶרֶץ,
וַהֲשִׁמּוֹתִי אֲנִי אֶת הָאָרֶץ.

טֻמְאָתָהּ טָפְלָה וְנָטָה קָו,[8]
וְלֹא נָסוֹג אָחוֹר מִקָּוָיו, **טוֹב יהוה לְקֹוָו.**
טָבְעוּ טִירוֹתַי וּפִי צַר דָּמַם,[9]
וְכָל עוֹבֵר עָלַי שָׁרַק וְשָׁמַם,[10] **טוֹב וְיָחִיל וְדוּמָם.**

---

(1) Cf. *Deuteronomy* 28:68. (2) See commentary to *kinnah* 11. (3) *Eichah* 3:20; as evidenced by the rhyme scheme, the *paytan* used the כְּתִיב, *Masoretic spelling,* in place of the קְרִי, *Masoretic pronunciation* (וְתָשִׂיחַ instead of וְתָשׁוּחַ or וְתָשׁוּחַ); nevertheless, most editions read וְתָשׁוּחַ. (4) Cf. *Jeremiah* 2:22. (5) Many editions omit the word in parentheses; if included, it refers to the walls of the *Beis HaMikdash.* (6) *Isaiah* 33:7. (7) Cf. 59:10. (8) *Eichah* 2:8. (9) Alternatively: *the tormentor's mouth was silent.* (10) Cf. *Jeremiah* 18:16, 19:8.

---

from the *Tochachah.*

In the complex format of this *kinnah*, each letter of the *aleph-beis* appears ten times in the following manner: The respective letter is represented by four three-line stanzas. The first word in stanza one of each four-stanza group is the first word of the corresponding verse in chapter one of *Eichah;* the next word begins with the

'To Egypt and to Kush,' said God, 'shall I return you;[1]
and I shall judge you in accordance with your scheming;
And I shall destroy your high altars.'

ז *He [God] remembered when [my sin with the Golden Calf] putrefied my nard.*
Therefore He told the bride,
"Descend from [your place of] honor!'
O remember my afflictions and my sorrow.

ז *He abandoned His Temple and stiffened His heart,*
[because] of His anger with the anointed one [King Josiah].[2]
[My soul] remembers well, and makes me despondent.[3]

ז *I shall bring My ancestors' merit and their achievement [to God's attention],*
because my path was justly breached [due to my iniquity].
This I bear in mind [therefore I still hope].

Our forefathers cried and were annihilated because of the [spies'] slander;
and when our wickedness multiplied, [He proclaimed,]
'I shall lay waste to your cities.'

ח *He saw sin [within me], for I was stained by iniquity;[4]*
for we filthied ourselves in the Wilderness, exchanging [God for the Golden Calf].
[Yet,] HASHEM's kindness surely has not ended.

ח *The one who plowed over me planned to tear down [the wall of][5] the precious ones,*
and [the angels] who perceive my wounds cry bitterly,[6]
[the angels] who are renewed every morning.

ח *He deprived [the priests] who bring [offerings to] my [Altar] fire of their prophetic vision,*
like the sightless, I must grope for the wall.[7]
[Nevertheless,] 'HASHEM is my portion,' says my soul.

[The Babylonian soldier-]slaves prevented us from repairing the breach,
because He had spoken sharply with harsh admonition,
And I Myself shall bring the land to desolation.

ט *She [Zion] attached her [idolatrous] impurity [to the Temple], so [God] stretched out the measuring line [of retribution].[8]*
Yet He did not turn away from those who sincerely hope to Him;
[for] HASHEM is good to those who trust in Him.

ט *My turrets sank into the earth, and my mouth became silenced with tribulation.[9]*
and whoever passed me whistled [in amazement] and wondered [what I did to deserve such punishment].[10]
[Still, I declare,] 'It is good to hope submissively [for HASHEM's salvation].'

טוֹבִים טַפִּים נִכְּלוּ בְּהוֹסִיפִי לִמְעוֹל,
וּכְמַעֲלָלַי חָרָה בִּי לִפְעוֹל, **טוֹב לַגֶּבֶר כִּי יִשָּׂא עוֹל.**
בְּנַפְשֵׁנוּ נָבִיא טֶרֶף נִכְרֶה,[1]
כִּי כְמוֹ בָּרַחַת וּבַמִּזְרֶה,[2]
נָם וְאֶתְכֶם אֱזָרֶה.

יָדוֹ יָרָה בִּי אוּר כַּסְדוֹם,
וְעַל כָּל אֵלֶּה הוֹנָאַתְנִי בַּת אֱדוֹם, **יֵשֵׁב בָּדָד וְיִדֹּם.**
יֵשְׁבוּ יְגוֹנִים בָּנַי עֲלֵי חוֹפֵיהוּ,
כִּי כָבֵד עָלַי אַכְפֵּהוּ,[3] **יִתֵּן בֶּעָפָר פִּיהוּ.**
יְדֵי יוֹסְרֵי שָׁתוּ בִּי מֹחִי,
וְקָשַׁבְתִּי מִפִּי צַר שְׂחִי, **יִתֵּן לְמַכֵּהוּ לֶחִי.**
עוֹרֵנוּ יוּעַם כְּחֶרֶשׁ בַּקֶּרֶץ,
וּגְוִיּוֹתֵינוּ שַׂמְנוּ כָּאָרֶץ,[4]
אָז תִּרְצֶה הָאָרֶץ.

כָּל כְּבוֹד תַּאֲרֵנוּ הָכְלָם,
וְצוּר אוֹרְחוֹתָיו חֶסֶד[5] כֻּלָּם, **כִּי לֹא יִזְנַח לְעוֹלָם.**
כָּלוּ[6] כִּמְעַט כִּי בִי נִלְחָם,
וְעַל הָרָעָה הוּא נִחָם,[7] **כִּי אִם הוֹגָה וְרִחַם.**
כִּלָּה כַעְסוֹ וְהִצִּית לְהָבוֹ,
וּבְתַכְלִית שִׁשָּׁה מְאוֹרֵי אוֹר* כָּבוּ,
כִּי לֹא עִנָּה מִלִּבּוֹ.

נָשִׁים כִּפְרוּעוֹת יוֹשְׁבוֹת שַׁמָּה,
בְּכָל שָׁנָה וְשָׁנָה מַזְכִּירוֹת אַשְׁמָה,
כָּל יְמֵי הָשַּׁמָּה.

---

(1) Some editions read טֶרֶף נִבְרֶה, *our food is supplied.* (2) *Isaiah* 30:24.
(3) Cf. *Job* 33:7; some editions read אַפֵּהוּ, *His [God's] anger.*
(4) Cf. *Isaiah* 51:23; some editions read בָּאָרֶץ, *(we placed our bodies) on the ground.*
(5) Cf. *Psalms* 25:10. (6) Some editions read כָּלִינוּ, which includes the interpolated 'we' of the translation; however, since this stich corresponds to *Eichah* 2:11, it should begin כָּלוּ.
(7) Cf. *Joel* 2:13.

---

same letter of the alphabet. Stanza two follows the same format but the first word is from chapter two of *Eichah*. And in stanza three the first word is from chapter four. The third stich of each of these three stanzas is the opening phrase from the respective verses of chapter three (which has three verses for each letter). Thus, the group's *aleph-beis* letter appears three times in each of these stanzas: the first two words of line one and the first word of line three, for a total of nine times. The fourth stanza of each group begins with the first word of the respective verse in chapter five of *Eichah*. This is followed by a word beginning with the group's code letter (its

ט *The finest infants were exterminated*
when I continued to sin even more,
and in proportion to my misdeeds, [God's anger]
flared against me, to act.
It is good for a man that he bear the yoke [of discipline in his youth,
so that he not stray when he is older].
With [danger to] our lives is our food purchased,[1]
and [we are tossed about] as if with
a winnowing shovel or a pitchfork,[2]
[thus fulfilling the curse,] 'And [like grain in the field]
shall I scatter you [among the nations].'

י *His hand shot fire at me as [He did] against Sodom,*
and in addition to all that, He caused the [Roman]
daughter of Edom to torment me.
Let one sit in solitude and be submissive [for it is God
Who has laid His hand upon him].
י *My children sit in anguish over His sheltering canopy,*
because His [God's] burden weighs heavily upon them.[3]
[Therefore] let him put his mouth to the dust
[in absolute submission to God, as there may yet be hope].
י *The hands of those who punish me shower me with blows,*
and I have heard from the mouth of the tormentor, Bend low,
offer a cheek to his smiter.'
Our skin has become dark like earthenware
because of pogroms,
and we [submissively] made our bodies like the ground.[4]
Thus, the land will be appeased.

כ *[Although] all the splendor of our features has been humiliated,*
[we have faith that] all of the Creator's paths reflect total kindness;[5]
For [the Lord] does not reject forever.
כ *[We] were almost annihilated,*[6] *He Himself waged war against us,*
but then He reconsidered the evil[7] *[with which He afflicted us].*
[For,] even if He afflicts [at first], He [later] pities.
כ *He spent His anger when He lit his flame,*
*which had been cooling for six [annual cycles of the] luminaries,**
for He does not torment capriciously.
Women sat devastated with their hair unkempt,
and each and every year [on Tishah B'Av] they recall
[and confess] the sins [that brought about the Destruction].
As long as it lies desolate.

---

tenth appearance). The final stich of this stanza is the opening phrase of the corresponding verse from *Leviticus* 26:25-46. [Some commentators assume that this *kinnah* is a companion to *kinnah* 9, in which the stanzas end with the first phrases of the verses from *Leviticus* 26:3-24.]

שִׁשָּׁה מְאוֹרֵי אוֹר — *Six [annual cycles of the] luminaries.* When the nation's sinfulness reached the maximum that God would overlook, He commanded the angel Gabriel to throw two coals from the celestial fires upon the city of Jerusalem (see *Ezekiel* 10:2). For six years, Gabriel allowed

לֹא אֲלֵיכֶם לוֹחֲצֵי גִילָיו,

וְעַל בָּנָיו הֶעֱבִיר גַּלָּיו,[1] **לְדַכֵּא תַּחַת רַגְלָיו.**

לְאֻמּוֹתָם עֵת כָּמֹהוּ מִשֶּׁבֶר,

יַעַן כִּי גָרוֹן פָּתְּחוּ כְּקֶבֶר,[2] **לְהַטּוֹת מִשְׁפַּט גָּבֶר.**

לֹא לִמְחוֹת[3] פֶּץ לְעַם קְרוֹבוֹ,

וְאֵיךְ מִתְּעַר הוֹצִיא חַרְבּוֹ,[4] **לְעַוֵּת אָדָם בְּרִיבוֹ.**

שָׂרִים לְכוּדִים הוֹצִיא מִשְּׁעָרִים,

תֵּת כַּתְּאֵנִים הַשּׁוֹעָרִים,[5]

לְעוֹלֵל אֶת **הַנִּשְׁאָרִים.**[6]

מִמָּרוֹם מְגִלָּה כָּתַב וָנֶהִי,

קִינִים וָהֶגֶה וָהִי,[7] **מִי זֶה אָמַר וַתֶּהִי.**

מָה אֲעִידֵךְ מְאוּמָה מִלְּהֶרָצֶה,[8]

נְתוּנָה בְּיַד מֵרִיב וּמִתְנַצֶּה,[9]

מִפִּי עֶלְיוֹן לֹא תֵצֵא.

מֵחַטֹּאת מַדִּיחֵי שָׁוְא[10] אֲקוֹנֵן,

מְנַחֲמִי כְּמִיַּיִן מִתְרוֹנֵן,[11] **מַה יִּתְאוֹנֵן.**

בַּחוּרִים מוּטָּטוּ כְּשֶׁל בִּי לְהָרֵב,

וּשְׁכִינָה הוּעֲלָה מִקֶּרֶב,

וְכָשְׁלוּ אִישׁ בְּאָחִיו כְּמִפְּנֵי חָרֶב.

נִשְׂקַד נֵטֶל עוֹל פּוֹרְכֵינוּ,

וַיִּתָעֵב שַׁי עוֹרְכֵינוּ, **נַחְפְּשָׂה דְרָכֵינוּ.**

נְבִיאַיִךְ נֹאֲצוּ לִקְרוֹץ עַפְעַפַּיִם,[12]

וְאַכְזָרוּ עָלֵינוּ אֶרֶךְ אַפַּיִם, **נִשָּׂא לְבָבֵנוּ אֶל כַּפָּיִם.**

נָעוּ וְנָדוּ רֹאשׁ[13] בְּמַהֲמוֹרֵינוּ,

רְשָׁעִים מַפִּילִים בְּמִכְמוֹרֵינוּ,[14] **נַחְנוּ פָּשַׁעְנוּ וּמָרִינוּ.**

---

(1) Cf. *Psalms* 42:8. (2) Cf. 5:10. (3) Cf. *II Kings* 14:27. (4) Cf. Ezekiel 21:8. (5) *Jeremiah* 29:17. (6) Cf. 6:9. (7) Cf. *Ezekiel* 2:9. (8) See commentary to *kinnah* 9. (9) Cf. *Isaiah* 58:4. (10) Cf. *Eichah* 2:14. (11) Cf. *Psalms* 78:65. (12) Cf. *Proverbs* 10:10. (13) Cf. *Jeremiah* 18:16. (14) Cf. *Psalms* 141:10.

---

the coals to cool in his hands before he actually threw them. He was certain that Israel's repentance would soon be forthcoming. When he realized that the people were steadfast in their evil ways, he decided to cast the fire upon them in a way that would wipe them out without a trace remaining. But God intervened, 'Gabriel, Gabriel, take your time; take your time, for among them there are some who treat one another righteously.'

But then an accusing angel appeared before the Throne of Glory and said, 'Master of the universe, will this wicked man be permitted to say haughtily, "I have destroyed God's Home,

ל *[God did] not [bring suffering] upon you*
who tyrannize those who emulate [God's ways]!
Rather, upon his own sons did God cause
His [destructive] waves to roll.[1]
To crush [them] under His feet.

ל *[Children cried out] to their mothers when they were pining for food,*
[The children were punished] because
their [parents'] throats had gaped like an open grave,[2]
to deny another man justice.

ל *He did not declare that His intimate people be eradicated.*[3]
How then did He draw His sword from its sheath,[4]
to wrong a man in his conflict?
The captive noblemen were removed
from the gateways [of Jerusalem],
and they were ill-treated like rotten figs,[5]
to be harvested to their very remainder.[6]

מ *From Above He wrote a scroll while moaning,*
lament, murmuring and woe.[7]
[For] who [other than the Lord] can say something,
and it will be fulfilled?

מ *What slightest example can I adduce for you*
[of another nation's suffering] to bring consolation?[8]
[Has any other nation] been delivered into
the hand of antagonist and foe?[9]
Has it not issued from the mouth of the Most High?

מ *I shall lament over the sins of the worthless,*[10] *deceptive [soothsayers].*
Yet my Comforter [has not forsake me; rather,]
He is as one arousing Himself from wine.[11]
So what is there to complain about?
Youths crumbled, they increasingly stumbled within me,
while the Divine Presence ascended
[and departed] from our midst.
And they stumble over one another
as if [running] before the sword.

נ *Heavy upon us is the yoke of those who crush us,*
for He has rejected our well-ordered prayers.
[Therefore,] let us search [and examine] our ways
[to see where we erred].

נ *Your [false] prophets with winking eyelids caused abomination,*[12]
therefore, He Who is slow to anger treated us harshly.
Let us lift our hearts to [the One Who dwells above] the clouds!

נ *Everyone shook and wagged their heads*[13]
[in disbelief] at the deep pits [of our woes];
even the wicked who made us fall into our nets
[were amazed by the enormity of our tragedy].[14]
[All because] we have transgressed and rebelled
[but God has not yet forgiven].

זְקֵנִים וְנִינָם לָרֹב סְגוּיִם,
אֲכָלוּם וְהֶשִׁיתוּם מָשָׁל בַּגּוֹיִם,[9]
כְּנָם **וַאֲבַדְתֶּם בַּגּוֹיִם.**

סֹלָה שָׂמֵי קְטוֹרָה בְּאַף,[10]*
וָאֶפְעַר פִּי וָאֶשְׁאַף,[11] **סַכּוֹתָה בָאַף.**
סָפְקוּ שׂוֹטְנַי כַּף וָאֶשְׁתּוֹנָן,
וָאֶזְעַק חָמָס[1] וָאֶתְאוֹנָן, **סַכּוֹתָה בֶעָנָן.**
סוּרוּ טָמֵא סָחוּ מֵאֲשִׁימֵינוּ,
בְּהִנָּתֵן כַּבַּרְזֶל שָׁמֵינוּ, **סְחִי וּמָאוֹס תְּשִׂימֵנוּ.**
שָׁבַת מְשׂוֹשׂ שִׂמְחַת מְשׁוֹרְרִים,
וְרוֹדְפֵי קַלּוּ מִנְּשָׁרִים,
לְאַבֵּד הַנִּשְׁאָרִים.

עַל אֵלֶּה עֲשָׁקוּנוּ בְּחֵרוּפֵיהֶם,
וְהִגְדִּילוּ שְׁאוֹן גִּדּוּפֵיהֶם, **פָּצוּ עָלַי פִּיהֶם.**
פָּצוּ פָּעֲרוּ פֶה מִבְּאֵר שַׁחַת,
וְאִטְּרוּ עָלַי בְּתוֹכַחַת, **פַּחַד וָפָחַת.**
פְּנֵי פְאֵר חֻפַּת מְעוֹנִי,
הִקְמִיל וְהֵקִים מְעַנִּי, **פַּלְגֵי מַיִם תֵּרַד עֵינִי.**
נָפְלָה עֲטֶרֶת עֹז מַשְׁעֵנָם,
וְצָר[2] בְּשִׁבְעָה דִינִים דָּנָם,[3]
וְהִתְוַדּוּ אֶת עֲוֹנָם.

פֵּרְשָׂה פוֹצְצָה אוֹי כִּי סֻגָּרָה,
תְּמוּר עֹז מָתְנֶיהָ בְּשַׂק חָגְרָה, **עֵינִי נִגְּרָה.**
עָשָׂה עֶבְרָתוֹ וַיֶּחֱרֶה,
וְעָרַף אֶת מָדוֹן מְגָרֶה,[4] **עַד יַשְׁקִיף וְיֵרֶא.**
עוֹדֵנוּ עָף כָּבוֹד וְעָלָה,
וְעֶשֶׂר מַסָּעוֹת הוּעֲלָה, **עֵינִי עוֹלְלָה.**

---

(1) *Psalms* 44:15. (2) Cf. *Deuteronomy* 33:10. (3) Cf. *Psalms* 119:131. (4) *Job* 19:7.
(5) See *Eichah* 2:4. (6) See *Leviticus* 26:18, 24, 28. (7) Cf. *Proverbs* 15:18.

---

and burned His Sanctuary?'''
Immediately, God replied, 'If so, let fire descend from above and burn it!' (*Midrash Eichah* 1:41).

שָׂמֵי קְטוֹרָה בְּאַף — *[The Kohanim] who offered incense . . . in fury.* The *paytan* plays on the dual meaning of the word אַף. The Torah verse that this stich paraphrases reads, יָשִׂימוּ קְטוֹרָה בְּאַפֶּךָ,

Grandparents and their offspring increased abundantly,
[the conquerors] devoured them and made them
into a simile [for misfortune] amongst the nations.[9]
As He had said, 'You will become lost among the nations.'

ס *[The Kohanim] who offered incense were trampled in fury,*[10]*
while my mouth opened wide and I gasped [in bewilderment][11]
[for] You have enveloped Yourself in anger.

ס *My accusers clapped hands [with glee over my sorrows]*
and caused me sharp pain,
and I would scream out over the corruption
[perpetrated against me][1] *and I mourned,*
[because] You wrapped Yourself in a cloud
[that no prayer can pierce].

ס *'Away, unclean one,' our persecutors said,*
when our skies were rendered as hard as iron [allowing no rainfall].
[Thus,] You made us as filth and refuse [among the nations].
The joyous jubilation of the singers has ceased,
for those who chased me were swifter than eagles
to destroy the remnant.

ע *Because of these [sins] they abused us with their curses,*
and they intensified the din of their blasphemies,
[when] they opened their mouths against us.

פ *They opened their mouth wider than the Well of Destruction*
they closed me in with rebuke,
panic and pitfall [were ours].

פ *The majestic appearance of my canopied Temple*
he cut down. He stood my oppressor erect.
[Therefore,] my eye sheds streams of water.
Fallen is their crown of strength, their [pillar of] support;
for God[2] *afflicted them with seven harsh punishments.*[3]
[This would bring them] to confess their sin.

פ *[Zion] spread [her arms in distress], she cried,*
'Woe!' for she was locked [into captivity]!
Instead of [girding] her loins with power,
she now girds herself with sackcloth.
My eye will flow [with endless tears].

ע *[God] smote with His fury and it continued to burn,*
and He beheaded those [evildoers] who instigated
the strife [that alienated God from Israel].[4]
[Yet, how long must we wait] until [HASHEM] looks down
and takes notice [of our shame].

ע *[Divine] Glory soared continually heavenward,*
[away from the Temple] it ascended in ten stages
[to provide Israel with ten opportunities to repent].
[Over this] my eyes have brought me grief.

עַל זֶה פָּסַק נוֹי נָעֳמָם,
וְשָׁח לֹא אֶעֶזְבֵם בְּכַף זוֹעֲמָם,
אַף אֲנִי אֵלֵךְ עִמָּם.

צַדִּיק צָר צְעָדַי לִסְפּוֹר,[1]
וּכְעִקַּלְתִּי יֹשֶׁר וָאֶכְפּוֹר, **צוֹד צָדְוּנִי כַּצִּפּוֹר.**
צָעַק צוֹרִי וְסִכֵּךְ מֵעֲבוֹר,
וּבְחִלְּלִי עֵרֶךְ לִשְׁבּוֹר, **צָמְּתוּ בַבּוֹר.**
צָדוּ צְעָדַי וְסָע דוֹרְשִׁי,
וְכַעֲלוֹתָם עָלַי לְדוֹרְשִׁי,[2] **צָפוּ מַיִם עַל רֹאשִׁי.**
עַל הַר צִיּוֹן צָבְאוּ לְהַכְרִיתִי,
וְצוּר שָׁח אֶחְמוֹל עַל שְׁאֵרִיתִי,
וְזָכַרְתִּי אֶת בְּרִיתִי.

קָרָאתִי קְשׁוֹב חֶרְפַּת מוֹנַי,
עַל הַלֶּחִי מַכִּים בָּנַי, **קָרָאתִי שִׁמְךָ יהוה.**
קוּמִי קִרְאִי כִּי לֹא יִכָּלֵם,
עַל יֶתֶר לְמַקְנִיאַי יְשַׁלֵּם,[3] **קוֹלִי שָׁמָעְתָּ אַל תַּעְלֵם.**
קַלִּים קְדָחוּנִי וְעַלַּמְתָּ מַרְאֶךָ,
הָשֵׁב בַּגּוֹיִם מוֹרָאֶךָ,[4] **קָרַבְתָּ בְּיוֹם אֶקְרָאֶךָּ.**
אַתָּה יהוה קֵץ אַל תְּכַזֵּב,[5]
עַד מָתַי כְּחֹרֶשׁ אֵעָזֵב,[6]
וְהָאָרֶץ תֵּעָזֵב.

רְאֵה רֹגֶז מַכַּת אֱנוּשִׁי,
וָאוֹמַר בְּהִנָּטְשִׁי בַּנֶּשִׁי, **רַבְתָּ אֲדֹנָי רִיבֵי נַפְשִׁי.**
רְאֵה רֹב בְּעָתוּתִי,
הֲשִׁמּוֹתָ כָּל עֲדָתִי, **רָאִיתָה יהוה עַוָּתָתִי.**

---

(1) Cf. *Job* 31:4. (2) Some editions read כַּיָּם לְגָרְשִׁי, *to drive me away like the [rolling] sea.* (3) Some editions read וְיִתְעַנְּגוּ לְרֹב שָׁלוֹם, *and may they delight in abundant peace,* cf. *Psalms* 37:11. (4) Cf. 9:21. (5) Cf. *Habakkuk* 2:3. (6) Cf. *Isaiah* 17:9.

They shall place incense before You. The literal meaning of בְּאַפֶּךָ is *in Your nose*, hence *before You*. The word אַף can also mean *anger* or *fury*, for flaring nostrils are a sign of anger (see *Rashi* to *Exodus* 15:8). Thus, *Malbim* expounds regarding the Scriptural verse: Both anger and incense enter through the nose, one to torment the soul, the other to restore it.

For this the beauty of their pleasant [Temple shrine] has ended,
although the Creator stated, 'I shall never abandon them into the hands of [the enemies] who frustrate them,
[nevertheless,] even I shall behave towards them [in a punitive manner].'

צ *The Righteous One once [lovingly] observed my footsteps and counted them,*[1]
but ever since I corrupted the straight and denied [God's sovereignty],
I have been ensnared like a bird.

צ *My Rock shouted [a command] and sealed [the heavens] [to prevent my entreaties] from passing through;*
and when I profaned [God's sanctity], He prepared to break [me].
So they cut off [my life] in a pit.

צ *[The enemy hounded] my footsteps, but the One Who had sought my welfare departed;*[2]
and when [the enemy] overpowered me and sought [my downfall],
waters flowed over my head.

On Mount Zion [the enemy legions] assembled to cut me down,
but the Creator said, 'I will take pity on My [people's] remnant
and I will remember My covenant [with them].'

ק *I called out, 'Listen carefully [O God] to my detractors' insults!' [See how] they smack my sons on the cheek!*
I called Your Name, HASHEM.'

ק *Arise! Call out [O Israel to your God], for He will not shame you!*
He will surely repay the haughtiness of those who disturbed me.[3]
You have heard my voice; do not shut [Your ear from my prayer].

ק *Vulgar barbarians burnt me, but You were oblivious to what You saw,*
re-establish Your fear over the nations[4]
You would always draw near on the day I would call You.

O You, HASHEM, do not misrepresent the [time of the] End,[5]
O how long shall I be abandoned like a [lonely] forest?[6]
[As You stated,] 'The land will be bereft.'

ר *Behold the turmoil caused by my mortal wound,*
yet [even though] I seem to be forsaken and forgotten, I shall [still] say,
'You always championed my cause, O my Lord.'

ר *Behold my extraordinary terror,*
because You have ruined my entire flock,
You have seen, HASHEM, the injustices I suffer.

רְוּחַ **רָ**פְּתָה[1] בִּי מֵאֵימָתָם,
לְבַלְּעֵי הֶעֱלוּ חֲמָתָם, **רָאִיתָה כָּל נִקְמָתָם.**
לָמָּה בְּרָחוֹק תַּעֲמוֹד[2] בְּדַבְּרָם עַזּוֹת,[3]
נַמְתָּ הַנְּשָׁמָה אוֹשִׁיב פְּרָזוֹת,[4]
וְאַף גַּם זֹאת.

שָׁמְעוּ שֶׁנּוֹקַשְׁתִּי בִּדְחִיפָתָם,
וּכְיֶלֶק עָלָה עֵיפָתָם, **שָׁמַעְתָּ חֶרְפָּתָם.**
שָׁכְבוּ שׁוֹחֲחִים בְּנֵי מִיגוֹנָם,
וְשׁוֹבֵיהֶם גָּאָה מְאֹד גְּאוֹנָם, **שִׂפְתֵי קָמַי וְהֶגְיוֹנָם.**
שֵׁישִׁי שׁוֹסֵיתִי כִּי בִי יַד מָטָה,
מֻשְׁפֶּלֶת עַד[5] שְׁאוֹל מָטָּה, **שִׁבְתָּם וְקִימָתָם הַבִּיטָה.**
הֲשִׁיבֵנוּ שָׁלֵם שִׁלּוּם שָׁנִים,
וְתֹאמַר אֶפְדֵּם מִשְּׁאוֹנִים,
וְזָכַרְתִּי לָהֶם בְּרִית רִאשׁוֹנִים.

תָּבֹא תָּשׁוּר מְעַנַּי לָמוֹל,
הֵם שָׁגְבוּ חַיִל וְאוּוְיָךְ אָמוּל, **תָּשִׁיב לָהֶם גְּמוּל.**
תִּקְרָא תְּגַלֶּה יוֹם כָּמוּס בְּלֵב,
וּמְחַפְּשֵׂי עוֹלוֹת לִפְעוֹל מִלֵּב,[6]
תִּתֵּן לָהֶם מְגִנַּת לֵב.

תַּם תַּכְלִית תָּקְפָּם לְלָכְדֵם,
יִפְּלוּ בְּלִי לְהַעֲמִידָם.[7] **תִּרְדּוֹף בְּאַף וְתַשְׁמִידֵם.**
כִּי תָמִיד דּוֹקְרִים וְשׁוֹחֲקִים,
וּמִתּוֹרָתְךָ אָנוּ לֹא רוֹחֲקִים,
הֲשִׁיבֵנוּ וְהוֹרֵנוּ **אֵלֶּה הַחֻקִּים.**

ר *My spirit sagged[1] within me because of their intimidation,*
for they stirred up their wrath in order to swallow me.
You have seen all their vengeance.

Why do You stand aloof[2] when they speak brazenness?[3]
Have You not said, I shall restore the desolate [city of Jerusalem and it will be secure] without walls?[4]
For despite all this [that they have done, I shall not annul My covenant with them].

ש *They [the enemy] heard that I was battered from their shoving,*
so they rose against me like a locust plague.
Haven't You heard their insults [regarding me]?

ש *My sons lay bent and cringing from their agony,*
while their captors' haughtiness grew ever more powerful,
the speech and thoughts of my enemies.

ש *Rejoice, O You who plundered me,*
for the [punishing] hand of [God] has fallen upon me,
and I have been dragged down to the grave.[5]
Observe their sitting down [to plot against me]
and their rising up [to take action].

Return us to [Jeru]salem and repay [us for the] years [we suffered in exile].
And say, 'I shall release them from the roaring masses!
I shall remember for their sake the covenant of the ancients.'

ת *Come and observe those who torment me in order to cut me down,*
they performed mighty military feats
in order to destroy Your desirous [Temple].
Pay them back their due.

ת *Divulge and publicize the date [of redemption] sealed in [Your] heart.*
But as for those who search their hearts[6] to work evil,
give them a broken heart.

ת *Let the gist of their power cease,*
let them be humbled, never to be permitted to rise,[7]
pursue them in anger and destroy them.

Because [our enemies] stab and scorn us continuously,
yet we are not alienated from Your Torah,
O bring us back and guide us [on the path of] these decrees
[that HASHEM gave at Mount Sinai, through Moses].

(1) Cf. *Judges* 8:3. (2) Cf. *Psalms* 10:1. (3) Cf. *Proverbs* 18:23. (4) Cf. *Zechariah* 2:8. (5) Cf. *Isaiah* 57:9. (6) Some editions read וְהֵטִיבָה לָּנוּ לְהָסִיר מֶנּוּ מְגִינַּת לֵב, *be good to us, to remove from us a broken heart.* (7) Some editions read תַּצִּילֵנִי מִמּוֹקְשֵׁי בְּנֵי אָדָם, *save me from the snares of humankind,* / שׁוֹטְנִים לְהַפִּיל בְּלִי לְהַעֲמִידָם, *to humble accusers that they never be permitted to arise;* some editions read תִּשְׁלַח חִישׁ עֶזְרֶךָ, *swiftly dispatch Your assistance,* / וְרַחֵם עַל בָּנֶיךָ, *and have mercy on Your sons,* / הַמְצַפִּים לִישׁוּעָתֶךָ, *who long for Your salvation.*

טז.

זָכוֹר* אֲשֶׁר עָשָׂה צַר בִּפְנִים,[1]*
שָׁלַף חַרְבּוֹ וּבָא לִפְנֵי וְלִפְנִים,
נַחֲלָתֵנוּ בְּעֵת כְּטִמֵּא לֶחֶם הַפָּנִים,
וְגִדֵּר פָּרֹכֶת בַּעֲלַת שְׁתֵּי פָנִים.[2]*

יְתוֹמִים גֹּעַל בְּמָגֵן מְאָדָּם,[3]*
וַיְמַדֵּד קָו[4] כְּמַרְאֵה אֲדַמְדָּם,
מֵימֵינוּ דָּלַח וְהִשְׁכִּיר חִצָּיו מִדָּם,[5]
כְּיָצָא מִן הַבַּיִת וְחַרְבּוֹ מְלֵאָה דָם.

עַל הֲגוֹתוֹ הַוּוֹת גָּבֵר,
וְנָטָה אֶל אֵל יָדוֹ לְמוּלוֹ לְגַבֵּר,[6]
מִצְרַיִם וְכָל לְאוֹם אִם בָּם גָּבַר,
אֲנִי בְּתוֹךְ אִוּוּיוֹ אָרוּץ אֵלָיו בְּצַוָּאר.[7]*

אֲבוֹתֵינוּ זָרָה כְּהִכְנִיסוֹ[9] בַּחוּרָיו אָכְלָה אֵשׁ,[8]

◆§ זָכוֹר —*Remember.* The Roman general Titus — whose words and actions represent the unique arrogance and ruthlessness of the entire Roman nation, the seed of the proud and bloodthirsty Esau — destroyed the Second Temple. The Talmud *(Gittin* 56b) relates that he began his assault on Jerusalem with an insolent declaration of war — not merely against the Jews — but against the Almighty, God of Israel, Himself! Titus shouted out the verse from Scripture: אֵי אֱלֹהֵימוֹ צוּר חָסָיוּ בוֹ, *Where is their God, the Rock in Whom they have trusted? (Deuteronomy* 32:37).

Avos d'Rabbi Nosson (1:6) states that King David had Titus in mind when he supplicated before God: אַל תְּבוֹאֵנִי רֶגֶל גַּאֲוָה, *Let not the foot of the arrogant overtake me (Psalms* 36:12), because Titus' insufferable arrogance against God was unsurpassed. When he entered the Temple sanctuary he banged on the altar and taunted: "O Wolf! O Wolf! You are a monarch and I am a monarch! Come, let us do battle with one another!'

Nor was Titus alone in this defiance. He was merely continuing the attitude of his father Vespasian, who had begun the siege against Jerusalem and had continued it until he was elected Emperor of Rome. Then he appointed his son Titus to complete the destruction of the city. Therefore many Midrashim which describe the destruction refer to one or the other of these wicked men, or to both.

God allowed the brutal Roman legions to vanquish their Jewish victims. Jerusalem was reduced to rubble; the Temple was destroyed. The human toll was staggering: 'The number of captives was 97,000. The number of those who perished (from starvation or pestilence) or were slaughtered by the sword was one million and one hundred thousand' (Josephus, *Wars of the Jews* VI, 9:3). Even after Jerusalem fell, the Romans relentlessly hunted down every Jew they could find. Thus, they supplied victims for cruel torture for the amusement of Titus and his cohorts in sensational celebrations throughout the Roman Empire.

To emphasize how important this victory over the Jews was, a special coin was minted and issued to commemorate this event. On one side appears the head of Vespasian garlanded by a victory wreath, the reverse side depicts a Roman legionnaire leaning on his spear, while a forlorn figure representing the Jews weeps pitifully under a palm tree. The inscription reads, *Judea Capta* — Judah is a captive! Moreover, Titus had a huge monument erected to mark this great triumph, an arch upon which are engraved scenes of the sacred vessels being plundered from the *Beis HaMikdash.* This Arch of Titus, which has endured for almost 2000 years, is one of the most dramatic structures of the Imperial Capital, and is a constant reminder to us that we have not yet fully repented the sins that vouchsafed to Titus the power to destroy our *Beis HaMikdash.*

This *kinnah,* by R' Elazar HaKalir, depicts

16.

א *Remember* what the tormentor [Titus]*
*perpetrated in the Temple;[1]**
he unsheathed his sword and entered
the innermost chamber [the Holy of Holies].

ב *He struck terror throughout [the land of] our heritage*
when he desecrated the show bread,
*and he impaled the two-sided[2] Curtain.**

ג *He besmirched the orphaned [nation] with a red [bloody] shield;[3]**
and measured them [for death][4] along a blood-red line.

ד *He muddied our waters, and inebriated his arrows with blood,[5]*
as he emerged from the Temple with his blood-soaked sword.

ה *[We mourn] because of the evil plans and words of the man*
who stretched his hand out against God,
attempting to vanquish Him.[6]

ו *[He bragged,] '[Despite the downfall of] Egypt and the other nations,*
*that He conquered, I shall rush with [haughty] neck[7]**
within His own desirable Temple.'

ז *[In the times of] our ancestors, fire consumed His young men[8]*
[Aaron's sons Nadab and Abihu] when they brought
an alien [fire into the Tabernacle],[9]

(1) Cf. *Zechariah* 14:10; some editions read בִּפְנִים, *within.* (2) Some editions read בְּבַעֲלַת שְׁתֵּי פָנִים, *with a double-edged [blade].* (3) Cf. *Nahum* 2:4. (4) Cf. *II Samuel* 8:2. (5) Cf. *Deuteronomy* 32:42. (6) Cf. *Job* 15:25. (7) 15:26. (8) *Psalms* 78:63. (9) See *Leviticus* 10:1-2.

Titus' wicked acts when he entered and destroyed the Temple. The first and third line of each quatrain begin with the opening words of the corresponding verses in chapter five of *Eichah* and appear in bold type. The second words of those lines form an *aleph-beis* acrostic.

זְכוֹר אֲשֶׁר עָשָׂה צַר בִּפְנִים — *Remember what the tormentor perpetrated in the Temple.* The Talmud (*Gittin* 56b) relates that when Titus entered the Holy Temple he cursed and blasphemed the God of Israel. He dragged a prostitute into the Holy of Holies and unrolled a holy Torah scroll and committed unspeakably lewd acts upon it. He then unsheathed his sword (already bloodied with the blood of countless Jewish victims) and slashed the פָּרוֹכֶת, *Curtain* (that separated the Sanctuary from the Holy of Holies), to shreds. A miracle occurred and blood began to flow from the curtain. Thus Titus imagined that he had actually pierced and slain God Himself!

פָּרֹכֶת בַּעֲלַת שְׁתֵּי פָנִים — *The two-sided Curtain.* The *Paroches* was woven in an intricate manner with various designs depicted on each of its sides. Two views are stated in the Talmud: (a) 'A lion on one side, and a lion on the other,' i.e., the same picture was visible from either side (or, as some explain, the front view of the lion on the front of the curtain, and the back view of the same lion on the reverse); or, (b) 'a lion on one side, and an eagle on the other,' i.e., totally different scenes on each side (*Yerushalmi Shekalim* 8:2).

יְתוֹמִים גֹּעַל בְּמָגֵן מְאָדָּם — *He besmirched the orphaned [nation] with a red [bloody] shield.* Josephus (*Wars of the Jews* VI, 5:1) described the misery and destruction brought about by Titus:

'There was a shout of the Roman legions as they marched together, and a sad clamor of the people, now surrounded by fire and sword ... Many who were worn away by starvation so that their mouths were almost closed, when they saw the Holy House on fire they exerted their last strength and broke out in groans and outcry. The mountains around the city returned the echo and increased the noise... The Temple Mount was seething with fire in every part, and the blood was even more than the fire. . .for the ground was not visible because of the dead bodies that covered it; the soldiers went over heaps of those bodies in pursuit of the fleeing.'

בְּצַוָּאר — *With [haughty] neck.* The translation is based upon *Rashi's* interpretation of this phrase in *Job* 15:26 (see also *Psalms* 75:6). Alternatively, it is an allusion to the Temple and Altar both of which are compared to the straight neck of stately stature (see commentaries to *Song of Songs* 4:4 and 7:5).

וְזֶה זוֹנָה צוֹעָה הִכְנִיס[1] וְלֹא נִכְוָה בָּאֵשׁ,*
עֲבָדִים חִתּוּ בְּתוֹכוֹ לַבַּת אֵשׁ,
וְעַל מֶה בְּבֵית אֵשׁ,[2] מִמָּרוֹם שָׁלַח אֵשׁ.[3]*

בְּנַפְשֵׁנוּ טָבַעְנוּ כְּהוֹצִיא כְּלֵי שָׁרֵת,
וְשָׁמָם בָּאֳנִי שַׁיִט בָּם לְהַשָּׁרֵת,
עוֹרֵנוּ נָמַק כְּהִשְׁכִּים מְשָׁרֵת,
וְלֹא מָצָא תִּשְׁעִים וּשְׁלֹשָׁה כְּלֵי שָׁרֵת.*

נָשִׁים כְּשָׁרוּ כִּי בָא עָרִיץ,
בְּקַרְקַע הַבַּיִת נְעָלָיו הֶחֱרִיץ,[4]
שָׂרִים* לְפָתוּ כְּבוֹא פָרִיץ,
בְּבֵית קֹדֶשׁ הַקֳּדָשִׁים צַחֲנָתוֹ הִשְׁרִיץ.

בַּחוּרִים מִבַּחוּץ צָגוּ מְחֻזָּקִים,
וְתָרוּ כִּי יוּזַק בְּשִׁשִּׁים רִבּוֹא מַזִּיקִים,*
זְקֵנִים נִבְעֲתוּ כְּהִרְשׁוּהוּ מִשְׂחָקִים[5]
עֲשׂוֹת רְצוֹנוֹ וְהוּא אָסוּר בָּזִקִּים.[6]

שָׁבַת סוֹטֵן וַיָּבֹא אַדְמוֹן,
וַיְסַבֵּב חוֹמָה וַיְעַוֵּת הֲמוֹן,
נָפְלָה עֶבְרָה עַל נִינֵי פִּצֵּל לַח וְלוּז וְעַרְמוֹן,[7]
עַד כִּי נָטַשׁ מְדוֹק אַרְמוֹן.

בַּחוּרָיו אָכְלָה אֵשׁ ... וְלֹא נִכְוָה בָּאֵשׁ — *Fire consumed His young men [Aaron's sons Nadab and Abihu]... yet he [Titus] was not burnt by the fire.* These two eldest sons of Aaron were pious and holy but they erred in their service on the very day of the Tabernacle's inauguration, Rosh Chodesh Nissan 2449. Bolts of fire burst forth from the Holy of Holies, entered their nostrils and consumed their innards, yet their outer flesh and garments remained perfectly intact. The fact that they were punished so severely for their error, while Titus who intentionally committed every form of atrocity and sacrilege was left unscathed, demonstrates that they entered the House of God when it was at the height of its sanctity, and God's Presence permeated its environs with unsurpassed intimacy and intensity. Therefore, the slightest deviation caused a serious flaw in the awesome level of sanctity maintained at that moment. Titus, however, entered the Temple only after God's Presence departed in anger over the sins of Israel. Therefore, his victory was truly a hollow one, because he destroyed an empty shell, a meaningless facade. Although Titus' intentions were entirely evil, God left him unharmed. This demonstrated that Titus was unwittingly a tool of the Divine will to destroy the Temple from which the sins of Israel had chased the protective *Shechinah.*

בְּבֵית אֵשׁ — *In the House of [God, the All-consuming] Fire.* Alternatively, the *Beis HaMikdash* is the House of the Altar and Menorah fires, both of which had miraculous elements: The Altar fire was never extinguished, even though it stood in the open air (see *Avos* 5:7); the נֵר מַעֲרָבִי, *western lamp,* of the Menorah would still be burning, long after the other lamps (with the same amount of oil and same size wicks) had gone out (see *Shabbos* 22b).

וְעַל מֶה... מִמָּרוֹם שָׁלַח אֵשׁ — *Why ... did He send a fire from on high?* The translation treats the

while this man [Titus] brought a reclining harlot[1]
*inside [the Holy of Holies], yet he was not burnt by the fire.**

ח *[A lowly] slave-nation stoked the flames within it;*
Why upon this House of [God, the All-consuming] Fire,[2]
did He send a fire from on high?[3]*

ט *Our souls sank, when he removed the service vessels,*
and placed them on oared ships,
that he might be served with them.
Our very skin seemed to melt away [in agony]
when the ministering priest arose early
*and didn't find the [full complement of] ninety-three service vessels.**

כ *The women were terrified when they saw the ruthless one enter*
and riddle the Temple floor with his [hob-nailed] boots.[4]

ל *Princes** *cringed in [helpless] fear when the wanton one entered,*
he splattered the Holy of Holies with his foul stench.

מ *Outside, young men [Jewish defenders] stood firm,*
they thought he [Titus] would be harmed by the
*six hundred thousand demons [they saw entering with him].**

נ *Elders panicked when he [Titus] was given free reign by heaven*[5]
to do as he pleased, while He [God] appeared
to be shackled in chains.[6]

ס *When the Satanic one [Babylon] withdrew,*
the ruddy one [Rome] arrived;
he surrounded the wall and shocked the populace.

ע *The wrath [of God] fell upon the descendants of he [Jacob]*
who had peeled fresh [branches of] almond and chestnut,[7]
to the point where the palace was abandoned by heaven.

---

(1) Cf. *Jeremiah* 2:20. (2) Cf. *Deuteronomy* 4:24. (3) *Eichah* 1:13. (4) See *kinnah* 13. (5) Some editions read מֵחֲזָקִים, *from the powerful [heavens].* (6) *Jeremiah* 40:1. (7) See *Genesis* 30:37.

---

entire line as a rhetorical question. Alternatively, it comprises a question and answer: *How could this happen to the House of Fire? — He sent a fire from on high!*

תִּשְׁעִים וּשְׁלֹשָׁה כְּלֵי שָׁרֵת — *Ninety-three service vessels.* Each morning, the *Kohanim* of the day's watch would remove exactly ninety-three vessels needed for the Temple service (*Tamid* 3:4). On the morning of the day on which the *Beis HaMikdash* was to fall, the *Kohanim* could not find all ninety-three vessels — something that had never happened before.

שָׂרִים — *Princes.* This refers either to the nobility of Jerusalem, or to the heavenly angels who are called שָׂרִים. When the sinful were admonished that Jerusalem would be destroyed unless they would mend their ways, they replied, 'We know the Divine Names that are the lifeblood of the various angels appointed over the elements. Should we be attacked, we will call upon the angels to surround us with walls of water, or fire, or iron.' But God confounded them by exchanging each angel's role with another's. Thus, when the people called upon the angels that formerly protected them, the answer was always the same, 'That is no longer within my realm.' These angels now cringed because they were unable to help Israel (*Yalkut Shimoni II*:1023).

וְתָרוּ כִּי יוּזַק בְּשִׁשִּׁים רִבּוֹא מַזִּיקִים — *They thought he [Titus] would be harmed by the six hundred thousand demons.* When the Roman enemies came to destroy Jerusalem, six hundred thousand demons waited at the gateway of the Temple to attack and harm them. However, the demons realized that God Himself witnessed the atrocities the Romans perpetrated, yet remained silent, as it is written: *He withdrew His right hand in the presence of the enemy.* Therefore the demons said, 'If God does not interfere, we too will not interfere!' (*Devarim Rabbah* 1:17).

עַל פֶּתַח הַר הַבַּיִת הֵחֵל לָבֹא,
בְּיַד אַרְבָּעָה רָאשֵׁי טַפְסְרָיו לְהַחֲרִיבוֹ,
עַל צַד מַעֲרָבִי לְזֵכֶר הִשְׁרִיד בּוֹ,*
וְצָג אַחַר כָּתְלֵנוּ וְלֹא רָב רִיבוֹ.

אַתָּה קָצַפְתָּ וְהִרְשֵׁיתָ לְפַנּוֹת,
יְלָדִים אֲשֶׁר אֵין בָּהֶם כָּל מְאוּם מִשָּׁם לְהַפְנוֹת,[1]
לָמָּה רָגְשׁוּ גוֹיִם[2] וְלֹא שַׁעְתָּ אֶל הַמִּנְחָה פְּנוֹת,[3]
וְשִׁלְּחוּם בְּאֶרֶץ עוּץ בְּשָׁלֹשׁ סְפִינוֹת.*

הֲשִׁיבֵנוּ שִׁוְּעוּ כְּבָאוּ בְּנִבְכֵי יָם,[4]
וְשִׁתְּפוּ עַצְמָם יַחַד לִנְפּוֹל בַּיָּם,
שִׁיר וְתִשְׁבָּחוֹת שׁוֹרְרוּ כְּעַל יָם,
כִּי עָלֶיךָ הוֹרַגְנוּ[5] בִּמְצוּלוֹת יָם.

כִּי תְהוֹמוֹת בָּאוּ עַד נַפְשָׁם,
כָּל זֹאת בָּאַתְנוּ וְלֹא שְׁכַחֲנוּךָ חִלּוּ לְמַמָּשָׁן,[6]
תִּקְוָתָם נָתְנוּ לְמֵשִׁיב מִבָּשָׁן,[7]
וּבַת קוֹל נִשְׁמְעָה עוּרָה לָמָּה תִישָׁן.[8]

(1) *Daniel* 1:4. (2) *Psalms* 2:1. (3) Cf. *Malachi* 2:13. (4) Cf. *Job* 38:16.
(5) *Psalms* 44:23. (6) Cf. 44:21. (7) Cf. 68:23. (8) 44:24.

עַל צַד מַעֲרָבִי לְזֵכֶר הִשְׁרִיד בּוֹ — *On the Western Side, as a memorial, they left over a remnant of it.* The Midrash states: When Vespasian besieged Jerusalem, he assigned four different generals to raze the four sections of the city. The western sector fell to the lot of a general named Pangar. In heaven it was decreed that the Western Wall of the Temple Mount should not be destroyed and, indeed, while the other three generals destroyed their sectors, Pangar allowed the Western Wall to stand intact. Vespasian summoned him and demanded an explanation, to which Pangar responded, 'I swear that my intention is only to glorify your reputation, O royal master! Had I obliterated every last vestige of this metropolis of Jerusalem, later generations would have no idea of the scope of your victory, for they might think that Jerusalem was no more than a tiny town. But now that I have left over this massive Western Wall as a memorial, it will be known for all time that your majesty conquered a major city of colossal proportions!'

The Emperor said to him, 'You have defended yourself very well, nevertheless, since you failed to follow my command you must climb to the top of a tower and throw yourself off. If you survive, I will let you live; but if you die, then indeed you will have received the death penalty you deserve!' Pangar threw himself off the top of a tower and was killed, for Rabban Yochanan ben Zakkai had uttered a curse against him saying, 'Your own heart knows what your real intentions are! You claim to have preserved the Western Wall for the glory of Vespasian, but in your heart you know full well that you desire a memorial to commemorate the utter defeat and destruction of the Jewish people!' (*Midrash Eichah* 1:32).

וְשִׁלְּחוּם בְּאֶרֶץ עוּץ בְּשָׁלֹשׁ סְפִינוֹת — *They sent them [the children] away to the land of Uz in three ships.* This is based on the narrative related in the Talmud *(Gittin* 57b) and the Midrash *(Midrash Eichah)* and presented here in composite form: Vespasian (or Titus) filled three galleys with four hundred of the finest youths of Jerusalem, boys and girls, and sent

פ *Upon the entrance of the Temple Mount*
he [Titus] began to advance,
to destroy it through the hand of his four chief commanders.

צ *On the Western side, as a memorial,*
*they left over a remnant of it,**
and He [God] stood behind our wall,
but did not fight on its behalf.

ק *You [God] were so enraged that You allowed them to empty*
[the Temple of its contents],
and to remove from there [Jerusalem]
the unblemished children.[1]

ר *Why do You allow the nations to gather [against me]?*[2]
while You ignore my offering, paying it no attention?[3]
They sent them [the children] away
*to the land of Uz in three ships.**

ש *'Bring us back!' [to life in the Hereafter] they cried out*
as they sunk into the sea's depths,[4]
as they united themselves with a solemn pact
to cast themselves into the sea as one.
They sang song and praises as [Israel did] at the Sea of Reeds,
chanting, 'Because for Your sake we are killed[5]
in the depths of the Sea!'

ת *Even as the depths were about to take their souls,*
they prayed to the Real One, saying,
'All this has befallen us, yet we have not forgotten You!'[6]
They placed their hope in the One [Who promised]
to bring them back from Bashan,[7]
and a heavenly voice was heard, 'Awaken!
Why do You seem to sleep?'[8]

---

them off to Rome for immoral purposes. The children realized this and preferred taking their own lives to living in sin, yet they were uncertain whether suicide is permissible under such circumstances. They feared they might forfeit their share in the World to Come. God inspired them with a holy spirit to expound a verse from Scripture which gave them guidance and comfort: *My Lord promised, 'I will bring back from Bashan* (i.e. those threatened by בּוּשָׁה, *immoral disgrace*), *I will bring back from the depths of the sea'* (i.e. God will resurrect and reward those who drown themselves in the sea in order to preserve their purity and to sanctify God's name) (*Psalms* 68:23). Upon hearing this, all the maidens leaped into the sea without any hesitation. The youths immediately followed their inspiring example.

As they performed this ultimate act of *Kiddush Hashem*, Sanctification of God's Holy Name, those on the first ship cried out, *'Have we forgotten the Name of our God and extended our hands to a strange god?'* (ibid. 44:21). Those on the second ship cried out, *'Is it not so that God can examine this? For He knows the secrets of the heart!'* (44:22). Those on the third ship cried out, *'Because for Your sake we are killed all the time, we are considered as sheep for slaughter'* (44:23).

Concerning these young and innocent martyrs Jeremiah laments: *'Over these people I weep; my eyes run with water ... My children have been destroyed, because the enemy has prevailed'* (*Lamentations* 1:16). And about them does the remainder of this *kinnah* speak.

יז.

אִם* תֹּאכַלְנָה נָשִׁים פִּרְיָם עוֹלְלֵי טִפּוּחִים,[1] אַלְלַי לִי.[2]
אִם תְּבַשֵּׁלְנָה נָשִׁים רַחֲמָנִיּוֹת יְלָדִים[3]
הַמְּדוּדִים טְפָחִים טְפָחִים,* אַלְלַי לִי.
אִם תְּגֻזָּנָה פְּאַת רֹאשָׁם וְתִקָּשַׁרְנָה לְסוּסִים פּוֹרְחִים,* אַלְלַי לִי.
אִם תִּדְבַּק לְשׁוֹן יוֹנֵק לְחֵיךְ[4] בְּצִמָּאוֹן צְחִיחִים, אַלְלַי לִי.
אִם תְּהוֹמֶינָה זוֹ לְעֻמַּת זוֹ
בּוֹאִי וּנְבַשֵּׁל אֶת בָּנֵינוּ צוֹרְחִים, אַלְלַי לִי.
אִם תִּוָּעַדְנָה זוֹ לְזוֹ
תְּנִי בְנֵךְ וְהוּא חָבוּי מְנֻתָּח נְתָחִים,[5] אַלְלַי לִי.
אִם תְּזַמֵּנָה בְּשַׂר אָבוֹת לַבָּנִים* בִּמְעָרוֹת וְשִׁיחִים, אַלְלַי לִי.
אִם תְּחַיֵּבְנָה בָּנוֹת אֶל חֵיק אִמּוֹתָם נִתְפָּחִים,[6] אַלְלַי לִי.
אִם תָּטֹסְנָה רוּחוֹת עוֹלְלִים
בִּרְחוֹבוֹת קִרְיָה תְּפוּחִים,[7] אַלְלַי לִי.
אִם תְּיַקֵּרְנָה בְּשִׁכּוּל רֶחֶם וְצִמּוּק שָׁדָיִם[8]
וְאֵם עַל בָּנִים שָׁחִים, אַלְלַי לִי.
אִם תְּכַשַּׁלְנָה שְׁמוֹנֶה מֵאוֹת מָגִנִּים בַּעֲרַב אֱלוּחִים, אַלְלַי לִי.

---

(1) *Eichah* 2:20. (2) *Job* 10:15. (3) Cf. *Eichah* 4:10. (4) Cf. 4:4; *Psalms* 137:6.
(5) See *II Kings* 6:28-29. (6) Cf. *Eichah* 2:12. (7) Cf. 2:11. (8) Cf. *Hosea* 9:14.

⁂ **אם** — *If [it could happen that.]* This *kinnah* describes in horrible detail how the scope of the Destruction was not merely confined to material objects. Rather, this event ripped out the very moral fiber of the people and utterly distorted their essential personality traits. The Talmud teaches that the Jewish nation is identified by three basic qualities, they are רַחְמָנִים, בַּיְשָׁנִים, וְגוֹמְלֵי חֲסָדִים, *compassionate, modest, and performers of kindness* (*Yevamos* 79a). The intense suffering of the Destruction crazed the Jewish People and stripped them of the most elementary, normal human feelings and emotions, to the point where mothers relished the opportunity to cook the flesh of their own babes in order to still their hunger, and children were not revolted to consume the remains of their dead parents.

Concurrently, the heathen conquerors, already barbaric, were roused to an unprecedented level of cruelty and depravity and perpetrated every form of unspeakable atrocity against their Jewish victims.

In the closing stanza of this *kinnah*, the author, R' Elazar HaKalir, reveals the true reason for this atmosphere of utter inhumanity. It all stemmed from the astonishing crime which the Jewish nation committed as a whole. Two hundred and fifty years before the destruction of the Temple, in the reign of King Joash, the prophet and priest Zechariah ben Jehoiada admonished the nation in the Temple courtyard on Yom Kippur. So perverted were the people that instead of heeding the rebuke of their spiritual leader, they cold-bloodedly stoned and murdered their holiest leader, on the holiest day of the year, in the holiest location on earth. It was this crime which totally corrupted the Jewish people and distorted their nature and for this God exacted terrible vengeance at the time of the Temple's Destruction.

Each line of the *kinnah* begins with . . . אִם תּ, *if,* followed by the third person feminine prefix. The second letters of the second words of each line form the *aleph-beis*. The letters א מ ת spell the word אֱמֶת, *truth* or *it is true*. Perhaps this is an allusion to that which the *paytan* writes in the closing stanza, namely, that God was in full accord with the punishments described in the first twenty-two verses of the *kinnah*. Similarly, we find that when the Sages wished to eradicate the overpowering *yetzer hara* of idolatry from Israel, a note fell from heaven on which was written אֱמֶת, *it is true*. This proved that God

17.

א *If [it could happen that]* women ate the fruit of their own [womb], the babes of their care —[1] alas unto me![2]*

ב *If [it could happen that] compassionate women cooked [their own] children[3] whom they had so carefully measured handbreadth by handbreadth* — alas unto me!*

ג *If [it could happen that] the locks of their hair were torn from their heads when they were tied [by their hair] to fleet horses* — alas unto me!*

ד *If [it could happen that] the tongue of the nursing babe would adhere to its palate[4] through unmitigated thirst — alas unto me!*

ה *If [it could happen that] one [mother] cried out to another, 'Come, let us cook our screeching children!' — alas unto me!*

ו *If [it could happen that after devouring one of their babies,] the two met [and the mother of the eaten child said], 'Give your son!' But he was already cut to pieces and hidden away [for his mother to enjoy alone] —[5] alas unto me!*

ז *If [it could happen that] fathers' flesh was waiting for [their] sons* [to eat] in caves and ditches — alas unto me!*

ח *If [it could happen that] daughters were condemned to die in their mother's bosom, swollen [with hunger] —[6] alas unto me!*

ט *If [it could happen that] the spirits of infants soared [heavenward] from their swollen corpses [which were lying] in the city's streets —[7] alas unto me!*

י *If [it could happen that] women were weighed down by miscarriage of womb and dryness of breast,[8] and that mother [lamented] over dying sons — alas unto me!*

כ *If [it could happen that] eight hundred [young Kohanim who bore decorative gold] shields were trapped; in Arabia [they fell to] foul decay — alas unto me!*

---

agreed to their plan, for אֱמֶת is the signet of God (*Yoma* 69b; *Sanhedrin* 63a).

The significance of these letters is that they come at the beginning, middle and end of the *aleph-beis.* Thus they allude to the fact that God is the First, the Last and has no equal or partner (*Yerushalmi Sanhedrin* 1:1). Accordingly, with this scheme, as with the alphabetical arrangement, the *paytan* intimates that the sins of the generation ran the gamut from א to ת.

טְפָחִים טְפָחִים — *Handbreadth by handbreadth.* The Talmud relates that when Doeg ben Yosef died, his widow was left with a young son. Each year, she would measure his growth by handbreadths and donate an equivalent amount of gold coins to the Temple treasury in honor of her son. But when the siege intensified against Jerusalem, she was caught in the throes of starvation until she slaughtered and ate her precious son (*Yoma* 38b).

וְתִקְשַׁרְנָה לְסוּסִים פּוֹרְחִים — *When they were tied [by their hair] to fleet horses.* The Midrash recounts how, after the Destruction, Miriam bas Baisos, wife of the *Kohen Gadol* Yehoshua ben Gamla, was tied by her hair to the tails of Arabian steeds and was dragged from Jerusalem to Lud (*Midrash Eichah* 1:47).

בְּשַׂר אָבוֹת לְבָנִים — *Fathers' flesh ... for [their] sons.* When the siege was at its peak and the hunger most intense, one man of a group went out to find a corpse they could scavenge. When he chanced upon his own father's body, he buried it in a shallow grave and made a sign to enable him to recognize the spot. Then he returned empty-handed to his comrades. They sent out a second man to seek food. He returned with a corpse which they proceeded to eat. Later the first scout asked, 'I was unable to find anything to eat. Where did you find this body?' The second described how he had exhumed it from a freshly dug grave which was marked in such and such a manner. And the first screamed, 'Woe is me! For

אִם תְּלַהֲטְנָה רוּחָם בְּמִינֵי מְלוּחִים וְנוֹדוֹת נְפוּחִים,* אַלְלַי לִי.
אִם תְּמָעַטְנָה מֵאֶלֶף מֵאָה
וּמִמֵּאָה עֲשָׂרָה עַד אֶחָד[1] לְמַפָּחִים, אַלְלַי לִי.
אִם תָּנְסְנָה לְמָסַךְ הֵיכָל שְׁמוֹנִים אֶלֶף כֹּהֲנִים פִּרְחִים, אַלְלַי לִי.
אִם תִּשָּׂרַפְנָה שָׁם כָּל אוֹתָם הַנְּפָשׁוֹת
כְּקוֹצִים כְּסוּחִים, אַלְלַי לִי.
אִם תֵּעָרַפְנָה עַל דָּם נָקִי
שְׁמוֹנִים אֶלֶף כֹּהֲנִים מְשׁוּחִים,[2] אַלְלַי לִי.
אִם תִּפַּחְנָה נְפָשׁוֹת מְדֻקָּרִים מֵרֵיחַ תְּנוּבוֹת שִׂיחִים,[3] אַלְלַי לִי.
אִם תִּצָּבַרְנָה עַל אֶבֶן אַחַת
תִּשְׁעָה קַבִּין מוֹחֵי יְלָדִים מֻנָּחִים, אַלְלַי לִי.
אִם תּוּקַעְנָה שְׁלֹשׁ מֵאוֹת יוֹנְקִים
עַל שׂוֹכָה אַחַת מְתוּחִים, אַלְלַי לִי.
אִם תֵּרָאֶינָה רַכּוֹת וַעֲנֻגּוֹת[4] כְּבוּלוֹת
עַל יַד רַב טַבָּחִים, אַלְלַי לִי.
אִם תִּשְׁכַּבְנָה בֵּין שְׁפַתַּיִם[5]* בְּנוֹת נְדִיבִים מְשֻׁבָּחִים, אַלְלַי לִי.
אִם תִּתְעַלַּפְנָה הַבְּתוּלוֹת וְהַבַּחוּרִים
בְּצִמָּאוֹן צְחִיחִים, אַלְלַי לִי.
וְרוּחַ הַקֹּדֶשׁ לְמוּלָם מַרְעִים,
הוֹי עַל כָּל שְׁכֵנַי הָרָעִים,
מַה שֶּׁהִקְרָאָם מוֹדִיעִים,
וְאֵת אֲשֶׁר עָשׂוּ לֹא מוֹדִיעִים,
אִם תֹּאכַלְנָה נָשִׁים פִּרְיָם מַשְׁמִיעִים,
וְאִם יֵהָרֵג בְּמִקְדַּשׁ יהוה כֹּהֵן וְנָבִיא לֹא מַשְׁמִיעִים.

(1) Cf. *Amos* 5:3. (2) See *kinnah* 34. (3) Cf. *Eichah* 4:9.
(4) Cf. *Deuteronomy* 28:56. (5) Cf. *Psalms* 68:14; *Genesis* 49:14.

I have eaten my father's flesh!' (*Midrash Eichah* 1:45).

וְנוֹדוֹת נְפוּחִים — *Wineskins [deviously] inflated with [hot, stale] air.* Various Midrashim describe how, when the captives were led through the lands of Arabia, the Ishmaelites met them on the way and appeared to be friendly and sympathetic. They offered bread and other foods all of which had been oversalted. Soon the Jews asked for something to drink. The Ishmaelites offered them leather canteens that they had filled with air and left hanging in the sun. Thinking they were full of refreshing liquid, the unfortunate captives — whose hands were tied behind their back — bit off the plugs with their teeth. The hot, stagnant air in the bags filled their lungs and killed them (*Tanchuma Yisro* 5; *Midrash Eichah*; *Yerushalmi Taanis* 4:5).

בֵּין שְׁפַתָּיִם — *On the open roadsides* [lit., *between the borders*]. The translation and interpretation follow *Rashi* (*Genesis* 49:14 and *Psalms* 68:14). The captive women were not permitted to sleep

ל *If [it could happen that] their breath was set on fire*
with a variety of salty foods and [they died while trying to drink from] wineskins [deviously] inflated with [hot, stale] air —*
alas unto me!

מ *If [it could happen that] they were decimated*
from one thousand to one hundred, from one hundred to ten, until but one [remained][1] — a source of terrible sorrow —
alas unto me!

נ *If [it could happen that] eighty thousand fledgling priests*
fled to the sheltering Sanctuary — alas unto me!

ס *If [it could happen that] all those souls*
were burned there like dry thorn cuttings — alas unto me!

ע *If [it could happen that] eighty thousand anointed priests*
were beheaded over the innocent blood [of Zechariah] —[2]
alas unto me!

פ *If [it could happen that] the souls [of the starving defenders] were swollen and stricken by the [tantalizing] aroma of the fruits of the field [that they could not attain] —[3] alas unto me!*

צ *If [it could happen that] heaped on one stone*
were nine kab-measures of children's brains — alas unto me!

ק *If [it could happen that] three hundred suckling babes*
were hung [to die], stretched out on a single branch —
alas unto me!

ר *If [it could happen that] delicate, pampered women[4]*
were seen in iron chains, under the hand of the chief butcher —
alas unto me!

ש *If [it could happen that] the daughters of distinguished royalty*
took their rest on the open roadsides —[5] alas unto me!*

ת *If [it could happen that] young maidens and young men*
fainted from the dehydrating thirst — alas unto me!

But the Holy Spirit raged back at them:
'Woe unto all my wicked neighbors!
Those [tragedies] which befell them, they publicize,
but that [evil] which they perpetrated, they do not publicize.
If [it happened that] women ate the fruit of their own [womb],
they let it be heard,
but if [it happened that] they murdered a Prophet-Priest
in God's Sanctuary,
they did not let that be heard!'

---

in the cities they passed on their way to Babylon, but had to sleep out in the open, exposed to the elements. Some interpret that these women were publicly violated when they were made to lie on the roadsides.

Various other interpretations of this phrase are possible: The noble daughters were forced to work as kitchen slaves and had to sleep among the racks of pots (see *Ibn Ezra* to *Psalms* 68:14); they were forced to till the soil and sleep between the furrows (see *Rashbam* to *Genesis* 49:14); they were forced to carry heavy double burdens and collapsed under their weight (see *Sforno* ibid.). None of these views are mutually exclusive, for all of these atrocities may have been perpetrated against the captives.

יח.

וְאַתָּה אָמַרְתָּ* הֵיטֵב אֵיטִיב עִמָּךְ,[1]
וְנִפְלֵינוּ אֲנִי וְעַמָּךְ,[2]
וְלָמָּה בְּנֵי בְלִיַּעַל חִלְּלוּ שְׁמָךְ,
וְלֹא שָׁפַכְתָּ עֲלֵיהֶם זַעְמָךְ.

אַתָּה גִּדַּלְתָּ וְרוֹמַמְתָּ בָּנִים[3] לְהָנֵק,
כַּאֲשֶׁר יִשָּׂא הָאוֹמֵן אֶת הַיּוֹנֵק,[4]
וְלָמָּה דוֹדָנִים רָצוּ לְזַנֵּק,
וְאַרְיֵה גּוֹרוֹתָיו לְחַנֵּק.[5]

אַתָּה הֵינַקְתָּ דְּבַשׁ מִסֶּלַע,[6]
וַתּוֹצִיא נוֹזְלִים מִסֶּלַע,[7]
וְלָמָּה שׁוֹפְטֵיהֶם נִשְׁמְטוּ בִידֵי סֶלַע,[8]
וְעוֹלְלֵיהֶם נֻפְּצוּ אֶל הַסָּלַע.[9]

אַתָּה זָנַחְתָּ וַתִּמְאַס[10] כָּל גּוֹי,
לָקַחַת גּוֹי מִקֶּרֶב גּוֹי,[11]
וְלָמָּה חָשׁ וְעָלָה עַל אַרְצִי גּוֹי,
וְאָמְרוּ לְכוּ וְנַכְחִידֵם מִגּוֹי.[12]

אַתָּה טֵאטֵאתָ שִׁשִּׁים וּשְׁמוֹנִים,
לְהָבִיא גּוֹי שׁוֹמֵר אֱמוּנִים,
וְלָמָּה יָזְמוּ מוֹאָבִים וְעַמּוֹנִים,
לְעַם זוּ[13] בַּכְּרוּבִים מוֹנִים.*

אַתָּה כּוֹנַנְתָּ לָשֶׁבֶת הוֹדֶךָ,[14]
הַר זֶה קָנְתָה יְמִינְךָ וְיָדֶךָ,[15]

וְאַתָּה אָמַרְתָּ ❧ — *And You have said.* The stark contrast between God's extremely close relationship with the Jewish people in early times and His aloofness at the time of the Destruction is highlighted in this *kinnah,* by R' Elazar HaKalir. Each odd-numbered line begins with the word אַתָּה, *You,* and describes some aspect of the closeness that permeated the relationship in the past. Each even-numbered line begins וְלָמָּה, *so why* have You, O God, permitted such drastic change? The second words of the respective lines form an alphabetical acrostic. The final stanza acknowledges that God is righteous in all His deeds, and we must accept responsibility for the bitter tragedies that are the consequences of our misguided action.

It is not clear why the first stanza begins with a connective ו, *and,* while the remaining stanzas do not. If anything, the opposite would be expected. Indeed, many old editions omit the opening ו.

שִׁשִּׁים וּשְׁמוֹנִים — *The sixty and the eighty.* This is based on the verse: שִׁשִּׁים הֵמָּה מְלָכוֹת וּשְׁמֹנִים פִּילַגְשִׁים, *There are sixty queens and eighty concubines* (*Song of Songs* 6:8). *Rashi* (ibid.), based on the Midrash, explains that *sixty queens* refers to the offspring of Abraham who were noble people, when compared to the rest of the world. The family heads directly descended from

18.

א *And You have said,* 'I will surely do good with you!'[1]*
[And You acquiesced when Moses requested,]
'Let us be differentiated [from all the nations], I and Your people.'[2]

ב *So, why, when worthless men desecrated Your Name,*
did you fail to pour out Your fury upon them?

ג *You have reared and raised children,[3]*
nurturing [with the milk and honey of the Holy Land],
as a nurse who carries the suckling babe.[4]

ד *So, why did You allow [their Ishmaelite] cousins to prance with joy*
as the leonine [Nebuchadnezzar of Babylon]
strangled their young cubs?[5]

ה *You have caused [Israel] to suck honey from the rock,[6]*
and You brought forth flowing waters from the rock.[7]

ו *So, why did their judges go astray through [their hearts] of stone[8]*
and cause their infants to be smashed against the rock?[9]

ז *You have abandoned and rejected[10] every nation,*
but have taken one nation from the midst of another nation.[11]

ח *So, why did [You allow] a [heathen] nation*
to arise speedily against my land, saying,
'Come let us cut them off from nationhood.'[12]

ט *You have swept away the sixty and the eighty**
in order to bring forth the one nation which guards the faith.

י *So, why did You allow the Moabites and Ammonites*
to conspire against this nation,[13] to denounce them
*because of the Cherubim?**

כ *You aligned [Your earthly Temple] with Your majestic Throne,[14]*
on the mountain You acquired with Your right hand.[15]

---

(1) *Genesis* 32:13. (2) Cf. *Exodus* 33:16. (3) Cf. *Isaiah* 1:2. (4) *Numbers* 11:12. (5) Cf. *Nahum* 2:13. (6) Cf. *Deuteronomy* 32:13. (7) Cf. *Psalms* 78:16. (8) Cf. 141:6. (9) Cf. 137:9. (10) Cf. 89:39. (11) Cf. *Deuteronomy* 4:34. (12) *Psalms* 83:5. (13) See commentary to *kinnah* 11. (14) See commentary to *kinnah* 5. (15) Cf. *Psalms* 78:54.

---

him were: the sixteen of Keturah; Isaac and his two children; Ishmael and his twelve family heads; the twelve sons of Jacob; and the sixteen family heads of Esau; a total of sixty. The vast majority of these nations were rejected by God in favor of Israel. *Eighty concubines* refers to Noah and his descendants until Abraham. The family heads descending from those leaving the Ark to rebuild and repopulate the earth add up to eighty. And just as queens are superior to concubines, so are Abraham and his descendants more esteemed than all others.

בִּכְרוּבִים מוֹנִים — *To denounce them because of the Cherubim.* The Midrash relates that when the Babylonian hordes entered into the Holy Temple the troops of Ammon and Moab joined them. However, whereas all the marauders greedily looted silver, gold and precious treasures, the Ammonites and Moabites turned their attention exclusively towards destroying the Torah which states: *No Ammonite or Moabite shall enter into the congregation of* HASHEM (*Deuteronomy* 23:4). Furthermore, they burst into the Holy of Holies and seized the two golden Cherubs which were atop the Ark-cover. They placed them on display in an open cage and paraded them all around Jerusalem. They mocked the Jews with derision and scorn, saying, 'Didn't you all think that the Jews were special because they spurned idolatry? Look what we found in their holiest inner sanctum! Graven images! They are no better than the rest of us!' (*Midrash Eichah* intro. 9; 1:4).

וְלָֽמָּה **לְ**אָחוֹר הֵשַׁבְתָּ יְמִין יָדֶֽךָ,[1]
וַתְּנַבֵּל כִּסֵּא כְבוֹדֶֽךָ.[2]

אַתָּה **מָ**רוֹם לְעוֹלָם יהוה[3] וְרִאשׁוֹן,
כּוֹנַנְתָּ מָרוֹם מֵרִאשׁוֹן,[4]
וְלָֽמָּה **נ**ִאֵץ רָשָׁע[5] בְּפֶה וְלָשׁוֹן,
עַד כִּי נָגַע צַר בְּאִישׁוֹן.

אַתָּה **שַׂ**שְׂתָּ לְטוֹב עָלֵימוֹ,
בְּשִׂיחַ תְּבִאֵמוֹ וְתִטָּעֵמוֹ,[6]
וְלָֽמָּה **עָ**רִיץ* חֵרֵף וְאָמַר אֵי אֱלֹהֵימוֹ,[7]
אֲשֶׁר יֹאכַל חֵלֶב זְבָחֵימוֹ.

אַתָּה **פ**וֹרַרְתָּ בְעָזְּךָ יָם,[8]*
וַתָּסֶךְ בִּדְלָתַיִם יָם,[9]
וְלָֽמָּה **צָ**לַלְתִּי עַד נִבְכֵי יָם,[10]
וַיִּגְדַּל שִׁבְרִי כַּיָּם.[11]

וְאַתָּה **קָ**דוֹשׁ יוֹשֵׁב תְּהִלּוֹת קְדוֹשִׁים,[12]
בְּקֶרֶב יְשִׁישִׁים הַמְּקֻדָּשִׁים,
וְלָֽמָּה **רָ**גְשׁוּ גוֹיִם עַם קְדֹשִׁים,[13]
וְהֵשִׁימוּ בֵּית קֹדֶשׁ הַקֳּדָשִׁים.

וְאַתָּה **שְׁ**מַע אֱלֹהֵינוּ כִּי הָיִינוּ חֶרְפָּה,
וְסֻכָּתְךָ בָּאֵשׁ נִשְׂרְפָה,
וְלָֽמָּה **תְ**בַלַּע נַחֲלַת[14] חֻפָּה,
תַּצְמִיחַ תְּרוּפָה וְעָלֵינוּ חוֹפְפָה.

וְאַתָּה צַדִּיק עַל כָּל הַבָּא,[15]
לְךָ אֲדֹנָי הַצְּדָקָה וְנַצְדִּיקָךְ בְּחִבָּה,
וְלָֽמָּה נָהִינוּ וְלָֽנוּ הַדִּבָּה,
כִּי כָל זֹאת בָּאַתְנוּ בְּחוֹבָה.

עָרִיץ — *The ruthless oppressor*. According to the Talmud (*Gittin* 56b), the wicked Titus shouted, *'Where is their God?'* as he desecrated the inner sanctum of the Temple (see commentary to *kinnah* 16).

Beis Levi says that afterwards, Titus and his soldiers offered animal sacrifices to their pagan gods in the ruins of our Holy Temple. All the while they mocked the God of Israel, saying, 'Since He allows us to worship other gods in His Temple, He must venerate our gods too. Why, then, does He not come to partake of the

ל *Why, then, did You withdraw Your majestic right hand[1]*
and allow Your Throne of Glory to be derogated?[2]

מ *You remain exalted forever,* HASHEM*![3] and You are the very first.*
Indeed, you established the exalted [Temple]
from the first [even before Creation].[4]

נ *So, why did You allow the wicked to revile You[5]*
with his mouth and tongue,
until the tormentor attacked [the Temple,] the apple of Your eye?

ס *You rejoiced to bestow goodness upon them,*
as the statement 'You shall bring them,
and implant them (on the mount of Your heritage).'[6]

ע *So, why did You allow the ruthless oppressor**
to blaspheme and taunt, 'Where is their God[7]
Who would eat the fats of their slaughter?'

פ *'You shattered the sea with Your might,'[8]**
then You held back the seawaters with double doors.[9]

צ *So, why am I now drowning [in tragedy]*
unto the very depths of the sea,[10]
and my ruination has grown as huge as the ocean?[11]

ק *You are the Holy One, enthroned upon the praises of the holy ones[12]*
You dwell in the counsel of the sacred elders
(the seventy sages of the Sanhedrin).

ר *So, why do the profligate nations gather[13]*
to lay waste to the Temple's Holy of Holies?

ש *And You, our God, hear how we have been disgraced*
while Your Tabernacle was burnt in fire.

ת *So, why do You swallow up the heritage[14] You once sheltered?*
Cause a healing balm to blossom forth
and hover protectively over us!

But You are righteous in all that happens;[15]
Yours, My Lord, is the righteousness,
and we shall proclaim Your righteousness with love.
So, why do we moan, when the [evil] words are ours?
For all this has befallen us as a result of [our] guilt!

---

(1) Cf. *Eichah* 2:3. (2) Cf. *Jeremiah* 14:21. (3) Cf. *Psalms* 92:9. (4) Cf. *Jeremiah* 17:12. (5) Cf. *Psalms* 10:13. (6) *Exodus* 15:17. (7) *Deuteronomy* 32:37. (8) *Psalms* 74:13. (9) Cf. *Job* 38:8. (10) 38:16. (11) Cf. *Eichah* 2:13. (12) Cf. *Psalms* 22:4; some editions omit the prefix ו from this and the next two verses that begin וְאַתָּה. (13) Cf. 2:1. (14) Cf. *II Samuel* 20:19. (15) *Nehemiah* 9:33.

---

choicest of our sacrifices?'

אַתָּה פּוֹרַרְתָּ בְעָזְּךָ יָם — *You shattered the sea with Your might.* You split the Sea of Reeds so Israel could cross on dry land. When the Egyptians entered, You returned the waters to their natural condition to drown them, yet You kept Israel safe from the raging, flooding waters, by holding them back as if with a dike of double doors.

יט.

לְךָ אֲדֹנָי הַצְּדָקָה* **בְּא**וֹתוֹת אֲשֶׁר הִפְלֵאתָ מֵאָז וְעַד עָתָּה,
וְלָנוּ בֹּשֶׁת הַפָּנִים **בִּב**ְחִינָה אֲשֶׁר נִצְרַפְנוּ[1] וְאוֹתָנוּ תִּעַבְתָּ.
לְךָ אֲדֹנָי הַצְּדָקָה **בְּג**וֹי מִקֶּרֶב גּוֹי לָקַחַת בְּמַסּוֹת,[2]
וְלָנוּ בֹּשֶׁת הַפָּנִים **בְּד**ֹפִי אֲשֶׁר נִמְצָא בָנוּ כְּמַעֲשֵׂיהֶם עֲשׂוֹת.
לְךָ אֲדֹנָי הַצְּדָקָה **בְּה**ָלְכוּ אֱלֹהִים לִפְדּוֹת לוֹ לְעָם,[3]
וְלָנוּ בֹּשֶׁת הַפָּנִים **בְּו**ַיַּמְרוּ עַל יָם בְּיַם סוּף[4] גּוֹי בֵּאלֹהָיו בְּפָשְׁעָם.
לְךָ אֲדֹנָי הַצְּדָקָה **בְּז**ֵכֶר וְאַתֶּם עֵדַי וַאֲנִי אֱלֹהִים,[5]
וְלָנוּ בֹּשֶׁת הַפָּנִים **בְּח**ָרְפֵנוּ יהוה בְּסִין קוּם עֲשֵׂה לָנוּ אֱלֹהִים.[6]
לְךָ אֲדֹנָי הַצְּדָקָה **בְּט**ַעַם שֶׁהִטְעַמְתָּנוּ כְּצַפִּיחִית בִּדְבָשׁ,[7]
וְלָנוּ בֹּשֶׁת הַפָּנִים **בְּי**וֹם הִקְרַבְנוּ לְפָנָיו סֹלֶת וְשֶׁמֶן וּדְבָשׁ.[8]*
לְךָ אֲדֹנָי הַצְּדָקָה **בְּכ**ִלְכּוּל מָן וּבְאֵר וְעַמּוּד עָנָן,
וְלָנוּ בֹּשֶׁת הַפָּנִים **בְּל**ֶחֶם הַקְּלֹקֵל[9]* אֲבוֹתֵינוּ בְּאָהֳלֵיהֶם בְּרָגְנָן.[10]
לְךָ אֲדֹנָי הַצְּדָקָה **בַּמ**ִּדְבָּר לֹא חָסַרְנוּ דָּבָר,[11]
וְלָנוּ בֹּשֶׁת הַפָּנִים **בְּנ**ַאֲצוֹת לָבָן וַחֲצֵרוֹת וְדִי זָהָב[12]* כַּמִּדְבָּר.
לְךָ אֲדֹנָי הַצְּדָקָה **בְּס**ִיחוֹן וְעוֹג[13] וְכָל מַמְלְכוֹת כְּנָעַן,[14]

---

(1) Cf. *Jeremiah* 9:6. (2) *Deuteronomy* 4:34. (3) *II Samuel* 7:23. (4) *Psalms* 106:7.
(5) Cf. *Isaiah* 43:12. (6) *Exodus* 32:1. (7) 16:31. (8) Cf. *Ezekiel* 16:19. (9) *Numbers* 21:5.
(10) Cf. *Deuteronomy* 1:27. (11) Cf. 2:7. (12) 1:1. (13) See *Numbers* 21:21-35. (14) See *Joshua* ch. 12.

לְךָ ה׳ הַצְּדָקָה — *Yours, my Lord, is the righteousness.* R' Elazar HaKalir based this *kinnah* on the Midrash (*Tanchuma, Re'eh* 16) which expounds on the verse continuing the theme expressed in the preceding *kinnah's* conclusion — *Yours, my Lord, is the righteousness* (*Daniel* 9:7). R' Elazar HaKalir illustrates a number of applications of this verse. Each odd-numbered line begins with the opening phrase of the Scriptural verse לְךָ ה׳ הַצְּדָקָה, *Yours, my Lord, is the righteousness,* and each even-numbered line begins with the phrase וְלָנוּ בֹּשֶׁת הַפָּנִים, *and ours is the shamefacedness.* The next word of each line begins with the respective letter of the *aleph-beis* after the prefix בְּ, *because of* or *in regard to.*

הִקְרַבְנוּ לְפָנָיו סֹלֶת וְשֶׁמֶן וּדְבָשׁ — *We brought it an offering of fine flour with oil and honey.* Regarding Israel's sinfulness with idolatry, the prophet Ezekiel admonishes that their betrayal is all the more shocking because God's own special gifts to Israel were used as offerings to idols. *My bread which I gave you — fine flour, oil and honey did I feed you — you placed it before them ...* (*Ezekiel* 16:19). *Rashi* cites a Midrash that this refers to the *manna* that was placed in worship before the Golden Calf. *Rashi* there cites the verses from *Nehemiah* (9:18-19) that state: *Although they had made themselves a molten calf ... You, in Your great compassion, did not forsake them in the Wilderness ...*

בְּלֶחֶם הַקְּלֹקֵל — *About ... the destructive bread.* The word קְלוֹקֵל means either *destructive* (see *Metzudos* to *Jeremiah* 4:24) or *extremely light* (see *Ibn Ezra* to *Numbers* 21:5). *Rashi* (*Numbers* 21:5 and *Avodah Zarah* 5b) explains that since the *manna* is perfect food, it is digested in its entirety, producing no waste material. After a period of eating nothing but *manna*, the people no longer had the need to defecate. Instead of showing thankfulness for this miraculous food, they complained, 'This bread will destroy us. It enters our bodies but does not leave. Eventually we will be bloated and become sick and die.' The Talmud (*Avodah Zarah* 5a-b) cites this as an example of כְּפוּי טוֹבָה, *ingratitude.*

לָבָן וַחֲצֵרוֹת וְדִי זָהָב — *Laban, Hazeroth and Di-zahab.* Moses began his reprimand to the nation before his death with a seemingly inno-

19.

א *Yours, my Lord, is the righteousness,* because of*
the wondrous signs You have displayed from then until now;
ב *and ours is the shamefacedness, because of the trials*
with which You sought to refine us,[1]
[but as a result of our failure] You despised us.

ג *Yours, my Lord, is the righteousness,*
because You have taken [our] nation
from amidst another nation, with miracles;[2]
ד *and ours is the shamefacedness, because of the hypocrisy*
to be found within us as we emulated [Egypt's abominable] deeds.

ה *Yours, my Lord is the righteousness, because God went out*
to redeem us as a people unto Himself;[3]
ו *and ours is the shamefacedness,*
because they [our forefathers] rebelled
on the shore of the Sea of Reeds,[4]
the nation sinning against its God!

ז *Yours, my Lord, is the righteousness,*
when we recall the proclamation,
'You are witnesses, and I am God!'[5]
ח *and, ours is the shamefacedness,*
because we blasphemed HASHEM *in*
[the Wilderness of] Sin [when we demanded of Aaron],
'Arise and create a god for us!'[6]

ט *Yours, my Lord, is the righteousness,*
because You fed us [the manna]
that tasted like dough fried in honey;[7]
י *and ours is the shamefacedness,*
because on the day [we made the Golden Calf],
we brought it an offering of fine flour with oil and honey.[8]*

כ *Yours, my Lord, is the righteousness,*
because You provided us with the manna,
the well and the pillar of clouds;
ל *and ours is the shamefacedness,*
because our forefathers grumbled in their tents[10]
about [the manna and called it] the destructive bread.[9]*

מ *Yours, my Lord, is the righteousness,*
because in the wilderness we lacked for nothing;[11]
נ *and ours is the shamefacedness, because we defied You*
at Laban, Hazeroth and Di-zahab[12]* *as related [by Moses].*

ס *Yours, my Lord, is the righteousness, because of*
[how You waged war for us with] Sihon and Og[13]
and all the kings of Canaan;[14]

וְלָנוּ בֹּשֶׁת הַפָּנִים בְּעָכָן אֲשֶׁר מָעַל בְּחֵרֶם בְּלִי מְצֹא מַעַן.[1]
לְךָ אֲדֹנָי הַצְּדָקָה בְּפֹעַל אֲשֶׁר פָּעַלְתָּ בְּאַרְבָּעָה עָשָׂר מוֹשִׁיעִים,*
וְלָנוּ בֹּשֶׁת הַפָּנִים בְּצֶלֶם מִיכָה כִּי בוֹ אֲנַחְנוּ פוֹשְׁעִים.[2]
לְךָ אֲדֹנָי הַצְּדָקָה בְּקִימַת שִׁילֹה וְנוֹב וְגִבְעוֹן* וּבֵית עוֹלָמִים,
וְלָנוּ בֹּשֶׁת הַפָּנִים בְּרֶשַׁע שֶׁנִּמְצָא בָנוּ שֶׁחָרְבוּ וּבָם אָנוּ נִכְלָמִים.
לְךָ אֲדֹנָי הַצְּדָקָה בִּשְׁנֵי חֻרְבָּנוֹת שֶׁחָרְבוּ בְּבִצְעֵנוּ וַאֲנַחְנוּ קַיָּמִים,
וְלָנוּ בֹּשֶׁת הַפָּנִים בְּשׁוּבֵנוּ אֵלֶיךָ בְּכָל לֵב שֶׁתָּשׁוּב אֵלֵינוּ בְּרַחֲמִים.
לְךָ אֲדֹנָי הַצְּדָקָה בְּתְשַׁע מֵאוֹת שָׁנָה* שֶׁהָיְתָה שְׁנָאָה כְּבוּשָׁה מִלְּהַשָּׁמַע,
וְלָנוּ בֹּשֶׁת הַפָּנִים כְּתָבַע אִישׁ חֲמוּדוֹת, הַטֵּה אֱלֹהַי אָזְנְךָ וּשְׁמַע.[3]

(1) See *Joshua* 7:10-26. (2) See *Judges* chs. 17-18. (3) *Daniel* 9:18.

cent recollection of their itinerary through the Wilderness. Close inspection reveals a deeper meaning to Moses' words. Firstly, not all the place names enumerated by Moses appear elsewhere in the Torah. This raises the question of why they were omitted from the list of encampments given in *Numbers* (ch. 33). Secondly, at each of the places mentioned by Moses that does appear earlier, the nation struck a rebellious pose. Three of the names on Moses' litany are לָבָן, *Laban*, חֲצֵרוֹת, *Hazeroth*, and דִי זָהָב, *Di-zahab* (*Deuteronomy* 1:1). *Rashi* cites a Midrash that לָבָן is not a place name but means *white* and refers to the *manna* which the Torah describes as white (*Exodus* 16:31). Thus, Laban alludes to the Israelites' ingratitude when they grumbled about the *manna*.

חֲצֵרוֹת is mentioned elsewhere and was the site of both Korah's uprising and Miriam's *tzaraas* punishment when she spoke slanderously about her brother Moses (see *Numbers* 12:14-16).

ע *and ours is the shamefacedness, because of Achan*
who appropriated for himself from the forbidden booty
[of Jericho] and found no excuse [for his crime].[1]

פ *Yours, my Lord, is the righteousness,*
because of all that You accomplished through
*the fourteen savior[—Judges];**

צ *and ours is the shamefacedness, because of*
Micah's idol through which we transgressed.[2]

ק *Yours, my Lord, is the righteousness,*
*because You erected [Tabernacles] at Shiloh, Nob, Gibeon**
and the Eternal Temple [in Jerusalem];

ר *and ours is the shamefacedness,*
because the evil in our midst
caused each one's destruction,
and in their loss we have been humiliated.

ש *Yours, my Lord, is the righteousness,*
because although the Destructions of the two Temples
were caused by our corruption, we ourselves were spared;

ש *and ours is the shamefacedness,*
because we should have repented to You wholeheartedly,
so that You would return to us with compassion.

ת *Yours, my Lord, is the righteousness*
*because of the [almost] nine centuries**
throughout which You withheld Your anger
[over our sins] and didn't broadcast it;

ת *and ours is the shamefacedness,*
because [Daniel] the man of delights pleaded with You
[to end the Babylonian Exile after a mere seventy years,
even though we were not worthy,] saying,
'Incline Your ear, O my God, and hear!'[3]

דִי זָהָב, literally, *sufficient gold,* is also not a place name. Rather, it alludes to the Golden Calf made by the nation because God had endowed them with abundant gold (see also *Hosea* 2:10).

בְּאַרְבָּעָה עָשָׂר מוֹשִׁיעִים — *The fourteen savior[-Judges].* These are the fourteen leaders of Israel from the death of Moses until the era of the prophets which began with Samuel. They were called שׁוֹפְטִים, *Judges,* and their tenures are the subject of the Scriptural Book of that name.

שִׁילֹה וְנוֹב וְגִבְעוֹן — *Shiloh, Nob, Gibeon.* These were the successive sites of the Tabernacle before the בֵּית עוֹלָמִים, *Eternal Temple,* was erected by King Solomon.

בְּתְשַׁע מֵאוֹת שָׁנָה — *Because of the [almost] nine centuries.* When Israel left Egypt, some of the nation carried out idols with them. For close to nine hundred years, God remained silent. But when idolatry became rampant in the days of Ezekiel, God revived the memory of that treachery and admonished the nation for it (*Vayikra Rabbah* 7:1; cited by *Rashi* to *Ezekiel* 20:5).

כ.

הַטֵּה אֱלֹהַי אָזְנְךָ,[1]*
לְתִפְלֶצֶת מְנַאֶצֶת מִי לִי בַשָּׁמָיִם,[2]*
וּשְׁמַע
שַׁאֲגַת צוֹרְרֶיךָ הָאֹמְרִים עָרוּ עָרוּ עַד הַיְסוֹד[3] שַׁעַר הַשָּׁמָיִם.[4]*
הַטֵּה אֱלֹהַי אָזְנְךָ,
לְרִגְשַׁת הַדּוֹבֶרֶת עַל צַדִּיק עָתָק,[5]*
וּשְׁמַע
קוֹל שָׁאוֹן מֵעִיר[6] בְּחֵמָה שְׁפוּכָה לְשַׁתֵּק.
הַטֵּה אֱלֹהַי אָזְנְךָ,
לְצִיר שֻׁלַּח וְנָם קוּמוּ וְנָקוּמָה עָלֶיהָ לַמִּלְחָמָה,[7]
וּשְׁמַע
פַּלָּצוּת הוֹמִים בָּא הָעֵת אִתּוֹ בְּבֵיתוֹ לְהִלָּחֵמָה.
הַטֵּה אֱלֹהַי אָזְנְךָ,
לְעָצוּ עֵצָה וְחָשְׁבוּ מְזִמָּה בַּל יוּכָלוּ,
וּשְׁמַע
שִׂיחַת נוֹעֲצוּ לֵב יַחְדָּו עָלֶיךָ[8] עֲלוֹת נִסְתַּכָּלוּ.
הַטֵּה אֱלֹהַי אָזְנְךָ,
לְנִאֲצוּ וְשִׁלְּחוּ בָאֵשׁ מִקְדַּשׁ מוֹרָא,[9]
וּשְׁמַע
מְחָרְפֶיךָ מַדְמִימֵי תוֹדָה וְקוֹל זִמְרָה.[10]
הַטֵּה אֱלֹהַי אָזְנְךָ,
לְלֵצִים לָצוֹן חָמְדוּ לָהֶם,[11]
וּשְׁמַע
כָּל חֶרְפָּתָם אֲשֶׁר חֵרְפוּךָ[12] וְהַפֵּל אֵימָתְךָ עֲלֵיהֶם.

הַטֵּה אֱלֹהַי אָזְנְךָ — *Incline Your ear, my God.* As in the preceding *kinnah,* R' Elazar HaKalir based this composition on a verse from the Book of *Daniel, Incline Your ear, my God, and hear* (9:18). The contention of this lament is that the gentile marauders, who are supposedly God's agents to punish Israel and to destroy the Temple, are not merely enemies of the Jewish people; rather, they are the enemies of God Himself. This is vividly and unquestionably evident by the way in which they curse, blaspheme and taunt God. Therefore Israel argues with God, 'How can You, O God, allow these heathens to continue unchecked? They claim that since the Temple site remains desolate it proves that God was destroyed together with His Abode! You, O God, must stop them because they are far greater enemies of heaven than we

20.

ת *Incline Your ear, my God,*[1]* *to the licentious ones who blaspheme saying, 'Whom do I have [to fear] in heaven?'*[2]*

ש *And hear the roaring of Your enemies who declare, 'Destroy! Destroy! unto the very foundation*[3] *of [the Temple which is] the gateway to heaven.'*[4]*

ר *Incline Your ear, my God, to the gathering of those who speak falsehood against** *the Righteous One;*[5]

ק *and hear the sound of tumult [arising] from the [conqueror's capital] city,*[6] *silence it with an outpouring of rage.*

צ *Incline Your ear, my God, to the emissary [Obadiah who was] sent [to rally the gentile nations] and proclaim, 'Arise! Let us arise against her [the Roman Empire] in war!'*[7]

פ *And hear the horrifying sound of those who scream, 'The time has come to wage war [against God] in His own Temple!'*

ע *Incline Your ear, my God, to those who conspired and concocted an evil scheme that was impossible to carry out;*

ס *and hear the uttering of those who singleheartedly take counsel [against You],*[8] *and foolishly rise up against You.*

נ *Incline Your ear, my God, to those who blasphemed and set fire to the awe-inspiring Temple;*[9]

מ *and hear [the curses] of those who deride You, who silence the sound of thanksgiving and song.*[10]

ל *Incline Your ear, my God, to the scorners who relish ridicule,*[11]

כ *and hear all the disgrace with which they disgrace You,*[12] *and make Your fear befall them.*

---

(1) *Daniel* 9:18. (2) *Psalms* 73:25. (3) 137:7. (4) *Genesis* 28:17.
(5) Cf. *Psalms* 31:19. (6) *Isaiah* 66:6. (7) *Obadiah* 1:1. (8) *Psalms* 83:6.
(9) Cf. 74:7. (10) *Isaiah* 51:3. (11) Cf. *Proverbs* 1:22. (12) *Psalms* 79:12.

---

are, despite our sins. Therefore we beseech You, O God, to return, rebuild the Temple and demonstrate how mistaken they are!'

In each stanza the first line begins הַטֵּה אֱלֹהַי אָזְנְךָ לְ . . ., *Incline Your ear, my God, to . . .*, and the second line begins וּשְׁמַע, *and hear*. These phrases are followed by a word beginning with the respective letter of the reverse-alphabetical formulation known as תַּשְׁרַ״ק.

מִי לִי בַשָּׁמַיִם — *'Whom do I have [to fear] in heaven?'* According to the translation, these words were spoken by the Roman soldier in direct defiance of God, as if to say, 'I need fear none in heaven.' Alternatively, these are Israel's words: The heathens ask *whom I have in heaven* to protect me. They claim that even God has forsaken me.

שַׁעַר הַשָּׁמָיִם — *The gateway to heaven.* When Jacob awoke from his prophetic vision of the angels ascending and descending a ladder stretching from earth to heaven, he declared, *'How awesome is this place! This is none other than the House of God and this is the gateway to heaven!'* (*Genesis* 28:17).

עָתָק — *Falsehood.* The translation follows *Rashi's* first interpretation of this word (*Psalms* 31:19). In an alternate explanation, *Rashi* has *harsh*; thus, in this *kinnah*, *'those who speak harshly about the Righteous One.'*

הַטֵּה אֱלֹהַי אָזְנְךָ,
לְיָהֲרוּ וְהוֹצִיאוּ כְּרוּבִים בִּרְחוֹבוֹת מְחַזְּרִים,
וּשְׁמַע
טַרְחוֹת טִנּוּפָם* כְּהֶעֱלוּ עַל מִזְבַּחֲךָ חֲזִירִים.
הַטֵּה אֱלֹהַי אָזְנְךָ,
לְחִלְּלוּ וְטִנְּפוּ בֵּית קֹדֶשׁ הַקֳּדָשִׁים,
וּשְׁמַע
זֵדִים מְזָרְקִים לְמוֹלֶךְ מִילוֹת קְדוֹשִׁים.*
הַטֵּה אֱלֹהַי אָזְנְךָ,
לְלוֹעֲזִים מְעִיזִים מֶצַח לְכוּ וְנִלָּחֲמָה אִתּוֹ בְּבֵיתוֹ,
וּשְׁמַע
הַוּוֹת הוֹלְלִים מְהַלְּלִים כִּי אֵין הָאִישׁ בְּבֵיתוֹ.[1]
הַטֵּה אֱלֹהַי אָזְנְךָ,
לְדוֹבֶרֶת אֲנִי וְאַפְסִי עוֹד,[2]
וּשְׁמַע
גִּדּוּפֶיהָ וְחֵרוּפֶיהָ מִשְׁתַּחֶצֶת עַד כִּסְאֲךָ עוֹד.
הַטֵּה אֱלֹהַי אָזְנְךָ,
לְבוֹזָה וּמַלְעֶגֶת[3] מַה תּוֹחִילִי וְאֵינוֹ נִבְנֶה,
וּשְׁמַע
בְּכִיַּת מַסְפִּידִים וְקוֹרְאִים[4] וּמְחַכִּים מָתַי יִבָּנֶה.
הַטֵּה אֱלֹהַי אָזְנְךָ,
לְאוֹמְרִים עָזַב וְשָׁכַח וְנָטַשׁ וְלָעַד שׁוֹמֵם,
וּשְׁמַע
אֶנְקָתֵנוּ, וְקַנֵּא קִנְאָתֵנוּ,
וְהָאֵר פָּנֶיךָ עַל מִקְדָּשְׁךָ הַשָּׁמֵם.[5]

טִנּוּפָם — *Their filth.* Idolatrous offerings are considered nothing more than filth, as the prophet (*Isaiah* 28:8) declares: *For all the tables [i.e., altars] are full of vomit and excrement, without the Omnipresent* (See *Avos* 3:4). Moreover, the idols themselves are so considered, as it is written: צֵא תֹּאמַר לוֹ, *Say unto him [the idol], 'You are excrement!'* (ibid. 30:22; see *Radak* there, and *Maharshal* to *Shabbos* 82a).

מִילוֹת קְדוֹשִׁים — *The circumcised organs ... from the holy ones.* The Amalekites would

י *Incline Your, ear, my God, to those*
who haughtily removed the Cherubim
[from the Ark Cover in the Holy of Holies]
and paraded them around the streets;

ט *and hear how they burdened You with their filth**
when they offered up swine on Your Altar.

ח *Incline Your ear, my God, to those who desecrated*
and filthied the chamber of the Holy of Holies;

ז *and hear how the wanton ones*
flung at You the circumcised organs
*[they cruelly severed] from the holy ones.**

ו *Incline Your ear, my God, to the*
brazen-browed foreigners [who declare],
'Let us go forth and wage war with Him in His own House';

ה *and hear the treacherous mockery of the scorners,*
'The Man is not in His House!'[1]

ד *Incline Your ear, my God, to those who boast,*
'I am [everything] and anything else is nothing!'[2]

ג *And hear the curses and disgraces [of the nation]*
whose arrogance reaches up to Your very Throne.

ב *Incline Your ear, my God,*
to the disparagement and ridicule,[3]
'Where is your hope? Your Temple will never be rebuilt!'

ב *And hear the weeping of those who mourn and cry out*[4]
and yearn, 'When will it be built [again]?'

א *Incline Your ear, my God, to those who claim*
that [the Temple] is abandoned, forgotten and cast aside,
forever will it be desolate.

א *And hear our anguished cry and zealously take up our cause;*
and let Your countenance shine upon
Your desolate Sanctuary.[5]

---

(1) *Proverbs* 7:19. (2) *Isaiah* 47:8. (3) Cf. *Nehemiah* 2:19.
(4) Some editions read וְקוֹרְעִים, *and rend [their garments],*
in place of וְקוֹרְאִים, *and cry out.* (5) *Daniel* 9:17.

---

mutilate their Jewish victims, then throw their organs skyward while calling out blasphemously to God, 'Here, this is what You have chosen! Take what is Yours!' (*Midrash Tanchuma, Ki Seitzei* 10).

כא.

אַרְזֵי הַלְּבָנוֹן* אַדִּירֵי הַתּוֹרָה,
בַּעֲלֵי תְרֵיסִין* בְּמִשְׁנָה וּבִגְמָרָא,
גִּבּוֹרֵי כֹחַ* עֲמֵלֶיהָ בְּטָהֳרָה,
דָּמָם נִשְׁפַּךְ וְנָשְׁתָה גְבוּרָה,
הִנָּם קְדוֹשֵׁי הֲרוּגֵי מַלְכוּת עֲשָׂרָה,
וְעַל אֵלֶּה אֲנִי בוֹכִיָּה וְעֵינִי נִגָּרָה.
זֹאת בְּזָכְרִי אֶזְעַק בְּמָרָה,
חֶמְדַּת יִשְׂרָאֵל כְּלֵי הַקֹּדֶשׁ נֵזֶר וַעֲטָרָה,
טְהוֹרֵי לֵב קְדוֹשִׁים מֵתוּ בְּמִיתָה חֲמוּרָה,
יַדּוּ גוֹרָל* מִי רִאשׁוֹן לַחֶרֶב בְּרוּרָה,
כִּנְפוֹל גוֹרָל עַל רַבָּן שִׁמְעוֹן* פָּשַׁט צַוָּארוֹ וּבָכָה כִּנְגְזָרָה גְזֵרָה,*
לְרַבָּן שִׁמְעוֹן[2] חָזַר הַהֶגְמוֹן לְהָרְגוֹ בְּנֶפֶשׁ נְצוּרָה,
מִזֶּרַע אַהֲרֹן* שָׁאַל בְּבַקָּשָׁה לִבְכּוֹת עַל בֶּן הַגְּבִירָה,

---

⚜ **אַרְזֵי הַלְּבָנוֹן** — *Cedars of Lebanon.* This *kinnah,* whose author is unknown [although some ascribe it to יְחִיאֵל בֶּן מֵאִיר, whose name may appear in the acrostic], is a dramatic highlight of the Tishah B'Av service. It depicts the tragic execution of the עֲשָׂרָה הֲרוּגֵי מַלְכוּת, *Ten Martyrs.*

Numerous *piyutim, kinnos* and *selichos* have been written about the Ten Martyrs, all of which seemingly place them as contemporaneous. It should be noted, however, that while all ten of these righteous men were murdered by the Romans during the Mishnaic period, their executions did not take place at the same time, nor could they have, since two of the ten did not even live in the same generation as the other eight. Namely, Rabban Shimon ben Gamliel and Rabbi Yishmael the *Kohen Gadol* lived before the Destruction of the Second Temple, and were murdered shortly thereafter, while the others were all killed after the Bar Kochba revolt, more than sixty years later. The liturgical accounts of the martyrdom were not meant as historical records, but as dramatic accounts of the story, in order to evoke feelings of loss and repentance on the part of the congregation.

The Talmud teaches: 'The death of the righteous is a tragedy equal to the burning of the Temple of our God' (*Rosh Hashanah* 18a). Thus, it is appropriate to mourn the loss of these righteous sages on Tishah B'Av, the day our Temple was destroyed in fire.

In the *chazzan's* repetition of the *Amidah* during *Mussaf* on Yom Kippur, the Day of Atonement, we read another *piyut* describing the death of the Ten Martyrs titled אֵלֶּה אֶזְכְּרָה, *These shall I recall.* It is included in the Yom Kippur service because the Talmud (*Moed Katan* 28a) states: 'The death of the righteous atones for the sins of Israel,' and it is on Yom Kippur that we seek to arouse the merit of the martyrs. The Yom Kippur version of this story is lengthier and explains that the death of the Ten Martyrs was an atonement for the sin of the ten sons of Jacob who were involved in the sale of Joseph into slavery (see *Genesis* ch. 37). That heartless deed sowed the seeds of future dissension and senseless hatred in Israel. But it was not until the Second Temple was destroyed due to שִׂנְאַת חִנָּם, *baseless hatred,* that Israel reaped the bitter fruits of that deed (*Yoma* 9b). Then, after the Temple's destruction, God brought about the death of ten holy martyrs who sanctified His Name in atonement for the sin of the ten brothers. For it was the still-present influence of their act that continued to prevent their offspring from living in brotherhood and harmony.

This *kinnah* lists only eight of the Ten Martyrs. In the Yom Kippur liturgy and other sources the other two are given as Rabbi Chanina ben Chachinai, one of Rabbi Akiva's earlier disciples and Rabbi Yehudah (or Elazar) ben Dama. Some versions add the name of Rabbi Yehudah HaNachtom in place of ben Dama.

אַרְזֵי הַלְּבָנוֹן — *Cedars of Lebanon.* The righteous are thus described by the psalmist: *A righteous man will flourish like a date palm,* כְּאֶרֶז בַּלְּבָנוֹן יִשְׂגֶּה, *like a cedar in Lebanon he will grow tall* (*Psalms* 92:13).

בַּעֲלֵי תְרֵיסִין — *Shield-carriers* [lit., *masters of the shields*]. The Talmud uses this when referring to the sages in the academy of Rabban Gamliel,

21.

א *Cedars of Lebanon,* giants of Torah,*
ב *shield-carriers* of Mishnah and Gemara,*
ג *powerful warriors,* exerting themselves over it in purity,*
ד *their blood was spilt and [their] greatness removed [from us].*
ה *Behold, they are the holy Ten Martyrs executed by the [Roman] government,*
ו *and for these do I weep and my eye overflows.*[1]
ז *When I remember this I scream in bitterness.*
ח *The most desirable in Israel, the holy vessels, crown and tiara,*
ט *pure of heart and consecrated, they suffered a harsh death.*
י *They cast lots* to determine whom to put to the sword first.*
כ *When the lot fell on Rabban Shimon [ben Gamliel],* he stretched out his neck and wept as the decree was issued.**
ל *The overlord, with soul steeped in evil, turned to slay Rabban Shimon.*[2]
מ *[Rabbi Yishmael, the Kohen Gadol,] the scion of Aaron* asked permission to cry over this son of royalty.*

(1) Cf. *Eichah* 1:16; 3:49. (2) Some editions read רַבִּי יִשְׁמָעֵאל, *Rabbi Yishmael.*

nassi of Israel and son of Rabban Shimon, the first of the Ten Martyrs. Among those described with this title was Rabbi Chutzpis the Interpreter, ninth of the Martyrs (*Berachos* 27b). They are called shield-carriers either because they metaphorically do battle with each other in debating the fine points of Torah law, or because of their role in enforcing the law as interpreted by the *nassi* and his academy (*Aruch*).

גִּבּוֹרֵי כֹחַ — *Powerful warriors.* Perhaps this is an even greater accolade than earlier ones, for the psalmist depicts the angels with this term (see *Psalms* 103:20).

יַדּוּ גוֹרָל — *They cast lots.* Rabban Shimon ben Gamliel and Rabbi Yishmael the *Kohen Gadol* were seized by the Romans at the time of the Temple's destruction. When they were about to be killed, each begged the executioner, 'Please kill me first, so that I will not be forced to witness the death of my beloved colleague!' The executioner was amazed by the pure love for one another and said, 'In that case we will cast lots to decide who should die first!'

רַבָּן שִׁמְעוֹן — *Rabban Shimon* [*ben Gamliel*], the נָשִׂיא, *Prince,* of Israel, a great grandson of Hillel and a direct descendant of the royal family of King David. He was the first of the Ten Martyrs to die. *Mishnah Berurah* (53:35) quotes *Sefer Chassidim* who relates that when Rabban Shimon ben Gamliel was about to die he asked Rabbi Yishmael, 'My dear brother, why am I being subjected to die such an ignominious death [like a common criminal]?'

Rabbi Yishmael replied, 'Perhaps when you preached in public before the masses you were filled with too much personal pleasure and you thereby benefited personally from words of Torah?' Rabban Shimon responded, 'My brother, you have comforted and consoled me!'

וּבָכָה כִּנְגְזְרָה גְזֵרָה — *And wept as the decree was issued.* The much more detailed version in the *piyut* אֵלֶּה אֶזְכְּרָה (see above) relates that the Roman ruler informed the martyrs that they would be executed as retribution for the sale of Joseph by his brothers. They asked for a three-day period during which they would determine whether their deaths had been decreed by the Heavenly Tribunal. Rabbi Yishmael the *Kohen Gadol* uttered God's secret Name by which miracles can be performed, and ascended to heaven. There he met the angel Gabriel who told him, 'Accept it upon yourselves . . . for I have heard . . . that you have been destined for this.'

The *kinnah* informs us that Rabban Shimon wept as he heard Rabbi Yishmael report that their deaths had been decreed in heaven.

מִזֶּרַע אַהֲרֹן — *The scion of Aaron.* Although his name is not mentioned in this *kinnah,* other sources identify him as Rabbi Yishmael ben Elisha the *Kohen Gadol* (see *kinnah* 23). According to those sources, the Roman governor who condemned Rabbi Yishmael to death had a daughter who was impressed with the Rabbi's appearance, for he was as handsome as Joseph in his prime. She begged her father to spare the Rabbi for her personal gratification. Her father replied, 'If it is his face that impresses you, we can preserve it.' In an incredible display of cruelty, the governor gave orders that Rabbi Yishmael be skinned alive and the skin on his face be mounted like a trophy and preserved in fragrant balsam. They flayed the flesh off his face until they reached the top of his head where *tefillin* were

נָטַל רֹאשׁוֹ וּנְתָנוֹ עַל אַרְכֻּבוֹתָיו מְנוֹרָה הַטְּהוֹרָה,*
שָׂם עֵינָיו עַל עֵינָיו וּפִיו עַל פִּיו בְּאַהֲבָה גְמוּרָה,
עָנָה וְאָמַר פֶּה הַמִּתְגַּבֵּר בַּתּוֹרָה,
פִּתְאוֹם נִקְנְסָה עָלָיו מִיתָה מְשֻׁנָּה וַחֲמוּרָה,
צִוָּה לְהַפְשִׁיט אֶת רֹאשׁוֹ בְּתַעַר הַשְּׂכִירָה,
קִיֵּם בְּעוֹרוֹ אָמְרוּ לְנַפְשֵׁךְ שְׁחִי וְנַעֲבֹרָה.[1]
רָשָׁע הַפּוֹשֵׁט עֵת הִגִּיעַ לִמְקוֹם תְּפִלִּין מִצְוַת בָּרָה,
צָעַק צְעָקָה* וְנִזְדַּעְזְעָה עוֹלָם וְאֶרֶץ הִתְפּוֹרָרָה.
מֵאַחֲרָיו הֵבִיאוּ אֶת רַבִּי עֲקִיבָא*
עוֹקֵר הָרִים וְטוֹחֲנָן זוּ בְּזוּ בִּסְבָרָה,
וְסָרְקוּ אֶת בְּשָׂרוֹ בְּמַסְרֵק שֶׁל בַּרְזֶל לְהִשְׁתַּבְּרָה,
יָצְתָה נִשְׁמָתוֹ בְּאֶחָד וּבַת קוֹל אָמְרָה,
אַשְׁרֶיךָ רַבִּי עֲקִיבָא גּוּפְךָ טָהוֹר בְּכָל מִינֵי טָהֳרָה.
בֶּן בָּבָא רַבִּי יְהוּדָה* אַחֲרָיו, הֵבִיאוּ בְּשִׁבְרוֹן לֵב וְאַזְהָרָה,
נֶהֱרַג בֶּן שִׁבְעִים שָׁנָה בִּידֵי אֲרוּרָה,
יוֹשֵׁב בְּתַעֲנִית הָיָה נָקִי וְחָסִיד בִּמְלַאכְתּוֹ לְמַהֲרָה.
רַבִּי חֲנִינָא[2] בֶּן תְּרַדְיוֹן* אַחֲרָיו מַקְהִיל קְהִלּוֹת בְּצִיּוֹן שֶׁעְרָה,

positioned. Until that point Rabbi Yishmael bore the excruciating physical pain in silence, but when they stripped him of this precious spiritual possession he let out a terrifying scream.

The Talmud relates that once every seventy years the Romans would reenact the following scene: A healthy man (representing Esau) would ride on the back of a cripple (symbolic of Jacob, who had a temporary limp after doing battle with the angel — see *Genesis* 32:24-32). 'Esau' would be wearing the garments once worn by Adam and later the property of Esau and would hold aloft the preserved head of Rabbi Yishmael. All this, to prove Esau's continued supremacy over Jacob, i.e., Israel (*Avodah Zarah* 11b with *Rashi*).

מְנוֹרָה הַטְּהוֹרָה — *'O pure Menorah!'* Torah scholars are beacons of light that guide people along the paths that lead to heaven. Or, in the words of King Solomon: נֵר מִצְוָה וְתוֹרָה אוֹר, *A mitzvah is a lamp and the Torah is light* (*Proverbs* 6:23).

צָעַק צְעָקָה — *He ... let such a scream.* For some reason the alphabetical acrostic is discontinued after the first twenty letters and omits the letter ש and ת. Perhaps some lines of the original composition have been lost or removed by the censors.

רַבִּי עֲקִיבָא — *Rabbi Akiva.* Rabbi Akiva's death at the age of one hundred and twenty took place about sixty years after the destruction of the Temple (circa 135 C.E.). After Bar Kochba's unsuccessful uprising against the Romans, they enacted extremely harsh decrees proscribing the practice of Judaism in general and prohibiting the study and teaching of Torah in particular. Rabbi Akiva believed that without Torah study the Jewish people suffer a demise worse than death, so he ignored the Roman decree and taught Torah at massive public gatherings. The Romans imprisoned him and finally executed him on Yom Kippur.

Rabbi Akiva was tortured to death in this barbaric manner:

It was the time of the morning *Shema* reading when R' Akiva was taken out to be murdered publicly. During his frightful ordeal he accepted God's sovereignty upon himself by reciting the *Shema* joyously, oblivious to the pain. Turnus Rufus, the Roman commander who ordered the barbarous execution, was flabbergasted. 'Have you no feeling of pain that you can laugh in the face of such intense suffering!' he exclaimed. Even R' Akiva's own students wondered, 'Our teacher, even to this extent?'

The dying sage explained, 'All my life I was concerned over a phrase of the Torah. We are taught in the *Shema* to accept God's sovereignty and decrees upon ourselves, בְּכָל נַפְשְׁךָ, *with all your soul* (*Deuteronomy* 6:5) — this implies that we must serve God even if it means forfeiting our life. I used to wonder if I would ever have the

נ *He took [Rabban Shimon's severed] head and placed it on his lap [and lamented], 'O pure Menorah!'**

ס *He placed his eyes upon his eyes, and his mouth upon his mouth in absolute love.*

ע *He cried out and said, 'O mouth that strengthened itself in Torah,*

פ *how suddenly a violent and cruel death has been inflicted upon you!'*

צ *He [the overlord] ordered them to strip the skin off [Rabbi Yishmael's] head with a sharp razor.*

ק *With his skin he fulfilled the prophecy: 'They [the enemy] said to your soul, "Prostrate yourself that we may walk over you!"'*[1]

ר *When the wicked one who flayed him reached the place of the tefillin, the brilliant mitzvah,*
He [Rabbi Yishmael] let out such a scream that the whole world quaked and the earth crumbled into little pieces.*
After him they brought forth Rabbi Akiva who uprooted mountains [of halachic problems] and ground them one against the other by thorough analysis.*
They combed his flesh with an iron comb in order to break him. His soul departed while he declared, '[God is] One' and a heavenly voice proclaimed,
'Fortunate are you, Rabbi Akiva; your body has been purified with every type of purity!'
After him they brought forth Rabbi Yehudah ben Bava, a man of humble heart, and scrupulous [in avoiding sin],*
he was killed at age seventy by the hands of the cursed [nation].
He was immersed in fasting; clean and pious, alacritous in his service.
Rabbi Chanina[2] *ben Teradyon* came after him, [condemned because] he assembled crowds [to study Torah] within the gates of Zion.*

(1) *Isaiah* 51:23. (2) Some editions read חֲנַנְיָה or חֲנַנְיָא, *Chananiah.*

privilege of serving God to such a degree. Now that the chance has come to me, shall I not grasp it with joy?'

He repeated the first verse of *Shema* — *Hear, O Israel,* HASHEM *is our God,* HASHEM *is One* — and as he drew out the word אֶחָד, *One,* his soul left him.

A heavenly voice was heard saying, 'You are praiseworthy, Rabbi Akiva, for your soul left you as you proclaimed God's Oneness! ... You are praiseworthy, Rabbi Akiva, for you are ready to enter the life of the World to Come' (*Berachos* 61b; *Yerushalmi Berachos* 9:5).

רַבִּי יְהוּדָה בֶּן בָּבָא — *Rabbi Yehudah ben Bava.* Moses ordained his disciple Joshua, thus investing him with the God-given authority to render halachic judgments and to impose certain fines. The chain of *Semichah* ordination remained unbroken, handed down from teacher to disciple, for almost fifteen centuries until the Romans issued a decree prohibiting Rabbis (under pain of death) from ordaining their students. Rabbi Yehudah ben Bava was determined to guarantee the perpetuation of the chain of *Semichah*. He secretly ordained five of his greatest disciples near a mountain pass in a secluded area between the cities of Usha and Shefaram. These illustrious students were: Rabbi Meir, Rabbi Yehudah bar Illai, Rabbi Shimon bar Yochai, Rabbi Yossi ben Chalafta and Rabbi Elazar ben Shamua, the tenth martyr (other opinions add a sixth disciple, Rabbi Nechemiah, see *Sanhedrin* 13b-14a).

Unfortunately, the Romans heard about this convocation and sent troops to execute the master and his disciples. Seventy-year-old Rabbi Yehudah ben Bava commanded his students, 'Run away, my sons, and I will stand firm before them like an immovable boulder.' Rabbi Yehudah blocked the narrow mountain path with his body and the Romans could not budge him. Only after they pierced his body with three hundred iron spears and made him like a sieve did he fall dead.

רַבִּי חֲנִינָא בֶּן תְּרַדְיוֹן — *Rabbi Chanina ben Teradyon.* The Talmud (*Avodah Zarah* 18a)

יוֹשֵׁב וְדוֹרֵשׁ וְסֵפֶר תּוֹרָה עִמּוֹ, וְהִקִּיפוּהוּ בְּחַבְלֵי זְמוֹרָה,
אֶת הָאוּר הִצִּיתוּ בָהֶם וּכְרָכוּהוּ בְּסֵפֶר תּוֹרָה,
סְפוּגִין שֶׁל צֶמֶר הִנִּיחוּ עַל לִבּוֹ שֶׁלֹּא יָמוּת מְהֵרָה.
חָסִיד רַבִּי יֶשֵׁבָב הַסּוֹפֵר* הֲרָגוּהוּ עַם עֲמוֹרָה,
זְרָקוּהוּ וְהִשְׁלִיכוּהוּ לַכְּלָבִים וְלֹא הֻקְבַּר בִּקְבוּרָה,
יָצְתָה בַּת קוֹל עָלָיו שֶׁלֹּא הִנִּיחַ כְּלוּם מִתּוֹרַת מֹשֶׁה לְשָׁמְרָה.
וְאַחֲרָיו רַבִּי חוּצְפִּית* בְּיוֹם עֶבְרָה,
עוֹף הַפּוֹרֵחַ נִשְׂרַף בַּהֲבֵל פִּיו כְּבַמְּדוּרָה.
צַדִּיק רַבִּי אֶלְעָזָר בֶּן שַׁמּוּעַ* בָּאַחֲרוֹנָה נֶהֱרַג בְּמַדְקִירָה,
יוֹם עֶרֶב שַׁבָּת הָיָה זְמַן קִדּוּשׁ וַיְקַדֵּשׁ וַיִּקְרָא,
חֶרֶב שָׁלְּפוּ עָלָיו וְלֹא הִנִּיחוּהוּ בַּחַיִּים לְגָמְרָה,
יָצְתָה נִשְׁמָתוֹ בְּבָרָא אֱלֹהִים[1] יוֹצֵר וְצָר צוּרָה.
כָּהֵנָּה וְכָהֵנָּה הוֹסִיפוּ בְּנֵי עַוְלָה לְעַנּוֹת בִּגְעָרָה,
בִּסְקִילָה שְׂרֵפָה הֶרֶג וְחֶנֶק מִי יוּכַל לְשַׁעֲרָה,
נוֹתֶרֶת מִמֶּנָּה יֹאכְלוּ אֲרָיוֹת שֶׂה פְזוּרָה,[2]
חֲזֵה הַתְּנוּפָה וְשׁוֹק הַתְּרוּמָה[3]* טָרְפוּ אַרְיֵה וְהַכְּפִירָה,
יֵיטִיב יהוה וְלֹא יוֹסִיף עוֹד לְיַסְּרָה,[4]
אַמֵּיץ בִּרְכַּיִם כּוֹשְׁלוֹת[5] חֵלֶק יַעֲקֹב[6] וּמוֹשִׁיעַ בְּעֵת צָרָה,[7]
לְצֶדֶק יִמְלֹךְ מֶלֶךְ,[8] יֹאמַר שָׁלְמוּ יְמֵי אֶבְלֵךְ,[9] לְאוֹרוֹ נִסַּע וְנֵלֵךְ.

(1) *Genesis* 2:3. (2) Cf. *Jeremiah* 50:17. (3) Cf. *Leviticus* 7:34. (4) Cf. 26:18.
(5) Cf. *Isaiah* 35:3. (6) *Jeremiah* 10:16. (7) Cf. 14:8. (8) *Isaiah* 32:1. (9) 60:20.

teaches that the pretext to execute Rabbi Chanina was that he violated the Roman edict against teaching the Torah publicly. The Romans wrapped him in the Torah Scroll that he always kept with him and set it afire. To prolong his agony, they packed his chest with water-soaked wool. To his horrified daughter and student, Rabbi Chanina said, 'The parchment is consumed, but the letters fly up in the air.' The Roman executioner was deeply moved by Rabbi Chanina's holiness and asked, 'If I remove the wool from your heart, will I have a share in the World to Come?' Rabbi Chanina promised that he would, whereupon the Roman removed the wet wool and put more wood on the fire, so that the agony would end quickly. Then, the Roman threw himself into the fire and died. A heavenly voice proclaimed, 'Rabbi Chanina and his executioner are about to enter the World to Come.'

רַבִּי יֶשֵׁבָב הַסּוֹפֵר — *Rabbi Yeshevav the Scribe.* Rabbi Yeshevav was Rabbi Akiva's colleague. It was said of him that he was as great as Moses in every respect other than prophecy. The Romans murdered him while he was reciting the *Shema*, as he was reading the portion dealing with the *mitzvah* of the *tzitzis* fringes. He died on a high level of purity for he had been fasting all that day, but the Romans were determined to subject his remains to degradation. They refused to allow him to be buried; instead, they had wild dogs drag his pure and holy body through the streets.

רַבִּי חוּצְפִּית — *Rabbi Chutzpis.* In Talmudic times, a מְתוּרְגְּמָן, literally, *interpreter*, would repeat and explain the lecture of the *rosh yeshivah*. Rabbi Chutzpis was one day short of his 130th birthday and his last wish was for one more day of life in order to recite the *Shema* for another evening and morning. But his wish was not granted.

The Romans devised a particularly sadistic barbarism for Rabbi Chutzpis. Since he was renowned for his rhetorical skill and his golden tongue, before they killed him they cut out his tongue and tossed it into the trash heap. This was a particularly disturbing torture, for Rabbi Chutzpis never used his tongue to speak anything other than words of Torah. The Talmud

While he sat with a Torah Scroll and taught,
they surrounded him with bundles of vines.
They set them on fire, and wrapped him in the Torah Scroll
[from which he taught].
They placed tufts of [water-soaked] wool on his heart,
so that he would not die quickly.
The pious one, Rabbi Yeshevav the Scribe, was killed*
by the descendants of [Sodom and] Amorah.
They threw him down and flung him to the dogs,
so he was not buried in a proper grave.
A heavenly voice went forth [and said] that he did not fail
to observe any detail of the Torah of Moses.
*And after him on the day of wrath, they [killed] Rabbi Chutzpis,**
[who taught Torah with such fiery zeal that a] bird
flying [above him] would be burnt
by the breath of his mouth as if on the Altar pyre.
The righteous Rabbi Elazar ben Shamua was the last;*
he was killed by stabbing.
It was on a Friday as the day turned to the holy Sabbath,
so he began the Kiddush and recited [the opening passage].
They unsheathed a sword over him,
and did not allow him to live to finish it.
His soul departed with [the words] 'which God created,'[1]
[thereby acknowledging Him as] the Creator
Who fashioned every creature's form.
Again and again in this manner, the sons of iniquity
continued to torture [us] with rebuke.
With stoning, burning, beheading and strangling —
who can calculate [the enormity of the tragedy]?
What remained of it, the scattered flock, the lions consumed.[2]
The breast of the waving and the thigh of the raising-up[3]*
the lion and his daughter tore to pieces.
May HASHEM *show [His] benevolence [to us]*
and never again make us suffer.[4]
Strengthen the faltering knees,[5] *O You Who are Jacob's portion,*[6]
and his savior in times of distress.[7]
For the sake of righteousness He [God] shall reign as king.[8]
He will say [to Israel], 'The days of your mourning have come to
an end!'[9] *Then we shall venture forth and walk in His light!*

---

relates that when Elisha ben Avuyah, a well-known Sage of Mishnaic times, saw Rabbi Chutzpis' tongue being chewed up by a swine in the trash heap, he could not fathom that a just God would allow such 'injustice,' and he turned heretic. The Talmud, however, explains Rabbi Chutzpis' degradation as proof that שְׂכַר מִצְוָה בְּהַאי עָלְמָא לֵיכָּא, *reward for mitzvah observance is not forthcoming in this world,* but in the World to Come (*Kiddushin* 39b).

רַבִּי אֶלְעָזָר בֶּן שַׁמּוּעַ — *Rabbi Elazar ben Shamua.* One of the five great disciples ordained by Rabbi Yehudah ben Bava (see above), he was the last of the Ten Martyrs. He was killed at the age of one hundred and five.

חֲזֵה הַתְּנוּפָה וְשׁוֹק הַתְּרוּמָה — *The breast of the waving and the thigh of the raising-up.* The flesh of these innocent victims was regarded as the choicest and finest of the priestly sacrificial gifts.

כב.

הַחֲרִישׁוּ מִמֶּנִּי* וַאֲדַבְּרָה, וְיַעֲבוֹר עָלַי מָה,[1]
חָמָס אֶזְעַק וְשׁוֹד[2] לְךָ שׁוֹכֵן שָׁמַיְמָה,
הֱצִיקַתְנִי רוּחִי וְלֹא אוּכַל אֶדְּמָה,
כְּיוֹלֵדָה אֶפְעֶה אֶשְׁאַף וְאֶשְׁמָּה,[3]
מִסְפֵּד מַר אֶעֱשֶׂה וַאֲקוֹנֵן בִּנְהִימָה,
דִּבְרֵי שַׁאֲגוֹתַי יִתְּכוּ כְּיַמָּה,[4]
סִפְדִי עַל עֲדָתִי אֲשֶׁר נִתְּנָה לְשַׁמָּה,
אָרִיד בְּשִׂיחִי וְאָהִימָה,[5] וְקוֹל נְהִי אָרִימָה.
אֵיךְ שָׁבַת מָשׂוֹשׂ וְעָרְבָה שִׂמְחָה,
כָּל פָּנִים פָּארוּר[6] וְכָל רֹאשׁ קָרְחָה,
וְכָל זָקָן גְּרוּעָה[7] וְעַל כָּל לֵב אֲנָחָה,
מֵאָז נִתְעוֹרֵר גּוֹי עַז דּוֹרֵשׁ שׁוּחָה,[8]
סִלָּה אַבִּירַי[9] הוֹגֵי עֹז מִבְטֶחָה,
בְּתוּלוֹתַי וּבַחוּרַי נָסַח בִּנְסִיחָה,
בְּרֹאשׁ כָּל חוּצוֹת[10] נִבְלָתָן כַּסּוּחָה,[11]
עוֹלָלַי וְטַפַּי נֶחְשָׁבוּ כְּצֹאן טִבְחָה,[12]
אֵילִילָה עַל זֹאת[13] וְדִמְעָתִי עַל לֶחָה,[14]
הֵאָסְפוּ אֵלַי דְּוּוּיֵי צֹאן נִדָּחָה.
לְהַרְבּוֹת הַבְּכִי וּלְהָרִים צְוָחָה,
הֵילִילוּ שָׁמַיִם וְזַעֲקִי אֲדָמָה.
אָרִיד בְּשִׂיחִי וְאָהִימָה, וְקוֹל נְהִי אָרִימָה.
אֶרְאֶלִּים* צְאוּ וְצַעֲקוּ[15] מָרָה,
סִפְדוּ תַּמְרוּר הֵאָגְדוּ בַּחֲבוּרָה,[16]
קוֹל כַּחוֹלָה צָרָה כְּמַבְכִּירָה,[17]
הִתְאוֹנְנוּ עַל עֲדַת שֶׂה פְזוּרָה,
עָלֵימוֹ כִּי נִגְזְרָה גְזֵרָה, בָּחֳרִי אַף וָזַעַם וְעֶבְרָה,[18]
וְנִתְוַעֲדוּ בִּפְרִישׁוּת וּבְטָהֳרָה, לְקַדֵּשׁ שֵׁם הַגָּדוֹל וְהַנּוֹרָא,

---

§ **הַחֲרִישׁוּ מִמֶּנִּי** — *Be silent and leave me be.* In vivid prose and sharp detail this *kinnah*, of unknown authorship, captures the anguish of a survivor of an unknown massacred community whose emotions are still storming and seething and whose tears are not yet dry. It describes the untenable tragedy of loving parents forced to slaughter their cherished children by their own hand, to save them from excruciating torture and mutilation at the hand of the enemy. All this was

22.

Be silent and leave me be so that I may speak out;*
let whatever may befall me,[1]
I shall scream to You, Who dwells in the Heavens,
over the violence and pillage.[2]
My spirit presses me and I cannot remain still,
I shall cry like a woman in birth travail, I shall pant and gasp.[3]
I shall compose a bitter dirge and I shall lament as I moan.
The words of my roars shall roll out like [the waves of] the sea.[4]
I eulogize my community which has been given over to desolation.
I shall lament as I speak and I shall moan,[5]
and I shall raise the sound of lament.
O how joy is halted and gladness darkened;
every face is blackened[6] *and every head is bald,*
every beard is clipped[7] *and on every heart a sigh,*
ever since the powerful nation aroused itself to seek
[the means to cast us into] the pit,[8]
He trampled my heroes,[9] *those who study*
our secure stronghold [the Torah].
My maidens and my youths, he uprooted with devastation;
on every street corner[10] *their corpses lay like refuse.*[11]
My infants and my babes were treated like sheep for the slaughter.[12]
About this shall I wail,[13] *my tears on [my] cheek.*[14]
Gather around me, O suffering lost sheep,
to intensify [your] weeping and to scream even louder.
Howl, O Heaven, and shout out, O Earth.
I shall lament as I speak and I shall moan, and I shall raise the sound of lament.
O Erelim, go forth and shout*[15] *bitterly,*
assemble in groups for most bitter eulogy,[16]
cry like a woman in travail, with the pain
of one undergoing her first childbirth.[17]
Mourn for the flock of scattered sheep,
for the decree was issued against them
with blazing anger, rage and wrath.[18]
They gathered themselves in abstinence and purity
to sanctify the Great and Awesome Name,

(1) Cf. *Job* 13:13. (2) Cf. *Habakkuk* 1:2-3. (3) *Isaiah* 42:14. (4) Cf. *Job* 3:24. (5) *Psalms* 55:3. (6) Cf. *Joel* 2:6. (7) Cf. *Jeremiah* 48:37; some editions read גְּרוּעָה, *diminished,* which is the word used in Scriptures. (8) Some editions read כּוֹרֶה שׁוּחָה, *to dig a pit;* cf. *Jeremiah* 18:22. (9) Cf. *Eichah* 1:15. (10) 2:19. (11) Cf. *Isaiah* 5:25. (12) Cf. *Psalms* 44:23. (13) Cf. *Micah* 1:8. (14) Cf. *Eichah* 1:2. (15) Cf. *Isaiah* 33:7. (16) Cf. *Jeremiah* 6:26. (17) Cf. 4:31. (18) Cf. *Psalms* 78:49.

performed in a spirit of utmost piety and purity to sanctify the Name of God. Furthermore, it describes how the greatest Torah scholars were murdered and how their books and manuscripts were mercilessly consigned to the flames.

It concludes with a question and a challenge to God, 'How long will You continue to witness this indifferently? ... Will You not seek revenge for the blood spilled like gushing streams?'

The particular tragedy about which this *kinnah* was written is unknown. It very aptly describes any one of many massacres and pogroms that have formed a large part of Jewish history.

אֶרְאֶלִּים — *Erelim.* We lack the vocabulary to distinguish between the varieties of angels.

וְאִישׁ אֶת אָחִיו חִזְּקוּ בְּעֶזְרָה,[1]
לְהִדָּבֵק בְּיִרְאָה טְהוֹרָה, בְּלִי כְּרוֹעַ לַעֲבוֹדָה זָרָה,
וְלֹא חָסוּ גֶּבֶר וּגְבִירָה,
עַל בָּנִים צְפִירַת תִּפְאָרָה,
אֲבָל אָזְרוּ גְּבוּרָה יְתֵרָה,
לַהֲלוֹם רֹאשׁ וְלִקְרוֹץ שֶׁדְרָה,
וְאֵלִימוּ דִּבְּרוּ בַּאֲמִירָה,
לֹא זָכִינוּ לְגַדֶּלְכֶם לַתּוֹרָה,
נַקְרִיבְכֶם כְּעוֹלָה וְהַקְטָרָה,
וְנִזְכֶּה עִמָּכֶם לְאוֹרָה, הַצְּפוּנָה מֵעֵין כֹּל נַעֲלוּמָה.
אָרִיד בְּשִׂיחִי וְאָהִימָה, וְקוֹל נְהִי אָרִימָה.
אָז הִסְכִּימוּ גְּדוֹלִים וּקְטַנִּים,
לְקַבֵּל בְּאַהֲבָה דִּין שׁוֹכֵן מְעוֹנִים,
וּזְקֵנִים דְּשֵׁנִים וְרַעֲנַנִּים,[2] הֵם הָיוּ תְּחִלָּה נִדּוֹנִים,
וְיָצְאוּ לִקְרָאתָם עַזֵּי פָנִים, וְנֶהֶרְגוּ הֲמוֹנִים הֲמוֹנִים,
וְנִתְעָרְבוּ פְּרָדִים עִם פַּרְשְׁדוֹנִים,
וְהָאָבוֹת אֲשֶׁר הָיוּ רַחֲמָנִים,
נֶהֶפְכוּ לְאַכְזָר כַּיְּעֵנִים,[3]
וְהֵפִּיסוּ עַל אָבוֹת וְעַל בָּנִים,
וּמִי שֶׁגּוֹרָל עָלָה לוֹ רִאשׁוֹנִים,
הוּא נִשְׁחַט בַּחֲלָפוֹת וְסַכִּינִים,
וּבַחוּרִים עֲלֵי תוֹלָע אֱמוּנִים,[4]
הֵם לָחֲכוּ עָפָר כְּתַנִּינִים,[5]
וְהַכַּלּוֹת לְבוּשׁוֹת שָׁנִים, מְעֻלָּפוֹת בִּזְרוֹעוֹת חֲתָנִים,
מִתְנַחוֹת בְּחֶרֶב וְכִידוֹנִים,
זִכְרוּ זֹאת קְהַל עֲדַת נְבוֹנִים,
וְאַל תֶּחֱשׁוּ מֵהַרְבּוֹת קִינִים,
וְהַסְפִּידוּ עַל חֲסִידִים וַהֲגוּנִים,
אֲשֶׁר צָלְלוּ בַּמַּיִם הַזֵּידוֹנִים,
לְזֵכֶר זֹאת נַפְשִׁי עֲגוּמָה.

אָרִיד בְּשִׂיחִי וְאָהִימָה, וְקוֹל נְהִי אָרִימָה.

and each man encouraged the other with succor,[1]
[enabling him] to embrace [God] with pure awe,
and not to kneel to strange gods.
Neither a man nor a woman showed weakening pity
for the [children whose] faces were like a splendid tiara.
Instead, they girded themselves with abnormal courage
to smash the head and sever the spine.
Then they addressed them with these words,
'We merited not to raise you in the Torah['s ways],
let us then bring you nearer [to God],
like burnt-offering and incense.
May we merit sharing with you the light
that is concealed and hidden from the eyes of all.

I shall lament as I speak and I shall moan, and I shall raise the sound of lament.

Then young and old agreed
to accept lovingly the decision
of the One Who Dwells in the heavens.
The aged who were nevertheless still vigorous and fresh,[2]
it was they who were judged the first [to be executed].
The insolent [enemy] went forth against them
and slaughtered multitudes upon multitudes,
until there was a [gruesome heap] of
intermingled fats and intestinal wastes.
Then the Fathers who were once compassionate
turned cruel as ostriches,[3]
and they cast lots over parents and children
and whomever the lot came upon first,
he was slaughtered with blades and knives.
Youths brought up in scarlet clothing[4]
now licked the dust like serpents;[5]
and brides dressed in scarlet
swooned into the arms of their husbands,
[where they were] butchered by sword and spears.
Remember this, assembled congregation of the wise,
and dare not be silenced from abundant lamentations!
Eulogize the pious and proper ones
who sank in the treacherous waters.
At the memory of this, my soul is grieved.

I shall lament as I speak and I shall moan, and I shall raise the sound of lament.

(1) Cf. *Isaiah* 41:6. (2) Cf. *Psalms* 92:15. (3) Cf. *Eichah* 4:3. (4) Cf. 4:5. (5) Cf. *Micah* 7:17.

Rambam (*Yesodei HaTorah* 2:7) enumerates ten levels: *Chayos, Ofanim, Erelim, Chashmalim, Seraphim, Malachim, Elohim, Bnei Elohim, Cheruvim,* and *Ishim.*

תּוֹרָה תּוֹרָה חִגְרִי שַׂק וְהִתְפַּלְּשִׁי בָּאֲפָרִים,
אֵבֶל יָחִיד עֲשִׂי לָךְ וּמִסְפַּד תַּמְרוּרִים,[1]
עַל תּוֹפְשֵׂי מְשׁוּטַיִךְ וּפוֹרְשֵׂי מַכְמוֹרִים,
מַלָּחַיִךְ וְחוֹבְלַיִךְ בְּמַיִם אַדִּירִים,[2]
עוֹרְכֵי מַעֲרָכַיִךְ, מְיַשְּׁרֵי הַדּוּרִים,[3]
מְפַעַנְחֵי צְפוּנַיִךְ וּמְגַלֵּי מִסְתּוֹרִים,
מִי יְקַצֵּה בִּגְבָעוֹת וּמִי יְסַתֵּת בֶּהָרִים,
וּמִי יְפָרֵק הֲוָיוֹת וּמִי יְתָרֵץ שְׁבָרִים,
מִי יַפְלִיא נְזִירוֹת וּמִי יַעֲרוֹךְ נְדָרִים,
מִי יְשַׁדֵּד מַעֲמַקַּיִךְ וְחַתּוּ אִכָּרִים,
וּמִי יִלְחוֹם מִלְחַמְתֵּךְ וְיָשׁוּב לַשְּׁעָרִים,
כְּלֵי מִלְחָמָה אָבְדוּ וְנָפְלוּ גִבּוֹרִים.[4]
אַשְׁרֵיהֶם מַשְׂכִּילִים כָּרָקִיעַ זוֹהֲרִים,[5]
בִּמְנוּחוֹת שָׁלוֹם נָחוּ יְשָׁרִים, אוֹי וַאֲבוֹי שׁוֹד וָשֶׁבֶר לְנוֹתָרִים,
לְמְדִיבַת נֶפֶשׁ[6] וַחֲבָלִים וְצִירִים,
לְכִלְיוֹן עֵינַיִם[7] צַלְמָוֶת וְלֹא סְדָרִים,
עֶרֶב אוֹמְרִים מִי יִתֵּן צְפָרִים, וּבֹקֶר מְצַפִּים מִי יְגַלֶּה אוֹרִים,*
מִמַּרְאֵה עֵינֵימוֹ אֲשֶׁר הֵמָּה שָׁרִים,[8]
מִחוּץ שִׁכְּלָה חֶרֶב וְאֵימָה מֵחֲדָרִים,[9]*
עַד מָתַי תַּבִּיט רוֹאֶה כָּל סְתָרִים,
קַנֵּא לְתוֹרָתְךָ אֲשֶׁר שְׂרָפוּהָ זָרִים,
קְלָאוּהָ פְּרָעוּהָ קְרָעוּהָ לִגְזָרִים,
כְּסִירִים סְבוּכִים הִגְדִּילוּ הַמְּדוּרִים,
הַעַל אֵלֶּה תִתְאַפַּק[10] אֲדוֹן כָּל יְצוּרִים,
תִּנְקוֹם דָּם הַנִּשְׁפָּךְ כַּמַּיִם הַמֻּגָּרִים,
מִשּׁוֹד עֲנִיִּים מֵאֶנְקַת סְעוּרִים,[11]
עִם שָׁבֵי פֶשַׁע לְעוֹנִים וּמְרוּרִים רַחֲמָה,
אוֹתָם בַּל תַּחֲרִימָה, קַרְנָם הַגְבִּיהַּ וְהָרִימָה.

אָרִיד בְּשִׂיחִי וְאָהִימָה וְקוֹל נְהִי אָרִימָה.

מִי יְגַלֶּה אוֹרִים — *O who will remove the daylight [and bring on evening]?* The root גלה has two diametrically opposite meanings. It can mean *to exile, to remove,* or *to uncover, to reveal.* The translation uses the first meaning. Alternatively, the phrase may be translated according to the second meaning, *O who will reveal the night-time luminaries?*

Torah, O Torah, gird yourself in sackcloth and roll yourself in ashes,
make yourself mourn for your only son; [recite the] most bitter eulogy[1]
over those who hold the oars and spread the nets,
your sailors and those who man the ropes through
the mighty waters[2] *[of the sea of Talmud],*
[They are the ones] who organize [Torah themes according to]
logical arrangements that clarify complicated issues.[3]
who explain Your hidden [wisdom] and uncover its secrets.
Who will [now] cut through the heights,
and who will [now] carve through the mountains?
Who will [now] clarify the issues, and who will [now]
answer the [earth-]shattering [questions]?
Who will [now] interpret the [intricacies of] Nazirite vows, and who will
[now] arrange [the complex laws of] oaths [and their annulment]?
Who will plow through your depths when
the farmers have been cut down?
And who will wage your battles and return [Israel]
to the gates [of the House of Torah Study],
[now that] the weapons are lost, and the heroes have fallen?[4]
Fortunate are those wise [martyrs] who are radiant as the firmament,[5]
these upright ones rest in peaceful repositories.
Woe and wailing, plunder and devastation; for the survivors,
for those miserable of spirit,[6] *travail and torment;*
for those of failing eyes,[7] *the shadow of death and anarchy.*
Eveningtime they say, 'O who will make it morning!'
And morning they anxiously say, 'O who will remove the daylight
*[and bring on evening]?'**
[This,] because of the [frightful] sights their eyes behold.[8]
Outside the sword cuts down while terror reigns within;[9]*
O how long will You watch [indifferently],
You Who sees everything hidden?
Avenge Your Torah, which strangers have burnt;
they scorched it, they vandalized it, they ripped it to pieces.
They enlarged the pyre [with stacks of Torah volumes]
like piles of tangled thornbrush.
Shall You restrain Yourself[10] *over such deeds,*
O Master of everything created?
Seek revenge for the blood spilled like falling waters,
for the plundering of the poor, for the cry of the storm-tossed.[11]
Upon the people who repent transgression,
who are sated with wormwood and bitterness,
take pity; do not allow them to be annihilated.
Elevate and exalt their honor.

I shall lament as I speak and I shall moan, and I shall raise the sound of lament.

(1) Cf. *Jeremiah* 6:26. (2) Cf. *Ezekiel* 27:27-29. (3) Cf. *Isaiah* 45:2. (4) Cf. *II Samuel* 1:27. (5) Cf. *Daniel* 12:3. (7) Cf. *Deuteronomy* 28:65. (8) Cf. 28:67. (9) Cf. 32: 25. (10) *Isaiah* 64:11. (11) Cf. *Psalms* 12:6.

מִחוּץ ... מֵחֲדָרִים — *Outside ... within* [lit., *from the chambers*]. The translation follows one of the interpretations given by *Rashi* (*Deuteronomy* 32:25). According to *Rashi's* other interpre-

כג.

וְאֶת נָוִי חַטָּאתִי הִשְׁמִימָה,*
וְדִמְעָתִי עַל לֶחְיִי אַזְרִימָה.
וּבְיוֹם זֶה נְהִי נִהְיָה אָרִימָה,
וְאָהִימָה מִיָּמִים יָמִימָה.

אֵבֶל לֵב וְנִחוּם חָדַל חָדוֹל,
וּמִכָּל כְּאֵב צִירִי נִבְדַּל בָּדוֹל,
עַל בֵּן וּבַת רַבִּי יִשְׁמָעֵאל כֹּהֵן גָּדוֹל,
זִכְרָם יְקוֹד בִּלְבָבִי אָשִׂימָה.
וְאָהִימָה מִיָּמִים יָמִימָה.

עֵת נִשְׁבּוּ וְנָפְלוּ לִשְׁנֵי אֲדוֹנִים,
וְהֵם שְׁכֵנִים זֶה לְעֻמַּת זֶה חוֹנִים,
וַיְסַפְּרוּ זֶה לָזֶה עִנְיָנִים,
זֶה אָמַר מִשִּׁבְיַת צִיּוֹנִים,
שָׁבִיתִי שִׁפְחָה לְבוּשַׁת שָׁנִים,
כַּלְּבָנָה בְּזִיו וּקְלַסְתֵּר פָּנִים,
וּבְתֹאַר כִּקְצִיעָה וִימִימָה.*
וְאָהִימָה מִיָּמִים יָמִימָה.

רֵעֵהוּ סִפֵּר לוֹ בְּכִפְלַיִם,
הֵן אֲנִי מִשִּׁבְיֵי יְרוּשָׁלַיִם,
שָׁבִיתִי עֶבֶד יְפֵה עֵינַיִם,
כַּשֶּׁמֶשׁ בְּתָקְפּוֹ עֵת צָהֳרַיִם,
בֹּא וּנְזַוֵּג וּנְחַלְּקָה בִּנְתַּיִם,
בִּוְלָדוֹת כְּמוֹ כוֹכְבֵי שָׁמַיִם,
לִשְׁמַע זֹאת תְּצַלֶּנָה אָזְנַיִם,
לְזֵכֶר זֹאת אֶת מַדַּי אַפְרִימָה.
וְאָהִימָה מִיָּמִים יָמִימָה.

כְּהִסְכִּימוּ עַל זֹאת שְׁנֵיהֶם יַחַד,
לָעֶרֶב זִוּוּגוּם בְּחֶדֶר אֶחָד,
וְהָאֲדוֹנִים מִבַּחוּץ לִבָּם כְּאֶחָד,

23.

*My sin caused the destruction of my Temple,**
so I shall cause my tears to run down my cheeks;
and on this day I shall raise a doleful lament.
And I shall moan [about this] each year on this day.

The heart mourns, yet refuses consolation,
and from all other pain is my pain set apart,
upon [the fate of] the son and daughter of Rabbi Yishmael the Kohen Gadol;
I shall set their memory as a fire in my heart.
And I shall moan [about this] each year on this day.

When they were captured, they fell to two different masters,
who were neighbors dwelling across from one another;
they discussed their affairs between themselves.
One said, 'From the captivity of Zion
I have captured a maid-servant dressed in scarlet-wool,
[her] features as bright as the moon,
*as beautiful as Keziah and Jemimah!'**
And I shall moan [about this] each year on this day.

His neighbor responded with double [those praises],
'I [too] have come from the captivity of Jerusalem,
where I captured a man-servant with eyes so beautiful,
as the sun in its full splendor at high noon!
Come, let us pair them and divide between us
their children who will be abundant as the stars of the heavens!'
At these tidings all ears will ring;
to commemorate this, I shall rend my robe!
And I shall moan [about this] each year on this day.

Once the two of them had approved this [plan],
they paired [brother and sister] together that evening in one room.
The masters waited outside, their hearts as one,

---

tations: *Outside* refers to the battlefield outside the city, and *chambers* refers to the fugitives from the battlefield who succumbed to the terror throbbing in the chamber of their hearts; or *outside* alludes to overt idolatry (see, e.g., *Jeremiah* 11:13) and *chambers* to covert idolatry (see, e.g., *Ezekiel* 8:12).

⇐§ וְאֶת נָוִי חַטָּאתִי הִשְׁמִימָה — *My sin caused the destruction of my Temple.* The story of the son and daughter of R' Yishmael ben Elisha, the *Kohen Gadol,* (see *kinnah* 21) is related in the Talmud (*Gittin* 58a). It is interesting to note that the Midrash contains a very similar, though more complicated, narrative about the son and daughter of Tzaddok HaKohen (*Midrash Eichah* 1:46). In each case, the young pair's moral purity set an example of chastity and righteousness that became an example for future generations. Neither youth nor maiden complained about the personal tragedy each underwent. Rather, it was the *chillul Hashem,* the desecration of God's Holy Name, that was the point of their plaints. And it was for this reason that Jeremiah prophetically wailed and lamented for this brother and sister so many centuries earlier.

וּבְתֹאַר כִּקְצִיעָה וִימִימָה — *As beautiful as Keziah and Jemimah.* Job had three daughters:

וְהֵם בּוֹכִים בְּמַר נֶפֶשׁ וָפַחַד,
עַד בֹּקֶר בִּכְיָתָם לֹא הִדְמִימָה.
וְאָהֱימָה מִיָּמִים יָמֶימָה.

זֶה יִסְפּוֹד בְּחִיל וּבְקִיר לֵב יִמְסֶה,
נִין אַהֲרֹן אֵיךְ לְשִׁפְחָה יְהִי נוֹשֵׂא,
וְהִיא גַם הִיא תְּיַלֵּל בְּתִגְרַת שׁוֹסֶה,
בַּת יוֹכֶבֶד אֵיךְ לְעֶבֶד תִּנָּשֵׂא,
אוֹי כִּי זֹאת גָּזַר אוֹמֵר וְעֹשֶׂה,
לְזֹאת יִבְכּוּ עָשׁ וּכְסִיל וְכִימָה.[1]
וְאָהֱימָה מִיָּמִים יָמֶימָה.

אוֹר בֹּקֶר זֶה אֶת זֶה כְּהִכִּירוּ,
הוֹי אָחִי וְהוֹי אָחוֹת הִגְבִּירוּ.
וְנִתְדַּבְּקוּ יַחַד וְנִתְחַבְּרוּ,
עַד יָצְתָה נִשְׁמָתָם בִּנְשִׁימָה.
וְאָהֱימָה מִיָּמִים יָמֶימָה.

לָזֹאת יְקוֹנֵן יִרְמְיָהוּ בִּשְׁאִיָּה,
גְּזֵרָה זֹאת תָּמִיד אֲנִי בוֹכִיָּה,
וּבִלְבָבִי יֵקַד יְקוֹד וּכְוִיָּה,
עַל בֵּן וּבַת מִסְפַּד רַב אַרְעִימָה.[2]
אָרִיד בְּשִׂיחִי וְאָהֱימָה,
וְקוֹל נְהִי אָרִימָה.

Jemimah, Keziah and Keren-happuch. *And there were not to be found in all the land, women as beautiful as the daughter of Job* (Job 42:15).

but [the young couple] wept with bitter soul and fear,
their weeping was not stilled until the morning.
And I shall moan [about this] each year on this day.

He mourned all atremble; inside, his heart was melting,
'A scion of Aaron, can he be wed to a maid-servant?'
While she also bemoaned her captor's deal,
'A daughter of Yocheved, can she be wed to a slave?'
Woe! For this is the decree of [God],
Who says [something] and does [it].
Upon this [tragedy], even [the constellations] Ursa,
Orion and Pleiades[1] weep!
And I shall moan [about this] each year on this day.

At the light of dawn, they recognized one another,
they intensified [their cries], 'Woe! Brother!' and 'Woe! Sister!'
They embraced each other and were cleaved together,
until both their souls left them, in the very same breath.
And I shall moan [about this] each year on this day.

For this Jeremiah lamented amidst the Destruction,
'I shall weep continually,
and in my heart is kindled a flame and a burn,
for this son and daughter I will thunder forth a great lament.[2]
I shall lament as I speak, and I shall moan,
and I shall raise the sound of lament.'

(1) *Job* 9:9; see commentary to *kinnah* 5.
(2) Some editions read אַעֲצִימָה, but the meaning is the same.

כד.

עַל חֻרְבַּן בֵּית הַמִּקְדָּשׁ,
כִּי הוּרַס וְכִי הוּדַשׁ,
אֶסְפּוֹד בְּכָל שָׁנָה וְשָׁנָה מִסְפֵּד חָדָשׁ,
עַל הַקֹּדֶשׁ וְעַל הַמִּקְדָּשׁ.

תִּסָּתֵר לְאַלֵּם תַּרְשִׁישִׁים* מֵרוֹן,
כְּזִעֲזַעְתָּ עוֹלָם מִפְּנֵי חָרוֹן,
כְּלִהֲטָה הָאֵשׁ בֵּין שְׁנֵי בַּדֵּי אָרוֹן.

שְׁנֵי מִקְדָּשִׁים אֲשֶׁר בְּמַעְלָה וּבְמַטָּה,
זֶה עַל גַּב זֶה[1] הוּאֳפָלוּ בַּעֲלָטָה,
וְנַמְתָּ אַחֲרִישׁ וְאֶתְאַפַּק[2] וְאַבִּיטָה.

רָאשֵׁי הַבַּדִּים כְּנִגְנְזוּ* מִבֵּין הַפָּרוֹכוֹת,*
וְאַרְבַּע גֶּחָלִים* בִּדְבִיר מְהַלְּכוֹת,
וְאַרְבָּעִים יְסוֹד עַד תְּהוֹם מְלַחֲכוֹת.

קֹדֶשׁ הַקֳּדָשִׁים מִבֵּית קֹדֶשׁ כְּנִבְדַּד,
שַׁחְתָּ וְהֵילַלְתָּ אָהֳלֵי שֻׁדַּד,[3]
וְנַמְתָּ אַכֶּה כַּף עַל כַּף[4] וְאֶשְׁאַג הֵידָד.[5]

צְפִירַת תִּפְאַרְתָּךְ כְּנִתְּנָה בְּיַד צָר,
וְכָל כְּלֵי חֶמְדָּה אִוּוּי בֵּית הָאוֹצָר,[6]
וּלְךָ הַכֹּחַ וְהַגְּבוּרָה[7] וְנָמוּ עָצָר.

⊲§ עַל חֻרְבַּן בֵּית הַמִּקְדָּשׁ — *Over the Destruction of the Temple.* This *kinnah,* by Rabbi Elazar HaKalir, focuses on yet another tragic aspect of the Temple's Destruction. Not only was the Temple edifice destroyed but its furnishings, adornments and holy vessels were plundered too. Each one of these components was designed to reflect the celestial Temple in the heavens above where the ministering angels offer their fiery and awesome paeans of praise to the Almighty. Moreover, each corresponded to some particular natural phenomenon (such as rain or dew). Here we lament the fact that these very adornments and vessels were ignominiously vandalized by the vile hand of Nebuchadnezzar and then sent as gifts to adorn the pagan temples of the Babylonian Empire. Here we mourn this terrible degradation that befell both the terrestrial and celestial Temples. Here we grieve over the diminution of benefits derived from the phenomena of nature.

The *kinnah* follows a reverse-alphabetical format, beginning with the second stanza.

לְאַלֵּם תַּרְשִׁישִׁים — *To silence the celestial angels.* On three occasions when the angels in their heavenly array were about to begin their daily songs of God's praises, He stopped them: during the Flood in Noah's time; when the Egyptians were drowning in the Sea of Reeds; and at the Destruction of the *Beis HaMikdash* (*Midrash Eichah,* intro. 24, as interpreted by *Yefeh Anaf*). The *paytan* alludes to the Flood and the drowning with the words, *when You made the world shudder before Your fiery anger,* and to the Destruction with, *when the*

24.

Over the Destruction of the Temple,
that was torn down and trampled upon,
I shall lament with a new elegy every year,
for the holy [vessels] and for the Sanctuary.

ת *You hid Yourself in order to silence*
the celestial angels from their songs,*
When You made the world shudder before Your fiery anger,
[and] when the flames flared between the two poles of the Ark.

ש *When these two Temples, the one above and the one below —*
one directly over the other — were[1] both enshrouded in darkness,
You said, 'I will be silent, I will hold myself back,[2] I will observe.'

ר *When the heads of the poles were [removed*
from] behind the Curtains, and hidden,**
four [flaming] coals blazed in the Holy of Holies*
and the forty foundation pillars were burnt to the depths.

ק *When the Holy of Holies was desolated*
and ceased to be a holy habitation,
You proclaimed and wailed, 'My Tent is plundered!'[3]
And you said, 'I shall clap My hands,
one on the other,[4] and I shall roar, "O woe!"'[5]

צ *When the crown of Your glory [the Temple]*
was delivered into the hands of Your tormentors, —
with all the precious vessels,
the most desirable of the treasure house;[6]
You to Whom belongs the strength and the power[7]
allowed them to exult, 'He has been restrained!'

(1) See *kinnah* 5. (2) *Isaiah* 42:14. (3) *Jeremiah* 10:20. (4) Cf. *Ezekiel* 21:22.
(5) See *Jeremiah* 48:33 with *Rashi*. (6) Cf. *Hosea* 13:15. (7) Cf. *I Chronicles* 29:11.

flames flared between the two poles of the Ark (*Beis Levi*).

מִבֵּין הַפָּרוֹכוֹת — *Behind the Curtains.* Although the Torah speaks of only one *Paroches*-Curtain in the Tabernacle, there were two in the Second Temple (see *Yoma* 47a).

כְּנִגְנְזוּ — *When the ...were [removed ...] and hidden.* The Talmudic Sages discuss the fate of the Ark. Some maintain that it was taken by Nebuchadnezzar when he conquered the First Temple. Others hold, and this is the opinion of the *paytan*, that when King Josiah was informed by the prophets of the impending Destruction, he had the Ark removed from its place in the Holy of Holies and hidden in one of the underground passageways that Solomon had built beneath the *Beis HaMikdash* (*Yoma* 54b; *Shekalim* 6:2).

וְאַרְבַּע גֶּחָלִים — *Four [flaming] coals.* While the enemy was debating how to set fire to the *Beis HaMikdash*, the angels were debating with God (as it were) whether to permit the Destruction to take place. Finally, the Divine Attribute of Strict Justice came to the fore and said, 'Master of the world, do You want this wicked man to be able to boast, "I have destroyed God's Temple! I have burnt His Sanctuary!" No! It is better that a heavenly fire be sent down upon it ... Then, if the Babylonians claim supremacy because of their victory, Jerusalem will be able to retort, "You have slain an already dying lion! You have ground already milled flour! You have kindled an already burned city!"' (*Midrash Eichah* 1:41). Suddenly the conquerors looked up and saw four flaming coals descend from heaven upon the four corners of the Temple and set it afire (*Pesikta Rabbah* 27:6).

פְּנֵי הַכִּסֵּא אָז אֻמְלָּלוּ,
וְגָבְהֵי שָׁמַיִם לְקַדְרוּת הוּשְׁפָּלוּ,
יָכִין וּבוֹעַז[1] לְהִשְׁתַּבֵּר כְּנָפָלוּ,
עֲשָׂרָה שֻׁלְחָנוֹת[2]* אָז שֻׁלָּלוּ,
וּלְעוֹרְכֵיהֶם נָמוּ אַיֵּה אֲדוֹן אֵלּוּ,
לְאוֹצְרוֹת שִׁנְעָר לְקָדָשִׁים כְּהוּנְחָלוּ.
שְׂרָפִים עוֹמְדִים[3] נָעוּ מִמַּעֲמָד,
כְּנֶהֶרְסוּ מְכוֹנוֹת[4] מִתּוֹךְ מַחְמָד,
וְזֵדִים קָרְאוּ יְמֵי הַשְּׁמַד.
נְחֹשֶׁת יָם[5] וַעֲשָׂרָה כִּיּוֹרוֹת,[6]
כְּנִמְסְרוּ לְבֵל וְהִנָּם שְׁבוּרוֹת,*
וּשְׁנֵי הַמְּאוֹרוֹת מֵאָז קְדוֹרוֹת.[7]
מַעֲשֵׂה הָאוֹפַנִּים אֲשֶׁר בַּמֶּרְכָּבָה,[8]
כְּהוּרְדוּ לָאָרֶץ וְזֹהַר הָרָקִיעַ כָּבָה,
חוֹלֵשׁ עַל גּוֹיִם[9]* לִפְנֵי כְרוּבִים בָּא.
לוֹיוֹת הַמּוֹרָד[10] מֵעֵת הוּרָדוּ,
וְהַטְּלָלִים לִבְרָכָה לֹא יָרָדוּ,
אֲנָשִׁים רָעִים עַל בָּמֳתֵי עָב דָּדוּ.[11]
כָּל כְּלֵי כֶסֶף וּכְלֵי הַזָּהָב,
קֻצְּצוּ וְשֻׁסּוּ מִבֵּית הַלַּהַב,
בְּצֵאת הֶהָדָר שָׁחוּ עוֹזְרֵי רַהַב.[12]
יוֹם אֲשֶׁר נִקְרָא מְהוּמָה וּמְבוּכָה,[13]
לַהֲקַת מַלְאָכִים כְּאִשָּׁה מְצֵרָה נְבוֹכָה,
דִּבּוּר פָּתַח וְעָנוּ אַחֲרָיו אֵיכָה.

(1) See *I Kings* 7:21. (2) See *II Chronicles* 4:8. (3) See commentary to *kinnah* 22, s.v. אֶרְאֶלִּים, *Erelim.* (4) See *I Kings* 7:27ff. (5) See 7:23 ff. (6) See 7:38. (7) Cf. *Joel* 2:10. (8) Cf. *I Kings* 7:33. (9) *Isaiah* 14:12. (10) See *I Kings* 7:29. (11) Cf. *Isaiah* 14:14. (12) Cf. *Eichah* 1:6; *Job* 9:13. (13) Cf. *Isaiah* 22:5.

עֲשָׂרָה שֻׁלְחָנוֹת — *Ten Tables.* The Torah ordains that a Golden Table be placed in the Sanctuary, upon which the *Panim*-breads are arranged. When King Solomon built the *Beis HaMikdash,* he enhanced that Table by placing five more to its right and five to its left (see *Rashi* to *II Chronicles* 4:8). These should not be confused with the thirteen tables of the Second Temple (see *Shekalim* 6:4) which served an entirely different purpose.

וְהִנָּם שְׁבוּרוֹת — *And behold, they were broken.* When these sturdy copper vessels were brought to Babylon for idolatrous purposes, they suddenly broke apart of their own accord (*Arugas HaBosem*).

פ *Then [the heavens] facing the Throne [of Glory] were darkened,*
and the celestial heights were plunged into blackness,
when [the two Temple pillars called] Yachin and Boaz[1]
fell and were smashed.

ע *Ten Tables*[2]* *were then taken as booty;*
and to [the priests] who once set them, [the enemy] said,
'Where is the Master of these [tables]?'
when [they were taken] to the treasure houses
of Shinar [Babylon], and bequeathed to harlots.

ס *The stationary Seraphim*[3] *were removed from their positions,*
when the bases [of the washstands][4]
were demolished within the [Temple of God's] delight,
while strangers proclaimed [that period as]
'The Days of Destruction'.

נ *When the copper [pool known as 'the] Sea [of Solomon']*[5]
and the ten washbasins[6]
were given over to the [worshipers of the idol]
*Bel, and, behold, they were broken —**
and ever since then the two luminaries
[the sun and the moon] have darkened.[7]

מ *When [the copper bases] designed in the shape of*
the wheels of the [Celestial] Chariot,[8]
were lowered to the ground, the brilliance
of the firmament was dimmed,
because [Nebuchadnezzar] who cast lots over the nations[9]*
entered into the presence of the Cherubim [in the Holy of Holies].

ל *When the engravings of the entwined [cherubs]*[10]
were taken down [from the Temple walls],
the dew ceased descending from the skies for a blessing,
while the vicious dogs [Nebuchadnezzar's hordes]
ascended above the cloud-wreathed heights.[11]

כ *All the silver and golden vessels*
were hacked to pieces and pillaged
from the abode of the Eternal Flame.
and when the splendor departed,
the ministering angels were demoted.[12]

י *On the day which was called 'Chaos and Confusion,'*[13]
bands of angels were left perplexed like a woman in birth travail,
until [the Almighty Himself] began to speak
[in lament and the angels] answered 'Eichah' after Him.

חוֹלֵשׁ עַל גּוֹיִם — *[Nebuchadnezzar] who cast lots over the nations.* Nebuchadnezzar would degrade the kings of the lands he had captured, by making them his personal servants. Daily lots would be cast to determine which king would serve him each day. According to the Sages, he

טָסוּ עֲמּוֹנִים וּמוֹאָבִים, וְהוֹצִיאוּ הַכְּרוּבִים,
וּבִכְלִיבָה הָיוּ אוֹתָם מְסַבְּבִים,
הִנֵּה כְּכָל הַגּוֹיִם בֵּית יְהוּדָה חֲשׁוּבִים.[1]
חֵיל שַׂרְפֵי הַקֹּדֶשׁ[2] חֻלַּף מִגְּדֻלָּתוֹ,
וְאֵל אַדִּיר שְׁמוֹ לֹא אָבָה תְהִלָּתוֹ,[3]
לְגַלִּים הוּשַׂם בֵּית תְּפִלָּתוֹ.
זְמָרֵי שַׁחַק הֶחֱשׁוּ מִנֹּעַם,
וְנָם מַה לָּכֶם פֹּה אֵין הַיּוֹם טַעַם,
מַה תְּקַלְּסוּן לַמֶּלֶךְ בִּשְׁעַת הַזַּעַם.
וְהַכֹּהֲנִים וְהַלְוִיִּם עַל מִשְׁמְרוֹתָם נִשְׁחָטִים,
וְעַל מַחְלְקוֹתָם שַׁעֲטַת אִסְטַרְדִּיוֹטִים,
וְנָמוּ אַיֵּה מֶלֶךְ אָסוּר בָּרְהָטִים.[4]
הַכֵּלִים וְהַמְשַׁמְּשִׁים בַּשְּׁבִי הוֹלְכִים,
וְהַשָּׂרִים וְהַסְּגָנִים בַּכֶּבֶל מְשׁוּכִים,
וּתְמוּר בַּדִּים שַׂק חָגְרוּ מַלְאָכִים.
דָּץ לָבִיא וּפָקַח עֵינָיו,
וְהִנֵּה מִיכָאֵל מְהַלֵּךְ לְפָנָיו,
וְשָׂרִים* הוֹלְכִים כַּעֲבָדִים חָזוּ הֲמוֹנָיו.
גַּאֲוָה עָטָה וְכִבָּה הַמְּנוֹרָה,
וְנָטָה יָדוֹ אֶל אֵל[5] הַמּוֹרָא,
וַיַּחֲשִׁיךְ אוֹר עוֹטֶה אוֹרָה.[6]
בְּשַׁאֲגוֹ כָּאֲרִי בִּדְבִיר בֵּל,
בָּרַח דּוֹדִי וּכְעַל מֵת מִתְאַבֵּל,
פִּקְדוֹן הָרוּחוֹת בּוֹ בַּלַּיְלָה לֹא קִבֵּל.
אָמַר לַמַּשְׁחִיתִים חֲמָתִי הִתַּכְתִּי,[7]
אֶת יְדִידוּת נַפְשִׁי בְּכַף אוֹיְבֶיהָ נָתַתִּי,
עָזַבְתִּי אֶת בֵּיתִי וְאֶת נַחֲלָתִי נָטַשְׁתִּי.[8]

---

also used them for immoral purposes (*Rashi* to *Isaiah* 14:12).

וְשָׂרִים — *And ... [Jewish] nobles.* Alternatively, this alludes to the Midrash that tells how, when Nebuchadnezzar ordered crushing burdens placed on the captives' backs to break their noble stature, armies of angels descended to help the Jews bear their loads (*Midrash Tehillim* 137). Thus, the שָׂרִים are the *celestial princes.*

ט *The Ammonites and Moabites swept in and took out the Cherubim,*
and paraded them around [Jerusalem] in a cage,
saying, 'Behold, the House of Judah is to be considered
[idolatrous] like all the nations.'[1]

ח *The legions of holy Seraphim*[2] *were removed from their prominence,*
and God Whose Name is Mighty had no desire to be praised,[3]
when His House of Splendor was turned into piles of ruins.

ז *The angelic singers were silent from their pleasant [singing],*
because He said, 'What are you doing here? Today,
permission [to sing] has not been given!
How can you offer praise to the King at the time of fury?'

ו *The Kohanim and the Levites were slaughtered at their watches;*
they manned their posts despite the clamor
of the [Roman] commanders,
who asked, 'Where is the King who is bound under the roofbeams?'[4]

ה *The vessels and the ministers have gone into captivity,*
the nobles and the assistants were dragged away in shackles,
and instead of fine linen, the angels girded themselves in sackcloth.

ד *Lion[-like Nebuchadnezzar] rejoiced and opened up his eyes,*
and behold, [the archangel] Michael was going before him;
*and [Nebuchadnezzar's] hordes witnessed [Jewish] nobles**
going [into exile] like slaves.

ג *[Nebuchadnezzar] wrapped himself in arrogance*
and extinguished the Menorah,
then he stretched out his hand against God[5] *so Awesome,*
and darkened the light of God Who is enveloped in light.[6]

ב *When [Nebuchadnezzar who worshiped the idol] Bel*
roared like a lion in the Holy of Holies,
my Beloved fled and mourned as for the dead;
*on that night He did not accept the deposited souls.**

א *To the destructive angels, [God] said,*
'I have poured out My fury [over Jerusalem],[7]
I have placed the beloved of My soul [Israel]
into the hand of her enemies;
I have abandoned My Temple and forsaken My estate.'[8]

(1) Cf. *Ezekiel* 25:8. (2) Some editions read שַׂרְפֵי מַעְלָה, *celestial* or *exalted Seraphim.*
(3) See commentary above. (4) *Song of Songs* 7:6. (5) Cf. *Job* 15:25.
(6) Cf. *Psalms* 104:2. (7) Cf. *II Chronicles* 34:25. (8) Cf. *Jeremiah* 12:7.

פִּקְדוֹן הָרוּחוֹת בּוֹ בַּלַּיְלָה לֹא קִבֵּל — *On that night He did not accept the deposited souls.* Every night, when a person retires, his soul ascends to the heavens where it is held in safekeeping until morning (see *Psalms* 31:6). Moreover, it is invigorated and returned to its body in a fresh and renewed state — as it is stated: *They are new every morning; great is Your faithfulness* (*Eichah* 3:23). The *paytan* teaches us that on the night of the Destruction, God accepted no souls, for no one was able to sleep. Or, perhaps, no one could fall asleep, because God would not accept the souls.

כה.

מִי יִתֵּן רֹאשִׁי מַיִם* וְעֵינִי מְקוֹר נוֹזְלַי,
וְאֶבְכֶּה כָּל יְמוֹתַי וְלֵילַי,[1]
אֶת חַלְלֵי טַפִּי וְעוֹלָלַי, וִישִׁישֵׁי קְהָלַי,
וְאַתֶּם עֲנוּ אֲבוֹי אוֹי[2] וְאַלְלַי,
וּבְכֵן בָּכֹה בֶּכֶה[3] רַב וְהֶרֶב,
עַל בֵּית יִשְׂרָאֵל וְעַל עַם יהוה כִּי נָפְלוּ בֶּחָרֶב.[4]

וְדָמוֹעַ תִּדְמַע[5] עֵינִי וְאֵלְכָה לִי שְׂדֵה בוֹכִים,
וַאֲבַכֶּה עִמִּי מָרֵי לֵבָב הַנְּבוּכִים,
עַל בְּתוּלוֹת הַיָּפוֹת וִילָדִים הָרַכִּים,
בְּסִפְרֵיהֶם נִכְרָכִים וְלַטֶּבַח נִמְשָׁכִים,
אָדְמוּ עֶצֶם[6] מִפְּנִינִים סַפִּירִים וְנוֹפְכִים,
כְּמוֹ טִיט חוּצוֹת[7] נִדָּשִׁים וְנִשְׁלָכִים,
סוּרוּ טָמֵא קָרְאוּ לָמוֹ[8] מִלְּקָרֵב,
עַל בֵּית יִשְׂרָאֵל וְעַל עַם יהוה כִּי נָפְלוּ בֶּחָרֶב.

מִי יִתֵּן רֹאשִׁי מַיִם — *Would that my head were water.* Significantly, this is the first *kinnah* recited on the Ninth of Av that is clearly unrelated to the destruction of the two Temples. Indeed, this elegy mourns the calamity that befell the Jewish communities of the Rhineland — Worms, Speyer and Mainz (Mayence) — in the year 1096, during the First Crusade, over one thousand years after the destruction of the Second Temple. The inclusion of this lament in the Tishah B'Av ritual serves to demonstrate that the source and cause of all Jewish tragedies in exile can and must be traced back to the Destruction of our Temple. The following incident illustrates this concept vividly.

When the Jewish people became aware of the awesome devastation that befell our nation at the hands of the murderous Nazis in World War II, many sought to establish a new day of national mourning to commemorate *Churban Europa.* The contemporary Torah leaders were consulted. Among the responses was that of the *Brisker Rav, R' Yitzchak Zev Soloveitchik,* who said that the reply to this question lies in the *kinnah* before us. Why didn't the great Rabbis and Sages of that generation — among them the greatest of the *Rishonim,* including Rashi — establish a *new* day of national mourning to commemorate that *new* tragedy? The author of this *kinnah* addresses this question and offers this insight:

> Please take to your hearts to compose a bitter eulogy, / because their massacre is deservant of mourning and rolling in dust / as was the burning of the House of our God, its Hall and its Palace. / However, we cannot add a (new) day (of mourning) over ruin and conflagration, / nor may we mourn any earlier — only later. / Instead, today (on Tishah B'Av), I will arouse my sorrowful wailing, / and I will eulogize and wail and weep with a bitter soul, / and my groans are heavy from morning until evening.

Thus, the essential purpose of this *kinnah* is to drive home this lesson: There are really no *new* tragedies befalling Israel. All of our woes stem from one tragic source — the Destruction of the Temple on Tishah B'Av. To establish a new day of mourning would detract from the significance of Tishah B'Av and obscure its lesson and message. (See *Rashi* to *II Chronicles* 35:25.)

This *kinnah* also answers other major questions. Why does the exile continue? Why does God visit fresh calamities upon His people? Where have we gone astray?

One of the main reasons for the continuation of our exile is because Jews are often quite content and comfortable in their adopted, alien homelands and have all but lost their desire to return to the poverty and hardships of *Eretz Yisrael.* Slowly the Jew ceases to identify with his true home, the Holy Land, and begins to feel intense pride in his citizenship in his new country.

The destruction of the Jewish community of Worms in the German Rhineland was the work of the crusaders. How ironic! The crusaders were willing to leave everything behind — homes,

25.

*Would that my head were water,**
and my eye a fount of flowing tears,
that I might spend all my days and nights weeping,[1]
for my slaughtered children and infants,
and for the venerable oldsters of my congregation.
I call upon all of you to respond [to my cry], 'Vay! Ay![2] *Woe!'*
And cry profusely[3] *and intensify your weeping!*
Over the House of Israel and over the nation of HASHEM,
because they have fallen by the sword![4]

My eye shall be filled with copious tears,[5]
and I shall get me to the weeper's field.
I shall arouse the bitter of heart,
the confounded ones, to weep with me,
over the beautiful maidens and the tender lads,
wrapped in their scrolls and dragged to the slaughter.
Their appearance was ruddier[6] *than rubies,*
[more dazzling] than sapphires and gems,
yet they were trampled and discarded like the mud in the streets.[7]
'Turn away from the unclean [Jew]!'
they called to each other,[8] *lest they come too close.*
Over the House of Israel and over the nation of HASHEM,
because they have fallen by the sword!

(1) Cf. *Jeremiah* 8:23. (2) Cf. *Proverbs* 23:29. (3) Cf. *Ezra* 10:1. (4) Cf. *II Samuel* 1:12. (5) *Jeremiah* 13:17. (6) *Eichah* 4:7. (7) *II Samuel* 22:43. (8) *Eichah* 4:15.

families, occupations — in order to conquer the Holy Land they called Palestine, while the Jews themselves were filled with no such zeal to regain their own homeland! In heaven, this irony did not go unnoticed, but aroused a terrible denunciation against the Jewish people, and especially against the Jews of Worms and her neighboring communities.

The classic work on Jewish history, *Seder HaDoros,* by *R' Yechiel Halperin,* records the following observation in his entry for the year 5380 (1620):

> The author of the commentary *Sefer Meiras Eynayim (SMA)* on the *Shulchan Aruch* explained why the Jewish community of Worms suffered far more persecution, pogroms and evil decrees than other congregations. That *kehillah* was founded by Jewish exiles who made their way to Germany following the Destruction of the First Temple. After seventy years of exile, many Jews returned from Babylon to *Eretz Yisrael* and Jerusalem, but none returned from Worms. The community in Jerusalem wrote to the *kehillah* in Worms and urged them to join their new settlement in Jerusalem ... but the complacent Jews of Worms dismissed this invitation out of hand. Instead, they responded, 'You stay where you are in the great Jerusalem, and we will continue to stay where we are in our little Jerusalem!' This arrogant response was due to the prosperity and prestige the Jews of Worms enjoyed in the eyes of the local gentiles and their princes.

The success of Worms was its undoing! The prosperity of the Jew in exile is nothing more than a Divine test to see whether it will cause the Jew to forget his homeland and his heritage. Worms and the Rhineland failed and suffered bitterly. Before World War I a large portion of Germany's Jewish population failed because, as *Meshech Chochmah* (*Bechukosai*) observes, 'They began to call Berlin, Jerusalem!'

◆§ The Calamity of the First Crusade

On November 27, 1095, in Clermont (southeastern France) Pope Urban II called upon faithful Christians to join in arms to liberate the city of Jerusalem and its holy sites from the hands of the Moslem infidels who occupied it. Those who answered the call affixed crosses to their garments, and the campaign became known as *le Croisade* (from *croix,* French for cross), or the Crusade. At first, the Crusade seemed to pose no threat to the Jews who resided in peace with their Christian neighbors, but soon enough it became clear that the crusaders did not wish to wait until they reached far-off Palestine to 'avenge the

וְתֵרַד עֵינִי דִּמְעָה[1] וְאֵילִילָה וְאָנוּדָה,
וְלִבְכִּי וְלַחֲגוֹר שַׂק אֶקְרָא לְהַסְפִּידָה,
מִפָּז יְקָרָה וְזָהָב חֲמוּדָה,
פְּנִימָה כְּבוּדָה[2] כְּבוֹד כָּל כְּלִי חֶמְדָּה,
רְאִיתִיהָ קְרוּעָה שְׁכוּלָה וְגַלְמוּדָה,[3]
הַתּוֹרָה וְהַמִּקְרָא וְהַמִּשְׁנָה וְאַגָּדָה,
עֲנוּ וְקוֹנְנוּ זֹאת לְהַגִּידָה,
אֵי תוֹרָה תַּלְמִיד וְהַלּוֹמְדָהּ,
הֲלֹא הַמָּקוֹם מֵאֵין יוֹשֵׁב חָרֵב,[4]
עַל בֵּית יִשְׂרָאֵל וְעַל עַם יהוה כִּי נָפְלוּ בֶּחָרֶב.

וְעַפְעַפִּי יִזְּלוּ מַיִם דֶּמַע[5] לְהַגִּירָה,
וַאֲקוֹנֵן מַר עֲלֵי הֲרוּגֵי אַשְׁפִּירָה,*
בַּשֵּׁנִי בִּשְׁמוֹנָה בוֹ בְּיוֹם מַרְגּוֹעַ הַקְּרָה,
מֵרְגוֹעַ נֶחְלְפוּ לְהַבְעִירָה,
נֶהֶרְגוּ בַּחוּרֵי חֶמֶד[6] וִישִׁישֵׁי הֲדָרָה,
נֶאֶסְפוּ יַחַד נַפְשָׁם הִשְׁלִימוּ בְּמוֹרָא.
עַל יִחוּד שֵׁם הַמְּיֻחָד יִחֲדוּ שֵׁם בִּגְבוּרָה,
גִּבּוֹרֵי כֹחַ עוֹשֵׂי דְבָרוֹ[7] לְמַהֲרָה,
וְכֹהֲנֵי וְעֶלְמֵי נִגְוְעוּ כֻּלְּהֶם עֲשָׂרָה.

וּבְמַר יְגוֹנִי וְעָצְבִּי יֶלֶל אַחְבִּירָהּ,
קְהִלּוֹת הַקֹּדֶשׁ הֲרִיגָתָם הַיּוֹם בְּזָכְרָה,
קְהַל וַרְמַיְזָא* בְּחוּנָה וּבְחוּרָה,
גְּאוֹנֵי אֶרֶץ וּנְקִיֵּי טָהֳרָה,

blood of their savior.' In truth, it was their envy of the prosperous Jewish communities that incited the vulgar rabble and the greedy nobility to punish 'the murderers of their lord' wherever they passed. It was rumored that the French leader of the Crusades, Godfrey of Bouillon, had taken a solemn vow that he would avenge the blood of the crucifixion with the blood of the Jews and that he would not tolerate even one Jewish soul remaining alive.

Early in the year 1096, the French communities, threatened with extinction if they did not submit to baptism, called upon the great Jewish communities on the Rhine to ordain a day of public fasting and prayer. The Rhenish Jews complied and prayed fervently for the welfare of their French brethren. However, they themselves felt perfectly secure, enjoying as they did the special favor of the Emperor and the local nobility.

But all too soon, the frenzied mobs of crusaders poured into Germany, thirsty for Jewish blood, and hungry for Jewish riches.

In the early spring, in the weeks between Pesach and Shavuos, violence broke out and atrocities escalated. The three Jewish communities of Speyer, Worms and Mainz felt the main brunt of the carnage, and their calamity is described in this *kinnah* (see commentary below).

הֲרוּגֵי אַשְׁפִּירָה — *The slain victims of Speyer.* On the Sabbath, the eighth of Iyar [May 3, 1096], the crusaders surrounded the synagogue in Speyer. They were unable to breach its fortifications, and

My eyes will shed tears[1] and I will wail
and thus bestirring [friends to comfort me],
and I will call them to cry, to don sackcloth and to eulogize
that which is more precious than fine gold, more desirable than gold,
whose glory is concealed within,[2]
honored as the most cherished vessel,
and now I see it ripped, desolate, forlorn[3] —
[namely,] the Torah, the Scriptures, the Mishnah and the Aggadah.
Raise your voice and moan and make this pronouncement,
'Where is the Torah and the student who studied it?'
Behold, the place is desolate and no one dwells therein![4]
Over the House of Israel and over the nation of HASHEM,
because they have fallen by the sword!

Water will stream from my eyelids, running over with tears,[5]
*as I bitterly bemoan the slain victims of Speyer.**
It happened on the eighth day of the second month [Iyar],
on the day of tranquility [the Sabbath].
My calm was transformed into a destructive tempest.
Pleasant young men[6] were murdered
with splendid, venerable oldsters.
They assembled together and [decided]
to surrender their souls in reverence,
for the unification of the One and Only Name,
they declared the unity of God with fortitude.
Strong warriors, swift to fulfill His word.[7]
And my ministers and my youths expired
— altogether they numbered ten.

In my bitter agony and sadness, I compose elegies,
as I remember today the murder of the holy congregations;
the community of Worms, proven and chosen.*
Talmudic masters of the land, their purity unsullied.

(1) *Jeremiah* 13:17. (2) *Psalms* 45:14. (3) *Isaiah* 49:21. (4) Cf. *Jeremiah* 26:9.
(5) Cf. 9:17. (6) *Ezekiel* 23:12. (7) *Psalms* 103:20.

the assembled worshipers were able to repel their attack. Frustrated, the frenzied mob threw itself upon any Jew it could find outside the synagogue. Altogether they murdered ten men. In addition they attacked one woman who was given the choice of death or conversion. She gladly chose the former and died a martyr's death and proved to be an example for many other Jews who preferred to sanctify God's Name in death, rather than to abandon Him in life.

קְהַל וַרְמַיְזָא — *The community of Worms.* On the twenty-third of Iyar [Sunday, May 18, 1096] a large force of crusaders, led by Count Emicho, mercilessly attacked the Jews of Worms who had remained confidently in their homes. There they felt safe, relying on the promises of protection offered by their Christian neighbors. Many were slain by the crusaders and their small children were seized for forced baptism. Jewish homes were pillaged and destroyed. The greedy mob even stripped the clothing from their victims' corpses, leaving them naked. Eventually, some Jews who had found refuge in the bishop's palace managed to send clothes to cover their shame.

But for the Jews of Worms the suffering was not over. God had singled them out for double tragedy. On the following Sunday, Rosh Chodesh Sivan [May 25,] the crusaders and local rabble attacked the bishop's palace to kill the many Jews who had taken refuge there. After fierce combat the crusaders prevailed and slew every Jew they could find. When the attack came, the victims were in the midst of reciting *Hallel* (*Psalms* 113-118); with God's praises on

פַּעֲמַיִם קִדְּשׁוּ שֵׁם הַמְּיֻחָד בְּמוֹרָא.
בְּעֶשְׂרִים וּשְׁלֹשָׁה בְּחֹדֶשׁ זִיו[1] לְטַהֲרָה,
וּבְחֹדֶשׁ הַשְּׁלִישִׁי בִּקְרִיאַת הַלֵּל לְשׁוֹרְרָה,
הִשְׁלִימוּ נַפְשָׁם בְּאַהֲבָה קְשׁוּרָה,
אָהִימָה עֲלֵיהֶם בִּבְכִי יֶלֶל לְחַשְׁרָה,
כְּלוּלֵי כֶתֶר עַל רֹאשָׁם לַעֲטָרָה.

וְעַל אַדִּירֵי קְהַל מַגֶּנְצָא* הַהֲדוּרָה,
מִנְּשָׁרִים קַלּוּ מֵאֲרָיוֹת לְהִתְגַּבְּרָה,[2]
הִשְׁלִימוּ נַפְשָׁם עַל יִחוּד שֵׁם הַנּוֹרָא,
וַעֲלֵיהֶם זַעֲקַת שֶׁבֶר אֶשְׁעֲרָה,
עַל שְׁנֵי מִקְדָּשֵׁי יְסוֹדָם כְּהַיּוֹם עֶרְעָרָה,
וְעַל חָרְבוֹת מְעַט מִקְדָּשַׁי[3] וּמִדְרְשֵׁי הַתּוֹרָה.

בַּחֹדֶשׁ הַשְּׁלִישִׁי בַּשְּׁלִישִׁי נוֹסַף לְדַאֲבוֹן וּמְאֵרָה,
הַחֹדֶשׁ אֲשֶׁר נֶהְפַּךְ לְיָגוֹן וְצָרָה,
בְּיוֹם מַתַּן דָּת שִׁבַּרְתִּי לְהִתְאַשְּׁרָה,
וּבְיוֹם נְתִינָתָהּ כְּמוֹ כֵן אָז חָזְרָה,
עָלְתָה לָּהּ לַמָּרוֹם לִמְקוֹם מְדוֹרָהּ,
עִם תֵּיקָהּ וְנַרְתֵּקָהּ וְהַדּוֹרְשָׁהּ וְחוֹקְרָהּ,
לוֹמְדֶיהָ וְשׁוֹנֶיהָ בְּאִישׁוֹן כְּמוֹ בְאוֹרָה,
שִׂימוּ נָא עַל לְבַבְכֶם[4] מִסְפֵּד מַר לְקָשְׁרָה,
כִּי שְׁקוּלָה הֲרִיגָתָם לְהִתְאַבֵּל וּלְהִתְעַפְּרָה,
כִּשְׂרֵפַת בֵּית אֱלֹהֵינוּ הָאוּלָם וְהַבִּירָה,
וְכִי אֵין לְהוֹסִיף מוֹעֵד שֶׁבֶר וְתַבְעֵרָה,
וְאֵין לְהַקְדִּים זוּלָתִי לְאַחֲרָה,
תַּחַת כֵּן הַיּוֹם לִוְיָתִי אֲעוֹרֵרָה,
וְאֶסְפְּדָה וְאֵילִילָה וְאֶבְכֶּה בְּנֶפֶשׁ מָרָה,
וְאַנְחָתִי כָּבְדָה מִבֹּקֶר וְעַד עֶרֶב,
עַל בֵּית יִשְׂרָאֵל וְעַל עַם יהוה כִּי נָפְלוּ בֶּחָרֶב.

---

their lips they sanctified His Name. A youth named Simchah Cohen planned to avenge his father and seven brothers who had been murdered by the crusaders. He pretended that he would accept baptism, and was taken to the church. At the moment he was to receive the sacrament, he whipped out a concealed knife and lashed out at those around him, stabbing the bishop's nephew in the act. Needless to say, the brave youth was torn to pieces by the infuriated bystanders.

All told, eight hundred Jews fell victim to the

Twice they sanctified the One and Only Name in reverence.
On the twenty-third day of the month of Ziv [Iyar],[1]
they were purified,
and in the third month [Sivan],
while reciting the Hallel [on Rosh Chodesh] in song,
they surrendered their soul, bound up with love.
I moan over them with a wailing cry. Saturated [with tears]
those adorned with a perfect crown upon their heads.

For the towering personalities of
*the distinguished community of Mainz;**
quicker than eagles, stronger than lions,[2]
they surrendered their souls while declaring
[God's] unity and His awesome Name.
For them, I will scream out a shattering cry,
over my two Temples whose foundation were destroyed on this day,
and for the ruins of my miniature sanctuaries[3]
and houses of Torah study.

In the third month [Sivan], on the third day,
more misery and misfortune were added,
in this month which was turned into agony and grief.
I had hoped that on the day the Law was given [Shavuos]
I would renew my fortune [in the merit of the Torah],
but on the very day it was given it was returned.
It arose on high, [back to] its dwelling place,
together with its cover and its case, its expounder and its examiner,
those who study it and reviewed it in the darkness [of night]
as by the light [of day].

Please take to your hearts[4] *to compose a bitter eulogy,*
because their massacre is deserving of mourning and rolling in dust
as was the burning of the House of our God, its Hall and its Palace.
However, [we] cannot add a [new] day
[of mourning] over ruin and conflagration,
nor may [we] mourn any earlier — only later.
Instead, today [on Tishah B'Av], I will arouse my sorrowful wailing,
and I will eulogize and wail and weep with a bitter soul,
and my groans are heavy from morning until evening.

Over the House of Israel and over the nation of HASHEM,
because they have fallen by the sword!

---

(1) *I Kings* 6:1. (2) Cf. *II Samuel* 1:23. (3) Cf. *Ezekiel* 11:16. (4) Cf. *Chaggai* 2:18.

---

crusaders on those two Sundays in Worms.

קְהַל מַגֶנְצָא — *The ... community of Mainz.* Terribly alarmed by the massacre at Speyer and Worms, the Jews of Mainz petitioned for the bishop's protection and paid him 400 pieces of silver for his promise. However, on the third of Sivan [May 27, 1096], when Count Emicho and his multitudes arrived at the gates of the city, the burghers were only too happy to welcome the crusaders and join in their attack on the Jews. The populace led the crusaders to all the Jewish hiding places. The Jews, led by R' Klonimos ben R' Meshullam, valiantly resisted, but were outnumbered and weakened by their penitential fasting. After a brief struggle, a general massacre

וְעַל אֵלֶּה אֲנִי בוֹכִיָּה[1] וְלִבִּי נוֹהֵם נְהִימוֹת,
וְאֶקְרָא לַמְקוֹנְנוֹת וְאֶל הַחֲכָמוֹת,[2]
אֱלִי וְאֶלְיָה כֻּלָּם הוֹמוֹת,
הֲיֵשׁ מַכְאוֹב לְמַכְאוֹבִי[3] לְדַמּוֹת,
מִחוּץ תְּשַׁכֶּל חֶרֶב וּמֵחֲדָרִים אֵמוֹת,[4]
חַלְלֵי חַלְלֵי חֶרֶב מוּטָלִים עֲרֵמִים וַעֲרֵמוֹת,
נִבְלָתָם כְּסוּחָה[5] לְחַיַּת אֶרֶץ וְלַבְּהֵמוֹת,
יוֹנֵק עִם אִישׁ שֵׂיבָה[6] עֲלָמִים וַעֲלָמוֹת.

מִתְעַתְּעִים בָּמוֹ מוֹנַי וּמַרְבִּים כְּלִמּוֹת,
אֵי אֱלֹהֵימוֹ אָמְרוּ צוּר חָסָיוּ בוֹ[7] עַד מוֹת,
יָבֹא וְיוֹשִׁיעַ וְיַחֲזִיר נְשָׁמוֹת,
חֲסִין יָהּ מִי כָמוֹךָ[8] נוֹשֵׂא אֲלֻמּוֹת,[9]
תֶּחֱשֶׁה וְתִתְאַפַּק[10] וְלֹא תַחְגּוֹר חֵמוֹת,[11]
בֶּאֱמוֹר אֵלַי מַלְעִיגַי אִם אֱלֹהִים הוּא יָרֶב,[12]
עַל בֵּית יִשְׂרָאֵל וְעַל עַם יהוה כִּי נָפְלוּ בֶּחָרֶב.

עֵינִי עֵינִי יוֹרְדָה מַּיִם[13] כִּי נֶהְפַּךְ לְאֵבֶל[14] מְשׁוֹרֵר,
וְעֻגָבִי לְקוֹל בּוֹכִים[15] מִלְּהָפִיג וּלְקָרֵר,
מִי יָנוּד לִי[16] וּמִי מַחֲזִיק לְהִתְעוֹרֵר,[17]
חֵמָה בִּי יָצְאָה וְסַעַר מִתְגּוֹרֵר,[18]
אֲכָלַנִי הֱמָמַנִי[19] הַצַּר הַצּוֹרֵר,[20]
שִׁבַּר עַצְמוֹתַי[21] זוֹרֵר וּמְפָרֵר,
סִלָּה כָל אַבִּירַי[22] הַטָּבוּר וְהַשָּׁרֵר,
רְטִיָּה וּמָזוֹר אֵין לְבָרֵר,
מַכָּתִי אֲנוּשָׁה[23] בְּאֵין מַתְעִיל וּמְזוֹרֵר,
עַל כֵּן אָמַרְתִּי שְׁעוּ מֶנִּי אֲמָרֵר,
בִּבְכִי[24] דִּמְעָתִי עַל לֶחֱיִי[25] לְצָרֵב,
עַל בֵּית יִשְׂרָאֵל וְעַל עַם יהוה כִּי נָפְלוּ בֶּחָרֶב.

---

ensued. The victims, more than one thousand pure Jewish souls, were ignominiously thrown into nine large ditches for mass burial.

Throughout the spring and early summer, the crusaders continued to maraud and sack once proud and venerable Jewish communities, many of which had stood for over a thousand years. They brought death and destruction to Cologne, Trier, Regensburg, Metz and Prague. In all, it is estimated that over 5,000 Jews lost their lives during the First Crusade. But worse than that, the Crusades introduced the idea of organized, massive, widespread terror against the Jews on a vast, sweeping scale — an idea that would continue, and find its ultimate, horrible expression in the awesome Nazi Holocaust.

Over these I do cry[1] and my heart moans deeply,
and I summon the wailing-women and the skilled ones.[2]
'Ay li', 'Ay lay,' they all cry with intense feeling.
Is there any pain which compares with my pain?[3]
Outside the [avenging] sword renders parents childless,
while terror stalks the inner chambers.[4]
My dead bodies, corpses of the sword,
are strewn about naked, both male and female.
Their cadavers rotting[5] for the wild beasts of the land
and for the animals —
suckling baby with hoary old man,[6] young men and young maidens.
My tormentors ridicule them and humiliate them intensely.
'Where is their God,' taunt they,
'the Rock in Whom they sought refuge[7] until death?
Let Him come and save and restore souls!'
Who is like You, O strong One, God,[8]
Who patiently bears the bundles[9] [of their iniquities]?
Will You remain silent and hold back,[10]
not to gird Yourself in burning wrath,[11]
when those who mock me say, 'If indeed there is a God,
let Him fight[12] [on your behalf]!'
Over the House of Israel and over the nation of HASHEM,
because they have fallen by the sword!

My eyes, my eyes, run with water![13]
For our singer has turned to mourning,[14]
my flute has changed over to the sound of weeping,[15]
without relief or composure.
Who will bestir himself to console me?[16]
And is there none to revive me with a strong embrace?[17]
[God's] wrath went forth against me,
while a storm [of anger] gathered[18] [to harm me].
The cruel enemy[20] consumed and mutilated me.[19]
My bones he shattered,[21] strew and pulverized.
He trampled all my heroes,[22] [who were my] navel and umbilicus.
There is no bandage or medicine from which to choose.
[because] my wound is mortal,[23] beyond remedy or cure.
Therefore I said, 'Leave me alone with my bitterness,
so that with the weeping[24] of my tears, I will blister my cheeks.[25]
Over the House of Israel and over the nation of HASHEM,
because they have fallen by the sword!

---

(1) *Eichah* 1:16. (2) Cf. *Jeremiah* 9:16. (3) Cf. *Eichah* 1:12. (4) Cf. *Deuteronomy* 32:25. (5) *Isaiah* 5:25. (6) *Deuteronomy* 32:25. (7) Cf. 32:37. (8) Cf. *Psalms* 89:9. (9) Cf. 126:6. (10) Cf. *Isaiah* 42:14. (11) Cf. *Psalms* 76:11. (12) *Judges* 6:31. (13) *Eichah* 1:16. (14) 5:15. (15) *Job* 30:31. (16) Cf. *Isaiah* 51:19. (17) Cf. 64:6. (18) *Jeremiah* 30:23. (19) Cf. 51:34. (20) *Numbers* 10:9. (21) *Eichah* 3:4. (22) 1:15. (23) *Jeremiah* 15:18. (24) *Isaiah* 22:4. (25) *Eichah* 1:2.

כו.

אָז* בַּהֲלוֹךְ יִרְמְיָהוּ עַל* קִבְרֵי אָבוֹת,
וְנָם עֲצָמוֹת חֲבִיבוֹת, מָה אַתֶּם שׁוֹכְּבוֹת,
בְּנֵיכֶם גָּלוּ וּבָתֵּיהֶם חֲרֵבוֹת,
וְאַיֵּה זְכוּת אָבוֹת בְּאֶרֶץ תַּלְאוּבוֹת.*

גָּעוּ כֻּלָּם בְּקִינִים עַל חֶסְרוֹן בָּנִים,
דּוֹבְבוּ בְּקוֹל תַּחֲנוּנִים פְּנֵי שׁוֹכֵן מְעוֹנִים,
וְאַיֵּה הַבְטָחַת וְזָכַרְתִּי לָהֶם בְּרִית רִאשׁוֹנִים.[1]

הֵם הֵמִירוּ כְבוֹדוֹ בְתֹהוּ,[2] וְלֹא פָחֲדוּ וְלֹא רָהוּ,[3]
וְאַעְלִים עֵינַי מֵהֶם[4] וְלֹא שָׁבוּ וְלֹא נָהוּ,
וְאֵיךְ אֶתְאַפַּק עַל אֲמִירַת לֹא הוּא.[5]

זָעַק אַב הֲמוֹן[6] בַּעֲבוּרָם, וְחִנֵּן פְּנֵי אֵל רָם,
חִנָּם נִסֵּיתִי עֶשֶׂר בְּחִינוֹת עֲבוּרָם, וְהֵן חָזִיתִי שִׁבְרָם,
וְאַיֵּה הַבְטָחַת אַל תִּירָא אַבְרָם.[7]

טָעוּ לְהוֹרוֹת[8] בַּעֲבוֹדוֹת זָרוֹת,
יָעֲצוּ לַחְצוֹב בֹּארוֹת נִשְׁבָּרוֹת,[9]
וְאֵיךְ אֶתְאַפַּק עַל בִּטּוּל עֲשֶׂרֶת הַדִּבְּרוֹת.

כֹּה צָוַח יִצְחָק פְּנֵי שׁוֹכֵן שַׁחַק,
לַשָּׁוְא בִּי טֶבַח הוּחַק, וְהֵן זַרְעִי נִשְׁחַק וְנִמְחַק,
וְאַיֵּה הַבְטָחַת וְאֶת בְּרִיתִי אָקִים אֶת יִצְחָק.[10]
מָרוּ בְּיִרְמְיָה, וְטִמְּאוּ הַר הַמּוֹרִיָּה,

(1) *Leviticus* 26:45. (2) Cf. *Jeremiah* 2:11. (3) Cf. *Isaiah* 44:8. (4) Cf. 1:15. (5) *Jeremiah* 5:12. (6) Cf. *Genesis* 17:4. (7) 15:1. (8) Some editions read לְהִזָּרוֹת, *to become estranged.* (9) Cf. *Jeremiah* 2:13. (10) *Genesis* 17:21.

אָז — *Then.* In this work, R' Elazar HaKalir retells the Midrashic account (Midrash *Eichah* intro. 24) of God's reaction to the Destruction. When He saw the ruins of the burnt Sanctuary, God cried to Jeremiah, 'I feel like a father whose only son died on his wedding day! Go, summon Abraham, Isaac, Jacob, and Moses from their graves. They know how to weep (and perhaps they will arouse My mercy to return Israel to their land).' Jeremiah went to the Cave of Machpelah in Hebron to arouse the Patriarchs and to the banks of the Jordan river to awaken Moses. They all went to visit the ruins of the Temple. As they passed from gate to desolate gate, they wailed and cried and rent their garments in mourning. Yet, all their tears and pleas failed to arouse God's mercy, that He pledge to guarantee Israel's final redemption and return, for Israel had sinned terribly and God's fury was aroused.

God relented only after the Matriarchs led by Rachel joined in with their impassioned plea and God's response is recorded by the Prophet Jeremiah:

Thus says HASHEM, *'A voice is heard in Ramah, lamentation and bitter weeping, Rachel is weeping for her children, she refuses to be comforted*

26.

א *Then* when Jeremiah approached* the graves of the Patriarchs*
and said, 'O cherished bones, how can you lie still?
ב *Your sons have been exiled and their homes destroyed;*
*where is the merit of their ancestors in a parched wasteland?'**

ג *They all cried out in lamentations*
over the loss of their children;
ד *they spoke in a voice of supplication before [God]*
Who dwells in the high heavens,
"Where is the assurance, 'And I shall remember for their sake
the covenant of the ancients'?"[1]

ה *[God replied,] "They exchanged My honor for utter nothingness,*[2]
and they were neither awed nor afraid [of Me].[3]
ו *Then I averted My eyes from them*[4]*, yet they did not repent*
nor did they lament;
and how can I restrain [My anger] from the statement,
'He is not [the Lord]'?"[5]

ז *Then [Abraham] the father of the multitude*[6] *cried out*
on their behalf and pleaded before God, the Most High,
ח *"For nothing was I tried with ten tests for their sake,*
for behold, how I must witness their ruination!
Where is the assurance 'Fear not, O Abram!'?"[7]

ט *[God responded,] 'They erred by permitting*[8] *idolatrous worship.*
י *They devised plans to dig [for themselves] cisterns, broken cisterns,*[9]
and how can I restrain [My anger]
over the nullification of the Ten Commandments?'

כ *Then Isaac screamed before [God] Who dwells in heaven,*
ל *"Was it for nothing that I was inscribed [in the Torah]*
as being prepared for slaughter?
For behold how my seed is crushed and obliterated.
Where is the assurance,
'And I shall fulfill My covenant with Isaac'?"[10]

מ *[God responded,] 'They have defied Jeremiah*
and defiled Mount Moriah.

---

over her children for they are not here.' Thus says HASHEM, *'Restrain your voice from weeping and hold back your eyes from tears, for your efforts will be rewarded,' says* HASHEM, *'and they will return from the land of the enemy. And there is hope for your future,' says* HASHEM, *'for your children shall be restored to their own borders!'* (Jeremiah 31:14-16).

אָז בַּהֲלוֹךְ יִרְמְיָהוּ עַל — *Then when Jeremiah approached* [lit., *walked upon*]. Since Jeremiah was a *Kohen* (see *Jeremiah* 1:1), he was forbidden from contaminating himself to the dead. Therefore, he could not have entered the Cave of Machpelah (see *Rashi* to *Ezekiel* 37:2, where Ezekiel, also a *Kohen*, was led around a valley filled with bones to prophesy regarding those bones, but was not permitted to enter the valley). Thus, עַל, *upon*, has been translated according to its alternate meaning, *near* (see *Targum* and *Rashi* to *Numbers* 2:20) and the phrase . . . הֲלוֹךְ עַל is rendered *approached*.

בְּאֶרֶץ תַּלְאוּבוֹת — *In a parched wasteland*, an

נִלְאֵיתִי נְשׂוֹא[1] גְּעִיָּה, עוֹלָה לִי מִנְּשִׁיָּה,
וְאֵיךְ אֶתְאַפַּק עַל הֲרִיגַת זְכַרְיָה.[2]

סָח יֶלֶד בְּתֶלֶף, דְּמָעוֹת כְּתַנִּין זוֹלֵף,
עוֹלָלַי אֲשֶׁר טִפַּחְתִּי[3] בְּעֶלֶף,
וְאֵיךְ גָּזוּ מֶנִּי בְּחֵלֶף
וְאֵיךְ הֶפְרַע מֶנִּי דָּמִים בְּדָמִים כַּמָּה אֶלֶף.

פָּץ רוֹעֶה נֶאֱמָן, כָּפוּשׁ בְּאֵפֶר וּמְדְמָן,
צֹאן אֲשֶׁר בְּחֵיקִי הֶאֱמָן,[4] אֵיךְ גָּזוּ בְּלֹא זְמָן,
וְאַיֵּה הַבְטָחַת כִּי לֹא אַלְמָן.[5]

קוֹל בְּכִי לֵאָה מְתוֹפֶפֶת עַל לְבָבֶיהָ,[6]
רָחֵל אֲחוֹתָהּ מְבַכָּה עַל בָּנֶיהָ,[7]
וְזִלְפָּה מַכָּה פָּנֶיהָ, בִּלְהָה מְקוֹנֶנֶת בִּשְׁתֵּי יָדֶיהָ.

שׁוּבוּ תְמִימִים לִמְנוּחַתְכֶם,
מַלֵּא אֲמַלֵּא כָּל מִשְׁאֲלוֹתֵיכֶם,
שִׁלַּחְתִּי בָבֶלָה לְמַעַנְכֶם,[8]
הִנְנִי מְשׁוֹבֵב גָּלוּת בְּנֵיכֶם.

---

allusion to the Wilderness of Sinai where their ancestors accepted the Torah. As the prophet (*Jeremiah* 2:2) states: *So said* HASHEM, *'I shall remember for your sake the kindness of your younger days . . . how you followed Me in the Wilderness in an unsown land.'*

נ *I have become exhausted from bearing*[1]
the cry that rises from the land of oblivion;
and how can I restrain [My anger from avenging]
the murder of Zechariah?'[2]

ס *[Then Jacob] who was born to learning*
spoke with tears flowing [to the ground] like a [slithering] serpent,
ע *'My babes whom I have dandled [and reared]*[3]
to the point of exhaustion,
how they have been torn from me, to disappear!
How there has been exacted from me, for [Zechariah's] blood,
the blood of so many thousands!'

פ *The faithful shepherd [Moses] burst forth,*
while sunk in ashes and sullied in filth,
צ *'The lambs, who were nursed at my bosom,*[4]
O how were they cut off before their time!
Where is the assurance, "It [Israel] shall not be widowed"?'[5]

ק *The sound of Leah's weeping, as she pounds on her heart;*[6]
ר *Rachel, her sister, weeping for her sons;*[7]
Zilpah slapping her face;
and Bilhah lamenting with her two hands [outstretched].

ש־ת *[God responds,] 'Return, O wholesome ones, to your place of rest,*
I shall surely fulfill all your requests.
I was sent to Babylon, for your sake.[8]
Behold, I shall return your children from exile!'

(1) *Isaiah* 1:14. (2) See *kinnah* 34. (3) Cf. *Eichah* 2:22. (4) Cf. *Numbers* 11:12. (5) *Jeremiah* 51:5. (6) Cf. *Nahum* 2:8. (7) Cf. *Jeremiah* 31:14. (8) See *Minchas Shai* to *Isaiah* 43:14.

כז.

אָז בִּמְלֹאת סֶפֶק יָפָה כְּתִרְצָה,*
הֵן אֶרְאֶלָּם[1] צָעֲקוּ חוּצָה,[2]
בֶּן חִלְקִיָּהוּ מֵאַרְמוֹן כְּיָצָא,
אִשָּׁה יְפַת תֹּאַר מְנֻוֶּלֶת מָצָא.
גּוֹזַרְנִי עָלַיִךְ בְּשֵׁם אֱלֹהִים וְאָדָם,
אִם שֵׁד לַשֵּׁדִים אַתְּ אוֹ לִבְנֵי אָדָם,
דְּמוּת יָפְיֵךְ כְּבָשָׂר וָדָם,
פַּחְדֵּךְ וְיִרְאָתֵךְ כְּמַלְאָכִים לְבַדָּם.
הֵן לֹא שֵׁד אֲנִי וְלֹא גֹלֶם פַּחַת,
יְדוּעָה הָיִיתִי בְּשׁוּבָה וָנַחַת,
הֵן לְאֶחָד אֲנִי וְלִשְׁלֹשָׁה וְשִׁשִּׁים וְאַחַת,
וְלִשְׁנֵים עָשָׂר וּלְשִׁבְעִים וְאַחַת.
זֶה הָאֶחָד אַבְרָהָם הָיָה,
וּבֵין הַשְּׁלֹשָׁה אָבוֹת שְׁלִישִׁיָּה,
חֹק שְׁנֵים עָשָׂר הֵן הֵן שִׁבְטֵי יָהּ,
וְשִׁשִּׁים רִבּוֹא וְשִׁבְעִים וְאֶחָד סַנְהֶדְרֵי יָהּ.
טַעֲמִי הַקְשִׁיבִי וַעֲשִׂי תְשׁוּבָה,
יַעַן הֱיוֹתֵךְ כָּל כַּךְ חֲשׁוּבָה,
יָפָה לָךְ בְּעֶלֶץ וְלִשְׂמוֹחַ בְּטוֹבָה,
וְלֹא לִקָּרֵא עוֹד בַּת הַשּׁוֹבֵבָה.
כִּי אֵיךְ אֶשְׂמַח וְקוֹלִי מָה אָרִים,
הֵן עוֹלָלַי נִתְּנוּ בְּיַד צָרִים,
לָקוּ נְבִיאַי וְדָמָם מֻגָּרִים,
גָּלוּ מְלָכַי וְשָׂרַי וְכֹהֲנַי וַהֲרֵי הֵם בְּקוֹלָרִים.
מְלוֹן מִקְדָּשִׁי בַּעֲוֹנִי נֻדַּד,
דּוֹדִי מֵאָז נָדַד וַיִּדַּד,

אָז בִּמְלֹאת סֶפֶק — *Then, when the measure [of sin] was filled.* According to some versions this *kinnah* by R' Elazar HaKalir appears *before* the preceding *kinnah*. The end of this *kinnah* relates how Jeremiah awakened the Patriarchs at the Cave of Machpelah and thus serves as an appropriate introduction to *kinnah* 26 which narrates the pleas of the Patriarchs after they were aroused. According to our sequence, this *kinnah* comes later because its main theme is an

27.

א *Then, when the measure [of sin] was filled by [Israel]*
who is as beautiful as Tirtzah, the Erelim*[1] *cried out in public.*[2]

ב *As [Jeremiah] the son of Hilkiyah departed from the Temple,*
he met a woman of beautiful features who was filthy.

ג *[He said:] 'I command you, in the name of God and man,*
[to reveal] whether you are one of the demons or of humankind.

ד *Your graceful appearance resembles flesh and blood, but the terror and awe [etched on your features] is unique to the angels!'*

ה *'Behold', [she replied] 'I am neither demon,*
nor worthless lump [of clay].
Rather, I was once renowned for tranquility and serenity.
I am [the representative spirit of the Jewish people, the daughter] of one and of three,
[my offspring number] sixty with one [leader, Moses, over them]; [they stem]

ו *from twelve and [are ruled by] seventy-one!*

ז *This one [that I mentioned] was Abraham,*
and the three refers to the Patriarchs, a trio dedicated to God.

ח *The number twelve represents the tribes of God, who numbered sixty myriad. And the seventy-one are God's Sanhedrin.'*

ט *[Jeremiah responded,] 'Harken to my advice and repent,*
considering that you are truly so distinguished.

י *It is proper for you to celebrate and to rejoice in goodness,*
no longer to be referred to as the rebellious daughter!'

כ *'But how can I rejoice? How can I raise my voice [in song]?*
Behold, my babes are delivered into the hands of my tormentors!

ל *My prophets were beaten and their blood flowed. My kings,*
my princes and my priests were exiled and behold,
they are now in shackles.

מ *My Holy Dwelling was uprooted because of my iniquity,*
since then my Beloved has fled and withered.

(1) See commentary to *kinnah* 22. (2) *Isaiah* 33:7.

event that occurred after the Destruction, as related in *Pesikta Rabbosi* (27): When Jeremiah returned to Jerusalem he met a woman sitting on a mountaintop, clothed in black, her hair disheveled. 'Who will console me?' she cried out.

Jeremiah responded sternly, 'If you are a real woman, speak to me, but if you are a spirit, depart!'

'I am your mother, Zion!' the woman responded.

Jeremiah said to her, 'God, Himself, will console you! Mortal men built you and mortal men destroyed you. But in the future, God Himself will rebuild you as Scripture states: *The Builder of Jerusalem is HASHEM* (*Psalms* 147:2).

The *kinnah* follows an alphabetical format, and is a conversation between Jeremiah, Israel, God, and the Patriarchs.

יָפָה כְּתִרְצָה — *Beautiful as Tirtzah.* Israel is described with this phrase in *Song of Songs* (6:4).

נֹעַם אָהֳלִי בְּעַל כָּרְחִי שֻׁדַּד,
רַבָּתִי עָם אֵיכָה יָשְׁבָה בָדָד.[1]
שָׁחָה הָאִשָּׁה לַנָּבִיא יִרְמְיָה,
סַח לֵאלֹהֶיךָ בְּעַד מַכַּת סוֹעֲרָה עֲנִיָּה,
עַד יַעֲנֶה אֵל וְיֹאמַר דַּיָּהּ,
וְיַצִּילֵנִי מֵחֶרֶב וְשִׁבְיָה.
פִּלֵּל תְּחִנָּה לִפְנֵי קוֹנוֹ,
מָלֵא רַחֲמִים רַחֵם כְּאָב עַל בְּנוֹ,
צָעַק מַה לְּאָב שֶׁהֶגְלָה בְּנוֹ,
וְגַם אוֹי לַבֵּן שֶׁעַל שֻׁלְחַן אָב אֵינוֹ.
קוּם לָךְ יִרְמְיָה לָמָּה תֶּחֱשֶׁה,
לֵךְ קְרָא לְאָבוֹת וְאַהֲרֹן וּמֹשֶׁה,
רוֹעִים יָבֹאוּ קִינָה לְהִנָּשֵׂא,
כִּי זְאֵבֵי עֶרֶב טָרְפוּ אֶת הַשֶּׂה.
שׁוֹאֵג הָיָה יִרְמְיָהוּ הַנָּבִיא,
עַל מַכְפֵּלָה נוֹהֵם כְּלָבִיא,
תְּנוּ קוֹל בִּבְכִי אֲבוֹת הַצְּבִי,
תָּעוּ בְנֵיכֶם וַהֲרֵי הֵם בַּשֶּׁבִי.
וְאִם כְּאָדָם עָבְרוּ בְרִית,
אַיֵּה זְכוּת כְּרוּתֵי בְרִית.
מָה אֶעֱשֶׂה לָכֶם בָּנַי,
גְּזֵרָה הִיא מִלְּפָנַי.
שָׁמֵם מִקְדָּשׁ מִבְּלִי בָּאֵי מוֹעֵד,[2]
עַל כִּי יְדִידִים נִתְּנוּ לְהִמָּעֵד,
תְּשִׁיבֵם* כְּמֵאָז סוֹמֵךְ וְסוֹעֵד,
תְּרַחֵם צִיּוֹן כִּי בָא מוֹעֵד.[3]

The translation follows *Ibn Ezra* there, who explains that Tirtzah refers to the province of that name mentioned elsewhere in Scriptures (see, e.g., *I Kings* chs. 14-16). *Rashi*, however, translates homiletically, and understands כְּתִרְצָה as a contraction of כְּשֶׁאַתְּ רְצוּיָה, *when you find*

נ *My pleasant Tent was forcefully plundered.*
The city once great with people,
alas, she now sits in solitude!'[1]

ס *The woman spoke [further] to Jeremiah,*
"Pray to your God concerning the blows
inflicted upon the suffering, storm-tossed [people of Israel],

ע *Until God responds and says, 'Enough!'*
and saves me from sword and captivity."

פ *[Jeremiah] prayed in supplication before his Creator,*
'[O You Who are] full of compassion,
pity [us] as a father would [pity] his son!'

צ *[God] cried, 'How does a Father feel*
when he has exiled his son?
And woe unto the son,
who is absent from the father's table!

ק *Arise, Jeremiah! Why should you be silent?*
Go summon the Patriarchs, and Aaron and Moses!

ר *Let these shepherds come and arouse lamentation,*
because the wolves of the night have torn the lamb to pieces.'

ש *Jeremiah the prophet roared;*
at the [Cave of] Machpelah he growled like a lion,

ת *'Give forth [your] voice in weeping,*
O Patriarchs of the splendid [nation]!
Your children have strayed, and behold, they are in captivity!'
[The Patriarchs replied,]
'And if, indeed, like mortals they violated the Covenant,
where is the merit of [our deeds, for we are] the ones
with whom the covenant was signed?'
[God answered,]
'What can I do for you, My sons?
This is My irrevocable decree!
The Temple has been laid waste for lack of Festival pilgrims,[2]
because [My] beloved ones have faltered!'
'Return them as in days of yore,*
O Supporter and Sustainer, have mercy on Zion,
for the appointed time [of redemption] has come!'[3]

(1) Cf. *Eichah* 1:1. (2) 1:4. (3) Cf. *Psalms* 102:14.

favor; in other words, Israel is beautiful when it follows God's will and thereby finds favor in His eyes.

תְּשִׁיבֵם — *Return them.* It is unclear whether this last verse is spoken by Jeremiah, the Patriarchs, or the *paytan.*

כח.

אֵיךְ תְּנַחֲמוּנִי* הֶבֶל,[1] וְכִנּוֹרִי נֶהְפַּךְ לְאֵבֶל,[2]
בְּנַחֲלַת חֶבֶל,[3] כָּבֵד עָלַי עוֹל סֵבֶל, וְאֵיךְ אֶנָּחֵם.

בְּזֶה יוֹם בְּכָל שָׁנָה, עִדָּן עָלַי שִׁנָּה,
וְהִנְנִי עֲגוּמָה וַעֲגוּנָה, יוֹתֵר מֵאֶלֶף שָׁנָה,* וְאֵיךְ אֶנָּחֵם.

גָּבַר חָרוֹן, וְנִגְנַז אָרוֹן,[4]
בְּמִשְׁנֶה שִׁבָּרוֹן,[5] בִּמְסָרְבֵי מָרוֹן,[6] וְאֵיךְ אֶנָּחֵם.

דִּירָתִי חֳרֵבָה, וְעֶדְרִי נִשְׁבָּה,
וְרַבַּת אָהֳלִיבָה,[7] בָּדָד יָשְׁבָה,[8] וְאֵיךְ אֶנָּחֵם.

הוּעַל אַרְיֵה* מִסֻּבְּכוֹ,[9] עַל אֲרִיאֵל וְהִסְבִּיכוֹ,
וְהֶגְלָה מִסְּכוֹ, מִנְחָתוֹ וְנִסְכּוֹ, וְאֵיךְ אֶנָּחֵם.

וְהָרַג הֲמוֹנִים, מְשׁוּחֵי שְׁמָנִים,
בְּאִוּוּי נִמְנִים, פִּרְחֵי כֹהֲנִים, אֲלָפִים שְׁמוֹנִים, וְאֵיךְ אֶנָּחֵם.

זִנְּבָם כְּחִוּוּי[10] וְהִדְבִּיא, בְּעֶזְרַת הַמַּלְבִּיא,[11]
אַרְיוֹךְ* כְּמוֹ לָבִיא, עַל דַּם כֹּהֵן וְנָבִיא,[12] וְאֵיךְ אֶנָּחֵם.

---

(1) *Job* 21:34. (2) Cf. 30:31. (3) Cf. *Deuteronomy* 32:9.
(4) See commentary to *kinnah* 24. (5) Cf. *Jeremiah* 17:18.
(6) See commentary to *kinnah* 10. (7) See *kinnah* 4. (8) Cf. *Eichah* 1:1.
(9) Cf. *Jeremiah* 4:7. (10) Some editions read בְּאִוּוּי, *in the desirable [Temple].*
(11) Some editions read בַּעֲזָרַת, but the meaning is unchanged. (12) See *kinnah* 34.

איך תנחמוני — *How can you console me?* This alphabetical composition by R' Elazar HaKalir highlights the futility of our attempts to find consolation for the tragedy of Israel's destruction. The calamity was so enormous that it is absolutely unforgettable. Its harsh effects are still felt today, even though many centuries have elapsed. Indeed, the opening words of this *kinnah* declare that any attempt at comfort is futile. The burden of witnessing the desolation of *Eretz Yisrael* and the suffering of the Jewish people is beyond endurance. The *kinnah* ends with a proclamation that even though there can be no consolation as long as the nation remains in exile, there is always hope for redemption and ultimate consolation.

It is not clear from the context whether the speaker of this *kinnah* is God, the nation or the individual lamenter.

יוֹתֵר מֵאֶלֶף שָׁנָה — *For more than a thousand years.* This *kinnah* is usually ascribed to R' Elazar HaKalir, who lived, according to various opinions, somewhere between the second and seventh centuries C.E. In any case, he did not live a thousand years after the Destruction. Assumedly, this line originally read something like כַּמָּה מֵאוֹת שָׁנָה, *many hundreds of years,* but was changed by a later copyist who updated the *kinnah*. Alternatively, if he was (as *Tosafos* and the *Rosh* record) a second-century Tanna, then he may have had in mind the original Tishah B'Av of the Spies' slanderous report about *Eretz Yisrael*. That event would have preceded him by some fourteen centuries, a period of 'more than a thousand years.'

אַרְיֵה — *The lion [Nebuchadnezzar].* Throughout the Talmud and Midrash, and based on the Book of *Daniel* (ch. 8), Israel's long series of exiles and persecutions are always treated as four main periods of subjugation to foreign oppressors — either in *Eretz Yisrael* or in the Diaspora. These periods are known collectively as אַרְבַּע מַלְכֻיּוֹת, *the Four Kingdoms* (*Daniel* 8:22), and each is called by the name of the

28.

א *How can you console me* in vain,*[1]
when my harp has turned to mourning?[2]
Indeed, because of [the sins of Israel] the lot of [my] heritage,[3]
the yoke of the burden is heavy upon me!
So how can I be consoled?

ב *On this day, every year, times for me [are the worst],*
and behold I have been anguished and abandoned
*for more than a thousand years.** *So how can I be consoled?*

ג *Fury intensified and the Holy Ark was concealed;*[4]
disaster struck twice[5] *because of those*
who defiantly rebelled [against God].[6] *So how can I be consoled?*

ד *My dwelling is in ruins and my flock is captured,*
and once-teeming Oholivah [Jerusalem][7] *now sits in solitude!*[8]
So how can I be consoled?

ה *The lion [Nebuchadnezzar]* arose from his dense brush,*[9]
to attack God's leonine Temple;
and banished from His Tabernacle, His meal-offering and His libation.
So how can I be consoled?

ו *And he killed multitudes of blossoming Priests*
[who had been] anointed with oils.
[Their corpses] in the desirable [Temple]
were counted at eighty thousand. *So how can I be consoled?*

ז *He attacked from behind like a snake*[10] *and caused [their blood]*
to flow in the leonine [Temple's] Courtyard.[11]
Arioch [General Nebuzaradan] and the lion [King Nebuchadnezzar]*
both stood over the blood of the priest and prophet [Zechariah].[12]
So how can I be consoled?

---

empire dominant in the world at that particular time. The first, called גָּלוּת בָּבֶל, *the Babylonian Exile,* began when Nebuchadnezzar king of Babylon conquered the Land of Israel and destroyed the First Temple. The second, called גָּלוּת מָדַי וּפָרַס, *the Median-Persian Exile* (ibid. 8:20), began when that empire captured the Babylonians and became the leading world power. Although the Medes permitted the Jewish return to *Eretz Yisrael* and the building of the Second Temple, the early years of that *Beis HaMikdash* were still considered a part of the exile, because Israel was not sovereign in its Land. During the entire third period, גָּלוּת יָוָן, *the Greek Exile* (ibid. 8:21), paradoxically, Israel lived on its Land and the Temple stood. Nevertheless, it was a very turbulent era marked with civil strife, foreign domination, vicious anti-religious campaigns, and the rejection of Torah values by a large number of Jews who adopted Greek culture with all its abominations. The downfall of the Greek Empire and the rise of Rome marked the beginning of גָּלוּת אֱדוֹם, *the Edomite* or *Roman Exile.* It is this millennia-long exile that we are still in today. The *kinnah* now speaks of these Four Kingdoms and their respective atrocities.

אַרְיוֹךְ — *Arioch [General Nebuzaradan].* In *II Kings* (ch. 25) and in *Jeremiah* (chs. 39, 52, et al.), Nebuchadnezzar's general is called נְבוּזַרְאֲדָן רַב טַבָּחִים, *Nebuzaradan the chief executioner.* In *Daniel* (2:14), he is called אַרְיוֹךְ רַב טַבָּחַיָּא, *Arioch the chief executioner.* According to the Midrash, his name was Nebuzaradan, but he was called Arioch (a diminutive of *Ari,* lion) because he roared at the Jewish captives, giving them no rest until they reached the banks of the Euphrates (*Midrash Eichah* 5:5).

חָרַשׁ לְמַשּׁוּאוֹת, עִיר מְלֵאָה תְּשׁוּאוֹת,[1]
וּבָתֵּי סוֹפְרִים וּמִשְׁנִיּוֹת, יוֹתֵר מֵאַרְבַּע מֵאוֹת, **וְאֵיךְ אֶנָּחֵם.**

טָסָה מָדַי, לְאַבֵּד חֲמוּדַי,
וּמָשְׁלָה בְּמַחֲמַדַּי, בְּקָרְעֵי מַדַּי, **וְאֵיךְ אֶנָּחֵם.**

יָעֲצָה לְחַנֵּק, בְּנֵי גוּר מְזַנֵּק,[2]
בְּפֶה אֶחָד לְשַׁנֵּק, זָקֵן וְיָשִׁישׁ עוֹלֵל וְיוֹנֵק, **וְאֵיךְ אֶנָּחֵם.**

כָּבְדָה שְׁלִישִׁית, עַל קֹדֶשׁ רֵאשִׁית,[3]
בְּשֶׁצֶף חֲרִישִׁית, בָּתָּה לְהָשִׁית, **וְאֵיךְ אֶנָּחֵם.**

לָחֲצָה לְחַלֵּק, בְּנֵי חָלָק וְחוּלֵק,
שֶׁאֵין לָכֶם חֵלֶק, בְּשֵׁם אֵשׁ דּוֹלֵק,[4] **וְאֵיךְ אֶנָּחֵם.**

מָרְדָה אֱדוֹם, עֲדוּשַׁת אָדוֹם,
וְאָצָה בְּזָדוֹן, לְאַבֵּד כֵּס וַהֲדוֹם,[5] **וְאֵיךְ אֶנָּחֵם.**

נוֹעֲדוּ עִם אַדְמוֹן, מוֹאָב וְעַמּוֹן,
לְהַשְׁבִּית אָמוֹן,* וּלְהַחֲרִיב אַרְמוֹן, **וְאֵיךְ אֶנָּחֵם.**

סִלָּה כָּל אַבִּירַי,[6] וְעֶדְרֵי חֲבֵרַי,
וְהֶבְלָגוּ גִּבּוֹרַי, לְעֵין כָּל עוֹבְרַי, **וְאֵיךְ אֶנָּחֵם.**

עָיְפָה נַפְשִׁי לְהוֹרְגִים,[7] לְמִסְפַּר הַהֲרוּגִים,
כְּאַיָּל עוֹרְגִים,[8] וְעָלֶיךָ נֶהֱרָגִים,[9] **וְאֵיךְ אֶנָּחֵם.**

פֶּלְצוּ בְּיוֹם קְרָב, בְּמִזְרָח וּבְמַעֲרָב,
עַל דָּמָם מְעֹרָב, קָהָל וְעַם רָב,[10]* **וְאֵיךְ אֶנָּחֵם.**

צָרוֹת עַל צָרוֹת, זוּ מִזּוּ מְצִירוֹת,
גְּדוֹלוֹת וּבְצוּרוֹת[11] אֲרֻכּוֹת וְלֹא קְצָרוֹת, **וְאֵיךְ אֶנָּחֵם.**

---

(1) Cf. *Isaiah* 22:2. (2) Cf. *Deuteronomy* 33:22. (3) Cf. *Jeremiah* 2:3. (4) Some editions read אֵל דּוֹלֵק, *the fiery God.* (5) Cf. *Isaiah* 66:1; see also *Ezekiel* 43:7. (6) *Eichah* 1:15. (7) *Jeremiah* 4:31. (8) Cf. *Psalms* 42:2. (9) Cf. 44:23. (10) *Ezekiel* 26:7. (11) Cf. *Jeremiah* 33:3.

לְהַשְׁבִּית אָמוֹן — *To eradicate the nurturing Torah.* The Talmud relates that when the enemies entered the Temple, Ammonites and Moabites entered among them. While the others ran to plunder the silver and gold, the Ammonites and Moabites ran to plunder the Torah itself to erase the verse (*Deuteronomy* 23:4), לֹא יָבֹא עַמּוֹנִי וּמוֹאָבִי בִּקְהַל ה׳, *An Ammonite or Moabite shall not enter the Assembly of* HASHEM (*Yevamos* 13b). The intention of Ammon and Moab in performing this brazen act was not merely to expunge the verse. There were many other Torah Scrolls in the land which still contained that verse — tearing it from the Temple scroll would not have changed their forbidden status. Rather, their sole aim was to

ח *[The wicked Turnus Rufus] plowed [Jerusalem] to devastation; the city [once] filled with multitudes,*[1] *and more than four hundred schools studying Scripture and Mishnah.* *So how can I be consoled?*

ט *Media flew swiftly to annihilate my cherished ones; and ruled over my precious [Temple], when I rent my robes [in sorrow].* *So how can I be consoled?*

י *She took counsel [from Haman] to strangle the prancing lion cub,*[2] *with one bite to tear asunder the elderly, the aged, the infant and the nursing babe.* *So how can I be consoled?*

כ *The third kingdom was even more oppressive, [they came] upon the premier holy [nation]*[3] *like a deafening tempest, to devastate it.* *So how can I be consoled?*

ל *She [Greece] pressured to separate the sons of the smooth-skinned [Jacob] and [God] the One Who apportions [to each man his lot]; [she coerced them, saying, 'Declare that you have no portion in the Name of [the God you call] the Flaming Fire!'*[4] *So how can I be consoled?*

מ *Edom, [who took his name from] the red lentils, rebelled [against God], and they defiantly hastened to obliterate God's [celestial] throne and His [earthly] footstool.*[5] *So how can I be consoled?*

נ *Allied with Edom were Moab and Ammon, [who came] to eradicate the nurturing Torah,** *and to destroy the palatial Temple.* *So how can I be consoled?*

ס *He trampled all my heroes*[6] *and all the flocks of my comrades; all my warriors were vanquished in full view of all who passed me by.* *So how can I be consoled?*

ע *My spirit is exhausted by the killers,*[7] *by the number of the murder victims who call longingly like a deer,*[8] *and are slaughtered for Your sake.*[9] *So how can I be consoled?*

פ *They were horrified on the day of battle, in the East and in the West, [when] the [flowing] blood of congregation and great nation*[10]* *intermingled.* *So how can I be consoled?*

צ *Calamities upon calamities, each more tragic than the other, overwhelming and powerful,*[11] *enduring and not short lived.* *So how can I be consoled?*

---

defy God and His Torah with impunity (*Lechem Dimah*).

קָהָל וְעַם רָב — *Congregation and great nation.* Ironically, this phrase, used by the *paytan* to

קָשְׁרוּ צִנָּתָם, וְחָגְרוּ חֲנִיתָם וְאָסְפוּ מַחֲנוֹתָם,
וְהֶאֱרִיכוּ לְמַעֲנִיתָם,*[1] וְאֵיךְ אֶנָּחֵם.

רַבּוֹת אַנְחוֹתַי וַעֲצוּמוֹת קִינוֹתַי,
רַבּוּ נַהֲמוֹתַי, וְאַתָּה יהוה עַד מָתַי,[2] וְאֵיךְ אֶנָּחֵם.

שָׁמַעְתָּ חֶרְפָּתָם, חֵרְפוּנִי בִּשְׂפָתָם,
שִׁבְתָּם וְקִימָתָם, אֲנִי מַנְגִּינָתָם,[3] וְאֵיךְ אֶנָּחֵם.

תִּקְוַתְכֶם אֵיפוֹא, מַה לָּכֶם פֹּה,
חָרָה אַפּוֹ, וְאֵין עוֹד לִרְפֹּא, וְאֵיךְ אֶנָּחֵם.

תְּשׁוּבוֹתֵיכֶם נִשְׁאֲרָה מָעַל, הוֹנוּנִי עוֹבְדֵי הַבָּעַל,
עַד יַשְׁקִיף[4] מִמָּעַל, מוֹרִיד שְׁאוֹל וַיָּעַל,[5]* **וְאָז אֶנָּחֵם.**

(1) Cf. *Psalms* 129:3. (2) 6:4. (3) Cf. *Eichah* 3:61-63. (4) Cf. 3:50. (5) *I Samuel* 2:6.

describe the masses murdered by Nebuchadnezzar's hordes, is used by the prophet to describe those very hordes (see *Ezekiel* 26:7).

וְהֶאֱרִיכוּ לְמַעֲנִיתָם — *And lengthened their furrow.* The plowman never pauses while he is in the middle of a furrow, but waits until he reaches the end of the line. Thus, the longer the furrow, the longer the oxen must toil, without any respite. This alludes to Israel in exile who

ק *They tied on their armor and belted their spears;*
they gathered their camps
and lengthened their furrow.[1*] *So how can I be consoled?*

ר *My groans are many and my laments are powerful;*
my moanings are abundant,
so [I ask] You, HASHEM, *'Until when?'*[2] *So how can I be consoled?*

ש *You have heard their insults [as] they defamed me with their lips;*
when they sit and when they stand,
I am the theme of their derisive songs.[3] *So how can I be consoled?*

ת *'Where is your hope? What are you doing here?*
His fury has been aroused [against you],
and there is no longer any cure [for you]!' *So how can I be consoled?*

ת *'All your answers remain lies!'*
the worshipers of the Baal taunt me.
[And this will last] until He looks down and takes notice[4]
from above,
[until] He lowers [our enemies] to the grave,
and raises [us out of exile].[5*] *And then I will be consoled!*

---

suffered over a lengthy period, without relief (*Radak* to *Psalms* 129:3).

מוֹרִיד שְׁאוֹל וַיָּעַל — *[Until] He lowers [our enemies] to the grave, and raises [us out of exile].* Alternatively, this is a descriptive phrase: *He Who lowers to the grave, then raises.* Accordingly the paytan means: Just as God causes people to die and will eventually resurrect them, so has He caused us to sink to the depths of exile and will eventually redeem us.

כט.

אָמַרְתִּי* שְׁעוּ מִנִּי בִּבְכִי אֲמָרֵר,[1]
מַר נַפְשִׁי וְרוּחִי אֲקָרֵר,
עִם לִוְיָתָן* הָעֲתִידִים לְעוֹרֵר.[2]

בִּבְכִי יַעְזֵר[3]* עָלַי יְגוֹנֵךְ,
בַּת עַמִּי הִתְאַבְּכִי בְגִינֵךְ,
אַל תִּתְּנִי פוּגַת לָךְ, וְאַל תִּדּוֹם בַּת עֵינֵךְ.[4]

גְּעִי בִבְכִיָּה מְעֻטֶּרֶת בַּעֲלִיזוּת,
הָיִית מִקֶּדֶם וְהִנָּךְ לְבִזּוּת,
אֵיכָה נִהְיְתָה הָרָעָה הַזֹּאת.[5]

דָּמִי אַל תִּתְּנִי[6] פְּלֵטָה הַנִּשְׁאָרָה,
הָרִימִי קוֹל וְזַעֲקִי מָרָה,
כִּי שֶׁבֶר עַל שֶׁבֶר נִקְרָא.[7]

הֵן לְאֻמִּים עֵת נִקְבָּצוּ,
חַי עָלֶיךָ כְּרוֹת בְּרִית[8] כְּחָפְצוּ,
עַל עַמְּךָ יַעֲרִימוּ סוֹד וְיִתְיָעֲצוּ.[9]

וְנִבְלוּ מְזִמּוֹת נְטוֹת אֲשׁוּרַי לִמְעוֹד,
מִדְּאָגָה וּמִפַּחַד לִרְעוֹד,[10]
אָמְרוּ לְכוּ וְנַכְחִידֵם מִגּוֹי וְלֹא יִזָּכֵר שֵׁם יִשְׂרָאֵל עוֹד.[11]

זֹאת הִשְׁמִיעוּ בְּנֵי מִקְרָאָיו,
לוֹ נְיַחֵל אִם יִקְטְלֵנוּ[12] נַעֲרִיץ לְמוֹרָאָיו,
הֵכִין יהוה זֶבַח הִקְדִּישׁ קְרוּאָיו.[13]

חֲלָלַי אָז הִרְבּוּ וְהָרְגוּ טוֹבַי,
יִסְּרוּנִי קָשׁוֹת צָרַי וְאוֹיְבַי,
הַמַּכּוֹת הָאֵלֶּה הֻכֵּיתִי בֵּית מְאַהֲבָי.[14]

אָמַרְתִּי — *I said.* This *kinnah* is a bitter narrative that recounts the brave martyrdom and slaughter of innocent Jews at the hand of their enemy. It laments children being butchered cruelly for the sanctification of God's name while their fathers are forced to witness this scene, reciting the *Shema* to proclaim that despite these unspeakable tragedies their faith was not shaken. The author cries out to God to avenge the blood of Israel and to speedily bring the redemption.

Each stanza comprises three lines. The third line is a Scriptural verse fragment and determines the rhyme. The initial letters of the respective stanzas form the *aleph-beis*, followed by the composer's signature, קְלוֹנִימוֹס הַקָּטָן, *Klonimos the lesser.* Perhaps he is Klonimos Yehudah who composed *kinnah* 25. If so, the events described here occurred during the First Crusade, in 1096. It

29.

א *I said,* 'Turn away from me,*
while I express my bitterness with weeping.'[1]
I will soothe the bitterness of my soul and spirit [by crying]
with those who are prepared to arouse their lament.[2]*

ב *Assist in weeping*[3]* *over your agony,*
O daughter of my nation, weep over yourself!
Give yourself no rest, let not your eyes be silenced [from crying].[4]

ג *Burst out weeping, O you who had been crowned with joy,*
but now have been shamed.
Alas! How did this evil happen?[5]

ד *Do not hold yourself silent,*[6] *O you fugitive remnant,*
call out in loud voice and cry out bitterly,
because catastrophe occurs on [the heels] of catastrophe.[7]

ה *Behold, when all the nations gathered together*
at the designated time,
O Lifegiver, they entered into a covenant against You,[8]
as was their desire.
Against Your nation they plot deviously and take counsel.[9]

ו *They wove treacherous schemes, turning my steps to cause a fall;*
to make me tremble from anxiety and fear.[10]
They said, 'Come, let us cut them off from nationhood,
so Israel's name will not be remembered any more!'[11]

ז *The sons of His summoned ones proclaimed,*
'We place our trust in Him, even if He should slay us,[12]
we will revere His awesomeness,
for HASHEM *has prepared a sacrifice,*
He has consecrated His guests.'[13]

ח *They then multiplied my corpses and slaughtered my finest;*
my tormentors and my enemies tortured me intensively,
these are the wounds inflicted upon me
in the house of my [treacherous] lovers.[14]

(1) Cf. *Isaiah* 22:4. (2) Cf. *Job* 3:8 [7]. (3) Cf. *Isaiah* 16:9. (4) *Eichah* 2:18. (5) *Judges* 20:3. (6) Cf. *Isaiah* 62:7. (7) *Jeremiah* 4:20. (8) Cf. *Psalms* 83:6. (9) 83:4. (10) Some editions read אַחֲרֵי הַהֶבֶל לְהַהְבִּיל וּמִפָּנָיו לִרְעוֹד, *to misguide me after the futile [idolatry], and to tremble before it.* (11) *Psalms* 83:5. (12) Cf. *Job* 13:15. (13) *Zephaniah* 1:7. (14) Cf. *Zechariah* 13:6.

is not surprising, therefore, that the medieval censors laid a heavy hand on this *kinnah*, as is obvious from the number and genre of the variant readings for some of the stanzas.

לִוְיָתָן — *Their lament.* The translation follows *Ibn Ezra* (to *Job* 3:8 [7]) in his first explanation. Accordingly, the word is third person feminine plural possessive, a contraction of לִוְיָה שֶׁלָּהֶן. Alternatively, the word is a proper noun and refers to the huge sea creature *Leviathan*, as if the sailors on an about-to-capsize ship were bemoaning their fate to become food for the Leviathan (*Ibn Ezra* ibid.). *Rashi* (ibid.) understands the word as *their conjugality*, i.e., as bereaved partners mourning over the spouse of their youth. In the *kinnah* this alludes to Israel lamenting its wayward infidelity in worshiping idols and in forsaking her first Husband, God, Who, in return, banished her from His House.

בִּבְכִי יַעְזֵר — *Assist in weeping.* In the verses from

טוֹב וּמֵטִיב הַבֵּט בְּצָרוֹתֵינוּ,
הִשְׁמִידוּ גִּבּוֹרֵי בְּחֶתֶף מֵאַרְצֵנוּ,
כָּל נֵתַח טוֹב יָרֵךְ וְכָתֵף[1] וְכָל מַשְׁמַנֵּינוּ.[2]

יַחַד לָטֶבַח הוּבָלוּ כִּטְלָאִים וּגְדָיִים,[3]
בָּנוֹת מְחֻטָּבוֹת מִשְׁבְּצוֹת עֲדִי עֲדָיִים,
גְּמוּלֵי מֵחָלָב עַתִּיקֵי מִשָּׁדָיִם.[4]

כָּבַשׁ הָאָב רַחֲמָיו* לִזְבֹּחַ,
יְלָדָיו הַשְּׁלֵמִים כְּכָרִים לָטֶבַח,
הֵכִין לְבָנָיו מַטְבֵּחַ.[5]

לְאִמּוֹתָם נוֹאֲמִים הִנְנוּ נִשְׁחָטִים וְנִטְבָּחִים,
כְּהִקְדִּישׁוּם לָטֶבַח וְהִתִּיקוּם לַאֲבָחִים,[6]
נָשִׁים פִּרְיָם עוֹלְלֵי טִפּוּחִים.[7]

מִי יִשְׁמַע וְלֹא יִדְמַע,
הַבֵּן נִשְׁחַט וְהָאָב קוֹרֵא אֶת שְׁמַע,
מִי רָאָה כָזֹאת וּמִי שָׁמַע.[8]

נְוַת בַּיִת הַיָּפָה בְּתוּלַת בַּת יְהוּדָה,
צַוָּארָהּ פָּשְׁטָה וּמַאֲכֶלֶת הִשְׁחִיזָה וְחִדְּדָה,
עַיִן רָאֲתָה וַתְּעִידָהּ.[9]

סֻגְּפָה הָאֵם וּפָרְחָה רוּחָהּ,
וְנַפְשָׁהּ הִשְׁלִימָה לָטֶבַח אֲרוּחָה כְּאָרְחָה,
אֵם הַבָּנִים שְׂמֵחָה.[10]

עָלְצוּ הַבָּנוֹת כְּנוּסוֹת וַאֲרוּסוֹת,
לְאִבְחַת חֶרֶב לְקַדֵּם רָצוֹת וְשָׂשׂוֹת,
דָּמָם עַל צְחִיחַ סֶלַע לְבִלְתִּי הִכָּסוֹת.[11]*

פוֹנֶה הָאָב בִּבְכִי וִילָלָה,
עַצְמוֹ עַל חַרְבּוֹ לִדְקוֹר וּלְהַפִּילָה,
וְהוּא מִתְגּוֹלֵל בַּדָּם בְּתוֹךְ הַמְּסִלָּה.[12]

---

(1) *Ezekiel* 24:4. (2) Some editions have a variant reading of this entire stanza. טֶנֶף צַחֲנָתָם מֵאַנְתִּי בָּם לְהִשְׁתַּתֵּף, *I refused to become a partner to the smelly filth [of their idols],*/ הִשְׁמִידוּ גִּבּוֹרֵי כֻּלָּם בְּחֶתֶף, *in one fell swoop all our warriors were obliterated,*/ כָּל נֵתַח טוֹב יָרֵךְ וְכָתֵף, *[they were like] all the best cuts [of meat], thigh and shoulder.*
(3) Cf. *Isaiah* 53:7. (4) 28:9. (5) Cf. 14:21. (6) Cf. *Jeremiah* 12:3. (7) *Eichah* 2:20.
(8) *Isaiah* 66:8. (9) Cf. *Job* 29:11. (10) *Psalms* 113:9. (11) Cf. *Ezekiel* 24:8. (12) *II Samuel* 20:12.

ט *[O God] Who is good and does good, observe our misfortunes,*
for in one fell swoop our warriors were obliterated from our land,
[they were like] all the best cuts [of meat], thigh and shoulder,[1]
and all of our choicest [leaders].[2]

י *They were led to the slaughter together, like lambs and kids;*[3]
daughters perfectly formed, adorned with jewels and ornaments,
[and] just-weaned babies torn from the breast.[4]

כ *The father suppressed his compassion**
[to allow himself] to sacrifice.
He surrendered his children like fatted sheep to the slaughter.
He prepared the butchering block for his own sons.[5]

ל *To their mothers they said,*
'Behold we are slaughtered and butchered!'
when they prepared them for the slaughter
and dragged them from their place.[6]
Women [did this to] their own offspring,
the babes they carefully pampered.[7]

מ *Who can hear this and not shed tears?*
The son is slaughtered, and the father recites the Shema!
Who ever saw the likes of this, who ever heard of it?[8]

נ *The beautiful one who dwells within,*
the maiden daughter of Judah,
stretched her neck [for the slaughter] and honed
and sharpened the knife;
[God's] Eye saw and testified [to this unsurpassed devotion].[9]

ס *Tormented was the mother and her spirit flew off,*
she submitted her soul to the slaughter, [with the same love]
as if she were preparing a meal [for her family].
[And yet,] the mother of children rejoices.[10]

ע *The daughters exulted, those wed and those betrothed,*
they rushed joyfully and gladly to the whetted sword,
their blood [shed] on a smooth rock, never to be covered over.[11]*

פ *The father turns away with weeping and wailing,*
throwing himself on his sword to be stabbed.
He wallows in his own blood on the roadway.[12]

---

which this phrase is borrowed (*Isaiah* 16:9 and *Jeremiah* 48:32), the word יַעְזֵר is a proper noun, the name of a Moabite city. Nevertheless, the translation treats it as a derivative of the root עזר, *to help* or *assist*, because that interpretation seems more apt. Although the word's vowelization seems to contradict this view, it is not uncommon for *paytanim* to speak in wordplay and conundrum.

כָּבַשׁ הָאָב רַחֲמָיו — *The father suppressed his compassion.* The next series of stanzas describes how parents made the supreme sacrifice in sanctification of God's Name by offering their children to the crusader's sword, rather than to his baptismal font. And all the while affirming their faith in the One True God by reciting the *Shema.*

דָּמָם עַל צְחִיחַ סֶלַע לְבִלְתִּי הִכָּסוֹת — *Their blood [shed] on a smooth rock, never to be covered over.* The Scriptural verse from which this

צִדְקָה דִינָהּ פּוֹרִיָּה כְּהִקְרִיבָה עֲנָפֶיהָ,
וּתְמוּר מִזְרָק דָּם קִבְּלָה בִּכְנָפֶיהָ,
תִּתְיַפֵּחַ תְּפָרֵשׂ כַּפֶּיהָ.[1]

קוֹרוֹתַי מִי יָנוּד שׁוֹד וָשֶׁבֶר[2] יִשְׂתָּרֵג,
מַחֲמַד עֵינַי כְּנִמְסַר לְחֶרֶב וּלְהֶרֶג,
אִם כְּהֶרֶג הֲרוּגָיו הֹרָג.[3]

רַעְיוֹנַי נִבְהָלוּ וַאֲחָזַתְנִי פַּלָּצוּת וָשֶׁבֶר,
בְּאַחַת* נִמְצָא הַכָּתוּב בּוֹ תִּקְוָה וָשֶׁבֶר,
כִּי זֶה לְבַדּוֹ יָבֹא לְיָרָבְעָם אֶל קָבֶר.[4]

שָׁלֵם נִמְצָא בְּכָל פָּעֳלוֹ,
נַפְשׁוֹ לָטֶבַח הִשְׁלִים מִפַּחַד חֵילוֹ,
וְגַם קְבוּרָה לֹא הָיְתָה לּוֹ.[5]

תָּהּתִּי לִבִּי מְצֹא תֹּכֶן עִנְיָנָיו,
יָדַעְתִּי אֲנִי צֶדֶק וְיֹשֶׁר דִּינָיו,
וְטוֹב הוּא לְיִרְאֵי הָאֱלֹהִים שֶׁיִּירְאוּ מִלְּפָנָיו.[6]

קְדוֹשָׁיו לֹא יַאֲמִין[7]* הִשְׁלִים עֲוֹנוֹתָם לְשַׂעֲרָה,[8]
סִמָּן טוֹב לְאָדָם* שֶׁלֹּא נִסְפַּד וְנִקְבַּר כְּשׁוּרָה,
בְּיוֹם עֶבְרָה לֹא יִירָא.

לְזֹאת יֶחֱרַד לִבִּי יִתַּר בְּחַלְחָלָה,
גִּבּוֹרַי נִרְעֲצוּ וְנִכְנְעוּ לְהַשְׁפִּילָה,
כִּנְפוֹל לִפְנֵי בְנֵי עַוְלָה.[9]

---

fragment is borrowed reads in full: *In order to arouse fury, to incite vengeance, have I placed her blood on a smooth rock, never to be covered* (*Ezekiel* 24:8). *Rashi* explains that since the smooth rock will not absorb the blood as the soil would, the blood will remain a visible reminder that the murderer has not received his just desserts.

בְּאַחַת — *Because of one [good deed].* In *I Kings* (ch. 14), the prophet אֲחִיָּה, *Ahijah*, tells the wicked Jeroboam's wife that God would utterly cut off every male child from the House of Jeroboam, '*. . .and will sweep them away as one sweeps away dung . . . The dead of Jeroboam in the city, the dogs shall eat, and the dead in the field, the birds of the heaven shall eat.*' The only exception to this curse was Jeroboam's son אֲבִיָּה, *Abijah*, who merited a proper burial because he defied his father on one point. Jeroboam had stationed armed sentries on all the roads leading to Jerusalem to prevent any member of the Ten Tribes of Israel from making the pilgrimage to Jerusalem on the three Festivals. According to the Talmud (*Moed Kattan* 28b), Prince Abijah was on sentry duty, but deserted his post and went up to Jerusalem himself. Another opinion says that Abijah entirely abolished the sentry system his father had established.

קְדוֹשָׁיו לֹא יַאֲמִין — *He trusts not His holy ones.* When R' Yochanan would reach this verse (*Job* 15:15), he would weep. 'If He does not trust His holy ones, whom does He trust?' One day, he

צ *The fruitful [mother] proclaimed the righteousness of her judgment as she offered her scions.*
And instead of the [usual] consecrated basin [in which the sacrificial blood is caught], she caught [her children's blood] in the hem of her garments,
sobbing and spreading out her arms [in anguish].[1]

ק *Who will be stirred by my tragedies wherein ruination and destruction*[2] *knitted together,*
when my eye's delight was delivered to the sword and to the slaughter.
Was there ever a slaughter to compare with the murder of his victims?[3]

ר *My thoughts are confounded for I am seized by confusion and heartbreak;*
because of one [good deed] found in him, Scripture gives [Abijah] hope and confidence,*
for he alone of [the House of] Jeroboam shall come to the grave.[4]

ש *[Yet,] one found perfect in his every deed,*
who gave up his life to the slaughter in awe
of God's domain, for him there was no proper burial![5]

ת *I have set my heart to finding the inner meaning of His dealings.*
For this I do know: His judgments are righteous and just,
and it will be good for the God-fearing, that they may be awed in His Presence.[6]

ק *He trusts not His holy ones,*[7]* *rather He punishes their sins even to a hair.*[8]
Indeed, it is an auspicious omen for a man if he is not eulogized or buried properly.*
Therefore, let him not fear the day of wrath.

ל *Over this my heart shudders, it palpitates with convulsion,*
for my heroes are shattered and subdued, humbled
as they fall before the iniquitous.[9]

(1) *Jeremiah* 4:31. (2) Cf. *Isaiah* 51:19. (3) 27:7. (4) *I Kings* 14:13. (5) *Ecclesiates* 6:3. (6) 8:12. (7) Cf. *Job* 15:15. (8) Tractate *Bava Kamma* 50a. (9) *II Samuel* 3:34.

came upon a man picking not-yet-completely-ripe figs while leaving the ripe figs on the tree. He explained to R' Yochanan that he was going on a long journey. the not-yet-ripe fruits could be expected to last; but the already ripe could not. Said R' Yochanan, 'That must be the meaning of the verse!' Just as this man is apprehensive of how the ripe figs will fare later on, so is God apprehensive lest a young *tzaddik* spoil as he ages. Thus, He will sometimes take His holy ones from this world while they are still young, and not trust them to the vicissitudes that might break them of their righteousness (*Chagigah* 5a with *Rashi*).

סִמָן טוֹב לְאָדָם — *It is an auspicious omen for a man* ... The Talmud teaches that God will sometimes cause a righteous person anguish after his death, in order to fully purge him of any stain on his soul caused by sin. Thus, one who does not receive proper burial, or is not eulogized in accordance with his stature, or

וְעַד מָתַי תִּהְיֶה כְּגִבּוֹר לֹא יוּכַל לְהוֹשִׁיעַ,[1]
נִקְמַת דַּם עֲבָדֶיךָ תּוֹדִיעַ,[2]
אֵל נְקָמוֹת יהוה אֵל נְקָמוֹת הוֹפִיעַ.[3]
נְקוֹם נִקְמָתִי מֵאֵת מְעַנַּי,
עֵת נְקָמָה הִיא[4] לָדוּן דִּינַי,
אֵל קַנֹּא וְנוֹקֵם יהוה.[5]
יהוה כְּגִבּוֹר יֵצֵא[6] יְדֵי חוֹבָךְ פְּרַע,
שׁוֹבֵר כְּתוּב שְׁטַר חוֹב תִּקְרַע,
שְׁבוֹר גְּזַר דִּינֵנוּ הָרַע.[7]
מִמָּרוֹם כְּהִסִּיק אֵשׁ[8] בְּמַעֲזִיבָה וְתִקְרָה,
חוֹמַת אֵשׁ סָבִיב[9] שׁוֹמִירָה וּבֵית דִּירָה,
שַׁלֵּם יְשַׁלֵּם הַמַּבְעִיר אֶת הַבְּעֵרָה.[10]
וּכְעַל גְּמוּלוֹת נָא שַׁלֵּם,[11]
(אוֹיְבַי תַּפִּיל מְהֵרָה וּתְכַלֵּם,)[12]
כִּי אֵל גְּמוּלוֹת יהוה שַׁלֵּם יְשַׁלֵּם.[13]
(**שׁוֹ**נְאֶיךָ תַּצְמִית סַף רַעַל תַּשְׁקֵם,[14]
הַמֵּת תַּחַת יָדוֹ נָקֹם יִנָּקֵם,[15]
אִם בְּכָזֶה לֹא תִתְנַקֵּם.[16])[12]
הַעַל כֵּן נִקְרֵאתָ אִישׁ מִלְחָמָה,[17]
צָרֶיךָ לְכַלּוֹת וּבָהֶם לְהִנָּקְמָה,
נֹקֵם יהוה וּבַעַל חֵמָה.[18]
קַנֵּא לְשִׁמְךָ עֲבוּרְךָ הָאֵל,
וּלְדַם עֲבָדֶיךָ הַשָּׁפוּךְ[19] וּלְחָרְבוֹת אֲרִיאֵל,
וּנְקוֹם נִקְמַת בְּנֵי יִשְׂרָאֵל.[20]
טִפֵּי דָמָם אַחַת לְאַחַת מְנוּיוֹת,
וְיֵז נִצְחָם[21] עַל בְּגָדֶיךָ וּבְפוּרְפְּרָךְ הֱיוֹת,
יָדִין בַּגּוֹיִם מָלֵא גְוִיּוֹת.[22]
נִלְאֵיתִי נְשֹׂא אֶת כָּל הַתְּלָאָה,
מַהֵר גְּאֻלָּתִי וְתָחִישׁ הַמַּרְאָה,
כִּי יוֹם נָקָם בְּלִבִּי וּשְׁנַת גְּאוּלַי בָּאָה.[23]

---

whose unburied body is attacked by a wild beast, attains atonement through this degradation. Such a person will be spared the punishments of the next world (*Sanhedrin* 47a with *Rashi* and *Tosafos* [46b]).

ו *Until when will You continue to be like a warrior*
who is unable to save?[1]
Let [Your] vengeance for the blood of Your servants become known
[before our eyes and among the nations];[2]
O God of vengeance, HASHEM, O God of vengeance, appear![3]

נ *Take my revenge from those who tormented me,*
[for] it is a time of vengeance,[4] *to take up my grievance.*
A zealous and avenging God is HASHEM.[5]

י *HASHEM, go forth like mighty warrior*[6] *and pay Your obligation*
[to avenge the slaughtered];
write [Yourself] a receipt [acknowledging this action],
and rip up the note of [Israel's] indebtedness [for their iniquities].
Break the power of the wicked and the evil one.[7]

מ *From on high [God] kindled a fire*[8] *on the plaster and the beam,*
a wall of fire engulfed[9] *[everything from] the sentry box*
to the [Divine] Dwelling,
He who kindled the fire must surely make full restitution.[10]

ו *According to their [wicked] deeds, please do repay [them];*[11]
(humble my enemies speedily, and destroy them,)[12]
for HASHEM is a God of retribution, He will surely repay [them].[13]

ס *(Cut down Your enemies, give them to drink the cup of poison;*[14]
[as Scripture states,] 'If one dies under his hand, he shall
surely be avenged.'[15] *Will You not avenge such as these?*[16]*)*[12]

ה *Is this why You are called the Man of War,*[17] *because*
You destroy Your enemies as You wreak vengeance upon them?
HASHEM avenges and is Master of His fury.[18]

ק *Be zealous for Your Name, for Your sake, O God!*
And for the spilt blood of Your servants[19]
and for the ruins of the leonine Temple.
O avenge the vengeance of the Children of Israel.[20]

ט *The drops of my blood, counted one by one,*
drippings of their lifeblood[21] *on Your [royal] purple,*
let Him judge the nations [on a battlefield] filled with corpses.[22]

נ *I am tired from carrying all travail,*
hasten my redemption and speedily fulfill the vision:
For the day of vengeance is in my heart,
and the year of my redemption has arrived![23]

---

(1) Cf. *Jeremiah* 14:9. (2) Cf. *Psalms* 79:10; some editions include a longer segment of the verse and read . . . . . . לְעֵינֵינוּ בַּגּוֹיִם נִקְמַת; the translation includes this phrase in the interpolation. (3) 94:1. (4) *Jeremiah* 51:6. (5) *Nahum* 1:2. (6) Cf. *Isaiah* 42:13. (7) Cf. *Psalms* 10:15; some editions read שְׁבוֹר גְּזַר דִּינֵנוּ הָרַע, *Break the evil decree of our verdict.* (8) Cf. *Eichah* 1:13. (9) *Zechariah* 2:9. (10) *Exodus* 22:5. (11) Cf. *Isaiah* 59:18. (12) Some editions omit the passages in parentheses. (13) *Jeremiah* 51:56. (14) Cf. *Zechariah* 12:2. (15) Cf. *Exodus* 21:20. (16) Cf. *Jeremiah* 5:9, 29; 9:8. (17) *Exodus* 15:3. (18) *Nahum* 1:2. (19) Cf. *Psalms* 79:10. (20) Cf. *Numbers* 31:2. (21) Cf. *Isaiah* 63:3. (22) *Psalms* 110:6; some editions do not contain this stanza, but instead read: טוֹב וּמֵטִיב קַנֵּא לִשְׁמֶךָ, *O God One Who does good for others be zealous for Your Name,*/לְמַעַן יֵחָלְצוּן יְדִידֶיךָ, *so that Your beloved ones may be released*/ הוֹשִׁיעָה יְמִינְךָ, *save us with Your right hand* (*Psalms* 60:7). (23) *Isaiah* 63:4.

ל.

מְעוֹנֵי שָׁמַיִם,* שְׁחָקִים יְזְבֻלוּךָ, מְלֵאִים מֵהוֹדְךָ,
וְהֵם לֹא יְכַלְכְּלוּךָ, וְאַף כִּי הַבָּיִת.[1]

מַה טּוֹב וּמַה נָּעִים,[2] שִׁבְתְּךָ עִם רֵעִים, בְּכַנְפֵי צַעֲצוּעִים,[3]
יַעַן הָיָה עִם לְבָבְךָ[4] לִבְנוֹת הַבָּיִת.

נָאוֹר, אַהֲבָתְךָ הֶרְאֵיתָ לְעַמֶּךָ, כִּי הֵם נַחֲלָתֶךָ,
וְלֵידַע כִּי שִׁמְךָ נִקְרָא עַל הַבָּיִת.[5]

נָכְרִים שָׁם בָּאוּ, וְעַמִּים הַר יִקְרָאוּ, וְאוֹתוֹתָיו רָאוּ,
לְמַעַן יִרְאוּ כְּבוֹד יהוה עַל הַבָּיִת.[6]

חֲטָאַי כִּי עָצְמוּ, אֲכָלַתְנִי קִנְאָה,[7]* וְעָרָה צָר הַיְסוֹד,[8]
שָׂמַנִי שׁוֹאָה, וְנָתַץ אֶת הַבָּיִת.[9]

חֲמוּדֵי אוֹצְרֵיהֶם, הֵבִיאוּ בְּהֵיכְלֵיהֶם, מִלְּאוּ כְרֵסֵיהֶם,[10]
וְצִוָּה הַכֹּהֵן וּפִנּוּ אֶת הַבָּיִת.[11]

מַדּוּעַ נִתְּכָה, וְחֵמָה לֹא שָׁכָכָה, עַל מָה זֶה עָשָׂה צוּרֵנוּ כָּכָה,
לָאָרֶץ הַזֹּאת וְלַבָּיִת.[12]

מְקוֹם כֹּהֲנֵי נִגָּשׁוּ, וְשָׁם יִתְקַדָּשׁוּ, וְהֵן כָּעֵת רָפְסוּ,
הֲמוֹן גּוֹיִם רָגְשׁוּ,[13] נָסַבּוּ עַל הַבָּיִת.[14]

בַּת קוֹל הִיא עוֹנָה, מַה תִּתְמְהוּ פֶּגַע,
סֵמֶל הַקִּנְאָה[15] הֲבֵאתֶם, וּכְנֶגַע נִרְאָה לִי בַּבָּיִת.[16]

רְבִיצַת עוֹלָם מְלֹא, שׁוֹכֵן בְּהֵיכָלוֹ, הִתְעַשּׁוּ צָרָה* לוֹ,

(1) *I Kings* 8:27. (2) *Psalms* 133:1. (3) *II Chronicles* 3:10. (4) Cf. 6:8. (5) Cf. *I Kings* 8:43. (6) *II Chronicles* 7:3. (7) Cf. *Psalms* 69:10. (8) Cf. 137:7. (9) *Leviticus* 14:45. (10) Cf. *Jeremiah* 51:34. (11) *Leviticus* 14:36. (12) *II Chronicles* 7:21. (13) Cf. *Psalms* 2:1. (14) *Genesis* 19:4. (15) *Ezekiel* 8:3. (16) *Leviticus* 14:35.

מְעוֹנֵי שָׁמַיִם — *The celestial palaces.* There was a time when God was so eager to dwell in the midst of His beloved Jewish people that He contained His unlimited Being within the limited confines of the Temple's walls. His *Shechinah*-Presence was so manifest in the Temple that even a non-Jew who came to pray there could feel God's Presence. But later, Israel ignored God's Presence. They desecrated His earthly abode with abominable idolatry. To purify the Temple, God purged it with fiery flames that consumed it.

Today, Israel eagerly awaits God's return when He will surround the rebuilt Temple with a wall of protective fire so that it will never again be defiled or destroyed.

The acrostic of the stanzas spells the composer's name, מְנַחֵם בַּר יַעֲקֹב חֲזַק, *Menachem son of Yaakov, may he be strong.* (R' Menachem flourished in Worms, Germany, during the last decades of the 12th century.) The fourth, final stich of each stanza is a Scriptural fragment ending with the word בַּיִת, *house* or *Temple.*

30.

מ *The celestial palaces,* the heavens that house You,*
are filled with Your splendor, yet they cannot contain You.
How much less so the Temple?[1]

מ *How good and how pleasant*[2] *was Your dwelling amongst friends*
between the wings of the cherished Cherubim[3]
because it was Your heart's desire[4] *to [have us] build the Temple.*

נ *O Awesome One, You have displayed Your love to Your nation,*
for they are Your heritage, and You let it be known
that Your Name is identified with the Temple.[5]

נ *Gentiles [also] came there, and foreign nations*
summoned one another to the [Temple] mountain,
they saw its wondrous signs, in order that they
should see the glory of HASHEM *upon the Temple.*[6]

ח *However, when my sins became massive,*
jealous zeal consumed me,[7]* *and the tormentor*
[razed the Temple until he] laid bare its foundation,[8]
left me desolate, and smashed the Temple.[9]

ח *They [the heathens] brought into their palaces*
[Israel's] precious treasures,
they filled their bellies[10] *[with spoils].*
For the [supreme] Kohen [God] commanded
that they empty out the Temple.[11]

מ *Why was [God's] unrelenting fury*
poured out like molten metal?
Why did our Creator do such a thing
to this land and to the Temple?[12]

מ *The place where my priests would approach,*
there to sanctify themselves, behold,
it is now overrun [by] gentile hordes
who have gathered,[13] *surrounding the Temple.*[14]

ב *A [heavenly] echo replies, 'Why are you so bewildered*
by this visitation? [Have] you [not] brought
the image of jealousy[15] *in[to the Sanctuary],*
which seemed to me like a plague in the Temple?'[16]

ר *He whose resting place is the entire universe,*
yet dwelled in His palatial Temple,
how could you manufacture a rival to Him*

אֲכָלַתְנִי קִנְאָה — *Jealous zeal consumed me.* Various interpretations are given for this line. It refers to either: God's zealous anger at 'my sins' of the preceding line; or the sin of idolatry as represented by the סֶמֶל הַקִּנְאָה, *image of jealousy,* mentioned below; or the jealousy borne by the heathen nations against the *Beis HaMikdash* and which, because of my sins, they were permitted to vent by destroying the Temple.

צָרָה — *Rival.* A polygamous man's wives are called צָרוֹת, *rivals,* literally, *troubles,* to each other (see, e.g., *I Samuel* 1:6 and *Yevamos* 2a).

עִוֵּר וּפִסֵּחַ לֹא יָבֹא אֶל הַבָּיִת.[1]

יַעַן הִשְׁחַתֶּם מִצָּאוֹנְכֶם רָעוֹת, חִלֵּל הַמִּקְדָּשׁ וְהִנֵּה מִגְרָעוֹת נָתַן לַבָּיִת.[2]

קָדוֹשׁ יִתְעַשֵּׁת, אֱמֶת לָנוּ בֹּשֶׁת,[3] יִשְׁלַח תַּחְבֹּשֶׁת,
וְחֵטְא אַל יָשֶׁת,[4] וְחִטֵּא אֶת הַבָּיִת.[5]

בְּמָקוֹר הַנִּפְתָּח[6] וּמַעֲלֶה עַל שָׂפָה,[7] מְבַכֵּר לָחֳדָשָׁיו,
וְעָלֵהוּ לִתְרוּפָה, מִתַּחַת מִפְתַּן הַבָּיִת.

חֲמוֹל עִיר הַחֲרֵבָה, תְּמוּר מוֹקֵשׁ שְׁבִיבָהּ, חוֹמַת אֵשׁ סוֹבְבָהּ,
לְכָבוֹד תִּהְיֶה בָּהּ,[8] אֶל דְּבִיר הַבָּיִת.[9]

זְרֵה וְהַעֲבֵר טֻמְאָה מִבֵּיתְךָ מַלְכִּי, אֱלִיל כָּלִיל תַּחֲלוֹף,[10]
וְתִקְרָא אָנֹכִי פִּנִּיתִי הַבָּיִת.[11]

קַדֵּשׁ בֵּית מְעוֹנִי,* וְתָשׁוּב לִמְלוֹנִי, וְנִקְבְּצוּ לִגְיוֹנִי,
וְהִנֵּה כְּבוֹד יהוה, בָּא אֶל הַבָּיִת.[12]

(1) *II Samuel* 5:8. (2) *I Kings* 6:6. (3) *Daniel* 9:7. (4) Cf. *Numbers* 12:11. (5) *Leviticus* 14:52. (6) *Zechariah* 13:1. (7) Cf. *Ezekiel* 47:12. (8) Cf. *Zechariah* 2:9. (9) *I Kings* 8:6. (10) Cf. *Isaiah* 2:18. (11) *Genesis* 24:31. (12) *Ezekiel* 43:4.

קַדֵּשׁ בֵּית מְעוֹנִי — *Sanctify the House of My Dwelling.* The translation assumes that God is still speaking. Accordingly, God says, 'I have done My part by cleansing the Sanctuary of idolatrous defilement. Now you do your part by sanctifying yourself and your environs, and by

[especially in the place of which it is written],
'A blind man or a cripple shall not enter into the Temple.'[1]

יע *Because you grew immoral, evil has found you!*
The Sanctuary was defiled and [God] Himself
diminished [the stature of] the Temple.[2]

ק *May the Holy One reflect that shame is truly ours;*[3]
May He send a cure [for our wounds] and not hold sin[4]
[against us]. May He purge the Temple.[5]

ב *With the [newly] opened water source*[6]
[He will purify the Temple];
and on the bank [of this stream] will grow[7]
fruit trees that ripen each month
and whose leaves will have curative powers,
[because they are nurtured by the holy water]
flowing from under the threshold of the Temple.

ח *Have mercy on the devastated city!*
Instead of the flaming pyre [that destroyed it,
let] a [protective] wall of fire surround it,
and You shall be glorious within it,[8]
[when Your Presence returns] to the Holy of Holies of the Temple.[9]

ז *Cast out and throw away all impurity from your House,*
O my King! Let the idols utterly vanish,[10] *and cry out,*
'I alone have cleared out [the idols from] the Temple!'[11]

ק *So sanctify the House of My Dwelling,* and return to My Lodging;*
let My legions be gathered there [and let them proclaim],
'Behold the glory of HASHEM *has entered the Temple!'*[12]

---

returning your thoughts to My Lodging, so that I may return to My Dwelling.' Alternatively, this stanza contains Israel's plaint that God return to 'the House that I built for Your dwelling.'

לא.

אֵשׁ תּוּקַד בְּקִרְבִּי,* בְּהַעֲלוֹתִי עַל לִבִּי, — בְּצֵאתִי מִמִּצְרָיִם.
קִינִים אָעִירָה, לְמַעַן אַזְכִּירָה, — בְּצֵאתִי מִירוּשָׁלָיִם.
אָז יָשִׁיר מֹשֶׁה,[1] שִׁיר לֹא יִנָּשֶׁה, — בְּצֵאתִי מִמִּצְרָיִם.
וַיְקוֹנֵן יִרְמְיָה,* וְנָהָה נְהִי נִהְיָה,[2] — בְּצֵאתִי מִירוּשָׁלָיִם.
בֵּיתִי הִתְכּוֹנָן, וְשָׁכַן הֶעָנָן,[3] — בְּצֵאתִי מִמִּצְרָיִם.
וַחֲמַת אֵל שָׁכְנָה, עָלַי כַּעֲנָנָה, — בְּצֵאתִי מִירוּשָׁלָיִם.
גַּלֵּי יָם רָמוּ, וְכַחוֹמָה קָמוּ,[4] — בְּצֵאתִי מִמִּצְרָיִם.
זֵדוֹנִים שָׁטָפוּ, וְעַל רֹאשִׁי צָפוּ,[5] — בְּצֵאתִי מִירוּשָׁלָיִם.
דְּגַן שָׁמַיִם, וּמִצּוּר יָזוּבוּ מַיִם,[6] — בְּצֵאתִי מִמִּצְרָיִם.
לַעֲנָה וּמְרוֹרִים, וּמַיִם הַמָּרִים, — בְּצֵאתִי מִירוּשָׁלָיִם.
הַשְׁכֵּם וְהַעֲרֵב, סְבִיבוֹת הַר חוֹרֵב,* — בְּצֵאתִי מִמִּצְרָיִם.
קוֹרֵא אֵל אֵבֶל, עַל נַהֲרוֹת בָּבֶל,[7] — בְּצֵאתִי מִירוּשָׁלָיִם.
וּמַרְאֵה כְּבוֹד יהוה, כְּאֵשׁ אוֹכֶלֶת[8] לְפָנַי, — בְּצֵאתִי מִמִּצְרָיִם.
וְחֶרֶב לְטוּשָׁה, וּלְטֶבַח נְטוּשָׁה, — בְּצֵאתִי מִירוּשָׁלָיִם.
זֶבַח וּמִנְחָה, וְשֶׁמֶן הַמִּשְׁחָה, — בְּצֵאתִי מִמִּצְרָיִם.
סְגֻלַּת אֵל לְקוּחָה, כְּצֹאן לְטִבְחָה, — בְּצֵאתִי מִירוּשָׁלָיִם.
חַגִּים וְשַׁבָּתוֹת, וּמוֹפְתִים וְאוֹתוֹת, — בְּצֵאתִי מִמִּצְרָיִם.
תַּעֲנִית וְאֵבֶל, וּרְדוֹף הַהֶבֶל, — בְּצֵאתִי מִירוּשָׁלָיִם.

(1) *Exodus* 15:1. (2) *Micah* 2:4. (3) See *Numbers* 9:15,22. (4) Cf. *Exodus* 15:8. (5) Cf. *Eichah* 3:54. (6) Cf. *Psalms* 78:24,20. (7) 137:1. (8) *Exodus* 24:17.

אֵשׁ תּוּקַד בְּקִרְבִּי — *A fire . . . burns within me.* The Midrash cites numerous examples of the startling contrast between our triumphant Exodus from Egypt and our tragic exit from conquered Jerusalem (*Eichah Zuta* 19). When Israel left Egypt their hearts were aflame with a fire of love for God and an unquenchable desire to receive the Torah at Sinai. But as the defeated Jews trudged out of Jerusalem's ruins into captivity, their hearts were shrouded in gloom and lamentations were on their lips.

Another tragedy which occurred on Tishah B'Av was the expulsion of the Jews from Spain in 1492. At that time the Spanish rabbis allowed orchestras to play before them (even on Tishah B'Av itself), in order to strengthen the spirits of the unfortunate exiles and to thank God for giving them the courage and strength not to succumb to the pressure to convert. It was also the aim of these rabbis to teach the people that we never weep over departing from a country in exile. No matter how we prospered in that land, we weep only over our forced departure from Jerusalem (see *Sefer HaTodaah*).

The *kinnah*, of unknown authorship, follows an *aleph-beis* arrangement as the initial letters of the respective stanzas.

הַר חוֹרֵב — *Mount Horeb.* According to the Midrash (*Tanchuma, Bamidbar* 7), Scripture records six names for Mount Sinai: (a) הַר [הָ]אֱלֹהִים, *the Mountain of Elokim* (*Exodus* 3:1; 18:5; *Psalms* 68:16); (b) הַר בָּשָׁן, *Mount Bashan* (*Psalms* 68:16); (c) הַר גַּבְנֻנִּים, *Mount Gavnunim* (ibid.); (d) הָהָר חָמַד, *the Desired Mountain* (ibid. v. 17); (e) הַר חוֹרֵב, *Mount Horeb* (*Exodus* 3:1;

31.

א *A fire [of elation] burns within me,**
when I recall in my heart [what happened],
when I went forth from Egypt;
but I shall arouse lamentations,
so that I'll remember [what occurred],
when I went forth from Jerusalem.

א *Then Moses chose to sing*[1] *a song not to be forgotten,*
when I went forth from Egypt;
but Jeremiah lamented a doleful lament,*[2]
when I went forth from Jerusalem.

ב *My House [the Tabernacle] was established, and the cloud rested upon it,*[3]
when I went forth from Egypt;
but God's fury rested like a heavy cloud upon me,
when I went forth from Jerusalem.

ג *The waves of the Sea piled high, and stood up like a wall,*[4]
when I went forth from Egypt;
but the wanton enemy drowned me and poured over my head,[5]
when I went forth from Jerusalem.

ד *Heavenly grain and a rock from which flowed water,*[6]
when I went forth from Egypt;
wormwood and bitterness and the bitter waters,
when I went forth from Jerusalem.

ה *From dawn to dusk, encircling Mount Horeb,**
when I went forth from Egypt;
but a call to mourning by the rivers of Babylon,[7]
when I went forth from Jerusalem.

ו *And the appearance of the glory of* HASHEM
was like a fire consuming[8] *before me,*
when I went forth from Egypt;
but abandoned to the slaughter of the sharpened sword,
when I went forth from Jerusalem.

ז *Sacrifices and flour offerings, and the oil of anointment,*
when I went forth from Egypt;
but God's treasure was taken like sheep to the slaughter,
when I went forth from Jerusalem.

ח *Festivals and Sabbaths, and miracles and signs,*
when I went forth from Egypt;
but fasting and mourning and the pursuit of futility,
when I went forth from Jerusalem.

33:6; *I Kings* 19:8); and (f) הַר סִינַי, *Mount Sinai* (*Exodus* 19:18).

וַיְקוֹנֵן יִרְמְיָה — *But Jeremiah lamented.* This refers to the Book of *Eichah* that *Jeremiah*

טֹבוּ אֹהָלִים, לְאַרְבָּעָה דְּגָלִים,* בְּצֵאתִי מִמִּצְרָיִם.
וְאָהֳלֵי יִשְׁמְעֵאלִים, וּמַחֲנוֹת עֲרֵלִים, בְּצֵאתִי מִירוּשָׁלָיִם.

יוֹבֵל וּשְׁמִטָּה,[1] וְאֶרֶץ שׁוֹקֵטָה, בְּצֵאתִי מִמִּצְרָיִם.
מָכוּר לַצְּמִיתוּת, וְכָרוּת וְכָתוּת, בְּצֵאתִי מִירוּשָׁלָיִם.

כַּפֹּרֶת וְאָרוֹן,[2] וְאַבְנֵי זִכָּרוֹן,[3] בְּצֵאתִי מִמִּצְרָיִם.
וְאַבְנֵי הַקֶּלַע, וּכְלֵי הַבֶּלַע, בְּצֵאתִי מִירוּשָׁלָיִם.

לְוִיִּם וְאַהֲרֹנִים, וְשִׁבְעִים זְקֵנִים,[4] בְּצֵאתִי מִמִּצְרָיִם.
נוֹגְשִׂים וּמוֹנִים, וּמוֹכְּרִים וְקוֹנִים, בְּצֵאתִי מִירוּשָׁלָיִם.

מֹשֶׁה יִרְעֵנוּ, וְאַהֲרֹן יַנְחֵנוּ, בְּצֵאתִי מִמִּצְרָיִם.
נְבוּכַדְנֶצַּר, וְאַנְדְּרִיָּנוּס* קֵיסַר, בְּצֵאתִי מִירוּשָׁלָיִם.

נַעֲרוֹךְ מִלְחָמָה, וַיהוה שָׁמָּה,[5] בְּצֵאתִי מִמִּצְרָיִם.
רָחַק מִמֶּנּוּ, וְהִנֵּה אֵינֶנּוּ, בְּצֵאתִי מִירוּשָׁלָיִם.

סִתְרֵי פָּרֹכֶת,[6] וְסִדְרֵי מַעֲרֶכֶת,[7] בְּצֵאתִי מִמִּצְרָיִם.
חֵמָה נִתֶּכֶת, וְעָלַי סוֹכֶכֶת, בְּצֵאתִי מִירוּשָׁלָיִם.

עוֹלָה וּזְבָחִים, וְאִשֵּׁי נִיחוֹחִים, בְּצֵאתִי מִמִּצְרָיִם.
בְּחֶרֶב מְדֻקָּרִים, בְּנֵי צִיּוֹן הַיְקָרִים,[8] בְּצֵאתִי מִירוּשָׁלָיִם.

פְּאֵרֵי מִגְבָּעוֹת, לְכָבוֹד נִקְבָּעוֹת,[9] בְּצֵאתִי מִמִּצְרָיִם.
שְׁרִיקוֹת וּתְרוּעוֹת, וְקוֹלוֹת וּזְוָעוֹת, בְּצֵאתִי מִירוּשָׁלָיִם.

צִיץ הַזָּהָב,[10] וְהַמְּשֵׁל וָרָהַב, בְּצֵאתִי מִמִּצְרָיִם.
הֻשְׁלַךְ הַנֵּזֶר, וְאָפֵס הָעֵזֶר, בְּצֵאתִי מִירוּשָׁלָיִם.

---

(1) See *Leviticus* 25:1-24. (2) See *Exodus* 25:10-22. (3) See 28:9-12.
(4) See *Numbers* 11:16-17,24-25. (5) Cf. *Exodus* 14:13. (6) See 26:31-33.
(7) See *Leviticus* 24:5-9. (8) *Eichah* 4:2. (9) Cf. *Exodus* 39:28. (10) See 28:36-38.

---

composed as a lament over the Destruction.

לְאַרְבָּעָה דְּגָלִים — *[Encamped] under four flags.* The Israelite camp in the Wilderness was in the shape of a square with three tribes on each side. The Torah ordained four tribes as the head of their respective sides. Thus, for example, the tribes of Judah, Issachar and Zebulun camped on the Eastern side under the דֶּגֶל מַחֲנֵה יְהוּדָה, *flag of Judah's camp.* With a similar arrangement on each side, the nation camped under four flags (see Numbers ch. 2).

נְבוּכַדְנֶצַּר וְאַנְדְּרִיָּנוּס — *Nebuchadnezzar and Hadrian.* The *kinnah* bewails the Destruction of both the First Temple by Nebuchadnezzar of

ט *Goodly tents [encamped] under four flags,**
when I went forth from Egypt;
but tents of the Ishmaelites
and camps of the uncircumcised,
when I went forth from Jerusalem.

י *Jubilee and Sabbatical year,*[1] *and the land was tranquil,*
when I went forth from Egypt;
but I was sold for posterity; torn apart and cut to pieces,
when I went forth from Jerusalem.

כ *The Ark and [its] cover,*[2] *and the stones of remembrance*
[on the High Priest's shoulder],[3]
when I went forth from Egypt;
but stones from the catapult and weapons that devour,
when I went forth from Jerusalem.

ל *Levites and sons of Aaron and the seventy elders,*[4]
when I went forth from Egypt;
but tyrants and tormentors, [slave-]traders and buyers,
when I went forth from Jerusalem.

מ *Moses provided for us, and Aaron guided us,*
when I went forth from Egypt;
but Nebuchadnezzar and Hadrian the Emperor,*
when I went forth from Jerusalem.

נ *We arrayed for battle, and* HASHEM *was [with us] there,*[5]
when I went forth from Egypt;
but He was distant from us and indeed,
He seemed not to be present,
when I went forth from Jerusalem.

ס *The [Ark] concealed behind the Curtain,*[6]
and the [Tables's] Panim-bread arrangement,[7]
when I went forth from Egypt;
but fury poured out upon me, and hovered over me,
when I went forth from Jerusalem.

ע *Burnt offerings and sacrifices, and pleasing fire offerings,*
when I went forth from Egypt;
but stabbed with the sword were precious children of Zion,[8]
when I went forth from Jerusalem.

פ *Glorious turbans, designated for [the priests'] honor,*[9]
when I went forth from Egypt;
but whistle calls and trumpet blasts, fearsome cries and shuddering,
when I went forth from Jerusalem.

צ *[The High Priest's] golden Head Plate,*[10] *monarchy and sovereignty,*
when I went forth from Egypt;
but the tiara was thrown down and [Divine] help vanished,
when I went forth from Jerusalem.

קְדֻשָּׁה וּנְבוּאָה, וּכְבוֹד יהוה נִרְאָה,[1] בְּצֵאתִי מִמִּצְרָיִם.
נִגְאָלָה וּמוֹרָאָה,[2] וְרוּחַ הַטֻּמְאָה, בְּצֵאתִי מִירוּשָׁלָיִם.

רִנָּה וִישׁוּעָה, וַחֲצוֹצְרוֹת הַתְּרוּעָה, בְּצֵאתִי מִמִּצְרָיִם.
זַעֲקַת עוֹלָל, וְנַאֲקַת חָלָל, בְּצֵאתִי מִירוּשָׁלָיִם.

שֻׁלְחָן[3] וּמְנוֹרָה,[4] וְכָלִיל וּקְטוֹרָה, בְּצֵאתִי מִמִּצְרָיִם.
אֱלִיל וְתוֹעֵבָה, וּפֶסֶל וּמַצֵּבָה, בְּצֵאתִי מִירוּשָׁלָיִם.

תּוֹרָה וּתְעוּדָה, וּכְלֵי הַחֶמְדָּה, בְּצֵאתִי מִמִּצְרָיִם.
שָׂשׂוֹן וְשִׂמְחָה, וְנָס יָגוֹן וַאֲנָחָה,[5] בְּשׁוּבִי לִירוּשָׁלָיִם.

Babylon, and the Second Temple by the Romans, here represented by Hadrian, the emperor who crushed the Bar Kochba revolution some sixty years later.

ק *Sanctity and prophecy,*
and the glory of H*ASHEM* *was manifest,*[1]
when I went forth from Egypt;
but abomination and filth[2] *and impure spirit,*
when I went forth from Jerusalem.

ר *Joyous song and salvation, and the [triumphant] trumpet blasts,*
when I went forth from Egypt;
but the infant's wailing and the mortally wounded's groaning,
when I went forth from Jerusalem.

ש *[The Tabernacle's] Table*[3] *and Menorah,*[4]
burnt offering and incense,
when I went forth from Egypt;
but idol and abomination, graven image and [pagan] stele,
when I went forth from Jerusalem.

ת *Torah and Testimony, and the cherished vessels,*
when I went forth from Egypt;
gladness and joy, while anguish and sighing will flee,[5]
when I return to Jerusalem!

(1) Cf. *Exodus* 16:10. (2) Cf. *Zephaniah* 3:1. (3) See *Exodus* 25:23-30.
(4) See 25:31-40. (5) Cf. *Isaiah* 51:11.

לב.

אֶצְבְּעוֹתַי שָׁפְלוּ,* וְאַשְׁיוֹתַי נָפְלוּ,[1]	אְוֹיָה.
בְּנֵי צִיּוֹן גָּלוּ, וְכָל אוֹיְבַי שָׁלוּ,[2]	אוֹי מֶה הָיָה לָנוּ.
בַּיִת וַעֲזָרוֹת, בְּיוֹם אַף נִגָּרוֹת,[3]	אְוֹיָה.
פְּנֵי שָׂרִים וְשָׂרוֹת, כְּמוֹ שׁוּלֵי קְדֵרוֹת,	אוֹי מֶה הָיָה לָנוּ.
גֻּלַּת הַכּוֹתֶרֶת,[4] כְּנֵבֶל נִשְׁבֶּרֶת,[5]	אְוֹיָה.
עֲטֶרֶת תִּפְאֶרֶת, לָאָרֶץ נִגְרֶרֶת,	אוֹי מֶה הָיָה לָנוּ.
דַּרְכֵי עִיר אֲבֵלוֹת,[6] וַיֶּחְדְּלוּ הַקּוֹלוֹת[7]	אְוֹיָה.
אָרְחוֹת הַסְּלוּלוֹת, חֲשֵׁכוֹת וַאֲפֵלוֹת,	אוֹי מֶה הָיָה לָנוּ.
הֵיכָל וּכְתָלָיו, מֵעַי הָמוּ עָלָיו,[8]	אְוֹיָה.
וְעַל שֻׁלְחָן וְכֵלָיו, וּמְעִיל עַל שׁוּלָיו,	אוֹי מֶה הָיָה לָנוּ.
וָוֵי הָעַמּוּדִים,[9] בְּיַד בְּנֵי הָעֲבָדִים,	אְוֹיָה.
וְהֶקֵּף רוֹבְדִים, רַבִּים וְנִכְבָּדִים,	אוֹי מֶה הָיָה לָנוּ.
זְבָחִים וּמְנָחוֹת, לְמַשּׁוּאוֹת[10] וּמַדּוּחוֹת,[11]	אְוֹיָה.
הֲדַר מִזְבְּחוֹת, בְּיָגוֹן וַאֲנָחוֹת,	אוֹי מֶה הָיָה לָנוּ.
חֵיל וְהַסּוֹרֵג, לְחֶרֶב וּלְהֶרֶג,	אְוֹיָה.
בִּנְיָן הַנֶּאֱרָג, נִדַּשׁ בְּמוֹרָג,	אוֹי מֶה הָיָה לָנוּ.
טְלָאִים מְבֻקָּרִים, מֶנּוּ נֶעְדָּרִים,	אְוֹיָה.
וְטַבָּעוֹת סְדוּרִים, וְנַנָּסִין הַהֲדוּרִים,	אוֹי מֶה הָיָה לָנוּ.
יְפִי נִבְרֶכֶת, אֵיכָה נֶהְפֶּכֶת,	אְוֹיָה.
וְגֶפֶן וּפָרֹכֶת, וּמִנְחַת מֻרְבֶּכֶת,[12]	אוֹי מֶה הָיָה לָנוּ.
כִּיּוֹר עִם כַּנּוֹ, הֶתָעִיף בּוֹ וְאֵינוֹ,[13]	אְוֹיָה.
הַנֵּר עִם שַׁמְנוֹ, לֻקַּח מִמְּעוֹנוֹ,	אוֹי מֶה הָיָה לָנוּ.
לֶחֶם הַפָּנִים, שְׂאוּ עָלָיו קִינִים,	אְוֹיָה.
וְטוּרֵי רִמּוֹנִים, לְמִרְמָס נְתוּנִים,	אוֹי מֶה הָיָה לָנוּ.
מְנוֹרָה הַטְּהוֹרָה, אוֹרָהּ נֶעְדָּרָה,	אְוֹיָה.
וּמַגְרֵפָה יְקָרָה, נְטוּלָה וַחֲסֵרָה,	אוֹי מֶה הָיָה לָנוּ.

(1) Cf. *Jeremiah* 50:15. (2) *Eichah* 1:5. (3) Cf. *Job* 20:28. (4) *I Kings* 7:41. (5) Cf. *Isaiah* 30:14. (6) Cf. *Eichah* 1:4. (7) *Exodus* 9:33. (8) *Song of Songs* 5:4. (9) *Exodus* 27:10. (10) *Psalms* 73:18. (11) Cf. *Eichah* 2:14. (12) Cf. *Leviticus* 6:14. (13) Cf. *Proverbs* 23:5.

אֶצְבְּעוֹתַי שָׁפְלוּ — *My fingers are humbled.* Many beautiful aspects of Jerusalem and its crowning glory, the Temple, are described and their disappearance is mourned in this *kinnah.* The greatest misfortune of all is that we once had so many opportunities to show our devotion

32.

א *My fingers are humbled* and my foundations are crumbled[1] — O woe!*
The children of Zion are exiled while all my enemies are serene[2] — woe, what has befallen us!

ב *The Holy Temple and its courtyards are dragged under on the day of wrath[3] — O woe!*
The faces of princes and princesses are [blackened] like the bottoms of pots — woe, what has befallen us!

ג *The crown atop the colonnades[4] is shattered like a clay jug[5] — O woe!*
the majestic tiara is pulled to the ground — woe, what has befallen us!

ד *The city's roads mourn,[6] and the voices [of her inhabitants] ceased[7] — O woe!*
Her smoothly paved highways are darkened and gloomy — woe, what has befallen us!

ה *The Sanctuary with its walls, O how my stomach longs for them[8] — O woe!*
And for the Table and its vessels and for the [Kohen Gadol's] tunic [with bells] on its hem — woe, what has befallen us!

ו *The hooks of the [Tabernacle's] posts[9] are in the hand of the [Babylonian] slave-nation — O woe!*
As are the many stately rows of flooring stone. — woe, what has befallen us!

ז *Sacrificial slaughterings and flour offerings are destroyed[10] and pushed away[11] — O woe!*
The glorious altars are in agony and groaning — woe, what has befallen us!

ח *The cheil promenade and the [surrounding] fence [fell] to sword and to murder — O Woe!*
The edifice decorated with woven tapestries lies crushed under the threshing boards — woe, what has befallen us!

ט *The lambs that were examined [before being slaughtered] have been concealed from us — O woe!*
Along with the orderly rows of [animal] shackles and the flaying pillars — woe, what has befallen us!

י *The water pool, so lovely! O how it has been turned to ruin — O woe!*
[Together with] the [golden] grapevine, the Paroches curtain and the hot-water flour-offering[12] — woe, what has befallen us!

כ *The washbasin on its stand was gone in a blink[13] — O woe!*
The lamp with its oil has been taken from its dwelling place — woe, what has befallen us!

ל *For the Panim Bread, arouse lamentations — O woe!*
And for the rows of pomegranates [on the High Priest's tunic] given over to be stepped upon — woe, what has befallen us!

מ *The pure Menorah, its light has vanished — O woe!*
The [Altar's] heavy coal rake was carried off and is missing — woe, what has befallen us!

נוֹי יַם הַנְּחֹשֶׁת,[1] לְעוֹבְדִים לַבֹּשֶׁת, אֽוֹיָה.
וּמַעֲשֵׂה הָרֶשֶׁת, וַחַלּוֹת מַרְחֶשֶׁת,[2] אוֹי מֶה הָיָה לָֽנוּ.
סְלָתוֹת וּנְסָכִים, מֶנּוּ נֶחְשָׂכִים, אֽוֹיָה.
וּבֹֽעַז וְגַם יָכִין,[3] לָאָֽרֶץ נִשְׁלָכִים, אוֹי מֶה הָיָה לָֽנוּ.
עַל מַחְתָּה וּמִזְרָק, אוֹיֵב שֵׁן חָרַק,[4] אֽוֹיָה.
טֶֽנִי גַּם כּוּז זָרַק, וְאֶת חַרְבּוֹ הִבְרַק, אוֹי מֶה הָיָה לָֽנוּ.
פִּשְׁפָּשִׁים וּשְׁעָרִים, אַֽרְצָה נִגְרָרִים, אֽוֹיָה.
הַתֻּמִּים וְהָאוּרִים, אֵיכָה נִסְתָּרִים, אוֹי מֶה הָיָה לָֽנוּ.
צְפִירַת מַעֲטָפוֹת, בְּאֵיבָה נֶהְדָּפוֹת, אֽוֹיָה.
לְשָׁכוֹת הַיָּפוֹת, וּבֵית הַחֲלָפוֹת, אוֹי מֶה הָיָה לָֽנוּ.
קִיר מָגֵן עֵרָה,[5] וְקַרְקֵר הֶהָרָה,[6] אֽוֹיָה.
וְזָרְקוּ הַמָּרָה, וְשָׂרְפוּ הַבִּירָה, אוֹי מֶה הָיָה לָֽנוּ.
רָאשֵׁי מִשְׁמָרוֹת, סְבוּכִים בְּצָרוֹת, אֽוֹיָה.
וְשָׂרֵי הָעֲשָׂרוֹת, בְּיַד בַּעֲלֵי חֲטוֹטְרוֹת, אוֹי מֶה הָיָה לָֽנוּ.
שַֽׁעַר בַּת רַבִּים,[7] לִזְאֵבֵי עֲרָבִים,[8] אֽוֹיָה.
לָֽקְחוּ הַכְּרוּבִים, תֻּפִּים וַאֲבוּבִים, אוֹי מֶה הָיָה לָֽנוּ.
תָּאִים הַנָּאִים, לַבָּנִים הַשְּׂנוּאִים, אֽוֹיָה.
בַּפָּז מְסֻלָּאִים,[9] לְחֶלְדּוֹת הַסְּנָאִים, אוֹי מֶה הָיָה לָֽנוּ.
בָּנִים הַיְּקָרִים, בַּחֲרָבוֹת נִדְקָרִים, אֽוֹיָה.
לְוִיִּם הַמְשׁוֹרְרִים, וְכֹהֲנִים מַקְטִירִים, אוֹי מֶה הָיָה לָֽנוּ.
רוֹבִים וּפִרְחִים, לְחִצִּים וּשְׁלָחִים, אֽוֹיָה.
בְּכוּרוֹת וְטִפּוּחִים, בְּיָגוֹן נֶאֱנָחִים, אוֹי מֶה הָיָה לָֽנוּ.
וּמְפַתְּחוֹת זָרְקוּ, בְּשׁוּרָם כִּי לָקוּ, אֽוֹיָה.
בְּעָוֹן נָמַֽקּוּ,[10] וְכַפַּיִם סָפָֽקוּ,[11] אוֹי מֶה הָיָה לָֽנוּ.

(1) *II Kings* 25:13. (2) *Leviticus* 2:7. (3) See *I Kings* 7:21. (4) *Eichah* 2:17. (5) Cf. *Isaiah* 22:6. (6) Cf. 22:5. (7) *Song of Songs* 7:5. (8) *Jeremiah* 5:6. (9) Cf. *Eichah* 4:2. (10) Cf. *Leviticus* 26:39. (11) Cf. *Eichah* 2:15.

to God and to be close to Him in the Temple, but now we are distant and alienated.

The stanzas of this *kinnah* bear an alphabetical acrostic, followed by the author's signature, בָּרוּךְ חֲזַק, *Baruch, may he be strong.* The first line of each stanza contains two stiches, and ends with the plaintive cry, אוֹיָה, *O woe!* The second line's two stiches are followed by, אוֹי מֶה הָיָה לָנוּ, *Woe, what has befallen us!*

The author, R' Baruch [probably R' Baruch ben Shmuel (died, Mainz, Germany, 1221)], was one of the Tosafists (*Ba'alei HaTosafos*) and served on the Mainz *beis din.* He wrote commentary to various tractates of the Talmud. His work *Sefer HaChochmah* is no longer extant.

נ *The beautiful copper pool[1] [known as King Solomon's sea]*
[is in the hands] of those who worship ignominious idols — O woe!
Along with the [Altar's] network and the deep-fried
loaves offering[2] — woe, what has befallen us!

ס *Fine meal offerings and wine libations have been removed from us — O woe!*
And [the twin Temple columns called] Boaz and Yachin[3]
are thrown down to the ground — woe, what has befallen us!

ע *Over the fire pan and the blood basin, the enemy gnashed his*
teeth[4] — O woe!
Also, he threw down basket and jug, while he flashed his sword—
woe, what has befallen us!

פ *Small doors and large gates are dragged along the ground— O woe!*
The Urim V'Tumim, O where are they now hidden? —
woe, what has befallen us!

צ *The crown-like turbans were knocked off with malice — O woe!*
The beautiful chambers and the repository of the slaughtering
knives — woe, what has befallen us!

ק *[The citizenry of] Kir [in Assyria] uncovered its battle shield[5]*
[against Jerusalem], [and the Jerusalemites]
ran screaming into the mountains[6] — O woe!
They injected bitterness [into the people] and burnt down
the palatial Temple — woe, what has befallen us!

ר *The leaders of the [Temple] watches were entangled in troubles — O woe!*
And the captains of ten suffer at the hand of whippers —
woe, what has befallen us!

ש *The gate of the many-peopled city[7]*
[is abandoned to] the wolves of the wilderness[8] — O woe!
The Cherubim have been taken away, with the [Levites']
drums and flutes — woe, what has befallen us!

ת *The lovely chambers [of the Temple have been given over]*
to the despised sons — O woe!
[While Zion's children] who are comparable to fine gold,[9]
are now like weasels in the bush — woe, what has befallen us!

ב *[Zion's] precious children are run through by the sword — O woe!*
As are the Levite choristers and the priests who offer incense —
woe, what has befallen us!

ר *Youths and [priestly] blossoms [have fallen*
victim] to arrows and sabers — O woe!
Firstborn sons and pampered babies sigh in agony—
woe, what has befallen us!

ו *[The beleaguered priests] threw the keys [of the Temple heavenward]*
when they saw that they were beaten — O woe!
They melted in sin[10] and clapped [their] hands[11] [in anguish] —
woe, what has befallen us!

כַּפּוֹת וּבָזִיכִים, מֶנּוּ נִפְסָקִים, אְוֹיָה.
וּבָנֵי נֶאֱנָקִים, בְּאֶרֶץ מֶרְחַקִּים, אוֹי מֶה הָיָה לָנוּ.
חַי חוֹבוֹ גָּבָה, וְצִיץ טָהוֹר נִשְׁבָּה, אְוֹיָה.
נֵר מַעֲרָב כָּבָה, וְשִׂמְחַת בֵּית הַשּׁוֹאֵבָה, אוֹי מֶה הָיָה לָנוּ.
זֵדִים בְּנֵי עֲדִינָה, עַל בְּנֵי מִי מָנָה, אְוֹיָה.
פְּאֵר בִּגְדֵי כְהֻנָּה, בְּיָדָם נִתְּנָה, אוֹי מֶה הָיָה לָנוּ.
קְטֹרֶת נֶעְדֶּרֶת, וְאָרוֹן וְכַפֹּרֶת, אְוֹיָה.
תִּכֵּן בַּזֶּרֶת,[1] תְּקַבֵּץ נִפְזֶרֶת,[2] יְשׁוּעָה תְּהְיֶה לָנוּ.

(1) Cf. *Isaiah* 40:12. (2) Cf. *Jeremiah* 50:17.

כ *The incense spoons and ladles have been withdrawn from us — O woe!*
And my sons are screaming in a far-off land —
woe, what has befallen us!

ח *The Living One collected His debt, and the [Kohen Gadol's] forehead plate of pure [gold] was captured— O woe!*
The Western Lamp was snuffed out, as is the joy of the Drawing of the Water — woe, what has befallen us!

ז *The wanton sons spoiled by luxury overpowered the sons [of Israel] too numerous to be counted— O woe!*
The majestic priestly robes were given over into their hand — woe, what has befallen us!

ק *The incense offering has vanished, as have the Ark and its Cover— O woe!*
[O God] Who measures [the expanse of heaven] with a little finger,[1] gather the scattered[2] and be a salvation unto us!

לג.

אֵבֶל אֲעוֹרֵר, אֲנִינוּת אֲגָרֵר, אוֹיָה לִי.
בִּבְכִי אֲמָרֵר, בַּחֲמַת צוֹרֵר, דְּרָכַי סוֹרֵר,[1] אַלְלַי לִי.
גָּלוּת אָרַךְ, וְלִבִּי הֵרַךְ,[2] אוֹיָה לִי.
דָּרַךְ וּפָרַךְ, נָחַנִי נַחְשָׁרַךְ, וְצִידוֹ חָרַךְ, אַלְלַי לִי.
הַמְּעַט מִבְּאִישַׁי, חִלְּלוּ מִקְדָּשַׁי, אוֹיָה לִי.
וְהֵם בָּזוּ קֳדָשַׁי, הֵחֵלּוּ מִמִּקְדָּשַׁי,[3] וְזִלְזְלוּ קְדוֹשַׁי, אַלְלַי לִי.
זְמַן שְׁנַת תַּתְנ"וּ, בְּיָ"א לְמַחֲזוֹר רְנ"וּ,* אוֹיָה לִי.
חֲיָלוֹת זִיְּנוּ, מְקוֹמָם פִּנּוּ, כָּאַרְבֶּה נִמְנוּ, אַלְלַי לִי.
טֶרֶף בִּקְשׁוּ,[4] וְעָלַי הִקְשׁוּ,[5] אוֹיָה לִי.
יִרְאָתָם קִשְׁקְשׁוּ, וְאוֹתוֹת הִקִּישׁוּ, וְאוֹתִי עִקְּשׁוּ, אַלְלַי לִי.
כֹּפֶר מָאָסוּ, וּנְפָשׁוֹת חָמָסוּ, אוֹיָה לִי.
לְוִיַּי בּוֹסָסוּ, כֹּהֲנַי בּוֹשָׁסוּ, צְנוּעַי אָנָסוּ, אַלְלַי לִי.
מְתֵי חֶרֶב מְהֻדָּמִים, בְּאֶפֶס דָּמִים, אוֹיָה לִי.
נִבְלַת תְּמִימִים, בְּלִי מוּמִים, הָיוּ שׁוֹמֵמִים, אַלְלַי לִי.
סָחוֹב וְהַשְׁלֵךְ,[6] עֵרוֹם לְלַכְלֵךְ, אוֹיָה לִי.
עוֹבְרֵי בְּכָל פֶּלֶךְ,[7] חֵיל יָרֵב מֶלֶךְ,[8] וְרָדוּ בְּפֶלֶךְ, אַלְלַי לִי.
פְּרִיעָה וּפְרִימָה, עַל תּוֹרָה תְּמִימָה,[9] אוֹיָה לִי.
צָר בְּיָד רָמָה, הַמְּסֻכָּן תְּרוּמָה,[10] נָם לְהַחֲרִימָה, אַלְלַי לִי.
קוֹל בָּתֵּי כְנֵסִיּוֹת, וּבָתֵּי תוּשִׁיּוֹת, אוֹיָה לִי.

(1) *Eichah* 3:11. (2) Cf. *Job* 23:16. (3) Cf. *Ezekiel* 9:6.
(4) Some editions read טָעוּת בִּקְשׁוּ, *they sought to misguide me.*
(5) Some editions read וְעָלִי הִקְשׁוּ, *they made my yoke heavy.* (6) *Jeremiah* 22:19.
(7) Some editions read עוֹבְרֵי, *those who passed;* others read עוֹבְדֵי לַמֹּלֶךְ, *those who worshiped the Molech.* (8) Cf. *Hosea* 5:13. (9) Cf. *Psalms* 19:8. (10) *Isaiah* 40:20.

אֵבֶל אֲעוֹרֵר — *I shall arouse mourning.* This *kinnah* bemoans the atrocities and calamities which befell the Jewish people during the First Crusade in the year 1096 C.E. (4856 from Creation). These events have already been described in much greater detail in *kinnah* 25. The author's signature appears in the acrostic after the *aleph-beis;* it reads אָנֹכִי מְנַחֵם הֶעָלוּב בְּרַבִּי מָכִיר, *I am Menachem, the unworthy one, the son of R' Machir.* The author's father, R' Machir, was a brother to Rabbeinu Gershom *Meor HaGolah.* His Talmudic lexicon is quoted by Rashi. R' Menachem, together with his brother, compiled a halachic work called *Maaseh HaMachiri,* which is extensively cited in *Sefer HaPardes* and *Sefer HaOrah.* Although primarily a halachist, R' Menachem wrote other liturgical compositions, including: אָדָם בְּקוּם, recited in the *Selichos* for Taanis Esther; and כְּהוֹשַׁעְתָּ אָדָם, recited on the Sabbath of Succos.

שְׁנַת תַּתְנ״וּ בְּיָ״א לְמַחֲזוֹר רְנ״וּ — *The year 4856 ... in the eleventh year of the 256th cycle.* There is a period of about eleven days by which the solar year exceeds the lunar twelve months. The calendars can be brought into alignment by intercalating a thirteenth month (of thirty days) seven times every nineteen years. 255 of these nine

33.

א *I shall arouse mourning, I shall drag out grief.* *Woe unto me!*
ב *Through weeping, I am embittered,*
because of the fury of the tormentor,
who has strewn my path with thorns.[1] *Alas for me!*
ג *He [God] lengthened the exile,*
and my heart grew timid.[2] *Woe unto me!*
ד *[The enemy] trampled and shattered,*
[Esau] the hunter led me [into captivity],
and immobilized his prey. *Alas for me!*
ה *Is it then insignificant that those who sully me,*
also desecrated my Sanctuaries? *Woe unto me!*
ו *And they shamed my holy things,*
beginning with my holy people [the Kohanim],[3]
they profaned my holy ones. *Alas for me!*
ז *The time was the year 4856 [from Creation]*
in the eleventh year of the 256th cycle [of leap years]* *Woe unto me!*
ח *Troops of soldiers armed themselves,*
they emptied out of their places
as numerous as locusts *Alas for me!*
ט *While they sought provisions*[4]
they placed a severe burden on me[5] *Woe unto me!*
י *They gathered to their idols, wearing their [crucifix] symbols,*
and claimed that I was perverted. *Alas for me!*
כ *Ransom they rejected, but souls they snatched.* *Woe unto me!*
ל *My Levites they stomped, my priests they trampled,*
and my modest women they ravished. *Alas for me!*
מ *The victims of the sword were cut to pieces,*
without a whit of guilt. *Woe unto me!*
נ *The corpses of the perfectly righteous, unblemished [by any sin],*
were abandoned [without burial]. *Alas for me!*
ס *They were dragged around and thrown down*[6]
naked, to become filthy. *Woe unto me!*
ע *Those who trod over me through every district;*[7]
the army that fought with [God] the King[8]
and dominated all of the province *Alas for me!*
פ *Let your hair grow wild and rend your garments*
over the perfect Torah[9] *[desecrated by the enemy].* *Woe unto me!*
צ *The tormentor with upraised hand,*
accustomed to offering choice gifts [to his idols],[10]
now he announced [his intention] to demolish [the Torah]. *Alas for me!*
ק *The sound of [mourning is heard in] the synagogues*
and study halls. *Woe unto me!*

רַחֲמָנִיּוֹת בִּידֵיהֶן נְקִיּוֹת, זִבְחֵי רְאִיּוֹת, אַלְלַי לִי.
שְׁלָמִים וְעוֹלוֹת, חֲתָנִים וְכַלּוֹת, אוֹיָה לִי.
תּוֹדוֹת וּבְלִילוֹת, בַּחוּרִים וּבְתוּלוֹת, וְטוֹבֵי קְהִלּוֹת, אַלְלַי לִי.
אַחִים גַּם יָחַד, **נִ**שְׁפַּךְ דָּמָם כְּאֶחָד, אוֹיָה לִי.
כֵּן אֲחָיוֹת בְּפַחַד, **בְּ**יִרְאַת שֵׁם הַמְיֻחָד,
לַטֶּבַח לְהֵאָחֵד, אַלְלַי לִי.
הוֹגֵי **מִ**לְחֲמוֹת סֵפֶר, **נֶ**שֶׁף וָצֶפֶר, אוֹיָה לִי.
חֵיךְ אִמְרֵי שֶׁפֶר,[1] **מָ**לֵא חָצָץ וָאֵפֶר,[2]
וְאַיֵּה שׁוֹקֵל וְסוֹקֵר,[3] אַלְלַי לִי.
הֶהָיְתָה זֹּאת מֵאָז, **עָ**לָה עַם עָז, אוֹיָה לִי.
לְהַשְׁמִיד הוֹעַז, **וְ**אֻסַּף עַם נוֹעָז,[4] אֲרָם וְלוֹעֵז,[5] אַלְלַי לִי.
בְּקֵשׁ עֵקֶר, **רַ**ק לַעֲקוֹר וּלְעַקֵּר, אוֹיָה לִי.
(**בְּ**בַקָּר אַרְמָאִי מְשַׁקֵּר,)[6] **יָ**זַם הַזָּר[7] לְעַקֵּר,
וְלֹא לְגָרֵם לַבֹּקֶר,[8] אַלְלַי לִי.
מְקַיֵּם הַבְּרִית, לוּלֵי הוֹתִיר שְׁאֵרִית, בְּגֵיא נָכְרִית, (אוֹיָה לִי.)[6]
כְּשַׂר שַׁעֲרוּרִית, **יְ**דִידַת עִבְרִית,
רַחֵם מֵהַכְרִית, וְיֵשׁ תִּקְוָה לְאַחֲרִית.[9]

לוֹבֵשׁ נְקָמָה, עוּרָה וְקוּמָה,
הָרִים שִׁפְלֵי קוֹמָה,
יָדִין גְּוִיּוֹת רִקְמָה.
וּשְׁכִינָה קָמָה עַל מְקוֹמָהּ.

---

(1) Cf. *Genesis* 49:21. (2) Cf. *Eichah* 3:16. (3) Cf. *Isaiah* 33:18. (4) 33:19.
(5) Some editions read בְּנֵי נָבָל וְלוֹעֵז, *the children of the irrelevant and speakers of foreign tongues,* a reading that completes the acrostic of the author's signature [see commentary].
(6) Some editions omit the words in parentheses.
(7) Some editions read אֲרַמִּי, *the Aramean,* instead of הַזָּר, *the alien.*
(8) Cf. *Zephaniah* 3:3. (9) Cf. *Jeremiah* 31:16.

ר *Compassionate [mothers slaughtered their children]*
with their own innocent hands,
as if they were festival sacrifices. *Alas for me!*
ש *[Like] peace-offerings and burnt-offerings,*
grooms and brides [were butchered] *Woe unto me!*
ת *Like thanksgiving-offerings and mixed flour-offerings,*
youths and maidens and the elite community leaders
[were sacrificed]. *Alas for me!*
א *Brothers who lived in harmony,*
נ *their blood was shed as one.* *Woe unto me!*
כ *Similarly, sisters who shared*
י *reverence for the awesome Name of the One and Only God,*
now shared a common fate
as they were slaughtered together *Alas for me!*
מ *Those who struggled to comprehend the lessons of the [Torah] volumes*
נ *from dusk to dawn.* *Woe unto me!*
ח *The mouths which were filled with lovely [Torah] words*[1]
מ *were stuffed with dust and dirt;*[2] *and where are those who weighed*
and measured [every Torah letter]?[3] *Alas for me!*
ה *Has similar [tragedy] occurred since days of yore,*
ע *that such a brazen nation should rise up [against God]?* *Woe unto me!*
ל *With audacity to destroy [the Jews],*
ו *while they assembled fierce nations,*[4]
Aram and others who spoken foreign languages.[5] *Alas for me!*
ב *These unworthy nations attempted*
ר *to uproot [us] and to leave us barren.* *Woe unto me!*
ב *[With perverted justice the Aramean acted deceitfully]*[6]
י *and the alien*[7] *plotted to uproot me*
and to allow no bone to remain until the morning.[8] *Alas for me!*
מ *[O God] Who upholds the covenant,*
if not for Your faithfulness which allowed a remnant
to survive in the deep valley of foreign exile; *[Woe unto me!]*[6]
כ *When You observed the wretched misery*
י *of Your beloved Hebrews,*
ר *You mercifully saved [us] from annihilation*
and there yet is hope for our future![9]
[O You] Who dons the robes of revenge, awaken and arise
and elevate the stature of the downtrodden,
and do justice for the corpses
of elegant design [before being murdered],
and let the Divine Presence arise [and ascend] to its place.

---

nineteen-year cycles total 4845 years. Adding eleven years to this total brings us to 4856, the eleventh year in the 256th nineteen-year cycle.

לד.

יוֹם אַכְפִּי הִכְבַּדְתִּי,[1]* וַיִּכְפְּלוּ עֲוֹנִי,
בְּשָׁלְחִי יַד בְּדַם נָבִיא בַּחֲצַר אֵל מִקְדַּשׁ יהוה,
וְלֹא כִסִּתְהוּ אֲדָמָה עַד בֹּא חֶרֶב מוֹנָי,
וְלֹא שָׁקַט עֲדֵי הֶקַּם דַּם הַנָּבִיא זְכַרְיָה,
וַיֶּרֶב בְּבַת יְהוּדָה תַּאֲנִיָּה וַאֲנִיָּה.[2]

הָיָה הוֹלֵךְ וְסוֹעֵר, עַד בֹּא רַב טַבָּחִים,
וּבָא אֶל מִקְדַּשׁ יהוה, וּמָצָא דָמִים רוֹתְחִים,
וַיִּשְׁאַל בַּעֲבוּר זֶה, הַכֹּהֲנִים הַזּוֹבְחִים,
וַיַּעֲנוּהוּ כִּי זֶה הוּא, דַּם קָרְבַּן הַזְּבָחִים,
וַיְנַסֶּה בְּדַם פָּרִים וְדַם אֵילִים וְדַם מֵחִים,
וְגַם זָבַח זֶבַח רַב, לַחֲקוֹר מֶה הָיָה,
וַיֶּרֶב בְּבַת יְהוּדָה תַּאֲנִיָּה וַאֲנִיָּה.

וּבְכָל זֹאת לֹא שָׁקַט, וְעוֹדוֹ כַּיָּם נִגְרָשׁ,[3]
וַיְבֻקַּשׁ הַדָּבָר וַיִּמָּצֵא מְפֹרָשׁ,[4]
כִּי הוּא דַּם אִישׁ הָאֱלֹהִים עַל לֹא חָמָס[5] שֹׁרָשׁ,
וַיֹּאמֶר נְבוּזַרְאֲדָן, גַּם דָּמוֹ הִנֵּה נִדְרָשׁ,[6]
אִסְפוּ לִי הַכֹּהֲנִים, וְהוֹצִיאוּם מִבֵּית יָהּ,
כִּי לֹא אֶשְׁקוֹט, עַד יִשְׁקוֹט, דַּם הַנָּבִיא זְכַרְיָה,
וַיֶּרֶב בְּבַת יְהוּדָה תַּאֲנִיָּה וַאֲנִיָּה.

דָּקַר יְשִׁישִׁים לְמֵאוֹת וּבַחוּרִים לְרִבּוֹאוֹת,
וַיּוֹרֶד לָטֶבַח כֹּהֲנֵי יהוה צְבָאוֹת,
וְאֵין שֶׁקֶט לְדַם נָבִיא, וַיְהִי לְמוֹפֵת וָאוֹת,
וְהַבָּנִים נִשְׁחָטִים, וְעֵינֵי אָבוֹת רוֹאוֹת,

(1) Cf. *Job* 33:7. (2) *Eichah* 2:5. (3) Cf. *Isaiah* 57:20.
(4) Cf. *Esther* 2:23. (5) *Isaiah* 53:9. (6) Cf. *Genesis* 42:22.

יוֹם אַכְפִּי הִכְבַּדְתִּי — *On that day I increased my burden.* When Zechariah ben Jehoiada protested the introduction of a pagan idol into the Holy Temple, he was stoned to death in the Temple courtyard by the Jewish masses. This occurred during the time, and at the bidding, of the wicked King Joash. With this cold blooded murder the entire Jewish nation became guilty of a sevenfold crime: (1) The murder of an innocent person; (2) who was a *Kohen;* (3) a prophet; (4) and a judge; (5) the desecration of the Temple Courtyard; (6) on Yom Kippur, (7) which was also a Sabbath day (see *II Chronicles* 24:20-21 and *Koheles Rabbah* 3:20).

The blood of Zechariah lay uncovered on the stone floor of the Temple Courtyard for two

34.

י *On that day I increased my burden,[1]**
because I doubled my iniquity,
When I stretched out my hand to spill the blood of the prophet
in God's Courtyard, in HASHEM's Sanctuary.
But the earth would not cover it until the sword of
my tormentors entered;
nor was the blood silent,
until the blood of the prophet Zechariah was avenged.
And He increased within the daughter of Judah
moaning and mourning.[2]

ה *[The blood] continued to churn and roil*
until the chief executioner arrived,
He entered HASHEM's Sanctuary and found the blood boiling.
He inquired about this from the priests
who were slaughtering offerings.
And they answered him,
'Why, this is the blood of the sacrificial offerings.'
And he tested [the seething blood by comparing it] with the blood
of cows, the blood of rams, and the blood of fattened animals,
and he slaughtered many animals, to determine what had occurred.
And He increased within the daughter of Judah moaning and mourning.

ך *Despite all this, the blood was not silent,*
but continued like the troubled sea.[3]
The matter was investigated and clearly corroborated,[4]
that this was the blood of the man of God
who was ripped out by his roots for no reason.[5]
Nebuzaradan then declared, 'Behold,
his blood now demands [revenge]![6]
Gather unto me the priests and remove them from God's House,
for I shall not be silent, until the blood
of the prophet Zechariah remains silent.'
And He increased within the daughter of Judah moaning and mourning.

ד *He stabbed elders by the hundreds*
and youths by the tens of thousands,
and he dragged the priests of HASHEM, Master of Legions,
to the slaughter.
Yet the prophet's blood was not silent;
and this was an amazing wonder and a clear sign.
For the children were massacred
while their fathers' eyes watched,

וְאִמּוֹתָם לָטֶבַח, גַּם אַחֲרֵיהֶם בָּאוֹת,
וָאֹמַר לְנַפְשִׁי זֶה חַטָּאתֵךְ וְזֶה פִּרְיָהּ,
וַיֶּרֶב בְּבַת יְהוּדָה תַּאֲנִיָּה וַאֲנִיָּה.

הוֹסִיף לַהֲרוֹג נָשִׁים עִם יוֹנְקֵי שָׁדַיִם,
וְדָם עוֹלֶה בֵּינֵיהֶם, כְּדַם יְאוֹר מִצְרַיִם,
עֲדֵי נָשָׂא נְבוּזַרְאֲדָן לִבּוֹ לַשָּׁמַיִם,
וַיֹּאמֶר, הַאֵין דַּי בִּבְנוֹת יְרוּשָׁלַיִם,
הֲכָלָה אַתָּה עוֹשֶׂה לִשְׁאֵרִית[1] הַשְּׁבִיָּה,
וַיֶּרֶב בְּבַת יְהוּדָה תַּאֲנִיָּה וַאֲנִיָּה.

(לְךָ חָטָאנוּ אֱלֹהִים, הֶעֱוִינוּ וְהִרְשָׁעְנוּ,
וְהָרַגְנוּ נְבִיאֶךָ וְרִשְׁעֵנוּ יָדָעְנוּ,
יְהִי חַסְדְּךָ לְנַחֲמֵנוּ, כִּי מִשְּׁאוֹל שִׁוַּעְנוּ,
וּמִפְּרִי מַעֲלָלֵינוּ זֶה כַּמֶּה שָׂבָעְנוּ,
רַחֵם לֹא רֻחָמָה, הַסֹּעֲרָה עֲנִיָּה,
עֵינֶיהָ לְךָ תִשָּׂא, וְאֶת עֶזְרָתְךָ צוֹפִיָּה.)

---

hundred and fifty years during which it continued to seethe and bubble as a sign of God's fury against the nation. The blood thus pointed an accusing finger, and demanded the retribution described in this *kinnah*, which is based on the following Talmudic account:

The Babylonian general Nebuzaradan was spurred on by the sight of the blood of the murdered prophet Zechariah seething on the floor of the Temple. At first, the Jews sought to conceal the true story connected with the blood. Eventually, however, they had to confess that it was the blood of a prophet who had prophesied the Destruction of the Temple, and had been slain by the people for his candor.

'I,' said Nebuzaradan, 'will appease him.' He ordered the scholars of the kingdom to be executed on that bloody spot, then the school children, and at last the young priests — more

and their mothers, too, followed them to the slaughter.
And I said to myself,
'This is your sin and this is its fruit!'
And He increased within the daughter of Judah moaning and mourning.

ה *He continued slaying women with [their] nurslings.*
And the blood surged up among them like
the [Nile] river of Egypt [at flood stage],
until Nebuzaradan lifted his heart towards heaven
and said, 'Are the daughters of Jerusalem not enough?
Is it Your intention to annihilate the remainder[1] *of the captivity?'*
And He increased within the daughter of Judah moaning and mourning.

ל *(We have sinned to You, O God, we have been iniquitous and wicked;*
ו *we have murdered Your prophets and we recognize our evil.*
י *Let Your kindness comfort us, for we cry from the grave,*
and long have we been sated on the fruits of our misdeeds.
Be merciful with the unmercied, storm-tossed, afflicted one,
who lifts her eyes to You, and hopes for Your help.)

(1) Cf. *Ezekiel* 11:13.

than nine hundred forty thousand in all.

But the blood of the prophet went on seething until Nebuzaradan exclaimed: 'Zechariah, Zechariah! I have destroyed the flower of them. Do you wish me to massacre them all?'

Only then did the blood rest.

Thoughts of repentance came to Nebuzaradan's mind: If the Jews, who killed one person only, have been so severely punished, what will be my fate?

He left, and ultimately converted to Judaism (*Sanhedrin* 96b).

This *kinnah* was composed by R' Yehudah HaLevi (see commentary to *kinnah* 36), whose name יְהוּדָה forms the acrostic of the five stanzas. A sixth stanza (printed here in parentheses) appears in the Sefardic rite, and forms the acrostic לֵוִי, *Levi.*

לה.

שִׁכֹּרַת וְלֹא מִיַּיִן[1] **הַ**שְׁלִיכִי תֻפַּיִךְ,
קָרְחִי נָא וָגֹזִּי[2] וְהַשְׁחִיתִי אַפַּיִךְ,
שְׂאִי עַל שְׁפָיִם קִינָה[3] וְסֹבִּי אֲגַפַּיִךְ.
וְצַעֲקִי לִפְנֵי יהוה עַל חֹרֶב סִפַּיִךְ,
עַל חֹרֶב סִפַּיִךְ, עַל נֶפֶשׁ עוֹלָלַיִךְ,[4] שְׂאִי אֵלָיו כַּפַּיִךְ.

אֵיכָה בָּא צַר וְאוֹיֵב[5] בְּצִיּוֹן עִיר מַמְלֶכֶת,
אֵיכָה רֶגֶל זֵדִים אַדְמַת קֹדֶשׁ דּוֹרֶכֶת,
בְּבוֹאָם מָצְאוּ כֹּהֲנִים שׁוֹמְרֵי הַמַּעֲרֶכֶת,
וְעַל מִשְׁמְרוֹתָם עָמְדוּ וְלֹא עָזְבוּ הַמְּלֶאכֶת,
עַד אֲשֶׁר שֻׁפַּךְ דָּמָם כְּמֵימֵי הַמַּהְפֶּכֶת,
וּבָא עָרֵל וְטָמֵא[6] מִבֵּית לַפָּרֹכֶת,
לַמָּקוֹם אֲשֶׁר כֹּהֵן גָּדוֹל יָרֵא שָׁם לָלֶכֶת,
וְהֶחֱרִיבוּ סִפַּיִךְ וְחַלּוֹנֵי שְׁקוּפַיִךְ.[7]
וְצַעֲקִי לִפְנֵי יהוה עַל חֹרֶב סִפַּיִךְ,
עַל חֹרֶב סִפַּיִךְ, עַל נֶפֶשׁ עוֹלָלַיִךְ, שְׂאִי אֵלָיו כַּפַּיִךְ.

קוֹל יִלְלַת בַּת צִיּוֹן מֵרָחוֹק נִשְׁמַעַת,
תִּזְעַק זַעֲקַת חֶשְׁבּוֹן[8] תִּבְכֶּה בְּכִי מֵיפָעַת,[9]
אֲהָהּ כִּי כוֹס שָׁתִיתִי וּמַצִּיתִי קֻבַּעַת,[10]
אֲכָלוּנִי אֲרָיוֹת[11] חַדּוּדֵי מַלְתָּעַת,
בַּת בָּבֶל הַשְּׁדוּדָה וּבַת הַמַּרְשַׁעַת,
מַה תִּתְאוֹנְנִי צִיּוֹן וְחַטָּאתֵךְ נוֹדַעַת,
עַל רֹב עֲוֺנֵךְ[12] גָּלָה עַמֵּךְ מִבְּלִי דָעַת,[13]
עַל עָזְבֵךְ צוֹפַיִךְ וְשָׁמְעֵךְ קוֹל תְּרָפַיִךְ.
וְצַעֲקִי לִפְנֵי יהוה עַל חֹרֶב סִפַּיִךְ,
עַל חֹרֶב סִפַּיִךְ, עַל נֶפֶשׁ עוֹלָלַיִךְ, שְׂאִי אֵלָיו כַּפַּיִךְ.

(1) Cf. *Isaiah* 51:21. (2) Cf. *Micah* 1:16. (3) Cf. *Jeremiah* 7:29. (4) Cf. *Eichah* 2:19. (5) 4:12.
(6) Some editions read וּבָא כָּל עָרֵל וְטָמֵא, *Then all the uncircumsized and contaminated entered.*
(7) Cf. *I Kings* 6:4. (8) See *Jeremiah* 48:34.(9) See 48:21. (10) Cf. *Isaiah* 51:17.
(11) Some editions read . . . שִׁנֵּי אֲרָיוֹת, *the teeth of the sharp-fanged lions;* some read
שְׁנֵי אֲרָיוֹת, *the two . . . lions,* i.e., Babylon and Edom. (12) *Jeremiah* 30:14. (13) Cf. *Isaiah* 5:13.

שִׁכֹּרַת וְלֹא מִיַּיִן — *Drunk, but not from wine.* The prophet Isaiah foretells of the shock which will overcome Israel after the Destruction, a trauma that will delude their intellect:

Awaken! Awaken! Stand up, O Jerusalem! You who have drunk from the hand of HASHEM *the cup of His fury; you have drunk down to the very dregs the deep bowl which makes you*

35.

[O Israel] drunk, but not from wine,[1] throw down your tambourines!*
Tear out your hair now and cut it off![2] Mutilate your face!
Raise a lament upon the hills,[3] and circle around your borders.
And cry out before HASHEM about
the destruction of your [Temple's] gateways
about the destruction of your [Temple's] vessels,
about the life of your young children,[4]
lift your hands up to Him [in prayer].

O how was the enemy oppressor able to enter[5] Zion, the royal city;
how were the feet of the wanton able to tread on the holy ground?
When they entered they found the priests,
the guardians of the sacrificial order
standing at their guard, not abandoning the service,
until their blood was spilled like the waters of [the Nile]
that were changed [into blood].
Then the uncircumcised entered and contaminated[6]
[the Holy of Holies] within the Paroches curtain,
the place where the High Priest feared to go,
and they destroyed your entranceways
and your slotted windows.[7]
And cry out before HASHEM
about the destruction of your [Temple's] gateways
about the destruction of your [Temple's] vessels,
about the life of your young children,
lift your hands up to Him [in prayer].

The sound of Zion's daughter's wailing is heard from afar,
she cries out as Cheshbon once cried,[8]
she weeps as Mephaath once wept.[9]
'Ah, woe! For I have drunk deeply of the cup [of retribution]
and I have sucked out its bitter dregs![10]
The sharp-fanged lions[11] have consumed me,
the destructive daughter of Babylon,
and the wicked daughter of Edom.
Why do you complain, O Zion, when your sins are well known!
Because of your many iniquities,[12] your nation was exiled,
for your ignorance [of God's ways];[13]
because you abandoned your seers,
listened to the voice of your idolatrous oracles.
And cry out before HASHEM
about the destruction of your [Temple's] gateways
about the destruction of your [Temple's] vessels,
about the life of your young children,
lift your hands up to Him [in prayer].

אַל תִּשְׂמְחִי אוֹיַבְתִּי, עַל שֶׁבֶר קַרְנִי,
כִּי נָפַלְתִּי קָמְתִּי[1] וַיהוה עֲזָרָנִי,[2]
הִנֵּה יַאַסְפֵנִי אֵלִי אֲשֶׁר פְּזָרָנִי,
וְיִגְאָלֵנִי מִמֵּךְ צוּרִי אֲשֶׁר מְכָרָנִי,
וְגַם עָלַיִךְ תַּעֲבָר כּוֹס[3] אֲשֶׁר עֲבָרַנִי,
וְאָז בְּסַלְעֵי סְעִפַּיִךְ,
אֲנַפֵּץ אֶת טַפַּיִךְ.[4]

וְצַעֲקִי לִפְנֵי יהוה עַל חָרֶב סִפַּיִךְ,
עַל חָרֶב סִפַּיִךְ, עַל נֶפֶשׁ עוֹלָלַיִךְ, שְׂאִי אֵלָיו כַּפָּיִךְ.

---

stagger ... Therefore, now hear this, you who are afflicted, drunk, but not from wine!' (*Isaiah* 51:17,21). The author here vividly describes the terrible cruelties that befell Israel and the destruction that numbed their hearts and their minds.

The author's name שְׁלֹמֹה, *Shlomo*, appears in the first four words. He is usually identified as R' Shlomo ben Yitzchak of thirteenth-century Gerona, Spain.

Do not rejoice, O my enemy,
that my pride was broken,
for although I have fallen, I shall arise[1]
and HASHEM shall assist me.[2]
Behold, it is the Almighty Who dispersed me,
Who shall gather me in.
And my Creator Who sold me will redeem me from you.
Indeed, the cup [of retribution] that passed over me
will also pass over you,[3]
and then upon the jagged edges of your rocks
I will smash your infants [as you did mine].[4]

And cry out before HASHEM
about the destruction of your [Temple's] gateways
about the destruction of your [Temple's] vessels,
about the life of your young children,
lift your hands up to Him [in prayer].

(1) *Micah* 7:8. (2) *Psalms* 118:13. (30) Cf. *Eichah* 4:21. (4) Cf. *Psalms* 137:9.

לו.

צִיּוֹן הֲלֹא תִשְׁאֲלִי* לִשְׁלוֹם אֲסִירָיִךְ,
דּוֹרְשֵׁי שְׁלוֹמֵךְ[1] וְהֵם יֶתֶר עֲדָרָיִךְ.
מִיָּם וּמִזְרָח וּמִצָּפוֹן וְתֵימָן,[2]
שְׁלוֹם רָחוֹק וְקָרוֹב,[3] שְׂאִי מִכָּל עֲבָרָיִךְ.
וּשְׁלוֹם אֲסִיר תִּקְוָה,[4] נוֹתֵן דְּמָעָיו כְּטַל חֶרְמוֹן,[5]
וְנִכְסָף לְרִדְתָּם עַל הֲרָרָיִךְ.
לִבְכּוֹת עֱנוּתֵךְ אֲנִי תַנִּים,[6]
וְעֵת אֶחֱלוֹם שִׁיבַת שְׁבוּתֵךְ,[7] אֲנִי כִנּוֹר לְשִׁירָיִךְ.
לִבִּי לְבֵית אֵל, וְלִפְנֵי אֵל מְאֹד יֶהֱמֶה,
וּלְמַחֲנָיִם* וְכָל נִגְעֵי טְהוֹרָיִךְ.[8]
שָׁם הַשְּׁכִינָה שְׁכוּנָה לָךְ,
וְיוֹצְרֵךְ פָּתַח לְמוּל שַׁעֲרֵי שַׁחַק שְׁעָרָיִךְ.[9]
וּכְבוֹד יהוה לְבַד הָיָה מְאוֹרֵךְ,[10]
וְאֵין סַהַר וָשֶׁמֶשׁ וְכוֹכָבִים מְאוֹרָיִךְ.[11]
אֶבְחַר לְנַפְשִׁי לְהִשְׁתַּפֵּךְ,[12]
בִּמְקוֹם אֲשֶׁר רוּחַ אֱלֹהִים שְׁפוּכָה עַל בְּחִירָיִךְ.
אַתְּ בֵּית מְלוּכָה, וְאַתְּ כִּסֵּא כְבוֹד אֵל,[13]
וְאֵיךְ יָשְׁבוּ עֲבָדִים עֲלֵי כִסְאוֹת גְּבִירָיִךְ.
מִי יִתְּנֵנִי מְשׁוֹטֵט,
בִּמְקוֹמוֹת אֲשֶׁר נִגְלוּ אֱלֹהִים לְחוֹזַיִךְ וְצִירָיִךְ.
מִי יַעֲשֶׂה לִּי כְנָפַיִם[14] וְאַרְחִיק נְדוֹד,[15]

⁂ **צִיּוֹן הֲלֹא תִשְׁאֲלִי** — *O Zion, will you not inquire.* This very well-known *kinnah* was written by one of the greatest *paytanim* of all time, R' Yehudah (ben Shmuel) HaLevi. The beauty and passion of this *kinnah* reflects its author's life-long yearning to flee from the exile and to walk on the sacred soil of the Holy Land.

R' Yehudah HaLevi was born in Toledo, Spain (circa 1080) and received an intensive Torah education at the yeshivah of R' Yitzchak Alfasi (the *Rif*) in Lucena, Spain. In addition to studying Talmud, R' Yehudah became a master of literary style in Hebrew and Arabic. *Rashba* writes of him (Responsum 418): 'R' Yehudah HaLevi is foremost amongst all poetic singers in distinction and merit.' His greatest contribution to Torah knowledge was the *Kuzari*, a philosophical work telling of the king of the Khazar tribe who sought to determine the true religion by questioning a Christian, a Moslem and a Jewish scholar. The king was finally convinced of the authenticity of Judaism, which he, together with his entire kingdom, embraced as the true religion. In the course of the disputation, the Khazar king taunts the Jewish teacher that the Jews seem to pay insincere lip service to Zion, their homeland. They pray for the restoration of Zion three times daily, yet in practice they are not willing to leave behind the prosperity and comfort of the exile to live in *Eretz Yisrael.* Humiliated, the Jewish sage of the *Kuzari* resolves to tear himself away from the

36.

צִיּוֹן *O Zion, will you not inquire* about the welfare of your imprisoned,*
who seek your welfare,[1] for they are the remnants of your flocks.
From west and east, from north and south,[2] carry [in your heart]
the welfare of the distant and the near,[3] from your every side.
And the welfare of the prisoner who is yet full of hope,[4]
who gives forth his tears like the dew of [Mount] Hermon,[5]
and yearns to let them fall upon your hills.
Weeping over your suffering, I am like a sea monster,[6]
but when I dream of the return of your captivity,[7]
I am a harp for your songs.
My heart [longs] for God's Temple, and before God I long intensely,
and for the [three] encampments [of the Divine Presence,*
the Kohanim and Levites, the Israelites],
and for all who approach your purity.[8]
For there [in Zion] the Divine Presence resides,
and [there] your Creator has opened gates for you
opposite the gates of heaven.[9]
And only the glory of God was your lamp,[10]
but the moon, sun, and stars were not your luminaries.[11]
I would elect for my soul to be poured out[12] [in prayer],
in the place where the prophetic spirit of God
was poured out upon your chosen ones.
You are the royal palace and you are God's Throne of Glory.[13]
How have slaves sat upon the thrones of your heroes?
If only I could be set adrift in the places where God
was revealed to your seers and your emissaries.
Who shall make me wings[14] so that I might wander far away?[15]

(1) Cf. *Psalms* 122:6. (2) Cf. 107:3. (3) Cf. *Isaiah* 57:19. (4) Cf. *Zechariah* 9:12. (5) *Psalms* 133:3. (6) Cf. *Micah* 1:8. (7) Cf. *Psalms* 126:1. (8) Some editions read פִּגְעֵי טְהוֹרַיִךְ, *the places where your pure ones prayed,* or *where your pure ones met.* (9) Cf. *Genesis* 28:17. (10) Cf. *Isaiah* 60:1. (11) Cf. 60:19. (12) Cf. *Joel* 3:1. (13) Cf. *Jeremiah* 3:17. (14) Cf. *Proverbs* 23:5. (15) *Psalms* 55:8.

---

lands of the gentiles and to settle in *Eretz Yisrael.*

The author of the *Kuzari* took his own words to heart and prepared to make his way to the land for which he had always yearned. Had not Rabbi Yehudah HaLevi himself written, 'My heart is in the east while I am stranded in the farthest end of the west!' Despite many hardships he finally made his way to Damascus. An ancient manuscript states that R' Yehudah HaLevi composed this *kinnah* while journeying towards *Eretz Yisrael* and recited it when he reached Damascus, facing the direction of Zion. Although many historians believe that R' Yehudah HaLevi only got as far as Egypt (never even reaching Damascus), tradition has it that he finally reached Jerusalem (circa 1145). There he fell to the ground, in a state of ecstasy to fulfill the verse כִּי רָצוּ עֲבָדֶיךָ אֶת אֲבָנֶיהָ וְאֶת עֲפָרָהּ יְחֹנֵנוּ, *For Your servants had cherished her stones and been gracious to her dust* (*Psalms* 102:15). As he was kissing and embracing the dust near the Temple Mount he was trampled and killed by an Arab horseman.

לְבֵית אֵל וְלִפְנֵי אֵל ... וּלְמַחֲנַיִם — *For God's Temple, and before God ... and for the [three] encampments.* Some editions read, לְבֵית־אֵל וְלִפְנִיאֵל, *For Bethel and for Peniel,* treating these words as place names. If so, מַחֲנַיִם is also a place name, *Mahanaim.* Each of these three places was named by the Patriarch Jacob: Bethel, after his dream of angels ascending and descending a ladder (*Genesis* 28:19); Mahanaim, after his

אָנִיד לְבִתְרֵי לְבָבִי בֵּין בְּתָרָיִךְ.
אֶפֹּל לְאַפִּי עֲלֵי אַרְצֵךְ,
וְאֶרְצֶה אֲבָנַיִךְ לִמְאֹד וַאֲחוֹנֵן אֶת עֲפָרָיִךְ.[1]
אַף כִּי בְּעָמְדִי עֲלֵי קִבְרוֹת אֲבוֹתַי,
וְאֶשְׁתּוֹמֵם עֲלֵי חֶבְרוֹן, מִבְחַר קְבָרָיִךְ.
הַר הָעֲבָרִים[2] וְהֹר הָהָר,[3]
אֲשֶׁר שָׁם שְׁנֵי אוֹרִים גְּדוֹלִים מְאוֹרַיִךְ וּמוֹרָיִךְ.
חַיֵּי נְשָׁמוֹת אֲוִיר אַרְצֵךְ,*
וּמִמָּר דְּרוֹר אַבְקַת עֲפָרֵךְ, וְנֹפֶת צוּף נְהָרָיִךְ.
יִנְעַם לְנַפְשִׁי הָלוֹךְ עָרוֹם וְיָחֵף,[4]
עֲלֵי חָרְבוֹת שְׁמָמָה, אֲשֶׁר הָיָה דְּבִירָיִךְ.
בִּמְקוֹם אֲרוֹנֵךְ אֲשֶׁר נִגְנַז וּבִמְקוֹם כְּרוּבָיִךְ,
אֲשֶׁר שָׁכְנוּ חַדְרֵי חֲדָרָיִךְ.
אָגוֹז וְאַשְׁלִיךְ פְּאֵר נִזְרִי[5] וְאֶקֹּב זְמָן,
חִלֵּל בְּאֶרֶץ בָּבֶל[6] אֶת נְזִירָיִךְ.
אֵיךְ יֶעֱרַב לִי אֱכוֹל וְשָׁתוֹת בְּעֵת אֶחֱזֶה,
כִּי יִסְחֲבוּ הַכְּלָבִים אֶת כְּפִירָיִךְ.[7]
אוֹ אֵיךְ מְאוֹר יוֹם יְהִי מָתוֹק לְעֵינַי,[8]
בְּעוֹד אֶרְאֶה בְּפִי עוֹרְבִים פִּגְרֵי בְּשָׂרָיִךְ.[7]
כּוֹס הַיְגוֹנִים לְאַט, הַרְפִּי מְעַט,
כִּי כְבָר מָלְאוּ כְסָלַי וְנַפְשִׁי[9] מִמְּרוֹרָיִךְ.
עֵת אֶזְכְּרָה אָהֳלָה[10] אֶשְׁתֶּה חֲמָרֵךְ,
וְאֶזְכּוֹר אָהֳלִיבָה, וְאֶמְצֶה אֶת שְׁמָרָיִךְ.
צִיּוֹן כְּלִילַת יֹפִי,[11] אַהֲבָה וְחֵן עוֹרְרִי לִמְאֹד,[12]
וּבָךְ נִקְשְׁרוּ נַפְשׁוֹת חֲבֵרָיִךְ.
הֵם הַשְּׂמֵחִים לְשַׁלְוָתֵךְ,
וְהַכּוֹאֲבִים עַל שׁוֹמְמוּתֵךְ, וּבוֹכִים עַל שְׁבָרָיִךְ.
מִבּוֹר שְׁבִי שׁוֹאֲפִים נֶגְדֵּךְ,
וּמִשְׁתַּחֲוִים אִישׁ מִמְּקוֹמוֹ, עֲלֵי נוֹכַח שְׁעָרָיִךְ.

---

encounter with an encampment of angels as he returned to Canaan from Aram (ibid. 32:3); and Peniel, after he wrestled with the angel and prevailed (ibid. 32:31).

I would cause my shattered heart to wander
amidst your shattered ruins.
I would fall on my face upon your soil
and intensely cherish your stones and favor your dust.[1]
Even as I stand by the graves of my Patriarchs,
I behold in sheer wonderment the choicest burial sites in Hebron.
Mount Abarim[2] *and Mount Hor,*[3] *the resting places*
of your two great lights [Moses and Aaron],
your beacons and your guides.
*A breath of life for [our] souls is the air of your land;**
the powder of your dust is finer than flowing myrrh
and your river is like the honeycomb's drippings.
My soul would be pleased walking naked and barefoot[4]
among the desolate ruins, where your Holy of Holies once stood.
In the place of your Ark, which was [later] hidden, and in the place
of your Cherubim, which resided in your innermost chamber.
I will clip and throw away my glorious crown[5] *[of hair in mourning]*
and I will curse the time when your nazirim
were defiled in the land of Babylon.[6]
How can food and drink taste pleasant to me, when I witness
the dogs dragging away your leonine youth?[7]
Or how can the light of day be sweet to my eye[8] *when I must see*
the flesh of your corpses in the mouth of ravens?[7]
O cup of misery, slow down, give me some respite! For my thoughts
and my soul have already had their fill[9] *of your bitterness.*
When I remember Oholah [Shomron][10] *I will drink your wine; and*
when I recall Oholibah [Jerusalem] I shall sip it to the very lees.
O Zion, consummation of beauty,[11] *with love and charm*
have you aroused yourself[12] *greatly, and the souls*
of your dear friends are bound up with you.
It is they who rejoice over your serenity, and who are pained
by your destruction and weep over your devastation.
From the pit of captivity, they yearn for you, and everyone
at his place prostrates himself towards your gates.

(1) Cf. *Psalms* 102:15. (2) See *Deuteronomy* 32:49-50. (3) See *Numbers* 20:24-25. (4) *Isaiah* 20:2. (5) Cf. *Jeremiah* 7:29. (6) This seems to be the censor's emandation; some editions read בְּאֶרֶץ טְמֵאָה, *in an unclean land.* (7) Cf. *Jeremiah* 15:3. (8) Cf. *Ecclesiastes* 11:7. (9) Cf. *Psalms* 38:8. (10) See commentary to *kinnah* 4. (11) *Eichah* 2:15. (12) Some editions read עוֹדְדִי, *you invigorated yourself;* some editions read תִּקְשְׁרִי מֵאָז, *you have bound from yore.*

חַיֵּי נְשָׁמוֹת אֲוִיר אַרְצֵךְ — *A breath of life for [our] souls is the air of your land.* This stich can be interpreted two ways. It may refer to the souls of the living which receive an extra measure of vitality from the very air of the Holy Land. This is in accordance with the Talmudic dictum: The air of *Eretz Yisrael* makes one wise (*Bava Basra* 158b). Or it may refer to the souls of the dead who are buried in the Land of Israel. They will rise immediately at the time of the Resuscitation of the Dead. But those buried outside of the Land will not arise until underground passages

עֶדְרֵי הֲמוֹנֵךְ, אֲשֶׁר גָּלוּ,
וְנִתְפַּזְּרוּ מֵהַר לְגִבְעָה[1] וְלֹא שָׁכְחוּ גְּדֵרָיִךְ.
הַמַּחֲזִיקִים בְּשׁוּלַיִךְ וּמִתְאַמְּצִים לַעֲלוֹת,
וְלֶאֱחוֹז בְּסַנְסִנֵּי תְמָרָיִךְ.[2]
שִׁנְעָר וּפַתְרוֹס, הֲיַעַרְכוּךְ בְּגָדְלָם,
וְאִם הֶבְלָם יְדַמּוּ לְתֻמַּיִךְ וְאוּרָיִךְ.*
אֶל מִי יְדַמּוּ מְשִׁיחַיִךְ, וְאֶל מִי נְבִיאַיִךְ,
וְאֶל מִי לְוִיַּיִךְ וְשִׁירָיִךְ.
יִשַׁנֶּה וְיַחֲלוֹף כָּלִיל כָּל מַמְלְכוֹת הָאֱלִילִים,[3]
חָסְנֵךְ לְעוֹלָם לְדוֹר וָדוֹר נְזִירָיִךְ.[4]
אִוָּה לְמוֹשָׁב אֱלֹהָיִךְ,[5]
וְאַשְׁרֵי אֱנוֹשׁ יִבְחַר וְיִקְרַב וְיִשְׁכּוֹן בַּחֲצֵרָיִךְ.[6]
אַשְׁרֵי מְחַכֶּה וְיַגִּיעַ וְיִרְאֶה עֲלוֹת אוֹרֵךְ,
וְיִבָּקְעוּ עָלָיו שְׁחָרָיִךְ.[7]
לִרְאוֹת בְּטוֹבַת בְּחִירָיִךְ, לַעֲלוֹת בְּשִׂמְחָתֵךְ,
בְּשׁוּבֵךְ אֱלֵי קַדְמוּת נְעוּרָיִךְ.

---

are prepared for them to roll all the way to *Eretz Yisrael*, where they will be revived (see *Bereishis Rabbah* 96:5).

לְתֻמַּיִךְ וְאוּרָיִךְ — *To your Urim V'Tumim.* The חֹשֶׁן, *breastplate*, worn by the *Kohen Gadol* was made of linen; blue, purple and red wools; and gold threads. It was folded over and the *Urim V'Tumim* (see below) was inserted in the fold. Twelve precious stones were attached to the front of the breastplate in four rows of three stones each, with each stone inscribed with the name of one of the tribes. When the *Urim V'Tumim* was consulted, the letters etched on the stones lit up and spelled out a message. Since the letters חטצק do not appear in the names of the tribes, the stones were also engraved with the names of the Patriarchs אַבְרָהָם יִצְחָק יַעֲקֹב,

The flocks of your masses who were exiled and scattered
from mountain to hill,[1] *they did not forget your sheepfolds.*
Those who cling to your hems and exert themselves to climb
and grasp the branches of your date palm.[2]
Can Shinar [Babylon] and Pathros [Egypt] compare with you
despite their greatness, and can their worthless deities
*be likened to your Urim V'Tumim?**
To whom can your anointed ones be compared?
To whom your prophets?
And to whom your Levites and singers?
All idolatrous kingdoms shall pass on and disappear,[3]
while your firm power is forever; your leaders [shall endure]
for all generations.[4]
Your God desired you for His residence,[5]
and fortunate is the man who chooses and draws near
and dwells in your courtyards.[6]
Fortunate is he who waits and arrives and witnesses
the rising of your light when your dawn bursts forth over him.[7]
To behold the goodness of your chosen ones,
and exult in your joy when you return
to the youthfulness of early times.

(1) Cf. *Jeremiah* 50:6. (2) Cf. *Song of Songs* 7:9. (3) Cf. *Isaiah* 2:18.
(4) Cf. *Proverbs* 27:24. (5) Cf. *Psalms* 132:13. (6) Cf. 65:5. (7) Cf. *Isaiah* 58:8.

Abraham, Isaac, Jacob, and the phrase שִׁבְטֵי יְשֻׁרוּן, *tribes of Yeshurun* (another name for Israel). This accounted for all twenty-two letters of the *aleph-beis.*

According to *Rashi* the *Urim V'Tumim* was a slip of parchment upon which the שֵׁם הַמְּפוֹרָשׁ, *Ineffable Four-Letter Name* of *HASHEM,* was written. This was the power that lit up the letters on the breastplate. *Ramban* (*Exodus* 28:30) adds that this Name was written by Moses in a manner entrusted by God to him alone; it was considered a heavenly handicraft. *Ritva* maintains that it was Divinely written and given to Moses.

לז.

צִיּוֹן קְחִי* כָּל צֳרִי גִלְעָד[1] לְצִירָיִךְ,
אֵין דַּי, לְמַעַן כַּיָּם גָּדְלוּ שְׁבָרָיִךְ.[2]
אֶרֶץ צְבִי אַתְּ[3] בְּתוֹךְ גּוֹיִם נְתוּנָה,[4]*
וּמִן עֵדֶן מְקוֹם כָּל יָקָר יָצְאוּ נְהָרָיִךְ.[5]
וַיְהִי לְאוֹת, נַעֲמָן* רָחַץ בְּשָׂרוֹ בְּמֵי יַרְדֵּן,
אֲזַי נֶאֱסַף אַף כִּי טְהוֹרָיִךְ.
אַף לֹא יְסֻלֶּה עֲפַר אַרְצֵךְ בְּזָהָב וּפָז,[6]
יָקָר כְּמוֹ יָהֲלוֹם מַחְצַב הֲרָרָיִךְ.
כָּל תַּעֲנוּגִים* בְּבֹא בָסְרֵךְ,
לֹא קָהֲתָה הַשֵּׁן[7] וְאוּלָם כְּצוּף מָתְקוּ מְרוֹרָיִךְ.
פִּרְיֵךְ לְמַרְפֵּא, וְכָל עָלֶה תְעָלָה,
הֲלֹא כְּיַעֲרַת הַדְּבַשׁ[8] הָיוּ יְעָרָיִךְ.
עִם הַפְּתָנִים בְּרִית כָּרְתוּ מְתַיִךְ וְאֵין שָׂטָן,
אֲבָל הָשְׁלְמוּ לָהֶם כְּפִירָיִךְ.*
בָּךְ כָּל בְּהֵמָה וְעוֹף חָכְמוּ, עֲדֵי כַּחֲמוֹר הָיָה לְפָנִים,
לְבֶן יָאִיר* חֲמוֹרָיִךְ.
בָּךְ אֵל לְבַדּוֹ וְאֵין בִּלְתּוֹ, וַיֵּצֵא שְׁמֵךְ[9]
עַד כִּי אֱלֹהִים אֱמֶת נוֹדַע בְּשִׁירָיִךְ.

◆§ **צִיּוֹן קְחִי** — *O Zion, even if you took.* This beautiful composition illustrates the unique natural gifts with which the Holy Land is so abundantly blessed. Indeed, it is this country which is closest in nature to the Garden of Eden itself. The waters of the land are endowed with curative powers; the earth is filled with precious gems and metals and every type of essential resource; the fruits and grain of *Eretz Yisrael* are as delicious and nutritious as can be. In this blessed environment the Torah nation developed the most perfect society ever known to mankind. Law and order reigned throughout the land, capably governed by a noble king and taught by holy priests and prophets. Alas, all this has fallen into the rapacious hands of our enemies, but we yearn for this splendor to return!

Scholars are in dispute regarding the authorship of this *kinnah*. It is variously attributed to R' Shlomo ibn Gabirol, R' Avraham HaChozeh, R' Avraham ibn Ezra, and R' Elyah ben Menachem HaZaken.

אַתְּ בְּתוֹךְ גּוֹיִם נְתוּנָה — *You have been placed in the center of all nations. Eretz Yisrael* is positioned in the center of the world; Jerusalem is at the center of *Eretz Yisrael;* the Temple is at the center of Jerusalem; the *Heichal* hall is at the center of the Temple; and the Holy Ark is at the center of the *Heichal* (*Midrash Tanchuma, Kedoshim* 10).

נַעֲמָן — *Naaman. II Kings* chapter 5 relates the story of Naaman, the great and victorous commander-in-chief of the Aramean army. Because of his excessive pride, God afflicted him with a painful leprous disease of the skin for which he could find no cure. Finally, out of sheer desperation he came to the prophet Elisha for help. At first Naaman adamantly refused to follow Elisha's instructions to bathe himself in the waters of the Jordan, exclaiming, '*Are not Amanah and Parpar, the rivers of (my homeland) Damascus, better than all the waters of Israel?*' (ibid. v. 12). Finally, Naaman relented and humbly dipped himself seven times in the Jordan River and when he emerged, *his flesh was*

37.

ציּוֹן *O Zion, even if you took* all the balm of Gilead[1]*
it would not be enough for your wounds,
because your ruination is as vast as the sea.[2]
O most desirable land,[3] you have been placed in the center
of all nations,[4] and from Eden the source of*
all splendor your rivers emanated.[5]
And this is the proof: Naaman bathed his flesh in the waters*
of the Jordan and his affliction disappeared; how much
more effective [are these waters] for your own pure people.
Indeed, even the value of the dust of your land cannot be measured
in comparison with plain gold or the purest gold,[6]
for even the coarse rocks hewn from your mountains
are as precious as yahalom gems.
All the delights [of the world found their way to the Land of Israel]*
and even your unripe fruits set no tooth on edge;[7] rather,
your most bitter fruits were as sweet as honey.
Your fruits had healing powers, and within every leaf was a cure;
indeed, your forests were thickets filled with sweet honey.[8]
Your citizens entered into a covenant with the vipers and none
*were harmed; indeed, even your lions made peace with them.**
Within you every animal and bird grew wise, to the point where
*even the donkeys were as intelligent as the donkey of ben Yair.**
In your midst was God, Who is alone with none besides Him,
and your fame spread,[9] because the true God
was revealed through your songs.

(1) Cf. *Jeremiah* 8:22. (2) Cf. *Eichah* 2:13. (3) Cf. *Ezekiel* 20:6. (4) Cf. 5:5. (5) See *Genesis* 2:10. (6) Cf. *Job* 28:16. (7) Cf. *Jeremiah* 31:28; *Ezekiel* 18:2. (8) *I Samuel* 14:27. (9) Cf. *Ezekiel* 16:14.

restored like the flesh of a small child (ibid. v.14).

כָּל תַּעֲנוּגִים — *All the delights.* The finest agricultural area in the Land was adjacent to Lake Kineret and was called גִּינוֹסַר, *Ginnosar,* which is a contraction of גַּן שָׂרִים, *garden of Princes,* because its fruit and produce was desired by royalty the world over (see *Pesachim* 8b and *Rashi* to *Genesis* 49:21). The historian Josephus (*Wars of the Jews*, Book III, 10:8) reports that the soil of Ginnosar is so fruitful that every type of tree can grow on it: 'The temper of the air is so well mixed that it agrees well with all sorts, particularly walnuts, which require the coldest air, and flourish there in vast plenty; there are also palm trees which grow best in hot air. Fig trees and olive trees which require more temperate air grow near them. One may call this place the ambition of nature, where it forces those plants which are naturally enemies to abide together; it is a happy contention of the seasons as if everyone of them laid claim to the country at once.'

אֲבָל הִשְׁלְמוּ לָהֶם כְּפִירַיִךְ — *Even your lions made peace with them.* The Torah promised the Jews: *No man shall covet your land when you go to appear before* HASHEM *your God three times in the year* (*Exodus* 34:24). The Talmud relates many wondrous examples of how God protected the property that the pilgrims left behind. A man once left his granary unprotected when he went to spend the festival in Jerusalem. When he returned he found everything intact because a pride of lions was patroling his premises, scaring away intruders. Another time, a person left his chickens alone, unprotected from hungry wolves. When he returned from Jerusalem, he found dead wolves that had been torn apart by his chickens. Another man came home and found a deadly scorpion wrapped around the doorknobs of his home, frightening away all burglars (*Yerushalmi Peah* 3:7).

כַּחֲמוֹר... לְבֶן יָאִיר — *The donkey of ben Yair*. The *Talmud* relates that one night robbers stole R'

מַה טּוֹב וְנָעִים,[1] בְּבֹא שִׁבְטֵי בְנֵי יַעֲקֹב
שָׁלֹשׁ פְּעָמִים[2] בְּכָל שָׁנָה בִּשְׁעָרָיִךְ.
בָּךְ סוֹד הַתְּעוּדָה וְסוֹד חָכְמוֹת,
וּבָאוּ בְנֵי קֶדֶם[3] וְחַכְמֵי שְׁבָא לִכְתּוֹב סְפָרָיִךְ.
שׁוֹטְרִים בְּכָל הַגְּבוּל, שׁוֹפְטִים בְּכָל עִיר וָעִיר,[4]
זִקְנֵי אֱמֶת הֵם וְאֵין מוֹרֶה כְּמוֹרָיִךְ.
מֶלֶךְ בְּקִרְבֵּךְ, וּבָךְ שָׂרֵי חֲיָלִים בְּכָל נֶשֶׁק,
וְעַל כָּל לְאוֹם גָּבְרוּ גְבִירָיִךְ.
בִּימֵי בְחוּרוֹת, הֱיוֹת קֹדֶשׁ לָאֵל נִבְחָרוּ,
וּבְנֵי נְבִיאִים בְּנֵי אֵל חַי נְעָרָיִךְ.
בָּךְ הַתְּקוּפָה עֲלֵי קַו הָאֱמֶת נִשְׁקָלָה,
תְּכֶן שְׁנוֹת דּוֹר וָדוֹר[5] בִּשְׁנֵי אֲדָרָיִךְ.
מוֹלַד לְבָנָה כְּפִי אָרְכֵּךְ וְהַמַּחֲזֶה שׁוּמָה לְרָחְבֵּךְ,
וּבָהּ הֶרְאֵית סְתָרָיִךְ.
נִרְאֶה בְּתַמּוּז כְּסִיל[6] בָּךְ יַעֲלֶה,
כִּי שְׁאָר כָּל הֶחֳדָשִׁים לְבַד זֶה בַּחֲדָרָיִךְ.
אַיֵּה דְבִירֵךְ מְקוֹם אָרוֹן,
וְאַיֵּה הֲדַר הֵיכָל וְהַמִּזְבְּחוֹת, וְאַיֵּה חֲצֵרָיִךְ.
אַיֵּה מְשִׁיחֵךְ, בְּעַד עַמֵּךְ יְכַפֵּר,
וּמֶה הָיָה לְיַלְדֵי קְהָת, וְאַיֵּה נְזִירָיִךְ.
אֵיפֹה נְבִיאִים בְּנֵי עֶלְיוֹן וְכָל יוֹעֲצַיִךְ אָבָדוּ,
וְהָלְכוּ שְׁבִי מַלְכֵּךְ וְשָׂרָיִךְ.
הָיִית יְפֵה נוֹף[7] וְרֹאשׁ עַפְרוֹת תֵּבֵל,[8]
בְּרוּשֵׁךְ לְנֵס, חֶטְאֵךְ סְחָפֵךְ, הֲלֹא קָצַר קְצִירָיִךְ.
אֶרֶץ מְאָסֵךְ וּמֵי נָכְרִים שְׁטָפוּךְ,
וְכָל רוּחַ הֱפִיצֵךְ, וְאֵשׁ בָּעֲרָה בְּעָרָיִךְ.

(1) Cf. *Psalms* 133:1. (2) Cf. *Deuteronomy* 16:16. (3) *I Kings* 5:10. (4) Cf. *Deuteronomy* 16:18. (5) *Deuteronomy* 32:7. (65) See commentary to *kinnah* 5. (7) *Psalms* 48:3. (8) *Proverbs* 8:26.

Pinchas ben Yair's donkey. They hid the animal for three days during which it refused to eat a thing, because it would never eat stolen goods. In desperation, the robbers released her and she made her way home to the rabbi's house. The family gave her barley to eat but again the donkey refused to partake. R' Pinchas asked, 'Are you certain that this barley was properly tithed?' The family responded, 'Father, you yourself ruled that we may follow the lenient opinion that

How good and pleasant[1] it was
when the tribes the sons of Jacob entered your gates,
three times each year.[2]
You are the repository of the secrets of [Torah] tradition
and the secrets of wisdom, so the (wise) men of the Orient[3]
and the scholars of Sheba came to transcribe your books.
Law enforcement officers were [posted] within all your borders
and judges for each and every city;[4] these elders
were men of truth and no teacher equaled your teachers.
A king was in your midst, and fully equipped military officers
were in position; your warriors subdued every other nation.
In your youth, you were chosen to be consecrated unto God,
and even your youngsters were disciples of the prophets,
children of the Living God!
Through you the seasons of the year were balanced
on a perfect time-line;
the years were determined for generation upon generation[5]
by intercalating the two months of Adar.
The birth of the new moon [fixes the new month]
according to your longitude, and its visibility was measured
according to your latitude, and through it was revealed
your secret knowledge [of the heavens].
The constellation Orion[6] is visible everywhere [except in Israel]
in the month of Tammuz, for it only ascends above
you [Israel] during one of the other months [Sivan],
while [in Tammuz] it remains concealed in your inner chambers.
O where is your Holy of Holies, the resting place of the Holy Ark?
And where is the splendor of the Sanctuary and the Altars?
And where are your courtyards?
And where is your anointed [High Priest,]
who would effect atonement for your people?
And what happened to [the Levite] children of Kehath?
And where are your nazirites?
Where are the prophets, the sons of the Most High?
All of your advisors have perished;
your kings and nobles have gone into captivity.
You were the fairest of sites,[7] the first of the dusts of the earth,[8]
your cypress tree is a banner;
it is your sin that has drowned you,
that has cut down your assassinated men.
The land abominated you and the alien waters swept you away,
while every wind scattered you and fires raged in your cities.

מָרִית בְּצוּרֵךְ, אֲשֶׁר מִצָּר נְצָרֵךְ,
וְאָז זָרִים עֲכָרוּךְ, וְאַתְּ הָיִית בְּעוֹכְרָיִךְ.
אֵל הֶאֱמִירָךְ עֲדֵי נִקְרֵאת אֲרִיאֵל,*
וְאֵיךְ עָבַר בְּנָוֵךְ אֲרִי טוֹרֵף עֲדָרָיִךְ.
שׁוּבִי לָאֵל בּוֹעֲלֵךְ, אַל תִּתְּנִי לוֹ דֳּמִי[1]
עַד שׁוּב כְּבוֹדוֹ, עַד יִבְנֶה גְּדֵרָיִךְ.
נַפְשִׁי מְאֹד נִכְסְפָה[2] לִרְאוֹת בְּזִיו זָהֳרֵךְ,
שָׁלוֹם יְהִי לָךְ וְרֹב שָׁלוֹם לְעוֹזְרָיִךְ.[3]

---

exempts this type of produce from the tithe.' To this R' Pinchas responded, 'Indeed, I personally follow the lenient view, but what can I do if my donkey wishes to accept the stricter opinion?' (*Yerushalmi Shekalim* 5:1; see also *Chullin* 7a).

אֲרִיאֵל — *Ariel* [lit., *the lion of God*]. The Temple is described thus because just as the lion is broad in chest and small behind, so is the Temple wide in front and narrow at the back.

The Midrash states: A lion came, in the month of the lion and destroyed the lion of God.

'A lion came' refers to Nebuchadnezzar, the wicked King of Babylon, of whom it is written: *A lion came forth from his thicket (Jeremiah* 4:7).

'In the month of the lion,' means that the

You rebelled against your Creator, He who had protected you
from every foe. Therefore aliens distressed you,
but it was you who brought this distress upon yourself.
*O how God elevated you! Until he bestowed upon you the title Ariel!**
How then did He allow the lion to trespass your dwelling
to tear apart your flocks?
Return to God, your devoted spouse, give Him no rest[1]
[from entreaty], until His glory returns,
until He rebuilds your walls.
My soul yearns intensely[2] *to behold the splendor of your radiance;*
may peace be yours and abundant peace to those who help you![3]

(1) Cf. *Isaiah* 62:7. (2) *Psalms* 84:3. (3) *I Chronicles* 12:19.

Temple was destroyed in the month of Av whose symbol in the Zodiac is the lion.

'And destroyed the lion of God (Ariel)' refers to the Temple, as the prophet lamented: *'Woe Ariel, Ariel, the city where David encamped'* (*Isaiah* 29:1).

The Midrash continues: In the end of time a lion shall come in the month of the lion, and rebuild the lion of God.

'A lion shall come' refers to Almighty God Himself.

'In the month of the lion' refers to the month of Av which will be transformed from sorrow to rejoicing.

'And rebuild the lion of God' refers to the Temple, as it says, *The Builder of Jerusalem is* HASHEM, *He will gather in the outcasts of Israel* (*Psalms* 147:2; *Pesikta* 13).

לח.

צִיּוֹן עֲטֶרֶת צְבִי[1] שִׂמְחַת הֲמוֹנָיִךְ,
שָׁלוֹם כְּנָהָר[2] קְחִי מֵאֵת אֲדוֹנָיִךְ.
אֵילֵי שְׁחָקִים אֲשֶׁר שׁוֹמְרִים לְחוֹמוֹת[3] וָחֵל,[4]
לַיְלָה וָיוֹם יִדְרְשׁוּן[5] שָׁלוֹם לְמַחֲנָיִךְ.
גַּם הַנְּפוּצִים בְּכָל אַרְבַּע קְצָוֹת,
וְהֵם דּוֹרְשֵׁי שְׁלוֹמֵךְ, בְּנוֹתַיִךְ וּבָנָיִךְ.
שׁוֹכְנֵי קְבָרִים מְחַכִּים וּמְצַפִּים לְיוֹם יִשְׁעֵךְ,
וְאָז יִצְמְחוּ יִחְיוּ יְשֵׁנָיִךְ.
וַאֲנִי בְּשָׁאֲלִי שְׁלוֹמֵךְ אֶקְרָא קוֹל בְּרֹאשׁ הָרִים,
וְאֶדְמֶה לְעוֹף עַל רַעֲנָנָיִךְ.
שָׁלוֹם לְצִיּוֹן נְוֵה צֶדֶק[6] וְשָׁלוֹם עֲלֵי חֵילֵךְ
וְחוֹמוֹת יְקַר אַבְנֵי פְּנִינָיִךְ.
שָׁלוֹם לְאֶרֶץ צְבִי,[7]
שָׁלוֹם לְכָל הַגְּבוּל גִּלְעָד וְשׁוֹמְרוֹן, וְכָל יֶתֶר שְׁכֵנָיִךְ.
צִיּוֹן לְפָנִים הֲלֹא הָיִית יְפַת מַרְאֶה,
אֵיךְ נֶהֶפְכוּ לִשְׁחוֹר תָּאֳרֵךְ וּפָנָיִךְ.
כִּבְנוֹת מְלָכִים יְקַר עָטִית תְּהִלָּה,
וְאֵיךְ שַׂק תַּחְגְּרִי עַל חֲלָצַיִךְ וּמָתְנָיִךְ.
לַחְמִי אֲנָחָה[8] בְּעֵת תַּעְדִּי אֵפֶר תַּחַת פְּאֵר,
(אֶפְעֶה)[9] וְאֶשְׁתֶּה יְגוֹנִי עֲלֵי יְגוֹנָיִךְ.
קוּמִי וְנִשָּׂא נְהִי, נִבְכֶּה דְּמָעוֹת כַּיָּם,
יִזְּלוּ נְהָרוֹת, לְמִן עֵינַי לְעֵינָיִךְ.
עַל אַלְמְנוּתֵךְ אֲשֶׁר הָלַךְ יְדִידֵךְ,
וְהוּא הֶחֱרִיב דְּבִירוֹ וְכָל סִתְרֵי צְפוּנָיִךְ.
עֵת אֶרְאֶה יָפְיֵךְ אֶקְרָא מְשׁוֹרְרִים בְּשִׁיר,
עֵת אֶחֱזֶה עָנְיֵךְ אֶקְרָא מְקוֹנְנָיִךְ.
אֶבְחַר לְקָאַת וְקִפּוֹד[10] יִשְׁכְּנוּ בָךְ,

צִיּוֹן עֲטֶרֶת צְבִי — *O Zion, most desirable crown.* The Destruction of the *Beis HaMikdash* has deprived the universe of God's favorite location, His garden of delights, the Holy Temple. The composer of this *kinnah* [R' Elazar, the son of R' Moshe HaDarshan, of

38.

ציון *O Zion, most desirable crown,*[1] *joy for your multitudes;*
accept blessings of peace,
[endless] as the river['s flow],[2] *from your Lord.*
The celestial angels who guard your walls[3] *and cheil,*[4]
pray fervently by day and by night[5] *for the welfare of your camp.*
And those scattered to the four corners, they too beseech [God]
on your behalf, for they are your sons and daughters.
Even those interred in graves wait and hope for the day
of your salvation, and then those who slumber [in the earth]
shall sprout forth and come [back] to life.
As for me, when I pray for your welfare, I shall cry out
from the mountaintops, I shall be like a bird [singing aloud]
from your verdant treetops.
Peace unto Zion, where righteousness resides,[6]
and peace be upon your ramparts and walls
whose stones are more precious than gems.
Peace unto [you] O desirable land,[7] *and peace throughout*
all of your borders — reaching as far away as
Gilead and Samaria, and the rest of your dwellings.
O Zion, did you not once enjoy fine appearance?
How, then, has your form and your face
become transfigured into blackness?
You were swathed in precious robes like the daughters of kings,
O how you must gird yourself with sackcloth on your waist
and on your loins!
My sighs [replace] my bread,[8] *when you [Zion] cover yourself*
with ashes instead of splendor; (I shall cry out loud,)[9]
and quaff my [cupful of] anguish for your anguish.
Arise, and let us arouse a lamentation; let us shed tears like the sea,
let the tears flow like rivers, from my eyes to yours.
[I will cry over] your widowhood, for your Beloved has gone
and He has destroyed His Temple residence
and all the secret places of your concealment.
When I would behold your beauty, I would summon the singers
to make song; [but] now when I witness your pain
I summon those who chant your laments.
I would prefer that the pelican and porcupine[10]
would dwell in your midst;

(1) *Isaiah* 28:5. (2) Cf. 48:18. (3) Cf. 62:6. (4) Cf. *Eichah* 2:8. (5) Cf. *Isaiah* 58:2. (6) *Jeremiah* 50:7. (7) Cf. Ezekiel 20:6. (8) Cf. *Job* 3:24. (9) Some editions omit the term in parentheses. (10) This identification of these creatures of the wild may not be accurate.

Wurtzburg, Germany, early 13th century] describes how he, a lover of Zion, yearns and languishes to hear the herald of redemption and to witness the return of God to His Palace. He

וְאוֹי לִי אִם אֱדוֹם וַעֲרָב קִנְּנוּ בְּקִנֵּיִךְ.

עִיר הַמְּלוּכָה לְדָוִד וּשְׁלֹמֹה בְנוֹ* הָיִית בְּנוּיָה,

וְהֵם קֶדֶם מְכוֹנְנַיִךְ.

אַתְּ הִיא לְמִקְדָּשׁ לָאֵל, אַתְּ הִיא מְנוּחָה לְצוּר,

אַתְּ הִיא אֲשֶׁר יוֹם בְּיוֹם יָרַד לְגַנַּיִךְ.

שָׁם שֻׁלְחָן וּמְנוֹרָה, וַאֲרוֹן הַבְּרִית,*

אֵל בֵּין שְׁדַיִ* אַהֲבָה, לָן בִּמְלוֹנַיִךְ.

עַל מִזְבְּחֵךְ עָמְדוּ כֹּהֲנִים מְשָׁרְתִים,

בְּמוֹ זֶבַח וְעוֹלָה לְכַפֵּר עַל עֲוֹנַיִךְ.

רֹאשׁ הַכְּהֻנָּה אֲשֶׁר אָפוּד לְבוּשֵׁי יְקָר,

נִשְׁמַע בְּשׁוּלֵי מְעִיל קוֹל פַּעֲמוֹנָיִךְ.[1]

אַחַת בַּשָּׁנָה[2] פְּנִים הָלַךְ לְחַדְרֵי דְבִיר,

הֵבִיא קְטֹרֶת מְלֹא קֻמְצוֹ[3] וְחָפְנַיִךְ.[4]

קִדָּה וְקָנֶה, וְכָל רָאשֵׁי בְשָׂמִים,[5]

עֲדֵי עִיר הַתְּמָרִים, בְּבֹא רֵיחַ סַמָּנַיִךְ.[6]*

אַף הַלְוִיִּם אֲשֶׁר שׁוֹמְרִים שְׁעָרִים,

וְגַם הַמְשׁוֹרְרִים שִׁיר בְּפֶה עִם כָּל רְנָנַיִךְ.

---

calls upon all the angels in heaven above to join in the lament of the Jewish people who are scattered to the four corners of the earth.

לְדָוִד וּשְׁלֹמֹה בְּנוֹ — *For David and Solomon his son.* David made all the preparations for Jerusalem and the Temple. At first the entire city was in the hands of Aravna the Jebusite. David collected fifty shekels from each of the twelve tribes of Israel, and paid a total of six hundred gold shekels for the city (*Zevachim* 116b). David also brought the place of the altar from Aravna for fifty silver shekels. David dug the foundations of the Temple especially for the place of the Altar (*Sukkah* 53a) and he laid down and consecrated the Temple's floor (*Zevachim* 24a). David assembled all the necessary money and materials in preparation for construction and he handed down to Solomon a comprehensive master plan describing how the Temple should be built, to the most scrupulous detail.

שֻׁלְחָן וּמְנוֹרָה וַאֲרוֹן הַבְּרִית — *The Table, the Menorah and the Ark of the Covenant.* God performs revealed miracles as a display of His love for the beneficiary of those miracles. Thus the supernatural events that ocurred on a daily basis in the *Beis HaMikdash* were clear demonstrations of God's extraordinary love for His Jewish people. The *Panim*-Bread was baked on Friday and arranged on the Table on Saturday, where it remained until the following Saturday. In good times the bread remained fresh and steaming hot until the last day, even though it was at least eight full days since it left the baking oven. This manifested God's intense and burning love for His people. The *Talmud (Chagigah* 26b) says that on the festivals the *Kohanim* would hold the Table aloft so that all the pilgrims could see the steaming hot bread and the *Kohanim* would say, 'Behold how beloved you are to God!'

The Menorah, too, had a perpetual miracle. One of its seven lamps, called the נֵר מַעֲרָבִי, *western lamp,* would be filled with the same quantity of oil and same size wick as the other six, yet it would continue to burn throughout the following day, long after the other lights had died out in the morning. This, says the *Talmud (Shabbos* 22b), was a public demonstration to the entire world that God's Holy Spirit settled over the people of Israel and caused miracles to occur.

Finally, the *Talmud* (*Yoma* 54a) teaches that

but woe unto me
that Edom and Arabia make their home in your nest.
O Royal City! You were built expressly
*for David and Solomon his son,**
and they were the first to lay down your foundations.
It is you who were a Sanctuary unto God; it is you
who were a place of rest for the Creator; it is you,
for to your gardens God descended every day.
*There were the Table, the Menorah and the Ark of the Covenant;**
there God dwelled lovingly in your Lodge between
*the staves of the Holy Ark.**
Upon your Altar stood the priests in [Divine] service,
with animal sacrifices and burnt offerings
to atone for your iniquities.
The High Priest was garbed in precious garments,
from the edge of his tunic was heard the sound of your bells.[1]
Once a year [on Yom Kippur][2] *he entered into the Inner Chamber*
of the Sanctuary and offered [in addition to] his fistful[3]
[of frankincense that accompanied the flour-offering
of the tamid,] your double handful[4] *of incense.*
The scent of the kaneh, kiddah and other primary spices[5]
wafted to [Jericho] the City of Palms, where the
fragrance of your spices reached.[6]*
Also [the sound of] the opening of the Temple gates
by the Levite guards [was heard in Jericho],
as well as the voices of the [Levite] singers
who sang to the accompaniment of joyous instruments.

(1) See *Exodus* 28:33-35. (2) 30:10. (3) Cf. *Leviticus* 2:2. (4) Cf. 16:12.
(5) Cf. *Exodus* 30:23. (6) Some editions read שְׁמָנַיִךְ, *your oils.*

when God was pleased with the Jewish people that close love was symbolized by the golden *Cherubim* on top of the Holy Ark, for they would then embrace each other in a display of love and affection. However, when Israel's actions were contrary to the *mitzvos* of the Torah, the *Cherubim* would face away from one another.

בֵּין שָׁדַי — *Between the staves of the Holy Ark* [lit., *between the bosoms*]. The simile of שָׁדַיִם, *bosom*, and staves of the Ark is elaborated upon in the Talmud. Although the staves were very long they were *perceivable from without but could not be actually seen* (see *I Kings* 8:8), because the twin poles pressed against the Curtain from within, and only the twin bosom-like protrusions could be discerned from without (*Yoma* 54a; *Menachos* 98a).

The word לָן, *lodged*, infers a temporary situation as one who 'sleeps over' and then goes his way. Similarly, God 'lodged' within the Sanctuary, but when Israel sinned, the *Shechinah* departed to its 'heavenly abode' and took up its lodging there.

עֲדֵי עִיר הַתְּמָרִים בָּבָא רֵיחַ סַמָּנַיִךְ — *Wafted to [Jericho] the City of Palms, where the fragrance of your spices reached.* The Talmud lists many sounds and aromas from the Temple which were heard and smelled in Jericho, including the voice of the *Kohen Gadol* when he cried out God's name on Yom Kippur during the Temple service. *Raavad* (comm. ibid.) explains that the smell of the incense and the sounds of the Temple were only sensed in Jericho and not in any other areas around Jerusalem. This miracle was designed to demonstrate Jericho's special status and kinship to Jerusalem. Jericho was the first city to be conquered by Joshua so it achieved the sanctity of תְּרוּמָה, *the Kohen's due*, which is the first part of the crop that the Torah

נֶגְדָּם בְּנֵי מַעֲמָד* עוֹרְכִים תְּפִלָּה,
וְלוֹ יַעֲלֶה הֲמוֹנֵךְ בְּכָל פַּעֲמֵי זְמַנַּיִךְ.
בָּךְ הַנְּבִיאִים, הֲלֹא הָיוּ בְּסוֹד אֵל,[1]
וּבָךְ חַכְמֵי תְכוּנָה, וּבָךְ שִׁבְעִים זְקֵנַיִךְ.
אַרְצֵךְ מְלֵאָה בְּמוֹ עֶשֶׂר קְדֻשּׁוֹת,*
וְכָל מַעֲשַׂר תְּרוּמָה וְגַם מִבְחַר דְּגָנַיִךְ.
עַתָּה שְׁמָמָה בְּלִי בָנִים וּבָנוֹת,
וְאָן מַלְכֵּךְ נְבִיאַיִךְ לְוִיַּיִךְ וְכֹהֲנַיִךְ.
מָתַי יְשׁוּבוּן וְיָבוֹאוּ בְּתוֹךְ אָהֳלֵךְ,
הַמִּתְאַוִּים שְׁכוֹן תַּחַת עֲנָנַיִךְ.
(מִי יִתְּנֵנִי לְעֵת תֵּלְדִי יְלָדִים,
כְּמוֹ שִׁפְרָה וּפוּעָה מְיַלֶּדֶת בְּאָבְנָיִךְ.[2]
זֹאת אֶתְאַוֶּה לְיוֹם יָבֹא חֲתָנֵךְ,
וְאַתְּ כַּלָּה וְהִתְפָּאֲרִי בְּעֶדְיֵי עֲדָנַיִךְ.)[3]
לִבִּי יְאַוֶּה לְחַבֵּק בִּזְרוֹעוֹת עֲפַר אַרְצֵךְ,
וְאֶחְשׁוֹק בְּפִי נַשֵּׁק אֲבָנַיִךְ.
לוּ אֶרְאֵךְ בִּהְיוֹת נִבְנֵית בְּנֹפֶךְ וָפוּךְ,
יֵרָאוּ לְצָפוֹן וָיָם גֹּבַהּ קְרָנַיִךְ.
אֶכְסוֹף וְאֶחְמוֹד לְנֶחָמָה,
וְתִשְׁמַעְנָה דִּבְרֵי מְבַשֵּׂר בְּקוֹל, אָזְנֵי וְאָזְנַיִךְ.
הִתְעוֹרְרִי*[4] לִקְרַאת דּוֹדֵךְ וְהִתְנַעֲרִי מִן הָאֲדָמָה[5]
בְּשׁוּבוֹ אֶל מְעוֹנַיִךְ.

---

requires to be set aside. God wanted the inhabitants of Jericho to be aware of their city's status, so He gave them the ability to hear and smell things from Jerusalem which was many miles away.

בְּנֵי מַעֲמָד — *The maamad delegation.* The Mishnah explains that all the priests and the Levites were divided into twenty-four separate groups called *mishmaros* (watches; see commentary to *kinnah* 10) and each one served in the Temple for two weeks of the year and on the festivals. Corresponding to these *mishmaros*, all of the Israelites were divided into twenty-four groups. The Mishnah teaches: These are the *maamados*. Since the Torah states: *Command the Children of Israel and say to them, 'My sacrifice, My bread' (Numbers* 28:2). Now, a person's sacrifice cannot be offered if he is not present. [So we require that all of Israel be represented in the sacrificial procedure.] Therefore, the early prophets (Samuel and David) instituted twenty-four *mishmaros* (of Priests and Levites). Corresponding to every single *mishmar* there was a *maamad* in Jerusalem of *Kohanim*, Levites and Israelites. When the time came for the *mishmar* to ascend, the *Kohanim* and Levites ascended to Jerusalem while the Israelites assigned to that *mishmar* would assemble in their own (specially designated) cities and read sections from the Story of Creation (in

*Facing them were the members of the maamad delegation**
offering their prayers; and to [you,] your [pilgrim] masses
ascended at every pilgrimage season.
Within you were the prophets, those who were privy
to the secrets of God,[1]
and within you were the experts of intercalation,
together with your seventy elders.
Your land was permeated with holiness,
*with ten levels of sanctity;**
tithes and priest's due were brought from your land,
from the choicest of your grains.
But now you lie desolate, bereft of sons and daughters;
and where are your kings, your prophets,
your Levites and your priests?
O when will they return [from exile] and enter your tents,
those who yearn to dwell under your [sheltering] clouds?
(Would that He allowed me to bear children,
as [in the days of] Shifra and Puah,
the midwives at the birthstone.[2]
For this I yearn, the day that your bridegroom will arrive,
and you, the bride,
will adorn yourself in jeweled ornaments.)[3]
My heart pines to embrace with my arms
the very dust of your Land,
and my passion is to kiss your stones with my mouth!
Would that I shall see you when you will be rebuilt
with gemstones and jewels, when your lofty corner stones
will be visible from north and west.
I yearn and languish for consolation.
O that the loud proclamation of the herald [of redemption]
be heard in my ears and yours!
Wake up[4] *to greet your beloved!*
Shake yourself from the dust of the ground,[5]
when He [God] returns to your palace!

(1) Cf. *Amos* 3:7. (2) Cf. *Exodus* 1:15-16. (3) Some editions omit the two stanzas in parentheses. (4) *Isaiah* 51:17. (5) Cf. 52:2.

the Book of *Genesis*). Also, the men of the *maamad* would fast four days a week, from Monday through Thursday (*Taanis* 26a).

עֶשֶׂר קְדֻשּׁוֹת — *Ten levels of sanctity.* The Mishnah teaches that in the dimension of space there are ten levels of sanctity and enumerates them in ascending order: (1) [The Land of Israel and] its walled cities; (2) the area enclosed within the walls of Jerusalem; (3) the Temple Mount; (4) the enclosed area in front of the Temple Courtyard; (5) the Women's Courtyard; (6) the Israelites' courtyard; (7) the *Kohanim's* Courtyard; (8) the area between the Altar and the Sanctuary; (9) the great *Heichal* hall; and (10) the Holy of Holies.

לט.

צִיּוֹן תְּקוֹנְנִי* עֲלֵי בֵיתֵךְ אֲשֶׁר נִשְׂרַף,
צָרְחִי בְּמֶרֶר עֲלֵי שִׁמְמוֹת גְּפָנַיִךְ.*
צִיּוֹן תְּעוֹרְרִי כְּאַלְמָנָה אֲשֶׁר הָיְתָה לָמַס[1]
לְכָל עוֹבְרִים מֵרֹב עֲוֹנַיִךְ.
עַל הַגְּבָעוֹת שְׂאִי קִינָה וְתַמְרוּר,
וְגַם נְהִי בְּקוֹל רָם אֲשֶׁר הֻכּוּ הֲמוֹנַיִךְ.
אֵיכָה לְמוֹאָב בְּנֵי צִיּוֹן בְּאַף חֻלָּלוּ
עַל רֹב גְּאוֹנֵךְ, וְקִרְאִי אֶל מְקוֹנְנַיִךְ.
הֵילֵל וְקִינָה שְׂאִי צִיּוֹן בְּמַר וּנְהִי,
וּבְכִי שְׁמָמוֹת עֲלֵי שִׁמְמוֹת מְעוֹנַיִךְ.
קוֹנְנִי וְאַל תִּדְמִי קוֹלֵךְ בִּבְכִי שְׂאִי,
דֶּבֶר וְחֶרֶב אֲשֶׁר שֻׁלַּח לְמַחֲנַיִךְ.
צָדוּ כְּצִפּוֹר[2] וְאֵין עוֹזֵר לְנֶגְדּוֹ,
אֲשֶׁר פָּרְשׂוּ רְשָׁתוֹת[3] לְגַלּוֹת אֶת קְלוֹנַיִךְ.
וְאֵיךְ הִשְׁלִיךְ תִּפְאֶרֶת יִשְׂרָאֵל,[4]
וְלֹא זָכַר שְׁבוּעָה אֲשֶׁר כָּרַת לְאוֹמְנַיִךְ.
קוֹלֵךְ כְּקוֹל נַהֲמַת תַּנִּים,[5]
נְאוֹת יַעֲקֹב[6] בְּכִי וְקִינָה שְׂאִי, עַל רֹב תְּלוּנַיִךְ.
גָּזִּי נִזְרֵךְ וְהַשְׁלִיכִי[7] לְרֹאשֵׁךְ עֲלֵי אֶרֶץ,
וְשַׂק תִּקְשְׁרִי עָצְרִי בְּמָתְנַיִךְ.
קוֹנְנִי בְּפֶשַׁע, וְאַל תִּתְּנִי מְנוּחָה וְקוֹנְנֵךְ אֶל שְׁפָיִים,[7]
שְׂאִי מֵרֹב מְעַנַּיִךְ.
אֶרֶץ צְבִי צְבָאוֹת,[8] קִינָה וּנְהִי תְּעוֹרְרִי עַל שְׁפָיִים,
הֲלֹא תַּחַת שְׂשׂוֹנַיִךְ.

ציון תקונני ◆ — *O Zion, lament.* In this *kinnah,* by R' Asher HaKohen, we cry out to Zion herself and implore her to weep and to wail over her own destruction, at the hand of the barbaric enemy which trampled over every one of Zion's precious treasures. The author concludes with a plea to Zion to approach the graves of the Patriarchs and Matriarchs to beg them to petition God on her behalf.

גְּפָנַיִךְ — *Your vines.* This refers to the Jewish people who are often compared to grapevines. The prophet *Isaiah* (5:1-7) devotes a number of passages to an allegory comparing Israel to a vineyard as does the prophet *Ezekiel* (ch. 15).

The Sages compare Israel to a vine in three respects: (1) The vine is alive, yet it is supported by posts of dead wood; similarly, Israel is bolstered by the merit of its forefathers, who are

39.

צִיּוֹן *O Zion, lament* over your house which is burnt,*
*cry out bitterly over the ruination of your vines.**
O Zion, intensify your wailing like a [helpless] widow
who imposes a burden[1] [of charity] on all who pass her by;
thus shall you weep over your many sins.
On the hills arouse a lamentation and bitterness;
also moan very loud over your multitudes who were smitten.
Alas! For your sons of Zion are humiliated by Moab's fury
which was aroused by your outstanding prominence;
therefore summon those who will recite lamentations for you.
Arouse wailing and lamentation, O Zion,
with bitterness and moaning, cry incessantly
until you are devastated over the ruination of your palaces.
Lament and be not silent, raise your voice in weeping
over the plague and the sword which were
dispatched against your encampment.
The [enemy] ensnared you like a bird[2]
and no one came to your assistance against them,
when they spread out their nets[3] [to capture you]
and to uncover your shame.
O how did God cast away the majesty of Israel,[4]
while He failed to remember the oath of covenant
which He made to [the Patriarchs] who nursed you.
Raise your voice like the howling of the serpents,[5]
O congregation of Jacob;[6] arouse weeping and lamentation
[over the tragedy you brought upon yourself]
because of your many grievances.
Rip off your [crown of flowing] hair and throw[7] your head
upon the ground; tie on a sackcloth and bind it to your loins.
Lament over the treachery [of your allies who betrayed you]
and give yourself no rest [from mourning];
carry your lamentations up to the barren hills[7]
[and bemoan] the many who oppress you.
O land, desirable even to the host[8] [of gentile nations],
arouse lamentations and moaning on your barren hills,
indeed they now replace your former joys!

(1) *Eichah* 1:1. (2) Cf. 3:52. (3) Cf. 1:13. (4) Cf. 2:1. (5) Some editions read יְעֵנִים, *ostriches.* (6) *Eichah* 2:2. (7) *Jeremiah* 7:29. (8) Cf. 3:19.

long dead (*Shemos Rabbah* 44); (2) If the vine fails to thrive on a given plot of soil, the farmer will uproot it and replant it elsewhere; similarly, if Israel sins in one land, God will uproot them and replant them on foreign soil (ibid.); (3) The grapes of the vine produce both sweet wine and sour vinegar; similarly, the fate of Israel may be sweet or it may be bitter. Under all circum-

קוֹנְנוּ מְלָכִים, וְהֵילִילוּ קְצִינִים

וְכָל יוֹשְׁבֵי מַעֲרָב וּמִזְרָח, עַל שְׁמְלוֹנָיִךְ.

פִּשְׁטִי מְעִילֵךְ וְהַשְׁלִיכִי לָאָרֶץ,

וְחִגְרִי שַׂק וְגַם תֶּהֱמִי תַּחַת סְדִינָיִךְ.

בָּחוּר וְזָקֵן וְגַם עוֹלֵל וְיוֹנֵק,[1]

שְׂאוּ תַּמְרוּר נֶפֶשׁ, לְעֵינֵי כָּל זְקֵנָיִךְ.

צִיּוֹן שׁוֹשַׁנֵּךְ[2] הֲלֹא עָבַר כְּקוֹץ עֲלֵי מַיִם,

וְנֶהֶפְכוּ מֵרֹב זְדוֹנָיִךְ.

חָשְׁכוּ מְאוֹרוֹת וְגַם שְׁחָקִים,*

וְכָל דֶּרֶךְ מְלֹא נֶחְשַׁךְ, סָתוּם לְפָנָיִךְ.

כִּי הַשְּׁחָקִים מְאֹד זָרוּ וְאָסְפוּ לְאוֹרָם,[3]

לִפְנֵי כָּל שָׁאוֹן, עַל רֹב יְגוֹנָיִךְ.

צִיּוֹן בְּשׁוֹפָר תִּקַע,[4] עַל הַר וְגֶבַע רְאִי,

צָרְחִי בְּמַר וּבְכִי, עַל מוֹת סְרָנָיִךְ.

שִׁלְּחוּ שְׁלָלֵךְ בָּאֵשׁ, צִיּוֹן לְמִרְמָס,

הֲלֹא טָבְעוּ שְׁעָרַיִךְ[5] בְּתוֹךְ אֶרֶץ אֲדָנָיִךְ.

הִנֵּה לְמִרְמָס נְתוּנָה בַּת יְהוּדָה,

וְאֵין מֵשִׁיב לְנַפְשָׁהּ,[6] עֲלֵי שִׁמְּמוֹת שְׁמָנָיִךְ.

צִיּוֹן בְּמַר תִּבְכִּי מֵאֵין מְנַחֵם,[6]

אֲשֶׁר רָחַק מְאֹד מִקָּרוֹב נַחֵם בְּחוּנָיִךְ.

קוֹלֵךְ כְּקוֹל יָם וְגַם תַּנִּין וְיַעֲנָה,[7]

וְקוֹל נְהִי וּבְכִי אֲשֶׁר תַּחַת סְלוֹנָיִךְ.

צִיּוֹן לַמָּרוֹם שְׂאִי עֵינַיִךְ,[8]

וְגַם תִּרְאִי סִפְדִי וְהֵילִילִי, עֲלֵי עָזְבֵךְ תּוֹאֲנָיִךְ.

---

stances, however, Israel blesses God for doing as He sees best (*Vayikra Rabbah* 36).

R' S. R. Hirsch (Commentary to *Psalms* 80:9) notes also that of all fruits, only the grape is so crushed and extensively altered from its natural state. But this very abuse serves to transform the grape into something far above what it had been — from an ordinary fruit into valuable, and treasured wine. Ultimately, the finished product, wine, intoxicates and overpowers the one who mangled the grape.

Similarly, Israel in the crucible of exile will eventually overcome their captors and tormentors.

חָשְׁכוּ מְאוֹרוֹת וְגַם שְׁחָקִים — *The celestial luminaries are plagued in darkness together with the dazzling skies.* The *Talmud* teaches in the name of Rav Chisda; since the day that the Holy Temple was destroyed the sky has never appeared in its pure (color) as it says, *I cloak the heavens with blackness, I make sackcloth their covering* (*Isaiah* 50:3; *Berachos* 59a).

Lament, O kings! Wail, O commanders!
Together with all who dwell in east and west,
over the [loss of] your protective cloak [the Temple].
Strip off your tunic and cast it to the ground;
gird yourself with sackcloth instead of your
fine linen wraps and continue your moaning.
Youth and elder, and also infant and suckling,[1]
express the bitterness of your soul
in the presence of all of your elders.
O Zion, your rose[2] *has departed like a thorn in the water,*
so have you been transformed by
the enormity of your wanton deeds.
The celestial luminaries are plunged in darkness together
with the [once-dazzling] skies and every path*
is shrouded in deep darkness and sealed off before you.
For the heavens are deeply alienated [from mankind],
and therefore hold back their light[3]
from the masses of nations
as they [the skies] commiserate with your tremendous grief.
O Zion, sound the shofar's blast![4]
Look upon mountain and hill!
Scream bitterly and weep over the death of your leaders.
They cast your spoils into the fire and Zion to be trampled,
indeed your gates sank[5] *into the ground*
together with your foundations.
Behold, the beloved daughter of Judah [the city of Jerusalem]
has been given over to be trampled.
There is no one to restore her spirits[6]
[from the shock] of the destruction of your finest inhabitants.
O Zion, weep bitterly!
For there is none to offer you consolation;[6]
He Who once was close is now much too distant
to give comfort to [the Jews] who were so sorely tested.
Raise your [wailing] voice as loud as the raging sea,
as loud as the cry of the serpent and the ostrich;[7]
raise your voice in moaning and weeping
like someone lying under your thorn[-like captors].
O Zion, raise your eyes on high and see [God's glory];[8]
mourn and wail over your betrayal of your [God,]
the First Cause [of the creation].

---

(1) Cf. *Deut.* 32:25. (2) Some editions read שְׂשׂוֹנֵךְ, *your joy.* (3) Cf. *Joel* 2:10.
(4) Cf. 2:15. (5) Cf. *Eichah* 2:9. (6) Cf. 1:16. (7) Cf. *Micah* 1:8. (8) Cf. *Isaiah* 40:26.

צִיּוֹן תְּקוֹנְנִי עֲלֵי אָבוֹת וְשַׁאֲלִי מְכוֹן בֵּיתֵךְ,
וְגַם עֻזְרֵךְ, חֹסֶן קְצִינַיִךְ.
אֶל הַמְּעָרָה לְכִי, צָרְחִי בְּמַר וּבְכִי,
עִנּוּ בָנַיִךְ וּבְנוֹתַיִךְ וְנִינַיִךְ.
שָׂרָה כְּשָׁמְעָה לְקוֹלֵךְ, גַּם מְבַכָּה עֲלֵי בָנִים,
אֲשֶׁר נִשְׁבּוּ אֶל כָּל שְׁכֵנַיִךְ.
רָחֵל וְלֵאָה* בְּכוּ, בִּלְהָה וְזִלְפָּה הֲלֹא קוֹנְנוּ,
וְקָרְאוּ בְּקוֹל, מְחִי בְּפָנַיִךְ.
כִּי הָאֱלֹהִים הֲלֹא לָנֶצַח וְלֹא יִזְנַח,[1]
כִּי תִקְוָה הִיא וְרֹב שָׁלוֹם לְבָנַיִךְ.[2]

רָחֵל וְלֵאָה — *Rachel and Leah.* When the Temple was destroyed, even the merit of the Patriarchs and the Matriarchs was not enough to prevent it. However, the arguments and pleas of the Matriarch Rachel did elicit from God a solemn pledge that the exiles of Israel would someday return. The Midrash (*Pesichta* to *Eichah Rabbasi* §24) records the logical argument which Rachel put before God: 'You know that your servant Jacob loved me intensely and worked for seven hard years to earn my hand in marriage. But at the end of the seven long years of waiting, my father Laban wanted me to give up my rights to my beloved Jacob in favor of my older sister Leah. My heart ached, but I didn't want my sister to be humiliated. I suppressed all of my tender feelings and emotions and revealed to Leah all the secret identification signs that Jacob and I had agreed upon as guarantees that my father Laban would not trick him. Moreover, on

O Zion, lament to the Patriarchs [to seek]
for the reestablishment of your House,
for He is your Helper, the One Who strengthens your leaders.
א *Go to the Cave [of Machpelah], scream bitterly and cry*
[to the Patriarchs], because [the enemy] has tormented
their sons and daughters and the descendants of their line.
ש *Sarah [our Matriarch], when she hears your voice,*
she too will cry for [her] sons who were taken
into captivity amongst all your [hostile] neighbors.
ר *Rachel and Leah,* you cry too! Bilhah and Zilpah,*
surely you must lament! Cry out loud and beat on your faces.
For indeed, God endures for eternity and He will never [totally]
abandon us.[1] Therefore, there surely is hope
for abundant peace for your children.[2]

(1) *Eichah* 3:31. (2) Cf. *Isaiah* 54:13.

the wedding night I hid under the bed and spoke instead of Leah who was together with Jacob, so that he wouldn't recognize her voice and reject her. Now, dear God, see how I acted even though I am a weak mortal of mere flesh and blood. Nevertheless, I overcame my inclination to be jealous of my rival, my sister. Certainly, You, O God, who are Infinite and Eternal and filled with compassion, can forgive my children, the Children of Israel, and not be jealous of the idols they worshiped instead of worshiping You!'

צִיּוֹן יְדִידוּת יְדִיד* צָעִיר לְשָׂרָיִךְ,[1]
שָׁכַנְתְּ כְּתֵפָיו[2]* בְּרֹב עַנְוַת הֲדָרָיִךְ.
צִיּוֹן הֲדַר כָּל חֲדַר מִטּוֹת,
וְכָל מִשְׁכַּב דּוֹדִים יְדִידֵךְ בְּבֹא חַדְרֵי חֲדָרָיִךְ.
צִיּוֹן בְּרוּכָה בְּרָכָה עֶלְיוֹנָה עֲלֵי רֹאשֵׁךְ,
לְמוּלֵךְ מְחֻטָּבִים שְׁעָרָיִךְ.
צִיּוֹן יְרֻשַּׁת זְאֵב עֶרֶב,[3]*
שְׁבִי פְאֵרֵךְ בַּעֲדִי עֲדָיִים,[4] עֲדֵי עָלוּ כְתָרָיִךְ.
יָפִית בְּרֹב הוֹן וְהֵן רָבִית בְּדֵעוֹת,
וְהֵן מִזִּקְנֵי צוֹעֲנִים, חָכְּמוּ נְעָרָיִךְ.
הָיִית יְפֵה מִכְלָל,[5] נָאוָה בְּכָל מַהֲלָל,
עָלִית וְשָׁבִית שְׁלַל, מַלְכֵי מְגוּרָיִךְ.
בָּךְ בִּרְוָחָה אֱנוֹשׁ לָן* מִבְּלִי חֵטְא,
בָּךְ כֻּפַּר בְּקָרְבַּן תָּמִיד מְכַפְּרָיִךְ.

(1) Cf. *Psalms* 68:28. (2) Cf. *Deuteronomy* 33:12. (3) *Genesis* 49:27. (4) *Ezekiel* 16:7. (5) *Psalms* 50:2.

☙ **צִיּוֹן יְדִידוּת יְדִיד** — *O Zion, . . . the Beloved's beloved.* Again we have a composition that sings the praises of Jerusalem and Zion, this time emphasizing the idea that the Temple was constructed on the territory of Benjamin, the youngest of Jacob's sons. The Second Temple was destroyed because of the senseless hatred which divided one Jew from another. This lack of brotherhood had its roots in the hatred displayed by Jacobs' sons for their brother Joseph, many centuries earlier. The only one of the twelve brothers who had nothing to do with this bitter feud was young Benjamin, and for this reason he was especially beloved to God. And for this reason the Temple, a symbol of national unity and brotherhood, was built in Benjamin's province.

Moreover, the Second Temple was destroyed by the Romans who were descendants of Esau. When Jacob encountered Esau with his entire family, Jacob, his wives, and his sons all bowed before Esau. Only Benjamin who was not born yet did not bow. Therefore, the Temple was built in Benjamin's portion so that it would not bend before Esau's onslaught.

Nevertheless, Israel's sins were so great that none of these merits could protect Zion and the Temple, when God's fury was aroused and the awesome day of reckoning arrived.

The composer of this *kinnah* is the otherwise unknown R' Yaakov.

יְדִידוּת יְדִיד — *The Beloved's beloved.* The Talmud (*Menachos* 53a) teaches that when the *Beis HaMikdash* was to be built, God said: 'Let the יְדִיד, *beloved,* son of the יְדִיד, come and build the יְדִיד for the יְדִיד in the portion of the יְדִיד, in order to bring atonement for the יְדִידִים.' This means: Let Solomon, who is called יְדִיד (*II Samuel* 12:24) the son, [i.e., descendant] of Abraham who is called יְדִיד (*Jeremiah* 11:15), come and build the *Beis HaMikdash* which is called יְדִיד (*Psalms* 84:2), for the Holy One, Blessed is He, Who is called יְדִיד (*Isaiah* 5:1), in the portion of Benjamin who is called יְדִיד (*Deuteronomy* 33:12), to bring atonement for Israel who are called יְדִידִים (*Jeremiah* 12:7).

From the first moment when God began His creation, His prime desire was to establish a place which would allow Him to dwell in the midst of His creatures on earth: The Temple is His *beloved,* therefore, because it is, so to speak, the culmination of God's aspirations (*Alshich*).

שָׁכַנְתְּ כְּתֵפָיו — *You [God] rest unobtrusively between his shoulders.* Moses gave his final blessing to the tribes of Israel. *Of Benjamin he said: 'May Hashem's beloved dwell securely by Him; He hovers above him all day long; and rests His Presence between his shoulders* (*Deuteronomy* 33:12). The Talmud (*Zevachim* 118b) explains that in this world God's presence was not permanently entrenched over the Temple, but in the future Third Temple of the Messianic Era,

40.

צִיּוֹן *O Zion, [Your Temple is] the Beloved's* beloved*
[because it is situated in the territory of Benjamin]
the youngest of your [tribal] princes;[1] *You [God]*
rest unobtrusively between his shoulders[2]*
because your extreme humility is your greatest splendor.
O Zion, your splendor is that you are called 'the chamber of couches'
[for God's Divine Presence rests within you],
and when your beloved people [Israel]
enter your inner chambers it is there
that they rest in strong embrace [with God].
O Zion, you are blessed with the supreme celestial blessings
which descend upon your head, for the heavenly gates
are carved to be directly facing you.
O Zion, you are the heir [of Benjamin who is likened to]
the wolf who hunts at dusk,[3]* *your majestic tiara*
is encrusted with rows upon rows of gems,[4]
but your [spiritual] crowns [of Torah, priesthood
and monarchy] far surpass all jeweled adornment.
You are beautified by your abundant wealth,
but even more so are you enriched by your vast wisdom,
because even your youths are far wiser
than the venerable elders of Tzoan [Egypt].
You were the consummation of beauty,[5]
so lovely that you were worthy of every form of praise;
you overwhelmed and captivated the kings
who dwelled all around you.
*Those who lodged within you found ample space**
and were absolved from every sin, for the daily
Tamid sacrifices atoned for the sins
of all who required forgiveness.

God will dwell permanently and securely between the shoulders of Benjamin. Indeed, the Holy Spirit of God dwelled among the Israelites in three places and all three were in Benjamin's territory. First the Tabernacle was in Shiloh, then in Nob and Gibeon, and finally the Temple was built in Jerusalem on the land belonging not to Judah, but to the tribe of Benjamin. The Talmud (*Yoma* 12a) explains that more than any other tribe, Benjamin pined and yearned to host the Divine Presence in his territory and therefore he was granted his fervent wish. Elsewhere, the Talmud (*Sotah* 38a) says that at the Sea of Reeds the tribe of Benjamin displayed extraordinary faith and devotion to God. Even before the raging seawaters split, the Benjaminites eagerly jumped into the sea in response to God's command and in this merit the Divine Presence dwelled in their midst. Finally, *Sifri* observes that Benjamin's advantage was that he was the only one of Jacob's sons born on the holy soil of *Eretz Yisrael* and therefore merited to host God's holy *Shechinah*.

זְאֵב עֶרֶב — *[Benjamin . . .] the wolf who hunts at dusk.* In Jacob's blessing to his son Benjamin, he said: *Benjamin is a predatory wolf; in the morning he will devour prey and in the evening he will distribute spoils* (*Genesis* 49:2). According to *Targum Onkelos* this means that Benjamin hungered for the Divine Presence as a wolf hungers for its prey. Therefore the Temple, in which the *Kohanim* offered sacrifices each morning and divided the remaining sacred portions in the evening, stood in his territory.

בָּךְ בְּרֶוָחָה אָנוּשׁ לָן — *Those lodged within you found ample space.* The Mishnah (*Avos* 5:7) lists ten miracles that were performed for our ancestors in the Holy Temple. One was that no man ever said to his fellow, 'The space is insufficient

יְסַדְתְּ בְּזִיו לְפָאֵר, חָרַבְתְּ בְּתוֹךְ אָב
בְּאַף אֶשְׁאַף לְזֹאת אֶשְׁאַב, מֵימֵי תַמְרוּרָיִךְ.
נִרְאוּ בְּעִירֵךְ פְּנֵי קוֹנֶה,
בְּנֵי מַחֲנֶה רְצוֹן לְשׁוֹכְנִי סְנֶה,[1] בִּשְׁנֵי חֲצֵרָיִךְ.
עוֹשֵׂי מְלַאכְתֵּךְ בְּחוּט,
הִתְעַשְּׁרוּ בִּרְכוּשׁ כָּל הוֹן יָקָר נִמְצָא, לִקְהַל עֲשִׁירָיִךְ.
נִבְחַר מְקוֹמֵךְ לְצוּר בָּחַר בְּאוֹם בְּחוּרָיו,
בָּחַר בְּמוֹצָאֵךְ, וּבַכֹּהֲנִים בְּחִירָיִךְ.[2]
בָּךְ דָּר בְּגִיל נֶהְדָּר, אַדִּרֵךְ בְּכָל דּוֹר וָדוֹר,
עֶרְכֵּךְ בְּבֹא לַעֲדוֹר, עֶדְרֵי חֲבֵרָיִךְ.[3]
עָלָה גְּבוּלֵךְ[4] דְּבִיר צֶלַע יְבוּס,
לֹא לְעֵין עֵיטָם, לְבִלְתִּי שְׂאֵת כִּתְפוֹת דְּבִירָיִךְ.
קָרָא יהוה שְׁמֵךְ עַל שֵׁם שְׁנֵי כֹהֲנִים,*
דָּוִד מְצָאֵךְ בְּחִיל בִּשְׂדֵי יְעָרָיִךְ.[5]
בָּנָה מְעוֹנֵךְ בְּנוֹ, וַיְחַנְּכֵךְ שֵׁם בְּשֵׁם אָבִיו אֲשֶׁר קִדְּמוֹ,
נֶחְתַּם בְּשִׁירָיִךְ.[6]
וּבְמַחְשְׁבוֹת בּוֹרְאֵךְ עָלִית, בְּטֶרֶם בְּרֹא תֵבֵל,
וְשַׁחַק וְעוֹלָם* עַל עֲפָרָיִךְ.
וּבְמֵי מְרִיבָה בְּיוֹם זַעַם, אֲזַי טָהֳרָה אַרְצֵךְ,
וְלֹא גֻשְּׁמָה[7]* בִּכְלוֹת יְצוּרָיִךְ.
יָרַד בְּעִתּוֹ מְטַר אַרְצֵךְ, זְמַן לַיְלָה בָּא לִבְרָכָה,
וְטַל לָן בִּקְצִירָיִךְ.

---

for me to stay overnight in Jerusalem,' i.e., despite the multitudes convening in Jerusalem for the festivals, there were sufficient accommodations for them all. Moreover, because of the sanctity of the city, God provided for all residents of Jerusalem, so that no one ever had to move to another city to seek a livelihood.

קָרָא ה׳ שְׁמֵךְ עַל שֵׁם שְׁנֵי כֹהֲנִים — *HASHEM gave you the name [Jerusalem] based on the names [you were called] by the two priests [Shem and Abraham].* The *Midrash* (*Bereishis Rabbah* 5:1) notes that after the *Akeidah,* we read that *Abraham named that site 'HASHEM Yireh [Hashem will see]'* (*Genesis* 22:14), and earlier we read that Shem the son of Noah greeted Abraham in his role as *Malchizedek, King of Shalem* (*Genesis* 14:18). Both men were in the same location and gave it different names reflecting different aspects of the unique sanctity of the holy mountain. Thus, God made a synthesis of *Yireh* and *Shalem* and called the city *Yerushalem* [יִרְאֶה שָׁלֵם = יְרוּשָׁלַיִם].

בְּטֶרֶם בְּרֹא תֵבֵל וְשַׁחַק וְעוֹלָם — *Even before He created earth, heaven and the universe.* The Talmud lists seven things that were created before the world itself: the Torah, the concept of *teshuvah, Gan Eden, Gehinnom,* the Throne of Glory, the *Beis HaMikdash,* and the name of the Messiah (*Pesachim* 54a)

אֲזַי טָהֳרָה אַרְצֵךְ וְלֹא גֻשְּׁמָה — *Only your land was deemed to be pure and was not rained upon.* According to one view in the Talmud, the waters of Noah's Flood did not enter the area that was to become the Land of Israel (*Zevachim* 113a).

You were established in the bright [spring month of Iyar]
to be a splendor, and you were destroyed with fury
in the month of Av; therefore I gasp thirstily
and drink deeply of your bitter waters.
The children of your camp [the Israelites] appeared
in your city to be in the presence of your Maker;
they entered the two courtyards [of the Temple]
in order to find favor [in the eyes of] the One
Who dwelt in the Burning Bush.[1]
Even those who worked for you [in the Temple]
with the [weaver's] thread were enriched
with many possessions, and every precious treasure
was available for your community of prosperous people.
Your site was chosen for the One called 'the Rock',
He selected the 'Chosen Ones' [Israel] for His Nation;
He designated [David] whom He found [secluded with the sheep,
to be His king], and for His priests He chose the finest
[the seed of Aaron].[2]
Within you dwelt the One Who is majestic in joy,
He remained your splendor for generation after generation;
but your true value will be revealed when the flocks
of your beloved [Israel] return to your fold.[3]
The borders of your Divine Residence ascended[4]
only upward from the slopes of Yevus, but ultimately
[the Temple was not built on the highest point called]
the Fountain of Eitam so that the shoulders
of your Divine Residence should not soar too high.
HASHEM gave you the name [Jerusalem],
based on the names [you were called]
*by the two priests [Shem and Abraham].**
David discovered you to be encircled [by mountains],
in your forest fields.[5]
His son [King Solomon] built your palace [the Temple]
and he dedicated it with the name of his father
[David] who preceded him [and built the Temple's foundation]
as is sealed in the inscription of your songs.[6]
You were conceived in the thoughts of your Creator even before
He created earth, heaven and the universe from your dust.*
And on the day of wrath [at the time of the Flood] by the waters
of strife, only your land was deemed to be pure and was not
rained upon,[7]* *while the [rest of God's creations] ceased to be.*
The rain of your land descended in its proper time,
it even fell at night [not to disturb wayfarers] as a blessing,
and the dew came to rest [gently] on your harvests.

(1) Cf. *Deuteronomy* 33:16. (2) Cf. *I Samuel* 2:28. (3) Cf. *Song of Songs* 1:7.
(4) Cf. *Joshua* 15:8,9. (5) *Psalms* 132:6. (6) See *Psalms* 30:1. (7) Cf. *Ezekiel* 22:24.

הָיִית לְשִׁית חוּג יְסוֹד, מִמֵּךְ תְּעוּדָה[1]
וְסוֹד קָדוֹשׁ יַרְחִיק לְפִי עֵדִים מְעַבְּרָיִךְ.
בָּנִים וּבָנוֹת תְּשׁוּקָה, בַּשּׁוּק שׁוֹקְקוּ,
שָׂחֲקוּ וְהִשְׁתַּקְשְׁקוּ בְּסַךְ עוֹבְרָיִךְ.
בְּחַג פֶּסַח נִפְלָאוּ, פּוּרִים בְּפָז סֻלָּאוּ,[2]
טַל אוֹר וְחֵן נִמְלָאוּ, זַכּוּ נְזִירָיִךְ.[3]
אֵיךְ אֶשְׂמְחָה עוֹד בְּחַג, אֵיךְ אֶעֱלוֹז עוֹד בְּפוּר,
עַד כִּי יְבוֹאוּן, יְמֵי שָׂשׂוֹן לְפוּרָיִךְ.
אַרְצֵךְ חֲמוּדָה[4] מְאֹד, לֹא נֶחְמָדָה,[5]
בַּעֲלוֹת בָּנִים חֲמוּדִים, לְבֵית מַחְמַד מְגוּרָיִךְ.
נַעֲלָה עֲנַן הַקְּטֹרֶת, מִמְּקוֹם מִקְדָּשׁ יָצָא מְקוֹמוֹ,
עֲשַׁן אֵשׁ מְנַּחִירָיִךְ.
בִּקְרוֹב מְרֵעִים בָּעִיר,[6] שִׁלְּחוּ בְּכַרְמֵךְ בְּעִיר,[7]
עָרוּ וְעוֹרְרוּ,[8] בְּעִיר וְקַדִּישׁ[9] בְּעָרָיִךְ.
בַּרְזֶל בְּלִי נִשְׁמַע קוֹלוֹ[10] בְּעֵת נִבְנֵית,*
אֵיךְ חַרְבוֹת צוּרִים, בָּךְ תָּקְעוּ מְצִירָיִךְ.
עַל זֹאת בַּשַּׂק עוֹבְרִים עִבְרִים,
אֲבָל בּוֹטְחִים כִּי יִשְׂמְחוּ אַחֲרֵי חִתּוּךְ בְּתָרָיִךְ.[11]
לֵב מַדְוֶה יֶחֱלֶה, לְתַאֲוָה יִכְלֶה,
יִישָׁן עֲדֵי יַעֲלֶה, עַמּוּד שְׁחָרָיִךְ.
יְלֵל לְקוֹלִי, אֱלִי אֵיךְ תִּתְאַפְּקִי,
הֲלֹא קָרָא לְשַׂק וּבְכִי,[12] אַלּוּף נְעוּרָיִךְ.[13]
אָקוּם חֲצוֹת לַיְלָה,[14] עַל מִשְׁמְרוֹת מַאֲפֵל,
לִשְׁמוֹר לְאוֹר יֶאֱתֶה בֹּקֶר[15] לְשֹׁמְרָיִךְ.

---

(1) Cf. *Micah* 4:2. (2) Cf. *Eichah* 4:2. (3) Cf. 4:7. (4) Cf. *Jeremiah* 3:19. (5) Cf. *Exodus* 34:24. (6) Cf. *Psalms* 27:2. (7) Cf. *Exodus* 22:4. (8) Cf. *Psalms* 137:7. (9) *Daniel* 4:10. (10) *I Kings* 6:7. (11) Some editions read הַתּוֹר בְּתוֹרָיִךְ, *the turtledove [which was not severed] is your portion,* a reference to the Covenant Between the Parts (*Genesis* 15:9-10 with *Rashi*); some read הַתּוֹר בְּשׂוֹרָיִךְ, *the guide [i.e., the herald] will inform you [of the Messiah's arrival].* (12) Cf. *Isaiah* 22:12. (13) Cf. *Jeremiah* 3:4. (14) Cf. *Psalms* 119:62. (15) Cf. *Isaiah* 21:12.

בַּרְזֶל בְּלִי נִשְׁמַע קוֹלוֹ בְּעֵת נִבְנֵית — *The sound of iron [tools] was not heard while you were under construction.* When Solomon constructed the First Temple, it is stated: *And the House, when it was being constructed, was built of stone finished at the quarry, and there was neither hammer, nor axe, nor any tool of iron heard in the House while it was under construction* (*I Kings* 6:7). *Rashi* and *Radak* (based on *Sotah* 48b and *Gittin* 68a) explain that the stones for the Temple were hewn by a small, soft worm called שָׁמִיר, *shamir,* which has the amazing ability to cut through the hardest stones. The *shamir* was the size of a barleycorn and it was kept in a hollow lead pipe

You were the location of the Foundation Stone upon which the universe was established; from you went forth the [Torah] tradition.[1] The sanctification of the New Moon and the complexities of intercalation were determined [by the testimony] of your witnesses.
Darling sons and daughters merrily romped around the marketplace [bustling with pilgrims who journeyed there], they played amidst the clatter [of horses' hooves] and the [creaking of the] covered wagons of your [pilgrimage] travelers.
They displayed outstanding dedication [in braving the elements] to arrive for the Pesach celebration; from the Purim season they were already adorned with the finest of gold decoration;[2] thus dew and light and grace permeated them and purified your coronated people.[3]
O how can I rejoice any more on the festivals and how can I make merry on Purim day, until once again days of joy will return to your lot?
Although your land was most covetable,[4] [none dared] to usurp it [in the owner's absence during the festivals[5] when [your] coveted sons ascended to the coveted House where you took up residence.
The cloud of incense which once arose from your Holy Temple has now departed, in its place a furious flame smokes from your nostrils.
When evildoers approached the city,[6] they unleashed animals into your vineyards,[7] they aggravated and chased[8] the Alert Holy One[9] from your City.
The sound of iron [tools] was not heard[10] while you were under construction, [for the wondrous shamir worm hewed your stones], how then were your tormentors allowed to pierce you with their sharpened swords?*
For this, the Hebrews wander about in sackcloth; yet they maintain their firm faith that they are destined to rejoice when they see the one who decimated you cut down.[11]
The aching heart grows very sick, it pines away in [its] yearning, [therefore] it sinks into deep sleep until the breaking of your [Messianic] dawn.
[O all who hear] my voice, wail with me. How then [O Zion] can you restrain yourself? Has not the Mentor of your youth[12] ordained this day [Tishah B'Av] for sackcloth and crying?[13]
I will arise at midnight[14] during the gloomiest of the nightwatches, to keep vigil for the light which will arrive in the morning[15] for those who await you.

אָז תִּמְצְאִי צוּף דְּבַשׁ,[1] אָז לֹא תְקוֹנְנִי בְּרֹאשׁ,
כִּי תִתְכּוֹנְנִי בְּרֹאשׁ הָרִים הֲרָרַיִךְ.
יָבֹא כְּבוֹד הַלְּבָנוֹן לָךְ,[2]
וְתִתְלַבְּנִי כִּבְנֵי עֲדָרִים, בְּנֵי אֶדֶר גְּדָרַיִךְ.
עוּרִי וְהִתְנַעֲרִי[3] עֶרֶךְ יַעַר נוֹעָרִים,
נַעַר יִתָּו אוֹת, לְעֵץ יַעַר[4] חֲזִירַיִךְ.[5]
(קוּמִי וְאוֹרִי לְכָל חוֹשְׁקֵי מְאוֹרֵךְ,
וְהֵם הוֹלְכֵי בְּחֹשֶׁךְ עֲדֵי אוֹרוּ מְאוֹרָיִךְ.)[6]
צִיּוֹן לְצִיּוּן וָאוֹת, עֹז עוֹד תְּהִי וּלְנֵס עַמִּים,[7]
וְתִגְבַּהְנָה רַגְלֵי מְבַשְּׂרַיִךְ.[8]
נַצְּלִי עֲדִי הֶעֳנִי, וּתְנִי לְבוּשֵׁךְ שָׁנִי,
תּוֹלָע[9] כְּכַלָּה עֲדִי, לִקְשׁוֹר קִשּׁוּרַיִךְ.
אַל תֹּאמְרִי לִי, אֲשֶׁר זָקַנְתְּ הֱיוֹתֵךְ לְאִישׁ,[10]
עוֹד תִּתְעַדְּנִי חֲלוּץ הַשַּׁד לְגוּרַיִךְ.[11]
תֵּלְדִי בְּנֵי שַׁעֲשׁוּעַיִךְ בְּעֵת עֶדְנָה,
תִּתְחַדְּשִׁי בִּנְעוּרִים כִּנְשָׁרַיִךְ.[12]
יַטֶּה לְטוּב יִצְרֵךְ צוּר יוֹצְרֵךְ יְצָרֵךְ,
תְּהִי נְצוּרָה, כְּעִיר חֻבְּרָה[13] לְמוֹרַיִךְ.
יִגְאַל בְּעֹז מִשְּׁבִי, לְהָשִׁיב לְאֶרֶץ הַצְּבִי,
וִיהִי עֲטֶרֶת צְבִי[14] לִשְׁאָר עֲדָרַיִךְ.

filled with rags and bran flour. This remarkable creature could split an entire mountain in half. Moses used it to cut the gemstones on the High Priest's breastplate and it was brought to Solomon from the Garden of Eden by an eagle (see also *Midrash Shocher Tov*).

Then you will discover [a contentment] as sweet as dripping honey,[1]
no longer will you lament with [wormwood and] gall,
for you will be firmly established on the summit
of your foremost mountains.
י *The glory of Lebanon shall return to you,*[2]
and you will be whitened as a flock.
O children of [the Patriarchs who are] your [protective] walls.
ע *Awaken [O Zion] and shake your dust,*[3]
you who are now like a forest stripped of its leaves;
[in the future] a little child who can pen
no more than one stroke [will be able to record
the minuscule number of] your boarish enemies,[5]
who will be] like a lone tree in the forest.[4]
(קב *Arise and give light for all who seek your light,*
for they go in darkness, until your light will shine.)[6]
O Zion, you are destined to be an outstanding landmark
and a signpost [of Divinity to the world];
you will yet be a tower of strength and a banner unto the nations;[7]
and the footsteps of your heralds will be lifted on high.[8]
Remove the rags of your poverty and don your robes of scarlet,
swathe yourself in crimson[9] *like a bride*
and bedeck yourself with ornaments.
Do not say to me that you are too old to have a husband,[10]
for you will be rejuvenated and you will nurture your cubs.[11]
You will bear the children of your delight
when you return to delicate smoothness,
and you will renew your youth as do the eagles.[12]
The Creator, who fashioned all the inclinations
of our impulsive nature, will incline your desires exclusively
for the good, and you will be safeguarded [from evil]
like a [fortified] city; [and you will be] bound[13] *to your Master.*
He [God] will powerfully redeem [you] from captivity,
to return you to the desirable land,
and He will be a desirable crown[14] *for the remnants of your flock.*

---

(1) *Proverbs* 16:24. (2) Cf. *Isaiah* 60:13. (3) Cf. 52:1,2. (4) Cf. 10:19.
(5) *Psalms* 80:14. (6) Some editions omit the stanza in parentheses.
(7) *Isaiah* 11:10. (8) Cf. 52:7. (9) Cf. *Exodus* 25:4. (10) Cf. *Ruth* 1:12.
(11) Cf. *Eichah* 4:3. (12) Cf. *Psalms* 103:5. (13) Cf. 122:3. (14) *Isaiah* 28:5.

מא.

שַׁאֲלִי שְׂרוּפָה בָאֵשׁ,* לִשְׁלוֹם אֲבֵלָיִךְ, הַמִּתְאַוִּים שְׁכוֹן, בַּחֲצַר זְבוּלָיִךְ.

⁂ **שַׁאֲלִי שְׂרוּפָה בָאֵשׁ** — *O [Torah] by fire consumed, seek* ... Twenty-four cartloads of the Talmud and its commentaries were publicly burned in the streets of Paris, France in the year 1242. The events leading to this tragedy give us a glimpse of the terrible persecution which hounded our ancestors in those dark times.

The French king, Louis IX (1226-1270), was a fanatical religious zealot, so much so, in fact, that he earned himself the title of Saint Louis. His piety, however, did not extend to his Jewish subjects, against whom he enacted many harsh and discriminatory laws. The king's pious zeal manifested itself most clearly in the favor he extended to apostates who abandoned Judaism. To encourage conversion, the king himself would often attend their baptisms.

Nicholas Donin of La Rochelle was an apostate who was especially vicious in his hatred for his former co-religionists, and who caused the forced baptism of the Jews of Anjou and Poitiers. Five hundred Jews from these cities surrendered before the threat of death and were baptized, while the majority of Jews, 3,000 martyrs in all, chose to meet their death while sanctifying God's Name.

Donin realized that the bulwark of firm Jewish faith was the holy Talmud, the repository of our traditions and teachings. He felt that if he could destroy the Talmud he could easily eradicate the Jews. To that end, he went to Pope Gregory IX in Rome, where he presented a formal accusation against the Talmud. He charged that it contained blasphemies against God and against Christianity, and that it alone was the cause of the Jews' steadfast refusal to accept the 'true' faith.

The Pope issued orders for a seizure of all copies of the Talmud and for a thorough examination and evaluation of its contents. The churchmen of France were only too eager to obey this decree, so on March 3, 1240, while the Jews were in their synagogues, all of their sacred tomes were seized and confiscated. On June 12th of that year a public debate was held in Paris between Donin and four of the most eminent rabbinical authorities in France.

The Jewish deputation was led by R' Yechiel ben Yosef (died 1268) who headed the Yeshiva in Paris. Many of the major sages of that period studied under him. These include R' Yitzchok of Corbeil (his son-in-law) and Maharam of Rothenburg.

The other representatives were R' Moshe of Coucy, R' Yehudah ben David of Melun and R' Shmuel ben Shlomo of Falaise.

Although R' Yechiel and his colleagues displayed great scholarship, courage, and dignity in their defense of the Talmud, the official verdict against them was a foregone conclusion. The Talmud would have been immediately consigned to the flames if not for the lone staunch ally the Jews had amongst the churchmen, the bishop of Sens (Shantz), whose arguments and pleas averted any evil decree for one year. At the year's end, while the good bishop was standing in the presence of King Louis, he suddenly convulsed and died in a most grotesque fashion. The anti-Semitic priests convinced the gullible king that this was actually an act of Divine retribution against the bishop for his heresy in defending the blasphemous Talmud. A tribunal of church elders condemned the Talmud to be burnt. Their agents eagerly searched and confiscated over 1200 manuscripts of the Talmud and commentaries. We must bear in mind that this occurred two centuries before the invention of the printing press. Each one of these volumes was a handwritten manuscript which took months, even years to write, at tremendous effort and expense. Moreover, many of the more recent works such as novellae by the *Tosafists* of France and their correspondence and halachic decisions were transcribed only in a limited number of copies and would be lost forever.

R' Yechiel recognized that this tragedy threatened the very survival of the French Jewish community. He therefore recorded the proceedings of his disputation in a work called simply וִיכּוּחַ [*Vikuach*], *Debate*. In his introduction, paraphrasing the words of Jeremiah (*Eichah* 4:9), he states, כִּי הִנֵּה טוֹבִים חַלְלֵי חֶרֶב מֵהַיּוֹשְׁבִים שׁוֹמֵמִים בְּלִי תוֹרָה, *For those put to death by the sword were better off than those who sat in desolation without Torah.*

In 1242, on Friday, 6 Tammuz, the day before the *Shabbos* when *Parashas Chukas* would be read, twenty-four wagonloads of holy *sefarim* were burnt.

R' Tzidkiyah ben Avrohom HaRofeh, who lived at that time, writes:

> From Torah scholars who were involved, we heard that the Rabbis inquired of heaven by means of a dream (שְׁאֵלַת חֲלוֹם), to discover whether this terrible event had been so decreed by the Almighty. The heavenly reply was given in three words: 'דָּא גְּזֵרַת אוֹרַיְיתָא, *This is the decree of the Torah,*' the Aramaic version of the opening words of that week's Torah reading — (וזאת חֻקַּת הַתּוֹרָה). R' Tzidkiyah further notes that, in commemoration of this tragic event, some pious people customarily fast on Erev Shabbos of *Parashas Chukas* every year (*Shibbolei HaLeket* 263).

The Ashes of the Rambam's Works

R' Hillel of Verona, Italy was an eyewitness to these tragic events in Paris. He considered the burning of the Talmud as a clear sign of Divine

41.

שְׁאַלִי *O [Torah] by fire consumed, seek* the welfare of your mourners, of those who yearn to lodge in the courtyard of your dwelling;*

anger and retribution for the destruction of the works of R' Moshe ben Maimon, known as the *Rambam* (Maimonides).

There were many great scholars, especially in southern France, who did not agree with many of *Rambam's* opinions in his *Moreh Nevuchim* (*Guide for the Perplexed*) and his philosophical observations in the first book of his *Yad HaChazakah* (*Sefer HaMada*). Some went so far as to place a ban on studying or even owning these works. A tremendous controversy erupted and the situation got out of control. The hysteria reached its terrible climax when members of the anti-*Rambam* camp submitted copies of his philosophical writings to the monks of the Dominican Order for the sake of determining whether these works contained heretical ideas.

The Dominicans, of course, swiftly concluded that the *Rambam's* writings were blasphemous and false. They publicly burned all copies of *Moreh Nevuchim* and *Sefer HaMada* that they could lay their hands on. This was done in Montpelier France in 1234. In the year 1242, fanatical churchmen once again burnt the *Rambam's* works in the streets of Paris.

In a letter recording these events, R' Hillel of Verona makes the following observations:

> God looked down from heaven and avenged the honor of our holy master, *Rambam*, and his works. He poured His wrath upon the Jewish communities of France. You should not ask in wonderment, 'How did God disregard twelve hundred manuscripts of Talmud and Aggadah and allow them to be burnt as retribution for the *Moreh Nevuchim* and *Sefer HaMada?* Rather, you must bear in mind that R' Moshe ben Maimon was almost second in his generation to Moshe Rabbeinu, and the righteousness of the entire generation depended upon him ... If you ask; 'Who can be sure that the Talmud was burned because of the burning of the *Rambam's* works?' I will answer you. This is the sign and proof. Take note of this: Not even forty days passed between the conflagration of the works of our master and the burning of the Talmud. On the very spot where the *Rambam's* works were destroyed, the Talmud was later burnt! The ashes of the burnt Talmud mingled with the ashes of the *Rambam's* volumes, for those ashes still remained in that very place. This served as a clear lesson to one and all, Jew and gentile alike.

The destruction of the Talmud was a crushing blow to the venerable and ancient Jewish community of France. It marked the beginning of its very rapid decline and eventual disintegration.

With the conditions of the Jews in France steadily worsening, R' Yechiel emigrated to *Eretz Yisrael* in 1260 together with a large group of French Talmudists. He settled in Acre, where he established the Talmudic academy *Midrash HaGadol d' Paris*. He is believed to have died in 1267.

One of the participants in the great Talmudic debate in Paris, R' Shmuel of Falaise summed up the enormity of the tragedy in the following elegy:

> My spirit is gone, my strength is sapped, the light of my eyes has dimmed, because of the tyrant whose hand weighed very heavily upon us, when he seized the core of our soul and the delight of our eyes. Now we have no holy book in which to study and meditate. May the Almighty God avenge His people and may He say to our misery, 'It is enough!' (quoted in *Teshuvos Maharam MiRottenburg* 250).

In 1306, the glorious chapter of Jewish history in medieval France came an abrupt close, when King Philip IV (the Fair) expelled the Jews from all of France. French Jewry, which had enriched our eternal Torah legacy with the magnificent Talmudic commentaries of *Rashi* and *Tosafos*, was no longer.

The Maharam of Rothenburg

The author of this *kinnah* was R' Meir ben Baruch (1220-1293) better known as the Maharam of Rothenburg, who studied in the Yeshivah of Rabbeinu Yechiel of Paris and is said to have personally witnessed the tragic burning of the Talmud in 1242.

Born in Worms, Germany in the year 1220, Maharam first studied under the greatest *Tosafists* of that land including R' Yitzchak (author of *Or Zarua*) in Wurtzberg and R' Yehudah ben Moshe HaKohen of Mainz.

Maharam is considered to be one of the last important *Baalei Tosafos*, but his major contribution to Rabbinic literature was his prolific responsa in all areas of Halachah. Approximately one thousand of Maharam's responsa have been published and his rulings have been accepted by all subsequent generations as the opinion of a leading halachic authority.

From the seat of his rabbinate in Rothenburg, Maharam guided German Jewry throughout the second half of the thirteenth century. However, in his final years, he met with tragedy. The terrible burden of persecution was making life intolerable for the Jews of Germany. Taxation, pogroms, blood libels, harsh decrees — all of these spurred Jews to flee from this miserable exile and to make the arduous journey to *Eretz Yisrael*. Emperor Rudolph I did not wish to lose the Jews from whom he enjoyed extorting so much gold, so, in the year 1286, he declared the Jews to be his personal property — *Servi Camerae*, serfs of the Emperor's Treasury. He prohibited Jews from leaving Germany and confiscated the property of

הַשּׁוֹאֲפִים בַּעֲפַר אֶרֶץ,[1]* וְהַכּוֹאֲבִים הַמִּשְׁתּוֹמְמִים,
עֲלֵי מוֹקֵד גְּלִילַיִךְ.[2]
הוֹלְכִים חֲשֵׁכִים וְאֵין נֹגַהּ,[3] וְקוִֹים לְאוֹר יוֹמָם,
אֲשֶׁר יִזְרַח עֲלֵיהֶם וְעָלַיִךְ.
וּשְׁלוֹם אֱנוֹשׁ נֶאֱנָח בּוֹכֶה בְּלֵב נִשְׁבָּר,
תָּמִיד מְקוֹנֵן עֲלֵי צִירֵי חֲבָלַיִךְ.
וְיִתְאוֹנֵן כְּתַנִּים וּבְנוֹת יַעֲנָה,
וְיִקְרָא מִסְפֵּד מַר בִּגְלָלַיִךְ.
אֵיכָה נְתוּנָה בְּאֵשׁ אוֹכְלָה,[4]*
תְּאֻכַּל בְּאֵשׁ בָּשָׂר, וְלֹא נִכְווּ זָרִים בְּגֶחָלַיִךְ.
עַד אָן עֲדִינָה[5] תְּהִי שׁוֹכְנָה בְּרֹב הַשְׁקֵט,
וּפְנֵי פְרָחַי הֲלֹא כִסּוּ חֲרוּלַיִךְ.[6]
תֵּשֵׁב בְּרֹב גַּאֲוָה, לִשְׁפּוֹט בְּנֵי אֵל בְּכָל הַמִּשְׁפָּטִים,
וְתָבִיא בִּפְלִילַיִךְ.
עוֹד תִּגְזוֹר לִשְׂרוֹף דַּת אֵשׁ* וְחֻקִּים,
וְלָכֵן אַשְׁרֵי שֶׁיְּשַׁלֶּם לָךְ גְּמוּלַיִךְ.[7]
צוּרִי בְּלַפִּיד וָאֵשׁ,* הֲלְבַעֲבוּר זֶה נְתָנֵךְ כִּי בְאַחֲרִיתֵךְ,
תְּלַהֵט אֵשׁ בְּשׁוּלַיִךְ.
סִינַי הַעַל כֵּן בְּךָ בָּחַר אֱלֹהִים,
וּמָאַס בִּגְדוֹלִים* וְזָרַח בִּגְבוּלַיִךְ.

---

those who did.

Maharam vigorously opposed this decree and together with his family attempted to flee Germany. Unfortunately, when he reached the border with Lombardy, he was recognized by a Jewish apostate who reported him to the royal agents. The Emperor imprisoned Maharam in the Castle of Ensisheim. He demanded an exorbitant ransom from the Jewish community if they were to obtain their leader's release.

German Jewry, led by Maharam's disciple Rabbeinu Asher (the *Rosh*), began to amass the enormous sum of 23,000 talents of silver to redeem their Rav. However, Maharam refused to permit them to pay such an exorbitant sum, for the Mishnah (*Gittin* 45a) teaches; 'For the sake of public welfare it is prohibited to redeem Jewish captives for an exorbitant sum' (lest this encourage despots to kidnap other Jews for high ransom in the future).

R' Asher disagreed with his mentor's decision. He argued that the Mishnah's ruling did not apply to the generation's greatest Torah leader, for whom no amount could be considered exorbitant. Thus, he guaranteed the Emperor that he would personally raise the full ransom. However, Maharam died in prison in the year 1293, before R' Asher was able to raise the full amount. Fearing that he would now be held hostage in Maharam's place, R' Asher fled to Spain where he died in 1327.

Maharam died in prison in the year 1293, but his remains were not released for burial until they were ransomed fourteen years later by a wealthy Jew, Alexander Wimpfen, whose sole request was that he be buried near this great leader.

Maharam's noble act of self-sacrifice achieved its purpose. Never again in Jewish history were great Rabbinic leaders held hostage in order to extort enormous ransom payments from the Jews.

of those who long [to roll] in the dust of the [Holy] Land;[1]*
of those distressed and bewildered by the incineration of your scrolls;[2]
of those who walk in the darkness [of exile], deprived of illumination;[3]
of those who wait hopefully for the light of day,
which will shine upon them and upon you.
[Seek] the welfare of the sighing mortal who cries with a broken heart,
who constantly laments over the excruciating pains of your suffering;
who howls like a serpent and ostriches
and cries out a bitter eulogy on your behalf.
O how did it come to pass [O Holy Torah] that you who were given
[by God] the All-Consuming Fire,[4]* *should be consumed*
by man-made fires — and yet, those alien intruders
[who burned you] escaped unscathed from your flaming coals?
Until when, O pampered [gentile nations],[5] *will you lounge*
in excessive serenity, while the faces of my
blossoming youths are covered with thistles?[6]
You sit with overbearing arrogance to judge the children
of God for every libelous accusation, and you drag us
before your judges.
In addition, you issued a decree to burn the fiery Law and its statutes;*
therefore praiseworthy is he who will repay you
with the punishment you deserve.[7]
*O my Rock! [Who transmitted the Torah at Sinai] with flame and fire!**
Was it with this in mind that He [God] gave you [the Torah]
so that in the end the edges of your columns should be set ablaze?
O Sinai, was it for this reason that God chose you
while He spurned taller [mountains] and made His light shine*
within your boundaries?

---

(1) Cf. *Amos* 2:7. (2) Some editions read גְּוִילַיִךְ, *your parchments.* (3) Cf. *Isaiah* 50:10. (4) *Deut.* 9:3. (5) *Isaiah* 47:8. (6) Cf. *Proverbs* 24:31. (7) *Psalms* 137:8.

הַשּׁוֹאֲפִים בַּעֲפַר אֶרֶץ — *Of those who long [to roll] in the dust of the [Holy] Land.* The Talmud (*Kesubos* 112a) relates that Rav Chiya bar Ganda would actually roll around in the dust of *Eretz Yisrael* to fulfill the dictate of the verse, *For Your servants had cherished her stones, and been gracious to her dust* (*Psalms* 102:15).

אֵשׁ אוֹכְלָה — *The All-Consuming Fire.* Scripture refers to God as אֵשׁ אֹכְלָה, *an All-Consuming Flame* (*Deuteronomy* 9:3). The Talmud (*Yoma* 21b) identifies six types of fires which have different properties. The fire of the *Shechinah*, the Divine Presence, is so powerful that it can overwhelm any other flame — even that of the fiery ministering angels.

דַּת אֵשׁ — *The fiery Law.* The Torah was given, מִימִינוֹ אֵשׁ דָּת לָמוֹ, *From His right hand, the fiery Law unto them* (*Deuteronomy* 33:2). Rashi explains that when the Torah was given, the top of Mount Sinai was engulfed in flames; and the Torah itself (as it appears before God in the highest celestial spheres) is black fire (in the shape of the letters) imposed upon white fire (which serves as the parchment).

בְּלַפִּיד וָאֵשׁ — *[Who transmitted the Torah at Sinai] with flame and fire!* The Torah states: *And Mount Sinai was engulfed in smoke, because* HASHEM *descended upon it in fire; and its smoke ascended like the smoke from a furnace and the entire mountain shook greatly* (*Exodus* 19:18). Elsewhere it is stated: *And the appearance of the glory of* HASHEM *was like an All-Consuming Fire at the top of the mountain in the eyes of the Children of Israel* (ibid. 24:17).

סִינַי ... בָּךְ בָּחַר אֱלֹהִים וּמָאַס בִּגְדוֹלִים — *Sinai ... God chose you while He spurned taller (moun-*

לִהְיוֹת לְמוֹפֵת לְדָת, כִּי תִתְמַעֵט וְתֵרֵד מִכְּבוּדָהּ,
וְהֵן אֶמְשׁוֹל מְשָׁלֶיךָ.
מָשָׁל לְמֶלֶךְ, אֲשֶׁר בָּכָה לְמִשְׁתֵּה בְנוֹ,
צָפָה אֲשֶׁר יִגְוַע כֵּן אַתְּ בְּמִלֶּיךָ.
תַּחַת מְעִיל, תִּתְכַּס סִינַי לְבוּשֵׁךְ בְּשַׂק,
תַּעֲטֶה לְבוּשׁ אַלְמְנוּת, תַּחֲלִיף שְׂמָלֶיךָ.
אוֹרִיד דְּמָעוֹת, עֲדֵי יִהְיוּ כְנַחַל,[1]
וְיַגִּיעוּ לְקִבְרוֹת שְׁנֵי שָׂרֵי אֲצִילֶיךָ.
מֹשֶׁה וְאַהֲרֹן בְּהֹר הָהָר,
וְאֶשְׁאַל הֲיֵשׁ תּוֹרָה חֲדָשָׁה, בְּכֵן נִשְׂרְפוּ גְלִילֶיךָ.
חֹדֶשׁ שְׁלִישִׁי וְהֻקְשַׁר הָרְבִיעִי,
לְהַשְׁחִית חֶמְדָּתֵךְ, וְכָל יְפִי כְלִילֶיךָ.[2]
גָּדַע לְלֻחוֹת, וְעוֹד שָׁנָה בְּאִוַּלְתּוֹ,
לִשְׂרוֹף בָּאֵשׁ דָּת,[3] הֲזֶה תַּשְׁלוּם כְּפֶלֶיךָ.
אֶתְמַהּ לְנַפְשִׁי אֵיךְ יֶעֱרַב לְחִכִּי אֲכוֹל,
אַחֲרֵי רְאוֹתִי, אֲשֶׁר אָסְפוּ שְׁלָלֶיךָ.
אֶל תּוֹךְ רְחוֹבָהּ כְּנִדַּחַת,* וְשָׂרְפוּ שְׁלַל עֶלְיוֹן,
אֲשֶׁר תְּמָאֵס לָבֹא קְהָלֶיךָ.
לֹא אֵדְעָה לִמְצוֹא דֶּרֶךְ סְלוּלָה,[4]
הֲכִי הָיוּ אֲבֵלוֹת, נְתִיב יָשָׁר מְסִלֶּיךָ.
יִמְתַּק בְּפִי מִדְּבַשׁ, לִמְסוֹךְ בְּמַשְׁקֶה דְּמָעוֹת,
וּלְרַגְלֵי הֱיוֹת כָּבוּל כְּבָלֶיךָ.
יֶעֱרַב לְעֵינַי, שְׁאוֹב מֵימֵי דְּמָעַי,
עֲדֵי כָלוּ לְכָל מַחֲזִיק בִּכְנַף מְעִילֶיךָ.[5]
אַף יֶחֱרְבוּ בְּרִדְתָּם עַל לְחָיַי,
עֲבוּר כִּי נִכְמְרוּ רַחֲמַי לְנְדוֹד בְּעָלֶיךָ.

---

tains). The *Talmud* (*Sotah* 5a) teaches that God rejected lofty mountains and summits and rested His Holy Presence upon Sinai because it is the lowest of all peaks. This emphasizes that no quality is more beloved to God than genuine humility. Moreover, even after God designated Sinai for greatness, the mountain remained low and humble (see *Megillah* 29a).

לִשְׂרוֹף בָּאֵשׁ דָּת — *By incinerating the Law in fire.* This refers to the Talmud's statement (*Taanis* 26b) that on the seventeenth of Tammuz, the gentile general Apostumus committed the terrible sacrilege of burning a *Sefer Torah.*

כְּנִדַּחַת — *Like the [condemned property of] an apostate city.* If an individual Jew is guilty of

[Did God choose you, Sinai, the lowest mountain]
to be an ominous sign for the Torah Law that it would be belittled and forced to descend from its glory? Behold, I will illustrate your condition with appropriate parables!
This may be compared to the king who wept at his son's [wedding] feast because he foresaw his son's demise, so too, [O Sinai,] did you foretell your fate in your own words.
Therefore, O Sinai, instead of a royal robe, garb yourself in sackcloth, cloak yourself in widow's garb; change your attire!
And I will shed tears until they flow like a river[1] *that reaches to the gravesites of your two most noble princes.*
They are Moses and Aaron [who were] on Mount Hor.
And I will ask them if there is perhaps a new Torah, therefore your scrolls have been burnt!
[They accepted the Torah during Sivan,] the third month, but [Tammuz] the fourth month revolted [against your Torah], to destroy your delight and your most exquisite beauty.[2]
The Tablets of the Law were shattered [by Moses] and [Tammuz'] folly was repeated by incinerating the Law in fire.[3]
Is this the payment of your double reward?
I wonder to myself, 'How can food ever again be pleasant to my taste after I have seen what your plunderers gathered?'
Into the main public square [they heaped our Talmud scrolls] like [the condemned property of] an apostate city; there men, rejected from entering your congregation, burned exalted spoils.*
I know not how to find the straight road[4] *[which will lead me to fathom your ways]; has not your straight path become shrouded in mourning?*
It would be sweeter to my mouth than honey to mix tears into [my] drink, and to have my feet chained in your shackles [so that I might properly commiserate with your sorrow].
It would be pleasant to my eyes to absorb the waters of my tears, until [the tears] would disappear for all those who cling to edges of your robes.[5]
But they would evaporate as they rolled down my cheeks, because my compassion is intense over the wanderings of your Master.

---

(1) Cf. *Eichah* 2:18. (2) Cf. 2:15. (3) Cf. *Deuteronomy* 33:2.
(4) Cf. *Jeremiah* 18:15. (5) Cf. *I Samuel* 15:27.

---

idolatry, he is condemned to death by stoning. But if an entire city or a majority of its inhabitants are seduced by some of its citizens to worship idols, then this place is adjudged with the special laws of עִיר הַנִּדַּחַת, *an apostate city.* The idolaters are executed by the sword, whereas of the city the Torah says: *And you shall gather all of its contents into the middle of the main open place of the city and you shall burn with fire both the entire city and all of its contents, a total*

לָקַח צְרוֹר כַּסְפּוֹ,[1]* הָלַךְ בְּדֶרֶךְ לְמֵרָחוֹק,[2]
וְעִמּוֹ הֲלֹא נָסוּ צְלָלַיִךְ.[3]
וַאֲנִי כְּשָׁכוּל וְגַלְמוּד,[4] נִשְׁאַרְתִּי לְבַד מֵהֶם,
כְּתֹרֶן בְּרֹאשׁ הַר[5] מִגְּדוֹלַיִךְ.
לֹא אֶשְׁמַע עוֹד לְקוֹל שָׁרִים וְשָׁרוֹת,
עֲלֵי כִּי נִתְּקוּ, חֶבְלֵי תֻפֵּי חֲלִילַיִךְ.
אֶלְבַּשׁ וְאֶתְכַּס בְּשַׂק, כִּי לִי מְאֹד יָקְרוּ,
עַצְמוּ כְּחוֹל יִרְבְּיוּן, נַפְשׁוֹת חֲלָלַיִךְ.
אֶתְמַהּ מְאֹד עַל מְאוֹר הַיּוֹם,
אֲשֶׁר יִזְרַח אֶל כֹּל, אֲבָל יַחֲשִׁיךְ אֵלַי וְאֵלַיִךְ.
זַעֲקִי בְּקוֹל מַר לְצוּר, עַל שִׁבְרוֹנֵךְ וְעַל חָלְיֵךְ,
וְלוּ יִזְכּוֹר אַהֲבַת כְּלוּלַיִךְ.[6]
חִגְרִי לְבוּשׁ שַׂק[7] עֲלֵי הַהַבְעָרָה,
אֲשֶׁר יָצְתָה לְחַלֵּק וְסָפְתָה אֶת תְּלוּלַיִךְ.
כִּימֵי עֱנוּתֵךְ[8] יְנַחֲמֵךְ צוּר,
וְיָשִׁיב שְׁבוּת שִׁבְטֵי יְשֻׁרוּן,[9] וְיָרִים אֶת שְׁפָלַיִךְ.
עוֹד תַּעְדִּי[10] בַּעֲדִי שָׁנִי וְתֹף תִּקְחִי,
תֵּלְכִי בְּמָחוֹל, וְצַהֲלִי בִּמְחוֹלַיִךְ.
יָרוּם לְבָבִי בְּעֵת צוֹרֵךְ[11] לְאוֹר לָךְ,
וְיַגִּיהַּ לְחָשְׁכֵךְ וְיָאִירוּ אֲפֵלָיִךְ.

---

conflagration for HASHEM*, your God* (*Deuteronomy* 13:17). And that is just what happened to the Talmud volumes on that fateful Friday in Paris.

לָקַח צְרוֹר כַּסְפּוֹ — *[God] took His purseful of silver pieces.* The Talmud (*Sanhedrin* 96b) relates that Ammon and Moab are the most malicious enemies of the Jews. They heard that Nebuchadnezzar was apprehensive about destroying the Temple. He was afraid that he would meet with the same ruinous disaster as others had before him when they had attempted to harm God's Holy Sanctuary. So Ammon and

*[God] took His purseful of silver pieces[1]**
and embarked on a distant journey;[2] and behold,
when He departed, your sheltering shadows fled.[3]
And I am left behind like someone bereft of all his children,
utterly forlorn;[4] so have I been left all alone.
I am like a [lone] flagstaff planted
atop your towering mountain peak.[5]
No longer do I hear the sounds of [your] musicians, male and female,
because the strings of your musical instruments have been torn.
I will clothe and cover myself with sackcloth, because [your martyrs]
are very precious to me, and as powerful
and numerous as the sand are the souls of your corpses.
I am deeply perplexed by the light of day which shines brightly
towards everyone, yet towards you and me it casts only darkness.
O cry out to the Rock with bitter voice over your ruination
and your debilitation; O if only He would remember
the love of Your wedding day.[6]
Gird yourself with garments of sackcloth[7] over the conflagration
which burst out and tore you to pieces,
and wiped out your towering [Torah scholars].
May the Rock [of salvation] comfort you according to
the days of your affliction,[8] and may He return the
captivity of the Tribes of Jeshurun[9] and exalt your degraded ones.
Once again you will adorn yourself[10] with ornaments of scarlet,
and you will take up the tambourine and go out in a circle
dance and rejoice with your dancing.
At that time my heart will be uplifted, when your Rock will be a light
unto you, to brighten your darkness[11] and to illuminate your gloom.

(1) Cf. *Proverbs* 7:20. (2) 7:19. (3) Cf. *Song of Songs* 2:17.
(4) Cf. *Isaiah* 49:21. (5) Cf. 30:17. (6) Cf. *Jeremiah* 2:2. (7) Cf. 6:26.
(8) Cf. *Psalms* 90:15. (9) Cf. *Jeremiah* 30:3. (10) 31:3. (11) Cf. *II Samuel* 22:29.

Moab assured him that he had nothing to fear for the God of the Jews had already abandoned His Temple, as we read: *For the Man is not at home, He has gone on a faraway journey* (*Proverbs* 7:19). Still Nebuchadnezzar was reluctant. 'Perhaps there are still righteous men whose prayers will save the Jews and their Temple?' Again Ammon and Moab reassured him, for it is written, *He has taken a bag of silver with Him* (ibid. 7:20), i.e., in anticipation of the Destruction, God has removed the righteous who are as precious as silver coins!

מב.

צִיּוֹן צְפִירַת פְּאֵר[1]* חֶדְוַת אֲגוּדָיִךְ,
זַעֲקִי בְּרָמָה בְּקוֹלֵךְ[2] עַל **אֲ**בוּדָיִךְ.
אֶל הַבְּנוּיָה לְבַקֵּשׁ וּלְחַנֵּן לָאֵל,
שָׁלוֹם יִשְׁפּוֹת לָךְ[3] וְגַם לִבְנֵי **בְּ**חִירָיִךְ.
בְּעַל בְּחִירֵךְ אֲשֶׁר לָךְ אַהֲבָתוֹ,
לְזָר נֶהְפַּךְ לְנֶגְדֵּךְ וְגַם נֶגֶד **גְּ**דוּדָיִךְ.
גֶּלֶף וּפְתַח בְּלוּחַ לֵב, אֲזַי נִשְׁקַטְתְּ בֶּטַח
בְּשַׁלְוָה שְׁדוּכָה עַל **רְדִ**ידָיִךְ.
דַּבְּרִי נְכוֹחוֹת לְרֵעַיִךְ לְהָלִיץ עֲבוּרֵךְ,*
אַף תְּצַפְצְפִי לְהָרִים קוֹל **הֲ**דָרָיִךְ.
הָשֵׁב יְדִידֵךְ לְמִטָּתֵךְ וְלָלוּן בְּצִלֵּךְ,
וּלְטַיֵּל בְּסֻגַּת גַּן **וְ**רָדָיִךְ.
וְעַד בְּמֹהַר וְקִדּוּשִׁין וְגַם בִּכְתֻבָּה,
לָךְ וּלְעֶזְרֵךְ וְהֵם בָּרוּר **זְ**בָדָיִךְ.
זֶרַע וּבָנִים מְחֻטָּבִים לְאִישֵׁךְ הֲלֹא יָלַדְתְּ,
וְאֵיךְ נִשְׁכַּלְתְּ מִכָּל **חֲ**סִידָיִךְ.
חָמַק וְעָבַר[4] וְגָז מִמֵּךְ וְלֹא נִשְׁלַחַתְּ,
לֹא בָא בְיָדֵךְ, שְׁטַר סֵפֶר **טְ**רוּדָיִךְ.[5]
טוֹעֵן בְּטַעֲנַת מְמָאֶנֶת בְּמֶרֶד,
עֲלֵי כֵן נִתְקַלַּסְתְּ וְהֻשְׁפַּל עַם דּוֹדָיִךְ.
יוֹשַׁבְתְּ בְּדוּדָה דְּמוּיָה כִּי חֲשׂוּפָה קְלוֹן שׁוּלַיִךְ,
וְנִגְלֵית וְנִדְלַל **כְּ**בוּדָיִךְ.
כָּל מַחֲזִיקִים בְּנִזְרֵךְ, הֵם יְצָאוּךְ,
דְּחוּפִים וּבְהוּלִים[6] וְהֵם הָיוּ **לְ**בוּדָיִךְ.
לִבִּי הֲלֹא נֶחֱלַל[7] מֵאֵין הֲפוּגוֹת,[8]

(1) Cf. *Isaiah* 28:5. (2) Cf. *Jeremiah* 31:14. (3) Cf. *Isaiah* 26:12. (4) Cf. *Song of Songs* 5:6. (5) Cf. *Isaiah* 50:1. (6) Cf. *Esther* 8:14. (7) Cf. *Psalms* 109:22. (8) *Eichah* 3:49.

צִיּוֹן צְפִירַת פְּאֵר — *O Zion, crown of splendor.* The *paytan* urges terrestrial Zion to plead with its celestial counterpart that it intervene with the Heavenly Court to bring an end to Israel's exile and dispersion.

The *kinnah* is arranged according to an *aleph-beis* acrostic, each letter appearing twice: as the initial of the first word of a line, and of the last word of the preceding line. Then follows the author's signature מֵאִיר חֲזַק, *Meir, may he be strong,* in a similar manner. The composer is generally identified as R' Meir ben Elazar

42.

ציון *O Zion, crown of splendor,*[1]* *desire of your [diverse] groups,*
let your voice cry out to the highest [heavens][2]
over your lost [populace].

א *[Cry out] to the celestial Jerusalem built [on high],*
to beg and plead with God to settle you in peace,[3]
as well as your chosen children.

ב *[God,] the husband of your choice,*
Whose love was [once exclusively] for you, has turned
against you and against your soldiers like a total stranger.

ג *As long as He was chiseled and engraved*
upon the tablet of your heart, you were quiet,
confident and tranquil, relaxed on your mantle [the Holy Temple].

ד *So speak to your friends [the angels Michael and Gabriel,*
*and ask them] to intervene on your behalf,**
and sing [like a bird] yourself, raising your
splendid voice [in intensive prayer].

ה *[And entreat] your Beloved to return to your [Temple] couch,*
to rest in your shade and to stroll in the garden
hedged by your roses.

ו *Bound together [with God, is Israel] through dowry [the Sabbath]*
and betrothal [the Ten Commandments] and also
marriage contract [the Torah], [so that Israel is unto] you
[the Holy Land] and your helpmate [the Temple],
and they are your [choicest] portion.

ז *[O Israel!] Have you not borne fine children for your spouse,*
sons hewn to perfection? How, then,
are you now utterly bereft of your pious ones?

ח *He [God] disappeared and went away*[4]
and severed Himself from you, although
you were never formally released,
for no official bill of your divorce[5] *was placed in your hand.*

ט *He [God] charges you with defiance and rebelliousness,*
therefore you, your Beloved's nation,
are now disgraced and degraded.

י *Now you sit solitary and silent, for the shame of your hems*
has been uncovered, and your honor has been diminished.

כ *All who had supported your crown fled from you speedily*
and confused[6] *— even though they had been connected to you.*

ל *Behold, my heart is hollow*[7] *within me without relief,*[8]

Lombard HaDarshan who flourished early in the thirteenth century.

דַּבְּרִי נְכוֹחוֹת לְרֵעַיִךְ לְהָלִיץ עֲבוּרֵךְ — *So speak to your friends [the angels Michael and Gabriel and ask them] to intervene on your behalf.* This must not be misinterpreted as a prayer to the angels to pray on our behalf. *Rambam* and many others have clearly postulated that a Jew must pray to God directly without any intermediaries. Rather, *in addition* to our own fervent

אֲשֶׁר הוּמַר וְנֶחְלַף לְמַר מֶתֶק **מְ**גָדֶיךָ.
מְלֹא דְּמָעוֹת כַּמַּיִם נִשְׁטָפוּ,
נִמְלְאוּ דְמָעוֹת לְחָיַי וְכָל עֵינֵי **נְ**גִידַיִךְ.
נַפְשִׁי עֲטוּפָה[1] בְּעֵת זָכְרִי לְאִשֵּׁךְ הֲלֹא נִכְבָּה,
וְלֹא יָכְלוּ לֶאֱפוֹת **סְ**מִידַיִךְ.
סַמֶּךְ אֲשִׁישַׁי[2] עֵנָב מָהוּל בַּמַּיִם,[3]*
וּפַס מִן הָרְפָתִים, בְּקַר זִבְחֵי **עוֹ**בְדַיִךְ.
עֻדַּר וְנֶחֱרַשׁ יְסוֹדֵךְ* לְשָׂדֶה בוּר וְנִיר,
לְחָכָה וְאָכְלָה סְבִיבַיִךְ אֵשׁ **פְּ**לָדַיִךְ.[4]
פֶּלֶץ וְשָׁבָץ לְבָשׁוּנִי, בְּעֵת אֶחֱזֶה מוֹנֵי שְׁקֵטִים,
וְהֵם צָדוּ **צְ**עָדַיִךְ.[5]
צוֹעֵק אֲנִי לִמְקוֹנְנוֹת לִבְכּוֹת,
וּבְמַר לִזְעוֹק נְהִי נִהְיָה, הוֹי עַל **קְ**פָדַיִךְ.
קַלּוּ יְמֵי עָנְיִי, עֵת אֶחֱזֶה עָנְיֵךְ,
שׁוֹמְרִים מְצָאוּךְ, וְהֵם נָשְׂאוּ **רְ**דִידַיִךְ.[6]
רָחֲפוּ עֲצָמַי[7] עֲלֵי בָּנִים יְקָרִים
אֲשֶׁר כְּשִׂיד שְׂרוּפִים, בְּאוּר אוּדֵי **שְׂ**רִידַיִךְ.
שָׁקְדוּ וְיָקְדוּ גְּוִילֵי דַּת מְשַׂנְאַי,
אוֹי אֵיךְ נִמְשַׁלְתְּ לְפַטִּישׁ **תְּ**עוּדַיִךְ.
תּוֹהֶה לְבָבִי אֲשֶׁר נִרְצָה,
בְּאֶרֶץ טְמֵאָה לִנְדָבָה לִנְסוֹךְ יֵין תְּמִידַיִךְ.
צִיּוֹן עֲדֵי אָן מְשִׂימָה אַתְּ לְפֶה אֶת יָדֵךְ,[8]
אֵיכָה בְּיַד אוֹיְבַיִךְ נָפְלוּ נְגִידַיִךְ.

---

(1) Cf. *Psalms* 107:5. (2) Cf. *Song of Songs* 2:5. (3) *Isaiah* 1:22. (4) *Nahum* 2:4. (5) Cf. *Eichah* 4:18. (6) Cf. *Song of Songs* 5:7. (7) Cf. *Jeremiah* 23:9. (8) Cf. *Job* 40:4.

---

prayers addressed directly and exclusively to God, we summon the defending angels to testify in our favor before the Heavenly Tribunal and to bring our good deeds and merits to God's attention in the most forceful fashion.

עֵנָב מָהוּל בַּמָּיִם — *Grape wine ... intermingled with the water.* This refers to the ritual of נִיסּוּךְ הַמַּיִם, *the water libation,* which took place in the Temple on the Sukkos festival (see *Sukkah* 4:9). There were two bowls atop the Altar. A *Kohen* would pour wine into one bowl and water into the other. The liquids would flow out of the bowls into two holes in the Altar's top. Eventually, they would mingle deep under the Altar. *Vilna Gaon* explains that strong wine symbolizes God's Attribute of Strict Justice whereas sweet, pure water represents God's Attribute of Mercy. When the strong wine is diluted by the water it symbolizes God's desire to temper His Strict Justice with tender and compassionate Mercy.

עֻדַּר ... יְסוֹדֵךְ — *Your foundations were hacked away.* Five terrible tragedies befell the Jewish people on Tishah B'Av. They culminated with

because spoiled and turned into bitterness are your sweet fruit.

מ *Full of tears flowing like flooding waters, my cheeks, as well as the eyes of all your princes, have become filled with tears.*

נ *My spirit is weakened*[1] *when I remember*
your [Altar] fire that is now extinguished!
And no longer can they bake your fine-flour offerings.

ס *[Gone are] the pitchers*[2] *of grape wine [for the libations]*
that intermingled with the water [libation*[3]
during the Festival of Sukkos];
and absent from the pens are the cattle
for the sacrifices of those who serve You.

ע *Your foundations were hacked away**
and plowed under [by the Roman Turnus Rufus]
into a plowed yet fallow field; your tongues of flame
licked at you from every side.[4]

פ *I am clad with trembling and revulsion,*
when I observe my tormentors [lounging] in tranquility;
those [murderers] who hunted down
those who followed in Your footsteps.[5]

צ *I scream to the wailing-women to weep and to cry bitterly,*
'O woe! Alas! Ho!' for your [citizens who were] cut off.

ק *My days of suffering feel light, when I see your suffering;*
the [hostile] watchmen caught you
and they carried off your mantle.[6]

ר *A shudder passes through my bones*[7] *for the precious children*
who were burnt like limestone ash; those very survivors
who [originally were saved] like a firebrand from the fire.

ש *My avowed enemies made all haste*
to burn the parchments of the Law.
Woe! How did this befall you [O Torah]
who are likened to a hammer
[which destroys every obstacle in its path]?

ת *My heart is thrown into turmoil when I consider that You*
prefer to send beneficial rains down on the defiled lands
of the gentiles more than You desire the pouring
of the wine libations of the daily [Temple] sacrifice.

O Zion! How long will you clasp your hand to your mouth[8]
[to ensure your silence]? O how did you allow your princes
to fall into the hands of your foes?

---

the obliteration of every last vestige of the Temple by the wicked Roman governor Turnus Rufus some sixty years after the Temple was destroyed. He plowed over the Temple mount and its surroundings in fulfillment of the prophet's threat: צִיּוֹן שָׂדֶה תֵחָרֵשׁ, *Zion will be plowed over like a field* (*Micah* 3:12; *Taanis* 29a; *Rambam, Hilchos Taanis* 5:3).

מִמֵּךְ אֲבוּדִים יְלָדִים חֲמוּדִים כְּפָז,
עַל זֹאת בְּמֶרֶר בְּכִי יְלֵלַת **מְ**רוּדַיִךְ.
אֵיכָה מְעֻכָּב זְמַן לִדְתֵּךְ,
וְעַד אָן תְּהִי אַתְּ נִקְשֶׁרֶת בְּחִיל צִירֵי **אֲ**חוּדַיִךְ.
יוֹלְדוֹת לְתִשְׁעָה יְרָחִים עֵת נְשֵׁי כֹל,
וְאֵיךְ רַבּוּ שְׁנוֹתֵךְ אֲשֶׁר הָרִית **יְ**לָדַיִךְ.
רָנִּי לְשׁוֹמֵר לְאַיָּלָה[1] חֲבָלִים,
וְהוּא יַתִּיר לְצִירֵךְ עֲלֵי רֶבֶד **רְ**פִידַיִךְ.
חוֹשֵׁב זְמַן יַעֲלֵי סֶלַע[1] לְהַתִּיר,
וְלֹא חָשַׁב זְמַנֵּךְ לְהָסִיר כָּל **חֲ**רָדַיִךְ.
זְמַן בְּיָדוֹ פַּתֵּחַ אַרְבַּע נְעוּלִים,*
וְגַם כֵּן יִפְתַּח גִּנְזֵי אוֹצָר **זְ**בוּלַיִךְ.
קוֹל יַשְׁמִיעַ לְקַבֵּץ הָאֱמוּנִים,
וְאָז דְּלָתָיו פָּתוֹחַ יַפְקִידֵם עַל **קְ**לִידַיִךְ.
צִיּוֹן מְעֻשִּׂים בְּצַעֲרֵךְ וּבְיָפְיֵךְ מְעֻשָּׁתִים,
אֲשֶׁר יִזְרַח חֶרֶס חֲדוּדַיִךְ.[2]
צִיּוֹן בְּמִנְחָה יְכַפְּרוּן אֶת פְּנֵי זַעְמֵךְ,
אָז יִשְׁתַּחֲווּ לְכַף רַגְלֵךְ חֲרָדַיִךְ.
צִיּוֹן עֲדִי עֶדְיֵךְ[3] רִקְמַת בִּגְדֵךְ,[4]
וְגַם עֹז וּזְרוֹעַ[5] פְּאֵר בִּגְדֵי חֲמוּדַיִךְ.

בְּיָדוֹ פַּתֵּחַ אַרְבַּע נְעוּלִים — *In His hands are the keys to the four sealed [celestial] vaults.* The Talmud (*Taanis* 2a; *Sanhedrin* 113a) teaches that although God has entrusted all of the blessings of nature to angels intermediaries, three 'keys' remain in His hand because there natural phenomenon require intimate Divine Providence. The three are rainfall, resurrection and childbirth. *Tur Shulchan Aruch* (*Orach Chaim* #114, based on the *Jerusalem Talmud*) adds a fourth key — that of livelihood. *Tur* notes that the word מַפְתֵּחַ, *key*, is an acronym for these four blessings: מָטָר, *rainfall;* פַּרְנָסָה, *livelihood;* תְּחִיָּה, *resurrection;* and חַיָּה, *childbearing mother* (see ArtScroll, *Shemoneh Esrei*, p. 70).

מ *Your children, as precious as the finest gold, have vanished,*
therefore your anguished wailing is mixed with bitter weeping.

א *O how long will your rebirth be delayed? And until when will you*
be gripped by the excruciating travails of birth which grip you?

י *A birth process terminating in nine months is the norm for all women,*
why then have the years since you conceived
your children extended for so much longer?

ר *Cry out prayerfully to He Who even watches over the hind*[1]
in her birth travail, certainly He will release you from the pain
you suffer over [the loss of] your couch-like Temple.

ח *Although He even calculates with precision the moment*
the mountain goat delivers its offspring,[1]
He nevertheless refrained from determining the final time
[of your redemption] to spare you from [prolonged] terror.

ז *prepared in His hands are the keys to the four sealed*
[celestial] vaults; and also He [alone holds the key]*
to open the hidden treasures of the Temple Dwelling.

ק *He will issue a call to gather in the faithful,*
and then He will command the gatekeepers
to leave the doors [of Jerusalem] wide open.

O Zion! *Those who are heartbroken over your pains*
will be thrilled by your [future] beauty,
when the dazzling rays of your sun will shine.[2]

O Zion! *[The gentile nations] shall attempt*
to appease your wrath with a gift-offering,
then those who made you shudder with fear
will bow down to the bottoms of your feet.

O Zion! *Adorn yourself with ornaments,*[3]
with your embroidered robes,[4]
and gird yourself, too, with power and might[5]
and the splendor of your precious garments.

(1) Cf. *Job* 39:1. (2) Cf. 41:22. (3) Cf. *Jeremiah* 4:30. (4) Cf. *Ezekiel* 16:18. (5) *Isaiah* 51:9.

מג.

צִיּוֹן בְּמִשְׁפָּט* לְכִי לָךְ עִם מְעוֹנְנַיִךְ,
הִתְעוּךְ בְּכָזָב וְלֹא גִלּוּ עֲוֹנַיִךְ.[1]
אָכֵן בְּנֵי עַוְלָה עִנּוּךְ וִירָשׁוּךְ,
נְוֵה צֶדֶק[2] הָיִית אֶל כָּל שְׁכֵנַיִךְ.
בָּזִית מַמְלִיכֵךְ, וְלֹא הִקְשַׁבְתְּ לְמוֹרֵךְ לְטוֹב,
בִּשְׁכּוֹן בְּאַרְצֵךְ קְדוֹשֵׁךְ בִּמְלוֹנַיִךְ.
גִּלִּית קְלוֹנֵךְ וְטֻמְאָתֵךְ בְּשׁוּלֵךְ,[3]
וְגַם טִמֵּאת דְּרָכַיִךְ, מְאֹד הִרְבֵּית זְנוּנַיִךְ.
דֶּרֶךְ אֲחוֹתֵךְ הֲלֹא הָלַכְתְּ,
וְזָנִית בְּתַזְנוּתָהּ, וְהִזְנֵית בְּנוֹתַיִךְ וּבָנַיִךְ.
הֻכֵּית וְנֻגַּפְתְּ לְאֵין מַרְפֵּא,
וְהֻשְׁלַכְתְּ כְּטִיט חוּצוֹת,[4] וְהִנֵּךְ שְׂחוֹק לִבְנֵי מְעַנַּיִךְ.
וַתְּהִי נְגִינָה בְּפִי זֵדִים אֲרוּרִים,
אֲשֶׁר אָמְרוּ לְנַפְשֵׁךְ שְׁחִי[5] הֲרוֹס לְשִׁנַּיִךְ.
זִכְרִי עֲנִיָּה בְּלֵב נִשְׁבָּר,
וְזַעֲקִי עֲלֵי מַכֵּךְ וְנוֹגְשֵׂךְ אֲשֶׁר גָּדַע קְרָנַיִךְ.[6]
חַכִּי בֶּאֱמֶת לְאֵל צוּרֵךְ וּבוֹרְאֵךְ,
וְהוֹחִילִי לְמַלְכֵּךְ לְבַד כִּי הוּא אֲדוֹנַיִךְ.
טַהֲרִי לְבָבֵךְ וְכַפַּיִךְ,
וְשׁוּבִי עֲדֵי אִישֵׁךְ קְדוֹשֵׁךְ, וְלוֹ הַרְבִּי רְנָנַיִךְ.
יוֹמָם וָלַיְלָה תְּנִי קוֹל בִּבְכִי מַר,
עֲלֵי קִרְיַת מְלוּכָה[7] וְעַל תֵּל אַרְמוֹנַיִךְ.
כָּבוֹד וְהָדָר וְרֹב יֹפִי בְּתוֹכֵךְ,
הֲלֹא נִמְצָא פְּנֵי קְדוֹשֵׁךְ וְהֵן נִתַּן לְעוֹיְנַיִךְ.

(1) Cf. *Eichah* 2:14. (2) *Jeremiah* 31:22. (3) Cf. *Eichah* 1:9. (4) *Psalms* 18:43. (5) *Isaiah* 51:23. (6) Cf. *Eichah* 2:3. (7) Cf. *Psalms* 48:3.

צִיּוֹן בְּמִשְׁפָּט — *O Zion, enter into litigation.* This *kinnah* was written by R' Yosef bar Chaim HaKohen who highlights the tragic fact that the Jewish people were misguided and led to sin by false prophets and corrupt leaders. Indeed, corruption and perversion of justice was one of the primary causes of our nation's decline and ultimate banishment. As the Talmud (*Shabbos* 118b) graphically describes, the leaders and judges of the Temple era were afraid to offend the rich and the powerful so they twisted the law in their favor.

Isaiah the prophet lamented this, saying: *How has the faithful city become a harlot? It had*

43.

צִיּוֹן *O Zion, enter into litigation* against your false prophets who deliberately misled you with deceit and who failed to expose your iniquities[1] [and deprived you of an opportunity for repentance and salvation].*

א *Indeed, men of iniquity tortured and exploited you, even though you were once a haven of righteousness[2] for all of your neighbors.*

ב *[Because] you disgraced [God] Who invested you with sovereignty, and you did not listen to those who attempted to guide you towards goodness, while you were settled in your land and your sacred [God] dwelt in your abode [the Temple].*

ג *You uncovered your own shame and your impurity is spread out over your garments;[3] you even sullied your pathway, because you increased your acts of harlotry.*

ד *Have you not followed in the path of your sister [the Northern Kingdom], and strayed after her harlotry? Moreover, you even perverted the ways of your daughters and sons and caused them to take up harlotry.*

ה *Therefore, you were beaten and plagued beyond any cure, and were thrown out like mud in the streets,[4] and you have become a laughingstock for the sons of those who torment you.*

ו *And you were the butt of the taunting songs in the mouths of the accused wanton ones who said to you, 'Bend over[5] so that we may smash your teeth!'*

ז *Remember the impoverished one [Israel] with her broken heart, and cry out over your abusers and taskmasters who tore away your dignity.[6]*

ח *Look forward sincerely for [salvation at the hand of] God Who is your Rock and your Creator, and yearn exclusively for your King for only He is your Lord.*

ט *Purify your heart and your hands and return [in penitence] to your [Divine] Helpmate, your Holy One; and intensify towards Him your joyous songs.*

י *Day and night, raise your voice with bitter weeping over [Jerusalem] the city of royalty[7] and the heaped ruins of your Temple palace.*

כ *Glory and splendor and bountiful beauty were in your midst, all these were displayed before your holy one [Israel], but now they have been given over to your malicious enemies.*

---

been filled with justice, righteousness lodged in it; but now — murderers! (Isaiah 1:21). The prophet goes on to predict that in the future God will purge Jerusalem of its crooked leaders and

לָֽמָּה לְגַלִּים, מְעוֹן תַּנִּים,[1]
וּמוֹרַשׁ קָאַת וְקִפּוֹד,[2] וְגַם אַגְמֵי מַיִם מַעְיָנָֽיִךְ.
מֵאַנְתְּ שְׁמֽוֹעַ לְקוֹל מוּסַר מְיַסְּרֵךְ,
בְּכֵן שָׁתִית וּמָצִית,[3] שְׁמָנַֽיִךְ שְׁמָרָֽיִךְ.
נֹֽכַח פְּנֵי עֶלְיוֹן שִׁפְכִי לְבָבֵךְ[4] כְּמֵי נָהָר,
וְאַל תִּתְּנִי פוּגַת[5] לְעֵינָֽיִךְ.
סֹֽבִּי וְהוֹמִי בְּעִיר,[6] קִרְאִי מְקוֹנְנוֹת[7]
וְכָל נָשִׁים מְבַכּוֹת, בְּכִי גָדוֹל מְקוֹנְנָֽיִךְ.
עֲלֵי צְנִיף מַלְכֵּךְ[8] עַד אָן לְמִרְמָס יְהִי,
עַד מֶה בְּיַד צָר בְּנֵי שָׂרִים סְגָנָֽיִךְ.
פְּתַח לְבָנוֹן שְׁעָרָֽיִךְ,[9]* אֲשֶׁר טָבְעוּ בְּאֶרֶץ[10] נְשִׁיָּה,[11]
וְאֵין מָלוֹן לְכֹהֲנָֽיִךְ.
צִיּוֹן עֲלֵיהֶם נְהִי נִהְיָה,[12] וְלֹא תֶחֱשִׁי,
אִסְפִּי וְקַבְּצִי זְקֵנוֹת וּזְקֵנָֽיִךְ.
קָרְחִי וָגֹזִּי כַּנֶּשֶׁר עַל בְּנֵי תַּעֲנוּגָֽיִךְ,[13]
וְעַל כָּל נְשִׂיאַֽיִךְ וְרוֹזְנָֽיִךְ.
רָֽמוּ וְגָֽדְלוּ כְּמוֹ גַלִּים בְּלֶב יָם מְזוֹרָֽיִךְ,
בְּלֵיל שֻׁדְּדוּ[14] טוּרֵי אֲבָנָֽיִךְ.
שֻׁדַּד מְלוֹנֵךְ וְכָל מַחְמַד יְקָרֵךְ,
בְּאֵין אוּרִים וְתֻמִּים[15] אֲשֶׁר גִּלּוּ צְפוּנָֽיִךְ.
תָּבוֹר וְכַרְמֶל כְּהָרֵי גִלְבֹּֽעַ,*
בְּלִי טַלֵּךְ וּמִטְרֵךְ,[16] וְלֹא אוֹר עֲנָנָֽיִךְ.[17]
צִיּוֹן יְגוֹנֵךְ נְשִׁי, טַהֲרִי וְהִתְקַדְּשִׁי,
עֲדִי יְקָר לִבְשִׁי, תַּמְרוּק שְׁמָנָֽיִךְ.

---

that will lead to the redemption. *And I shall restore your judges as in earliest times and your counselors at first. Afterwards you shall be called the city of righteousness, the faithful city* (*Isaiah* 1:26).

This *kinnah* ends off on a note of hope that after Zion is purified it will once again be regarded as 'the most precious treasure of monarchs and kingdoms.'

פְּתַח לְבָנוֹן שְׁעָרָֽיִךְ — *Open your gates, O [Levanon,] Whitened One!* This is based on the words of the prophet who said: פְּתַח לְבָנוֹן דְּלָתֶֽיךָ, *Open your doors, O [Levanon] Whitened One!* (*Zechariah* 11:1). The Talmud (*Yoma* 39b) teaches that forty years before the destruction of the Second Temple, the Temple itself exhibited many signs and omens of its impending doom. One of the portents was that the Temple gates would swing open all by themselves as if to invite the enemy to enter and destroy it. Rabban Yochanan ben Zakkai saw this and addressed the Temple:. Sanctuary, O Sanctuary! Why do

ל *Why has it [Jerusalem] been turned into a mound of rubble,*
a den of serpents,[1] the domain of the wild birds of the night?[2]
Even your springs have turned into swamps.

מ *You stubbornly refused to heed the warning voice*
of those who admonished you, therefore you have drunk deep
and drained[3] the very grease and the lees.

נ *In the presence of the Exalted God, pour out your heart[4]*
like waters of the river and give no rest[5] to your eyes.

ס *Go around and moan all over the city.[6]*
Summon forth the wailing-women[7] and all the women
who know how to weep. Let your lamenters weep copiously!

ע *[To bemoan] your royal tiara,[8] O how long will it be trampled over?*
Until when will the children of your nobles, your ministers,
remain in the hands of your tormentors?

פ *Open your gates, O [Levanon,] Whitened One![9]**
The ones that sank into the forgotten[11] land[10]
for [now] there is no [longer] a lodging house for your priests.

צ *O Zion, engage in pitiful cries of doleful lamentation[12]*
over their plight and be not silent. Gather together
and assemble your old women and old men [to join in mourning].

ק *Make yourself bald as an eagle as you tear out your hair*
over the children of your pleasure[13]
and for all your princes and advisers.

ר *Your ugly wounds became swollen and bloated like billowing waves*
in the heart of the sea, on the night when the rows of your precious
gems were plundered[14] [from the High Priest's breastplate].

ש *Your lodging place [the Temple] was plundered together*
with your most precious treasures, you are bereft of
your Urim V'Tumim[15] which revealed all things hidden.

ת *Tabor and Carmel have become like the mountains of Gilboa**
which are devoid of your dew and your rain[16]
and deprived of the light of your [protective] clouds.[17]

י *O Zion! You will ultimately forget your agony.*
Purify and prepare yourself in sanctity!
Adorn yourself with precious jewels and with your perfumed oils.

(1) *Jeremiah* 9:10. (2) Cf. *Isaiah* 34:11. (3) Cf. 51:17. (4) Cf. *Eichah* 2:19. (5) 2:18. (6) Cf. *Isaiah* 23:16. (7) Cf. *Jeremiah* 9:16. (8) Cf. *Isaiah* 62:3. (9) Cf. *Zechariah* 11:1. (10) *Eichah* 2:9. (11) *Psalms* 88:13. (12) *Micah* 2:4. (13) Cf. 1:16. (14) Cf. *Isaiah* 15:1. (15) *Exodus* 28:30. (16) Cf. *II Samuel* 1:21. (17) Cf. *Job* 37:11.

you take such pains to terrify yourself? I know full well that you are destined to be destroyed as indeed the prophet Zechariah foretold when he said, *Open your doors, O [Levanon,] Whitened One, so that the fire many consume your cedars!* [But why must you fulfill this prophecy so early and prematurely?] The *Talmud* concludes: And why is the Temple referred to as לְבָנוֹן, *Levanon* [Whitened One]? Because it is there that the Jewish nation finds atonement and the stain of their sins is whitened and cleansed!

תָּבוֹר וְכַרְמֶל כְּהָרֵי גִלְבּוֹעַ — *Tabor and Carmel have become like the mountains of Gilboa.* Tabor and Carmel were fertile mountains cov-

צִיּוֹן **וְ**שָׁלְמוּ יְמֵי אֶבְלֵךְ[1] בְּשָׂשׂוֹן וְגִיל,
כִּי תַם עֲוֹנֵךְ וּמִשְׁנֶה שִׁבְרוֹנָיִךְ.
צִיּוֹן **סְ**גֻלַּת מְלָכִים וּמְדִינוֹת[2] תְּהִי עוֹד,
יִזְּלוּ מֵי מְנוּחוֹת[3] מַעְיָנָיִךְ.
צִיּוֹן **פְּ**דוּתֵךְ צְפִי, עוֹד יִקְרָאוּךְ צְפִירַת תִּפְאָרָה,[4]
בְּפִי יְשָׁרִים וְנוֹגְנָיִךְ.[5]
צִיּוֹן **בְּ**רָכָה **וְ**חַיִּים,[6] בָּךְ אֲבִיר יַעֲקֹב,[7]
צִוָּה לְעוֹלָם[6] וְעוֹד יֹאמְרוּ בְּאָזְנָיִךְ.
צִיּוֹן **הֲ**מוֹן **כֹּ**הֲנִים הֵמָּה יְשָׁרְתוּנֵךְ,
וְגַם יוֹסִיף יהוה קְנוֹת שֵׁנִית קְצִינָיִךְ.[8]

(1) *Isaiah* 60:20. (2) Cf. *Ecclesiates* 2:8. (3) *Psalms* 23:2. (4) *Isaiah* 28:5. (5) Cf. *Psalms* 68:26. (6) Cf. 133:3. (7) *Genesis* 49:24. (8) Cf. *Isaiah* 11:11.

ered with grass and trees. Gilboa, however, was cursed and barren for it was on Gilboa that King Saul died in his final battle with the Philistines. In his passionate eulogy for Saul, David cursed Mount Gilboa forever: *O mountains of Gilboa, let there be no dew nor rain upon you, nor shall*

ו *O Zion! Your era of mourning will come to an end*[1]
with joy and jubilation, for your sins will be entirely absolved
and your double Destruction will be concluded.

ס *O Zion! Once again you will be considered*
the most precious treasure
by all the monarchs and kingdoms,[2]
and tranquil waters[3] *will flow from your fountain springs.*

פ *O Zion! Look forward to your redemption!*
You will again be called a crown of splendor[4]
by the mouth of the upright and by your musicians [the Levites].[5]

O Zion! [God] the Mighty One of Jacob[7] *has decreed blessing*
and life for you forever[6] *and [mankind]*
is destined to say that in your ears.

— O Zion! A multitude of priests shall serve you!
And HASHEM *will once again take charge of your leaders.*[8]

---

your fields produce heave offerings for there the shield of the mighty was rejected, the shield of Saul was as though not anointed with oil [II Samuel 1:21].

מד.

צִיּוֹן גְּבֶרֶת* לְמַמְלָכוֹת[1] מְצִירָיִךְ,
רְבֵּי שְׁלוֹמִים שְׂאִי, מֵאֵת אֲסִירָיִךְ.
יֶחְמַץ לְבָבִי[2] לְקוֹל נָתְנוּ רְאֵמִים,
בְּנֵי שֵׂעִיר וּמוֹאָב, בְּתוֹךְ הֵיכַל דְּבִירָיִךְ.
לִבְּסוּ מְשִׁיחַי בְּדַם קָדְקֹד סְגָנִים,
טְרוּף[3] שׁוֹעַ וְקוֹעַ, רָמוּס עַמִּי בְּחִירָיִךְ.
עָרִים בְּצוּרוֹת תְּפוּשׂ דָּיֵק וְסוֹלָל שְׁפוּךְ,[4]
אַרְזֵי לְבָנוֹן כְּרוּת, מֵעֲצֵי יְעָרָיִךְ.
חָזוּ נְבִיאִים בְּשָׁוְא דִּבֵּר[5] בְּשֵׁם עִיר קְדוֹשׁ יַעֲקֹב[6] לְשָׁלוֹם,
וְלֹא חֶבְּשׁוּ מְזוֹרָיִךְ.
יִתַּר לְבָבִי עֲלֵי אָרוֹן וּמִשְׁכָּן וְצִיץ זָהָב וְאֵפוֹד,
וְשֵׁם קֹדֶשׁ סְתָרָיִךְ.
אִיִּים יְחַוּוּ לְרָז אוֹתוֹת וּמוֹפֵת,
עֲלֵי שִׁבְרֵךְ יְרַפְּאוּ, אֱלֵי מִשְׁנֶה שְׁבָרָיִךְ.[7]
שֶׁמֶשׁ וְכָל כּוֹכְבֵי שַׁחַק בְּעֵמֶק דָּמוּ,
קוֹלֵךְ בְּרָמָה שְׂאִי, קוֹל תַּמְרוּרָיִךְ.[8]
סַהַר וְכִימָה וְעָשׁ וּכְסִיל[9] לָזֹאת יִבְכּוּ,
נָגְהָם אֲשֶׁר אָסְפוּ,[10] כּוֹכְבֵי שְׁחָרָיִךְ.
מַטֵּה רְשָׁעִים[11] כְּקָם, שָׂרִים בְּיָדָם תְּלוּת,
שָׁבַת מְשׂוֹשֵׂךְ[12] וְגִיל וּכְלֵי זְמָרָיִךְ.
אָבַל לְבָנוֹן וְגִיל כַּרְמֶל בְּלִי נִשְׁמַע חָפְרוּ סְגָנִים,
בְּבֹא צָר בִּשְׁעָרָיִךְ.
חָכְמַת נְבוֹנִים[13] בְּיוֹם אָבְדָה וְאֶסְרוּ קְצִינַיִךְ,
וְשָׁחוּ בְּנֵי צִיּוֹן יְקָרָיִךְ.[14]

צִיּוֹן גְּבֶרֶת — *O Zion! You who were once the mistress.* In this *kinnah* we bemoan Zion's terrible fall from prominence to pitiful wretchedness. Once Zion was the center of the entire world, mistress to all the nations but now she lies downtrodden beneath the heel of her former vassals.

Indeed it seems as if God has lost all interest in Jerusalem (Zion) and has abandoned it to heathen marauders, but in truth, God still cares deeply for Israel and Jerusalem, only He is hidden from our view. For this reason we sing *kinnos* such as this one, to arouse God to reveal His Presence once more.

The Talmud (*Menachos* 87a) states that even after the destruction of Zion, God protected this sacred site by posting guardian angels around it. As the prophet says, *Upon your walls, O*

44.

ציון *O Zion! You who were once the mistress* over the nations[1]*
who are now your tormentors, accept abundant wishes
for peace from your captive [people].
My heart is in ferment[2] when I hear the roar of the royal monarchs,
the sons of Seir and Moab, inside the hall of your Sanctuary.
My anointed ones [the High Priest and the king] were besmirched
by the blood which splattered from the [smashed]
skulls of the slain [Jewish] princes.
Shoa and Koa [fierce gentile princes] tore them to pieces[3]
and trampled over my nation, your chosen ones.
They seized the fortified cities by building siege towers and by
paving assault roads;[4] they chopped down the cedars of
Lebanon from the woods of your forests [for construction materials].
The [corrupt] prophets prophesied falsely,[5]
saying in the Name of God that [Jerusalem]
the city of the Holy One of Jacob[6] would be left in peace.
Thus, your festering [spiritual] wounds were not bandaged
[and you did not repent].
My heart pounded [in terror] over the loss of the Ark, the Tabernacle,
the golden Headplate [of the High Priest], the sacred Ephod robe
and Your concealed Holy Name.
Even the inhabitants of the most remote islands
acknowledge your power to reveal secrets through the signs
[of the Urim V'Tumim breastplate] and the wonders
[of your prophets]. These [wondrous faces] could have cured
your wounds, now instead we wail over your two-fold devastation![7]
The sun and all the heavenly stars were plunged
into deepest silence, so raise up your voice in Ramah,
the voice of your bitter wailing.[8]
The moon and the constellations of Pleiades, Ursa and Orion,[9]
let them all weep over this, that your morning stars
have withheld their radiance.[10]
When the powerful staff of the wicked[11] arose,
they commanded the [Jewish] princes to be hung
by their own hands; at that moment your gladness
and joy ceased,[12] together with the instruments of your music.
Lebanon [the Temple] mourns, and the joy of Carmel [the Temple]
is no longer heard, the deputies were disgraced
when the enemy entered your gates.
The wisdom of the sages[13] vanished on that day
[of the Temple's destruction] and your leaders were imprisoned,
and your precious ones, the sons of Zion, were bent low.[14]

---

(1) Cf. *Isaiah* 47:5. (2) Cf. *Psalms* 73:21. (3) Cf. *Deuteronomy* 33:20. (4) Cf. *Ezekiel* 4:2. (5) Cf. *Eichah* 2:14. (6) *Isaiah* 29:23. (7) Cf. *Jeremiah* 17:18. (8) Cf. *Jeremiah* 31:14. (9) Cf. *Job* 9:9. (10) Cf. *Joel* 2:10. (11) *Isaiah* 14:5. (12) Cf. *Eichah* 5:15. (13) Cf. *Isaiah* 29:14. (14) Cf. *Eichah* 4:2.

מִכְּלַל מְלָכִים לְבוּשׁ בָּנוֹת רְעוּלוֹת,
פְּאֵר רָאמוֹת וְגָבִישׁ,[1] וְאַף סַפִּיר גְּזִירָיִךְ.[2]
בָּזְאוּ נְהָרִים[3] בְּתוֹךְ קִרְיָה עַלִּיזָה,[4]
לְאֵין קֵץ לִתְכוּנָה[5] וְסוֹף, פָּרְצוּ גְּדֵרָיִךְ.[6]
גִּבְעָה וְעֵץ רַעֲנָן,[7]
אֵלֶּה מְקוֹם פִּגּוּל מְלֵאִים מֵחֲלַל פְּגָרָיִךְ.
יֶהֱמוּ קְרָבַי כַּיָּם, יִזְּלוּ דְמָעַי כְּמֵי נִמְרִים,[8]
לְבָאִים בְּיוֹם טָרְפוּ כְּפִירָיִךְ.[9]
יִסְעַר לְבָבִי כְּמוֹ סוּפָה וָסַעַר,
כְּמוֹץ גֹּרֶן יְסוֹעֵר,[10] עֲלֵי אַשְׁמוֹת כְּמָרָיִךְ.
הוּמַר בְּשָׂרַי לְיוֹם נֹאֵר קְדוֹשׁ יַעֲקֹב
מִקְדָּשׁ וּמִזְבְּחוֹ,[11] בְּלִי בוֹא בַּחֲצֵרָיִךְ.
שׂוֹרֵק וּנְטַע נַעֲמָן[12] הָיִית,
וּבְבֹקֶר כְּצָץ פֶּרַח וְנִצָּה, תְּשַׂגְשְׂגִי זְמוֹרָיִךְ.
שׁוּבִי צְבִיָּה לְאֵל יוֹצְרֵךְ, יְכוֹנְנֵךְ לְדוֹר וָדוֹר,
בְּתוֹכֵךְ שְׁכוֹן בַּעַל נְעוּרָיִךְ.
אַרְיֵה בְּנָוֵךְ לְבַל יַעֲלֶה[13] מְסִלּוֹת,
וְצִי אַדִּיר וְשַׁיִט לְבַל יַעֲבוֹר[14] יְאוֹרָיִךְ.
נַפְשִׁי שְׁלוֹמֵךְ דְּרוֹשׁ אִוְּתָה כְּחוֹם צַח עֲלֵי אוֹר,
כְּעָב טַל בְּחוֹם[15] יוֹם, נֵד קְצִירָיִךְ.[16]
אֶשְׂמַח וְאָשִׂישׂ בְּיוֹם אֶשְׁמַע מְבַשֵּׂר בְּקוֹל,[17]
שָׁלוֹם מְנוּחָה דְּרוֹשׁ, וּשְׁלוֹם אֲסִירָיִךְ.

Jerusalem, I posted sentries all day and all night; they will ever be silent; all those who remember HASHEM be not still! (*Isaiah* 62:6). What do these angels say as they stand guard? Either they recite the verse, *'You will arise and show Zion mercy'* (*Psalms* 102:14), or they recite the verse, *'The builder of Jerusalem is HASHEM'* (ibid. 147:2).

What did the angels say before the destruction? They recited the verse, *'For HASHEM has chosen Zion, it He desired for His dwelling place'* (ibid. 132:13). And when the Temple is rebuilt, *Rashi* comments, they will recite that verse once again.

The crown of [Jewish] kings is now worn by gentile daughters;
[the crown] resplendent with precious stones,[1]
even [inlaid] with skillfully cut sapphires.[2]

Streams [of gentile hordes] utterly pillaged[3] *the [once] joyous city,*[4]
[multitudes] without end[5] *or limit to their numbers,*
and they breached your walls.[6]

On every hill and beneath every flourishing tree,[7]
all places where idolatrous abominations [once] stood,
are now filled with the corpses of your slaughtered.

My innards churn like the sea,
my tears flow like the waters of Nimrim,[8]
because of the [barbaric gentiles who attacked Jews like]
lions on the day they tore apart the [young Jewish] cubs.[9]

My heart is in turmoil as if struck by a tempest and a storm,
swirling like the chaff flying wildly from the threshing floor,[10]
because of the guilt of your idolatrous priests [who led Israel astray].

The appearance of my flesh has changed [by suffering] since the day
on which the Holy One of Jacob rejected the Temple and its Altar,[11]
and prevented our entry into Your courtyards.

[O Israel] at one time you were a sturdy vine, a choice planting,[12]
at the dawn [of your history] when your buds blossomed
and flowered, your vine's tendrils got entangled
[in the destructive thorns of sin].

Return, O lovely hind, to God, your Creator, and He will establish
you firmly for generation upon generation, when He,
the husband of your youth, will dwell in your midst.

The lion [Nebuchadnezzar] will no longer march up[13] *the highways*
[to attack] your Temple dwelling, nor will any mighty naval fleet
or any sailing vessel trespass[14] *your waterways.*

My soul yearns to seek your welfare [as people] long for a day
radiant with brilliant sunshine
or as [they pine] for a cloud of dew on the day of intense heat[15]
at the time of your harvest.[16]

I will rejoice and exalt on the day that I hear the herald who proclaims[17]
[the Redemption] out loud, and strives to bring tranquility and peace
and [above all] seeks the peace and welfare of your captives.

---

(1) *Job* 28:18. (2) Cf. *Eichah* 4:7. (3) *Isaiah* 18:7. (4) 22:2. (5) *Nahum* 2:10. (6) Cf. *Psalms* 80:13. (7) Cf. *Jeremiah* 2:20. (8) *Isaiah* 15:6. (9) Cf. *Nahum* 2:14. (10) Cf. *Hosea* 13:3. (11) Cf. *Eichah* 2:7. (12) Cf. *Jeremiah* 2:21. (13) Cf. *Jeremiah* 4:7. (14) Cf. 33:21. (15) 18:4. (16) Cf. 17:11. (17) Cf. 52:7.

קינה לזכרון הקדושים של חורבן איירופא

מאת הרב שלמה האלבערשטאם זצ״ל, האדמו״ר מבאבאב

זִכְרוּ נָא וְקוֹנְנוּ כָּל יִשְׂרָאֵל, קוֹלְכֶם יִשָּׁמַע בָּרָמָה,
כִּי הִשְׁמִידָה גֶּרְמַנְיָא אֶת עַמֵּנוּ בִּימֵי זַעַם הַמִּלְחָמָה,
בְּמִיתוֹת מְשֻׁנּוֹת אַכְזָרִיּוֹת, בָּרָעָב וּבַצָּמָא,
אַל תִּשְׁכְּחוּ בְּכָל הַדּוֹרוֹת, עֲדֵי תִזְכּוּ לִרְאוֹת בַּנֶּחָמָה.

צַעֲקָתָם וּבְכִיּוֹתֵיהֶם, צְפוּפִים וּסְגוּרִים בַּקְּרוֹנִים,
כַּצֹּאן לַטֶּבַח יוּבָלוּ, לִשְׂרֵפָה בַּכִּבְשׁוֹנִים,
קוֹל שַׁוְעָם יִזָּכֵר תָּמִיד לִפְנֵי שׁוֹכֵן מְעוֹנִים,
בְּקָרְאָם שְׁמַע יִשְׂרָאֵל, מָסְרוּ נַפְשָׁם לַאֲדוֹנֵי הָאֲדוֹנִים.

רָאשֵׁי יְשִׁיבוֹת וְתַלְמִידֵיהֶם, וַהֲמוֹנֵי עַמְּךָ שָׁמָּה,
הֶעֱבִידוּם בְּעִנּוּיִים קָשִׁים, וַהֲרָגוּם בְּיָד רָמָה,
דְּמֵי יְלָדִים רַכִּים צוֹעֲקִים אֵלֶיךָ מִן הָאֲדָמָה,
נְקוֹם נִקְמַת טַף וְנָשִׁים, לֹא תְחַיֶּה כָּל נְשָׁמָה.

עַל שְׂרֵפַת אַלְפֵי מִדְרָשׁוֹת וּבָתֵּי כְנֵסִיּוֹת,
רִבְבוֹת סִפְרֵי תוֹרָה וְלוֹמְדֶיהָ, נְקוֹנֵן בִּשְׁאִיּוֹת,
שִׁלְּחוּ בָאֵשׁ מִקְדְּשֵׁי אֵל, הִצִּיתוּ וְעֵינֵינוּ צוֹפִיּוֹת,
יְשַׁלֵּם הַמַּבְעִיר אֶת הַבְּעֵרָה, יָדִין בַּגּוֹיִם מָלֵא גְוִיּוֹת.

זַעֲקוּ שָׁמַיִם וַאֲדָמָה, עַל אַלְפֵי עֲיָרוֹת מִבְצְרֵי תוֹרָה,
אַרְצוֹת אֵירוֹפָּא וּקְהִלּוֹתֶיהָ, נוֹחֲלֵי וּמְקַיְּמֵי מְסוֹרָה,
צַדִּיקִים זְקֵנִים וַחֲסִידִים, דְּבֵקֵי אֱמוּנָה טְהוֹרָה,
מִיּוֹם גָּלִינוּ מֵאַרְצֵנוּ לֹא הָיָה כָּזֶה כִּלָּיוֹן נוֹרָא.

רַחֵם עַל שְׁאֵרִיתֵנוּ, הַבֵּט נָא מִשָּׁמַיִם,
לְמַחֲנוֹת הַקְּדוֹשִׁים, פִּי עֶשֶׂר כְּיוֹצְאֵי מִצְרַיִם,
קוֹמֵם בֵּית קָדְשֵׁנוּ, וְנַחֲמֵנוּ בְּכִפְלַיִם,
רוֹמְמֵנוּ, וַהֲבִיאֵנוּ לְצִיּוֹן וִירוּשָׁלָיִם.

זכרו נא — *Remember, please.* The destruction of European Jewry by the Nazis during World War II was the most massive calamity to befall our people since the Destruction of the Second Temple. As explained in the prefatory notes to *kinnah* 25, which laments the devastation of the Crusades, Torah Jews recognize that all Jewish misfortunes have their roots in the tragic events of Tishah B'Av. Therefore we designate no new days of mourning to commemorate later events, but include them in our Tishah B'Av *kinnos* service.

The Bobover Rav, Admor HaRav Shlomo Halberstam, זצ״ל, was a scion of Sanz, one of the most illustrious Rabbinic and Chassidic dynasties. The Rav lost everything in the Holocaust — family, friends, followers, disciples and students in the thousands. The Rebbe arrived in America after the war with nothing but the clothes on his back and a burning determination to rebuild what the Nazis destroyed. With the help of Hashem the glory of the House of Bobov has been restored and one will find dozens of Bobover institutions and thousands of Bobover Chassidim in every corner of the globe.

In 1984, the Bobover Rav composed a special

KINNAH IN MEMORY OF THE MARTYRS OF CHURBAN EUROPE

by Rabbi Shlomo Halberstam, זצ"ל, Bobover Rav

זִכְרוּ נָא *Remember, please, and lament, O all of Israel,*
let your voices be heard on high.
For Germany has destroyed our people, during stormy days of the World War;
with killings, horrible and cruel, with starvation and thirst.
For all generations, do not forget,
until you will merit witnessing the [ultimate] consolation.

[Remember] their screams and their weeping as they were
tightly packed and locked into the train's [cattle] cars.
Like sheep to the slaughter they were led to be
incinerated in the crematorium ovens.
May the sound of their pleading cries be eternally remembered,
by the One Who dwells in the Heavens.
When they proclaimed, 'Shema Yisrael'
they offered up their lives to the Lord of lords.

Roshei Yeshivah and their students, and the
multitudes of Your people were there.
They enslaved them with brutal tortures,
and they slaughtered them with high-handed arrogance.
The blood of tender babes cries out to You from the earth, [saying;]
'Exact vengeance for the children and the women;
let no living soul escape alive!'

For the burning of thousands of study halls and synagogues,
and for myriad of Torah scrolls and their students,
we shall lament with raised and screaming voices.
They set God's sanctuaries aflame, they ignited them,
and our eyes witnessed this.
Let those who lit the fire suffer retribution;
may God judge the corpse-filled nations.

Cry out loud, O heaven and earth, for the thousands of cities, citadels of Torah,
for the countries of Europe and their Jewish communities,
the heirs and trustees of our traditions,
for righteous tzaddikim, elders, pious chassidim,
all those who cleaved unto a faith so pure.
From the day we were exiled from our homeland,
there was never an annihilation as awesome as this.

Be compassionate with our remnant; look down upon us, please, from heaven,
at the [death] camps of the martyrs, ten times as many as those who left Egypt.
Rebuild our holy Temple, and provide us with double consolation,
Exalt us, and bring us back to Zion and Jerusalem.

---

kinnah to bemoan the tragedy of *Churban Europa,* and it is recited in many congregations. When the Rav was asked for permission to include his *kinnah* and its translation in this edition of *kinnos*, he graciously conceded. Then he explained why he had written it: 'For years I had wanted to express my grief over my personal loss and *Klal Yisrael's* loss, in a special *kinnah*, but I hesitated. I felt that in order to compose a *kinnah* one must be on the exalted level of R' Elazar HaKalir, who wrote with *Ruach HaKodesh,* Divine inspiration. Moreover, he was a master of Kabbalistic secrets and knew the mystical incantations of the ministering angels. Still, many

קינה לזכרון הקדושים של חורבן איירופא

מאת הרב שמעון שוואב זצ"ל, רב דקהל עדת ישורון

הַזּוֹכֵר* מַזְכִּירָיו, דּוֹר דּוֹר וּקְדוֹשָׁיו, מֵעֵת אֲשֶׁר אָז בְּחַרְתָּנוּ,
יִזְכּוֹר דֵּרָאוֹן, שֶׁל דּוֹר אַחֲרוֹן, אוֹיָה מֶה הָיָה לָּנוּ.

שְׁטוּפֵי מַבּוּל דָּם, שֶׁמָּסְרוּ נַפְשׁוֹתָם, כָּל שְׁקוּעֵי עִמְקֵי הַבָּכָא,
יִפְקְדֵם אֱלֹהִים, בְּאַרְצוֹת הַחַיִּים, וַעֲדֵי עַד זִכְרָם לִבְרָכָה.

שְׂאוּ אֵלָיו כַּפַּיִם, אֲהָהּ, אֵי שָׁמַיִם, הוֹי עַל מֵיטַב שִׁבְטֵי יִשְׂרָאֵל,
עֵדוֹת וּקְהִלּוֹת, עָרִים וּגְלִילוֹת, חֲבוּרוֹת, מוֹסָדוֹת, כָּל מוֹעֲדֵי אֵל.

מִי יִתֵּן פַּלְגֵי מַיִם, תֵּרַדְנָה עֵינַיִם, אֶל אַשְׁדוֹת נַחֲלֵי הַדְּמָעוֹת,
עֲלֵי אַלְפֵי אֲלָפִים, גּוּפִים נִשְׂרָפִים, בְּמוֹ אֵשׁ הַחֻרְבָּן וּזְוָעוֹת.

וְעַל שָׂרֵי הַתּוֹרָה, וּמַחֲזִיקֵי מָסוֹרָה, וְעַל פִּרְחֵי הַכְּהוּנָּה הַצְּעִירִים,
וְעַל חוֹבְשֵׁי מִדְרָשׁוֹת, וּמוֹרִים וּמוֹרוֹת, תִּינוֹקוֹת בֵּית רַבָּן יַקִּירִים.

עַל בָּנוֹת בּוֹטְחוֹת, וְסָבִים וְסָבוֹת, וְעַל זַרְעָם וְטַפָּם שֶׁיָּלְדוּ,
וְגַם לְרַבּוֹת, רִבְבוֹת נֶאֱהָבִים בַּחַיִּים, בְּמוֹתָם לֹא נִפְרָדוּ.

אֶת דָּמָם דְּרוֹשׁ, כִּי תִשָּׂא אֶת רֹאשׁ, שֶׁל כָּל נִדָּף לֶעָלִים הַטְּרוּפִים.
כָּל נַפְשׁוֹת מֵת, בִּימֵי שֶׁבֶר וָשֵׁאת, שִׁשָּׁה אַלְפֵי פְעָמִים אֲלָפִים.

שְׁלִישִׁיָּה לְבָעֵר, בִּבְרַק זַעַם סוֹעֵר, מִכַּרְמֵי הַחֶמֶד אָהָבְתָּ,
גּוֹאֵל הַדָּם, נָא זֶכֶר צַעֲרָם, אַל תִּמְחֶה מִסֵּפֶר כָּתָבְתָּ.

זְכוֹר הַנְּאָקוֹת, וְרַעַשׁ צְעָקוֹת, אָז יוּבְלוּ לָרֶצַח,
יְאוֹרֵי דְמֵיהֶם, וְדִמְעוֹת פְּנֵיהֶם, לֹא תִשָּׁכַחְנָה לָנֶצַח.

כָּל חִיל וּגְנִיחָה, וּנְהִי צְרִיחָה, מִשְּׁדוּדֵי לַהֲקוֹת הַכְּלָבִים,
זְכוֹר וּסְפוֹר, בְּנֹאדְךָ צְרוֹר, עַד עֵת נְקֹם עֶלְבּוֹן עֲלוּבִים.

---

chassidim requested a vehicle to convey their personal sorrow on this bitter day, but I held back, because I felt genuinely unworthy.

'Then, one day, I was studying the laws of Tishah B'Av in the book *Seder HaYom* [by R' Moshe ben Yehudah Makir, Rosh Yeshivah in Safed, and a colleague of the *Arizal* and *R' Yosef Karo*]. He writes as follows:

> Whoever can wail on this day should wail, and whoever can recite *kinnos* should recite *kinnos* — either those already recorded in the holy books, or the *kinnos* he himself composed with the intellect God has granted him. It is a *mitzvah* for each and every individual to compose *kinnos* for weeping and moaning and to recite them on this bitter day. One who does this is considered most righteous and is worthy of being described as one of Jerusalem's mourners and one of her holy men. But one who is *not* capable of composing his personal *kinnos*, should recite the *kinnos* written by others.

'When I read these words,' the Rav concluded, 'I saw a clear sign from heaven that the time had come to compose a *kinnah* over the last *churban*. For doesn't the *Seder HaYom* say clearly that any person, even the smallest, should express his own feelings in his original *kinnah*?'

הזוכר — *He Who remembers.* Rav Shimon Schwab, זצ"ל, widely recognized as an eloquent spokesman for Torah Jewry, joined the Rabbinate of Congregation K'hal Adas Jeshurun in the Washington Heights neighborhood of New York in 1958, in association with the late revered Rav Dr. Joseph Breuer, זצ"ל.

Rav Schwab was born in Frankfurt-am-Main, Germany in 1908, and studied at several well-known Eastern European *yeshivos*, including Telshe and Mir. In those years, Rav Schwab had

IN MEMORY OF THE MARTYRS OF CHURBAN EUROPE

by Rabbi Shimon Schwab, זצ"ל, Rav of K'hal Adas Jeshurun

הַזּוֹכֵר *He Who remembers those who remember Him,*
Each generation and its holy ones —
since the time You have chosen us —
May He remember the gruesome fate of the last generation.
Woe! what has happened to us!

Those who were swept away by the flood of blood —
who sacrificed their lives —
All who were submerged in valleys of tears,
May God think of them in the lands of eternal life.
May their memory be a blessing for all eternity.

Lift up your hands to Him, woe O you Heavens!
Woe over the best of Israel's tribes,
Communities and congregations, cities and districts,
fraternities, foundations, all rendezvous with God.

If only streams of water could pour down from eyes
towards waterfalls of the rivers of tears,
for the thousands times thousands of corpses
consumed in the fire of destructions and horrors.

For the princes of Torah, the pillars of tradition,
for the young flowers of the priesthood,
for the diligent scholars, the men teachers and women,
and the precious children in school.

The trusting daughters, the elderly grandparents, and their offspring,
and the infants whom they bore, everyone —
including the myriads beloved in life, not parted by death.

Seek out their blood when You take the count
of all the scattered, rent leaves, of every life perished
in the days of destruction and calamity — six thousand times a thousand.

An entire third to be destroyed, by the Blitzkrieg's fury,
of the cherished vineyards You dearly loved.
O Avenger of blood! The memory of their misery,
please do not erase from the book You have written.

Remember the moans and tumultuous screams,
when they were herded for slaughter —
May the rivers of their blood and the tears on their faces
not be forgotten forever.

Every tremble, every groan, every piercing cry
of those torn asunder by hoards of dogs,
remember and count them, collect them into Your flask,
Till the time the degraded ones' shame is avenged.

---

the opportunity to meet with and learn from the foremost *Gedolim* of the time, including the holy Chafetz Chaim of Radin.

In the early 1930's, Rav Schwab was an eyewitness to the rise of Hitler Nazism in Germany and the systematic oppression of the Jews. In 1936, the persecution of the Nazis forced him to leave his pulpit in Germany. He came to the United States where he assumed a position in the Baltimore Rabbinate.

Rav Schwab relates that in 1959, as Tishah B'Av approached, the late Rav Breuer made a re-

בְּמַחֲנוֹת הַפְּרָאִים, כְּאֵב וּנְגָעִים, וּפַחֵי נְפָשׁוֹת עֲגוּמוֹת,
חֲרָפוֹת וּצְחוֹק, כְּלִימוֹת וָרוֹק, פִּצְעֵי הַכָּאוֹת אֲיֻמּוֹת.

וּרְעָבוֹן, צִמָּאוֹן, שִׁגָּעוֹן, עִצָּבוֹן, וְכִשָּׁלוֹן נֶחֱשָׁלִים בְּלִי כֹחַ,
וְכָל נַאֲקוֹת חָלָל, מִכָּל יָחִיד אֻמְלָל, חָלִילָה לְךָ מִלִּשְׁכֹּחַ.

וְתִימְרוֹת עָשָׁן, וְקִיטוֹר מִכִּבְשָׁן, תִּלֵּי תִלִּים עֲצָמוֹת וְגִידִים,
וְחַדְרֵי הָרַעַל, קוֹל שְׁאָגוֹת מִקְּהַל הַנֶּחְנָקִים תּוֹךְ תָּאֵי הָאֵדִים.

וְסִרְחוֹן גּוּפוֹת, וּגְוִיּוֹת סְגוּפוֹת, גְּלַל דֹּמֶן אַדְמַת נוֹאֲצִים,
אֵיךְ הָפְכוּ טוֹרְפֵיהֶם, לְבֹרִית חֶלְבֵיהֶם, וְעוֹר אִישׁ לְקִשּׁוּטֵי הַנָּשִׁים.

וּקְרִיצַת אֶצְבָּעוֹת, שֶׁל רָאשֵׁי הַפְּרָעוֹת,
לְימִין שִׁעְבּוּד פֶּרֶךְ, צַלְמָוֶת לִשְׂמֹאול.
וְאֵיךְ יָרוּ יְרִיּוֹת עַל חוֹפְרֵי הַבּוֹרוֹת,
בְּיִסּוּרֵי חִבּוּט קֶבֶר הוֹרְדוּם שְׁאוֹל.

אֵיךְ עִנּוּ אַחְיוֹתֵינוּ, וְסֵרְסוּ בְּנוֹתֵינוּ,
כּוֹסוֹת תַּרְעֵלָה מִידֵי רוֹפְאִים אַכְזָרִים.
וּפְלִיטֵי הַשְּׂרִידִים בִּמְחִלּוֹת וּסְתָרִים,
וְטִמְיוֹן יְלָדִים בְּבָתֵּי שְׁמַד כְּמָרִים.

שֶׂה תָמִים לָעוֹלָה, דַּם בְּנֵי הַגּוֹלָה, הוֹי אֲרִיאֵל מִנִּבְלַת חֲסִידֶיךָ,
צֹאן קָדָשִׁים מִי יִמְנֶה, אֲשֶׁר אִשָּׁם לֹא תִכְבֶּה,
בְּחוּנֶיךָ הָיוּ מְקַדְּשֵׁי שְׁמֶךָ.

בְּקוֹל שְׁמַע יִשְׂרָאֵל, מָסְרוּ נֶפֶשׁ לָאֵל, שֶׁהוּא יַאַסְפֵם, וְעַד יוֹם אַחֲרוֹן,
הִצְדִּיקוּ דִין, וְאַף אֲנִי מַאֲמִין עָנוּ, וְשָׁרוּ שִׁירַת בִּטָּחוֹן.

וּבְכֵן נִשְׁאַר עָם, כְּיָתוֹם נִדְהָם, בְּלִי קְבָרִים לְהִשְׁתַּטֵּחַ,
וְלֹא מַצֵּבוֹת, אֵיפֹה לִבְכּוֹת, יְבָבוֹת לֵבָב רוֹתֵחַ.

רַק נִסְכֵי הַדָּם, אַזְכָּרוֹתָם, תּוֹסְסִים בְּלִי שׁוֹכֵחַ,
וְהָרֵי אֶפְרֵי עֲקֵדָתָם, תְּרוּמוֹת דִּשְׁנֵי מִזְבֵּחַ.

מִי יְמַלֵּל צַעַר יִשְׂרָאֵל, אֲשֶׁר דַּעְתּוֹ מִכְּאֵב נִטְרֶפֶת,
וּשְׁאֵרִית הַפְּאֵר, כִּמְעַט מִזְּעֵיר, וְאֵיךְ קוֹמָתָהּ הַיּוֹם נִכְפֶּפֶת.

אֵל חַי מְרַחֵם, עֲדָתְךָ נַחֵם, אֲשֶׁר לְךָ מְאֹד נִכְסֶפֶת,
אוֹר חָדָשׁ תַּזְרִיחַ, קַרְנֵי הוֹד תַּצְמִיחַ, וְרוּחַ אֱלֹהִים מְרַחֶפֶת.

---

quest of him, 'Please compose a special Tishah B'Av *kinnah* for our *kehillah*. Each and every one of us is either a refugee or a Holocaust survivor. We have all lost family and friends in this *churban*, and we German Jews bore the brunt of Hitler's fury. We must not forget, nor can we allow our children to forget. Eight centuries ago German Jewry was slaughtered by the Crusaders. According to historians, how many Jews were killed? Perhaps 5,000. In World War II more than

In the barbarians' camps were pain and sickness,
the anguish of mortified souls;
insults and mockery, shame and spit, searing wounds from horrible blows.

Hunger, thirst, frenzy, sorrow, the faint stumbling without any strength;
every death rattle of every forlorn one, far be it from You to forget.

The pillars of smoke, the fumes from furnace,
Piles and piles of bones and sinews, poison-filled halls,
the roaring sound of the multitude, choking in gas chamber.

The stench of the bodies, the tortured corpses,
fertilizers for the soil of the blasphemers.
How the tormentors turned their fat into soap,
and human skin into feminine adornments.

[Remember] the finger motions of the savage officers.
To the right — slave labor! To the left — the shadow of death.
[Remember] how the sharpshooters shot at those digging [their own] graves,
lowering them to the depths in the agony of the grave.

And how they afflicted our sisters and mutilated our daughters,
doses of poison from sadistic doctors,
And fugitive survivors in burrows and bunkers,
and the disappearance of children in houses of apostasy, in monasteries.

Unblemished sheep, completely consumed,
the blood of the Diaspora's children,
Woe! O Ariel, for the corpses of your devout ones.
Who could count the sacred flock, whose flame will never be extinguished,
Your tested ones were Sanctifiers of Your name.

With the cry of 'Shema Yisrael,' they gave up their lives for God,
so that He might gather them in.
And until the very last day, they justified His judgment,
and called out, 'I believe...' and sang a song of trust.

And now, a people is left, bewildered as an orphan —
without graves at which to pray, without tombstones
where to weep the laments of emotion-filled hearts.

Only blood libations are their memorials boiling, unforgettable —
and the mounds of ashes from their Akeidah,
are tributes from the Altar's ashes.

Who can express Israel's torment, whose mind is frenzied by misery?
The remnants of its splendor is a fraction of a bit,
how its pride is humbled today!

O Living God! Merciful One!
Comfort Your congregation that yearns for You so mightily,
Let new light shine, let rays of glory grow, And may God's spirit hover.

---

one thousand times that number were killed! In just one day at Auschwitz more than 5,000 Jews were brutally gassed and murdered. If German Jewry composed *kinnos* to commemorate the evil that befell us during the Crusades, how much more so must we compose one over the Holocaust!'

In deference to this request, Rav Schwab composed the following *kinnah* which, in Khal Adas Jeshurun, is recited by the Rav on Tishah B'Av night at the conclusion of the *kinnos* service before the passage which begins with תְּרַחֵם צִיּוֹן, *Have mercy on Zion.* Although Rav Schwab only composed this *kinnah* to be said in his *kehillah*,

מה.

The congregation rises and recites the following *kinnah* responsively with the *chazzan*.

אֱלִי צִיּוֹן* וְעָרֶיהָ, כְּמוֹ אִשָּׁה בְצִירֶיהָ,
וְכִבְתוּלָה חֲגֻרַת שַׂק עַל בַּֽעַל נְעוּרֶיהָ.[1]
עֲלֵי אַרְמוֹן אֲשֶׁר נִטַּשׁ בְּאַשְׁמַת צֹאן עֲדָרֶיהָ,
וְעַל בִּיאַת מְחָרְפֵי אֵל בְּתוֹךְ מִקְדַּשׁ חֲדָרֶיהָ,
אֱלִי צִיּוֹן וְעָרֶיהָ, כְּמוֹ אִשָּׁה בְצִירֶיהָ,
וְכִבְתוּלָה חֲגֻרַת שַׂק עַל בַּֽעַל נְעוּרֶיהָ.

עֲלֵי גָלוּת מְשָׁרְתֵי אֵל, מַנְעִימֵי שִׁיר זְמָרֶיהָ,[2]
וְעַל דָּמָם אֲשֶׁר שֻׁפַּךְ, כְּמוֹ מֵימֵי יְאוֹרֶיהָ,
אֱלִי צִיּוֹן וְעָרֶיהָ, כְּמוֹ אִשָּׁה בְצִירֶיהָ,
וְכִבְתוּלָה חֲגֻרַת שַׂק עַל בַּֽעַל נְעוּרֶיהָ.

עֲלֵי הֶגְיוֹן מְחוֹלֶיהָ, אֲשֶׁר דָּמַם בְּעָרֶיהָ,
וְעַל וַֽעַד אֲשֶׁר שָׁמֵם וּבִטּוּל סַנְהֶדְרֶיהָ,
אֱלִי צִיּוֹן וְעָרֶיהָ, כְּמוֹ אִשָּׁה בְצִירֶיהָ,
וְכִבְתוּלָה חֲגֻרַת שַׂק עַל בַּֽעַל נְעוּרֶיהָ.

עֲלֵי זִבְחֵי תְמִידֶיהָ, וּפִדְיוֹנֵי בְּכוֹרֶיהָ,*
וְעַל חִלּוּל כְּלֵי הֵיכָל וּמִזְבַּח קְטוֹרֶיהָ,
אֱלִי צִיּוֹן וְעָרֶיהָ, כְּמוֹ אִשָּׁה בְצִירֶיהָ,
וְכִבְתוּלָה חֲגֻרַת שַׂק עַל בַּֽעַל נְעוּרֶיהָ.

עֲלֵי טַפֵּי מְלָכֶיהָ, בְּנֵי דָוִד גְּבִירֶיהָ,
וְעַל יָפְיָם אֲשֶׁר חָשַׁךְ בְּעֵת סָרוּ כְתָרֶיהָ,
אֱלִי צִיּוֹן וְעָרֶיהָ, כְּמוֹ אִשָּׁה בְצִירֶיהָ,
וְכִבְתוּלָה חֲגֻרַת שַׂק עַל בַּֽעַל נְעוּרֶיהָ.

---

many other congregations have adopted the custom of reciting it on Tishah B'Av, either at night or by day, as a memorial of our most recent *churban*.

אֱלִי צִיּוֹן — *Wail, O Zion.* This final *kinnah* is chanted to a traditional heart-rending melody that expresses the full measure of our sorrow. Once again, in this last lament, we list all that we lost at the time of the Destruction, both materially and spiritually. However, the opening line of the *kinnah* (which is repeated either as a refrain after every second line, or once at the end of the *kinnah*) provides a ray of hope: 'Wail, O Zion and her cities, like a woman suffering from birth travail.' Israel's suffering is not in vain, rather the Destruction and Exile should be viewed as a period of embryonic development and gestation leading to the rebirth of our nation. No pain is more excruciating than birth travail, yet the mother accepts it because it heralds the exhilarating joy of birth. Similarly, Israel's suffering has been indescribable but we must accept it as the travail which precedes the glorious rebirth of our people.

45.

The congregation rises and recites the following *kinnah* responsively with the *chazzan*.

אֱלִי צִיּוֹן *Wail, O Zion* and her cities,*
like a woman suffering from birth travail,
and like a maiden girded in sackcloth,
[lamenting] for the husband of her youth. . .[1]

א *. . . for the palace that is abandoned because of*
the sin of the sheep of her flocks,
ב *and for the entrance of the blasphemers of God*
into the chambers of her Sanctuary.

Wail, O Zion and her cities, like a woman suffering from birth travail,
and like a maiden girded in sackcloth, [lamenting] for the husband of her youth. . .

ג *. . . for the exile of [the Kohanim,] the servants of God*
[and the Levites] who sweetly sang the song of her praise,[2]
ד *and for their blood that was spilt like the waters of her canals.*

Wail, O Zion and her cities, like a woman suffering from birth travail,
and like a maiden girded in sackcloth, [lamenting] for the husband of her youth. . .

ה *. . . for the lyrics of her dances, that have been stilled in her cities,*
ו *and for the assembly chamber that is abandoned,*
with the disbandment of her Sanhedrin.

Wail, O Zion and her cities, like a woman suffering from birth travail,
and like a maiden girded in sackcloth, [lamenting] for the husband of her youth. . .

ז *. . . for her daily [Tamid] offerings,*
*and for the redemption of her firstborn sons,**
ח *and for the desecration of the Temple's vessels and her incense Altar.*

Wail, O Zion and her cities, like a woman suffering from birth travail,
and like a maiden girded in sackcloth, [lamenting] for the husband of her youth. . .

ט *. . . for young children of her kings,*
the sons of David, her royal sovereigns,
י *and for their beauty which was darkened*
when her crowns were taken from her.

Wail, O Zion and her cities, like a woman suffering from birth travail,
and like a maiden girded in sackcloth, [lamenting] for the husband of her youth. . .

---

(1) *Joel* 1:8. (2) Cf. *II Samuel* 23:1.

עֲלֵי זִבְחֵי תְמִידֶיהָ וּפִדְיוֹנֵי בְּכוֹרֶיהָ — *. . . for her daily [Tamid] offerings, and for the redemption of her firstborn sons.* This statement is very puzzling. True, the daily *Tamid* offerings are dependent on the existence of the Temple, but the *mitzvah* of redeeming the firstborn son is not a function of the Temple. Indeed, it is in full force today and is practiced wherever Jews may live! This question has prodded some commentaries to suggest that the text be emended from פִּדְיוֹנֵי בְּכוֹרֶיהָ to פִּרְיוֹנֵי בִיכּוּרֶיהָ, *her bikkurim fruits,* i.e., the *mitzvah* of bringing the first fruits to the *Kohen* in the Temple is no longer possible.

Others explain that the redemption of the firstborn here alludes to the Levites who served as the original objects by which the firstborn Israelites were redeemed in the Wilderness (see *Numbers* 3:11-13, 44-51). Thus, the first stich of this line, זִבְחֵי תְמִידֶיהָ, refers to the *Kohanim* who offered the *Tamid,* while the second stich speaks of the *Leviim.*

However, the passage may also be explained in its simplest and most literal reading. Regarding the *mitzvah* of redeeming the firstborn, the

עֲלֵי **כָּ**בוֹד, אֲשֶׁר גָּלָה בְּעֵת חֻרְבַּן דְּבִירֶיהָ,
וְעַל **לוֹ**חֵץ אֲשֶׁר לָחַץ, וְשָׂם שַׂקִּים חֲגוֹרֶיהָ,
אֱלִי צִיּוֹן וְעָרֶיהָ, כְּמוֹ אִשָּׁה בְצִירֶיהָ,
וְכִבְתוּלָה חֲגֻרַת שַׂק עַל בַּעַל נְעוּרֶיהָ.

עֲלֵי **מַ**חַץ וְרֹב מַכּוֹת[1] אֲשֶׁר הֻכּוּ נְזִירֶיהָ,
וְעַל **נִ**פּוּץ עֲלֵי סֶלַע עוֹלָלֶיהָ[2] וּנְעָרֶיהָ,
אֱלִי צִיּוֹן וְעָרֶיהָ, כְּמוֹ אִשָּׁה בְצִירֶיהָ,
וְכִבְתוּלָה חֲגֻרַת שַׂק עַל בַּעַל נְעוּרֶיהָ.

עֲלֵי **שִׂ**מְחַת אוֹיְבֶיהָ, שָׂחֲקוּ עַל שְׁבָרֶיהָ,
וְעַל **עִ**נּוּי בְּנֵי חוֹרִין נְדִיבֶיהָ טְהוֹרֶיהָ,
אֱלִי צִיּוֹן וְעָרֶיהָ, כְּמוֹ אִשָּׁה בְצִירֶיהָ,
וְכִבְתוּלָה חֲגֻרַת שַׂק עַל בַּעַל נְעוּרֶיהָ.

עֲלֵי **פֶ**שַׁע אֲשֶׁר עִוְּתָה סְלוּל דֶּרֶךְ אֲשׁוּרֶיהָ,
וְעַל **צִ**בְאוֹת קְהָלֶיהָ שְׁזוּפֶיהָ שְׁחוֹרֶיהָ,
אֱלִי צִיּוֹן וְעָרֶיהָ, כְּמוֹ אִשָּׁה בְצִירֶיהָ,
וְכִבְתוּלָה חֲגֻרַת שַׂק עַל בַּעַל נְעוּרֶיהָ.

עֲלֵי **קוֹ**לוֹת מְחָרְפֶיהָ, בְּעֵת רַבּוּ פְּגָרֶיהָ,
וְעַל **רִ**גְשַׁת מְגַדְּפֶיהָ, בְּתוֹךְ מִשְׁכַּן חֲצֵרֶיהָ,
אֱלִי צִיּוֹן וְעָרֶיהָ, כְּמוֹ אִשָּׁה בְצִירֶיהָ,
וְכִבְתוּלָה חֲגֻרַת שַׂק עַל בַּעַל נְעוּרֶיהָ.

עֲלֵי **שִׁ**מְךָ אֲשֶׁר חֻלַּל בְּפִי קָמֵי מְצִירֶיהָ,
וְעַל **תַּ**חַן יְצַוְּחוּ לָךְ קְשׁוֹב וּשְׁמַע אֲמָרֶיהָ,
אֱלִי צִיּוֹן וְעָרֶיהָ, כְּמוֹ אִשָּׁה בְצִירֶיהָ,
וְכִבְתוּלָה חֲגֻרַת שַׂק עַל בַּעַל נְעוּרֶיהָ.

Torah states: כֹּל בְּכוֹר בָּנֶיךָ תִּפְדֶּה וְלֹא יֵרָאוּ פָנַי רֵיקָם, *Every firstborn of your sons you shall redeem, and none shall appear before Me empty* (*Exodus* 34:20). *Rabbeinu Bachya* (ibid.) comments: Why did the Torah juxtapose the *mitzvah* of redeeming the firstborn son with the *mitzvah* of appearing before God in the Temple on the festivals? To teach that the firstborn who is redeemed is assured that he will merit the privilege of seeing the construction of the Temple and he will witness God's presence therein.

כ *... for the [Divine] glory which was exiled*
at the time of the Destruction of her Temples,
ל *and for the tyrant who persecuted her*
and caused her to gird herself in sackcloth.

Wail, O Zion and her cities, like a woman suffering from birth travail,
and like a maiden girded in sackcloth, [lamenting] for the husband of her youth...

מ *... for the pounding and the numerous blows*[1]
with which her aristocrats were beaten,
נ *and for the smashing on the rock of her infants*[2] *and her youths.*

Wail, O Zion and her cities, like a woman suffering from birth travail,
and like a maiden girded in sackcloth, [lamenting] for the husband of her youth...

ס *... for the joy of her enemies when they made sport of her calamities,*
ע *and for the tormenting of her free-spirited men,*
her noble-minded and pure-hearted people.

Wail, O Zion and her cities, like a woman suffering from birth travail,
and like a maiden girded in sackcloth, [lamenting] for the husband of her youth...

פ *... for the sin which corrupted her,*
and diverted her footsteps from the straight path,
צ *and for the legions of her congregations*
whose [faces] now are wrinkled and blackened
[by the flames of the Temple's destruction].

Wail, O Zion and her cities, like a woman suffering from birth travail,
and like a maiden girded in sackcloth, [lamenting] for the husband of her youth...

ק *... for the cries of those who vilified her*
when the number of her corpses increased,
ר *and for the clamor of those who cursed her,*
inside the Courtyards of her Tabernacle.

Wail, O Zion and her cities, like a woman suffering from birth travail,
and like a maiden girded in sackcloth, [lamenting] for the husband of her youth...

ש *... for Your Name which was profaned by the mouth*
of those who arose to torment her,
ת *and to the pleaful prayer which they cry out to You,*
listen carefully and heed her words.

Wail, O Zion and her cities,
like a woman suffering from birth travail,
and like a maiden girded in sackcloth,
[lamenting] for the husband of her youth...

(1) Cf. *Isaiah* 30:26. (2) Cf. *Psalms* 137:9.

Thus, the purpose of the firstborn's redemption is to prepare him for an encounter with God in the Temple so that he will 'belong' to the Temple and be one of *her* firstborn sons. In this *kinnah*, we lament the fact that today, in the absence of the Temple, the firstborn sons cannot achieve this encounter, the ultimate purpose of their redemption.

מו.

שׁוֹמְרוֹן קוֹל תִּתֵּן מְצָאוּנִי עֲוֹנַי,[1]
לְאֶרֶץ אַחֶרֶת יְצָאוּנִי בָנַי,[2]
וְאָהֳלִיבָה תִּזְעַק נִשְׂרְפוּ אַרְמוֹנַי,[3]
וַתֹּאמֶר צִיּוֹן עֲזָבַנִי יהוה.[4]

לֹא לָךְ אָהֳלִיבָה חֲשׁוֹב עָנְיֵךְ כְּעָנְיִי,
הֲתַמְשִׁילִי חָלְיֵךְ לְשִׁבְרִי וּלְחָלְיִי,
אֲנִי אָהֳלָה סוּרָה בָּגַדְתִּי בְקָשְׁיִי,
וְקָם עָלַי כַּחֲשִׁי וְעָנָה בִי מֶרְיִי,[5]
וּלְמִקְצַת הַיָּמִים שִׁלַּמְתִּי נִשְׁיִי,
וְתִגְלַת פִּלְאֶסֶר[6] אָכַל אֶת פִּרְיִי,
חֶמְדָּתִי פָּשַׁט וְהִצִּיל אֶת עֶדְיִי,*[7]
וְלַחֲלַח וְחָבוֹר[8] נָשָׂא אֶת שִׁבְיִי,
דֹּמִּי אָהֳלִיבָה וְאַל תִּבְכִּי כְּבִכְיִי,
שְׁנוֹתַיִךְ אָרְכוּ וְלֹא אָרְכוּ שָׁנָי.*

וְאָהֳלִיבָה תִּזְעַק נִשְׂרְפוּ אַרְמוֹנַי,
וַתֹּאמֶר צִיּוֹן עֲזָבַנִי יהוה.

מְשִׁיבָה אָהֳלִיבָה אֲנִי כֵּן נֶעֱקַשְׁתִּי,
וּבְאַלּוּף נְעוּרַי[9] כְּאָהֳלָה בָּגַדְתִּי,
דֹּמִּי אָהֳלָה כִּי יְגוֹנִי זָכַרְתִּי,
נָדַדְתְּ אַתְּ אַחַת וְרַבּוֹת נָדַדְתִּי,
הִנֵּה בְּיַד הַכַּשְׂדִּים פְּעָמִים נִלְכַּדְתִּי,
וּשְׁבִיָּה עֲנִיָּה לְבָבֶל יָרַדְתִּי,

⇐§ **שומרון** — *Shomron.* This *kinnah* is based on chapter 23 of *Ezekiel*, where God bids the prophet to expose the sins of the Jewish people. Then unfolds the shocking parable of two faithless wives who seek fulfillment of their unnatural lusts through numerous lovers. Ezekiel tells of two sisters, אָהֳלָה, *Oholah*, and אָהֳלִיבָה, *Oholivah*, who are both married to the same man. Oholah is identified as Shomron [Samaria, capital of the Northern Kingdom, also called the Kingdom of Israel, which comprised ten of the tribes] and Oholivah as Jerusalem [capital of the Southern Kingdom, also called the Kingdom of Judah, which comprised Judah and Benjamin]. Both are 'wed' to one 'husband', God, but both brazenly betray Him.

The names, אָהֳלָה, *Oholah*, and אָהֳלִיבָה, *Oholivah*, are both derived from אֹהֶל, a *tent* or *dwelling place*. However, אָהֳלָה is a contraction of הָאֹהֶל שֶׁלָּהּ, *her tent*, because God had no part in the tabernacles of Shomron. They were 'her own tents' which she had dedicated to the golden calves Jeroboam ben Nevat had erected (see *I Kings* 12:28). On the other hand, אָהֳלִיבָה is

46.

שׁוֹמְרוֹן *Shomron gives forth [her] voice,*
'The deserts of my sins have found me![1]
My children have gone forth from me[2] *to another land!'*
Then Oholivah screams, 'My palaces were burnt down!'[3]
And Zion says, 'HASHEM has abandoned me!'[4]

ל *[Oholah:] 'It is not right for you, Oholivah,*
to consider your suffering as mine!
Can you compare your sickness to my fracture and sickness?
I, Oholah, [am now] displaced, I have rebelled in my stubbornness,
but now my deceitfulness has risen against me,[5]
and my defiance has testified against me,
and after a short time I paid my debts [for my sins].
[The Assyrian king] Tiglath-pileser[6] *devoured my [womb's] fruits,*
he stripped away my precious possessions
and confiscated my jewelry,[7]*
then [his successor Shalmaneser] carried away my captives
to Halah and Habor.[8]
[Therefore,] Oholivah be silent and weep not as I weep!
Your years [in the Land] were prolonged,
*but my years were not prolonged!'**

Then Oholivah screams, 'My palaces were burnt down!'
And Zion says, 'HASHEM has abandoned me!'

מ *Oholivah responds: 'I too deviated,*
and like Oholah, I betrayed [God,] the Mentor of my youth![9]
Be still, Oholah, for I remember my agony.
You were exiled but once, while I was exiled repeatedly.
Behold, by the hands of the Chaldeans I was taken twice;
as a miserable captive I descended to Babylon;

(1) Cf. *II Kings* 7:9. (2) Cf. *Jeremiah* 10:20. (3) Cf. *II Chronicles* 36:19. (4) *Isaiah* 49:14. (5) Cf. *Job* 16:8. (6) *II Kings* 15:29. (7) Cf. *Exodus* 33:6. (8) See *II Kings* 17:3-6. (9) Cf. *Jeremiah* 3:4.

a contraction of הָאֹהֶל שֶׁלִּי בָהּ, *My Tent is within her*, i.e., the Tent of God, the *Beis HaMikdash*. These names place Judah, in which God's Temple stood, in sharp contrast to Shomron.

The wicked city of Shomron, with the abominations of its citizens, epitomizes all of the evil of the Ten Tribes. That segment of Israel became so corrupted that to this day those tribes are lost in exile and the possibility of their ultimate return remains the subject of considerable Talmudic debate (see *Sanhedrin* 110b and *Ramban, Sefer HaGeulah, shaar* I).

In this *kinnah*, the author compares the tragedies which befell both Judah and Samaria by means of a debate raging between the two. Each capital claims — and vehemently defends its claim — that it suffered more at the hand of the marauding enemy.

The composer of the *kinnah*, R' Shlomo ibn Gabirol (11th-century Spain), used the letters of his name שְׁלֹמֹה to begin the respective stanzas.

חֶמְדָּתִי ... עֶדְיִי — *My precious possessions ... my jewelry.* Some commentators understand these expressions as allusions to the two Temples. We have rejected that interpretation because Oholah is the speaker, but the Temples had stood in Oholivah's estate.

שְׁנוֹתַיִךְ אָרְכוּ וְלֹא אָרְכוּ שָׁנַי — *Your years [in the Land] were prolonged, but my years were not prolonged!* Oholah, the Northern Kingdom of Samaria, was exiled more than one hundred

וְנִשְׂרַף הַהֵיכָל אֲשֶׁר בּוֹ נִכְבַּדְתִּי,
וּלְשִׁבְעִים שָׁנָה בְּבָבֶל נִפְקַדְתִּי,
וְשַׁבְתִּי לְצִיּוֹן עוֹד וְהֵיכָל יָסַדְתִּי,
גַּם זֹאת הַפַּעַם מְעַט לֹא עָמַדְתִּי,
עַד לְקָחַנִי אֱדוֹם וּכְמִעַט אָבַדְתִּי,
וְעַל כָּל הָאֲרָצוֹת נָפְצוּ הֲמוֹנַי.

וְאָהֳלִיבָה תִּזְעַק נִשְׂרְפוּ אַרְמוֹנַי,
וַתֹּאמֶר צִיּוֹן עֲזָבַנִי יהוה.

הַחוֹמֵל עַל דַּל חֲמוֹל עַל דַּלּוּתָם,*
וּרְאֵה שְׁמְמוֹתָם[1] וְאֹרֶךְ גָּלוּתָם,
אַל תִּקְצוֹף עַד מְאֹד[2] וּרְאֵה שִׁפְלוּתָם,
וְאַל לָעַד תִּזְכּוֹר עֲוֹנָם[2] וְסִכְלוּתָם,
רְפָא נָא אֶת שִׁבְרָם[3] וְנַחֵם אֲבֵלוּתָם,
כִּי אַתָּה סִבְרָם וְאַתָּה אֱיָלוּתָם,
חַדֵּשׁ יָמֵינוּ כִּימֵי קַדְמוֹנַי,[4]
כִּנְאֻמֶךָ בּוֹנֵה יְרוּשָׁלַיִם יהוה.[5]

תְּרַחֵם צִיּוֹן כַּאֲשֶׁר אָמַרְתָּ, וּתְכוֹנְנֶהָ כַּאֲשֶׁר דִּבַּרְתָּ, תְּמַהֵר יְשׁוּעָה וְתָחִישׁ גְּאֻלָּה, וְתָשׁוּב לִירוּשָׁלַיִם בְּרַחֲמִים רַבִּים. כַּכָּתוּב עַל יַד נְבִיאֶךָ, לָכֵן כֹּה אָמַר יהוה, שַׁבְתִּי לִירוּשָׁלַיִם בְּרַחֲמִים, בֵּיתִי יִבָּנֶה בָּהּ, נְאֻם יהוה צְבָאוֹת, וְקָו יִנָּטֶה עַל יְרוּשָׁלָיִם.[6]

וְנֶאֱמַר, עוֹד קְרָא לֵאמֹר, כֹּה אָמַר יהוה צְבָאוֹת, עוֹד תְּפוּצֶנָה עָרַי מִטּוֹב, וְנִחַם יהוה עוֹד אֶת צִיּוֹן, וּבָחַר עוֹד בִּירוּשָׁלָיִם.[7] וְנֶאֱמַר, כִּי נִחַם יהוה צִיּוֹן, נִחַם כָּל חָרְבוֹתֶיהָ, וַיָּשֶׂם מִדְבָּרָהּ כְּעֵדֶן, וְעַרְבָתָהּ כְּגַן יהוה, שָׂשׂוֹן וְשִׂמְחָה יִמָּצֵא בָהּ, תּוֹדָה וְקוֹל זִמְרָה.[8]

(1) Cf. *Daniel* 9:18. (2) Cf. *Isaiah* 64:8. (3) Cf. *Psalms* 60:4. (4) Cf. *Eichah* 5:21.
(5) *Psalms* 147:2. (6) *Zechariah* 1:16. (7) 1:17. (8) *Isaiah* 51:3.

and the Sanctuary by which I was honored
was burnt down.
After seventy years in Babylon I was recalled [by God];
I returned once again to Zion
and established the [Second] Temple.
This time, too, I did not last long
before Edom seized me and I was all but annihilated.
Through all the lands were my multitudes dispersed.'

Then Oholivah screams, 'My palaces were burnt down!'
And Zion says, 'HASHEM has abandoned me!'

ה *O You Who takes pity on the pauper,*
*take pity on their poverty.**
See their desolation[1] *and the length of their exile.*
Do not be overly angered,[2] *rather take note of their degradation.*
Do not eternally remember their sins[2] *and their foolishness.*
Please heal their wounds[3] *and assuage their mourning;*
for You are their Hope and You are their Strength.
Renew our days as the days of my youth;[4]
as You have said: 'The Builder of Jerusalem is HASHEM.'[5]

Show Zion mercy as You have said, and establish her as You have spoken. Hasten salvation and speed redemption and return to Jerusalem with abundant compassion.

As it is written by the hand of Your prophet: Therefore, thus says HASHEM, 'I shall return to Jerusalem with compassion, My House shall be rebuilt within it,' says HASHEM, Master of Legions, 'and a [measuring] string shall be stretched over Jerusalem.'[6]

And it is said: Call out again, saying, Thus says HASHEM, Master of Legions, 'My cities shall again overflow with beneficence, and again HASHEM will assuage Zion and again He will choose Jerusalem.'[7]

And it is said: For HASHEM comforts Zion, He comforts her ruins, and He will make her wilderness like Eden, and her wastes like a garden of HASHEM; gladness and joy shall be found there, thanksgiving and the sound of music.[8]

---

thirty years before Oholivah, the Southern Kingdom of Judah.

דַּלּוּתָם — *Their poverty.* Until this point, the *kinnah* has been a one-on-one debate between Oholah and Oholivah. Thus, the statements are all in first or second person singular. The last stanza, however, is the *paytan's* supplication for the restitution of both, and consequently is couched in third person plural. Finally, the last line prays for the reunification of the two Kingdoms with Jerusalem as the focal point as it was in 'the days of my youth.'

⁂ אשרי – ובא לציון ⁂

אַשְׁרֵי יוֹשְׁבֵי בֵיתֶךָ, עוֹד יְהַלְלְוּךָ סֶּלָה.[1] אַשְׁרֵי הָעָם שֶׁכָּכָה לּוֹ, אַשְׁרֵי הָעָם שֶׁיהוה אֱלֹהָיו.[2]

תהלים קמה

תְּהִלָּה לְדָוִד,

אֲרוֹמִמְךָ אֱלוֹהַי הַמֶּלֶךְ, וַאֲבָרְכָה שִׁמְךָ לְעוֹלָם וָעֶד.

בְּכָל יוֹם אֲבָרְכֶךָּ, וַאֲהַלְלָה שִׁמְךָ לְעוֹלָם וָעֶד.

גָּדוֹל יהוה וּמְהֻלָּל מְאֹד, וְלִגְדֻלָּתוֹ אֵין חֵקֶר.

דּוֹר לְדוֹר יְשַׁבַּח מַעֲשֶׂיךָ, וּגְבוּרֹתֶיךָ יַגִּידוּ.

הֲדַר כְּבוֹד הוֹדֶךָ, וְדִבְרֵי נִפְלְאֹתֶיךָ אָשִׂיחָה.

וֶעֱזוּז נוֹרְאוֹתֶיךָ יֹאמֵרוּ, וּגְדוּלָּתְךָ אֲסַפְּרֶנָּה.

זֵכֶר רַב טוּבְךָ יַבִּיעוּ, וְצִדְקָתְךָ יְרַנֵּנוּ.

חַנּוּן וְרַחוּם יהוה, אֶרֶךְ אַפַּיִם וּגְדָל חָסֶד.

טוֹב יהוה לַכֹּל, וְרַחֲמָיו עַל כָּל מַעֲשָׂיו.

יוֹדְוּךָ יהוה כָּל מַעֲשֶׂיךָ, וַחֲסִידֶיךָ יְבָרְכוּכָה.

כְּבוֹד מַלְכוּתְךָ יֹאמֵרוּ, וּגְבוּרָתְךָ יְדַבֵּרוּ.

לְהוֹדִיעַ לִבְנֵי הָאָדָם גְּבוּרֹתָיו, וּכְבוֹד הֲדַר מַלְכוּתוֹ.

מַלְכוּתְךָ מַלְכוּת כָּל עֹלָמִים, וּמֶמְשַׁלְתְּךָ בְּכָל דּוֹר וָדֹר.

סוֹמֵךְ יהוה לְכָל הַנֹּפְלִים, וְזוֹקֵף לְכָל הַכְּפוּפִים.

עֵינֵי כֹל אֵלֶיךָ יְשַׂבֵּרוּ, וְאַתָּה נוֹתֵן לָהֶם אֶת אָכְלָם בְּעִתּוֹ.

While reciting the verse פּוֹתֵחַ, concentrate intently on its meaning.

פּוֹתֵחַ אֶת יָדֶךָ,

וּמַשְׂבִּיעַ לְכָל חַי רָצוֹן.

צַדִּיק יהוה בְּכָל דְּרָכָיו, וְחָסִיד בְּכָל מַעֲשָׂיו.

קָרוֹב יהוה לְכָל קֹרְאָיו, לְכֹל אֲשֶׁר יִקְרָאֻהוּ בֶאֱמֶת.

רְצוֹן יְרֵאָיו יַעֲשֶׂה, וְאֶת שַׁוְעָתָם יִשְׁמַע וְיוֹשִׁיעֵם.

שׁוֹמֵר יהוה אֶת כָּל אֹהֲבָיו, וְאֵת כָּל הָרְשָׁעִים יַשְׁמִיד.

❖ תְּהִלַּת יהוה יְדַבֶּר פִּי, וִיבָרֵךְ כָּל בָּשָׂר שֵׁם קָדְשׁוֹ לְעוֹלָם וָעֶד.

וַאֲנַחְנוּ נְבָרֵךְ יָהּ, מֵעַתָּה וְעַד עוֹלָם, הַלְלוּיָהּ.[3]

PSALM 20, לַמְנַצֵּחַ, IS OMITTED.

(1) *Psalms* 84:5. (2) 144:15. (3) 115:8.

ASHREI – UVA L'TZION

אַשְׁרֵי *Praiseworthy are those who dwell in Your house; may they always praise You, Selah![1] Praiseworthy is the people for whom this is so, praiseworthy is the people whose God is HASHEM.[2]*

Psalm 145 *A psalm of praise by David:*

א *I will exalt You, my God the King,*
and I will bless Your Name forever and ever.
ב *Every day I will bless You, and I will laud Your Name forever and ever.*
ג *HASHEM is great and exceedingly lauded,*
and His greatness is beyond investigation.
ד *Each generation will praise Your deeds to the next*
and of Your mighty deeds they will tell.
ה *The splendrous glory of Your power*
and Your wondrous deeds I shall discuss.
ו *And of Your awesome power they will speak,*
and Your greatness I shall relate.
ז *A recollection of Your abundant goodness they will utter*
and of Your righteousness they will sing exultantly.
ח *Gracious and merciful is HASHEM,*
slow to anger, and great in [bestowing] kindness.
ט *HASHEM is good to all; His mercies are on all His works.*
י *All Your works shall thank You, HASHEM,*
and Your devout ones will bless You.
כ *Of the glory of Your kingdom they will speak,*
and of Your power they will tell;
ל *To inform human beings of His mighty deeds,*
and the glorious splendor of His kingdom.
מ *Your kingdom is a kingdom spanning all eternities,*
and Your dominion is throughout every generation.
ס *HASHEM supports all the fallen ones and straightens all the bent.*
ע *The eyes of all look to You with hope*
and You give them their food in its proper time;
פ *You open Your hand, and satisfy*
the desire of every living thing.

While reciting the verse, *'You open . . .'* concentrate intently on its meaning.

צ *Righteous is HASHEM in all His ways*
and magnanimous in all His deeds.
ק *HASHEM is close to all who call upon Him —*
to all who call upon Him sincerely.
ר *The will of those who fear Him He will do;*
and their cry He will hear, and save them.
ש *HASHEM protects all who love Him; but all the wicked He will destroy.*
ת Chazzan– *May my mouth declare the praise of HASHEM*
and may all flesh bless His Holy Name forever and ever.
We will bless God from this time and forever, Halleluyah![3]

PSALM 20, לַמְנַצֵּחַ, IS OMITTED.

The primary part of וּבָא לְצִיּוֹן is the *Kedushah* recited by the angels. These verses are presented in bold type and it is preferable that the congregation recite them aloud and in unison. However, the interpretive translation in Aramaic (which follows the verses in bold type) should be recited softly.

THE VERSE וַאֲנִי זֹאת, IS OMITTED.

וּבָא לְצִיּוֹן גּוֹאֵל, וּלְשָׁבֵי פֶשַׁע בְּיַעֲקֹב, נְאֻם יהוה. [. . .] ❖ וְאַתָּה קָדוֹשׁ יוֹשֵׁב תְּהִלּוֹת יִשְׂרָאֵל.[1] וְקָרָא זֶה אֶל זֶה וְאָמַר:

קָדוֹשׁ, קָדוֹשׁ, קָדוֹשׁ יהוה צְבָאוֹת, מְלֹא כָל הָאָרֶץ כְּבוֹדוֹ.[2]

וּמְקַבְּלִין דֵּין מִן דֵּין וְאָמְרִין:

קַדִּישׁ בִּשְׁמֵי מְרוֹמָא עִלָּאָה בֵּית שְׁכִינְתֵּהּ,

קַדִּישׁ עַל אַרְעָא עוֹבַד גְּבוּרְתֵּהּ,

קַדִּישׁ לְעָלַם וּלְעָלְמֵי עָלְמַיָּא, יהוה צְבָאוֹת,

מַלְיָא כָל אַרְעָא זִיו יְקָרֵהּ.[3]

❖ וַתִּשָּׂאֵנִי רוּחַ, וָאֶשְׁמַע אַחֲרַי קוֹל רַעַשׁ גָּדוֹל:

בָּרוּךְ כְּבוֹד יהוה מִמְּקוֹמוֹ.[4]

וּנְטָלַתְנִי רוּחָא, וְשִׁמְעֵת בַּתְרַי קָל זִיעַ סַגִּיא דִּמְשַׁבְּחִין וְאָמְרִין:

בְּרִיךְ יְקָרָא דַיהוה מֵאֲתַר בֵּית שְׁכִינְתֵּהּ.[5]

יהוה יִמְלֹךְ לְעֹלָם וָעֶד.[6]

יהוה מַלְכוּתֵהּ קָאֵם לְעָלַם וּלְעָלְמֵי עָלְמַיָּא.[7]

יהוה אֱלֹהֵי אַבְרָהָם יִצְחָק וְיִשְׂרָאֵל אֲבֹתֵינוּ, שָׁמְרָה זֹּאת לְעוֹלָם, לְיֵצֶר מַחְשְׁבוֹת לְבַב עַמֶּךָ, וְהָכֵן לְבָבָם אֵלֶיךָ.[8] וְהוּא רַחוּם, יְכַפֵּר עָוֹן וְלֹא יַשְׁחִית, וְהִרְבָּה לְהָשִׁיב אַפּוֹ, וְלֹא יָעִיר כָּל חֲמָתוֹ.[9] כִּי אַתָּה אֲדֹנָי טוֹב וְסַלָּח, וְרַב חֶסֶד לְכָל קֹרְאֶיךָ.[10] צִדְקָתְךָ צֶדֶק לְעוֹלָם, וְתוֹרָתְךָ אֱמֶת.[11] תִּתֵּן אֱמֶת לְיַעֲקֹב, חֶסֶד לְאַבְרָהָם, אֲשֶׁר נִשְׁבַּעְתָּ לַאֲבֹתֵינוּ מִימֵי קֶדֶם.[12] בָּרוּךְ אֲדֹנָי יוֹם יוֹם יַעֲמָס לָנוּ, הָאֵל יְשׁוּעָתֵנוּ סֶלָה.[13] יהוה צְבָאוֹת עִמָּנוּ, מִשְׂגָּב לָנוּ אֱלֹהֵי יַעֲקֹב סֶלָה.[14] יהוה צְבָאוֹת, אַשְׁרֵי אָדָם בֹּטֵחַ בָּךְ.[15] יהוה הוֹשִׁיעָה, הַמֶּלֶךְ יַעֲנֵנוּ בְיוֹם קָרְאֵנוּ.[16]

בָּרוּךְ הוּא אֱלֹהֵינוּ שֶׁבְּרָאָנוּ לִכְבוֹדוֹ, וְהִבְדִּילָנוּ מִן הַתּוֹעִים, וְנָתַן לָנוּ תּוֹרַת אֱמֶת, וְחַיֵּי עוֹלָם נָטַע בְּתוֹכֵנוּ. הוּא יִפְתַּח לִבֵּנוּ בְּתוֹרָתוֹ, וְיָשֵׂם בְּלִבֵּנוּ אַהֲבָתוֹ וְיִרְאָתוֹ וְלַעֲשׂוֹת רְצוֹנוֹ וּלְעָבְדוֹ בְּלֵבָב שָׁלֵם, לְמַעַן לֹא נִיגַע לָרִיק, וְלֹא נֵלֵד לַבֶּהָלָה.[17]

The primary part of וּבָא לְצִיּוֹן, *'A redeemer shall come . . .'*, is the *Kedushah* recited by the angels. These verses are presented in bold type and it is preferable that the congregation recite them aloud and in unison. However, the interpretive translation in Aramaic (which follows the verses in bold type) should be recited softly.

THE VERSE וַאֲנִי זֹאת, *'AND AS FOR ME . . .,'* IS OMITTED.

וּבָא לְצִיּוֹן *'A redeemer shall come to Zion and to those of Jacob who repent from willful sin,' the words of HASHEM.* [. . .] ∴ *You are the Holy One, enthroned upon the praises of Israel.*[1] *And one [angel] will call another and say:*

'Holy, holy, holy is HASHEM, Master of Legions, the whole world is filled with His glory.'[2]

And they receive permission from one another and say:
'Holy in the most exalted heaven, the abode of His Presence;
holy on earth, product of His strength;
holy forever and ever is HASHEM, Master of Legions —
the entire world is filled with the radiance of His glory.'[3]

∴ *And a wind lifted me; and I heard behind me the sound of a great noise:*

'Blessed is the glory of HASHEM from His place.'[4]

And a wind lifted me and I heard behind me the sound
of the powerful movement of those who praised saying:
'Blessed is the honor of HASHEM
from the place of the abode of His Presence.'[5]

HASHEM shall reign for all eternity.[6]

HASHEM — His kingdom is established forever and ever.[7]

HASHEM, God of Abraham, Isaac, and Israel, our forefathers, may You preserve this forever as the realization of the thoughts in Your people's heart, and may You direct their heart to You.[8] *He, the Merciful One, is forgiving of iniquity and does not destroy; frequently He withdraws His anger, not arousing His entire rage.*[9] *For You, my Lord, are good and forgiving, and abundantly kind to all who call upon You.*[10] *Your righteousness remains righteous forever, and Your Torah is truth.*[11] *Grant truth to Jacob, kindness to Abraham, as You swore to our forefathers from ancient times.*[12] *Blessed is my Lord for every single day, He burdens us with blessings, the God of our salvation, Selah.*[13] *HASHEM, Master of Legions, is with us, a stronghold for us is the God of Jacob, Selah.*[14] *HASHEM, Master of Legions, praiseworthy is the man who trusts in You.*[15] *HASHEM, save! May the King answer us on the day we call.*[16]

Blessed is He, our God, Who created us for His glory, separated us from those who stray, gave us the Torah of truth and implanted eternal life within us. May He open our heart through His Torah and imbue our heart with love and awe of Him and that we may do His will and serve Him wholeheartedly, so that we do not struggle in vain nor produce for futility.[17]

---

(1) *Psalms* 22:4. (2) *Isaiah* 6:3. (3) *Targum Yonasan* to *Isaiah* 6:3. (4) *Ezekiel* 3:12. (5) *Targum Yonasan* to *Ezekiel* 3:12. (6) *Exodus* 15:18. (7) *Targum Onkelos* to *Exodus* 15:18. (8) *I Chronicles* 29:18. (9) *Psalms* 78:38. (10) 86:5. (11) 119:142. (12) *Micah* 7:20. (13) *Psalms* 68:20. (14) 46:8. (15) 84:13. (16) 20:10. (17) Cf. *Isaiah* 65:23.

יְהִי רָצוֹן מִלְּפָנֶיךָ יהוה אֱלֹהֵינוּ וֵאלֹהֵי אֲבוֹתֵינוּ, שֶׁנִּשְׁמֹר חֻקֶּיךָ בָּעוֹלָם הַזֶּה, וְנִזְכֶּה וְנִחְיֶה וְנִרְאֶה וְנִירַשׁ טוֹבָה וּבְרָכָה לִשְׁנֵי יְמוֹת הַמָּשִׁיחַ וּלְחַיֵּי הָעוֹלָם הַבָּא. לְמַעַן יְזַמֶּרְךָ כָבוֹד וְלֹא יִדֹּם, יהוה אֱלֹהַי לְעוֹלָם אוֹדֶךָּ.[1] בָּרוּךְ הַגֶּבֶר אֲשֶׁר יִבְטַח בַּיהוה, וְהָיָה יהוה מִבְטַחוֹ.[2] בִּטְחוּ בַיהוה עֲדֵי עַד, כִּי בְּיָהּ יהוה צוּר עוֹלָמִים.[3] ❖ וְיִבְטְחוּ בְךָ יוֹדְעֵי שְׁמֶךָ, כִּי לֹא עָזַבְתָּ דֹּרְשֶׁיךָ, יהוה.[4] יהוה חָפֵץ לְמַעַן צִדְקוֹ, יַגְדִּיל תּוֹרָה וְיַאְדִּיר.[5]

The *chazzan* recites קַדִּישׁ שָׁלֵם בְּלֹא תִּתְקַבַּל.

יִתְגַּדַּל וְיִתְקַדַּשׁ שְׁמֵהּ רַבָּא. (.Cong – אָמֵן.) בְּעָלְמָא דִּי בְרָא כִרְעוּתֵהּ. וְיַמְלִיךְ מַלְכוּתֵהּ, בְּחַיֵּיכוֹן וּבְיוֹמֵיכוֹן וּבְחַיֵּי דְכָל בֵּית יִשְׂרָאֵל, בַּעֲגָלָא וּבִזְמַן קָרִיב. וְאִמְרוּ: אָמֵן.

(.Cong – אָמֵן. יְהֵא שְׁמֵהּ רַבָּא מְבָרַךְ לְעָלַם וּלְעָלְמֵי עָלְמַיָּא.)

יְהֵא שְׁמֵהּ רַבָּא מְבָרַךְ לְעָלַם וּלְעָלְמֵי עָלְמַיָּא.

יִתְבָּרַךְ וְיִשְׁתַּבַּח וְיִתְפָּאַר וְיִתְרוֹמַם וְיִתְנַשֵּׂא וְיִתְהַדָּר וְיִתְעַלֶּה וְיִתְהַלָּל שְׁמֵהּ דְּקֻדְשָׁא בְּרִיךְ הוּא (.Cong – בְּרִיךְ הוּא) — לְעֵלָּא מִן כָּל בִּרְכָתָא וְשִׁירָתָא תֻּשְׁבְּחָתָא וְנֶחֱמָתָא, דַּאֲמִירָן בְּעָלְמָא. וְאִמְרוּ: אָמֵן. (.Cong – אָמֵן.)

יְהֵא שְׁלָמָא רַבָּא מִן שְׁמַיָּא, וְחַיִּים עָלֵינוּ וְעַל כָּל יִשְׂרָאֵל. וְאִמְרוּ: אָמֵן. (.Cong – אָמֵן.)

Take three steps back. Bow left and say . . . עֹשֶׂה; bow right and say . . . הוּא; bow forward and say וְעַל כָּל . . . אָמֵן. Remain standing in place for a few moments, then take three steps forward.

עֹשֶׂה שָׁלוֹם בִּמְרוֹמָיו, הוּא יַעֲשֶׂה שָׁלוֹם עָלֵינוּ, וְעַל כָּל יִשְׂרָאֵל. וְאִמְרוּ: אָמֵן. (.Cong – אָמֵן.)

עלינו

Stand while reciting עָלֵינוּ.

עָלֵינוּ לְשַׁבֵּחַ לַאֲדוֹן הַכֹּל, לָתֵת גְּדֻלָּה לְיוֹצֵר בְּרֵאשִׁית, שֶׁלֹּא עָשָׂנוּ כְּגוֹיֵי הָאֲרָצוֹת, וְלֹא שָׂמָנוּ כְּמִשְׁפְּחוֹת הָאֲדָמָה. שֶׁלֹּא שָׂם חֶלְקֵנוּ כָּהֶם, וְגוֹרָלֵנוּ כְּכָל הֲמוֹנָם. (שֶׁהֵם מִשְׁתַּחֲוִים לְהֶבֶל וָרִיק, וּמִתְפַּלְּלִים אֶל אֵל לֹא יוֹשִׁיעַ.[6]) וַאֲנַחְנוּ כּוֹרְעִים וּמִשְׁתַּחֲוִים וּמוֹדִים, לִפְנֵי מֶלֶךְ מַלְכֵי הַמְּלָכִים הַקָּדוֹשׁ בָּרוּךְ הוּא. שֶׁהוּא נוֹטֶה שָׁמַיִם וְיֹסֵד אָרֶץ,[7] וּמוֹשַׁב יְקָרוֹ בַּשָּׁמַיִם מִמַּעַל, וּשְׁכִינַת עֻזּוֹ בְּגָבְהֵי מְרוֹמִים. הוּא

Bow while reciting וַאֲנַחְנוּ כּוֹרְעִים וּמִשְׁתַּחֲוִים.

May it be Your will, HASHEM, *our God and the God of our forefathers, that we observe Your decrees in This World, and merit that we live and see and inherit goodness and blessing in the years of Messianic times and for the life of the World to Come. So that my soul might sing to You and not be stilled,* HASHEM, *my God, forever will I thank You.*[1] *Blessed is the man who trusts in* HASHEM, *then* HASHEM *will be his security.*[2] *Trust in* HASHEM *forever, for in God,* HASHEM, *is the strength of the worlds.*[3] Chazzan– *Those knowing Your Name will trust in You, and You forsake not those Who seek You,* HASHEM.[4] HASHEM *desired, for the sake of its [Israel's] righteousness, that the Torah be made great and glorious.*[5]

The *chazzan* recites the following *Kaddish.*

יִתְגַּדַּל *May His great Name grow exalted and sanctified* (Cong.– *Amen.*) *in the world that He created as He willed. May He give reign to His kingship in your lifetimes and in your days, and in the lifetimes of the entire Family of Israel, swiftly and soon. Now respond: Amen.*

(Cong.– *Amen. May His great Name be blessed forever and ever.*)

May His great Name be blessed forever and ever.

Blessed, praised, glorified, exalted, extolled, mighty, upraised, and lauded be the Name of the Holy One, Blessed is He (Cong.– *Blessed is He*) — *beyond any blessing and song, praise and consolation that are uttered in the world. Now respond: Amen.* (Cong.– *Amen.*)

May there be abundant peace from Heaven, and life, upon us and upon all Israel. Now respond: Amen. (Cong.– *Amen.*)

Take three steps back. Bow left and say, *'He Who makes peace . . .';* bow right and say, *'may He . . .';* bow forward and say, *'and upon all Israel . . .'* Remain standing in place for a few moments, then take three steps forward.

He Who makes peace in His heights, may He make peace upon us, and upon all Israel. Now respond: Amen. (Cong.– *Amen.*)

ALEINU

Stand while reciting עָלֵינוּ, *'It is our duty . . .'*

עָלֵינוּ *It is our duty to praise the Master of all, to ascribe greatness to the Molder of primeval creation, for He has not made us like the nations of the lands, and has not emplaced us like the families of the earth; for He has not assigned our portion like theirs nor our lot like all their multitudes. (For they bow to vanity and emptiness and pray to a god which helps not.*[6]*) But we bend our knees, bow, and acknowledge our thanks before the King Who reigns over kings, the Holy One, Blessed is He. He stretches out heaven and establishes earth's foundation,*[7] *the seat of His homage is in the heavens above and His powerful Presence is in the loftiest heights. He*

Bow while reciting *'But we bend our knees.'*

(1) *Psalms* 30:13. (2) *Jeremiah* 17:7. (3) *Isaiah* 26:4.
(4) *Psalms* 9:11. (5) *Isaiah* 42:21. (6) *Isaiah* 45:20. (7) 51:13.

אֱלֹהֵינוּ, אֵין עוֹד. אֱמֶת מַלְכֵּנוּ, אֶפֶס זוּלָתוֹ, כַּכָּתוּב בְּתוֹרָתוֹ: וְיָדַעְתָּ הַיּוֹם וַהֲשֵׁבֹתָ אֶל לְבָבֶךָ, כִּי יהוה הוּא הָאֱלֹהִים בַּשָּׁמַיִם מִמַּעַל וְעַל הָאָרֶץ מִתָּחַת, אֵין עוֹד.[1]

עַל כֵּן נְקַוֶּה לְּךָ יהוה אֱלֹהֵינוּ לִרְאוֹת מְהֵרָה בְּתִפְאֶרֶת עֻזֶּךָ, לְהַעֲבִיר גִּלּוּלִים מִן הָאָרֶץ, וְהָאֱלִילִים כָּרוֹת יִכָּרֵתוּן, לְתַקֵּן עוֹלָם בְּמַלְכוּת שַׁדַּי. וְכָל בְּנֵי בָשָׂר יִקְרְאוּ בִשְׁמֶךָ, לְהַפְנוֹת אֵלֶיךָ כָּל רִשְׁעֵי אָרֶץ. יַכִּירוּ וְיֵדְעוּ כָּל יוֹשְׁבֵי תֵבֵל, כִּי לְךָ תִּכְרַע כָּל בֶּרֶךְ, תִּשָּׁבַע כָּל לָשׁוֹן.[2] לְפָנֶיךָ יהוה אֱלֹהֵינוּ יִכְרְעוּ וְיִפֹּלוּ, וְלִכְבוֹד שִׁמְךָ יְקָר יִתֵּנוּ. וִיקַבְּלוּ כֻלָּם אֶת עוֹל מַלְכוּתֶךָ, וְתִמְלֹךְ עֲלֵיהֶם מְהֵרָה לְעוֹלָם וָעֶד. כִּי הַמַּלְכוּת שֶׁלְּךָ הִיא וּלְעוֹלְמֵי עַד תִּמְלוֹךְ בְּכָבוֹד, כַּכָּתוּב בְּתוֹרָתֶךָ: יהוה יִמְלֹךְ לְעֹלָם וָעֶד.[3] ❖ וְנֶאֱמַר: וְהָיָה יהוה לְמֶלֶךְ עַל כָּל הָאָרֶץ, בַּיּוֹם הַהוּא יִהְיֶה יהוה אֶחָד וּשְׁמוֹ אֶחָד.[4]

Some congregations recite the following after עָלֵינוּ.

אַל תִּירָא מִפַּחַד פִּתְאֹם, וּמִשֹּׁאַת רְשָׁעִים כִּי תָבֹא.[5] עֻצוּ עֵצָה וְתֻפָר, דַּבְּרוּ דָבָר וְלֹא יָקוּם, כִּי עִמָּנוּ אֵל.[6] וְעַד זִקְנָה אֲנִי הוּא, וְעַד שֵׂיבָה אֲנִי אֶסְבֹּל, אֲנִי עָשִׂיתִי וַאֲנִי אֶשָּׂא, וַאֲנִי אֶסְבֹּל וַאֲמַלֵּט.[7]

קדיש יתום

In the presence of a *minyan,* mourners recite קַדִּישׁ יָתוֹם, the Mourner's *Kaddish* (see *Laws* §132-134).

יִתְגַּדַּל וְיִתְקַדַּשׁ שְׁמֵהּ רַבָּא. (.Cong – אָמֵן.) בְּעָלְמָא דִּי בְרָא כִרְעוּתֵהּ. וְיַמְלִיךְ מַלְכוּתֵהּ, בְּחַיֵּיכוֹן וּבְיוֹמֵיכוֹן וּבְחַיֵּי דְכָל בֵּית יִשְׂרָאֵל, בַּעֲגָלָא וּבִזְמַן קָרִיב. וְאִמְרוּ: אָמֵן.

(.Cong – אָמֵן. יְהֵא שְׁמֵהּ רַבָּא מְבָרַךְ לְעָלַם וּלְעָלְמֵי עָלְמַיָּא.)

יְהֵא שְׁמֵהּ רַבָּא מְבָרַךְ לְעָלַם וּלְעָלְמֵי עָלְמַיָּא.

יִתְבָּרַךְ וְיִשְׁתַּבַּח וְיִתְפָּאַר וְיִתְרוֹמַם וְיִתְנַשֵּׂא וְיִתְהַדָּר וְיִתְעַלֶּה וְיִתְהַלָּל שְׁמֵהּ דְּקֻדְשָׁא בְּרִיךְ הוּא (.Cong – בְּרִיךְ הוּא) – לְעֵלָּא מִן כָּל בִּרְכָתָא וְשִׁירָתָא תֻּשְׁבְּחָתָא וְנֶחֱמָתָא, דַּאֲמִירָן בְּעָלְמָא. וְאִמְרוּ: אָמֵן. (.Cong – אָמֵן.)

יְהֵא שְׁלָמָא רַבָּא מִן שְׁמַיָּא, וְחַיִּים עָלֵינוּ וְעַל כָּל יִשְׂרָאֵל. וְאִמְרוּ: אָמֵן. (.Cong – אָמֵן.)

Take three steps back. Bow left and say . . . עֹשֶׂה; bow right and say . . . הוּא; bow forward and say וְעַל כָּל . . . אָמֵן. Remain standing in place for a few moments, then take three steps forward.

עֹשֶׂה שָׁלוֹם בִּמְרוֹמָיו, הוּא יַעֲשֶׂה שָׁלוֹם עָלֵינוּ, וְעַל כָּל יִשְׂרָאֵל. וְאִמְרוּ: אָמֵן. (.Cong – אָמֵן.)

The recitation of שִׁיר שֶׁל יוֹם, *the Song of the Day,* is postponed until Minchah.
After midday it is permissible to sit on a regular seat.

is our God and there is none other. True is our King, there is nothing beside Him, as it is written in His Torah: 'You are to know this day and take to your heart that HASHEM is the only God — in heaven above and on the earth below — there is none other.'[1]

עַל כֵּן *Therefore we put our hope in You, HASHEM, our God, that we may soon see Your mighty splendor, to remove detestable idolatry from the earth, and false gods will be utterly cut off, to perfect the universe through the Almighty's sovereignty. Then all humanity will call upon Your Name, to turn all the earth's wicked toward You. All the world's inhabitants will recognize and know that to You every knee should bend, every tongue should swear.*[2] *Before You, HASHEM, our God, they will bend every knee and cast themselves down and to the glory of Your Name they will render homage, and they will all accept upon themselves the yoke of Your kingship that You may reign over them soon and eternally. For the kingdom is Yours and You will reign for all eternity in glory as it is written in Your Torah: HASHEM shall reign for all eternity.*[3] Chazzan– *And it is said: HASHEM will be King over all the world — on that day HASHEM will be One and His Name will be One.*[4]

Some congregations recite the following after *Aleinu*.

אַל תִּירָא *Do not fear sudden terror, or the holocaust of the wicked when it comes.*[5] *Plan a conspiracy and it will be annulled; speak your piece and it shall not stand, for God is with us.*[6] *Even till your seniority, I remain unchanged; and even till your ripe old age, I shall endure. I created you and I shall bear you; I shall endure and rescue.*[7]

MOURNER'S KADDISH

In the presence of a *minyan,* mourners recite קַדִּישׁ יָתוֹם, the Mourner's *Kaddish* (see *Laws* 132-134).
[A transliteration of this *Kaddish* appears on page 484.]

יִתְגַּדַּל *May His great Name grow exalted and sanctified* (Cong.– *Amen.*) *in the world that He created as He willed. May He give reign to His kingship in your lifetimes and in your days, and in the lifetimes of the entire Family of Israel, swiftly and soon. Now respond: Amen.*

(Cong.– *Amen. May His great Name be blessed forever and ever.*)

May His great Name be blessed forever and ever.

Blessed, praised, glorified, exalted, extolled, mighty, upraised, and lauded be the Name of the Holy One, Blessed is He (Cong.– *Blessed is He*) *— beyond any blessing and song, praise and consolation that are uttered in the world. Now respond: Amen.* (Cong.– *Amen*).

May there be abundant peace from Heaven, and life, upon us and upon all Israel. Now respond: Amen. (Cong.– *Amen.*)

Take three steps back. Bow left and say, *'He Who makes peace . . .';* bow right and say, *'may He . . .';* bow forward and say, *'and upon all Israel . . .'*
Remain standing in place for a few moments, then take three steps forward.

He Who makes peace in His heights, may He make peace upon us, and upon all Israel. Now respond: Amen. (Cong.– *Amen.*)

The recitation of שִׁיר שֶׁל יוֹם, *the Song of the Day,* is postponed until Minchah.
After midday it is permissible to sit on a regular seat.

---

(1) *Deuteronomy* 4:39. (2) Cf. *Isaiah* 45:23. (3) *Exodus* 15:18.
(4) *Zechariah* 14:9. (5) *Proverbs* 3:25. (6) *Isaiah* 8:10. (7) 46:4.

מנחה

The *Paroches* is returned to the Ark.

עטיפת טלית

Before donning the *tallis,* inspect the *tzitzis,* while reciting these verses:

בָּרְכִי נַפְשִׁי אֶת יהוה, יהוה אֱלֹהַי גָּדַלְתָּ מְּאֹד, הוֹד וְהָדָר לָבָשְׁתָּ. עֹטֶה אוֹר כַּשַּׂלְמָה, נוֹטֶה שָׁמַיִם כַּיְרִיעָה.[1]

Many recite the following declaration of intent before donning the *tallis:*

לְשֵׁם יִחוּד קֻדְשָׁא בְּרִיךְ הוּא וּשְׁכִינְתֵּהּ, בִּדְחִילוּ וּרְחִימוּ לְיַחֵד שֵׁם י״ה בְּו״ה בְּיִחוּדָא שְׁלִים, בְּשֵׁם כָּל יִשְׂרָאֵל.

הֲרֵינִי מִתְעַטֵּף גּוּפִי בַּצִּיצִת, כֵּן תִּתְעַטֵּף נִשְׁמָתִי וּרְמַ״ח אֵבָרַי וּשְׁסָ״ה גִידַי בְּאוֹר הַצִּיצִת הָעוֹלֶה תַרְיַ״ג. וּכְשֵׁם שֶׁאֲנִי מִתְכַּסֶּה בְּטַלִּית בָּעוֹלָם הַזֶּה, כַּךְ אֶזְכֶּה לַחֲלוּקָא דְרַבָּנָן וּלְטַלִּית נָאָה לָעוֹלָם הַבָּא בְּגַן עֵדֶן. וְעַל יְדֵי מִצְוַת צִיצִת תִּנָּצֵל נַפְשִׁי וְרוּחִי וְנִשְׁמָתִי וּתְפִלָּתִי מִן הַחִיצוֹנִים. וְהַטַּלִּית יִפְרוֹשׂ כְּנָפָיו עֲלֵיהֶם וְיַצִּילֵם כְּנֶשֶׁר יָעִיר קִנּוֹ, עַל גּוֹזָלָיו יְרַחֵף.[2] וּתְהֵא חֲשׁוּבָה מִצְוַת צִיצִת לִפְנֵי הַקָּדוֹשׁ בָּרוּךְ הוּא כְּאִלּוּ קִיַּמְתִּיהָ בְּכָל פְּרָטֶיהָ וְדִקְדּוּקֶיהָ וְכַוָּנוֹתֶיהָ וְתַרְיַ״ג מִצְוֹת הַתְּלוּיִם בָּהּ. אָמֵן סֶלָה.

Unfold the *tallis*, hold it in readiness to wrap around yourself, and recite the following blessing:

בָּרוּךְ אַתָּה יהוה אֱלֹהֵינוּ מֶלֶךְ הָעוֹלָם, אֲשֶׁר קִדְּשָׁנוּ בְּמִצְוֹתָיו, וְצִוָּנוּ לְהִתְעַטֵּף בַּצִּיצִת.

Wrap the *tallis* around your head and body, then recite:

מַה יָּקָר חַסְדְּךָ אֱלֹהִים, וּבְנֵי אָדָם בְּצֵל כְּנָפֶיךָ יֶחֱסָיוּן. יִרְוְיֻן מִדֶּשֶׁן בֵּיתֶךָ, וְנַחַל עֲדָנֶיךָ תַשְׁקֵם. כִּי עִמְּךָ מְקוֹר חַיִּים, בְּאוֹרְךָ נִרְאֶה אוֹר. מְשֹׁךְ חַסְדְּךָ לְיֹדְעֶיךָ, וְצִדְקָתְךָ לְיִשְׁרֵי לֵב.[3]

סדר הנחת תפילין

Many recite the following declaration of intent before putting on *tefillin:*

לְשֵׁם יִחוּד קֻדְשָׁא בְּרִיךְ הוּא וּשְׁכִינְתֵּהּ, בִּדְחִילוּ וּרְחִימוּ לְיַחֵד שֵׁם י״ה בְּו״ה בְּיִחוּדָא שְׁלִים, בְּשֵׁם כָּל יִשְׂרָאֵל.

הִנְנִי מְכַוֵּן בְּהַנָּחַת תְּפִלִּין לְקַיֵּם מִצְוַת בּוֹרְאִי, שֶׁצִּוָּנוּ לְהָנִיחַ תְּפִלִּין, כַּכָּתוּב בְּתוֹרָתוֹ: וּקְשַׁרְתָּם לְאוֹת עַל יָדֶךָ, וְהָיוּ לְטֹטָפֹת בֵּין עֵינֶיךָ[4] וְהֵם אַרְבַּע פַּרְשִׁיּוֹת אֵלּוּ – שְׁמַע, וְהָיָה אִם שָׁמֹעַ, קַדֶּשׁ,

MINCHAH

The *Paroches* is returned to the Ark.

DONNING THE TALLIS

Before donning the *tallis,* inspect the *tzitzis,* while reciting these verses:

בָּרְכִי נַפְשִׁי *Bless HASHEM, O my soul; HASHEM, my God, You are very great; You have donned majesty and splendor; cloaked in light as with a garment, stretching out the heavens like a curtain.*[1]

Many recite the following declaration of intent before donning the *tallis:*

לְשֵׁם יִחוּד *For the sake of the unification of the Holy One, Blessed is He, and His Presence, in fear and love to unify the Name — yud-kei with vav-kei — in perfect unity, in the name of all Israel.*

הֲרֵינִי *I am ready to wrap my body in tzitzis, so may my soul, my two hundred forty-eight organs and my three hundred sixty-five sinews be wrapped in the illumination of tzitzis which has the numerical value of six hundred thirteen. Just as I cover myself with a tallis in This World, so may I merit the rabbinical garb and a beautiful cloak in the World to Come in the Garden of Eden. Through the commandment of tzitzis may my life-force, spirit, soul, and prayer be rescued from the external forces. May the tallis spread its wings over them and rescue them like an eagle rousing his nest, fluttering over his eaglets.*[2] *May the commandment of tzitzis be worthy before the Holy One, Blessed is He, as if I had fulfilled it in all its details, implications, and intentions, as well as the six hundred thirteen commandments that are dependent upon it. Amen, Selah!*

Unfold the *tallis*, hold it in readiness to wrap around yourself, and recite the following blessing:

בָּרוּךְ *Blessed are You, HASHEM, our God, King of the universe, Who has sanctified us with His commandments and has commanded us to wrap ourselves in tzitzis.*

Wrap the *tallis* around your head and body, then recite:

מַה יָּקָר *How precious is Your kindness, O God! The sons of man take refuge in the shadows of Your wings. May they be sated from the abundance of Your house; and may You give them to drink from the stream of Your delights. For with You is the source of life — by Your light we shall see light. Extend Your kindness to those who know You, and Your charity to the upright of heart.*[3]

ORDER OF PUTTING ON TEFILLIN

Many recite the following declaration of intent before putting on *tefillin:*

לְשֵׁם יִחוּד *For the sake of the unification of the Holy One, Blessed is He, and His Presence, in fear and love, to unify the Name — yud-kei with vav-kei — in perfect unity, in the name of all Israel.*

הִנְנִי מְכַוֵּן *Behold, in putting on tefillin I intend to fulfill the commandment of my Creator, Who has commanded us to put on tefillin, as is written in His Torah: 'Bind them as a sign upon your arm and let them be tefillin between your eyes.'*[4] *These four portions [contained in the tefillin] — [1] 'Shema' (Deuteronomy 6:4-9); [2] 'And it will come to pass, if you will hearken' (Deuteronomy 11:13-21); [3] 'Sanctify' (Exodus 13:1-10)*

(1) *Psalms* 104:1-2. (2) *Deuteronomy* 32:11. (3) *Psalms* 36:8-11. (4) *Deuteronomy* 6:8.

וְהָיָה כִּי יְבִאֲךָ — שֶׁיֵּשׁ בָּהֶם יִחוּדוֹ וְאַחְדוּתוֹ יִתְבָּרַךְ שְׁמוֹ בָּעוֹלָם; וְשֶׁנִּזְכּוֹר נִסִּים וְנִפְלָאוֹת שֶׁעָשָׂה עִמָּנוּ בְּהוֹצִיאָנוּ מִמִּצְרָיִם; וַאֲשֶׁר לוֹ הַכֹּחַ וְהַמֶּמְשָׁלָה בָּעֶלְיוֹנִים וּבַתַּחְתּוֹנִים לַעֲשׂוֹת בָּהֶם כִּרְצוֹנוֹ. וְצִוָּנוּ לְהָנִיחַ עַל הַיָּד, לְזִכְרוֹן זְרוֹעַ הַנְּטוּיָה, וְשֶׁהִיא נֶגֶד הַלֵּב, לְשַׁעְבֵּד בָּזֶה תַּאֲוַת וּמַחְשְׁבוֹת לִבֵּנוּ לַעֲבוֹדָתוֹ, יִתְבָּרַךְ שְׁמוֹ. וְעַל הָרֹאשׁ נֶגֶד הַמּוֹחַ, שֶׁהַנְּשָׁמָה שֶׁבְּמוֹחִי, עִם שְׁאָר חוּשַׁי וְכֹחוֹתַי, כֻּלָּם יִהְיוּ מְשֻׁעְבָּדִים לַעֲבוֹדָתוֹ, יִתְבָּרַךְ שְׁמוֹ. וּמִשֶּׁפַע מִצְוַת תְּפִלִּין יִתְמַשֵּׁךְ עָלַי לִהְיוֹת לִי חַיִּים אֲרוּכִים, וְשֶׁפַע קֹדֶשׁ, וּמַחֲשָׁבוֹת קְדוֹשׁוֹת בְּלִי הַרְהוּר חֵטְא וְעָוֹן כְּלָל; וְשֶׁלֹּא יְפַתֵּנוּ וְלֹא יִתְגָּרֶה בָּנוּ יֵצֶר הָרָע, וְיַנִּיחֵנוּ לַעֲבֹד אֶת יהוה כַּאֲשֶׁר עִם לְבָבֵנוּ. וִיהִי רָצוֹן מִלְּפָנֶיךָ, יהוה אֱלֹהֵינוּ וֵאלֹהֵי אֲבוֹתֵינוּ, שֶׁתְּהֵא חֲשׁוּבָה מִצְוַת הֲנָחַת תְּפִלִּין לִפְנֵי הַקָּדוֹשׁ בָּרוּךְ הוּא כְּאִלּוּ קִיַּמְתִּיהָ בְּכָל פְּרָטֶיהָ וְדִקְדּוּקֶיהָ וְכַוָּנוֹתֶיהָ, וְתַרְיַ״ג מִצְוֹת הַתְּלוּיִם בָּהּ. אָמֵן סֶלָה.

Stand while putting on *tefillin*. Place the arm-*tefillin* upon the left biceps (or the right biceps of one who writes left-handed), hold it in place ready for tightening, then recite the following blessing:

בָּרוּךְ אַתָּה יהוה אֱלֹהֵינוּ מֶלֶךְ הָעוֹלָם, אֲשֶׁר קִדְּשָׁנוּ בְּמִצְוֹתָיו, וְצִוָּנוּ לְהָנִיחַ תְּפִלִּין.

Tighten the arm-*tefillin* and wrap the strap seven times around the arm. Without any interruption whatsoever, put the head-*tefillin* in place, above the hairline and opposite the space between the eyes. Before tightening the head-*tefillin* recite the following blessing:

בָּרוּךְ אַתָּה יהוה אֱלֹהֵינוּ מֶלֶךְ הָעוֹלָם, אֲשֶׁר קִדְּשָׁנוּ בְּמִצְוֹתָיו, וְצִוָּנוּ עַל מִצְוַת תְּפִלִּין.

Tighten the head-*tefillin* and recite:

בָּרוּךְ שֵׁם כְּבוֹד מַלְכוּתוֹ לְעוֹלָם וָעֶד.

After the head-*tefillin* is securely in place, recite:

וּמֵחָכְמָתְךָ אֵל עֶלְיוֹן, תַּאֲצִיל עָלַי; וּמִבִּינָתְךָ תְּבִינֵנִי; וּבְחַסְדְּךָ תַּגְדִּיל עָלַי; וּבִגְבוּרָתְךָ תַּצְמִית אֹיְבַי וְקָמַי. וְשֶׁמֶן הַטּוֹב תָּרִיק עַל שִׁבְעָה קְנֵי הַמְּנוֹרָה, לְהַשְׁפִּיעַ טוּבְךָ לִבְרִיּוֹתֶיךָ. פּוֹתֵחַ אֶת יָדֶךָ, וּמַשְׂבִּיעַ לְכָל חַי רָצוֹן.[1]

Wrap the strap around the middle finger and hand according to your custom. While doing this, recite:

וְאֵרַשְׂתִּיךְ לִי לְעוֹלָם, וְאֵרַשְׂתִּיךְ לִי בְּצֶדֶק וּבְמִשְׁפָּט וּבְחֶסֶד וּבְרַחֲמִים. וְאֵרַשְׂתִּיךְ לִי בֶּאֱמוּנָה, וְיָדַעַתְּ אֶת יהוה.[2]

and [4] *'And it will come to pass when He shall bring you' (Exodus 13:11-16) — contain His Oneness and Unity, may His Name be blessed, in the universe; so that we will recall the miracles and wonders that He did with us when He removed us from Egypt; and that He has the strength and dominion over those above and those below to do with them as He wishes. He has commanded us to put [tefillin] upon the arm to recall the 'outstretched arm' [of the Exodus] and that it be opposite the heart thereby to subjugate the desires and thoughts of our heart to His service, may His Name be blessed; and upon the head opposite the brain, so that the soul that is in my brain, together with my other senses and potentials, may all be subjugated to His service, may His Name be blessed. May some of the spiritual influence of the commandment of tefillin be extended upon me so that I have a long life, a flow of holiness, and holy thoughts, without even an inkling of sin or iniquity; and that the Evil Inclination will not seduce us nor incite against us, and that it permit us to serve HASHEM as is our hearts' desire. May it be Your will, HASHEM, our God and the God of our forefathers, that the commandment of putting on tefillin be considered as worthy before the Holy One, Blessed is He, as if I had fulfilled it in all its details, implications, and intentions, as well as the six hundred thirteen commandments that are dependent upon it. Amen, Selah.*

Stand while putting on *tefillin*. Place the arm-*tefillin* upon the left biceps (or the right biceps of one who writes left-handed), hold it in place ready for tightening, then recite the following blessing:

בָּרוּךְ *Blessed are You, HASHEM, our God, King of the universe, Who has sanctified us with His commandments and has commanded us to put on tefillin.*

Tighten the arm-*tefillin* and wrap the strap seven times around the arm. Without any interruption whatsoever, put the head-*tefillin* in place, above the hairline and opposite the space between the eyes. Before tightening the head-*tefillin* recite the following blessing:

בָּרוּךְ *Blessed are You, HASHEM, our God, King of the universe, Who has sanctified us with His commandments and has commanded us regarding the commandment of tefillin.*

Tighten the head-*tefillin* and recite:

Blessed is the Name of His glorious kingdom for all eternity.

After the head-*tefillin* is securely in place, recite:

וּמֵחָכְמָתְךָ *From Your wisdom, O supreme God, may You imbue me; from Your understanding give me understanding; with Your kindness do greatly with me; with Your power cut down my foes and rebels. [May] You pour goodly oil upon the seven arms of the menorah, to cause Your good to flow to Your creatures. [May] You open Your hand and satisfy the desire of every living thing.*[1]

Wrap the strap around the middle finger and hand according to your custom. While doing this, recite:

וְאֵרַשְׂתִּיךְ *I will betroth you to Me forever, and I will betroth you to Me with righteousness, justice, kindness, and mercy. I will betroth you to Me with fidelity, and you shall know HASHEM.*[2]

---

(1) *Psalms* 145:16. (2) *Hoshea* 2:21-22.

PORTIONS OMITTED FROM SHACHARIS (EXCEPT לַמְנַצֵּחַ AND תַּחֲנוּן) ARE RECITED HERE.

שיר של יום

A different psalm is assigned as the Song of the Day for each day of the week.

SUNDAY

הַיּוֹם יוֹם רִאשׁוֹן בַּשַּׁבָּת, שֶׁבּוֹ הָיוּ הַלְוִיִּם אוֹמְרִים בְּבֵית הַמִּקְדָּשׁ:

תהלים כד

לְדָוִד מִזְמוֹר, לַיהוה הָאָרֶץ וּמְלוֹאָהּ, תֵּבֵל וְיֹשְׁבֵי בָהּ. כִּי הוּא עַל יַמִּים יְסָדָהּ, וְעַל נְהָרוֹת יְכוֹנְנֶהָ. מִי יַעֲלֶה בְהַר יהוה, וּמִי יָקוּם בִּמְקוֹם קָדְשׁוֹ. נְקִי כַפַּיִם וּבַר לֵבָב, אֲשֶׁר לֹא נָשָׂא לַשָּׁוְא נַפְשִׁי, וְלֹא נִשְׁבַּע לְמִרְמָה. יִשָּׂא בְרָכָה מֵאֵת יהוה, וּצְדָקָה מֵאֱלֹהֵי יִשְׁעוֹ. זֶה דּוֹר דֹּרְשָׁיו, מְבַקְשֵׁי פָנֶיךָ יַעֲקֹב סֶלָה. שְׂאוּ שְׁעָרִים רָאשֵׁיכֶם, וְהִנָּשְׂאוּ פִּתְחֵי עוֹלָם, וְיָבוֹא מֶלֶךְ הַכָּבוֹד. מִי זֶה מֶלֶךְ הַכָּבוֹד, יהוה עִזּוּז וְגִבּוֹר, יהוה גִּבּוֹר מִלְחָמָה. ❖ שְׂאוּ שְׁעָרִים רָאשֵׁיכֶם, וּשְׂאוּ פִּתְחֵי עוֹלָם, וְיָבֹא מֶלֶךְ הַכָּבוֹד. מִי הוּא זֶה מֶלֶךְ הַכָּבוֹד, יהוה צְבָאוֹת, הוּא מֶלֶךְ הַכָּבוֹד סֶלָה.

The service continues with קַדִּישׁ יָתוֹם, *the Mourner's Kaddish* (page 412).

TUESDAY

הַיּוֹם יוֹם שְׁלִישִׁי בַּשַּׁבָּת, שֶׁבּוֹ הָיוּ הַלְוִיִּם אוֹמְרִים בְּבֵית הַמִּקְדָּשׁ:

תהלים פב

מִזְמוֹר לְאָסָף, אֱלֹהִים נִצָּב בַּעֲדַת אֵל, בְּקֶרֶב אֱלֹהִים יִשְׁפֹּט. עַד מָתַי תִּשְׁפְּטוּ עָוֶל, וּפְנֵי רְשָׁעִים תִּשְׂאוּ סֶלָה. שִׁפְטוּ דַל וְיָתוֹם, עָנִי וָרָשׁ הַצְדִּיקוּ. פַּלְּטוּ דַל וְאֶבְיוֹן, מִיַּד רְשָׁעִים הַצִּילוּ. לֹא יָדְעוּ וְלֹא יָבִינוּ, בַּחֲשֵׁכָה יִתְהַלָּכוּ, יִמּוֹטוּ כָּל מוֹסְדֵי אָרֶץ. אֲנִי אָמַרְתִּי אֱלֹהִים אַתֶּם, וּבְנֵי עֶלְיוֹן כֻּלְּכֶם. אָכֵן כְּאָדָם תְּמוּתוּן, וּכְאַחַד הַשָּׂרִים תִּפֹּלוּ. ❖ קוּמָה אֱלֹהִים שָׁפְטָה הָאָרֶץ, כִּי אַתָּה תִנְחַל בְּכָל הַגּוֹיִם.

The service continues with קַדִּישׁ יָתוֹם, *the Mourner's Kaddish* (page 412).

THURSDAY

הַיּוֹם יוֹם חֲמִישִׁי בַּשַּׁבָּת, שֶׁבּוֹ הָיוּ הַלְוִיִּם אוֹמְרִים בְּבֵית הַמִּקְדָּשׁ:

תהלים פא

לַמְנַצֵּחַ עַל הַגִּתִּית לְאָסָף. הַרְנִינוּ לֵאלֹהִים עוּזֵּנוּ, הָרִיעוּ לֵאלֹהֵי יַעֲקֹב. שְׂאוּ זִמְרָה וּתְנוּ תֹף, כִּנּוֹר נָעִים עִם נָבֶל. תִּקְעוּ בַחֹדֶשׁ שׁוֹפָר, בַּכֶּסֶה לְיוֹם חַגֵּנוּ. כִּי חֹק לְיִשְׂרָאֵל הוּא, מִשְׁפָּט לֵאלֹהֵי יַעֲקֹב. עֵדוּת בִּיהוֹסֵף שָׂמוֹ, בְּצֵאתוֹ עַל אֶרֶץ מִצְרָיִם, שְׂפַת לֹא יָדַעְתִּי אֶשְׁמָע. הֲסִירוֹתִי מִסֵּבֶל שִׁכְמוֹ, כַּפָּיו מִדּוּד תַּעֲבֹרְנָה. בַּצָּרָה קָרָאתָ, וָאֲחַלְּצֶךָּ, אֶעֶנְךָ בְּסֵתֶר רַעַם, אֶבְחָנְךָ עַל מֵי מְרִיבָה, סֶלָה. שְׁמַע עַמִּי וְאָעִידָה בָּךְ, יִשְׂרָאֵל אִם תִּשְׁמַע לִי. לֹא יִהְיֶה בְךָ אֵל זָר, וְלֹא תִשְׁתַּחֲוֶה לְאֵל נֵכָר. אָנֹכִי

PORTIONS OMITTED FROM SHACHARIS (EXCEPT תַּחֲנוּן AND לַמְנַצֵּחַ) ARE RECITED HERE.

SONG OF THE DAY

A different psalm is assigned as the Song of the Day for each day of the week.

SUNDAY

Today is the first day of the Sabbath,
on which the Levites would recite in the Holy Temple:

Psalm 24

לְדָוִד *Of David a psalm.* HASHEM*'s is the earth and its fullness, the inhabited land and those who dwell in it. For He founded it upon seas, and established it upon rivers. Who may ascend the mountain of* HASHEM*, and who may stand in the place of His sanctity? One with clean hands and pure heart, who has not sworn in vain by My soul and has not sworn deceitfully. He will receive a blessing from* HASHEM *and just kindness from the God of his salvation. This is the generation of those who seek Him, those who strive for Your Presence — Jacob, Selah. Raise up your heads, O gates, and be uplifted, you everlasting entrances, so that the King of Glory may enter. Who is this King of Glory? —* HASHEM*, the mighty and strong,* HASHEM*, the strong in battle.* Chazzan— *Raise up your heads, O gates, and raise up, you everlasting entrances, so that the King of Glory may enter. Who then is the King of Glory?* HASHEM*, Master of Legions, He is the King of Glory. Selah!*

The service continues with קַדִּישׁ יָתוֹם, *the Mourner's Kaddish* (p. 412).

TUESDAY

Today is the third day of the Sabbath,
on which the Levites would recite in the Holy Temple:

Psalm 82

מִזְמוֹר *A psalm of Assaf: God stands in the Divine assembly, in the midst of judges shall He judge. Until when will you judge lawlessly and favor the presence of the wicked, Selah? Judge the needy and the orphan, vindicate the poor and impoverished. Rescue the needy and destitute, from the hand of the wicked deliver them. They do not know nor do they understand, in darkness they walk; all foundations of the earth collapse. I said, 'You are angelic, sons of the Most High are you all.' But like men you shall die, and like one of the princes you shall fall.* Chazzan— *Arise, O God, judge the earth, for You allot the heritage among all the nations.*

The service continues with קַדִּישׁ יָתוֹם, *the Mourner's Kaddish* (p. 412).

THURSDAY

Today is the fifth day of the Sabbath,
on which the Levites would recite in the Holy Temple:

Psalm 81

לַמְנַצֵּחַ *For the Conductor, upon the gittis, by Assaf. Sing joyously to the God of our might, call out to the God of Jacob. Raise a song and sound the drum, the sweet harp with the lyre. Blow the shofar at the moon's renewal, at the time appointed for our festive day. Because it is a decree for Israel, a judgment day for the God of Jacob. He imposed it as a testimony for Joseph when he went forth over the land of Egypt — 'I understood a language I never knew!' I removed his shoulder from the burden, his hands let go of the kettle. In distress you called out, and I released you, I answered you with thunder when you hid, I tested you at the Waters of Strife, Selah. Listen, My nation, and I will attest to you; O Israel, if you would but listen to Me. There shall be no strange god within you, nor shall you bow before an alien god. I am*

יהוה אֱלֹהֶיךָ, הַמַּעַלְךָ מֵאֶרֶץ מִצְרָיִם, הַרְחֶב פִּיךָ וַאֲמַלְאֵהוּ. וְלֹא שָׁמַע עַמִּי לְקוֹלִי, וְיִשְׂרָאֵל לֹא אָבָה לִי. וָאֲשַׁלְּחֵהוּ בִּשְׁרִירוּת לִבָּם, יֵלְכוּ בְּמוֹעֲצוֹתֵיהֶם. לוּ עַמִּי שֹׁמֵעַ לִי, יִשְׂרָאֵל בִּדְרָכַי יְהַלֵּכוּ. כִּמְעַט אוֹיְבֵיהֶם אַכְנִיעַ, וְעַל צָרֵיהֶם אָשִׁיב יָדִי. מְשַׂנְאֵי יהוה יְכַחֲשׁוּ לוֹ, וִיהִי עִתָּם לְעוֹלָם. ❖ וַיַּאֲכִילֵהוּ מֵחֵלֶב חִטָּה, וּמִצּוּר דְּבַשׁ אַשְׂבִּיעֶךָ.

The service continues with קַדִּישׁ יָתוֹם, *the Mourner's Kaddish* (below).

קדיש יתום

In the presence of a *minyan,* mourners recite קַדִּישׁ יָתוֹם, the Mourner's *Kaddish* (see *Laws* §132-134):

יִתְגַּדַּל וְיִתְקַדַּשׁ שְׁמֵהּ רַבָּא. (.Cong – אָמֵן.) בְּעָלְמָא דִּי בְרָא כִרְעוּתֵהּ. וְיַמְלִיךְ מַלְכוּתֵהּ, בְּחַיֵּיכוֹן וּבְיוֹמֵיכוֹן וּבְחַיֵּי דְכָל בֵּית יִשְׂרָאֵל, בַּעֲגָלָא וּבִזְמַן קָרִיב. וְאִמְרוּ: אָמֵן.

(.Cong – אָמֵן. יְהֵא שְׁמֵהּ רַבָּא מְבָרַךְ לְעָלַם וּלְעָלְמֵי עָלְמַיָּא.)

יְהֵא שְׁמֵהּ רַבָּא מְבָרַךְ לְעָלַם וּלְעָלְמֵי עָלְמַיָּא.

יִתְבָּרַךְ וְיִשְׁתַּבַּח וְיִתְפָּאַר וְיִתְרוֹמַם וְיִתְנַשֵּׂא וְיִתְהַדָּר וְיִתְעַלֶּה וְיִתְהַלָּל שְׁמֵהּ דְּקֻדְשָׁא בְּרִיךְ הוּא (.Cong – בְּרִיךְ הוּא) – לְעֵלָּא מִן כָּל בִּרְכָתָא וְשִׁירָתָא תֻּשְׁבְּחָתָא וְנֶחֱמָתָא, דַּאֲמִירָן בְּעָלְמָא. וְאִמְרוּ: אָמֵן. (.Cong – אָמֵן.)

יְהֵא שְׁלָמָא רַבָּא מִן שְׁמַיָּא, וְחַיִּים עָלֵינוּ וְעַל כָּל יִשְׂרָאֵל. וְאִמְרוּ: אָמֵן. (.Cong – אָמֵן.)

Take three steps back. Bow left and say . . . עֹשֶׂה; bow right and say . . . הוּא; bow forward and say וְעַל כָּל . . . אָמֵן. Remain standing in place for a few moments, then take three steps forward.

עֹשֶׂה שָׁלוֹם בִּמְרוֹמָיו, הוּא יַעֲשֶׂה שָׁלוֹם עָלֵינוּ, וְעַל כָּל יִשְׂרָאֵל. וְאִמְרוּ: אָמֵן. (.Cong – אָמֵן.)

אַשְׁרֵי יוֹשְׁבֵי בֵיתֶךָ, עוֹד יְהַלְלוּךָ סֶּלָה.[1] אַשְׁרֵי הָעָם שֶׁכָּכָה לּוֹ, אַשְׁרֵי הָעָם שֶׁיהוה אֱלֹהָיו.[2]

תהלים קמה

תְּהִלָּה לְדָוִד,

אֲרוֹמִמְךָ אֱלוֹהַי הַמֶּלֶךְ, וַאֲבָרְכָה שִׁמְךָ לְעוֹלָם וָעֶד.

בְּכָל יוֹם אֲבָרְכֶךָּ, וַאֲהַלְלָה שִׁמְךָ לְעוֹלָם וָעֶד.

גָּדוֹל יהוה וּמְהֻלָּל מְאֹד, וְלִגְדֻלָּתוֹ אֵין חֵקֶר.

דּוֹר לְדוֹר יְשַׁבַּח מַעֲשֶׂיךָ, וּגְבוּרֹתֶיךָ יַגִּידוּ.

הֲדַר כְּבוֹד הוֹדֶךָ, וְדִבְרֵי נִפְלְאֹתֶיךָ אָשִׂיחָה.

וֶעֱזוּז נוֹרְאוֹתֶיךָ יֹאמֵרוּ, וּגְדוּלָּתְךָ אֲסַפְּרֶנָּה.

זֵכֶר רַב טוּבְךָ יַבִּיעוּ, וְצִדְקָתְךָ יְרַנֵּנוּ.

חַנּוּן וְרַחוּם יהוה, אֶרֶךְ אַפַּיִם וּגְדָל חָסֶד.

---

(1) *Psalms* 84:5. (2) 144:15.

HASHEM, your God, who elevated you from the land of Egypt, open wide your mouth and I will fill it. But My people did not heed My voice and Israel did not desire Me. So I let them follow their heart's fantasies, they follow their own counsels. If only My people would heed Me, if Israel would walk in My ways. In an instant I would subdue their foes, and against their tormentors turn My hand. Those who hate HASHEM lie to Him — so their destiny is eternal. Chazzan— *But He would feed him with the cream of the wheat, and with honey from a rock sate you.*

The service continues with קַדִּישׁ יָתוֹם, *the Mourner's Kaddish* (below).

MOURNER'S KADDISH

In the presence of a *minyan,* mourners recite קַדִּישׁ יָתוֹם, the Mourner's *Kaddish* (see *Laws* §132-134):
[A transliteration of this *Kaddish* appears on p. 484.]

יִתְגַּדַּל *May His great Name grow exalted and sanctified* (Cong.— *Amen.*) *in the world that He created as He willed. May He give reign to His kingship in your lifetimes and in your days, and in the lifetimes of the entire Family of Israel, swiftly and soon. Now respond: Amen.*

(Cong.— *Amen. May His great Name be blessed forever and ever.*)
May His great Name be blessed forever and ever.

Blessed, praised, glorified, exalted, extolled, mighty, upraised, and lauded be the Name of the Holy One, Blessed is He (Cong.— *Blessed is He*) — *beyond any blessing and song, praise and consolation that are uttered in the world. Now respond: Amen.* (Cong.— *Amen*).

May there be abundant peace from Heaven, and life, upon us and upon all Israel. Now respond: Amen. (Cong.— *Amen.*)

Take three steps back. Bow left and say, *'He Who makes peace . . .';* bow right and say, *'may He . . .';* bow forward and say, *'and upon all Israel . . .'* Remain standing in place for a few moments, then take three steps forward.

He Who makes peace in His heights, may He make peace upon us, and upon all Israel. Now respond: Amen. (Cong.— *Amen.*)

אַשְׁרֵי *Praiseworthy are those who dwell in Your house; may they always praise You, Selah!*[1] *Praiseworthy is the people for whom this is so, praiseworthy is the people whose God is HASHEM.*[2]

Psalm 145 *A psalm of praise by David:*

א *I will exalt You, my God the King,*
and I will bless Your Name forever and ever.
ב *Every day I will bless You,*
and I will laud Your Name forever and ever.
ג *HASHEM is great and exceedingly lauded,*
and His greatness is beyond investigation.
ד *Each generation will praise Your deeds to the next*
and of Your mighty deeds they will tell.
ה *The splendrous glory of Your power*
and Your wondrous deeds I shall discuss.
ו *And of Your awesome power they will speak,*
and Your greatness I shall relate.
ז *A recollection of Your abundant goodness they will utter*
and of Your righteousness they will sing exultantly.
ח *Gracious and merciful is HASHEM,*
slow to anger, and great in [bestowing] kindness.

טוֹב יהוה לַכֹּל, וְרַחֲמָיו עַל כָּל מַעֲשָׂיו.
יוֹדוּךָ יהוה כָּל מַעֲשֶׂיךָ, וַחֲסִידֶיךָ יְבָרְכוּכָה.
כְּבוֹד מַלְכוּתְךָ יֹאמֵרוּ, וּגְבוּרָתְךָ יְדַבֵּרוּ.
לְהוֹדִיעַ לִבְנֵי הָאָדָם גְּבוּרֹתָיו, וּכְבוֹד הֲדַר מַלְכוּתוֹ.
מַלְכוּתְךָ מַלְכוּת כָּל עֹלָמִים, וּמֶמְשַׁלְתְּךָ בְּכָל דּוֹר וָדֹר.
סוֹמֵךְ יהוה לְכָל הַנֹּפְלִים, וְזוֹקֵף לְכָל הַכְּפוּפִים.
עֵינֵי כֹל אֵלֶיךָ יְשַׂבֵּרוּ, וְאַתָּה נוֹתֵן לָהֶם אֶת אָכְלָם בְּעִתּוֹ.
פּוֹתֵחַ אֶת יָדֶךָ,
וּמַשְׂבִּיעַ לְכָל חַי רָצוֹן.

While reciting the verse פּוֹתֵחַ, concentrate intently on its meaning.

צַדִּיק יהוה בְּכָל דְּרָכָיו, וְחָסִיד בְּכָל מַעֲשָׂיו.
קָרוֹב יהוה לְכָל קֹרְאָיו, לְכֹל אֲשֶׁר יִקְרָאֻהוּ בֶאֱמֶת.
רְצוֹן יְרֵאָיו יַעֲשֶׂה, וְאֶת שַׁוְעָתָם יִשְׁמַע וְיוֹשִׁיעֵם.
שׁוֹמֵר יהוה אֶת כָּל אֹהֲבָיו, וְאֵת כָּל הָרְשָׁעִים יַשְׁמִיד.
❖ תְּהִלַּת יהוה יְדַבֶּר פִּי, וִיבָרֵךְ כָּל בָּשָׂר שֵׁם קָדְשׁוֹ לְעוֹלָם וָעֶד.
וַאֲנַחְנוּ נְבָרֵךְ יָהּ, מֵעַתָּה וְעַד עוֹלָם, הַלְלוּיָהּ.[1]

The *chazzan* recites Half-*Kaddish*:

יִתְגַּדַּל וְיִתְקַדַּשׁ שְׁמֵהּ רַבָּא. (Cong. – אָמֵן.) בְּעָלְמָא דִּי בְרָא כִרְעוּתֵהּ. וְיַמְלִיךְ מַלְכוּתֵהּ, בְּחַיֵּיכוֹן וּבְיוֹמֵיכוֹן וּבְחַיֵּי דְכָל בֵּית יִשְׂרָאֵל, בַּעֲגָלָא וּבִזְמַן קָרִיב. וְאִמְרוּ: אָמֵן.

(Cong. – אָמֵן. יְהֵא שְׁמֵהּ רַבָּא מְבָרַךְ לְעָלַם וּלְעָלְמֵי עָלְמַיָּא.)

יְהֵא שְׁמֵהּ רַבָּא מְבָרַךְ לְעָלַם וּלְעָלְמֵי עָלְמַיָּא.

יִתְבָּרַךְ וְיִשְׁתַּבַּח וְיִתְפָּאַר וְיִתְרוֹמַם וְיִתְנַשֵּׂא וְיִתְהַדָּר וְיִתְעַלֶּה וְיִתְהַלָּל שְׁמֵהּ דְּקֻדְשָׁא בְּרִיךְ הוּא (Cong. – בְּרִיךְ הוּא) – לְעֵלָּא מִן כָּל בִּרְכָתָא וְשִׁירָתָא תֻּשְׁבְּחָתָא וְנֶחֱמָתָא, דַּאֲמִירָן בְּעָלְמָא. וְאִמְרוּ: אָמֵן. (Cong. – אָמֵן.)

הוצאת ספר תורה

From the moment the Ark is opened until the Torah is returned to it, one must conduct himself with the utmost respect, and avoid unnecessary conversation. It is commendable to kiss the Torah as it is carried to the *bimah* [reading table] and back to the Ark. All rise and remain standing until the Torah is placed on the *bimah*. The Ark is opened. Before the Torah is removed the congregation recites:

וַיְהִי בִּנְסֹעַ הָאָרֹן וַיֹּאמֶר מֹשֶׁה, קוּמָה יהוה וְיָפֻצוּ אֹיְבֶיךָ וְיָנֻסוּ מְשַׂנְאֶיךָ מִפָּנֶיךָ.[2] כִּי מִצִּיּוֹן תֵּצֵא תוֹרָה, וּדְבַר יהוה מִירוּשָׁלָיִם.[3] בָּרוּךְ שֶׁנָּתַן תּוֹרָה לְעַמּוֹ יִשְׂרָאֵל בִּקְדֻשָּׁתוֹ.

ט *HASHEM is good to all; His mercies are on all His works.*
י *All Your works shall thank You, HASHEM,*
and Your devout ones will bless You.
כ *Of the glory of Your kingdom they will speak,*
and of Your power they will tell;
ל *To inform human beings of His mighty deeds,*
and the glorious splendor of His kingdom.
מ *Your kingdom is a kingdom spanning all eternities,*
and Your dominion is throughout every generation.
ס *HASHEM supports all the fallen ones and straightens all the bent.*
ע *The eyes of all look to You with hope*
and You give them their food in its proper time;
פ *You open Your hand,*
and satisfy the desire of every living thing.

While reciting the verse, *'You open . . .'* concentrate intently on its meaning.

צ *Righteous is HASHEM in all His ways*
and magnanimous in all His deeds.
ק *HASHEM is close to all who call upon Him —*
to all who call upon Him sincerely.
ר *The will of those who fear Him He will do;*
and their cry He will hear, and save them.
ש *HASHEM protects all who love Him; but all the wicked He will destroy.*
ת Chazzan– *May my mouth declare the praise of HASHEM*
and may all flesh bless His Holy Name forever and ever.
We will bless God from this time and forever, Halleluyah![1]

The *chazzan* recites Half-*Kaddish:*

יִתְגַּדַּל *May His great Name grow exalted and sanctified* (Cong.– *Amen.*) *in the world that He created as He willed. May He give reign to His kingship in your lifetimes and in your days, and in the lifetimes of the entire Family of Israel, swiftly and soon. Now respond: Amen.*

(Cong.– *Amen. May His great Name be blessed forever and ever.*)
May His great Name be blessed forever and ever.

Blessed, praised, glorified, exalted, extolled, mighty, upraised, and lauded be the Name of the Holy One, Blessed is He (Cong.– *Blessed is He*) — *beyond any blessing and song, praise and consolation that are uttered in the world. Now respond: Amen.* (Cong.– *Amen.*)

REMOVAL OF THE TORAH FROM THE ARK

From the moment the Ark is opened until the Torah is returned to it, one must conduct himself with the utmost respect, and avoid unnecessary conversation. It is commendable to kiss the Torah as it is carried to the *bimah* [reading table] and back to the Ark. All rise and remain standing until the Torah is placed on the *bimah*. The Ark is opened. Before the Torah is removed the congregation recites:

וַיְהִי בִּנְסֹעַ *When the Ark would travel, Moses would say, 'Arise, HASHEM, and let Your foes be scattered, let those who hate You flee from You.'*[2] *For from Zion the Torah will come forth and the word of HASHEM from Jerusalem.*[3] *Blessed is He Who gave the Torah to His people Israel in His holiness.*

(1) *Psalms* 115:18. (2) *Numbers* 10:35. (3) *Isaiah* 2:3.

זוהר ויקהל שסט:א

בְּרִיךְ שְׁמֵהּ דְּמָרֵא עָלְמָא, בְּרִיךְ כִּתְרָךְ וְאַתְרָךְ. יְהֵא רְעוּתָךְ עִם עַמָּךְ יִשְׂרָאֵל לְעָלַם, וּפֻרְקַן יְמִינָךְ אַחֲזֵי לְעַמָּךְ בְּבֵית מַקְדְּשָׁךְ, וּלְאַמְטוּיֵי לָנָא מִטּוּב נְהוֹרָךְ, וּלְקַבֵּל צְלוֹתָנָא בְּרַחֲמִין. יְהֵא רַעֲוָא קֳדָמָךְ, דְּתוֹרִיךְ לָן חַיִּין בְּטִיבוּתָא, וְלֶהֱוֵי אֲנָא פְקִידָא בְּגוֹ צַדִּיקַיָּא, לְמִרְחַם עָלַי וּלְמִנְטַר יָתִי וְיַת כָּל דִּי לִי, וְדִי לְעַמָּךְ יִשְׂרָאֵל. אַנְתְּ הוּא זָן לְכֹלָּא, וּמְפַרְנֵס לְכֹלָּא, אַנְתְּ הוּא שַׁלִּיט עַל כֹּלָּא. אַנְתְּ הוּא דְשַׁלִּיט עַל מַלְכַיָּא, וּמַלְכוּתָא דִּילָךְ הִיא. אֲנָא עַבְדָּא דְקֻדְשָׁא בְּרִיךְ הוּא, דְּסָגֵידְנָא קַמֵּהּ וּמִקַּמָּא דִּיקַר אוֹרַיְתֵהּ בְּכָל עִדָּן וְעִדָּן. לָא עַל אֱנָשׁ רָחֵיצְנָא, וְלָא עַל בַּר אֱלָהִין סָמֵיכְנָא, אֶלָּא בֶּאֱלָהָא דִשְׁמַיָּא, דְּהוּא אֱלָהָא קְשׁוֹט, וְאוֹרַיְתֵהּ קְשׁוֹט, וּנְבִיאוֹהִי קְשׁוֹט, וּמַסְגֵּא לְמֶעְבַּד טַבְוָן וּקְשׁוֹט. בֵּהּ אֲנָא רָחֵיץ, וְלִשְׁמֵהּ קַדִּישָׁא יַקִּירָא אֲנָא אֵמַר תֻּשְׁבְּחָן. יְהֵא רַעֲוָא קֳדָמָךְ, דְּתִפְתַּח לִבָּאִי בְּאוֹרַיְתָא, וְתַשְׁלִים מִשְׁאֲלִין דְּלִבָּאִי, וְלִבָּא דְכָל עַמָּךְ יִשְׂרָאֵל, לְטַב וּלְחַיִּין וְלִשְׁלָם. (אָמֵן.)

The Torah is removed from the Ark and presented to the *chazzan,* who accepts it in his right arm. He then turns to the Ark, bows while raising the Torah, and recites:

גַּדְּלוּ לַיהוה אִתִּי וּנְרוֹמְמָה שְׁמוֹ יַחְדָּו.[1]

The *chazzan* turns to his right and carries the Torah to the *bimah,* as the congregation responds:

לְךָ יהוה הַגְּדֻלָּה וְהַגְּבוּרָה וְהַתִּפְאֶרֶת וְהַנֵּצַח וְהַהוֹד כִּי כֹל בַּשָּׁמַיִם וּבָאָרֶץ, לְךָ יהוה הַמַּמְלָכָה וְהַמִּתְנַשֵּׂא לְכֹל לְרֹאשׁ.[2] רוֹמְמוּ יהוה אֱלֹהֵינוּ, וְהִשְׁתַּחֲווּ לַהֲדֹם רַגְלָיו, קָדוֹשׁ הוּא. רוֹמְמוּ יהוה אֱלֹהֵינוּ, וְהִשְׁתַּחֲווּ לְהַר קָדְשׁוֹ, כִּי קָדוֹשׁ יהוה אֱלֹהֵינוּ.[3]

אַב הָרַחֲמִים הוּא יְרַחֵם עַם עֲמוּסִים, וְיִזְכֹּר בְּרִית אֵיתָנִים, וְיַצִּיל נַפְשׁוֹתֵינוּ מִן הַשָּׁעוֹת הָרָעוֹת, וְיִגְעַר בְּיֵצֶר הָרָע מִן הַנְּשׂוּאִים, וְיָחֹן אוֹתָנוּ לִפְלֵיטַת עוֹלָמִים, וִימַלֵּא מִשְׁאֲלוֹתֵינוּ בְּמִדָּה טוֹבָה יְשׁוּעָה וְרַחֲמִים.

The Torah is placed on the *bimah* and prepared for reading. The *gabbai* uses the following formula to call a *Kohen* to the Torah:

וְתִגָּלֶה וְתֵרָאֶה מַלְכוּתוֹ עָלֵינוּ בִּזְמַן קָרוֹב, וְיָחֹן פְּלֵיטָתֵנוּ וּפְלֵיטַת עַמּוֹ בֵּית יִשְׂרָאֵל לְחֵן וּלְחֶסֶד וּלְרַחֲמִים וּלְרָצוֹן. וְנֹאמַר אָמֵן. הַכֹּל הָבוּ גֹדֶל לֵאלֹהֵינוּ וּתְנוּ כָבוֹד לַתּוֹרָה. כֹּהֵן° קְרָב, יַעֲמֹד (insert name) הַכֹּהֵן.

°If no *Kohen* is present, the *gabbai* says: „אֵין כָּאן כֹּהֵן, יַעֲמֹד (name) יִשְׂרָאֵל (לֵוִי) בִּמְקוֹם כֹּהֵן.”

Zohar, Vayakhel 369a

בְּרִיךְ שְׁמֵהּ *Blessed is the Name of the Master of the universe, blessed is Your crown and Your place. May Your favor remain with Your people Israel forever; may You display the salvation of Your right hand to Your people in Your Holy Temple, to benefit us with the goodness of Your luminescence and to accept our prayers with mercy. May it be Your will that You extend our lives with goodness and that I be numbered among the righteous; that You have mercy on me and protect me, all that is mine and that is Your people Israel's. It is You Who nourishes all and sustains all; You control everything. It is You Who controls kings, and kingship is Yours. I am a servant of the Holy One, Blessed is He, and I prostrate myself before Him and before the glory of His Torah at all times. Not in any man do I put trust, nor on any angel do I rely — only on the God of heaven Who is the God of truth, Whose Torah is truth and Whose prophets are true and Who acts liberally with kindness and truth. In Him do I trust, and to His glorious and holy Name do I declare praises. May it be Your will that You open my heart to the Torah and that You fulfill the wishes of my heart and the heart of Your entire people Israel for good, for life, and for peace. (Amen.)*

The Torah is removed from the Ark and presented to the *chazzan,* who accepts it in his right arm. He turns to the Ark, bows while raising the Torah, and recites:

Declare the greatness of HASHEM with me, and let us exalt His Name together.[1]

The *chazzan* turns to his right and carries the Torah to the *bimah,* as the congregation responds:

לְךָ *Yours, HASHEM, is the greatness, the strength, the splendor, the triumph, and the glory; even everything in heaven and earth; Yours, HASHEM, is the kingdom, and the sovereignty over every leader.*[2] *Exalt HASHEM, our God, and bow at His footstool; He is Holy! Exalt HASHEM, our God, and bow to His holy mountain; for holy is HASHEM, our God.*[3]

אַב הָרַחֲמִים *May the Father of compassion have mercy on the nation that is borne by Him, and may He remember the covenant of the spiritually mighty. May He rescue our souls from the bad times, and upbraid the evil inclination to leave those borne by Him, graciously make us an eternal remnant, and fulfill our requests in good measure, for salvation and mercy.*

The Torah is placed on the *bimah* and prepared for reading.
The *gabbai* uses the following formula to call a *Kohen* to the Torah:

וְתִגָּלֶה *And may His kingship over us be revealed and become visible soon, and may He be gracious to our remnant and the remnant of His people the Family of Israel, for graciousness, kindness, mercy, and favor. And let us respond, Amen. All of you ascribe greatness to our God and give honor to the Torah. Kohen,°approach. Stand* (name) *son of* (father's name) *the Kohen.*

°If no *Kohen* is present, the *gabbai* says: *'There is no Kohen present, stand* (name) *son of* (father's name) *an Israelite (Levite) in place of the Kohen.'*

---

(1) *Psalms* 34:4. (2) *I Chronicles* 29:11. (3) *Psalms* 99:5,9.

בָּרוּךְ שֶׁנָּתַן תּוֹרָה לְעַמּוֹ יִשְׂרָאֵל בִּקְדֻשָּׁתוֹ. (תּוֹרַת יהוה תְּמִימָה מְשִׁיבַת נָפֶשׁ, עֵדוּת יהוה נֶאֱמָנָה מַחְכִּימַת פֶּתִי. פִּקּוּדֵי יהוה יְשָׁרִים מְשַׂמְּחֵי לֵב, מִצְוַת יהוה בָּרָה מְאִירַת עֵינָיִם.[1] יהוה עֹז לְעַמּוֹ יִתֵּן, יהוה יְבָרֵךְ אֶת עַמּוֹ בַשָּׁלוֹם.[2] הָאֵל תָּמִים דַּרְכּוֹ, אִמְרַת יהוה צְרוּפָה, מָגֵן הוּא לְכֹל הַחוֹסִים בּוֹ.[3])

Congregation, then *gabbai:*

וְאַתֶּם הַדְּבֵקִים בַּיהוה אֱלֹהֵיכֶם, חַיִּים כֻּלְּכֶם הַיּוֹם.[4]

The reader shows the *oleh* (person called to the Torah) the place in the Torah. The *oleh* touches the Torah with a corner of his *tallis,* or the belt or mantle of the Torah, and kisses it. He then begins the blessing, bowing at בָּרְכוּ, and straightening up at 'ה.

בָּרְכוּ אֶת יהוה הַמְּבֹרָךְ.

Congregation, followed by *oleh,* responds, bowing at בָּרוּךְ, and straightening up at 'ה.

בָּרוּךְ יהוה הַמְּבֹרָךְ לְעוֹלָם וָעֶד.

Oleh continues:

בָּרוּךְ אַתָּה יהוה אֱלֹהֵינוּ מֶלֶךְ הָעוֹלָם, אֲשֶׁר בָּחַר בָּנוּ מִכָּל הָעַמִּים, וְנָתַן לָנוּ אֶת תּוֹרָתוֹ. בָּרוּךְ אַתָּה יהוה, נוֹתֵן הַתּוֹרָה. (Cong.– אָמֵן.)

After his Torah portion has been read, the *oleh* recites:

בָּרוּךְ אַתָּה יהוה אֱלֹהֵינוּ מֶלֶךְ הָעוֹלָם, אֲשֶׁר נָתַן לָנוּ תּוֹרַת אֱמֶת, וְחַיֵּי עוֹלָם נָטַע בְּתוֹכֵנוּ. בָּרוּךְ אַתָּה יהוה, נוֹתֵן הַתּוֹרָה. (Cong.– אָמֵן.)

PRAYER FOR A SICK PERSON / מי שברך לחולה

מִי שֶׁבֵּרַךְ אֲבוֹתֵינוּ אַבְרָהָם יִצְחָק וְיַעֲקֹב, מֹשֶׁה אַהֲרֹן דָּוִד וּשְׁלֹמֹה,

for a man

הוּא יְבָרֵךְ וִירַפֵּא אֶת הַחוֹלֶה (patient's name) בֶּן (mother's name) בַּעֲבוּר שֶׁ(supplicant's name) יִתֵּן לִצְדָקָה בַּעֲבוּרוֹ.°° בִּשְׂכַר זֶה, הַקָּדוֹשׁ בָּרוּךְ הוּא יִמָּלֵא רַחֲמִים עָלָיו, לְהַחֲלִימוֹ וּלְרַפֹּאתוֹ לְהַחֲזִיקוֹ וּלְהַחֲיוֹתוֹ, וְיִשְׁלַח לוֹ מְהֵרָה רְפוּאָה שְׁלֵמָה מִן הַשָּׁמַיִם, לִרְמַ״ח אֵבָרָיו, וּשְׁסָ״ה גִּידָיו, בְּתוֹךְ

for a woman

הוּא יְבָרֵךְ וִירַפֵּא אֶת הַחוֹלָה (patient's name) בַּת (mother's name) בַּעֲבוּר שֶׁ(supplicant's name) יִתֵּן לִצְדָקָה בַּעֲבוּרָהּ.°° בִּשְׂכַר זֶה, הַקָּדוֹשׁ בָּרוּךְ הוּא יִמָּלֵא רַחֲמִים עָלֶיהָ, לְהַחֲלִימָהּ וּלְרַפֹּאתָהּ וּלְהַחֲזִיקָהּ וּלְהַחֲיוֹתָהּ, וְיִשְׁלַח לָהּ מְהֵרָה רְפוּאָה שְׁלֵמָה מִן הַשָּׁמַיִם, לְכָל אֵבָרֶיהָ, וּלְכָל גִּידֶיהָ, בְּתוֹךְ

שְׁאָר חוֹלֵי יִשְׂרָאֵל, רְפוּאַת הַנֶּפֶשׁ, וּרְפוּאַת הַגּוּף, הַשְׁתָּא, בַּעֲגָלָא וּבִזְמַן קָרִיב. וְנֹאמַר: אָמֵן. (Cong.– אָמֵן.)

°°Many congregations substitute:

בַּעֲבוּר שֶׁכָּל הַקָּהָל מִתְפַּלְּלִים בַּעֲבוּרוֹ (בַּעֲבוּרָהּ)

Blessed is He Who gave the Torah to His people Israel in His holiness. (The Torah of HASHEM is perfect, restoring the soul; the testimony of HASHEM is trustworthy, making the simple one wise. The orders of HASHEM are upright, gladdening the heart; the command of HASHEM is clear, enlightening the eyes.[1] HASHEM will give might to His nation; HASHEM will bless His nation with peace.[2] The God Whose way is perfect, the promise of HASHEM is flawless, He is a shield for all who take refuge in Him.[3])

Congregation, then *gabbai:*

You who cling to HASHEM, your God, you are all alive today.[4]

The reader shows the *oleh* (person called to the Torah) the place in the Torah. The *oleh* touches the Torah with a corner of his *tallis,* or the belt or mantle of the Torah, and kisses it. He then begins the blessing, bowing at *'Bless,'* and straightening up at 'HASHEM.'

Bless HASHEM, the blessed One.

Congregation, followed by *oleh,* responds, bowing at 'Blessed,' and straightening up at 'HASHEM.'

Blessed is HASHEM, the blessed One, for all eternity.

Oleh continues:

בָּרוּךְ *Blessed are You, HASHEM, our God, King of the universe, Who selected us from all the peoples and gave us His Torah. Blessed are You, HASHEM, Giver of the Torah.* (Cong.– *Amen.*)

After his Torah portion has been read, the *oleh* recites:

בָּרוּךְ *Blessed are You, HASHEM, our God, King of the universe, Who gave us the Torah of truth and implanted eternal life within us. Blessed are You, HASHEM, Giver of the Torah.* (Cong.– *Amen.*)

PRAYER FOR A SICK PERSON

מִי שֶׁבֵּרַךְ *He Who blessed our forefathers Abraham, Isaac and Jacob, Moses and Aaron, David and Solomon — may He bless and heal the sick person (* patient's Hebrew name*) son/daughter of (* patient's mother's Hebrew name*) because (* name of supplicant*) will contribute to charity on his/her behalf.°° In reward for this, may the Holy One, Blessed is He, be filled with*

for a man

compassion for him to restore his health, to heal him, to strengthen him, and to revivify him. And may He send him speedily a complete recovery from heaven for his two hundred forty-eight organs and three hundred sixty-five blood vessels, among the other

for a woman

compassion for her to restore her health, to heal her, to strengthen her, and to revivify her. And may He send her speedily a complete recovery from heaven for all her organs and all her blood vessels, among the other

sick people of Israel, a recovery of the body and a recovery of the spirit, may a recovery come speedily, swiftly and soon. Now let us respond: Amen.

(Cong.—*Amen.*)

°°Many congregations substitute:

because the entire congregation prays for him (her)

(1) *Psalms* 19:8-9. (2) 29:11. (3) 18:31. (4) *Deuteronomy* 4:4.

❧ קריאת התורה ❧

שמות לב:יא-יד; לד:א-י

Upon reaching the phrases in bold type, the reader pauses.
The congregation recites the phrases, after which they are recited by the reader.

כהן – וַיְחַ֣ל מֹשֶׁ֔ה אֶת־פְּנֵ֖י יהו֣ה אֱלֹהָ֑יו וַיֹּ֗אמֶר לָמָ֤ה יהוה֙ יֶחֱרֶ֤ה אַפְּךָ֙ בְּעַמֶּ֔ךָ אֲשֶׁ֤ר הוֹצֵ֙אתָ֙ מֵאֶ֣רֶץ מִצְרַ֔יִם בְּכֹ֥חַ גָּד֖וֹל וּבְיָ֥ד חֲזָקָֽה: לָ֣מָּה יֹאמְר֣וּ מִצְרַ֗יִם לֵאמֹ֗ר בְּרָעָ֤ה הֽוֹצִיאָם֙ לַהֲרֹ֤ג אֹתָם֙ בֶּֽהָרִ֔ים וּ֨לְכַלֹּתָ֔ם מֵעַ֖ל פְּנֵ֣י הָֽאֲדָמָ֑ה שׁ֚וּב מֵחֲר֣וֹן אַפֶּ֔ךָ **וְהִנָּחֵ֥ם עַל־הָרָעָ֖ה לְעַמֶּֽךָ:** זְכֹ֡ר לְאַבְרָהָם֩ לְיִצְחָ֨ק וּלְיִשְׂרָאֵ֜ל עֲבָדֶ֗יךָ אֲשֶׁ֨ר נִשְׁבַּ֜עְתָּ לָהֶם֮ בָּךְ֒ וַתְּדַבֵּ֣ר אֲלֵהֶ֔ם אַרְבֶּה֙ אֶֽת־זַרְעֲכֶ֔ם כְּכוֹכְבֵ֖י הַשָּׁמָ֑יִם וְכָל־הָאָ֣רֶץ הַזֹּ֗את אֲשֶׁ֤ר אָמַ֙רְתִּי֙ אֶתֵּ֣ן לְזַרְעֲכֶ֔ם וְנָחֲל֖וּ לְעֹלָֽם: וַיִּנָּ֖חֶם יהו֑ה עַל־הָ֣רָעָ֔ה אֲשֶׁ֥ר דִּבֶּ֖ר לַעֲשׂ֥וֹת לְעַמּֽוֹ:

לוי – וַיֹּ֤אמֶר יהוה֙ אֶל־מֹשֶׁ֔ה פְּסָל־לְךָ֛ שְׁנֵֽי־לֻחֹ֥ת אֲבָנִ֖ים כָּרִֽאשֹׁנִ֑ים וְכָתַבְתִּי֙ עַל־הַלֻּחֹ֔ת אֶת־הַ֨דְּבָרִ֔ים אֲשֶׁ֥ר הָי֛וּ עַל־הַלֻּחֹ֥ת הָרִֽאשֹׁנִ֖ים אֲשֶׁ֥ר שִׁבַּֽרְתָּ: וֶהְיֵ֥ה נָכ֖וֹן לַבֹּ֑קֶר וְעָלִ֤יתָ בַבֹּ֙קֶר֙ אֶל־הַ֣ר סִינַ֔י וְנִצַּבְתָּ֥ לִ֛י שָׁ֖ם עַל־רֹ֥אשׁ הָהָֽר: וְאִישׁ֙ לֹא־יַעֲלֶ֣ה עִמָּ֔ךְ וְגַם־אִ֥ישׁ אַל־יֵרָ֖א בְּכָל־הָהָ֑ר גַּם־הַצֹּ֤אן וְהַבָּקָר֙ אַל־יִרְע֔וּ אֶל־מ֖וּל הָהָ֥ר הַהֽוּא:

מפטיר – וַיִּפְסֹ֡ל שְׁנֵֽי־לֻחֹ֨ת אֲבָנִ֜ים כָּרִֽאשֹׁנִ֗ים וַיַּשְׁכֵּ֨ם מֹשֶׁ֤ה בַבֹּ֙קֶר֙ וַיַּ֙עַל֙ אֶל־הַ֣ר סִינַ֔י כַּאֲשֶׁ֛ר צִוָּ֥ה יהו֖ה אֹת֑וֹ וַיִּקַּ֣ח בְּיָד֔וֹ שְׁנֵ֖י לֻחֹ֥ת אֲבָנִֽים: וַיֵּ֤רֶד יהוה֙ בֶּֽעָנָ֔ן וַיִּתְיַצֵּ֥ב עִמּ֖וֹ שָׁ֑ם וַיִּקְרָ֥א בְשֵׁ֖ם יהוֽה: וַיַּעֲבֹ֨ר יהו֥ה ׀ עַל־פָּנָיו֮ וַיִּקְרָא֒ **יהו֣ה ׀ יהו֔ה אֵ֥ל רַח֖וּם וְחַנּ֑וּן אֶ֥רֶךְ אַפַּ֖יִם וְרַב־חֶ֥סֶד וֶאֱמֶֽת: נֹצֵ֥ר חֶ֙סֶד֙ לָאֲלָפִ֔ים נֹשֵׂ֥א עָוֹ֛ן וָפֶ֖שַׁע וְחַטָּאָ֑ה וְנַקֵּה֙ לֹ֣א יְנַקֶּ֔ה** פֹּקֵ֣ד ׀ עֲוֹ֣ן אָב֗וֹת עַל־בָּנִים֙ וְעַל־בְּנֵ֣י בָנִ֔ים עַל־שִׁלֵּשִׁ֖ים וְעַל־רִבֵּעִֽים: וַיְמַהֵ֖ר מֹשֶׁ֑ה וַיִּקֹּ֥ד אַ֖רְצָה וַיִּשְׁתָּֽחוּ: וַיֹּ֡אמֶר אִם־נָא֩ מָצָ֨אתִי חֵ֤ן בְּעֵינֶ֙יךָ֙ אֲדֹנָ֔י יֵֽלֶךְ־נָ֥א אֲדֹנָ֖י בְּקִרְבֵּ֑נוּ כִּ֤י עַם־קְשֵׁה־עֹ֙רֶף֙ ה֔וּא **וְסָלַחְתָּ֛ לַעֲוֹנֵ֥נוּ וּלְחַטָּאתֵ֖נוּ וּנְחַלְתָּֽנוּ:** וַיֹּ֗אמֶר הִנֵּ֣ה אָנֹכִי֮ כֹּרֵ֣ת בְּרִית֒ נֶ֤גֶד כָּֽל־עַמְּךָ֙ אֶעֱשֶׂ֣ה נִפְלָאֹ֔ת אֲשֶׁ֛ר לֹֽא־נִבְרְא֥וּ בְכָל־הָאָ֖רֶץ וּבְכָל־הַגּוֹיִ֑ם וְרָאָ֣ה כָל־הָ֠עָם אֲשֶׁר־אַתָּ֨ה בְקִרְבּ֜וֹ אֶת־מַעֲשֵׂ֤ה יהוה֙ כִּֽי־נוֹרָ֣א ה֔וּא אֲשֶׁ֥ר אֲנִ֖י עֹשֶׂ֥ה עִמָּֽךְ:

◆§ Torah Reading

The afternoon Torah reading for Tishah B'Av is the same as that read on the other fast days. Rather than an admonition that outlines the national weaknesses that cause the sorts of tragedy commemorated by the fast day, this reading might be described as an 'antidote' to the calamity.

TORAH READING

Exodus 32:11-14; 34:1-10

Kohen – *Moses prayed before* HASHEM, *his God, and he said, "Why,* HASHEM, *shall Your wrath burn against Your people, whom You have taken out of Egypt with great might and with a strong hand? Why should Egypt say as follows, 'Under an evil fate did He take them out to kill them in the mountains and to exterminate them from upon the face of the earth?' Turn back from Your burning wrath and relent from this evil to Your people. Remember for the sake of Abraham, Isaac, and Jacob, Your servants, what You swore to them by Your Person, and You spoke to them, 'I shall multiply your offspring like the stars of heaven, and this entire land of which I spoke I shall give to your offspring, and they shall have it as a heritage forever.'"*

HASHEM *relented over the evil that He had said He would do to His people.*

Levi – HASHEM *said to Moses, 'Carve for yourself two stone tablets like the first ones, and I shall write upon the tablets the words that were on the first tablets, which you smashed. And be ready in the morning; you shall ascend in the morning to Mount Sinai and stand before Me there on the mountaintop. No man shall ascend with you, nor shall any man be seen on the entire mountain, even the sheep and cattle shall not graze opposite that mountain.'*

Maftir – *He carved two stone tablets like the first ones; and Moses arose early in the morning and ascended Mount Sinai, as* HASHEM *had commanded him; and in his hand he took two stone tablets.* HASHEM *descended in a cloud and stood there with him, and He called out with the Name* HASHEM. *And* HASHEM *passed before him and proclaimed, '*HASHEM, HASHEM, *God, Compassionate and Gracious, Slow to anger, and Abundant in Kindness and Truth. Preserver of kindness for thousands of generations, Forgiver of iniquity, willful sin, and error; and Cleanses but does not cleanse [entirely], remembering the iniquity of parents upon children and grandchildren to the third and fourth generations.'*

Moses hastened and bowed his head and prostrated himself. He said, 'If I have now found favor in Your eyes, my Lord, may my Lord go among us, for it is a stiff-necked people. May You forgive our iniquities and our errors and make us Your heritage.'

He said, 'Behold! I seal a covenant: Before all your people I shall perform such wonders as have never been created in all the world or in any nation; and the entire people in whose midst you are will recognize the handiwork of HASHEM *that it is awesome, that I perform with you.'*

While Moses was on Mount Sinai receiving the Torah and the Tablets of the Law, his people in the Wilderness were making the Golden Calf and giving it their allegiance. God told Moses that the purpose of his mission no longer existed; he was the representative of Israel, but his nation had betrayed God. He told Moses that He would destroy the nation, and begin anew with Moses and his offspring. But in making this chilling declaration to Moses, God asked Moses to 'permit Him' to do so — this implied that Moses could prevent the destruction of Israel (see *Rashi*

הגבהה וגלילה

The Torah Scroll is raised and each person looks at the Torah and recites aloud:

וְזֹאת הַתּוֹרָה אֲשֶׁר שָׂם מֹשֶׁה לִפְנֵי בְּנֵי יִשְׂרָאֵל,[1] עַל פִּי יהוה בְּיַד מֹשֶׁה.[2]

Some add:

עֵץ חַיִּים הִיא לַמַּחֲזִיקִים בָּהּ, וְתֹמְכֶיהָ מְאֻשָּׁר.[3] דְּרָכֶיהָ דַרְכֵי נֹעַם, וְכָל נְתִיבוֹתֶיהָ שָׁלוֹם.[4] אֹרֶךְ יָמִים בִּימִינָהּ, בִּשְׂמֹאלָהּ עֹשֶׁר וְכָבוֹד.[5] יהוה חָפֵץ לְמַעַן צִדְקוֹ, יַגְדִּיל תּוֹרָה וְיַאְדִּיר.[6]

After the Torah Scroll has been wound, tied and covered, he *maftir* recites the *Haftarah* blessings.

ברכה קודם ההפטרה

בָּרוּךְ אַתָּה יהוה אֱלֹהֵינוּ מֶלֶךְ הָעוֹלָם, אֲשֶׁר בָּחַר בִּנְבִיאִים טוֹבִים, וְרָצָה בְדִבְרֵיהֶם הַנֶּאֱמָרִים בֶּאֱמֶת, בָּרוּךְ אַתָּה יהוה, הַבּוֹחֵר בַּתּוֹרָה וּבְמֹשֶׁה עַבְדּוֹ, וּבְיִשְׂרָאֵל עַמּוֹ, וּבִנְבִיאֵי הָאֱמֶת וָצֶדֶק: (Cong. – אָמֵן.)

הפטרה

ישעיה נה:ו-נו:ח

[Although the Divine Name יהוה is pronounced as if it were spelled אֲדֹנָי, when it is vowelized יֱהֹוִה, it is pronounced as if it were spelled אֱלֹהִים.]

דִּרְשׁוּ יהוה בְּהִמָּצְאוֹ קְרָאֻהוּ בִּהְיוֹתוֹ קָרוֹב: יַעֲזֹב רָשָׁע דַּרְכּוֹ וְאִישׁ אָוֶן מַחְשְׁבֹתָיו וְיָשֹׁב אֶל־יהוה וִירַחֲמֵהוּ וְאֶל־אֱלֹהֵינוּ כִּי־יַרְבֶּה לִסְלוֹחַ: כִּי לֹא מַחְשְׁבוֹתַי מַחְשְׁבוֹתֵיכֶם וְלֹא דַרְכֵיכֶם דְּרָכָי נְאֻם יהוה: כִּי־גָבְהוּ שָׁמַיִם מֵאָרֶץ כֵּן גָּבְהוּ דְרָכַי מִדַּרְכֵיכֶם וּמַחְשְׁבֹתַי מִמַּחְשְׁבֹתֵיכֶם: כִּי כַּאֲשֶׁר יֵרֵד הַגֶּשֶׁם וְהַשֶּׁלֶג מִן־הַשָּׁמַיִם וְשָׁמָּה לֹא יָשׁוּב כִּי אִם־הִרְוָה אֶת־הָאָרֶץ וְהוֹלִידָהּ וְהִצְמִיחָהּ וְנָתַן זֶרַע לַזֹּרֵעַ וְלֶחֶם לָאֹכֵל: כֵּן יִהְיֶה דְבָרִי אֲשֶׁר יֵצֵא מִפִּי לֹא־יָשׁוּב אֵלַי רֵיקָם כִּי אִם־עָשָׂה אֶת־אֲשֶׁר חָפַצְתִּי וְהִצְלִיחַ אֲשֶׁר שְׁלַחְתִּיו: כִּי־בְשִׂמְחָה תֵצֵאוּ וּבְשָׁלוֹם תּוּבָלוּן הֶהָרִים וְהַגְּבָעוֹת יִפְצְחוּ לִפְנֵיכֶם רִנָּה וְכָל־עֲצֵי הַשָּׂדֶה יִמְחֲאוּ־כָף:

---

to *Exodus* 32:10). From this, Moses understood that his prayers could save Israel, and he immediately begged God to spare them.

The first portion of this reading is his prayer on the mountain; after returning to the camp, he smashed the Tablets and took charge of a mass repentance, which made Israel worthy to receive the Second Tablets. The rest of the reading skips to God's command that Moses fashion a pair of tablets, upon which God would inscribe the Ten Commandments a second time. In the context of the fast days, the significance of the passage is that in it God taught Moses the Thirteen Attributes of Mercy, which are now the central theme of the fast-day *Selichos* (except for Tishah B'Av) and of the evening and *Neilah* services of Yom Kippur. According to R' Yochanan (*Rosh Hashana* 17b), Moses thought that Israel's sin was so grievous that there was no possibility for him to intercede on their behalf. Thereupon God appeared to him in the form of a *chazzan* wrapped in a *tallis* and taught him the Thirteen Attributes. God said, 'Whenever Israel sins, let them recite this in its proper order and I shall

HAGBAHAH AND GELILAH

The Torah Scroll is raised and each person looks at the Torah and recites aloud:

This is the Torah that Moses placed before the Children of Israel,[1] upon the command of HASHEM, through Moses' hand.[2]

Some add:

עֵץ *It is a tree of life for those who grasp it, and its supporters are praiseworthy.[3] Its ways are ways of pleasantness and all its paths are peace.[4] Lengthy days are at its right; at its left are wealth and honor.[5] HASHEM desired, for the sake of its [Israel's] righteousness, that the Torah be made great and glorious.[6]*

After the Torah Scroll has been wound, tied and covered, the *maftir* recites the *Haftarah* blessings.

BLESSING BEFORE THE HAFTARAH

בָּרוּךְ *Blessed are You, HASHEM, our God, King of the universe, Who has chosen good prophets and was pleased with their words that were uttered with truth. Blessed are You, HASHEM, Who chooses the Torah; Moses, His servant; Israel, His nation; and the prophets of truth and righteousness.* (Cong.— *Amen.*)

HAFTARAH

Isaiah 55:6-56:8

Seek HASHEM when He can be found; call Him when He is near. Let the wicked one forsake his way and the iniquitous man his thoughts; and let him return to HASHEM and He will show him mercy, to our God for He will be abundantly forgiving. For My thoughts are not your thoughts, and your ways are not My ways, the words of HASHEM. As high as the heavens over the earth, so are My ways higher than your ways, and My thoughts than your thoughts. For just as the rain and snow descend from heaven and will not return there, but it waters the earth and causes it to produce and sprout, and gives seed to the sower and food to the eater; so shall be My word that emanates from My mouth, it shall not return to Me unfulfilled unless it will have accomplished what I desired and brought success where I sent it. For in gladness shall you go out and in peace shall you arrive, the mountains and hills will break out in glad song before you, and all the trees of the field will clap hands.

(1) *Deuteronomy* 4:44. (2) *Numbers* 9:23. (3) *Proverbs* 3:18. (4) 3:17. (5) 3:16. (6) *Isaiah* 42:21.

forgive them.' Thus the appeal found in this Torah reading reassures us that repentance is always possible and that God always awaits our return.

Since it is axiomatic that punishment and exile are always the result of Jewish shortcomings, and as Rambam teaches, we fast to remind ourselves that no Jewish suffering is coincidental, this Torah reading teaches us the way to curtail the suffering and end the exile.

◈ The Haftarah

As noted above, fast days represent a call to repentance and the Torah reading is the encouraging message that God is always ready — indeed, anxious — to accept our prayers. The Haftarah is an eloquent expression of that theme. It begins by urging us to seek God where He can be found and when He is near. The commentators explain that these times are before He brings punishment upon us, for then He longs for us to repent and thereby remove the root of His anger; and they are also times when we are ready to seek Him with all our hearts.

God declares that we should not project our own base, human frailties onto our perceptions of Him. God is merciful. He guarantees us that everyone who is sincere and ready to serve Him wholeheartedly has a place at His table. Even those who are barren — literally or figuratively — will blossom if they join themselves to Him. The aliens who leave their origins to become Jews

תַּ֤חַת הַנַּֽעֲצוּץ֙ יַעֲלֶ֣ה בְר֔וֹשׁ וְתַ֥חַת הַסִּרְפַּ֖ד יַעֲלֶ֣ה הֲדַ֑ס וְהָיָ֤ה לַֽיהוה֙ לְשֵׁ֔ם לְא֥וֹת עוֹלָ֖ם לֹ֥א יִכָּרֵֽת׃ כֹּ֚ה אָמַ֣ר יהוה שִׁמְר֥וּ מִשְׁפָּ֖ט וַעֲשׂ֣וּ צְדָקָ֑ה כִּֽי־קְרוֹבָ֤ה יְשֽׁוּעָתִי֙ לָב֔וֹא וְצִדְקָתִ֖י לְהִגָּלֽוֹת׃ אַשְׁרֵ֤י אֱנוֹשׁ֙ יַעֲשֶׂה־זֹּ֔את וּבֶן־אָדָ֖ם יַחֲזִ֣יק בָּ֑הּ שֹׁמֵ֤ר שַׁבָּת֙ מֵֽחַלְּל֔וֹ וְשֹׁמֵ֥ר יָד֖וֹ מֵעֲשׂ֥וֹת כָּל־רָֽע׃ וְאַל־יֹאמַ֣ר בֶּן־הַנֵּכָ֗ר הַנִּלְוָ֤ה אֶל־יהוה֙ לֵאמֹ֔ר הַבְדֵּ֧ל יַבְדִּילַ֛נִי יהוה מֵעַ֣ל עַמּ֑וֹ וְאַל־יֹאמַר֙ הַסָּרִ֔יס הֵ֥ן אֲנִ֖י עֵ֥ץ יָבֵֽשׁ׃ כִּי־כֹ֣ה ׀ אָמַ֣ר יהוה לַסָּֽרִיסִים֙ אֲשֶׁ֤ר יִשְׁמְרוּ֙ אֶת־שַׁבְּתוֹתַ֔י וּבָֽחֲר֖וּ בַּאֲשֶׁ֣ר חָפָ֑צְתִּי וּמַחֲזִיקִ֖ים בִּבְרִיתִֽי׃ וְנָתַתִּ֨י לָהֶ֜ם בְּבֵיתִ֤י וּבְחוֹמֹתַי֙ יָ֣ד וָשֵׁ֔ם ט֖וֹב מִבָּנִ֣ים וּמִבָּנ֑וֹת שֵׁ֤ם עוֹלָם֙ אֶתֶּן־ל֔וֹ אֲשֶׁ֖ר לֹ֥א יִכָּרֵֽת׃ וּבְנֵ֣י הַנֵּכָ֗ר הַנִּלְוִ֤ים עַל־יהוה֙ לְשָׁ֣רְת֔וֹ וּֽלְאַהֲבָה֙ אֶת־שֵׁ֣ם יהוה לִהְי֥וֹת ל֖וֹ לַעֲבָדִ֑ים כָּל־שֹׁמֵ֤ר שַׁבָּת֙ מֵֽחַלְּל֔וֹ וּמַחֲזִיקִ֖ים בִּבְרִיתִֽי׃ וַהֲבִיאוֹתִ֞ים אֶל־הַ֣ר קָדְשִׁ֗י וְשִׂמַּחְתִּים֙ בְּבֵ֣ית תְּפִלָּתִ֔י עוֹלֹתֵיהֶ֧ם וְזִבְחֵיהֶ֛ם לְרָצ֖וֹן עַל־מִזְבְּחִ֑י כִּ֣י בֵיתִ֔י בֵּית־תְּפִלָּ֥ה יִקָּרֵ֖א לְכָל־הָעַמִּֽים׃ נְאֻם֙ אֲדֹנָ֣י יֱהֹוִ֔ה מְקַבֵּ֖ץ נִדְחֵ֣י יִשְׂרָאֵ֑ל ע֛וֹד אֲקַבֵּ֥ץ עָלָ֖יו לְנִקְבָּצָֽיו׃

ברכות לאחר ההפטרה

After the *Haftarah* is read, the *oleh* recites the following blessings.

בָּרוּךְ אַתָּה יהוה אֱלֹהֵינוּ מֶלֶךְ הָעוֹלָם, צוּר כָּל הָעוֹלָמִים, צַדִּיק בְּכָל הַדּוֹרוֹת, הָאֵל הַנֶּאֱמָן הָאוֹמֵר וְעֹשֶׂה, הַמְּדַבֵּר וּמְקַיֵּם, שֶׁכָּל דְּבָרָיו אֱמֶת וָצֶדֶק. נֶאֱמָן אַתָּה הוּא יהוה אֱלֹהֵינוּ, וְנֶאֱמָנִים דְּבָרֶיךָ, וְדָבָר אֶחָד מִדְּבָרֶיךָ אָחוֹר לֹא יָשׁוּב רֵיקָם, כִּי אֵל מֶלֶךְ נֶאֱמָן (וְרַחֲמָן) אָתָּה. בָּרוּךְ אַתָּה יהוה, הָאֵל הַנֶּאֱמָן בְּכָל דְּבָרָיו.

(Cong. – אָמֵן.)

רַחֵם עַל צִיּוֹן כִּי הִיא בֵּית חַיֵּינוּ, וְלַעֲלוּבַת נֶפֶשׁ תּוֹשִׁיעַ בִּמְהֵרָה בְיָמֵינוּ. בָּרוּךְ אַתָּה יהוה, מְשַׂמֵּחַ צִיּוֹן בְּבָנֶיהָ.

(Cong. – אָמֵן.)

שַׂמְּחֵנוּ יהוה אֱלֹהֵינוּ בְּאֵלִיָּהוּ הַנָּבִיא עַבְדֶּךָ, וּבְמַלְכוּת בֵּית דָּוִד מְשִׁיחֶךָ, בִּמְהֵרָה יָבֹא וְיָגֵל לִבֵּנוּ, עַל כִּסְאוֹ לֹא יֵשֶׁב זָר וְלֹא יִנְחֲלוּ עוֹד אֲחֵרִים אֶת כְּבוֹדוֹ, כִּי בְשֵׁם קָדְשְׁךָ נִשְׁבַּעְתָּ לּוֹ, שֶׁלֹּא יִכְבֶּה נֵרוֹ לְעוֹלָם וָעֶד. בָּרוּךְ אַתָּה יהוה, מָגֵן דָּוִד.

(Cong. – אָמֵן.)

In place of the thorn-bush, a cypress will rise; and in place of the nettle, a myrtle will rise. This will be a monument to HASHEM, *an eternal sign never to be cut down.*

So said HASHEM: *Observe justice and perform righteousness, for My salvation is at hand to come and My righteousness to be revealed. Praiseworthy is the man who does this and the son of man who grasps it tightly: Whoever guards the Sabbath against desecration and guards his hand against doing any evil.*

Let not the alien, who has joined himself to HASHEM, *say: '*HASHEM *shall utterly separate me from His people;' and let not the barren one say: 'Behold I am a shriveled tree.' For so says* HASHEM *to the barren ones who observe My Sabbaths and choose what I desire, and grasp My covenant tightly. In My House and within My walls I shall give them a place and renown, better than sons and daughters; eternal renown shall I give them, never to be cut down; and the aliens who join* HASHEM *to serve Him and to love the Name of* HASHEM *to become His servants, whoever guards the Sabbath against desecration and grasps My covenant tightly — I shall bring them to My holy mountain, and I shall gladden them in My house of prayer, their elevation-offerings and their feast-offerings will find favor on My Altar, for My House shall be a house of prayer for all the peoples.*

The words of my Lord, HASHEM/ELOHIM, *Who gathers in the dispersed of Israel, 'I shall gather to him even more than those already gathered.'*

BLESSINGS AFTER THE HAFTARAH

After the *Haftarah* is read, the *oleh* recites the following blessings.

בָּרוּךְ *Blessed are You,* HASHEM, *King of the universe, Rock of all eternities, Righteous in all generations, the trustworthy God, Who says and does, Who speaks and fulfills, all of Whose words are true and righteous. Trustworthy are You,* HASHEM, *our God, and trustworthy are Your words, not one of Your words is turned back to its origin unfulfilled, for You are God, trustworthy (and compassionate) King. Blessed are You,* HASHEM, *the God Who is trustworthy in all His words.* (Cong.– *Amen.*)

רַחֵם *Have mercy on Zion for it is the source of our life; to the one who is deeply humiliated bring salvation speedily, in our days. Blessed are You,* HASHEM, *Who gladdens Zion through her children.*

(Cong.– *Amen.*)

שַׂמְּחֵנוּ *Gladden us,* HASHEM, *our God, with Elijah the prophet, Your servant, and with the kingdom of the House of David, Your anointed, may he come speedily and cause our heart to exult. On his throne let no stranger sit nor let others continue to inherit his honor, for by Your holy Name You swore to him that his heir will not be extinguished forever and ever. Blessed are You,* HASHEM, *Shield of David.*

(Cong.– *Amen.*)

---

are no longer aliens. To the contrary, they will be the forerunners of the masses who will flock to the truth when the time of redemption finally arrives.

הכנסת ספר תורה

Chazzan takes the Torah in his right arm and recites:

יְהַלְלוּ אֶת שֵׁם יהוה, כִּי נִשְׂגָּב שְׁמוֹ לְבַדּוֹ –

Congregation responds:

– הוֹדוֹ עַל אֶרֶץ וְשָׁמָיִם. וַיָּרֶם קֶרֶן לְעַמּוֹ, תְּהִלָּה לְכָל חֲסִידָיו, לִבְנֵי יִשְׂרָאֵל עַם קְרֹבוֹ, הַלְלוּיָהּ.[1]

As the Torah is carried to the Ark, congregation recites Psalm 24, לְדָוִד מִזְמוֹר.

לְדָוִד מִזְמוֹר, לַיהוה הָאָרֶץ וּמְלוֹאָהּ, תֵּבֵל וְיֹשְׁבֵי בָהּ. כִּי הוּא עַל יַמִּים יְסָדָהּ, וְעַל נְהָרוֹת יְכוֹנְנֶהָ. מִי יַעֲלֶה בְהַר יהוה, וּמִי יָקוּם בִּמְקוֹם קָדְשׁוֹ. נְקִי כַפַּיִם וּבַר לֵבָב, אֲשֶׁר לֹא נָשָׂא לַשָּׁוְא נַפְשִׁי וְלֹא נִשְׁבַּע לְמִרְמָה. יִשָּׂא בְרָכָה מֵאֵת יהוה, וּצְדָקָה מֵאֱלֹהֵי יִשְׁעוֹ. זֶה דּוֹר דֹּרְשָׁיו, מְבַקְשֵׁי פָנֶיךָ, יַעֲקֹב, סֶלָה. שְׂאוּ שְׁעָרִים רָאשֵׁיכֶם, וְהִנָּשְׂאוּ פִּתְחֵי עוֹלָם, וְיָבוֹא מֶלֶךְ הַכָּבוֹד. מִי זֶה מֶלֶךְ הַכָּבוֹד, יהוה עִזּוּז וְגִבּוֹר, יהוה גִּבּוֹר מִלְחָמָה. שְׂאוּ שְׁעָרִים רָאשֵׁיכֶם, וּשְׂאוּ פִּתְחֵי עוֹלָם, וְיָבֹא מֶלֶךְ הַכָּבוֹד. מִי הוּא זֶה מֶלֶךְ הַכָּבוֹד, יהוה צְבָאוֹת הוּא מֶלֶךְ הַכָּבוֹד, סֶלָה.

As the Torah is placed into the Ark, congregation recites the following verses:

וּבְנֻחֹה יֹאמַר, שׁוּבָה יהוה רִבְבוֹת אַלְפֵי יִשְׂרָאֵל.[2] קוּמָה יהוה לִמְנוּחָתֶךָ, אַתָּה וַאֲרוֹן עֻזֶּךָ. כֹּהֲנֶיךָ יִלְבְּשׁוּ צֶדֶק, וַחֲסִידֶיךָ יְרַנֵּנוּ. בַּעֲבוּר דָּוִד עַבְדֶּךָ אַל תָּשֵׁב פְּנֵי מְשִׁיחֶךָ.[3] כִּי לֶקַח טוֹב נָתַתִּי לָכֶם, תּוֹרָתִי אַל תַּעֲזֹבוּ.[4] ❖ עֵץ חַיִּים הִיא לַמַּחֲזִיקִים בָּהּ, וְתֹמְכֶיהָ מְאֻשָּׁר.[5] דְּרָכֶיהָ דַרְכֵי נֹעַם, וְכָל נְתִיבֹתֶיהָ שָׁלוֹם.[6] הֲשִׁיבֵנוּ יהוה אֵלֶיךָ וְנָשׁוּבָה, חַדֵּשׁ יָמֵינוּ כְּקֶדֶם.[7]

חצי קדיש

The Ark is closed and the *chazzan* recites חֲצִי קַדִּישׁ.

יִתְגַּדַּל וְיִתְקַדַּשׁ שְׁמֵהּ רַבָּא. (–Cong. אָמֵן.) בְּעָלְמָא דִּי בְרָא כִרְעוּתֵהּ. וְיַמְלִיךְ מַלְכוּתֵהּ, בְּחַיֵּיכוֹן וּבְיוֹמֵיכוֹן וּבְחַיֵּי דְכָל בֵּית יִשְׂרָאֵל, בַּעֲגָלָא וּבִזְמַן קָרִיב. וְאִמְרוּ: אָמֵן.

(–Cong. אָמֵן. יְהֵא שְׁמֵהּ רַבָּא מְבָרַךְ לְעָלַם וּלְעָלְמֵי עָלְמַיָּא.)

יְהֵא שְׁמֵהּ רַבָּא מְבָרַךְ לְעָלַם וּלְעָלְמֵי עָלְמַיָּא.

יִתְבָּרַךְ וְיִשְׁתַּבַּח וְיִתְפָּאַר וְיִתְרוֹמַם וְיִתְנַשֵּׂא וְיִתְהַדָּר וְיִתְעַלֶּה וְיִתְהַלָּל שְׁמֵהּ דְּקֻדְשָׁא בְּרִיךְ הוּא (–Cong. בְּרִיךְ הוּא) – לְעֵלָּא מִן כָּל בִּרְכָתָא וְשִׁירָתָא תֻּשְׁבְּחָתָא וְנֶחֱמָתָא, דַּאֲמִירָן בְּעָלְמָא. וְאִמְרוּ: אָמֵן. (–Cong. אָמֵן.)

(1) *Psalms* 148:13-14. (2) *Numbers* 10:36. (3) *Psalms* 132:8-10.
(4) *Proverbs* 4:2. (5) 3:18. (6) 3:17. (7) *Lamentations* 5:21.

RETURNING THE TORAH

Chazzan takes the Torah in his right arm and recites:

Let them praise the Name of HASHEM, for His Name alone will have been exalted –

Congregation responds:

— His glory is above earth and heaven. And He will have exalted the pride of His people, causing praise for all His devout ones, for the Children of Israel, His intimate nation. Halleluyah![1]

As the Torah is carried to the Ark, congregation recites Psalm 24, *'Of David a psalm.'*

לְדָוִד *Of David a psalm.* HASHEM*'s is the earth and its fullness, the inhabited land and those who dwell in it. For He founded it upon seas, and established it upon rivers. Who may ascend the mountain of* HASHEM, *and who may stand in the place of His sanctity? One with clean hands and pure heart, who has not sworn in vain by My soul and has not sworn deceitfully. He will receive a blessing from* HASHEM *and just kindness from the God of his salvation. This is the generation of those who seek Him, those who strive for Your Presence — Jacob, Selah. Raise up your heads, O gates, and be uplifted, you everlasting entrances, so that the King of Glory may enter. Who is this King of Glory? —* HASHEM, *the mighty and strong,* HASHEM, *the strong in battle. Raise up your heads, O gates, and raise up, you everlasting entrances, so that the King of Glory may enter. Who then is the King of Glory?* HASHEM, *Master of Legions, He is the King of Glory. Selah!*

As the Torah is placed into the Ark, congregation recites the following verses:

וּבְנֻחֹה *And when it rested he would say, 'Return,* HASHEM, *to the myriad thousands of Israel.'[2] Arise,* HASHEM, *to Your resting place, You and the Ark of Your strength. Let Your priests be clothed in righteousness, and Your devout ones will sing joyously. For the sake of David, Your servant, turn not away the face of Your anointed.[3] For I have given you a good teaching, do not forsake My Torah.[4]* Chazzan– *It is a tree of life for those who grasp it, and its supporters are praiseworthy.[5] Its ways are ways of pleasantness and all its paths are peace.[6] Bring us back to You,* HASHEM, *and we shall return, renew our days as of old.[7]*

HALF KADDISH

The Ark is closed and the *chazzan* recites Half-*Kaddish.*

יִתְגַּדַּל *May His great Name grow exalted and sanctified* (Cong.– *Amen.*) *in the world that He created as He willed. May He give reign to His kingship in your lifetimes and in your days, and in the lifetimes of the entire Family of Israel, swiftly and soon. Now respond: Amen.*

(Cong.– *Amen. May His great Name be blessed forever and ever.*)

May His great Name be blessed forever and ever.

Blessed, praised, glorified, exalted, extolled, mighty, upraised, and lauded be the Name of the Holy One, Blessed is He (Cong.– *Blessed is He*) *— beyond any blessing and song, praise and consolation that are uttered in the world. Now respond: Amen.* (Cong.– *Amen*.)

שמונה עשרה – עמידה

Take three steps backward, then three steps forward. Remain standing with feet together while reciting *Shemoneh Esrei*. Recite it with quiet devotion and without interruption, verbal or otherwise. Although it should not be audible to others, one must pray loudly enough to hear himself.

כִּי שֵׁם יהוה אֶקְרָא, הָבוּ גֹדֶל לֵאלֹהֵינוּ.[1]
אֲדֹנָי שְׂפָתַי תִּפְתָּח, וּפִי יַגִּיד תְּהִלָּתֶךָ.[2]

אבות

Bend the knees at בָּרוּךְ; bow at אַתָּה; straighten up at ה׳.

בָּרוּךְ אַתָּה יהוה אֱלֹהֵינוּ וֵאלֹהֵי אֲבוֹתֵינוּ, אֱלֹהֵי אַבְרָהָם, אֱלֹהֵי יִצְחָק, וֵאלֹהֵי יַעֲקֹב, הָאֵל הַגָּדוֹל הַגִּבּוֹר וְהַנּוֹרָא, אֵל עֶלְיוֹן, גּוֹמֵל חֲסָדִים טוֹבִים וְקוֹנֵה הַכֹּל, וְזוֹכֵר חַסְדֵי אָבוֹת, וּמֵבִיא גוֹאֵל לִבְנֵי בְנֵיהֶם, לְמַעַן שְׁמוֹ בְּאַהֲבָה. מֶלֶךְ עוֹזֵר וּמוֹשִׁיעַ וּמָגֵן.

Bend the knees at בָּרוּךְ; bow at אַתָּה; straighten up at ה׳.

בָּרוּךְ אַתָּה יהוה, מָגֵן אַבְרָהָם.

גבורות

אַתָּה גִּבּוֹר לְעוֹלָם אֲדֹנָי, מְחַיֵּה מֵתִים אַתָּה, רַב לְהוֹשִׁיעַ. מְכַלְכֵּל חַיִּים בְּחֶסֶד, מְחַיֵּה מֵתִים בְּרַחֲמִים רַבִּים, סוֹמֵךְ נוֹפְלִים, וְרוֹפֵא חוֹלִים, וּמַתִּיר אֲסוּרִים, וּמְקַיֵּם אֱמוּנָתוֹ לִישֵׁנֵי עָפָר. מִי כָמוֹךָ בַּעַל גְּבוּרוֹת, וּמִי דּוֹמֶה לָּךְ, מֶלֶךְ מֵמִית וּמְחַיֶּה וּמַצְמִיחַ יְשׁוּעָה. וְנֶאֱמָן אַתָּה לְהַחֲיוֹת מֵתִים. בָּרוּךְ אַתָּה יהוה, מְחַיֵּה הַמֵּתִים.

During the *chazzan's* repetition, *Kedushah* (below) is recited at this point.

קדושה

When reciting *Kedushah,* one must stand with his feet together and avoid any interruptions. One should rise on his toes when saying the words קָדוֹשׁ, קָדוֹשׁ, קָדוֹשׁ; בָּרוּךְ (of בָּרוּךְ כְּבוֹד); and יִמְלֹךְ.

Cong. then *Chazzan* – **נְקַדֵּשׁ** אֶת שִׁמְךָ בָּעוֹלָם, כְּשֵׁם שֶׁמַּקְדִּישִׁים אוֹתוֹ בִּשְׁמֵי מָרוֹם, כַּכָּתוּב עַל יַד נְבִיאֶךָ, וְקָרָא זֶה אֶל זֶה וְאָמַר:

All – קָדוֹשׁ קָדוֹשׁ קָדוֹשׁ יהוה צְבָאוֹת, מְלֹא כָל הָאָרֶץ כְּבוֹדוֹ.[3]

Chazzan – לְעֻמָּתָם בָּרוּךְ יֹאמֵרוּ:

All – בָּרוּךְ כְּבוֹד יהוה, מִמְּקוֹמוֹ.[4]

Chazzan – וּבְדִבְרֵי קָדְשְׁךָ כָּתוּב לֵאמֹר:

All – יִמְלֹךְ יהוה לְעוֹלָם, אֱלֹהַיִךְ צִיּוֹן לְדֹר וָדֹר, הַלְלוּיָהּ.[5]

Chazzan only concludes – לְדוֹר וָדוֹר נַגִּיד גָּדְלֶךָ וּלְנֵצַח נְצָחִים קְדֻשָּׁתְךָ נַקְדִּישׁ, וְשִׁבְחֲךָ אֱלֹהֵינוּ מִפִּינוּ לֹא יָמוּשׁ לְעוֹלָם וָעֶד, כִּי אֵל מֶלֶךְ גָּדוֹל וְקָדוֹשׁ אָתָּה. בָּרוּךְ אַתָּה יהוה, הָאֵל הַקָּדוֹשׁ.

Chazzan continues . . . אַתָּה חוֹנֵן (page 430).

SHEMONEH ESREI – AMIDAH

Take three steps backward, then three steps forward. Remain standing with feet together while reciting *Shemoneh Esrei*. Recite it with quiet devotion and without interruption, verbal or otherwise. Although it should not be audible to others, one must pray loudly enough to hear himself.

When I call out the Name of HASHEM, ascribe greatness to our God.[1]
My Lord, open my lips, that my mouth may declare Your praise.[2]

PATRIARCHS

Bend the knees at *'Blessed'*; bow at *'You'*; straighten up at *'HASHEM.'*

בָּרוּךְ *Blessed are You, HASHEM, our God and the God of our forefathers, God of Abraham, God of Isaac, and God of Jacob; the great, mighty, and awesome God, the supreme God, Who bestows beneficial kindnesses and creates everything, Who recalls the kindnesses of the Patriarchs and brings a Redeemer to their children's children, for His Name's sake, with love. O King, Helper, Savior, and Shield.*

Bend the knees at *'Blessed'*; bow at *'You'*; straighten up at 'HASHEM.'

Blessed are You, HASHEM, Shield of Abraham.

GOD'S MIGHT

אַתָּה *You are eternally mighty, my Lord, the Resuscitator of the dead are You; abundantly able to save. Who sustains the living with kindness, resuscitates the dead with abundant mercy, supports the fallen, heals the sick, releases the confined, and maintains His faith to those asleep in the dust. Who is like You, O Master of mighty deeds, and who is comparable to You, O King Who causes death and restores life and makes salvation sprout! And You are faithful to resuscitate the dead. Blessed are You, HASHEM, Who resuscitates the dead.*

During the *chazzan's* repetition, *Kedushah* (below) is recited at this point.

KEDUSHAH

When reciting *Kedushah*, one must stand with his feet together and avoid any interruptions. One should rise on his toes when saying *Holy, holy, holy; Blessed is;* and *HASHEM shall reign.*

Cong. then Chazzan – **נְקַדֵּשׁ** *We shall sanctify Your Name in this world, just as they sanctify it in heaven above, as it is written by Your prophet, "And one [angel] will call another and say:*

All – *'Holy, holy, holy is HASHEM, Master of Legions, the whole world is filled with His glory.' "*[3]

Chazzan – *Those facing them say 'Blessed':*

All – *'Blessed is the glory of HASHEM from His place.'*[4]

Chazzan – *And in Your holy Writings the following is written:*

All – *'HASHEM shall reign forever — your God, O Zion, from generation to generation — Halleluyah!'*[5]

Chazzan only concludes – *From generation to generation we shall relate Your greatness and for infinite eternities we shall proclaim Your holiness. Your praise, our God, shall not leave our mouth forever and ever, for You, O God, are a great and holy King. Blessed are You, HASHEM, the holy God.*

Chazzan continues אַתָּה חוֹנֵן, *You graciously endow . . .* (page 430).

---

(1) *Deuteronomy* 32:3. (2) *Psalms* 51:17. (3) *Isaiah* 6:3. (4) *Ezekiel* 3:12. (5) *Psalms* 146:10.

קדושת השם

אַתָּה קָדוֹשׁ וְשִׁמְךָ קָדוֹשׁ, וּקְדוֹשִׁים בְּכָל יוֹם יְהַלְלְוּךָ סֶּלָה. בָּרוּךְ אַתָּה יהוה, הָאֵל הַקָּדוֹשׁ.

בינה

אַתָּה חוֹנֵן לְאָדָם דַּעַת, וּמְלַמֵּד לֶאֱנוֹשׁ בִּינָה. חָנֵּנוּ מֵאִתְּךָ דֵּעָה בִּינָה וְהַשְׂכֵּל. בָּרוּךְ אַתָּה יהוה, חוֹנֵן הַדָּעַת.

תשובה

הֲשִׁיבֵנוּ אָבִינוּ לְתוֹרָתֶךָ, וְקָרְבֵנוּ מַלְכֵּנוּ לַעֲבוֹדָתֶךָ, וְהַחֲזִירֵנוּ בִּתְשׁוּבָה שְׁלֵמָה לְפָנֶיךָ. בָּרוּךְ אַתָּה יהוה, הָרוֹצֶה בִּתְשׁוּבָה.

סליחה

Strike the left side of the chest with the right fist while reciting the words חָטָאנוּ and פָּשָׁעְנוּ.

סְלַח לָנוּ אָבִינוּ כִּי חָטָאנוּ, מְחַל לָנוּ מַלְכֵּנוּ כִּי פָשָׁעְנוּ, כִּי מוֹחֵל וְסוֹלֵחַ אָתָּה. בָּרוּךְ אַתָּה יהוה, חַנּוּן הַמַּרְבֶּה לִסְלוֹחַ.

גאולה

רְאֵה בְעָנְיֵנוּ, וְרִיבָה רִיבֵנוּ, וּגְאָלֵנוּ[1] מְהֵרָה לְמַעַן שְׁמֶךָ, כִּי גוֹאֵל חָזָק אָתָּה. בָּרוּךְ אַתָּה יהוה, גּוֹאֵל יִשְׂרָאֵל.

During his repetition the *chazzan* recites עֲנֵנוּ at this point. See *Laws* §61-63. [If he forgot to recite it at this point, he may insert it in שְׁמַע קוֹלֵנוּ, p. 434].

עֲנֵנוּ יהוה עֲנֵנוּ, בְּיוֹם צוֹם תַּעֲנִיתֵנוּ, כִּי בְצָרָה גְדוֹלָה אֲנָחְנוּ. אַל תֵּפֶן אֶל רִשְׁעֵנוּ, וְאַל תַּסְתֵּר פָּנֶיךָ מִמֶּנּוּ, וְאַל תִּתְעַלַּם מִתְּחִנָּתֵנוּ. הֱיֵה נָא קָרוֹב לְשַׁוְעָתֵנוּ, יְהִי נָא חַסְדְּךָ לְנַחֲמֵנוּ, טֶרֶם נִקְרָא אֵלֶיךָ עֲנֵנוּ, כַּדָּבָר שֶׁנֶּאֱמַר: וְהָיָה טֶרֶם יִקְרָאוּ וַאֲנִי אֶעֱנֶה, עוֹד הֵם מְדַבְּרִים וַאֲנִי אֶשְׁמָע.[2] כִּי אַתָּה יהוה הָעוֹנֶה בְּעֵת צָרָה, פּוֹדֶה וּמַצִּיל בְּכָל עֵת צָרָה וְצוּקָה. בָּרוּךְ אַתָּה יהוה, הָעוֹנֶה בְּעֵת צָרָה.

רפואה

רְפָאֵנוּ יהוה וְנֵרָפֵא, הוֹשִׁיעֵנוּ וְנִוָּשֵׁעָה, כִּי תְהִלָּתֵנוּ אָתָּה,[3] וְהַעֲלֵה רְפוּאָה שְׁלֵמָה לְכָל מַכּוֹתֵינוּ, °°כִּי אֵל מֶלֶךְ רוֹפֵא נֶאֱמָן וְרַחֲמָן אָתָּה. בָּרוּךְ אַתָּה יהוה, רוֹפֵא חוֹלֵי עַמּוֹ יִשְׂרָאֵל.

°°At this point one may interject a prayer for one who is ill:

יְהִי רָצוֹן מִלְּפָנֶיךָ יהוה אֱלֹהַי וֵאלֹהֵי אֲבוֹתַי, שֶׁתִּשְׁלַח מְהֵרָה רְפוּאָה שְׁלֵמָה מִן הַשָּׁמַיִם, רְפוּאַת הַנֶּפֶשׁ וּרְפוּאַת הַגּוּף

לַחוֹלֶה—for a male (patient's name) בֶּן (mother's name) בְּתוֹךְ שְׁאָר חוֹלֵי יִשְׂרָאֵל.

לַחוֹלָה—for a female (patient's name) בַּת (mother's name) בְּתוֹךְ שְׁאָר חוֹלֵי יִשְׂרָאֵל.

Continue—כִּי אֵל . . .

HOLINESS OF GOD'S NAME

אַתָּה *You are holy and Your Name is holy, and holy ones praise You every day, forever. Blessed are You,* HASHEM, *the holy God.*

INSIGHT

אַתָּה *You graciously endow man with wisdom and teach insight to a frail mortal. Endow us graciously from Yourself with wisdom, insight, and discernment. Blessed are You,* HASHEM, *gracious Giver of wisdom.*

REPENTANCE

הֲשִׁיבֵנוּ *Bring us back, our Father, to Your Torah, and bring us near, our King, to Your service, and influence us to return in perfect repentance before You. Blessed are You,* HASHEM, *Who desires repentance.*

FORGIVENESS

Strike the left side of the chest with the right fist while reciting the words *'erred'* and *'sinned.'*

סְלַח *Forgive us, our Father, for we have erred; pardon us, our King, for we have willfully sinned; for You pardon and forgive. Blessed are You,* HASHEM, *the gracious One Who pardons abundantly.*

REDEMPTION

רְאֵה *Behold our affliction, take up our grievance, and redeem us*[1] *speedily for Your Name's sake, for You are a powerful Redeemer. Blessed are You,* HASHEM, *Redeemer of Israel.*

During his repetition the *chazzan* recites עֲנֵנוּ, *'Answer us,'* at this point. See *Laws* §61-63. [If he forgot to recite it at this point, he may insert it in שְׁמַע קוֹלֵנוּ, *'Hear our voice'* (p. 434).]

עֲנֵנוּ *Answer us,* HASHEM, *answer us, on this day of our fast, for we are in great distress. Do not pay attention to our wickedness; do not hide Your Face from us; and do not ignore our supplication. Please be near to our outcry; please let Your kindness comfort us — before we call to You answer us, as it is said: 'And it will be that before they call, I will answer; while they yet speak, I will hear.'*[2] *For You,* HASHEM, *are the One Who responds in time of distress, Who redeems and rescues in every time of distress and woe. Blessed are You,* HASHEM, *Who responds in time of distress.*

HEALTH AND HEALING

רְפָאֵנוּ *Heal us,* HASHEM *— then we will be healed; save us — then we will be saved, for You are our praise.*[3] *Bring complete recovery for all our ailments,* °°*for You are God, King, the faithful and compassionate Healer. Blessed are You,* HASHEM, *Who heals the sick of His people Israel.*

°°At this point one may interject a prayer for one who is ill:

May it be Your will, HASHEM, *my God, and the God of my forefathers, that You quickly send a complete recovery from heaven, spiritual healing and physical healing to the patient* (name) *son/daughter of* (mother's name) *among the other patients of Israel.*

Continue: *For You are God ...*

(1) Cf. *Psalms* 119:153-154. (2) *Isaiah* 65:24. (3) Cf. *Jeremiah* 17:14.

ברכת השנים

בָּרֵךְ עָלֵינוּ יהוה אֱלֹהֵינוּ אֶת הַשָּׁנָה הַזֹּאת וְאֶת כָּל מִינֵי תְבוּאָתָהּ לְטוֹבָה, וְתֵן בְּרָכָה עַל פְּנֵי הָאֲדָמָה, וְשַׂבְּעֵנוּ מִטּוּבֶךָ, וּבָרֵךְ שְׁנָתֵנוּ כַּשָּׁנִים הַטּוֹבוֹת. בָּרוּךְ אַתָּה יהוה, מְבָרֵךְ הַשָּׁנִים.

קיבוץ גליות

תְּקַע בְּשׁוֹפָר גָּדוֹל לְחֵרוּתֵנוּ, וְשָׂא נֵס לְקַבֵּץ גָּלֻיּוֹתֵינוּ, וְקַבְּצֵנוּ יַחַד מֵאַרְבַּע כַּנְפוֹת הָאָרֶץ.[1] בָּרוּךְ אַתָּה יהוה, מְקַבֵּץ נִדְחֵי עַמּוֹ יִשְׂרָאֵל.

דין

הָשִׁיבָה שׁוֹפְטֵינוּ כְּבָרִאשׁוֹנָה, וְיוֹעֲצֵינוּ כְּבַתְּחִלָּה,[2] וְהָסֵר מִמֶּנּוּ יָגוֹן וַאֲנָחָה, וּמְלוֹךְ עָלֵינוּ אַתָּה יהוה לְבַדְּךָ בְּחֶסֶד וּבְרַחֲמִים, וְצַדְּקֵנוּ בַּמִּשְׁפָּט. בָּרוּךְ אַתָּה יהוה, מֶלֶךְ אוֹהֵב צְדָקָה וּמִשְׁפָּט.

ברכת המינים

וְלַמַּלְשִׁינִים אַל תְּהִי תִקְוָה, וְכָל הָרִשְׁעָה כְּרֶגַע תֹּאבֵד, וְכָל אֹיְבֶיךָ מְהֵרָה יִכָּרֵתוּ, וְהַזֵּדִים מְהֵרָה תְעַקֵּר וּתְשַׁבֵּר וּתְמַגֵּר וְתַכְנִיעַ בִּמְהֵרָה בְיָמֵינוּ. בָּרוּךְ אַתָּה יהוה, שׁוֹבֵר אֹיְבִים וּמַכְנִיעַ זֵדִים.

צדיקים

עַל הַצַּדִּיקִים וְעַל הַחֲסִידִים, וְעַל זִקְנֵי עַמְּךָ בֵּית יִשְׂרָאֵל, וְעַל פְּלֵיטַת סוֹפְרֵיהֶם, וְעַל גֵּרֵי הַצֶּדֶק וְעָלֵינוּ, יֶהֱמוּ רַחֲמֶיךָ יהוה אֱלֹהֵינוּ, וְתֵן שָׂכָר טוֹב לְכָל הַבּוֹטְחִים בְּשִׁמְךָ בֶּאֱמֶת, וְשִׂים חֶלְקֵנוּ עִמָּהֶם לְעוֹלָם, וְלֹא נֵבוֹשׁ כִּי בְךָ בָּטָחְנוּ. בָּרוּךְ אַתָּה יהוה, מִשְׁעָן וּמִבְטָח לַצַּדִּיקִים.

בנין ירושלים

וְלִירוּשָׁלַיִם עִירְךָ בְּרַחֲמִים תָּשׁוּב, וְתִשְׁכּוֹן בְּתוֹכָהּ כַּאֲשֶׁר דִּבַּרְתָּ, וּבְנֵה אוֹתָהּ בְּקָרוֹב בְּיָמֵינוּ בִּנְיַן עוֹלָם, וְכִסֵּא דָוִד מְהֵרָה לְתוֹכָהּ תָּכִין.

נַחֵם יהוה אֱלֹהֵינוּ אֶת אֲבֵלֵי צִיּוֹן, וְאֶת אֲבֵלֵי יְרוּשָׁלָיִם, וְאֶת הָעִיר הָאֲבֵלָה וְהַחֲרֵבָה וְהַבְּזוּיָה וְהַשּׁוֹמֵמָה. הָאֲבֵלָה מִבְּלִי בָנֶיהָ, וְהַחֲרֵבָה מִמְּעוֹנוֹתֶיהָ, וְהַבְּזוּיָה מִכְּבוֹדָהּ, וְהַשּׁוֹמֵמָה מֵאֵין יוֹשֵׁב. וְהִיא יוֹשֶׁבֶת וְרֹאשָׁהּ חָפוּי כְּאִשָּׁה עֲקָרָה שֶׁלֹּא יָלָדָה. וַיְבַלְּעוּהָ

YEAR OF PROSPERITY

בָּרֵךְ *Bless on our behalf — O HASHEM, our God — this year and all its kinds of crops for the best, and give a blessing on the face of the earth, and satisfy us from Your bounty, and bless our year like the best years. Blessed are You, HASHEM, Who blesses the years.*

INGATHERING OF EXILES

תְּקַע *Sound the great shofar for our freedom, raise the banner to gather our exiles and gather us together from the four corners of the earth.[1] Blessed are You, HASHEM, Who gathers in the dispersed of His people Israel.*

RESTORATION OF JUSTICE

הָשִׁיבָה *Restore our judges as in earliest times and our counselors as at first;[2] remove from us sorrow and groan; and reign over us — You, HASHEM, alone — with kindness and compassion, and justify us through judgment. Blessed are You, HASHEM, the King Who loves righteousness and judgment.*

AGAINST HERETICS

וְלַמַּלְשִׁינִים *And for slanderers let there be no hope; and may all wickedness perish in an instant; and may all Your enemies be cut down speedily. May You speedily uproot, smash, cast down, and humble the wanton sinners — speedily in our days. Blessed are You, HASHEM, Who breaks enemies and humbles wanton sinners.*

THE RIGHTEOUS

עַל הַצַּדִּיקִים *On the righteous, on the devout, on the elders of Your people the Family of Israel, on the remnant of their scholars, on the righteous converts and on ourselves — may Your compassion be aroused, HASHEM, our God, and give goodly reward to all who sincerely believe in Your Name. Put our lot with them forever, and we will not feel ashamed, for we trust in You. Blessed are You, HASHEM, Mainstay and Assurance of the righteous.*

REBUILDING JERUSALEM

וְלִירוּשָׁלַיִם *And to Jerusalem, Your city, may You return in compassion, and may You rest within it, as You have spoken. May You rebuild it soon in our days as an eternal structure, and may You speedily establish the throne of David within it.*

O HASHEM, our God, console the mourners of Zion and the mourners of Jerusalem, and the city that is mournful, ruined, scorned, and desolate: mournful without her children, ruined without her abodes, scorned without her glory, and desolate without inhabitant. She sits with covered head like a barren woman who never gave birth. Legions have devoured

(1) Cf. *Isaiah* 11:12. (2) Cf. 1:26.

לִגְיוֹנוֹת, וַיִּירָשְׁוּהָ עוֹבְדֵי זָרִים, וַיָּטִילוּ אֶת עַמְּךָ יִשְׂרָאֵל לֶחָרֶב, וַיַּהַרְגוּ בְזָדוֹן חֲסִידֵי עֶלְיוֹן. עַל כֵּן צִיּוֹן בְּמַר תִּבְכֶּה, וִירוּשָׁלַיִם תִּתֵּן קוֹלָהּ. לִבִּי לִבִּי עַל חַלְלֵיהֶם, מֵעַי מֵעַי עַל חַלְלֵיהֶם, כִּי אַתָּה יהוה בָּאֵשׁ הִצַּתָּהּ, וּבָאֵשׁ אַתָּה עָתִיד לִבְנוֹתָהּ, כָּאָמוּר: וַאֲנִי אֶהְיֶה לָּהּ, נְאֻם יהוה, חוֹמַת אֵשׁ סָבִיב וּלְכָבוֹד אֶהְיֶה בְתוֹכָהּ.[1] בָּרוּךְ אַתָּה יהוה, מְנַחֵם צִיּוֹן וּבוֹנֵה יְרוּשָׁלָיִם.

מלכות בית דוד

אֶת צֶמַח דָּוִד עַבְדְּךָ מְהֵרָה תַצְמִיחַ, וְקַרְנוֹ תָּרוּם בִּישׁוּעָתֶךָ, כִּי לִישׁוּעָתְךָ קִוִּינוּ כָּל הַיּוֹם. בָּרוּךְ אַתָּה יהוה, מַצְמִיחַ קֶרֶן יְשׁוּעָה.

קבלת תפלה

שְׁמַע קוֹלֵנוּ יהוה אֱלֹהֵינוּ, חוּס וְרַחֵם עָלֵינוּ, וְקַבֵּל בְּרַחֲמִים וּבְרָצוֹן אֶת תְּפִלָּתֵנוּ, כִּי אֵל שׁוֹמֵעַ תְּפִלּוֹת וְתַחֲנוּנִים אָתָּה. וּמִלְּפָנֶיךָ מַלְכֵּנוּ רֵיקָם אַל תְּשִׁיבֵנוּ,

During the silent *Shemoneh Esrei* the following is recited.
[If forgotten, *Shemoneh Esrei* is not repeated. See *Laws* §61-63.]

עֲנֵנוּ יהוה עֲנֵנוּ, בְּיוֹם צוֹם תַּעֲנִיתֵנוּ, כִּי בְצָרָה גְדוֹלָה אֲנָחְנוּ. אַל תֵּפֶן אֶל רִשְׁעֵנוּ, וְאַל תַּסְתֵּר פָּנֶיךָ מִמֶּנּוּ, וְאַל תִּתְעַלַּם מִתְּחִנָּתֵנוּ. הֱיֵה נָא קָרוֹב לְשַׁוְעָתֵנוּ, יְהִי נָא חַסְדְּךָ לְנַחֲמֵנוּ, טֶרֶם נִקְרָא אֵלֶיךָ עֲנֵנוּ, כַּדָּבָר שֶׁנֶּאֱמַר: וְהָיָה טֶרֶם יִקְרָאוּ וַאֲנִי אֶעֱנֶה, עוֹד הֵם מְדַבְּרִים וַאֲנִי אֶשְׁמָע.[2] כִּי אַתָּה יהוה הָעוֹנֶה בְּעֵת צָרָה, פּוֹדֶה וּמַצִּיל בְּכָל עֵת צָרָה וְצוּקָה.

During the silent *Shemoneh Esrei* one may insert either or both of these prayers at this point.

For forgiveness:

אָנָּא יהוה, חָטָאתִי עָוִיתִי וּפָשַׁעְתִּי לְפָנֶיךָ, מִיּוֹם הֱיוֹתִי עַל הָאֲדָמָה עַד הַיּוֹם הַזֶּה (וּבִפְרַט בַּחֵטְא ....). אָנָּא יהוה, עֲשֵׂה לְמַעַן שִׁמְךָ הַגָּדוֹל, וּתְכַפֶּר לִי עַל עֲוֹנַי וַחֲטָאַי וּפְשָׁעַי שֶׁחָטָאתִי וְשֶׁעָוִיתִי וְשֶׁפָּשַׁעְתִּי לְפָנֶיךָ, מִנְּעוּרַי עַד הַיּוֹם הַזֶּה. וּתְמַלֵּא כָּל הַשֵּׁמוֹת שֶׁפָּגַמְתִּי בְּשִׁמְךָ הַגָּדוֹל.

For livelihood:

אַתָּה הוּא יהוה הָאֱלֹהִים, הַזָּן וּמְפַרְנֵס וּמְכַלְכֵּל מִקַּרְנֵי רְאֵמִים עַד בֵּיצֵי כִנִּים. הַטְרִיפֵנִי לֶחֶם חֻקִּי, וְהַמְצֵא לִי וּלְכָל בְּנֵי בֵיתִי מְזוֹנוֹתַי קוֹדֶם שֶׁאֶצְטָרֵךְ לָהֶם, בְּנַחַת וְלֹא בְצַעַר, בְּהֶתֵּר וְלֹא בְאִסּוּר, בְּכָבוֹד וְלֹא בְבִזָּיוֹן, לְחַיִּים וּלְשָׁלוֹם, מִשֶּׁפַע בְּרָכָה וְהַצְלָחָה, וּמִשֶּׁפַע בְּרֵכָה עֶלְיוֹנָה, כְּדֵי שֶׁאוּכַל לַעֲשׂוֹת רְצוֹנֶךָ וְלַעֲסוֹק בְּתוֹרָתֶךָ וּלְקַיֵּם מִצְוֹתֶיךָ. וְאַל תַּצְרִיכֵנִי לִידֵי מַתְּנַת בָּשָׂר וָדָם. וִיקֻיַּם בִּי מִקְרָא שֶׁכָּתוּב: פּוֹתֵחַ אֶת יָדֶךָ, וּמַשְׂבִּיעַ לְכָל חַי רָצוֹן.[3] וְכָתוּב: הַשְׁלֵךְ עַל יהוה יְהָבְךָ וְהוּא יְכַלְכְּלֶךָ.[4]

Continue — כִּי אַתָּה . . .

her, and idolaters have conquered her; they have cast Your people Israel to the sword and wantonly murdered the devout servants of the Supreme One. Therefore, Zion weeps bitterly and Jerusalem raises her voice. My heart, my heart — [it aches] for their slain! My innards, my innards — [they ache] for their slain! For You HASHEM, *with fire You consumed her and with fire You will rebuild her, as it is said: 'I will be for her, the words of* HASHEM, *a wall of fire around and I will be glorious in her midst.'*[1] *Blessed are You,* HASHEM, *Who consoles Zion and rebuilds Jerusalem.*

DAVIDIC REIGN

אֶת צֶמַח *The offspring of Your servant David may You speedily cause to flourish, and enhance his pride through Your salvation, for we hope for Your salvation all day long. Blessed are You,* HASHEM, *Who causes the pride of salvation to flourish.*

ACCEPTANCE OF PRAYER

שְׁמַע *Hear our voice,* HASHEM *our God, pity and be compassionate to us, and accept — with compassion and favor — our prayer, for God Who hears prayers and supplications are You. From before Yourself, our King, turn us not away empty-handed,*

During the silent *Shemoneh Esrei* the following is recited.
[If forgotten, *Shemoneh Esrei* is not repeated. See *Laws* §61-63.]

עֲנֵנוּ *Answer us,* HASHEM, *answer us, on this day of our fast, for we are in great distress. Do not pay attention to our wickedness; do not hide Your Face from us; and do not ignore our supplication. Please be near to our outcry; please let Your kindness comfort us — before we call to You answer us, as it is said: 'And it will be that before they call, I will answer; while they yet speak, I will hear.'*[2] *For You,* HASHEM, *are the One Who responds in time of distress, Who redeems and rescues in every time of distress and woe.*

During the silent *Shemoneh Esrei* one may insert either or both of these prayers at this point.

For forgiveness:

אָנָּא *Please, O* HASHEM, *I have erred, been iniquitous, and willfully sinned before You, from the day I have existed on earth until this very day (and especially with the sin of . . .). Please,* HASHEM, *act for the sake of Your Great Name and grant me atonement for my iniquities, my errors, and my willful sins through which I have erred, been iniquitous, and willfully sinned before You, from my youth until this day. And make whole all the Names that I have blemished in Your Great Name.*

For livelihood:

אַתָּה *It is You,* HASHEM *the God, Who nourishes, sustains, and supports, from the horns of re'eimim to the eggs of lice. Provide me with my allotment of bread; and bring forth for me and all members of my household, my food, before I have need for it; in contentment but not in pain, in a permissible but not a forbidden manner, in honor but not in disgrace, for life and for peace; from the flow of blessing and success and from the flow of the Heavenly spring, so that I be enabled to do Your will and engage in Your Torah and fulfill Your commandments. Make me not needful of people's largesse; and may there be fulfilled in me the verse that states, 'You open Your hand and satisfy the desire of every living thing'*[3] *and that states, 'Cast Your burden upon* HASHEM *and He will support you.'*[4]

Continue: *For You hear the prayer . . .*

(1) *Zechariah* 2:9. (2) *Isaiah* 65:24. (3) *Psalms* 145:16. (4) 55:23.

כִּי אַתָּה שׁוֹמֵעַ תְּפִלַּת עַמְּךָ יִשְׂרָאֵל בְּרַחֲמִים. בָּרוּךְ אַתָּה יהוה, שׁוֹמֵעַ תְּפִלָּה.

עבודה

רְצֵה יהוה אֱלֹהֵינוּ בְּעַמְּךָ יִשְׂרָאֵל וּבִתְפִלָּתָם, וְהָשֵׁב אֶת הָעֲבוֹדָה לִדְבִיר בֵּיתֶךָ. וְאִשֵּׁי יִשְׂרָאֵל וּתְפִלָּתָם בְּאַהֲבָה תְקַבֵּל בְּרָצוֹן, וּתְהִי לְרָצוֹן תָּמִיד עֲבוֹדַת יִשְׂרָאֵל עַמֶּךָ.

וְתֶחֱזֶינָה עֵינֵינוּ בְּשׁוּבְךָ לְצִיּוֹן בְּרַחֲמִים. בָּרוּךְ אַתָּה יהוה, הַמַּחֲזִיר שְׁכִינָתוֹ לְצִיּוֹן.

הודאה

Bow at מוֹדִים; straighten up at ה'. In his repetition the *chazzan* should recite the entire מוֹדִים aloud, while the congregation recites מוֹדִים דְּרַבָּנָן softly.

מוֹדִים אֲנַחְנוּ לָךְ, שָׁאַתָּה הוּא יהוה אֱלֹהֵינוּ וֵאלֹהֵי אֲבוֹתֵינוּ לְעוֹלָם וָעֶד. צוּר חַיֵּינוּ, מָגֵן יִשְׁעֵנוּ אַתָּה הוּא לְדוֹר וָדוֹר. נוֹדֶה לְּךָ וּנְסַפֵּר תְּהִלָּתֶךָ[1] עַל חַיֵּינוּ הַמְּסוּרִים בְּיָדֶךָ, וְעַל נִשְׁמוֹתֵינוּ הַפְּקוּדוֹת לָךְ, וְעַל נִסֶּיךָ שֶׁבְּכָל יוֹם עִמָּנוּ, וְעַל נִפְלְאוֹתֶיךָ וְטוֹבוֹתֶיךָ שֶׁבְּכָל עֵת, עֶרֶב וָבֹקֶר וְצָהֳרָיִם. הַטּוֹב כִּי לֹא כָלוּ רַחֲמֶיךָ, וְהַמְּרַחֵם כִּי לֹא תַמּוּ חֲסָדֶיךָ,[2] מֵעוֹלָם קִוִּינוּ לָךְ.

מודים דרבנן

מוֹדִים אֲנַחְנוּ לָךְ, שָׁאַתָּה הוּא יהוה אֱלֹהֵינוּ וֵאלֹהֵי אֲבוֹתֵינוּ, אֱלֹהֵי כָל בָּשָׂר, יוֹצְרֵנוּ, יוֹצֵר בְּרֵאשִׁית. בְּרָכוֹת וְהוֹדָאוֹת לְשִׁמְךָ הַגָּדוֹל וְהַקָּדוֹשׁ, עַל שֶׁהֶחֱיִיתָנוּ וְקִיַּמְתָּנוּ. כֵּן תְּחַיֵּנוּ וּתְקַיְּמֵנוּ, וְתֶאֱסוֹף גָּלֻיּוֹתֵינוּ לְחַצְרוֹת קָדְשֶׁךָ, לִשְׁמוֹר חֻקֶּיךָ וְלַעֲשׂוֹת רְצוֹנֶךָ, וּלְעָבְדְּךָ בְּלֵבָב שָׁלֵם, עַל שֶׁאֲנַחְנוּ מוֹדִים לָךְ. בָּרוּךְ אֵל הַהוֹדָאוֹת.

וְעַל כֻּלָּם יִתְבָּרַךְ וְיִתְרוֹמַם שִׁמְךָ מַלְכֵּנוּ תָּמִיד לְעוֹלָם וָעֶד.

Bend the knees at בָּרוּךְ; bow at אַתָּה; straighten up at ה'.

וְכֹל הַחַיִּים יוֹדוּךָ סֶּלָה, וִיהַלְלוּ אֶת שִׁמְךָ בֶּאֱמֶת, הָאֵל יְשׁוּעָתֵנוּ וְעֶזְרָתֵנוּ סֶלָה. בָּרוּךְ אַתָּה יהוה, הַטּוֹב שִׁמְךָ וּלְךָ נָאֶה לְהוֹדוֹת.

ברכת כהנים

The *chazzan* recites the following during his repetition.
He faces right at וְיִשְׁמְרֶךָ; faces left at אֵלֶיךָ וִיחֻנֶּךָּ; faces the Ark for the rest of the blessings.

אֱלֹהֵינוּ, וֵאלֹהֵי אֲבוֹתֵינוּ, בָּרְכֵנוּ בַבְּרָכָה הַמְּשֻׁלֶּשֶׁת בַּתּוֹרָה הַכְּתוּבָה עַל יְדֵי מֹשֶׁה עַבְדֶּךָ, הָאֲמוּרָה מִפִּי אַהֲרֹן וּבָנָיו, כֹּהֲנִים עַם קְדוֹשֶׁךָ, כָּאָמוּר: יְבָרֶכְךָ יהוה, וְיִשְׁמְרֶךָ. (.Cong – כֵּן יְהִי רָצוֹן)

יָאֵר יהוה פָּנָיו אֵלֶיךָ וִיחֻנֶּךָּ. (.Cong – כֵּן יְהִי רָצוֹן)

יִשָּׂא יהוה פָּנָיו אֵלֶיךָ וְיָשֵׂם לְךָ שָׁלוֹם.[3] (.Cong – כֵּן יְהִי רָצוֹן)

for You hear the prayer of Your people Israel with compassion. Blessed are You, HASHEM, Who hears prayer.

TEMPLE SERVICE

רְצֵה *Be favorable, HASHEM, our God, toward Your people Israel and their prayer and restore the service to the Holy of Holies of Your Temple. The fire-offerings of Israel and their prayer accept with love and favor, and may the service of Your people Israel always be favorable to You.*

וְתֶחֱזֶינָה *May our eyes behold Your return to Zion in compassion. Blessed are You, HASHEM, Who restores His Presence to Zion.*

THANKSGIVING [MODIM]

Bow at *'We gratefully thank You'*; straighten up at *'HASHEM.'* In his repetition the *chazzan* should recite the entire *Modim* aloud, while the congregation recites *Modim of the Rabbis* softly.

מוֹדִים *We gratefully thank You, for it is You Who are HASHEM, our God and the God of our forefathers for all eternity; Rock of our lives, Shield of our salvation are You from generation to generation. We shall thank You and relate Your praise[1] — for our lives, which are committed to Your power and for our souls that are entrusted to You; for Your miracles that are with us every day; and for Your wonders and favors in every season — evening, morning, and afternoon. The Beneficent One, for Your compassions were never exhausted, and the Compassionate One, for Your kindnesses never ended[2] — always have we put our hope in You.*

MODIM OF THE RABBIS

מוֹדִים *We gratefully thank You, for it is You Who are HASHEM, our God and the God of our forefathers, the God of all flesh, our Molder, the Molder of the universe. Blessings and thanks are due Your great and holy Name for You have given us life and sustained us. So may You continue to give us life and sustain us and gather our exiles to the Courtyards of Your Sanctuary, to observe Your decrees, to do Your will and to serve You wholeheartedly. [We thank You] for inspiring us to thank You. Blessed is the God of thanksgivings.*

For all these, may Your Name be blessed and exalted, our King, continually forever and ever.

Bend the knees at *'Blessed'*; bow at *'You'*; straighten up at *'HASHEM.'*

Everything alive will gratefully acknowledge You, Selah! and praise Your Name sincerely, O God of our salvation and help, Selah! Blessed are You, HASHEM, Your Name is 'The Beneficent One' and to You it is fitting to give thanks.

THE PRIESTLY BLESSING

The *chazzan* recites the following during his repetition.

אֱלֹהֵינוּ *Our God and the God of our forefathers, bless us with the three-verse blessing in the Torah that was written by the hand of Moses, Your servant, that was said by Aaron and his sons, the Kohanim, Your holy people, as it is said:*

May HASHEM bless you and safeguard you. (Cong.— *So may it be.*)

May HASHEM illuminate His countenance for you and be gracious to you. (Cong.— *So may it be.*)

May HASHEM turn His countenance to you and establish peace for you.[3] (Cong.— *So may it be.*)

(1) Cf. *Psalms* 79:13. (2) Cf. *Lamentations* 3:22. (3) *Numbers* 6:24-26.

שלום

שִׂים שָׁלוֹם, טוֹבָה, וּבְרָכָה, חֵן, וָחֶסֶד וְרַחֲמִים עָלֵינוּ וְעַל כָּל יִשְׂרָאֵל עַמֶּךָ. בָּרְכֵנוּ אָבִינוּ, כֻּלָּנוּ כְּאֶחָד בְּאוֹר פָּנֶיךָ, כִּי בְאוֹר פָּנֶיךָ נָתַתָּ לָּנוּ, יהוה אֱלֹהֵינוּ, תּוֹרַת חַיִּים וְאַהֲבַת חֶסֶד, וּצְדָקָה, וּבְרָכָה, וְרַחֲמִים, וְחַיִּים, וְשָׁלוֹם. וְטוֹב בְּעֵינֶיךָ לְבָרֵךְ אֶת עַמְּךָ יִשְׂרָאֵל, בְּכָל עֵת וּבְכָל שָׁעָה בִּשְׁלוֹמֶךָ. בָּרוּךְ אַתָּה יהוה, הַמְּבָרֵךְ אֶת עַמּוֹ יִשְׂרָאֵל בַּשָּׁלוֹם.

יִהְיוּ לְרָצוֹן אִמְרֵי פִי וְהֶגְיוֹן לִבִּי לְפָנֶיךָ, יהוה צוּרִי וְגֹאֲלִי.[1]

Chazzan's repetition of *Shemoneh Esrei* ends here. Individuals continue below:

אֱלֹהַי, נְצוֹר לְשׁוֹנִי מֵרָע, וּשְׂפָתַי מִדַּבֵּר מִרְמָה,[2] וְלִמְקַלְּלַי נַפְשִׁי תִדּוֹם, וְנַפְשִׁי כֶּעָפָר לַכֹּל תִּהְיֶה. פְּתַח לִבִּי בְּתוֹרָתֶךָ, וּבְמִצְוֹתֶיךָ תִּרְדּוֹף נַפְשִׁי. וְכֹל הַחוֹשְׁבִים עָלַי רָעָה, מְהֵרָה הָפֵר עֲצָתָם וְקַלְקֵל מַחֲשַׁבְתָּם. עֲשֵׂה לְמַעַן שְׁמֶךָ, עֲשֵׂה לְמַעַן יְמִינֶךָ, עֲשֵׂה לְמַעַן קְדֻשָּׁתֶךָ, עֲשֵׂה לְמַעַן תּוֹרָתֶךָ. לְמַעַן יֵחָלְצוּן יְדִידֶיךָ, הוֹשִׁיעָה יְמִינְךָ וַעֲנֵנִי.[3]

Some recite the following at *Minchah:*

רִבּוֹן כָּל הָעוֹלָמִים, גָּלוּי וְיָדוּעַ לְפָנֶיךָ, בִּזְמַן שֶׁבֵּית הַמִּקְדָּשׁ קַיָּם אָדָם חוֹטֵא וּמֵבִיא קָרְבָּן, וְאֵין מַקְרִיבִים מִמֶּנּוּ אֶלָּא חֶלְבּוֹ וְדָמוֹ, וְאַתָּה בְּרַחֲמֶיךָ הָרַבִּים מְכַפֵּר. וְעַכְשָׁו יָשַׁבְתִּי בְתַעֲנִית, וְנִתְמַעֵט חֶלְבִּי וְדָמִי. יְהִי רָצוֹן מִלְּפָנֶיךָ שֶׁיֵּהָא מִעוּט חֶלְבִּי וְדָמִי שֶׁנִּתְמַעֵט הַיּוֹם, כְּאִלּוּ הִקְרַבְתִּיו לְפָנֶיךָ עַל גַּב הַמִּזְבֵּחַ, וְתִרְצֵנִי.

Some recite verses pertaining to their names here. See page 480.

יִהְיוּ לְרָצוֹן אִמְרֵי פִי וְהֶגְיוֹן לִבִּי לְפָנֶיךָ, יהוה צוּרִי וְגֹאֲלִי.[1]

Bow and take three steps back. Bow left and say . . . עֹשֶׂה; bow right and say . . . הוּא יַעֲשֶׂה; bow forward and say . . . וְעַל כָּל.

עֹשֶׂה שָׁלוֹם בִּמְרוֹמָיו, הוּא יַעֲשֶׂה שָׁלוֹם עָלֵינוּ, וְעַל כָּל יִשְׂרָאֵל. וְאִמְרוּ: אָמֵן.

יְהִי רָצוֹן מִלְּפָנֶיךָ יהוה אֱלֹהֵינוּ וֵאלֹהֵי אֲבוֹתֵינוּ, שֶׁיִּבָּנֶה בֵּית הַמִּקְדָּשׁ בִּמְהֵרָה בְיָמֵינוּ, וְתֵן חֶלְקֵנוּ בְּתוֹרָתֶךָ. וְשָׁם נַעֲבָדְךָ בְּיִרְאָה, כִּימֵי עוֹלָם וּכְשָׁנִים קַדְמוֹנִיּוֹת. וְעָרְבָה לַיהוה מִנְחַת יְהוּדָה וִירוּשָׁלָיִם, כִּימֵי עוֹלָם וּכְשָׁנִים קַדְמוֹנִיּוֹת.[4]

THE INDIVIDUAL'S RECITATION OF *SHEMONEH ESREI* ENDS HERE.

The individual remains standing in place until the *chazzan* reaches *Kedushah* — or at least until the *chazzan* begins his repetition — then he takes three steps forward. The *chazzan* himself, or one who is praying alone, should remain in place for a few moments before taking three steps forward.

PEACE

שִׂים שָׁלוֹם *Establish peace, goodness, blessing, graciousness, kindness, and compassion upon us and upon all of Your people Israel. Bless us, our Father, all of us as one, with the light of Your countenance, for with the light of Your countenance You gave us, HASHEM, our God, the Torah of life and a love of kindness, righteousness, blessing, compassion, life, and peace. And may it be good in Your eyes to bless Your people Israel at every time and every hour with Your peace. Blessed are You, HASHEM, Who blesses His people Israel with peace.*

May the expressions of my mouth and the thoughts of my heart find favor before You, HASHEM, my Rock and my Redeemer.[1]

Chazzan's repetition of *Shemoneh Esrei* ends here. Individuals continue below:

אֱלֹהַי *My God, guard my tongue from evil and my lips from speaking deceitfully.*[2] *To those who curse me, let my soul be silent; and let my soul be like dust to everyone. Open my heart to Your Torah, then my soul will pursue Your commandments. As for all those who design evil against me, speedily nullify their counsel and disrupt their design. Act for Your Name's sake; act for Your right hand's sake; act for Your sanctity's sake; act for Your Torah's sake. That Your beloved ones may be given rest; let Your right hand save, and respond to me.*[3]

Some recite the following at *Minchah:*

רִבּוֹן *Master of all the worlds, it is revealed and known before You that in the time when the Holy Temple existed, if someone sinned, he brought an offering — yet nothing of it was offered [on the Altar] except for its fat and blood, yet You in Your abundant mercy would atone. Now I have engaged in a fast and my own fat and blood have been diminished. May it be Your will that the diminution of my fat and blood that was diminished today should be as if I had offered it upon the Altar and may You show me favor.*

Some recite verses pertaining to their names at this point. See page 480.

May the expressions of my mouth and the thoughts of my heart find favor before You, HASHEM, my Rock and my Redeemer.[1] °°*He Who makes peace in His heights, may He make peace upon us, and upon all Israel. Now respond: Amen.*

Bow and take three steps back. Bow left and say, *'He Who makes peace . . .';* bow right and say, *'may He make peace . . .';* bow forward and say, *'and upon . . . Amen.'*

יְהִי רָצוֹן *May it be Your will, HASHEM, our God and the God of our forefathers, that the Holy Temple be rebuilt, speedily in our days. Grant us our share in Your Torah, and may we serve You there with reverence, as in days of old and in former years. Then the offering of Judah and Jerusalem will be pleasing to HASHEM, as in days of old and in former years.*[4]

THE INDIVIDUAL'S RECITATION OF *SHEMONEH ESREI* ENDS HERE.

The individual remains standing in place until the *chazzan* reaches *Kedushah* — or at least until the *chazzan* begins his repetition — then he takes three steps forward. The *chazzan* himself, or one who is praying alone, should remain in place for a few moments before taking three steps forward.

---

(1) *Psalms* 19:15. (2) Cf. 34:14. (3) 60:7; 108:7. (4) *Malachi* 3:4.

קדיש שלם

The *chazzan* recites קַדִּישׁ שָׁלֵם.

יִתְגַּדַּל וְיִתְקַדַּשׁ שְׁמֵהּ רַבָּא. (Cong. – אָמֵן.) בְּעָלְמָא דִּי בְרָא כִרְעוּתֵהּ. וְיַמְלִיךְ מַלְכוּתֵהּ, בְּחַיֵּיכוֹן וּבְיוֹמֵיכוֹן וּבְחַיֵּי דְכָל בֵּית יִשְׂרָאֵל, בַּעֲגָלָא וּבִזְמַן קָרִיב. וְאִמְרוּ: אָמֵן.

(Cong. – אָמֵן. יְהֵא שְׁמֵהּ רַבָּא מְבָרַךְ לְעָלַם וּלְעָלְמֵי עָלְמַיָּא.)

יְהֵא שְׁמֵהּ רַבָּא מְבָרַךְ לְעָלַם וּלְעָלְמֵי עָלְמַיָּא.

יִתְבָּרַךְ וְיִשְׁתַּבַּח וְיִתְפָּאַר וְיִתְרוֹמַם וְיִתְנַשֵּׂא וְיִתְהַדָּר וְיִתְעַלֶּה וְיִתְהַלָּל שְׁמֵהּ דְּקֻדְשָׁא בְּרִיךְ הוּא (Cong. – בְּרִיךְ הוּא) — לְעֵלָּא מִן כָּל בִּרְכָתָא וְשִׁירָתָא תֻּשְׁבְּחָתָא וְנֶחֱמָתָא, דַּאֲמִירָן בְּעָלְמָא. וְאִמְרוּ: אָמֵן. (Cong. – אָמֵן.)

(Cong. – קַבֵּל בְּרַחֲמִים וּבְרָצוֹן אֶת תְּפִלָּתֵנוּ.)

תִּתְקַבֵּל צְלוֹתְהוֹן וּבָעוּתְהוֹן דְּכָל בֵּית יִשְׂרָאֵל קֳדָם אֲבוּהוֹן דִּי בִשְׁמַיָּא. וְאִמְרוּ: אָמֵן. (Cong. – אָמֵן.)

(Cong. – יְהִי שֵׁם יהוה מְבֹרָךְ, מֵעַתָּה וְעַד עוֹלָם.[1])

יְהֵא שְׁלָמָא רַבָּא מִן שְׁמַיָּא, וְחַיִּים עָלֵינוּ וְעַל כָּל יִשְׂרָאֵל. וְאִמְרוּ: אָמֵן. (Cong. – אָמֵן.)

(Cong. – עֶזְרִי מֵעִם יהוה, עֹשֵׂה שָׁמַיִם וָאָרֶץ.[2])

Take three steps back. Bow left and say . . . עֹשֶׂה; bow right and say . . . הוּא; bow forward and say וְעַל כָּל . . . אָמֵן. Remain standing in place for a few moments, then take three steps forward.

עֹשֶׂה שָׁלוֹם בִּמְרוֹמָיו, הוּא יַעֲשֶׂה שָׁלוֹם עָלֵינוּ, וְעַל כָּל יִשְׂרָאֵל. וְאִמְרוּ: אָמֵן. (Cong. – אָמֵן.)

עלינו

Stand while reciting עָלֵינוּ.

עָלֵינוּ לְשַׁבֵּחַ לַאֲדוֹן הַכֹּל, לָתֵת גְּדֻלָּה לְיוֹצֵר בְּרֵאשִׁית, שֶׁלֹּא עָשָׂנוּ כְּגוֹיֵי הָאֲרָצוֹת, וְלֹא שָׂמָנוּ כְּמִשְׁפְּחוֹת הָאֲדָמָה. שֶׁלֹּא שָׂם חֶלְקֵנוּ כָּהֶם, וְגוֹרָלֵנוּ כְּכָל הֲמוֹנָם. (שֶׁהֵם מִשְׁתַּחֲוִים לְהֶבֶל וָרִיק, וּמִתְפַּלְּלִים אֶל אֵל לֹא יוֹשִׁיעַ.[3]) וַאֲנַחְנוּ כּוֹרְעִים וּמִשְׁתַּחֲוִים וּמוֹדִים, לִפְנֵי מֶלֶךְ מַלְכֵי הַמְּלָכִים הַקָּדוֹשׁ בָּרוּךְ הוּא. שֶׁהוּא נוֹטֶה שָׁמַיִם וְיֹסֵד אָרֶץ,[4] וּמוֹשַׁב יְקָרוֹ בַּשָּׁמַיִם מִמַּעַל, וּשְׁכִינַת עֻזּוֹ בְּגָבְהֵי מְרוֹמִים. הוּא אֱלֹהֵינוּ, אֵין עוֹד. אֱמֶת מַלְכֵּנוּ, אֶפֶס זוּלָתוֹ, כַּכָּתוּב בְּתוֹרָתוֹ: וְיָדַעְתָּ הַיּוֹם וַהֲשֵׁבֹתָ אֶל לְבָבֶךָ, כִּי יהוה הוּא הָאֱלֹהִים בַּשָּׁמַיִם מִמַּעַל וְעַל הָאָרֶץ מִתָּחַת, אֵין עוֹד.[5]

Bow while reciting וַאֲנַחְנוּ כּוֹרְעִים וּמִשְׁתַּחֲוִים.

FULL KADDISH

The *chazzan* recites the Full *Kaddish.*

יִתְגַּדַּל *May His great Name grow exalted and sanctified* (Cong.– *Amen.*) *in the world that He created as He willed. May He give reign to His kingship in your lifetimes and in your days, and in the lifetimes of the entire Family of Israel, swiftly and soon. Now respond: Amen.*

(Cong.– *Amen. May His great Name be blessed forever and ever.)*

May His great Name be blessed forever and ever.

Blessed, praised, glorified, exalted, extolled, mighty, upraised, and lauded be the Name of the Holy One, Blessed is He (Cong.– *Blessed is He*) *— beyond any blessing and song, praise and consolation that are uttered in the world. Now respond: Amen.* (Cong.– *Amen.*)

(Cong.– *Accept our prayers with mercy and favor.*)

May the prayers and supplications of the entire Family of Israel be accepted before their Father Who is in Heaven. Now respond: Amen. (Cong.– *Amen.*)

(Cong.– *Blessed be the Name of* HASHEM, *from this time and forever.*[1])

May there be abundant peace from Heaven, and life, upon us and upon all Israel. Now respond: Amen. (Cong.– *Amen.*)

(Cong.– *My help is from* HASHEM, *Maker of heaven and earth.*[2])

Take three steps back. Bow left and say, *'He Who makes peace . . .';* bow right and say, *'may He . . .';* bow forward and say, *'and upon all Israel . . .'* Remain standing in place for a few moments, then take three steps forward.

He Who makes peace in His heights, may He make peace upon us, and upon all Israel. Now respond: Amen. (Cong.– *Amen.*)

ALEINU

Stand while reciting עָלֵינוּ, *'It is our duty . . .'*

עָלֵינוּ *It is our duty to praise the Master of all, to ascribe greatness to the Molder of primeval creation, for He has not made us like the nations of the lands, and has not emplaced us like the families of the earth; for He has not assigned our portion like theirs nor our lot like all their multitudes. (For they bow to vanity and emptiness and pray to a god which helps not.*[3]*) But we bend our knees, bow, and acknowledge our thanks before the King Who reigns over kings, the Holy One, Blessed is He. He stretches out heaven and establishes earth's foundation,*[4] *the seat of His homage is in the heavens above and His powerful Presence is in the loftiest heights. He is our God and there is none other. True is our King, there is nothing beside Him, as it is written in His Torah: 'You are to know this day and take to your heart that* HASHEM *is the only God — in heaven above and on the earth below — there is none other.'*[5]

Bow while reciting *'But we bend our knees.'*

(1) *Psalms* 113:2. (2) 121:2. (3) *Isaiah* 45:20. (4) 51:13. (5) *Deuteronomy* 4:39.

עַל כֵּן נְקַוֶּה לְּךָ יהוה אֱלֹהֵינוּ לִרְאוֹת מְהֵרָה בְּתִפְאֶרֶת עֻזֶּךָ, לְהַעֲבִיר גִּלּוּלִים מִן הָאָרֶץ, וְהָאֱלִילִים כָּרוֹת יִכָּרֵתוּן, לְתַקֵּן עוֹלָם בְּמַלְכוּת שַׁדַּי. וְכָל בְּנֵי בָשָׂר יִקְרְאוּ בִשְׁמֶךָ, לְהַפְנוֹת אֵלֶיךָ כָּל רִשְׁעֵי אָרֶץ. יַכִּירוּ וְיֵדְעוּ כָּל יוֹשְׁבֵי תֵבֵל, כִּי לְךָ תִּכְרַע כָּל בֶּרֶךְ, תִּשָּׁבַע כָּל לָשׁוֹן.[1] לְפָנֶיךָ יהוה אֱלֹהֵינוּ יִכְרְעוּ וְיִפֹּלוּ, וְלִכְבוֹד שִׁמְךָ יְקָר יִתֵּנוּ. וִיקַבְּלוּ כֻלָּם אֶת עוֹל מַלְכוּתֶךָ, וְתִמְלֹךְ עֲלֵיהֶם מְהֵרָה לְעוֹלָם וָעֶד. כִּי הַמַּלְכוּת שֶׁלְּךָ הִיא וּלְעוֹלְמֵי עַד תִּמְלוֹךְ בְּכָבוֹד, כַּכָּתוּב בְּתוֹרָתֶךָ: יהוה יִמְלֹךְ לְעֹלָם וָעֶד.[2] ❖ וְנֶאֱמַר: וְהָיָה יהוה לְמֶלֶךְ עַל כָּל הָאָרֶץ, בַּיּוֹם הַהוּא יִהְיֶה יהוה אֶחָד וּשְׁמוֹ אֶחָד.[3]

Some congregations recite the following after עָלֵינוּ:

אַל תִּירָא מִפַּחַד פִּתְאֹם, וּמִשֹּׁאַת רְשָׁעִים כִּי תָבֹא.[4] עֻצוּ עֵצָה וְתֻפָר, דַּבְּרוּ דָבָר וְלֹא יָקוּם, כִּי עִמָּנוּ אֵל.[5] וְעַד זִקְנָה אֲנִי הוּא, וְעַד שֵׂיבָה אֲנִי אֶסְבֹּל, אֲנִי עָשִׂיתִי וַאֲנִי אֶשָּׂא, וַאֲנִי אֶסְבֹּל וַאֲמַלֵּט.[6]

קדיש יתום

In the presence of a *minyan,* mourners recite קַדִּישׁ יָתוֹם, the Mourner's *Kaddish* (see *Laws* §132-133).

יִתְגַּדַּל וְיִתְקַדַּשׁ שְׁמֵהּ רַבָּא. (.Cong – אָמֵן.) בְּעָלְמָא דִּי בְרָא כִרְעוּתֵהּ. וְיַמְלִיךְ מַלְכוּתֵהּ, בְּחַיֵּיכוֹן וּבְיוֹמֵיכוֹן וּבְחַיֵּי דְכָל בֵּית יִשְׂרָאֵל, בַּעֲגָלָא וּבִזְמַן קָרִיב. וְאִמְרוּ: אָמֵן.

(.Cong – אָמֵן. יְהֵא שְׁמֵהּ רַבָּא מְבָרַךְ לְעָלַם וּלְעָלְמֵי עָלְמַיָּא.)

יְהֵא שְׁמֵהּ רַבָּא מְבָרַךְ לְעָלַם וּלְעָלְמֵי עָלְמַיָּא.

יִתְבָּרַךְ וְיִשְׁתַּבַּח וְיִתְפָּאַר וְיִתְרוֹמַם וְיִתְנַשֵּׂא וְיִתְהַדָּר וְיִתְעַלֶּה וְיִתְהַלָּל שְׁמֵהּ דְּקֻדְשָׁא בְּרִיךְ הוּא (.Cong – בְּרִיךְ הוּא) — לְעֵלָּא מִן כָּל בִּרְכָתָא וְשִׁירָתָא תֻּשְׁבְּחָתָא וְנֶחֱמָתָא, דַּאֲמִירָן בְּעָלְמָא. וְאִמְרוּ: אָמֵן. (.Cong – אָמֵן.)

יְהֵא שְׁלָמָא רַבָּא מִן שְׁמַיָּא, וְחַיִּים עָלֵינוּ וְעַל כָּל יִשְׂרָאֵל. וְאִמְרוּ: אָמֵן. (.Cong – אָמֵן.)

Take three steps back. Bow left and say . . . עֹשֶׂה; bow right and say . . . הוּא; bow forward and say וְעַל כָּל . . . אָמֵן. Remain standing in place for a few moments, then take three steps forward.

עֹשֶׂה שָׁלוֹם בִּמְרוֹמָיו, הוּא יַעֲשֶׂה שָׁלוֹם עָלֵינוּ, וְעַל כָּל יִשְׂרָאֵל. וְאִמְרוּ: אָמֵן. (.Cong – אָמֵן.)

עַל כֵּן *Therefore we put our hope in You, HASHEM, our God, that we may soon see Your mighty splendor, to remove detestable idolatry from the earth, and false gods will be utterly cut off, to perfect the universe through the Almighty's sovereignty. Then all humanity will call upon Your Name, to turn all the earth's wicked toward You. All the world's inhabitants will recognize and know that to You every knee should bend, every tongue should swear.[1] Before You, HASHEM, our God, they will bend every knee and cast themselves down and to the glory of Your Name they will render homage, and they will all accept upon themselves the yoke of Your kingship that You may reign over them soon and eternally. For the kingdom is Yours and You will reign for all eternity in glory as it is written in Your Torah: HASHEM shall reign for all eternity.[2]* Chazzan– *And it is said: HASHEM will be King over all the world — on that day HASHEM will be One and His Name will be One.[3]*

Some congregations recite the following after *Aleinu.*

אַל תִּירָא *Do not fear sudden terror, or the holocaust of the wicked when it comes.[4] Plan a conspiracy and it will be annulled; speak your piece and it shall not stand, for God is with us.[5] Even till your seniority, I remain unchanged; and even till your ripe old age, I shall endure. I created you and I shall bear you; I shall endure and rescue.[6]*

MOURNER'S KADDISH

In the presence of a *minyan,* mourners recite קַדִּישׁ יָתוֹם, the Mourner's *Kaddish* (see *Laws* 132-133).
[A transliteration of this *Kaddish* appears on page 484.]

יִתְגַּדַּל *May His great Name grow exalted and sanctified* (Cong.– *Amen.*) *in the world that He created as He willed. May He give reign to His kingship in your lifetimes and in your days, and in the lifetimes of the entire Family of Israel, swiftly and soon. Now respond: Amen.*

(Cong.– *Amen. May His great Name be blessed forever and ever.*)
May His great Name be blessed forever and ever.

Blessed, praised, glorified, exalted, extolled, mighty, upraised, and lauded be the Name of the Holy One, Blessed is He (Cong.– *Blessed is He*) *— beyond any blessing and song, praise and consolation that are uttered in the world. Now respond: Amen.* (Cong.– *Amen*).

May there be abundant peace from Heaven, and life, upon us and upon all Israel. Now respond: Amen. (Cong.– *Amen.*)

Take three steps back. Bow left and say, *'He Who makes peace . . .';* bow right and say, *'may He . . .';* bow forward and say, *'and upon all Israel . . .'* Remain standing in place for a few moments, then take three steps forward.

He Who makes peace in His heights, may He make peace upon us, and upon all Israel. Now respond: Amen. (Cong.– *Amen.*

(1) Cf. *Isaiah* 45:23. (2) *Exodus* 15:18. (3) *Zechariah* 14:9. (4) *Proverbs* 3:25. (5) *Isaiah* 8:10. (6) 46:4.

מעריב למוצאי תשעה באב

Congregation, then *chazzan:*

וְהוּא רַחוּם יְכַפֵּר עָוֹן וְלֹא יַשְׁחִית, וְהִרְבָּה לְהָשִׁיב אַפּוֹ, וְלֹא יָעִיר כָּל חֲמָתוֹ.[1] יהוה הוֹשִׁיעָה, הַמֶּלֶךְ יַעֲנֵנוּ בְיוֹם קָרְאֵנוּ.[2]

In some congregations the *chazzan* chants a melody during his recitation of בָּרְכוּ, so that the congregation can then recite יִתְבָּרַךְ.

Chazzan bows at בָּרְכוּ and straightens up at ה׳.

בָּרְכוּ אֶת יהוה הַמְּבֹרָךְ.

Congregation, followed by *chazzan,* responds, bowing at בָּרוּךְ and straightening up at ה׳.

בָּרוּךְ יהוה הַמְּבֹרָךְ לְעוֹלָם וָעֶד.

יִתְבָּרַךְ וְיִשְׁתַּבַּח וְיִתְפָּאַר וְיִתְרוֹמַם וְיִתְנַשֵּׂא שְׁמוֹ שֶׁל מֶלֶךְ מַלְכֵי הַמְּלָכִים, הַקָּדוֹשׁ בָּרוּךְ הוּא. שֶׁהוּא רִאשׁוֹן וְהוּא אַחֲרוֹן, וּמִבַּלְעָדָיו אֵין אֱלֹהִים.[3] סֹלּוּ, לָרֹכֵב בָּעֲרָבוֹת, בְּיָהּ שְׁמוֹ, וְעִלְזוּ לְפָנָיו.[4] וּשְׁמוֹ מְרוֹמָם עַל כָּל בְּרָכָה וּתְהִלָּה.[5] בָּרוּךְ שֵׁם כְּבוֹד מַלְכוּתוֹ לְעוֹלָם וָעֶד. יְהִי שֵׁם יהוה מְבֹרָךְ, מֵעַתָּה וְעַד עוֹלָם.[6]

ברכות קריאת שמע

בָּרוּךְ אַתָּה יהוה אֱלֹהֵינוּ מֶלֶךְ הָעוֹלָם, אֲשֶׁר בִּדְבָרוֹ מַעֲרִיב עֲרָבִים, בְּחָכְמָה פּוֹתֵחַ שְׁעָרִים, וּבִתְבוּנָה מְשַׁנֶּה עִתִּים, וּמַחֲלִיף אֶת הַזְּמַנִּים, וּמְסַדֵּר אֶת הַכּוֹכָבִים בְּמִשְׁמְרוֹתֵיהֶם בָּרָקִיעַ כִּרְצוֹנוֹ. בּוֹרֵא יוֹם וָלָיְלָה, גּוֹלֵל אוֹר מִפְּנֵי חֹשֶׁךְ וְחֹשֶׁךְ מִפְּנֵי אוֹר. וּמַעֲבִיר יוֹם וּמֵבִיא לָיְלָה, וּמַבְדִּיל בֵּין יוֹם וּבֵין לָיְלָה, יהוה צְבָאוֹת שְׁמוֹ. ❖ אֵל חַי וְקַיָּם, תָּמִיד יִמְלוֹךְ עָלֵינוּ, לְעוֹלָם וָעֶד. בָּרוּךְ אַתָּה יהוה, הַמַּעֲרִיב עֲרָבִים. (Cong. – אָמֵן.)

אַהֲבַת עוֹלָם בֵּית יִשְׂרָאֵל עַמְּךָ אָהָבְתָּ. תּוֹרָה וּמִצְוֹת, חֻקִּים וּמִשְׁפָּטִים, אוֹתָנוּ לִמַּדְתָּ. עַל כֵּן יהוה אֱלֹהֵינוּ, בְּשָׁכְבֵנוּ וּבְקוּמֵנוּ נָשִׂיחַ בְּחֻקֶּיךָ, וְנִשְׂמַח בְּדִבְרֵי תוֹרָתֶךָ, וּבְמִצְוֹתֶיךָ לְעוֹלָם וָעֶד. ❖ כִּי הֵם חַיֵּינוּ, וְאֹרֶךְ יָמֵינוּ, וּבָהֶם נֶהְגֶּה יוֹמָם וָלָיְלָה. וְאַהֲבָתְךָ, אַל תָּסִיר מִמֶּנּוּ לְעוֹלָמִים. בָּרוּךְ אַתָּה יהוה, אוֹהֵב עַמּוֹ יִשְׂרָאֵל. (Cong. – אָמֵן.)

שמע

Immediately before its recitation, concentrate on fulfilling the positive commandment of reciting the *Shema* twice daily. It is important to enunciate each word clearly and not to run words together. For this reason, vertical lines have been placed between two words that are prone to be slurred into one and are not separated by a comma or a hyphen. See *Laws* §95-109.

MAARIV FOR THE CONCLUSION OF TISHAH B'AV

Congregation, then *chazzan:*

וְהוּא רַחוּם *He, the Merciful One, is forgiving of iniquity and does not destroy. Frequently He withdraws His anger, not arousing His entire rage.[1] HASHEM, save! May the King answer us on the day we call.[2]*

In some congregations the *chazzan* chants a melody during his recitation of *Borchu,* so that the congregation can then recite *'Blessed, praised . . .'*

Chazzan bows at *'Bless,'* and straightens up at *'HASHEM.'*

Bless HASHEM, the blessed One.

Congregation, followed by *chazzan,* responds, bowing at *'Blessed'* and straightening up at *'HASHEM.'*

Blessed is HASHEM, the blessed One, for all eternity.

Blessed, praised, glorified, exalted and upraised is the Name of the King Who rules over kings — the Holy One, Blessed is He. For He is the First and He is the Last and aside from Him there is no god.[3] Extol Him — Who rides the highest heavens — with His Name, YAH, and exult before Him.[4] His Name is exalted beyond every blessing and praise.[5] Blessed is the Name of His glorious kingdom for all eternity. Blessed be the Name of HASHEM from this time and forever.[6]

BLESSINGS OF THE SHEMA

בָּרוּךְ *Blessed are You, HASHEM, our God, King of the universe, Who by His word brings on evenings, with wisdom opens gates, with understanding alters periods, changes the seasons, and orders the stars in their heavenly constellations as He wills. He creates day and night, removing light before darkness and darkness before light. He causes day to pass and brings night, and separates between day and night — HASHEM, Master of Legions, is His Name.* Chazzan— *May the living and enduring God continuously reign over us, for all eternity. Blessed are You, HASHEM, Who brings on evenings.* (Cong.— *Amen.)*

אַהֲבַת *With an eternal love have You loved the House of Israel, Your nation. Torah and commandments, decrees and ordinances have You taught us. Therefore HASHEM, our God, upon our retiring and arising, we will discuss Your decrees and we will rejoice with the words of Your Torah and with Your commandments for all eternity.* Chazzan— *For they are our life and the length of our days and about them we will meditate day and night. May You not remove Your love from us forever. Blessed are You, HASHEM, Who loves His nation Israel.* (Cong.— *Amen.)*

THE SHEMA

Immediately before its recitation, concentrate on fulfilling the positive commandment of reciting the *Shema* twice daily. It is important to enunciate each word clearly and not to run words together. See *Laws* §95-109.

(1) *Psalms* 78:38. (2) 20:10. (3) Cf. *Isaiah* 44:6. (4) *Psalms* 68:5.
(5) Cf. *Nehemiah* 9:5. (6) *Psalms* 113.2.

When praying without a *minyan,* begin with the following three-word formula:

אֵל מֶלֶךְ נֶאֱמָן.

Recite the first verse aloud, with the right hand covering the eyes, and concentrate intently upon accepting God's absolute sovereignty.

שְׁמַע | יִשְׂרָאֵל, יהוה | אֱלֹהֵינוּ, יהוה | אֶחָד:[1]

In an undertone – בָּרוּךְ שֵׁם כְּבוֹד מַלְכוּתוֹ לְעוֹלָם וָעֶד.

While reciting the first paragraph (דברים ו:ה-ט), concentrate on accepting the commandment to love God.

וְאָהַבְתָּ אֵת | יהוה | אֱלֹהֶיךָ, בְּכָל־לְבָבְךָ, וּבְכָל־נַפְשְׁךָ, וּבְכָל־מְאֹדֶךָ: וְהָיוּ הַדְּבָרִים הָאֵלֶּה, אֲשֶׁר | אָנֹכִי מְצַוְּךָ הַיּוֹם, עַל־לְבָבֶךָ: וְשִׁנַּנְתָּם לְבָנֶיךָ, וְדִבַּרְתָּ בָּם, בְּשִׁבְתְּךָ בְּבֵיתֶךָ, וּבְלֶכְתְּךָ בַדֶּרֶךְ, וּבְשָׁכְבְּךָ וּבְקוּמֶךָ: וּקְשַׁרְתָּם לְאוֹת | עַל־יָדֶךָ, וְהָיוּ לְטֹטָפֹת בֵּין | עֵינֶיךָ: וּכְתַבְתָּם | עַל־מְזֻזוֹת בֵּיתֶךָ, וּבִשְׁעָרֶיךָ:

While reciting the second paragraph (דברים יא:יג-כא), concentrate on accepting all the commandments and the concept of reward and punishment.

וְהָיָה, אִם־שָׁמֹעַ תִּשְׁמְעוּ אֶל־מִצְוֹתַי, אֲשֶׁר | אָנֹכִי מְצַוֶּה | אֶתְכֶם הַיּוֹם, לְאַהֲבָה אֶת־יהוה | אֱלֹהֵיכֶם וּלְעָבְדוֹ, בְּכָל־לְבַבְכֶם, וּבְכָל־נַפְשְׁכֶם: וְנָתַתִּי מְטַר־אַרְצְכֶם בְּעִתּוֹ, יוֹרֶה וּמַלְקוֹשׁ, וְאָסַפְתָּ דְגָנֶךָ וְתִירֹשְׁךָ וְיִצְהָרֶךָ: וְנָתַתִּי | עֵשֶׂב | בְּשָׂדְךָ לִבְהֶמְתֶּךָ, וְאָכַלְתָּ וְשָׂבָעְתָּ: הִשָּׁמְרוּ לָכֶם, פֶּן־יִפְתֶּה לְבַבְכֶם, וְסַרְתֶּם וַעֲבַדְתֶּם | אֱלֹהִים | אֲחֵרִים, וְהִשְׁתַּחֲוִיתֶם לָהֶם: וְחָרָה | אַף־יהוה בָּכֶם, וְעָצַר | אֶת־הַשָּׁמַיִם, וְלֹא־יִהְיֶה מָטָר, וְהָאֲדָמָה לֹא תִתֵּן אֶת־יְבוּלָהּ, וַאֲבַדְתֶּם | מְהֵרָה מֵעַל הָאָרֶץ הַטֹּבָה | אֲשֶׁר | יהוה נֹתֵן לָכֶם: וְשַׂמְתֶּם | אֶת־דְּבָרַי | אֵלֶּה, עַל־לְבַבְכֶם וְעַל־נַפְשְׁכֶם, וּקְשַׁרְתֶּם | אֹתָם לְאוֹת | עַל־יֶדְכֶם, וְהָיוּ לְטוֹטָפֹת בֵּין | עֵינֵיכֶם: וְלִמַּדְתֶּם | אֹתָם | אֶת־בְּנֵיכֶם, לְדַבֵּר בָּם, בְּשִׁבְתְּךָ בְּבֵיתֶךָ, וּבְלֶכְתְּךָ בַדֶּרֶךְ, וּבְשָׁכְבְּךָ וּבְקוּמֶךָ: וּכְתַבְתָּם | עַל־מְזוּזוֹת בֵּיתֶךָ, וּבִשְׁעָרֶיךָ: לְמַעַן | יִרְבּוּ | יְמֵיכֶם וִימֵי בְנֵיכֶם, עַל הָאֲדָמָה | אֲשֶׁר נִשְׁבַּע | יהוה לַאֲבֹתֵיכֶם לָתֵת לָהֶם, כִּימֵי הַשָּׁמַיִם | עַל־הָאָרֶץ:

במדבר טו:לז-מא

וַיֹּאמֶר | יהוה | אֶל־מֹשֶׁה לֵּאמֹר: דַּבֵּר | אֶל־בְּנֵי | יִשְׂרָאֵל, וְאָמַרְתָּ אֲלֵהֶם, וְעָשׂוּ לָהֶם צִיצִת, עַל־כַּנְפֵי בִגְדֵיהֶם לְדֹרֹתָם, וְנָתְנוּ | עַל־צִיצִת הַכָּנָף, פְּתִיל תְּכֵלֶת: וְהָיָה לָכֶם לְצִיצִת, וּרְאִיתֶם | אֹתוֹ, וּזְכַרְתֶּם | אֶת־כָּל־מִצְוֹת | יהוה, וַעֲשִׂיתֶם | אֹתָם,

When praying without a *minyan,* begin with the following three-word formula:
God, trustworthy King.
Recite the first verse aloud, with the right hand covering the eyes, and concentrate intently upon accepting God's absolute sovereignty.

Hear, O Israel: HASHEM is our God, HASHEM, the One and Only.[1]

In an undertone— *Blessed is the Name of His glorious kingdom for all eternity.*

While reciting the first paragraph (*Deuteronomy* 6:5-9), concentrate on accepting the commandment to love God.

וְאָהַבְתָּ *You shall love HASHEM, your God, with all your heart, with all your soul and with all your resources. Let these matters that I command you today be upon your heart. Teach them thoroughly to your children and speak of them while you sit in your home, while you walk on the way, when you retire and when you arise. Bind them as a sign upon your arm and let them be tefillin between your eyes. And write them on the doorposts of your house and upon your gates.*

While reciting the second paragraph (*Deuteronomy* 11:13-21), concentrate on accepting all the commandments and the concept of reward and punishment.

וְהָיָה *And it will come to pass that if you continually hearken to My commandments that I command you today, to love HASHEM, your God, and to serve Him, with all your heart and with all your soul — then I will provide rain for your land in its proper time, the early and late rains, that you may gather in your grain, your wine, and your oil. I will provide grass in your field for your cattle and you will eat and be satisfied. Beware lest your heart be seduced and you turn astray and serve gods of others and bow to them. Then the wrath of HASHEM will blaze against you. He will restrain the heaven so there will be no rain and the ground will not yield its produce. And you will swiftly be banished from the goodly land which HASHEM gives you. Place these words of Mine upon your heart and upon your soul; bind them for a sign upon your arm and let them be tefillin between your eyes. Teach them to your children, to discuss them, while you sit in your home, while you walk on the way, when you retire and when you arise. And write them on the doorposts of your house and upon your gates. In order to prolong your days and the days of your children upon the ground that HASHEM has sworn to your ancestors to give them, like the days of the heaven on the earth.*

Numbers 15:37-41

וַיֹּאמֶר *And HASHEM said to Moses saying: Speak to the Children of Israel and say to them that they are to make themselves tzitzis on the corners of their garments, throughout their generations. And they are to place upon the tzitzis of each corner a thread of techeiles. And it shall constitute tzitzis for you, that you may see it and remember all the commandments of HASHEM and perform them;*

(1) *Deuteronomy* 6:4.

וְלֹא־תָתֻ֗רוּ | אַחֲרֵ֤י לְבַבְכֶם֙ וְאַחֲרֵ֣י | עֵֽינֵיכֶ֔ם, אֲשֶׁר־אַתֶּ֥ם זֹנִ֖ים | אַחֲרֵיהֶֽם: לְמַ֣עַן תִּזְכְּר֔וּ, וַעֲשִׂיתֶ֖ם | אֶת־כָּל־מִצְוֺתָ֑י, וִהְיִיתֶ֥ם קְדֹשִׁ֖ים לֵאלֹהֵיכֶֽם: אֲנִ֞י יְהוָ֣ה | אֱלֹהֵיכֶ֗ם, אֲשֶׁ֨ר הוֹצֵ֤אתִי | אֶתְכֶם֙ | מֵאֶ֣רֶץ מִצְרַ֔יִם, לִהְי֥וֹת לָכֶ֖ם לֵאלֹהִ֑ים, אֲנִ֖י | יְהוָ֣ה | אֱלֹהֵיכֶֽם: אֱמֶת —

Concentrate on fulfilling the commandment of remembering the Exodus from Egypt.

Although the word אֱמֶת belongs to the next paragraph, it is appended to the conclusion of the previous one.

—Chazzan repeats **יהוה אֱלֹהֵיכֶם אֱמֶת.**

וֶאֱמוּנָה כָּל זֹאת, וְקַיָּם עָלֵינוּ, כִּי הוּא יהוה אֱלֹהֵינוּ וְאֵין זוּלָתוֹ, וַאֲנַחְנוּ יִשְׂרָאֵל עַמּוֹ. הַפּוֹדֵנוּ מִיַּד מְלָכִים, מַלְכֵּנוּ הַגּוֹאֲלֵנוּ מִכַּף כָּל הֶעָרִיצִים. הָאֵל הַנִּפְרָע לָנוּ מִצָּרֵינוּ, וְהַמְשַׁלֵּם גְּמוּל לְכָל אֹיְבֵי נַפְשֵׁנוּ. הָעֹשֶׂה גְדֹלוֹת עַד אֵין חֵקֶר, וְנִפְלָאוֹת עַד אֵין מִסְפָּר.[1] הַשָּׂם נַפְשֵׁנוּ בַּחַיִּים, וְלֹא נָתַן לַמּוֹט רַגְלֵנוּ.[2] הַמַּדְרִיכֵנוּ עַל בָּמוֹת אוֹיְבֵינוּ, וַיָּרֶם קַרְנֵנוּ עַל כָּל שׂנְאֵינוּ. הָעֹשֶׂה לָּנוּ נִסִּים וּנְקָמָה בְּפַרְעֹה, אוֹתוֹת וּמוֹפְתִים בְּאַדְמַת בְּנֵי חָם. הַמַּכֶּה בְעֶבְרָתוֹ כָּל בְּכוֹרֵי מִצְרָיִם, וַיּוֹצֵא אֶת עַמּוֹ יִשְׂרָאֵל מִתּוֹכָם לְחֵרוּת עוֹלָם. הַמַּעֲבִיר בָּנָיו בֵּין גִּזְרֵי יַם סוּף, אֶת רוֹדְפֵיהֶם וְאֶת שׂוֹנְאֵיהֶם בִּתְהוֹמוֹת טִבַּע. וְרָאוּ בָנָיו גְּבוּרָתוֹ, שִׁבְּחוּ וְהוֹדוּ לִשְׁמוֹ. ❖ וּמַלְכוּתוֹ בְּרָצוֹן קִבְּלוּ עֲלֵיהֶם. מֹשֶׁה וּבְנֵי יִשְׂרָאֵל לְךָ עָנוּ שִׁירָה, בְּשִׂמְחָה רַבָּה, וְאָמְרוּ כֻלָּם:

מִי כָמֹכָה בָּאֵלִים יהוה, מִי כָּמֹכָה נֶאְדָּר בַּקֹּדֶשׁ, נוֹרָא תְהִלֹּת, עֹשֵׂה פֶלֶא.[3] ❖ מַלְכוּתְךָ רָאוּ בָנֶיךָ בּוֹקֵעַ יָם לִפְנֵי מֹשֶׁה, זֶה אֵלִי[4] עָנוּ וְאָמְרוּ:

יהוה יִמְלֹךְ לְעֹלָם וָעֶד.[5] ❖ וְנֶאֱמַר: כִּי פָדָה יהוה אֶת יַעֲקֹב, וּגְאָלוֹ מִיַּד חָזָק מִמֶּנּוּ.[6] בָּרוּךְ אַתָּה יהוה, גָּאַל יִשְׂרָאֵל.

(*—Cong.* אָמֵן.)

הַשְׁכִּיבֵנוּ יהוה אֱלֹהֵינוּ לְשָׁלוֹם, וְהַעֲמִידֵנוּ מַלְכֵּנוּ לְחַיִּים, וּפְרוֹשׂ עָלֵינוּ סֻכַּת שְׁלוֹמֶךָ, וְתַקְּנֵנוּ בְּעֵצָה טוֹבָה מִלְּפָנֶיךָ, וְהוֹשִׁיעֵנוּ לְמַעַן שְׁמֶךָ. וְהָגֵן בַּעֲדֵנוּ, וְהָסֵר מֵעָלֵינוּ אוֹיֵב, דֶּבֶר, וְחֶרֶב, וְרָעָב, וְיָגוֹן, וְהָסֵר שָׂטָן מִלְּפָנֵינוּ וּמֵאַחֲרֵינוּ, וּבְצֵל כְּנָפֶיךָ תַּסְתִּירֵנוּ,[7] כִּי אֵל שׁוֹמְרֵנוּ וּמַצִּילֵנוּ אָתָּה, כִּי אֵל

and not explore after your heart and after your eyes after which you stray. So that you may remember and perform all My commandments;

Concentrate on fulfilling the commandment of remembering the Exodus from Egypt.

and be holy to your God. I am HASHEM, *your God, Who has removed you from the land of Egypt to be a God to you; I am* HASHEM *your God — it is true —*

Although the word אֱמֶת, *'it is true,'* belongs to the next paragraph, it is appended to the conclusion of the previous one.

Chazzan repeats: **HASHEM, your God, is true.**

וֶאֱמוּנָה *And faithful is all this, and it is firmly established for us that He is* HASHEM *our God, and there is none but Him, and we are Israel, His nation. He redeems us from the power of kings, our King Who delivers us from the hand of all the cruel tyrants. He is the God Who exacts vengeance for us from our foes and Who brings just retribution upon all enemies of our soul; Who performs great deeds that are beyond comprehension, and wonders beyond number.*[1] *Who set our soul in life and did not allow our foot to falter.*[2] *Who led us upon the heights of our enemies and raised our pride above all who hate us; Who wrought for us miracles and vengeance upon Pharaoh; signs and wonders on the land of the offspring of Ham; Who struck with His anger all the firstborn of Egypt and removed His nation Israel from their midst to eternal freedom; Who brought His children through the split parts of the Sea of Reeds while those who pursued them and hated them He caused to sink into the depths. When His children perceived His power, they lauded and gave grateful praise to His Name.* Chazzan– *And His Kingship they accepted upon themselves willingly. Moses and the Children of Israel raised their voices to You in song with abundant gladness — and said unanimously:*

מִי כָמֹכָה *Who is like You among the heavenly powers,* HASHEM! *Who is like You, mighty in holiness, too awesome for praise, doing wonders!*[3] Chazzan– *Your children beheld Your majesty, as You split the sea before Moses: 'This is my God!'*[4] *they exclaimed, then they said:*

יהוה *'*HASHEM *shall reign for all eternity!'*[5] Chazzan– *And it is further said: 'For* HASHEM *has redeemed Jacob and delivered him from a power mightier than he.'*[6] *Blessed are You,* HASHEM, *Who redeemed Israel.*

(Cong.– *Amen.*)

הַשְׁכִּיבֵנוּ *Lay us down to sleep,* HASHEM *our God, in peace, raise us erect, our King, to life; and spread over us the shelter of Your peace. Set us aright with good counsel from before Your Presence, and save us for Your Name's sake. Shield us, remove from us foe, plague, sword, famine, and woe; and remove spiritual impediment from before us and behind us, and in the shadow of Your wings shelter us*[7] *— for God Who protects and rescues us are You; for God,*

(1) *Job* 9:10. (2) *Psalms* 66:9. (3) *Exodus* 15:11. (4) 15:2. (5) 15:18. (6) *Jeremiah* 31:10. (7) Cf. *Psalms* 17:8.

מֶלֶךְ חַנּוּן וְרַחוּם אָתָּה.[1] ❖ וּשְׁמוֹר צֵאתֵנוּ וּבוֹאֵנוּ, לְחַיִּים וּלְשָׁלוֹם מֵעַתָּה וְעַד עוֹלָם.[2] בָּרוּךְ אַתָּה יהוה, שׁוֹמֵר עַמּוֹ יִשְׂרָאֵל לָעַד. (.Cong – אָמֵן.)

Some congregations omit the following prayers and continue with Half-*Kaddish* (p. 452).

בָּרוּךְ יהוה לְעוֹלָם, אָמֵן וְאָמֵן.[3] בָּרוּךְ יהוה מִצִּיּוֹן, שֹׁכֵן יְרוּשָׁלָיִם, הַלְלוּיָהּ.[4] בָּרוּךְ יהוה אֱלֹהִים אֱלֹהֵי יִשְׂרָאֵל, עֹשֵׂה נִפְלָאוֹת לְבַדּוֹ. וּבָרוּךְ שֵׁם כְּבוֹדוֹ לְעוֹלָם, וְיִמָּלֵא כְבוֹדוֹ אֶת כָּל הָאָרֶץ, אָמֵן וְאָמֵן.[5] יְהִי כְבוֹד יהוה לְעוֹלָם, יִשְׂמַח יהוה בְּמַעֲשָׂיו.[6] יְהִי שֵׁם יהוה מְבֹרָךְ, מֵעַתָּה וְעַד עוֹלָם.[7] כִּי לֹא יִטֹּשׁ יהוה אֶת עַמּוֹ בַּעֲבוּר שְׁמוֹ הַגָּדוֹל, כִּי הוֹאִיל יהוה לַעֲשׂוֹת אֶתְכֶם לוֹ לְעָם.[8] וַיַּרְא כָּל הָעָם וַיִּפְּלוּ עַל פְּנֵיהֶם, וַיֹּאמְרוּ, יהוה הוּא הָאֱלֹהִים, יהוה הוּא הָאֱלֹהִים.[9] וְהָיָה יהוה לְמֶלֶךְ עַל כָּל הָאָרֶץ, בַּיּוֹם הַהוּא יִהְיֶה יהוה אֶחָד וּשְׁמוֹ אֶחָד.[10] יְהִי חַסְדְּךָ יהוה עָלֵינוּ, כַּאֲשֶׁר יִחַלְנוּ לָךְ.[11] הוֹשִׁיעֵנוּ יהוה אֱלֹהֵינוּ, וְקַבְּצֵנוּ מִן הַגּוֹיִם, לְהוֹדוֹת לְשֵׁם קָדְשֶׁךָ, לְהִשְׁתַּבֵּחַ בִּתְהִלָּתֶךָ.[12] כָּל גּוֹיִם אֲשֶׁר עָשִׂיתָ יָבוֹאוּ וְיִשְׁתַּחֲווּ לְפָנֶיךָ אֲדֹנָי, וִיכַבְּדוּ לִשְׁמֶךָ. כִּי גָדוֹל אַתָּה וְעֹשֵׂה נִפְלָאוֹת, אַתָּה אֱלֹהִים לְבַדֶּךָ.[13] וַאֲנַחְנוּ עַמְּךָ וְצֹאן מַרְעִיתֶךָ, נוֹדֶה לְּךָ לְעוֹלָם, לְדוֹר וָדֹר נְסַפֵּר תְּהִלָּתֶךָ.[14] בָּרוּךְ יהוה בַּיּוֹם. בָּרוּךְ יהוה בַּלָּיְלָה. בָּרוּךְ יהוה בְּשָׁכְבֵנוּ. בָּרוּךְ יהוה בְּקוּמֵנוּ. כִּי בְיָדְךָ נַפְשׁוֹת הַחַיִּים וְהַמֵּתִים. אֲשֶׁר בְּיָדוֹ נֶפֶשׁ כָּל חָי, וְרוּחַ כָּל בְּשַׂר אִישׁ.[15] בְּיָדְךָ אַפְקִיד רוּחִי, פָּדִיתָה אוֹתִי, יהוה אֵל אֱמֶת.[16] אֱלֹהֵינוּ שֶׁבַּשָּׁמַיִם יַחֵד שִׁמְךָ, וְקַיֵּם מַלְכוּתְךָ תָּמִיד, וּמְלוֹךְ עָלֵינוּ לְעוֹלָם וָעֶד.

יִרְאוּ עֵינֵינוּ וְיִשְׂמַח לִבֵּנוּ וְתָגֵל נַפְשֵׁנוּ בִּישׁוּעָתְךָ בֶּאֱמֶת, בֶּאֱמֹר לְצִיּוֹן מָלַךְ אֱלֹהָיִךְ.[17] יהוה מֶלֶךְ,[18] יהוה מָלָךְ,[19] יהוה יִמְלֹךְ לְעֹלָם וָעֶד.[20] ❖ כִּי הַמַּלְכוּת שֶׁלְּךָ הִיא, וּלְעוֹלְמֵי עַד תִּמְלוֹךְ בְּכָבוֹד, כִּי אֵין לָנוּ מֶלֶךְ אֶלָּא אָתָּה. בָּרוּךְ אַתָּה יהוה, הַמֶּלֶךְ בִּכְבוֹדוֹ תָּמִיד יִמְלוֹךְ עָלֵינוּ לְעוֹלָם וָעֶד, וְעַל כָּל מַעֲשָׂיו. (.Cong – אָמֵן.)

the Gracious and Compassionate King, are You.[1] Chazzan– *Safeguard our going and coming, for life and for peace from now to eternity.*[2] *Blessed are You, HASHEM, Who protects His people Israel forever.*

(Cong.– *Amen.*)

Some congregations omit the following prayers and continue with Half-*Kaddish* (p. 452).

בָּרוּךְ *Blessed is HASHEM forever, Amen and Amen.*[3] *Blessed is HASHEM from Zion, Who dwells in Jerusalem, Halleluyah!*[4] *Blessed is HASHEM, God, the God of Israel, Who alone does wondrous things. Blessed is His glorious Name forever, and may all the earth be filled with His glory, Amen and Amen.*[5] *May the glory of HASHEM endure forever, let HASHEM rejoice in His works.*[6] *Blessed be the Name of HASHEM from this time and forever.*[7] *For HASHEM will not cast off His nation for the sake of His Great Name, for HASHEM has vowed to make you His own people.*[8] *Then the entire nation saw and fell on their faces and said, 'HASHEM — only He is God! HASHEM — only He is God!'*[9] *Then HASHEM will be King over all the world, on that day HASHEM will be One and His Name will be One.*[10] *May Your kindness, HASHEM, be upon us, just as we awaited You.*[11] *Save us, HASHEM, our God, gather us from the nations, to thank Your Holy Name and to glory in Your praise!*[12] *All the nations that You made will come and bow before You, My Lord, and shall glorify Your Name. For You are great and work wonders; You alone, O God.*[13] *Then we, Your nation and the sheep of Your pasture, shall thank You forever; for generation after generation we will relate Your praise.*[14] *Blessed is HASHEM by day; Blessed is HASHEM by night; Blessed is HASHEM when we retire; Blessed is HASHEM when we arise. For in Your hand are the souls of the living and the dead. He in Whose hand is the soul of all the living and the spirit of every human being.*[15] *In Your hand I shall entrust my spirit, You redeemed me, HASHEM, God of truth.*[16] *Our God, Who is in heaven, bring unity to Your Name; establish Your kingdom forever and reign over us for all eternity.*

יִרְאוּ *May our eyes see, our heart rejoice and our soul exult in Your salvation in truth, when Zion is told, 'Your God has reigned!'*[17] *HASHEM reigns,*[18] *HASHEM has reigned,*[19] *HASHEM will reign for all eternity.*[20] Chazzan– *For the kingdom is Yours and for all eternity You will reign in glory, for we have no King but You. Blessed are You, HASHEM, the King in His glory — He shall constantly reign over us forever and ever, and over all His creatures.* (Cong.– *Amen.*)

(1) Cf. *Nehemiah* 9:31. (2) Cf. *Psalms* 121:8. (3) 89:53. (4) 135:21. (5) 72:18-19.
(6) 104:31. (7) 113:2. (8) *I Samuel* 12:22. (9) *I Kings* 18:39. (10) *Zechariah* 14:9.
(11) *Psalms* 33:22. (12) 106:47. (13) 86:9-10. (14) 79:13. (15) *Job* 12:10. (16) *Psalms* 31:6.
(17) Cf. *Isaiah* 52:7. (18) *Psalms* 10:16. (19) 93:1 et al. (20) *Exodus* 15:18.

The *chazzan* recites חֲצִי קַדִּישׁ.

יִתְגַּדַּל וְיִתְקַדַּשׁ שְׁמֵהּ רַבָּא. (.Cong – אָמֵן.) בְּעָלְמָא דִּי בְרָא כִרְעוּתֵהּ, וְיַמְלִיךְ מַלְכוּתֵהּ, בְּחַיֵּיכוֹן וּבְיוֹמֵיכוֹן וּבְחַיֵּי דְכָל בֵּית יִשְׂרָאֵל, בַּעֲגָלָא וּבִזְמַן קָרִיב. וְאִמְרוּ: אָמֵן.

(.Cong – אָמֵן. יְהֵא שְׁמֵהּ רַבָּא מְבָרַךְ לְעָלַם וּלְעָלְמֵי עָלְמַיָּא.)

יְהֵא שְׁמֵהּ רַבָּא מְבָרַךְ לְעָלַם וּלְעָלְמֵי עָלְמַיָּא.

יִתְבָּרַךְ וְיִשְׁתַּבַּח וְיִתְפָּאַר וְיִתְרוֹמַם וְיִתְנַשֵּׂא וְיִתְהַדָּר וְיִתְעַלֶּה וְיִתְהַלָּל שְׁמֵהּ דְּקֻדְשָׁא בְּרִיךְ הוּא (.Cong – בְּרִיךְ הוּא) – לְעֵלָּא מִן כָּל בִּרְכָתָא וְשִׁירָתָא תֻּשְׁבְּחָתָא וְנֶחֱמָתָא, דַּאֲמִירָן בְּעָלְמָא. וְאִמְרוּ: אָמֵן. (.Cong – אָמֵן.)

❧ שמונה עשרה – עמידה ❧

Take three steps backward, then three steps forward. Remain standing with the feet together while reciting *Shemoneh Esrei.* Recite it with quiet devotion and without interruption, verbal or otherwise. Although its recitation should not be audible to others, one must pray loudly enough to hear himself.

אֲדֹנָי שְׂפָתַי תִּפְתָּח, וּפִי יַגִּיד תְּהִלָּתֶךָ.[1]

אבות

Bend the knees at בָּרוּךְ; bow at אַתָּה; straighten up at ה׳.

בָּרוּךְ אַתָּה יהוה אֱלֹהֵינוּ וֵאלֹהֵי אֲבוֹתֵינוּ, אֱלֹהֵי אַבְרָהָם, אֱלֹהֵי יִצְחָק, וֵאלֹהֵי יַעֲקֹב, הָאֵל הַגָּדוֹל הַגִּבּוֹר וְהַנּוֹרָא, אֵל עֶלְיוֹן, גּוֹמֵל חֲסָדִים טוֹבִים וְקוֹנֵה הַכֹּל, וְזוֹכֵר חַסְדֵי אָבוֹת, וּמֵבִיא גוֹאֵל לִבְנֵי בְנֵיהֶם, לְמַעַן שְׁמוֹ בְּאַהֲבָה. מֶלֶךְ עוֹזֵר וּמוֹשִׁיעַ וּמָגֵן.

Bend the knees at בָּרוּךְ; bow at אַתָּה; straighten up at ה׳.

בָּרוּךְ אַתָּה יהוה, מָגֵן אַבְרָהָם.

גבורות

אַתָּה גִּבּוֹר לְעוֹלָם אֲדֹנָי, מְחַיֵּה מֵתִים אַתָּה, רַב לְהוֹשִׁיעַ. מְכַלְכֵּל חַיִּים בְּחֶסֶד, מְחַיֵּה מֵתִים בְּרַחֲמִים רַבִּים, סוֹמֵךְ נוֹפְלִים, וְרוֹפֵא חוֹלִים, וּמַתִּיר אֲסוּרִים, וּמְקַיֵּם אֱמוּנָתוֹ לִישֵׁנֵי עָפָר. מִי כָמוֹךָ בַּעַל גְּבוּרוֹת, וּמִי דּוֹמֶה לָּךְ, מֶלֶךְ מֵמִית וּמְחַיֶּה וּמַצְמִיחַ יְשׁוּעָה. וְנֶאֱמָן אַתָּה לְהַחֲיוֹת מֵתִים. בָּרוּךְ אַתָּה יהוה, מְחַיֵּה הַמֵּתִים.

קדושת השם

אַתָּה קָדוֹשׁ וְשִׁמְךָ קָדוֹשׁ, וּקְדוֹשִׁים בְּכָל יוֹם יְהַלְלוּךָ סֶּלָה. בָּרוּךְ אַתָּה יהוה, הָאֵל הַקָּדוֹשׁ.

בינה

אַתָּה חוֹנֵן לְאָדָם דַּעַת, וּמְלַמֵּד לֶאֱנוֹשׁ בִּינָה. חָנֵּנוּ מֵאִתְּךָ דֵּעָה בִּינָה וְהַשְׂכֵּל. בָּרוּךְ אַתָּה יהוה, חוֹנֵן הַדָּעַת.

The *chazzan* recites Half-*Kaddish*.

יִתְגַּדַּל *May His great Name grow exalted and sanctified (*Cong.– *Amen.) in the world that He created as He willed. May He give reign to His kingship in your lifetimes and in your days, and in the lifetimes of the entire Family of Israel, swiftly and soon. Now respond: Amen.*

*(*Cong.– *Amen. May His great Name be blessed forever and ever.)*

May His great Name be blessed forever and ever.

*Blessed, praised, glorified, exalted, extolled, mighty, upraised, and lauded be the Name of the Holy One, Blessed is He (*Cong.– *Blessed is He) — beyond any blessing and song, praise and consolation that are uttered in the world. Now respond: Amen. (*Cong.– *Amen.)*

❧ SHEMONEH ESREI – AMIDAH ❧

Take three steps backward, then three steps forward. Remain standing with the feet together while reciting *Shemoneh Esrei*. Recite it with quiet devotion and without interruption, verbal or otherwise. Although its recitation should not be audible to others, one must pray loudly enough to hear himself.

My Lord, open my lips, that my mouth may declare Your praise.[1]

PATRIARCHS

Bend the knees at '*Blessed*'; bow at '*You*'; straighten up at '*HASHEM*.'

בָּרוּךְ *Blessed are You, HASHEM, our God and the God of our forefathers, God of Abraham, God of Isaac, and God of Jacob; the great, mighty, and awesome God, the supreme God, Who bestows beneficial kindnesses and creates everything, Who recalls the kindnesses of the Patriarchs and brings a Redeemer to their children's children, for His Name's sake, with love. O King, Helper, Savior, and Shield.*

Bend the knees at '*Blessed*'; bow at '*You*'; straighten up at 'HASHEM.'

Blessed are You, HASHEM, Shield of Abraham.

GOD'S MIGHT

אַתָּה *You are eternally mighty, my Lord, the Resuscitator of the dead are You; abundantly able to save. Who sustains the living with kindness, resuscitates the dead with abundant mercy, supports the fallen, heals the sick, releases the confined, and maintains His faith to those asleep in the dust. Who is like You, O Master of mighty deeds, and who is comparable to You, O King Who causes death and restores life and makes salvation sprout! And You are faithful to resuscitate the dead. Blessed are You, HASHEM, Who resuscitates the dead.*

HOLINESS OF GOD'S NAME

אַתָּה *You are holy and Your Name is holy, and holy ones praise You every day, forever. Blessed are You, HASHEM, the holy God.*

INSIGHT

אַתָּה *You graciously endow man with wisdom and teach insight to a frail mortal. Endow us graciously from Yourself with wisdom, insight, and discernment. Blessed are You, HASHEM, gracious Giver of wisdom.*

---

(1) *Psalms* 51:17.

תשובה

הֲשִׁיבֵנוּ אָבִינוּ לְתוֹרָתֶךָ, וְקָרְבֵנוּ מַלְכֵּנוּ לַעֲבוֹדָתֶךָ, וְהַחֲזִירֵנוּ בִּתְשׁוּבָה שְׁלֵמָה לְפָנֶיךָ. בָּרוּךְ אַתָּה יהוה, הָרוֹצֶה בִּתְשׁוּבָה.

סליחה

Strike the left side of the chest with the right fist while reciting the words חָטָאנוּ and פָּשָׁעְנוּ.

סְלַח לָנוּ אָבִינוּ כִּי חָטָאנוּ, מְחַל לָנוּ מַלְכֵּנוּ כִּי פָשָׁעְנוּ, כִּי מוֹחֵל וְסוֹלֵחַ אָתָּה. בָּרוּךְ אַתָּה יהוה, חַנּוּן הַמַּרְבֶּה לִסְלֹחַ.

גאולה

רְאֵה בְעָנְיֵנוּ, וְרִיבָה רִיבֵנוּ, וּגְאָלֵנוּ[1] מְהֵרָה לְמַעַן שְׁמֶךָ, כִּי גוֹאֵל חָזָק אָתָּה. בָּרוּךְ אַתָּה יהוה, גּוֹאֵל יִשְׂרָאֵל.

רפואה

רְפָאֵנוּ יהוה וְנֵרָפֵא, הוֹשִׁיעֵנוּ וְנִוָּשֵׁעָה, כִּי תְהִלָּתֵנוּ אָתָּה,[2] וְהַעֲלֵה רְפוּאָה שְׁלֵמָה לְכָל מַכּוֹתֵינוּ, °°כִּי אֵל מֶלֶךְ רוֹפֵא נֶאֱמָן וְרַחֲמָן אָתָּה. בָּרוּךְ אַתָּה יהוה, רוֹפֵא חוֹלֵי עַמּוֹ יִשְׂרָאֵל.

ברכת השנים

בָּרֵךְ עָלֵינוּ יהוה אֱלֹהֵינוּ אֶת הַשָּׁנָה הַזֹּאת וְאֶת כָּל מִינֵי תְבוּאָתָהּ לְטוֹבָה, וְתֵן בְּרָכָה עַל פְּנֵי הָאֲדָמָה, וְשַׂבְּעֵנוּ מִטּוּבֶךָ, וּבָרֵךְ שְׁנָתֵנוּ כַּשָּׁנִים הַטּוֹבוֹת. בָּרוּךְ אַתָּה יהוה, מְבָרֵךְ הַשָּׁנִים.

קיבוץ גליות

תְּקַע בְּשׁוֹפָר גָּדוֹל לְחֵרוּתֵנוּ, וְשָׂא נֵס לְקַבֵּץ גָּלֻיּוֹתֵינוּ, וְקַבְּצֵנוּ יַחַד מֵאַרְבַּע כַּנְפוֹת הָאָרֶץ.[3] בָּרוּךְ אַתָּה יהוה, מְקַבֵּץ נִדְחֵי עַמּוֹ יִשְׂרָאֵל.

דין

הָשִׁיבָה שׁוֹפְטֵינוּ כְּבָרִאשׁוֹנָה, וְיוֹעֲצֵינוּ כְּבַתְּחִלָּה,[4] וְהָסֵר מִמֶּנּוּ יָגוֹן וַאֲנָחָה, וּמְלוֹךְ עָלֵינוּ אַתָּה יהוה לְבַדְּךָ בְּחֶסֶד וּבְרַחֲמִים, וְצַדְּקֵנוּ בַּמִּשְׁפָּט. בָּרוּךְ אַתָּה יהוה, מֶלֶךְ אוֹהֵב צְדָקָה וּמִשְׁפָּט.

°°At this point one may interject a prayer for one who is ill:

יְהִי רָצוֹן מִלְּפָנֶיךָ יהוה אֱלֹהַי וֵאלֹהֵי אֲבוֹתַי, שֶׁתִּשְׁלַח מְהֵרָה רְפוּאָה שְׁלֵמָה מִן הַשָּׁמַיִם, רְפוּאַת הַנֶּפֶשׁ וּרְפוּאַת הַגּוּף

לַחוֹלֶה—for a male (patient's name) בֶּן (mother's name) בְּתוֹךְ שְׁאָר חוֹלֵי יִשְׂרָאֵל.

לַחוֹלָה—for a female (patient's name) בַּת (mother's name) בְּתוֹךְ שְׁאָר חוֹלֵי יִשְׂרָאֵל.

continue—כִּי אֵל . . .

REPENTANCE

הֲשִׁיבֵנוּ *Bring us back, our Father, to Your Torah, and bring us near, our King, to Your service, and influence us to return in perfect repentance before You. Blessed are You,* HASHEM, *Who desires repentance.*

FORGIVENESS

Strike the left side of the chest with the right fist while reciting the words *'erred'* and *'sinned.'*

סְלַח *Forgive us, our Father, for we have erred; pardon us, our King, for we have willfully sinned; for You pardon and forgive. Blessed are You,* HASHEM, *the gracious One Who pardons abundantly.*

REDEMPTION

רְאֵה *Behold our affliction, take up our grievance, and redeem us*[1] *speedily for Your Name's sake, for You are a powerful Redeemer. Blessed are You,* HASHEM, *Redeemer of Israel.*

HEALTH AND HEALING

רְפָאֵנוּ *Heal us,* HASHEM *— then we will be healed; save us — then we will be saved, for You are our praise.*[2] *Bring complete recovery for all our ailments,* °°*for You are God, King, the faithful and compassionate Healer. Blessed are You,* HASHEM, *Who heals the sick of His people Israel.*

YEAR OF PROSPERITY

בָּרֵךְ *Bless on our behalf — O* HASHEM, *our God — this year and all its kinds of crops for the best, and give a blessing on the face of the earth, and satisfy us from Your bounty, and bless our year like the best years. Blessed are You,* HASHEM, *Who blesses the years.*

INGATHERING OF EXILES

תְּקַע *Sound the great shofar for our freedom, raise the banner to gather our exiles and gather us together from the four corners of the earth.*[3] *Blessed are You,* HASHEM, *Who gathers in the dispersed of His people Israel.*

RESTORATION OF JUSTICE

הָשִׁיבָה *Restore our judges as in earliest times and our counselors as at first;*[4] *remove from us sorrow and groan; and reign over us — You,* HASHEM, *alone — with kindness and compassion, and justify us through judgment. Blessed are You,* HASHEM, *the King Who loves righteousness and judgment.*

°°At this point one may interject a prayer for one who is ill:

May it be Your will, HASHEM, *my God, and the God of my forefathers, that You quickly send a complete recovery from heaven, spiritual healing and physical healing to the patient* (name) *son/daughter of* (mother's name) *among the other patients of Israel.*

Continue: *For You are God . . .*

(1) Cf. *Psalms* 119:153-154. (2) Cf. *Jeremiah* 17:14. (3) Cf. *Isaiah* 11:12. (4) Cf. 1:26.

ברכת המינים

וְלַמַּלְשִׁינִים אַל תְּהִי תִקְוָה, וְכָל הָרִשְׁעָה כְּרֶגַע תֹּאבֵד, וְכָל אֹיְבֶיךָ מְהֵרָה יִכָּרֵתוּ, וְהַזֵּדִים מְהֵרָה תְעַקֵּר וּתְשַׁבֵּר וּתְמַגֵּר וְתַכְנִיעַ בִּמְהֵרָה בְיָמֵינוּ. בָּרוּךְ אַתָּה יהוה, שׁוֹבֵר אֹיְבִים וּמַכְנִיעַ זֵדִים.

צדיקים

עַל הַצַּדִּיקִים וְעַל הַחֲסִידִים, וְעַל זִקְנֵי עַמְּךָ בֵּית יִשְׂרָאֵל, וְעַל פְּלֵיטַת סוֹפְרֵיהֶם, וְעַל גֵּרֵי הַצֶּדֶק וְעָלֵינוּ, יֶהֱמוּ רַחֲמֶיךָ יהוה אֱלֹהֵינוּ, וְתֵן שָׂכָר טוֹב לְכָל הַבּוֹטְחִים בְּשִׁמְךָ בֶּאֱמֶת, וְשִׂים חֶלְקֵנוּ עִמָּהֶם לְעוֹלָם, וְלֹא נֵבוֹשׁ כִּי בְךָ בָּטָחְנוּ. בָּרוּךְ אַתָּה יהוה, מִשְׁעָן וּמִבְטָח לַצַּדִּיקִים.

בנין ירושלים

וְלִירוּשָׁלַיִם עִירְךָ בְּרַחֲמִים תָּשׁוּב, וְתִשְׁכּוֹן בְּתוֹכָהּ כַּאֲשֶׁר דִּבַּרְתָּ, וּבְנֵה אוֹתָהּ בְּקָרוֹב בְּיָמֵינוּ בִּנְיַן עוֹלָם, וְכִסֵּא דָוִד מְהֵרָה לְתוֹכָהּ תָּכִין. בָּרוּךְ אַתָּה יהוה, בּוֹנֵה יְרוּשָׁלָיִם.

מלכות בית דוד

אֶת צֶמַח דָּוִד עַבְדְּךָ מְהֵרָה תַצְמִיחַ, וְקַרְנוֹ תָּרוּם בִּישׁוּעָתֶךָ, כִּי לִישׁוּעָתְךָ קִוִּינוּ כָּל הַיּוֹם. בָּרוּךְ אַתָּה יהוה, מַצְמִיחַ קֶרֶן יְשׁוּעָה.

קבלת תפלה

שְׁמַע קוֹלֵנוּ יהוה אֱלֹהֵינוּ, חוּס וְרַחֵם עָלֵינוּ, וְקַבֵּל בְּרַחֲמִים וּבְרָצוֹן אֶת תְּפִלָּתֵנוּ, כִּי אֵל שׁוֹמֵעַ תְּפִלּוֹת וְתַחֲנוּנִים אָתָּה. וּמִלְּפָנֶיךָ מַלְכֵּנוּ רֵיקָם אַל תְּשִׁיבֵנוּ,°°

°°During the silent *Shemoneh Esrei* one may insert either or both of these personal prayers.

For forgiveness:

אָנָּא יהוה, חָטָאתִי עָוִיתִי וּפָשַׁעְתִּי לְפָנֶיךָ, מִיּוֹם הֱיוֹתִי עַל הָאֲדָמָה עַד הַיּוֹם הַזֶּה (וּבִפְרַט בַּחֵטְא ....). אָנָּא יהוה, עֲשֵׂה לְמַעַן שִׁמְךָ הַגָּדוֹל, וּתְכַפֶּר לִי עַל עֲוֹנַי וַחֲטָאַי וּפְשָׁעַי שֶׁחָטָאתִי וְשֶׁעָוִיתִי וְשֶׁפָּשַׁעְתִּי לְפָנֶיךָ, מִנְּעוּרַי עַד הַיּוֹם הַזֶּה. וּתְמַלֵּא כָּל הַשֵּׁמוֹת שֶׁפָּגַמְתִּי בְּשִׁמְךָ הַגָּדוֹל.

For livelihood:

אַתָּה הוּא יהוה הָאֱלֹהִים, הַזָּן וּמְפַרְנֵס וּמְכַלְכֵּל מִקַּרְנֵי רְאֵמִים עַד בֵּיצֵי כִנִּים. הַטְרִיפֵנִי לֶחֶם חֻקִּי, וְהַמְצֵא לִי וּלְכָל בְּנֵי בֵיתִי מְזוֹנוֹתַי קוֹדֶם שֶׁאֶצְטָרֵךְ לָהֶם, בְּנַחַת וְלֹא בְצַעַר, בְּהֶתֵּר וְלֹא בְאִסּוּר, בְּכָבוֹד וְלֹא בְבִזָּיוֹן, לְחַיִּים וּלְשָׁלוֹם, מִשֶּׁפַע בְּרָכָה וְהַצְלָחָה, וּמִשֶּׁפַע בְּרֵכָה עֶלְיוֹנָה, כְּדֵי שֶׁאוּכַל לַעֲשׂוֹת רְצוֹנֶךָ וְלַעֲסוֹק בְּתוֹרָתֶךָ וּלְקַיֵּם מִצְוֹתֶיךָ. וְאַל תַּצְרִיכֵנִי לִידֵי מַתְּנַת בָּשָׂר וָדָם. וִיקֻיַּם בִּי מִקְרָא שֶׁכָּתוּב: פּוֹתֵחַ אֶת יָדֶךָ, וּמַשְׂבִּיעַ לְכָל חַי רָצוֹן.[1] וְכָתוּב: הַשְׁלֵךְ עַל יהוה יְהָבְךָ וְהוּא יְכַלְכְּלֶךָ.[2]

—Continue ... כִּי אַתָּה

AGAINST HERETICS

וְלַמַּלְשִׁינִים *And for slanderers let there be no hope; and may all wickedness perish in an instant; and may all Your enemies be cut down speedily. May You speedily uproot, smash, cast down, and humble the wanton sinners — speedily in our days. Blessed are You,* HASHEM, *Who breaks enemies and humbles wanton sinners.*

THE RIGHTEOUS

עַל הַצַּדִּיקִים *On the righteous, on the devout, on the elders of Your people the Family of Israel, on the remnant of their scholars, on the righteous converts and on ourselves — may Your compassion be aroused,* HASHEM, *our God, and give goodly reward to all who sincerely believe in Your Name. Put our lot with them forever, and we will not feel ashamed, for we trust in You. Blessed are You,* HASHEM, *Mainstay and Assurance of the righteous.*

REBUILDING JERUSALEM

וְלִירוּשָׁלַיִם *And to Jerusalem, Your city, may You return in compassion, and may You rest within it, as You have spoken. May You rebuild it soon in our days as an eternal structure, and may You speedily establish the throne of David within it. Blessed are You,* HASHEM, *the Builder of Jerusalem.*

DAVIDIC REIGN

אֶת צֶמַח *The offspring of Your servant David may You speedily cause to flourish, and enhance his pride through Your salvation, for we hope for Your salvation all day long. Blessed are You,* HASHEM, *Who causes the pride of salvation to flourish.*

ACCEPTANCE OF PRAYER

שְׁמַע *Hear our voice,* HASHEM *our God, pity and be compassionate to us, and accept — with compassion and favor — our prayer, for God Who hears prayers and supplications are You. From before Yourself, our King, turn us not away empty-handed,*°°

°°During the silent *Shemoneh Esrei* one may insert either or both of these personal prayers.

For forgiveness:

אָנָּא *Please, O* HASHEM, *I have erred, been iniquitous, and willfully sinned before You, from the day I have existed on earth until this very day (and especially with the sin of . . .). Please,* HASHEM, *act for the sake of Your Great Name and grant me atonement for my iniquities, my errors, and my willful sins through which I have erred, been iniquitous, and willfully sinned before You, from my youth until this day. And make whole all the Names that I have blemished in Your Great Name.*

For livelihood:

אַתָּה *It is You,* HASHEM *the God, Who nourishes, sustains, and supports, from the horns of re'eimim to the eggs of lice. Provide me with my allotment of bread; and bring forth for me and all members of my household, my food, before I have need for it; in contentment but not in pain, in a permissible but not a forbidden manner, in honor but not in disgrace, for life and for peace; from the flow of blessing and success and from the flow of the Heavenly spring, so that I be enabled to do Your will and engage in Your Torah and fulfill Your commandments. Make me not needful of people's largesse; and may there be fulfilled in me the verse that states, 'You open Your hand and satisfy the desire of every living thing'*[1] *and that states, 'Cast Your burden upon* HASHEM *and He will support you.'*[2]

Continue: *For You hear the prayer . . .*

(1) *Psalms* 145:16. (2) 55:23.

כִּי אַתָּה שׁוֹמֵעַ תְּפִלַּת עַמְּךָ יִשְׂרָאֵל בְּרַחֲמִים. בָּרוּךְ אַתָּה יהוה, שׁוֹמֵעַ תְּפִלָּה.

עבודה

רְצֵה יהוה אֱלֹהֵינוּ בְּעַמְּךָ יִשְׂרָאֵל וּבִתְפִלָּתָם, וְהָשֵׁב אֶת הָעֲבוֹדָה לִדְבִיר בֵּיתֶךָ. וְאִשֵּׁי יִשְׂרָאֵל וּתְפִלָּתָם בְּאַהֲבָה תְקַבֵּל בְּרָצוֹן, וּתְהִי לְרָצוֹן תָּמִיד עֲבוֹדַת יִשְׂרָאֵל עַמֶּךָ.

וְתֶחֱזֶינָה עֵינֵינוּ בְּשׁוּבְךָ לְצִיּוֹן בְּרַחֲמִים. בָּרוּךְ אַתָּה יהוה, הַמַּחֲזִיר שְׁכִינָתוֹ לְצִיּוֹן.

הודאה

Bow at מוֹדִים; straighten up at 'ה.

מוֹדִים אֲנַחְנוּ לָךְ שָׁאַתָּה הוּא יהוה אֱלֹהֵינוּ וֵאלֹהֵי אֲבוֹתֵינוּ לְעוֹלָם וָעֶד. צוּר חַיֵּינוּ, מָגֵן יִשְׁעֵנוּ אַתָּה הוּא לְדוֹר וָדוֹר. נוֹדֶה לְּךָ וּנְסַפֵּר תְּהִלָּתֶךָ[1] עַל חַיֵּינוּ הַמְּסוּרִים בְּיָדֶךָ, וְעַל נִשְׁמוֹתֵינוּ הַפְּקוּדוֹת לָךְ, וְעַל נִסֶּיךָ שֶׁבְּכָל יוֹם עִמָּנוּ, וְעַל נִפְלְאוֹתֶיךָ וְטוֹבוֹתֶיךָ שֶׁבְּכָל עֵת, עֶרֶב וָבֹקֶר וְצָהֳרָיִם. הַטּוֹב כִּי לֹא כָלוּ רַחֲמֶיךָ, וְהַמְרַחֵם כִּי לֹא תַמּוּ חֲסָדֶיךָ,[2] מֵעוֹלָם קִוִּינוּ לָךְ.

וְעַל כֻּלָּם יִתְבָּרַךְ וְיִתְרוֹמַם שִׁמְךָ מַלְכֵּנוּ תָּמִיד לְעוֹלָם וָעֶד.

Bend the knees at בָּרוּךְ; bow at אַתָּה; straighten up at 'ה.

וְכֹל הַחַיִּים יוֹדְוּךָ סֶּלָה, וִיהַלְלוּ אֶת שִׁמְךָ בֶּאֱמֶת, הָאֵל יְשׁוּעָתֵנוּ וְעֶזְרָתֵנוּ סֶלָה. בָּרוּךְ אַתָּה יהוה, הַטּוֹב שִׁמְךָ וּלְךָ נָאֶה לְהוֹדוֹת.

שלום

שָׁלוֹם רָב עַל יִשְׂרָאֵל עַמְּךָ תָּשִׂים לְעוֹלָם, כִּי אַתָּה הוּא מֶלֶךְ אָדוֹן לְכָל הַשָּׁלוֹם. וְטוֹב בְּעֵינֶיךָ לְבָרֵךְ אֶת עַמְּךָ יִשְׂרָאֵל, בְּכָל עֵת וּבְכָל שָׁעָה בִּשְׁלוֹמֶךָ. בָּרוּךְ אַתָּה יהוה, הַמְּבָרֵךְ אֶת עַמּוֹ יִשְׂרָאֵל בַּשָּׁלוֹם.

יִהְיוּ לְרָצוֹן אִמְרֵי פִי וְהֶגְיוֹן לִבִּי לְפָנֶיךָ, יהוה צוּרִי וְגֹאֲלִי.[3]

אֱלֹהַי, נְצוֹר לְשׁוֹנִי מֵרָע, וּשְׂפָתַי מִדַּבֵּר מִרְמָה,[4] וְלִמְקַלְלַי נַפְשִׁי תִדּוֹם, וְנַפְשִׁי כֶּעָפָר לַכֹּל תִּהְיֶה. פְּתַח לִבִּי בְּתוֹרָתֶךָ, וּבְמִצְוֹתֶיךָ תִּרְדּוֹף נַפְשִׁי. וְכֹל הַחוֹשְׁבִים עָלַי רָעָה, מְהֵרָה הָפֵר עֲצָתָם וְקַלְקֵל מַחֲשַׁבְתָּם. עֲשֵׂה לְמַעַן שְׁמֶךָ, עֲשֵׂה לְמַעַן יְמִינֶךָ, עֲשֵׂה לְמַעַן קְדֻשָּׁתֶךָ, עֲשֵׂה לְמַעַן תּוֹרָתֶךָ. לְמַעַן יֵחָלְצוּן יְדִידֶיךָ, הוֹשִׁיעָה יְמִינְךָ וַעֲנֵנִי.[5]

for You hear the prayer of Your people Israel with compassion. Blessed are You, HASHEM, Who hears prayer.

TEMPLE SERVICE

רְצֵה *Be favorable, HASHEM, our God, toward Your people Israel and their prayer and restore the service to the Holy of Holies of Your Temple. The fire-offerings of Israel and their prayer accept with love and favor, and may the service of Your people Israel always be favorable to You.*

וְתֶחֱזֶינָה *May our eyes behold Your return to Zion in compassion. Blessed are You, HASHEM, Who restores His Presence to Zion.*

THANKSGIVING [MODIM]

Bow at *'We gratefully thank You'*; straighten up at *'HASHEM.'*

מוֹדִים *We gratefully thank You, for it is You Who are HASHEM, our God and the God of our forefathers for all eternity; Rock of our lives, Shield of our salvation are You from generation to generation. We shall thank You and relate Your praise[1] — for our lives, which are committed to Your power and for our souls that are entrusted to You; for Your miracles that are with us every day; and for Your wonders and favors in every season — evening, morning, and afternoon. The Beneficent One, for Your compassions were never exhausted, and the Compassionate One, for Your kindnesses never ended[2] — always have we put our hope in You.*

For all these, may Your Name be blessed and exalted, our King, continually forever and ever.

Bend the knees at *'Blessed'*; bow at *'You'*; straighten up at *'HASHEM.'*

Everything alive will gratefully acknowledge You, Selah! and praise Your Name sincerely, O God of our salvation and help, Selah! Blessed are You, HASHEM, Your Name is 'The Beneficent One' and to You it is fitting to give thanks.

PEACE

שָׁלוֹם *Establish abundant peace upon Your people Israel forever, for You are King, Master of all peace. May it be good in Your eyes to bless Your people Israel at every time and every hour with Your peace. Blessed are You, HASHEM, Who blesses His people Israel with peace.*

May the expressions of my mouth and the thoughts of my heart find favor before You, HASHEM, my Rock and my Redeemer.[3]

אֱלֹהַי *My God, guard my tongue from evil and my lips from speaking deceitfully.[4] To those who curse me, let my soul be silent; and let my soul be like dust to everyone. Open my heart to Your Torah, then my soul will pursue Your commandments. As for all those who design evil against me, speedily nullify their counsel and disrupt their design. Act for Your Name's sake; act for Your right hand's sake; act for Your sanctity's sake; act for Your Torah's sake. That Your beloved ones may be given rest; let Your right hand save, and respond to me.[5]*

(1) Cf. *Psalms* 79:13. (2) Cf. *Lamentations* 3:22. (3) *Psalms* 19:15. (4) Cf. 34:14. (5) 60:7; 108:7.

Some recite verses pertaining to their names here. See page 480.

יִהְיוּ לְרָצוֹן אִמְרֵי פִי וְהֶגְיוֹן לִבִּי לְפָנֶיךָ, יהוה צוּרִי וְגֹאֲלִי.[1]

Bow and take three steps back. Bow left and say . . . עֹשֶׂה; bow right and say . . . הוּא יַעֲשֶׂה; bow forward and say וְעַל כָּל . . . אָמֵן.

עֹשֶׂה שָׁלוֹם בִּמְרוֹמָיו, הוּא יַעֲשֶׂה שָׁלוֹם עָלֵינוּ, וְעַל כָּל יִשְׂרָאֵל. וְאִמְרוּ: אָמֵן.

יְהִי רָצוֹן מִלְּפָנֶיךָ יהוה אֱלֹהֵינוּ וֵאלֹהֵי אֲבוֹתֵינוּ, שֶׁיִּבָּנֶה בֵּית הַמִּקְדָּשׁ בִּמְהֵרָה בְיָמֵינוּ, וְתֵן חֶלְקֵנוּ בְּתוֹרָתֶךָ. וְשָׁם נַעֲבָדְךָ בְּיִרְאָה, כִּימֵי עוֹלָם וּכְשָׁנִים קַדְמוֹנִיּוֹת. וְעָרְבָה לַיהוה מִנְחַת יְהוּדָה וִירוּשָׁלָיִם, כִּימֵי עוֹלָם וּכְשָׁנִים קַדְמוֹנִיּוֹת.[2]

SHEMONEH ESREI ENDS HERE.

Remain standing in place for at least a few moments before taking three steps forward.

Chazzan recites קַדִּישׁ שָׁלֵם.

יִתְגַּדַּל וְיִתְקַדַּשׁ שְׁמֵהּ רַבָּא. (Cong. – אָמֵן.) בְּעָלְמָא דִּי בְרָא כִרְעוּתֵהּ. וְיַמְלִיךְ מַלְכוּתֵהּ, בְּחַיֵּיכוֹן וּבְיוֹמֵיכוֹן וּבְחַיֵּי דְכָל בֵּית יִשְׂרָאֵל, בַּעֲגָלָא וּבִזְמַן קָרִיב. וְאִמְרוּ: אָמֵן.

(Cong. – אָמֵן. יְהֵא שְׁמֵהּ רַבָּא מְבָרַךְ לְעָלַם וּלְעָלְמֵי עָלְמַיָּא.)

יְהֵא שְׁמֵהּ רַבָּא מְבָרַךְ לְעָלַם וּלְעָלְמֵי עָלְמַיָּא.

יִתְבָּרַךְ וְיִשְׁתַּבַּח וְיִתְפָּאַר וְיִתְרוֹמַם וְיִתְנַשֵּׂא וְיִתְהַדָּר וְיִתְעַלֶּה וְיִתְהַלָּל שְׁמֵהּ דְּקֻדְשָׁא בְּרִיךְ הוּא (Cong. – בְּרִיךְ הוּא) – לְעֵלָּא מִן כָּל בִּרְכָתָא וְשִׁירָתָא תֻּשְׁבְּחָתָא וְנֶחֱמָתָא, דַּאֲמִירָן בְּעָלְמָא. וְאִמְרוּ: אָמֵן. (Cong. – אָמֵן.)

(Cong. – קַבֵּל בְּרַחֲמִים וּבְרָצוֹן אֶת תְּפִלָּתֵנוּ.)

תִּתְקַבֵּל צְלוֹתְהוֹן וּבָעוּתְהוֹן דְּכָל בֵּית יִשְׂרָאֵל קֳדָם אֲבוּהוֹן דִּי בִשְׁמַיָּא. וְאִמְרוּ: אָמֵן. (Cong. – אָמֵן.)

(Cong. – יְהִי שֵׁם יהוה מְבֹרָךְ, מֵעַתָּה וְעַד עוֹלָם.[3])

יְהֵא שְׁלָמָא רַבָּא מִן שְׁמַיָּא, וְחַיִּים עָלֵינוּ וְעַל כָּל יִשְׂרָאֵל. וְאִמְרוּ: אָמֵן. (Cong. – אָמֵן.)

(Cong. – עֶזְרִי מֵעִם יהוה, עֹשֵׂה שָׁמַיִם וָאָרֶץ.[4])

Take three steps back. Bow left and say . . . עֹשֶׂה; bow right and say . . . הוּא; bow forward and say וְעַל כָּל . . . אָמֵן. Remain standing in place for a few moments, then take three steps forward.

עֹשֶׂה שָׁלוֹם בִּמְרוֹמָיו, הוּא יַעֲשֶׂה שָׁלוֹם עָלֵינוּ, וְעַל כָּל יִשְׂרָאֵל. וְאִמְרוּ: אָמֵן. (Cong. – אָמֵן.)

The congregation stands while reciting עָלֵינוּ.

עָלֵינוּ לְשַׁבֵּחַ לַאֲדוֹן הַכֹּל, לָתֵת גְּדֻלָּה לְיוֹצֵר בְּרֵאשִׁית, שֶׁלֹּא עָשָׂנוּ כְּגוֹיֵי הָאֲרָצוֹת, וְלֹא שָׂמָנוּ כְּמִשְׁפְּחוֹת הָאֲדָמָה. שֶׁלֹּא שָׂם חֶלְקֵנוּ כָּהֶם, וְגוֹרָלֵנוּ כְּכָל הֲמוֹנָם. (שֶׁהֵם מִשְׁתַּחֲוִים לְהֶבֶל וָרִיק, וּמִתְפַּלְלִים אֶל אֵל לֹא יוֹשִׁיעַ.[5]) וַאֲנַחְנוּ כּוֹרְעִים וּמִשְׁתַּחֲוִים וּמוֹדִים, לִפְנֵי מֶלֶךְ מַלְכֵי הַמְּלָכִים הַקָּדוֹשׁ בָּרוּךְ הוּא. שֶׁהוּא נוֹטֶה שָׁמַיִם וְיֹסֵד אָרֶץ,[6] וּמוֹשַׁב יְקָרוֹ בַּשָּׁמַיִם

Bow while reciting וַאֲנַחְנוּ כּוֹרְעִים וּמִשְׁתַּחֲוִים.

Some recite verses pertaining to their names at this point. See page 480.

May the expressions of my mouth and the thoughts of my heart find favor before You, HASHEM, my Rock and my Redeemer.[1] *He Who makes peace in His heights, may He make peace upon us, and upon all Israel. Now respond: Amen.*

Bow and take three steps back. Bow left and say, *'He Who makes peace . . .'*; bow right and say, *'may He make peace . . .'*; bow forward and say, *'and upon . . . Amen.'*

יְהִי רָצוֹן *May it be Your will, HASHEM, our God and the God of our forefathers, that the Holy Temple be rebuilt, speedily in our days. Grant us our share in Your Torah, and may we serve You there with reverence, as in days of old and in former years. Then the offering of Judah and Jerusalem will be pleasing to HASHEM, as in days of old and in former years.*[2]

SHEMONEH ESREI ENDS HERE.

Remain standing in place for at least a few moments before taking three steps forward.

Chazzan recites the Full *Kaddish.*

יִתְגַּדַּל *May His great Name grow exalted and sanctified* (Cong.– *Amen.*) *in the world that He created as He willed. May He give reign to His kingship in your lifetimes and in your days, and in the lifetimes of the entire Family of Israel, swiftly and soon. Now respond: Amen.*

(Cong.– *Amen. May His great Name be blessed forever and ever.*)

May His great Name be blessed forever and ever.

Blessed, praised, glorified, exalted, extolled, mighty, upraised, and lauded be the Name of the Holy One, Blessed is He (Cong.– *Blessed is He*) — *beyond any blessing and song, praise and consolation that are uttered in the world. Now respond: Amen.* (Cong.– *Amen.*)

(Cong.– *Accept our prayers with mercy and favor.*)

May the prayers and supplications of the entire Family of Israel be accepted before their Father Who is in Heaven. Now respond: Amen. (Cong.– *Amen.*)

(Cong.– *Blessed be the Name of HASHEM, from this time and forever.*[3])

May there be abundant peace from Heaven, and life, upon us and upon all Israel. Now respond: Amen. (Cong.– *Amen.*)

(Cong.– *My help is from HASHEM, Maker of heaven and earth.*[4])

Take three steps back. Bow left and say, *'He Who makes peace . . .'*; bow right and say, *'may He . . .'*; bow forward and say, *'and upon all Israel . . .'*

Remain standing in place for a few moments, then take three steps forward.

He Who makes peace in His heights, may He make peace upon us, and upon all Israel. Now respond: Amen. (Cong.– *Amen.*)

The congregation stands while reciting עָלֵינוּ, *'It is our duty . . .'*

עָלֵינוּ *It is our duty to praise the Master of all, to ascribe greatness to the Molder of primeval creation, for He has not made us like the nations of the lands, and has not emplaced us like the families of the earth; for He has not assigned our portion like theirs nor our lot like all their multitudes. (For they bow to vanity and emptiness and pray to a god which helps not.*[5]*) But we bend our knees, bow, and acknowledge our thanks before the King Who reigns over kings, the Holy One, Blessed is He. He stretches out heaven and establishes earth's foundation,*[6] *the seat of His homage is in the heav-*

Bow while reciting *'But we bend our knees.'*

(1) *Psalms* 19:15. (2) *Malachi* 3:4. (3) *Psalms* 113:2.
(4) 121:2. (5) *Isaiah* 45:20. (6) 51:13.

מִמַּעַל, וּשְׁכִינַת עֻזּוֹ בְּגָבְהֵי מְרוֹמִים. הוּא אֱלֹהֵינוּ, אֵין עוֹד. אֱמֶת מַלְכֵּנוּ, אֶפֶס זוּלָתוֹ, כַּכָּתוּב בְּתוֹרָתוֹ: וְיָדַעְתָּ הַיּוֹם וַהֲשֵׁבֹתָ אֶל לְבָבֶךָ, כִּי יהוה הוּא הָאֱלֹהִים בַּשָּׁמַיִם מִמַּעַל וְעַל הָאָרֶץ מִתָּחַת, אֵין עוֹד.[1]

עַל כֵּן נְקַוֶּה לְּךָ יהוה אֱלֹהֵינוּ לִרְאוֹת מְהֵרָה בְּתִפְאֶרֶת עֻזֶּךָ, לְהַעֲבִיר גִּלּוּלִים מִן הָאָרֶץ, וְהָאֱלִילִים כָּרוֹת יִכָּרֵתוּן, לְתַקֵּן עוֹלָם בְּמַלְכוּת שַׁדַּי. וְכָל בְּנֵי בָשָׂר יִקְרְאוּ בִשְׁמֶךָ, לְהַפְנוֹת אֵלֶיךָ כָּל רִשְׁעֵי אָרֶץ. יַכִּירוּ וְיֵדְעוּ כָּל יוֹשְׁבֵי תֵבֵל, כִּי לְךָ תִּכְרַע כָּל בֶּרֶךְ, תִּשָּׁבַע כָּל לָשׁוֹן.[2] לְפָנֶיךָ יהוה אֱלֹהֵינוּ יִכְרְעוּ וְיִפֹּלוּ, וְלִכְבוֹד שִׁמְךָ יְקָר יִתֵּנוּ. וִיקַבְּלוּ כֻלָּם אֶת עוֹל מַלְכוּתֶךָ, וְתִמְלֹךְ עֲלֵיהֶם מְהֵרָה לְעוֹלָם וָעֶד. כִּי הַמַּלְכוּת שֶׁלְּךָ הִיא וּלְעוֹלְמֵי עַד תִּמְלוֹךְ בְּכָבוֹד, כַּכָּתוּב בְּתוֹרָתֶךָ: יהוה יִמְלֹךְ לְעֹלָם וָעֶד.[3] ❖ וְנֶאֱמַר: וְהָיָה יהוה לְמֶלֶךְ עַל כָּל הָאָרֶץ, בַּיּוֹם הַהוּא יִהְיֶה יהוה אֶחָד וּשְׁמוֹ אֶחָד.[4]

אַל תִּירָא מִפַּחַד פִּתְאֹם, וּמִשֹּׁאַת רְשָׁעִים כִּי תָבֹא.[5] עֻצוּ עֵצָה וְתֻפָר, דַּבְּרוּ דָבָר וְלֹא יָקוּם, כִּי עִמָּנוּ אֵל.[6] וְעַד זִקְנָה אֲנִי הוּא, וְעַד שֵׂיבָה אֲנִי אֶסְבֹּל, אֲנִי עָשִׂיתִי וַאֲנִי אֶשָּׂא, וַאֲנִי אֶסְבֹּל וַאֲמַלֵּט.[7]

קדיש יתום

Mourners recite קַדִּישׁ יָתוֹם.

יִתְגַּדַּל וְיִתְקַדַּשׁ שְׁמֵהּ רַבָּא. (.Cong – אָמֵן.) בְּעָלְמָא דִּי בְרָא כִרְעוּתֵהּ. וְיַמְלִיךְ מַלְכוּתֵהּ, בְּחַיֵּיכוֹן וּבְיוֹמֵיכוֹן וּבְחַיֵּי דְכָל בֵּית יִשְׂרָאֵל, בַּעֲגָלָא וּבִזְמַן קָרִיב. וְאִמְרוּ: אָמֵן.

(.Cong – אָמֵן. יְהֵא שְׁמֵהּ רַבָּא מְבָרַךְ לְעָלַם וּלְעָלְמֵי עָלְמַיָּא.)

יְהֵא שְׁמֵהּ רַבָּא מְבָרַךְ לְעָלַם וּלְעָלְמֵי עָלְמַיָּא.

יִתְבָּרַךְ וְיִשְׁתַּבַּח וְיִתְפָּאַר וְיִתְרוֹמַם וְיִתְנַשֵּׂא וְיִתְהַדָּר וְיִתְעַלֶּה וְיִתְהַלָּל שְׁמֵהּ דְּקֻדְשָׁא בְּרִיךְ הוּא (.Cong – בְּרִיךְ הוּא) — לְעֵלָּא מִן כָּל בִּרְכָתָא וְשִׁירָתָא תֻּשְׁבְּחָתָא וְנֶחֱמָתָא, דַּאֲמִירָן בְּעָלְמָא. וְאִמְרוּ: אָמֵן. (.Cong – אָמֵן.)

יְהֵא שְׁלָמָא רַבָּא מִן שְׁמַיָּא, וְחַיִּים עָלֵינוּ וְעַל כָּל יִשְׂרָאֵל. וְאִמְרוּ: אָמֵן. (.Cong – אָמֵן.)

Take three steps back. Bow left and say . . . עֹשֶׂה; bow right and say . . . הוּא; bow forward and say וְעַל כָּל . . . אָמֵן. Remain standing in place for a few moments, then take three steps forward.

עֹשֶׂה שָׁלוֹם בִּמְרוֹמָיו, הוּא יַעֲשֶׂה שָׁלוֹם עָלֵינוּ, וְעַל כָּל יִשְׂרָאֵל. וְאִמְרוּ: אָמֵן. (.Cong – אָמֵן.)

---

(1) *Deuteronomy* 4:39. (2) Cf. *Isaiah* 45:23. (3) *Exodus* 15:18.
(4) *Zechariah* 14:9. (5) *Proverbs* 3:25. (6) *Isaiah* 8:10. (7) 46:4.

ens above and His powerful Presence is in the loftiest heights. He is our God and there is none other. True is our King, there is nothing beside Him, as it is written in His Torah: 'You are to know this day and take to your heart that HASHEM *is the only God — in heaven above and on the earth below — there is none other.'*[1]

עַל כֵּן *Therefore we put our hope in You,* HASHEM, *our God, that we may soon see Your mighty splendor, to remove detestable idolatry from the earth, and false gods will be utterly cut off, to perfect the universe through the Almighty's sovereignty. Then all humanity will call upon Your Name, to turn all the earth's wicked toward You. All the world's inhabitants will recognize and know that to You every knee should bend, every tongue should swear.*[2] *Before You,* HASHEM, *our God, they will bend every knee and cast themselves down and to the glory of Your Name they will render homage, and they will all accept upon themselves the yoke of Your kingship that You may reign over them soon and eternally. For the kingdom is Yours and You will reign for all eternity in glory as it is written in Your Torah:* HASHEM *shall reign for all eternity.*[3] Chazzan– *And it is said:* HASHEM *will be King over all the world — on that day* HASHEM *will be One and His Name will be One.*[4]

אַל תִּירָא *Do not fear sudden terror, or the holocaust of the wicked when it comes.*[5] *Plan a conspiracy and it will be annulled; speak your piece and it shall not stand, for God is with us.*[6] *Even till your seniority, I remain unchanged; and even till your ripe old age, I shall endure. I created you and I shall bear you; I shall endure and rescue.*[7]

MOURNER'S KADDISH

Mourners recite the Mourners' *Kaddish. See Laws* §132-134.
[A transliteration of this *Kaddish* appears on page 490.]

יִתְגַּדַּל *May His great Name grow exalted and sanctified* (Cong.– *Amen.*) *in the world that He created as He willed. May He give reign to His kingship in your lifetimes and in your days, and in the lifetimes of the entire Family of Israel, swiftly and soon. Now respond: Amen.*

(Cong.– *Amen. May His great Name be blessed forever and ever.*)

May His great Name be blessed forever and ever.

Blessed, praised, glorified, exalted, extolled, mighty, upraised, and lauded be the Name of the Holy One, Blessed is He (Cong.– *Blessed is He*) *— beyond any blessing and song, praise and consolation that are uttered in the world. Now respond: Amen.* (Cong.– *Amen.*)

May there be abundant peace from Heaven, and life, upon us and upon all Israel. Now respond: Amen. (Cong.– *Amen.*)

Take three steps back. Bow left and say, *'He Who makes peace . . .';* bow right and say, *'may He . . .';* bow forward and say, *'and upon all Israel . . .'* Remain standing in place for a few moments, then take three steps forward.

He Who makes peace in His heights, may He make peace upon us, and upon all Israel. Now respond: Amen. (Cong.– *Amen.*)

הבדלה

When Tishah B'Av falls on Sunday *Havdalah* is recited. Spices and a flame are not used.

סַבְרִי מָרָנָן וְרַבָּנָן וְרַבּוֹתַי:

בָּרוּךְ אַתָּה יהוה אֱלֹהֵינוּ מֶלֶךְ הָעוֹלָם, בּוֹרֵא פְּרִי הַגָּפֶן.

(all present respond — אָמֵן.)

בָּרוּךְ אַתָּה יהוה אֱלֹהֵינוּ מֶלֶךְ הָעוֹלָם, הַמַּבְדִּיל בֵּין קֹדֶשׁ לְחוֹל, בֵּין אוֹר לְחֹשֶׁךְ, בֵּין יִשְׂרָאֵל לָעַמִּים, בֵּין יוֹם הַשְּׁבִיעִי לְשֵׁשֶׁת יְמֵי הַמַּעֲשֶׂה. בָּרוּךְ אַתָּה יהוה, הַמַּבְדִּיל בֵּין קֹדֶשׁ לְחוֹל.

(all present respond — אָמֵן.)

The one who recited *Havdalah,* or someone else present for *Havdalah,* should drink most of the wine from the cup.

קידוש לבנה

תהלים קמח:א-ו

הַלְלוּיָהּ, הַלְּלוּ אֶת יהוה מִן הַשָּׁמַיִם, הַלְּלוּהוּ בַּמְּרוֹמִים. הַלְלוּהוּ כָל מַלְאָכָיו, הַלְלוּהוּ כָּל צְבָאָיו. הַלְלוּהוּ שֶׁמֶשׁ וְיָרֵחַ, הַלְלוּהוּ כָּל כּוֹכְבֵי אוֹר. הַלְלוּהוּ שְׁמֵי הַשָּׁמָיִם, וְהַמַּיִם אֲשֶׁר מֵעַל הַשָּׁמָיִם. יְהַלְלוּ אֶת שֵׁם יהוה, כִּי הוּא צִוָּה וְנִבְרָאוּ. וַיַּעֲמִידֵם לָעַד לְעוֹלָם, חָק נָתַן וְלֹא יַעֲבוֹר. הֲרֵינִי מוּכָן וּמְזוּמָן לְקַיֵּם הַמִּצְוָה לְקַדֵּשׁ הַלְּבָנָה. לְשֵׁם יִחוּד קֻדְשָׁא בְּרִיךְ הוּא וּשְׁכִינְתֵּיהּ עַל יְדֵי הַהוּא טָמִיר וְנֶעְלָם, בְּשֵׁם כָּל יִשְׂרָאֵל.

One should look at the moon before reciting this blessing:

בָּרוּךְ אַתָּה יהוה, אֱלֹהֵינוּ מֶלֶךְ הָעוֹלָם, אֲשֶׁר בְּמַאֲמָרוֹ בָּרָא שְׁחָקִים, וּבְרוּחַ פִּיו כָּל צְבָאָם. חֹק וּזְמַן נָתַן לָהֶם שֶׁלֹּא יְשַׁנּוּ אֶת תַּפְקִידָם. שָׂשִׂים וּשְׂמֵחִים לַעֲשׂוֹת רְצוֹן קוֹנָם, פּוֹעֵל אֱמֶת שֶׁפְּעֻלָּתוֹ אֱמֶת. וְלַלְּבָנָה אָמַר שֶׁתִּתְחַדֵּשׁ, עֲטֶרֶת תִּפְאֶרֶת לַעֲמוּסֵי בָטֶן, שֶׁהֵם עֲתִידִים לְהִתְחַדֵּשׁ כְּמוֹתָהּ, וּלְפָאֵר לְיוֹצְרָם עַל שֵׁם כְּבוֹד מַלְכוּתוֹ. בָּרוּךְ אַתָּה יהוה, מְחַדֵּשׁ חֳדָשִׁים.

Recite three times — בָּרוּךְ יוֹצְרֵךְ, בָּרוּךְ עוֹשֵׂךְ, בָּרוּךְ קוֹנֵךְ, בָּרוּךְ בּוֹרְאֵךְ.

Upon reciting the next verse, rise on the toes as if in dance:

Recite three times — כְּשֵׁם שֶׁאֲנִי רוֹקֵד כְּנֶגְדֵּךְ וְאֵינִי יָכוֹל לִנְגּוֹעַ בָּךְ כַּךְ לֹא יוּכְלוּ כָּל אוֹיְבַי לִנְגּוֹעַ בִּי לְרָעָה.

Recite three times — תִּפֹּל עֲלֵיהֶם אֵימָתָה וָפַחַד, בִּגְדֹל זְרוֹעֲךָ יִדְּמוּ כָּאָבֶן.[1]

Recite three times — כָּאָבֶן יִדְּמוּ זְרוֹעֲךָ בִּגְדֹל וָפַחַד אֵימָתָה עֲלֵיהֶם תִּפֹּל.

Laws of Kiddush Levanah

It is preferable that *Kiddush Levanah* be recited: (a) under the open sky; (b) with a *minyan;* (c) at the departure of the Sabbath. When these optimal conditions are not feasible, they may be waived (e.g., a shut-in may recite it indoors if he

HAVDALAH

When Tishah B'Av falls on Sunday *Havdalah* is recited. Spices and a flame are not used.

By your leave, my masters and teachers:

בָּרוּךְ *Blessed are You, HASHEM, our God, King of the universe, Who creates the fruit of the vine.* (All present respond– *Amen.)*

בָּרוּךְ *Blessed are You, HASHEM our God, King of the universe, Who separates between holy and secular, between light and darkness, between Israel and the nations, between the seventh day and the six days of labor. Blessed are You, HASHEM, Who separates between holy and secular.* (All present respond– *Amen.)*

The one who recited *Havdalah,* or someone else present for *Havdalah,* should drink most of the wine from the cup.

SANCTIFICATION OF THE MOON/KIDDUSH LEVANAH

Psalms 148:1-6

הַלְלוּיָהּ *Halleluyah! Praise HASHEM from the heavens; praise Him in the heights. Praise Him, all His angels; praise Him, all His legions. Praise Him, sun and moon; praise Him, all bright stars. Praise Him, the most exalted of the heavens and the waters that are above the heavens. Let them praise the Name of HASHEM, for He commanded and they were created. And He established them forever and ever, He issued a decree that will not change. Behold I am prepared and ready to perform the commandment to sanctify the moon. For the sake of the unification of the Holy One, Blessed is He, and His Presence, through Him Who is hidden and inscrutable — [I pray] in the name of all Israel.*

One should look at the moon before reciting this blessing:

בָּרוּךְ *Blessed are You, HASHEM, our God, King of the Universe, Who with His utterance created the heavens, and with the breath of His mouth all their legion. A decree and a schedule did He give them that they not alter their assigned task. They are joyous and glad to perform the will of their Owner — the Worker of truth Whose work is truth. To the moon He said that it should renew itself, which will be a crown of splendor for those borne [by Him] from the womb, those who are destined to renew themselves like it, and to glorify their Molder for the name of His glorious kingdom. Blessed are You, HASHEM, Who renews the months.*

Recite three times – *Blessed is your Molder; blessed is your Maker; blessed is your Owner; blessed is your Creator.*

Upon reciting the next verse, rise on the toes as if in dance:

Recite three times – *Just as I dance toward you but cannot touch you, so may none of my enemies be able to touch me for evil.*

Recite three times – *Let fall upon them fear and terror; at the greatness of Your arm, let them be still as stone.*[1]

Recite three times – *As stone let them be still, at Your arm's greatness; terror and fear, upon them let fall.*

(1) *Exodus* 15:16.

---

can see the moon through a window or door; one who cannot form a *minyan;* the sky is cloudy at the departure of the Sabbath).

The earliest time for reciting *Kiddush Levanah* is seventy-two hours after the *molad* (new moon), although some authorities delay its recitation until seven full days after the *molad.* The latest time is mid-month, i.e., fourteen days, eighteen hours and twenty-two minutes (some authorities extend this limit to fifteen full days) after the *molad.* Those who follow the latter opinion do not recite *Kiddush Levanah* during the month of Sivan until after Shavuos.

Kiddush Levanah should not be recited on a

Recite three times – דָּוִד מֶלֶךְ יִשְׂרָאֵל חַי וְקַיָּם.

Extend greetings to three different people – שָׁלוֹם עֲלֵיכֶם –

who, in turn, respond – עֲלֵיכֶם שָׁלוֹם.

Recite three times – סִמָּן טוֹב וּמַזָּל טוֹב יְהֵא לָנוּ וּלְכָל יִשְׂרָאֵל. אָמֵן.

קוֹל דּוֹדִי הִנֵּה זֶה בָּא מְדַלֵּג עַל הֶהָרִים מְקַפֵּץ עַל הַגְּבָעוֹת. דּוֹמֶה דוֹדִי לִצְבִי אוֹ לְעֹפֶר הָאַיָּלִים הִנֵּה זֶה עוֹמֵד אַחַר כָּתְלֵנוּ, מַשְׁגִּיחַ מִן הַחַלֹּנוֹת, מֵצִיץ מִן הַחֲרַכִּים.[1]

תהלים קכא

שִׁיר לַמַּעֲלוֹת, אֶשָּׂא עֵינַי אֶל הֶהָרִים, מֵאַיִן יָבֹא עֶזְרִי. עֶזְרִי מֵעִם יהוה, עֹשֵׂה שָׁמַיִם וָאָרֶץ. אַל יִתֵּן לַמּוֹט רַגְלֶךָ, אַל יָנוּם שֹׁמְרֶךָ. הִנֵּה לֹא יָנוּם וְלֹא יִישָׁן, שׁוֹמֵר יִשְׂרָאֵל. יהוה שֹׁמְרֶךָ, יהוה צִלְּךָ עַל יַד יְמִינֶךָ. יוֹמָם הַשֶּׁמֶשׁ לֹא יַכֶּכָּה וְיָרֵחַ בַּלָּיְלָה. יהוה יִשְׁמָרְךָ מִכָּל רָע, יִשְׁמֹר אֶת נַפְשֶׁךָ. יהוה יִשְׁמָר צֵאתְךָ וּבוֹאֶךָ, מֵעַתָּה וְעַד עוֹלָם.

תהלים קנ

הַלְלוּיָהּ, הַלְלוּ אֵל בְּקָדְשׁוֹ, הַלְלוּהוּ בִּרְקִיעַ עֻזּוֹ. הַלְלוּהוּ בִגְבוּרֹתָיו, הַלְלוּהוּ כְּרֹב גֻּדְלוֹ. הַלְלוּהוּ בְּתֵקַע שׁוֹפָר, הַלְלוּהוּ בְּנֵבֶל וְכִנּוֹר. הַלְלוּהוּ בְתֹף וּמָחוֹל, הַלְלוּהוּ בְּמִנִּים וְעֻגָב. הַלְלוּהוּ בְצִלְצְלֵי שָׁמַע, הַלְלוּהוּ בְּצִלְצְלֵי תְרוּעָה. כֹּל הַנְּשָׁמָה תְּהַלֵּל יָהּ, הַלְלוּיָהּ.

תָּנָא דְבֵי רַבִּי יִשְׁמָעֵאל: אִלְמָלֵי לֹא זָכוּ יִשְׂרָאֵל אֶלָּא לְהַקְבִּיל פְּנֵי אֲבִיהֶם שֶׁבַּשָּׁמַיִם פַּעַם אַחַת בַּחֹדֶשׁ, דַּיָּם. אָמַר אַבַּיֵּי: הִלְכָּךְ צָרִיךְ לְמֵימְרָא מְעֻמָּד. מִי זֹאת עֹלָה מִן הַמִּדְבָּר מִתְרַפֶּקֶת עַל דּוֹדָהּ.[2]

וִיהִי רָצוֹן מִלְּפָנֶיךָ יהוה אֱלֹהַי וֵאלֹהֵי אֲבוֹתַי, לְמַלְּאוֹת פְּגִימַת הַלְּבָנָה, וְלֹא יִהְיֶה בָּהּ שׁוּם מִעוּט, וִיהִי אוֹר הַלְּבָנָה כְּאוֹר הַחַמָּה, וּכְאוֹר שִׁבְעַת יְמֵי בְרֵאשִׁית[3] כְּמוֹ שֶׁהָיְתָה קוֹדֶם מִעוּטָהּ, שֶׁנֶּאֱמַר: אֶת שְׁנֵי הַמְּאֹרֹת הַגְּדֹלִים.[4] וְיִתְקַיֵּם בָּנוּ מִקְרָא שֶׁכָּתוּב: וּבִקְשׁוּ אֶת יהוה אֱלֹהֵיהֶם, וְאֵת דָּוִיד מַלְכָּם.[5] אָמֵן.

תהלים סז

לַמְנַצֵּחַ בִּנְגִינֹת מִזְמוֹר שִׁיר. אֱלֹהִים יְחָנֵּנוּ וִיבָרְכֵנוּ, יָאֵר פָּנָיו אִתָּנוּ סֶלָה. לָדַעַת בָּאָרֶץ דַּרְכֶּךָ, בְּכָל גּוֹיִם יְשׁוּעָתֶךָ. יוֹדוּךָ עַמִּים אֱלֹהִים, יוֹדוּךָ עַמִּים כֻּלָּם. יִשְׂמְחוּ וִירַנְּנוּ לְאֻמִּים, כִּי תִשְׁפֹּט עַמִּים מִישֹׁר, וּלְאֻמִּים בָּאָרֶץ תַּנְחֵם סֶלָה. יוֹדוּךָ עַמִּים אֱלֹהִים, יוֹדוּךָ עַמִּים כֻּלָּם. אֶרֶץ נָתְנָה יְבוּלָהּ, יְבָרְכֵנוּ אֱלֹהִים אֱלֹהֵינוּ. יְבָרְכֵנוּ אֱלֹהִים, וְיִירְאוּ אוֹתוֹ כָּל אַפְסֵי אָרֶץ.

In most congregations, עָלֵינוּ (page 460), followed by the Mourner's *Kaddish,* is recited at this point.

Recite three times – *David, King of Israel, is alive and enduring.*
Extend greetings to three different people – *Peace upon you—*
who, in turn, respond – *Upon you, peace.*
Recite three times – *May there be a good sign and a good fortune for us and for all Israel. Amen.*

קוֹל *The voice of my beloved — Behold! It came suddenly, leaping over mountains, skipping over hills. My beloved is like a gazelle or a young hart. Behold! He was standing behind our wall, observing through the windows, peering through the lattices.*[1]

Psalm 121

שִׁיר לַמַּעֲלוֹת *A song to the ascents. I raise my eyes to the mountains; whence will come my help? My help is from HASHEM, Maker of heaven and earth. He will not allow your foot to falter; your Guardian will not slumber. Behold, He neither slumbers nor sleeps — the Guardian of Israel. HASHEM is your Guardian; HASHEM is your Shade at your right hand. By day the sun will not harm you, nor the moon by night. HASHEM will protect you from every evil; He will guard your soul. HASHEM will guard your departure and your arrival, from this time and forever.*

Psalm 150

הַלְלוּיָהּ *Halleluyah! Praise God in His Sanctuary; praise Him in the firmament of His power. Praise Him for His mighty acts; praise Him as befits His abundant greatness. Praise Him with the blast of the shofar; praise Him with lyre and harp. Praise Him with drum and dance; praise Him with organ and flute. Praise Him with clanging cymbals; praise him with resonant trumpets. Let all souls praise God, Halleluyah!*

תָּנָא *The Academy of Rabbi Yishmael taught: Had Israel not been privileged to greet the countenance of their Father in Heaven except for once a month — it would have sufficed them. Abaye said: Therefore one must recite it while standing. Who is this who rises from the desert clinging to her Beloved!*[2] *May it be Your will, HASHEM, my God and the God of my forefathers, to fill the flaw of the moon that there be no diminution in it. May the light of the moon be like the light of the sun and like the light of the seven days of creation,*[3] *as it was before it was diminished, as it is said: 'The two great luminaries.'*[4] *And may there be fulfilled upon us the verse that is written: They shall seek HASHEM, their God, and David, their king.*[5] *Amen.*

Psalm 67

לַמְנַצֵּחַ *For the Conductor, upon Neginos, a psalm, a song. May God favor us and bless us, may He illuminate His countenance with us, Selah. To make known Your way on earth, among all the nations Your salvation. The peoples will acknowledge You, O God, the peoples will acknowledge You, all of them. Nations will be glad and sing for joy, because You will judge the peoples fairly and guide the nations on earth, Selah. Then peoples will acknowledge You, O God, the peoples will acknowledge You, all of them. The earth has yielded its produce, may God, our own God, bless us. May God bless us and may all the ends of the earth fear Him.*

In most congregations, *Aleinu* (page 460), followed by the Mourner's *Kaddish,* is recited at this point.

(1) *Song of Songs* 2:8-9. (2) 8:5. (3) Cf. *Isaiah* 30:26. (4) *Genesis* 1:16. (5) *Hosea* 3:5.

Sabbath or a Festival unless it is the last remaining night before the mid-month deadline.

If one cannot recite *Kiddush Levanah* with a *minyan,* he should try to do so in the presence of at least three others. If this, too, is not possible, he may recite it by himself.

❧ Selected Tishah B'Av Laws and Customs

compiled by Rabbi Hersh Goldwurm

Although most of the applicable laws are cited in the main text of the prayers, in some cases they are too involved or too lengthy to be given fully where they apply. A selection of such laws is compiled here. This digest cannot cover all eventualities and should be regarded merely as a guide; in case of doubt, one should consult a competent halachic authority. When a particular *halachah* is in dispute, we generally follow the ruling of the *Mishnah Berurah*. On occasion, however (usually when *Mishnah Berurah* does not give a definitive ruling or when a significant number of congregations do not follow *Mishnah Berurah's* ruling), we cite more than one opinion. As a general rule, each congregation is bound by its tradition and the ruling of its authorities.

These laws and customs have been culled, in the main, from the most widely accepted authorities: the *Shulchan Aruch Orach Chaim* [here abbreviated *O.C.*] and *Mishnah Berurah* [*M.B.*]. We have also included many of the general laws of prayer that also apply to Tishah B'Av. They are meant only as a learning and familiarizing tool. For halachic questions, one should consult the *Shulchan Aruch* and its commentaries and/or a halachic authority.

EREV TISHAH B'AV — TISHAH B'AV EVE

❧ The Afternoon

1. The afternoon before the Tishah B'Av fast takes on some of the mourning aspects of the fast day itself. One should not go on a pleasure trip or even on a pleasurable stroll. [Rather, one should devote his time to reflect on the theme of the upcoming day.] (*Rama O.C.* 553:2).

2. Similarly, from the hour of noon before the fast it is customary to learn only the Torah subjects that one may learn on Tishah B'Av itself (see §38), i.e. matters that pertain to the fast or to mourning. Therefore, even when Tishah B'Av falls on the Sabbath (so that the fast is observed on Sunday) or Sunday, it is customary to refrain from learning matters other than those permitted on Tishah B'Av on the Sabbath afternoon before the fast; the recitation of *Pirkei Avos* is deferred to the following week (*Rama O.C.* 553:2). However, many *poskim* point out that the custom has no Talmudic basis and argue that it is better to study whatever Torah subjects one wishes, rather than to desist from learning altogether. Therefore if one wishes to be lenient in this matter we do not deter him (*M.B.* 553:8).

❧ Minchah

3. The *Minchah* prayer should be recited early enough to allow time to eat a small meal — the *se'udah hamafsekes* (see §5) — between the prayer and the beginning of the fast.

4. *Minchah* is recited in the usual manner, *Tachanun* is omitted. Since Tishah B'Av itself has the status of a quasi-festival on which *Tachanun* is omitted, it is also omitted at *Minchah* of the preceding afternoon (*O.C.* 552:2).

❧ The Se'udah Hamafsekes

5. The meal that immediately precedes the fast — the *se'udah hamafsekes*, literally the *meal that interposes* — should reflect the mourning theme of the impending fast day. The *Gemara* (*Taanis* 30a) relates that on the eve of Tishah B'Av, the Tanna R' Yehudah bar Ilai's meal consisted only of stale bread with salt and a jug of water, which he would consume while seated between the oven and the stove. *Rambam* writes (*Taanis* 5:9): 'The following was the practice of the devout people of ancient times: On the eve of Tishah B'Av one would be served dry bread . . . and after it, drink a jug of water, in sadness, desolation, and with tears, like one who has the body of a dear one in his presence. This, or [a practice] resembling this, should be the practice of Torah scholars. In all my life I have not eaten a cooked dish on the eve of Tishah B'Av — even one of lentils — except when [Tishah B'Av or its eve] falls on the Sabbath.'

6. The above practices, however, were the stringent practices of the extremely devout; they are not binding upon every Jew. The *halachah* follows the Mishnah (*Taanis* 26b), which states that at the final meal before the fast, one may not eat more than one cooked dish. Meat and wine are entirely forbidden. (The ban upon meat and wine need not concern us, since it is customary to refrain from these foods from Rosh Chodesh Av.) It should be noted that in this context fish is also categorized as meat.Thus, even fish may not be eaten at the *se'udah hamafsekes* (*O.C.* 352:2).

7. The *Gemara* (30a) applies two qualifications to the food restrictions in the meals of Tishah B'Av eve: (a) They apply only to meals eaten after the hour of noon; and (b) only to the meal that immediately precedes the fast — hence, the restrictions apply only to the *se'udah hamafsekes*, provided it is eaten in the afternoon. Hence, if one eats more than one meal in the afternoon, the restrictions apply to the final full meal of the day, and if one's last meal was eaten before noon, it is not subject to these restrictions (*O.C.* 552:9).

8. One may eat even many different types of raw fruit and vegetables (*O.C.* 552:4), but not

two cooked fruit or vegetable dishes; even if they are also fit to be eaten raw (e.g. apple sauce), they qualify as cooked dishes (*O.C.* 552:3). Therefore, some poskim prohibit hot coffee or tea at the *se'udah hamafsekes* (in addition to one cooked dish). Some permit this, arguing that the prohibition applies only to solid foods, not to drinks (*Shaarei Teshuvah* 552:1).

9. Roasted (and fried) foods are considered cooked dishes in this regard (*O.C.* 552:3), as are also pickled foods (*Shaarei Teshuvah* 552:1).

10. Even two batches of the same food could be considered two dishes in this regard: if they were cooked in two different pots and thereby differ in some way, even if the difference is only in consistency, e.g. one has a thick texture while the other is more watery. But if both batches are identical they are considered one food (*O.C.* 552:3 with *M.B.* §8).

11. Two foods that were cooked together are considered two dishes, unless it is customary to cook these foods together year round, e.g. peas with onions (*O.C.* 552:3).

12. One should also curtail one's pleasure at this meal, by cutting down on the amount and type of drinks consumed. Beer and other intoxicating drinks should be avoided completely. One should not eat salads after the meal, as is the custom year round (*O.C.* 552:1).

13. The prevalent custom, which is also the ancient Ashkenazic custom, is to eat a regular meal in the afternoon before *Minchah*. There are no restrictions on this meal, and it is customary to eat well at this meal so that fasting will not be difficult the next day. However, if one feels that the fast will not harm him and he wishes to be stringent in this matter, he is to be commended. After *Minchah*, the *seudah hamafsekes* is eaten, subject to the restrictions noted above (*Rama O.C.* 552:9). Moreover, one should take care not to overeat at the first meal, because if one has no appetite to eat afterwards, the meal may be considered as inconsequential, so that the first meal will be the actual *se'udah hamafsekes*.

◆§ Customs of the Se'udah Hamafsekes

14. At the *se'udah hamafsekes* it is customary to eat [bread and] a hard-boiled egg, because eggs are a mourner's food. At the conclusion of the meal one dips a piece of bread in ashes and says, 'This is the Tishah B'Av meal' (*O.C.* 552:5, 6, with *M.B.*).

15. The meal is eaten sitting on the ground or a low seat, but one need not remove one's shoes. After the meal, however, one may sit on a chair (*O.C.* 552:7).

16. Three males should not sit together during the meal, so that they will not have to recite *Birkas Hamazon* together with *zimun*. Even if they did eat together, they should nevertheless not say *zimun* (*O.C.* 552:8 with *M.B.*).

◆§ After the Se'udah Hamafsekes

17. After the meal has been concluded and *Birkas Hamazon* been recited, until sundown one may still eat and do other things that are prohibited on the fast itself (*O.C.* 553:1).

18. If, however, one explicitly (i.e. orally) expressed the resolve not to eat anymore, he is considered to have taken the fast upon himself, and is obligated to observe all the strictures of the fast (eating, drinking, washing, etc.) — except for the wearing of shoes, which is permitted until sundown (*O.C.* 553:1 with *M.B.* §4). The same is true if one did not mention 'eating,' but said that he accepts the fast upon himself (*M.B.* §1).

19. The above-mentioned acceptance of the fast is valid only if it is done before *plag haminchah*, i.e. within approximately one and one half hours before sundown (or more precisely, 5/48 of the time between sunrise and sunset). Consequently, if the resolve not to eat was expressed prior to that time, one need not observe *all* the strictures of the fast, but, in accordance with his explicit vow, one is forbidden to eat (*M.B.* §4).

20. According to the *Shulchan Aruch* (*O.C.* 553:1) only an oral declaration has validity, so that if one resolved only mentally not to eat or to accept the fast, one may still eat thereafter. Some *poskim* dispute this ruling, however, and obligate one to fast even if he made merely a mental resolution to *fast;* but if he resolved mentally not to *eat*, the resolution is not binding. In view of the above, it is advisable to declare (either orally or mentally) at the conclusion of the meal that one does not wish to accept the fast prematurely (*M.B.* §2).

21. Immediately upon sundown, the fast takes effect, and all of its strictures apply. Therefore one must take care to stop eating and drinking before sundown, but there is no obligation to 'add' from the daytime to the fast, as there is on the eve of the Sabbaths and festivals (*O.C.* 553:2 with *M.B.* §3).

22. Since wearing shoes is prohibited on Tishah B'Av, one must take off his shoes before sundown. Moreover if *Maariv* is recited before sundown, the shoes should be taken off before *borchu* (i.e. the beginning of the service) is recited. Some advise that the shoes be taken off before one goes to the synagogue. However, once the sun sets one must remove them even if one has not yet gone to the synagogue (*O.C.* 553:2 with *M.B.* §5).

◆§ Tishah B'Av Eve on the Sabbath

23. When Tishah B'Av occurs on Sunday or on the Sabbath itself (so that the fast is

observed on Sunday), none of the strictures regarding the *se'udah hamafsekes* apply. One may eat meat and drink wine and set the table 'as King Solomon did in his time.' Moreover, it is a sin to deprive oneself of these foods if one does so in observance of the mourning of Tishah B'Av (*O.C.* 552:10 with *M.B.* §23). [It goes without saying that customs such as sitting on the ground, eating a hard-boiled egg and dipping the bread in ashes are not observed.]

24. Some say that one should not eat the third meal of Sabbath — the *se'udah shlishis* — together with a group, but others argue that if one always eats this meal together with his associates (e.g. the group meets in the synagogue for a public *se'udah shlishis*), one must also do so now, for to refrain would be a public observance of mourning on the Sabbath. All agree that at home the meal should be eaten with the family sitting together, and that *Birkas Hamazon* be recited with *zimun* (*O.C.* 552:10 with *M.B.* §23).

25. As on a weekday, the fast begins at sundown (*O.C.* 552:10 with *M.B.* §24). At this time all eating, drinking, etc. must stop, and the five restrictions are observed. However, wearing of shoes is permitted until *borchu* is recited. The members of the congregation remove their shoes after the recitation and the *chazzan* does so before it; they should first recite the formula: בָּרוּךְ הַמַּבְדִּיל בֵּין קוֹדֶשׁ לְחוֹל, *Blessed is He Who separates between holy and secular* (*O.C.* 553:2). [Nowadays it is customary in many congregations to recite *Maariv* some time after the Sabbath has ended, so that people will have time to remove their shoes and change into their weekday clothing at home, before they go to the synagogue. They should of course recite the above-mentioned formula first.]

26. Regarding Torah study on Tishah B'Av eve when it occurs on the Sabbath, see above §2.

27. The verses of צִדְקָתְךָ, *Tzidkas'cha*, which are said at the conclusion of the *chazzan's* repetition of the Sabbath *Minchah*, are omitted (*O.C.* 552:12).

☙ Tishah B'Av on the Sabbath

28. Even when Tishah B'Av falls on the Sabbath itself, none of the restrictions of the fast day apply, because to observe them would be a public manifestation of mourning on the Sabbath. Regarding marital relations see *O.C.* 554:19. *M.B.* §39-40.

29. Torah study is permitted until noon (*M.B.* 553:9). Thereafter, the restrictions are the same as those of a Tishah B'Av eve that falls on the Sabbath; see above §2.

30. The prayer *Av Harachamim* is recited after the Torah reading (*M.B.* 552:30).

THINGS PROHIBITED ON THE FAST DAY

☙ The Five Restrictions

31. Fasting on Tishah B'Av is a broader concept than mere abstention from food and drink. It includes abstention from five activities: (1) eating and drinking; (2) washing one's body; (3) anointing oneself; (4) wearing leather shoes; and (5) marital relations. It is not within the scope of this summary to discuss in detail the ramifications of the restrictions that do not pertain to the prayer service. However, a few words about the restriction on washing, especially about washing the hands before a prayer service, are appropriate here.

32. It is absolutely forbidden to wash even a minute part of the body, whether in hot or cold water, or even to dip one's finger in water (*O.C.* 554:7). However, one may wash his hands three times upon arising in the morning [נְטִילַת יָדַיִם] except that one may wash only the minimum-required area — the fingers, but not the palm of the hand (*O.C.* 554:10).

33. If one has performed his bodily functions and is returning to his prayers (i.e. to recite the *Shemoneh Esrei*), he may also wash his fingers (as above; *O.C.* 554:9, 613:2, *M.B.* 4). If it is his custom all year round to wash three times, he may wash his fingers three times (*Matteh Ephraim* 613:5). One may also wash his hands in preparation for *Minchah* (*M.B.* 554:21).

34. However, if one has merely urinated and will not recite the *Shemoneh Esrei*, it is questionable whether he may wash his hands. In order to avoid this problem, one should touch a covered part of the body, thus incurring an unquestionable obligation to wash his hands before reciting the blessing of אֲשֶׁר יָצַר (see *O.C.* 613:3, *M.B.* 4,6).

35. One who merely entered a bathroom may not wash his hands, even if this is one's practice throughout the year. Rather one should wipe his hands, on a clean cloth or board, in lieu of washing (*M.E.* 613:7). However, if one is upset at praying with unwashed hands, one may wash them (*Eleph LaMatteh* 613:7). [Presumably the device of touching oneself on a covered part of the body is applicable here too.]

36. If one has touched a covered part of the body and wishes to pray or recite a blessing, one should wash all the fingers of that hand. But if one has touched dirt or mud, he may wash only the soiled area (*O. C.* 554:9, *M.B.* 613:6).

37. Although it is customary to wash one's face and rinse one's mouth every morning before praying, it is forbidden to do so on Tishah B'Av. However, if one has mucous on his eyes, he may moisten his fingers and rub them over his eyes (O.C. 554:11).

☙ Other Prohibitions

38. Though we cannot detail all the laws of Tishah B'Av here, the following is a brief listing: One may not study Torah, except for things pertaining to mourning of Tishah B'Av, because the study of Torah brings joy. One may study, with commentary, the Biblical books of *Job*, the 'unpleasant' passages in *Jeremiah* (omitting the verses of consolation), and *Eichah*. One may also study the Midrash to *Eichah*, the third chapter of *Moed Kattan* (which discusses the laws of mourning), the passages in the Talmud (*Gittin* 55b-58a) that discuss the destruction of the Temple, and the story of the destruction of the Temple in the book of *Yossipon* (O.C. 554:1-2, *M.B.* §3).

39. One does not greet his fellows on Tishah B'Av; not even to say good morning. If one is greeted by someone who is unaware of this law, one should answer quietly and with a serious mien. It is better to tell him that on Tishah B'Av one does not extend greetings. One should also not give a present on Tishah B'Av (O.C. 554:20; *M.B.* 41-2).

40. Work should be avoided until noon. See O.C. 554:22-4. If possible, one should refrain from smoking on Tishah B'Av. If this is very difficult, one may smoke in private after the hour of noon (*M.B.* 555:8).

41. On the night of Tishah B'Av and on the morning, until noon, one sits on the ground or on a low stool (O.C. 559:3; *M.B.* §3).

MAARIV

42. *Maariv* begins in the usual manner. After בָּרְכוּ the congregation sits on the floor or on low stools and the lights are dimmed. The *paroches* is removed from the front of the Holy Ark. On Tishah B'Av the prayers are said slowly and tearfully, in the manner of mourners (O.C. 559:1).

43. The regular *Maariv* service is recited [on Saturday night with the addition of אַתָּה חוֹנַנְתָּנוּ]. After *Shemoneh Esrei* the Full *Kaddish* is recited [including the verse תִּתְקַבַּל] (*M.B.* 559:4).

44. On Saturday night, although *Havdalah* is not recited [see below], a multi-wicked candle is lit and the blessing בּוֹרֵא מְאוֹרֵי הָאֵשׁ is recited (O.C. 556:1).

45. *Eichah* (the Book of *Lamentations*) is chanted aloud by the reader. The prevalent custom is that the entire congregation reads along in an undertone (see *M.B.* 559:15. See also *Taz*, *Magen Avraham*, and *Pri Megadim* to 559:4). After *Eichah* has been concluded, the evening *Kinnos* are recited.

46. After the *Kinnos*, the congregation recites וְאַתָּה קָדוֹשׁ, omitting the verse וַאֲנִי זֹאת בְּרִיתִי; the reader recites the Full *Kaddish*, but omits the verse תִּתְקַבַּל; and the congregation recites עָלֵינוּ, followed by the Mourner's *Kaddish*. [At the end of the Sabbath, וִיהִי נֹעַם and וְיִתֶּן לְךָ are omitted, and *Havdalah* is postponed until Sunday night.]

SHACHARIS

47. Candles are not lit at the *chazzan's* lectern for *Shacharis*, but they are lit for *Minchah* (*M.B.* 559:15).

48. Donning of the *tallis* and *tefillin* is postponed until *Minchah*. The *tallis kattan* (*tzitzis*) is worn, however, but the accompanying blessing is omitted. (O.C. 555:1)

49. The morning blessings (p. 72) are recited as usual. Although the blessing שֶׁעָשָׂה לִי כָּל צָרְכִּי was instituted to thank God for providing us with shoes, it is the general custom among Ashkenazim to recite it even though shoes are not worn on Tishah B'Av (*M.B.* 554:31, see *Shaarei Teshuvah* and *Pri Megadim* to O.C. 46:8). However, Sephardim omit the blessing (see *Kaf HaChaim* 46:17), and the Vilna Gaon (*Maaseh Rav*) is reported to have recited the blessing only at night, after the fast.

50. The entire prayer service which precedes פְּסוּקֵי דְזִמְרָה (the *Verses of Praise*), including אֵיזֶהוּ מְקוֹמָן, may be said [Although *Eizehu Mekoman* is a chapter of Mishnah — which may not be studied on Tishah B'Av — it is part of the regular prayer order, and is therefore not omitted.] (O.C. 554:4, *M.B.* 7). However, *Rama* states (O.C. 559:4) that פִּטּוּם הַקְּטֹרֶת is omitted (because, *M.B.* explains, its recitation is not considered to be sufficiently widespread for it to be considered part of the 'order of the day').

Mishnah Berurah (554:7) maintains that according to *Rama's* view, the passage of *Tamid* is the only Scriptural passage referring to offerings that may be recited. Nevertheless, in many communities the entire service is recited, without omission, as already indicated.

51. Individuals recite *Shemoneh Esrei* at *Shacharis* as usual, without any additions.

The *chazzan*, however, inserts the blessing עֲנֵנוּ in his repetition. See §61 for laws pertaining to this blessing. *Birkas Kohanim* is omitted (see *Dagul Merevavah* to O.C. 559) as is *tachanun.*

52. The prayer service continues with reading from the Torah, followed by the Half *Kaddish* and *Haftarah.* The Torah is returned to the Ark and *Kinnos* are recited. It is preferable that their recitation extend until close to noon (O.C. 559:2).

53. After the recitation of *Kinnos*, the prayer service continues with אַשְׁרֵי and וּבָא לְצִיּוֹן (with the omission of the verse . . . וַאֲנִי זֹאת), the Full *Kaddish*, with the omission of תִּתְקַבַּל; followed by עָלֵינוּ and the Mourner's *Kaddish.* The Song of the Day is deferred until *Minchah.*

54. During the recitation of *Kinnos*, one should not talk about extraneous matters nor leave the synagogue, in order to fully concentrate on mourning for the destruction of the Temple (O.C. 559:5).

55. It is commendable that every individual read *Eichah* again during the daytime (*Shelah* cited by *Magen Avraham*, beginning of 559).

MINCHAH

56. Candles are lit at the *chazzan's* lectern for *Minchah* (*Pri Megadim* in *Eishel Avraham* 559:3). The *paroches* [*Ark* curtain] is put back in place (*Kaf HaChaim* 559:19).

57. The *talis* and *tefillin* are donned (O.C. 555:1), and the remainder of the *Shacharis* prayer is said.

58. *Minchah* on Tishah B'Av is the same as that of a regular fast day (except that נַחֵם, *Nacheim*, is inserted in the Shemoneh Esrei (see §64). The Torah reading and the *Haftarah* are identical to that of a regular fast day, with the exception of *Avinu Malkeinu* and *tachanun*, which are omitted.

59. In *Shemoneh Esrei*, עֲנֵנוּ, *Aneinu*, [*Answer us*] is inserted, as on other fast days. In addition, נַחֵם, *Nacheim*, [*comfort*] is inserted. See below §64.

60. The *chazzan* repeats the *Shemoneh Esrei* as usual and inserts the above two prayers (see below). He also recites the Priestly Blessing, as on other fast days (*Kitzur Shulchan Aruch* 124:19). The *Shemoneh Esrei* is followed by the Full *Kaddish* (with תִּתְקַבַּל), then עָלֵינוּ, and the Mourner's *Kaddish.*

⁂ עֲנֵנוּ / Aneinu

61. A special fast-day prayer — עֲנֵנוּ — is interjected both in the silent *Shemoneh Esrei* and in the *chazzan's* repetition. This prayer may be recited only by one who is fasting; for someone not fasting to recite this prayer which refers specifically to 'our public fast' would be fraudulent (see O.C. 565:3 in *Rama*). This insertion is made by the *chazzan* in his repetition of both *Shacharis* and *Minchah*, but in the silent *Shemoneh Esrei* it is recited only during *Minchah* (O.C. 565:3). In the *chazzan's* prayer, *Aneinu* takes the form of a complete benediction, concluding with . . . בָּרוּךְ הָעוֹנֶה בְּעֵת צָרָה, *Blessed . . . Who responds in time of distress* (O.C. 566:1), . . . רְפָאֵנוּ and גּוֹאֵל יִשְׂרָאֵל. The individual's recitation is included in the benediction שְׁמַע קוֹלֵנוּ (O.C. 565:1). In order for the *chazzan* to recite the blessing in his repetition of the *Shemoneh Esrei*, there must be ten congregants who are fasting. Some authorities rule that it is sufficient that there be seven fasting individuals (O.C. 566:3, M.B. §14). Individuals recite *Aneinu* in their own *Shemoneh Esrei* even if no one else is fasting.

62. If an individual forgot to insert עֲנֵנוּ in its proper place and has already said the word *HASHEM* in the concluding blessing of שְׁמַע קוֹלֵנוּ, he must conclude with שׁוֹמֵעַ תְּפִלָּה and continue with רְצֵה. He may insert עֲנֵנוּ at the end of the *Shemoneh Esrei* before אֱלֹהַי נְצוֹר. If he finished *Shemoneh Esrei* before realizing his error, he should not repeat the *Shemoneh Esrei* (M.B. 119:16,19).

63. If the *chazzan* forgot to insert עֲנֵנוּ in its proper place, but has not yet said the word *HASHEM* of the concluding blessing of רְפָאֵנוּ, he should interrupt his recitation, and recite עֲנֵנוּ. Thereafter he should begin רְפָאֵנוּ again and continue. If he has already uttered the word *HASHEM*, he must conclude the blessing רוֹפֵא חוֹלֵי and continue his prayer as usual. In this case, the *chazzan* inserts עֲנֵנוּ in the benediction שְׁמַע קוֹלֵנוּ, as do individuals in the silent prayer, but omits the concluding formula בָּרוּךְ הָעוֹנֶה בְּעֵת צָרָה. If he realized his error after he uttered the word *HASHEM* in the concluding formula of שְׁמַע קוֹלֵנוּ, he must continue with שׁוֹמֵעַ תְּפִלָּה. In that case, he may recite עֲנֵנוּ (omitting the concluding blessing) after הַמְבָרֵךְ אֶת עַמּוֹ יִשְׂרָאֵל בַּשָּׁלוֹם (O.C. 119:4 M.B. §16,19).

⁂ נַחֵם / Nacheim

64. In addition to עֲנֵנוּ, a special prayer (נַחֵם, *Comfort*), mourning the destruction of the Holy Temple and supplicating that it be rebuilt, is inserted in the benediction וְלִירוּשָׁלַיִם, *and to Jerusalem* (both in the silent and *Chazzan's Shemoneh Esrei*) of *Minchah.* The concluding blessing of וְלִירוּשָׁלַיִם is changed (both for individuals and for the *chazzan*) to . . . בָּרוּךְ מְנַחֵם צִיּוֹן וּבוֹנֵה יְרוּשָׁלָיִם, *Blessed . . . Who consoles Zion and rebuilds Jerusalem.* If one forgot to recite this prayer in its appropriate place, he inserts it in

the benediction רְצֵה, before the word וְתֶחֱזֶינָה, but in that case one omits the concluding formula ... מְנַחֵם צִיּוֹן (O.C. 557:1, M.B. §2). However, if one recited נַחֵם erroneously in the benediction שְׁמַע קוֹלֵנוּ, it need not be repeated in רְצֵה (Be'ur Halachah). If one has already concluded the רְצֵה benediction with הַמַּחֲזִיר שְׁכִינָתוֹ לְצִיּוֹן (or even said the word Hashem), he continues his prayer, and need not repeat *Shemoneh Esrei* (O.C. 557).

AFTERNOON

65. Although some restrictions are relaxed in the afternoon, e.g. one may sit on a chair etc., this applies only to practices that are based on custom. However, all halachic strictures that apply to the fast, i.e. eating, drinking, wearing shoes, studying Torah, et al., are in force until nightfall, when stars become visible (*M.B.* 553:3).

MAARIV

66. The regular *Maariv* is recited. On Sunday night, *Havdalah* is recited, with the following exceptions: a) *Havdalah* commences with the blessing over wine; the preliminary verses that are reciting at the end of the Sabbath are omitted; b) The blessings over spices and the candles are omitted. Even those who do not drink the *Havdalah* wine during the nine days may do so now; they need not give the wine to a child to drink. [One should not eat before reciting *Havdalah*.] (*O.C.* 556:1, *M.B.* §3).

☙ Kiddush Levanah

67. According to *Rama* (*O.C.* 426:2), *Kiddush Levanah* should not be recited on the night following Tishah B'Av, because it should be recited joyously, but we are still in mourning. However, many *poskim* dispute this ruling and permit the recitation of *Kiddush Levanah*. Nevertheless, one should first eat something and don his shoes (*M.B.* §11). However, if this is the only time he will be able to recite *Kiddush Levanah* with a *minyan*, some permit its recitation even if one has not yet broken his fast (*Shaar HaTziyun* §9).

☙ The Night After the Fast

68. The strictures that were observed during the Nine Days apply also to the night following Tishah B'Av and the next day until noon. Thus, one does not eat meat, take a haircut, launder clothing, etc. until noon of the next day (O.C. 558:1, M.B. §3).

However if Tishah B'Av was on Thursday, one may wash clothing and take a haircut or shave on Friday morning in preparation for the Sabbath (M.B. 558:3), *Shaarei Teshuvah* §2).

69. If Tishah B'Av fell on the Sabbath so that the fast was observed on the tenth of Av, one need not observe the strictures of the Nine Days [e.g., bathing, haircut, laundering] on the night after the fast. However, one should abstain from meat and wine [except for the *Havdalah* wine] on the night itself (*O.C.* 558:1, M.B. §4).

GENERAL LAWS OF PRAYER

☙ The Obligation

70. Prayer is a major ingredient of every Jew's daily religious life. The Sages teach us that in the post-Temple era, prayer was substituted for the Temple service, and according to some authorities it is a Scriptural obligation to pray every single day (see *Rambam, Hil. Tefillah* 1:1).

71. Before praying, one should set aside a few minutes to collect his thoughts and to prepare himself mentally to stand before his Maker. Also, one should not rush away immediately after ending his prayer so as not to give the impression that he regards prayer as a burdensome task (*O.C.* 93:1).

72. Before beginning to pray, one should meditate upon God's infinite greatness and man's insignificance, and thereby remove from his heart any thoughts of physical pleasure (*O.C.* 98:1). By pondering God's works, man recognizes His infinite wisdom and comes to love and laud Him. This makes man cognizant of his own puny intelligence and flawed nature and puts him in a proper frame of mind to plead for God's mercy (*Rambam, Yesodei HaTorah* 2:2).

73. The prayers should be said with a feeling of awe and humility, and surely not in an atmosphere of levity, frivolity, or mundane concerns, nor should one pray while angry. Rather, one should pray with the feeling of happiness brought on by the knowledge of God's historic kindness to Israel and His mercy to all creatures (*O.C.* 93:2).

☙ Concentration on the Prayers

74. During *Shemoneh Esrei* one should imagine that he is in the Holy Temple and concentrate his feelings and thoughts toward Heaven, clearing his mind of all extraneous matters (*O.C.* 95:2). His eyes should be directed downward, either closed or reading from the *machzor* (*O.C.* 95:2, *M.B.* 5). One should not look up during *Shemoneh Esrei*, but when he feels his

concentration failing, he should raise his eyes heavenward to renew his inspiration (*M.B.* 90:8).

75. One should know the meaning of his prayers. If one had an audience with a human ruler he would take the utmost care in his choice of words and be aware of their meaning. Surely, therefore, when one stands before the King of kings Who knows his innermost thoughts, he must be careful how he speaks (O.C. 98:1). Especially in regard to the benedictions of *Shemoneh Esrei,* one should at least meditate on the meaning of the concluding sentence of each benediction, which summarizes its theme (e.g., בָּרוּךְ... הָאֵל הַקָּדוֹשׁ, *Blessed ... the holy God; M.B.* 101:1). The first benediction of the *Shemoneh Esrei* is treated with special stringency in this regard. According to the *halachah* as stated in the Talmud, this benediction must be repeated if it was said without concentration on its meaning (*O.C.* 101:1). However, *Rama* (loc. cit.) rules that it is best *not* to repeat the benediction because it is likely that one will not concentrate properly even during the repetition. *Chayei Adam* (cited in *M.B.* 101:4) advises that if one realized his inattentiveness before saying the word HASHEM in the concluding formula of the first blessing (בָּרוּךְ... מָגֵן אַבְרָהָם), he should start over from אֱלֹהֵי אַבְרָהָם. Thus, it is of utmost importance that one learn the meaning of the prayers in order to develop his power of concentration (*M.B.* 101:2).

76. On Tishah B'Av a lengthy selection of lamentation liturgy — *Kinnos* — is a central part of the *Shacharis* service. It is important that one familiarize himself with these prayers prior to the fast day, some of which use unfamiliar language and contain numerous allusions to Midrashic sources.

Women's Obligation to Pray

77. Women are obligated to pray, and according to *Rambam* and *Shulchan Aruch* (O.C. 106:1) this obligation has Scriptural status. However, there are various opinions regarding the extent of their obligation.

According to the views preferred by *M.B.* (106:4), women are required to recite the *Shemoneh Esrei* of *Shacharis* and *Minchah;* they must recall the Exodus by reciting אֱמֶת וְיַצִּיב, *true and certain* (the prayer after the *Shacharis* recitation of *Shema*), and אֱמֶת וֶאֱמוּנָה, *true and faithful* (the parallel prayer after the *Maariv* recitation of *Shema*), because it recalls the Exodus (*M.B.* 70:2); and it is urged that they recite at least the first verse of *Shema* because it constitutes קַבָּלַת עוֹל מַלְכוּת שָׁמַיִם, *acceptance of God's sovereignty* (O.C. 70:1).

Some authorities rule that women should also recite all the morning benedictions. According to one view, *Pesukei D'zimrah* is introductory to *Shemoneh Esrei* and, consequently, is obligatory upon women too (*M.B.* 70:2).

Women should recite בִּרְכַּת הַתּוֹרָה, *blessings of the Torah* (O.C. 47:14, see *Be'ur Halachah*).

According to *Magen Avraham* (O.C. 106:2), women are required by the Torah to pray once a day and they may formulate the prayer as they wish. In many countries, this ruling became the basis for the custom that women recite a brief prayer early in the morning and do not recite any of the formal prayers from the *Siddur*.

Miscellaneous Laws

78. One may not pray in the presence of immodestly clad women, or facing a window through which they can be observed (see O.C. 75 for details).

79. It is forbidden to pray while one feels the need to discharge his bodily functions (O.C. 92:1-3).

80. One must wash his hands before praying, but no benediction is required (O.C. 92:4).

On Tishah B'Av, certain strictures must be observed when washing one's hands before prayer; see §32-36.

PRAYER WITH THE CONGREGATION

Prayer with a Minyan of Ten

81. One should do his utmost to pray in the synagogue together with the congregation (O.C. 90:9), for the Almighty does not reject the prayer of the many. Contrary to the popular misconception that it is sufficient to respond to בָּרְכוּ and קְדוּשָּׁה, the main objective of prayer with a *minyan* is to recite *Shemoneh Esrei* with the *minyan.* Therefore one must arrive at the synagogue early enough to keep up with the congregation (*M.B.* §28).

Instructions for Latecomers

82. If one arrived at the synagogue too late to recite the entire order of the prayer and still recite the *Shemoneh Esrei* together with the congregation, he may omit certain parts of the service and recite them after the end of *Shacharis.* If time is extremely short, it suffices to recite the benedictions אֱלֹהַי נְשָׁמָה; אֲשֶׁר יָצַר; עַל נְטִילַת יָדָיִם; the benedictions over the Torah; בָּרוּךְ שֶׁאָמַר; אַשְׁרֵי; and from יִשְׁתַּבַּח through *Shemoneh Esrei.* If time permits, the following sections (listed in descending order of importance) should be recited:

(1) הַלְלוּיָהּ הַלְלוּ אֵל בְּקָדְשׁוֹ;

(2) הַלְלוּיָהּ הַלְלוּ אֶת ה׳ מִן הַשָּׁמַיִם;

(3) the other three הַלְלוּיָהּ psalms;

(4) from וַיְבָרֶךְ דָּוִיד until לְשֵׁם תִּפְאַרְתֶּךָ;

(5) וְהוּא רַחוּם until הודו;

(6) the rest of *Pesukei D'zimrah* (O.C. 52:1, *M.B.* 4, *Ba'er Heitev* §3).

83. The above is only an emergency solution. One should not rely on this to arrive late

for the *Pesukei D'zimrah*, because the proper order of the prayers is of utmost importance. Indeed, some authorities contend that recitation of the prayers in their proper order takes priority over the obligation to recite *Shemoneh Esrei* together with the congregation (*M.B.* 52:1).

RESPONSES DURING THE PRAYER

☙ During Pesukei D'zimrah

84. Other than the exceptions noted below, it is prohibited to interrupt from the beginning of בָּרוּךְ שֶׁאָמַר until the conclusion of the *Shemoneh Esrei* (*O.C.* 51:4). Wherever one may not talk, it is forbidden to do so even in Hebrew (*M.B.* 51:7).

85. With the exception of *Shemoneh Esrei*, parts of *Shacharis* may be interrupted for certain responses to the *chazzan* or for certain blessings, but the rules vary widely, depending on the section of *Shacharis* and the response. In this regard, the most lenient part of *Shacharis* is *Pesukei D'zimrah*, i.e., the unit that includes the verses between בָּרוּךְ שֶׁאָמַר and יִשְׁתַּבַּח. There, one may respond with *Amen* to any benediction, but may not say בָּרוּךְ הוּא וּבָרוּךְ שְׁמוֹ. It is permitted to respond to *Kedushah* and מוֹדִים (in the repetition of *Shemoneh Esrei*), בָּרְכוּ, and *Kaddish*. If the congregation is reciting the *Shema*, one should recite the first verse (*Shema Yisrael* . . .) together with them. If one discharged his bodily functions, he may recite the benediction אֲשֶׁר יָצַר (*M.B.* 51:8).

86. If one did not yet recite the *Shema* and calculates that the congregation will reach it after the deadline (see §109 below) or if he had forgotten to say the daily *berachos* on the Torah, he should say them in the *Pesukei D'zimrah* (*M.B.* 51:10).

☙ During the Pesukei D'zimrah Blessings

87. The second level of stringency regarding interruptions includes the two benedictions of *Pesukei D'zimrah* — בָּרוּךְ שֶׁאָמַר and יִשְׁתַּבַּח.

בָּרוּךְ שֶׁאָמַר is composed of three parts:

(a) From בָּרוּךְ שֶׁאָמַר until the first בָּרוּךְ אַתָּה ה׳ is but a preamble; all responses are permitted.

(b) From the first בָּרוּךְ אַתָּה ה׳ until the final one, all the interruptions permitted in §85 for the rest of *Pesukei D'zimrah* are also permitted here. However, the following interruptions are *not* permitted at this point: אֲשֶׁר יָצַר and the *Amen* after the benedictions בָּרוּךְ שֶׁאָמַר and יִשְׁתַּבַּח.

(c) The last, brief blessing, בָּרוּךְ . . . בַּתִּשְׁבָּחוֹת, during which no interruption at all is permitted (*M.B.* 51:2).

יִשְׁתַּבַּח is composed of two parts:

(a) From the beginning of יִשְׁתַּבַּח to בָּרוּךְ אַתָּה ה׳, which has the same rules as (b) above.

(b) From בָּרוּךְ אַתָּה ה׳ to the end, which has the same rules as (c) above (*M.B.* 51:2, 65:11, 54:11).

☙ Between the Shema Blessings of Shacharis and Maariv

88. The third level of stringency concerns the 'intervals' between the various sections of the *Shema* and the benedictions bracketing it. The intervals are as follows: After בָּרוּךְ . . . יוֹצֵר הַמְּאוֹרוֹת; after בָּרוּךְ . . . בְּאַהֲבָה; and after the first and second sections of the *Shema*. [The end of the *Shema* is immediately followed by the first word of the following paragraph (אֱמֶת) so that there is no 'interval' there. Similarly, it is forbidden to interrupt between the benediction גָּאַל יִשְׂרָאֵל and *Shemoneh Esrei* (*O.C.* 66:5,9).]

Corresponding 'intervals' exist in *Maariv* following each blessing and after the first and second sections of the *Shema* (*M.B.* 66:27; *Be'ur Halachah* there).

89. During the 'intervals' one may respond with *Amen* to all benedictions (*M.B.* 66:23). Regarding קַדִּישׁ, קְדוּשָּׁה, בָּרְכוּ, and other interruptions, the 'intervals' are treated in the same way as are interruptions in the fourth level (see below §90). During the interval between בְּאַהֲבָה and שְׁמַע, however, only the *Amen* after בְּאַהֲבָה is permitted (*Derech HaChaim;* see *M.B.* 59:25).

☙ During the Shema and Its Blessings in Shacharis and Maariv

90. The fourth level concerns the *Shema* itself and the benedictions bracketing it. The benedictions may be separated into two parts for this purpose: (1) During the concluding, brief blessing, and during the verses of שְׁמַע . . . אֶחָד and בָּרוּךְ שֵׁם, no interruption whatever is permitted (*O.C.* 66:1; *M.B.* §11, 12). (2) During the rest of the fourth level, one may respond with *Amen* only to the two blessings הָאֵל הַקָּדוֹשׁ and שׁוֹמֵעַ תְּפִלָּה in *Shemoneh Esrei*. It is permitted to respond to בָּרְכוּ of both the *chazzan* and one who is called up to the Torah. In *Kaddish* one may respond with אָמֵן יְהֵא שְׁמֵהּ רַבָּא . . . and with the *Amen* to דַּאֲמִירָן בְּעָלְמָא. In *Kedushah* one may say only the verses beginning קָדוֹשׁ and בָּרוּךְ. To *Modim*, one may respond only with the three words מוֹדִים אֲנַחְנוּ לָךְ (*O.C* 66:3; *M.B.* §17,18).

A person who is reciting the *Shema* or its benedictions should not be called up to the Torah, even if he is the only *Kohen* or Levite present; in such a case it is preferable that he leave the room. However, if he *was* called up to the Torah, he may recite the benedictions, but should not read along with the reader. If possible he should attempt to get to an 'interval' in his prayers before doing so (*M.B.* 66:26).

If one had to discharge his bodily functions he should merely wash his hands and defer the recitation of אֲשֶׁר יָצַר until after *Shemoneh Esrei* (*M.B.* 66:23).

91. If one has not yet responded to בָּרְכוּ, קְדוּשָּׁה or מוֹדִים and is nearly up to *Shemoneh Esrei*, he should stop before שִׁירָה

חֲדָשָׁה in order to make the responses. If he has already said שִׁירָה חֲדָשָׁה, but has not yet concluded the benediction, he may respond, but after the response he should start again from שִׁירָה חֲדָשָׁה (*M.B.* 66:52).

92. Regarding גָּאַל יִשְׂרָאֵל of *Shacharis, Rama,* followed by most Ashkenazic congregations, rules that it is permitted to answer *Amen,* while others, particularly Chassidic congregations, follow R' Yosef Caro's ruling against *Amen* at this point. To avoid the controversy, many individuals recite the blessing in unison with the *chazzan* (*O.C.* 66:7, *M.B.* §35).

93. The fifth level concerns the *Shemoneh Esrei* prayer. Here, any interruption is forbidden. Even motioning to someone is prohibited (*O.C.* 104:1; *M.B.* §1). If the *chazzan* is up to קַדִּישׁ, קְדוּשָׁה, or בָּרְכוּ, one should stop and listen silently to the *chazzan's* recitation; his own silent concentration is considered as if he had responded (*O.C.* 104:7; *M.B.* §26-28).

94. From the time one has concluded the last benediction of *Shemoneh Esrei* with בַּשָּׁלוֹם until the end of the standard prayers (i.e., יִהְיוּ לְרָצוֹן at the end of אֱלֹהַי נְצוֹר), one is restricted to the responses listed in level four. However, whenever possible, one should hurry to say the verse יִהְיוּ לְרָצוֹן . . . וְגוֹאֲלִי before making any kind of response. It is preferable to take the usual three steps backward before making the responses (*O.C.* 122:1; *M.B.* §2-4). [Once one has concluded the *Shemoneh Esrei* by taking three steps backward, he may make any response, even if he has not yet recited אֱלֹהַי נְצוֹר.]

LAWS OF RECITING THE SHEMA

95. It is a Scriptural precept to recite the *Shema* twice daily, once in the morning and again in the evening. When one recites the *Shema* he must have in mind that he is fulfilling a Scriptural precept; otherwise it must be repeated (*O.C.* 60:4). However, if the circumstances make it obvious that the intention was present — e.g., he recited it during the prayer with the benedictions preceding and following it — he need not repeat the *Shema* even if he did not make a mental declaration of purpose (*M.B.* 60:10).

96. The third section of *Shema,* whose recitation is Rabbinical in origin according to almost all authorities, contains a verse whose recitation fulfills the Scriptural obligation to commemorate the Exodus from Egypt twice daily (see *Berachos* 12b; *Rambam, Hil. Kerias Shema* 1:3). The above rule concerning a mental declaration of intent applies here, too.

97. One should concentrate on the meaning of all the words, and read them with awe and trepidation (*O.C.* 61:1). He should read the *Shema* as if it were a new proclamation containing teachings never yet revealed (*O.C.* 61:2). The first verse of *Shema* is the essential profession of our faith. Therefore, the utmost concentration on its meaning is necessary. If one said it without such concentration, he has not fulfilled his obligation and must repeat it (*O.C.* 60:5, 63:4), but he should repeat the verse quietly, for one may not (publicly) say the first verse of *Shema* repeatedly (ibid.).

98. While reciting the first verse, it is customary to cover the eyes with the right hand to avoid distraction and to enhance concentration (*O.C.* 61:5).

99. Although *Shema* may be recited quietly, one should recite it loudly enough to hear himself. However, one has discharged his obligation even if he does not hear himself, as long as he has enunciated the words (*O.C.* 62:3).

100. The last word of the first verse, אֶחָד, must be pronounced with special emphasis, while one meditates on God's exclusive sovereignty over the seven heavens and earth, and the four directions — east, south, west, and north (*O.C.* 61:6).

101. Some consider it preferable to recite the entire *Shema* aloud (except for the passage בָּרוּךְ שֵׁם) while others say it quietly; our custom follows the latter usage. However, the first verse should be said aloud in order to arouse one's full concentration (*O.C.* 61:4,26). It is customary for the *chazzan* to lead the congregation in the recitation of the first verse so that they all proclaim the Kingdom of Heaven together (*Kol Bo* cited in *Darkei Moshe* to *O.C.* 61; *Levush*).

102. Every word must be enunciated clearly and uttered with the correct grammatical pronunciation (*O.C.* 62:1, 61:23, 16-19). It is especially important to enunciate each word clearly and to avoid run-on words by pausing briefly between words ending and beginning with the same consonant, such as וַאֲבַדְתֶּם מְהֵרָה, בְּכָל לְבַבְכֶם, and to pause between a word that ends with a consonant and the next one that begins with a silent letter [i.e., א or ע], such as אֲשֶׁר אָנֹכִי, הַיּוֹם עַל, וּרְאִיתֶם אֹתוֹ (*O.C.* 61:20, 21).

103. Although it is not the universal custom to chant the *Shema* with the cantillation melody used during the synagogue Torah reading, it is laudable to do so, unless one finds that such chanting interferes with his concentration. In any event, the proper punctuation must be followed so that words are grouped into the proper phrases in accordance with the syntax of each word-group and verse (*O.C.* 61:24, *M.B.* §37,38).

104. While reciting the first two portions of the *Shema,* one may not communicate with someone else by winking or motioning with his lips or fingers (*O.C.* 63:6, *M.B.* §18).

105. It is incumbent that each paragraph of the *Shema* be read word for word as it

appears in the Torah. If one erred and skipped a word, he must return to the place of his error and continue the section from there (*O.C.* 64:1-2).

106. The *Shema* should be said in one uninterrupted recitation, but, if one interrupted, whether by talking or waiting silently, he does not have to repeat the *Shema*. However, if the interruption was involuntary in nature [e.g., one had to relieve himself], and the interruption was long enough for him to have recited all three paragraphs of the *Shema* at his own normal speed, he must repeat the entire *Shema* (*Rama O.C.* 65:1). Multiple interruptions interspersed in the recitation of *Shema* are not added together to constitute one long, invalidating interruption (*M.B.* 65:4).

107. If one is present in the synagogue when the congregation recites the *Shema*, he must recite at least the first verse and the verse בָּרוּךְ שֵׁם together with them. If he is in the midst of a prayer that he may not interrupt (see above §87-92), he should at least give the appearance of saying *Shema* by praying loudly in the tune the congregation uses for the *Shema* (*O.C.* 65:2,3; *M.B.* §10).

108. During morning services, one ordinarily gathers together the four *tzitzis* when he says the words וַהֲבִיאֵנוּ לְשָׁלוֹם מֵאַרְבַּע כַּנְפוֹת הָאָרֶץ, *Bring us in peacefulness from the four corners of the earth*, in the paragraph preceding the *Shema*. [The *tzitzis* are then held in the hand and kissed at specific points of the *Shema* recitation and the blessing which follows it. On Tishah B'Av, however, this is not done.]

109. It is absolutely required that the *Shema* be recited within the requisite time — the first quarter of the day. There are various opinions among the *poskim* as to how to calculate the first quarter of a day, and these are noted in many Jewish calendars. If the congregation begins *Shacharis* late, one should be careful to check the deadline for *K'rias Shema* and, if necessary, recite all three passages of the *Shema* before the communal prayers.

◆§ The Chazzan's Repetition of the Shemoneh Esrei

110. The *chazzan's* repetition of *Shemoneh Esrei* is a congregational, rather than an individual, worship. By definition, a 'congregation' consists of a *minyan* (quorum of at least ten males over *bar mitzvah*, including the *chazzan*), present and listening to the recitation. If the congregants do not pay attention, it is almost as if the *chazzan* were taking God's Name in vain. Every person should imagine that there are only ten congregants present and that he is one of the nine whose attentive listening is vital to the recitation (*O.C.* 124:4).

If one of the ten is in the middle of the silent *Amidah*, he may still be counted as part of the *minyan*. However, it is preferable that not more than one such person be included (*M.B.* 55:32-34).

111. One should respond with *Amen* to every benediction he hears, and should teach his young children to do so (*O.C.* 124:6,7).

112. When one says *Amen*, it is important to enunciate all of the vowels and consonants distinctly. One should not respond until the *chazzan* has concluded the benediction, and then the response should be immediate (*O.C.* 124:8). *Mishnah Berurah* (§17) cautions even against Torah study or recitation of psalms and other prayers during the *chazzan's* recitation of the *Shemoneh Esrei*.

113. It is absolutely forbidden to talk during the repetition of *Shemoneh Esrei* even if one makes sure to respond with *Amen* at the conclusion of each benediction (*O.C.* 124:7).

THE READING OF THE TORAH

114. On Tishah B'Av, as on every fast day, three people are called to the Torah at the *Shacharis* prayer, and three at the *Minchah* prayer. One may not add to the prescribed amount of *aliyos* (*O.C.* 282:1, *M.B.* §6).

115. The first *aliyah* belongs to a *Kohen* and the second to a *Levi* (if any are present). If no *Kohen* is present, there is no obligation to call a *Levi* in his place, but if no *Levi* is present the same *Kohen* who has been called for his own *aliyah* is called again to replace the *Levi*. He recites both blessings again (*O.C.* 135:10; *M.B.* §35).

◆§ Procedure of the Aliyah

116. Before the person called to the Torah for an *aliyah* recites the benediction, he must open the Torah and find the passage that will be read for him (*O.C.* 139:4). In order to dispel any notion that he is reading the benedictions from the Torah, one should avert his face while reciting them; it is preferable to turn to the left side (*Rama* there). Some authorities maintain that it is better to face the Torah while saying the benedictions but to close his eyes (*M.B.* §19). Others say that it is better to close the Torah during the recitation of the benedictions (*Be'ur Halachah* there). All three modes are practiced today in various congregations.

117. In many congregations it is customary to touch the Torah with a *tallis* (or the Torah's mantle or girdle) at the beginning of the passage to be read, and to kiss the edge which touched the Torah (*Sha'arei Ephraim* 4:3). One should be careful not to rub on the Torah script forcefully for this can cause words to become erased and thus invalidate the Torah scroll.

118. It is extremely important that the benedictions be said loud enough for the congregation to hear (O.C. 139:6). If the congregation did not hear the recitation of בָּרְכוּ, they may not respond with בָּרוּךְ . . . וָעֶד (*Be'ur Halachah* to O.C. 57:1). However, if the congregation (or at least a *minyan*) heard בָּרְכוּ, then even someone who has not heard בָּרְכוּ may respond along with the congregation (*M.B.* 57:2).

119. While reciting the benedictions, one should hold the poles (*atzei chaim*) upon which the Torah is rolled. During the reading, the reader holds one pole and the person called to the Torah holds the other one (O.C. 139:11; *M.B.* §35). *Arizal* says one should hold the *atzei chaim* with both hands during the benedictions and with the right hand only during the reading (cited in *Magen Avraham* 139:13).

120. Upon completion of the reading it is customary for the person who has been called up to touch the Torah with a *tallis* (or the Torah's mantle or girdle) and to kiss the edge that has touched the Torah (see *M.B.* 139:35).

121. After the Torah passage has been read, he closes the Torah scroll and then recites the benediction (*Rama* O.C. 139:5). If the Torah reading will not be resumed immediately (e.g., a מִי שֶׁבֵּרַךְ is said), then a covering should be spread out over the Torah (*M.B.* 139:21).

122. In Talmudic times the person called for an *aliyah* would also read aloud from the Torah. This practice was still followed in Greek and Turkish communities up to the sixteenth century (see *Beis Yosef* to *Tur* O.C. 141), and the tradition persists to this day in Yemenite communities. However, since ancient times the Ashkenazic custom has been for a designated reader (*baal korei*) to read the Torah aloud to the congregation (see *Rosh* cited in *Tur* loc. cit). Nevertheless, the person who recites the benedictions should read quietly along with the reader (O.C. 141:2).

123. The reader and the one called up to the Torah must stand while reading the Torah in public. It is forbidden even to lean upon something (O.C. 141:1).

124. When going up to the *bimah* to recite the benedictions one should pick the shortest route possible, and when returning to his seat, he should take a longer route. If two routes are equidistant, one should go to the *bimah* via the route which is to his right and descend via the opposite route (O.C. 141:7).

125. After one has finished reciting the concluding benediction he should not return to his place at least until the next person called up to the Torah has come to the *bimah* (O.C. 141:7). However, it is customary to wait until the next person has finished his passage of the Torah (*M.B.* §26).

126. It is forbidden to talk or even to discuss Torah topics while the Torah is being read (O.C. 146:2).

127. It is forbidden to leave the synagogue while the Torah is being read (O.C. 146:1), even if one has already heard the reading of the passage elsewhere (*M.B.* §1). However, if necessary, one may leave during the pause between one portion and the next (O.C. 146:1), provided that a *minyan* remains in the synagogue (*M.B.* §2).

KADDISH

128. The conclusion of a section of prayer is usually signified by the recitation of the *Kaddish*. Many of these *Kaddish* recitations are the privilege of mourners (within the eleven months following the death or burial of a parent, or in some instances, of other close relatives), or of those observing *yahrzeit*, i.e., the anniversary of the death of a parent (and in some congregations, of a grandparent who has no living sons; see *Matteh Ephraim, Dinei Kaddish* 3:14). However, many recitations of *Kaddish* are exclusively the prerogative of the *chazzan*.

129. Basically there are four types of *Kaddish:*

(a) חֲצִי קַדִּישׁ, Half-*Kaddish*, which ends with דַּאֲמִירָן בְּעָלְמָא וְאִמְרוּ אָמֵן;

(b) קַדִּישׁ יָתוֹם, the Mourner's *Kaddish*, which consists of the Half-*Kaddish*, with the addition of יְהֵא שְׁלָמָא and עוֹשֶׂה שָׁלוֹם;

(c) קַדִּישׁ שָׁלֵם, the Full *Kaddish*, the same as the Mourner's *Kaddish* with the addition of תִּתְקַבַּל before יְהֵא שְׁלָמָא; and

(d) קַדִּישׁ דְּרַבָּנָן, the Rabbis' *Kaddish*, the same as the Mourner's *Kaddish* with the addition of עַל יִשְׂרָאֵל.

130. The function of the Half-*Kaddish* is to link different segments of the prayer, e.g., it is recited between *Pesukei D'zimrah* and the *Shema* benedictions, between *Shemoneh Esrei* (or *Tachanun*) and the prayers that conclude the service (*Pri Megadim* in *Mishbetzos Zahav, Orach Chaim* 55:1). Thus, it is recited by the *chazzan*.

Nevertheless, in some congregations it is customary for a mourner to recite the *Kaddish* following the reading of the Torah if he has been called to the Torah for the concluding segment (*Sha'arei Ephraim* 10:9). The rationale for this custom is that the person called to the Torah is also a *chazzan* of sorts, since he too must read from the Torah, albeit quietly. In some congregations, a mourner recites this *Kaddish* even if he was not called to the Torah.

131. The Full *Kaddish* is recited only after the communal recitation of *Shemoneh Esrei* (or *Selichos*). It includes the *chazzan's* prayer that the just-concluded service be accepted by God. Consequently it must be recited by the *chazzan*.

132. The Mourner's *Kaddish* is recited after the recital of Scriptural verses that supplement the main body of prayer. The recital of *Kaddish* after this portion of the service is not obligatory, and is not recited if no mourners are present. Since *Kaddish* in these parts of the service is recited exclusively by mourners, it has become customary that one whose parents are living should not recite it, since this would be a mark of disrespect to his parents (see *Rama O.C.* 132:2; *Pis'chei Teshuvah, Yoreh Deah* 376:4).

If no mourners are present, the Mourner's *Kaddish* is not recited, with one exception. After *Aleinu,* which also contains Scriptural verses, *Kaddish* should be recited even if no mourner is present. In such a case, it should be recited by the *chazzan* or one of the congregants, preferably one whose parents are no longer alive, or one whose parents have not explicitly expressed their opposition to his recitation of *Kaddish (O.C.* 132:2 with *M.B.* §11).

133. Ideally, each Mourner's *Kaddish* should be recited by only one person. Where more than one mourner is present, the *poskim* developed a system of rules establishing an order of priorities for those who must recite *Kaddish* (see *M.B.* in *Be'ur Halachah* to *O.C.* 132, et al.). However, since adherence to these rules can often cause discord in the congregation, it has become widely accepted for all the mourners to recite the *Kaddish* simultaneously (see *Aruch HaShulchan O.C.* 132:8; *Siddur R' Yaakov Emden; Teshuvos Chasam Sofer, O. C.* 159).

134. In many congregations it is customary that someone observing a *yahrzeit* is given the exclusive privilege of reciting a *Kaddish,* usually the one after *Aleinu.* In that case, an additional psalm (usually *Psalm* 24) is recited at the conclusion of the services so that all the mourners can recite *Kaddish* after it.

135. The Rabbis' *Kaddish (Kaddish D'Rabbanan)* is recited after segments of the Oral Torah (e.g., Talmud) have been studied or recited by a quorum of ten adult males *(Rambam, Seder Tefilos Kol HaShanah).* The Talmud *(Sotah* 49a) refers to the great significance of יְהֵא שְׁמֵיהּ רַבָּא (a reference to *Kaddish)* that is said after *Aggadah,* indicating that this *Kaddish* has a special relevance to the Midrashic portion of the Torah. Therefore, it is customary to append a brief Aggadic selection to Torah study and then to recite the Rabbis' *Kaddish* (*M.B.* 54:9).

136. Although *Kaddish D'Rabbanan* is not reserved for mourners and may be recited even by one whose parents are alive *(Pis-chei Teshuvah, Yoreh Deah* 376:4), it is generally recited by mourners. However, when one celebrates the completion of a tractate of the Talmud, or when the rabbi delivers a *derashah* (homiletical discourse), it is customary for the celebrant or the rabbi to recite the *Kaddish* himself.

VERSES FOR PEOPLE'S NAMES / פסוקים לשמות אנשים

Kitzur Sh'lah teaches that it is a source of merit to recite a Scriptural verse symbolizing one's name before יִהְיוּ לְרָצוֹן at the end of *Shemoneh Esrei*. The verse should either contain the person's name, or else begin and end with the first and last letters of the name.

Following is a selection of first and last letters of names, with appropriate verses:

א...א אָנָּא יהוה הוֹשִׁיעָה נָּא, אָנָּא יהוה הַצְלִיחָה נָּא.[1]

א...ה אַשְׁרֵי מַשְׂכִּיל אֶל דָּל, בְּיוֹם רָעָה יְמַלְּטֵהוּ יהוה.[2]

א...ו אַשְׁרֵי שֶׁאֵל יַעֲקֹב בְּעֶזְרוֹ, שִׂבְרוֹ עַל יהוה אֱלֹהָיו.[3]

א...י אֲמָרַי הַאֲזִינָה יהוה, בִּינָה הֲגִיגִי.[4]

א...ך אָמַרְתְּ לַיהוה, אֲדֹנָי אָתָּה, טוֹבָתִי בַּל עָלֶיךָ.[5]

א...ל אֶרֶץ רָעָשָׁה, אַף שָׁמַיִם נָטְפוּ מִפְּנֵי אֱלֹהִים; זֶה סִינַי, מִפְּנֵי אֱלֹהִים אֱלֹהֵי יִשְׂרָאֵל.[6]

א...ם אַתָּה הוּא יהוה הָאֱלֹהִים, אֲשֶׁר בָּחַרְתָּ בְּאַבְרָם, וְהוֹצֵאתוֹ מֵאוּר כַּשְׂדִּים, וְשַׂמְתָּ שְׁמוֹ אַבְרָהָם.[7]

א...ן אֵלֶיךָ יהוה אֶקְרָא, וְאֶל אֲדֹנָי אֶתְחַנָּן.[8]

א...ע אָמַר בְּלִבּוֹ בַּל אֶמּוֹט, לְדֹר וָדֹר אֲשֶׁר לֹא בְרָע.[9]

א...ר אֵלֶּה בָרֶכֶב וְאֵלֶּה בַסּוּסִים, וַאֲנַחְנוּ בְּשֵׁם יהוה אֱלֹהֵינוּ נַזְכִּיר.[10]

ב...א בְּרִיתִי הָיְתָה אִתּוֹ הַחַיִּים וְהַשָּׁלוֹם, וָאֶתְּנֵם לוֹ מוֹרָא וַיִּירָאֵנִי, וּמִפְּנֵי שְׁמִי נִחַת הוּא.[11]

ב...ה בַּעֲבוּר יִשְׁמְרוּ חֻקָּיו, וְתוֹרֹתָיו יִנְצֹרוּ, הַלְלוּיָהּ.[12]

ב...ז בְּיוֹם קָרָאתִי וַתַּעֲנֵנִי, תַּרְהִבֵנִי בְנַפְשִׁי עֹז.[13]

ב...ך בָּרוּךְ אַתָּה יהוה, לַמְּדֵנִי חֻקֶּיךָ.[14]

ב...ל בְּמַקְהֵלוֹת בָּרְכוּ אֱלֹהִים, אֲדֹנָי מִמְּקוֹר יִשְׂרָאֵל.[15]

ב...ן בָּרוּךְ יהוה אֱלֹהֵי יִשְׂרָאֵל מֵהָעוֹלָם וְעַד הָעוֹלָם, אָמֵן וְאָמֵן.[16]

ב...ע בְּחֶסֶד וֶאֱמֶת יְכֻפַּר עָוֹן, וּבְיִרְאַת יהוה סוּר מֵרָע.[17]

ג...ה גּוֹל עַל יהוה דַּרְכֶּךָ, וּבְטַח עָלָיו וְהוּא יַעֲשֶׂה.[18]

ג...ל גַּם אֲנִי אוֹדְךָ בִכְלִי נֶבֶל אֲמִתְּךָ אֱלֹהָי, אֲזַמְּרָה לְךָ בְכִנּוֹר, קְדוֹשׁ יִשְׂרָאֵל.[19]

ג...ן גַּם בְּנֵי אָדָם גַּם בְּנֵי אִישׁ, יַחַד עָשִׁיר וְאֶבְיוֹן.[20]

ד...ב דִּרְשׁוּ יהוה בְּהִמָּצְאוֹ, קְרָאֻהוּ בִּהְיוֹתוֹ קָרוֹב.[21]

ד...ד דִּרְשׁוּ יהוה וְעֻזּוֹ, בַּקְּשׁוּ פָנָיו תָּמִיד.[22]

ד...ה דְּאָגָה בְלֶב אִישׁ יַשְׁחֶנָּה, וְדָבָר טוֹב יְשַׂמְּחֶנָּה.[23]

ד...ל דָּן יָדִין עַמּוֹ, כְּאַחַד שִׁבְטֵי יִשְׂרָאֵל.[24]

ה...א הַצּוּר תָּמִים פָּעֳלוֹ, כִּי כָל דְּרָכָיו מִשְׁפָּט, אֵל אֱמוּנָה וְאֵין עָוֶל, צַדִּיק וְיָשָׁר הוּא.[25]

ה...ה הַסְתֵּר פָּנֶיךָ מֵחֲטָאָי, וְכָל עֲוֹנֹתַי מְחֵה.[26]

ה...ל הַקְשִׁיבָה לְקוֹל שַׁוְעִי מַלְכִּי וֵאלֹהָי, כִּי אֵלֶיךָ אֶתְפַּלָּל.[27]

ז...ב זֵכֶר צַדִּיק לִבְרָכָה, וְשֵׁם רְשָׁעִים יִרְקָב.[28]

ז...ה זֹאת מְנוּחָתִי עֲדֵי עַד, פֹּה אֵשֵׁב כִּי אִוִּתִיהָ.[29]

ז...ח זָכַרְתִּי יָמִים מִקֶּדֶם, הָגִיתִי בְכָל פָּעֳלֶךָ, בְּמַעֲשֵׂה יָדֶיךָ אֲשׂוֹחֵחַ.[30]

ז...ן זְבוּלֻן לְחוֹף יַמִּים יִשְׁכֹּן, וְהוּא לְחוֹף אֳנִיֹּת, וְיַרְכָתוֹ עַל צִידֹן.[31]

ח..ה חָגְרָה בְעוֹז מָתְנֶיהָ, וַתְּאַמֵּץ זְרוֹעֹתֶיהָ.[32]

---

(1) *Psalms* 118:25. (2) 41:2. (3) 146:5. (4) 5:2. (5) 16:2. (6) 68:9. (7) *Nehemiah* 9:7. (8) *Psalms* 30:9. (9) 10:6. (10) 20:8. (11) *Malachi* 2:5. (12) *Psalms* 105:45. (13) 138:3. (14) 119:12. (15) 68:27. (16) 41:14. (17) *Proverbs* 16:6. (18) *Psalms* 37:5. (19) 71:22. (20) 49:3. (21) *Isaiah* 55:6. (22) *Psalms* 105:4. (23) *Proverbs* 12:25. (24) *Genesis* 49:16. (25) *Deuteronomy* 32:4. (26) *Psalms* 51:11. (27) 5:3. (28) *Proverbs* 10:7. (29) *Psalms* 132:14. (30) 143:5. (31) *Genesis* 49:13. (32) *Proverbs* 31:17.

ח...ך חֲצוֹת לַיְלָה אָקוּם לְהוֹדוֹת לָךְ, עַל מִשְׁפְּטֵי צִדְקֶךָ.[1]

ח...ם חֹנֶה מַלְאַךְ יהוה סָבִיב לִירֵאָיו, וַיְחַלְּצֵם.[2]

ט...א טוֹב יַנְחִיל בְּנֵי בָנִים, וְצָפוּן לַצַּדִּיק חֵיל חוֹטֶא.[3]

ט...ה טָמְנוּ גֵאִים פַּח לִי וַחֲבָלִים, פָּרְשׂוּ רֶשֶׁת לְיַד מַעְגָּל, מֹקְשִׁים שָׁתוּ לִי סֶלָה.[4]

י...א יִשְׂרָאֵל בְּטַח בַּיהוה, עֶזְרָם וּמָגִנָּם הוּא.[5]

י...ב יַעַנְךָ יהוה בְּיוֹם צָרָה, יְשַׂגֶּבְךָ שֵׁם אֱלֹהֵי יַעֲקֹב.[6]

י...ד יָסַד אֶרֶץ עַל מְכוֹנֶיהָ, בַּל תִּמּוֹט עוֹלָם וָעֶד.[7]

י...ה יהוה הַצִּילָה נַפְשִׁי מִשְּׂפַת שֶׁקֶר, מִלָּשׁוֹן רְמִיָּה.[8]

י...י יהוה לִי בְּעֹזְרָי, וַאֲנִי אֶרְאֶה בְשֹׂנְאָי.[9]

י...ל יְמִין יהוה רוֹמֵמָה, יְמִין יהוה עֹשָׂה חָיִל.[10]

י...ם יַעְלְזוּ חֲסִידִים בְּכָבוֹד, יְרַנְּנוּ עַל מִשְׁכְּבוֹתָם.[11]

י...ן יָשֵׂם נְהָרוֹת לְמִדְבָּר, וּמֹצָאֵי מַיִם לְצִמָּאוֹן.[12]

י...ע יָחֹס עַל דַּל וְאֶבְיוֹן, וְנַפְשׁוֹת אֶבְיוֹנִים יוֹשִׁיעַ.[13]

י...ף יהוה יִגְמֹר בַּעֲדִי, יהוה חַסְדְּךָ לְעוֹלָם, מַעֲשֵׂי יָדֶיךָ אַל תֶּרֶף.[14]

י...ץ יְבָרְכֵנוּ אֱלֹהִים, וְיִירְאוּ אוֹתוֹ כָּל אַפְסֵי אָרֶץ.[15]

י..ק יוֹצִיאֵם מֵחֹשֶׁךְ וְצַלְמָוֶת, וּמוֹסְרוֹתֵיהֶם יְנַתֵּק.[16]

י...ר יהוה שִׁמְךָ לְעוֹלָם, יהוה זִכְרְךָ לְדֹר וָדֹר.[17]

י...ת יהוה שֹׁמֵר אֶת גֵּרִים, יָתוֹם וְאַלְמָנָה יְעוֹדֵד, וְדֶרֶךְ רְשָׁעִים יְעַוֵּת.[18]

כ...ב כִּי לֹא יִטֹּשׁ יהוה עַמּוֹ, וְנַחֲלָתוֹ לֹא יַעֲזֹב.[19]

כ...ל כִּי מֶלֶךְ כָּל הָאָרֶץ אֱלֹהִים, זַמְּרוּ מַשְׂכִּיל.[20]

ל...א לֹא תִהְיֶה מְשַׁכֵּלָה וַעֲקָרָה בְּאַרְצֶךָ, אֶת מִסְפַּר יָמֶיךָ אֲמַלֵּא.[21]

ל...ה לְדָוִד, בָּרוּךְ יהוה צוּרִי, הַמְלַמֵּד יָדַי לַקְרָב, אֶצְבְּעוֹתַי לַמִּלְחָמָה.[22]

ל...י לוּלֵי תוֹרָתְךָ שַׁעֲשֻׁעָי, אָז אָבַדְתִּי בְעָנְיִי.[23]

ל...ת לַמְנַצֵּחַ עַל שֹׁשַׁנִּים לִבְנֵי קֹרַח, מַשְׂכִּיל שִׁיר יְדִידֹת.[24]

מ..א מִי כָמֹכָה בָּאֵלִם יהוה, מִי כָּמֹכָה נֶאְדָּר בַּקֹּדֶשׁ, נוֹרָא תְהִלֹּת עֹשֵׂה פֶלֶא.[25]

מ...ה מַחֲשָׁבוֹת בְּעֵצָה תִכּוֹן, וּבְתַחְבֻּלוֹת עֲשֵׂה מִלְחָמָה.[26]

מ...ו מַה דּוֹדֵךְ מִדּוֹד הַיָּפָה בַּנָּשִׁים, מַה דּוֹדֵךְ מִדּוֹד שֶׁכָּכָה הִשְׁבַּעְתָּנוּ.[27]

מ...י מָה אָהַבְתִּי תוֹרָתֶךָ, כָּל הַיּוֹם הִיא שִׂיחָתִי.[28]

מ...ל מַה טֹּבוּ אֹהָלֶיךָ יַעֲקֹב, מִשְׁכְּנֹתֶיךָ יִשְׂרָאֵל.[29]

מ...ם מְאוֹר עֵינַיִם יְשַׂמַּח לֵב, שְׁמוּעָה טוֹבָה תְּדַשֶּׁן עָצֶם.[30]

מ...ר מִי זֶה הָאִישׁ יְרֵא יהוה, יוֹרֶנּוּ בְּדֶרֶךְ יִבְחָר.[31]

נ...א נַפְשֵׁנוּ חִכְּתָה לַיהוה, עֶזְרֵנוּ וּמָגִנֵּנוּ הוּא.[32]

נ...ה נָחַלְתִּי עֵדְוֹתֶיךָ לְעוֹלָם, כִּי שְׂשׂוֹן לִבִּי הֵמָּה.[33]

נ...י נִדְבוֹת פִּי רְצֵה נָא יהוה, וּמִשְׁפָּטֶיךָ לַמְּדֵנִי.[34]

נ...ל נֶחְשַׁבְתִּי עִם יוֹרְדֵי בוֹר, הָיִיתִי כְּגֶבֶר אֵין אֱיָל.[35]

נ...ם נַחֲמוּ נַחֲמוּ עַמִּי, יֹאמַר אֱלֹהֵיכֶם.[36]

נ...ן נֵר יהוה נִשְׁמַת אָדָם, חֹפֵשׂ כָּל חַדְרֵי בָטֶן.[37]

---

(1) *Psalms* 119:62. (2) 34:8. (3) *Proverbs* 13:22. (4) *Psalms* 140:6. (5) 115:9. (6) 20:2. (7) 104:5. (8) 120:2. (9) 118:7. (10) 118:16. (11) 149:5. (12) 107:33. (13) 72:13. (14) 138:8. (15) 67:8. (16) 107:14. (17) 135:13. (18) 146:9. (19) 94:14. (20) 47:8. (21) *Exodus* 23:26. (22) *Psalms* 144:1. (23) 119:92. (24) 45:1. (25) *Exodus* 15:11. (26) *Proverbs* 20:18. (27) *Song of Songs* 5:9. (28) *Psalms* 119:97. (29) *Numbers* 24:5. (30) *Proverbs* 15:30. (31) *Psalms* 25:12. (32) 33:20. (33) 119:111. (34) 119:108. (35) 88:5. (36) *Isaiah* 40:1. (37) *Proverbs* 20:27.

ס...ה סֹבּוּ צִיּוֹן וְהַקִּיפוּהָ, סִפְרוּ מִגְדָּלֶיהָ.[1]

ס...י סֵעֲפִים שָׂנֵאתִי, וְתוֹרָתְךָ אָהָבְתִּי.[2]

ע...א עַתָּה אָקוּם, יֹאמַר יהוה, עַתָּה אֵרוֹמָם, עַתָּה אֶנָּשֵׂא.[3]

ע...ב עַד אֶמְצָא מָקוֹם לַיהוה, מִשְׁכָּנוֹת לַאֲבִיר יַעֲקֹב.[4]

ע...ה עָזִּי וְזִמְרָת יָהּ, וַיְהִי לִי לִישׁוּעָה.[5]

ע...ל עַל דַּעְתְּךָ כִּי לֹא אֶרְשָׁע, וְאֵין מִיָּדְךָ מַצִּיל.[6]

ע...ם עֲרֹב עַבְדְּךָ לְטוֹב, אַל יַעַשְׁקֻנִי זֵדִים.[7]

ע...ר עֹשֶׂה גְדֹלוֹת וְאֵין חֵקֶר, נִפְלָאוֹת עַד אֵין מִסְפָּר.[8]

פ...ה פִּתְחוּ לִי שַׁעֲרֵי צֶדֶק, אָבֹא בָם אוֹדֶה יָהּ.[9]

פ...ל פֶּן יִטְרֹף כְּאַרְיֵה נַפְשִׁי, פֹּרֵק וְאֵין מַצִּיל.[10]

פ...ס פֶּלֶס וּמֹאזְנֵי מִשְׁפָּט לַיהוה, מַעֲשֵׂהוּ כָּל אַבְנֵי כִיס.[11]

פ...ץ פִּנִּיתָ לְפָנֶיהָ, וַתַּשְׁרֵשׁ שָׁרָשֶׁיהָ, וַתְּמַלֵּא אָרֶץ.[12]

צ...ה צִיּוֹן בְּמִשְׁפָּט תִּפָּדֶה, וְשָׁבֶיהָ בִּצְדָקָה.[13]

צ...ח צִיּוֹן יִשְׁאָלוּ דֶּרֶךְ הֵנָּה פְנֵיהֶם, בֹּאוּ וְנִלְווּ אֶל יהוה, בְּרִית עוֹלָם לֹא תִשָּׁכֵחַ.[14]

צ...י צַר וּמָצוֹק מְצָאוּנִי, מִצְוֹתֶיךָ שַׁעֲשֻׁעָי.[15]

צ...ל צַהֲלִי וָרֹנִּי יוֹשֶׁבֶת צִיּוֹן, כִּי גָדוֹל בְּקִרְבֵּךְ קְדוֹשׁ יִשְׂרָאֵל.[16]

ק...ל קַמְתִּי אֲנִי לִפְתֹּחַ לְדוֹדִי, וְיָדַי נָטְפוּ מוֹר וְאֶצְבְּעֹתַי מוֹר עֹבֵר עַל כַּפּוֹת הַמַּנְעוּל.[17]

ק...ן קוֹלִי אֶל יהוה אֶזְעָק, קוֹלִי אֶל יהוה אֶתְחַנָּן.[18]

ק...ת קָרוֹב אַתָּה יהוה, וְכָל מִצְוֹתֶיךָ אֱמֶת.[19]

ר...ה רִגְזוּ וְאַל תֶּחֱטָאוּ, אִמְרוּ בִלְבַבְכֶם עַל מִשְׁכַּבְכֶם, וְדֹמּוּ סֶלָה.[20]

ר...ל רְאוּ עַתָּה כִּי אֲנִי אֲנִי הוּא, וְאֵין אֱלֹהִים עִמָּדִי, אֲנִי אָמִית וַאֲחַיֶּה, מָחַצְתִּי וַאֲנִי אֶרְפָּא, וְאֵין מִיָּדִי מַצִּיל.[21]

ר...ן רְאֵה זֶה מָצָאתִי, אָמְרָה קֹהֶלֶת, אַחַת לְאַחַת לִמְצֹא חֶשְׁבּוֹן.[22]

ר...ת רָאוּךָ מַּיִם אֱלֹהִים, רָאוּךָ מַּיִם יָחִילוּ, אַף יִרְגְּזוּ תְהֹמוֹת.[23]

ש...א שַׂמֵּחַ נֶפֶשׁ עַבְדֶּךָ, כִּי אֵלֶיךָ אֲדֹנָי נַפְשִׁי אֶשָּׂא.[24]

ש...ה שְׂאוּ יְדֵכֶם קֹדֶשׁ, וּבָרְכוּ אֶת יהוה.[25]

ש...ח שָׁמַע יהוה תְּחִנָּתִי, יהוה תְּפִלָּתִי יִקָּח.[26]

ש...י שָׂנֵאתִי הַשֹּׁמְרִים הַבְלֵי שָׁוְא, וַאֲנִי אֶל יהוה בָּטָחְתִּי.[27]

ש...ל שָׁלוֹם רָב לְאֹהֲבֵי תוֹרָתֶךָ, וְאֵין לָמוֹ מִכְשׁוֹל.[28]

ש...ם שְׁמָר תָּם וּרְאֵה יָשָׁר, כִּי אַחֲרִית לְאִישׁ שָׁלוֹם.[29]

ש...ן שִׁיתוּ לִבְּכֶם לְחֵילָה, פַּסְּגוּ אַרְמְנוֹתֶיהָ, לְמַעַן תְּסַפְּרוּ לְדוֹר אַחֲרוֹן.[30]

ש...ר שְׂפַת אֱמֶת תִּכּוֹן לָעַד, וְעַד אַרְגִּיעָה לְשׁוֹן שָׁקֶר.[31]

ש...ת שִׁיר הַמַּעֲלוֹת, הִנֵּה בָּרְכוּ אֶת יהוה כָּל עַבְדֵי יהוה, הָעֹמְדִים בְּבֵית יהוה בַּלֵּילוֹת.[32]

ת...ה תַּעֲרֹךְ לְפָנַי שֻׁלְחָן נֶגֶד צֹרְרָי, דִּשַּׁנְתָּ בַשֶּׁמֶן רֹאשִׁי, כּוֹסִי רְוָיָה.[33]

ת...י תּוֹצִיאֵנִי מֵרֶשֶׁת זוּ, טָמְנוּ לִי, כִּי אַתָּה מָעוּזִּי.[34]

ת...ם תְּנוּ עֹז לֵאלֹהִים, עַל יִשְׂרָאֵל גַּאֲוָתוֹ, וְעֻזּוֹ בַּשְּׁחָקִים.[35]

---

(1) *Psalms* 48:13. (2) 119:113. (3) *Isaiah* 33:10. (4) *Psalms* 132:5. (5) 118:14. (6) *Job* 10:7. (7) *Psalms* 119:122. (8) *Job* 5:9. (9) *Psalms* 118:19. (10) 7:3. (11) *Proverbs* 16:11. (12) *Psalms* 80:10. (13) *Isaiah* 1:27. (14) *Jeremiah* 50:5. (15) *Psalms* 119:143. (16) *Isaiah* 12:6. (17) *Song of Songs* 5:5. (18) *Psalms* 142:2. (19) 119:151. (20) 4:5. (21) *Deuteronomy* 32:39. (22) *Ecclesiastes* 7:27. (23) *Psalms* 77:7. (24) 86:4. (25) 134:2. (26) 6:10. (27) 31:7. (28) 119:165. (29) 37:37. (30) 48:14. (31) *Proverbs* 12:19. (32) *Psalms* 134:1. (33) 23:5. (34) 31:5. (35) 68:35.

THE RABBIS' KADDISH / KADDISH D'RABBANAN

TRANSLITERATED WITH ASHKENAZIC PRONUNCIATION

Yisgadal v'yiskadash sh'mei rabbaw (Cong. – *Amein).*
B'allmaw dee v'raw chir'usei v'yamlich malchusei,
b'chayeichon, uv'yomeichon, uv'chayei d'chol beis yisroel,
ba'agawlaw u'vizman kawriv, v'imru: Amein.
(Cong. – *Amein. Y'hei sh'mei rabbaw m'vawrach l'allam u'l'allmei allmayaw.)*
Y'hei sh'mei rabbaw m'vawrach, l'allam u'l'allmei allmayaw.

Yis'bawrach, v'yishtabach, v'yispaw'ar, v'yisromam, v'yis'nasei,
v'yis'hadar, v'yis'aleh, v'yis'halawl
sh'mei d'kudshaw b'rich hu (Cong. – *b'rich hu).*
L'aylaw min kol bir'chawsaw v'shirawsaw,
tush'b'chawsaw v'nechemawsaw,
da'ami'rawn b'allmaw, v'imru: Amein (Cong. – *Amein).*

Al yisroel v'al rabaw'nawn v'al talmidei'hon,
v'al kol talmidei salmidei'hon,
v'al kol mawn d'awskin b'oray'saw,
dee v'as'raw haw'dain, v'dee b'chol asar va'asar.
Y'hei l'hon u'l'chon shlaw'maw rabbaw,
chee'naw v'chisdaw v'rachamin,
v'chayin arichin, u'm'zonei r'vichei,
u'furkawnaw min kaw'dawm a'vu'hone dee vi'sh'ma'yaw
v'imru: Amein (Cong. – *Amein).*

Y'hei shlawmaw rabbaw min sh'mayaw,
v'chayim awleinu v'al kol yisroel, v'imru: Amein (Cong. – *Amein).*

Take three steps back, bow left and say, *'Oseh. . .'*; bow right and say, *'hu b'rachamawv ya'aseh. . .'*; bow forward and say, *'v'al kol yisroel v'imru: Amein.'*

Oseh shawlom bim'ro'mawv,
hu b'rachamawv ya'aseh shawlom awleinu,
v'al kol yisroel v'imru: Amein (Cong. – *Amein).*

Remain standing in place for a few moments, then take three steps forward.

THE MOURNER'S KADDISH

TRANSLITERATED WITH ASHKENAZIC PRONUNCIATION

Yisgadal v'yiskadash sh'mei rabbaw (Cong. – *Amein*).
B'allmaw dee v'raw chir'usei v'yamlich malchusei,
b'chayeichon, uv'yomeichon, uv'chayei d'chol beis yisroel,
ba'agawlaw u'vizman kawriv, v'imru: Amein.
(Cong. – *Amein. Y'hei sh'mei rabbaw m'vawrach l'allam u'l'allmei allmayaw.*)
Y'hei sh'mei rabbaw m'vawrach, l'allam u'l'allmei allmayaw.

Yis'bawrach, v'yishtabach, v'yispaw'ar, v'yisromam, v'yis'nasei,
v'yis'hadar, v'yis'aleh, v'yis'halawl
sh'mei d'kudshaw b'rich hu (Cong. – *b'rich hu*).
L'aylaw min kol bir'chawsaw v'shirawsaw,
tush'b'chawsaw v'nechemawsaw,
da'ami'rawn b'allmaw, v'imru: Amein (Cong. – *Amein*).

Y'hei shlawmaw rabbaw min sh'mayaw,
v'chayim awleinu v'al kol yisroel, v'imru: Amein (Cong. – *Amein*).

Take three steps back, bow left and say, *'Oseh. . .'*; bow right and say, *'hu ya'aseh. . .'*; bow forward and say, *'v'al kol yisroel v'imru: Amein.'*

Oseh shawlom bim'ro'mawv,
hu ya'aseh shawlom awleinu,
v'al kol yisroel v'imru: Amein (Cong. – *Amein*).

Remain standing in place for a few moments, then take three steps forward.